THE WORLD BOOK

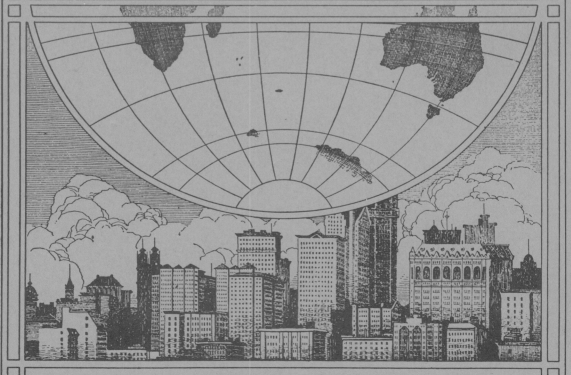

F Volume 7

The World Book Encyclopedia

World Book, Inc.
a Scott Fetzer company

Chicago London Sydney Toronto

The World Book Encyclopedia

Copyright © 1990, U.S.A.
by
World Book, Inc.

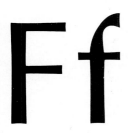

F is the sixth letter of our alphabet. Historians believe that the letter came from a symbol used by the Semites, who once lived in Syria and Palestine. They named it *waw,* meaning *hook.* The ancient Greeks later took the symbol into their own alphabet and called it *digamma.* They used it to represent the sound of *w* in English. The Romans were the first to use the letter to represent our sound for *f.* See **Alphabet.**

Uses. *F* or *f* is about the 15th most frequently used letter in books, newspapers, and other material printed in English. When used on a report card, *F* usually means failure in a school subject. In music, it names one note of the scale. As an abbreviation, *F* shows that a temperature reading is in Fahrenheit degrees. *F* means *fluorine* in chemistry, *function* in mathematics, *fluid* in pharmacy,

free energy in physics, and *frequency* in statistics. In photography, *f* refers to the focal length of the lens divided by its actual opening. The *f* also stands for *franc* (in France).

Pronunciation. In English, a person pronounces the *f* by placing the lower lip against the edges of the upper front teeth and forcing the breath out. A person pronounces *ff* as a single *f,* except when the letter appears in combinations of two words, such as *self-fed.* In some English nouns, such as *knife,* the *f* becomes a *v* in the plural form of the word. The *f* in French, Italian, Spanish and German words resembles the English *f* sound. The Latin pronunciation of *f* was also similar to the English *f* sound. Marianne Cooley

See **Pronunciation.**

Development of the letter F

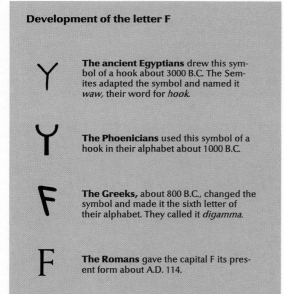

The ancient Egyptians drew this symbol of a hook about 3000 B.C. The Semites adapted the symbol and named it *waw,* their word for *hook.*

The Phoenicians used this symbol of a hook in their alphabet about 1000 B.C.

The Greeks, about 800 B.C., changed the symbol and made it the sixth letter of their alphabet. They called it *digamma.*

The Romans gave the capital F its present form about A.D. 114.

The small letter f developed about A.D. 500 from Roman writing. Monks who copied manuscripts modified the letter during the 800's. By about 1500, the f had its present shape.

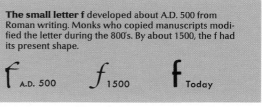

A.D. 500   1500   Today

Special ways of expressing the letter F

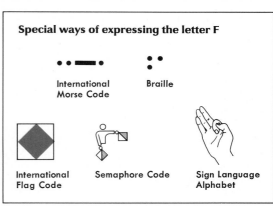

International Morse Code

Braille

International Flag Code

Semaphore Code

Sign Language Alphabet

Common forms of the letter F

Handwritten letters vary from person to person. *Manuscript* (printed) letters, *left,* have simple curves and straight lines. Cursive letters, *right,* have flowing lines.

Roman letters have small finishing strokes called *serifs* that extend from the main strokes. The type face shown above is Baskerville. The italic form appears at the right.

Sans-serif letters are also called *gothic letters.* They have no serifs. The type face shown above is called Futura. The italic form of Futura appears at the right.

Computer letters have special shapes. Computers can "read" these letters either optically or by means of the magnetic ink with which the letters may be printed.

Faber, *FAY buhr,* **Eberhard,** *EHB ur hahrd* (1822-1879), an American businessman born in Bavaria, built the first mass-production pencil factory in the United States. His great-grandfather had started making pencils in Bavaria in 1761. Faber moved to New York City in 1848 and opened a branch of the family firm there the next year. He sold pencils from Bavaria and exported cedar boards from Florida to European pencil manufacturers.

Faber had to pay a tariff on the pencils he imported, and so he decided it would be cheaper to make them himself. He developed labor-saving machinery to avoid high production costs and, in 1861, built a pencil factory in New York City. Faber later expanded the business to include pens, erasers, and other stationery products. Faber was born in Stein, near Nuremberg in what is now West Germany.   Barry W. Poulson

Fabergé, *FAB uhr ZHAY,* **Peter Carl** (1846-1920), was a Russian goldsmith and jeweler who won international fame for his design of decorative objects. His imaginative creations included cigarette cases, picture frames, parasol handles, and miniature flowers and animals, as well as clocks and other traditional items.

The Resurrection Egg (about 1889), by Peter Carl Fabergé. Gold, diamonds, and pearls, with enameled figures. The Forbes Magazine Collection

A Fabergé egg

Fabergé's objects were made from gold, silver, and various gemstones native to Russia. He decorated many items with a brilliantly colored enamel that was characteristic of his work. Fabergé's most famous pieces are the beautifully crafted Easter eggs he made for Czars Alexander III and Nicholas II.

Fabergé was born in St. Petersburg (now Leningrad). He received his first training from his father, a successful jeweler, and inherited the small family business at the age of 24. He expanded the business into a company with workshops in the Russian cities of Kiev, Moscow, Odessa, and St. Petersburg, and eventually in London. Czar Alexander III appointed him imperial jeweler in 1884. The Soviet government took over Fabergé's firm after the Bolshevik Revolution of 1917. Fabergé fled to Switzerland, where he died.   Marilyn Pfeifer Swezey

Fabian Society, *FAY bee uhn,* is a group of British socialists. The society was founded in 1884. It was named for Quintus Fabius Maximus, a Roman general who avoided defeat by refusing to fight any decisive battles against Hannibal. The Fabians teach that socialism can be achieved gradually, through a series of reforms (see **Socialism**). They differ from the Communists, who believe that the people can gain ownership of the means of production only through revolution. Noted Fabians have included George Bernard Shaw, H. G. Wells, and Sidney and Beatrice Webb. Fabian ideas became the basis of the British Labour Party (see **Labour Party**). Today, the society sponsors and publishes research on political and social issues. See also **Webb, Sidney and Beatrice.**   Chris Cook

Fable is a brief fictitious story that teaches a moral. In most fables, one or more of the characters is an animal, plant, or thing that talks and acts like a person. A fable may be told in prose or in verse. In many fables, the moral is told at the end in the form of a proverb.

Famous fables include "The Fox and the Grapes," "The City Mouse and the Country Mouse," and "The Wolf in Sheep's Clothing." These tales have been told and retold for more than 2,000 years. They remain popular because they illustrate truths that almost anyone can recognize. In "The Fox and the Grapes," for example, a fox decides that some grapes growing too high for him to reach are probably sour anyway. A person who hears the tale recognizes the fox's attitude as a common human failing. The moral of the fable—that people often express a dislike for what they cannot have—is summed up in the expression "sour grapes."

Nearly all ancient peoples invented folk tales in which animals had human traits. The fox was often pictured as sly, and the owl as wise. In time, people began to tell the stories to teach morals. The tales thus became fables.

Most of the fables that are popular in Western countries can be traced back to ancient Greece and India. The majority of the Greek fables are credited to Aesop, a Greek slave who lived about 600 B.C. Aesop had a reputation for telling wise, witty tales about animals, but scholars know little else about him. The fables known as "Aesop's fables" probably came from several ancient sources. Some of the stories originated in India.

The fables of the people of India were influenced by their belief that after death, human beings might be reborn as animals. Indian storytellers made up many tales of such rebirths and used them to teach a variety of morals. Some of these fables had reached the West by the start of the Christian era and were included in early collections of Aesop's fables. During the 200's B.C. or

Engraving (1879) by William Salter Herrick. (Bettmann Archive)

The fable "The Fox and the Grapes" tells of a fox who wants to eat a bunch of grapes on a vine. After he finds he can't reach the grapes, he decides that they were probably sour anyway.

after, the Indians collected their best-known fables in a work called the *Panchatantra.*

Through the centuries, many writers have retold the ancient fables. The most famous such writer was Jean de La Fontaine, a French poet of the 1600's. La Fontaine retold Aesop's fables in elegant verse and expanded their meanings. Fables had always made fun of human follies, but La Fontaine turned such satire into biting social criticism. In "The Fox and the Crow," for example, a fox robs a crow of some cheese by telling him what a fine singing voice he must have. As the flattered crow opens his mouth to caw, the cheese drops from his beak. Earlier versions of the fable poked fun at the crow for being fooled by the fox's flattery. La Fontaine's version includes the trickery of the fox and ends with a thoughtful moral: "Every flatterer lives at the expense of his listeners." La Fontaine wrote his fables mainly for adults, but they have long been favorites of French children.

La Fontaine has had many imitators. One of the most successful was Ivan Krylov, a Russian poet of the early 1800's. Krylov translated La Fontaine's fables into Russian and also wrote many of his own. Krylov intended his stories mainly for adults. But they have become the most popular children's stories in Russia.

During the 1900's, writers have continued to develop the fable as a literary form. The Irish novelist James Joyce wove "The Fox and the Grapes" and "The Ant and the Grasshopper" into his *Finnegans Wake.* The fables help create the mood of fantasy that characterizes this novel. The American humorist James Thurber revived the fable as a form of social criticism. His fables are noted for their stinging portrayal of the anxieties of modern life.   Darcy O'Brien

See also **Aesop's fables; Allegory; Folklore; La Fontaine, Jean de; Literature for children** (Folk literature).

Additional resources

Level I
Ginsburg, Mirra. *Three Rolls and One Doughnut: Fables from Russia Retold.* Dial, 1970.
Martin, Rafe. *The Hungry Tigress and Other Traditional Asian Tales.* Shambhala, 1984.
Level II
Jacobs, Joseph. *The Fables of Aesop.* Schocken, 1966. First published in 1894.
La Fontaine, Jean de. *The Fables of La Fontaine.* Trans. by Marianne Moore. Viking, 1954.

Fabre, *FAH buhr,* **Jean Henri Casimir,** *zhahn ahn REE ka zee MEER* (1823-1915), a French naturalist, spent his life observing insects and spiders. He wrote simply of what he saw in the gardens and fields near his home. He received the ribbon of The Legion of Honor, but was fired from his teaching position because he allowed girls to attend his science classes. Fabre was almost unknown outside of France until he was nearly 80. Then the great scientific societies recognized his work. He wrote a 10-volume *Souvenirs Entomologiques.* Fabre was born in St. Léon.   Carolyn Merchant

Fabric. See Textile.

Face is the front part of a person's head. It consists of the forehead, eyes, nose, mouth, cheeks, and chin. The face is covered with muscles and skin. The eyes are protected from glare and dust by the eyelids, lashes, and eyebrows. The tip of the nose is made up of cartilage and skin, which act as a flexible cushion. The channels of the nose are covered with tiny hairs which strain out dust and dirt in the air going through the nose. The mouth includes the lips, teeth, tongue, and roof, and is lined with mucous membrane. The lower jaw is the only bony part of the face that moves.

The facial skeleton is made up of 14 bones and 32 teeth. The *frontal bone* forms part of the forehead. The *nasal bones* and *lacrimal bones* combine to support the bridge and base of the nose. The middle portion of the face, including the cheekbones and upper jawbones, is formed by the *zygomatic bones* and *maxillae.* The *mandible* forms the jaw. The *vomer bones, ethmoid bones,* and *palatine bones* lie deeper in the face. There are also a number of muscles in the face. There is a circular muscle around the mouth and one around each eye. Other muscles spread out over the face from the edges of the circular muscles.

The face is the most distinctive part of a human being. It differs in each person because of variations in the nose, eyes, and other parts of the face. It is because of these variations that we recognize each other and tell one another apart. Much of what goes on in our mind finds expression in our face. Our facial muscles often show the kind of emotions we feel. We cannot always control our expression.   Charles W. Cummings

See also **Bell's palsy; Blushing; Head; Mandible.**

Face fly is an annoying pest for livestock. Groups of adult face flies feed on the fluid around the eyes, noses, and mouths of livestock, especially cattle. They also feed on blood from the wounds that other flies make on cattle. Face flies do not bite and are not known to carry germs that cause human diseases. But they can transmit diseases to horses, donkeys, and cattle. The face fly looks like the common house fly, but they differ in their habits.

The female face fly lays eggs in fresh cow manure. Face fly *larvae* (maggots) develop faster than house fly larvae. Mature face fly larvae are yellowish instead of white, but otherwise resemble house fly maggots. Face flies hibernate in barns, houses, and other shelters.

WORLD BOOK illustration by Shirley Hooper, Oxford Illustrators Limited
Face fly

The first known face flies in North America were discovered in Nova Scotia in 1952. They probably came from Europe. The flies soon spread throughout most of the United States.

Scientific classification. The face fly is in the order Diptera. It belongs to the house fly family, Muscidae. It is *Musca autumnalis.*   E. W. Cupp

Facet. See Diamond (How diamonds are cut to make jewels; pictures).

Facsimile, *fak SIHM uh lee,* often called *fax,* is a way of transmitting text and pictures over telephone lines. News services often use facsimile to send news stories and photographs to newspapers and television stations. Banks, law firms, and other businesses use facsimile to send copies of documents to clients, branch offices, and other organizations.

A facsimile machine transmits images over telephone lines. This woman is receiving an image sent on another machine.

A device called a *facsimile machine* is used for transmitting and receiving images. Facsimile machines resemble small photocopiers. However, they are equipped with a telephone or are connected to one. To send a document, the user inserts it into the machine and dials the telephone number of the receiving fax machine. After the connection is made, an electronic scanner on the transmitting machine moves across the page and converts the image into a set of electric signals. These signals travel over the telephone line to the receiving fax machine. That machine converts the electric signals back into an image of the original document and then prints a copy.

Some business people use small desktop fax machines or portable models at home or when they travel. A personal computer can also be used to send and receive documents if it is equipped with a special electronic circuit board called a *fax board.*

Many inventors in Europe and the United States worked on facsimile in the late 1800's and early 1900's. News services began using fax machines to transmit photographs in the 1930's. At that time, fax machines used radio waves instead of telephone lines for transmission. Facsimile became increasingly popular in business in the 1980's after manufacturers developed machines that were smaller, less costly, and faster. Today, most machines fit on a desktop. Many can transmit two or three pages of information a minute.   Eileen Feretic

See also **Telephoto.**

Factor. The factors of a number are the numbers which when multiplied together give the original number. For example, the numbers 3 and 4 are factors of 12 because 3 × 4 = 12. The other whole number factors of 12 are 2 and 6, and 1 and 12. *Factoring* (determining factors) provides insight into one of the many relationships among numbers.

Every whole number, except 1, can be expressed as the product of at least two factors. A number that has exactly two different factors, itself and 1, is called a *prime number.* The number 7 is prime because 1 and 7 are its only factors. The eight smallest primes are 2, 3, 5, 7, 11, 13, 17, and 19. A number that has more than two factors is called a *composite number.* The number 4 is composite because it has three factors, 1, 2, and 4. The eight smallest composite numbers are 4, 6, 8, 9, 10, 12, 14, and 15. The number 1 is neither composite nor prime.

Prime factors of a number are those prime numbers which when multiplied together equal the number. Each number is a product of only one set of prime numbers. For example, 24 can only be expressed as a product of prime numbers as 2 × 2 × 2 × 3 (in any order). The *prime factorization* of 24 is 2 × 2 × 2 × 3 and the *prime factors* of 24 are 2 and 3.

To find the prime factors of a number, divide the number by any *prime number* that goes into it evenly. It is usually easiest to use the smallest prime number that divides the number evenly. For example, to find the prime factors of 220, begin by dividing by 2 (220 ÷ 2 = 110). Continue dividing the *quotient* (the number obtained) by 2 until it is no longer divisible by 2 (110 ÷ 2 = 55). But 55 cannot be divided by 2 without leaving a remainder. The next prime, 3, does not divide 55 without a remainder either. But the next greater prime, 5, does divide 55 equally (55 ÷ 5 = 11). The number 11, like 2 and 5, is a prime number. Therefore the prime factorization of 220 is 2 × 2 × 5 × 11 and the prime factors are 2, 5, and 11. The product 2 × 2 × 5 × 11 (in any order) is the only way 220 can be expressed as the product of prime numbers. The process may be written like this:

$$
\begin{array}{r}
2\,|\,\underline{220} \\
2\,|\,\underline{110} \\
2\,|\,\underline{55} \\
\end{array}
$$

(leaves a remainder)

$$3\,|\,\underline{55}$$

(leaves a remainder)

$$
\begin{array}{r}
5\,|\,\underline{55} \\
11 \quad \text{(prime)}
\end{array}
$$

The only factors of a prime number are the number itself and 1.

Common factors. If a number is a factor of two or more numbers, it is called a *common factor* of those numbers. For example, 1, 3, 5, and 15 are the factors of 15; and 1, 2, 4, 5, 10, and 20 are the factors of 20. One and 5 are common to both these sets of factors.

If two numbers have more than one common factor, the greatest one is called the *greatest common factor.* It is also the *greatest common divisor* since a factor of a number is also a divisor of that number. For example, the numbers 30 and 45 have four common factors: 1, 3, 5, and 15. The greatest common factor is 15. To find the greatest common factor of two or more numbers, first find the set of all the factors for each number. Then select the largest factor which is in all the sets. The greatest common factor of 18, 30, and 42 is in this example:

Number	Set of factors
18	1, 2, 3, 6, 9, 18
30	1, 2, 3, 5, 6, 10, 15, 30
42	1, 2, 3, 6, 7, 14, 21, 42

The number 6 is the greatest factor common to all the sets, so 6 is the greatest common factor of 18, 30, and 42.

Relative primes. Two numbers that have no common factors other than 1 are *relatively prime* or *prime in relation to each other.* For example, the factors of 12 are 1, 2, 3, 4, 6, and 12. The factors of 35 are 1, 5, 7, and 35. Twelve and 35 have no common factors other than 1. They are relatively prime.

Algebraic factors. *Algebraic expressions* (2x + 4 is an algebraic expression) also have factors. For example, *1, 3, a, b,* and *ab* are factors of *3ab.* The expressions *1, a, a^2, b* and *a^2b* are factors of *a^2b.* The factors of algebraic expressions are found in the same way as the factors of whole numbers. Multiplying *2ab* by *(a + 2b)* gives *$2a^2b$ + $4ab^2$.* Therefore, *2ab* and *a + 2b* are factors of *$2a^2b$ + $4ab^2$.* The other factors of *$2a^2b$ + $4ab^2$* are *1, 2, a, b,* and *ab.* The expression *$a^2 + b^2$* cannot be factored using real numbers only. Its factors are *complex numbers.* A complex number is the sum of a real number and an *imaginary number* (the square root of a negative number).

John M. Smith

See also **Algebra** (Factoring); **Numeration systems** (The decimal system).

Factory is a building or group of buildings in which products are manufactured. Factories range in size from home garages to groups of buildings covering whole city blocks. Inside, workers and machines turn raw materials and parts into finished products. Factories make almost all the products people use except food. But numerous factories treat, prepare, or package food products. Factories employ about a fifth of the labor force in both the United States and Canada.

Kinds of factories. Factories use the principle of *division of labor*—that is, they divide the required work into a number of separate operations. There are three main kinds of factories: (1) repetitive factories, (2) job factories, and (3) job-lot factories.

Repetitive factories make many units of the same product. Automobile makers use a repetitive approach called the *assembly-line* method, in which the auto frame moves on a conveyor through the factory. As the

frame moves, parts arrive on other conveyors and get attached to the frame until the car is completed. See **Automobile** (illustration: Assembling an automobile).

Job factories, also called *project factories,* make only a small number of units of the same product. They include aircraft factories. In aircraft plants, the product cannot be moved because of its great size. Instead, workers and equipment must be moved to the product. Completing one item may take months.

Job-lot factories combine repetitive factory and job factory methods. Machines are set up to make a certain number of units of a product. Once that number is finished, the machines make another kind of product.

Location and design. Most manufacturers build their factories in suburban areas, where land costs less than in central cities. Many new plants have a one-story structure, which permits materials to move easily through them.

To make factories more efficient, some manufacturers use computers to link operations of various machines and to control the flow of work through the plant. These computers enable a few technicians to survey and operate the entire factory. Such factories may use robots and computer-controlled machine tools. These devices often provide safer, more efficient ways to perform tiring or dangerous tasks. Such tasks include welding, spray painting, and transporting heavy machinery.

History. Before the development of factories, workers made most manufactured products in homes or shops. The development of power-driven machines in the 1700's and 1800's made the modern factory system possible (see **Industrial Revolution**). Until the 1900's, factories were often dirty and poorly lighted, and many were dangerous places in which to work. Most of them stood crowded together in industrial sections of large cities. Today, most factories have good lighting and ventilation. Many provide music, cafeterias, and medical staffs for their employees.   Ronald G. Askin

Related articles in *World Book* include:

Automation	Labor force
Electricity (In industry)	Manufacturing
Industrial relations	Mass production
Industrial Revolution	Sweatshop
Industry	Technology
Invention	Workers' compensation

Factory Act. See **Great Britain** (The era of reform).

Faeroe Islands, *FAIR oh,* also spelled *Faroe* and *Føroyar,* are a group of 18 islands and some reefs in the North Atlantic Ocean. They lie between Iceland and the Shetland Islands. The group has an area of 540 square miles (1,399 square kilometers), and a population of about 42,000. Major islands are Streymoy, Eysturoy, Vágar, Sudhuroy, and Sandoy.

The 140-mile (225-kilometer) coastline is steep and deeply indented. Treacherous currents

Lockheed-California Company

An airplane factory brings together skilled workers and sophisticated equipment to build a modern jet plane, *above.*

WORLD BOOK map

Location of Faeroe Islands

along the shores of the islands make navigation difficult. The islanders are hardy people of Norse origin who fish and raise sheep. They also sell the eggs and feathers of the many sea birds that nest on the cliffs. The islanders do little farming.

Norway ruled over the Faeroe Islands from the 800's until 1380, when the islands came under the control of Denmark. British forces occupied the islands during World War II (1939-1945), but the civil government remained the same. In 1948, Denmark granted the Faeroes self-government. The islanders have their own parliament, or *Lagting,* and send representatives to the Danish parliament in Copenhagen. The Faeroe Islands seat of government is Tórshavn on Streymoy.

M. Donald Hancock

See also **Europe** (picture: Special political units).

Fagin, *FAY guhn,* was a receiver of stolen goods and a trainer of young thieves. He was a character in the novel *Oliver Twist,* by Charles Dickens.

Fahd (1923-   ) became king and prime minister of Saudi Arabia in 1982. He came to power following the death of his half-brother King Khalid. When Khalid became king in 1975, he named Fahd crown prince and first deputy prime minister of Saudi Arabia. Fahd ran the day-to-day affairs of the government because Khalid was not in good health and he lacked Fahd's detailed experience of government functions. Fahd has tried to maintain Saudi Arabia's traditional Islamic moral values while continuing the process of rapid modernization made possible by the country's great oil wealth.

Fahd was born in Riyadh. His full name is Fahd ibn Abd al-Aziz Al Saud. From 1953 to 1960, Fahd served as Saudi Arabia's first minister of education. In 1962, he was appointed as the nation's minister of the interior. In 1967, he also became second deputy prime minister.

Malcolm C. Peck

Fahrenheit, Gabriel Daniel (1686-1736), a German physicist, developed the Fahrenheit temperature scale. He also made the thermometer more accurate by using mercury instead of mixtures of alcohol and water in the thermometer tube (see **Thermometer**).

Fahrenheit determined three fixed temperatures: 0° for the freezing point of ice, salt, and water; 32° for the freezing point of pure water; and 212° F. for the boiling point of water. These three temperatures, from lowest to highest, are equal to $-18°$, 0°, and 100° on the Celsius temperature scale. Fahrenheit was born in Danzig (now Gdańsk, Poland).   Margaret J. Osler

Faïence, *fy AHNS* or *fay AHNS,* is a kind of earthenware. Faïence is glazed with tin oxide to produce a creamy white color. The ware can be decorated with other metallic oxides that turn various colors when the pottery is *fired* (baked). Faïence is related to two other types of earthenware, majolica and delft. But the three have different forms of decoration and also assumed their characteristic style in different countries. Faïence came from France, majolica from Italy, and delft from the Netherlands.

The French named faïence for Faenza, Italy, which was the center for the production of tin oxide-glazed pottery during the 1500's. Today, potters in Germany, the Scandinavian countries, and Spain produce tin oxide-glazed wares that are known as faïence.

William C. Gates, Jr.

WORLD BOOK photo by Steinkamp/Ballogg

A fainting spell can be relieved by having the person lie on the floor with the legs slightly elevated, *above.* The person should be given plenty of room and air.

Fainting is a temporary loss of consciousness. The fainting person becomes pale, begins to perspire, and then loses consciousness and collapses. The person also has a weak pulse and breathes irregularly. Fainting usually lasts only a few minutes. As the fainting passes, the muscles become firm, the pulse is stronger, and breathing becomes regular.

Fainting occurs when there is an insufficient supply of blood to the brain for a short period of time. This condition results from a *dilation* (widening) of the blood vessels in the body followed by a drop in heart rate and blood pressure. It is usually triggered by a frightening event.

Fainting should be treated by letting the person lie stretched out with the head slightly lower than the body. The person's clothing should be loosened, and the individual should be given plenty of room and air. In some cases, a person can be revived by bathing the face with cool water or by passing a whiff of ammonia under the nostrils.

A physician should be called if a person does not recover from a fainting spell promptly. A person who feels weak or dizzy may prevent a fainting spell by lying down or sitting with the head level with the knees.

Carlotta M. Rinke

See also **First aid** (Fainting).

Fair is an event held for the presenting or viewing of exhibits. Depending on the theme of the fair, the exhibits presented may be agricultural, commercial, industrial, or artistic.

Some fairs are called *expositions* or *exhibitions.* Small

Granger Collection

A faïence dish and plate show the elaborate decoration that made this kind of French pottery famous. The bird-shaped dish was made during the 1700's. The plate, which has a delicate snowflake design, also dates from that period.

fairs last just a few days and involve exhibitors and visitors from a local area. The largest fairs run for months and attract exhibitors and visitors from many countries.

Fairs are a major industry in the United States and Canada. More than 3,200 fairs are held annually in the two countries, and they earn more than $1.7 billion for the areas in which they are held.

There are three basic types of fairs—agricultural fairs, trade fairs, and world's fairs. This article discusses agricultural and trade fairs. For information on world's fairs, see the **World's fair** article.

Agricultural fairs are the most common type of fair in the United States and Canada. Such fairs hold contests for the best examples of crops, livestock, poultry, and other farm products. Most agricultural fairs organize competitions for various home-prepared foods. Companies exhibit and demonstrate agricultural machinery and other equipment. Farm youth groups and adult organizations also participate.

Agricultural fairs provide amusements and entertainment for visitors. For example, many agricultural fairs provide a carnival midway with rides and games. At large fairs, famous entertainers perform before large audiences in a grandstand or coliseum. Visitors can purchase many kinds of food and souvenirs at concession stands. Sports events are also popular at some fairs. These events include harness racing, horse racing, automobile racing, and rodeos. Each day's activities may end with a fireworks display.

Agricultural fairs can be divided into three general categories, primarily based on their size. These categories are, from smallest to largest, county fairs, regional or district fairs, and state fairs. Some regional fairs, however, are larger than state fairs. The smallest fairs may cover only a few acres or hectares of open space near a town. The biggest fairs are held at permanent fairgrounds that include large buildings and such special facilities as grandstands and race tracks.

County fairs normally last from two to five days and are operated by a volunteer staff. County fairs mainly attract exhibitors and visitors from the local area. Regional fairs serve a larger geographical area than county fairs. They have a permanent staff and may last as long as two weeks. Every state and province holds an annual fair. The fair is usually held in the late summer or autumn and is generally the major fair or exhibition in the area. State fairs are sometimes operated by a department of the state government. However, a number of state fairs are operated by nonprofit organizations.

Trade fairs normally center on a specific product or industry. For example, a trade fair may confine itself to the computer industry or to book publishing. Generally, trade fairs are intended to provide commercial exposure for the products of the exhibitors. Some of these fairs limit admission only to people within the field covered by the fair. Other trade fairs encourage attendance by the general public.

Most trade fairs are held in large exhibition halls in major cities. Fairs are often held in a different city each year. Guest performers may entertain visitors at special shows, but the fair has no carnival midway.

History. Fairs date back to Biblical times. The book of Ezekiel, which was written in the 500's B.C., has several references to fairs. During the early centuries of Chris-

© Bob Daemmrich

State fairs are held every summer and fall throughout the United States. Exhibits, games, and exciting rides attract large crowds to a state fair midway, *above.*

tianity, the church took an active part in sponsoring fairs as part of the observance of religious holidays and seasons. During the mid-1500's, the church stopped participating in and promoting fairs. As a result, fairs lost their religious associations and became events devoted to commercial exhibits and entertainment.

In 1641, the government of New Netherland authorized the first annual fair in the American colonies, to be held in New Amsterdam (now New York City). By the mid-1700's, fairs had become common throughout the colonies. They were primarily agricultural and served as an important showcase for the farm products of the local area. The first state fairs were held in New Jersey and New York about 1840.   H. Lewis Miller

Related articles in *World Book.* For the dates and locations of fairs in the United States and Canada, see the *Annual events* section of the state and province articles. See also **City** (picture: Trade fairs); **Future Farmers of America** (picture); **Toronto** (Other interesting places to visit); **World's fair; Yugoslavia** (picture: A rural fair).

Fair Deal is the name President Harry S. Truman gave to his domestic legislative program. He said it offered to the American people "the promise of equal rights and equal opportunities." See also **Truman, Harry S.** (Domestic program).

Fair employment practices. See Equal Employment Opportunity Commission.

Fair housing laws. See Open housing.

Fair Labor Standards Act is a law that sets the minimum wage and the length of the standard workweek for most employees in the United States. It applies to employees of firms that do business in more than one state and have annual sales of at least $250,000. It also sets minimum age requirements for all workers. The act was passed in 1938 and has been amended many times. A 1963 amendment, the Equal Pay Act, requires that men and women be paid equally for doing equal work. The Employment Standards Administration of the U.S. Department of Labor enforces the act.

Congress passed the Fair Labor Standards Act as part of the *New Deal,* President Franklin D. Roosevelt's program to end the Great Depression. The act originally set a minimum wage of 25 cents an hour. Amendments have raised the wage repeatedly. An amendment passed in 1977 provided for yearly increases, bringing the minimum wage to $3.35 an hour by 1981.

The act at first limited the standard workweek to 44 hours, but provided for it to be reduced to 40 hours—the current length—by 1940. For *overtime,* or the time worked beyond the 40-hour limit, employees are entitled to be paid at a rate of $1\frac{1}{2}$ times their regular rate.

The Fair Labor Standards Act bans the employment of children less than 14 years old, except for limited employment in certain agricultural jobs. Children 14 or 15 years old are prohibited from working in factories or during school hours. People less than 18 years old may not work in jobs declared hazardous by the U.S. secretary of labor. Such occupations include mining and certain factory jobs.   James G. Scoville

See also **Child labor; Minimum wage; Wages and hours.**

Fair-trade laws were designed to prevent large retail stores from selling certain merchandise at extremely low prices in attempts to drive their smaller competitors out of business. Such laws are also called *resale price maintenance laws.* Many U.S. states once had such laws. However, fair-trade laws have been illegal in the United States since 1975.

In some states, if any retailer agreed with a manufacturer to sell an item at a particular price, the state's fair-trade laws required all retailers to sell the item at that price. Other states allowed merchants to sell an item either at a price specified by the manufacturer or at a higher price. Goods covered by fair-trade laws included television sets, stereo equipment, clothing, watches, bicycles, and jewelry.

In 1931, California became the first state to pass a fair-trade law. By 1950, 45 states had such laws. Ordinarily, price fixing would violate federal antitrust laws (see **Antitrust laws**). But two federal laws, the Miller-Tydings Act of 1937 and the McGuire Act of 1952, made such price fixing legal. Opponents of fair-trade laws argued that the laws cost consumers millions of dollars a year in higher prices. In time, many states repealed such laws. The U.S. Congress abolished the remaining ones in 1975 by repealing the Miller-Tydings and McGuire acts.

Jay Diamond

Fairbanks (pop. 22,645) is the second largest city in Alaska. Only Anchorage has more people. Fairbanks lies

Steve McCutcheon

Fairbanks, Alaska, the chief financial and trade center of the interior of Alaska, lies on the banks of the Chena River, *center.* Fairbanks is in the heart of a great gold-mining region.

150 miles (240 kilometers) south of the Arctic Circle. It is a transportation and supply center for the interior and the Arctic area of Alaska (see **Alaska** [political map]).

Fairbanks is often called the *Golden Heart City,* a name it received when it was the center of a gold mining region. It is centrally located along the Trans-Alaska Pipeline, which transports oil from the northern to the southern coast of Alaska. The Chena River runs through Fairbanks. Tourism, the main campus of the University of Alaska, a U.S. Air Force base, and a U.S. Army post help support the economy. Fairbanks' architecture includes modern office and residential buildings, as well as old log cabins.

Temperatures in the city average about 60° F. (16° C) in June and about −11° F. (−23° C) in January. Fairbanks receives an average of about 65 inches of snow (165 centimeters) yearly. It has about 22 hours of daylight at *summer solstice* (the longest day of the year) and less than 4 hours at *winter solstice* (the shortest day).

Felix Pedro, an Italian immigrant, found gold 12 miles (19 kilometers) north of Fairbanks in 1902. The city developed as a supply center for other mining towns around it. It was named after Charles W. Fairbanks, a U.S. senator from Indiana who became Vice President of the United States in 1905. In 1967, a flood in Fairbanks killed 6 people and caused $200 million in damage. The discovery of oil at Prudhoe Bay in 1968 and the construction of the Trans-Alaska Pipeline between 1974 and 1977 caused the city's population to increase by 50 per cent between 1970 and 1980.   Claus-M. Naske

Fairbanks, Charles Warren (1852-1918), served as Vice President of the United States from 1905 to 1909 under President Theodore Roosevelt. He hoped to be the Republican presidential candidate in 1908. But he did not get along well with Roosevelt, and the President helped William Howard Taft win the nomination. Fairbanks again was the Republican vice presidential candidate in 1916. However, Fairbanks and presidential candidate Charles Evans Hughes lost the 1916 election to

Woodrow Wilson and his running mate, Thomas R. Marshall.

He was born on a farm near Unionville Center, Ohio, and was graduated from Ohio Wesleyan University. He became a successful railroad lawyer in Indianapolis, Ind. Fairbanks served as a U.S. senator from Indiana from 1897 to 1905. He headed the American delegation to the Joint High Commission that tried to settle all outstanding difficulties with Canada in 1898. Fairbanks rejected an offer from Mark Hanna, Republican political leader, to be William McKinley's running mate in the 1900 presidential campaign.   Irving G. Williams

Culver

Charles W. Fairbanks

Fairbanks, Douglas, Sr. (1883-1939), was an American motion-picture actor who became famous for his acrobatic acting in colorful adventure films. All of Fairbanks' notable movies were silent films. They included *The Mark of Zorro* (1920), *Robin Hood* (1922), *The Thief of Bagdad* (1924), and *The Black Pirate* (1926). Fairbanks' name is still associated with the exaggerated, romantic style of such motion pictures.

Fairbanks was born in Denver. His real name was Douglas Elton Ullman. For several years, he starred in

Bettmann Archive

Douglas Fairbanks, Sr., was a famous motion-picture actor of the 1920's. In 1929, he starred with his wife, Mary Pickford, in William Shakespeare's comedy *The Taming of the Shrew, above.*

comedies on Broadway. Fairbanks made his movie debut in 1915. He helped found the United Artists studio in 1919 with actor Charlie Chaplin, actress Mary Pickford, and director D. W. Griffith. Fairbanks married Pickford in 1920.   James MacKillop

Fairbanks, Douglas, Jr. (1909-   ), is an American

motion-picture actor. His father was Douglas Fairbanks, Sr., a star of silent films. Fairbanks performed in a variety of roles, ranging from romantic heroes to troubled weaklings. His best-known movies include *The Prisoner of Zenda* (1937) and *Gunga Din* (1939). He also made several romantic adventure films in the style of his father. They include *The Corsican Brothers* (1941), *Sinbad the Sailor* (1947), and *The Fighting O'Flynn* (1949).

Douglas Elton Fairbanks, Jr., was born in New York City. He made his movie debut in 1923 and retired in the early 1950's. His autobiography, *The Salad Days* (1988), describes his life to the age of 30.   James MacKillop

Fairbanks, Thaddeus (1796-1886), invented the platform scale in 1831. It replaced the large hooks and lifting apparatus necessary for weighing heavy loads.

Fairbanks was born in Brimfield, Mass. He suffered from poor health as a boy, and had little formal education. He established a small iron foundry in St. Johnsbury, Vt., in 1823, and, over a period of 60 years, made many improvements in such products as plows and stoves.   Robert P. Multhauf

Fairburn, William Armstrong. See Match (The First Matches).

Fairchild, David Grandison (1869-1954), an American botanist and explorer, brought more than 200,000 species of plants to the United States. He helped found the Section of Foreign Seed and Plant Introduction in the U.S. Department of Agriculture, and directed that section from 1906 to 1928. He established the Fairchild Tropical Garden, 12 miles (19 kilometers) south of Miami, Fla., in 1938. It became the largest botanical garden in the United States. Fairchild wrote such books as *Garden Islands of the Great East* and *The World Grows Round My Door.*

Fairchild was born in Lansing, Mich. He studied at Kansas State and Iowa State colleges, and at Rutgers University.   C. B. Baker

Fairchild, Sherman Mills (1896-1971), an American inventor and businessman, was called the "father of aerial mapping photography." He invented many cameras and an automatic photoengraver. Fairchild invented the Fairchild Flight Analyzer Camera in 1953. It was the first camera to take pictures without distortion in a continuous sequence of action. It has been used to track guided missiles and to study the take-offs and landings of missiles and planes.

Fairchild developed the FC-1 and FC-2 planes, the first to have enclosed cockpits. He built the C-119 transport plane so that equipment could be rolled in or out of its rear cargo doors. He also developed a radio compass and hydraulic landing gear. Fairchild was born in Oneonta, N.Y.   R. E. Westmeyer

Fairfield, Cicily Isabel. See West, Dame Rebecca.

Fairless, Benjamin Franklin (1890-1962), was an American industrialist. He was president of U.S. Steel Corporation from 1938 to 1953 and chairman of the board from 1952 to 1955. He held several positions with the American Iron and Steel Institute and served as its president from 1955 until his death. Fairless received the Bessemer Medal in 1951 for distinguished service to the iron and steel industry. He was born Benjamin F. Williams in Pigeon Run, Ohio. He took the name Fairless from an uncle who adopted him. He graduated from Ohio Northern University.   W. H. Baughn

Detail of an oil painting on canvas (1847) by Sir Joseph Noel Paton; National Gallery of Scotland (Granger Collection)

The king and queen of the fairies were named Oberon and Titania in many tales. William Shakespeare featured them in his comedy *A Midsummer Night's Dream.*

Detail of a pen and ink drawing (1891) by Henry Justice Ford (Granger Collection)

Rumpelstiltskin was a wicked fairy in German folklore. He spun gold from straw for a girl in exchange for her promise to give him her first child after she married a king. In this picture, Rumpelstiltskin arrives to collect his debt from the girl.

Fairy is an imaginary creature that appears in the folklore of Western Europe. Fairies have magic powers, which they use to perform both good and bad deeds. Fairies are usually helpful, but they often behave mischievously and occasionally act cruelly.

There are several kinds of fairies, and each lives in a certain area. For example, *brownies, buccas,* and *pixies* live in England; *goblins* in France; *kobolds* and *nixes* in Germany; and *elves* and *trolls* in the Scandinavian countries. Although the word *fairy* generally refers to various characters in Western European folklore, fairylike creatures exist in the folklore of many other parts of the world. Hawaiian folklore includes stories about dwarfs called *Menehune,* who work at night. Japanese folk stories tell of a water demon known as the *kappa.*

Fairies make themselves invisible to human beings. However, some people have the power to see fairies and the places where they live. Sometimes fairies become visible to a person who steps into a *fairy ring.* Fairy rings are dark green circles found in a field or meadow. Fairies enjoy dancing and use fairy rings as dancing places.

Fairies appear in two kinds of folk stories—*legends* and *fairy tales.* Legends take place in the real world, and fairy tales occur in some imaginary land. Legends are told as true stories, but fairy tales are told as fiction. Actually, fairies appear in few fairy tales. Most stories about fairies are really legends.

A number of beliefs and stories about fairies have been popular for hundreds of years. For example, many children believe that the *sandman* comes each night and puts "sleepy dust" in their eyes to help them sleep. American children especially like the *tooth fairy.* After losing a baby tooth, a child puts it under a pillow or in a glass of water. During the night, while the youngster is asleep, the tooth fairy takes the tooth and leaves money. The *bogeyman,* an evil fairy, kidnaps boys and girls who leave home without permission. The *bogey beast,* also called the *bug-a-boo,* carries off children who have been naughty.

No one knows how the belief in fairies began. In some stories, fairies were angels who were forced to leave heaven because of some wrongdoing. In other stories, fairies were spirits of the dead. Some scholars believe that fairies began as ancient nature spirits, such as the spirits of mountains, streams, and trees. Many stories about fairies represent attempts to explain various happenings. For example, if a cow goes dry for no apparent reason, a farmer may blame fairies for stealing her milk.

What fairies look like. Fairies vary in size, but the majority of them are smaller than adult human beings. Most fairies have various human features. Some fairies, including pixies, have great beauty. Other fairies have misshapen faces or deformed bodies. For example, trolls are short, ugly men with crooked noses and humped backs. Leprechauns are wrinkled little men. The *banshees,* who live in Ireland and Scotland, have long, streaming hair, and their eyes are fiery red from continual crying. Many fairies wear green or white clothing with red caps. Brownies usually wear brown cloaks and hoods.

Where fairies live. Fairies may live alone or in a large group. The banshee is an example of a fairy that lives alone. In Scotland, she can be heard wailing by a river as she washes the clothes of a person who soon will die. In Ireland, banshees often live near a particular family. The sound of a wailing banshee means that someone in the family will soon die.

Large groups of fairies live in fairyland, a fairy society with its own government and territory. In most stories, a king and queen rule fairyland, with the queen having the most power. Queen Mab is a famous fairy queen in Irish folklore. Oberon is king of the fairies in many legends. Fairyland may be under the earth, inside a hollow hill, or beneath a lake. The entrance may be a door in a hill or under the roots of trees.

Life in fairyland closely resembles life in the human world. Fairies work, marry, and have children. But time passes extremely slowly in fairyland, and so there is no old age or death. Many legends describe the difference between time in fairyland and in the human world. In one legend, a man spends what he believes is one night in fairyland. But after he returns to his home, he discovers that hundreds of years have passed—and no one remembers him.

In fairyland, fairies often have trouble giving birth. A common type of fairy legend tells how fairies kidnap a human woman and take her to fairyland to help deliver a baby. The fairies blindfold the woman before she enters and leaves fairyland so that the entrance to the fairy society will remain secret. Fairies nearly always pay the woman well for her help.

Fairies and human beings. People and fairies sometimes marry. A man might go to fairyland to live with his bride, or he might bring his fairy wife back to his home. In many stories, the human being must follow strict rules to remain married to a fairy. For example, a human husband must never scold or strike his fairy wife or refer to her being a fairy. If he does, the fairy immediately returns to fairyland.

Fairies often aid people in various ways. They might help with the housework or with such farmwork as reaping and threshing. In some cases, a person is not allowed to thank the fairy, to offer it gifts, or even to watch it work. If the person breaks one of these rules, the fairy runs away and never returns.

Sometimes fairies reward people for doing them a favor. According to one story, a farmer who mends a fairy oven or chair will receive delicious food in return. Grateful fairies also may leave money for people who have treated them well.

However, fairies are not always helpful and kind. They may steal grain or lead travelers astray. Occasionally, fairies commit cruel acts. In one legend, a woman helps deliver a fairy baby. As she puts some magic ointment on the baby's eye, she accidentally rubs some on one of her own eyes. The ointment enables her to see fairies who are normally invisible to human beings. Later, the woman sees a fairy in a market place and speaks to him. The fairy asks which eye the woman sees him with. After she tells him, he blinds her in that eye.

Fairies sometimes try to trick women into caring for fairy babies. The fairies may exchange their babies, called *changelings,* for healthy newborn human infants. Usually a human mother can see that a changeling has been substituted for her child because the fairy baby has some ugly physical feature or habit. If the mother threatens to burn the changeling, it may leave and give back the woman's own child.

Many people believe in fairies and have developed ways to win their favor or to protect themselves from evil ones. Fairies love milk, and so people may pour milk into the ground for them. Parents may hang an open pair of scissors over a child's crib as a charm to prevent fairies from stealing the infant. Parents also may place a cross or a container of holy water beside the baby for protection. If travelers lose their way because of what they believe is a fairy's spell, they try to break the spell by turning a piece of their clothing inside out and burning it.

Fairies in literature. For hundreds of years, authors have written about fairies in novels, plays, and stories. The English playwright William Shakespeare used fairies as major characters in his comedy *A Midsummer Night's Dream.* This play includes Oberon and Titania, the king and queen of the fairies, and the mischievous fairy Puck. Shakespeare may have based Puck on any of several fairies from British folklore, including *Pooka* of Ireland, *Pwca* of Wales, and *Robin Goodfellow* of England. A fairy named Ariel is an important character in Shakespeare's *The Tempest.* The playwright also wrote a famous description of Queen Mab in *Romeo and Juliet.*

In 1697, the French author Charles Perrault published a collection of folk stories called *Tales of Mother Goose.* This book included some stories that are still popular. In one tale, Cinderella's fairy godmother changes a pumpkin into a carriage and mice into horses—and changes them back again. In another story, an evil fairy condemns Sleeping Beauty to death. But a good fairy changes the curse from death to sleep, so a handsome prince can awaken the girl with a kiss.

In the early 1800's, two German scholars, the brothers Jakob and Wilhelm Grimm, published a collection of folk stories called *Grimm's Fairy Tales.* Only a few of the stories include fairies. One tale, "Rumpelstiltskin," tells of a fairy who spins gold from straw.

Some authors have made up their own stories about fairies. The Danish writer Hans Christian Andersen wrote several volumes of stories from 1835 until his death in 1875. In one tale, "Little Tiny," the main character springs from a magic flower. The Italian author Carlo Collodi wrote *Pinocchio* (1883), a famous children's novel that has a fairy character. *Peter Pan* (1904), a popular children's play by the English writer Sir James M. Barrie, has a number of fairies, including one of the main characters.

The English author J. R. R. Tolkien included fairies and other imaginary creatures in his works. In *The Hobbit* (1937) and the three-volume *The Lord of the Rings* (1954-1955), Tolkien described a race of wise and gifted elves. They live in the Undying Lands, where nothing ever ages or dies.   Alan Dundes

Related articles in *World Book* include:

Andersen, Hans Christian	Gremlin
Brownie	Grimm's Fairy Tales
Elf	Nix
Folklore	

For a list of collections of fairy tales, see **Literature for children** (Books to read [Folk literature—Fairy tales]).

Fairy Falls is a waterfall in Mount Rainier National Park in western Washington. It stands 5,500 feet (1,676

meters) above sea level at the head of Stevens Canyon. Fairy Falls is 700 feet (213 meters) high. It is one of the highest U.S. waterfalls.   Wallace E. Akin

Fairy tale. See Fairy.

Faisal, FY suhl, also spelled Feisal, is the name of two kings of Iraq, grandfather and grandson. They were members of the Hashemite family, which traced its descent from the Prophet Muhammad (see **Muhammad**).

Faisal I (1885-1933) became the first king of Iraq after the British took Iraq from the Ottoman Empire during World War I. He was elected king in 1921, while the country was a British mandate under the League of Nations. Faisal and the British cooperated in overthrowing the ruling Ottoman Turks during the war. The famed Lawrence of Arabia was a close friend of Faisal. Under Faisal's rule, Iraq gained independence in 1932.

Faisal II (1935-1958) became king in 1939 at the age of three when his father, Ghazi I, was killed in an automobile accident. His uncle, Prince Abdul Ilah, ruled Iraq as regent during Faisal's youth. Faisal II began his reign on May 2, 1953. He and his uncle were killed by revolutionaries on July 14, 1958.   Sydney N. Fisher

See also Iraq (History).

Faisal, FY suhl, also spelled Feisal (1906?-1975), was king of Saudi Arabia from 1964 to 1975. He became an important world leader because of his control over Saudi Arabia's vast oil resources. In 1975, Faisal was assassinated by one of his nephews.

Faisal used government profits from oil for such things as industrialization projects and the expansion of public education in Saudi Arabia. During the early 1970's, he brought about an oil embargo against the United States, the Netherlands, and other nations friendly to Israel. He also favored sharp price increases for petroleum exports.

Faisal ibn Abdul Aziz al Faisal al Saud was born in Riyadh. He was crown prince from 1953 to 1964, and served as prime minister from 1953 to 1960 and from 1962 to 1964 when his brother Saud was king of Saudi Arabia.   Frank Tachau

See also **Saudi Arabia** (History).

Faith. See Religion.

Fakir, fuh KIHR or FAY kuhr, is a Muslim or Hindu man who practices extreme self-denial as part of his religion. Fakir is an Arabic word meaning poor, especially poor in the sight of God. Fakirs usually live on charity and spend most of their lives in religious contemplation. Some fakirs can actually perform such feats of will power as walking on hot coals. But they also frequently practice deception. Some fakirs live in religious communities. Others wander about alone. People whose way of life resembles that of fakirs include Muslim dervishes and Hindu yogis.   Richard C. Martin

See also **Asceticism; Dervish; Yoga.**

Falange Española, FAY lanj, or fah LAHNG hay, ehs pahn YOH lah, also called Spanish Phalanx, was the only legal political party in Spain under dictator Francisco Franco. The Falange Española was founded in 1933 as a fascist group that attempted to overthrow the republic through violence. José Antonio Primo de Rivera, son of former dictator Miguel Primo de Rivera, founded the party. Falangists supported Franco during the Spanish Civil War. In 1937, Franco took control of the party. After 1945, the party was known as the National Movement. In 1977, after Franco's death, the democratic government of Spain abolished it.   Stanley G. Payne

Falcon is a type of bird closely related to hawks. Falcons are found in a variety of habitats throughout the world. They live in grasslands, forests, deserts, and Arctic tundras, and along seacoasts. Falcons probably first appeared thousands of years ago in the grasslands of Africa. Today, there are about 40 species, about half of them found in Africa. The best-known North American species include the American kestrel, the peregrine falcon, and the gyrfalcon.

Like hawks, falcons have a hooked beak and powerful feet with strong claws. Falcons differ from hawks in having dark eyes, long, pointed wings that curve back in a sickle shape, and beaks that have a "tooth" on each side. Most measure from 8 to 24 inches (20 to 60 centimeters) long. Females are larger than males.

Falcons are exceptionally powerful fliers. They often make spectacular stoops (steep descents) from great heights to capture prey. They use their feet to either grasp or strike at their prey. Unlike hawks, falcons kill the prey with a powerful bite to the head or neck. Hawks normally kill prey with their claws.

Falcons do not build nests. Females lay their eggs on the ground, on rocky ledges, in abandoned nests, or in holes in trees, cliffs, or even buildings. They usually lay three to five eggs that are buff or whitish in color and heavily marked with brown, red, or purple spots or blotches. In most species, the female incubates (sits on and warms) the eggs, with regular help from the male. Most falcon eggs require about 30 days of incubation. For the first few weeks after the young have hatched, the male provides nearly all the food for the family. Many falcons die during the first year of life. The falcons that survive the first year typically live for 10 years or more.

The American kestrel is the smallest and most common North American falcon. The adult measures about 8 inches (20 centimeters) long. American kestrels range from Alaska through South America. They live in grasslands, woodlands, and even cities. The male has a reddish-brown back and tail and grayish-blue wings. The wings of the female are brown.

American kestrels prey on insects, lizards, and mice, and on other birds. American kestrels typically hunt their prey from perches. However, on windy days, they may hover (stay in one place) in the air while hunting. In some areas, American kestrels migrate south for the winter.

The peregrine falcon is one of nature's flying marvels. It can stoop for prey at a speed of nearly 200 miles (320 kilometers) per hour. This falcon measures up to 20 inches (50 centimeters) long. It is dark blue or bluish-gray above and has white to reddish underparts marked with blackish-brown bars. Peregrine falcons live along cliffs near seacoasts, rivers, and lakes, or in the mountains. They once were found throughout most of the world but are now rare or absent in many areas. Scientists have reintroduced peregrine falcons into many of their present and former habitats, including a number of large cities. These falcons feed chiefly on other birds.

The gyrfalcon is the largest species of falcon. The gyrfalcon grows to a length of 2 feet (61 centimeters). It lives in Arctic regions of North America, Europe, and

Merlin
Falco columbarius
Nests in northern North America, winters in the Southern United States, Mexico, and South America
Body length: 12 inches (30 centimeters)

WORLD BOOK illustration by John F. Eggert

Aplomado falcon
Falco femoralis
Found in Central and South America and the extreme Southwestern United States
Body length: 16 inches (41 centimeters)

American kestrel
Falco sparverius
Found throughout the Western Hemisphere
Body length: 10 inches (25 centimeters)

Gyrfalcon
Falco rusticolus
Found near the Arctic Circle
Body length: 24 inches (61 centimeters)

WORLD BOOK illustrations, except for the Merlin, by Walter Linsenmaier

© Ron Austing, Photo Researchers

Peregrine-gyrfalcon hybrids, like the one above, are bred for the sport of falconry. Both peregrines and gyrfalcons are prized for their speed and their breathtaking dives after prey.

Asia. Most gyrfalcons have white or gray coloring.

Other North American falcons include the *merlin,* the *prairie falcon,* and the *Aplomado falcon.* The merlin lives in open woodlands and other open areas, and along coastal areas, of northern North America. It migrates to the Southern United States, Mexico, and South America for the winter. The prairie falcon inhabits deserts or dry grasslands in western North America. The Aplomado falcon is found in high deserts and tropical

Ron Austing

The peregrine falcon dives at speeds close to 200 miles (320 kilometers) per hour. This photo shows a peregrine falcon that has been trained to hunt. The trainer keeps the bird from escaping by holding the *jesses* (straps) hanging from its legs.

lowlands. Its range extends from South America north to the extreme Southwestern United States, where it is extremely rare.

Scientific classification. True falcons belong to the family Falconidae. They make up the genus *Falco.* The American kestrel is *F. sparverius;* the peregrine falcon, *F. peregrinus;* and the gyrfalcon, *F. rusticolus.*   Thomas G. Balgooyen

See also **Bird** (picture: Interesting facts about birds; How birds see); **Falconry; Hawk; Kestrel.**

Falconry, once the "sport of kings," is the art of training falcons, hawks, or eagles to hunt game. A *falconer* is a person who hunts with trained birds of prey.

Training the birds requires patience and persistence. Basically, a hunting bird must be tamed, or "manned," and taught to return to the falconer's fist or to a lure. Special devices aid the falconer. A hood covers the eyes of the bird, keeping it calm. Small bells or radio transmitters are placed on the bird to help locate it when lost. Leg straps called *jesses* restrict the bird's movement when it is on the falconer's hand or perch. A heavy glove protects the falconer's hand from the bird's claws.

The ancient Chinese and the ancient Persians independently began the sport of falconry more than 3,000 years ago. Falconry flourished in Europe during the Middle Ages. Each social class was assigned a certain falcon or hawk to fly as a symbol of rank. Kings flew majestic gyrfalcons and serfs flew goshawks. In the 1700's, the wide use of firearms nearly brought an end to falconry. The sport, however, continues to attract many followers, especially in North America, Europe, and the Middle East. Because of successful breeding programs, falconry has entered a new era in which the domesticated ancestries of hawks and falcons are becoming established.   Thomas G. Balgooyen

Falkland Islands, *FAWK lund,* make up a dependency of Great Britain in the South Atlantic Ocean. The islands lie about 320 miles (515 kilometers) east of the southern coast of Argentina (see **South America** [political map]). They form the southernmost part of the British Empire outside the British Antarctic Territory. Argentina also claims ownership of the Falkland Islands. Argentina calls the islands the *Islas Malvinas.*

The dependency includes two large islands, East and West Falkland, and about 200 smaller ones. East Falkland covers 2,580 square miles (6,682 square kilometers) and West Falkland covers 2,038 square miles (5,278 square kilometers). All the islands together have a coastline of 610 miles (982 kilometers). The climate is damp and cool. Strong winds limit the growth of trees on the islands.

Most of the approximately 2,000 inhabitants are of British origin. About half the people live in Stanley, the capital and chief town. Stanley is on East Falkland Island. The Falkland Islands' main source of income comes from the sale of fishing licenses to foreign fishing fleets. Many of the islanders raise sheep and export wool. The sale of postage stamps and coins, primarily to collectors, also contributes to the economy.

A governor rules the dependency, aided by an executive and legislative council. The government provides schools which children must attend. Traveling teachers instruct children in isolated settlements.

The English explorer John Davis sighted the Falklands in 1592. British Captain John Strong first landed on the islands in 1690. He named them for Viscount Falkland, the British treasurer of the navy. France, Spain, and Argentina later laid claim to the islands. British rule was established in the islands in 1833, and the Falklands are now an important British base. The British won a great naval victory over Germany near the Falklands in 1914.

Argentina has continued to claim the Falkland Islands. In April 1982, Argentine troops invaded and occupied the islands. Britain responded by sending troops, ships, and planes to the Falklands. Air, sea, and land battles broke out between Argentina and Britain. The Argentine forces surrendered in June 1982.

A vast area of islands and ocean became dependencies of Britain in 1908. Known as the Falkland Island Dependencies, they were administered by the Falkland Islands. The main islands included South Orkney, South Shetland, South Georgia, and South Sandwich. The South Orkney and South Shetland island groups became part of the British Antarctic Territory in 1962. In 1985, the islands of South Georgia and South Sandwich became the British dependency of South Georgia and the South Sandwich Islands.   Richard W. Wilkie

Fall. See Autumn.

Fall, Albert B. See Harding, Warren G. (Government scandals); Teapot Dome.

Fall line is a series of waterfalls and rapids formed where hard rock meets softer rock. The falls and rapids develop as erosion by a river or stream wears away some of the softer rock, creating a ledge over which the water flows. In the Eastern United States, a Fall Line stretches from southern New York to Alabama. It formed as water carried away some of the soft sediments of the Atlantic Coastal Plain, leaving behind the harder rocks of

WORLD BOOK map

The Fall Line in the Eastern United States extends from New Jersey to Alabama. A series of waterfalls lies along the Fall Line and provides electric power to many cities on the line.

the Piedmont—the plateau east of the Appalachian Mountains. Nearly every stream on the Fall Line has rapids or waterfalls.

The Fall Line of the Eastern United States is a great source of electric power. The falling water can be used to turn turbines to generate electricity. Also, the Fall Line generally marks the farthest point inland a ship can go. For these reasons, many important cities are found along the Fall Line.   Donald F. Eschman

See also **Piedmont Region; Plain; Waterfall.**

Fall River (pop. 92,574; met. area pop. 157,222) is an industrial city in southeastern Massachusetts. It lies in a hilly area where the Taunton River flows into Mount Hope Bay. For location, see **Massachusetts** (political map). The Quequechan River flows through the city. The city's name comes from *Falling Water*, the translation of Quequechan, an Indian name.

From the 1870's until the 1920's, Fall River was the largest center in the United States for the manufacture of cotton textiles. The number of mills declined sharply after 1929. However, garment making and the finishing of textile fabrics are still important industries in Fall River (see **Textile** [Finishing the fabric]). Other industries include the manufacture of rubber products, plastics, and textile machinery.

Many granite buildings stand along the Quequechan River in the city. Formerly cotton mills, they now house various industries. The World War II battleship U.S.S. *Massachusetts*, docked in Battleship Cove in Mount Hope Bay, is a major tourist attraction.

Settlers from Plymouth Colony purchased part of what is now Fall River from the Wampanoag Indians in 1659. In the Battle of Fall River, fought in 1778 during the Revolutionary War, the townspeople put up a strong defense against a British force. The settlement was incorporated as a town in 1803. From 1804 to 1834, the town was called Troy. The name was changed to Fall River in 1834. It was the site of the famous Lizzie Borden murder trial in 1893 (see **Borden, Lizzie**). Fall River has a mayor-council form of government.   Herman P. Mello

Falla, *FAH yuh* or *FAH lyah*, **Manuel de,** *mah NWEHL deh* (1876-1946), was a Spanish composer who gained international recognition for his success in developing a modern Spanish style of music. He based many of his compositions on Spanish folklore, folk music, and literary traditions. His best-known work, the music for the ballet *The Three-Cornered Hat* (1919), is based on popular folk music.

Falla's opera *La Vida Breve* won a contest for the best opera by a Spanish composer in 1905, but it was not performed until 1913. His other important works include the music for the ballet *El Amor Brujo* (1915), with its famous "Ritual Fire Dance," and *Nights in the Gardens of Spain* (1916), a composition for piano and orchestra. Falla's puppet opera *Master Peter's Puppet Show* (1923) was based on an episode from the famous Spanish novel *Don Quixote. Fantasia Bética* (1920) is his major work for solo piano. Falla was born in Cádiz. He lived in Argentina from 1939 until his death.   Vincent McDermott

Fallacy is an error in reasoning. Many fallacies appear persuasive and may lead people to false conclusions. *Logicians* (persons who study logic) divide fallacies into two main groups, *formal* and *informal.*

A formal fallacy is an argument which has a faulty

structure or form. The following incorrect argument is an example of a formal fallacy: Since only seniors have their pictures in the book, and since John is a senior, then John's picture is in the book.

Informal fallacies are errors other than violations of the rules of formal logic. Logicians disagree about the number and kinds of informal fallacies. One informal fallacy, called *hasty generalization*, is the assumption that what is true of a few cases is true in general. The assumption that what is true of parts is also true of the whole is a fallacy based on a *presumption* or *silent assumption*. A fallacy of *relevance* is an argument in which the truth of the conclusion does not depend on the claims made by the premises.   Morton L. Schagrin

See also **Logic**.

Fallen Timbers, Battle of. See **Indian wars** (Other Midwestern conflicts); **Indiana** (Territorial days); **Wayne, Anthony**.

Falling bodies, Law of. Several laws, or rules, tell what an object does when it is allowed to fall to the ground without anything stopping it. These are called the laws of falling bodies. From the time of Aristotle to the end of the 1500's, people believed that if two bodies of different mass were dropped from the same height at the same time, the heavier one would hit the ground first. The great Italian scientist Galileo did not believe this was true. He reasoned that if two bricks of the same mass fall at the same speed, side by side, they ought to fall at the same speed even when cemented together. Therefore, a single brick would fall just as fast as the heavier two bricks cemented together.

Other scientists disagreed with Galileo. According to a story that probably is not true, he proved his theory about 1590 in an experiment at the famous Leaning Tower of Pisa. Galileo is supposed to have gone to the top of the tower with two cannon balls, one large and the other small. He dropped them both at the same instant, and they reached the ground at nearly the same time. There was a small difference, but not nearly so great as the difference between their weights. Galileo concluded that it was the resistance of the air which caused the difference in time of fall between the two cannon balls. Whether or not Galileo actually conducted

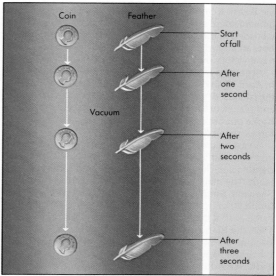

WORLD BOOK diagram by Laura Lee Lizak

Bodies falling freely in a vacuum descend at the same speed regardless of their size, shape, or weight. But different objects falling through air may descend at different speeds. This is because objects of different shape meet different amounts of air resistance as they fall.

this experiment, his reasoning about the result was correct.

The dispute was not finally settled until the air pump was invented about 1650. Then it was shown that if the air were pumped from a long tube, and a feather and a coin were dropped down the tube at the same instant, they would fall side by side and reach the bottom together. The force which draws bodies toward the earth is called *gravity* (see **Gravitation**).

It has been found that this force of gravity acts on all bodies alike, regardless of shape, size, or density. The earth attracts bodies toward its center, so all bodies fall in a direct line toward that point. This is the direction called *down*, and it is exactly perpendicular to the surface of still water.

There are three things to consider in studying the laws of falling bodies. One is the *distance* the body travels when it falls. The second is its *velocity*, or speed. The third is its *acceleration*, the rate at which its speed increases as it falls (see **Motion** [Velocity and acceleration]). The abbreviations of these three terms are d, v, and a.

The longer a freely falling body falls, the *faster* it travels. The first law of falling bodies says that, under the influence of gravity alone, all bodies fall with equal acceleration. If the bodies start from rest, and their velocity increases at the same rate, they fall at the same velocity.

Actually, when various kinds of bodies fall through the air, they fall at different velocities. The air *resists* the falling bodies, so they are not falling under the influence of gravity alone. You can test this resistance by dropping two sheets of newspaper, one unfolded and the other crushed into a ball. Both pieces have the same weight, so they give a perfect illustration that the difference of *shape* and not of *mass* causes the difference in

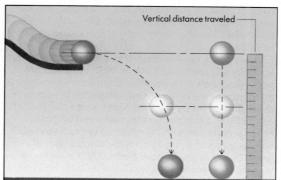

WORLD BOOK diagram by Laura Lee Lizak

Falling bodies descend at the same rate, regardless of horizontal motion, when their fall is caused by gravity. Although the blue ball travels farther than the red ball, they both hit the ground at the same time. The blue ball's horizontal motion, caused by the chute, does not affect its vertical speed.

the speed at which various kinds of bodies fall.

The acceleration of a falling body is the same for each second. There are no spurts in its "pickup," and its fall is described as *uniformly accelerated* motion. This is true if gravity is the only force acting on the body. Gravity acting on a body that falls from rest *increases* its velocity during *each* second of fall by the same amount of velocity that the body had at the end of its *first* second of fall. The velocity at the end of the first second is 32.16 feet (9.802 meters) per second (at the latitude of New York City). The speed of the body increases at a rate of 32.16 feet per second for each second it falls. The body's acceleration is expressed as *32.16 feet per second per second.* This figure is used in most calculations.

At the end of the 1st second $v = (0(\text{rest})+32.16) =$ 32.16 feet a second.
At the end of the 2nd second $v = (32.16+32.16) =$ 64.32 feet a second.
At the end of the 3rd second $v = (64.32+32.16) =$ 96.48 feet a second.
At the end of the 4th second $v = (96.48+32.16) =$ 128.64 feet a second.

A simple formula to get the velocity of a falling body at the end of any second is to multiply 32.16 feet per second per second by the number of seconds the body has fallen.

There is also a simple formula to find the distance a body falls in a given second. Multiply the distance it falls the first second by twice the total number of seconds, minus 1. Since the distance fallen during the first second is always 16.08 feet (4.901 meters), the distance fallen during the third second is $[(2 \times 3)-1] \times 16.08 = 80.40$. The distance fallen during the fourth second equals $[(2 \times 4)-1] \times 16.08 = 112.56$.

By adding the distance during any given second to the distances for all the preceding seconds, you can find the total distance traveled at the end of that given second. For instance, at the end of the third second, a body has fallen $16.08 + 48.24 + 80.40$ feet, which adds up to 144.72 feet. Now 144.72 can also be divided up this way: $3 \times 3 \times 16.08$. The total distance fallen in 4 seconds, 257.28 feet, can be divided this way: $4 \times 4 \times 16.08$. So a shorter formula has been worked out which says that the distance a falling body travels in a given time is 16.08 times the square of the number of seconds.

The laws just stated can be written in the form of equations. For velocity at the end of any second:

$$v = 32.16 \times t$$

For distance traveled during any second:

$$d = \left(\frac{32.16}{2}\right) \times (2t-1) = 16.08 \times (2t-1)$$

For total distance traveled at the end of any second:

$$d = \left(\frac{32.16}{2}\right) \times t^2 = 16.08 \times t^2$$

These three equations are true not only for falling bodies, but for any bodies that have uniformly accelerated motion. Any other acceleration, *a*, can be substituted in place of 32.16 feet per second per second. Then we are able to use the more general equations: $v=at$, and $d=\frac{1}{2}at^2$.   Gregory Benford

Falling sickness is another name for epilepsy. See Epilepsy.

Falling star. See Meteor.

Fallout is radioactive material that settles over the earth's surface following a nuclear explosion in the atmosphere. It consists of atoms known as *radioactive isotopes* or *radioisotopes.* These isotopes form from the *fission* (splitting) of uranium or plutonium in a nuclear weapon. Radioisotopes also form when radiation that results from the explosion causes other atoms nearby to become radioactive.

After the explosion, the radioisotopes in the air, on the ground, and in the bodies of human beings and other organisms *decay* (break down) into more stable isotopes. They do so by emitting radiation in the form of alpha particles, beta particles, and gamma rays. Exposure to large amounts of radiation can result in immediate sickness and even death. Exposure to radiation over longer periods can cause cancer and damage genes.

The testing of nuclear weapons in the atmosphere once produced large amounts of fallout. Today, fallout has been almost eliminated by underground testing. However, a serious accident in a nuclear reactor can release the same radioisotopes that occur in fallout. In 1986, an explosion and fire at the Chernobyl nuclear power plant in the Soviet Union released radioisotopes that scattered across the Western Hemisphere.

How fallout is produced. All nuclear explosions produce a giant fireball of intensely hot gases. Everything inside the fireball or in contact with it is *vaporized* (turned into a gas). When an explosion occurs close to the earth's surface, the fireball vaporizes soil, vegetation, and buildings. It then begins to rise, carrying the vaporized material with it. As the fireball rises, a low-pressure area forms beneath it. Air rushes in to fill this partial vacuum carrying along with it dust, dirt, and other small particles. Much of this debris may be lifted up through the atmosphere along with the fireball.

As the vaporized materials rise and cool, some of them condense into solid particles. Atoms of the various radioactive elements produced by the explosion cling to these particles. These radioisotopes eventually return to the earth as fallout. Fallout particles range in size from fine invisible dust to ash of snowflake size.

The fallout pattern. Fallout is described as either *local* or *distant,* depending on how far from the blast site it settles to the earth.

Local fallout consists of the larger and heavier particles that fall to earth within a few hundred miles or kilometers of the blast site. The time it takes for these particles to reach the earth, and the distance they travel from the blast site depend on a number of factors. These factors include (1) their size and composition, (2) the altitude the particles reach before they begin to fall, (3) the pattern of the winds that carry them, (4) the latitude at which the explosion takes place, and (5) the time of year. When a nuclear device explodes on the earth's surface, over half of the total fallout produced is local fallout.

Local fallout may settle over an irregularly shaped area, depending upon the winds that carry it. In general, the intensity of radiation within this area decreases as the distance from the blast site increases. But there may be *hot spots* (areas of intense radioactivity) scattered within the zone of fallout.

Distant fallout consists of fine radioactive material that may be scattered by winds to any part of the world. Winds traveling through the *troposphere,* the lowest

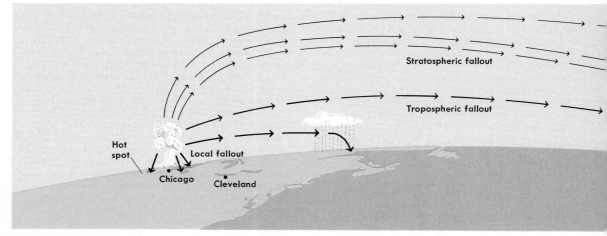

Fallout can be local or distant, depending on how far it is carried by the wind. *Local fallout* settles near the blast site. *Distant fallout* is carried by winds in two layers of the atmosphere—the troposphere and the stratosphere. Much of this high-altitude fallout may descend to the earth with rain, snow, and fog. But some of it may remain in the stratosphere for years before it settles.

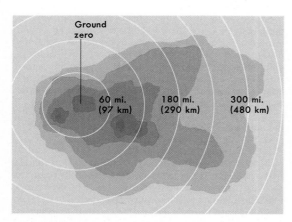

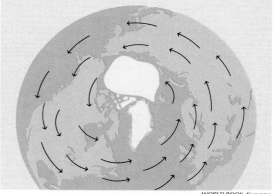

WORLD BOOK diagrams

Local fallout settles in an irregularly shaped pattern. The reddish areas in this diagram indicate relative strength of radiation from a 15-megaton blast. The darkest red areas are "hot spots."

Distant fallout may be scattered by winds in the stratosphere to any part of the world. The arrows show how fallout from a bomb blast in Chicago would be carried over northern Europe.

layer of the atmosphere, carry some distant fallout for periods of a few days to a few weeks. Winds near the earth's surface change their direction. But at about 50,000 feet (15,000 meters) in the upper troposphere, winds generally blow in an eastward direction. Fallout carried to this height circles the earth within a week or two. Most of the fallout returns to earth within a band around the globe near the latitude of the fallout's origin. Rain and other precipitation may carry it to the earth.

In the most powerful nuclear explosions, much of the fallout may rise to the *stratosphere,* the layer of atmosphere above the troposphere. There, fallout becomes widely scattered and may take from several months to several years to settle on the earth.

The fallout hazard. Fallout can be dangerous to plants, animals, and people because of the radioactive elements it contains (see **Radiation sickness**). These elements include about 200 isotopes of more than 30

chemical elements produced by a nuclear explosion.

The radioisotopes in fallout give off radiation for varying periods of time. Most fallout radioactivity dies off in a matter of hours or days. As a result, the radioactivity at the end of two weeks is only one-thousandth as strong as the radioactivity one hour after the nuclear explosion. But even at the end of two weeks, local fallout can be so intense that it remains a serious hazard. A few of the fallout elements continue to give off radiation over a long period. For example, the radioisotope strontium 90 loses half its radioactive strength every 28 years, and the radioisotope cesium 137 loses half its strength every 30 years (see **Radioactivity** [Half life]).

The possibility of nuclear war has caused people to think about the danger of local fallout. This type of fallout involves a twofold problem. First, there is the danger of radiation that is emitted by the radioactive debris on the ground. People can best protect themselves from

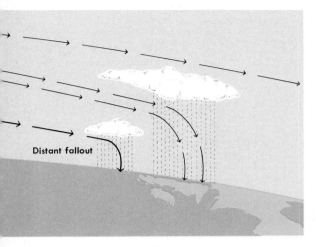

Distant fallout

this radiation by taking refuge in underground fallout shelters. For example, 3 feet (91 centimeters) of earth overhead will reduce the radiation's intensity to one-thousandth of its original intensity. See **Fallout shelter**.

Second, there is the danger that certain fallout elements may enter the human body through breathing and eating. For example, milk is a route by which the radioisotopes iodine 131 and strontium 90 enter the body. First, fallout descends on grass. Next, cows eat the grass. Some of the radioisotopes are then transferred to the cows' milk. Anyone who drinks the contaminated milk takes in iodine 131, which collects in the thyroid, and strontium 90, which is absorbed by the bones.

Foods are contaminated by the direct deposit of fallout on plants and by the slow uptake of radioisotopes in soil by the plants' roots. The behavior of radioisotopes in the environment depends partly on the chemical properties of the element. For example, bones in the body can absorb strontium-90 because strontium and calcium have certain similar chemical properties.

History. From the mid-1940's to the early 1960's, the United States, the Soviet Union, and a few other nations exploded many experimental nuclear weapons. As a result, distant fallout increased to alarming levels. In 1963, more than 100 nations, including the United States and the Soviet Union, signed a treaty that banned the testing of nuclear weapons everywhere but underground. Fallout then decreased greatly. China and France did not sign the treaty. They later stopped testing nuclear weapons aboveground.   B. G. Bennett

See also **Civil defense; Isotope; Nuclear weapon** (Residual nuclear radiation); **Radiation** (How radiation affects health).

Additional resources

Clayton, Bruce D. *Fallout Survival: A Guide to Radiological Defense.* Paladin Press, 1984.
Harwell, Mark A. *Nuclear Winter: The Human and Environmental Consequences of Nuclear War.* Springer-Verlag, 1984.
Miller, Richard L. *Under the Cloud: The Decades of Nuclear Testing.* Free Press, 1986.
Williams, Gene B. *Nuclear War, Nuclear Winter.* Watts, 1987.

Fallout shelter is a building or an underground area that protects people from fallout. A nuclear explosion scatters bits of radioactive material into the air. Within a

few hours, the fallout particles settle on an area of hundreds of square miles or kilometers. Fallout gives off radiation that can cause burns, illness, or even death. The particles of radioactive material could endanger almost everyone in the United States in the event of a nuclear attack.

People can protect themselves from fallout by taking shelter in a building made of thick layers of a heavy material, such as brick, concrete, or stone. Any such building blocks radiation and can serve as a fallout shelter. Underground areas, including mines and tunnels, also provide protection from fallout.

The United States government has designated many buildings and underground areas as public fallout shelters. Some families have their own fallout shelter. An emergency fallout shelter, which can be constructed quickly of heavy materials at hand, provides some protection from radiation.

The United States public fallout shelter program began in 1961. Civil defense agencies urge people without a public shelter nearby to build a home fallout shelter or to locate and improve protective areas already in their home. These agencies also provide instructions for building emergency shelters. The nation has thousands of public shelters and an unknown number of private ones.

Various agencies of the federal government have administered national programs concerned with the designation and construction of fallout shelters. These programs are now the responsibility of the Federal Emergency Management Agency (FEMA), an independent agency established in 1979. Public fallout shelters have also been established by the governments of many other countries. These countries include Canada, Denmark, Finland, the Soviet Union, Sweden, Switzerland, and West Germany.

Public shelters. The majority of public fallout shelters have been set up in the basement of apartment and office buildings, factories, schools, and other large

WORLD BOOK photo by Steinkamp/Ballogg
A black-and-yellow sign, such as the one shown above, marks the entrance to every public fallout shelter in the United States.

Kinds of home fallout shelters   These drawings show four types of fallout shelters that can be built in or near the home. The emergency shelter shown below probably would not provide complete protection from fallout, but it might block enough radiation to save lives. A permanent shelter, which provides better protection, can be built in a basement or outdoors—either above or below the ground.

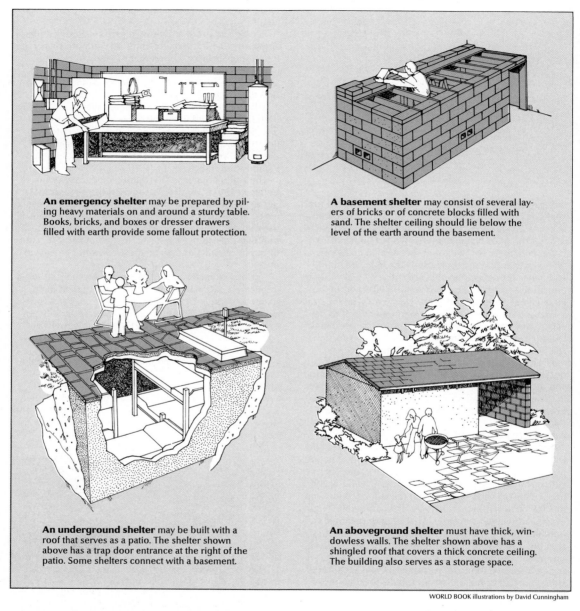

An emergency shelter may be prepared by piling heavy materials on and around a sturdy table. Books, bricks, and boxes or dresser drawers filled with earth provide some fallout protection.

A basement shelter may consist of several layers of bricks or of concrete blocks filled with sand. The shelter ceiling should lie below the level of the earth around the basement.

An underground shelter may be built with a roof that serves as a patio. The shelter shown above has a trap door entrance at the right of the patio. Some shelters connect with a basement.

An aboveground shelter must have thick, windowless walls. The shelter shown above has a shingled roof that covers a thick concrete ceiling. The building also serves as a storage space.

WORLD BOOK illustrations by David Cunningham

structures, or in windowless central areas aboveground. A number of such public fallout shelters consist of a subway-train tunnel or some other underground area. In the United States, every public fallout shelter is marked by a black and yellow sign. This sign appears near the entrance to the building or underground area in which the fallout shelter occurs.

Many public fallout shelters in the United States have radiation detection instruments and emergency medical and sanitation kits. Local civil defense agencies plan to make food, water, and other necessities available to people in public fallout shelters if nuclear war becomes likely. In some cases, people going to an unstocked shelter might be asked to bring food and other essential items. Civil defense agencies would supplement those supplies.

Most of the public fallout shelters in the United States are in cities. Suburban and rural areas have few public shelters. The government urges architects and engineers to design buildings that include public fallout shelter areas. In many cases, a building can be designed to provide such protection at little or no increase in the cost of construction.

Home shelters. A family may build its own home fallout shelter, or several families may share in constructing a shelter. A basement makes a good place for a home fallout shelter because the earth around the building helps block radiation. Two walls of a shelter could be provided by a windowless basement corner. Two more walls and a ceiling would complete the structure. A fallout shelter may also be built outside the home. Such a shelter may be aboveground or partly or completely underground. In most cases, an underground shelter provides the most protection.

A shelter can be built with any heavy construction material. For example, a basement shelter may consist of walls and ceiling made of solid concrete 8 inches (20 centimeters) thick, brick 10 inches (25 centimeters) thick, or wood 32 inches (81 centimeters) thick. An aboveground outdoor shelter would require walls of solid concrete about 20 inches (50 centimeters) thick and a ceiling of the same material about 8 inches (20 centimeters) thick. An underground outdoor shelter should have at least 8 inches (20 centimeters) of concrete or 14 inches (35 centimeters) of earth above it. Any additional thickness improves the protection provided by the shelter.

Any fallout shelter should have at least 10 square feet (0.9 square meter) of floor space for each person who uses it. It also should have a drain, an electrical outlet, and adequate ventilation. An underground shelter should have a mechanical blower to provide fresh air. An aboveground shelter or a basement shelter can be ventilated by leaving an open doorway. But a wall must be built just outside the doorway and parallel to it. This wall would help keep fallout and radiation from entering the doorway.

A home shelter should be stocked with a two-week supply of food and water. Equipment and supplies for medical, sanitation, and personal hygiene needs must also be provided. A battery-powered radio is necessary to receive information and instructions from civil defense officials. An outside antenna may have to be installed to provide good radio reception in the fallout shelter.

Other important supplies for a shelter include batteries, bedding, clothing, fire-fighting equipment, flashlights, tools, and eating utensils. If space permits, various items may be provided to make shelter life more pleasant. They include reading and writing materials, toys and games, and nonessential foods.

Plans for various kinds of home shelters may be obtained from the Federal Emergency Management Agency, Washington, DC 20472. Instructions are also available for building an emergency shelter in a few hours.

Emergency shelters. Most emergency shelters provide less protection from fallout than do permanent shelters. But an emergency shelter may block enough radiation to save lives. Such a shelter may be built if better protection is not available, and if fallout will not reach a community for at least several hours.

An emergency shelter should be in a basement or storm cellar if possible. Otherwise, an emergency shelter can be built in an inner room of a building. First, one or more large, sturdy tables are moved to the area where the shelter is to be constructed. Next, various heavy materials are piled on and around the tables as a shield against radiation. An opening is left among the piles of shielding materials to serve as the doorway of the shelter. Such materials might include books and magazines, bricks, firewood and lumber, metal appliances, paving stones from a patio, and containers filled with earth or gravel. The containers could be boxes, strong sacks, or even dresser drawers. After the shelter has been stocked with water and other supplies, the doorway should be blocked from the inside with some of the shielding materials.

Living in a shelter need not be difficult if the proper preparations have been made and if reasonable rules of conduct are followed. The daily routine in the shelter must be supervised, and everyone should share in such tasks as preparing food and keeping the shelter clean. Food and water should be rationed carefully, and cleanliness maintained at all times. Someone in the shelter should know how to administer first aid. Fire must be guarded against, and gasoline or other explosive fuels should not be used for cooking or heating. If a mechanical blower ventilates the shelter, it should be operated on a regular schedule.

Every person should stay in the shelter until radio broadcasts announce that radiation in the area has decreased to a safe level. Fallout loses much of its radioactivity fairly quickly. In most areas, people would have to remain in the shelter for only two or three days. They then could go outside safely, at least for short periods. Even in areas of heavy fallout, people could probably leave their shelter after a week or two to perform emergency tasks. Such tasks would include obtaining food or medical care.

Critically reviewed by the Federal Emergency Management Agency

See also **Civil defense; Fallout; Radiation sickness.**

Falls. See Waterfall.

Falls of Saint Anthony are waterfalls in the upper Mississippi River. They were sighted by Father Louis Hennepin in 1680 on the site of present Minneapolis. They are 49 feet (15 meters) high. See also **Hennepin, Louis; Minneapolis.**

False imprisonment is any unlawful restraint of a person, whether by confinement in a jail or elsewhere, by threats, or by force. An unlawful arrest, called a *false arrest,* is a form of false imprisonment. But false imprisonment also may follow a legal arrest. False imprisonment is an offense against both the victim and the state. The victim may sue for damages, charge the offender with a crime, or both.   James O. Finckenauer

False teeth. See Dentistry (Prosthodontics).

Falstaff, Sir John. See Shakespeare, William (*Henry IV;* picture; *The Merry Wives of Windsor*).

Fame, Hall of. See Hall of Fame; Baseball (table: National Baseball Hall of Fame).

Family, in biology, is a unit of scientific classification. Organisms are classified in seven major groups called kingdoms, phyla, classes, orders, families, genera, and species. Members of a family are more closely related than members of an order, but not so closely related as members of a genus. See also **Classification, Scientific** (table).   Theodore J. Crovello

A single-parent American family

Jonathan T. Wright, Bruce Coleman Inc.

A nuclear Soviet family

Doug Wilson, Black Star

U.S. Department of Agriculture

A childless Chinese couple

Edward S. Ross

An extended Namibian family

People of all known cultures live in family groups. Such groups range from two people to *extended families,* in which grandparents, parents, and children share a home. The most common family unit is the *nuclear family,* consisting of a mother, a father, and their children.

Family

Family is one of the oldest and most common human institutions. Since prehistoric times, the family has been an important organization in society. Most people grow up in a family and, as adults, establish a family of their own.

In the United States and Canada, the term *family* commonly means a group of related persons who share a home. There are about 65 million such families in the United States and about 7 million in Canada. The word *family* also refers to all a person's ancestors and other relatives. Most families are based on *kinship*—that is, the members belong to the family through birth, marriage, or adoption. However, some groups that are not based on kinship think of themselves as a family because they share a home or feel ties of affection. For example, foster children and their foster parents are not related by adoption, birth, or marriage. But they live together and consider themselves a family.

American and Canadian families consist, on the average, of a mother, a father, and one or two children. However, there are many other types of family structures. The smallest family unit consists of two persons, such as a parent and child or a couple who share a home and companionship. When a couple have children, the parents and their children make up a *nuclear family.* If married children and their offspring live with the parents, the family is called an *extended family.* An extended family's household might also include aunts, uncles, and cousins. Such relatives, along with grandparents, grandchildren, and others, form part of an extended family group even if they live in separate homes. Some cultures recognize a large kinship unit called the *clan.* A clan consists of all people who are descended from a common ancestor through their mother's or father's side of the family.

The family fulfills many important functions in society, but the kinds of functions vary from one culture to an-

Nona Glazer, the contributor of this article, is Professor of Sociology and Women's Studies at Portland State University. She is the author of Old Family/New Family *and coeditor of* Woman in a Man-Made World.

other. In most societies, the family is the social unit into which children are born. The family also provides protection and training for the children. Human beings are born helpless and need care for several years after birth. Family life also helps children learn the culture of their society.

The family provides economic support for its members. Commonly, the adults receive income from jobs, investments, public welfare, or other sources. This money is then shared with the other members of the family. In some cases, the family functions as a group to make a living. All family members work together at farming or some other economic activity. The family may also be a means of preserving property. The children become heirs to their parents' land and other wealth. One function of the family in industrialized societies is to meet certain emotional and social needs of family members. Each member is expected to provide the others with affection, emotional support, and a sense of belonging.

This article deals mainly with families that share a household. It concentrates on families in the United States, but much of the information also applies to families in Canada and other industrialized nations whose economies are based on capitalism.

Family relationships

People are related to one another by *blood* (through birth), by *affinity* (through marriage), or through adoption. Most nuclear families consist of a mother, a father, and their *biological children* (the children born to them). Many other nuclear families have members who are included through adoption or remarriage. When a couple adopt a child, the child becomes a member of their family. The adopted child gains all the legal rights of a member of that family. When a divorced or widowed parent remarries, the parent's new *spouse* (husband or wife) becomes the children's *stepfather* or *stepmother*. The children become the new parent's *stepchildren*. Children from the couple's previous marriages become

Edward S. Ross

Touring places of interest is a popular family activity throughout the world. In Thailand, many families enjoy visiting their country's beautiful temples, such as this one in Bangkok.

stepbrothers and *stepsisters* to one another. *Half brothers* and *half sisters* share either the same biological mother or the same biological father.

The parents of a person's mother or father are that person's *grandparents. Great-grandparents* are the parents of a person's grandparents. An *aunt* is the sister of a person's mother or father. An *uncle* is a parent's brother. An uncle's wife is also called aunt, and an aunt's husband is also called uncle, but they are not a person's blood relatives. A *first cousin* is the child of a person's aunt or uncle. The child of a first cousin is a person's *first cousin once removed.* Children of first cousins are *second cousins* to each other, and children of second cousins are *third cousins.* The child of a second cousin is a person's *second cousin once removed.*

When people marry, they gain a new set of relatives, called *in-laws.* The mother of a person's spouse is called a *mother-in-law,* the brother is called a *brother-in-law,* and so on throughout the rest of the family.

Some families consider certain friends as family members because they feel special affection for them. Such friends are *fictive kin,* and family members might call them by family names. For example, children might call their parents' best friends "aunt" and "uncle."

Almost all societies prohibit *incest*—that is, marriage or sexual relations between certain relatives. They especially forbid sexual relations between all members of a nuclear family except the husband and wife. Most societies also prohibit marriage between such relatives as grandparent and grandchild or uncle and niece, and some extend the ban to first cousins.

Family living

In the United States, as in other industrialized countries, many people are turning away from traditional family patterns. They are adopting new roles for family members and various kinds of family structures. Many of these changes reflect scientific, economic, and social developments and changing attitudes. For example, modern birth control methods enable couples to limit the size of their family and to space their children. Many young people are postponing marriage and childbearing, and many couples want to have fewer children than people had in the past.

The number of employed married women has been growing dramatically. In the United States, the percentage of married women who work outside the home has risen from about 15 per cent in 1940 to about 55 per cent today. This increase has led to many changes in family life. It has contributed to the ideal of the *equalitarian family,* in which each member is respected and neither parent tries to be the head of the family.

Divorce has become more and more common. In the United States, statistics indicate that about half the marriages that took place during the 1970's are likely to end in divorce. But divorced Americans often remarry. This fact suggests that many people have not given up on family life. Instead, they believe they can find happiness in marriage with a new partner.

Home life. The home is the center of family activities. These activities include caring for the children, playing games, watching television, keeping house, and entertaining friends. In the home, children learn basic social skills, such as how to talk and how to get along with others. They also learn health and safety habits there. In addition, family meals can be a major source of nutrition for family members.

A family's home life is influenced by which members live in the home and by the roles each member plays. Home life can also be affected by relatives who live outside the family's home. Traditions, laws, and social conditions help determine who lives in a home and the place each family member holds.

Traditions, which are based on a family's cultural background, strongly influence family life. American families vary because they represent many cultural heritages. For example, some Americans have little contact with relatives outside the nuclear family. But many others—especially those who belong to such cultural groups as Chinese Americans and Mexican Americans—feel strong ties to such relatives and see them often. Aunts, uncles, and cousins traditionally are important in the lives of these people.

Laws regulate family behavior in various ways. In the United States, each state has its own family laws. Generally, these laws set forth the legal rights and responsibilities people have as husbands, wives, parents, and children. The laws forbid abuse of children by parents, and of one spouse by the other. Family laws also deal with marriage, divorce, and adoption.

Social conditions can affect family life in many ways. For example, many black American men have been discriminated against in getting well-paying jobs. Thus, black wives have been more likely than white wives to work outside the home to help support the family. As a result, many black wives have tended to have more authority in family affairs than have white wives.

The nuclear family, consisting of a husband, a wife, and their children, is considered the traditional American family. As husband and wife, the couple hope to share companionship, love, and a sexual relationship. As parents, they are required by law to feed, clothe, shelter, and educate their children.

Children depend on their parents for love and the basic necessities of life. The children, in turn, give emotional support to their parents and to their brothers and sisters. As the children grow older, they may be given various household chores. Most grown children eventually leave their parents' home.

Under the laws of most states, the father is required to support his wife and children. The mother is expected to run the home and care for the children. In many families, the father alone makes the major family decisions and is considered the head of the family.

Today, however, many Americans are turning away from these traditional family roles and toward an equalitarian relationship. The parents make family decisions together. They hold the authority in the family but try to consider the children's opinions. The children may express their desires and opinions, and they have much freedom within the family. In most such families, both parents probably work outside the home. The father may help out more in taking care of the children. The father and children may share in chores that were traditionally performed by the mother alone, such as washing clothes, cleaning the house, and cooking.

Other family patterns. Not all people choose to marry and live in a nuclear family. For example, some married couples decide not to have children. Also, some couples *cohabit* (live together without marrying). They want the companionship of another person but, for various reasons, prefer not to marry. Some such couples have children and live as a nuclear family, and some cohabiting couples eventually do marry. Although an increasing number of couples are deciding to cohabit, some people object to cohabitation because it conflicts with their moral standards.

In some cases, divorced or widowed parents choose not to remarry. Instead, they and their children live together as a *single-parent family.* In most cases of divorce, the children stay with their mother, but they may visit their father regularly. A judge might require the father to help support his minor children. However, more divorced fathers are sharing with the mother custody of their children. In many such cases, working mothers must contribute to their children's support. Increasingly, never-married fathers and mothers are deciding to raise their biological or adopted children in a single-parent family. In some families, children of unwed mothers are raised by their grandparents.

Some groups of people live together as *communal families.* The members of a communal family might include married and unmarried couples, single adults, and children. They might share child care, housework, and living expenses.

Family problems. Almost every family has problems as a normal part of living together. Many problems can be worked out in the home. But some problems are difficult to solve. Unsolved problems may result in unhappiness and lead to a breakdown of the family.

The question of divorce can be one of the most serious problems a family may face. Divorce can affect every member of the family deeply. The husband and wife must make a new life for themselves, and the children may grow up in a fatherless or motherless home. Today, divorced women and their children make up an increasing proportion of the poor. But many experts believe that living with only one parent may be better for children than living with both parents in an unhappy home.

Couples get divorced for numerous reasons. One of the main reasons is that they expect a great deal from family life. Many Americans expect the family to be a constant source of love and personal satisfaction. However, family members spend much of their time at work, in school, and at other places outside the home. Thus, they have limited time together to give one another emotional support. Their experiences outside the home affect their behavior in the family. They might not always feel as loving as they are expected to be.

Other problems may result from remarriages by divorced or widowed people. Such remarriages create the *blended family* of wife, husband, and each of their own children. Quarrels between the new couple over their children are sources of conflict and new divorces. Children naturally have mixed feelings about their new family. They become painfully certain that their biological parents will not be reunited. Children who were very close to the single parent may feel displaced and jealous because the stepparent has a special and private relationship with their parent. Children also may feel fondness and love for their new family but be scared that the new marriage also will end in divorce or death. In addition, children may see their feelings of love as a mark of disloyalty to the absent parent.

The rights and obligations between stepparent and stepchildren may seem different than those taken for granted between biological parents and children. Parents may recognize such differences, for example, in their right to discipline. Thus, stepparents and children are generally challenged to deal with many feelings that are not present in biological families.

Treatment of family problems. Many families can receive help with some of their problems by consulting a trained family counselor, a member of the clergy, a social worker, or a psychologist. Many such specialists use a technique called *family therapy.* They meet with the entire family as a group to help them work out their problems together. Various public welfare agencies offer guidance and economic aid. Other organizations counsel family members who have a specific problem. An organization called Alateen helps teen-agers who have an alcoholic parent. Other groups aid runaway children or battered children and wives.

Many Americans tend to view the family as separate from society. They think all family problems can be solved by dealing only with the family. They fail to realize that the family is part of society and that society influences family life. Such social problems as drugs, poor housing, and unemployment directly affect family life.

Increasingly, sociologists are finding that alcoholism, child abuse, runaway children, unhappy marriages, and certain other family problems are related to problems in society. They believe that such family problems can be reduced by dealing with the social conditions that help promote them. For example, programs that create new jobs, improve housing, or restrict drug traffic help support family life. With such programs, the family is no longer solely responsible for overcoming all the social problems that affect it.

History of the family

Early families. Scientists believe that family life began among prehistoric people more than 300,000 years ago. It may have developed because of the infant's need of care and the mother's ability to nurse the child.

The earliest prehistoric people probably lived in groups made up of several families. They moved from place to place, hunting animals and gathering wild plants for food. Everyone worked for the survival of the group by searching for food. At first, the early people hunted small animals. In time, they developed the means to kill or capture large animals. Some researchers think that the hunting of large game eventually led to a division of labor between men and women. Such hunting required the hunters to be away from the camp for hours or days. The women probably found such hunting difficult during pregnancy and, after giving birth, stayed near home to nurse their young. But the men could go off to hunt large game. The women probably gathered plants and hunted near the camp.

The division of labor between men and women may have helped the men gain power within the family. In many cultures, the women raised crops, and the men turned from hunting to the herding of goats, sheep, and other animals. A family's wealth depended on its herd because the animals provided a steady source of food and could also be traded for other goods. The father controlled the family's herd and thus its wealth. This control gave the father economic power within his family, and he came to be considered the head of the family. A family in which the father has the most power is called a *patriarchal family.*

Patriarchal families were common in early civilizations. Among the ancient Hebrews, who lived in the Middle East during Biblical times, the father had the power of life and death over his wife and children. He also controlled the family's property. Strong patriarchal societies also existed in ancient China, Egypt, Greece, and Rome and among Hindu people in India.

The family in Western culture developed from the traditions of the ancient Hebrews and other patriarchal societies. The father remained the most powerful figure in the family. The nuclear family was common throughout history. But some households included other rela-

Photograph (1908) by Lewis Wickes Hine; International Museum of Photography, Rochester, N.Y.

A family of the early 1900's made artificial flowers in their home to sell, *left.* Working as a group to earn a living was an important function of the family everywhere before the Industrial Revolution began in the 1700's. But by the time this photograph was taken, few families in industrial societies still worked together at home to support themselves.

tives, servants, or an apprentice, who lived with the family and learned the father's trade.

Until the Industrial Revolution began in the 1700's, most of the people of Europe lived in rural villages or small towns. Families produced their own food and made most of their clothing, furniture, and tools. Most manufactured goods were produced under the *domestic system,* also called *cottage industry.* Under this system, an entire family worked together in the home to make clothing, textiles, or other products for market.

Among the pioneers in America, the whole family worked together to clear the land and to plant, cultivate, and harvest crops. At about 6 years of age, children had to begin doing chores. Many settlers wanted, and needed, a large family to help with the work. In addition, older children could hunt and help protect the family against Indian attacks, fire, and other dangers.

In rural areas of Europe and America, the family also served as a center of education, religious instruction, health care, and recreation. Girls learned how to cook, sew, spin, and weave from their mother. Boys learned farming or a trade from their father or were apprenticed to a skilled worker. In many families, the children also received religious training from their parents. Old, orphaned, and sick relatives were cared for in the home. In addition, much of a family's social life took place there. For example, family members might gather in the evening for games or conversation or to entertain neighboring families.

In Western societies, the family served as a means for passing land and other wealth from one generation to the next. Commonly, property was inherited through the male line. Families hoped for sons, who would carry on the father's name and inherit his property.

As Western nations became increasingly industrialized, many rural people moved to the cities to seek factory work. Family life in the city differed from that in rural areas because people had to leave home each day to work. Commonly, the mother and children also held a job to help support the family. Family members had little time together, and the home became less central to family life. Hospitals, schools, and other social institutions took over many family functions. In addition, families could look to police and fire departments to help protect their lives and property.

Traditional families in other cultures. Most early non-Western civilizations probably also had a patriarchal family system. Some may have had an *equalitarian system,* which gave women and men equal power in the family. Researchers have found no evidence of a truly *matriarchal system,* in which the mother headed the family and held the most power in society. But in some cultures, the mother was especially honored.

Throughout history, most Western and non-Western societies have practiced a form of marriage called *monogamy.* Monogamy means a person has only one spouse at a time. But many other cultures, especially non-Western ones, have permitted *polygamy.* Polygamy allows a person to have more than one spouse at a time. There are two kinds of polygamy, *polyandry* and *polygyny.* Polyandry permits a woman to have more than one husband at a time, and polygyny allows a man more than one wife.

Today, many people in non-Western cultures follow

Edward S. Ross
Bushmen families in southwestern Africa live much as their ancestors did centuries ago. The women and young children gather wild plants for food, *above,* and the men hunt.

family patterns that are probably similar to those their ancestors practiced centuries ago. Most such traditional families live in remote rural areas. The following discussion describes some non-Western family patterns of the past and the present.

Hunter and gatherer societies still exist among the Pygmies and Bushmen of Africa; among various groups of Eskimos, Australian Aborigines, and South American Indians; and among certain other peoples. The people live in bands of about 20 to 200 members. The nuclear family is the main family structure in many groups, but some groups live in extended families. The men hunt, and the women gather wild plants. The women also practice, and probably invented, such crafts as weaving, basketry, and pottery making.

The Chinese. From ancient times to the mid-1900's, the Chinese worshiped their ancestors and felt great loyalty to their father's clan. The family was a strong patriarchal unit, and women had little freedom. The father decided whom his children should marry. Commonly, a bride went to live in her in-laws' home. She was considered an outsider because she came from another clan. The only way she could gain respect was to bear many sons and so increase her husband's clan.

In 1949, the Communists gained control of China's government. They began a program to make China a strong, industrialized nation. As part of the program, they tried to abolish many ancient family customs. Today, many Chinese people live in nuclear families much as do people in other industrialized countries.

The Muslim Arabs have had an extended, patriarchal family system for centuries. Family ties are extremely strong, and many related families commonly live near one another. The culture allows polygyny, but few men practice it. Women have little freedom and live in separate women's quarters in the house. If a husband divorces his wife, their children remain in his home.

Increasingly, the family patterns of some Muslim Arab communities are changing and coming to resemble those of Western cultures. This change is most common in the large, industrialized cities, where the people are exposed to Western ideas.

North American Indians practiced a variety of family customs before whites arrived. After the Indians were forced onto reservations, most tribes tried to keep their family customs. However, more and more Indians turned away from their traditional way of life and adopted family patterns of the white American culture.

Some tribes, such as the Hopi of the Southwestern United States, still follow their traditional way of life. To the Hopi, women are the center of family life. The oldest woman is honored as the head of the family, but her brother or maternal uncle commonly holds the most authority in the family.

In many cases, a woman shares her home with her unmarried children and her married daughters and their families. A husband lives in his wife's household. But he considers his mother's or his sister's house as his home and often returns there for family ceremonies.

Children are considered part of their mother's *line,* or ancestral family. The mother's brother, as a member of her line, has the most authority over her children. Her husband gives his children love but has little authority over them. Instead, he disciplines and has authority over his sisters' children.   Nona Glazer

Related articles. See the *Way of life* or *Family life* section of various country articles, such as **Mexico** (Way of life). See also the articles on groups of people, such as **Eskimo** and **Indian, American.** Other related articles in *World Book* include:

Children

Adolescent	Baby	Child welfare	Growth
Adoption	Child	Children's Bureau	

Family life through history

Colonial life in America	Greece, Ancient (Family life)	Prehistoric people
Egypt, Ancient (Family life)	Pioneer life in America	Rome, Ancient (Family life)

Family needs

Clothing	Food	Housing	School
Cooking	Home economics	Nutrition	

Parents

Divorce	Guardian	Parent
Foster parent	Marriage	Parent education

Other related articles

Adoption	Cousin	Planned Parenthood Federation of America
Birth control	Family Service America	
Budget	Genealogy	Polygamy
Clan	Health	Tribe
Community		

Outline

I. Family relationships
II. Family living
    A. Home life
    B. The nuclear family
    C. Other family patterns
    D. Family problems
    E. Treatment of family problems
III. History of the family
    A. Early families
    B. The family in Western culture
    C. Traditional families in other cultures

Questions

What is a *patriarchal family?*
How was family life affected as Western nations became increasingly industrialized?
What responsibilities do parents have toward their children?
How are *second cousins* related to each other?
What is a *nuclear family?* An *extended family?*
Who are *in-laws?*
What are some functions the family fulfills in society?
What are some reasons for the changes in traditional family patterns?
What is an *equalitarian family?*
How do some researchers think the division of labor between men and women developed in prehistoric times?

Reading and Study Guide

See *Family* in the Research Guide/Index, Volume 22, for a *Reading and Study Guide.*

Additional resources

Level I
Gay, Kathlyn. *Changing Families: Meeting Today's Challenges.* Enslow, 1988.
Rossel, Seymour. *Family.* Watts, 1980.
Worth, Richard. *The American Family.* Watts, 1984.

Level II
Changing Images of the Family. Ed. by Virginia Tufte and Barbara Myerhoff. Yale, 1979.
Mintz, Steven, and Kellogg, Susan. *Domestic Revolutions: A Social History of American Family Life.* Free Press, 1988.
Voth, Harold M. *Families: The Future of America.* Regnery Gateway, 1984.
Zollar, Ann C. *A Member of the Family: Strategies for Black Family Continuity.* Nelson-Hall, 1984.

Family name. See Name.

Family planning. See Birth control; Planned Parenthood Federation of America.

Family Service America is a national federation of about 300 social work-counseling agencies. These agencies provide professional help for personal and family problems. They serve about a million people each year in communities throughout North America. The organization was founded in 1911. It publishes two magazines, *Social Casework* and *Family Service Highlights.* Its headquarters are at 44 East 23rd Street, New York, NY 10010.

Critically reviewed by Family Service America

Family tree. See Genealogy.

Famine is a prolonged food shortage that causes widespread hunger and death. Throughout history, famine has struck at least one area of the world every few years. Most of the developing nations of Africa, Asia, and Latin America have barely enough food for their people. Roughly a half billion people on the earth are seriously malnourished, either from having too little food or from eating the wrong food. When food production or imports drop, famine may strike and thousands or millions of people may die.

Causes of famine

Many famines have more than one cause. For example, the great Bengal famine of 1943 in eastern India was caused by both historical and natural events. World War II created a general food shortage and led to the cutoff of rice imports from Burma, which was occupied by the Japanese. Then a cyclone destroyed much farmland. Famine struck, and more than $1\frac{1}{2}$ million people died.

Nearly all famines result from crop failures. The chief causes of crop failure include (1) *drought* (prolonged lack of rain), (2) too much rainfall and flooding, and (3) plant diseases and pests. Many other factors may also help create a famine.

Drought ranks as the chief cause of famine. Certain regions of Africa, China, India, and the Soviet Union

© W. Campbell, Sygma

Famine victims receive food and other emergency aid from their government and such international agencies as the Red Cross and United Nations (UN). These people are victims of a famine that struck Ethiopia in the mid-1980's.

have always been those hardest hit by famine. All have large areas near deserts, where the rainfall is light and variable. In a dry year, crops in those areas fail and famine may strike. In the 1870's, for example, dry weather in the Deccan plateau of southern India caused a famine that took about 5 million lives. During the same period, a famine in China killed more than 9 million people.

In the late 1960's and early 1970's, lack of rain produced widespread famine in a region of Africa called the Sahel. The Sahel lies just south of the Sahara. Famine again struck this part of Africa and also parts of southern Africa during the mid-1980's. The famine was especially devastating in Ethiopia, where a civil war hampered relief efforts. Since the late 1960's, millions of Africans have died of malnutrition or hunger-related causes. But many have been saved by international assistance.

Too much rainfall may also bring famine. Rivers swollen by heavy rains overflow their banks and destroy farmland. Other crops rot in the field because of the excess water. In the 1300's, several years of heavy rains created widespread famine in western Europe. The Huang He River in northern China is called *China's Sorrow* because it often floods, ruining crops and bringing famine. In 1929 and 1930, flooding along this river caused a famine that killed about 2 million people.

Plant diseases and pests sometimes produce famine. During the 1840's, a plant disease destroyed most of Ireland's potato crop. Between 1841 and 1851, Ireland's population dropped by about $2\frac{1}{2}$ million through starvation, disease, and emigration. From time to time, swarms of locusts cause widespread destruction of crops and vegetation in the Sahel and other areas of Africa.

Other causes of famine include both natural and human ones. Such natural disasters as cyclones, earthquakes, early frosts, and tidal waves may affect a large area, destroying enough crops to create a famine. War may result in a famine if many farmers leave their fields and join the armed forces. In some cases, an army has deliberately created a famine to starve an enemy into

surrender. The army destroys stored food and growing crops and sets up a blockade to cut off the enemy's food supply. Blockades prevented shipments of food from reaching the region of Biafra during the Nigerian civil war (1967-1970). A famine resulted, and more than a million Biafrans probably starved.

Poor transportation may also contribute to a famine because of the difficulty of shipping food where it is most needed. Many famines result largely from primitive transportation. A famine in what is now the state of Uttar Pradesh in northern India killed about 800,000 people in 1837 and 1838. Lack of transportation prevented the shipment of grain from other areas of India.

Effects of famine

The chief effects of famine include (1) death and disease, (2) destruction of livestock and seed, (3) crime and other social disorders, and (4) migration.

Death and disease are the main and most immediate effects of famine. People who lack sufficient food lose weight and grow extremely weak. Many famine victims become so feeble that they die from diarrhea or some other ailment. The weakened condition of a starvation victim is called *marasmus*. Old people and young children usually are the first to die.

Children who have some food but do not receive enough protein develop a condition called *kwashiorkor*. One of its symptoms is *edema* (puffy swelling of the face, forearms, and ankles). Changes in the color and texture of the hair and skin also may occur. Young victims who do not die from kwashiorkor or starvation may grow up with severe mental and physical handicaps.

Famines also increase the possibility of epidemics. Cholera, typhus, and other diseases take many lives because people weakened by hunger do not recover easily from disease. Large numbers of the victims have fled from their homes and live in crowded refugee camps where disease spreads quickly. People frequently must drink impure water, which can carry disease.

Destruction of livestock and seed during a famine prolongs the disaster. Many farm animals die or are killed for food. Farmers, to avoid starvation, may have to eat all their seed before the planting season begins. Such damaging losses hinder them from returning to a normal life and may lower production levels.

Crime and other social disorders increase during a famine. Such crimes as looting, prostitution, and theft multiply. Desperate people steal food and other items they could not obtain otherwise. They may sell stolen goods to buy something to eat. There may be scattered outbreaks of violence, particularly near food distribution centers.

Migration. Large numbers of famine victims leave their homes in rural areas and flock to cities or refugee camps where food may be available. In the confusion, parents and children may be separated.

Prolonged famine may result in emigration. The potato famine in Ireland caused about a million people to settle in other countries, chiefly the United States.

Fighting famine

The United Nations (UN) and several other international organizations provide emergency help for famine victims. Various agencies also work to increase the world's food supply and thus prevent future famines. Many nations hope to prevent famine by increasing their food production. If a nation can build up a large enough reserve of food, regional crop failures will not cause disastrous shortages. For additional information about world food programs and methods of producing more food, see the *World Book* articles on **United Nations** (Fighting hunger) and **Food supply** (Methods to increase the food supply; Food supply programs).

If a nation's population grows as fast as its food production, little food will be left over to build up a reserve. For this reason, many nations have promoted birth control programs to limit their population growth (see **Birth control** [In other countries]). However, such programs have had limited success in areas where large numbers of people remain poor. Many poor people want large families so the children can help with the work and, later, care for the parents.   John A. Harrington, Jr.

Fan. Long ago, people learned they could make themselves feel cooler on hot days by waving a leaf through the air and creating an artificial breeze. The early Assyrians and Egyptians used hand fans made of palm leaves. Wealthy people had servants fan them with these huge leaves.

Historians believe that the folding fan was invented in Japan about A.D. 700. The inventor may have made the

The Metropolitan Museum of Art, New York City, Gift of Miss Ella Mabel Clark, 1948

A French fan from the 1800's is decorated with a winter scene. It is made of paper, silk, lace, and mother-of-pearl.

fan after noticing the way in which a bat folds its wings. Japanese artists often painted fans with bright colors and used them in ceremonial dances.

The Chinese soon began using the folding fan, and in the 1500's the Portuguese brought it to Europe. European women adopted and used painted fans. For a short time, during the reign of Louis XV of France, men also carried dainty folding fans.

In the 1800's, noted artists painted fans which sold for high prices. They made the more expensive ones from asses' skin, parchment, or silk. They also made fine fans from lace, gauze, ostrich feathers, and peacock feathers. They mounted the fans on beautifully carved handles of ivory, tortoise shell, horn, bone, or sandalwood.

As a device for keeping cool, the electric fan has largely replaced the hand fan.   Lois M. Gurel

Faneuil, *FAN uhl* or *FAN yuhl,* **Peter** (1700-1743), a Boston merchant, built Faneuil Hall for the city of Boston as a public market and meeting place. It was completed in 1742. Fire gutted the hall in 1761, and repairs were

completed in 1763. Faneuil Hall now has historical paintings, a library, and a military museum. A huge grasshopper weathervane on top of the building has become a Boston landmark. The hall became known as the *Cradle of Liberty* because of the historic meetings there during the Revolutionary and Civil wars. Faneuil was born in New Rochelle, N.Y., and moved to Boston at the age of 12 to live with an uncle. He inherited his uncle's fortune in 1738. See also **Boston** (Downtown Boston; picture: Historic Faneuil Hall).   John B. McFerrin

Fang. See **Dog** (Body structure); **Snake** (Fangs and venom glands; diagram); **Spider** (Chelicerae).

Fannie Mae. See **Federal National Mortgage Association.**

Fanon, *fah NAWN,* **Frantz Omar** (1925-1961), was a political theorist who became a leader of Algeria's struggle to gain independence from France. A black, he also supported other African independence movements and helped strengthen ties between Arabs and black nationalists of Africa.

Fanon was born in the French colony of Martinique, in the French West Indies. As a young man, he studied psychiatry and medicine in France. He later worked in a hospital in Blida, Algeria. In 1956, Fanon joined the Algerian independence movement. For a time, he represented the movement as a diplomat in Ghana.

Fanon's first book, *Black Skin, White Masks* (1952), is a psychological study of problems black people face because of racism. In *L'An V de la révolution algérienne* (1959)—published in English in 1965 as *Studies in a Dying Colonialism*—Fanon described the Algerians' struggle for independence as both a social revolution resulting in changes in society and a nationalist movement. Fanon's book *The Wretched of the Earth* (1961) made him famous. In it, Fanon argued that Algerians could achieve independence only through violent revolution.   Emmanuel Hansen

Fantasia, *fan TAY zhee uh,* is an instrumental musical composition that has no fixed form or style. Instead, it depends on the composer's imagination.

Some fantasias are written in such a free style that they sound as though the performer is making up the composition as he or she plays. Such fantasias are composed mainly for organ or piano. In the 1700's, Johann Sebastian Bach and his son Carl Philipp Emanuel were masters of this type of fantasia. Another type, called a *fantasy piece,* is a short, dreamlike composition. Robert Schumann wrote many fantasy pieces. Longer fantasias resemble a sonata, but they are much freer in form. Schumann, Franz Schubert, and Frédéric Chopin composed a number of longer fantasias in the 1800's. In England during the 1500's and 1600's, composers wrote pieces for instrumental ensembles that were called fantasias or *fancies.*   R. M. Longyear

Fantasy. See **Literature for children** (Fiction).

FAO. See **Food and Agriculture Organization.**

Far East is a term that is sometimes used for the easternmost part of Asia. Traditionally, the term has been used to refer to China, Hong Kong, Macao, Japan, Korea, Taiwan, and eastern Siberia in the Soviet Union. This region, excluding eastern Siberia, is now often called East Asia. The meaning of the term Far East is sometimes extended to also include Southeast Asia. The nations of Southeast Asia are Brunei, Burma, Indonesia, Kampuchea, Laos, Malaysia, the Philippines, Singapore, Thailand, and Vietnam. Europeans created the term Far East. The region lies far to the east of Europe.

For more information on the Far East, see **Asia** (Way of life in East Asia; Way of life in Southeast Asia). See also the articles on the nations and other political units mentioned in this article.

Farad, *FAR uhd,* is a unit used to measure electrical capacitance. It is named for the English physicist Michael Faraday, and its symbol is F.

The electric charge in a capacitor is directly proportional to the *potential difference* (voltage) applied to it. If 1 coulomb of charge gives a capacitor a potential difference of 1 volt, the capacitance is a farad. In electronics, the *microfarad* and the *picofarad* are usually used to measure capacitance. A microfarad ($m\mu F$) is one-millionth of a farad, and a picofarad (pF) is one-millionth of a microfarad.   Hugh D. Young

See also **Capacitance; Capacitor; Coulomb; Volt.**

Faraday, *FAIR uh day,* **Michael** (1791-1867), one of the greatest English chemists and physicists, discovered the principle of electromagnetic induction in 1831 (see **Electromagnetism**). He found that moving a magnet through a coil of copper wire caused an electric current to flow in the wire. The electric generator and the electric motor are based on this principle. Joseph Henry, an American physicist, discovered induction shortly before Faraday, but failed to publish his findings (see **Henry, Joseph**).

Faraday's work in electrochemistry led him to discover a mathematical relationship between electricity and the *valence* (combining power) of a chemical element. Faraday's law states this relationship. It gave the first clue to the existence of electrons (see **Electron**). Faraday introduced ideas that would become the basis of field theory in physics. He maintained that magnetic, electric, and gravitational forces are passed from one body to another through *lines of force,* or strains in the area between the two bodies.

Faraday was born near London. He was first apprenticed to a bookbinder. He became Sir Humphry Davy's assistant at the Royal Institution in London in 1813, and remained there for 54 years. Faraday was a popular lecturer. He gave scientific lectures for children every Christmas. The most famous of these lectures is "The Chemical History of a Candle."   Seymour Harold Mauskopf

See also **Electricity** (Electromagnetism).

Farce. See **Comedy** (with picture); **Drama** (Forms of drama [Comedy]; Farces and interludes).

Fargo (pop. 61,383), is the largest city in North Dakota. It lies in the valley of the Red River of the North, one of the nation's great farming regions (see **North Dakota** [political map]). Fargo and Moorhead, Minn., together form a metropolitan area with 137,574 people. For Fargo's rainfall and monthly temperatures, see **North Dakota** (Climate).

The city's products include tractors, sugar beet harvesters and cultivators, metal products, furniture and cabinets, computer software, and dairy and other food products. The stockyards in suburban West Fargo are among the largest in the country. Fargo is a wholesale distribution center and is known as the *Transportation Hub of the Northwest.* Railroad passenger trains and freight lines serve the city. Airlines and bus lines link

Fargo with other cities. North Dakota State University is located in Fargo.

The city was founded in 1871, and was named for William G. Fargo of the famed Wells, Fargo & Company express. Fargo has a commission form of government.   John F. Lohman

Fargo, William George (1818-1881), was a partner in the gold rush express company of Wells, Fargo & Company (see **Wells, Fargo & Company**). His company's stagecoaches provided the best and fastest transportation between the East and the West in the mid-1800's. The city of Fargo, N. Dak., is named after him.

In Buffalo, N.Y., as a young man, Fargo served as a messenger with Wells and Company. Later, he became part owner. This was the first express company to go west of Buffalo. Wells and Company joined with two other companies to form the American Express Company in 1850. Fargo became its secretary. But the new firm was not equipped to handle the difficult gold rush business. So a new company, under the name of Wells, Fargo & Company, was formed to carry freight and express across the continent to San Francisco.

Wells, Fargo operated in most parts of the country. When the transcontinental rail line was completed in 1869, the railroad took most of the express business.

Fargo was born in Pompey, N.Y. He served as mayor of Buffalo from 1862 to 1866.   Thomas D. Clark

Farigoule, Louis. See **Romains, Jules.**

Farjeon, *FAHR juhn,* **Eleanor** (1881-1965), was a British author who became famous for her stories and poems for children. Her best-known works are noted for their combination of humor and fantasy.

Farjeon's popular collection *The Little Bookroom* (1955) contains her personal choices from among the many stories she wrote for children. The title refers to a special small room where the author read as a child. Farjeon's other collections of stories include *Jim at the Corner and Other Stories* (1934) and *Martin Pippin in the Daisy-Field* (1937).

Farjeon selected a number of favorite poems from her works for the collection *The Children's Bells* (1934). The book includes poems on such subjects as fairies, the seasons, and the experiences of childhood. Many of her poems were also published in *Eleanor Farjeon's Poems for Children* (1951).

Farjeon was born in London. During her long writing career, she produced more than 100 books and plays, including a few for adults.   Marilyn Fain Apseloff

Farley, *FAHR lee,* **James Aloysius,** *AL oh IHSH uhs* (1888-1976), a politician and businessman, served as postmaster general of the United States from 1933 to 1940. During his term he greatly improved airmail service. He was also chairman of the Democratic National Committee from 1932 to 1940. Farley managed the national presidential campaigns of Franklin D. Roosevelt during the elections of 1932 and 1936. He resigned before the 1940 election campaign. Farley also served as chairman of the New York State Democratic Committee from 1930 until he resigned in 1944.

Farley was born in Grassy Point, N.Y., and entered the building supply business. He became chairman of the Coca-Cola Export Corporation in 1940. He wrote two books about his career, *Behind the Ballots* (1940) and *Jim Farley's Story* (1948).   Harvey Wish

Grant Heilman

The vast farmlands of the United States are among the most productive in the world. Efficient management and the use of labor-saving machinery help account for the high productivity.

Farm and farming

Farm and farming. Farming is the most important occupation in the world. People cannot live without food, and nearly all the food they eat comes from crops and livestock raised on farms. Various industrial materials, such as cotton and wool, also come from plants and animals raised on farms.

Farming was once the chief way of life in nearly every country. For example, the typical American family of the 1700's and early 1800's lived on a small farm. The family raised cattle, chickens, and hogs and grew corn, fruits, garden vegetables, hay, and wheat. Everyone in the family worked long and hard, but the results were often disappointing. Most families produced barely enough food for themselves. This situation began to change during the last half of the 1800's—and it has changed remarkably during the 1900's.

Scientific advances since the 1800's have made farming increasingly productive. The development of better plant varieties and fertilizers has helped double and even triple the yields of some major crops. Scientific livestock care and breeding have helped increase the amount of meat that animals produce. At the same time, the use of tractors and other modern farm machines has sharply reduced the need for farm labor.

Lester V. Boone, the contributor of this article, is an agronomist at the University of Illinois at Urbana-Champaign.

Farming is no longer the chief way of life in countries where farmers use scientific methods and labor-saving machinery. In these countries, farmers produce more food than ever before, and most of the people live and work in urban areas. These changes have occurred in all industrialized nations and have been dramatic in the United States. In 1850, each farmer in the United States produced, on the average, enough food for 4 people. Most Americans lived on farms. Today, each farmer produces enough food for over 80 people, and less than 3 per cent of all Americans live on farms. But even with the great decrease in the number of farmers, the nation's farms produce more food than the American people use. The surplus has enabled the United States to become the world's chief food exporter. About a sixth of all food exports come from American farms.

As farming has become less important as a way of life in the United States, it has become more and more important as a business. The successful farmers of today are expert not only in agriculture but also in accounting, marketing, and financing. Farms that are not run in a businesslike way have great difficulty surviving.

This article deals mainly with farms and farming in the United States. It discusses the various kinds of U.S. farms and the methods that American farmers use to raise crops and livestock scientifically. The article also discusses farming as a business. Much of the information about American farming also applies to such countries as Canada, Australia, and New Zealand. For information about farming in other countries and about the history of farming, see **Agriculture**.

Farms in the United States can be divided into two main groups: (1) specialized farms and (2) mixed farms. A specialized farm concentrates on a particular type of crop or livestock. A mixed farm raises a variety of crops and livestock.

Specialized farming is profitable only if there are large commercial markets for farm products. The United States had few such markets before the late 1800's because the majority of the people lived on farms and raised their own food. Most U.S. farms, therefore, were mixed farms. Specialized farming was important mainly in the South. Unlike the North, the South has a long enough *growing season* (frost-free period) to raise such warm-weather crops as cotton, rice, and sugar cane. The North provided a large commercial market for these products, and many Southern farmers specialized in raising them.

The surpluses from mixed farms could feed the relatively few people who lived in U.S. cities and towns before the mid-1800's. But the urban areas began to grow rapidly during the last half of the 1800's, creating a demand for larger and larger food supplies. Farmers started to meet the demand by specializing. During the 1900's, specialized farms have increased at nearly the same rapid rate as the population of U.S. cities and towns. Today, about 95 per cent of the nation's farms are specialized farms.

Specialized farms

Farmers who practice specialized farming raise the kind of crop or livestock that is best suited to their region. For example, corn is often the most profitable crop to grow in regions that have level land, fertile soil, and a warm, moist growing season. Wheat grows best in a drier and somewhat cooler climate. Dairy farming is often the most profitable kind of farming in regions with rolling land, rich pastures, and a short growing season. Much of the western half of the United States is too dry for any crops to grow without irrigation. But the West has vast grasslands, which farmers use to graze beef cat-

tle and sheep. Irrigated farms in the West specialize in such crops as citrus fruits, cotton, rice, or vegetables. For more information on how soils and climate influence the kinds of crops and livestock that a farmer can raise, see the article on **Agriculture** (Agriculture around the world).

In the United States, a farm is classed as a specialized farm if it earns more than half its income from the sale of one kind of crop or livestock. Many specialized farms raise other products in addition to their main one. Numerous crop farms, for example, also raise livestock, and many livestock farms also raise crops.

Specialized crop farms make up about 50 per cent of all the farms in the United States. Most of them raise *field crops.* Field crops are crops that must be grown on a relatively large amount of land to be profitable. They include nearly all crops except nuts and most vegetables and fruits. Nuts and most vegetables and fruits have a higher market value than do field crops. They may therefore be raised profitably on as little as 1 to 2 acres (0.4 to 0.8 hectare) of land. However, such vegetables and fruits as potatoes and pineapples must be grown in large fields to produce a crop big enough to be profitable. They are thus classed as field crops.

The most important field crops are *cereal grains.* Foods made from grain make up a large part of the American diet. In addition, grain is a major ingredient in livestock feed, and so it is essential to large-scale egg, meat, and milk production. The chief cereal grains grown in the United States are, in order of value, corn, wheat, sorghum, rice, barley, oats, and rye. Farmers raise these crops either to sell or to feed to their livestock. A farm that concentrates on raising grain for sale is called a *cash grain* farm.

Cash grain farms mainly raise cereal grains. However, farms that specialize in dry field beans, dry peas, or soybeans are also considered to be cash grain farms. These crops are *legumes* (members of the pea family), not grains. But they are grown much like cereal grains and, in many cases, on the same farms.

Mississippi Agricultural and Industrial Board

A mechanical cotton picker, *above,* can harvest as much cotton as 80 workers picking the crop by hand. Farms throughout the southern half of the United States grow this important crop.

Grant Heilman

Vegetable farming uses both machines and hand labor. This machine on a California farm cuts and gathers tomato plants. Workers then remove the tomatoes from the stems by hand.

Some cash grain farmers raise dry field beans, dry peas, rice, sorghum, or soybeans as their principal crop. However, most cash grain farmers specialize in corn or wheat. The majority of the nation's wheat farms are in the Great Plains region and the Pacific Northwest. Most farms that specialize in corn are in the Midwest and the South. Wheat is the only cash crop that most farmers in the Great Plains region grow. But in sections of the plains that have enough rainfall, many wheat farmers raise a secondary cash crop of corn or sorghum. Many corn farmers grow another grain or soybeans as a secondary cash crop.

Other field crop farms specialize in such crops as cotton, peanuts, pineapples, potatoes, sugar cane, sugar beets, or tobacco. All the cotton and peanut farms in the United States are in the southern half of the nation. Farms in Hawaii produce all the nation's commercial pineapple crop. California and the states that border Canada, especially Idaho and Maine, have most of the potato farms. Sugar cane is grown in Florida, Hawaii, and Louisiana. Farms in various parts of the country specialize in sugar beets. Most of the tobacco farms are in the South.

Vegetable farms raise such produce as cucumbers, green beans, lettuce, sweet corn, and tomatoes. Many of these farms grow only one kind of vegetable. Most vegetable farms are relatively small, but some of the larger ones cover 2,000 acres (810 hectares) or more. About half the nation's vegetable farms are in seven states—California, Florida, Michigan, New Jersey, New York, Texas, and Wisconsin.

Fruit and nut farms concentrate on raising tree fruits, berries, grapes, and nuts. Tree fruits are the most common fruit crops by far. These fruits include apples, cherries, citrus fruits, peaches, pears, and plums. Most fruit and nut farms raise only fruits or nuts. Many of them specialize in one crop, such as grapes, oranges, or pecans. About three-fourths of the farms are in five states—California, Florida, Michigan, New York, and Washington.

Other specialized crop farms raise flowers, nursery products, or forest products. Flower farms and nurseries are found throughout the United States. About half the farms that specialize in forest products are in the South.

Specialized livestock farms account for about 45 per cent of all U.S. farms. They can be divided into three main groups: (1) beef cattle, hog, and sheep farms, (2) dairy farms, and (3) poultry farms.

Beef cattle, hog, and sheep farms produce most of the nation's meat animals. The majority of the farms specialize in one kind of animal. In the eastern half of the United States, many livestock farmers raise crops to feed their animals. However, most livestock farmers in the western half of the nation engage in ranching—that is, they graze beef cattle and sheep on rangeland.

Milt and Joan Mann

An orange picker in Florida is one of thousands of workers hired by U.S. fruit farms each year at harvesttime. Fruits bruise easily, and so they are harvested mainly by hand.

Nicholas deVore III, Bruce Coleman Inc.

Cattle ranching is the main type of farming on the Western grasslands of the United States. This Montana ranch has fairly rich grazing land. Many other ranches are located in dry regions of the West. They must cover a huge area to provide enough grass for large numbers of cattle.

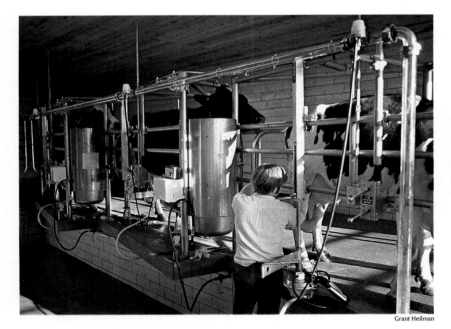

Machines milk cows in a milking parlor, *left.* The majority of U.S. dairy farms use milking machines. Because it is expensive to ship milk great distances, most large dairy farms are located near big-city markets.

Grant Heilman

Most of the rangeland is dry. In many areas, a rancher needs as many as 125 acres (51 hectares) of land to provide enough grass for one animal. A ranch must therefore cover a huge area to make a profit. Ranches are by far the largest kind of farm. They average nearly 3,350 acres (1,356 hectares) in size, and some cover 40,000 acres (16,000 hectares) or more.

Dairy farms specialize in raising milk cows. Most of the farms are concentrated near big-city markets. Many dairy farmers buy all or some of the feed they require from commercial suppliers. However, farmers in the Northeast and the Great Lakes region have large areas

Ray Atkeson, DPI

Poultry farming requires relatively little land—about 70 acres (28 hectares) for a typical farm. Most poultry farmers buy the grain to feed their birds. This farm in Oregon raises turkeys.

of pastureland that are ideal for the grazing of dairy cattle. The two regions have long been the nation's chief centers of dairy farming.

Poultry farms raise chickens, turkeys, and other poultry for meat. They also raise laying hens for eggs. Most of the farms specialize in broiler chickens or eggs. The broiler industry is centered in the South. Egg farms are scattered throughout the country. Nearly half the poultry farms grow no crops. The great majority of poultry farms buy most or all of their feed.

Other specialized livestock farms raise horses, mules, goats, rabbits, minks, chinchillas, bees, or fish. Usually, only *domesticated* (tame) animals are regarded as livestock. Minks, chinchillas, bees, and fish are not domesticated. But farms that raise them are often classed as livestock farms.

Farmers raise horses mainly for riding and racing. They raise mules to be work animals. Goats are raised for milk and wool, and rabbits for meat and fur. Farmers raise minks and chinchillas for their valuable fur. They keep bees for honey. Fish farms produce food fish, especially catfish, pompano, and trout. Farmers raise the fish in ponds and use special feeding methods to make them grow bigger and faster than they do in the wild.

Mixed farms

About 5 per cent of the farms in the United States produce a variety of crops and livestock. These mixed, or *diversified,* farms differ greatly from the mixed farms of the 1700's and 1800's. Like specialized farms, today's mixed farms are operated for profit and raise the kinds of crops and livestock that are best suited to their region. In the Midwest, for example, the typical mixed farm raises beef cattle, hogs, and cash grains. The typical mixed farm in the South produces beef cattle, peanuts, and tobacco.

This section discusses how farmers grow field crops scientifically. Field crops are grown on more than 95 per cent of the harvested cropland in the United States, and most of them are raised in a similar manner. The science of field crop production is called *agronomy*. In many cases, farmers must use special methods to grow fruits, vegetables, and nuts. The science of growing these crops is called *horticulture*. The articles **Fruit** and **Gardening** discuss horticultural methods. But fruits and vegetables grown in large fields are raised in much the same way as any field crop.

Basic principles of crop production

All crops require *nutrients* (nourishing substances) and water to grow. Soil supplies most of the nutrients. It also stores the water that the crops need. Crops take root in the soil and absorb the nutrients and water through their roots.

Crops differ, however, in the amount of nutrients and water they require for healthy growth. A farmer must therefore make sure that the soil and water resources meet the needs of each crop. A farmer must also plan measures to control pests, which could damage or ruin a crop. Most farmers plan their methods of soil and water management and of pest control well in advance of the growing season.

Soil management. Soil consists chiefly of mineral particles mixed with decaying *organic* (plant and animal) matter. Chemical reactions involving these substances produce most of the nutrients that crops need. But some of the most important chemical reactions, such as the decay of organic matter, require the help of certain microbes. To be fertile, therefore, soil must consist of the right mixture of minerals, organic matter, and helpful microbes. It must also have the proper amounts of air and water. A plant's roots need air to function properly, and some microbes need air to survive. Too much water in the soil reduces the supply of air and so drowns the plant roots and destroys helpful microbes. Too little water deprives crops of moisture.

Plants need 16 nutrients for healthy growth. The major nutrients are the elements calcium, carbon, hydrogen, magnesium, nitrogen, oxygen, phosphorus, potassium, and sulfur. Most crops require relatively large amounts of these elements. Elements needed in lesser amounts are called *trace* elements. They are boron, chlorine, copper, iron, manganese, molybdenum, and zinc. Water and air supply all the necessary carbon, hydrogen, and oxygen. The 13 other nutrients must come from the soil. But plants differ somewhat in their food requirements, and so the need for particular nutrients varies from one kind of crop to another.

After deciding which crops to grow, farmers analyze their soil to learn if any nutrients are insufficient or lacking. To get an accurate analysis, most farmers send samples of the soil to a soil-testing laboratory. The test results help farmers plan a scientific fertilizer program for their crops. Chemical companies provide fertilizers for almost any crop requirement. Most crops absorb large amounts of nitrogen, phosphorus, and potassium, and so most commercial fertilizers consist chiefly of these elements.

The richest soil lies at and just below the surface. If this topsoil is not protected, it may be blown away by strong winds or washed away by heavy rains—a process called *erosion*. Effective soil management therefore also includes methods of soil conservation. These methods are discussed later in this section.

Water management. Crops cannot grow without water. In most cases, farmers rely entirely on rainfall for the necessary moisture. In extremely dry areas, however, farmers must irrigate their crops. For a detailed discussion of irrigation techniques, see the **Irrigation** article.

Where rainfall is light or uncertain, many farmers practice *dry farming*. In dry farming, part of the cropland is left *fallow* (unplanted) each year. The fallow soil can store moisture for a crop the following year. Wheat is the main crop grown by dry farming.

Many farms often have too much water rather than too little. In most instances, the problem is greatest on low-lying land and on land crossed by streams or rivers. Fields that tend to collect water must have a drainage system. Most drainage systems consist of lengths of tile pipe buried 3 to 4 feet (0.9 to 1.2 meters) below the surface of the field. Excess moisture filters through cracks

Grant Heilman

Irrigation systems enable farmers to grow crops in dry regions. These Nebraska cornfields are watered by a *center-pivot* system. In each circular field, a central well supplies water to a series of sprinklers on a long arm. The arm rotates around the well and distributes water evenly throughout the field.

in the pipe and then flows to open drainage ditches at the edge of the field.

Pest control. Agronomists use the word *pests* in referring to weeds, plant diseases, and insects that threaten crops. Most farmers control pests with chemicals called *pesticides.* Scientists have developed hundreds of pesticides for use on farms. Each one is designed to fight certain types of weeds, plant diseases, or harmful insects. All pesticides must be used with extreme care. If they are used improperly, they may pollute the environment or the food supply and so endanger people's health. To help prevent this problem, the U.S. government sets and enforces standards for the manufacture, sale, and use of pesticides.

Farmers also use other methods of pest control in addition to pesticides. For example, turning the soil with a plow or mechanical cultivator kills most weeds. However, special pesticides called *herbicides* control weeds more thoroughly than does soil turning. Some herbicides remain active in the soil for some time and so kill weed seedlings as they develop. Plant scientists have developed varieties of corn, wheat, and other crops that are more resistant to diseases and insects than were earlier varieties.

Basic methods of crop production

Crop farming involves at least five separate operations: (1) preparing the soil, (2) planting, (3) cultivating, (4)

Tillage and planting equipment

These drawings show some of the equipment that farmers use to *till* (work) the soil and to plant crops. Plows are used for *primary tillage*—the original turning over of the soil each year. Harrows further break up plowed soil to prepare it for planting. Harrows may also be used for light primary tillage. Planting machines, called *planters* and *seed drills,* plant seeds in rows. Cultivators till the soil between the rows and so control weeds that appear while a crop is growing.

WORLD BOOK illustrations by Robert Keys

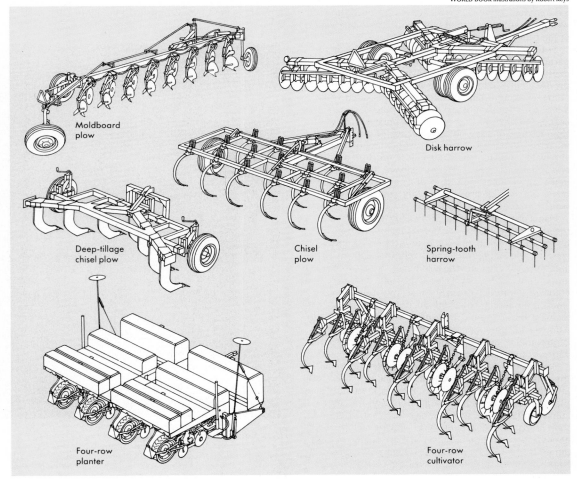

Moldboard plow

Disk harrow

Deep-tillage chisel plow

Chisel plow

Spring-tooth harrow

Four-row planter

Four-row cultivator

harvesting, and (5) processing and storage. Modern farm equipment can perform each of these operations easily and quickly. One of the most important items of equipment is the tractor, which is used to pull or push other field machinery. The use of modern farming equipment—and of improved plant varieties and fertilizers—has enabled American farmers to produce bigger and bigger harvests with less and less labor. In the early 1900's, a farmer had to work about 135 hours, on the average, to produce 100 bushels of corn. Today, a farmer can produce 200 bushels of corn with only 12 hours work.

Preparing the soil. The main purpose of soil preparation is to make a *seedbed*—that is, an area of soil in which seeds can be planted and in which they will sprout, take root, and grow. Most farmers make the seedbed by an age-old process called *tillage.* Tillage involves digging into the soil and mixing it.

Tillage loosens the soil, kills weeds, and improves the circulation of the water and air in the soil. Plows are the chief tillage devices. The most widely used plows are *moldboard* plows. The bottom of a moldboard plow is built to turn over about the top 8 inches (20 centimeters) of soil. This *clean* plowing buries most weeds and other plant matter that were on the surface. See **Plow** (The moldboard plow bottom).

At plowing time, most farm fields are scattered with dead stalks, leaves, and other plant wastes from the preceding crop. Other fields may have a *cover crop,* such as alfalfa or grass. Plant wastes and cover crops help protect soil from erosion. They also enrich the soil with nutrients if they are plowed under. Microbes cause the buried plant matter to decay. The decayed matter provides nutrients.

In many areas, the topsoil is too thin or too fragile for clean plowing. Farmers then use special plows that break up the soil without turning it over completely. This method kills fewer weeds than clean plowing does. But it leaves more plant matter on the surface and so helps reduce erosion. This kind of plowing is called *conservation tillage.* Some farmers prepare a seedbed with no or little tilling. Such methods are called *no-till* or *reduced tillage.*

Other plowing methods also help conserve soil. On sloping land, for example, farmers plow across, rather than up and down, the slope. The plowed soil forms ridges across the slope, which helps prevent erosion by rainwater. Such plowing is called *contour* plowing.

Soil that has been completely turned over in plowing often remains stuck together in large chunks. Most farmers therefore go over the plowed field with a device called a *harrow.* Harrows have sharp metal teeth or disks that break the chunks into smaller pieces and so smooth the surface for planting. Many farmers add fertilizers and pesticides to the soil during harrowing. The chemicals may be distributed by equipment attached to the harrow. In some cases, fertilizers and pesticides are applied before the soil is plowed.

No-till and reduced tillage. In the no-till system, wastes from the preceding crop are left on the field as a covering called a *mulch.* Farmers spray the mulch with a herbicide and apply fertilizer. Rainwater washes the

Grant Heilman

A special method of plowing called *conservation tillage* leaves some of the wastes from the previous crop on the surface of the soil. The wastes help prevent soil erosion. This tractor is pulling a chisel plow, a chief tool of conservation tillage.

chemicals down through the mulch and into the soil. In most cases, no further soil preparation is necessary. The seedbed is ready for planting.

The no-till method improves on traditional tillage systems in several ways. For example, the mulch helps prevent erosion and helps keep moisture in the soil. By eliminating plowing and harrowing, the method saves both time and tractor fuel. However, no-till may have certain disadvantages. Some weeds are not killed by herbicides, and so weed control may become a problem. Planting may be delayed because the mulch tends to keep fields cooler and moister than is desirable at the start of the growing season. In addition, the heavy use of herbicides may cause environmental problems.

Few U.S. farmers used no-till until herbicides became readily available in the 1960's. Today, a growing number of farmers use the method. Many other farmers have adopted a reduced or conservation tillage system. In this method, the plowing is done with a chisel plow, a harrow, or a cultivator. These devices leave more plant wastes on the surface, and so their use helps control erosion. Experts believe that more and more farmers will adopt no-till or reduced tillage systems.

Planting. American farmers plant certain types of barley, oats, and wheat in the fall. The plants begin to develop before the growing season ends and then rest during the winter. The young plants start to grow again in the spring and are ready to be harvested by midsummer. Except in the warmest regions of the country, however, farmers plant most crops in the spring after the danger of frost has passed.

Nearly all the field crops grown in the United States are planted by machines called *planters* or *drills.*

Larry Lefever, Grant Heilman

A seed drill plants seeds. It cuts furrows, drops seeds into them, and then covers the seeds with soil. The largest drills, such as the one shown above, can plant 12 or more rows at a time. Some drills also apply a herbicide, which kills weeds.

These machines cut furrows in the soil, drop seeds into each furrow, and cover the seeds with soil—all in one operation. Planters plant several rows of corn, cotton, and sorghum seeds at a time. These rows are 20 inches (50 centimeters) or more apart. Drills plant crops in closely spaced rows. These crops include the *small* grains, such as barley, oats, and wheat. Soybeans can be planted in either narrow or wide rows. Planters and drills designed for no-tillage operations are similar to conventional drills. However, they also have sharp blades that slice through the mulch so that the furrows can be dug.

Farmers use special planting methods to help conserve soil. On sloping land, for example, crops are often planted in long strips between bands of thick clover or grass. The clover or grass helps slow the flow of rainwater down the slope. This method of planting is called *strip cropping*.

Some fertilizers and pesticides are applied to the soil during planting. Equipment to distribute the chemicals may be attached to the seed drill just as it is to a harrow or a plow.

Cultivating. Herbicides applied before or during planting kill many kinds of weeds but not all. Some weeds may therefore develop with the crops. In most cases, weeds are not a problem in small-grain fields because the plants grow close together. In fields where row crops are grown, however, weeds can multiply rapidly between rows. Farmers control such weeds with cultivators. These devices stir the soil between rows and so uproot and bury any weeds.

J.C. Allen and Son

A cultivator stirs the soil between rows of corn, *above*. This process, used on crops planted in broadly spaced rows, uproots any weeds that herbicides have not controlled.

Grant Heilman

A combine cuts and threshes grain in one operation. Combines replaced machinery that only cut or only threshed a grain crop. This combine is harvesting sorghum.

Harvesting. Nearly all farmers in the United States harvest their field crops with machines. They use combines to harvest most grain and seed crops, including barley, corn, rice, soybeans, and wheat. A combine performs several tasks. First, it cuts the plant stalks. Then, it *threshes* the cuttings—that is, separates the grain or seeds from the straw and other wastes. The combine returns the wastes to the ground and collects the grain or seeds in a tank or bin. Some farmers harvest corn with special machines. The machines pick the ears from the stalks but do not remove the grain from the ears. The grain is removed later. The grain is then processed to make livestock feed. In the case of sweet corn, the ears are left whole and sold for human consumption.

Special machines are also used to harvest other field crops, including peanuts, potatoes, and sugar beets. Some machines mow such crops as alfalfa and clover. The mowed crops are left on the ground, where they dry and become hay. Machines called *hay balers* gather the hay and bind it into bales.

Some farmers harvest green grain or grass to make a kind of livestock feed called *silage.* To make silage, the entire plant is harvested and then chopped up. Some silage machines harvest the crop and chop up the plants in one operation.

Processing and storage. Crops raised to supply food for human beings are called *food crops.* Many food crops tend to spoil quickly, and so farmers ship these crops to market as soon as possible after harvesting. Food grains, however, can be stored for months on farms that have the proper facilities. Before grain is stored, it must be dried. Most farms that store large amounts of grain have grain-drying equipment and large storage bins.

Crops raised to supply feed for livestock are called *feed crops.* Hay, silage, soybeans, and such grains as corn and sorghum are the principal feed crops. Corn, wheat, and soybeans are used for both food and livestock feed. Hay must be kept dry until it is used, and so it is usually stored in barns. Unlike hay, silage must be kept moist. Most farmers store it in airtight structures called *silos.* Soybeans must be specially processed to produce meal for livestock feed. Most farmers buy soybean meal ready-made from commercial suppliers who have removed the oil from the soybeans to use it for food products and other purposes (see **Soybean** [How soybeans are used]). Many farmers have equipment for milling feed grains other than soybeans. Corn is often fed to hogs without any processing.

Special crop-growing methods include (1) organic farming and (2) hydroponics. Organic farming is the practice of raising crops without the use of synthetic chemicals. Hydroponics is the science of growing crops in water.

Organic farming. American farmers depend heavily on chemical fertilizers and pesticides. However, these

An automated grain storage system

Grain can be stored for months after harvesting if it has been dried to prevent spoilage. Many farms that store large quantities of grain have an automated system for drying the grain and for transferring it to and from storage bins. The drawings below show how such a system works.

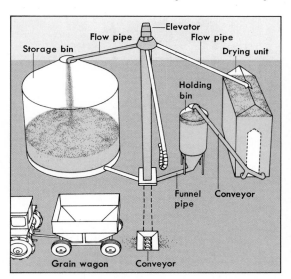

Drying and storage. Grain is brought from the fields by grain wagon and dumped on a conveyor, which carries it to an elevator. The elevator lifts the grain and releases it through a flow pipe into the drying unit. Here, hot forced air dries the grain. The dried grain, represented by the gold-colored areas, is moved by a conveyor to a holding bin. The grain funnels from the bin onto the elevator, which lifts it to a flow pipe at the top of the elevator. The grain then flows into the storage bin.

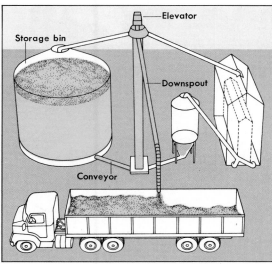

WORLD BOOK diagrams by Robert Keys

Unloading from storage. Farmers often store grain in hopes that the market price will rise. An automated storage system enables a farmer to ship stored grain to market quickly in case of a sudden increase in prices. To ship the stored grain, the farmer activates a conveyor at the foot of the storage bin. The conveyor removes grain from the bin and carries it to the elevator. The elevator lifts the grain and releases it into a downspout. The grain flows through the spout and into a waiting truck.

chemicals can cause soil and water pollution if they are overused or used improperly (see **Environmental pollution** [Water pollution; Soil pollution]). In extreme cases, the chemicals may also enter the food or water supply and so directly endanger people's health. For these reasons, some people believe that farmers should use organic farming methods whenever possible.

Organic farming relies on natural substances rather than on synthetic chemicals to fertilize the soil and control pests. *Manure* (wastes from animals) is the most widely used organic fertilizer. It is readily available on farms that raise livestock. However, most specialized crop farms raise too few livestock to provide enough manure for fertilizer.

Many farmers rotate their crops from year to year to reduce the need for chemical fertilizers. The rotation crop is usually a legume, such as alfalfa or soybeans. Unlike corn, wheat, and most other crops, legumes restore nitrogen to the soil. If corn or wheat is grown in a field one year, a legume may be grown in the field the

next year to replace part of the nitrogen used by the corn or wheat. See **Nitrogen cycle.**

Crop rotation also helps control insect pests and plant diseases. Most insects and disease-causing microbes are attracted only to particular crops. If the same kind of crop is grown in the same field year after year, the insects and microbes attracted to that crop can multiply out of control. But they gradually die out if a crop they are not attracted to is grown in the field for several years.

Hydroponics involves growing crops in large tanks filled either with water or with sand or gravel covered with water. Chemicals added to the water provide the nutrients that crops normally get from soil. Hydroponics has certain advantages over the growing of crops in soil. For example, the tanks can be kept in a greenhouse, and so crop losses due to pests or bad weather can largely be prevented. But hydroponics is unsuited to large-scale crop production. Its commercial importance is therefore limited. See **Hydroponics.**

An automated livestock farm   The farm in this drawing uses a variety of automatic machinery to mass-produce beef cattle. The farm also grows corn, hay, and silage to feed the animals. After the feed crops are harvested, they are loaded into the tall storage structures at the left through blower pipes. Conveyors remove them from storage as they are needed and carry them to a feed preparation room in the livestock building. Here, machinery mixes the feed and sends it by conveyor to the feeding trough in the main livestock room. The cattle remain in this room most of the time. Machinery scrapes their manure from the floor and pumps it into the outdoor storage tank at the right. The manure is used as fertilizer. As the cattle grow fat enough for slaughter, they are shipped to market in trucks.

WORLD BOOK diagram by Robert Addison; with technical assistance of A. O. Smith Harvestore Products, Inc.

In the past, almost all the chores on livestock farms were done by hand. These chores included milking the cows, gathering eggs, feeding all the animals, and cleaning the livestock buildings of animal wastes. Farmers had to do many of these tasks once or twice a day every day of the year.

The chores on a livestock farm must still be done regularly. However, farmers now have machines to do most of the work. On most large farms, cows are milked by machines, and eggs roll into collection troughs automatically as soon as they are laid. Feed is distributed to the livestock buildings by conveyor belts or other machinery. Similar machinery keeps the buildings cleared of wastes.

The use of machines has enabled livestock farmers to raise many more animals than they could in the past. In addition, improvements in livestock breeds and in livestock care have greatly increased the amount of eggs, meat, or milk that an animal can produce. The output of livestock and livestock products in the United States has more than doubled since the early 1900's—and with less than one-fourth the labor.

Basic principles of livestock production

To raise livestock successfully, farmers must provide the animals with the proper care. They must also select certain animals for *breeding* (reproductive) purposes to replace the animals that are marketed or that outgrow their usefulness.

Livestock care consists of providing feed and shelter for the animals and safeguarding their health. The success of a livestock farm largely depends on how skillfully the farmer does each of these jobs.

Feed. Livestock feeds can be divided into two main groups: (1) forage and (2) feed concentrates. Forage consists of plants that livestock graze on or that have been cut to make hay or silage. Forage supplies livestock mainly with *roughage* (coarse food). Feed concentrates consist chiefly of feed grains, such as corn and sorghum, and soybean meal. They supply much food energy and little roughage. In most cases, the grain is milled and mixed with vitamins and minerals. Some farmers also add synthetic *hormones* (growth-regulating chemicals) to feed concentrates to stimulate their animals' growth. Some farmers produce their own concentrates. Others buy them from commercial suppliers.

The digestive system of cattle and sheep enables them to convert forage into the protein and other nutrients they require. These animals can therefore live mainly on forage. Sheep get most of their forage by grazing. Cattle can also get forage by grazing. If either cattle or sheep are kept indoors, however, they are fed hay or silage. Although cattle and sheep can live on forage, farmers also feed them concentrates to ensure a balanced diet. Cattle and sheep that are being prepared for slaughter are usually fed large amounts of concentrates. The high-energy content of such a diet helps *finish* (fatten) the animals quickly. Unlike cattle and sheep, hogs and poultry cannot digest forage efficiently. They are therefore raised chiefly on concentrates.

Most livestock farms require great quantities of prepared feed. A herd of about 40 dairy cows, for example, may eat as much as 2 short tons (1.8 metric tons) of hay and other feed each day. An egg farm with about 20,000 laying hens uses about $2\frac{1}{2}$ short tons (2.3 metric tons) of feed concentrates daily.

Shelter. Most kinds of livestock need protection against extremely cold weather. Mature beef cattle and sheep, however, are less affected by the cold than are the majority of livestock. Ranchers may keep these animals on open rangeland throughout the year. Most other farmers provide shelter for their animals at least part of the time. Some livestock, including most poultry, are raised entirely indoors.

Health care for livestock has been made much easier by the development of vaccines and other modern drugs. Before these drugs were available, such diseases as anthrax and hog cholera killed large numbers of livestock. Farmers now prevent many kinds of diseases by having their animals vaccinated. Animals that have infectious diseases can be treated with penicillin and other germ-killing *antibiotics.* Farmers sometimes add antibiotics to livestock feed as a preventive measure.

Livestock breeding. Most farm animals are raised to provide livestock products. However, farmers also raise *breeding stock*—that is, animals of superior quality which are used mainly to produce offspring. In many cases, the offspring will inherit their parents' qualities, such as superior size and weight or exceptional milk- or egg-producing ability. Farmers select animals to be breeding stock on the basis of their qualities and those of their offspring. For example, a cow that gives much

Grant Heilman

Baby hogs depend on their mother's milk. Many hog farmers keep the babies partially separated from the mother while they are nursing, *above,* to prevent them from being crushed.

Rugged grazing land, such as this ranch land in Colorado, is well suited to raising sheep. Sheep are among the hardiest of livestock. They need little food other than grass.

A modern egg farm raises hundreds or thousands of hens in a *confinement building, above.* The birds are kept in small cages to conserve their energy and to make egg-gathering easier.

milk and whose daughter does the same may be removed from the milk herd and placed in the breeding herd. Over a period of years, such *selective breeding* can greatly improve the quality of all the animals on a farm. For detailed information about livestock breeding, see **Livestock** (Breeding livestock).

Basic methods of livestock production

Livestock production involves three main types of operations. They are (1) livestock grazing, (2) livestock finishing, and (3) confinement operations.

Livestock grazing. About 55 per cent of all U.S. farmland is used for the grazing of livestock, especially beef cattle and sheep. Most of this land is native grassland. The rest is pasture. Pastures are fields of cultivated grasses or other forage crops. They are used mainly to graze dairy cattle. In regions with enough rainfall, many farmers who raise beef cattle or sheep also have pastures for their animals.

Most of the grassland used to graze beef cattle and sheep is on ranches in the western half of the United States. However, ranches do not produce enough grain or other high-energy feed to finish the animals for slaughter. Most ranchers therefore ship their meat animals to other farms for finishing after the animals are 5 to 12 months old. Sheep raised for wool live mainly on grass, and so these animals remain on the ranch.

Dairy cows do not have to be fattened. In most cases, they are allowed to graze in pastures when the weather permits. Dairy farmers supply the cows with any additional feed they need for efficient milk production.

Livestock finishing, or fattening, depends on the large-scale use of feed concentrates. Most livestock finishing therefore takes place in major grain-producing areas. Hog farms, for example, are highly specialized finishing operations. The great majority of these farms are in the chief corn-producing states, especially Iowa and Illinois.

Some farmers finish beef cattle, hogs, or sheep that they have raised from birth. Many others sell their young animals for finishing, either to farmers who have excess feed grain or to *feed lots.* Feed lots specialize in finishing young beef cattle or sheep. The animals are kept in pens and fed large amounts of feed concentrates. The largest feed lots finish hundreds of animals at a time.

Confinement operations mass-produce certain kinds of livestock and livestock products. The largest operations produce poultry and eggs. Feed lots are a form of confinement operation. However, most feed lots are simply areas of open land that have been fenced in and divided into large pens. The animals can roam about freely inside the pens. In a full confinement operation, the animals are kept inside a building in small pens or cages that limit their movements. The animals therefore use less energy by not moving about and so produce more meat or other products.

Many confinement buildings have enclosures for hundreds or even thousands of animals. Most of these buildings are equipped with automatic machinery that brings feed to the animals and clears away their wastes. In the United States, nearly all broiler chickens and a large share of laying hens are raised in confinement. A growing number of American farmers also use confinement techniques to raise hogs, beef cattle, and dairy cattle.

The United States today has about 2,300,000 farms, compared with about 6,500,000 in the 1930's. Yet the nation's total farm output is far greater today than ever before. Much of this increase in production is due to efficient management. Businesslike farming therefore not only earns profits for farmers but also helps meet, and even exceed, the ever-increasing demand for food.

Farm owners and farm operators

Since 1945, the average size of U.S. farms has more than doubled—from 195 acres (79 hectares) to 440 acres (178 hectares). At the same time, the average cost of a farm has increased nearly 20 times. Today, the typical farm requires an investment of $300,000 to $600,000 or more, depending on the type and location of the farm. Most of the investment is in real estate. The rest is chiefly in supplies and equipment.

Most of the nation's farms are owned by individuals. In many cases, the owners also operate their farms. Other owners rent all or part of their land. More than half of all U.S. farmland is rented. Some farmers, called *tenant* farmers, rent all their land. Many other farmers rent part of their land and own the rest.

Some farms are owned by business partnerships or by corporations rather than by individuals. In a partnership, two or more people combine their resources to buy and operate a business. The partners then share the profits or the losses. The majority of farm partnerships consist of two or more members of a farm family.

Farms owned by corporations are called *corporate farms*. Most corporate farms, like most farm partnerships, are formed by farm families. A family corporate farm provides certain tax benefits that individual ownership and partnerships do not offer. The benefits are usually small, however, unless a farm has an exceptionally high income. The majority of family corporate farms have an income well above the average.

Some corporate farms are owned by stock corporations, such as food-processing firms and feed manufacturers. The food processors and feed manufacturers own such farms to supply the products that the companies process. The farms are operated by hired managers or by tenants and have a high average income.

Farm management

Farm management includes everything that farmers do to make farming profitable. To make a profit, farmers must sell their goods for more money than it costs to produce them. Farmers try to keep production costs as low as possible. They also try to find the highest-paying markets for their products. However, farm production costs have been increasing much faster than market prices. Farmers regularly borrow money to finance their operations. As farm production costs increase, the average debt per farm also increases.

Expert management helps lessen some of the finan-

Changes in U.S. farming since 1900

	1900	1925	1950	1975
Farm population	29,875,000	31,190,000	23,048,000	8,253,000
Total land in farms (in acres*)	839,000,000	924,000,000	1,202,000,000	905,600,000
Number of farms	5,737,000	6,471,000	5,648,000	2,314,000
Average size of farms (in acres*)	146	143	213	440
Average assets per farm†	unknown	unknown	$23,436	$185,396
Average crop production per acre* (index numbers**)	50	62	77	122
Average annual gross income per farm	$1,306	$2,120	$5,718	$34,956

*One acre equals 0.4047 hectare.
†Includes value of land, buildings, livestock, motor vehicles, machinery, stored crops, and household furnishings.
**The index numbers show changes in relation to the base year of 1967, which equals 100.
Sources: U.S. Department of Agriculture, U.S. Department of Commerce.

cial risks of farming. But farmers have little or no control over risks caused by the weather. Crops can be damaged or ruined by heavy rains at planting time or during the harvest season. A drought, flood, severe hail, or frost can destroy a crop at any time. A sudden cold spell or violent storm can endanger livestock on ranges or in pastures. Hazards like these can wipe out an entire year's profit. They thus make efficient farm management all the more important. An efficiently run farm should earn enough profit in most years to survive an occasional loss because of bad weather.

Managing production costs. The average cost of running a farm in the United States increased over 300 per cent from 1950 to 1978—and the cost continues to climb rapidly. The steep rise in farm expenses was caused partly by inflation, until inflation reached more moderate levels in the mid-1980's. Higher prices for farm *inputs* (purchased production materials and equipment, and interest paid on borrowed money) add to the cost of farming. But the rising costs are mainly due to the fact that farmers have greatly increased their use of such inputs as chemical fertilizers and pesticides, fuel, and machinery. Farmers depend on these inputs to expand production, and so their costs cannot be sharply reduced without lowering productivity. Farmers must thus manage their production costs carefully to ensure a profit.

Production costs are usually figured in terms of the *cost per unit* of the product. To find this figure, farmers add up the estimated cost of all the inputs they will need to produce a certain amount of their product—for example, 1,000 bushels of corn. They then divide the total cost by 1,000 to find the cost per bushel. Farmers compare the estimated cost per unit with the estimated selling price per unit to learn if the product can earn a profit. Sometimes, the unit cost may have to be reduced to show a profit. Farmers reduce unit costs by cutting expenses and by making their farms more productive.

Many farmers lower expenses by joining a *purchasing cooperative.* Purchasing cooperatives provide their members with farm materials and equipment at reduced prices. Nevertheless, most modern farm equipment is still increasingly expensive. Many farmers therefore rent equipment that they use only once or twice a year. Such equipment includes seed drills and combines.

In many cases, farmers have to increase their inputs to increase productivity. They can often make up for the added expense of the inputs if they make better use of their resources. For example, efficient methods of soil and water management can help expand a farm's total output at little or no added cost. The higher output lowers the cost per unit and thus raises the profit.

Marketing farm products. Some farmers sell directly to food processors, stores, or consumers. This marketing method is not particularly desirable, however, because a farmer may have difficulty finding the highest-paying buyers. For this reason, many farmers belong to *marketing cooperatives.* A marketing cooperative finds the best markets for its members' products.

Cooperatives assure farmers of a market, but they do not usually guarantee a specific selling price. If the supply of a product exceeds the demand, the price normally falls. American farms often produce a surplus, and so

© Frozen Images

Bookkeeping is an important part of farm management. This farmer uses a personal computer to keep track of his farm's income and his expenses for production materials and equipment.

farmers risk having their profit reduced or wiped out by falling prices.

Farmers can nearly eliminate marketing risks by an arrangement called *contract farming.* In contract farming, a farmer signs a contract with a food-processing or food-distributing firm. In most cases, the firm agrees to pay a certain price for a specified amount of the farmer's product. Much of the nation's broiler chickens, eggs, fruits, milk, and vegetables are produced under such agreements. However, contract farming has not won enthusiastic approval of all farmers. Many contracts specify which farming methods the farmer must use. Most farmers prefer to make such decisions themselves. In addition, farmers who sell on contract cannot benefit if market prices rise.

Many farmers sell beef cattle, hogs, and sheep at *auction markets.* The buyers at a livestock auction bid on the animals, and the animals are sold to the highest bidder. For more information about livestock marketing methods, see **Livestock** (Marketing livestock).

Financing farm operations. Production costs are so high that most American farmers cannot afford to pay them all out of annual earnings. Instead, they must regularly borrow money to finance their operations. About 10 per cent of U.S. farms have a *debt to asset ratio* (relationship of money owed to property owned) of 40 per cent or more. This figure indicates that these farms may be in serious financial trouble. Farmers pay back part of their debt each year, plus interest. The interest becomes an added production expense. Several farms are sold or go bankrupt each year, and a serious financial crisis has developed in the American farming community.

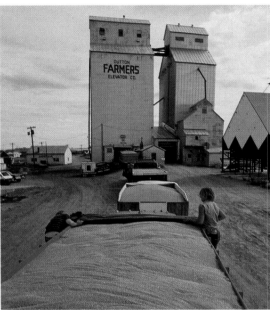

Nicholas deVore III, Bruce Coleman Inc.

A grain dealer buys truckloads of wheat from local farmers. The wheat is stored in elevators, *background.* It is later resold through a grain exchange or directly to a milling company.

Grant Heilman

Bidding at a cattle auction determines the price of animals offered for sale. The cattle are sold to the highest bidder. Farmers often sell hogs and sheep, as well as cattle, at auctions.

Farmers often borrow small sums from commercial banks. For large loans, most farmers deal with cooperatives. A farmer who belongs to a lending cooperative can borrow funds at reduced interest. The largest cooperatives are part of a nationwide system supervised by the Farm Credit Administration, an agency of the federal government. For more information on these cooperatives, see **Farm Credit System.** Another federal agency, the Farmers Home Administration, provides small, low-interest loans for farmers who cannot get funds from other sources (see **Farmers Home Administration**).

Many farmers buy insurance policies for protection against severe financial losses. Most of the policies insure farmers against crop losses due to bad weather or other natural hazards. The federal government provides such insurance through the Federal Crop Insurance Corporation. However, most crop insurance policies give farmers only partial protection. A serious crop loss is costly even to insured farmers.

Obtaining management assistance. To manage a farm successfully, a person needs a variety of skills. A crop farmer must have thorough knowledge of agronomy, including soil science and plant biology. Livestock farmers must know the principles of animal nutrition, animal breeding, and veterinary medicine. Every farmer has to be familiar with bookkeeping and other accounting techniques and with agricultural economics, including marketing and financing. Farmers need engineering skills to operate and service modern farm machinery. Farming requires so much specialized knowledge that most young people who plan to become farmers attend an agricultural college.

J. C. Allen and Son

Keeping farm equipment in working condition is a major task on today's highly mechanized farms. This farmer is servicing his combine, *right,* and its special corn-picking attachment, *left.*

Management assistance for farmers is provided by a variety of organizations. This course in the use of pesticides is sponsored by the U.S. Environmental Protection Agency.

Even the best-trained farmers occasionally need help in solving management problems. Farmers can get such assistance from various public and private agencies. Every state has an *extension service* and nearly every county in the United States has *extension agents,* which provide management help for farmers. Both are part of the Cooperative Extension System, a partnership of the federal, state, and county governments. Many farmers go to a county agent for up-to-date information about farming methods. County agents get much of their information from research centers sponsored by state agricultural colleges and the United States Department of Agriculture.

A growing number of private firms provide management assistance for farmers. Unlike government agencies, a private consulting firm charges a fee for its services. Several hundred agricultural periodicals are published in the United States. Some of them print articles of general interest to farmers. However, most deal with specialized subjects, from poultry breeding to soil conservation.

Farm income

Farm income consists chiefly of earnings from the sale of products plus payments from government farm programs. In the mid-1980's, the annual income per farm in the United States averaged about $5,000 after the payment of all expenses. Many farms have an income well above the average, but the majority have a below-average income or no income after expenses.

Most farm families cannot live on the money they make from farming. As a result, the great majority of farmers have other sources of income in addition to their farm earnings. Many farmers hold jobs as factory workers, truckdrivers, salespeople, teachers, or business executives. Farmers also earn outside income from the rental of property and from other investments. About two-thirds of all farmers earn at least half their personal income from nonfarm sources.

Federal farm programs

During the 1900's, U.S. farmers have often produced surpluses of corn, wheat, and other major crops. Such surpluses can help lower consumer food prices somewhat. However, the lower prices can reduce farm income so severely that many farmers cannot remain in business. The nation might then face a food shortage. To help prevent such a crisis, the U.S. government sets minimum prices that farmers receive for certain products. The government keeps prices from falling below the minimum levels through *price support programs.*

Most price support programs establish minimum prices for selected key farm products, such as corn, milk, and wheat. The government buys the products at these prices from farmers if the market prices fall much below the minimum, or support, levels. The government uses most of its food purchases for public aid and disaster relief programs.

Price support programs are often tied to *acreage allotments.* To take part in the programs, farmers must restrict the acreage they use to grow certain crops, such as corn and wheat. In addition to qualifying for price supports, these farmers receive payments for the crops they might grow, but do not.

The chief purpose of acreage allotments is to balance farm production with U.S. and worldwide demand. When the worldwide demand for grain and other crops is high, American farmers can sell their surpluses in other countries. At such times, the government may change acreage allotments and adjust price supports for various crops. Acreage allotments may be revised and price support payments may increase if the supply once again greatly exceeds the demand.

Farm programs have become complicated and expensive. As a result, the government is seeking alternative methods of ensuring adequate supplies of food without endangering the nation's agricultural community.

Farm organizations

A number of private organizations work to promote the interests of American farmers. Some of the organizations represent the interests of farmers in general. These general farm organizations include the American Farm Bureau Federation, the National Farmers Organization, the National Farmers Union, and the National Grange. Farmers who specialize in a particular product have formed *commodity organizations* to promote their interests. Each commodity organization represents a certain group of farmers, such as cattle producers or wheat growers. The general farm organizations and the commodity organizations both work to promote farm programs and legislation that they consider favorable.

Several labor unions represent the interests of hired farm workers. Many such workers are *migrants.* Migrant laborers move from one farming region to another to help harvest crops, especially vegetables and fruits. The United Farm Workers of America is the chief labor union for migrant workers.   Lester V. Boone

Related articles in *World Book*. See **Agriculture** and its list of *Related articles*. See also the *Agriculture* section of the state, province, country, and continent articles. Additional related articles include:

Kinds of farming

Aquaculture	Gardening	Plantation
Dairying	Horticulture	Ranching
Floriculture	Hydroponics	Tree farming
Fur (Fur ranching)	Nursery	Truck farming

Major crops

Alfalfa	Rice
Barley	Rye
Bean	Sorghum
Corn	Soybean
Cotton	Sugar
Fruit	Tobacco
Oats	Vegetable
Peanut	Wheat
Potato	

Chief kinds of livestock

Cattle	Horse
Chicken	Poultry
Duck	Rabbit
Goat	Sheep
Hog	Turkey

Farm buildings and equipment

Barn	Milking machine	Silo
Combine	Plow	Threshing ma-
Drill	Pump	chine
Greenhouse	Rake	Tractor
Harness	Reaper	Truck
Harrow	Scythe	Windmill

Methods and problems

Breeding	Fertilizer	Irrigation
Conservation	Fumigation	Migrant labor
Cropping system	Fungicide	Rainmaking
Drainage	Herbicide	Shelter belt
Dry farming	Hybrid	Weed
Erosion	Insecticide	

Government agencies and programs

Agricultural Stabilization and Conservation Service	Land Management, Bureau of
Agriculture, Department of	Reclamation, Bureau of
Commodity Credit Corporation	Rural Electrification Administration
Cooperative Extension System	Soil Bank
Farm Credit System	Soil Conservation Service
Farmers Home Administration	
Federal Crop Insurance Corporation	

Farm organizations

American Farm Bureau Federation	National Farmers Organization
Cooperative	National Farmers Union
4-H	United Farm Workers of America
Future Farmers of America	
Grange, National	

Other related articles

Agribusiness	Food
Agricultural education	Food supply
Agricultural experiment station	Grain
Agronomy	Land-grant university
Airplane (Special-purpose planes)	Livestock
County agricultural extension agent	Soil
	Tenant farming

Outline

I. Kinds of farms
  A. Specialized farms
  B. Mixed farms
II. Modern crop production
  A. Basic principles of crop production
  B. Basic methods of crop production
III. Modern livestock production
  A. Basic principles of livestock production
  B. Basic methods of livestock production
IV. Farming as a business
  A. Farm owners and farm operators
  B. Farm management
  C. Farm income
  D. Federal farm programs
  E. Farm organizations

Questions

What is the largest kind of farm? What do farms of this type raise?

Why do farmers use special crop-growing methods on sloping land? What are two such methods?

What are the two main kinds of farms? Which is more important in the United States today?

Why can farmers today produce more food with less labor than in the past?

What kinds of skills are required to manage a farm successfully?

Why must soil contain certain microbes in order for it to remain fertile?

What are *field crops*? Which ones are the most important?

How do livestock farmers improve the quality of their animals?

How does crop rotation help enrich the soil and control plant diseases and harmful insects?

Why has the cost of running a farm risen rapidly since the mid-1900's?

Reading and Study Guide

See *Farm and farming* in the Research Guide/Index, Volume 22, for a *Reading and Study Guide*.

Additional resources

Level I
Benson, Christopher. *Careers in Agriculture*. Lerner, 1974.
Demuth, Patricia. *Joel: Growing Up a Farm Man*. Dodd, 1982.
Marston, Hope I. *Machines on the Farm*. Dodd, 1982.
Patent, Dorothy H. *Farm Animals*. Holiday House, 1984.
Roth, Charles E., and Froehlich, R. J. *The Farm Book*. Harper, 1975.
Sallows, Reuben, and de Visser, John. *The Farm*. Methuen (Toronto), 1984. Photographic history of Ontario agriculture.

Level II
The Farm and the City: Rivals or Allies? Ed. by Archibald M. Woodruff. Prentice-Hall, 1980.
Fite, Gilbert C. *American Farmers: The New Minority*. Indiana Univ. Press, 1981.
Martin, John H., and others. *Principles of Field Crop Production*. 4th ed. Macmillan, 1986.
McMillen, Wheeler. *Feeding Multitudes: A History of How Farmers Made America Rich*. Interstate, 1981.
National Geographic Society. *Life in Rural America*. The Society, 1974.
Our Forgotten Past: Seven Centuries of Life on the Land. Ed. by Jerome Blum. Thames & Hudson, 1982.
U.S. Department of Agriculture. *Yearbook of Agriculture*. U.S. Government Printing Office. Published annually.

Farm Bureau Federation, American. See American Farm Bureau Federation.

Farm Credit System is the nationwide system of cooperatively owned banks and associations in the United States. The system is the nation's largest agricultural lender. It provides loans to farmers and ranchers and their marketing, purchasing, and business service-cooperatives in the United States and Puerto Rico. It also provides loans to people in the fishing industry. The federal government supplied the original capital for the system. But farmers gradually replaced the government's capital, and they now own all the stock in the system's cooperatives. The system obtains most of its loan funds from the sales of securities to the public.

The Farm Credit System is supervised and regulated by the Farm Credit Administration (FCA), an independent United States government agency. A three-member Federal Farm Credit Board sets FCA policies. Members are appointed by the President. One member serves as chief executive officer of the agency.

Organization. The nation is divided into 12 Farm Credit districts. Each district has a Federal Land Bank, a Federal Intermediate Credit Bank, and a Bank for Cooperatives.

Federal Land Banks provide long-term loans to farmers. These loans run from 5 to 40 years. Farmers may receive loans for general agricultural purposes, such as buying land and constructing or remodeling farm buildings. To be eligible for a loan, farmers must be members of a Federal Land Bank Association. The borrower buys stock in the association equal to at least 5 per cent of the loan. The association then buys the same amount of stock in its district bank. When the loan is repaid, the stock in the bank is retired.

Federal Intermediate Credit Banks do not lend money directly to farmers and ranchers. Instead, they provide funds to Production Credit Associations. These associations offer loans for agricultural purposes for periods of up to 10 years. They also provide loans to people in the fishing industry for up to 15 years. A person must belong to a Production Credit Association to obtain a loan. The borrower buys stock in the association equal to at least 5 per cent of the loan. Federal Intermediate Credit Banks also make loans to other institutions that lend money to farmers. Loans range up to seven years.

Banks for Cooperatives make loans to farmer cooperatives. To be eligible to borrow, a cooperative must be an association in which farmers act together to market farm products, purchase farm supplies, or furnish farm business services. The Central Bank for Cooperatives in Denver makes loans to the 12 district banks and participates in loans that exceed the limits of the district banks.

The Farm Credit System Capital Corporation allocates funding to all banks in the system and buys delinquent loans from financially troubled bank districts. It is owned by the district banks. The corporation has a five-member board. Three members are selected by the district banks, and two are appointed by the FCA. If federal funds are added to the Farm Credit System, the secretary of agriculture names a sixth board member. A seventh member is then elected by the other six.

History. Congress authorized Federal Land Banks in 1916. By 1947, government capital invested in these banks was repaid. Federal Intermediate Credit Banks were authorized in 1923. The FCA was established in 1933, and Production Credit Associations and banks for cooperatives were authorized that same year.

Since the early 1980's, many farmers have experienced serious financial difficulties due to high interest rates, a loss of international markets, and other related problems. As a result, the Farm Credit System has had record losses. Because of these losses, Congress restructured parts of the Farm Credit System through the Farm Credit Assistance Act of 1985. Under this act, Congress may appropriate federal funds for the system if both the FCA and the secretary of the treasury agree that it is necessary.   Raymond J. Miller

Farm machinery. See Farm and farming and its list of *Related articles.*

Farmer. See Farm and farming; Agriculture (Careers in U.S. agriculture).

Farmer, James Leonard (1920-   ), an American civil rights leader, was assistant secretary of the Department of Health, Education, and Welfare in 1969 and 1970. He helped set up the Congress of Racial Equality (CORE) in 1942, and was its national director until 1966. He guided CORE through the freedom marches and sit-ins of the 1960's (see **Congress of Racial Equality**).

Farmer served as program director of the National Association for the Advancement of Colored People (NAACP) from 1959 to 1961. He was a professor of social welfare at Lincoln (Pa.) University in 1966 and 1967. In 1968, he ran unsuccessfully for a seat in the United States House of Representatives from Brooklyn. In 1976, Farmer became associate director of the Coalition of American Public Employees, a group of labor and professional organizations.

Wide World
James L. Farmer

Farmer was born in Marshall, Tex. He graduated from Wiley College in 1938, and from the Howard University School of Religion in 1941.   C. Eric Lincoln

Farmer-Labor Party was a leading Minnesota political party. It was founded in 1918 and later took over the work of the Nonpartisan League (see **Nonpartisan League**). Its platform included government ownership of some industries, social security laws, and protection for farmers and labor union members. The party's outstanding leader was Floyd B. Olson, Minnesota governor from 1931 to 1936. The party elected candidates to state and national offices. In 1944, the party merged with the Minnesota Democratic Party to form the Democratic-Farmer-Labor Party. The Farmer-Labor Party was also the name of an organization formed in Chicago in 1919. It lasted until 1924, but elected no candidates.

Donald R. McCoy

Farmers Home Administration is an agency of the U.S. Department of Agriculture. The agency coordinates a nationwide rural development program and promotes cooperation between the federal government and state and local rural-development projects. It offers credit designed to improve the income of the small farm owner. It also provides financing for business and industrial development, community facilities, and housing in rural areas. Farmers may receive loans for farm supplies, land purchases, living needs, and special disaster relief. Community loans are made for such improvements as fire protection, medical facilities, and waste disposal systems. In most cases, financing becomes available when the applicant has no other source of credit. Repayment terms range from short periods to up to 40 years. Congress established the agency in 1946.

Critically reviewed by the Farmers Home Administration

Farmers of America, Future. See Future Farmers of America.

Farmers Organization, National. See National Farmers Organization.

Farmers Union, National. See National Farmers Union.

Farming. See Agriculture; Farm and farming.

Farnese Bull, *fahr NAY say,* is a famous ancient group sculpture that portrays an episode in Greek mythology. Its name comes from the Farnese Palace in Rome, where the sculpture was once kept. The *Farnese Bull* is a striking marble copy of a lost sculpture made in the 100's

Museo Nazionale, Naples (SCALA/Art Resource)

The *Farnese Bull* is a marble copy made in the A.D. 200's of the original Greek sculpture—now lost—carved in the 100's B.C.

B.C. by the Greek sculptors Apollonios and Tauriskos of Tralles. Unknown Roman sculptors made the copy in the A.D. 200's, adding their own elements to the original plan of the sculpture. The copy was discovered during an excavation in Rome in the 1500's, and lost portions of it were restored by Renaissance artists.

The sculpture shows two young men tying Dirce, the wife of King Lycus of Thebes, to a bull. Dirce had cruelly mistreated and imprisoned Antiope, who was Lycus' niece and, according to some stories, had been his first wife. Dirce planned to kill Antiope by binding her to a bull's horns. But Antiope's twin sons tied Dirce to the bull instead.   Warren G. Moon

Farnsworth, Philo Taylor, *FY loh* (1906-1971), an American inventor, was a pioneer in television technology. While still a teen-ager, he created an electronic television system that was superior to the mechanical discs used experimentally at the time. At the age of 20,

Farnsworth applied for a patent for an electronic television camera tube that became known as an *image dissector.* It created an image by producing an electronic signal that corresponded to the brightness of the objects being televised. Farnsworth demonstrated the image dissector in 1927. In 1939, Radio Corporation of America (RCA) obtained a license from Farnsworth to produce electronic television transmission systems that combined his technology with theirs. Farnsworth later conducted research on radar and nuclear energy. He was born in Beaver, Utah.   Joseph H. Udelson

Faroe Islands. See Faeroe Islands.

Farouk I. See Faruk I.

Farquhar, *FAHR kwuhr,* **George** (1678-1707), is a transitional figure in the history of English drama. His plays contain the wit found in Restoration comedy of the late 1600's and the emphasis on character and plot found in English plays of the 1700's.

Farquhar wrote eight comedies during his brief life, and is best known for two of them. In *The Beaux' Stratagem* (1707), two young Londoners visit a country town seeking rich wives in order to regain their wasted fortunes. Both have comic adventures, and one wins an heiress. *The Recruiting Officer* (1706) describes the adventures of army recruiters in an English country town.

Farquhar was born in Londonderry, Ireland, and worked briefly as an actor in Dublin before going to London to write comedy. A careless young man, he lived in constant need.   Jack D. Durant

Farragut, *FAR uh guht,* **David Glasgow,** *GLAS goh* (1801-1870), an American naval officer, won fame at the Civil War battle of Mobile Bay with the slogan: "Damn the torpedoes! Full speed ahead!" Congress created the rank of full admiral for him in 1866.

Farragut showed his loyalty to the Union when he gave up his home in Norfolk, Va., at the start of the Civil War to fight on the Northern side. He took command of the important Western Gulf Blockading Squadron, and cooperated brilliantly with General B. F. Butler and General E. R. S. Canby in operations against New Orleans and the forts at Mobile Bay. He

The Smithsonian Institution

David G. Farragut

won the nickname of *Old Salamander* when he ran his boats under heavy gunfire between the New Orleans forts on April 24, 1862, and the Mobile Bay forts on Aug. 5, 1864.

Farragut sailed up the Mississippi River with his heavy seagoing ships to bombard Vicksburg in 1862, a year before Grant captured the city by land. Farragut led a fleet that attacked Mobile in 1864. He forced his way into the bay, captured or destroyed enemy ships, and occupied the forts.

Farragut was born near Knoxville, Tenn., on July 5, 1801. He took the name David after his adoption in 1810 by Captain David Porter. He served under Porter as a midshipman on board the U.S.S. *Essex* in that vessel's famed battle with the British *Phoebe* and *Cherub.* Later, he fought pirates in the West Indies, took part in the war with Mexico, and helped establish the Mare Island Naval Shipyard in San Pablo Bay. He became a captain in 1855.   Richard S. West, Jr.

See also **Civil War** (Battle of Mobile Bay); **Porter** (David Dixon).

Farrell, *FAIR uhl,* **James T.** (1904-1979), was an American writer best known for his novels about lower middle-class life in a decaying neighborhood of a large city. Farrell followed the theory of naturalism in his early works, believing that people are influenced overwhelmingly by their environment (see **Naturalism**). Farrell's best-known work is the *Studs Lonigan* trilogy which consists of *Young Lonigan* (1932), *The Young Manhood of Studs Lonigan* (1934), and *Judgment Day* (1935). These novels are written largely in the language of Lonigan, a young tough. They explore the impact of urban industrial life on a boy growing up in a poor Chicago neighborhood.

James Thomas Farrell was born and raised in Chicago. After attending the University of Chicago, he became a writer. Following the Lonigan series, he wrote five novels featuring Danny O'Neill, a stronger and more sensitive hero than Lonigan. The O'Neill stories show Farrell's newly found faith in the ability of people to deal with their circumstances. The first O'Neill novel was *A World I Never Made* (1936).   Joseph N. Riddel

Farrier. See Blacksmith.

Farsightedness, also called *longsightedness,* is a visual defect in which a person can see distant objects clearly, but near vision may be blurred. Doctors call this condition *hyperopia.* In most cases of farsightedness, the eyes are too short from front to back. As a result, light rays from an object reach the retina before they can be brought into focus.

The eye may be able to correct its own farsightedness through a process called *accommodation.* In accommodation, certain muscles in the eye contract, making the lens of the eye rounder and thicker. The lens then has a greater ability to focus. The lens of a normal eye accommodates only to bring nearby objects into focus. But the lens of a farsighted eye must also accommodate for sharp distance vision. Although a farsighted eye receives sharp images of distant objects, the excessive accommodation may cause eyestrain and headaches. In addition, the lens may not accommodate enough for sharp near vision.

Young people and mildly farsighted individuals can accommodate enough for sharp vision at both near and far distances. As a person grows older, however, the lens begins to lose its ability to accommodate. Many individuals who are farsighted first notice the condition at that time.

Farsightedness cannot be cured. However, it can be corrected by glasses or contact lenses.

Ronald A. Krefman

See also **Eye** (Farsightedness).

Farthing was a bronze coin of the lowest value in British currency. It was worth one-fourth of a penny, or the 960th part of a pound sterling (see **Pound**). The farthing was first issued in 1279, in the reign of King Edward I (1272-1307). It remained a silver coin until 1613. The British government withdrew the farthing from circulation on Jan. 1, 1961. The word *farthing* is sometimes used to

mean a measure of land.   Fred Reinfeld

Farthingale. See Clothing (The Renaissance).

Faruk I, *fah ROOK* (1920-1965), also spelled *Farouk,* was the last king of Egypt. He became king in 1936, succeeding his father, Fuad I. Faruk enjoyed great popularity at the beginning of his reign. However, he shirked his duties and followed a life of luxury and dissipation. A group of rebels, directed by General Muhammad Naguib, forced Faruk to abdicate in July 1952. The group charged there was corruption in the government. Faruk went into exile in Europe. He was born in Cairo.

T. Walter Wallbank

See also **Egypt** (History); **Nasser, Gamal Abdel.**

Fasces, *FAS eez,* were a symbol of power in the days of the Roman Republic, of the Roman Empire, and, later, of Benito Mussolini's Fascist government in Italy. Fasces consisted of a bundle of birch or elm rods bound together by a red strap. The blade of an ax projected from the bundle. Servants called *lictors* carried these bundles ahead of such officials as magistrates, governors,

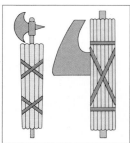

WORLD BOOK illustration by Lisa Wilkinson
Fasces

and emperors. The fasces stood for the official's power to punish people or put them to death, and also symbolized unity. Fasces also appear on the back of some American dimes.   Alexander J. Groth

Fascism, *FASH ihz uhm,* is a form of government headed, in most cases, by a dictator. It involves total government control of political, economic, cultural, religious, and social activities.

Fascism resembles Communism. But unlike Communism, which calls for the government to own all industry, fascism allows industry to remain in private ownership, though under government control. Other important features of fascism include extreme patriotism, warlike policies, and persecution of minorities.

The word *fascism* also describes any governmental system or political belief that resembles those of Benito Mussolini and Adolf Hitler. Fascist governments ruled Italy under Mussolini from 1922 to 1943, and Germany under Hitler from 1933 to 1945.

Fascism has varied from country to country. This arti-

WORLD BOOK photo by James Simek
The farthing was a British coin. One side showed the British monarch. The other side pictured a perching wren. The photograph has been greatly enlarged to show the details.

cle discusses fascism mainly as it existed in Italy under Mussolini and in Germany under Hitler.

Life under fascism

Political life. In most cases, fascists have come to power after a nation has suffered an economic collapse, a military defeat, or some other disaster. The fascists win mass support by promising to revive the economy and to restore national pride. They may also appeal to a fear of Communism or a hatred of Jews and other minorities. In time, the fascists may gain control of the government—through peaceful elections or by force.

After the fascist party takes power, its members replace the men and women in the executive, judicial, and legislative branches of the government. In most cases, one individual—usually a dictator with great popular appeal—becomes the leader of the government. Sometimes, a committee of party members holds the government leadership. Fascists permit no other political party and no opposition to their policies.

The fascist desire for national glory leads to an increase in military spirit and a build-up of the armed forces. After the military forces become strong enough, they may invade and occupy other countries.

Economic life. A fascist government permits and even encourages private enterprise—as long as such activity serves the government's goals. However, the government maintains strict control of industry to make sure it produces what the nation needs. The government discourages imports by putting high tariffs on certain essential products or by banning imports of those products. It does not want to depend on other countries for such vital products as oil and steel.

The government also forbids strikes so that production will not be interrupted. Fascism outlaws labor unions and replaces them with a network of organizations in the major industries. These organizations, which consist of both workers and employers, are called *corporations,* but they differ from those in other countries. Fascist corporations supposedly represent both labor and management. In reality, these corporations are controlled by the government. Through the corporations, the government determines wages, hours, and production goals. As a result, a fascist country is sometimes called a *corporative state.*

Personal liberty is severely limited under a fascist government. For example, the government limits travel to other countries and restricts any contact with their people. The government also controls the newspapers, radio, and other means of communication in its country. It issues propaganda to promote its policies, and it practices strict censorship to silence opposing views. All children are required to join youth organizations, where they exercise, march, and learn fascist beliefs. A secret police force crushes any resistance. Opposition may lead to imprisonment, torture, and death.

Fascists consider all other peoples inferior to those of their own nationality group. As a result, a fascist government may persecute or even kill Gypsies, Jews, or members of other minority groups.

History

The word *fascism* comes from ancient Roman symbols of authority called *fasces* (see **Fasces**). Many historians trace the beginning of modern fascism to Napoleon I, who ruled France as a dictator during the early 1800's. Napoleon carried out many liberal reforms and was not a true fascist. But fascists later adopted many of his methods. Napoleon promised his people that he would restore the glory of France through military conquest. To prevent opposition, he established one of the first secret police systems. Napoleon also controlled the French press and used propaganda and strict censorship to win support of his programs.

Fascism in Italy. Italy was on the winning side when World War I ended in 1918, but the war left the nation in poor economic condition. In addition, the peace treaties gave Italy far less territory than it had expected to receive. Benito Mussolini's Fascist Party promised to give Italians prosperity and to restore the prestige Italy had held during the days of the Roman Empire. The party gained the support of many landowners, business and military leaders, and members of the middle class. By 1922, the Fascists had become powerful enough to force the king of Italy to make Mussolini prime minister. Mussolini, who became known as *Il Duce* (the leader), soon began to create a dictatorship. He abolished all political parties in Italy except the Fascist Party and seized control of the nation's industries, newspapers, police, and schools.

In 1940, under Mussolini's leadership, Italy entered World War II on the side of Nazi Germany. The Fascist government was overthrown in 1943, when Italy surrendered to the Allies.

Fascism in Germany. Germany was defeated in World War I and lost much of its territory under the peace treaties. The treaties also forced Germany to disarm and to pay heavy penalties for war damages. Severe inflation during the 1920's, followed by a worldwide depression in the early 1930's, left the German economy in ruins.

A fascist party called the National Socialist German Workers' Party, or Nazi Party, gained strength rapidly during the postwar period of crisis. By 1933, the Nazis were the strongest party in the nation. Their leader, Adolf Hitler, became the head of the government that year. Hitler soon overthrew the constitution and began to make Germany a fascist state. His secret police wiped out any opposition.

Hitler, who was called *der Führer* (the leader), preached that Germans were superior people and that Jews, Slavs, Gypsies, and other minorities were inferior. His followers used these beliefs to justify the brutal Nazi persecution of Jews and other groups. The Nazis eventually killed about 6 million Jews.

Hitler vowed to extend Germany's borders and to avenge the nation's humiliation in World War I. He began to build up the armed forces and prepare for war. In 1939, World War II began when German armies invaded Poland. The Allies defeated Germany in 1945, and the Nazi government crumbled.

Fascism in other countries. In Hungary, a fascist party called the Arrow Cross gained much support in the late 1930's. During the same period, a fascist organization called the Iron Guard became the strongest political party in Romania. Fascist groups also gained considerable strength in Japan in the 1930's. All these fascist movements disappeared after the Nazi defeat in 1945.

During the Spanish Civil War (1936-1939), a fascist group that was called the Falange Española supported the rightist forces that were led by Francisco Franco. Franco's forces won the war, and he ruled Spain as a dictator from 1939 until his death in 1975. Some people consider the Franco government to have been fascist. However, most historians and political scholars believe that the Franco government lacked essential features of fascism.

Today, the rulers of many developing nations are following fascist policies in an effort to promote industrial growth and national unity. But because of the association of fascism with racism—and with Mussolini and Hitler—these leaders deny any similarity to fascist dictators.   Stanley G. Payne

Related articles in *World Book* include:

Black Shirt	Nazism
Fasces	Police state
Germany (Nazi Germany)	Romania (Depression and fascism)
Hitler, Adolf	
Italy (Italy under Mussolini)	Totalitarianism
Mussolini, Benito	World War II (The rise of dictatorships)
Nationalism	

See also *Fascism* in the Research Guide/Index, Volume 22, for a *Reading and Study Guide.*

Additional resources

Ebenstein, William, and Fogelman, Edwin. *Today's Isms: Communism, Fascism, Capitalism, Socialism.* 9th ed. Prentice-Hall, 1985.
Fascism: A Reader's Guide—Analyses, Interpretations, Bibliography. Ed. by Walter Z. Laqueur. Univ. of California Press, 1976.
Forman, James D. *Fascism: The Meaning and Experience of Reactionary Revolution.* Dell, 1974. Suitable for younger readers.
Payne, Stanley G. *Fascism: Comparison and Definition.* Univ. of Wisconsin Press, 1980.

Fashion is a term commonly used to describe a style of clothing worn by most of the people of a country. However, popular styles of automobiles, furniture, homes, and many other products are also fashions. The kinds of art, music, literature, and sports that many people prefer can likewise be fashions. Thus, a fashion is—or reflects—a form of behavior accepted by most people in a society.

A fashion remains popular for a few months or years before being replaced by yet another fashion. A product or activity is *in fashion* or is *fashionable* during the period of time that a large segment of society accepts it. After a time, however, the same product or activity becomes *old-fashioned* when the majority of people no longer accept it.

Most people do not easily accept extreme changes in fashion. Therefore, most new fashions closely resemble those they replace.

A clothing style may be introduced as a fashion, but its use becomes a *custom* if it is handed down from generation to generation. For example, in the early 1800's, long trousers replaced knee-length pants and stockings as the fashion in men's clothing in the United States and Europe. Today, wearing long trousers is a custom for men in most countries. But fashionable variations in the color and shape of trousers have occurred through the years.

A fashion that quickly comes and goes is frequently called a *fad.* The majority of people do not accept fads. Some people may become involved in faddish behavior because fads can be widely publicized. Fads of the mid-1900's included playing with such toys as hula hoops and skateboards.

Why people follow fashion

Before the 1800's, some nations had laws that regulated the clothing fashions of people in certain social classes. Many of these *sumptuary laws* were designed to preserve the class system. Sometimes, they forced people to buy products manufactured in their own country. An English law of the 1600's required men of the lower classes to wear woolen caps made in England. However, this same law permitted men of high position to wear velvet hats from France and Italy.

Today, people follow fashion for various reasons. For example, they may want to identify with a select group of people. New fashions may be adopted immediately by well-known people, including athletes, motion-picture stars, and political figures. Then, other people may follow these fashions so that they can identify with this privileged group. Some people think that fashionable clothes and surroundings raise their status in life.

Following fashion provides a way for people to gain acceptance from others. This adoption of fashion applies more to clothes and social behavior than to cars, houses, and other items that most people cannot afford to replace frequently. During the 1960's, many young people identified with one another's political and social beliefs by wearing blue jeans. After a while, blue jeans became a fashion that was accepted by a wide variety of people.

People also follow fashion to make themselves more attractive. Standards of beauty change through the years, and people decorate themselves to fit their society's changing standards. Ideas of beauty also vary from culture to culture. For example, people in many countries use cosmetics to increase their attractiveness. In some countries, people use tinted cream on their cheeks. In other countries, people decorate themselves with tattoos and with scars filled with colored clay.

Men and women have always enjoyed changing their appearance. Following new fashions in clothes, hair styles, and makeup allows people to alter their appearance in a generally accepted way.

What causes fashion to change

Major changes in fashion occurred infrequently before the 1300's. Since then, the political and social conditions of a nation, plus technological developments, have influenced fashion in various ways.

Political and social conditions. During the 1300's, the rulers of many European nations began to set fashions that were followed by the members of their courts. In the mid-1600's, King Louis XIII of France began wearing a wig to hide his baldness. Fashionable Frenchmen soon began to shave their heads and wear wigs. In the mid-1800's, English women are said to have copied Queen Victoria's stout figure by wearing puffy dresses with padding underneath.

Some fashion changes have accompanied a breakdown in the system of social classes. The members of the nobility lost much of their power during the 1300's, when rigid class systems were weakened in Europe. The nobility began to dress more elaborately to distinguish themselves from the middle classes.

Bettmann Archive

Brown Brothers

Fashions in clothing, furniture, and interior decoration change through the years. The decorative styles of the 1890's, *left*, gradually gave way to the simpler fashions of the 1940's, *right*.

During the mid-1800's, mass production of clothing made fashionable clothes available to more people at lower prices. People of all social classes began to wear similar styles of clothing. Today, it is easier to identify an expensive garment by the quality of its fabric and manufacture than by its style.

Through the years, fashions in games and sports have influenced the way people dress. During the 1700's, people in England adopted simpler clothing styles after they became interested in fox hunting and other outdoor sports. Today, many people wear special clothing for such activities as golf, horseback riding, hunting, and tennis.

Wars have also affected the style of dress in a country. European soldiers returning from the crusades during the 1100's and 1200's brought back various Eastern ideas of dress styles. The crusaders also returned with rich silk and other textiles that were not available in Europe.

During the French Revolution (1789-1795), the elegant dress styles associated with the French nobility were replaced by plainer fashions. After Napoleon became emperor in 1804, he brought back elaborate fashions in clothing for the court.

During World War II (1939-1945), the shortage of fabrics limited new fashions. The governments of many countries restricted the amount of fabric that could be used in various garments. Nylon stockings were also scarce during World War II, and many women began wearing leg paint.

Technological developments. The development of new dyes, machinery, and textiles has greatly affected most areas of fashion, especially clothing. The style of dress has changed frequently in countries that have highly mechanized production systems.

During the early 1700's, new dyes made new color combinations possible in clothes. In the late 1700's, the invention of the toothed cotton gin, the power loom, and other machines sped up the production of fabric and yarn. Industrial mass production of clothing began after the development of improved sewing machines during the mid-1800's. The production of many identical garments resulted in a more uniform clothing style for many people. Since that time, the garment industry has influenced the design of new clothing fashions.

In the early 1900's, manufacturers began to make clothing and other products from synthetic fabrics. These materials have become popular because they are easier to care for and less expensive than some natural fibers. People began to wear lighter-weight clothing in the 1900's, following the development of more efficient heating systems.

At one time, changes in fashion spread very slowly from one country to another. Today, however, various communication systems keep people informed on current fashion developments in all parts of the world.

Mary Ellen Roach

Related articles in *World Book* include:

Brummell, George B.	Hat
Clothing	Modeling
Hairdressing	Shoe

Additional resources

Boucher, François, and Deslandres, Yvonne. *20,000 Years of Fashion: The History of Costume and Personal Adornment.* Rev. ed. Abrams, 1987.

Dolber, Roslyn. *Opportunities in Fashion Careers.* National Textbook, 1986. Suitable for younger readers.

Ewing, Elizabeth. *History of Twentieth Century Fashion.* Rev. ed. Barnes & Noble, 1986.

O'Hara, Georgina. *The Encyclopaedia of Fashion.* Abrams, 1986.

Fast is abstinence from food, or certain kinds of food, for a period of time. The origin of *fasting* is unknown. But the custom of fasting has played a part in the practices of every major religious group at some time.

There are many purposes for fasting. It has often been a way in which people have sought pardon for their misdeeds. In some religions, people fast during times of mourning. In others, the people believe that fasting will take their minds away from physical things, and produce a state of spiritual joy and happiness.

There are important fast days in Judaism, Christianity, and Islam. Jewish law orders a yearly fast on *Yom Kippur,* the Day of Atonement. Many orthodox Jews follow the custom of having the bride and groom fast on the day before their wedding. Many Christians fast during Lent, the period of 40 days from Ash Wednesday until Easter, commemorating the 40 days that Jesus spent fasting in the wilderness. In general, for Christians, fasting seldom means doing without all food for an entire day at a time. In addition, people who are not well can usually receive permission from their religious leaders allowing them not to fast.

Muslims fast from dawn to sunset every day during Ramadan, the ninth month of their year. During these hours, Muslims abstain from food and beverage, even though this month often comes during the hottest season of the year. Buddhists and Hindus also fast.

Most people have fasted at some time during their lives, either for religious reasons, for initiation ceremonies, or for help in developing magical powers or control over the body. In some religions, such as Zoroastrianism, religious leaders have protested against fasting from food. They claim that the food fast actually has no moral value, when compared with "fasting from evil" with eyes, hands, tongue, or feet.

Sometimes, personal or political goals are sought through fasting. Mohandas Gandhi of India used fasting both as a penance and as a means of political protest (see **Gandhi, Mohandas Karamchand**).

People have also fasted for health reasons. Scientists have studied the effects of fasting on the body and found that the intake of food increases the body's metabolism (see **Metabolism**). After fasting, metabolism can become as much as 22 per cent lower than the normal rate. But research has also shown that, after long periods of fasting, the body tends to adjust itself by lowering the rate of metabolism itself. After fasting, a person should gradually resume eating. Religious groups do not intend fasting to be harmful. They believe that it promotes self-control and strengthens the will.

Jonathan Z. Smith

Fat is any of a group of chemical compounds found in both animals and plants. Fats are composed of carbon, hydrogen, and oxygen. They are one of the three main classes of food essential to the body. The others are carbohydrates and proteins.

An animal fat or plant fat that is liquid at room temperature is called an *oil.* Fats and oils are insoluble in water, but they can be dissolved in alcohols, chloroform, ether, and gasoline. Beef tallow and some other fats are hard at room temperature. Such fats as butter, lard, and margarine, are soft at room temperature.

Fat has many important uses. It is a concentrated source of food energy for animals and plants. Fat is stored under the surface of the skin of most kinds of animals, including human beings. These fat deposits act as insulation against heat loss. Deposits of fat around the eyeballs and other organs of animals serve as cushions against injury. In plants, most of the fat is stored in the seeds. Many industries use both animal and plant fats in the manufacture of various products.

Nutritional importance. Fat is an important energy source in the diet and is a more efficient fuel than either carbohydrates or proteins. Fat can produce about 4,000 calories of energy per pound (9 calories per gram). Carbohydrates and proteins can each produce about 1,800 calories per pound (4 calories per gram), or less than half the energy produced by fat.

Because of its high energy content, fat is the body's most efficient form of stored fuel. The body can store fat that is almost dry, but large amounts of water are necessary to store carbohydrates and proteins. The body converts carbohydrates and proteins into *adipose* (fatty) tissue for storage. When extra fuel is needed, the body draws on this stored fat.

Fats are composed of substances called *fatty acids* and an alcohol called *glycerol.* Certain fatty acids, known as *essential fatty acids,* are necessary for the growth and maintenance of the body. The body cannot manufacture essential fatty acids, and so they must be included in the diet.

Essential fatty acids are building blocks for the membranes that make up the outer border of every cell in the body. They also form many of the complicated structures inside body cells. Essential fatty acids are a main part of the membranes of the *retina,* the part of the eye that turns light into nerve impulses. *Synapses,* the junctions between the body's individual nerve cells, are also rich in essential fatty acids.

Dietary fats can be divided into two general groups, *visible fats* and *invisible fats.* Most people are aware of the visible fats they eat, such as the fat in meat, butter, and salad oils. But some individuals may not be aware of the invisible fats in such foods as milk, eggs, fish, and nuts. Invisible fats are spread finely throughout certain animals and plants. Many such fats are especially rich in essential fatty acids.

Fats and disease. Many scientists believe that controlling the consumption of fats can help reduce the risk of developing *coronary heart disease.* This disease results when deposits of *cholesterol,* a white waxy substance, build up on the inner walls of the arteries that nourish the heart. The artery walls may eventually become hard, rough, and narrow. Many heart attacks

Sources of fats and oils

Vegetable oils account for about three-fourths of the world's production of fats and oils. Animal fats make up the remainder.

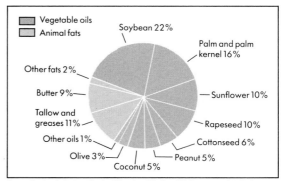

Source: *Foreign Agriculture Circular: Oilseeds and Products,* U.S. Department of Agriculture, August 1986.

The structure of fats

A molecule of fat includes three fatty acid chains, each of which consists of a chain of carbon atoms with hydrogen atoms attached. The structural diagram at the top of this illustration shows one molecule of a *saturated fat.* The fatty acid chains are saturated with hydrogen—that is, each carbon atom is linked to as many hydrogen atoms as possible. The bottom diagram shows one of the three chains of a *polyunsaturated fat.* Several of the carbon atoms in this chain are linked to only one hydrogen atom.

A molecule of a saturated fat

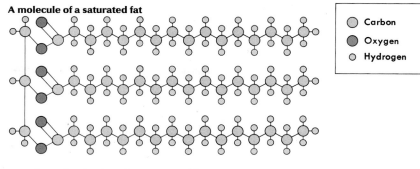

⬤	Carbon
⬤	Oxygen
○	Hydrogen

Part of a molecule of a polyunsaturated fat

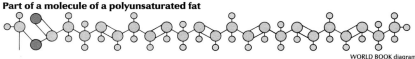

WORLD BOOK diagram

result from a blood clot that blocks a narrowed coronary artery.

Certain kinds of fats, called *saturated fats,* seem to increase the amount of cholesterol in the blood. Many scientists recommend limiting the intake of foods high in cholesterol and saturated fats. Instead, they recommend diets high in *unsaturated fats* and *polyunsaturated fats,* which seem to lower the cholesterol in the blood. In 1984, researchers reported evidence that lowering high blood levels of cholesterol reduces heart disease. But many scientists agree that other factors—such as smoking, stress, lack of exercise, or being overweight—contribute at least as much as diet to the development of coronary heart disease. See **Cholesterol.**

An excessive accumulation of fat in adipose tissue is called *obesity.* Obesity can be caused by too much food, too little exercise, or glandular disorders. Some diseases, such as appendicitis, cirrhosis of the liver, coronary heart disease, and diabetes, can be more difficult to treat if the patient is obese.

Structure. Most fats consist of one molecule of glycerol, also called *glycerin,* combined with three molecules of fatty acids. Each of these fatty acids is a long chain of carbon atoms with hydrogen atoms attached to them. The fatty acid chains are linked to the glycerol molecule to form a molecule of fat.

A saturated fatty acid has as many hydrogen atoms as possible attached to its carbon chain. The carbon atoms of the chain are linked together by single bonds. *Stearic acid* is an example of a saturated fatty acid.

In an unsaturated fatty acid, at least one pair of carbon atoms is joined by a double bond. For each such bond, the carbon chain is missing a pair of hydrogen atoms. *Oleic acid* is one unsaturated fatty acid.

A fatty acid that has more than one double bond is called polyunsaturated. The most highly polyunsaturated fatty acid in the body is known as *22:6.* It has a chain of 22 carbon atoms and 6 double bonds.

The hardness of a fat decreases as the number of double bonds in its fatty acid chains increases. The length of the carbon chain in the fatty acid also influences the hardness of a fat. Hard fats are less unsaturated than soft fats. Most liquid fats, such as vegetable oils and fish oils, are polyunsaturated.

A fat can be hardened by artificially adding hydrogen to the double bonds of the fatty acid, making the fatty acid less unsaturated. This process is called *hydrogenation* (see **Hydrogenation**).

Industrial uses. Fats from a wide variety of plants and animals supply many of the raw materials in manufacturing. The hydrogenation of various vegetable oils, such as corn, cottonseed, and soybean oils, produces margarines and shortenings. Linseed oil is used in making paints that have an oil base. Manufacturers use coconut oil in making hydraulic-brake fluid, lipstick, soap, and chocolate coating for ice cream bars. Beef fat, called *tallow,* is an important ingredient in soaps, cosmetics, and lubricants.   Cliffe D. Joel

Related articles in *World Book* include:

Blubber	Oil
Butter	Perfume
Detergent and soap	Stearic acid
Glycerol	Suet
Lard	Tallow
Margarine	Vegetable oil
Nutrition (Fats)	

Fatalism, *FAY tuh lihz uhm,* is the belief that events are determined by forces that human beings cannot control. Although all fatalists accept this general belief, they hold different views about the kinds of forces that determine events. In Greek mythology, for example, three goddesses called the Fates controlled human destiny. Theological fatalists believe that God determines what will happen. Scientific fatalists, generally called *determinists,* believe events are caused by physical, chemical, and biological forces described in scientific theories.

Fatalists may also hold differing views about whether all events are predetermined as part of a universal plan or order, or whether only some events are destined to occur. Those who base their fatalism on science generally hold the universal form of fatalism. Because fatalists believe some or all future events are as unchangeable as past events, they often believe it is possible to predict the future.   Stephen Nathanson

See also **Predestination; Free will; Fates.**

Fates were three goddesses who ruled people's lives. According to Greek and Roman mythology, the goddesses spun and cut the thread of life. They were called

Parcae among the Romans and *Moirai* among the Greeks. Clotho was the spinner of the thread and Lachesis decided how long it was to be. Atropos cut the thread.

The Fates were stern and gloomy goddesses. Nothing could make them change their minds. People offered them gifts to escape death, but never to thank them for any kind of blessings.

Ancient artists represented Clotho as holding the spindle of thread. Lachesis carries rods which she shakes to decide a person's fate. Atropos holds a tablet on which she writes the decision.   Padraic Colum

See also **Norns.**

Father Abraham was a popular name for Abraham Lincoln. See **Lincoln, Abraham.**

Father Divine. See **Divine, Father.**

Father of medicine. See **Hippocrates.**

Father of the Constitution. See **Madison, James.**

Father's Day is a day on which the people of many countries express gratitude and appreciation for their fathers by giving them gifts or greeting cards. In the United States and Canada, Father's Day falls on the third Sunday in June.

Sonora Louise Smart Dodd of Spokane, Wash., got the idea to set aside a special day to honor fathers in 1909, after listening to a sermon on Mother's Day. She wanted to honor her father, William Jackson Smart. Smart's wife died in 1898, and he raised their six children on his own. Dodd drew up a petition recommending adoption of a national father's day. The Spokane Ministerial Association and the local Young Men's Christian Association (YMCA) supported it. Through Sonora Dodd's efforts, Spokane celebrated the first Father's Day on June 19, 1910. Over the years, many resolutions to make the day an official national holiday were introduced. Finally, in 1972, President Richard M. Nixon signed Father's Day into law.   Sharron G. Uhler

Fathers of Confederation. See **Confederation of Canada** (table; picture).

Fathom, *FATH uhm,* is a unit of length used to measure ropes or cables and the depths of water. One fathom is equal to 6 feet (1.8 meters). Navigators mark a rope in fathoms and drop it into the water in order to measure the depth. Sailors of average height often measured fathoms roughly by extending both arms and measuring the rope from finger tip to finger tip.

E. G. Straus

Fathometer, *fa THAHM uh tuhr,* is an instrument used on ships to measure the depth of the water. It works by sending a sound down through the water to be echoed back from the bottom. Navigators can measure the depth below the ship by measuring the time it takes the sound to return. The speed of sound in water is known. Continuous soundings of this kind can be taken all during a voyage. The fathometer contains two parts, a *submarine oscillator,* which produces the sound, and a hydrophone *echo receiver.* The echo is amplified and sent to a *depth indicator* and a *recorder* near the bridge. The reliability of a fathometer depends on a number of factors, including the depth, temperature, and saltiness of the water. See also **Sonar.**

Robert F. Beck

Fatigue, *fuh TEEG,* is another name for tiredness. People often say they are "fatigued" when they feel tired. If we work hard, play hard, or go without rest or sleep, we expect to feel fatigued. In such cases, fatigue is normal. We know from experience that this feeling will disappear after we rest. But sometimes fatigue is a symptom of illness. Physically ill people often become fatigued after even a slight amount of work or exertion. Such people need a great deal of rest, often much more than they would need if they were well. Doctors have found that fatigue occurs frequently during many kinds of illnesses.

Fatigue may be one of the symptoms of a physical illness. It may also be a symptom of such mental illnesses as *panic disorder* and *depression* (see **Mental illness** [Affective disorders; Anxiety disorders]). In either case, rest helps a person feel less tired. But no amount of rest will cure the tendency to become tired easily. This tendency will disappear or improve only if the physical or mental illness that causes the fatigue is improved or cured.

Doctors do not know exactly what causes fatigue. They do not know why a person feels tired after exertion or mental effort. However, they do know that psychological as well as physical factors contribute to fatigue. The effect of fatigue has been closely studied. Research workers have shown that people who spend long hours at things that bore them or at tasks they do not want to do soon develop fatigue. If the person's *morale* (general attitude) and *incentive* (promise of reward) are good, it takes longer for fatigue to develop. But, no matter how good morale or incentive might be, a person who works

A fathometer is a marine instrument that sends sound pulses from a vessel to the sea bottom to determine the water's depth. Depth measurements are traced on a recorder aboard ship.

or plays long enough or hard enough will develop a feeling of fatigue. Paula J. Clayton

See also **Health.**

Fatigue, Metal. See Metal fatigue.

Fátima, *FAT uh muh* (pop. 3,464), is a town in west-central Portugal and the site of a famous religious shrine. For location, see **Portugal** (political map). The Virgin Mary, also called Our Lady of Fátima, reportedly appeared near Fátima in 1917. On May 13 of that year, three children told of seeing a vision of a lady near Fátima while they were tending sheep. They said that the lady, dressed in a white gown and veil, told them to come there on the 13th day of each month until the following October when she would tell them who she was. On October 13, she said that she was Our Lady of the Rosary, and told the children to recite the rosary every day. She called for people to reform their lives and asked that a chapel be built in her honor.

In 1930, the Roman Catholic Church authorized devotion to Our Lady of Fátima. Since then, millions of people have made pilgrimages to Fátima. Francis L. Filas

Fatimid dynasty, *FAT uh mihd,* was a line of Muslim *caliphs* (rulers) who held power from A.D. 909 to 1171. The caliphs claimed descent from Fatima, the daughter of the Prophet Muhammad, and her husband, Ali, a cousin of the Prophet. The Fatimids belonged to the Shiite branch of Islam, and to a sect called the Seveners. In 909, they gained control over territory that had been held by the larger group of rival Sunni Muslims and rose to power in north Africa. At various times, their empire included Sicily, Syria, and parts of Arabia and Palestine.

For many years, the Fatimids made their capitals in what are now the cities of Al Qayrawan and Al Mahdiyah, Tunisia. But after winning control of Egypt in 969, they founded a new capital, Cairo. There, they built many beautiful buildings and established Al-Azhar University. Today, this university is one of the oldest universities in the world and the most influential religious school in Islam. The Fatimids also established great libraries in Cairo and in Tripoli, Lebanon.

The Fatimid caliphs were good leaders, but as time went on, they became lazy and lost their authority. Members of the court struggled for power in the 1160's, and Nur al-Din, a Syrian leader, became involved. The last Cairo caliph asked Nur al-Din for protection against an invasion in 1168. Nur al-Din sent a strong force that included Saladin, a soldier who overthrew the Fatimid dynasty in 1171. Richard C. Martin

See also **Muhammad; Saladin; Shiites; Cairo** (History).

Faucet. See Plumbing.

Faulkner, *FAWK nuhr,* **William** (1897-1962), ranks among the leading authors in American literature. He gained fame for his novels about the fictional "Yoknapatawpha County" and its county seat of Jefferson. Faulkner patterned the county after the area around his hometown, Oxford, Miss. He explored the county's geography, history, economy, and social and moral life. Faulkner received the 1949 Nobel Prize for literature. He won Pulitzer Prizes in 1955 for *A Fable* and in 1963 for *The Reivers.*

Faulkner's work is characterized by a remarkable range of technique, theme, and tone. In *The Sound and the Fury* (1929) and *As I Lay Dying* (1930), he used stream-of-consciousness, in which the story is told through the seemingly chaotic thoughts of a character. In *Requiem for a Nun* (1951), Faulkner alternated sections of prose fiction with sections of a play. In *A Fable* (1954), he created a World War I soldier whose experiences parallel the Passion of Jesus Christ. Faulkner was skillful in creating complicated situations that involve a variety of characters, each with a different reaction to the situation. He used this technique to dramatize the complexity of life and the difficulty of arriving at truth.

The traditions and history of the South were a favorite Faulkner theme. *Sartoris* (1929) and *The Unvanquished* (1938) tell the story of several generations of the Sartoris family. *The Reivers* (1962) is a humorous story of a young boy's adventures during a trip from Mississippi to Memphis. Faulkner examined the relationship between blacks and whites in several works, including *Light in August* (1932); *Absalom, Absalom!* (1936); and *Go Down, Moses* (1942). Here, he was especially concerned with people of mixed racial background and their problems in establishing an identity.

Most of Faulkner's novels have a serious, even tragic, tone. But in nearly all of them, tragedy is profoundly mixed with comedy. Faulkner's comic sense was the legacy of Mark Twain and other earlier writers. Twain was a direct influence on him. *The Hamlet* (1940), *The Town* (1957), and *The Mansion*

Wide World

William Faulkner

(1959) make up the Snopes Trilogy. These novels form a tragicomic chronicle of the Snopes family and their impact on Yoknapatawpha County. Faulkner's short stories have the same range of technique, theme, and tone as his novels. His stories appear in *The Collected Stories of William Faulkner* (1950) and *The Uncollected Stories of William Faulkner* (published in 1979, after his death).

Faulkner was born in New Albany, Miss., and spent most of his life in Oxford. He worked occasionally in Hollywood as a film scriptwriter from 1932 to 1954.

Many early critics of Faulkner denounced his books for their emphasis on violence and abnormality. *Sanctuary* (1931), a story involving rape and murder, was most severely criticized. Later, many critics recognized that Faulkner had been criticizing the faults in society by showing them in contrast to what he called the "eternal verities." These verities are universal values such as love, honor, pity, pride, compassion, and sacrifice. Faulkner said it is the writer's duty to remind readers of these values. Noel Polk

Additional resources

Blotner, Joseph L. *Faulkner: A Biography.* Rev. ed. Random House, 1984.

Brooks, Cleanth. *William Faulkner: The Yoknapatawpha Country.* Yale, 1963. A standard work.

Friedman, Alan W. *William Faulkner.* Ungar, 1985.

Millgate, Michael. *The Achievement of William Faulkner.* Univ. of Nebraska Press, 1978. First published in 1966.

Fault. See Earthquake (Why earthquakes occur; illustration: An earthquake focus); **San Andreas Fault.**

Faun, *fawn,* was a half-human and half-animal spirit of the woods and herds in Roman mythology. The fauns corresponded to Greek satyrs. Like the satyrs, they enjoyed drinking, playing tricks, and chasing lovely maidens called *nymphs.*

Fauns were followers of Bacchus, the god of wine. The name faun comes from Faunus, whom the Romans

Bronze statue (A.D. 1-99) from Pompeii, Italy (Ronald Sheridan)

A faun was a half-human god of the woods in Roman mythology. A faun commonly had pointed ears, short horns, and a tail.

identified with Pan, the Greek god of fields and woods. See also **Satyr.**   Elaine Fantham

Fauna, *FAW nuh,* is the name given to the animal life of a certain period of time or of a certain part of the world. It corresponds to the word *flora,* which means the plant life of a certain place or time. Thus we may speak of the fauna and flora (animals and plants) of North America or of a past geological period. The term *fauna* comes from the name of a Roman goddess of fields and flocks.   George B. Johnson

Fauré, *foh RAY,* **Gabriel Urbain,** *ga bree EHL oor BAN* (1845-1924), was a French composer. He was an important composer of French songs and *song cycles* (series of songs). Fauré also composed extensively for solo piano and for chamber groups. Fauré's style is characterized by his adventurous use of harmony.

Fauré's major compositions include *Requiem* (1900), a work for chorus and orchestra; and two song cycles, *La Bonne Chanson* (1894) and *La Chanson d'Eve* (1906-1910). Fauré also wrote the orchestral suite *Pelléas et Melisande* (1898) and two operas, *Prométhée* (1900) and *Pénélope* (1913).

Fauré was born in Pamiers, near Toulouse. He worked primarily as a church organist until 1896, when he was appointed professor of composition at the Paris Conservatory. He served as director of the conservatory from 1905 to 1920.   Vincent McDermott

Faust, *fowst,* also called Faustus, *FOWS tuhs,* was a German astrologer and magician who became an important figure in legend and literature. Little is known about the historical Faust, but he probably lived from about 1480 to 1540. Germans of the time considered him

a fraud and a criminal. Martin Luther, the founder of Protestantism, believed that Faust possessed devilish powers.

In 1587, a crude legendary biography appeared, called *The History of Johann Faust,* or the *Faustbook.* The unknown author borrowed many sensational legends about other magicians. In the *Faustbook,* Faust sells his soul to the devil Mephistopheles for 24 years in exchange for whatever he wishes. Faust flies throughout Europe performing magic, and finally goes to hell, horrified by his damnation. The book was translated into many languages and rewritten three times in the next 125 years.

The first artistic version of the *Faustbook* was *The Tragical History of Doctor Faustus* (about 1588), a verse tragedy by the English playwright Christopher Marlowe. In the play, Faustus is a scholar who yearns to know all human experience. He often wavers about his bargain with the devil and finally wants to repent, but he cannot.

Many popular plays and puppet shows about Faust appeared during the 1600's and 1700's, mainly in Germany. These works were influenced by Marlowe's play but were gruesome and silly with little literary merit.

The greatest literary version of the Faust story was a poetic drama by Johann Wolfgang von Goethe, a German writer. Goethe wrote *Faust* in two parts (published in 1808 and 1832), changing the story radically. In Goethe's version, Faust is finally saved by God.

There have been many later versions of the Faust story. They all were influenced by Goethe's interpretation, except that in each version Faust goes to hell. Dorothy Sayers of England, Thomas Mann of Germany, and Paul Valéry of France are among the writers who have adapted the legend of Faust in their works during the 1900's.   David S. Chamberlain

See also **Goethe, Johann Wolfgang von; Marlowe, Christopher; Mann, Thomas; Mephistopheles; Opera** (*Faust*).

Fauves, *fohvz,* were a group of French artists who painted in a style that emphasized intense color and rapid, vigorous brushstrokes. Fauvism flourished from about 1903 to 1907. Henri Matisse led the movement, and members included André Derain, Raoul Dufy, Maurice de Vlaminck, and Georges Rouault.

The Fauves tried to express as directly as possible the vividness and excitement of nature. The group was influenced by the bright colors, bold patterns, and brushwork of such artists of the 1880's and 1890's as Paul Cézanne, Paul Gauguin, Georges Seurat, and Vincent van Gogh.

The word *fauves* means *wild beasts* in French. An art critic gave the painters this name because of the unusual boldness of their style. Most of the Fauves changed their style of painting by about 1907. But the movement had great influence throughout Europe, especially on German expressionism.   Marcel Franciscono

Each artist mentioned in this article has a biography in *World Book.* See also **Painting** (Fauvism).

Fawkes, *fawks,* **Guy** (1570-1606), helped lead a group who tried to blow up King James I and the Parliament on Nov. 5, 1605, to avenge the persecution of Roman Catholics in England (see **Gunpowder Plot**). Fawkes is the person most closely identified with the plot because it was his task to set off the explosion. Fawkes was born in

York, England. He was hanged in 1606, after the plot failed. England observes Guy Fawkes Day each November 5. Parliament proclaimed this day an annual day of thanksgiving shortly after Fawkes's arrest.

Roger Howell, Jr.

Fawn. See **Deer** (with picture).

Fax. See **Facsimile.**

FBI. See **Federal Bureau of Investigation.**

FCC. See **Federal Communications Commission.**

FDA. See **Food and Drug Administration.**

FDIC. See **Federal Deposit Insurance Corporation.**

Fear. See **Emotion; Phobia.**

Feast of Weeks. See **Shavuot.**

Feasts and festivals are special times of celebration. Most of them take place once a year and may last for one or more days. Many feasts and festivals honor great leaders, saints, or gods or spirits. Others celebrate a harvest, the beginning of a season or of a year, or the anniversary of a historical event. Most are joyous occasions, but some involve mourning and repentance.

During some feasts and festivals, adults stay away from their jobs, and children stay home from school. Some people celebrate happy events by decorating their homes and streets, wearing special clothes, and exchanging gifts. Many of these celebrations include special meals, dancing, and parades. Solemn occasions may be observed with fasts, meditation, and prayer.

In the past, nearly all feasts and festivals were religious. Today, many of them celebrate nonreligious events. This article discusses feasts and festivals in five major religions. For a discussion of nonreligious celebrations, see **Holiday.**

In Christianity, the most important festivals recall major events in the life of Jesus Christ. These festivals include Christmas, which celebrates His birth; and Easter, His Resurrection. Other Christian festivals honor the Virgin Mary, various saints, and the founding of the church.

Christians celebrate feasts and festivals both in church and at home. The celebrations vary widely among different groups. Many Protestants and Roman Catholics consider Christmas the most joyous and elaborate festival. Members of the Eastern Orthodox Churches regard Easter as their most important celebration. Some feasts and festivals are celebrated only in certain parts of the world. For example, a town may hold a festival for its patron saint.

In Judaism, the most sacred festivals are Rosh Ha-Shanah, the Jewish New Year; and Yom Kippur, the Day of Atonement. According to Jewish tradition, people are judged on Rosh Ha-Shanah for their deeds of the past year. On Yom Kippur, Jews fast, express their regret for past sins, and declare their hope to perform good deeds during the coming year.

Many Jewish festivals commemorate major events in Jewish history. For example, Passover celebrates the Exodus of the Jews from Egypt. Hanukkah is a celebration of a Jewish victory over the Syrians in 165 B.C. Purim honors the rescue of the Jews of Persia (now Iran) from a plot to kill them. Jews celebrate these festivals both in synagogues and at home.

Oil painting; the Museum of Modern Art, New York City

Fauve paintings show the emphasis of this group of painters on intense color and bold brushstrokes. André Derain, a leader of the Fauves, painted *London Bridge* in 1906.

In Islam. All followers of Islam, who are called Muslims, observe two celebrations—the Great Festival and the Lesser Festival. The Great Festival, or Festival of Sacrifice, traditionally takes place at the end of pilgrimages to the holy city of Mecca. During the Great Festival, which occurs in the last month of the Muslim year, Muslims sacrifice an animal and usually give the meat to the poor.

The Lesser Festival, or Festival of the Breaking of the Fast, marks the end of the month of Ramadan. During this month, Muslims fast from dawn to sunset. Many Muslims celebrate the birthday of the Prophet Muhammad and of various saints. Muslims who belong to the Shi'ite sect mourn the death of Husain, the grandson of Muhammad.

In Buddhism. Buddhists hold two principal kinds of festivals. The first type commemorates events in the life of Buddha—chiefly his birth, enlightenment, and death. Buddhists in different parts of the world observe these events in a variety of ways. In Japan, for example, Buddhists celebrate Buddha's birthday by decorating temples with flowers and pouring sweet tea over statues of the infant Buddha.

The second type of Buddhist festival honors the community of Buddhist monks. One such festival marks the end of the monks' annual retreat. During this celebration, groups of villagers perform a ceremony called the *kathina,* in which they give robes to the monks.

In Hinduism. Hindus hold festivals to honor each of the hundreds of Hindu gods and goddesses. Most of these festivals are local celebrations at the temples and honor specific divinities.

A few festivals are observed by all Hindus, chiefly in their homes and villages. These festivals, which include Holi and Divali, combine religious ceremonies with feasts, fireworks, parades, and other traditional amusements. Holi, the spring festival, is a boisterous celebration in which people throw colored water at one another. During the festival of Divali, which honors the goddess of wealth and beauty, Hindus decorate their houses and streets with lights.   Nancy E. Auer Falk

Related articles in *World Book* include:

All Saints' Day	Easter
Ash Wednesday	Epiphany
Assumption	Fair
Candlemas Day	Good Friday
Christmas	Guadalupe Day
Doll (Doll festivals	Halloween
and customs)	Hanukkah

Photri

A Shinto religious festival in Kyoto, Japan, features a parade of giant floats. The festival started in A.D. 876.

Steve Vidler, De Wys, Inc.

A religious procession by villagers in Sri Lanka honors the birthday of Buddha, the founder of their religion, Buddhism.

Steve Vidler, De Wys, Inc.

Local fairs called *ferias* are held throughout Spain and Latin America. The Spanish feria above celebrates a grape harvest.

Bettina Cirone, Photo Researchers

Guadalupe Day is Mexico's most important religious festival. People wear colorful Indian costumes on this holiday.

Holiday	Passover
Islam (Customs and ceremo- nies)	Pentecost Purim
Judaism (Holy days and festivals)	Rosh Ha-Shanah
Mardi Gras	Sabbath
Maundy Thursday	Saturnalia
May Day	Shavuot
Michaelmas	Simhat Torah
New Year's Day	Sukkot
Olympic Games	Tishah be-av
Palm Sunday	Yom Kippur

Additional resources

For other resources, see the list at the end of the *World Book* article on **Holiday.**

Chaudhuri, Nirad C. *Hinduism, A Religion to Live By.* Oxford, 1979. Includes information on Hindu festivals and observances.

Gaer, Joseph. *Holidays Around the World.* Little, Brown, 1953. Includes holidays and festivals celebrated by Buddhists, Christians, Hindus, Jews, and Muslims.

Strassfeld, Michael. *The Jewish Holidays: A Guide and Commentary.* Harper, 1985.

Von Grunebaum, Gustave E. *Muhammadan Festivals.* Interlink Pub. Group, 1988. First published in 1951.

Weiser, Francis. *Handbook of Christian Feasts and Customs.* Harcourt, 1958.

Feather is one of the light, thin growths that cover a bird's body. Feathers consist chiefly of *keratin,* a substance also found in the hair of mammals and the scales of fish and reptiles. Unlike hair and scales, feathers have a complicated branching pattern.

Kinds and parts of feathers. Birds have two chief kinds of feathers: (1) contour and (2) down. The parts of a feather vary somewhat, depending on the kind of feather.

Contour feathers grow on a bird's body only in special areas called *pterylae.* From the pterylae, the relatively large contour feathers fan out to cover the bird almost completely.

A typical contour feather has a broad, flat *vane* attached to a long central *shaft.* The shaft consists of two parts. A hollow, rounded base, called the *calamus* or *quill,* extends from the bird's skin to the vane. The solid, tapering upper part of the shaft, called the *rachis,* runs through the vane. The vane is formed by *barbs* that branch from the sides of the rachis and *barbules* that branch from the barbs. Hooks on the barbules link neighboring barbs, giving the vane both strength and flexibility. A sudden blow to the vane is more likely to separate the hooks from neighboring barbs than to tear or break the feather. The bird can refasten the hooks by pressing the barbs together with its beak.

Down feathers, unlike contour feathers, grow all over a bird's body. They have an extremely short rachis, so the barbs branch from almost the same point near the top of the shaft. The barbules of a down feather have no hooks. Thus, the vane is loose and fluffy.

Functions of feathers. Feathers enable a bird to fly and help it maintain a constant body temperature. Feathers also may provide coloring that helps the bird hide from its enemies or attract a mate. Although feathers are remarkably durable, they gradually wear out. Birds shed their feathers and grow a new set at least once a year. This process is called *molting.*

How people use feathers. People have used feathers for a variety of purposes. For hundreds of years, American Indians used feathers to make arrows and

Parts of a contour feather

WORLD BOOK illustration by Samantha Carol Smith

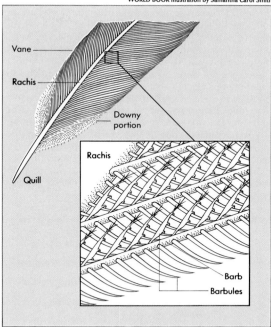

headdresses. Until the mid-1800's, when pens with steel points became popular, most people wrote with quill pens. Today, manufacturers use feathers as stuffing in pillows and furniture. Down feathers provide excellent insulation in jackets, quilts, and sleeping bags. Designers decorate hats and other garments with feathers.

Some uses of feathers, however, have come under heavy criticism. For example, the overuse of feathers for women's hats has endangered the survival of many kinds of birds. Laws forbid the importation of bird feathers into the United States.　　　Edward H. Burtt, Jr.

Related articles in *World Book* include:

Bird (Feathers; pic- ture: External fea- tures) Bird of paradise	Egret Molting Ostrich	Peacock Pen Pheasant

Feather star. See Sea lily.

Febold Feboldson, *FEE bohld FEE bohld suhn,* is a giant Swedish hero of many tall tales of Kansas and Nebraska. Feboldson performed fantastic feats that reflect the clever ways in which the American pioneers solved various problems. In one story Feboldson started tree planting in the Great Plains region by tossing handfuls of cottonwood seeds into prairie-dog holes. Another tale tells how he devised a way of digging postholes by using a creature called the happy auger. When the happy auger sat down, it spun around on its drill-like tail, forming a perfect posthole.

Feboldson may be based on an actual Swedish pioneer of the 1800's. The character was developed in the late 1920's by two Nebraska journalists, Don Holmes and Wayne T. Carroll. Paul R. Beath, a Nebraska lawyer, compiled *Febold Feboldson: Tall Tales from the Great Plains* (1948, 1962).　　　Harry Oster

February is the second month of the year according to the Gregorian calendar, which is used in almost all the world today. It is also the shortest month. According to legend, the first calendar of the ancient Romans had only 10 months. In about 700 B.C., the ruler Numa Pompilius added two months, making February the last month of the year. The month takes its name from the Latin word *februare,* meaning *to purify.* The Romans purified themselves in February to prepare for festivals at the start of the new year. In 46 B.C., the Roman statesman Julius Caesar moved the beginning of the year from March to January, making February the second month.

February usually has 28 days. But it has one extra day in every leap year. February had 30 days until the time of Julius Caesar. Caesar took one day off to add to the month named after him, July. According to tradition, the Roman emperor Augustus took another day off to add to August, the month named after him.

February is usually cold and stormy in the northern half of the world. But sunny days now and then show that spring is not far off. February is not nearly so dark and gloomy as the other winter months. The air is often crisp and clear. People in the Southern Hemisphere enjoy mid-summer weather during February.

Special days. People in most Western countries celebrate Valentine's Day on February 14. Many schools hold Valentine's Day parties when the children make special decorations for their classrooms. Old and young alike exchange Valentine cards with their friends. The custom of exchanging greetings on Valentine's Day goes back hundreds of years. Scholars have found records of Valentine notes that date from the 1400's.

Two of America's greatest leaders, George Washington and Abraham Lincoln, were born during February. Washington's birthday is celebrated as a federal holiday on the third Monday in February. Some states also honor Lincoln and other American Presidents on this day and call the holiday President's Day.

The Roman Catholic Church celebrates February 2 as Candlemas Day. The candles used in the church dur-

Important February events

1 Supreme Court of the United States met for the first time, 1790.
— Louis S. St. Laurent, second French-Canadian prime minister of Canada, born 1882.
— American writer Langston Hughes born 1902.
2 Ground-Hog Day.
— By the Treaty of Guadalupe Hidalgo, Mexico gave New Mexico and California to the United States, 1848.
— James Joyce, Irish novelist and poet, born 1882.
— Violinist Jascha Heifetz born 1901.
— The last German troops surrendered in the Stalingrad pocket, completing the Soviet Union's victory at Stalingrad, during World War II, 1943.
3 German composer Felix Mendelssohn born 1809.
— Horace Greeley, American publisher, born 1811.
4 Confederate States of America organized by a temporary committee that met at Montgomery, Ala., 1861.
— Philippine Rebellion against the United States began, 1899.
— Charles A. Lindbergh, American aviator, born 1902.
— Yalta Conference began, 1945.
— Amendment 24 to the U.S. Constitution, banning poll tax, proclaimed, 1964.
5 Evangelist Dwight L. Moody born 1837.
6 Queen Anne of England born 1665.
— Aaron Burr, American political leader, born 1756.
— Massachusetts ratified the Constitution, 1788.
— Home run king "Babe" Ruth born 1895.
— The United States Senate ratified the peace treaty ending the Spanish-American War, 1899.

— Ronald Reagan, 40th President of the United States, born in Tampico, Ill., 1911.
— Princess Elizabeth became Queen Elizabeth II of Great Britain, 1952.
— Amendment 20 to the United States Constitution, moving Inauguration Day to January 20, proclaimed, 1933.
7 British novelist Charles Dickens born 1812.
— Nobel Prize-winning novelist Sinclair Lewis born 1885.
8 Mary, Queen of Scots, executed, 1587.
— College of William and Mary, second oldest college in the United States, chartered, 1693.
— John Ruskin, English essayist and critic, born 1819.
— William T. Sherman, Union Army general in the Civil War, born 1820.
— Jules Verne, French novelist, born 1828.
— Russo-Japanese War began, 1904.
— Boy Scouts of America incorporated, 1910.
9 William Henry Harrison, ninth President of the United States, born in Charles City County, Virginia, 1773.
10 France surrendered Canada to Great Britain by the Treaty of Paris, 1763.
— English essayist and critic Charles Lamb born 1775.
11 Thomas A. Edison, American inventor, born 1847.
12 Thaddeus Kosciusko, Polish patriot, born 1746.
— Abraham Lincoln, 16th President of the United States, born near present-day Hodgenville, Ky., 1809.
— Charles Darwin, British naturalist, born 1809.
— John L. Lewis, American labor leader, born 1880.
13 Talleyrand, French statesman, born 1754.
— Grant Wood, American painter, born 1891.

Feb. birthstone— amethyst

Feb. flower— primrose

Four U.S. Presidents born in February—Washington, Feb. 22; W. H. Harrison, Feb. 9; Lincoln, Feb. 12; Reagan, Feb. 6

ing the rest of the year are blessed on February 2.

Popular beliefs. People often refer to the second day of February as Ground-Hog Day. According to many old stories, the ground hog, or woodchuck, comes out of its burrow on February 2 to look for its shadow. If the sun is shining and the ground hog can see its shadow, it goes back to sleep for a while, and winter is not over. If the ground hog cannot see its shadow, it begins its springtime activities. Only superstitious people believe this story.

February symbols. Many people consider the primrose the special flower for February. The amethyst is the birthstone for February.　　Sharron G. Uhler

Quotations

The February sunshine steeps your boughs,
And tints the buds and swells the leaves within.

William Cullen Bryant

I crown thee king of intimate delights,

Fireside enjoyments, home-born happiness,
And all the comforts that the lowly roof
Of undisturb'd retirement, and the hours
Of long uninterrupted evening know.

William Cowper

Hail to thy returning festival, old Bishop Valentine!
Like unto thee, assuredly, there is no other mitred
father in the calendar.

Charles Lamb

Thirty days hath September,
April, June, and November;
All the rest have thirty-one,
Excepting February alone
Which hath but twenty-eight, in fine,
Till leap year gives it twenty-nine.

Old saying

Related articles in *World Book* include:

Amethyst	Ground-Hog Day	Primrose
Calendar	Leap year	Valentine's Day
Candlemas Day		

Important February events

14 Valentine's Day.
　—Oregon became the 33rd state to join the Union, 1859.
　—John Barrymore, American actor, born 1882.
　—Arizona became the 48th state, 1912.
15 Galileo, Italian astronomer and physicist, born 1564.
　—Inventor Cyrus McCormick born 1809.
　—Susan B. Anthony, American woman suffrage leader, born 1820.
　—Elihu Root, U.S. statesman and lawyer, born 1845.
16 Henry Adams, American historian, born 1838.
17 Thomas Robert Malthus, British economist, born 1766.
　—Marian Anderson, American singer, born 1902.
18 Mary I, first reigning queen of England, born 1516.
　—John Bunyan's *Pilgrim's Progress* was licensed for publication, 1678.
　—Jefferson Davis took the oath as provisional President of the Confederate States of America, 1861.
　—Wendell Willkie, American political leader, born 1892.
　—San Francisco's Golden Gate International Exposition opened, 1939.
19 Polish astronomer Nicolaus Copernicus born 1473.
　—David Garrick, English actor, born 1717.
　—Thomas A. Edison patented the phonograph, 1878.
20 Astronaut John H. Glenn, Jr., became first American to orbit the earth, 1962.
21 Richard M. Nixon became first U.S. President to visit China, 1972.
22 George Washington, first U.S. President, born in Westmoreland County, Va., 1732.
　—German philosopher Arthur Schopenhauer born 1788.

22 James Russell Lowell, American poet, born 1819.
　—The United States acquired the Florida territory from Spain, 1819.
23 Samuel Pepys, English diarist, born 1633.
　—English composer George Frideric Handel born 1685.
　—W. E. B. Du Bois, American civil rights leader, historian, and sociologist, born 1868.
　—Amendment 25 to the U.S. Constitution, on presidential succession, proclaimed, 1967.
24 Winslow Homer, American painter, born 1836.
25 José de San Martín, liberator of Argentina, Chile, and Peru, born 1778.
　—Enrico Caruso, Italian singer, born 1873.
　—Amendment 16 to the Constitution, setting up the income tax, proclaimed, 1913.
　—President Ferdinand Marcos of the Philippines resigned from office and fled the country, 1986.
26 Victor Hugo, French poet and novelist, born 1802.
　—Napoleon escaped from island of Elba, 1815.
　—American frontiersman William Frederick Cody, better known as "Buffalo Bill," born 1846.
27 Henry Wadsworth Longfellow, American poet, born 1807.
28 American author Ben Hecht, born 1894.
　—Vincent Massey took the oath as the first Canadian-born governor general of Canada, 1952.
29 Marquis de Montcalm, French commander in Quebec, born 1712.
　—Gioacchino Antonio Rossini, Italian composer, born 1792.

WORLD BOOK illustrations by Mike Hagel

Feb. 6—Elizabeth II becomes queen of Great Britain

Feb. 14—Valentine's Day

Feb. 20—John Glenn orbits the earth

Feb. 23—W. E. B. Du Bois born

Federal Aviation Administration (FAA) is an agency in the United States Department of Transportation. It controls air traffic; certifies aircraft, airports, and pilots and other personnel; and operates navigation aids. The FAA writes and enforces air safety regulations and air traffic procedures. It requires airlines and airport operators to provide antihijacking security. The agency also conducts aviation research and promotes the safety and development of civil aviation. Its research and development services deal with air traffic, airway facilities, flight standards, logistics, security, and systems.

Founded in 1958, the FAA absorbed the Civil Aeronautics Administration, Airways Modernization Board, and safety rule-making functions of the Civil Aeronautics Board. An administrator appointed by the President directs the FAA.

Critically reviewed by Federal Aviation Administration

Federal Bureau of Investigation (FBI) is the chief investigating branch of the United States Department of Justice. The FBI investigates more than 180 kinds of federal crimes, including bank robbery and kidnapping. It also collects evidence in lawsuits that involve the federal government. In addition, the bureau gathers *intelligence* (information) about individuals or groups that it believes are dangerous to national security. FBI investigators are called *special agents.*

A director, appointed by the President with the approval of the Senate, supervises the FBI from headquarters in Washington, D.C. The FBI has about 60 offices in the United States and Puerto Rico and 15 offices in other countries. It employs more than 19,000 men and women, of whom about 7,750 are special agents. It has an annual budget of about $750 million.

FBI operations

Criminal investigation. The FBI investigates such federal crimes as assault on the President, bank robbery, bombing, hijacking, and kidnapping. It handles cases involving stolen money, property, or vehicles that have been taken from one state to another. The bureau fights organized crime and, at the request of state or local authorities, it helps capture fleeing criminals. The FBI also examines reported violations of civil rights laws. In addition, it works with the federal Drug Enforcement Administration to investigate violations of federal criminal drug laws. In all criminal investigations, the FBI gives its findings to the Justice Department, which determines whether to take further action.

Intelligence operations of the FBI consist of gathering information about individuals or organizations engaged in activities that may endanger national security. These operations include the investigation of rebellions, riots, spy activities, treason, and threats to overthrow the government. The FBI reports to the President, Congress, or the Justice Department for action.

Other services. The FBI provides various services to law enforcement agencies throughout the United States and in other countries. Such agencies may request help from the FBI Identification Division, the FBI Laboratory, and the National Crime Information Center (NCIC). The bureau also trains selected police officials in advanced methods of fighting crime.

The FBI Identification Division has the world's largest collection of fingerprints. Its files contain about 169 mil-

Federal Bureau of Investigation

The FBI Academy in Quantico, Va., trains future agents in the use of firearms and other crime-fighting methods.

lion prints. Police officials use these prints to identify over 40,000 suspects annually.

The FBI Laboratory is the world's finest crime laboratory. FBI scientists examine over 600,000 pieces of evidence yearly, including bullets, handwriting samples, and tire prints. They are often asked to testify in court.

The NCIC is a computerized information system that stores almost 5 million records concerning criminal suspects and stolen property. A network of about 90 computer terminals links the NCIC with law agencies in the United States, Puerto Rico, and Canada. The NCIC daily handles more than 170,000 requests for information, or replies to questions.

The FBI issues an annual publication called *Uniform Crime Reports for the United States,* which includes a record of rates and trends in major crimes. The bureau also distributes a list with descriptions of its *Ten Most Wanted Fugitives.* The FBI Academy in Quantico, Va., provides training in advanced methods of fighting crime for more than 5,000 police officials annually.

FBI agents

Men and women who wish to be special agents must be U.S. citizens between 23 and 35 years old and in excellent physical condition. There are five entry programs, all requiring a college degree: law, accounting, language, engineering/science, and diversified (any discipline, plus three years of work experience).

Future agents go through a 15-week training program at the FBI National Academy. They study crime detection, evidence, constitutional and criminal law, and methods of investigation. They also learn self-defense and how to use firearms. Agents later receive periodic refresher training to keep them up to date.

History

In 1908, Attorney General Charles J. Bonaparte organized a group of special investigators in the Justice Department. This group, called the Bureau of Investigation, investigated such offenses as illegal business practices and land sales. Its first director was Stanley W. Finch, an attorney. J. Edgar Hoover, a Justice Department lawyer, became director of the bureau in 1924 and headed it until his death in 1972. Congress gave the bureau its present name in 1935.

A wave of bank robberies, kidnappings, and other violent crimes broke out in the United States during the 1930's. Congress passed laws giving the FBI increased authority to combat this lawlessness. FBI agents, who were nicknamed *G-Men,* or *Government Men,* became admired for tracking down such gangsters as John Dillinger and George "Machine Gun" Kelly.

During World War II (1939-1945), the FBI broke up enemy spy rings in the United States. In the 1950's and 1960's, special agents arrested Communist spies who had stolen secret atomic and military information. The bureau also investigated protest organizations in the 1960's and early 1970's. Clarence M. Kelley, a former special agent, became director of the FBI in 1973.

In 1975, a Senate committee reported that the FBI had acted illegally or improperly in a number of cases. The committee revealed that FBI agents had committed burglaries during some investigations and had spied illegally on U.S. citizens. The Senate investigators also charged that Hoover had given certain Presidents damaging personal information about some of their political opponents. In 1976, Kelley apologized for the FBI's past abuses of power. He said some of the bureau's activities under Hoover had been "clearly wrong and quite indefensible." The Justice Department set up guidelines to prevent further abuses by the FBI. William H. Webster, a federal judge, became director of the bureau in 1978.

George T. Felkenes

See also **Hoover, J. Edgar; Abscam; Crime.**

Additional resources

Powers, Richard G. *G-Men: Hoover's FBI in American Popular Culture.* Southern Illinois Univ. Press, 1983.
Tully, Andrew. *Inside the FBI: From the Files of the Federal Bureau of Investigation and Independent Sources.* McGraw, 1980.
Ungar, Sanford J. *FBI.* Little, Brown, 1976. Covers the bureau's history and role.

Federal Communications Commission (FCC) is an independent agency of the United States government. The FCC was created in 1934 to centralize the regulation of U.S. interstate and foreign communication by radio, wire, and cable. It also regulates radio and television stations, without censorship authority.

The FCC (1) approves or disapproves interstate rate increases for telephone and telegraph systems; (2) allocates bands of frequencies for different types of radio and television operations; (3) assigns specific frequencies, power, and call letters; (4) issues licenses to stations and operators of stations; and (5) monitors radio broadcasts to detect unlicensed operations and technical violations, and to assist ships and planes in distress. It also regulates the Communications Satellite Corporation, a private corporation that owns and operates the U.S. portion of the global satellite system.

About 13 million stations hold FCC licenses. They operate about 50 million transmitters in 70 categories of services. The transmitters are used for communication by aircraft, ships, land transportation services, the national medical emergency service, police and fire departments, individuals, business and industry, AM and FM radio, television broadcast services, and telephone and telegraph systems.

The FCC has five commissioners. The President, with Senate approval, appoints them for five-year terms.

Critically reviewed by Federal Communications Commission

See also **Radio** (Government regulation); **Television** (Government regulations); **Monitoring station.**

Federal court. See Court; United States, Government of the (The judicial branch).

Federal Crop Insurance Corporation (FCIC) is an agency of the U.S. Department of Agriculture. It offers farmers insurance against loss of crops because of such natural hazards as drought, flood, or freeze. Federal Crop Insurance does not guarantee a profit, nor does it cover losses that result from bad farming practices. The FCIC was created in 1938.

Critically reviewed by Federal Crop Insurance Corporation

Federal Deposit Insurance Corporation (FDIC) insures the deposits of about 97 per cent of the banks in the United States. If an insured bank fails and is not taken over by another insured bank, the FDIC pays the depositors up to $100,000 each. It also provides financial assistance to reopen closed insured banks or to keep insured banks from closing. The FDIC has authority to examine all insured banks to make sure they are using safe banking practices. It also passes on bank mergers and acts on applications of nonmembers of the Federal Reserve System to change location or establish branches.

A board of three directors manages the FDIC. The President appoints two directors for six-year terms. The comptroller of the currency, who is appointed by the President, is an ex-officio member. The FDIC was created in 1933 to help end the banking crisis of the 1930's. Its funds come from assessments paid by insured banks and from earnings on U.S. government securities.

Critically reviewed by the Federal Deposit Insurance Corporation

Federal district is a tract of land which a country sets apart as the seat of its national capital. The U.S. District of Columbia is a federal district. Other countries that have a federal district include Australia, Brazil, Malaysia, Mexico, and Venezuela. In Australia, it is called a *capital territory* and in Malaysia it is known as a *federal territory.* See also **Canberra; Mexico City; Washington, D.C.**

Federal Election Commission is an independent agency of the United States government. The commission enforces the Federal Election Campaign Act, which governs campaign financing for election to federal offices. The act includes requirements to disclose campaign contributions and expenses, restrictions on the amounts any individual or group may contribute to a candidate, and prohibitions on the use of corporation and labor union funds for contributions. The commission also administers the public financing of presidential campaigns and national party nominating conventions.

The agency has the power to conduct investigations and audits of campaign funds. It serves as a national clearing house for information and research about the administration of elections.

The commission was established by Congress in 1974. It has six members who are appointed by the President, subject to the approval of the Senate. No more than three members may belong to the same political party.

Critically reviewed by the Federal Election Commission

Federal government. See Federalism.

Federal Hall, in New York City, was the first Capitol of the United States under the Constitution. City Hall, the original building on the site, was erected in 1699. It also housed the Stamp Act Congress (1765), and the Congress of the Confederation from 1785 to 1789. On April 30, 1789, George Washington took the oath as President there. The present structure was built in 1842. Federal Hall became a national memorial in 1955.

Marshall Smelser

See also L'Enfant, Pierre C.

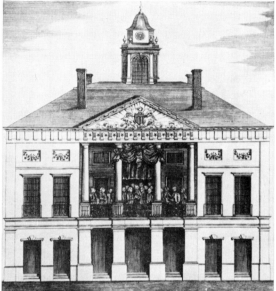

Engraving (1790) by Amos Doolittle; National Park Service

Federal Hall, New York. George Washington was inaugurated President on the balcony of this building in 1789.

Federal Highway Administration (FHWA) is an agency of the United States Department of Transportation. It supervises federal aid for highway construction and improvement. This program involves about 835,000 miles (1,344,000 kilometers) of highways out of a total of about 3,880,000 miles (6,244,000 kilometers) of roads and streets in the United States. The program costs billions of dollars annually.

The federal government pays 90 per cent of the cost of construction or improvement in the interstate highway system, and the states pay 10 per cent. For work involving state or local highways, the government pays 75 per cent and the states pay 25 per cent.

The FHWA, which is directed by an administrator appointed by the President, has offices in every state. Congress established the FHWA in 1966. The agency replaced the Bureau of Public Roads.

Critically reviewed by the Federal Highway Administration

Federal Home Loan Bank Board is an independent federal agency that supervises most savings and loan associations in the United States. It directs the Federal Home Loan Bank System, which provides credit to member institutions that issue mortgages. It also directs the Federal Savings and Loan Insurance Corporation, which insures the savings of depositors in member associations for up to $100,000.

The board has three members, whom the President appoints to four-year terms. Nominees are subject to confirmation by the Senate. The board was created in 1932. Critically reviewed by the Federal Home Loan Bank Board

Federal Housing Administration (FHA) is a United States government agency that works with private industry to provide good housing. The FHA insures mortgages on private homes, multifamily rental housing projects, cooperative and condominium housing, nursing homes, and hospitals. The FHA also insures loans to improve property and provides special programs for elderly people, military veterans, and disaster victims. The loans are made by banks, building associations, mortgage firms, and other approved lending institutions. The borrower applies to the lender for the loans. Most FHA operations are paid for by the agency's income from fees, insurance premiums on loans, and interest on investment of insurance reserves.

The FHA also determines minimum property standards for housing, analyzes local housing markets, and makes appraisals, land-planning surveys, and technical studies. Created in 1934, the FHA forms part of the Department of Housing and Urban Development. A commissioner heads the FHA and also serves as assistant secretary for housing.

Critically reviewed by the Federal Housing Administration

Federal Land Bank. See Farm Credit System.

Federal Maritime Commission is an independent agency of the United States government that administers the nation's shipping laws. It regulates the rates, services, and agreements of U.S. shipping firms. It also regulates ocean freight forwarders and terminal operators.

The commission requires evidence of financial responsibility from owners and charterers of vessels that carry 50 or more passengers and that sail from U.S. ports. This policy ensures that the owners and charterers can pay any claims involving accidental injuries and deaths. It also ensures that they can refund fares if a voyage is canceled.

The Federal Maritime Commission was established in 1961. The President appoints the commission's five members with the advice and consent of the Senate. The President also designates one of the five commissioners to serve as chairman of the commission.

Critically reviewed by the Federal Maritime Commission

Federal Mediation and Conciliation Service (FMCS) is an independent agency of the United States government. It helps prevent or settle disputes between labor unions and management that affect interstate commerce. Another government agency, the National Mediation Board, handles such disputes in the airline and railroad industries. *Mediation* involves giving both sides in a dispute various solutions to consider in working for a compromise.

The law requires either management or a union to give 60-day notice of any intention to end or change a labor contract. If the employer and the union do not reach an agreement within 30 days after such a notice, they must notify the FMCS. The service then investigates the case and decides whether to intervene. In most disputes, the FMCS intervenes at the request of one or more of the opposing parties. But it may intervene in any dispute without such a request. The FMCS does not

The **Federal Reserve System** is the national banking system of the United States. The nation is divided into 12 districts, each with a Federal Reserve Bank. These banks issue Federal Reserve notes, which make up nearly all the paper money in circulation. A number on each note identifies the bank that issued it. The system also includes 25 Federal Reserve branch banks throughout the country.

★ Federal Reserve Bank

• Federal Reserve Branch Bank

WORLD BOOK map

serve as a law enforcement or regulatory agency. It depends on persuasion.

The FMCS has about 250 mediators in 76 offices in principal industrial areas. The agency also maintains a roster of qualified private citizens who *arbitrate* (judge) labor-contract disputes (see **Arbitration** [Industrial, or labor, arbitration]). The FMCS was established under the Taft-Hartley Act of 1947.

Critically reviewed by the Federal Mediation and Conciliation Service

Federal National Mortgage Association is a private corporation chartered by the United States government. It is commonly referred to as *Fannie Mae.* The corporation helps assure that enough money is available for home mortgages. Fannie Mae buys mortgages from such institutions as banks, savings and loan associations, mortgage companies, and insurance companies. It purchases conventional mortgages and mortgages insured or guaranteed by such government agencies as the Federal Housing Administration (FHA) and the Department of Veterans Affairs. Fannie Mae also issues and guarantees mortgage-backed securities.

Fannie Mae was established in 1938 as a government-owned corporation and was placed under the Housing and Home Finance Agency in 1950. In 1954, Fannie Mae was reorganized as a corporation owned jointly by the government and private stockholders. It became a totally private corporation in 1970.

Critically reviewed by the Federal National Mortgage Association

Federal Reserve Bank. See Federal Reserve System.

Federal Reserve System (FRS) is an independent agency of the United States government that helps oversee the nation's banking system. The FRS, nicknamed the *Fed,* is known as the *central bank* of the United States. Its most important job is to manage the country's supply of money and credit. The FRS also performs many financial services for the federal government and provides numerous services to commercial banks in the United States.

Organization. The FRS has 12 Federal Reserve Banks and 25 Federal Reserve Bank branches. Each Federal Reserve Bank (FRB) operates in one of the country's 12 Federal Reserve districts. Most districts have from one to five FRB branches, each of which offers many of the services that FRB's provide. Banks in the FRS use the FRB in their district much as people use a bank in their community.

All national commercial banks are required by law to be members of the FRS. Membership is optional for state-chartered banks. But all deposit-taking institutions are subject to FRS requirements regarding a certain amount of deposits that cannot be used for loans.

Two main committees direct FRS policies. They are the *Board of Governors* and the *Federal Open Market Committee.*

The Board of Governors administers the system. It has seven members. Each member is appointed by the President of the United States to a 14-year term, subject to the consent of the U.S. Senate. The President names one member to serve as chairman for four years.

The Federal Open Market Committee makes the main decisions on FRS monetary policies. It sets the FRS policy for trading government securities, such as treasury bills, bonds, and notes. The committee consists of the FRS governors, the president of the New York City FRB, and the presidents of four other FRB's. It meets formally eight times a year and is in telephone contact between meetings when necessary.

Two other organizations assist the FRS board. The Federal Advisory Council advises the board on business and financial conditions. The Consumer Advisory Council advises the board on its responsibilities under consumer credit protection laws.

The FRS operates more independently of the President and Congress than do typical government agencies. A President may appoint no more than two FRS governors during a four-year period unless additional governors resign or die. The FRS does not rely on Congress for funding. It raises all its operating expenses from investment income and fees for its own services. The FRS reports to Congress about its proposed policies but has considerable freedom in policy decisions.

Managing the money supply. The FRS can influence the flow of credit and money three main ways. It can conduct *open-market operations,* change the *discount rate,* or change *reserve requirements.*

Open-market operations are the sale or purchase of government securities by the FRS. The FRS sells securities to dealers if it wants to decrease the quantity of money that banks have available to loan. Funds issued to pay for these securities are drawn on banks. Thus, the banks have less money to loan, and the amount of money and credit in the economy is reduced. To increase the money supply and provide more money for loans, the FRS buys securities.

The discount rate is the interest rate banks pay when they borrow money from an FRB. By raising the discount rate, the FRS can decrease the ability of banks to make loans and thus reduce the flow of credit and money. Lowering the rate has the opposite effect.

Reserve requirements are percentages of deposits that almost all deposit-taking institutions must set aside either as currency in their vaults or as deposits in their district FRB. An institution can use the rest of its deposits to make loans. Raising the reserve requirement reduces the money an institution has available for loans and shrinks the money supply. Lowering the requirement enables institutions to make more loans and increases the money supply.

Other FRS activities. The FRS has several jobs besides controlling the money supply. It works with the U.S. Department of the Treasury to put new coins and paper currency into circulation by issuing them to banks. It also processes checks and holds deposits for the Treasury and other federal agencies. The FRS also sets *margin requirements* for the purchase of certain securities by investors. A margin requirement is a percentage of the security's price that must be paid in cash.

The FRS also serves and supervises banks. It holds their cash reserves, lends them money, and exchanges checks for them. It enforces regulations set under consumer protection laws. The FRS reviews the operating procedures of state member banks. It also supervises the activities of member banks in other countries and regulates certain firms that deal in international finance.

For a detailed explanation of how the FRS influences the economy of the United States, see **Money** (How the money supply is determined; The role of the Federal Reserve System).

History. Congress established the FRS in 1913 to provide a flexible currency for the nation and to strengthen the supervision of the banking system. In the mid-1930's Congress gave the FRS authority to set reserve and margin requirements. Later laws made it easier for the FRS to expand credit when a financial disaster seemed likely. Through the years, the FRS promoted economic stability chiefly by working to keep interest rates low in recessions and allowing them to rise in periods of rapid economic expansion.

During the 1940's and 1970's, interest rates were kept too low and the resulting inflation hurt the economy. In 1979, the FRS adopted a policy aimed at controlling the money supply more directly instead of interest rates. This policy slowed the growth of the money supply, limited the expansion of credit, and led to a low rate of inflation. But it also contributed to two recessions in the early 1980's. In 1982, the FRS deemphasized the controls on money supply growth and began working to bring about lower interest rates.   William G. Dewald

See also **Bank; Inflation** (Monetary policy); **Volcker, Paul Adolph.**

Federal style. See **Furniture** (Early American furniture; picture: The Federal style).

Federal system. See **Federalism.**

Federal Trade Commission (FTC) is an independent U.S. government agency that works to (1) maintain free and fair competition in the economy and (2) protect consumers from unfair or misleading practices.

The FTC issues *cease and desist orders* against companies or individuals that it believes engage in unlawful practices. The firms or persons must then stop such practices unless a court decision sets aside the orders. The FTC also issues trade regulation guides for business and industry and conducts a wide variety of consumer-protection activities. Congress created the FTC in 1914. The President appoints the five FTC commissioners, subject to Senate approval, to seven-year terms.

Critically reviewed by the Federal Trade Commission

See also **Advertising** (Regulation of advertising); **Monopoly and competition** (History).

Federalism is a system in which political power is divided between a *central* (national) government and smaller governmental units. The central government is often called the *federal government,* and the smaller units, *states* or *provinces.* The division of powers is usually defined in a constitution. The United States, Canada, Australia, and Switzerland have federal systems. To a degree, so do Mexico and India.

Federal systems of government differ from *unitary* systems. In a unitary system, all power legally derives from the central government. States or provinces have only those powers that the central government gives them. Some nations that appear to use the federal system really use the unitary system. Their provinces are administrative units rather than political units with separate powers. The Soviet Union outwardly has a federal system, but domination of the government and society by the Communist Party make Soviet federalism illusory.

In a true federal system, some powers are constitutionally reserved for the states or provinces. The central government has direct authority over the people concerning powers granted to it in the constitution. This feature distinguishes a federal system from a loose grouping of states, commonly called a *confederation.* A confederation can only act through its individual member states.   Alexander J. Groth

See also **Government; State government; Canada, Government of; United States, Government of the;** and the *Government* section of the countries mentioned. For a *Reading and Study Guide,* see *Federalism* in the Research Guide/Index, Volume 22.

Additional resources

Goode, Stephen. *The New Federalism: States' Rights in American History.* Watts, 1983. Suitable for younger readers.
Henig, Jeffrey R. *Public Policy and Federalism: Issues in State and Local Politics.* St. Martin's, 1985.
Smiley, Donald V. *Canada in Question: Federalism in the Eighties.* 3rd ed. McGraw (Scarborough, Ont.), 1980.

Federalist, The, is a series of 85 letters written to newspapers by Alexander Hamilton, James Madison, and John Jay. The letters urge ratification of the Constitution. The letters sought to influence the New York ratifying convention. All except eight of the essays appeared during 1787 and 1788 under the signature "Publius." They appeared in the *Independent Journal,* a semiweekly New York newspaper. Hamilton wrote 51 of the essays, Madison 29, and Jay 5. The collected essays appeared in book form as *The Federalist.*

The Federalist authors used both logical argument and appeal to prejudice. They emphasized the weaknesses in the Articles of Confederation, the dangers in British sea power and Spanish intrigue, the desirability and need of a stronger central government, and the safeguards of the new Constitution.

The authors did not defend every point in the proposed Constitution. But they argued that it was the best document on which agreement could be reached. They asserted that the check and balance system of the Constitution would create a strong government and still protect the states' rights. The Federalist papers greatly influenced acceptance of the Constitution. They are still important in interpreting it.   Marshall Smelser

Federalist Party was one of the first political organizations in the United States. The members of the Federalist Party favored a strong central government.

After George Washington became President, a political division soon appeared between those who favored a strong federal government and those who opposed it. The Federalist Party developed under the leadership of Alexander Hamilton, Washington's secretary of the treasury. Hamilton believed that the Constitution should be loosely interpreted to build up federal power. He had aristocratic views and favored the interests of business. He wanted the new federal government on a sound financial basis, and sponsored a national bank.

Thomas Jefferson opposed Hamilton. Jefferson's followers called themselves Republicans. Historians often use the name Democratic-Republicans for Jefferson's party. The Democratic-Republicans believed that the Constitution should be strictly interpreted, and that the states and the citizens should retain as many of their powers and rights as possible. The Federalists controlled the national government until 1801, when Jefferson became President. They continued to oppose Democratic-Republican policies until their party broke up soon after the election of 1816.

The term *Federalists* also is used to indicate those persons who fought for the adoption of the Constitution in 1787 and 1788.   John R. Alden

See also **Political party** (Development of parties in the United States); **Adams, John** (Vice President; Adams' Administration); **Anti-Federalists; Democratic-Republican Party; Hamilton, Alexander.**

Fee, in modern property law, describes the kind of ownership that may pass to an owner's heirs on his or her death. A *fee simple absolute* is complete ownership of land. A *fee simple determinable* is ownership that is automatically lost if the property is used in a way prohibited by the previous owner. A *fee simple conditional* gives the previous owner a choice of whether to retake land used in a certain way. A *fee tail* is ownership that must pass in a certain way, as from father to eldest son. The term *fee,* or *fief,* also referred to land ownership under the English feudal system. A fief was also the piece of land that a lord granted to a servant in return for certain services (see **Feudalism**).   Sherman L. Cohn

Feed is a term for food given to farm animals. *Roughage feeds* (coarse foods) include soybeans, cowpeas, and pasture plants such as grass and alfalfa. Some of these plants are dried and fed to livestock as hay. Farmers often preserve whole corn plants and other crops, and use them as a feed called *silage.* Grains of corn, grain sorghum, or barley can be ground and mixed with other ingredients to make another kind of feed.

Farmers also give livestock extra and unused products from milling, brewing, meat packing, and other industries. Farmers give animals a combination of feeds to make sure the livestock get the nutrients necessary for good health.   Robert Allen Alexander

Related articles in *World Book* include:

Alfalfa	Farm and farming	Grass
Cattle (Feeding)	(Livestock care; il-	Hay
Chicken	lustration: An auto-	Hog (Raising hogs)
Corn (Livestock feed)	mated livestock	Silo
Cotton (Uses)	farm)	Soybean
Dairying (Feeding)	Grain	

Feed crop. See Farm and farming (Processing and storage).

Feedback. See Automation; Cybernetics.

Feet. See Foot.

Feininger, *FY nihng uhr,* **Lyonel** (1871-1956), was an American painter whose works combine qualities of cubism and expressionism. The subject matter of his mature work is based on nature, and is characterized by flat crystalline planes of color and thin straight lines.

Feininger was born in New York City. His parents were musicians. In 1887, he went to Germany to join his

Oil painting (1930); Neue Staatsgalerie, Munich, Germany

Feininger's *The Market Church in Halle* shows how the artist used straight lines to divide forms and space into flat planes.

parents, who were on tour. Feininger stayed in Europe and was a political and satirical cartoonist in Berlin and Paris from 1894 to 1908. He then turned to painting and soon earned an international reputation for his work while living in Germany. In 1919 Feininger became the first professor chosen by Walter Gropius for the Bauhaus school of art and design in Germany. He returned to the United States in 1937, after the Nazis labeled him a "degenerate artist." George Ehrlich

See also **Bauhaus.**

Feinstein, *FYN styn,* **Dianne** (1933-), was mayor of San Francisco from 1978 to 1988. Feinstein, a Democrat, became one of the most prominent women in American politics. In 1984, Democratic presidential nominee Walter F. Mondale considered Feinstein as a vice presidential nominee, but chose Representative Geraldine A. Ferraro of New York.

Feinstein was born in San Francisco and graduated from Stanford University. From 1969 to 1978, she served on the San Francisco Board of Supervisors. Feinstein was board president from 1970 to 1972, from 1974 to 1976, and in 1978. She succeeded to the office of mayor in 1978, when Mayor George R. Moscone was assassinated. Feinstein was elected mayor in 1979 and re-elected in 1983.

©Tom Gibbons

Dianne Feinstein

In April 1983, before the end of her first term, Feinstein easily won a *recall election*—that is, a vote to decide whether she should be removed from office. Feinstein's sponsorship of a ban on handguns had led to a petition for the recall. Her accomplishments as mayor included such projects as redeveloping downtown San Francisco, rebuilding the city's cable car system, and eliminating a deficit in the city budget. June Sochen

Feisal. See Faisal.

Feke, *feek,* **Robert** (1707?-1752?), was the earliest noteworthy American-born painter. His *Portrait of Isaac Royall and His Family* (1741) combines a knowledge of English portrait poses and the clear outlines of American primitive painting. The portrait is reproduced in **Colonial life in America** (Arts and sciences).

Feke was born in Oyster Bay, Long Island, N.Y. Little is known about his life. By 1741 he was painting portraits in Boston. He was married in 1742 in Newport, R.I., where he lived until 1750. Like many colonial artists, Feke traveled frequently in search of commissions. In 1744, a visiting Scot wrote in his journal that he had met Feke. The Scot described Feke as "the most extraordinary genius ever I knew for he does pictures tolerably well by force of genius, never having had any teaching."
Elizabeth Garrity Ellis

Feldspar is any of the most abundant group of minerals on the surface of the earth. These minerals make up about 60 per cent of the earth's crust. Feldspars occur in most *igneous rocks* and in many *metamorphic* and *sedimentary rocks* (see **Rock**). Extremely large feldspar crystals are found in a coarse-grained igneous rock called *pegmatite.* Feldspars rank among the hardest minerals (see **Hardness**). Feldspars range in color from clear white or gray to shades of blue, green, or pink.

All feldspars contain alumina and silica. The minerals may be classified into two general groups, *alkali feldspars* and *plagioclase feldspars,* according to the other elements they contain. All alkali feldspars contain potassium, and most contain sodium. The most common minerals in this group are *microcline, orthoclase,* and *sanidine.* Most plagioclase feldspars, such as *andesine* and *labradorite,* contain both sodium and calcium. Some feldspar crystals, called *perthites,* consist of combinations of alkali and plagioclase feldspars.

Feldspar is used in making glass and pottery. Feldspar crystals of especially beautiful color and luster may be used as gemstones, ornaments, and architectural decorations. The most popular of these crystals are *moonstone* (milky-white perthite), *Amazon stone* (green microcline), and rainbow-colored labradorite.

A process called *weathering* breaks down feldspars into other minerals, chiefly clay minerals and salts. *Kaolin,* the most important of these clay minerals, is used in making fine chinaware. Feldspar in the form of clay is also used as a coating and filler in the production of paper. Mary Emma Wagner

See also **Earth** (Weathering); **Granite; Moonstone; Crystal** (picture).

Fellahin. See **Egypt** (Rural life).

Feller, Bob (1918-), became the strikeout king of baseball while pitching for the Cleveland Indians. His blazing fast ball earned him the nickname "Rapid Robert." A right-handed pitcher, Feller struck out 2,581 batters in 570 games from 1936 through 1956. He led the American League seven times in strikeouts. Feller won 266 games during his career. He won 20 or more games in six seasons, leading the league in victories each time. His finest season was 1940, when he won 27 games and lost 11. Known for his durability, Feller led the league five times in number of innings pitched. He pitched three no-hit games, and struck out 348 batters in 1946.

Robert William Andrew Feller was born in Van Meter, Iowa. He joined the Indians after graduating from high school. In 1962, he was elected to the National Baseball Hall of Fame. Dave Nightingale

Fellini, Federico (1920-), is a famous Italian motion-picture director. He originates his own ideas for his movies, usually developing the story as the film is being made. Many of his films blend realism and social satire with fantasy. They rely heavily on the use of symbolism and imagery, which create dreamlike sequences that are sometimes deliberately obscure.

Fellini was born in Rimini. As a child, he ran away to the circus for a few days, and the experience inspired much of his work. He collaborated with Alberto Lattuada on his first motion picture, *Variety Lights* (1951). Fellini's first international success, *La Strada* (1954), won an Academy Award as best foreign film and established his wife, Julietta Masina, as a star. This grimly realistic, yet poetic film describes the relationship between a brutal circus strongman and a half-witted young girl.

Fellini's *La Dolce Vita* (1959) is an autobiographical and complex study of moral corruption in Italian society of the day. He also used autobiographical material in *8 $\frac{1}{2}$* (1963). *Amarcord* (1974) won another Academy Award as best foreign language film. Fellini's other major motion pictures include *I Vitelloni* (1953), *Nights of Cabiria* (1957), *Juliet of the Spirits* (1965), *Fellini's Roma* (1972), and *The City of Women* (1979). Rachel Gallagher

Fellowship is a sum of money given to scholars so they can continue their studies. Some fellowships are for specified periods of time, but others are for life. Fellowships have been made since the Middle Ages.

Today, fellowships are usually given by universities, foundations, learned societies, corporations, and governments. Universities give fellowships for graduate work. Sometimes fellows teach classes. Foundations and learned societies give fellowships for graduate study and individual research in such areas as education, medicine, and international relations. Large foundation and learned society fellowship programs in the United States include those of the Alfred P. Sloan Foundation, the American Council of Learned Societies, the John D. and Catherine T. MacArthur Foundation, the John Simon Guggenheim Memorial Foundation, and the Social Science Research Council. Corporation fellowships often encourage study and research in fields of interest to the sponsoring corporation. The federal government conducts fellowship programs in the arts, humanities, and sciences through the National Endowment for the Arts, the National Endowment for the Humanities, and the National Science Foundation.

In the United States, fellowships are usually granted for one or two years. The amount of money given may vary from a few hundred to several thousand dollars. In Great Britain, the grants are often given for three to five years. Joseph C. Kiger

See also **Foundations; Scholarship.**

Fellowship of Christian Athletes is a nondenominational organization of athletes, coaches, and clergy that promotes Christian ideals. The Fellowship, often called the FCA, sponsors athletic clinics; banquets; and national conferences, rallies, and retreats. Athletes are divided into groups, including *huddles* for students in high school and college and *chapters* for interested adults and coaches. The FCA maintains a National Conference Center near Marshall, Ind., for leadership training, conferences, sports camps, and retreats. The organization publishes a bimonthly magazine called *Sharing the Victory.*

The FCA was founded in 1954. It is a nonprofit organization supervised by a national board of trustees. National headquarters are at 8701 Leeds Road, Kansas City, MO 64129.

Critically reviewed by the Fellowship of Christian Athletes

Felony, *FEHL uh nee,* is a crime for which punishment is death or imprisonment for a year or more. Felonies include murder, robbery, burglary, kidnapping, treason, and certain other serious crimes. A violation of law less serious is called a *misdemeanor* and is punishable by a fine or jail sentence (see **Misdemeanor**).

The person directly injured by a felony may agree not to prosecute in return for some payment or other valuable consideration. For example, a person may promise not to prosecute a thief who gives back the stolen goods. This is called *compounding a felony* and is a crime punishable by fine or imprisonment.

Charles F. Wellford

See also **Burglary; Robbery.**

Felt is a fabric made of wool fibers or animal hair matted together by steam and pressure. Felt varies greatly in weight, thickness, and value. Manufacturers use felt to make hats, chalkboard erasers, rug pads, slippers, and billiard-table covers. Felt is usually made 72 inches (183 centimeters) wide. Keith Slater

Female. See **Reproduction; Sex.**

Feminine gender. See **Gender.**

Feminism, *FEHM uh nihz uhm,* is the belief that women should have economic, political, and social equality with men. The term *feminism* also refers to a political movement that works to gain such equality. This movement is sometimes called the *women's liberation movement* or *women's rights movement.*

Feminist beliefs have existed throughout history, but feminism did not become widespread in Europe and the United States until the mid-1800's. At that time, many people regarded women as inferior and less important than men. Such people believed a woman's proper place was in the home. The law reflected this opinion. For example, women were barred by law from voting in elections or serving on juries. Most institutions of higher education and most professional careers were also closed to women. Despite strong opposition, feminism grew in power during the 1800's and 1900's and won a number of new rights for women. Many people regard the feminist movement—and the resulting changes in the status of women—as a turning point in the history of society.

One of the first feminist books was *A Vindication of the Rights of Woman* (1792) by the British writer Mary Wollstonecraft. In this book, Wollstonecraft described the state of ignorance in which society kept women. She also pleaded for better educational opportunities. Another early feminist writer was the American antislavery leader Sarah M. Grimké. She wrote a pamphlet called *Letters on the Equality of the Sexes and the Condition of Woman* (1838). Grimké presented a powerful argument against religious leaders who claimed to find support in the Bible for the inferior position of women.

At first, the feminist movement concentrated on gaining legal equality—especially the right to vote, called

Culver

Feminism, the movement to gain equal rights for women, concentrated at first on winning *suffrage,* the right to vote. In 1915, women marched in a suffrage parade in New York City, *above.*

suffrage. Women in the United States and many European nations finally obtained the vote during the early 1900's. See **Woman suffrage.**

The feminist movement nearly disappeared after women received the right to vote. During the mid-1900's, however, increasing numbers of women entered the labor force. They found that many high-paying jobs were closed to them. A new concern with economic and social equality helped create a revival of the feminist movement in the 1960's. The National Organization for Women (NOW) and other feminist groups fought to end educational and job discrimination against women. Large numbers of women entered law, medicine, politics, business, and other traditionally male fields. Feminists worked for wider availability of birth control information and legalized abortion. They also called for men and women to share child care and other family responsibilities.   Miriam Schneir

See also **Women's movements.**

Additional resources

Bassnett, Susan. *Feminist Experiences: The Women's Movement in Four Cultures.* Allen & Unwin, 1986.

Cott, Nancy F. *The Grounding of Modern Feminism.* Yale, 1987.

Eisenstein, Hester. *Contemporary Feminist Thought: An Assessment.* G. K. Hall, 1983.

Feminism: Opposing Viewpoints. Ed. by Andrea Hinding. Greenhaven, 1986.

Rupp, Leila J., and Taylor, Verta. *Survival in the Doldrums: The American Women's Rights Movement, 1945 to the 1960s.* Oxford, 1987.

Femur. See **Leg.**

Fencing is the art and sport of swordsmanship using blunted weapons. Fencers use one of three types of weapons—the foil, the epee, or the sabre. Fencing meets are conducted as individual or team events, though even in team events, only two fencers compete against each other at one time.

Fencing is the only combative sport open to both men and women. But men and women do not compete against each other. Men's competition may include any of the three weapons. Women use the foil or the epee.

There is evidence that fencing competitions date back

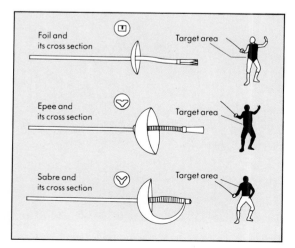

Fencing weapons and their target areas

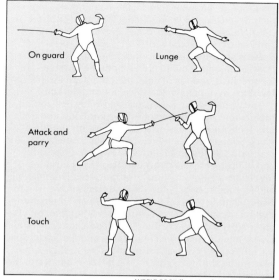

WORLD BOOK illustrations by David Cunningham

Fencing moves follow a sequence. Competition begins with fencers *on guard.* One fencer uses a *lunge* to *attack.* The defender blocks the attack with a *parry.* A *touch* ends the action.

at least 5,000 years to ancient Egypt and Japan. In Europe, modern swordsmanship dates back to about 1400. Fencing schools became popular in Italy and traveling Italian fencing masters spread the technique of swordsmanship to England, France, and Spain. By the late 1800's, fencing had become part of the education of a gentleman. Fencing was one of the original sports included in the modern Olympic Games.

To prevent injuries, fencers wear heavy wire-mesh masks with thick canvas bibs to protect the head and neck. They also wear thick canvas or nylon jackets and knickers and a padded glove on the hand holding the weapon.

The foil has a slender, flexible quadrilateral blade and a small, circular guard. The blade is 90 centimeters (3 feet) long. Foil fencers try to score touches or hits by touching their opponent's torso with the point.

Foil fencers must follow a certain sequence of moves, called *conventions.* The fencer who first *attacks* has the *right of way* or *priority* in scoring until the defender *parries* (blocks) the attack. The defender is then allowed to *riposte* (counterattack) and holds the right of way until parried. This alternation of action continues until a fencer scores a touch or the action becomes too confused for the chief official, the president, to follow.

If the fencer touches the opponent outside the torso area, no touch is scored and action resumes. If a fencer touches the opponent on the torso, then a touch is scored. If both fencers touch each other and the president cannot determine who had the right of way, there is no score. Most foil bouts have a 6-minute time limit. The first fencer to score five touches wins.

The epee has a rigid triangular blade with a bell-shaped guard. The blade is 90 centimeters long. Epee fencing has no conventions of right of way. Touches on any part of the body count. However, touches must

WORLD BOOK illustration by David Cunningham

The fencing area is 2 meters (6 feet 7 inches) wide and 14 meters (46 feet) long. An electronic device activates a light when a fencer scores a touch. A scorekeeper, timekeeper, and signaling apparatus operator sit at a table. The chief official, called the *president,* stands while observing the action.

be scored with the point of the weapon. If both fencers touch each other at the same time, both touches count. Most epee bouts have a 6-minute time limit. Five touches win the bout. Epee fencing for one touch is part of a five-sport competition called the modern pentathlon (see **Pentathlon**).

The sabre has a flexible triangular blade with a guard that curves around the knuckles. The blade is 88 centimeters (2 feet 11 inches) long. In sabre fencing, touches may be scored on any part of the body above the hips, including the head and arms, either with the point or with one of the two cutting edges. Sabre fencing follows the same conventions of right of way as foil fencing. Most sabre bouts have a 6-minute time limit. Five touches win the bout.

Fencing organizations. The United States Fencing Association (USFA) administers fencing in the United States. The USFA is the U.S. member of the International Fencing Federation (FIE). The FIE conducts the world championships and the fencing events of the Olympic Games. The FIE also establishes the official rules of the sport.   Jeffrey R. Tishman

See also **Olympic Games** (table: Fencing); **Sword.**

Additional resources

Alaux, Michel. *Modern Fencing: Foil, Epee, Sabre, from Initiation to Competition.* Scribner, 1975.
Shaff, Jo. *Fencing.* Atheneum, 1982. An instructional manual.
Thomas, Art. *Fencing Is for Me.* Lerner, 1982. For younger readers.

Fénelon, *fayn LAWN,* **François de Salignac de la Mothe-,** *frahn SWAH duh sa lee NYAK duh la MAWT* (1651-1715), was a French author and a Roman Catholic archbishop. He became known for his advanced political, social, and educational ideas.

Fénelon's *Treatise on the Education of Girls* (1687)

shows his keen understanding of child psychology. His best-known work is *Telemachus* (1695-1699), a novel written to instruct the Duke of Burgundy, grandson of King Louis XIV. The book is about a young man who observes the governments of many countries. It was intended to teach the duke the duties of high office. Fénelon's criticism of absolute monarchy was implied in *Telemachus* and clearly stated in a *Letter to Louis XIV,* published after Fénelon's death. The main ideas described in *Telemachus* had been foreshadowed by his *Dialogs of the Dead* (1692). In *Maxims of the Saints* (1697), Fénelon favored *quietism,* a religious movement that denied the value of conventional religious practices. The church condemned the *Maxims,* and Fénelon lost his influence in religious life and court life.

Fénelon was born at Périgord. He was ordained about 1675 and was appointed Archbishop of Cambrai in 1695.
          Robert B. Griffin

Fenian movement, *FEE nee uhn,* was a struggle by Irish nationalists to free Ireland from English rule. In the late 1850's, a group of Irish patriots called *Fenians* began to plan a revolution. The Fenians took their name from the *Fianna,* a band of mythical Irish warriors (see **Irish literature** [Heroic tales, romances, and sagas]).

Most Fenians belonged to a secret society called the Irish Republican Brotherhood (IRB), which was founded in the United States in 1858. In 1866 and 1867, the Fenians attacked police stations in Ireland and set off bombs in England. But the English authorities put down the rebellion and imprisoned hundreds of suspected rebels.

Many people who had emigrated from Ireland to the United States supported the Fenian movement. In the late 1860's, Irish-American Fenians staged three unsuccessful raids on Canada, then a member of the British Empire. The Fenians hoped to take over Canada and hold it as a "hostage" to force England to grant Ireland independence. The Fenian goal of independence through revolution was adopted by later Irish republican movements. Ireland became independent in 1921, after several years of guerrilla warfare.   L. Perry Curtis, Jr.

Fennec, *FEHN ehk,* is a small fox that lives in the deserts of North Africa and Arabia. Fennecs rest in burrows in the daytime. At night, they seek such food as

Anthony Mercieca, Photo Researchers

The fennec is a small fox with large ears and a black-tipped tail. The animal rests in a burrow during the day and hunts food at night. Fennecs live in North Africa and Arabia.

birds and birds' eggs, insects, lizards, rodents, and various bulbs and fruits. Fennecs have pale reddish-orange, sandy, or white fur. The tail has a black tip. A fennec weighs about $3\frac{1}{2}$ pounds (1.6 kilograms). Its exceptionally large ears may grow as long as 6 inches (15 centimeters). Fennecs live in family groups with two to five young.

Scientific classification. The fennec belongs to the dog family, Canidae. It is *Fennecus zerda.*   Anne Innis Dagg

See also **Fox** (Fennecs).

Fennel, *FEHN uhl,* is an herb related to parsley. It grows wild as a perennial plant in southern Europe. Fennel is cultivated annually or every two years in the United States, India, and Japan and in various areas of Europe.

The fennel plant has fragrant, finely divided leaves and yellow flowers. Its seeds also are fragrant, and they have a licorice taste. The leaves and seeds are used to flavor candy, liqueurs, medicines, and fish and other foods. Oil of fennel, which is made from the seeds, is used in giving soaps and perfumes a pleasing fragrance. In Italy,

WORLD BOOK illustration by Lorraine Epstein
Fennel

young shoots of one variety of fennel are served as a vegetable.

A group of plants called *fennelflowers* are related to buttercups but not to fennel. Fennelflowers grow in western Asia and in the region of the Mediterranean Sea. One variety of them has black and brown seeds that are used as seasoning for breads and pastries.

Scientific classification. Fennel is a member of the parsley family, Umbelliferae. It is *Foeniculum vulgare.* Fennelflower belongs to the crowfoot family, Ranunculaceae. It is *Nigella hispanica.*   J. B. Hanson

Fer-de-lance, *FAIR duh LAHNS,* is one of the largest and deadliest of the poisonous snakes. It lives in tropical North and South America. It has velvety scales, marks of rich brown and gray, and a yellowish throat. The fer-de-lance lives in both wet and dry places, in forests as well

WORLD BOOK illustration by Richard Lewington, The Garden Studio
The fer-de-lance is a large, poisonous snake that lives in tropical regions of North and South America.

as open country. It eats birds and small animals. There may be over 60 young snakes in one brood. The baby snakes are about 1 foot (30 centimeters) long. They have fully formed fangs at birth, and can give a poisonous bite. A fer-de-lance strikes swiftly. The snake may grow to be 8 feet (2.4 meters) long. Its name is French and means *lance head.* See also **Viper.**

Scientific classification. The fer-de-lance belongs to the viper family, Viperidae. It is *Bothrops atrox.*   Clifford H. Pope

Ferber, Edna (1885-1968), an American novelist and playwright, wrote many books about the colorful American life of the 1800's. She won the 1925 Pulitzer Prize for fiction for her first best-selling novel, *So Big* (1924). She also wrote *Show Boat* (1926), *Cimarron* (1930), *Saratoga Trunk* (1941), *Giant* (1952), and *Ice Palace* (1958). *Show Boat* was made into a popular musical comedy, and all of these books became successful motion pictures. She said that she intended her books to be social criticism as well as good stories. She often wrote about strong women characters. Ferber's other novels include *Dawn O'Hara* (1911), her first book; *The Girls* (1921); and *Come and Get It* (1935). *Roast Beef, Medium* (1913) is a collection of stories. She had considerable success with the plays she wrote with George S. Kaufman. The best known of these are *The Royal Family* (1927), *Dinner at Eight* (1932), and *Stage Door* (1936).

Doubleday
Edna Ferber

Ferber was born in Kalamazoo, Mich., but she grew up in Appleton, Wis. Ferber's first ambition was to become an actress. However, at the age of 17, when her father went blind, she took a newspaper job with the *Appleton Daily Crescent.* Ferber told her life story in two books, *A Peculiar Treasure* (1939) and *A Kind of Magic* (1963).   Bert Hitchcock

Ferdinand II (1578-1637) ruled the Holy Roman Empire from 1619 until his death. A devout Roman Catholic, Ferdinand dedicated his reign to restoring Catholicism to its former dominant position in the Protestant German states of the empire.

Ferdinand was the son of Archduke Charles of Styria, a province in what is now Austria. Ferdinand belonged to the Habsburg (or Hapsburg) family, which had long controlled the empire. He became emperor during the Thirty Years' War (1618-1648). The war had begun as a conflict between Protestants and Catholics, and Ferdinand defeated many rebel Protestant nobles.

To limit Ferdinand's power, leaders from several European countries began to help the rebels. Catholic nobles in the empire also grew to fear Ferdinand's power. In 1635, Ferdinand forced both Catholic and Protestant nobles to sign the Peace of Prague, increasing his authority over them. But expansion of the war quickly ended his dominance.   John P. Spielman, Jr.

Ferdinand III (1608-1657) ruled the Holy Roman Empire from 1637 until his death. Ferdinand tried to promote his authority over the German states of the empire and strengthen the Roman Catholic Church in those states.

Ferdinand was a member of the House of Habsburg (or Hapsburg), a Catholic family that had long dominated the empire. He succeeded his father, Ferdinand II, as emperor and continued his father's policies in the Thirty Years' War (1618-1648). During this war, Ferdinand III sought to increase his authority over the German states, promote Catholicism in Germany, and expand Habsburg power in Europe. But the war exhausted his resources. Following several military defeats, he signed the Peace of Westphalia in 1648. This agreement ended the war. It weakened Ferdinand's authority in the empire, but strengthened his control over the Habsburg family's lands.   John P. Spielman, Jr.

Ferdinand V (1452-1516), king of Castile and Aragon, married his cousin, Isabella I, in 1469. This marriage led to the unification of Castile and Aragon, Spain's two largest kingdoms (see **Isabella I**). The two rulers increased Spain's power by conquering the Moors in 10 years of war and by sending Christopher Columbus to America. After Isabella's death in 1504, Ferdinand added Naples and the province of Navarre to his kingdom. He was also known as Ferdinand II of Aragon and Sicily, and as Ferdinand III of Naples. He was born in Sos, Aragon. See also **Castile and Aragon; Columbus, Christopher** (Success in Spain); **Spain** (Union of the Spanish Kingdoms).   Franklin D. Scott

Ferdinand, Archduke. See World War I (The assassination of an archduke).

Ferlinghetti, *fur lihn GEHT ee,* **Lawrence** (1919-   ), is an American poet best known as a leader of the *beat movement* of the 1950's. The beats were writers who condemned commercialism and middle-class American values.

Ferlinghetti writes in a colloquial free-verse style. His poetry describes the need to release literature and life from conformity and timidity. He believes drugs, Zen Buddhism, and emotional and physical love are ways of opening the soul to truth and beauty. The grotesque and a feeling of euphoria are closely interwoven in his work, especially in his most famous poem, *A Coney Island of the Mind* (1958). The poem is also a satiric criticism of American culture. Ferlinghetti published *Selected Poems* in 1981. He has also composed *oral messages*—poems to be spoken to jazz accompaniment.

Ferlinghetti was born in Yonkers, N.Y. He publishes and sells the works of beat and *avant-garde* (experimental) authors in his San Francisco book store and publishing company, City Lights.   Bonnie Costello

Fermat, *fehr MAH,* **Pierre de** (1601-1665), a French mathematician, won fame for his work in the theory of numbers or integers. He also shared in the invention of analytic geometry and calculus. He formulated the least-time law to explain the *diffraction* (bending) of light, and also developed an equation for the graph of a straight line. His "last theorem" has never been proved or disproved. Fermat knew integral solutions of the equation $x^2 + y^2 = z^2$ (for example, $3^2 + 4^2 = 5^2$). His theorem held that there was no whole number solution of $x^n + y^n = z^n$ if the exponent, n, is larger than 2. Fermat and Blaise Pascal are credited with originating the theory of probability. Today, the theory of probability is widely used in insurance and statistics (see **Probability**).

Fermat practiced law in Toulouse and studied mathematics only as a hobby. He was born in Beaumont-de-Lomagne.   Phillip S. Jones

Fermentation, *FUR mehn TAY shuhn,* is a chemical process that breaks down organic materials. This process is carried out by such microbes as bacteria, molds, and yeasts. For example, molds or fungi act upon mixtures of molasses and mineral salts to produce penicillin. Yeast breaks down sugar obtained from malted grain into ethyl alcohol and carbon dioxide gas for use in beer. Sugar from grape juice is broken down in the same way for use in wine. Fermentation also is essential in the production of bread, cheese, and yogurt. In some cases, fermentation can be unhealthy. For example, fermented milk turns sour.

Fermented products useful to human beings are manufactured in large quantities. Although a variety of substances are produced by fermentation, the basic processes are similar. First, large stainless steel tanks are filled with a watery solution of nutrients. This solution is sterilized with steam to kill unwanted germs. Certain microbes then are added to the solution, and they ferment the nutrients over a period of several days. Workers carefully control the temperature and acid quality of the material in the tanks. Finally, the tanks are drained, and the desired product is separated from the rest of the mixture by extraction, filtration, or some other means. In most cases, this product makes up only about 5 per cent of the mixture in the tanks, so purification is often extremely complicated.

Fermentation has been used to make alcoholic beverages since ancient times. People who lived along the Nile River brewed beer around 3000 B.C. It was not until the A.D. 1800's, however, that scientists—particularly the French scientist Louis Pasteur—discovered how microbes cause fermentation in beer, milk, and wine.

In the 1900's, other types of fermentation were developed. Fermentation of a bacterium produced ingredients for explosives during World War I (1914-1918). Since 1943, the most important application of fermentation has been in the production of *antibiotics* (disease-killing drugs), especially penicillin. Fermentation also is used in certain other drugs, in vitamins, and in some types of chemicals.   Arthur J. Ashe III

See also **Alcoholic Beverage; Brewing** (Fermentation; picture); **Enzyme; Pasteur, Louis; Wine** (How wine is made).

Fermi, *FUR mee* or *FEHR mee,* **Enrico,** *ehn REE koh* (1901-1954), an Italian-born American physicist, designed the first atomic pile and produced the first nuclear chain reaction in 1942. He later worked on the atomic bomb project at Los Alamos, N. Mex. Fermi won the 1938 Nobel Prize for physics for his work on nuclear processes. He also made important contributions to quantum theory and other areas of physics.

Fermi began bombarding many elements with neutrons in 1934. He proved that slow neutrons

University of Chicago Press
Enrico Fermi

are very effective in producing radioactive atoms. This discovery was particularly important, because slow neutrons can split U-235. As a result of these experiments, Fermi announced in 1934 what he thought were elements lying beyond uranium, not realizing that he had actually split the atom. Otto Hahn and Fritz Strassmann of Germany performed a similar experiment in 1938. Lise Meitner and Otto Frisch showed that the uranium atom had been split, and named the process *nuclear fission* (see **Meitner, Lise**).

Fermi was born in Rome. He received a doctor's degree from the University of Pisa in 1922. He then returned to Rome, where he became professor of theoretical physics at the University of Rome in 1927. Fermi left Italy in 1938 to escape the Fascist regime, and settled in the United States. He became a professor of physics at Columbia University in 1939. He moved to the University of Chicago as a professor of physics in 1942. Fermi led the work on the first nuclear chain reaction. He became an American citizen in 1944. After World War II, he pioneered in research on high energy particles.

Roger H. Stuewer

See also **Nuclear energy** (Development).

Additional resources

Fermi, Laura. *Atoms in the Family: My Life with Enrico Fermi.* Univ. of Chicago Press, 1954. A biography by Enrico Fermi's wife.
Segrè, Emilio G. *Enrico Fermi: Physicist.* Univ. of Chicago Press, 1970.

Fermi National Accelerator Laboratory, *FUR mee* or *FEHR mee,* is a physics research laboratory near Batavia, Ill. Its name honors Enrico Fermi, the Italian-American physicist who produced the first nuclear chain reaction. Scientists from all over the world come to the laboratory to study mesons, neutrinos, protons, and other atomic particles. The laboratory is commonly called *Fermilab.*

The laboratory's main instrument is a particle accelerator, or atom smasher, called a *synchrotron.* One of the world's largest accelerators, it lies in an underground tunnel that forms a circle $1\frac{1}{4}$ miles (2 kilometers) in diameter. The synchrotron accelerates protons almost to the speed of light. The protons reach an energy of up to 900 *giga* (billion) electronvolts. Scientists direct a beam of protons at a target and study the result of the collision.

The United States Department of Energy pays for the operation of the Fermi National Accelerator Laboratory. Universities Research Association, Incorporated, a group of 56 universities in the United States and Canada, manages it.   Francis T. Cole

See also **Particle accelerator; Synchrotron; Meson; Proton.**

Fermium, *FUR mee uhm* (chemical symbol, Fm) is an artificially created radioactive element. Its atomic number is 100. Fermium has 18 known isotopes. Its most stable isotope has a mass number of 257 and a half-life of 100 days (see **Radioactivity** [Half-life]). A team of American scientists led by Albert Ghiorso discovered fermium in 1953. They found it in radioactive debris produced by the first hydrogen bomb explosion in 1952. Fermium was named for Enrico Fermi, the Italian nuclear physicist who produced the first controlled nuclear chain reaction (see **Fermi, Enrico**).

Extremely small amounts of fermium are produced in nuclear reactors for scientific research. Chemical compounds of fermium have not been produced in weighable amounts. Therefore, its chemical properties are not completely known to scientists.   Richard L. Hahn

See also **Einsteinium; Element, Chemical; Radioactivity; Transuranium element.**

Fern is a green, nonflowering plant that grows in most parts of the world. Ferns vary widely in size and form. Some ferns look like mosses and measure about 1 inch (2.5 centimeters) in length. Others resemble palm trees and grow more than 65 feet (20 meters) tall. Ferns have some of the most beautiful and varied leaves in the plant world. The leaves of many ferns are long and lacy and consist of hundreds of tiny leaflets. Other ferns have simple, rounded leaves.

Ferns can be found in all parts of the world except the driest deserts and coldest regions. There are approximately 10,000 species of ferns worldwide. Most ferns grow in damp, shady areas. The best places to look for ferns are along streams in woods and in the cracks and overhangs of rock cliffs. In tropical regions, ferns are common on the trunks and branches of trees. In the United States, most ferns are found in the Southeast and in the forests of the Pacific Northwest.

Ferns are among the oldest kinds of plants that live on land. Scientists believe that ferns appeared on earth more than 350 million years ago. Like mosses and other nonflowering plants, ferns reproduce by means of microscopic cells called *spores.* Most ferns produce spores on the underside of their leaves.

People enjoy ferns mainly for their beauty. Ferns are grown in many gardens, especially as background in shady areas. Several ferns are popular as house plants. Vast numbers of ferns are used each year as greenery in flower arrangements at weddings and funerals, and for Christmas decorations.

Parts of a fern. Ferns have well-developed stems, roots, and leaves. The stem of a fern stores food that the plant needs to grow. As long as the stem is alive, the fern will continue to grow and make new leaves and roots. The stem may grow upright above the ground, horizontally along the ground, or even underground. A stem that grows along the ground or underground is called a *rhizome.* The stems of ferns often form branches. A large clump of ferns forms if a stem branches many times. Fern stems usually grow slowly and may live for 100 years or more.

The roots also may live a long time. They anchor the stem to the ground and absorb water and nutrients.

Unlike the stem and roots, the leaves of a fern usually live only one or two years. A new set of leaves grows from the tip of the stem every year. A young fern leaf is coiled like the top of a violin. It uncurls as it grows. The leaf is attached to the stem by a stalk called the *stipe.* The fern leaf is often called a *frond.*

Fern leaves make food for the plant by a process called *photosynthesis* (see **Photosynthesis**). Many fern leaves also carry the tiny structures that produce spores. These structures, called *sporangia,* have a stalk and a capsule filled with spores. Usually, sporangia are found in clusters on the underside of fern leaves. Each cluster of sporangia is called a *sorus,* and all the clusters on a fern are the *sori.* Ferns are the only plants that have sori and so they are easy to identify.

Terry E. Eiler, Stock, Boston

L. West, Bruce Coleman Inc.

O. Franken, Stock, Boston

Ferns grow in a variety of habitats. Western sword ferns, *upper left*, grow in forests along the Pacific coast of North America. Bracken, *lower left*, is found in fields throughout most of the world. Tree ferns, such as the one shown at the right, grow in the tropics.

Life cycle of a fern. Ferns grow and reproduce in two stages—*sexual* and *asexual*. This kind of life cycle, called *alternation of generations*, involves two distinct forms of the fern plant.

During the asexual stage, the fern plant is called a *sporophyte*. The sporophyte produces leaves with sporangia and is the plant commonly recognized as the fern. After the sporangia mature, they split open in dry air and release their spores. A sporophyte may produce millions of spores. But only some of the spores land in places suitable for growth. Most fern spores grow best in shaded, moist soil. A fern spore develops into a tiny, heart-shaped plant that is called a *gametophyte*.

The growth of the gametophyte begins the sexual stage of the fern's life cycle. The gametophyte of a fern is usually called a *prothallium*. After a few weeks, the prothallium develops organs that produce male and female sex cells, called *gametes*. The male sex organ, called the *antheridium*, produces sperm. The female sex organ, the *archegonium*, contains an egg. In most ferns, both antheridia and archegonia are produced on the same prothallium. When the sperm are mature and the prothallium is wet, the antheridia split open and the sperm swim out. The sperm may swim into an archegonium on the same prothallium or on another prothallium. There, a sperm joins with the egg to form a single cell, called a *zygote*.

The zygote begins to grow inside the archegonium, forming a mass of cells called an *embryo*. Part of the embryo absorbs food from the prothallium. Other parts of the embryo develop into the first leaf, the first root, and the stem of a new sporophyte. The embryo draws its en-

ergy from the prothallium until the root enters the soil and the sporophyte can live on its own. At this point, the prothallium shrivels and dies, completing the life cycle.

North American ferns. More than 300 species of ferns grow in North America. Among the best-known species are (1) bracken, (2) the royal fern, and (3) the Western sword fern.

Bracken is probably the most common North American fern. It is common in most other parts of the world

Bill Tronca, Tom Stack & Assoc.

Robert and Linda Mitchell

Reproduction in ferns involves two forms of the fern plant. The mature plant, called a *sporophyte*, bears tiny *sporangia* on its leaves, *left*. The sporangia release spores, which grow into *gametophytes*, *right*. Gametophytes produce male and female sex cells that unite and develop into sporophytes.

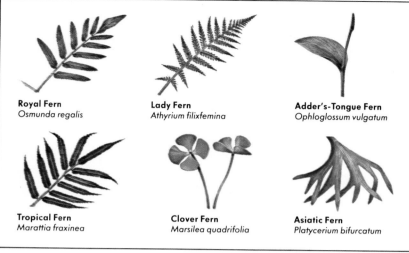

Royal Fern
Osmunda regalis

Lady Fern
Athyrium filixfemina

Adder's-Tongue Fern
Ophloglossum vulgatum

Tropical Fern
Marattia fraxinea

Clover Fern
Marsilea quadrifolia

Asiatic Fern
Platycerium bifurcatum

The leaves of ferns vary widely in shape among different species. These drawings show the leaves of six species. The scientific name of each species is given in italics.

WORLD BOOK illustrations by Chris Skilton

as well. It has large, triangular fronds that grow from a cordlike underground rhizome. It is found in open areas, especially along roadsides and in abandoned fields. Bracken is considered a nuisance in pastures because it is poisonous to livestock. It is hard to get rid of because its rhizome reaches deep underground.

The royal fern is a particularly beautiful species found in swampy areas of forests in eastern North America. It has a short, thick stem, with many fronds growing around the top of the stem like a basket. The fronds may grow up to 6 feet (2 meters) long and are divided into many narrow leaflets.

The Western sword fern grows in forests of the Pacific Coast. A redwood forest would seem empty without these ferns. Like the royal fern, the Western sword fern has fronds that grow in a circle from a short stem. Each year's fronds last until late in the following season. As a result, this fern is green throughout the year. Florists use the Western sword fern as greenery because fronds cut from it last for a long time in cold storage.

Scientific classification. Ferns make up the division Pterophyta. Bracken is *Pteridium aquilinum*, the royal fern is *Osmunda regalis*, and the Western sword fern is *Polystichum munitum*. David H. Wagner

See also **Epiphyte; Fossil** (picture: A carbonized fossil of a fern); **Plant** (pictures); **Spore.**

Fernando Po. See Equatorial Guinea.

Ferraro, *fuhr RAH roh,* **Geraldine Anne** (1935-   ), became the Democratic nominee for Vice President of the United States in 1984. She was the first woman chosen as a vice presidential candidate by a major American political party. Ferraro and her presidential running mate, former Vice President Walter F. Mondale, were defeated by their Republican opponents, President Ronald Reagan and Vice President George Bush. Previously, Ferraro had served three terms in the United States House of Representatives.

Ferraro was born in Newburgh, N.Y. She received a Bachelor of Arts degree from Marymount Manhattan College in 1956 and a law degree from Fordham University in 1960. Also in 1960, she married John A. Zaccaro.

Professionally, she continued to use her maiden name. She and her husband had three children. From 1961 to 1974, Ferraro occasionally handled legal matters for her husband's real estate business. She started her career in government service in 1974, when she became an assistant district attorney in Queens County, New York.

In 1978, Ferraro was elected to her first term in the U.S. House of Representatives. She represented a district in Queens, from which she won reelection in 1980 and 1982. Ferraro served on the House committees on post office and civil service, public works and transportation, and budget. In 1981, she became a member of the Democratic Steering and Policy Committee, which controls committee assignments for Democrats in the House. In Congress, Ferraro was known for her liberal views on domestic issues. She regularly voted for bills designed to benefit workers,

Rocco Galatioto

Geraldine A. Ferraro

women, and the elderly, and opposed efforts to ban abortion. Lee Thornton

Ferret is a small mammal that belongs to the weasel family. There are three species of ferrets: the *black-footed ferret,* found in the western Great Plains of North America; the *steppe polecat,* found in the plains of central Asia; and the *European polecat,* found throughout Europe. The terms *polecat* and *ferret* are often used interchangeably. See **Polecat.**

Ferrets prey mainly on rodents. They will also eat birds, eggs, reptiles, amphibians, and some plants and berries. Ferrets have long slim bodies and short legs. If frightened, they can discharge a strong-smelling fluid from scent glands under their tails.

Black-footed ferrets are dull yellow with black feet and tail tips, and a "mask" of black hair around their

WORLD BOOK illustration by John F. Eggert

The black-footed ferret, one of the rarest mammals of North America, is found in small numbers in the western Great Plains. It is a shy, secretive animal that lives in underground burrows.

eyes. Males measure 15 to 16 inches (38 to 41 centimeters) long, not including a tail of 4 to 5 inches (11 to 13 centimeters). Females are smaller.

The black-footed ferret is an endangered species. These ferrets depend on prairie dogs as a food source and live in the underground burrows that the prairie dogs make. However, farmers and cattle ranchers consider prairie dogs a pest, and so they have killed millions of them. The decrease in the number of prairie dogs is probably the main reason black-footed ferrets have become extremely rare.

Steppe polecats resemble black-footed ferrets, but wild European polecats have a longer and darker coat. The European polecat has been *domesticated* (tamed) and trained to hunt rats and rabbits. Domestic European polecats vary in color from *albino* (white) to black.

Scientific classification. Ferrets belong to the weasel family, Mustelidae. The black-footed ferret is classified as *Mustela nigripes.*   Barbara L. Clauson and Robert M. Timm

Ferris wheel is an entertainment device used at fairs, carnivals, and amusement and theme parks. A Ferris wheel is a power-driven vertical wheel with a steel frame. Passenger cabs are mounted on the rim of the wheel. Present-day Ferris wheels stand about 40 to 45 feet (12 to 14 meters) high and carry from 12 to 16 passenger cabs.

© Harald Sund

A ferry can carry people, vehicles, and freight across rivers, lakes, bays, and other bodies of water.

Ferris wheels were originally called *pleasure wheels.* The largest wheel was built by George W. Gale Ferris, a mechanical engineer in Galesburg, Ill. Ferris built it for the World's Columbian Exposition in Chicago in 1893. The wheel was 250 feet (76 meters) in diameter. Each of its 36 cabs could hold 60 people. This Ferris wheel was

Chicago Historical Society

The Ferris wheel at the World's Columbian Exposition in Chicago in 1893 was the largest ever built. Its 36 passenger cabs could carry 2,160 people.

used at the Louisiana Purchase Exposition in St. Louis in 1904 and then was sold for scrap metal.

In 1900, William E. Sullivan began making portable versions of the Ferris wheel in Jacksonville, Ill., for the Eli Bridge Co. In England, a Ferris wheel is called an *Eli wheel* or a *big wheel.*   Don B. Wilmeth

Ferrous sulfate, *FEHR us SUL fayt* (chemical formula, $FeSO_4 \cdot 7H_2O$), is a substance which occurs in light-green crystals. The crystals turn rusty brown when they react with oxygen in moist air. Ferrous sulfate is an iron salt of sulfuric acid. It can be made by combining iron with sulfuric acid or by oxidizing *iron pyrites,* a compound of iron and sulfur. Ferrous sulfate is used to dye fabrics and leather and to make ink. It is also used to purify water, and as a disinfectant, wood preservative, and weed killer.   Marianna A. Busch

Ferry is a boat used to carry persons, vehicles, and freight across narrow bodies of water. Most ferries have a large opening at each end so they can be loaded and unloaded without being turned around.

People have used ferries for hundreds of years. Early ferries included rafts and small boats that were rowed, sailed, or moved by poles across water. Many ferries were guided by cables stretched between shores, and were pulled by ferry workers on the shore of destination. Some cable-guided ferries are pushed by motorboats. Most large ferries in use today are powered by their own engines.

Bridges and tunnels have replaced many ferries. Ferries still operating include those between Manhattan and Staten islands in New York, and between New Jersey and New York.   Joseph A. Gutierrez, Jr.

See also **Ship** (Other passenger vessels).

Fertile Crescent was a crescent-shaped region in Asia. This historic region began at the Mediterranean Sea, stretched between the Tigris and Euphrates rivers, and ended at the Persian Gulf. In this area, the Sumerians developed the world's first civilization about 5,500

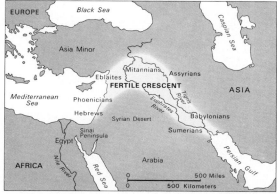

WORLD BOOK map

The Fertile Crescent was a historic region that curved around the Syrian Desert in Asia. The Sumerians developed the world's first civilization there about 5,500 years ago. Other advanced ancient cultures also developed in the region.

years ago. James H. Breasted, an American archaeologist, named the region the *fertile crescent* because these people and their successors created rich, irrigated farmlands. The Assyrians, Babylonians, Eblaites, Israelites, Mitannians, and Phoenicians also lived and ruled in the Fertile Crescent.   John A. Brinkman

See also **Asia** (History); **Syria** (introduction).

Fertility drug. See Fertilization; Multiple birth.

Fertilization, *FUR tuh luh ZAY shuhn,* is the process by which male and female sex cells unite to form a new individual. It is the first step in sexual reproduction. The male reproductive system produces sex cells called *spermatozoa,* or *sperm.* The female reproductive system produces sex cells called *eggs,* or *ova.* A fertilized egg, which results from the union of a sperm and an egg, is called a *zygote.* As the zygote develops further, it becomes an *embryo.* This article discusses fertilization among animals. For information about fertilization among plants, see **Plant** (How plants reproduce).

Among animals, fertilization may be external or internal. During external fertilization, male and female sex cells unite outside the female's body. This process occurs in water. The male releases sperm into the water at about the same time that the female releases eggs. Some sperm come into contact with eggs and fertilize them. Almost all aquatic invertebrates and some vertebrates, including the majority of fish and amphibians, reproduce in this way.

Internal fertilization occurs when the male deposits sperm directly into the female's body. Most land animals, including insects, reptiles, birds, and mammals, reproduce in this way. In almost all mammals and some reptiles, the embryo develops inside the female's body

after fertilization. However, in birds and many reptiles, the embryo develops outside her body. The female lays an egg in which the embryo develops. The egg is protected by a shell and contains material that nourishes the growing embryo.

Scientists have developed methods of promoting fertilization in mammals, including human beings. For example, *fertility drugs* increase a female's chances of becoming pregnant. In addition, eggs may be fertilized by a process called *artificial insemination.* In this process, sperm are collected from the male and later injected into the female by artificial methods.

Scientists have also united mammalian sperm and eggs *in vitro*—that is, in an artificial environment outside the female's body. The zygote must then be transferred into the female reproductive system to develop further. The human infants that have resulted from in vitro fertilization are sometimes called "test-tube babies."   Kelly Selman

See also **Breeding; Embryo** (Fertilization); **Infertility; Pollen; Reproduction.**

Fertilizer is a substance that is added to soil to help plants grow. Farmers use various kinds of fertilizers to produce abundant crops. Home gardeners use fertilizers to raise large, healthy flowers and vegetables. Landscapers spread fertilizers on lawns and golf courses to help grow thick, green grass.

Fertilizers contain *nutrients* (nourishing substances) that are essential for plant growth. Some fertilizers are made from organic waste, such as manure or sewage. Others are manufactured from certain minerals or from synthetic compounds produced in factories.

People have used fertilizer for thousands of years—even though at one time they did not know why it was beneficial for plants. Long before they gained an understanding of plant nutrition, people noticed that animal droppings, wood ashes, and certain minerals helped plants thrive. During the 1800's and early 1900's, scientists discovered that certain chemical elements were essential for plant nutrition.

Today, farmers throughout the world use billions of dollars worth of fertilizer yearly. Increased production resulting from the use of fertilizer probably accounts for about a fourth of the world's total crop production. Without fertilizer, greater amounts of land and labor would be needed to produce the same quantity of food and fiber.

The importance of fertilizer

Green plants produce the food they use. They produce it by means of the process of photosynthesis (see **Photosynthesis**). This process requires large amounts of nine chemical elements—carbon, hydrogen, oxygen, phosphorus, potassium, nitrogen, sulfur, calcium, and magnesium. It also requires smaller amounts of several other elements. These elements, called *micronutrients* because so little of each is needed, include boron, copper, iron, manganese, molybdenum, and zinc.

Air and water provide most of the carbon, hydrogen, and oxygen that green plants need for growth. The other elements must come chiefly from the soil.

The elements plants receive from soil are normally provided by decaying plant and animal matter and dissolved minerals. But sometimes soil does not have enough of these substances, resulting in a need for fertilizer. The harvest of crops, for example, involves removing plants from the soil before they die and decay. The soil does not receive the mineral elements contained in the crops, and so fertilizer must be added to supply them. Nitrogen, phosphorus, and potassium are the elements in which soil is most frequently deficient.

Kinds of fertilizers

There are two chief kinds of fertilizers, *mineral* and *organic.* Manufacturers produce mineral fertilizers from certain minerals or synthetic substances. Organic fertilizers come from decayed plant or animal matter.

Mineral fertilizers are the most widely used fertilizers. They supply three main elements: (1) nitrogen, (2) phosphorus, and (3) potassium.

Nitrogen fertilizers, the most widely used mineral fertilizers, are produced mainly from ammonia gas. Manufacturers use ammonia in making such liquid fertilizers as anhydrous ammonia and aqua ammonia. They also use it in producing solid fertilizers, such as ammonium sulfate, ammonium nitrate, ammonium phosphate, and an organic compound called *urea.* Each of these fertilizers provides the soil with large amounts of nitrogen. Some, including ammonium sulfate and ammonium phosphate, furnish other elements as well as nitrogen.

Phosphorus fertilizers, also called *phosphates,* are made from the mineral apatite. Finely ground apatite may be applied to soil as a solid fertilizer called *rock phosphate.* Apatite also may be treated with sulfuric acid or phosphoric acid to make liquid fertilizers called *superphosphates.*

Potassium fertilizers come largely from deposits of potassium chloride. Manufacturers mine the deposits or extract them with water to produce such fertilizers as potassium chloride, potassium nitrate, and potassium sulfate.

Other mineral fertilizers provide soil with various elements. Those made from gypsum, for example, supply sulfur. Manufacturers also produce fertilizers that provide specific micronutrients.

Organic fertilizers are made from a variety of substances, including manure, plant matter, sewage water, and packing house wastes. These fertilizers contain a smaller percentage of nutrients than do mineral fertilizers. Therefore, they must be used in larger quantities to obtain the same results. Some organic fertilizers may also cost more. But they solve a disposal problem because organic waste has few uses other than as fertilizer. Plant matter is used as fertilizer in two main ways, (1) as a compost pile or (2) as green manure.

A compost pile consists of alternate layers of plant matter and soil. Fertilizer mixed with lime is also usually added. The pile is allowed to decay for several months before being used as fertilizer. See **Compost.**

Green manure consists of certain crops that farmers use as fertilizer. For example, some plants have bacteria in *nodules* (knotlike growths) on their roots. These bacteria take nitrogen out of the air. Such plants, called *legumes,* include alfalfa, beans, and clover. Farmers may plant a crop of legumes and then plow the young plants into the soil. As the plants decay, nitrogen returns to the soil and enriches it so it can nourish other crops.

The fertilizer industry

The United States manufactures more fertilizer than any other country. It produces about $5\frac{1}{2}$ billion worth of fertilizer annually and exports about $680 million of it.

Commercial fertilizer containing nitrogen, phosphorus, and potassium helped produce the healthy green corn on the left. The weak, brown corn on the right received no fertilizer.

About 95 per cent of the fertilizer produced in the world is used on farm crops.

Raw materials for fertilizer come from several sources. Ammonia, the basic source of nitrogen fertilizer, is formed by combining nitrogen from the air with hydrogen from natural gas. Several oil firms in the United States produce ammonia because they have supplies of natural gas.

The United States has about 40 per cent of the world's supply of phosphate rock. The main sources are in Florida, Idaho, Missouri, Montana, North Carolina, Tennessee, Utah, and Wyoming. Morocco and the Soviet Union rank as the chief suppliers after the United States.

The largest deposits of potassium chloride, the major source of potassium fertilizer, occur in Canada and the Soviet Union. Canada furnishes about 75 per cent of the potassium chloride used in the United States. Potassium chloride is mined in several states, including California, New Mexico, and Utah.

Production and sale. Fertilizer is produced in four basic forms. *Straight goods fertilizer* is any chemical compound that contains one or two fertilizer elements. *Bulk blend fertilizer* is a mixture of straight goods in certain proportions. *Manufactured fertilizer* consists of two or more chemicals that are mixed and then formed into small grains. Each grain contains nitrogen, phosphorus, and potassium and perhaps certain micronutrients. *Liquid fertilizer* consists of one or more fertilizer materials dissolved in water. It may be sprayed on plants or soil, injected into soil, or added to irrigation water.

Most fertilizers release their plant nutrients into the soil almost immediately. Manufacturers also produce a special type of fertilizer, called *slow-release fertilizer,* that gives up its nutrients gradually. This type has been found useful when plants need a constant supply of nutrients over a long period of time.

Problems of the fertilizer industry. Every year, large amounts of fertilizer must be produced to meet the world's growing need for food. The fertilizer industry tries to match its production with this need. If it does not do so, severe food shortages might result.

A shortage of raw materials could cause a low supply of fertilizer. Some materials, such as natural gas and phosphorus, have uses other than in making fertilizer. Their use by other industries could cause a shortage for fertilizer manufacturers.

The mining and processing of the raw materials needed to make fertilizer may damage the environment. Many minerals used in making fertilizer come from open-pit mines, which cause large unproductive areas unless properly landscaped. In addition, the excessive use of fertilizer can contribute to water pollution. For example, erosion may carry fertilized soil into lakes and streams. The nutrient elements in the soil then increase the growth of simple plants called *algae* in the water. When the algae die, they produce large amounts of waste. As the waste decays, it uses up the oxygen supply of the water.   Frederick R. Troeh

Related articles in *World Book* include:

Fertilizer materials

Ammonia	Ash	Guano
Anhydrous ammonia	Calcium	Lime
	Compost	Limestone
Manure	Nitrogen	Potassium
Marl	Phosphate	Sulfur
Mulch	Phosphoric acid	Urea
Nitrate	Phosphorus	

Other related articles

Agricultural education	Eutrophication
Agriculture (New agricultural chemicals)	Soil (Characteristics of soils)
Agronomy	Water pollution

Fès. See Fez (city).

Fescue, *FEHS kyoo,* is the name of a group of grasses that grow in the United States and other temperate regions. Most fescue grasses tend to grow in tufts, or bunches. Fescue may grow to a height of 6 to 48 inches (15 to 122 centimeters) or more. Many perennial fescues serve as important foods for livestock in the grazing regions of the West. These include *Arizona fescue, Idaho fescue, greenleaf fescue,* and *Thurber fescue. Alpine fescue* is a variety of *sheep fescue* that grows above the timber line from the Rocky Mountains westward.

Farmers in humid areas of Tennessee, Missouri, and Kansas use *Kentucky 31* and *alta fescue* for hay and pasture. Sheep fescue and *red fescue* may be grown in lawns and pastures in the eastern United States. Creeping red fescue and *chewings,* a variety of red fescue, grow in a thick mat of fine leaves ideal for lawns.

Alan Pitcairn from Grant Heilman
Fescue grass

Scientific classification. The fescue grasses belong to the grass family, Gramineae. Arizona fescue is genus *Festuca,* species *F. arizonica.* Idaho fescue is *F. idahoensis;* greenleaf fescue, *F. viridula;* Thurber fescue, *F. thurberi.* Kentucky 31 and alta fescue are *F. arundinacea;* sheep fescue is *F. ovina;* and red fescue is *F. rubra.*   Wayne W. Huffine

See also **Grass.**

Fessenden, *FEHS uhn duhn,* **William Pitt** (1806-1869), a United States senator from Maine, helped found the Republican Party in the 1850's. He served in the Senate from 1854 to 1864, and from 1865 to 1869. He was secretary of the treasury under Abraham Lincoln in 1864. Fessenden opposed slavery and favored harsh measures against the South after the Civil War. However, he voted "not guilty" at the impeachment trial of President Andrew Johnson in 1868. Johnson had opposed Congress' harsh treatment of the South. Fessenden was born in Boscawen, N.H.   Robert M. York

Festival. See Feasts and festivals.

Festival of Light. See Sweden (Holidays).

Festival of Lights. See Hanukkah.

Fetish, *FEE tihsh* or *FEHT ihsh,* is an object that supposedly has magic powers. Many peoples worship bones, carved statues, unusual stones, and other objects as fetishes. In some societies, people carry such fetishes as a rabbit's foot or a "lucky" penny to bring them good luck.

© Odyssey Productions

Fetishes can take the form of such common objects as stones and bones, *above*. These fetishes belong to a Kikuyu witch doctor of Kenya. The Kikuyu believe that spirits control the fetishes and that a witch doctor can predict the future by tossing them.

Europeans first learned about *fetishism* (the worship of fetishes) when Portuguese explorers colonized Africa during the late 1400's. Many African peoples had fetishes and treated them with great devotion and respect. Fetishism is a type of *animism,* the belief that lifeless things have a spirit (see **Animism**). Fetish worshipers believe that the spirit protects them from evil and brings good luck. A fetish may become an *idol,* the image of a god, if word of its power spreads beyond the community (see **Idolatry**).

Psychiatrists use the term *fetishist* for a person who has an abnormal sexual attachment for a lifeless object. Such objects may include a lock of hair, a shoe, or a piece of clothing.   Alan Dundes

See also **Mythology** (African mythology); **Sculpture** (African); **Superstition**.

Fetus. See **Baby** (The developing baby); **Pregnancy** (The baby during pregnancy).

Feud is a long and sometimes murderous conflict between individuals, families, or groups. Feuds often occur in societies that lack a police force, other government law enforcement agency, or other form of central authority. They are also common in regions far from the center of authority or where central authority is hard to enforce because of rugged terrain or harsh climate. In addition, people inclined to take the law into their own hands frequently become involved in feuds. For example, feuds often occur among city youth gangs.

Most feuds begin when a member of one group or family insults or harms a member of another group or family. Then members of the victim's group seek revenge. If members seek to avenge a murder, they will probably kill the murderer or a member of the murderer's family. One such attack leads to another, and the feud continues. Families may keep fighting for years. Often, no person of either family can remember why the feud began, but new acts of violence keep it alive.

Many feuds have occurred in the mountains of Afghanistan; on the islands of Corsica and Sicily; on the Balkan Peninsula; and among such isolated African herding societies as the Masai and the Nuer. Feuds also have frequently occurred in the Appalachian Mountains of the United States. Feuds still break out occasionally in the Appalachian area of eastern Kentucky. The bloody quarrel between the Hatfield and McCoy families was the most famous Appalachian feud. At least 20 people died in this conflict, which began in the 1860's and lasted about 30 years. It became the subject of many local stories and songs.   Jennie Keith

See also **Vendetta**.

Feudalism is the general term used to describe the political and military system of western Europe during the Middle Ages. At that time, there was no strong central government and little security, but feudalism fulfilled the basic need for justice and protection.

Feudalism is often confused with *manorialism.* Manorialism was the system of organizing agricultural labor. It refers to the economic relationship between the lord of a manor and his peasant tenants (see **Manorialism**). Feudalism, on the other hand, was mainly a political and military system. Both the lord and his subjects, called *vassals,* were aristocrats. The lord gave vassals land in return for military and other services. The lord and the vassals were bound through ceremonies and oaths to be faithful to each other and to observe their obligations. The peasants had no part in such arrangements.

The word *feudal* comes from a Latin term for *fief.* The fief was the estate or land granted by a lord in return for a vassal's loyalty and service. Some fiefs were large enough to support one knight. Others were great provinces of a kingdom, such as the province of Normandy in France. The church, which owned large fiefs, was also part of the feudal system.

Feudalism developed to meet the needs of its time. In the A.D. 400's, Germanic tribes conquered the West Roman Empire and divided it into many kingdoms. The Germanic peoples—called *barbarians* by the Romans—were loyal only to their tribal chiefs or to their families. Thus, the strong central and local governments of the Romans disappeared. In addition, barbarian customs replaced many Roman laws. Such changes and further invasions resulted in general disorder and constant warfare in the years following the barbarian conquest of the West Roman Empire. Feudalism helped establish order in Europe under these conditions.

Feudalism began to appear in the 700's. By the 1100's, it had spread from France into England, Spain, and other parts of the Christian world. The crusaders organized their states in the Near East according to the feudal system. Feudalism reached its height between the 800's and 1200's. By the 1400's, it was disappearing or becoming an outdated system.

The beginnings of feudalism. Feudalism had two main roots. One was the relationship of honor that existed among the Germanic war bands that wandered over much of Europe in the early Middle Ages. The leader and warriors of these bands pledged their loyalty to each other. The warriors fought for the honor of their leader and were expected to remain with him even to death. In turn, the leader was responsible for his men and rewarded them with treasures and glory.

The second main root of feudalism was the system of *tenure* (landholding). Under this system, a lord would

A knight armed for battle in the 1200's carried a cross-hilted sword and a kite-shaped shield. His helmet completely covered his head. Other knights could identify him only by his heraldic symbol. The symbol of the Flemish lion that appears on the shield and horse's coverlet in this seal identifies the knight as Guy de Dampierre, the Count of Flanders.

grant land to a person on certain conditions or in return for services other than rent or payment. People who owned land might turn it over to a lord in return for protection. The lord allowed the people to stay on the land as tenants. These tenants became the peasants of the manorial system. Although they lost their independence, having the protection of a powerful local lord was more important to them. The system of tenure was already in use in the former provinces of the Roman Empire when the Germanic invaders settled there in the A.D. 400's.

By the 700's, the Muslims had spread from Africa to Spain, and their new empire threatened all of western Europe. Kings and important nobles began giving fiefs to free and noble warriors in return for military service. These fiefs included land, the buildings on it, and the peasants who lived and worked on it. The warriors who received the fiefs were called *vassals,* from a Latin word meaning *military retainer.* By the 800's, the relationship of honor and loyalty that existed between leader and warrior in the Germanic war bands was combined with a system for holding land and providing services in exchange. This combination was feudalism.

The principles of feudalism. Only noblemen or aristocratic warriors could take part in feudal practices. A saying of the time stated, "No land without a lord, and no lord without land." A man became a vassal of the lord in a ceremony called *homage.* The future vassal promised to be loyal, fight for the lord, and become his *man* (*homo* in Latin). The lord promised to treat the vassal with honor. See **Homage.**

After performing homage, the new vassal was *invested with* (given the rights to) his fief. This was done in an *investiture* ceremony. At the ceremony, the lord often gave his vassal a clod of dirt, a stick, or some other such object as a symbol of the fief.

The vassal received only the use or possession of the fief, not ownership of it. He held the fief in return for services he had promised. As long as the vassal held the fief, he received what the land—and the peasants—produced, collected taxes, held court, administered justice, and managed the peasants' labor. When the vassal died, his son usually took over the fief. The son provided the same services as his father.

By 1100, it had become the custom for a man's oldest son to inherit the fief. This custom was called *primogeniture* (the right of the first-born). Primogeniture ensured that the fief would not be broken up among many sons and that one heir would assume responsibility for the services to the lord. See **Primogeniture.**

If a vassal died without heirs, the fief *escheated* (went back) to the lord. The lord could then grant it to another person as he wished. If the dead vassal's heir was a young child, the lord had the right of *wardship* and became the protector of the *ward* (child). The lord could grant the wardship to another vassal, who held the fief and its profits until the young heir came of age. In many cases, the lord also had a right to choose marriage partners for his wards and for the daughters or widows of his vassal. If a woman inherited a fief, her husband performed homage and became the lord's vassal. Such rights of the lord were called feudal *incidents.* They were sources of power and profit for the lord.

The lord had other rights called *aids.* All vassals had to make a special payment when the lord's oldest son was knighted and when his oldest daughter married. If the lord was captured and held for ransom, the vassals had to pay the ransom. However, feudal aids and rights were limited. For example, a lord could not require new conditions or levy higher taxes on his vassals. In addition, the lord was supposed to consult with his vassals before making major decisions, such as whether or not to go to war.

Knighthood under feudalism. A vassal's main service to his lord was military. By the 700's, vassals had to supply a certain number of knights to serve the lord for a certain number of days, usually 40. Knights were armored warriors on war horses. The larger the fief held by a vassal, the more knights the vassal had to provide.

It became the custom for a vassal to divide his own fief and distribute parts of it to his knights. The knights then became his vassals. This practice of dividing fiefs was called *subinfeudation.* By the 1200's, it had developed so far that several layers of feudal relations might separate a simple knight at the bottom from a great baron or a king. At each level, a noble was both lord and vassal.

Justice under feudalism. Quarrels among vassals were settled at the lord's *court,* which consisted of all the vassals. Many of the legal customs developed at the feudal court have become part of the legal systems of Great Britain and the United States. For example, the lord presided over feudal courts. In courts today, a judge presides. A vassal received judgment from other vassals who were his *peers* (social equals). Today, citizens receive judgment from their peers on a jury. Other judicial customs of feudal days have disappeared. One such custom was *trial by combat,* which involved a fight between the vassals involved in a dispute. The winner of the fight was also declared the winner of the case. It was

From the Harley Manuscript of *Froissart's Chronicles,* The British Library, London

Feudal courts settled differences among nobles. This miniature shows England's King Richard II presiding over his royal court. The king gave the final verdict on the advice of his vassals, who were nobles and church officials. This court settled a dispute in 1398 between Thomas Mowbray and Henry of Bolingbroke (later King Henry IV) by banishing both men from England.

accepted that God gave victory to the honest vassal or correct side. See **Trial by combat.**

A vassal had to answer the *summons* (order to appear) of a feudal court. If the vassal failed to appear or did not obey the court's decision, the lord could take back the vassal's fief. A rebellious vassal was declared a *felon.*

The lord was expected to seek the advice and consent of his vassals before making laws. In time, this practice led to the idea that no ruler can make laws without the consent of the people being governed. Modern parliaments in Europe developed from the meetings of vassals summoned by a lord or a king.

The decline of feudalism. By the 1200's, several events in Europe led to the decline of feudalism. An economic revival put more money back into use. Because soldiers could be paid, fewer lords relied on vassals to provide the services of knights. The invention of gunpowder and of such weapons as the longbow and the cannon lessened the dominance of knights. Foot soldiers from Flemish cities defeated French knights at the battle of Courtrai in 1302. English longbowmen beat the French cavalry in battles at Crécy in 1346, Poitiers in 1356, and Agincourt in 1415. Stone castles occupied by feudal lords no longer could stand against cannons. Cities grew wealthier and became more important, and rulers had less need of the aristocracy. People trained in

government service took over the functions that vassals had performed on their fiefs.   Joel T. Rosenthal

Related articles in *World Book* include:

Castle	Manorialism
Clothing (Middle Ages;	Middle Ages
Renaissance)	Primogeniture
Homage	Serf
Knights and knighthood	Trial by combat

See also *Feudalism* in the Research Guide/Index, Volume 22, for a *Reading and Study Guide.*

Additional resources

Bloch, Marc L. *Feudal Society.* 2 vols. University of Chicago Press, 1961.
Brown, R. Allen. *Origins of English Feudalism.* Barnes & Noble, 1973.
Stephenson, Carl. *Mediaeval Feudalism.* Cornell Univ. Press, 1956. First published in 1942. A standard introduction.

Feuerbach, *FOY uhr bahk,* **Ludwig Andreas,** *LOOT vihk ahn DRAY uhs* (1804-1872), was a German philosopher. He studied under G. W. F. Hegel, but later turned from Hegel's philosophical idealism and instead stressed the scientific study of humanity.

In *Thoughts on Death and Immortality* (1830), Feuerbach challenged Christian doctrines. However, Feuerbach actually placed a high value on religion, because he thought it expressed, in an inverted form, humanity's idea of its true essence. Feuerbach presented this idea in his major work, *The Essence of Christianity* (1841).

Feuerbach argued that though religion represents human creative activity as if it depends on God, in reality God is just the projection of an ideal image of humanity's own capacities.

Feuerbach also believed philosophers such as Hegel had an excessively abstract view of human nature, and had missed the significance of concrete physical experience. Thus he declared that *Der Mensch isst was er ist* (Man is what he eats). These ideas influenced Karl Marx. However, Marx and other radicals attacked Feuerbach for merely criticizing views of the human condition, rather than acting directly to improve it. Feuerbach was born in Landshut.   Karl Ameriks

Fever is a condition in which the brain maintains the body temperature at a higher than normal level. It is one of the most common symptoms of disease. When fever is the main symptom of a disease, it may be part of the disease's name, as in *scarlet fever* or *yellow fever.*

Not every rise in body temperature is a fever. For example, exercising in the heat or sitting in a sauna can produce an above-normal body temperature. But in these cases, unlike what happens in a fever, the brain instructs the body to decrease its temperature by sweating and increasing skin blood flow, and the individual feels the urge to be in a cool place.

Fever results when an infection or an allergic or toxic reaction causes the brain's temperature setting to rise. For example, when a flu virus enters the human body, white blood cells release a protein called *endogenous pyrogen* or *leucocyte pyrogen.* This protein travels through the blood to the *hypothalamus,* the part of the brain mainly responsible for regulating body temperature. The protein triggers the release of chemical compounds called *prostaglandins.* Prostaglandins act on nerve cells to produce a sensation of coldness. This causes the hypothalamus to increase body temperature by making the body burn fat, decrease skin blood flow, shiver, and develop an urge to stay warm. *Antipyretic drugs,* such as aspirin and acetaminophen, reduce fever by slowing the production of prostaglandins.

Medical research has shown that fevers speed up the body's defenses against invading viruses and bacteria. Because fever thus can help fight infection, some medical experts advise against reducing a moderate fever. In human beings, a body temperature of 98.6° F. (36.9° C) is normal. A moderate fever generally ranges from 100° F. (37.7° C) to 102° F. (38.9° C). Most experts agree that fevers probably should be reduced if they rise above 102° F. (38.9° C), or if they occur in pregnant women, people with heart disease, or the elderly. When deciding how to handle a fever, it is wise to consult a doctor.

Fever occurs in all *vertebrates* (animals with backbones). Fever first appeared at least 300 million years ago as a means of fighting disease. Among warm-blooded vertebrates—that is, birds and mammals—fever is achieved by physical and behavioral changes. Cold-blooded vertebrates, such as fish and reptiles, achieve fevers by moving into the heat, where they can maintain a high body temperature.   Matthew J. Kluger

Fever blister. See Cold sore; Herpes.

Feverfew is a low, hardy plant that requires little attention. Its cluster of small, white, daisylike flowers appears in late summer. The leaves of the plant have a strong scent when crushed. People once believed that feverfew

WORLD BOOK illustration by Christabel King

The feverfew is so named because people once believed the plant could cure fever.

could cure fever. Its name means *to put fever to flight.*

Scientific classification. Feverfew is a member of the composite family, Compositae. It is classified as *Chrysanthemum parthenium.*   Robert W. Schery

Few, William (1748-1828), a lawyer, judge, and banker, was a Georgia signer of the Constitution of the United States. At the Constitutional Convention of 1787, Few supported the establishment of a strong national government. He later helped win *ratification* (approval) of the Constitution by Georgia.

Few was born near Baltimore. He was largely self-educated. In 1776, Few moved to Georgia. He became a lawyer and soon afterward entered politics. He was elected to the Georgia state assembly in 1777, 1779, 1783, and 1793. Few was a member of the Second Continental Congress and the Congress of the Confederation from 1780 to 1788. He served in the U.S. Senate from 1789 to 1793. From 1796 to 1799, Few was a judge of the U.S. Circuit Court. He served in the New York state legislature from 1802 to 1805. Few later became president of City Bank of New York.   Joan R. Gundersen

Feynman, *FYN muhn,* **Richard Phillips** (1918-1988), of the United States, shared the 1965 Nobel Prize in physics with Julian S. Schwinger and Sin-itiro Tomonaga. Working independently, the three men developed an improved theory of quantum electrodynamics in the late 1940's. *Quantum electrodynamics* is the study of the interaction of atomic particles and electromagnetic radiation. The theory enables scientists to predict accurately the effects of electrically charged particles on each other in a radiation field.

Feynman was born in New York City. He earned a Ph.D. degree from Princeton University in 1942. From 1942 to 1945, he worked on the atomic bomb project at Los Alamos, N. Mex. He became a professor of theoretical physics at Cornell University in 1945. He served on the faculty of the California Institute of Technology from 1951 until his death in 1988.   Roger H. Stuewer

Fez, also spelled *Fès* (pop. 325,327), is the religious center of Morocco and one of its traditional capitals. It boasts the Mosque of Mulai Idris, a noted Muslim shrine, and Karaouiyine University, one of the oldest universities in the world. The university was founded in 859.

Fez lies in the deep valley of the Fez River in northern Morocco. For the location of Fez, see **Morocco** [map]). Railroads connect it with other North African cities. It is noted for its silk, woolen, and leather goods. The Moorish ruler Idris II founded Fez as his capital in 808. The city declined in the 1600's, when Sultan Ismail built his palace in Meknès. But it again became the capital from 1728 until the French occupation of Morocco in 1912.
Keith G. Mather

Fez is a tall, red, brimless cap with a colored tassel of silk or wool. It is worn in Egypt and in North Africa where it is sometimes called a *tarboosh.* All fezzes were once colored with a dye made from the juice of red berries found only in Morocco. This same color can now be produced by chemical dyes. The fez was first made in Fez, Morocco.   Lois M. Gurel

FHA. See **Federal Housing Administration.**

Fianna Fáil. See **Ireland** (The Irish Free State).

Fiat, *FY at* or *FEE aht,* in government, is an executive order or decree that requires obedience but is not a law. Many legal scholars consider a fiat to be an order that is issued for purposes other than to carry out legislation. Such orders sometimes come into conflict with one or more laws. In many cases, these conflicts are resolved by the courts. The term *fiat* comes from Latin. Its Latin meaning is *let it be done.*   Anthony D'Amato

Fiber is a hairlike strand of a substance that is extremely long in relation to its width. A fiber is at least 100 times longer than it is wide. Fibers are flexible and may be spun into yarn and made into fabrics. A fiber is the smallest visible unit of any textile product. Manufacturers use fibers in clothing and in such home furnishings as carpets, drapes, and upholstery. They also use fibers in many industrial products, including parachutes, fire hoses, insulation, and space suits. In medicine, fibers are used to make artificial arteries and tendons.

Some fibers occur in nature, and others are manufactured. Most natural fibers come from plants and animals. These fibers include cotton, silk, and wool. There are two types of manufactured fibers. *Regenerated fibers* are made from natural materials. Manufacturers process these materials to form a fiber structure. *Synthetic fibers* are made entirely from chemicals.

No one knows when human beings learned to spin natural fibers into yarn to make fabrics. Evidence of wool fabrics dates from approximately 4200 B.C. Cotton was used in 3000 B.C. The Chinese discovered silk in 2640 B.C. The first practical manufactured fiber, rayon, was developed in 1885. See **Textile** (History).

All natural fibers except silk are limited in length from about $\frac{1}{2}$ inch to 8 inches (1.3 to 20 centimeters). The length of a silk fiber depends upon the size of the silkworm's cocoon. Fibers of limited length are called *staple fibers.* Manufacturers spin these fibers into yarn. Manufactured fibers are unlimited in length. They are produced in long, continuous strands called *filament fibers.* They can be used singly as yarns or blended with other filament fibers. When they are blended with natural fibers, filaments are cut into staple lengths.

The properties of a particular fiber depend on its chemical composition and physical structure. Manufacturers use fibers that have properties suited to their products. For example, fibers used in clothing must feel pleasant to the touch, be absorbent, have a good luster, and drape to fit the body. For industrial use, a fiber's strength and durability are important. One fiber, SPECTRA-900, is 10 times stronger than steel. Another class of fibers, *spandex,* can stretch like rubber.

Natural fibers

Natural fibers are obtained mainly from plants and animals. They account for more than half the fibers produced in the world yearly.

Plant fibers. *Cotton* is the most widely used natural fiber. Staple fibers from cotton *bolls* (seed pods) are spun into yarns for clothing, and household and industrial fabrics. Cotton cloth is absorbent, soft, and comfortable to wear. *Flax,* a strong fiber from the stems of flax plants, is used to make clothing and linen products. *Hemp, jute,* and *sisal* are coarse plant fibers used in cords, ropes, and rough fabrics.

Animal fibers include fur and hair. *Wool,* the hair sheared from sheep and certain other animals, is popular in clothing and home furnishings. Wool fibers have a scalelike surface that resembles shingles on a roof. Manufacturers mat wool fibers together in a process known as *felting.* This process produces air pockets within the matted fibers. Air trapped in these pockets acts as an insulator. This is one reason wool clothing keeps a person warm. *Silk* is the strongest natural fiber. Manufacturers unwind silk filaments from silkworm cocoons and make silk yarn for clothing and decorative fabrics.

Manufactured fibers

The study of plastics has helped chemists learn how to combine chemicals to create fibers that have specific properties. Machines melt the chemicals or mix them in various liquids. The machines then force streams of the chemicals through tiny holes. The streams harden into filament fibers that are wound onto spools or cut into staple lengths.

Manufactured fibers account for more than two-thirds of the fibers processed by textile mills in the United States. The variety and qualities of these fibers

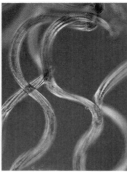

Science Photo Library from Photo Researchers   © Michael Abbey, Photo Researchers

Wool and nylon fibers show the difference between organic and synthetic fibers. Organic wool fibers, *left,* have a scaly structure similar to human hair. Synthetic nylon fibers, *right,* have a smooth surface that makes them resistant to wear.

make them popular with consumers and manufacturers. See **Textile** (table: Manufactured fibers).

The two main groups of manufactured fibers are re-generated fibers and synthetic fibers.

Regenerated fibers are also called *cellulosics* because they are derived from the cellulose in cotton and wood pulp. Manufacturers process cotton and wood pulp to make such cellulosics as *rayon,* the first successful manufactured fiber. Rayon has many properties that resemble those of cotton. Cellulose treated with acetic acid produces *acetate,* a fiber that is silkier than rayon. Rayon and acetate are used in clothing, and rayon also is used in tires.

Synthetic fibers are manufactured from chemicals. Most synthetic fibers are stronger than either natural or regenerated fibers. Synthetic fibers, as well as the re-generated fiber acetate, are *thermoplastic* (softened by heat). Manufacturers are able to shape these fibers at high temperatures, adding such features as pleats and creases. These fibers also will melt if touched with too hot an iron. The most widely used kinds of synthetic fibers are (1) nylon, or polyamide, fibers, (2) polyester fibers, (3) acrylic fibers, and (4) olefin fibers.

Nylon fibers, or *polyamide* fibers, were the first synthetic fibers. They are lightweight and strong and are widely used in carpets, hosiery, ropes, and tires.

Polyester fibers, such as Dacron, Fortrel, Kodel, and Trevira, are durable and quickly regain their shape after being stretched or wrinkled. They are used in clothing and bedding. Clothing fabrics are often made from a blend of polyester and cotton fibers. The polyester fibers provide wash-and-wear characteristics, and the cotton fibers make the fabrics comfortable to wear. Manufacturers also use polyester fibers in filters, sails, and other industrial fabrics.

Acrylic fibers, including Acrilan, Creslan, and Orlon, are soft and durable. A number of acrylic yarns resemble wool and are used in clothing, especially sweaters. Many artificial furs also are made from acrylic fibers.

Olefin fibers are strong and resist stains. These properties make Herculon, Marvess, and other olefin fibers useful in carpets, upholstery, and ropes.

Other synthetic fibers. Yarns called *Lastex* are made from manufactured rubber fibers wrapped in cotton, nylon, or other fibers. Lastex and *spandex,* a group of elastic fibers including Lycra and Glospan, add stretch to garments. Special metal treatments produce *metallic fibers,* such as gold and silver filaments, that can be used to decorate fabrics.   Robert A. Barnhardt

Related articles in *World Book* include:

Natural fibers

Abacá	Flax	Jute	Silk
Asbestos	Hemp	Kapok	Sisal
Bast	Henequen	Ramie	Wool
Cotton			

Manufactured fibers

Acrylic	Nylon	Rayon
Fiberglass	Polyester	

Other related articles

Agriculture (Natural fibers)	Mohair	Textile
	Palm	Thread
Cellulose	Plastics	Wallboard
Linen		

Corning Glass Works

A thin optical fiber can transmit as much information as a larger, traditional copper cable, *above.* There are two basic kinds of optical fibers, *below.* A *multi-mode fiber* has a wide core that allows light to travel along many paths. The narrow core of a *single-mode* fiber confines light to a central path.

WORLD BOOK diagram by Zorica Dabich

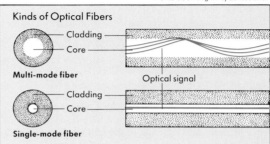

Kinds of Optical Fibers
Cladding
Core
Multi-mode fiber
Optical signal
Cladding
Core
Single-mode fiber

Fiber optics is a branch of physics based on the transmission of light through transparent fibers of glass or plastic. These *optical fibers* can carry light over distances ranging from a few inches or centimeters to more than 100 miles (160 kilometers). Such fibers work individually or in bundles. Some individual fibers measure less than 0.001 inch (0.025 millimeter) in diameter.

Optical fibers have an extremely pure core of glass or plastic surrounded by a covering called a *cladding.* Light from a laser, a light bulb, or some other source enters one end of the optical fiber. As the light travels through the core, it is typically kept inside it by the cladding. The cladding is designed so that it bends—inward—light rays that strike its inside surface. At the other end of the fiber, the light is received by a detector, such as a photosensitive device or the human eye.

There are two basic kinds of optical fibers—*single-mode fibers* and *multi-mode fibers.* Single-mode fibers are used for long-distance transmissions. They have extremely small cores, and they accept light only along the axis of the fibers. As a result, single-mode fibers require the use of special lasers as a light source, and they need to be precisely connected to the laser, to other fibers in the system, and to the detector. Multi-mode fibers have cores larger than those of single-mode fibers, and they accept light from a variety of angles. Multi-mode fibers can use more types of light sources and cheaper connectors than can single-mode fibers, but they cannot be used over long distances.

Optical fibers have a number of uses. In fiber-optic communication systems, special lasers transmit coded messages by flashing on and off at extremely high speeds. The messages travel through optical fibers to interpreting devices that decode the messages, converting them back into the form of the original signal. Fiber-optic communication systems have a number of features that make them superior to systems that use traditional copper cables. For example, they have a much larger information-carrying capacity and are not subject to electrical interference. In addition, signals sent over long-distance fiber-optic cables need less amplification than do signals sent over copper cables of equal length. As a result, many telephone and other communication companies have begun to replace copper cables with fiber-optic cables.

Bundles of optical fibers form part of gastroscopes and certain other medical instruments. These instruments enable physicians to view internal body parts without performing surgery (see **Gastroscope**). Surgical lasers and devices for measuring temperature or pressure also use optical fibers.   Nathan M. Denkin

See also **Communication** (Communication of the future; picture: Fiber-optic communication); **Laser; Telecommunication; Telephone** (Recent developments).

Fiberboard is a building material made of wood or other plant fibers pressed into sheets. Builders use it as insulation, as wall covering, and as a base for plastering and floor covering. It is also used for making furniture. Manufacturers make fiberboard chiefly from wood, but also use waste paper, straw, sugar cane, and cornstalks. Other materials, such as asphalt and rosin, may be added to increase strength or resistance to fire, decay, or moisture. See also **Wallboard**.   George W. Washa

Fiberglass, also called *fibrous glass,* is glass in the form of fine *fibers* (threads). The fibers may be many times finer than human hair, and may look and feel like silk. The flexible glass fibers are stronger than steel, and will not burn, stretch, rot, or fade.

Uses. Manufacturers use fiberglass to make a variety of products. Fiberglass is woven into cloth to make such products as curtains and tablecloths. The cloth does not change its properties when dyed. It will not wrinkle or soil easily, and needs no ironing after washing. Fiberglass textiles are also used for electrical insulation. In

bulk form, fiberglass is used for air filters and for heat and sound insulation. Air trapped between the fibers makes it a good insulator.

Fiberglass reinforced plastics are extremely strong and light in weight. They can be molded, shaped, twisted, and poured for many different uses. Manufacturers use fiberglass reinforced plastics to make automobile bodies, boat hulls, building panels, fishing rods, and aircraft parts. The fibers used to strengthen plastic may be woven or matted together, or they may be individual strands. The form used depends on the nature and price of the final product.

How fiberglass is made. Fiberglass is made from sand and other raw materials used to make ordinary glass (see **Glass** [Recipes for making glass]). Strands of fiberglass may be made in different ways. In one method, the raw materials are heated and formed into small glass marbles so workers can examine them for impurities. The marbles are then melted in special electric furnaces. The melted glass runs down through tiny holes at the bottom of the furnace. A spinning drum catches the fibers of hot glass and winds them on bobbins, like threads on spools. Because the drum revolves much faster than the glass flows, tension pulls the fibers and draws them out into still finer strands. The drum can pull out 2 miles (3.2 kilometers) of fibers in a minute. Up to 95 miles (153 kilometers) of fiber can be drawn from one marble $\frac{5}{8}$ inch (16 millimeters) in diameter. The fiber can be twisted together into yarns and cords. The yarns may be woven into cloth, tape, and other kinds of fabrics. In another method, called the *direct melt process,* the marble-making steps are omitted.

Bulk fiberglass, or *fiberglass wool,* is made somewhat differently. Sand and other raw materials are melted in a furnace. The melted glass flows from tiny holes in the furnace. Then high-pressure jets of steam catch it and draw it into fine fibers from 8 to 15 inches (20 to 38 centimeters) long. The fibers are gathered on a conveyor belt in the form of a white wool-like mass.

History. The Egyptians used coarse glass fibers for decorative purposes before the time of Christ. Edward Drummond Libbey, an American glass manufacturer, exhibited a dress made of fiberglass and silk at the Columbian Exposition in Chicago in 1893. During World War I, fiberglass was made in Germany as a substitute for asbestos. Finally, in experiments conducted from 1931 to 1939, the Owens Illinois Glass Company (now called Owens-Illinois, Inc.) and the Corning Glass Works developed practical methods of making fiberglass commercially.   Richard F. Blewitt

Fibonacci, *FEE boh NAHT chee,* **Leonardo,** *LAY oh NAHR doh* (1175?-1240?), was an Italian mathematician who helped introduce the Hindu-Arabic numerals (0, 1, 2, 3, 4, 5, 6, 7, 8, 9) into Western Europe. He is also known as the originator of a special series of numbers, now called the Fibonacci sequence or the Fibonacci numbers.

Fibonacci was born in Pisa and he is sometimes known as Leonardo of Pisa. In his youth, he traveled widely in the Middle East, where he learned the Hindu-Arabic numeral system. In 1202, Fibonacci published *Liber Abaci* (*Book of the Abacus*), in which he explained the Hindu-Arabic numerals, including methods of arithmetic and applications to commercial problems. At the

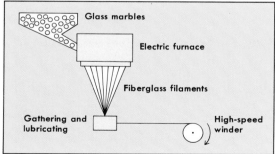

Glass marbles

Electric furnace

Fiberglass filaments

Gathering and lubricating

High-speed winder

WORLD BOOK diagram

Fiberglass is often made by melting glass marbles in a furnace. The melted glass flows through tiny holes at the bottom of the furnace and comes out as fine filaments. The filaments are then gathered together, lubricated, and wound around a reel.

time, European merchants were using the Roman numeral system (see **Decimal system** [History]).

In *Liber Abaci*, Fibonacci also explained his famous sequence. This sequence consists of the numbers 1, 1, 2, 3, 5, 8, 13, and so on. Each number after the first two numbers (1, 1) equals the sum of the two numbers before it—that is, $1 + 1 = 2, 1 + 2 = 3, 2 + 3 = 5$, and so on. Since their introduction, these numbers have been much studied by mathematicians.   Arthur Gittleman

Fibrillation. See Heart (Fibrillation).

Fibrin, *FY bruhn,* is a white, fibrous protein substance that makes up the most important part of a blood clot. The formation of a clot is called *coagulation.* Fibrin is formed from *fibrinogen,* a protein that is present in *plasma* (the liquid portion of the blood). When blood flows out of a cut area, molecules of fibrinogen unite to become long fibers of fibrin. These fibers make a mesh-like plug over the cut area. Red blood cells become caught in the mesh and help form the blood clot. Clots may also form inside blood vessels.   Douglas W. Huestis

Fichte, *FIHK tuh,* **Johann Gottlieb,** *YOH hahn GAWT leep* (1762-1814), was a German philosopher. He strongly influenced German metaphysics, aesthetics, and social thought. Fichte also influenced the ideas of philosophers Friedrich Schelling and G. W. F. Hegel.

Fichte was a follower of the idealism of German philosopher Immanuel Kant. Fichte believed that the mind is the essence of the universe. Our ideas, he maintained, do not come from experience of the material world. Instead, our minds are part of the universal creative mind. Fichte dealt with these ideas in his *Foundation of the Complete Theory of Knowledge* (1794). His chief political work is the patriotic *Addresses to the German Nation* (1808). In it, Fichte expressed his faith in German culture and national spirit. The book had a major impact on German nationalism. See **Education** (The rise of universal public schools).

Fichte was born in Rammenau, near Bautzen. He taught at the University of Jena from 1794 to 1799. He was a popular lecturer but lost his position after being accused of atheism. He served on the faculty of the University of Berlin from 1810 until his death.   Karl Ameriks

Fiction is a story created from an author's imagination. It may be written in prose or verse. Novels and short stories are the most popular forms of fiction. Other forms include dramas and *narrative poems* (poems that tell a story). Fiction differs from biographies, histories, and other *nonfiction,* which is created entirely from facts. The word *fiction* comes from the Latin word *fictio,* which means *a making* or *a fashioning.*

Characteristics of fiction. All fiction contains elements that are partly or entirely imaginary. Such elements include characters and settings. In some fiction, the imaginary elements are obvious. For example, *Alice's Adventures in Wonderland* (1865), by the English author Lewis Carroll, has wildly unrealistic characters and events. But fiction does not necessarily differ much from reality. Many fictional works feature true-to-life characters and realistic settings, and some fiction is based on real people and real events. For example, Napoleon's invasion of Russia in 1812 is the background of *War and Peace* (1869), a novel by the Russian writer Leo Tolstoy. The factual elements in fiction are always combined with imaginary situations and incidents.

The chief purpose of most fiction is to entertain. But a serious work of fiction also stimulates the mind. By creating characters, placing them in specific situations, and establishing a point of view, writers of serious fiction set forth judgments. These judgments may involve moral, philosophical, psychological, or social problems. They also may concern the nature of fiction. For example, an author may deliberately baffle the reader regarding how fiction should be presented.

History. Storytelling is as old as humanity. Prehistoric people passed on legends and myths from generation to generation by word of mouth. Fiction has appeared in a wide variety of forms since the development of writing about 5,000 years ago. But certain general forms have been dominant during various eras.

The most popular forms of fiction in ancient times included the *epic* and the *fable.* Epics are long narrative poems about heroes or gods. Two of the most famous epics, the *Iliad* and the *Odyssey,* were probably written by the Greek poet Homer in the 700's B.C. Fables are brief tales with a moral. Among the best-known fables are the animal stories attributed to the Greek slave Aesop, who lived about 600 B.C. See **Epic; Fable.**

From the 1100's to the 1400's, during the Middle Ages, the *romance* became the leading form of fiction. Most medieval romances tell about adventures of knights or other court figures. Many of these stories have supernatural characters and events. See **Romance.**

Since the mid-1700's, the chief forms of fiction have been the novel and the short story (see **Novel; Short story**). In some modern works, the authors have abandoned traditional storytelling devices, such as organized plots and clear-cut characters. For example, the novels of the French author Alain Robbe-Grillet feature precise descriptions of events and objects as experienced or seen by the characters. Such works intentionally confuse the reader.   Marcus Klein

Related articles. See the articles on national literatures, such as **American literature** and **French literature.** See also:

Detective story	Pulitzer Prizes (table: Fiction)
Drama	Science fiction
Literature for children (Fiction)	Writing (Fiction)
Poetry	

Additional resources

Gardner, John. *The Art of Fiction: Notes on Craft for Young Writers.* Random House, 1984.

Kenney, William P. *How to Analyze Fiction.* Simon & Schuster, 1982. First published in 1966.

Morris, Wright. *About Fiction: Reverent Reflections on the Nature of Fiction with Irreverent Observations on Writers, Readers, & Other Abuses.* Harper, 1975.

Fiddler crab is a burrowing animal that lives along sandy or muddy beaches and salt marshes in tropical and temperate regions. It belongs to the class Crustacea. The male has a huge front *pincer* (claw) that he moves back and forth much as a fiddler moves his or her arm when playing a violin. This claw is used for courting females and for fighting with other males. The fiddler crab feeds on water plants, called *algae,* mixed with mud. In the fall, the crabs in cold regions close their burrows and hibernate.

Scientific classification. The fiddler crab belongs to the order Decapoda. It makes up the genus *Uca.* There are various species.   J. Laurens Barnard

See also **Biological clock** (Other rhythms); **Crab.**

Fiedler, *FEED luhr,* **Arthur** (1894-1979), conducted the Boston Pops Orchestra from 1930 to 1979. He organized and conducted the Boston Sinfonietta, later known as the Arthur Fiedler Sinfonietta, and the Boston Esplanade Concerts. Fiedler was born in Boston, and studied at the Royal Academy of Music in Berlin. He taught at Boston University.   David Ewen

Fief. See Feudalism; Fee.

Field was the family name of three distinguished sons of David Dudley Field (1781-1867), a well-known Congregational clergyman and the author of several histories of Massachusetts.

David Dudley Field, Jr. (1805-1894), a brilliant lawyer, won recognition for his work as a reformer of legal procedure. He started work on a code of legal procedure in 1847. His code formed the basis for legal procedure reforms in many states and in England.

David became the first president of the International Law Association, founded in Brussels in 1873 to reform and codify international law. He was born in Haddam, Conn., and studied at Williams College.

Stephen Johnson Field (1816-1899) was an associate justice of the Supreme Court of the United States from 1863 to 1897. He handed down many opinions that helped develop United States constitutional law. He also served on the Electoral Commission in 1877 (see **Electoral Commission**). Stephen was born in Haddam, Conn., and graduated from Williams College.

Cyrus West Field (1819-1892) promoted the first telegraph cable across the Atlantic (see **Cable**). The first fully successful cable was laid in 1866, after four previous attempts.

The first cable, laid in 1857, broke 360 miles (579 kilometers) from shore. An attempt in June 1858 also failed. Field promoted a successful effort to lay a cable between Ireland and Newfoundland in August 1858. Technical carelessness ruined the cable's insulation, and it failed four weeks later. In 1865, Field attempted to lay a new cable. The cable broke when the project was almost done. The project succeeded in 1866, with the laying of a new cable and the repair of the old.

Field later promoted the New York elevated railroad. He also wanted to lay a cable to the Hawaiian Islands, Asia, and Australia. Field was born in Stockbridge, Mass.

Daniel J. Dykstra and Richard D. Humphrey

Field is the name of an American family that became prominent in merchandising, publishing, and philanthropy.

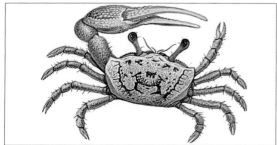

WORLD BOOK illustration by James Teason

The fiddler crab lives in sandy or muddy soil. The male, *above,* uses its huge front claw in fighting other males.

Marshall Field I (1834-1906), was a highly successful merchant. He established Marshall Field & Company, a world-famous Chicago department store.

Field was born in Conway Township, Mass. He went to Chicago in 1856 and got a job with a drygoods firm. About 1865, Field bought an interest in a rival business. He bought out his partners by 1881, and the firm became known as Marshall Field & Company.

Field introduced several new merchandising policies. He marked prices on the merchandise and let customers exchange goods if they were dissatisfied. Field's slogan was "Give the Lady What She Wants," and he made a special effort to attract women to his store. Marshall Field & Company was the first store to sell goods in its basement. The department store also led in developing advertising techniques and window displays to attract customers.

Field's philanthropic activities included a gift of 10 acres (4 hectares) of ground as a site for a new University of Chicago. He also contributed about $9 million for the establishment of the Field Museum of Natural History, which is in Chicago.

Marshall Field II (1868-1905), was the son of Marshall Field I. Poor health prevented him from taking part in the family enterprises.

Marshall Field III (1893-1956), the son of Marshall Field II, began the family publishing business. In 1940, he helped found *PM,* a New York City daily newspaper that carried no advertising. He founded *The Chicago Sun* in 1941 and purchased control of another Chicago paper, the *Daily Times,* in 1947. The next year, he merged the two newspapers into the *Chicago Sun-Times.*

Field consolidated his communications activities under Field Enterprises, Inc. These activities included the *Sun-Times; The World Book Encyclopedia* and *Childcraft,* which became Field Enterprises Educational Corporation; *Parade,* a Sunday newspaper supplement; the book-publishing houses of Simon & Schuster and Pocket Books; and several radio stations.

In 1940, Field established the Field Foundation to deal with problems relating to education, child welfare, and social and racial relations. See **Field Foundation.**

Field was born in Chicago. He attended Trinity College at Cambridge University in England.

Marshall Field IV (1916-1965), the son of Marshall Field III, expanded the Field publishing enterprises. He became editor and publisher of the *Chicago Sun-Times* in 1950 and was named president of Field Enterprises in 1956. He later became chairman of the board. In 1959, Field bought the *Chicago Daily News.* He served as editor and publisher of both the morning *Sun-Times* and the afternoon *Daily News.*

In 1963, Field formed Publishers Newspaper Syndicate, now called News America Syndicate. In 1965, he formed Field Communications Corporation.

Field was publisher of Field Enterprises Educational Corporation, now World Book, Inc. *The World Book Year Book* began publication in 1962. *The World Book Dictionary* started publication in 1963, and *Science Year* in 1965.

Field was born in New York City. He graduated from Harvard University and the University of Virginia Law School.

Marshall Field V (1941-   ), son of Marshall Field IV, served as chairman of the board of Field Enterprises from 1972 to 1984. That year, he and his half brother, Frederick W. Field, who co-owned Field Enterprises, dissolved the company. Marshall Field then founded the Field Corporation to manage his existing businesses and to acquire new ones.

Field was publisher of the *Sun-Times* from 1969 to 1980, and of the *Daily News* from 1969 until the newspaper ceased publication in 1978. In 1978, Field Enterprises sold World Book, Inc., to The Scott & Fetzer Company. Field Enterprises acquired Cabot, Cabot & Forbes, Incorporated, a national commercial real estate developer, in 1979.

In 1984, Field Enterprises sold the *Sun-Times*. That same year, Field became chairman of the board of the new Field Corporation and of Cabot, Cabot & Forbes. In 1984, the Field Corporation acquired Manistique Papers, Inc., a manufacturer of newsprint and specialty papers. It also purchased Pioneer Press, the publisher of 30 suburban Chicago newspapers and of *Q*, a quarterly magazine.

Marshall Field V was born in Charlottesville, Va. He graduated from Harvard University.   Virginia Butts

Field, Eugene (1850-1895), was a popular American author and journalist who is best known today as a writer of children's literature. Many of his poems and stories are highly fanciful and sentimental. Field's most famous works are probably "Wynken, Blynken, and Nod," a whimsical lullaby; and "Little Boy Blue," a poem about the death of a child.

Besides writing for children, Field worked as a newspaper columnist in Kansas City and Denver. In 1883, he moved to Chicago to write a humorous column called "Sharps and Flats" for the morning edition of the Chicago *Daily News*. Field's writings strongly influenced the development of humorous newspaper columns in the United States. His columns also introduced poetry and other literary material to the thousands of poorly educated people who read newspapers.

Field was born in St. Louis. He attended Williams College, Knox College, and the University of Missouri but never graduated.

Many of Field's poems and stories for children were collected in *A Little Book of Western Verse* (1889), *With Trumpet and Drum* (1892), *The Holy Cross and Other Tales* (1893), and *Lullaby-land,* which was published in 1897, after his death.   Eugene K. Garber

Additional resources

Conrow, Robert. *Field Days: The Life, Times & Reputation of Eugene Field.* Scribner, 1974.
Dennis, Charles H. *Eugene Field's Creative Years.* Scholarly, 1971. First published in 1924.
Thompson, Slason. *Life of Eugene Field: The Poet of Childhood.* R. West, 1927.

Field, Marshall. See Field (family).
Field, Rachel (1894-1942), an American author, is best known for her books for children. She won a Newbery Medal in 1930 for *Hitty, Her First Hundred Years* (1929), a story of a doll's adventures. Some critics consider *Calico Bush* (1931) to be Field's best book. This story describes the experiences of a French servant girl in pioneer Maine.

Field's other works include *Taxis and Toadstools*

(1926) and other books of poetry; several children's plays; and books for adults, including the novels *All This and Heaven Too* (1938) and *And Now Tomorrow* (1942). She was born in New York City.   Eloise Rue

Field, Stephen Johnson. See Field (family).
Field Enterprises, Inc. See Field (Marshall).
Field event. See Track and field.
Field Foundation, Inc., is an organization that administers a fund set aside for charitable, educational, and scientific purposes. The Field Foundation was established in 1940 by the American publisher and philanthropist Marshall Field III. The foundation's grants total about $3 million a year. Grants are made to organizations with programs to fight discrimination, poverty, and the wrongful uses of governmental power. The foundation is particularly interested in child welfare.

The Field Foundation was chartered in New York as a nonprofit membership corporation. It has its office at 100 E. 85th Street, New York, NY 10028.
    Critically reviewed by the Field Foundation, Inc.

See also **Field** (Marshall Field III); **Foundations** (Welfare).

Field glasses. See Binoculars.
Field hockey is a fast and exciting team sport in which players use sticks to try to hit a ball into their opponents' goal. In the United States, field hockey is played primarily by girls and women, but it is a popular male sport in many other countries.

The field and equipment. The teams compete on a smooth grass or artificial turf field 100 yards (91 meters) long and 60 yards (55 meters) wide. Various lines divide the field into sections. A *goal line* runs along the width of the field at each end. A wide arc called a *striking circle* extends from each goal line. A center line, also called a *50-yard line,* parallel to the goal lines divides the field in half.

A goal cage stands in the center of each goal line. The cage has two goal posts 7 feet (2.13 meters) high and 12 feet (3.66 meters) apart. The posts are connected by a crossbar. A net is attached to the posts and crossbar. A backboard 18 inches (46 centimeters) high and 4 yards (3.7 meters) long is placed inside the net. Sideboards the size of the backboard are attached to the backs of the goal posts at right angles to the goal line.

David Madison, Bruce Coleman Inc.
Field hockey is a fast-moving team sport. Players try to hit a ball toward their opponents' goal, using sticks curved at one end. A goalkeeper tries to block shots before they go into the goal.

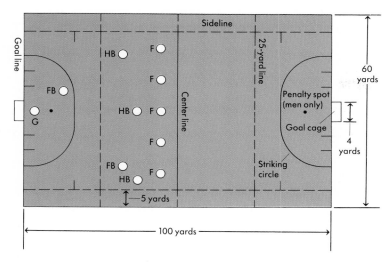

A field hockey field is divided into two halves by a solid center line. Two broken 25-yard lines run parallel to the center line and to a goal line at each end of the field. A broken line runs the length of the field 5 yards from each sideline. In a game, goals must be scored from within the striking circle.

WORLD BOOK diagram

Each player carries a stick with a curved end that is flat on its left side and rounded on its right. Only the flat side may be used to hit the ball. Most players use sticks that vary from 34 to 37 inches (86 to 94 centimeters) in length. The ball is about 9 inches (23 centimeters) in circumference and weighs about $5\frac{1}{2}$ ounces (160 grams). It has a cork and twine center and a leather or synthetic covering.

The game is divided into two halves and varies in length from 30 to 70 minutes. Older and more skillful players compete in the longer games. Each team has 11 players. The basic formation consists of five forwards, three halfbacks, two fullbacks, and a goalkeeper. Two umpires supervise the game, sometimes assisted by one or two timekeepers.

Players try to move the ball using only their sticks until they are in a position to shoot it into the other team's goal. Each goal counts 1 point. A goal is scored each time an offensive player hits the ball from within the striking circle so it crosses the goal line between the goal posts.

The game starts with a *passback*. A player from one team hits or pushes the ball with the stick from the 50-yard line to a teammate. At the time of the passback, no players of the opposing team may be within 5 yards (4.6 meters) of the ball. All players except the one executing the passback must remain in their own half of the field. The ball may not cross the center line. Play resumes with a passback after each goal.

The rules allow no body contact or dangerous hitting and prohibit a player from playing a ball above shoulder height with any part of the stick. The goalkeeper may kick the ball or stop it with any part of the body, including the hand, but only when the ball is inside the striking circle.

History. The origin of field hockey is not known. Ancient Greek carvings show players using crooked sticks to hit a small object. Only men played field hockey for many years. In 1889, the All England Women's Hockey Association was established. Constance M. K. Applebee of the British College of Physical Education promoted field hockey in the United States during the early 1900's. The United States Field Hockey Association (USFHA) for

women was organized in 1922. The Field Hockey Association of America (FHAA) for men was established in 1930.

Men's field hockey has been part of the Summer Olympics since 1908. Women's field hockey became an Olympic sport at the 1980 Summer Games. Rules are made by the International Hockey Rules Board and are the same for men and women.   Beatrice Toner

See also Hockey.

Field-ion microscope. See Ion microscope.

Field magnet. See Electric motor (Parts of an electric motor).

Field marshal. See Marshal.

Field Museum of Natural History, in Chicago, is one of the largest and best-known natural history museums in the world. It contains more than 13 million objects in four major fields—anthropology, botany, geology, and zoology.

Each year, more than a million people view the museum's collections. Its department of education provides lectures, short courses, and workshops. The museum also conducts natural history tours and sends traveling exhibits to schools. Its library has over 185,000 volumes for the use of scientists and the general public. The museum is privately supported. But it receives some funds from the city, state, and federal governments.

Exhibits. The museum has a number of outstanding anthropology exhibits. These exhibits include collections from the civilizations of the ancient Egyptians and of North American Indians. There are also collections of gems and jewels, primitive art, and Chinese jade.

The museum's botany department includes a world-famous collection of plant models. The geology exhibits are classified in two groups, one illustrating the scientific, and the other showing the economic and industrial relations of mineral products of the earth. The museum's geology department is noted for its great hall of paleontology, which has many fossil displays, including a number of dinosaurs. The geology department also has the most extensive collection of meteorites in the world. Another large exhibit in the museum represents a life-sized section of a forest of the coal age. The zoology exhibits include displays of the mammals of the world in habitat

WORLD BOOK photo by Odyssey Productions

The Field Museum of Natural History, in Chicago, is one of the world's largest and most famous museums of its kind.

groups. Other exhibits illustrate facts and theories about animals in their relation to each other and to human beings.

History. The Chicago merchant and philanthropist Marshall Field I founded the museum in 1893 and gave it more than $9 million during his lifetime. The museum was first called the Columbian Museum of Chicago. Within a year of its founding, its name was changed to the Field Columbian Museum. In 1905, the museum received its present name. But from 1943 to 1966, it was called the Chicago Natural History Museum.

Critically reviewed by the Field Museum of Natural History

Field of force. See Force.

Field spaniel is a hunting dog. For many years, owners separated field spaniels from cockers and other kinds of spaniels on the basis of size alone. The dog they called the field spaniel stands about 18 inches (46 centimeters) high and weighs 35 to 50 pounds (16 to 23 kilograms). It has a flat, glossy coat, usually black or some other solid color.

The field spaniel breed originated in England in the 1700's, but it has never been popular in the United States. This spaniel is intelligent and has great perseverance.   Maxwell Riddle

Fielding, Henry (1707-1754), an English author, wrote *The History of Tom Jones, a Foundling* (1749), one of the world's great novels. The book is an exciting, humorous story of an orphan and his adventures. Although it begins when Tom is a baby, most of the story concerns the hero as a young man. Tom's many adventures include a variety of love affairs, ranging from passing encounters to his true love for Sophia Western.

In *Tom Jones,* Fielding did more than create a humorous adventure story. He skillfully incorporated the plot's many twists into a unified structure, beginning each of the novel's 18 *books* (chapters) with a brilliant and re-

lated essay. He filled his story with unforgettable characters whom he described in a sophisticated and lively style. These qualities greatly influenced later novelists, as did Fielding's realistic, basically unsentimental attitude toward life. Fielding ridiculed hypocrites and selfish people but avoided a preaching tone. His tongue-in-cheek irony makes *Tom Jones* an outstanding satire on society.

Detail of an engraving by William Hogarth; The British Museum, London

Henry Fielding

Fielding's novel *Joseph Andrews* (1742) is a *parody* (mock imitation) of *Pamela,* Samuel Richardson's serious novel about the rewards of a virtuous life. *The Life of Jonathan Wild the Great* (1743) is fictional, but its criminal hero was a real person whom Fielding treated ironically to contrast "greatness" with "goodness."

Fielding's last novel, *Amelia* (1751), is a relatively sober work. It attacks social evils more directly than *Tom Jones* does. However, *Amelia* is less successful as a novel.

Early in his career, Fielding supported himself by writing plays. The most enjoyable is *The Tragedy of Tragedies; or, The Life and Death of Tom Thumb the Great* (1730-1731), a burlesque of English heroic drama. *Pasquin* (1736) and *The Historical Register for The Year 1736* (1737) attack Prime Minister Robert Walpole. These satires helped bring about the Licensing Act of 1737, which resulted in strict control and censorship of the London theater.

Fielding was also an excellent journalist and essayist. In 1752, he published the *Covent Garden Journal,* a satirical review of society and literature of his time that appeared twice a week. His *Journal of a Voyage to Lisbon,* published in 1755 after his death, describes a trip he made to Portugal.

Fielding was born near Glastonbury in Somerset. He attended Eton College and then studied law. He be-

Walter Chandoha

The field spaniel has a glossy coat.

came a justice of the peace in 1748. Throughout his life, Fielding fought for social and legal reforms, both as a writer and as a magistrate.   Frank W. Wadsworth

See also **Police** (History).

Additional resources

Dircks, Richard J. *Henry Fielding.* G. K. Hall, 1983.
Hassall, Anthony J. *Henry Fielding's "Tom Jones."* International Specialized Book, 1979.
Rogers, Pat. *Henry Fielding: A Biography.* Scribner, 1979.

Fields, W. C. (1879-1946), was an American motion-picture comedian. Fields incorporated his personal prejudices into his films, and it became difficult to separate his real personality from his film characters. In his movies, Fields often played swindling characters. He was at war with the world, battling both people and objects. He hated children, and they hated him. Fields' trademarks included a top hat, a monstrous nose, and a distinctive

Penguin Photo

W. C. Fields was a popular stage and motion-picture comedian. He and Mae West starred in the film *My Little Chickadee, above.*

side-of-the-mouth manner of speaking.

Fields made his film debut in 1915 in a brief role in a comedy. He was in several silent films but did not win fame until the emergence of sound films. His major movies include *The Old-Fashioned Way* (1934), *It's a Gift* (1934), *The Man on the Flying Trapeze* (1935), *David Copperfield* (1935), *You Can't Cheat an Honest Man* (1939), *My Little Chickadee* (1940), *The Bank Dick* (1940), and *Never Give a Sucker an Even Break* (1941).

William Claude Dukenfield, Fields' real name, was born in Philadelphia. He began a vaudeville and musical comedy career at the age of 14.   Rachel Gallagher

Additional resources

Fields, Ronald J. *W. C. Fields: A Life on Film.* St. Martin's, 1984.
Fields, W. C. *W. C. Fields by Himself: His Intended Autobiography.* Prentice-Hall, 1973.
Taylor, Robert L. *W. C. Fields: His Follies and Fortunes.* Amereon, 1986. First published in 1949.

Fiesta. See **Latin America** (Recreation); **Mexico** (Holidays).

Fife is a small woodwind instrument that belongs to the flute family. It consists of a wooden tube that has from six to eight finger holes along its length and a mouth hole near one end. A player holds the fife in a horizontal position and blows across the mouth hole. The fife produces a shrill, penetrating sound. The player covers and uncovers the finger holes to produce different notes.

The fife originated in Switzerland in the 1500's. It was later used throughout western Europe and in the United States. Traditionally, fifes were played with drums in military units and were associated with patriotic groups. They are now played primarily in ceremonial fife and drum corps.   Thomas C. Slattery

Fifteenth Amendment to the United States Constitution guarantees that an American citizen shall not be discriminated against in exercising the right to vote. It states that the federal and state governments cannot bar a citizen from voting because the person had been a slave or because of race.

Amendment 15 was ratified on Feb. 3, 1870. Seven Southern states tried to bypass it by adding *grandfather clauses* to their constitutions. One such clause gave the right to vote to people who could vote on Jan. 1, 1867, and to their family descendants. In 1915, the Supreme Court of the United States declared grandfather clauses unconstitutional. For information on recent legislation protecting the right to vote, see **Voting** (Restrictions on voting).   Charles V. Hamilton

See also **Grandfather clause; Constitution of the United States.**

Fifth Amendment to the United States Constitution guarantees that people cannot be forced to testify against themselves in a criminal case. It also provides that a person cannot be placed in jeopardy twice for the same offense. Amendment 5 also guarantees that (1) a person cannot be deprived of life, liberty, or property without due process of law; (2) a person cannot be held to answer for a "capital, or otherwise infamous crime" unless he or she has been indicted by a grand jury, except that military personnel are subject to court-martial; (3) property cannot be taken from a person without just compensation. Amendment 5 is a part of the Bill of Rights ratified on Dec. 15, 1791. See also **Bill of rights; Due process of law; Constitution of the United States.**

James O. Finckenauer

Fifth column refers to undercover agents operating within the ranks of an enemy to undermine its cause. The agents pave the way for military or political invasion. They may work in an army, political party, or industry. Their activities include spying, sabotage, economic subversion, propaganda, agitation, infiltration, and even, assassination, terror, and revolt. The term *fifth column* was first used during the Spanish Civil War (1936-1939) to describe the work of Francisco Franco's followers in Loyalist Madrid. Emilio Mola, a general under Franco, said, "I have four columns moving against Madrid, and a fifth will rise up inside the city itself."   Douglas L. Wheeler

Fifty-Four Forty or Fight was a slogan used during a boundary dispute between the United States and Great Britain. An 1818 treaty allowed both nations to occupy the Oregon Country, lying between 42° and 54°40' north latitude. In the 1830's and 1840's, American expansionists wanted to take the whole area, by force if necessary. When James K. Polk became President, the United

States made a new treaty that set 49° as a boundary, except for Vancouver Island. The United States secured the land south of the line, and Great Britain obtained the land to the north.   Oscar O. Winther

See also **British Columbia** (The border dispute); **Polk, James Knox** ("Oregon fever").

Fig is a fruit that has probably been cultivated for more than 5,000 years. It originated in the Mediterranean region, and ancient Greek, Roman, and Egyptian documents describe its popularity as a food.

Figs are small and round or pear-shaped. They have green, yellow, pink, purple, brown, or black skins, depending on the variety. They have a high sugar content, and people eat them fresh, dried, canned, or preserved in sugar.

Figs grow on trees of the same name. Fig trees thrive in climates with hot, dry summers and cool, moist winters. Important fig-producing countries include Portugal, Italy, Greece, and Turkey. California produces most of the figs grown in the United States.

Most fig trees grow to less than 33 feet (10 meters) tall and have a trunk about $3\frac{1}{4}$ feet (1 meter) in diameter. The trees have deeply lobed leaves. The fruit develops from podlike structures that grow on the branches and that contain hundreds of tiny flowers. As the fruits develop, these structures enlarge and become fleshy. Fig trees bear two or three crops of fruit each year.

There are four main types of figs: (1) caprifigs, (2) Smyrna figs, (3) common figs, and (4) San Pedro figs. The wild caprifig trees seldom produce edible fruit. Small fig wasps live inside the caprifigs. When the wasps leave the figs, they carry pollen from the flowers. The Smyrna fig depends on these pollen-carrying wasps to pollinate its flowers. All varieties of Smyrna figs require pollen from caprifigs in order to bear fruit. The common fig does not require pollination to produce fruit. The San Pedro fig produces two types of fig crops each year. The first crop, harvested in early summer, develops without pollination, like the common fig. The second crop, which matures in late summer, must be pollinated by the fig wasp like the Smyrna fig.

Growers produce new fig trees from branches cut

WORLD BOOK illustration by Kate Lloyd-Jones, Linden Artists Ltd.
Figs are the fruit of the fig tree, which generally grows in warm climates. The plant's flowers grow inside the fruit.

from other fig trees. In most cases, the new trees bear fruit two to four years later. Mediterranean fruit flies and tiny worms called *nematodes* are among the fig tree's most troublesome pests.

Ripe figs spoil easily and cannot be shipped long distances to market. For this reason, most growers dry their crop—either in the sun or in ovens—before shipping.

Scientific classification. Fig trees belong to the mulberry family, Moraceae. They are *Ficus carica.*   Michael G. Barbour

Figaro. See **Beaumarchais, Pierre A. C. De.**

Fightingfish is a small, quarrelsome fish that lives in the waters around the Malay Archipelago. It is often called the *Betta* or *Siamese fightingfish.* It has been bred

© Heather Angel, Biophotos
Fightingfish grow about $2\frac{1}{2}$ inches (6.4 cm) long. The male, *bottom,* displays its beautiful tail and fins to the female, *top.*

to develop long waving tails and fins. When the male is excited, it becomes colored with reds, greens, purples, and blues. Only the male is a fighter. Fightingfish dash at one another, biting the opponent's fins until one of the fish is exhausted. One fightingfish will even attack its own image in a mirror. Watching fights between male fightingfish is a popular sport among the people of Thailand.

Scientific classification. The fightingfish belongs to the family Anabantidae. It is *Betta splendens.*   John E. McCosker

See also **Fish** (pictures: Fish of tropical fresh waters; A male Siamese fightingfish).

Figure of speech is the use of words in certain conventional patterns of thought and expression. For example, we might read that "The spy was cornered *like a rat* . . . The crowd *surged* forward . . . The *redcoats* withdrew . . . Justice *hung her head* . . . Here was *mercy* indeed! . . . The *entire nation* screamed vengeance."

Each of these figures of speech has its own name. The first is *simile,* when the spy is compared with a rat, using the connective word *like.* The second is *metaphor,* when the author compares the movement of the crowd to that of an oncoming wave without using the connective words *like* or *as.* The third is *metonomy,* when the word *redcoats* stands for the soldiers who wear them. The fourth, *personification,* speaks of justice as though it were a person. The fifth is *irony,* because the author means the opposite of mercy. The sixth is *hyperbole,* or exaggeration for special effect.

Figures of speech are the flowers of rhetoric. They give to poetry much of its beauty and fragrance, its sweetness and germinal power. John Milton wrote, in "On His Being Arrived at the Age of Twenty-Three,"

How soon hath Time, the subtle thief of youth,
Stolen on his wing my three and twentieth year!
My hasting days fly on with full career,
But my late spring no bud or blossom shew'th.

Without consciously analyzing the personification, metonymy, and metaphor used, the reader still senses the richness of imagery and poetic thought. Everyday speech also uses many such figures.   Marianne Cooley

See also **Irony; Metaphor; Metonymy; Simile.**

Figure skating. See Ice skating.

Figwort family, also called *Scrophulariaceae*, SKRAHF yuh LAIR ee AY see ee, is a group of about 3,000 species of herbs, shrubs, and small trees. Some of these plants are used in medicines. They have bell-shaped flowers that are divided into two lips. The flowers grow at the top of a slender stem, while the leaves often grow in pairs on the stem. The family flourishes especially in temperate regions. It includes wild flowers and weeds such as mullein, butter-and-eggs, speedwell, and louse-wort. The cultivated varieties include foxglove, snapdragon, and calceolaria. Certain figworts live partially as parasites on other plants. The drug *digitalis,* used for heart ailments, comes from a kind of foxglove. Scrophularia, from which the family is named, is a medicinal figwort. People at one time believed that it would cure scrofula (see **Scrofula**).   Harold Norman Moldenke

Related articles in *World Book* include:

Beardtongue	Mullein
Digitalis	Slipperwort
Foxglove	Snapdragon
Indian paintbrush	Toadflax
Monkey flower	

Fiji, *FEE jee,* is a country in the South Pacific Ocean. It is made up of more than 800 scattered islands. Fiji has a total land area of 7,056 square miles (18,274 square kilometers). The island of Viti Levu (Big Fiji) covers about half this area, and Vanua Levu (Big Land) occupies about a third of the area. Many of the other islands of Fiji are merely piles of sand on coral reefs. Suva, Fiji's capital and largest city, lies on Viti Levu's southern coast (see **Suva**).

Fiji has about 772,000 people, of whom about 45 per cent are native Fijians of chiefly Melanesian descent. About 50 per cent of the people are descendants of laborers imported from India. The remaining 5 per cent—Fiji's so-called "general" population group—have Chinese, European, Micronesian, or Polynesian ancestry. Fiji became independent in 1970 after being a British crown colony since 1874.

Government. In 1987, military leaders overthrew Fiji's civilian government and abolished the Constitution. Later that year, the military leaders returned Fiji to civilian rule. They set up an interim government to rule the country until a new Constitution is completed. This government has a president, who was appointed by the military leaders before they gave up power. The president is the head of state. The president appointed a prime minister to serve as head of government. The prime minister appointed a 20-member Cabinet to help carry out government operations.

People. Slightly more than half of native Fijians live in rural areas. They follow such traditional customs as the ceremonial drinking of *kava,* a beverage made from pepper plants. Kava is called *yaqona* in Fiji. The men

Fiji

	Road
✈	Airport
⊛	National capital
•	Other city or town
+	Elevation above sea level

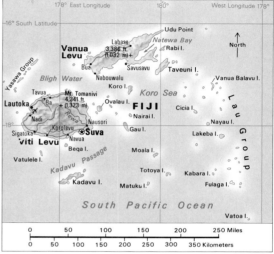

WORLD BOOK map

wear skirts called *sulus,* and the women wear bright cotton dresses or occasionally grass skirts. Most native Fijians are Christians.

Most of the Indians are descendants of about 60,000 laborers brought from India between 1879 and 1916 to work on Fiji's sugar plantations. Many Indians still work in the cane fields, but others have become prosperous shopkeepers or business people. Indians control much of Fiji's business and industry. The Indian women wear the *sari,* the traditional dress of India. Most of the Indians are Muslims or Hindus.

Facts in brief

Capital: Suva.
Official language: English.
Area: 7,056 sq. mi. (18,274 km²). *Greatest distances*—north-south, 364 mi. (586 km); east-west, 334 mi. (538 km). *Coastline*—925 mi. (1,489 km).
Elevation: *Highest*—Mount Tomanivi, on Viti Levu, 4,341 ft. (1,323 m) above sea level. *Lowest*—sea level.
Population: *Estimated 1990 population*—772,000; density, 109 persons per sq. mi. (42 per km²); distribution, 56 per cent rural, 44 per cent urban. *1986 census*—715,375. *Estimated 1995 population*—869,000.
Chief products: *Agriculture*—coconuts, forest products, sugar. *Manufacturing*—beer, cement, cigarettes. *Mining*—gold.
National Anthem: *God Bless Fiji.*
Flag: The British Union Jack appears in the upper left on a light blue field. On the right is the shield from Fiji's coat of arms with a British lion, a dove, coconut palms, and such agricultural products as bananas and sugar cane. Adopted on Oct. 10, 1970. See **Flag** (color picture: Flags of Asia and the Pacific).
Money: *Basic unit*—Fiji dollar.

Cal Harbert, DPI

Cal Harbert, DPI

Suva, the capital and largest city of Fiji, is also the nation's chief port and commercial center. Suva lies on the southern coast of Viti Levu, the largest of Fiji's islands. Many government buildings, such as the one above, stand along the city's shoreline.

Sugar cane is one of Fiji's chief agricultural products. Workers load sugar cane stalks onto a wagon, *above*. Bananas and coconuts also grow well in Fiji's tropical climate.

English, the official language of Fiji, is used in the schools. But the country also has two other main languages, Fijian and Hindi. The law does not require children to go to school, but more than 85 per cent of those from 6 to 13 years old do so. Most Fijian and Indian youngsters attend separate schools. The University of the South Pacific in Suva, the country's only university, serves students who come from many of the Pacific Island groups.

Land. Most of the Fiji islands were formed by volcanoes. Coral reefs surround nearly all the islands. The larger islands have high volcanic peaks, rolling hills, rivers, and grasslands. Tropical rain forests cover more than half the total area of Fiji. The islands also have fertile coastal plains and river valleys.

Cool winds make Fiji's tropical climate relatively comfortable. Temperatures range from about 60° F. (16° C) to 90° F. (32° C). Heavy rains and tropical storms occur frequently between November and April.

Economy of Fiji is based primarily on agriculture. Most Fijians grow such crops as sugar cane and coconuts. Gold is the country's chief mineral. Tourism is a major economic activity, and it employs many islanders. Sugar, coconut products, and gold account for about three-fourths of Fiji's exports. The country also exports timber. Manufactured products include beer, building materials, cement, and cigarettes.

Fiji has been called the "crossroads of the South Pacific." The airport at Nadi, on Viti Levu, is a busy terminal for planes flying the Pacific. Fiji also lies on major shipping routes and has several excellent harbors.

History. Melanesians migrated to Fiji thousands of years ago, probably from Indonesia. A small group of

Polynesians settled there during the A.D. 100's. In 1643, Abel Tasman, a Dutch navigator, became the first European to see Fiji. Captain James Cook, a British explorer, visited Vatoa, one of the southern islands, in 1774. During the 1800's, traders, Methodist missionaries, and escaped Australian convicts came to visit or settle there.

The Fijians were cannibals, and various tribes fought one another until 1871, when a chief named Cakobau extended his influence over much of Fiji. With the help of King George Tupou I of nearby Tonga, Cakobau was able to bring peace to Fiji. To protect the country from outside interference, Cakobau asked Britain to make Fiji a crown colony. Britain did so on Oct. 10, 1874. Fiji remained a colony until, at its own request, it became an independent nation on Oct. 10, 1970, with Ratu Sir Kamisese Mara as prime minister.

Since independence, the government has encouraged tourism and the development of manufacturing and forestry. It has also promoted the production of new crops to reduce Fiji's dependence on sugar cane and coconuts.

Although Indians control much of Fiji's economy, Fijians traditionally have held more power in the government. In April 1987, an Indian-backed coalition won a majority in parliament. The coalition leader, Timoci Bavadra, replaced Mara as prime minister. Bavadra appointed Indians to a majority of the Cabinet posts.

Many Fijians resented this increase of Indian political power. Military officers led by Colonel Sitiveni Rabuka overthrew Bavadra's government. Rabuka abolished the Constitution, named himself head of state and government, and declared the right of Fijians to govern the nation. In December 1987, Rabuka appointed a president and returned Fiji to civilian rule.   Stuart Inder

See also **Flag** (picture: Flags of Asia and the Pacific).

Filaria, *fih LAIR ee uh,* is a long threadlike roundworm that lives as a parasite in the bodies of human beings and animals. Filariae are commonly found in tropical and subtropical countries. The male worm is shorter than the female and it has a curved tail.

The *larvae* (young worms) are born alive. They can be seen in the blood near the body surface of the *host* (the animal in which the larvae live). When a blood-sucking fly or mosquito bites an infected person, it takes up the larvae with the blood. The larvae develop in the mosquito's or fly's head near the mouth. Then when the insect bites another animal, the larvae enter the wound and infect a new host.

E. R. Degginger

Filaria, shown here under a microscope, is a parasite common in tropical countries.

Wuchereria bancrofti is a filaria harmful to human beings. It is found in Africa, South America, and the Far East. The adult worms live in the *lymph,* a body fluid (see **Lymphatic system**). When the worms block the flow of lymph, a disease called *elephantiasis* results. This disease is characterized by severe swelling of the limbs, usually the legs (see **Elephantiasis**). Wuchereria bancrofti can be eliminated by controlling the mosquitoes that carry the larvae. Other kinds of filariae infect such animals as cattle and dogs.

Scientific classification. Filariae are members of the round-worm phylum, Nematoda.   David F. Oetinger

See also **Manson, Sir Patrick; Roundworm.**

Filbert is the name for both the nut and the plant of a group of trees and shrubs closely related to the birches. The nuts are also called *hazelnuts* and *cobnuts* (see **Hazel**). Some filberts grow 60 feet (18 meters) tall. Others are shrubs that normally grow from 2 to 30 feet (0.6 to 9 meters) high. Filberts are native to North America, Europe, and Asia. They thrive in orchards in the Pacific Northwest in the United States and in southern Europe. Larger nuts grow on the cultivated trees than on the wild ones. The seeds taste better roasted than they do raw.

The nuts form in compact clusters, with each nut encased within its own husk. The nuts have smooth, hard, but thin and brittle shells. The kernels are single.

Scientific classification. Filberts belong to the birch family, Betulaceae. Most cultivated varieties are *Corylus avellana.*
     Richard A. Jaynes

Filibuster, *FIHL uh BUHS tuhr,* originally meant a pirate of the 1600's. The word comes from the Dutch *Vrijbuiter,* which means *freebooter.* Beginning about 1850, *filibuster* came to mean an adventurer who organized an armed expedition against a nation with which the adventurer's own country was at peace.

During the mid-1800's, many adventurers led filibustering expeditions from the United States to attack various Latin-American countries. In 1850 and 1851, Narciso López, a former officer of the Spanish army, led two unsuccessful attempts to end Spanish rule in Cuba. The most notorious American filibuster, a Californian named William Walker, organized invasions of Lower California, Nicaragua, and Honduras (see **Walker, William**).
     John Donald Hicks

Filibustering, *FIHL uh BUHS tuhr ihng,* is the practice by which a minority in a legislature uses extended debate to block or delay action on a proposed bill. Members of the minority make long speeches, demand roll calls, propose useless motions, and use other delaying tactics. If they can keep the bill from coming to a vote, they can defeat it even if the majority is in favor of it.

The United States Senate has a tradition of unlimited debate. A senator who holds the floor may speak without interruption. The Senate can end a filibuster by reaching informal compromise with the filibusterers, or by invoking the *cloture rule* to end debate. This rule was adopted in 1917 and strengthened in 1979 and 1986. Under the cloture rule, a vote of 60 senators, three-fifths of the Senate membership, can limit each senator to one hour of debate on most bills. The rule also prevents senators from introducing large numbers of amendments. Final action on a bill is required within 30 hours after the cloture rule has been invoked. However, filibusters on proposed changes in the Senate rules can be stopped only by a two-thirds majority of the members who are present and voting.

From 1917 to 1962, Southerners opposed to civil rights bills staged most filibusters. During these years, cloture was invoked only four times. Today, filibusters and clotures occur routinely on a wide range of bills. See **Cloture.**

A filibuster against the civil rights bill of 1964 lasted 75 days, the longest since the cloture rule was adopted. In 1957, Senator Strom Thurmond of South Carolina filibustered 24 hours and 18 minutes in a debate over another civil rights bill.

The word *filibuster* originally meant *pirate.* Some members of Congress charged that the use of delaying tactics to block the will of the majority was like *filibustering* (piracy).   Roger H. Davidson

Filipinos. See **Philippines** (introduction; The people); **Races, Human** (table: Geographical races [Asian]).

WORLD BOOK illustration by Stuart Lafford, Linden Artist Ltd.

Filberts, or hazelnuts, grow in tight clusters.

13th President of
the United States 1850-1853

Taylor
12th President
1849-1850
Whig

Fillmore
13th President
1850-1853
Whig

Pierce
14th President
1853-1857
Democrat

National Portrait Gallery, Smithsonian Institution, Washington, D.C.

Fillmore, Millard (1800-1874), the second Vice President of the United States to inherit the nation's highest office, became President when Zachary Taylor died. During Fillmore's 32 months in office as President, his most important action was his approval of the Compromise of 1850. This series of laws helped delay the Civil War for more than 10 years.

A self-made man, Fillmore had been a poor boy who was once a clothmaker's apprentice. He studied law, then won election to the New York state legislature and to Congress. He became known nationally only after the Whig Party chose him to be Taylor's vice presidential running mate in 1848.

As Vice President, Fillmore presided coolly over the heated Senate debates between slavery and antislavery forces. The Compromise of 1850, which he helped achieve, had been opposed by President Taylor because of its concessions to the South. But when Taylor died, Fillmore urged passage of the compromise and quickly signed it into law. Fillmore personally did not approve of slavery. But he loved the Union and preferred compromise to the risk of war.

Important dates in Fillmore's life

1800 (Jan. 7) Born in Locke, N.Y.
1826 (Feb. 5) Married Abigail Powers.
1832 Elected to U.S. House of Representatives.
1848 Elected Vice President of the United States.
1850 (July 10) Sworn in as President.
1852 Defeated in bid for presidential nomination.
1853 Mrs. Abigail Fillmore died.
1856 Defeated in presidential election.
1858 (Feb. 10) Married Mrs. Caroline McIntosh.
1874 (March 8) Died in Buffalo, N.Y.

Fillmore faithfully enforced the compromise, including its provision for the return of runaway slaves. This policy lost him the support of most Northerners, and he was not nominated for President in 1852.

A conservative dresser, Fillmore always wore a dark frock coat and a high-collared shirt with a black silk neckcloth tied in a bow in front. He had kindly blue eyes and a gracious, courteous manner. People admired his modesty. When Great Britain's Oxford University offered him an honorary degree, Fillmore replied that he had done nothing to deserve the honor and would not accept the degree.

Early life

Millard Fillmore was born in Locke, N.Y., on Jan. 7, 1800. He was the second child in a family of three girls and six boys. His parents, Nathaniel and Phoebe Millard Fillmore, had moved to the frontier from Bennington, Vt. The elder Fillmore had hoped to improve his fortune, but he lost his farm through a faulty title. He then moved to another part of Cayuga County, where he rented a heavily wooded piece of land. Millard helped his father clear timber and work the farm.

Education. Millard attended school for only short periods, but he learned reading, spelling, arithmetic, and geography. His father owned two books, the Bible and a hymnbook.

At the age of 14, Millard was apprenticed to a clothmaker. His master treated Millard so badly that the boy once threatened him with an ax. He found a new master, but he bought his freedom from the apprenticeship in 1819 for $30. In the same year, he also purchased the first book he had ever owned, a dictionary. Fillmore decided to become a lawyer. He taught school while he

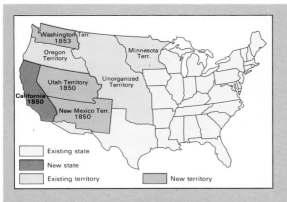

Existing state

New state

Existing territory

New territory

California became the 31st state in 1850. Three new territories were formed during Fillmore's presidency—New Mexico and Utah in 1850 and Washington in 1853.

The United States flag had 31 stars during most of Fillmore's presidency. California became the 31st state on Sept. 9, 1850, two months after Fillmore took office.

The world of President Fillmore

The "underground railroad" enabled many slaves to escape to the Northern States or to Canada during the mid-1800's. The underground railroad—neither underground nor a railroad—was an informal system of routes to freedom. Many people who opposed slavery provided hiding places and other assistance to slaves traveling along these routes. *Uncle Tom's Cabin,* a novel about slavery by Harriet Beecher Stowe, was first published in serial form in 1851 and 1852, then in book form in 1852. The novel aroused Northern sentiment against the South and angered many Southerners, who considered it an unjust portrayal of slavery.
Swedish soprano Jenny Lind made a triumphant tour of the United States from 1850 to 1852. She was known as the *Swedish Nightingale.*
Herman Melville's *Moby-Dick* was published in 1851. This highly symbolic novel was poorly received by critics and the public, but later was recognized as a literary masterpiece.
The Taiping Rebellion erupted in China in 1851 and threatened the power of the Qing dynasty. Millions of people died during the revolt, which lasted until 1864.
"Go West, young man" was a phrase made popular by Horace Greeley, editor of the *New York Tribune,* around 1851. Greeley used the phrase as advice to the unemployed of New York City.
Expanding railroads encouraged settlement of the Midwest. Direct rail lines linked New York and Chicago in 1852.
Louis Napoleon proclaimed himself emperor of France in 1852 and ruled as a dictator until he was overthrown in 1870.

WORLD BOOK map

studied with a local judge. In 1823, he opened a law office in East Aurora, N.Y.

Fillmore's family. During one of his periods of schooling, Fillmore's teacher was Abigail Powers (March 13, 1798-March 30, 1853), the daughter of a Baptist minister. He was then 19 years old, and she was 21. They fell in love and were married in 1826. Mrs. Fillmore continued to teach until 1828. The couple had two children, Millard Powers Fillmore (1828-1889) and Mary Abigail Fillmore (1832-1854). In 1830, the family moved to Buffalo, N.Y.

Political and public career

Fillmore won election to the New York House of Representatives in 1828 with the help of Thurlow Weed, an Albany publisher who helped form the Whig Party. Fillmore was twice reelected.

Congressman. In 1832, Fillmore was elected to the U.S. House of Representatives. He served from 1833 to 1835 and from 1837 to 1843. He generally favored the nationalistic policies of Henry Clay. As chairman of the Ways and Means Committee, Fillmore was the chief author of the tariff of 1842, which raised duties on manufactured goods. He ran for governor of New York in 1844 but was defeated and returned to his law practice. In 1846, he became the first chancellor of the University of Buffalo. The next year, he was elected comptroller of New York.

Vice President. The Whigs nominated Fillmore for Vice President in 1848 on a ticket headed by General Zachary Taylor, the hero of the Mexican War. The Democrats nominated Senator Lewis Cass of Michigan for President and former Congressman William O. Butler of Kentucky for Vice President. During the campaign, the

Democrats split over the slavery issue, and many voted for the Free Soil ticket (see **Free Soil Party**). Taylor and Fillmore won the election by a margin of 36 electoral votes.

Fillmore presided over the Senate debate on the

Buffalo and Erie County Historical Society
Abigail Powers Fillmore, the President's first wife, was one of his teachers before they married. She was two years older than he. Poor health restricted her activities as first lady.

As Vice President, Fillmore presided over major Senate debates on slavery. This picture shows him seated on the upper center platform while Daniel Webster addresses the chamber.

Library of Congress

Compromise of 1850 (see **Compromise of 1850**). Before the issue was settled, President Taylor died on July 9, 1850. Fillmore was sworn in as the new President the next day.

Fillmore's Administration (1850-1853)

Accomplishments. After becoming President, Fillmore came forth strongly in favor of compromise on slavery. As his first act, he replaced Taylor's Cabinet with men who had led the fight for compromise.

In September, Congress passed the series of laws that made up the Compromise of 1850. Fillmore promptly signed them. The compromise admitted California as a free state and organized territorial governments for Utah and New Mexico. These territories could decide for themselves whether or not to allow slavery. The compromise also settled a Texas boundary dispute, abolished the slave trade in the District of Columbia, and established a stricter fugitive slave law (see **Fugitive slave laws**).

Also during Fillmore's Administration, Congress reduced the basic postal rate from 5 to 3 cents. Later in 1852, the President sent Commodore Matthew C. Perry on an expedition to the Far East. Two years later, after Fillmore had left the presidency, this voyage resulted in the first trade treaty with Japan.

Life in the White House. Abigail Fillmore found her responsibilities as first lady a heavy burden on her health. Her 18-year-old daughter, Mary, took over many official tasks. Mrs. Fillmore arranged for the purchase of the first cooking stove in the White House. She also set up the first White House library. When the Library of

Congress burned in 1851, Fillmore and his Cabinet helped fight the blaze.

Election of 1852. When the Whigs met to nominate a presidential candidate in 1852, they were divided between friends and foes of the Compromise of 1850. Southerners supported Fillmore. But most Northerners rejected him, and a small group of pro-Compromise delegates from New England supported Secretary of State Daniel Webster. General Winfield Scott, an antislavery candidate, was finally nominated. He lost the election.

Later years

Mrs. Fillmore died less than a month after her husband left office. She was buried in Washington, D.C.

Fillmore returned to Buffalo and resumed his law practice. The Know-Nothing and the Whig parties nominated him for President in 1856. But the Republicans, who nominated General John C. Frémont, cut into his support. Democrat James Buchanan won. Fillmore ran third, carrying only Maryland.

In 1858, Fillmore married Mrs. Caroline Carmichael McIntosh (Oct. 21, 1813-Aug. 11, 1881), a widow. During the Civil War, he opposed many of Abraham Lincoln's policies. After the war, he favored the Reconstruction program of President Andrew Johnson. Fillmore died on March 8, 1874, and was buried in Forest Lawn Cemetery in Buffalo.   Michael F. Holt

Related articles in *World Book* include:

Clay, Henry   Perry (Matthew C.)   Taylor, Zachary
Know-Nothings   President of the U.S.   Whig Party

Fillmore's Cabinet

Secretary of state	* Daniel Webster
	* Edward Everett (1852)
Secretary of the treasury	Thomas Corwin
Secretary of war	Charles M. Conrad
Attorney general	John J. Crittenden
Postmaster general	Nathan K. Hall
	Samuel D. Hubbard (1852)
Secretary of the Navy	William A. Graham
	John P. Kennedy (1852)
Secretary of the interior	Thomas M. T. McKennan
	Alexander H. H. Stuart (1850)

*Has a separate biography in *World Book*.

Questions

What did Fillmore do that is credited with delaying the Civil War for 10 years?
How did Fillmore meet his first wife?
Why did Fillmore support some proslavery measures even though he opposed slavery?

Why did he refuse a degree from Oxford University?
How did the argument over slavery help Zachary Taylor and Fillmore win office in 1848?

Additional resources

Grayson, Benson L. *The Unknown President: The Administration of President Millard Fillmore.* Univ. Press of America, 1981.
Hamilton, Holman. *Prologue to Conflict: The Crisis and Compromise of 1850.* Univ. Press of Kentucky, 1964. A standard work.
Potter, David M. *The Impending Crisis, 1848-1861.* Harper, 1976. A political history that includes the years of Fillmore's Administration.
Rayback, Robert J. *Millard Fillmore: Biography of a President.* Easton Press, 1986. First published in 1959.

Film. See Motion picture (Film); **Photography** (Developing and printing; pictures).

Filmstrip is a related series of still pictures on 35 mm. film. A projector flashes one after another of these pictures on a screen. Teachers use filmstrips for instruction. They are easier to use, can be stored in less space, and cost less than slides.

Filmstrips are black and white or in color. A record player or tape recorder attached to the projector may provide sound for the filmstrips. The recording explains the film and sometimes has music and sound effects. Some recordings can change pictures automatically by transmitting a silent signal to a special type of projector. Other types give a beep when the operator should change pictures. But teachers often prefer to explain the picture themselves or to have a pupil do it. In this way, the picture can be changed whenever desired. Students can ask questions immediately instead of waiting until the end of the picture. Robert A. Sobieszek

Filter is a device that removes unwanted quantities from the flow of liquids or gases, or from the transmission of electric currents, beams of light, and sound waves. Filters that remove solid particles or other impurities from liquids or gases are made from paper, cloth, charcoal, porcelain, fiberglass, or some other porous material. Glass or gelatin filters are used on cameras to filter out certain light rays (see **Photography** [Filters]).

Internal combustion engines use various types of filters to remove impurities from air, lubricating oils, or fuel. Dry-paper filters on carburetors remove impurities from air before it enters the engine. Most oil filters also are made of fibrous paper. Many fuel filters have a stack of ceramic or metal disks separated by narrow spaces, but a few consist of wire screen. Some high-temperature engines also use magnetic filters. The filters attract metallic particles smaller than 1 micron (0.001 millimeter, or 0.000039 inch).

Cigarette filters, usually made of cellulose acetate, remove some of the tar and nicotine particles from cigarette smoke. Air conditioners use filters made of fiber glass or metal, coated with an adhesive, to remove dust and pollen from the air. Almost all large cities have filtration plants to filter water. Evan Powell

See also **Air conditioning** (Cleaning the air); **Aquarium** (picture).

Filtration. See Water (City water systems).

Finance. See Economics; Bank; Budget; Money.

Finance bill. See Bill of exchange.

Finance company is a firm that loans money to people who promise to repay the loan with interest in a specified period of time. Borrowers must offer some guarantee that they will repay the loan, such as a lien on

their salary or personal possessions (see **Lien**). Some finance companies also offer credit card services that let the holder buy merchandise. They also make loans to merchants and manufacturers. A merchant may offer the finance company a purchaser's contract to buy goods on installment payments as security for cash loans (see **Installment plan**). Some finance companies buy these contracts. Business people who need a loan can offer property, merchandise, or unpaid bills due to them as security. See also **Loan company.** Joanna H. Frodin

Finch is a general term applied to any small seed-eating songbird. Finches include towhees, goldfinches, buntings, and grosbeaks. They live on all continents except Antarctica and on most ocean islands. Their stout cone-shaped bills, strong skulls, large jaw muscles, and grinding gizzards enable these birds to eat hard seeds.

In North America, the term *finch* usually refers to members of the family Fringillidae. Many of these finches have striking red and yellow colors. These birds also sing beautifully, often while in flight. Finches build closely woven, cup-shaped nests in the branches of trees and shrubs. The female lays three to six bluish eggs that are usually streaked or spotted. She sits on and warms the eggs until they hatch, and the male finds food. Both sexes care for the young.

Scientific classification. Finches belong to five families: Emberizidae, Fringillidae, Passeridae, Ploceidae, and Estrildidae. Edward H. Burtt, Jr.

Related articles in *World Book* include:

Bird (pictures)	Cardinal	Grosbeak	Pine siskin
Bullfinch	Crossbill	Junco	Sparrow
Bunting	Goldfinch	Linnet	Towhee
Canary			

Finch, Robert Hutchison (1925-), was United States secretary of health, education, and welfare (HEW) under President Richard M. Nixon in 1969 and 1970. From 1970 to 1972, Finch served as counselor to the President—a post with Cabinet rank—and a member of the Domestic Council.

Finch was one of Nixon's closest friends and most trusted political advisers. He was Nixon's administrative assistant from 1958 to 1960, while Nixon was Vice President. He directed Nixon's unsuccessful campaign for President in 1960. He became lieutenant governor of California in 1967. When Nixon was elected President in 1968, he offered Finch his choice of Cabinet posts.

Finch was born in Tempe, Ariz., and grew up in southern California. He graduated from Occidental College and the University of Southern California Law School. Finch served as a Marine, both in World War II and the Korean War. David S. Broder

Fine is a payment of money ordered by a court from a person who has been found guilty of violating a law. The word comes from the Latin *finem facere,* which means *to put an end to.* The term originated in England in 1275, when the courts began to permit convicts to be released from prison when they paid a required amount of money. A fine is often the punishment for a *misdemeanor* (minor crime). But a fine and a prison sentence can be the penalty for a major crime. People who cannot pay a fine assessed against them are usually ordered to serve a prison sentence. James O. Finckenauer

Fine arts are concerned with making or performing beautiful products or products that appeal in some way to a person's aesthetic tastes. People expect to enjoy a poem, a painting, or a symphony for its own sake, not merely as a means to something else. People also expect a great work of art to develop their minds by expressing and clarifying the best thoughts of great people.

Grouping the arts. In a broad sense, the fine arts include music, literature, opera, and ballet, as well as painting, sculpture, architecture, and the decorative arts. Here the word *fine* is often taken to mean *beautiful* or *aesthetically pleasing.* But artists do not always try to make things beautiful or pleasing. Sometimes they try instead to shock or arouse the public to indignation or pity. They may do this by showing the tragic, evil, or ugly sides of life.

In a narrower sense, the fine arts include only the arts that appeal to aesthetic taste through the sense of sight. These arts include painting, sculpture, architecture, landscape design, furniture, ceramics, jewelry, and textile design. Many colleges have departments of "fine arts" that cover only these arts. But most authorities now prefer to call these the *visual arts.* They classify music and spoken literature, as in a dramatic performance, as *auditory arts.* Some authorities group music, dance, and the theater arts together as *performing arts,* because they must be performed, either by living artists or by mechanical means such as films and phonograph records. Many art authorities group painting, sculpture, and architecture together as *plastic arts,* because they consist of solid objects. Works of art that do not move, including most paintings, sculptures, and architecture, are called *static.* Those works that do move are called *mobile,* as in mobile sculptures and animated films. Perfume and cooking are sometimes called *lower-sense arts,* but they are rarely classed as fine arts.

Older groupings. Many people believe that there are seven fine arts. This idea developed in the Middle Ages. Scholars at that time grouped together seven kinds of learning, most of which we call sciences today. This group included grammar, dialectic (a kind of logic), rhetoric, arithmetic, geometry, music, and astronomy.

Another ancient idea is that fine arts can be separated from useful arts, because fine arts are only supposed to be beautiful, not to be useful. This idea developed in ancient times, when people believed that gentlemen and ladies could not use their hands for any useful work. But few people in democratic societies today believe that this is true. We regard architecture, furniture design, and ceramics as fine arts, even though their products are useful, when artists use good design and make their objects satisfying to our eyes, ears, and minds. The Greeks and Romans called all useful skills arts, including agriculture, mining, and medicine. But we regard the hundreds of arts as those which are concerned with beauty and aesthetic appeal, regardless of their practical use.   Thomas Munro

Related articles in *World Book* include:

Aesthetics	Furniture
Architecture	Literature
Art and the arts	Muses
Ballet	Music
Dancing	Painting
Drama	Poetry
Drawing	Sculpture

Fine Arts, Commission of, is an independent United States government agency. It advises the federal government and District of Columbia agencies on questions of architecture, art, and design. It reviews proposals for public buildings, monuments, parks, and other landmarks that affect the appearance of the nation's capital. It also reviews building permit applications for private property in such historic areas of Washington as Georgetown. The commission also makes recommendations on designs for coins, medals, and insignia. The commission has seven members, each appointed by the President for a four-year term.

Finger. See Hand.

Finger, Charles Joseph (1871-1941), an American adventure writer, won the 1925 Newbery Medal for his children's book, *Tales from Silver Lands.* The book is a collection of South American Indian legends.

Finger's colorful adventures as a young man furnished him with rich background material for the 35 books he wrote during his life. His works include *Courageous Companions* (1929), *Heroes from Hakluyt* (1927), *Tales Worth Telling* (1927), *A Dog at His Heel* (1935), and *Golden Tales from Far and Near* (1935).

Finger left home when he was 16. He roamed Africa, Alaska, and the Antarctic, and explored much of the United States. He spent 10 exciting years in South America, hunting gold, herding sheep, and living with Indians, sailors, miners, and *gauchos* (cowboys). When he was past 50, he bought a farm in the Ozark hills of Arkansas and began to write stories.

Finger was born in Willesden, England. He studied in England and Germany.   Evelyn Ray Sickels

Finger alphabet. See Sign language (picture).

Finger counting. See Chisanbop.

Finger Lakes are a group of long, narrow lakes in west-central New York. They received their name because they are shaped somewhat like the fingers of a hand. For the location of the lakes, see **New York** (physical map).

Geographers differ on how many lakes should be included in the group. Most experts include 11 lakes, however. The lakes are, from east to west, Otisco, Skaneateles, Owasco, Cayuga, Seneca, Keuka, Canandaigua, Honeoye, Canadice, Hemlock, and Conesus.

The most common explanation for how the lakes were formed is that glacial ice sheets deepened valleys that already existed in the area. Water from melting glaciers filled the valleys, which were dammed at their southern ends by glacial deposits of soil and rock.

Seneca is the largest of the Finger Lakes. It is 37 miles (60 kilometers) long and 3 miles (4.8 kilometers) wide at its broadest point. This lake lies 446 feet (136 meters) above sea level and is 600 feet (180 meters) deep at some points. Watkins Glen, a famous summer resort, is located at the head of Seneca Lake.

Cayuga Lake is 40 miles (64 kilometers) long, 1 to 3 miles (1.6 to 4.8 kilometers) wide, 435 feet (133 meters) deep, and lies 380 feet (116 meters) above sea level. Taughannock Falls (215 feet, or 66 meters), near the head of Cayuga Lake, is one of the highest falls east of the Rocky Mountains. Seneca and Cayuga lakes are connected at their northern ends by the Cayuga and Seneca Canal, part of the New York State Barge Canal System.

Most of the Finger Lake Valley lies in rolling country, with rounded hills from 60 to 800 feet (18 to 240 meters) above the level of the lakes. Thick woods, vineyards, orchards, and dairy farms cover most of the lake shores. Streams that run through many gorges and glens empty onto the lakes.   Michael K. Heiman

Finger painting is a method of painting pictures using the fingers, hands, and arms to apply the paint. A finger painter works with a thick, pasty paint and, in most cases, a wet piece of paper. The painter spreads, rolls, or pats the paint on the paper. The surfaces of the fingers, hands, and arms produce different designs.

Finger painting is enjoyed by both children and adults. The activity appeals especially to youngsters because it is easy and fun. Finger painting provides many adults with a relaxing hobby. It is used as a form of therapy for mentally ill people because it helps them express their feelings. It is also a practical activity for partially sighted persons because it stresses movement and does not require attention to visual details.

The standard paper used in finger painting is large and has a glazed side, on which the paint is applied. The paper should be soaked in water and then placed on a smooth, hard surface made of Formica, Masonite, plastic, or another material that can be washed easily. The painter smooths out all wrinkles and air bubbles from the paper and puts about two tablespoons of paint in the center of the paper. Beginners should work with one or two colors until they learn the techniques of finger painting. If the paint is too thick or begins to dry, it may be mixed with a few drops of water. Paint can be removed from the paper and hands with a wet sponge or cloth. If a second color of paint is used, it should be mixed with water to give it the same consistency as the first color.

Most finger painters work from a standing position, which allows them to move freely. The artist can spread the paint on the paper any way he or she chooses. Some

WORLD BOOK photo

A young artist applies finger paint to a piece of damp paper. Children enjoy finger painting because it is easy to learn and allows them to use their imagination to create countless designs.

finger painters work in rhythm with music. Artists may create abstract designs, or realistic pictures of birds, flowers, mountains, trees, or other subjects.

After the painting is finished, it should be lifted by the corners and placed on a newspaper to dry. Drying takes about an hour. If the painting wrinkles, press a warm iron against the back to flatten it out. Some artists paint on waterproofed canvas, glass, or other materials that last longer than paper.

No one knows for certain when finger painting began. As early as A.D. 750, Chinese artists created finger paintings.   Margaret A. Wolff

Finger spelling. See Deafness (Special aids and communication techniques); **Sign language.**

Finger painting by Margaret A. Wolff (WORLD BOOK photo)

A finger painting, *left,* shows an arrangement of plantlike forms. The picture is an example of the detailed designs that a skilled finger painter can create. The artist used the fingertips, palm, and other parts of the hand and arm to paint this picture.

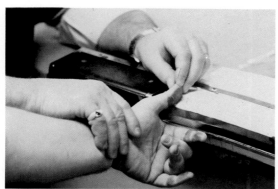

Chicago Police Department (WORLD BOOK photo by Dan Miller)

Fingerprinting is a positive method of identification because no two people have the same fingerprints. Fingerprinting is used by law enforcement officers in criminal investigations.

Fingernail. See Nail (finger).

Fingerprinting is a process of identification based on the impressions made by the ends of the fingers and thumbs. These impressions consist of patterns formed by the ridges that cover the skin of the fingertips. Fingerprints provide the most reliable method of identification because no person's prints are identical to those of another individual. Even identical twins have different fingerprints. In almost all cases, fingerprints remain the same throughout a person's lifetime. The ridges on the fingertips change only as the result of surgery, disease, or an accident.

Fingerprints are often used in the investigation of crimes. Prints found at the scene of a crime may help investigators identify suspects. Fingerprints that match those in police records serve as strong evidence in

Chicago Police Department (WORLD BOOK photo by Dan Miller)

A special computer can compare a person's fingerprints with those in a central file. This type of computer is used at police departments, U.S. military bases, and at some banks.

How fingerprints are classified

Ridges on the finger form three main groups of patterns—the arch, *below;* the loop, *upper right;* and the whorl, *lower right.* There are eight subclassifications of the main types of patterns.

Loop

Arch

Whorl

FBI

court. Fingerprinting may also help prevent crime. For example, some banks, military bases, and government buildings have computers that check the fingerprints of employees before these people are admitted into certain areas. Fingerprints also help identify victims of war; of such disasters as fires, epidemics, and airplane crashes; and of other tragedies. A number of states allow children to be fingerprinted to help identify them if they are reported missing.

How fingerprints are recorded. Fingerprints are recorded by means of a piece of glass or metal coated with a special ink. The fingertips are pressed into the ink with a rolling motion from one side of the fingernail to the other. The inked fingers are pressed on a white card, producing a copy of the prints.

Fingerprints are either visible or *latent* (hidden). Most visible fingerprints are made by fingers soiled with blood, dirt, or other substances. Latent fingerprints are made by the perspiration and oils that accumulate naturally on the fingers.

Visible prints can be photographed immediately, but latent prints must first be *developed* (made visible). Colored powder is used to develop most latent prints found on nonabsorbent surfaces, such as wood or metal. The powder is *dusted* (brushed) onto the surface, and it sticks to the oils in the prints. The prints are lifted from the surface by pressing a piece of sticky tape against the powder. They are then photographed from the tape. Chemicals are used to develop most latent fingerprints left on absorbent surfaces, such as paper or cloth. The chemicals react with substances in the perspiration left in a fingerprint and form a colored image of the print. This image is photographed.

Some latent fingerprints can be developed only with a *laser,* a device that produces a powerful beam of light. This light causes the perspiration in a fingerprint to shine with a yellow color so it can be photographed.

How fingerprints are classified. Fingerprint experts classify fingerprints according to *classification formulas.*

Mike Fink was a colorful American folk hero. He gained fame for his exploits as an Indian fighter on the Pennsylvania frontier and as a keelboater on the Ohio and Mississippi rivers. A famous story tells how Fink shot the scalp lock off an Indian named Proud Joe as a prank, *left.* Later, Proud Joe tried to get revenge on Fink, but killed one of Fink's companions by mistake. Fink killed Proud Joe during the fight.

Bettmann Archive

Most of these formulas are based on fingerprint patterns and on the number of ridges between certain points within the patterns.

There are four main types of fingerprint patterns. In a *loop pattern,* the most common type, the ridges begin on one side of the finger, curve back sharply, and end on the same side. The ridges in a *whorl pattern* have a circular form. In an *arch pattern,* the ridges extend from one side of the finger to the other, rising in the center. An *accidental pattern* has no specific form. Many combine loops, whorls, and arches.

History. Before the development of fingerprinting, people identified some criminals and slaves by branding or tattooing them, or by amputating one of their limbs. Other early methods were less reliable though more humane. They included photography and the *Bertillon system,* a technique based on the measurements of the arms, legs, and other parts of the body.

Fingerprinting became a scientific method of identification in the 1880's with the research of Sir Francis Galton, a British anthropologist. Galton calculated mathematically that no two persons could have exactly the same fingerprint patterns.

During the 1890's, two police officers, Juan Vucetich of Argentina and Sir Edward R. Henry of Great Britain, developed fingerprint classification systems. The Henry system became the basis of the fingerprint systems used in the United States and many other countries. Today, newer systems use computers to classify and compare fingerprints. Some crime laboratories also use evidence called a DNA "fingerprint." This evidence is based on genes from white blood cells and is used to make identifications in civil and criminal cases.   John I. Thornton

See also **Crime laboratory; Footprinting.**

Finite series. See Series (Working with finite series).

Fink, Mike (1770-1823), was an American frontier fighter and boatman whose adventures became the subject of many stories and legends. Fink's great strength, boastful nature, and skill with his rifle and his fists made him a hero on the frontier. He also was notorious for playing cruel pranks. One story tells how Fink punished his wife for flirting with another man by making her lie in a pile of dry leaves, which he then set on fire.

Fink was born at or near Fort Pitt (now Pittsburgh), Pa. As a youth, he gained fame for his expert marksmanship while fighting the British and Indians on the Pennsylvania frontier. During the early 1800's, Fink became the most famous of the rugged keelboaters who worked on the Ohio and Mississippi rivers. After steamboats replaced keelboats, Fink joined the Rocky Mountain Fur Company as a boatman and trapper. On his first expedition, he was killed by a companion.

Many stories have been told about how Fink died. But nearly all the tales agree that he died as a result of a shooting match. Fink and a friend named Carpenter were taking turns shooting a cup off each other's head. According to one story, Carpenter shot first and accidentally grazed Fink's scalp. Fink became enraged and shot his friend through the forehead. In revenge, one of Carpenter's friends shot Fink in the heart.   Harry Oster

Finland

Embassy of Finland

Thick forests and island-dotted lakes cover most of Finland. This small farm lies in the scenic Lake District, a land region that occupies the central part of the country.

Finland is a country in northern Europe famous for its scenic beauty. Thousands of lovely lakes dot Finland's landscape, and thick forests cover almost two-thirds of the land. The country has a long, deeply indented coast, marked by colorful red and gray granite rocks. Thousands of scenic islands lie offshore.

Sweden lies to the west of Finland, northern Norway to the north, and the Union of Soviet Socialist Republics (U.S.S.R.) to the east. The Gulf of Finland and the Gulf of Bothnia, two arms of the Baltic Sea, border Finland on the south and southwest. The northernmost part of the country lies inside the Arctic Circle in a region called the *Land of the Midnight Sun*. In this region of Finland, the sun shines 24 hours a day for long periods each summer. Helsinki, the country's capital and largest city, is located in the south on the Gulf of Finland.

Most of Finland's people live in the southern part of the country, where the climate is mildest. Finns love the outdoors and the arts. They have a high standard of living and receive many welfare benefits from the government. Most of Finland's wealth comes from its huge forests. They form the basis of the country's thriving forest-products industry, which includes woodworking and the manufacture of paper and pulp.

Finland's location between the U.S.S.R. on the east and Sweden on the west has played an important role in the country's history. In the 1000's, Sweden and Russia (the name for the U.S.S.R. before 1922) began to battle for possession of Finland. Sweden gradually gained control in the 1100's and 1200's, but conflict between Sweden and Russia over Finland continued for hundreds of years. Today, Swedish remains equal with Finnish as an official language of Finland. Russia controlled the country from 1809 until 1917, when Finland declared its independence. The nation became a republic with a president and parliament. During World War II (1939-1945), Finland fought two wars with the U.S.S.R. Today, Finland tries to maintain friendly relations with both the U.S.S.R. and Western nations by remaining strictly neutral in foreign affairs.

Government

Finland is a democratic republic. Its Constitution, adopted in 1919, guarantees the people such rights as freedom of speech, freedom of worship, and equality before the law. All Finns 18 years and older may vote.

Facts in brief

Capital: Helsinki (in Swedish, Helsingfors).
Official languages: Finnish and Swedish.
Official name: Republic of Finland. Finland's name in Finnish is *Suomi.*
Area: 130,559 sq. mi. (338,145 km²), including 12,943 sq. mi. (33,522 km²) of inland water. *Greatest distances*—east-west, 320 mi. (515 km); north-south, 640 mi. (1,030 km). *Coastline*—1,462 mi. (2,353 km).
Elevation: *Highest*—Mount Haltia, 4,344 ft. (1,324 m) above sea level. *Lowest*—sea level.
Population: *Estimated 1990 population*—4,981,000; density, 38 persons per sq. mi. (15 per km²); distribution, 68 per cent

urban, 32 per cent rural. *1980 census*—4,784,710. *Estimated 1995 population*—5,056,000.
Chief products: *Agriculture*—milk, hogs, beef cattle, barley, sugar beets, potatoes, oats. *Forestry*—birch, pine, spruce. *Manufacturing*—paper products, machinery, ships, wood products, chemicals. *Mining*—iron ore, copper, zinc.
National anthem: "Maamme" (in Finnish) or "Vårt Land" (in Swedish), meaning "Our Land."
Money: *Basic unit*—markka. For its price in U.S. dollars, see **Money** (table: Exchange rates).

The president is Finland's head of state and chief executive. The president is elected to a six-year term by the Electoral College, whose 301 members are chosen by the people. A president may be reelected any number of times. The president may issue orders that do not violate existing laws, *veto* (reject) bills passed by the parliament, and dissolve the parliament and call for new elections. The president handles foreign relations and acts as head of the armed forces. But the parliament must approve decisions concerning war and peace.

The prime minister and Cabinet. The president appoints the prime minister, who is head of government. The prime minister, with the president's approval, forms a Cabinet made up of members of several political parties. The political parties involved must agree on the Cabinet selections. Cabinet members head the government departments. The prime minister presides over the Cabinet and works with it in setting government programs, which must be acceptable to the parliament.

The parliament of Finland is a one-house legislature called the *Eduskunta* (in Swedish, the *Riksdag*). The people elect its 200 members to four-year terms. But the president may dissolve the Eduskunta and call for new elections at any time. The parliament, in turn, may force the Cabinet to resign by not supporting its programs. The Eduskunta can also repass a bill by a simple majority vote after the president has vetoed it.

Local government. For purposes of local government, Finland is divided into 12 provinces. The president appoints a governor to administer each province. The provinces are subdivided into more than 500 *communes*. They range in size from thinly populated rural areas to large cities. A council elected by the people governs each commune. Communes collect their own taxes to support hospitals, schools, police and fire departments, and other local institutions.

Political parties. Election to the Eduskunta is based on a system called *proportional representation*. This system gives a political party a share of seats in the parliament according to its share of the total votes cast in an election. The system encourages small parties to put up candidates and makes it hard for any one party to win a majority. As a result of proportional representation, a number of parties usually have seats in the Eduskunta. See **Proportional representation.**

The Social Democratic Party, supported mostly by working-class and lower-middle-class voters, generally receives the most votes. Other parties include the Center Party, Christian League, Liberal People's Party, National Coalition (Conservative) Party, People's Democratic League, Rural Party, and Swedish People's Party.

Courts. Finland's highest court of appeal is the Supreme Court. Four regional courts hear appeals from lower courts. Special courts handle such matters as impeachment of government officials and labor disputes.

Armed forces. Finland has about 34,400 people in its army, navy, and air force. Healthy men between 17 and 60 must serve 8 to 11 months in the armed forces.

People

Ancestry and population. More than 90 per cent of Finland's people are Finnish by descent, and most of

Kay Honkanen from Carl Östman

Parliament Building in Helsinki is the meeting place of Finland's one-house legislature, the *Eduskunta*. The Eduskunta has 200 members, elected by the people to four-year terms.

Finland's state flag, used by the government, was adopted in 1918. The national flag has no coat of arms.

The Finnish coat of arms was adopted in its present form in 1918. But its basic design dates back to the 1500's.

WORLD BOOK map

Finland is a northern European nation bordering Norway, the U.S.S.R., and Sweden. Its coastline stretches along the Baltic Sea.

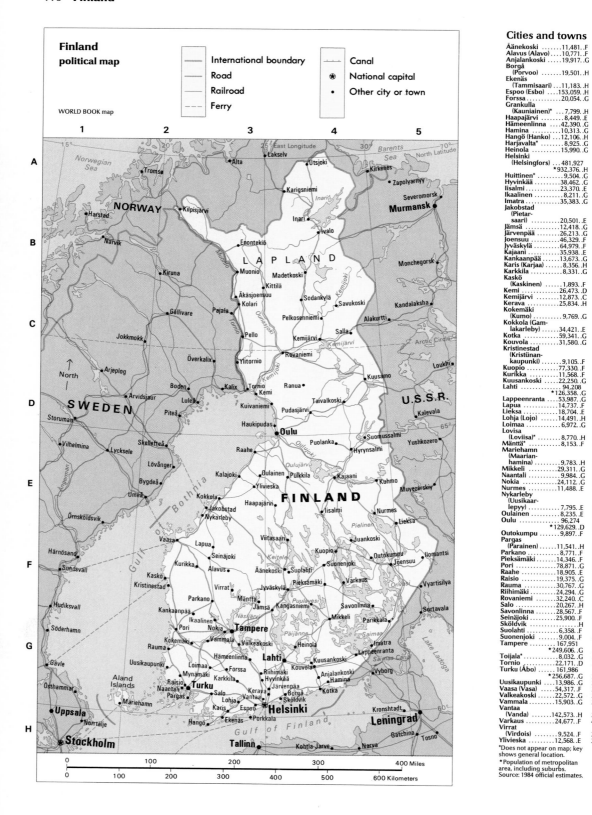

Finland
political map

— International boundary
— Road
— Railroad
— — Ferry

⌶ Canal
⊛ National capital
• Other city or town

WORLD BOOK map

Cities and towns

Äänekoski ....11,481..F 3
Alavus (Alavo) ....10,771..F 3
Anjalankoski .....19,917..G 4
Borgå
 (Porvoo) ....19,501..H 3
Ekenäs
 (Tammisaari) ..11,183..H 3
Espoo (Esbo) ..153,059..H 3
Forssa ....20,054..G 3
Grankulla
 (Kauniainen)* ...7,799..H 3
Haapajärvi ....8,449..E 3
Hämeenlinna ....42,390..G 3
Hamina ....10,313..G 4
Hangö (Hanko) ..12,106..H 3
Harjavalta* ....8,925..G 2
Heinola ....15,990..G 3
Helsinki
 (Helsingfors) ..481,927
          *932,376..H 3
Huittinen* ....9,504..G 2
Hyvinkää ....38,462..G 3
Iisalmi ....23,370..E 4
Ikaalinen ....8,211..G 2
Imatra ....35,383..G 4
Jakobstad
 (Pietar-
 saari) ....20,501..E 3
Jämsä ....12,418..G 3
Järvenpää ....26,213..G 3
Joensuu ....46,329..F 5
Jyväskylä ....64,979..F 4
Kajaani ....35,938..E 4
Kankaanpää .....13,673..G 2
Karis (Karjaa) ....8,356..H 3
Karkkila ....8,331..G 3
Kaskö
 (Kaskinen) ......1,893..F 2
Kemi ....26,473..D 3
Kemijärvi ....12,873..C 4
Kerava ....25,834..H 3
Kokemäki
 (Kumo) ....9,769..G 2
Kokkola (Gam-
 lakarleby) .....34,421..E 3
Kotka ....59,341..G 3
Kouvola ....31,580..G 4
Kristinestad
 (Kristiinan-
 kaupunki) ....9,105..F 2
Kuopio ....77,330..F 4
Kurikka ....11,568..F 2
Kuusankoski ....22,250..G 4
Lahti 94,208
          *126,358..G 3
Lappeenranta ...53,987..G 4
Lapua ....14,737..F 2
Lieksa ....18,704..E 5
Lohja (Lojo) ....14,491..H 3
Loimaa ....6,972..G 3
Lovisa
 (Loviisa)* ....8,770..H 4
Mänttä* ....8,153..F 3
Mariehamn
 (Maarian-
 hamina) ....9,783..H 4
Mikkeli ....29,311..G 4
Naantali ....9,984..G 2
Nokia ....24,112..G 3
Nurmes ....11,488..E 5
Nykarleby
 (Uusikaar-
 lepyy) ....7,795..E 2
Oulainen ....8,235..E 3
Oulu 96,274
          *129,629..D 3
Outokumpu ....9,897..F 4
Pargas
 (Parainen) .....11,541..H 2
Parkano ....8,771..F 3
Pieksämäki .....14,346..F 4
Pori ....78,871..G 2
Raahe ....18,905..E 3
Raisio ....19,375..G 2
Rauma ....30,767..G 2
Riihimäki ....24,294..G 3
Rovaniemi ....32,240..C 3
Salo ....20,267..H 3
Savonlinna ......28,567..F 5
Seinäjoki ....25,900..F 3
Sköldvik ....H 3
Suolahti ....6,358..F 3
Suonenjoki ....9,004..F 4
Tampere 167,951
          *249,606..G 3
Toijala* ....8,032..G 3
Tornio ....22,171..D 3
Turku (Åbo) ...161,986
          *256,687..G 2
Uusikaupunki ...13,986..G 2
Vaasa (Vasa) ...54,317..F 2
Valkeakoski .....22,572..G 3
Vammala ....15,903..G 3
Vantaa
 (Vanda) ......142,573..H 3
Varkaus ....24,677..F 4
Virrat
 (Virdois) ....9,524..F 3
Ylivieska ....12,568..E 3

*Does not appear on map; key
shows general location.

* Population of metropolitan
area, including suburbs.

Source: 1984 official estimates.

Volker von Bonin

The gleaming lights of downtown Helsinki, heart of Finland's capital and largest city, brighten the 18-hour nights of midwinter. The rest of Finland, like Helsinki, is also dark most of the time in winter. About a fifth of the nation's people live in Helsinki and its suburbs.

the rest are Swedish. Most people in both groups are tall, with fair skin, blue or gray eyes, and blond or light brown hair.

About 6,000 Lapps live in northern Finland. The ancestors of these short, stocky people lived in Finland long before the first Finns arrived thousands of years ago (see **Lapland**). Finland also has about 6,000 Gypsies and small groups of Jews and Turks.

Finland has a total population of about 5 million. Most of the people live in the south, and about two-thirds live in cities and towns. Helsinki, Finland's capital and largest city, has about 500,000 people. About a fifth of the nation's people live in Helsinki and its suburbs. Finland has two other çities—Tampere and Turku—with more than 150,000 people each. See **Helsinki; Tampere.**

Languages. Finland has two official languages—Finnish and Swedish. About 95 per cent of the people speak Finnish, and about 5 per cent speak Swedish. Most of the Swedish-speaking people live on the south and west coasts and on the offshore Aland Islands. Finnish and Swedish belong to different language families. The Lapps speak a language related to Finnish. See **Language** (Language families).

Way of life. In Finland's cities, most people own or rent apartments. Most people in rural areas live in one-family homes on farms or in villages.

The Finns enjoy fish, especially herring, perch, pike, and salmon. Popular meats include beef, veal, pork, and sausage. Smoked reindeer is a special treat. Boiled potatoes covered with butter and dill sprigs make up a favor-

ite side dish. Butter and milk are important parts of the Finnish diet.

The most famous feature of Finnish life is a special kind of bath called a *sauna.* Most Finns take a sauna at least once a week for cleansing and relaxation. In a sauna room or bathhouse, stones are heated over a stove or furnace. The temperature in the sauna rises to between 176° and 212° F. (80° and 100° C). Bathers sit or lie on wooden benches until they begin to perspire freely. After a while, they may throw water on the stones to produce vapor and make the sauna feel even hotter. The bathers may beat themselves gently with leafy birch twigs to stimulate circulation. Finally, they take a cold shower or plunge into a lake. After repeating the entire cycle, they lie down to rest until their body returns to normal temperature.

Social welfare. The government of Finland provides the people with many welfare services. Since the 1920's, maternity and child welfare centers have given free health care to pregnant women, mothers, and children. Since 1948, families have received an allowance every time they have had a new baby as well as a yearly allowance for each child under the age of 16.

In 1939, Finland began an old-age and disability insurance program. This program guarantees monthly pensions to people 65 years and older and to permanently disabled citizens. In 1963, Finland set up a health insurance program for all citizens.

The government began to guarantee workers annual holidays in the 1920's. Today, workers who remain in the

Bob and Ira Spring, FPG

Lapp schoolchildren in northernmost Finland place their skis against a rack after skiing to school. The Lapp people lived in Finland long before the Finns arrived thousands of years ago.

Embassy of Finland

A Finnish farmwife uses a wood-burning stove for baking. Such stoves are common in rural Finland, where forests provide plentiful wood. About a third of the people live in rural areas.

Keystone

Family camping vacations are popular among the Finns, who love the outdoors. Other summer activities include boating; hiking; and playing *pesäpallo,* a Finnish form of baseball.

Bud Guyon, Keystone

Finnish glassware is internationally prized for its high quality and simplicity of design. These women are admiring beautiful glass objects on display in a Helsinki store.

same job for one year receive a 26-day annual vacation. After 10 years, they receive 36 days.

Recreation. The Finns love outdoor sports. In winter, they enjoy ice hockey, ice-skating, ski-jumping, cross-country skiing, and downhill skiing. Popular summer sports include *pesäpallo* (a Finnish form of baseball), swimming, boating, and hiking. In summer, thousands of city families flock to their cottages and saunas on lakes, the seacoast, or the offshore islands. Favorite spectator sports include track-and-field events and ice hockey matches. The Finns also enjoy ballets, concerts, motion pictures, plays, and operas.

Education. Almost all adult Finns can read and write. All elementary school students and most other students go to public schools. The rest attend private schools, which may charge a small tuition fee. Elementary school students receive free one meal a day, books, and medical and dental care.

Finland has a *comprehensive school system.* Under this system, children are required to attend elementary schools called *basic schools* for nine years. They begin at the age of 7. They attend the lower level of the schools for six years and the upper level for three years.

After completing basic school, students may choose to enter an *upper secondary school* or a *vocational school.* Upper secondary schools, which offer three-year courses, emphasize academic subjects. Vocational schools, most of which offer two-year courses, emphasize education in skilled manual work.

Most vocational school students enter the job market after graduating. Graduates of upper secondary schools may apply to a *vocational institute* or a university. Vocational institutes chiefly prepare students for careers in managerial business jobs. The universities offer a wide variety of higher-education programs.

Finland has 13 universities and 26 other institutions of higher learning. The University of Helsinki is the country's largest university.

Religion. The Evangelical Lutheran Church is the state church of Finland, and the national government has supreme authority over it. But the people have com-

The new town of Tapiola, within the city of Espoo, has become a world-famous model for city planning. A private organization developed it as an entirely new community in the 1950's.

plete freedom of worship. More than 95 per cent of all Finns are Evangelical Lutherans. The Eastern Orthodox Church makes up the next largest religious group, with about 1 per cent of the population. Finland also has other, smaller Protestant groups as well as small groups of Jews, Muslims, and Roman Catholics.

The arts. Finland has a rich folk culture, which is reflected in the country's crafts, literature, music, and painting. The person most responsible for preserving Finland's oral folklore was Elias Lönnrot, a country doctor. He collected the centuries-old song-poems and chants of the Finnish peasants and published them in 1835. This huge collection, called the *Kalevala,* became Finland's national epic.

During the 1800's and 1900's, the *Kalevala* inspired many artists. Akseli Gallen-Kallela used its themes in many paintings. Composer Jean Sibelius based most of his symphonic poems on the work. American poet Henry Wadsworth Longfellow patterned the rhythm of his poem *The Song of Hiawatha* on the *Kalevala.*

In the early 1800's, Johan Ludvig Runeberg became known as Finland's national poet. His poem "Vårt Land" is the country's national anthem. Other writers of the 1800's include the novelist Aleksis Kivi and the playwright Minna Canth, an early champion of women's rights. In the 1900's, the novelists Frans Eemil Sillanpää and Mika Waltari gained international fame. Sillanpää won the Nobel Prize for literature in 1939.

Finnish glassware, ceramics, furniture, and textiles are world famous for the simple beauty of their design. This same simplicity of line and shape can be seen in the works of Finland's best-known architects—Eliel Saarinen and Alvar Aalto. Saarinen's famous designs include the railroad station and the National Museum in Helsinki. Aalto gained fame not only as an architect, but also as a town planner and furniture designer.

The land

Finland covers 130,559 square miles (338,145 square kilometers). This area includes 12,943 square miles (33,522 square kilometers) of inland water. Finland is largely a plateau broken by small hills and valleys and low ridges and hollows. The land rises gradually from south-southwest to north-northeast, but the average altitude is only 400 to 600 feet (120 to 180 meters) above sea level. Mount Haltia, the country's highest point, stands 4,344 feet (1,324 meters) above sea level in the far northwestern region of Finland. About 60,000 lakes are scattered throughout the country, and forests cover almost two-thirds of the land.

Land regions. Finland has four main land regions: (1) the Coastal Lowlands, (2) the Lake District, (3) the Upland District, and (4) the Coastal Islands.

The Coastal Lowlands lie along the Gulf of Bothnia and Gulf of Finland. Finland's coastline is 1,462 miles (2,353 kilometers) long. Many small lakes lie in the Coastal Lowlands. The region has less forestland and a milder climate than the Lake and Upland districts have. The lowlands also have some of the country's most fertile soil. As a result, the region offers the best conditions farming. The Coastal Lowlands of the south have the mildest climate and the most productive farms. Most of Finland's people live in this area.

The Lake District occupies central Finland north and east of the Coastal Lowlands. The region has thousands

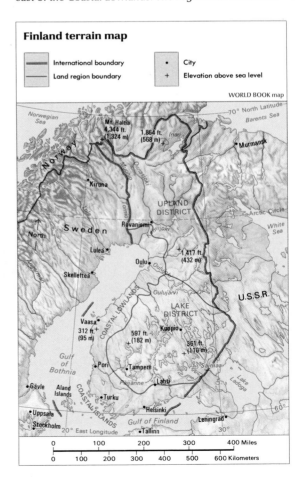

Finland terrain map

International boundary

Land region boundary

City

Elevation above sea level

WORLD BOOK map

The Coastal Lowlands along the Gulf of Finland are the home of most of the Finnish people. The town of Borgå, *above,* with its centuries-old wooden buildings, lies in this region.

The Upland District is Finland's northernmost, hilliest, and least densely populated region. Several rivers in the region provide energy for hydroelectric power stations.

of island-dotted lakes. The lakes cover about half the total area of the district. Narrow channels or short rivers connect many of the lakes. Saimaa, the largest lake in Finland, covers about 680 square miles (1,760 square kilometers) in the southeastern part of the region. The Saimaa Lake System, which is about 185 miles (298 kilometers) long, links several lakes in the area. A fleet of steamers travels the system, stopping at towns on the shores of the lakes. Forests of birch, pine, and spruce cover most of the land in the Lake District. Most farmlands in the region lie in the southwestern part of the Lake District.

The Upland District is Finland's northernmost and least densely populated region. It covers about 40 per cent of the country. The Upland District has a harsher climate and less fertile soil than the other regions have. As one travels north through the Upland District, plant life becomes increasingly scarce. Stunted pines and arctic birches grow in parts of the district. However, the northernmost part makes up a *tundra*—a frozen, treeless plain.

Most of Finland's hills rise in the Upland District. Swamps and marshlands separate the hills. Several rivers in the region provide energy for hydroelectric power stations.

The Coastal Islands consist of thousands of islands in the Gulf of Bothnia and Gulf of Finland. The great majority of these islands are small and uninhabited. The thin, rocky soil on many of Finland's islands cannot support much plant life, but many kinds of plants thrive on a few of the larger islands. People who fish for a living reside on some of the islands. However, Finland's islands serve chiefly as summer recreation areas. Many Finns have cottages or saunas on them.

The most important islands are the Aland group, which consists of about 6,500 islands off Finland's southwest coast. People, almost all of whom speak Swedish, live on about 80 of these islands. The land area of the Aland Islands totals 572 square miles (1,481 square kilometers). The main island, also called Aland, is Finland's largest island. Aland covers 285 square miles (738 square kilometers) and is an important tourist and shipping center.

Rivers Finland's longest river is the Kemijoki. It rises in the Upland District near the U.S.S.R. border and winds southwestward 340 miles (547 kilometers) to the Gulf of Bothnia. The Kemijoki and its chief branch, the Ounasjoki, provide important logging routes and rich salmon catches. Several hydroelectric stations have been built along both rivers.

The Muonio River begins about 60 miles (97 kilometers) southeast of the point where the Norwegian, Swedish, and Finnish borders meet. The river flows south about 110 miles (177 kilometers), forming part of the border between Sweden and Finland. The Muonio provides a logging route. The Oulujoki rises in the northern part of the Lake District and empties into the Gulf of Bothnia. The river is only about 80 miles (130 kilometers) long. But it serves as an important logging route. Its 105-foot (32-meter) Pyhä Falls provides power for a major hydroelectric plant.

Climate

Finland has a much milder climate than most other regions of the world that lie as far north. In January, for example, Helsinki's temperatures often average 25° to 35° F. (14° to 18° C) higher than the temperatures in parts of Canada at the same latitude. Finland's climate is influenced chiefly by the Gulf Stream, a warm ocean current that flows off Norway's west coast. Finland's many lakes and the gulfs of Bothnia and Finland help give the country a relatively mild climate.

July temperatures in Finland average 55° to 63° F. (13° to 17° C). The temperature reaches 50° F. (10° C) or higher on 110 to 122 days a year in the south and on 50 to 85 days a year in the north. February is usually Finland's coldest month, with temperatures averaging from −7° F. (−22° C) to 26° F. (−3° C). In northern Finland, winter temperatures sometimes drop as low as −22° F. (−30° C).

The amount of *precipitation* (rain, melted snow, and other forms of moisture) varies between southern and northern Finland. The south receives about 27 inches (69 centimeters) a year, and the north only about 16 inches (41 centimeters). August usually has the heaviest amount of rainfall.

Snow covers the ground in southern Finland from December to April, and northern Finland is snowbound from October to April. Most of the country is icebound in winter, but special icebreaking boats keep the major Finnish ports open so passenger traffic and shipping can continue.

Northern Finland lies in the *Land of the Midnight Sun,* and so has continuous daylight during part of the summer (see **Midnight sun**). At the country's northernmost point, constant daylight lasts for about $2\frac{1}{2}$ months. The period of midnight sun decreases southward. Southern Finland never has continuous daylight, but it averages 19 hours of daylight a day in midsummer. In winter, Finland has similar periods of continuous darkness. The sun never rises above the horizon in the northernmost areas of Finland for about 2 months in the winter. Southern areas only receive about 6 hours of sunlight a day in midwinter. The winter night sky—especially in northern Finland—often becomes glorious with bright displays of the *aurora borealis,* or northern lights (see **Aurora**).

Economy

Finland's economy is based mostly on private ownership. However, the national government has a monopoly in certain businesses, such as the railway and postal systems. In forestry and certain other industries, government-owned businesses compete with private companies.

Service industries account for 57 per cent of Finland's *gross national product* (GNP). The GNP is the total value of all goods and services produced in a country within a year. Manufacturing accounts for 26 per cent of the GNP; construction, 8 per cent; and mining, 1 per cent. Agriculture, forestry, and fishing—taken together—account for 8 per cent of the GNP.

Natural resources. Finland's greatest natural resource is its widespread forests. They cover almost two-thirds of the land—a higher percentage than in any other European country. But Finland's other resources are limited. Its soil is poor, and the crop-growing season short. The country has no deposits of oil, natural gas, or coal. Water power produces much of the country's electricity. Finland's most important mineral is zinc. The country also has important deposits of cobalt, copper, and iron.

Forestry plays a leading role in Finland's economy. Forestry and forest-products industries provide about 35 per cent of Finland's exports. The government owns about a third of Finland's forests, chiefly in the north. But these northern forests make up only about 15 per cent of the country's annual forest growth because of the short growing season in the north. Most private forests are owned by individual farmers. They work their farmland in summer and cut trees in their forests throughout the year. Pine, spruce, and birch trees cover much of the forest land.

Service industries are those economic activities that produce services rather than goods. Government is a leading type of service industry in Finland. The government provides people with extensive social programs, especially in the areas of health care and education. The government also controls several large companies. Trade is another important service industry. The wholesale trade of forest products, automobiles, and processed foods earns much income. Other service industries include finance, insurance, and real estate; community, social, and personal services; transportation and communication; and utilities.

Manufacturing. Woodworking, pulp and paper production, and other forest-based industries are Finland's chief manufacturing industries. Finland ranks as the world's top producer of plywood. The country is also a leading producer of paper and paperboard. Other major forest products include wood paneling and *prefabricated houses,* which are erected in factory-made sections.

Finland's metalworking industry has expanded rapidly since the 1940's. The chief metal products include farm machinery and equipment, electric motors and generators, and machinery for use in the paper and lumber industries. Finland also produces buses, ships, and other transportation equipment. The shipbuilding industry is especially known for its sturdy, powerful icebreakers and its ferries. Other manufactured products include chemicals, metals, processed foods, telephones, and textiles and clothing.

Agriculture. Most of Finland's farmland lies in the south and west. The farms are small, averaging about 29 acres (12 hectares). The Finnish government owns less than 2 per cent of the farmland.

Dairy farming and livestock production account for about 70 per cent of Finland's farm income. Finland's farmers produce all the milk, eggs, and meat needed by the people. They also produce almost all the bread grains needed in Finland. Barley and oats are the main grain crops. Other crops include potatoes, sugar beets and wheat.

Foreign trade. Finland depends heavily on foreign trade. It imports large quantities of fruits, vegetables, industrial raw materials, manufactured goods not produced in Finland, and petroleum and petroleum products. Paper, pulp, and wood products make up about 35 per cent of the country's exports. Other major exports include products of the metalworking industry, such as machinery and ships.

Finland does more than 80 per cent of its trade with European nations, especially Great Britain, Sweden,

Herbert Fristedt from Carl Östman

Stacks of lumber await loading onto ships at Kotka, a city on Finland's south coast. Lumber and other forest products make up about 35 per cent of the country's exports.

Herbert Fristedt from Carl Östman

Shipbuilding plays an important role in Finland's economy. The industry produces cargo and passenger ships but is best known for its icebreakers. This shipyard is in Helsinki.

Finland's gross national product

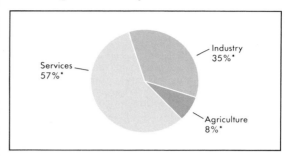

The gross national product (GNP) is the total value of goods and services produced by a country in a year. The GNP measures a nation's total economic performance and can also be used to compare the economic output and growth of countries. Finland's GNP was $53,090,000,000 in 1984.

Production and workers by economic activities

Economic activities	Per cent of GDP* produced	Employed workers	
		Number of persons	Per cent of total
Manufacturing	26	562,000	23
Government	17	123,000	5
Finance, insurance, & real estate	15	147,000	6
Trade	11	342,000	14
Agriculture, forestry, & fishing	8	294,000	12
Construction	8	183,000	8
Transportation & communication	7	180,000	8
Community, social, & personal services	4	541,000	22
Utilities	3	27,000	1
Mining	1	10,000	1
Total	100	2,409,000	100

*Based on gross domestic product (GDP). GDP is the total value of goods and services produced within the country in a year.
Sources: Nordic Council; World Bank.

West Germany, and the U.S.S.R. The U.S.S.R. is the chief importer of Finnish machinery and other metal products. Western European countries are the main customers for forest products. Finland is a member of the European Free Trade Association (EFTA), an economic organization of European nations. EFTA members have eliminated most tariffs on imports of manufactured goods from one another. Finland extends EFTA policies to its trade with the U.S.S.R. In 1973, EFTA members entered into free trade agreements with another economic group, the European Community. See **European Free Trade Association; European Community.**

Transportation. The government owns most of Finland's railroads. The country has a good network of roads and highways. Finland has an average of about one automobile for every three people. The main airport is at Helsinki. The Finnish airline, Finnair, is owned mostly by the government. It offers international and domestic flights. As a result of the great distances between many major Finnish communities and the watery nature of the land, Finland has one of Europe's busiest and most extensive domestic air networks. Helsinki Airport is the country's busiest airport.

A system of inland waterways connects various lakes and seaports. Sköldvik, near Helsinki, is the country's busiest port.

Communication. Finland publishes about 65 daily newspapers. The largest dailies include *Helsingin Sanomat* of Helsinki, *Aamulehti* of Tampere, and *Turun Sanomat* of Turku. Finland has an average of about one radio for every two people and about one television set for every three people. The government owns about 90 per cent of the stock in the main radio and television network. Telegraph and telephone lines connect all areas of Finland. The government owns the telegraph system. The government also owns a large part of the telephone services. Most families have a telephone.

History

Early years. The earliest-known inhabitants of Finland were the Lapps. These people lived as *nomadic* (wandering) hunters. Thousands of years ago, the ancestors of present-day Finns began to move into the country from the south shores of the Gulf of Finland. Their original homeland may have been between the Volga River and the Ural Mountains in what is now the U.S.S.R. The Finns gradually pushed the Lapps farther and farther north. The early Finns were divided into three loosely organized tribes that often fought one another. They lived by farming, hunting, and fishing.

In the 1000's, Sweden and Russia began a struggle for control of Finland. Both nations wanted to extend their boundaries. In addition, Sweden wanted to convert the Finns to Roman Catholicism, and Russia wanted to convert them to Eastern Orthodoxy.

Swedish rule. In the 1100's and 1200's, Sweden gradually conquered all Finland and established Catholicism as the official religion. Many Swedes settled in Finland, and Swedish became the official language. But Finns shared equal rights with Swedes. About 1540, the Swedish king made Lutheranism the official religion.

From the 1500's through the 1700's, Sweden and Russia fought several wars over Finland. Russia won the Finnish province of Vyborg after the Great Northern War (1700-1721), which was known in Finland as the *Great Wrath.* For several years during that war and from 1741 to 1743, Russia occupied all Finland. Sweden and Russia fought over Finland again from 1788 to 1790. After the 1788-1790 war, some Finns began to think Sweden could not protect their land. But a plot to create an independent Finland under Russian protection failed to win wide support.

Control by Russia. In 1808, Russia again invaded Finland. It conquered the country in 1809 and made it an independent grand duchy, but with the czar as grand duke. The duchy had local self-rule based on government systems developed during Swedish control. Russia returned Vyborg to the duchy.

During the 1800's, Finns began to develop feelings of nationalism as they took increasing pride in their country and its culture. In 1835, Elias Lönnrot published the *Kalevala,* whose heroic themes strengthened the growing sense of nationalism. Many Finnish leaders began to urge that Finnish be made an official language equal with Swedish. But Finnish did not become a fully equal official language until 1902.

In 1899, Czar Nicholas II began a program to force the Finns to accept Russian government and culture. He took away most of Finland's powers of self-rule and disbanded the Finnish national army. Russian was made the official language. In 1903, the Russian governor suspended Finland's constitution and became dictator. Finnish resistance reached a peak in 1905 with a six-day nationwide strike. The czar then restored much of Finland's self-government. In 1906, the Finns created their first parliament elected by all adult citizens, women as

Important dates in Finland

1100's-1200's Sweden gradually conquered all Finland.

1500's-1700's Sweden and Russia fought several wars for possession of Finland.

1809 Finland became a grand duchy of the Russian Empire.

1917 Finland declared its independence from Russia.

1918 Finnish socialists and nonsocialists fought a civil war.

1919 Finland adopted a republican constitution.

1939-1940 The U.S.S.R. defeated Finland in the Winter War.

1941-1944 The U.S.S.R. defeated Finland in the Continuation War.

1946 Finland established a policy of neutrality in international politics.

1955 Finland joined the United Nations (UN) and the Nordic Council.

1973 Finland and other EFTA members entered into free trade agreements with the European Community.

1981 President Urho Kekkonen resigned from office because of poor health. He had served as president since 1956.

well as men. During the next several years, Russia again tried to Russianize Finland.

Finland stayed out of World War I (1914-1918). But its merchant ships were blockaded in the Gulf of Bothnia, and the country suffered food shortages and unemployment. In 1917, a revolution in Russia overthrew the czar. Finland then decided to declare its freedom.

The new republic. Finland declared its independence from Russia on Dec. 6, 1917. Russia's new Bolshevik (Communist) government recognized the new nation, but some Russian troops remained in Finland. In preparing for independence, the Finns had become divided into two groups—socialists, who formed armed units called the Red Guard, and nonsocialists, who formed armed units called the White Guard. Both groups had demanded Finnish independence, but the socialists also wanted revolutionary social changes.

In January 1918, the White Guard, led by Carl Gustaf Mannerheim, began operations in western Finland to expel the Russian troops. Meanwhile, the Red Guard attempted to take over the Finnish government in Helsinki. A bloody civil war broke out between the two groups. The Whites received aid from Germany, and the Reds from Russia. The war ended in a White victory in May 1918.

In 1919, Finland adopted a republican constitution, and Kaarlo Juho Ståhlberg became the first president. But Finland's relations with Sweden and Russia remained unsettled. Finland and Sweden quarreled over possession of the Åland Islands. In 1921, the League of Nations awarded the islands to Finland. Disputes with Russia centered on Karelia, a large region east of present-day Finland. Finland demanded that the eastern part of Karelia be made part of Finland, like the rest of Karelia, or that it be made independent of Russia. Russia did not accept either of these demands, and relations between the two countries remained tense for years.

World War II (1939-1945). Although Finland never officially allied itself with any nation in World War II, the U.S.S.R. invaded the country twice. The *Winter War* began on Nov. 30, 1939, when Soviet troops marched into Finland. Mannerheim led the strong Finnish resistance, which included troops on skis. But Finland had to agree to a peace treaty in March 1940. Under the peace treaty, Finland was forced to give up the southern part of Karelia, where 12 per cent of the Finnish people lived. The area made up a tenth of Finland's territory and included Lake Ladoga and Finland's second largest city, Viipuri (now Vyborg). The U.S.S.R. also received a naval base at Hangö in the southwestern part of Finland.

In 1941, Finland allowed Germany to station troops in northern Finland and to move them through the region to attack the U.S.S.R. The U.S.S.R. then bombed Finland, beginning the *Continuation War.* Finnish troops recaptured southern Karelia. But in 1944, Soviet troops pushed farther and farther into Finland, and the country had to give up. On Sept. 19, 1944, Finland and the U.S.S.R. signed an armistice. As the German troops retreated from northern Finland, they burned towns, villages, and forests behind them.

The destruction by the Germans was only part of Finland's heavy war losses. About 100,000 Finns died, and about 50,000 were permanently disabled. The U.S.S.R. regained southern Karelia and won other Finnish territories as well. The U.S.S.R. also leased a military base at Porkkala, near Helsinki, but gave up its base at Hangö. About 420,000 Karelians fled to Finland, where the government gave them new land. Finland also had to pay the U.S.S.R. large *reparations* (payment for damages). See Russo-Finnish wars.

Postwar developments. Mannerheim became Finland's president in 1944, but he retired in 1946 because of poor health. Juho K. Paasikivi finished Mannerheim's term and was elected to a full term in 1950. Paasikivi set a policy of Finnish neutrality in international politics. Under him, Finland also developed close economic and cultural ties with the U.S.S.R. and the Scandinavian countries—Denmark, Norway, and Sweden. In 1955, the U.S.S.R. returned Porkkala to Finland, and the two nations renewed a 1948 treaty of friendship and assistance.

Also in 1955, Finland joined both the United Nations (UN) and the Nordic Council, which includes Denmark, Iceland, Norway, and Sweden. Citizens of Nordic Council countries may work and receive social benefits in any member nation and travel among member nations without a passport or visa. As a result, many Finns have moved to Sweden, which has a more developed economy and more social welfare benefits than Finland has.

In 1956, Urho Kekkonen was elected president. He continued to emphasize neutrality in international affairs and was reelected in 1962 and 1968.

Finland today stresses friendship with all nations, especially the U.S.S.R., and cooperation with Scandinavia. In late 1973, Finland and the other members of EFTA entered into agreements with another economic group, the European Community. The agreements reduced tariffs among all the nations of both groups. Earlier, in January 1973, Finland's parliament passed a special bill to extend Kekkonen's term from 1974 to 1978. Parliament hoped the bill would assure the U.S.S.R. that Kekkonen's policies of neutrality would not change because of the economic agreement with the European Community. President Kekkonen was reelected again in 1978. In September 1981, he took a medical leave from office and Prime Minister Mauno Koivisto became acting presi-

dent. Kekkonen resigned from office in October 1981 because of poor health. Koivisto was elected president in January 1982. Kekkonen died in 1986. In 1988, Koivisto was reelected.

During the late 1970's and early 1980's, Finland completed construction of four nuclear power plants. These plants supply more than a third of the nation's energy needs. Finland hopes to improve the economy in the underdeveloped north and so relieve overcrowding in the booming south.   Pekka Kalevi Hamalainen

Related articles in *World Book* include:

Biographies

Aalto, Alvar	Mannerheim,	Saarinen (family)
Kekkonen, Urho	Carl G.	Sibelius, Jean

Other related articles

City planning (picture: Tapiola, Finland)	Russo-Finnish wars
	Sauna
Helsinki	Tampere
Lapland	Tapiola

Outline

I. Government
  A. The president
  B. The prime minister and Cabinet
  C. The parliament
  D. Local government
  E. Political parties
  F. Courts
  G. Armed forces

II. People
  A. Ancestry and population
  B. Languages
  C. Way of life
  D. Social welfare
  E. Recreation
  F. Education
  G. Religion
  H. The arts

III. The land
  A. Land regions
  B. Rivers

IV. Climate

V. Economy
  A. Natural resources
  B. Forestry
  C. Service industries
  D. Manufacturing
  E. Agriculture
  F. Foreign trade
  G. Transportation
  H. Communication

VI. History

Questions

What are Finland's two official languages?
In which region of Finland do most of the people live?
How has Finland's location between the U.S.S.R. and Sweden influenced its history?
What are the chief manufacturing industries in Finland?
What is the *Kalevala?* How has it affected Finnish arts?
Why does Finland have a much milder climate than most other regions of the world that lie as far north?
What did the U.S.S.R. receive from Finland after the Winter War?
What is a *sauna?*
What are some of Finland's social welfare policies?
About how many lakes does Finland have?

Additional resources

American University. *Area Handbook for Finland.* U.S. Government Printing Office, 1974.
Hintz, Martin. *Finland.* Childrens Press, 1983. For younger readers.
Mead, William R. *Finland.* Praeger, 1968. A historical and geographical survey.
Nagel's Encyclopedia Guide: Finland. National Textbook, 1987. First published in 1980.
Rajanen, Aini. *Of Finnish Ways.* Dillon Press, 1981.

Finlay, Carlos Juan (1833-1915), was the first person to report evidence that yellow fever might be transmitted by the bite of the *Stegomyia* mosquito (*Aëdes aegypti*). The American Yellow Fever Commission went to Havana, Cuba, in 1900, and Finlay convinced its members that his theory was correct. Finlay was born in Puerto Principe (now Camagüey), Cuba. He was chief sanitary officer of Cuba from 1902 to 1908. He studied at Jefferson Medical College in Philadelphia. See also **Yellow fever.**   Noah D. Fabricant

Finn MacCool, *FIHN muh KOOL,* was the leader of the Fianna, an Irish band of warriors who appear in the Fenian cycle of ancient Irish tales. His name is also spelled *MacCumhal.* The tales are set in the province of Leinster about A.D. 200. Finn is also a familiar figure in Irish folk tales, sometimes portrayed as a giant. Several tales tell how Finn burned his thumb while cooking the salmon of knowledge. He put his thumb in his mouth to ease the pain. From that day, he had only to put his thumb in his mouth when he was perplexed to discover the solution to a problem. See also **Mythology** (Celtic mythology [The Fenian cycle]).

Fenian tales focus not only on Finn but also on his son, Oisin, and his grandson, Oscar. Finn and Oisin appear as Fingal and Ossian in the Ossianic poems published by the Scottish poet James Macpherson from 1760 to 1765. Macpherson claimed he had translated the poems from originals written by Ossian, but Macpherson was revealed as the actual author of at least some of them. Finn and Oisin also appear in the work of writers of the Irish Literary Renaissance of the late 1800's, notably in the poem *The Wanderings of Oisin* (1889) by William Butler Yeats. Finn as a giant is also the model for the character of Finn in James Joyce's experimental novel *Finnegans Wake* (1939).   Janet Egleson Dunleavy

Finnish spitz is a strong, sturdy dog related to the Siberian husky, the Samoyed, and other Arctic dogs. A Finnish spitz looks somewhat like a fox. The dog has a thick, red-gold coat; erect, pointed ears; and dark brown eyes. Its bushy, curled tail falls over its hindquarters. The male Finnish spitz stands from $17\frac{1}{2}$ to 20 inches (44.5 to

The Finnish spitz is the national dog of Finland.

51 centimeters) tall at the shoulder and weighs about 30 pounds (14 kilograms). The female is slightly smaller.

The Finnish spitz is the national dog of Finland. It is descended from dogs used for hunting by the early Finns. Finns still use the dog to hunt game birds. Outside Finland, however, the Finnish spitz is kept primarily

as a pet. The dog is intelligent and good-tempered.
Critically reviewed by the Finnish Spitz Club of America

Finns. See Finland (People).

Fiord, *fyawrd,* also spelled *fjord,* is a long, narrow, winding inlet or arm of the sea. *Fiord* is a Norwegian word, applied to the deep bays and inlets along the ragged and mountainous coastline of Norway. Geologists believe that rivers cut these fiords, and glaciers deepened them millions of years ago. Most fiords have steep, rocky walls with thick woods and foaming, roaring waterfalls. Most fiords also have shallow *sills* (underwater ridges) at their mouths that become more deeply submerged further inland. Small stretches of fertile farmland lie below some of the fiord walls.

The coasts of Alaska, Maine, British Columbia, Greenland, and New Zealand contain inlets like Norway's fiords. *Sea loch* or *firth* is the name for such an inlet in Britain.   William C. Mahaney

See also **Firth; Norway** (Coast and islands; picture).

Fir is a common name for a number of handsome evergreen trees that belong to the pine family. Nine types of firs grow in the United States. Two grow in the East and seven in the mountains of the West. The *Douglas-fir,* a valuable timber tree, is not a true fir. It belongs to a separate *genus* (group) in the pine family (see **Douglas-fir**).

When it grows in the open, the fir tree is shaped somewhat like a pyramid. It has dense foliage. Its needle-shaped leaves do not grow in clusters like pine needles, but are distributed evenly all around the

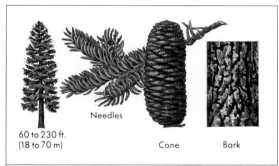

Needles

60 to 230 ft.
(18 to 70 m)   Cone   Bark

The California red fir grows in the mountains of western North America from Canada to southern California.

branch. They are usually soft, blunt, and fragrant. In many species the needles are dark green above, with two light-colored lines on the bottom surface. Firs have distinctive cylinder-shaped cones that grow upright on the branches. When the cones mature, they shed their scales, leaving a bare, spinelike axis. The bark of the young trees contains blisters that are filled with a resin called *balsam.*

Because of their attractive shape and fragrance, true firs are widely used as Christmas trees. Especially popular firs include the *balsam fir* and the *Fraser fir.* The balsam fir grows in northeastern North America and in the states bordering the Great Lakes. Its bark is a source of *Canada balsam,* a substance used in medicine and varnish. The Fraser fir is found in the mountains of Virginia, North Carolina, and Tennessee.

The California red fir and some other western firs grow quite large and are valuable for their timber. One California red fir grew 230 feet (70) meters high and 6½ feet (2 meters) in circumference.

Scientific classification. Firs belong to the pine family, Pinaceae, and make up the genus *Abies.* The balsam fir is *A. balsamea* and the Fraser fir is *A. fraseri.* The California red fir is *A. magnifica.*   Douglas G. Sprugel

See also **Balsam; Conifer; Tree** (Familiar broadleaf and needleleaf trees [picture]).

Firdausi, *fehr DOW see* (940?-1020?), was the pen name taken by Abul Qasim Mansur, the greatest epic poet of Persia. His name is also spelled Firdusi.

The major work of Firdausi is the *Shah-Nameh (Book of Kings),* which traces the history of Persia from the creation of the world to the Muslim conquest in the A.D. 600's. The poem runs more than 50,000 lines long. The central character of much of the first two-thirds of the epic poem is Rostam, who is the chief folk hero of Iran.
Dick Davis

Fire. The earliest use people made of fire was to keep warm. As civilizations advanced, people learned to use fire in many other ways. People learned to use fire to cook food, to shape weapons and tools, to change clay into pottery, and to furnish light. But early peoples had extremely slow and unsatisfactory ways of kindling fires. Today, we have not only improved the methods of kindling fires, but we also use fire in many more ways. Fire furnishes the energy to drive machines, and keeps industries running. It supplies the power to drive trains, ships, and planes; and it generates electricity. Fire is also sometimes used to remove and destroy waste materials. In addition, fire is used in separating most metals from their ores, as well as in forging and shaping metals into useful things.

Controlled fire is useful. But fire can also be destructive. Uncontrolled fire kills thousands of people and destroys billions of dollars worth of property each year. Fires burned down large parts of London in 1666, Chicago in 1871, and Tokyo in 1923. Fires also destroy large areas of trees and brush every year.

What is fire?

Fire is the heat and light that comes from burning substances. In 1777, Antoine Lavoisier, a French chemist, proved that burning is the result of the rapid union of oxygen with other substances (see **Lavoisier, Antoine L.**). As a substance burns, heat and light are produced. Burning is also called *combustion.* Often oxygen unites with other substances at such a slow rate that little heat and no light are given off. When this happens, we call the process *oxidation,* rather than *burning* or *combustion.* Oxidation takes place whenever oxygen unites with other substances either rapidly or slowly. For example, when oxygen unites with gasoline, the action takes place rapidly and heat and light are given off. This process may be described by any of the three words, burning, combustion, or oxidation. When oxygen unites with iron and causes it to rust, burning, or combustion, does not take place, but oxidation does.

Kinds of fire. All substances do not burn in the same manner. Charcoal, for example, gives off heat with a faint glow. But other substances, such as coal, gas, magnesium, oil, and wood, give off heat with a flame. The color of the flame depends chiefly on the kind of material being burned and on the temperature.

Substances may burn in different ways, but they all require oxygen to burn. Sometimes old rags soaked with oil or paint are thrown aside and forgotten. Oxygen from the air may slowly unite with the oil in the rags. At first, there will not be a fire. But as oxidation gradually takes place, enough heat accumulates to set the rags on fire. This type of burning, called *spontaneous combustion,* causes many fires.

Very rapid burning may cause explosions like those produced by gunpowder and dynamite. Here, oxidation takes place so rapidly that great volumes of gases are produced. These require many hundreds of times the

Jones & Laughlin Steel Corp.

Controlled fire is essential in various industrial processes, especially in the manufacture of steel, shown here. Intense flames melt scrap iron, iron ore, and other raw materials in an open-hearth furnace to produce molten steel.

© Chuck O'Rear, West Light

Uncontrolled fire, like this house fire, can be extremely destructive. Such fire kills thousands of people and destroys billions of dollars of property every year. Water puts out fire by cooling the burning materials.

space that was formerly occupied by the gunpowder or dynamite before it was oxidized. These gases expand so rapidly and violently that they produce an explosion.

How fire is produced. Three conditions must exist before a fire can be made. There must be a fuel or a substance that will burn. The fuel must be heated to its *ignition temperature*. This is the lowest temperature at which combustion can begin and continue. Finally, there must be plenty of oxygen, which usually comes from the surrounding air.

Fuels are of three classes, solids, liquids, and gases. Coal and wood are examples of solids. Oil and gasoline are liquid fuels. Natural gas and hydrogen are gaseous fuels.

The burning of a solid fuel often depends on the form of the fuel. For example, you may not be able to light a large log with a match, but a small twig from the same tree may catch fire easily with the same match. This is because heat flows to the inside of the log, and the log cannot maintain a high enough temperature to keep burning. But when several logs are burned together, heat also flows from each log to the others and keeps the fire going. This explains why it is easy to start a fire with splinters or shavings.

The ignition temperatures of fuels differ. For a solid or liquid fuel to ignite, some of the fuel must first be heated to the temperature at which it *vaporizes* (turns to a gas). Solids generally have higher ignition temperatures than liquids because they vaporize at higher temperatures. For example, the ignition temperatures of most woods and plastics range from about 500° to 900° F. (260° to 480° C). A liquid fuel such as gasoline can ignite at a temperature as low as −36° F. (−38° C).

In addition, every fuel has two ignition temperatures. At one temperature, combustion can occur with the help of an outside energy source, such as a match. At another, higher temperature, combustion can occur spontaneously—that is, without outside help.

How fires behave. A candle burning in a room without drafts produces a steady flame. The flame's heat vaporizes just enough candle wax to keep the flame burning at the same height.

Uncontrolled fires, on the other hand, fuel themselves by vaporizing the solid or liquid materials they find in their path. A house fire or forest fire may begin with easily ignitible materials. As the fire grows, it radiates more heat. The heat contributes to further growth, and the process accelerates as long as fuel and oxygen remain available. In a house fire, a phenomenon known as *flashover* occurs when all the surfaces in a room reach their ignition temperature. At this point, a relatively small fire suddenly ignites the remaining materials, filling the room with flames. In a forest fire, leaves, twigs, and other materials along the ground usually make up the fuel. But wind and certain types of terrain may cause a forest fire to spread along the tops of trees. Because fires can grow quickly and suddenly, professional fire fighters should be called immediately to control them.

We can control the fire in a furnace by regulating the supply of fuel and oxygen it receives. But only winds and the flow of air created by the fire regulate the rate of burning of an uncontrolled fire.

Fireproof materials. The term *fireproof* suggests that a material has been treated with a substance that will prevent it from burning. But no material is truly fireproof. Even such incombustible materials as concrete and stone can become damaged by an intense fire.

Materials can, however, be treated with a *fire retardant* to reduce their ability to burn. Most fire retardants act to raise the ignition temperature of a material or to reduce the heat produced by combustion. Such treatments can slow combustion but they do not eliminate it. See **Fireproofing.**

Methods of starting fires. There are several methods of starting a fire, but in each of them the three necessary conditions for a fire must be present. Before matches were invented, the flint and steel method was used. This method required a piece of steel, a flint (hard rock), and a tinder. The tinder was generally made from cotton or linen cloth, or from dried, powdered bark from certain trees. It was heated in an oven until it was nearly ready to burn. It was then placed in a tinderbox to keep it perfectly dry. When the fire was to be started, tinder was placed on the ground and the flint struck against the steel. Some of the sparks made by the flint and steel would fly into the tinder and light it.

Another early method of starting fires was by friction. This method consisted of whirling a stick in a notch in a board until the wood powder that was produced began to glow. Enough oxygen to turn the glow into a blaze was supplied by blowing carefully on the glowing powder.

The first match was invented in 1827 by the English pharmacist John Walker. The tip of this match was coated with a mixture of antimony sulfide and potassium chlorate that was held on the wooden matchstick by gum arabic and starch. When this tip was rubbed on a rough surface, friction produced enough heat to ignite the chemicals. The burning chemicals then produced enough heat to ignite the matchstick. Safer and more efficient matches were developed later. See **Match** (History).

What fire produces

An entire piece of wood or coal will not burn, even if there is sufficient oxygen present. Most of us have taken the ashes from a charcoal grill or fireplace. The ash, generally a mixture of minerals, is present in the fuel, but will not unite with the oxygen. Some fuels have a lower ash content than others. This is important to remember when buying charcoal or wood because you want the fuel with the lowest ash content, provided that it is good in other respects.

Often the bottom of a pan or a skillet becomes black when it is placed over a fire. This discoloration occurs because of soot. Soot is primarily unburned carbon. The skillet becomes coated because it cools the flame, preventing the temperature from getting high enough to burn the fuel completely. If a furnace produces great quantities of soot, some of the carbon of the fuel is not being burned, and is wasted. This problem can be remedied by seeing that sufficient air is supplied to burn all the carbon in the fuel.

Gases. Substances that burn in air are nearly always composed of two elements, carbon and hydrogen, or their compounds. For example, coal, coke, and charcoal are mostly carbon. Natural gas, gasoline, and fuel oils consist of many compounds of hydrogen and carbon.

When these fuels burn, the oxygen of the air unites with the carbon and hydrogen to form carbon dioxide gas and water vapor. These usually mix with the air and disappear. The uniting of the oxygen with the hydrogen and the carbon is what produces the heat and flame of the fire.

Often, a deadly gas called carbon monoxide forms when there is not enough oxygen to burn the fuel completely. For example, when gasoline burns in an automobile engine, some of this gas forms and comes out the exhaust pipe. If you are in a closed garage when this happens, you are in danger of breathing this gas. Death may result. A person should never run the engine of an automobile in a closed garage.

Most people who are killed in fires in buildings die from inhaling carbon monoxide. Both smoldering fires and too little oxygen following flashover can promote the production of this gas.

Smoke is a mixture of soot and other particles with the gases produced by combustion. Smoke from fires can contain carbon monoxide and other poisonous gases. The soot and particles hamper vision and thus can make it difficult to escape from fires. In general, smoke results from incomplete combustion, which wastes energy and pollutes the environment.

Light. Most of the energy caused by a fire goes into heat, but some of it goes into light. The light results either because the carbon particles in the flame become so hot that they give off light energy, or because the gas that is burning is a type that gives off light.

Ever since fire was discovered, people have been trying to convert more energy from heat into light energy. People first used flaming pieces of wood as torches. They later discovered that if the wood was dipped into pitch before lighting it, the light lasted longer and was much brighter. Years afterward, people poured oil in a dish, placed a wick in it, and lighted the wick. This gave a better light. Later, the tallow candle, which people could conveniently carry around, was invented. The kerosene lamp, with its chimney to help control the air currents, was a big improvement over the candle. After electricity was made usable, the American inventor Thomas A. Edison sent an electric current through a carbon *filament* (wire) until the filament became so hot that it gave off light.

Fire in legend and religion

We can only guess that prehistoric people may have gained a knowledge of fire from observing things in nature, such as lightning, the fire of volcanoes, and the heat of the sun. They also must have noticed that sparks fly when stones are struck upon one another, or when the hoofs or claws of an animal strike some hard substance.

In Persian literature, there is a story of the discovery of fire in a fight with a dragon. One of the stones which the hero used as weapons missed the monster and struck a rock. Light shone forth and human beings saw fire for the first time. The mythology of nearly all early peoples contains some account of accidental or supernatural happenings which first revealed fire to human beings. Early peoples regarded fire as a true gift of the gods.

Fire was considered sacred because it was so essen-

tial to the welfare of people. Fire worship and sun worship have existed since very early times. Because fire was so hard to produce, the custom soon became common of keeping a public fire, which was never allowed to die out. These fires were kept in every village among the Egyptians, Persians, Greeks, and Romans. They were often in the civic center of the community.

The Temple of Vesta in Rome was an outstanding example of the importance of fire to the Romans. Vesta was originally the goddess of the hearth, and her shrine was in every home. But when religion became an affair of state, a temple was erected in which the sacred fire was kept burning at all times. See **Vesta.**

James G. Quintiere

Related articles in *World Book* include:

Camping (Building a campfire)	Fire department	Fireproofing
	Fire extinguisher	Match
Combustion	Fire prevention	Prometheus

Additional resources

Level I
Adler, Irving. *Fire in Your Life*. Harper, 1955.
O'Donnell, James J. *Fire! Its Many Faces and Moods*. Messner, 1980.
Pringle, Laurence P. *Natural Fire: Its Ecology in Forests*. Morrow, 1979.

Level II
Lyons, John W. *Fire*. Scientific American Books, 1985.
Pyne, Stephen J. *Fire in America: A Cultural History of Wildland and Rural Fire*. Princeton, 1982.

Fire alarm. See **Fire department.**

Fire ant is any of several species of ants that inflict painful, burning stings. Five species of fire ants are found in the Southeastern United States. One of these, the red imported fire ant, is a major pest. Red imported fire ants build large dirt mounds that measure up to 2 feet (0.6 meter) high. The mounds are so hard they can damage farm machinery. Hundreds of thousands of fire ants may inhabit one mound. If a person or animal disturbs the activities of a mound, the ants swarm out to attack the intruder. The red imported fire ant's sting leaves a small, pus-filled, itchy bump that is easily infected. Some people experience severe—in rare cases, fatal—reactions to fire ant venom.

Red imported fire ants range in color from red to brown, and measure about $\frac{1}{4}$ inch (6 millimeters) long. This species is native to South America. It probably entered the United States by accident aboard freight shipped through Mobile, Ala., during the 1930's. It has since spread rapidly and now inhabits an area that stretches from southern North Carolina to central Texas. In the 1980's, scientists developed fire ant baits that contain soybean oil, which is used to attract the insects. An ingredient in the baits disrupts the development of the larva. The use of such baits may help control the population of fire ants.

The four other species of fire ants in the Southeastern United States do not pose major agricultural or health problems. Three of these species are native to this region. The fourth—the black imported fire ant—is a South American species that probably entered the United States in 1918.

Scientific classification. Fire ants belong to the order Hymenoptera. The red imported fire ant is classified as *Solenopsis invicta*.   S. Bradleigh Vinson

Fire blight. See **Pear** (Diseases); **Blight.**

Fighting fires is one of the most important tasks of a fire department. Many fire fighters and a variety of equipment are needed to put out a large building fire, such as the one shown above.

Fire department

Fire department is one of the most important organizations in a community. Fire departments battle fires that break out in homes, factories, office buildings, stores, and other places. Fire fighters risk their lives to save people and protect property from fires. They have one of the most dangerous of all occupations. In the United States, a higher percentage of fire fighters are killed or injured on the job than are workers in any other occupation.

The men and women who work for fire departments also help people in many kinds of emergencies besides fires. For example, they rescue persons who may be trapped in cars or trains after an accident. They aid victims of such disasters as tornadoes and floods.

Fire departments work to prevent fires by enforcing fire safety laws. They also teach people about possible fire dangers in their homes and places of work. People cause most fires through carelessness. They could prevent these fires if they knew about fire hazards and followed certain safety measures. Every year in the United States, fires kill about 6,000 people, injure about 28,000 others, and destroy more than $7 billion worth of property. To reduce the damage caused by fires, local fire departments need the support of the people in the community.

In colonial America, fires often destroyed whole settlements. When a fire broke out, all the people in the community rushed to the scene. They formed a row from a source of water to the fire and passed buckets of water from one person to another to put the fire out. As cities and towns grew larger, volunteer and paid fire departments were organized. Today, U.S. fire departments have well-trained men and women and a variety of modern fire-fighting equipment.

The work of a fire department

Fire fighting. The two basic fire-fighting units in most fire departments are *engine companies* and *ladder companies*. Engine companies operate trucks called *pumpers,* which carry a pump and hoses for spraying water on a fire. Ladder companies use *ladder trucks,* which carry an extension ladder or elevating platform to rescue people through the windows of buildings. Ladder trucks also have other rescue equipment and fire-fighting tools. In most large cities, each neighborhood fire station has at least one engine company and one ladder company. At a fire, the members of the engine and ladder companies work together as a team under the direction of an officer.

Fire departments must handle many types of fires. Each type requires a different plan of action to put it out. For example, the methods used to fight a building fire differ greatly from those used to fight a forest or grassland fire. The following discussion describes how fire fighters battle the two types.

Fighting a building fire. After an alarm is received, the engine and ladder companies speed to the fire. They often arrive within a few minutes after receiving the alarm. The officer in command quickly sizes up the situation and directs the fire fighters into action.

James W. Smith, the contributor of this article, is coauthor of Analytic Approaches to Public Fire Protection. *The article was critically reviewed by the United States Fire Administration.*

The members of the engine company first connect a hose from the pump to a nearby fire hydrant. They then stretch hose lines from the pump to the building on fire and try to locate the fire within the building. Their first concern is to keep the fire from spreading. The fire fighters spray water on any nearby buildings that are in danger of catching fire. They then direct water on the fire itself until it is out.

Meanwhile, the members of the ladder company search for people who may be trapped in the building. In some buildings, they use ladders to rescue people through windows. However, the ladders on most trucks extend up to only about eight stories. Fire fighters must use elevators or stairs to get to persons trapped on floors above the reach of the ladders.

Ladder company members must also ventilate the building to let out the smoke, heat, and gases that build up during a fire. They open or break windows and sometimes cut holes in the roof or walls. If the building were not ventilated, the heat and the pressure of the gases could cause an explosion.

The ladder company tries to save any furniture or other property not damaged by the fire. The members spread canvas or rubber covers over such property to prevent water damage. Finally, the ladder company searches the building for hidden sparks that might cause another blaze.

After the fire is out, the fire fighters try to find out exactly where and how the fire started. The officer in charge makes out a report that gives all the important facts about the fire. The report includes information on the number of persons killed, if any; the cause of the fire; and the estimated cost of damage.

Fighting a grassland or forest fire. Many grassland and forest fires occur in areas that are hard to reach and far from a source of water. Local fire departments have trucks that carry water and can travel over rough land. Observers in helicopters or airplanes may fly over the fire and report on its size and behavior. Sometimes, helicopters or airplanes are also used to carry fire fighters to the fire or to drop chemicals that slow the spread of the fire.

Grassland and forest fires often spread rapidly and are difficult to put out. Fire fighters try to keep the fire within the smallest area possible, and so they may first create a *firebreak,* or *fireline.* The fire fighters clear a strip of land some distance in front of the racing flames. They cut down the grass or trees and scrape away some of the soil with shovels or a bulldozer. The fire fighters may then set a *backfire* to burn the area between the firebreak and the onrushing fire. The firebreak and the backfire prevent the flames from spreading. After the fire has been contained, the fire fighters spray water or throw dirt on the flames until the fire is out.

Emergency rescue operations. Large fire departments have rescue companies to handle nonfire emergencies. For example, rescue workers may be called to free persons trapped under the wreckage of a fallen building or in a car after an accident. Rescue workers sometimes have to break through walls or cut through metal doors to reach an injured person.

Rescue companies also go to major fires. At a building fire, for example, the rescue workers help the ladder company get people out of the building. They give first aid to people overcome by smoke or suffering from burns and then rush them to a hospital.

Some fire departments have *paramedic units,* which give on-the-scene medical care in an emergency. Fire fighters trained as paramedics treat heart attack victims and other persons needing emergency attention. The paramedics operate ambulances that carry medical equipment, drugs, and a two-way radio for contact with a nearby hospital. See **Paramedic.**

Fire prevention and fire safety. To help prevent fires and reduce fire losses, local fire departments inspect public buildings and private homes. They also

Fire fighters ventilate a building by chopping holes in the roof, if necessary. Ventilation lets out smoke and gases that build up during a fire and that could cause an explosion.

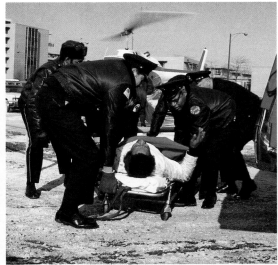

Chicago Fire Department

Fire department paramedics treat persons needing emergency medical care and rush them to a hospital. The paramedics operate ambulances that carry medical equipment and drugs.

teach people about fire safety and conduct *arson* investigations. Arson is the crime of purposely setting fire to a building or other property. Many fire departments have a separate division that carries out fire prevention and fire safety programs.

Public building inspections. Most cities have a fire safety code that applies to such buildings as theaters, department stores, schools, and hospitals. Under these codes, the buildings may not be constructed of materials that burn easily. The codes also require portable fire extinguishers, a certain number of exits, and other fire safety features in public buildings.

Fire department officials inspect public buildings from time to time to enforce the local code. The officials check the condition of the electrical equipment and the heating system. They note the number and location of exits and fire extinguishers. The inspection also covers housekeeping conditions and many other matters that affect fire safety. Fire department inspectors may also review plans for a new building to make sure it meets the safety code.

Home inspections. Most of the deaths caused by fires occur in private homes. For this reason, many fire departments have home safety programs. They will send a fire fighter to inspect a private home if asked by the owner. After the inspection, the fire fighter recommends ways to make the home safer from fire.

During home inspections, fire fighters check the heating and air-conditioning systems and the cooking equipment. They look for unsafe practices, such as overloading electrical outlets or running electrical cords under a rug. The fire fighters also instruct families on what to do if a fire breaks out. To leave the home safely and quickly in case of fire, families are advised to make escape plans and to practice fire drills. For other recommended instructions, see the table *What to do in case of fire* on this page.

Most fire departments advise people to install *smoke detectors* in their homes. Smoke detectors are devices that sound an alarm if smoke builds up in a room. The devices are atttached to the ceiling or wall in several areas of the home. Most home fires that result in deaths occur at night when the family is asleep. Smoke detectors will awaken the family before the fire and the smoke build up to the point where escape is impossible. *Heat detectors,* which sound an alarm if the temperature rises to a certain point, are also available. However, smoke detectors generally give an earlier warning than do most heat detectors.

Fire departments also recommend that people have portable fire extinguishers in their homes. A person must be sure, however, to use the right kind of extinguisher for the type of fire involved. For example, a water extinguisher cannot put out a grease fire. Such a fire can be fought with a special gas extinguisher. For more information on the kinds of fires and extinguishers, see the article **Fire extinguisher.**

Public education programs. Many fire departments work with other local agencies to teach people how to prevent fires and what procedures to follow during a fire. In some communities, fire department officials serve as instructors or advisers in fire safety courses in the schools. They also supervise school fire drills.

Arson investigations. Many fire departments have a

What to do in case of fire

1. **Leave the building immediately.** Do not try to fight the fire unless it is confined to a small area.
2. **Never open a door that feels hot.** Before opening any door, place your hand on it. If the door feels hot, the fire on the other side may be blazing fiercely. You could be killed by the heat and smoke if you opened the door. Try another escape route or wait for help.
3. **Crawl on the floor when going through a smoky area.** Smoke and heated gases tend to rise, and so they will be thinnest near the floor.
4. **Do not run if your clothes catch fire.** Running fans and spreads flames. Roll on the floor to smother the flames.
5. **Do not return to the building for any reason.** After you have escaped, call the fire department. If people are still trapped in the building, wait for the fire department to rescue them.

---

squad of specially trained investigators who gather evidence in cases where arson is suspected. Fire department officials in some cities estimate that nearly half the fires in their cities are purposely set.

Fire department equipment

The most important equipment of a fire department includes (1) communication systems, (2) fire trucks, and (3) special fire vehicles. In addition, the fire fighters themselves require protective clothing.

Communication systems are necessary to alert fire departments to the outbreak of a fire. Most fire alarms are telephoned to the fire department. Other alarms are sent from (1) fire alarm boxes or (2) automatic signaling devices. All alarms go to the department's *alarm headquarters,* which then quickly alerts the neighborhood station closest to the fire.

Milt and Joan Mann

The alarm headquarters of a fire department receives all alarms reporting the outbreak of a fire. An operator alerts the nearest fire station, which sends fire fighters to the scene.

Fire alarm boxes stand on street corners in some cities. Most of these boxes contain a telephone or two-way radio that can be used to talk directly to operators at alarm headquarters. Other boxes operate by telegraph and send a coded signal to the alarm center when a person pulls a lever. The signal indicates the location of the box.

Automatic signaling devices are installed in many public buildings. These devices include smoke and heat detectors that are wired to send an alarm automatically to alarm headquarters. A *sprinkler system* can also be wired to alert the fire department automatically. Such a system consists of a network of pipes installed throughout a building. The pipes carry water to nozzles in the ceiling. The heat from a fire causes the nozzles directly above the fire to open and spray water. When the water starts to flow through the pipes, an alarm is automatically sent to the fire department.

Alarm headquarters in a small fire department may consist of one switchboard operator. Some large fire departments have a computerized system of receiving alarms and notifying fire stations.

After fire fighters arrive at a fire, they advise alarm headquarters how serious the situation is and, if necessary, ask for more help. With each call for additional help, more equipment and companies are sent to the fire. Each fire truck has a two-way radio for communication with headquarters.

Fire trucks. Fire departments have several types of fire trucks. The main kinds are (1) pumpers, (2) ladder trucks, and (3) rescue trucks.

Pumpers have a large pump that takes water from a fire hydrant or other source. The pump boosts the pressure of the water and forces it through hose lines. The pump size is determined by the amount of water it can discharge per minute. The most common sizes deliver 750 to 1,500 gallons (2,840 to 5,680 liters) per minute.

Pumpers carry several sizes of hoses and nozzles. Many pumpers also have a small-diameter hose called a *booster line,* which is wound on a reel. The booster line

Three kinds of fire trucks   The illustrations below show an elevating platform truck, a pumper, and an aerial ladder truck. All three trucks are used to spray water on a fire. Elevating platform and aerial ladder trucks can also be used to rescue people through the windows of a burning building.

WORLD BOOK illustrations by George Suyeoka

is used chiefly to put out small outdoor fires. Pumpers used for fighting grass or brush fires carry a tank of water and such tools as shovels and rakes.

Ladder trucks. There are two kinds of ladder trucks— *aerial ladder* and *elevating platform.* An aerial ladder truck has a metal extension ladder mounted on a turntable. The ladder can be raised as high as 100 feet (30 meters), or about eight stories. An elevating-platform truck, commonly called a *snorkel,* has a cagelike platform that can hold several persons. The platform is attached to a lifting device, either an *articulating boom* or a *telescoping boom,* which is mounted on a turntable. The boom on the largest trucks can extend 150 feet (46 meters). A built-in hose runs the length of the boom and is used to direct water on a fire.

Ladder trucks are equipped with portable ladders, stretchers, and first-aid kits. They also carry *forcible entry tools* to break into a building or a room. These tools include axes, power saws, and sledge hammers.

Rescue trucks are enclosed vehicles equipped with many of the same kinds of forcible entry tools that ladder trucks carry. But rescue trucks also carry additional equipment for unusual rescues. They have such tools as oxyacetylene torches, for cutting through metal, and hydraulic jacks, for lifting heavy objects. They also carry scuba gear, fire-resistant suits, and emergency medical supplies and equipment.

Special fire vehicles include *airport crash trucks* and *fireboats.* Airport crash trucks are pumpers that spray foam or dry chemicals on burning aircraft. Water is ineffective against many aircraft fires, such as those that involve jet fuel, gasoline, or certain aircraft metals. Fireboats fight fires on ships and piers and in waterfront buildings. These boats have pumps that draw water from a river, lake, or ocean. Large seagoing fireboats can pump about 10,000 gallons (38,000 liters) of water per minute.

Protective clothing. Fire fighters require special clothing for protection against flames, falling objects, and other hazards. They wear knee-length coats made of fire-resistant material and protective pants and shirts. Other clothing includes specially made boots, gloves, and helmets. Fire fighters also use masks to avoid inhaling smoke and toxic gases. The masks are connected to small air cylinders strapped on the back.

On certain rare occasions, fire fighters must walk through flames. For instance, they may do so when rescuing passengers from a burning airplane. They then wear *heat-reflective suits.* These suits are fire resistant and coated with aluminum to reflect heat. They cover the whole body, leaving no part unprotected.

Kinds of fire departments

The main kinds of fire departments are (1) volunteer, (2) paid, and (3) special purpose. About 27,000 volunteer and paid fire departments protect communities in the United States. Most of these departments are volunteer organizations. Special-purpose departments are maintained by certain government agencies and some private industries.

Volunteer departments provide protection mainly in small towns and rural communities. They are staffed by men and women who serve part time. Some departments have a few paid fire fighters but rely chiefly on

Some equipment carried on fire trucks

Fire trucks carry a variety of *forcible entry tools,* such as axes and crowbars, which are used to break into a building or room. Other equipment on fire trucks includes first-aid kits, air cylinders and masks, and smoke ejectors.

WORLD BOOK illustrations by David Cunningham

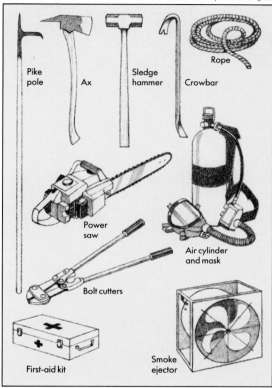

Pike pole
Ax
Sledge hammer
Crowbar
Rope
Power saw
Air cylinder and mask
Bolt cutters
First-aid kit
Smoke ejector

Chicago Fire Department

Protective clothing worn by fire fighters includes helmets, knee-length coats, gloves, and boots. The clothing protects fire fighters from flames, water, and other job hazards.

Owens-Corning Fiberglas Corporation

Heat-reflective suits are worn by fire fighters in special cases when they have to walk through flames. The suits are fire resistant and coated with aluminum to reflect heat.

volunteers. When a fire breaks out in the community, the volunteers leave their jobs or homes and rush to the fire station. In some departments, the volunteers are paid for their work, but in others they receive no pay.

Many volunteer departments have only enough equipment and volunteers for routine fires. In case of a major fire, departments from neighboring communities help one another. Most volunteer departments are headed by a fire chief, who is either appointed by the mayor or elected by members of the department.

Paid departments serve chiefly in larger cities. Some departments are organized on a county, district, or regional level. Paid departments are staffed by full-time fire fighters.

Paid fire departments in large cities have many fire-fighting companies, which operate from neighborhood fire stations. Each company is commanded by a captain or a lieutenant. Several companies make up a *battalion* or a *district*. Battalions may be further grouped into *divisions*. Large departments also have separate staffs that work in such areas as fire prevention, training, communications, and arson investigations. A fire chief, who is appointed by the mayor or some other city official, directs the entire fire department.

Special-purpose departments. The U.S. government maintains fire departments at all military bases and other large federal installations. These departments are trained to handle fires and other emergencies unique to a particular installation, as well as routine fires. For example, Air Force bases train fire fighters to battle aircraft fires, and nuclear power installations train fire fighters to deal with radiation emergencies. Certain federal and state agencies maintain fire-fighting units to watch for and put out forest fires.

Some industrial plants, such as those that manufacture fuels or explosives, organize their own fire departments. In addition, all major airports have a fire department to fight aircraft fires.

History

One of the first fire-fighting organizations was established in ancient Rome. Augustus, who became emperor in 27 B.C., formed a group called the *vigiles.* The vigiles patrolled the streets to watch for fires. They also served as the police force in Rome.

Scholars know little else about the development of fire-fighting organizations in Europe until after the Great Fire of London in 1666. This fire destroyed much of the city and left thousands of people homeless. Before the fire, London had no organized fire protection system. After the fire, insurance companies in the city formed private *fire brigades* to protect their clients' property.

The development of U.S. fire protection. The early American colonists fought building fires by forming *bucket brigades.* One row of volunteers passed buckets from a source of water to the fire. Another row passed back the empty buckets. The fire fighters also pulled down buildings next to the burning structure with iron hooks attached to ropes. In this way, they created a separation between the buildings to help prevent the fire from spreading.

Peter Stuyvesant, the governor of a colony that included what is now New York, made one of the first efforts to establish a fire prevention system. In 1648, he appointed four fire wardens to inspect homes in New Amsterdam, which later became New York City. The wardens' chief duty was to inspect chimneys for fire hazards. In 1658, Stuyvesant began one of the first community alarm systems. He appointed a number of men to patrol the streets at night and watch for fires. The men were called the *rattle watch* because they shook wooden rattles to alert the townspeople whenever a fire was discovered.

In 1679, Boston established the first paid fire department in the American Colonies. It consisted of a crew of men who operated a hand pump. In 1736, Benjamin Franklin founded the colonies' first volunteer fire department in Philadelphia.

By the early 1800's, many U.S. cities had volunteer fire departments. The departments required numerous volunteers to pull and operate the hand pumps and hose wagons. In many cities, the most prominent citizens belonged to the volunteer departments, which became powerful social and political organizations.

In the mid-1800's, steam pumpers pulled by horses began to replace hand pumps. The steam pumpers required fewer persons to operate them. About this time, many of the larger cities changed from volunteer to paid fire departments. During the early 1900's, steam pumpers were replaced by gasoline fire engines. Since then, many improvements have been made in the equipment and methods used in fire fighting.

Recent developments. During the 1970's, the U.S. government encouraged fire departments to devote more time and money to fire prevention activities. In 1974, the government established the National Fire Prevention and Control Administration, which became the United States Fire Administration (USFA) in 1978. The

Brown Bros.

Steam pumpers pulled by horses were used by fire departments from the mid-1800's to the early 1900's. At the time, they were a major improvement over the hand pumps formerly used.

USFA serves as an information center for fire departments in the United States. It also develops new fire prevention and control techniques for use by local departments. It also operates the National Academy for Fire Prevention and Control in Washington, D.C. The academy develops training programs for fire fighters and others who work in the field of fire prevention and control.

Since the 1960's, U.S. fire departments have been faced with drastic increases in arson. Between the mid-1960's and 1977, the arson rate increased about 300 per cent. In efforts to reduce the problem, some fire departments have hired more arson investigators and pushed for stronger laws against arson.

False alarms have also become a serious problem. In some United States cities, a third or more of all alarms received by the fire department are false alarms. Some fire departments have removed alarm boxes from areas with a long record of false alarms. Other departments send fewer companies to answer alarms during peak false alarm periods.

A number of paid fire departments began to hire women as fire fighters in the 1970's. Women had served in volunteer fire departments since the 1800's but were not admitted into any paid departments until the 1970's.

Careers

The requirements for becoming a paid fire fighter vary among fire departments. In general, an applicant must be at least 18 years old and in excellent physical condition. An applicant must also pass a written test.

After being accepted by a fire department, a probationary fire fighter takes a training program that lasts one to three months. The program covers such subjects as fire behavior, fire-fighting tactics and strategy, and forcible entry techniques. The entire probationary pe-

riod usually lasts one year. After the probationary period, a fire fighter may receive specialized training in such areas as rescue work, fire prevention, or emergency medical care.

Many fire departments provide continuing education programs for fire fighters. In addition, about 300 community colleges in the United States offer courses in subjects related to fire protection. James W. Smith

Critically reviewed by the United States Fire Administration

Related articles in *World Book* include:

Arson	Fire prevention	Safety
Fire	Fireproofing	Smoke detector
Fire drill	Forestry (Fire)	Thermography
Fire extinguisher	Paramedic	

Outline

I. The work of a fire department
  A. Fire fighting
  B. Emergency rescue operations
  C. Fire prevention and fire safety
II. Fire department equipment
  A. Communication sys-   C. Special fire vehicles
    tems   D. Protective clothing
  B. Fire trucks
III. Kinds of fire departments
  A. Volunteer departments   C. Special-purpose
  B. Paid departments   departments
IV. History
V. Careers

Questions

What rules should a person follow in case of fire?
What service does the United States Fire Administration provide?
How did the early American colonists fight fires?
What is the purpose of firebreaks and backfires?
What duties does an engine company perform at a building fire? A ladder company?
Why do fire departments inspect buildings and homes?
What are *paramedic units*?
How do smoke and heat detectors work?
Why must fire fighters ventilate a burning building?
Who founded the first volunteer fire department in the American Colonies?

Additional resources

Level I
Feldman, Anne. *Firefighters.* McKay, 1979.
Loeper, John J. *By Hook and Ladder: The Story of Fire Fighting in America.* Scribner, 1981.
Smith, Betsy. *A Day in the Life of a Firefighter.* Troll, 1981.
Wolf, Bernard. *Firehouse.* Morrow, 1983.

Level II
Earnest, Ernest P. *The Volunteer Fire Company: Past and Present.* Stein & Day, 1979.
Smith, Dennis. *Dennis Smith's History of Firefighting in America: 300 Years of Courage.* Dial, 1978.
Zurier, Rebecca. *The American Firehouse: An Architectural and Social History.* Abbeville, 1982.

Fire drill is an exercise to teach people to leave a place safely and speedily if fire breaks out. Without the practice a fire drill provides, people may become frightened and confused when they have to leave a burning area. Fire drills are important exercises at home, work, and school. In public buildings and many businesses, signs tell people the escape routes for the building. Fire drills are also practiced on ships and at such places as airports and oil refineries.

Many states have laws that require regular school fire drills. In most schools, each classroom has directional signs. Signs and red lights in halls show the nearest exit for children who are not in a classroom when the fire bell rings. When the alarm is given, the teacher sees that the class leaves the school in a quiet and orderly manner, usually in single file.

Studies show that families that practice fire drills at home are better prepared to save their lives when a fire occurs there. Fire prevention authorities have developed a program called Exit Drills in the Home (EDITH). They promote it during Fire Prevention Week each year.

Critically reviewed by the National Fire Protection Association

Fire engine. See **Fire department** (Fire department equipment).

Fire extinguisher is a metal container filled with water or chemicals used to put out fires. Fire extinguishers are portable and easy to operate and can be used to put out small fires before the flames spread.

In the United States, state and local fire laws require that extinguishers be installed in easily seen places in public buildings. Such buildings include factories, schools, stores, and theaters. School buses, boats, and most public vehicles also must have extinguishers.

There are many kinds of fire extinguishers. The kind used depends on the type of fire involved. Fire prevention experts divide fires into four classes—A, B, C, and D—depending on the burning material. *Class A* fires involve such ordinary combustible materials as cloth, paper, rubber, or wood. *Class B* fires involve flammable gases or such flammable liquids as cooking grease, gasoline, or oil. *Class C* fires involve motors, switches, or other electrical equipment through which electric current is flowing. *Class D* fires involve combustible metals, such as magnesium chips or shavings. Most extinguishers are labeled with the class, or classes, of fire for which they can be used.

Class D fires require special extinguishers designed for specific metals. But most other fire extinguishers can be classified, by their contents, as one of four main types: (1) water, (2) foam, (3) liquefied gas, and (4) dry chemical.

Water extinguishers are used to fight only class A fires. Water conducts electricity, and so it must never be used on a fire involving electrical equipment. A water extinguisher is operated by a lever or a hand pump, depending on the model. Either action shoots the water through a hose attached to the container.

Foam extinguishers are used for class A and class B fires. A foam extinguisher contains water and a foaming agent. One type of foam puts out fires that involve combustible liquids by depositing a film between the liquid and the flame.

Liquefied gas extinguishers may be used on class B and class C fires. There are two main kinds—*carbon dioxide extinguishers,* which contain carbon dioxide gas; and *Halon extinguishers,* which contain a gas called *Halon.* Larger Halon extinguishers can also be used to fight class A fires. Both carbon dioxide extinguishers and Halon extinguishers have the gas in liquid form under pressure in the container. When the operator squeezes a handle, the liquid flows out of the container and becomes a gas that covers the fire. Liquefied gas extinguishers leave no water or powder as do other extinguishers. For this reason, the gas types are the most suitable for class C fires involving computers or other delicate electrical equipment that could be damaged by other types of extinguishers.

Dry chemical extinguishers are used on class B and class C fires. One type, the *multipurpose dry chemical extinguisher,* also can be used against class A fires. Dry chemical extinguishers contain a chemical powder and a gas under pressure. The gas may be stored either with the powder in the extinguisher's main compartment or by itself in a separate cartridge or cylinder. If the gas is stored separately, the user must enable the gas to flow into the main compartment before the extinguisher can be used. The user does this either by turning a valve or by operating a lever that punctures the compartment in which the gas is stored.

Critically reviewed by the National Fire Protection Association

Fire fighting. See **Fire department** (Fire fighting).

Fire prevention is a term for the many safety measures used to keep harmful fires from starting. Each year, about $2\frac{1}{2}$ million fires are reported to fire departments in the United States. The fires cause about 6,000 deaths and billions of dollars worth of damage. In Canada, about 65,000 fires cause more than 600 deaths annually. More than a fourth of all the people killed or injured by fire are children.

Individuals, groups, and communities work to pre-

Kinds of fire extinguishers

The chief kinds of fire extinguishers are *water, foam, liquefied gas,* and *dry chemical.* To operate most extinguishers, a person pulls the locking pin and squeezes the operating lever while aiming the nozzle at the base of the fire and moving the nozzle with a sweeping motion across the fire's base.

Water extinguishers are filled with water. They are used to fight class A fires, which involve wood, paper, cloth, or other combustible solids. Water extinguishers must never be used for fires that involve electrical equipment.

Foam extinguishers contain water and a foaming agent. They are used for class A fires and for class B fires. Class B fires involve flammable gases or such flammable liquids as gasoline or cooking grease.

Liquefied gas extinguishers contain either carbon dioxide gas or a gas called *Halon.* They are used for class B fires and for class C fires, which involve electrical equipment through which electric current is flowing. Larger Halon extinguishers are also used for class A fires.

Dry chemical extinguishers contain a chemical powder. They are used on class B or C fires. A type called multipurpose dry chemical can also be used on class A fires.

Parts of a fire extinguisher

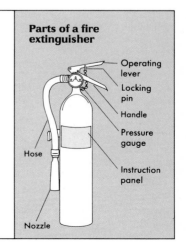

Operating lever

Locking pin

Handle

Pressure gauge

Hose

Instruction panel

Nozzle

vent fires. They use three main methods: (1) laws and regulations, (2) inspection of buildings and other property, and (3) public education about fire safety.

Most cities and states have codes and standards that require certain types of fire retardant materials and electric wiring to be used in buildings. Fire departments and other public agencies inspect public buildings for fire hazards and recommend corrective action. In some communities, homeowners may agree to have their homes inspected for fire hazards. Education is a vital part of fire prevention programs because people cause—and could prevent—almost all fires. Fire departments, community groups, and schools teach children and adults about fire hazards and work to reduce fires throughout the community.

In homes and schools, trash, old clothes, drapes, and furniture should be discarded, not stored in attics, basements, or closets. They could quickly catch fire in those places. Such liquids as gasoline and paint burn easily and should be stored in tightly closed cans, away from heat. Gasoline should not be stored indoors, and it must never be used to start a barbecue fire or bonfire.

In old homes and schools, an electrician should regularly check electric wiring and replace any that appears weak or worn. An electrician should also replace cords on electric appliances as soon as the outside coverings become worn. Cords should never be run under carpeting, where they might become damaged and set the carpeting on fire. A fire can also result from overloading one outlet with several appliances. See **Safety** (Safety at home; Safety at school).

Many types of fabrics burn easily. Wise parents teach children to avoid clothing fires by not standing near lighted stoves or bonfires and not playing with matches. Playing with matches causes loss of life and thousands of dollars in damage yearly in the United States.

Many school programs train children to be alert to fire hazards. Young children may learn these dangers by coloring sheets of pictures, rhymes, and slogans about fire prevention. Many older children visit fire departments. Fire fighters or teachers also may give talks and demonstrations for classes and assemblies. School and

Fire hazards in the home

Every 13½ seconds, a fire breaks out in the United States. Many of these fires start in homes, and most are caused by carelessness. These pictures show careless habits that can result in fire.

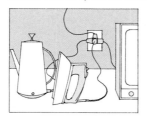

Smoking in bed can cause linen or clothing to catch fire if the smoker falls asleep.

An overloaded electrical outlet can cause overheated wires to burn.

Playing with matches can result in rugs, clothing, and other items being set aflame.

Storing flammable liquids near a furnace can cause escaping fumes to catch fire.

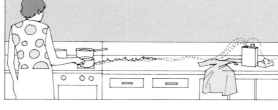
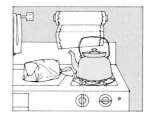

Gasoline should not be used to start fires. It is too flammable and uncontrollable.

A flashback fire can begin when fumes escape from cleaning fluid or some other flammable liquid and come in contact with a flame. A flashback fire travels along the path of the fumes.

Dish towels and other burnable items can be set ablaze if placed too near a stove.

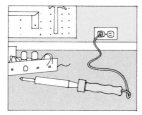
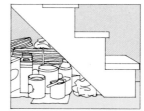

Throwing away cigarettes that are still burning can start a wastebasket fire.

A soldering iron can set a workbench on fire if not disconnected after being used.

Stored rags soaked with grease, oil, or paint can quickly burst into flame.

WORLD BOOK illustrations by David Cunningham

Space heaters located too close to blowing curtains can cause the fabric to catch fire.

Dept. of Fire Technology, Southwest Research Institute

A flammability test determines how fast a substance burns. This scientist is measuring the speed at which fire travels on the surface of a material that has been ignited inside a tunnel.

community groups sponsor children's clubs, called junior fire departments, to promote fire safety at home.

In the community, fire departments and other public agencies work to improve fire prevention through laws, inspections, and educational programs. Such groups as chambers of commerce and youth clubs promote fire prevention through newspapers, pamphlets, posters, and radio and television appeals.

Some groups sponsor programs to alert the community to fire hazards that occur during various seasons. For example, the number of fires in homes increases every winter, when heating equipment comes into use. Some of this equipment has not been kept in good condition or has been misused. In many communities, organizations put safety tags on Christmas trees. In addition, Halloween programs stress the dangers of bonfires, candles, and costumes that burn easily.

Local clean-up weeks encourage homeowners, stores, and factories to discard rubbish and eliminate other fire hazards. Each year, the United States and Canada observe National Fire Prevention Week during the week including October 9, the anniversary of the Chicago Fire of 1871. Most communities have laws that require regular inspections of commercial, public, and some residential buildings. Fire department officials conduct these inspections for fire dangers.

In industry, fire prevention presents special problems because fire must be used for so many jobs. Fire performs such tasks as melting metals, heating chemicals, and generating electricity. Machines and furnaces used for these jobs must be carefully designed to keep the flames under control. Inspectors check for fire hazards near machines and in other areas of a factory. Employers teach workers to operate machines safely and to report any problems that could cause fire.

Workers must take special care when using dry or liquid chemicals and oils. Some liquids give off easily ignited vapors and have to be stored in metal safety cans. Spilled chemicals, and dust and chips from flammable materials, must be cleaned up immediately.

Many industries sponsor special classes and demonstrations to teach workers how to prevent fire at their jobs. Factory bulletin boards, pamphlets, and articles in company magazines also promote fire safety.

Fire prevention laws began with building regulations established in ancient times. About 18 B.C., the Roman Emperor Augustus set maximum heights for houses and minimum thicknesses for their walls. Later laws required minimum separations between buildings to prevent fires from spreading from one structure to the next. In the A.D. 300's, Emperor Julian issued controls on the work of blacksmiths and other tradespeople who used fire. For example, he banned smoking chimneys that could cause roof fires. Princes in parts of Italy and Germany used some of these laws as late as the 1600's.

In the American Colonies, the earliest fire laws dealt with fighting, rather than preventing, fires. But newspapers sometimes advised readers about fire hazards.

In 1896, the National Fire Protection Association was formed to develop national fire codes and standards. The first Fire Prevention Day was observed in the United States in 1911. In 1922, the United States and Canada observed National Fire Prevention Week, the first campaign to educate the public in fire safety. Since then, public education programs have become important supplements to fire prevention laws and inspection programs. Many such programs operate the year around.

Australia, Great Britain, the Netherlands, and Sweden also stress public education in fire prevention. But most industrialized nations rely more on laws, inspections, and worker training. In many countries, insurance requirements form the basis of fire prevention programs.

Critically reviewed by the National Fire Protection Association

See also **Combustion; Fire department; Fire drill; Fire extinguisher; Fireproofing.**

Additional resources

Blair, William. *Fire! Survival & Prevention.* Barnes & Noble, 1983.
Dean, Anabel. *Fire! How Do They Fight It?* Westminster, 1978. For younger readers.
Fire Protection Handbook. Ed. by Gordon P. McKinnon and others. 16th ed. National Fire Protection Association, 1986.
Glenn, Gary A., and Peggy. *Don't Get Burned! A Family Fire-Safety Guide.* Aames-Allen, 1982.

Fire worship is an ancient religious practice based on the idea that fire is sacred. Since early times, people have worshiped fire because it destroys, purifies, and gives heat and light. Some people believe a god or spirit inhabits fire. The Parsis of India and other followers of a religion called Zoroastrianism use fire as a divine symbol. The ancient Greeks and Romans considered fire one of the major elements that made up the world. Today, many people build bonfires on various occasions. This practice probably developed from the ancient tradition of fire worship. See also **Parsis; Vesta.**

Christopher McIntosh

Firearm is any weapon that uses gunpowder to fire a bullet or shell. Generally, the term is used for light firearms, such as rifles, shotguns, and pistols. They are often called *small arms.* Heavier firearms are generally referred to as *artillery.*

Mechanism. Any firearm, large or small, has four essential parts: (1) barrel, (2) chamber, (3) breech mechanism, and (4) firing mechanism. The *barrel* is a long tube. It may be smooth, as in a shotgun, or with spiral grooves on the inner surface, as in a rifle. The *chamber*

Types of firearms

Automatic pistol

Chamber
Firing mechanism
Barrel
Breech
Grip

Revolver

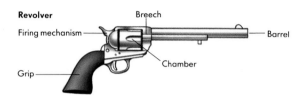

Breech
Firing mechanism
Barrel
Chamber
Grip

Bolt-action rifle

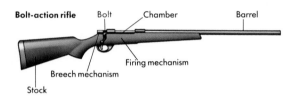

Bolt
Chamber
Barrel
Firing mechanism
Breech mechanism
Stock

Breechblock rifle

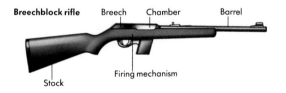

Breech
Chamber
Barrel
Firing mechanism
Stock

Shotgun

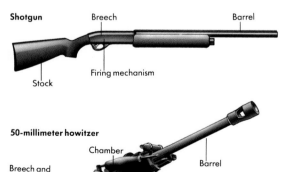

Breech
Barrel
Firing mechanism
Stock

50-millimeter howitzer

Chamber
Barrel
Breech and
firing mechanism

WORLD BOOK illustrations by Oxford Illustrators Limited

is a widened hole at the *breech* (rear) end of the barrel. It holds the *cartridge* (explosive charge). The *breech mechanism* closes the rear end of the barrel, holding the cartridge in the chamber. Every up-to-date firearm has some way by which the breech can be opened for loading and locked for safety in firing. Artillery uses screw plugs or breechblocks. Machine guns, rifles, and other small arms usually have a metal cylinder, or *bolt,* that is locked when the gun is fired, and drawn back to eject the empty cartridge case and to reload. The *firing mechanism* may be electric, as in some large artillery pieces. In small arms, a spring drives a pointed firing pin through the breech bolt against a sensitive *primer* in the cartridge. The firing pin is *cocked* (drawn back) against a hook called the *sear.* When the trigger is pulled, the sear releases the firing pin, which in turn leaps forward to strike the primer. A jet of flame from the primer ignites the rest of the powder, forming a gas. This explosive gas propels the bullet from the barrel.

In World War II, American soldiers carried semiautomatic Garand rifles that fired and ejected cases automatically with each pull of the trigger. The M1 carbine used a less powerful cartridge, but was quite similar. Both the Garand rifle and M1 carbine fired .30-caliber bullets. Soldiers and officers also used .45-caliber semiautomatic pistols.

History. Europeans first learned of gunpowder in the 1200's. By the 1300's, they discovered that it could be used to propel an object with great force. Firearms as we know them were then developed. The first firearms were cannons, but people soon developed firearms that they could carry.

The invention of firearms led to great changes in warfare. Bullets could penetrate armor. Castles had easily withstood the attacks of people armed with battle-axes, swords, spears, and bows and arrows. But they crumbled before the assault of new weapons such as cannon balls. Soldiers used pistols, blunderbusses, and muskets. They had to load their hand-held firearms from the muzzle, and found these weapons heavy and clumsy. But, clumsy as they were, they revolutionized warfare.

The rifle was invented about 1500. It had spiral grooves inside the barrel that made it more accurate than any previous firearm. Smokeless powder was developed in the 1800's. Breechloading systems replaced dangerous muzzle loading. Many improvements since have resulted in high-powered firearms.

Frances M. Lussier

Related articles in *World Book* include:

Ammunition	Cannon	Gun	Mortar
Armor	Carbine	Handgun	Musket
Artillery	Explosive	Harquebus	Rifle
Bazooka	Flintlock	Machine gun	Shotgun
Blunderbuss	Garand rifle		

Fireball is a meteor that burns brightly as it plunges through the earth's atmosphere. If the fireball explodes at the end of its path, it is generally called a *bolide.* Some pieces may survive the explosion, and fall to the earth. Only brightness makes a fireball different from an ordinary meteor. A fireball is as bright as Jupiter or Venus. In rare cases, it may be as bright as a full moon. A sound like thunder occasionally accompanies the passage of a fireball. See also **Meteor.**   Lee J. Rickard

Firebird. See Baltimore oriole.

WORLD BOOK illustration by Christabel King

The firecracker flower has narrow leaves and a long, thin stalk topped by a cluster of red and green tubelike blossoms.

Firecracker flower is a perennial plant of the amaryllis family. It grows in California. Its low, narrow leaves look like blades of grass. The slender stalk may grow to be 3 feet (91 centimeters) high. The tube-shaped flowers are scarlet, tipped with green. They grow in a cluster at the top of the stalk. The plant grows best in partial shade in deep, loose, well-drained soil with some leaf mold.

   Scientific classification. The firecracker flower belongs to the amaryllis family, Amaryllidaceae. It is *Dichelostemma idamaia.*   Donald Wyman

Firedamp. See Damp.
Firefly is any member of one particular family of soft-bodied beetles known for producing glowing or flashing light. Fireflies are also called *lightning bugs.* There are about 1,900 *species* (kinds) of fireflies. Members of the firefly family live on all the continents except Antarctica. In the United States and Canada, there are about 140 species. The pyralis firefly, one of the most familiar North American species found east of the Rocky Mountains, is active in the early evening. These fireflies can be seen floating silently over meadows and lawns, flashing their yellow lights.

   Not all members of the firefly family give off light as adults. For example, adults of most North American spe-

James E. Lloyd,
University of Florida

Fireflies have a flat, oblong body, and most have light organs on the underside of the abdomen. The species shown here are *Photinus pyralis, above,* and *Pyractomena ecostata, right.*

cies found west of the Rocky Mountains do not produce light. However, the *larvae* (young) of all firefly species and the eggs of some species give off light. The glowing larvae and the flightless females of some species are often called *glowworms.*

   Body. Adult fireflies are flattish, oblong insects about one-quarter to three-quarters of an inch (5 to 20 millimeters) long. Most are dull brown or black, with red, orange, or yellow markings. Like all beetles, fireflies have two pairs of wings but use only the second pair for flying. The first pair, the *elytra,* form a cover over the second pair. The females of many firefly species do not fly, and their wings and elytra are very short or absent.

   Firefly light organs are usually located on the underside of the *abdomen*—the last section of an insect's body. A chemical reaction that takes place in the light organs produces the firefly's light. This kind of heatless light is known as *bioluminescence.*

   Life. Fireflies use their lights to find mates. Each firefly species has its own light signal. Female fireflies perch on the ground or in the bushes and wait until a male flies nearby flashing the correct signal. She then answers him with her own light.

   Fireflies lay their eggs in moist places on or in the ground. The eggs hatch into flightless larvae that are often seen glowing on damp lawns and along streams. The larvae take one or two years to develop. They then pass through a brief *pupal* state, during which they change into adults. The adults live for 5 to 30 days. Firefly larvae eat snails, earthworms, and other insect larvae. They kill their prey by injecting poison into them. Adult fireflies may feed on nectar or eat nothing. However, the females of some firefly species prey on the males of other species. They lure the males by imitating the mating signals of the other species. The enemies of fireflies include various birds, frogs, lizards, and spiders.

   Scientific classification. Fireflies are in the class Insecta, order Coleoptera. They make up the firefly family, Lampyridae. The pyralis firefly is *Photinus pyralis.*   James E. Lloyd

   See also **Beetle** (picture); **Bioluminescence.**
Fireman. See Fire department (Careers).
Fireplace. See Heating (Local heating systems); **Pioneer life in America** (picture: A frontier home).
Fireproofing is the popular name for the coatings and methods used to protect paper, plastic, textiles, wood, and other materials against fire. Fire prevention experts, however, consider the term *fireproofing* misleading because even such incombustible materials as steel and concrete are affected to some degree by intense fire. Steel can weaken or melt and concrete can crack. Experts instead refer to materials that have been protected against fire as *fire resistant* or *fire retarded.* They call the substances that are used to protect such materials *fire retardants.*

   Fire retardants help prevent materials from burning or being severely damaged when exposed to fire. Some increase the time it takes for treated articles to burst into flame. Others cause a material to extinguish itself if it is ignited by a brief fire, thereby preventing the fire from spreading to surrounding objects.

   Fire results from the combination of fuel, heat, and oxygen. Fire retardants help materials resist fire by interfering with *combustion chemistry*—that is, the reactions of these elements with one another. For example, a combustible surface may be protected against fire by being covered with a special fire-retardant *intumescent coating.* Upon exposure to fire, an intumescent coating swells up to form a thick layer of insulating foam between the surface (the fuel) and the fire (the heat).

Many fire retardants produce physical or chemical changes in a flammable material in order to make it less flammable. Some, for example, cause a material, when exposed to fire, to release gases. The gases interfere with combustion chemistry, thereby quenching the flame. Retardants that alter the flammability of materials are applied in a number of ways. For example, textile manufacturers obtain nearly permanent fire resistance in natural and synthetic fabrics used in making carpets, clothing, draperies, and upholstery through processes that molecularly bond retardant compounds to the fabric. Temporary fire retardation can be obtained by soaking fabrics in solutions of such chemicals as borax, boric acid, diammonium phosphate, and ammonium sulfate. Paper manufacturers often add similar chemicals to paper and cardboard.

In the United States, materials used to build houses, schools, and other buildings are required to meet fire-resistance standards. These standards are set by local governments. The Revised Flammable Fabrics Act of 1967, a federal law, prohibits the sale of fabrics that burn rapidly. This law also enforces federal regulations requiring that children's sleepwear be treated with fire retardants. Norman J. Alvares

Firestone, Harvey Samuel (1868-1938), was an American industrial leader who pioneered in the field of automobile tires. He founded the Firestone Tire & Rubber Company in Akron, Ohio, in 1900. He served as president of this company from 1903 to 1926, and was chairman of the board of directors until his death.

The company produced its first tires, made of solid rubber, in 1903. Firestone's keen interest in technical progress caused his company to lead in numerous improvements. It developed and, in 1931, became the first to market a practical air-filled tire for farm machinery.

In 1924, Firestone took over a small plantation in Liberia to produce rubber. In 1926, he signed an agreement with the Liberian government to lease 1 million acres (400,000 hectares) of land for the development of rubber plantations. He made large loans to Liberia, and built for it a new and improved harbor. Firestone also led in investigating the rubber resources of the Philippines and South America, and he encouraged American investment in rubber-growing countries. He also helped organize rubber production for World War I (1914-1918).

Firestone was born and grew up on an Ohio farm. His first jobs were as a clerk and a bookkeeper. He became interested in rubber tires while he was working for a carriage factory. This lifetime interest caused him to carry on extensive rubber research and publish two books on the subject. In 1927, he joined Henry Ford and Thomas A. Edison in projects searching for substitutes for natural rubber. W. H. Baughn

Fireweed, also called *willow herb,* is an erect plant that thrives in the North Temperate Zone. It gets its name because it springs up so quickly after a forest fire. It grows about 3 to 6 feet (0.9 to 1.8 meters) high and looks like a long wand. The narrow leaves are 2 to 6 inches (5 to 15 centimeters) long. In the summer, clus-ters of rose-purple flowers bloom along the upper stalk. The slender fruits are four-sided pods. Fireweed is the official flower of the Yukon Territory.

Scientific classification. Fireweeds belong to the evening primrose family, Onagraceae. They are *Epilobium angustifolium.*
Earl L. Core

Firewood. See Camping (Building a campfire).

Fireworks are combinations of gunpowder and other ingredients that explode with loud noises and colorful sparks and flames when they burn. Fireworks are also called *pyrotechnics.* Fireworks that only make a loud noise are called *firecrackers.* Fireworks are dangerous because they contain gunpowder. They should be handled only by experts. Fireworks handled improperly can explode and cause serious injury to the untrained user. Most states prohibit the use of fireworks by individuals. The federal government limits the explosive power of fireworks that can be used by individuals.

Most fireworks are made by packing gunpowder in hollow paper tubes. A coarse gunpowder tightly packed is used to *propel* (drive) rockets into the air. A finer and more loosely packed gunpowder explodes the rocket once it is in the air. See **Gunpowder.**

Manufacturers add small amounts of special chemicals to the gunpowder to create colors. They add sodium compounds to produce yellow, strontium compounds for red, and copper and barium compounds for blue and green. Charcoal is another substance that can be added. It gives the rocket a sparkling, flaming tail.

How fireworks work. Fireworks rockets, also called *skyrockets,* operate on a principle close to that used in large military rockets. A *fuse* ignites the coarse gunpowder charge, which forms gases that stream out of the end of the paper tube. This propels the rocket into the air. When the rocket is near its highest point of flight, the coarse gunpowder ignites the finer charge, and the finer charge explodes. The explosion breaks up the rocket and ignites many small firecrackers in the *nose* (forward section) of the rocket.

Roman candles have gunpowder charges separated by inactive material so they shoot out separate groups of sparks and colored flames with series of booming noises. *Pinwheels* have a gunpowder charge packed in a long, flexible tube. The tube is attached to the outside edge of a cardboard disk that has a hole in its center. A stick is placed in the hole. As the charge ignites and burns, it makes the disk whirl around the stick, throwing off sparks and flames. *Lances* are thin paper tubes filled with color-producing fireworks. They are arranged in a pattern on a wooden frame so that when set afire they outline a scene, a portrait, or a flag.

Other uses of fireworks. Fireworks also have serious uses. A device called a *fusee* burns with a bright red flame and is used as a danger signal on highways and railroads. Railroads use giant firecrackers called *torpedoes.* The torpedoes explode while the train is passing over them to warn the engineer of danger ahead.

People can signal for help by using a *Very* pistol. The pistol shoots a flare into the air that can be seen far away. *Parachute flares* are used to light up landing areas. A kind of fireworks rocket can be used to shoot lifelines to shipwrecks. *Star shells* are used in wartime to light up battlefields. James E. Kennedy

See also **Explosive; Independence Day.**

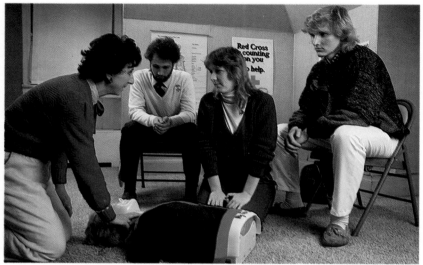

A first aid course teaches the proper emergency treatment for a variety of injuries and illnesses. In this picture, a student uses a *manikin* (model) of the head and upper torso of the human body to show how to check for a pulse.

First aid

First aid is the immediate care given to a victim of an accident, sudden illness, or other medical emergency. Proper first aid can save a victim's life, especially if the victim is bleeding heavily, has stopped breathing, or has been poisoned. First aid also can prevent the development of additional medical problems that might result from an injury or illness.

Emergency treatment should be administered by the person on the scene who has the best knowledge of first aid. The treatment should be continued until professional medical help is available. First aid also involves reassuring a victim, relieving the pain, and moving the victim, if necessary, to a hospital or clinic.

This article describes some basic first-aid techniques for common medical emergencies. People interested in taking a first-aid training course should contact their local chapter of the American Red Cross.

General rules for first aid

Analyze the situation quickly and decide whether you can help the victim. If you decide to treat the victim, begin at once. But if you are confused or unsure of yourself, do *not* attempt to give treatment. In many cases, the wrong treatment causes more damage than no treatment at all. For professional help in giving first aid, call a hospital, an emergency medical service, the fire department, or the police.

The general steps to take in any situation requiring first aid include the following: (1) call a local emergency medical service or a physician for assistance, (2) provide urgent care for life-threatening emergencies, (3) exam-

ine the victim for injuries, and (4) treat the victim for shock.

Call for assistance. Send someone else to call for a doctor, an ambulance, or other help while you care for the victim. If you are alone with the victim, you must decide when you can safely leave to call for assistance. Always treat the victim for any life-threatening conditions before leaving to summon aid.

When telephoning for help, be ready to describe the nature of the victim's illness or injury, the first aid measures you have taken, and the exact location of the victim. Also be prepared to write down any instructions a physician may give you. Repeat the instructions and ask questions to clarify orders you do not understand.

If you decide to take the victim to a hospital emergency room, first telephone the hospital to say you are coming. The hospital staff will then be better prepared to treat the victim's particular problems.

Every home should have a list of emergency phone numbers posted on or near the telephone. However, if such numbers are not available, the operator can assist you in contacting the proper person or emergency unit.

Provide urgent care. Certain medical emergencies require immediate care to save the victim's life. If the victim is bleeding severely, has been poisoned, or has stopped breathing, treatment must begin at once. A delay of even a few minutes can be fatal in these cases. The treatments for these emergencies are discussed in this article in the sections on *First aid for bleeding, Treatment for poisoning,* and *Restoring breathing.*

Do not move a victim who may have a broken bone, internal injuries, or damage to the neck or spine, unless absolutely necessary to prevent further injury. If the victim is lying down, keep the person in that position. Do not allow the victim to get up and walk about. Never give food or liquid to a person who may need surgery.

Carlotta M. Rinke, the contributor of this article, is a physician in private practice and a Clinical Assistant Professor of Medicine at Loyola University of Chicago.

If the victim is unconscious, turn the head to one side to help prevent the person from choking on blood, saliva, or vomit. But do *not* move the head of a person who may have a broken neck or a spinal injury. Never pour a liquid into the mouth of an unconscious person.

Make certain that the victim has an open airway. The *airway* consists of the nose, mouth, and upper throat. These passages must remain open in order for the victim to breathe. For information on keeping the airway open, see the section of this article on *Giving artificial respiration.*

Examine the victim for injuries only after treating the person for any life-threatening emergencies. Then treat the individual injuries. The victim may suffer from diabetes, heart trouble, or some other disease that can cause sudden illness. Many persons with such medical problems carry a medical tag or card. The tag or card lists instructions for care that should be followed exactly. If you must examine the victim's identification papers to look for a medical card, you should do so in the presence of a witness, if possible.

Make the victim comfortable, but handle the person as little as possible. If necessary, shade the victim from the sun or cover the victim to prevent chilling. Loosen the person's clothing. But do not pull on the victim's belt, because this pressure could damage an injured spine.

Remain calm and reassure the victim. Explain what has happened and what is being done. Ask any spectators to stand back.

Treat for shock. Shock results from the body's failure to circulate blood properly. Any serious injury or illness can cause a victim to suffer from shock. Shock most often occurs after an injury that causes blood loss, when there is a probability of heart attack, or during overwhelming infection. When a person is in shock, the blood fails to supply enough oxygen and food to the brain and other organs. The most serious form of shock may result in death.

A victim in shock may appear fearful, light-headed, confused, weak, and extremely thirsty. In some cases, the victim may feel nauseous. The skin appears pale and feels cold and damp. The pulse is rapid and breathing is quick and shallow or deep and irregular. It is best to treat a seriously injured person for shock even if these signs are not present. The treatment will help prevent a person from going into shock.

To treat shock, place the victim on his or her back, with the legs raised slightly. If the victim has trouble breathing in this position, place the person in a half-sitting, half-lying position. Warm the victim by placing blankets over and under the body.

First aid for bleeding

Severe *hemorrhage* (bleeding) can cause death within minutes. Bleeding from most small wounds stops by itself in a short time, after the blood begins to *clot* (thicken). But clotting alone cannot stop the flow of blood from large wounds. When treating a bleeding victim, you should attempt to stop the bleeding, protect the victim from further injury, and prevent shock. As with any situation involving first aid, medical assistance should be called for immediately. Emergency treatments for severe bleeding include such techniques as (1) direct pressure on the wound and (2) pressure on arteries carrying blood to the wound.

Direct pressure. The most effective way of controlling heavy bleeding is to press directly on the wound itself. If possible, have the victim lie down and elevate the bleeding part above the rest of the body. Then place a sterile dressing over the wound and press firmly on it with your hand. If you do not have a sterile dressing, use

How to control bleeding These photographs show how to stop bleeding from an arm or leg. The person giving the treatment applies pressure directly to the wound and raises it above the rest of the body. With his other hand, he helps control the bleeding by pressing on the arteries that supply blood to the affected limb. The diagram indicates the pressure points for the arteries of the arms and legs.

WORLD BOOK photos by Ralph Brunke

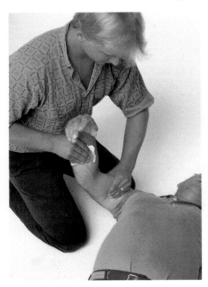
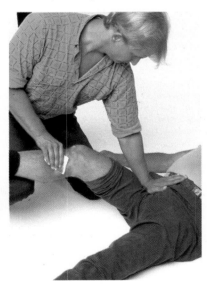
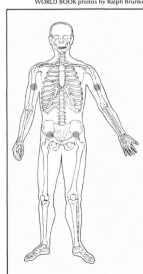

a clean handkerchief, towel, or other cloth folded to make a pad. If no cloth is available, press your hand directly on the wound while someone else obtains the necessary material. Apply constant pressure to the wound for about 10 to 15 minutes, or until professional help arrives.

If the victim bleeds through the first dressing, add another on top of it and apply firmer pressure. Do not remove the first dressing. After the hemorrhage has stopped, secure the dressing with a bandage.

Pressure on arteries. Sometimes, direct pressure and elevation fail to stop severe bleeding. If such bleeding is from an arm or leg, you may be able to stop it by applying pressure to the artery that supplies blood to the injured limb. The illustrations in this article on *How to control bleeding* show the points at which pressure should be applied to these arteries. Pressure on arteries should be used in addition to—not instead of—direct pressure and elevation.

Treatment for poisoning

There are four ways in which a victim may become poisoned. The poison may be swallowed, inhaled, injected, or absorbed through the skin.

If a poison victim is unconscious, having difficulty breathing, or having seizures, call for an ambulance immediately. If necessary, perform artificial respiration. If the victim has become poisoned by injection, keep the affected area lower than the level of the heart to slow the spread of the poison.

If a person has been poisoned by taking a drug, keep the person's breathing passage open. Quickly try to identify the drug, and then immediately call a physician or emergency medical service for help.

Swallowed poisons. A person who has swallowed a poisonous substance may die within minutes if not treated. The first step in treating the victim is to identify the poison. Identification of the poison helps determine the proper procedure for treating the victim. Immediately call a poison control center or a physician for advice. If the victim has swallowed a commercial product, take the container to the phone when you make the call so that you can provide information about the product. The poison control center or physician will tell you what to do. Do not put anything in the victim's mouth unless you have been told to do so by medical professionals.

The poison control center or physician may advise you to make the victim vomit. The most reliable way of making a person vomit is to use a drug called *syrup of ipecac*. To induce vomiting, give 1 tablespoon (15 milliliters) of syrup of ipecac mixed in half a glass of water. Afterward, have the victim drink as much water as possible. Keep the victim moving about, because activity promotes vomiting. If vomiting does not occur within 15 to 20 minutes, administer another dose of syrup of ipecac. Do not repeat a third time.

When a victim vomits, lay the person on his or her side. This position will help keep the airway open and will prevent the victim from inhaling the poisoned vomit into the lungs. Catch the vomit in a pan so that it can be examined by a physician.

Inhaled poisons. If the victim has inhaled a poison, such as carbon monoxide or chlorine gas, move the person to fresh air immediately. Open all windows and doors to ventilate the area. Then call a poison control center or a physician for advice.

Injected poisons include those transmitted by insect stings or bites and snakebite. For information on the treatment of snakebite, see the section on *Snakebite* in this article.

To treat a spider bite, apply cold compresses to the affected area. Afterward, apply a soothing lotion, such as calamine lotion, to the area.

When a person is bitten by a tick, the tick often adheres to the skin or scalp. Remove the tick at once. Pull the tick out steadily and firmly, not suddenly. Do not use your bare hands. Use a glove, a piece of plastic wrap or paper, or even a leaf. If you have tweezers, grasp the tick's mouthparts as close to the skin as possible. Do not attempt to remove the tick by burning it off, by coating it with petroleum jelly, or by putting oil on it. Clean the bite area with soap and water. Save the tick in a small, sealed container for possible identification. If a rash or flulike symptoms develop within the next several weeks, contact your physician.

When a bee stings a person, the insect's stinger remains in the wound. The person should scrape the stinger off immediately, taking care not to pinch or squeeze the sting. This action reduces the amount of poison that enters the wound.

A victim may experience a severe allergic reaction to a bite or sting. You should either call a physician for advice or take the victim to the nearest location that provides emergency medical treatment.

Poisons on the skin. Poisons can be absorbed through the skin as a result of contact with poisonous plants or chemical substances, such as insecticides. If a victim's skin has been exposed to a poison, remove all contaminated clothing and flush the skin with water for about 10 minutes. Afterward, wash the affected area with soap and water and then rinse it. Wear protective gloves to avoid exposing yourself to the poison.

Restoring breathing

Begin artificial respiration as soon as possible for any victim whose breathing has stopped. Two or three minutes without breathing can cause permanent brain damage, and six minutes can be fatal. Signs of breath stoppage include the lack of regular chest movements and a blue color in lips, tongue, or fingernails.

Removing the cause of breathing failure. The steps you take before administering artificial respiration depend on why the victim's breathing has stopped. For example, if the victim's airway is blocked, you must remove the obstruction before beginning artificial respiration.

Electric shock also can cause respiratory failure. In cases of electric shock, free the victim from contact with the current before attempting artificial respiration. Turn off the current if possible. Do not touch the victim with your bare hands or with a wet or metal object until the contact has been broken. If you cannot turn off the current, free the victim from contact by using a dry stick, rope, or cloth. Be sure to stand on a dry surface that will not conduct electricity.

Respiratory failure can also result from breathing air that lacks sufficient oxygen. Such air may be present in storage bins, poorly ventilated mines, and closed vaults.

How to give artificial respiration

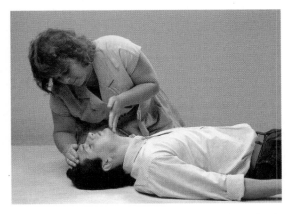

Open the airway. Place one hand on the victim's forehead and the other under the chin. Then tilt the victim's head back and lift the lower jaw.

For the mouth-to-mouth method, pinch the victim's nostrils shut. Take a deep breath, place your mouth tightly over the victim's mouth, and blow until the victim's chest rises.

WORLD BOOK photos by Steven Spicer

Listen for air being exhaled. Remove your mouth and release the victim's nose to allow the victim to breathe out. Repeat the procedure every five seconds for an adult.

Breathing also may stop because the victim has inhaled large quantities of carbon-monoxide, a substance that interferes with the blood's ability to carry oxygen. In any of these cases, move the victim into fresh air before beginning artificial respiration.

Giving artificial respiration. The most efficient method of artificial respiration is *mouth-to-mouth resuscitation.* To administer mouth-to-mouth resuscitation, place the victim on his or her back, on a firm surface if possible. Kneel down near the head and, using your fingers or a handkerchief, quickly remove such objects as dentures, food, or vomit from the mouth. Place one of your hands under the victim's chin and the other on the forehead. Tilt the victim's head back by lifting with the hand under the chin and pressing down with the one on the forehead. This position—with the chin pointing upward and the neck arched—opens the airway.

To treat an infant or small child, take a breath and place your mouth over both the mouth and nose. Blow gently into the child's mouth and nose. Then remove your mouth and listen for air to flow back out of the child's lungs. Take a breath and blow again. Repeat this procedure every three seconds.

If the victim is an older child or an adult, pinch the nostrils shut with the hand you have placed on the forehead. Take a deep breath, cover the mouth tightly with your own, and blow hard enough to make the chest rise. Then remove your mouth and listen for the return air flow. Repeat this procedure every five seconds.

If the victim's mouth is too large for you to make a tight seal over it with your own, or if victim has suffered a severe mouth injury, use mouth-to-nose resuscitation. Maintain the head-tilt position, and use the hand under the victim's chin to hold the mouth tightly shut. Then blow into the victim's nose.

If the victim's chest does not rise when you blow in, check the mouth again to be sure that there is nothing in it. Also make certain that the head is tilted back far enough and that the lower jaw is pulled upward. If you still cannot make the victim's chest expand, it may mean that an object is blocking the airway. The recommended technique for removing an object from the throat is the *Heimlich maneuver.* This technique is described in the *Choking* section of this article. After the object has been forced out of the throat, continue artificial respiration until the victim starts to breathe or until professional help arrives.

Other first-aid procedures

Animal bites or stings. Bites made by nonpoisonous animals can result in serious infections and diseases if left untreated. Wash the area of the bite thoroughly with soap and water. Rinse the wound and cover it with a gauze dressing. Call a physician. If possible, the animal should be kept under observation by a veterinarian to determine if it has rabies.

Bites by poisonous animals include those of some spiders, insects, and snakes. Such bites require medical attention. For information regarding such treatment, see the sections in this article on *Injected poisons* and *Snakebite.*

Burns. The first-aid treatment of burns depends on the severity of the injury. Burns are classified, in order of increasing severity, as first-, second-, or third-degree.

First-degree burns produce a reddening of the top layer of skin. *Second-degree burns* damage deeper skin layers. These burns give the injured skin a red or spotted appearance and cause blisters. *Third-degree burns* destroy tissues in the deepest layer of skin. The injury has a white or charred appearance.

To treat first- and second-degree burns, apply dressings soaked in iced, sterile solution to the injured area for about 20 or 30 minutes. Then dress the injured area with sterile bandages. Victims suffering first- or second-degree burns on the face or over an area larger than the size of the hand should receive professional medical attention.

A person who receives third-degree burns should not be treated at home. The person should instead be treated by a physician immediately. Large burns may be wrapped in a clean sheet or towel, or in plastic bags or kitchen wrap. Plastic bags or wrap should never be placed over the face. Clothing stuck to the wound should not be pulled away.

In treating any kind of burn, do not open blisters, and do not smear the injury with petroleum ointment, butter, or any greasy substance. If the victim has suffered burns around the face or has been exposed to smoke, watch for respiratory difficulties. If the victim has trouble breathing, give artificial respiration. Severe burns cause much pain and a loss of body fluids and may send the victim into shock. In such cases, take the first-aid measures to prevent or treat shock.

Chemical burns should be flushed with large amounts of water. Use a hose, shower, or bucket. Wash the injury for at least 10 minutes. Remove any clothing that has been covered by the chemical and cover the burn with a sterile dressing. Take the victim to a physician immediately.

Sunburn, in most cases, is a first-degree burn. Extremely deep sunburn may cause second-degree burns, with blistering. Do not open any blisters. Apply cool compresses to relieve pain. Consult a physician in cases of severe sunburn.

Choking occurs when food or some other object blocks the *trachea* (windpipe). A person who is choking cannot breathe or speak. After a short time, the victim's skin turns blue and he or she collapses. If the object is not removed in 4 to 6 minutes, death can occur.

An effective way to remove an object blocking the windpipe is a technique called the *Heimlich maneuver.* To perform this maneuver, stand behind the victim and place your arms around the victim's waist. Make a fist and place it so that the thumb is against the victim's abdomen, slightly above the navel and below the ribcage. Grasp your fist with your other hand and then press your fist into the victim's abdomen with a quick upward thrust. This thrusting action forces air out of the victim's lungs and blows the object from the trachea.

If the victim has collapsed or is too large for you to support or place your arms around, lay the person on his or her back. Then face the victim and kneel straddling the hips. Place one of your hands over the other, with the heel of the bottom hand on the victim's abdomen, slightly above the navel and below the ribcage. Then press your hands into the victim's abdomen with a quick upward thrust.

When applying the Heimlich maneuver, be careful not to apply pressure on the victim's ribs. Such pressure may break the ribs of a child or an adult.

Concussion is a head injury that results from a violent blow or shock. If the injury has knocked the victim unconscious, place the victim flat on his or her back, taking care not to move the neck. Give artificial respiration if the breathing stops. Get medical assistance as soon as possible.

Victims of a violent head blow might not lose consciousness at the time of the injury. However, they should be watched closely for the next 12 to 24 hours. They may develop delayed symptoms that should be treated by a physician. Such delayed symptoms include loss of consciousness, repeated vomiting, severe headache, pale appearance, weakness in the arms or legs, unsteady walking, convulsions, unusual behavior, difficulty in talking, pupils of unequal size, double vision, watery discharge from the ears or nose, and excessive drowsiness. Check the victim for alertness every 15 minutes immediately following the injury and awaken him or her every 3 hours during that night. If signs of a concussion appear, consult a physician.

Convulsion and epileptic seizure. A person who is suffering a convulsion experiences violent, completely involuntary contractions of the muscles. Major convulsions, particularly those that are associated with epileptic seizures, also involve loss of consciousness. The victim falls to the ground. The muscles twitch and jerk, or

WORLD BOOK photos by Dan Miller

A treatment for choking on an object stuck in the trachea can be applied to a standing victim, *left,* or one who is lying down, *right.* In this technique, called the *Heimlich maneuver,* the person giving the treatment presses sharply on the victim's abdomen. The pressure forces air out of the victim's lungs and blows the blockage from the trachea.

they become rigid. Most attacks last a few minutes.

Try to prevent the victim from being injured during the attack. Leave the victim in the position in which he or she falls, but move aside objects that the victim might strike during the seizure. Do not attempt to restrain the victim, and do not attempt to move the head. You may, however, loosen the victim's clothing. Put a folded handkerchief between the teeth to prevent the victim from biting the tongue. But be careful not to place your fingers in the victim's mouth because the person could bite them. After the attack, if there is no evidence that the victim may have fallen or may have injured the spine, turn the victim's head to one side to prevent choking in case vomiting occurs.

Eye injury. If acids or alkalis have been splashed into the eye, immediately flush the eye with water. Flush continuously at least 10 minutes for acids and 20 minutes for alkalis. Use a continuous stream of water from a tap or a hose, or pour the water from a cup or other container. Flush the eye from the inside corner outward, to avoid washing the chemical into the other eye. Cover the eye with sterile gauze or a clean pad and take the victim to an eye doctor.

Dust particles or other foreign objects can be removed from the eye by gently flushing with water. Or they can be removed with the corner of a clean handkerchief. However, do not wipe across the *cornea* (clear central part of the eye) with a handkerchief or any other material. Seriously injured victims should have the eyes examined at the emergency department of a hospital.

Fainting is a brief, sudden period of unconsciousness. It occurs when blood pressure falls to the point where the brain does not receive enough oxygen. In most cases, fainting occurs when a person is standing. The victim falls to the ground while losing consciousness. Leave the victim lying down. Loosen the clothing and raise the feet slightly. Blood will flow back into the head, and the victim should regain consciousness promptly. Should the victim fail to do so, lay the person on his or her side and make certain the airway remains open. Call a physician.

Just before fainting, a person may feel weak or numb. Other symptoms include nausea, light-headedness, blurred vision, pale appearance, sweating, or excessive yawning. A person experiencing these symptoms should lie down or sit with the head between the knees. If the victim has a heart or lung problem, fainting may be a serious condition related to the ailment. The conditions of such patients should be evaluated in a hospital's emergency department.

Fractures and dislocations. A *fracture* is a break in a bone. A *dislocation* occurs when the end of a bone is forced out of its normal position in a joint. Fractures and dislocations frequently result from automobile and sports accidents.

Signs of fractures and dislocations include pain, an unusual position of a joint or bone, and tenderness and swelling around the injury. The victim may also experience a grating sensation, caused by fragments of broken bone rubbing together. The victim may be unable to use a hand or a foot.

Keep the victim quiet and treat for shock. Whenever possible, do not move the person until expert help arrives. Improper handling of an injured bone or joint may

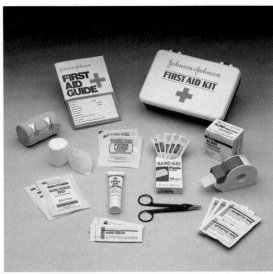

WORLD BOOK photo by Steven Spicer

A first-aid kit contains a variety of items that can be used to treat minor injuries. These items commonly include adhesive bandages, gauze, antiseptic wipes, and medicated creams.

seriously damage arteries, muscles, or nerves. It may also increase the severity of the fracture or dislocation.

If you must move the victim before help arrives, apply a splint to the injured area. The splint prevents broken or dislocated bones from moving. You can make a splint from any material that will support the injured part without bending. For fractures of the arm or leg, the splint should be long enough to prevent movement of joints above and below the injury. Pad the splint surfaces that touch the body. Do not try to correct any deformities before splinting. Do not push bone fragments back into an open wound.

Use strips of cloth to tie the splint above and below the point of injury. Do not tie the splint so tightly that it interferes with circulation. Blueness or swelling in fingers, for example, indicates that a splint has been tied too tightly to an arm.

Do not move a person who may have suffered a broken neck or other spinal injury. A person may receive such an injury by diving into shallow water, falling from a considerable height, or striking the head in an auto accident. Moving such an accident victim may cause permanent paralysis or death.

Frostbite may occur when the skin is exposed to extreme cold. It most frequently affects the skin of the cheeks, chin, ears, fingers, nose, or toes.

Frostbitten skin appears whitish and feels numb. It should be handled gently. Never massage frostbitten skin, and do not rub it with snow or bathe it in cold water. Warm the affected area with the heat of your hand or cover it with a heavy cloth until you can get the victim indoors. Thaw the affected skin by soaking it in lukewarm water. The temperature of this water should be between 102° and 105° F. (39° and 41° C). Keep the temperature in this range by adding more warm water as needed. Never use water hotter than 105° F. (41° C). If warm water is not available, wrap the frostbitten area with blankets. Obtain medical assistance as quickly as possible. If a victim of frostbite must be moved, protect the person from additional exposure.

Never treat frostbite with heat from a stove or with a heating pad, hot water bottle, or heat lamp. Such treatment may produce temperatures that can damage frostbitten tissue. If frostbite blisters occur, do not break them. Bandage them to prevent infection.

Heart attack. Most heart attacks begin with a crushing tightness or intense pressure behind the *sternum* (breastbone). This pain may spread across the chest, affecting the arms, the neck, the jaw, or the pit of the stomach. In most cases, it lasts more than five minutes. The victim appears worried, has difficulty breathing, and may perspire heavily and experience feelings of weakness and nausea. He or she may vomit.

Call a physician or summon an ambulance that has oxygen equipment. Stay calm and reassure the victim that help is on the way. The victim should not be picked up or allowed to move. Place him or her in the most comfortable sitting or half-sitting, half-lying position. Do not give the victim liquids without a doctor's orders.

In severe heart attacks and serious accidents, the victim's heart may stop beating temporarily. An effective method of treatment in such cases is *cardiopulmonary resuscitation,* commonly called *CPR.* CPR consists of artificial respiration and artificial circulation of the blood. It should be performed only by someone trained in the technique. See **Cardiopulmonary resuscitation.**

Heatstroke and heat exhaustion can occur when the body becomes overheated. Heatstroke is the more serious of the two conditions. A person suffering heatstroke feels hot but cannot sweat. The skin becomes hot, dry, and red. The body temperature rises so high that it can cause brain damage if not lowered quickly. Undress the victim. Either place the victim in a tub of cool water or apply cold, wet towels to the entire body. Get medical attention as quickly as possible.

A person suffering heat exhaustion, also called *heat prostration,* displays many of the symptoms of shock. Such symptoms include faintness, headache, and nausea. The skin is cold, gray, and wet with perspiration. In most cases, the body temperature remains about normal. Treat the victim as if he or she were in shock. Place the victim on his or her back, with the legs raised slightly. If the victim has trouble breathing in this position, place the person in a half-sitting, half-lying position. Take the victim to a hospital, in an air-conditioned vehicle if possible.

Nosebleed. To control a nosebleed, have the victim sit up and lean forward. Then press the nostrils firmly together for 5 to 10 minutes. Consult a physician if the bleeding does not stop within 10 to 15 minutes.

Snakebite. The treatment of a snakebite depends on whether or not the snake is poisonous. If the snake is nonpoisonous, the bite should be washed thoroughly with soap and water.

A person bitten by a poisonous snake requires medical attention. Most poisonous snakebites cause deep, burning pain along with swelling and discoloration. Within minutes the victim may begin to feel numb and have difficulty breathing. Call a physician or take the victim to a hospital. If possible, kill the snake and bring it along for identification.

Keep the victim motionless and quiet, because activity increases the spread of the poison. Place the bitten portion of the body at a level below that of the heart. If the bite is on an arm or a leg, tie a band above the wound, between it and the heart. The band should be loose enough for you to slip your finger under it. Release the band for 90 seconds every 10 minutes to prevent damage from lack of circulation. For more information on emergency treatment of snakebite, see **Snakebite.**

Transporting the victim

Moving a seriously injured person to a medical facility requires great care. Rough or careless handling can make the victim's injuries even more serious. If a victim must be moved, call for an ambulance.

If you must transport the victim yourself, be sure that you have thoroughly examined the person to determine the full extent of the injuries. All bleeding should be under control, and breathing should be satisfactory and comfortable. Treat the victim for shock and splint any fractures and dislocations. If the victim must be lifted, get someone to help you, in order to avoid rough handling. Whenever possible, use a stretcher to carry a seriously injured person.

If a person may have suffered a back or neck injury, wait for professional help. Move such a victim only if it is necessary to save the person's life. Take great care not to bend or twist the body or neck. Carry the victim on a wide, hard surface, such as a lightweight door.

During transport, drive safely. If possible, two persons should transport the victim. One can ensure that the victim's airway remains open and give comfort while the other drives.   Carlotta M. Rinke

Related articles in *World Book* include:

Conditions requiring first aid

Asphyxiation	Hemorrhage
Bee (Sting)	Hypothermia
Bleeding	Nosebleed
Blister	Poison
Bruise	Poison ivy
Burns and scalds	Rabies
Dislocation	Shock
Drowning	Snakebite
Fainting	Stroke
Fracture	Sunburn
Frostbite	Sunstroke

Other related articles

Ambulance	Cardiopulmonary	Respirator
Antidote	resuscitation	Safety
Antiseptic	Emetic	Tourniquet
Bandage	Red Cross	

Outline

I. General rules for first aid
    A. Call for assistance   C. Examine the victim
    B. Provide urgent care   D. Treat for shock
II. First aid for bleeding
    A. Direct pressure   B. Pressure on arteries
III. Treatment for poisoning
    A. Swallowed poisons   C. Injected poisons
    B. Inhaled poisons   D. Poisons on the skin
IV. Restoring breathing
    A. Removing the cause of breathing failure
    B. Giving artificial respiration
V. Other first-aid procedures
    A. Animal bites or stings   C. Choking
    B. Burns   D. Concussion

E. Convulsion and epileptic seizure
F. Eye injury
G. Fainting
H. Fractures and dislocations
I. Frostbite
J. Heart attack
K. Heatstroke and heat exhaustion
L. Nosebleed
M. Snakebite
VI. Transporting the victim

Questions

What is syrup of ipecac? When should it be used?
Why should an animal that has bitten a person be kept under observation by a veterinarian?
What is the purpose of a splint?
What information should a person administering first aid tell a doctor called in an emergency?
Why is it especially important to keep a snakebite victim motionless?
Why should a victim be examined for a medical tag or medical identification card?
What are the three types of burns? Which type should always be treated by a physician immediately?
What techniques should be used to stop severe bleeding in an arm or leg?
What are some of the signs that indicate a person may have suffered a concussion?
What kinds of injuries may cause the condition called *shock*?

Additional resources

American Medical Association. *The American Medical Association's Handbook of First Aid and Emergency Care.* Random House, 1980.
American Red Cross. *Advanced First Aid and Emergency Care.* 2nd ed. Semline, 1979. *Basic First Aid.* 1979. *Standard First Aid and Personal Safety.* 3rd ed. 1981. *Lifesaving: Rescue and Water Safety.* 1982.
Greenbank, Anthony. *A Handbook for Emergencies: Coming Out Alive.* Doubleday, 1976. For younger readers.
Heimlich, Henry J., and Galton, L. N. *Dr. Heimlich's Home Guide to Emergency Medical Situations.* Simon & Schuster, 1980.
Rosenberg, Stephen N. *The Johnson and Johnson First Aid Book.* Warner Books, 1985.
Smith, Bradley, and Stevens, Gus. *The Emergency Book: You Can Save a Life!* Simon & Schuster, 1980.

First Amendment. See **Constitution of the United States** (Amendment 1).

First Continental Congress. See **Continental Congress.**

First ladies. See pictures of the first ladies in the separate biographies of each President of the United States. See also the separate articles **Adams, Abigail Smith; Lincoln, Mary Todd; Madison, Dolley Payne; Roosevelt, Eleanor; Washington, Martha Custis.**

First National City Bank. See **Citibank.**

First Riel Rebellion. See **Red River Rebellion.**

Firth is an arm of the sea or the opening of a river into the sea. The term is used mostly in Scotland, where many rivers open into firths. Firths are similar to *fiords*. But most fiords have high walls, and the walls of firths may be low. See also **Fiord.**

Firth of Clyde is the broad, irregularly shaped mouth of the River Clyde in southwestern Scotland. The firth is a large bay 50 miles (80 kilometers) long and more than 30 miles (48 kilometers) wide in places. The North Channel connects it with the Atlantic Ocean and with the Irish Sea. Shipping from Glasgow, which lies inland on the River Clyde, has an outlet through the firth.   A. S. Mather

Firth of Forth is the large mouth of the River Forth on the east coast of Scotland. The baylike firth connects with the North Sea (see **Great Britain** [physical map]). The Firth of Forth is 50 miles (80 kilometers) long and 30 miles (48 kilometers) wide at its widest point.

One of the world's longest suspension bridges spans the firth at Queensferry. The bridge was completed in 1964. It is 8,244 feet (2,513 meters) long and has a 3,300-foot (1,006-meter) center span. A cantilever railroad bridge 1 mile (1.6 kilometers) long also crosses the firth at Queensferry. It was completed in 1890.   A. S. Mather

Fischer, Bobby (1943-   ), became the first American to win the official world chess championship. Fischer won the title in 1972 by defeating defending world chess champion Boris Spassky of the Soviet Union in the most publicized chess match in history. In 1975, the World Chess Federation took away Fischer's title after he refused to defend his championship by playing Soviet challenger Anatoly Karpov under rules set by the federation.

Robert James Fischer was born in Chicago and raised in New York City. In 1958, at the age of 14, he won his first United States chess championship. Fischer held the title until 1968, except in 1962, when he passed up the tournament. At 15, Fischer became the youngest international grandmaster in the history of chess.
Herman Weiskopf

Fischer, Emil (1852-1919), a German chemist, won the 1902 Nobel Prize in chemistry for his wide research. He discovered a method of identifying sugars, and did basic research on proteins, enzyme actions, and purine derivatives such as uric acid and caffeine. He also won fame for his work on dyes. During World War I, he conducted research on carbon, rubber, oils, fats, and other materials. Fischer was born in northern Germany. He taught at the University of Berlin from 1892 until his death.   K. L. Kaufman

Fischer, Ernst. See **Nobel Prizes** (table: Nobel Prizes for chemistry—1973).

Fischer-Dieskau, *FIHSH uhr DEE skow,* **Dietrich** (1925-   ), a German baritone, is considered one of the finest singers of *lieder* (German art songs) of his time (see **Lieder**). Fischer-Dieskau won international fame for his concerts and his many phonograph recordings. He has sung with many important conductors, and he frequently performed with the noted piano accompanist Gerald Moore. Fischer-Dieskau has also achieved great success in opera, performing with the world's leading companies. He has sung a wide range of baritone roles in works by most of the major opera composers.

Fischer-Dieskau was born in Berlin and studied music there. He made his debut in 1947 in Johannes Brahms's *A German Requiem.* He made his United States debut in 1955 with the Cincinnati Symphony Orchestra.

Fischer-Dieskau collected and introduced over 750 songs in *The Fischer-Dieskau Book of Lieder* (1977). He also wrote *Schubert's Songs: A Biographical Study* (1977).
Charles H. Webb

W. Neumeister, Colbert Artists Management
Dietrich Fischer-Dieskau

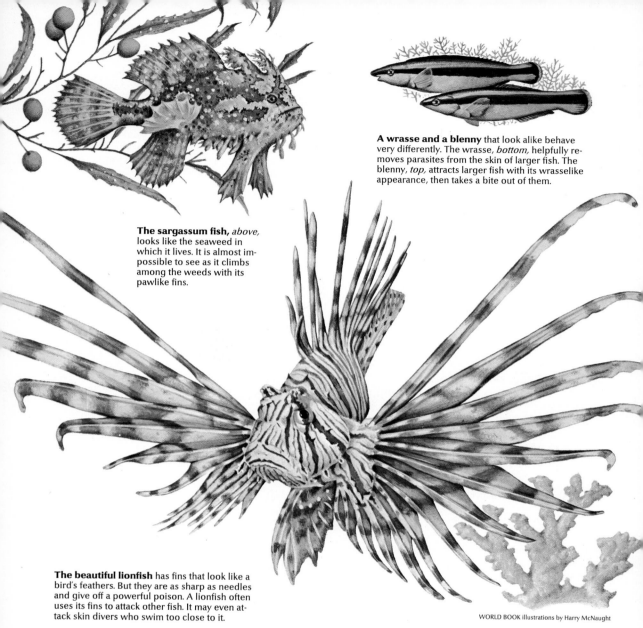

A wrasse and a blenny that look alike behave very differently. The wrasse, *bottom,* helpfully removes parasites from the skin of larger fish. The blenny, *top,* attracts larger fish with its wrasselike appearance, then takes a bite out of them.

The sargassum fish, *above,* looks like the seaweed in which it lives. It is almost impossible to see as it climbs among the weeds with its pawlike fins.

The beautiful lionfish has fins that look like a bird's feathers. But they are as sharp as needles and give off a powerful poison. A lionfish often uses its fins to attack other fish. It may even attack skin divers who swim too close to it.

WORLD BOOK illustrations by Harry McNaught

Fish

Fish are *vertebrates* (backboned animals) that live in water. There are more kinds of fish than all other kinds of water and land vertebrates put together. The various kinds of fish differ so greatly in shape, color, and size that it is hard to believe they all belong to the same group of animals. For example, some fish look like lumpy rocks, and others like wriggly worms. Some fish are nearly as flat as pancakes, and others can blow themselves up like balloons. Fish have all the colors of the rainbow. Many have colors as bright as the most

C. Lavett Smith, the contributor of this article, is Curator in the Department of Ichthyology at the American Museum of Natural History and coauthor of The Hidden Sea.

brightly colored birds. Their rich reds, yellows, blues, and purples form hundreds of beautiful patterns, from stripes and lacelike designs to polka dots.

The smallest fish is the pygmy goby of the Philippines, which grows less than $\frac{1}{2}$ inch (13 millimeters) long. The largest fish is the whale shark, which may grow more than 40 feet (12 meters) long and weigh over 15 short tons (14 metric tons). It feeds on small sea animals and plants and is completely harmless to most other fish and to human beings. The most dangerous fish weigh only a few pounds or kilograms. They include the deadly stonefish, whose poisonous spines can kill a human being in a matter of minutes.

Fish live almost anywhere there is water. They are found in the near-freezing waters of the Arctic and in the steaming waters of tropical jungles. They live in roaring mountain streams and in quiet underground

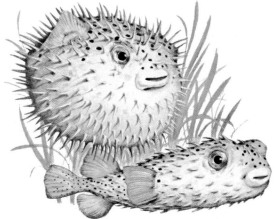

The **porcupinefish** is covered with protective spines. For added protection, the fish fills itself with water to change from its normal appearance, *bottom,* to that of a prickly balloon, *top.*

Roy Pinney, Globe

An **archerfish** catches an insect resting above the surface by spitting drops of water at it. The drops strike with enough force to knock the insect into the water, where the fish can eat it.

rivers. Some fish make long journeys across the ocean. Others spend most of their life buried in sand on the bottom of the ocean. Most fish never leave water. Yet some fish are able to survive for months in dried-up riverbeds.

Fish have enormous importance to human beings. They provide food for millions of people. Fishing enthusiasts catch them for sport, and people keep them as pets. In addition, fish are important in the *balance of nature.* They eat plants and animals and, in turn, become food for plants and animals. Fish thus help keep in balance the total number of plants and animals on the earth.

All fish have two main features in common. (1) They have a backbone, and so they are vertebrates. (2) They breathe mainly by means of gills. Nearly all fish are also *cold-blooded* animals—that is, they cannot regulate their body temperature, which changes with the temperature of their surroundings. In addition, almost all fish have fins, which they use for swimming. All other water animals differ from fish in at least one of these ways. Dol-

Interesting facts about fish

The smallest fish is the pygmy goby of the Philippines. It measures less than ½ inch (13 millimeters) when fully grown.

The largest fish is the whale shark. It may weigh more than 15 short tons (14 metric tons) —over twice as much as an African elephant. This fish is harmless to people. It eats small sea plants and animals.

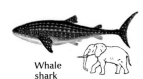

Whale shark

A four-eyed fish, the anableps, has eyes divided in two. When the fish swims just below the surface, the top half of each eye sees above the surface and the bottom half sees underwater.

Anableps

The black swallower can swallow fish twice its own size. Its jaws have "hinges" that enable them to open wide, and its stomach can stretch to several times its normal size. A fish swallowed whole is gradually digested.

Black swallower

The flying hatchet fish is one of the few fish that can really fly. A hatchet fish can take off from the water's surface and fly as far as 10 feet (3 meters). The fish uses its side fins as wings.

Flying hatchet fish

The walking catfish lives for days out of water and even "walks" on land from one lake to another. The fish has special air-breathing organs and uses its side fins and tail to help it crawl on the ground.

Walking catfish

The largest group of fish are bristlemouths, a kind of tiny salt-water fish. Scientists believe that bristlemouths number in the billions of billions.

phins, porpoises, and whales look like fish and have a backbone and fins, but they are *mammals* (animals that feed their young with the mother's milk). Mammals breathe with lungs rather than gills. They are also *warm-blooded*—their body temperature remains about the same when the air or water temperature changes. Some water animals are called *fish,* but they do not have a backbone and so are not fish. These animals include jellyfish and starfish. Clams, crabs, lobsters, oysters, scallops, and shrimps are called *shellfish.* But they also lack a backbone.

The first fish appeared on the earth about 500 million years ago. They were the first animals to have a backbone. Most scientists believe that these early fish became the ancestors of all other vertebrates.

The importance of fish

Fish benefit people in many ways. Fish make up a major part of the people's diet in Japan and Norway. In other countries, the people eat fish to add variety to their meals. For thousands of years, people have also enjoyed fishing for sport. Many people keep fish as pets. Fish are also important in the balance of nature.

Food and game fish. Fish rank among the most nourishing of all foods. Fish flesh contains about as much protein as meat does. Each year, millions of tons of cod, herring, tuna, and other ocean food fish are caught commercially. Commercial fishing also takes place in inland waters, where such freshwater food fish as perch and trout are caught. The *World Book* article on **Fishing industry** discusses commercial fishing throughout the world.

Businesses called *fish farms* raise certain types of fish for food. Fish farms in the United States raise catfish, salmon, and trout. In other countries, they raise carp and milkfish. Fish farmers raise the fish in ponds and use special feeding methods to make the fish grow larger and faster than they grow in the wild.

Some persons enjoy fishing simply for fun. Many of these people like to go after *game fish.* Game fish are noted for their fighting spirit or some other quality that adds to the excitement of fishing. They include such giant ocean fish as marlin and swordfish and such freshwater fish as black bass and rainbow trout. Most game fish are also food fish. See the article on **Fishing** for detailed information on sport fishing.

Other useful fish. Certain fish, such as anchovettas and menhaden, are caught commercially but are not good to eat. Industries process these fish to make glue, livestock feed, and other products. Scientists often

Fish in the balance of nature

Fish help keep the number of organisms on the earth in balance. Fish feed on some aquatic organisms and themselves become food for others. This process is called a *food chain.* Fish are part of many food chains, as shown in the diagram below. The blue symbols represent various aquatic organisms that fish eat. The red symbols represent living things that eat fish or are nourished by the matter that remains after fish die and decay.

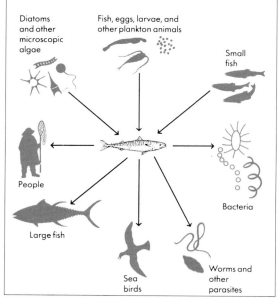

WORLD BOOK diagram

Jen & Des Bartlett, Bruce Coleman Inc.

Fish hatcheries raise fish that are used to stock rivers. The workers at the left are removing the eggs from a female salmon. The eggs are then fertilized with *milt* from a male salmon, *center.* The fertilized eggs are kept in an *incubator, right,* until they hatch into baby salmon.

use goldfish and other small fish as experimental animals in medical research. They do not require as much space or as much care as do other experimental animals. Some fish produce substances used as medicines. For example, a chemical produced by puffers is used to treat asthma. Many people enjoy keeping fish as pets in home aquariums (see **Aquarium**). Popular aquarium fish include goldfish, guppies, and tetras.

Harmful fish. Few species of fish will attack a human being. They include certain sharks, especially hammerhead and white sharks, which occasionally attack swimmers. Barracudas and moray eels may also attack a swimmer if provoked. Certain types of piranhas are bloodthirsty fish with razor-sharp teeth. A group of them can strip the flesh from a human being or an alligator or other large animal in minutes or even seconds. Some other fish, including sting rays and stonefish, have poisonous spines that can injure or kill anything that comes in contact with them. The flesh of filefish, puffers, and some other fish is poisonous and can cause sickness or death if eaten.

A few species of fish have become pests after being introduced into certain waters. For example, sea lampreys that entered the Great Lakes and Asian catfish introduced into inland waters of Florida have become threats to native fish.

Fish in the balance of nature. All the fish in a particular environment, such as a lake or a certain area of the ocean, make up a *fish community*. The fish in a community are parts of a system in which energy is transferred from one living thing to another in the form of food. Such a system is called a *food chain*. Every food chain begins with the energy from sunlight. Plants use this energy to make their food. In the ocean and in fresh water, the most important kinds of plant life are part of the *plankton*—the great mass of tiny plants and animals that drifts near the surface. Certain fish eat plankton and are in turn eaten by other fish. These fish may then be eaten by still other fish. Some of these fish may also be eaten by people or by birds or other animals. Many fish die naturally. Their bodies then sink and decay. The decayed matter provides nourishment for water plants and animals.

Every fish community forms part of a larger natural community made up of all the plants and animals in an area. A natural community includes numerous food chains, which together are called a *food web*. The complicated feeding patterns involved in a food web keep any one form of life from becoming too numerous and so preserve the balance of nature.

The balance of a community may be upset if large numbers of one species in the community are destroyed. People may upset the balance in this way by catching too many fish of a particular kind. Or they may pollute the water so badly that certain kinds of plants and animals, including certain fish, can no longer live in it. To learn how people conserve fish, see **Fishing industry** (Fishery conservation).

Kinds of fish

Scientists have named and described about 21,700 kinds of fish. Each year, they discover new species, and so the total increases continually. Fish make up more than half of all known species of vertebrates.

Scientists who study fish are called *ichthyologists* (pronounced *IHK thee AHL uh jihsts*). They divide fish into two main groups: (1) *jawed* and (2) *jawless.* Almost all fish have jaws. The only jawless species are lampreys and hagfish. Jawed fish are further divided into two groups according to the composition of their skeletons. One group has a skeleton composed of a tough, elastic substance called *cartilage*. Sharks, rays, and chimaeras make up this group. The other group has a skeleton composed largely or partly of bone. Members of this group, called *bony fish,* make up by far the largest group of fish in the world.

The section of this article called *A classification of fish* lists the major subgroups into which bony fish are divided. This section discusses the chief characteristics of (1) bony fish; (2) sharks, rays, and chimaeras; and (3) lampreys and hagfish.

Bony fish

Bony fish can be divided into two main groups according to the composition of their skeletons. One group consists of *modern bony fish,* whose skeletons are composed largely of bone. The second group consists of *primitive bony fish,* whose skeletons are partly bone and partly cartilage.

Modern bony fish include about 20,000 species. They make up about 95 per cent of all known kinds of fish. Some have bony skeletons. They are called *teleosts,* which comes from two Greek words meaning *complete* and *bone.* Nearly all food fish, game fish, and aquarium fish are teleosts. They include such well-known groups of fish as bass, catfish, cod, herring, minnows, perch, trout, and tuna. Each group of fish consists of a number of species. For example, Johnny darters, walleyes, and yellow perch are all kinds of perch.

Thousands of species of teleosts are not so well known. Many live in jungle rivers or coral reefs. Some are deep-sea species seldom seen by human beings. They include more than 150 kinds of deep-sea anglers. These small, fierce-looking fish have fanglike teeth and flashing light organs. They live in the ocean depths and seldom if ever come to the surface. Many teleosts have unusual names and are as strange and colorful as their names. For example, the elephant-nose mormyrid has a snout shaped much like an elephant's trunk. The fish uses its snout to hunt for food along river bottoms. Another strange fish, the upside-down catfish, regularly swims on its back.

Many millions of years ago, there were only a few species of teleosts. They were greatly outnumbered by sharks and the ancestors of certain present-day bony fish. The early teleosts looked much alike and lived in only a few parts of the world. Yet they became the most numerous, varied, and widespread of all fish mainly be-

Bill Noel Kleeman, Tom Stack & Associates

A leaping trout, *above,* is a sight familiar to many people. But some species of fish are seldom seen. Many kinds of fish live in such places as jungle rivers or deep parts of the ocean.

cause they were better able than other fish to *adapt* (adjust) to changes in their environment. In adapting to these changes, their bodies and body organs changed in various ways. Such changes are called *adaptations.*

Today, the various species of teleosts differ from one another in so many ways that they seem to have little in common. For example, many teleosts have flexible, highly efficient fins, which have helped them become excellent swimmers. Sailfish and tuna can swim long distances at high speed. Many teleosts that live among coral reefs are expert at darting in and out of the coral. But a number of other teleosts swim hardly at all. Some anglerfish spend most of their adult life lying on the ocean floor. Certain eellike teleosts are finless and so are poor swimmers. They burrow into mud on the bottom and remain there much of the time. Many teleosts have fins that are adapted to uses other than swimming. For example, flying fish have winglike fins that help them glide above the surface of the water. The mudskipper has muscular fins that it uses to hop about on land.

Other modern bony fish include sturgeons, paddlefish, gars, and bowfins. Sturgeons rank as the largest of all freshwater fish. The largest sturgeon ever caught weighed more than 2,800 pounds (1,300 kilograms). Instead of scales, sturgeons have an armorlike covering consisting of five rows of thick, bony plates. Some sturgeons live in salt water but return to fresh water to lay their eggs. Paddlefish are strange-looking fish found only in China and the Mississippi Valley of the United States. They have huge snouts shaped somewhat like

canoe paddles. Bowfins and gars are extremely fierce fish of eastern North America. They have unusually strong jaws and sharp teeth.

Primitive bony fish include about 15 species of bichirs, coelacanths, and lungfish. They make up less than 1 per cent of all fish species. These odd-looking fish are related to fish that lived many millions of years ago.

All the primitive bony fish except the coelacanths live in fresh water. Coelacanths live off the southeast coast of Africa. They are not closely related to any other living fish, and there is only one known species of coelacanth.

Bichirs live in tropical Africa. They are slow-moving fish with a long, thin body and thick scales. Lungfish live in Africa, Australia, and South America. They breathe with lunglike organs as well as gills. The African and South American species can go without food and water longer than any other vertebrates. They live buried in dry mud for months at a time, during which they neither eat nor drink.

Sharks, rays, and chimaeras

Sharks, rays, and chimaeras total about 790 species, or about 3 per cent of all known fish. All have jaws and a skeleton of cartilage rather than bone. Almost all live in salt water. Sharks and rays are the most important members of the group and make up about 760 species.

Most sharks have a torpedo-shaped body. The bodies of most rays are shaped somewhat like pancakes. A large, winglike fin extends outward from each side of a ray's flattened head and body. But the angel shark has a flattened body, and the sawfish and a few other rays are torpedo shaped. As a result, the best way to tell a shark from a ray is by the position of the *gill slits.* In sharks and rays, gill slits are slotlike openings on the outside of the body, leading from the gills. A shark's gill slits are on the sides of its head just back of the eyes. A ray's are underneath its side fins.

Chimaeras, or ratfish, include about 30 species. They are medium-sized fish with large eyes and a long, slender, pointed tail. They live near the ocean bottom. Several species have long, pointed snouts.

Lampreys and hagfish

Lampreys and hagfish are the most primitive of all fish. There are about 30 species of lampreys and about 15 kinds of hagfish. They make up less than 1 per cent of all fish species. Lampreys live in both salt water and fresh water. Hagfish live only in the ocean.

Lampreys and hagfish have slimy, scaleless bodies shaped somewhat like the bodies of eels. But they are not closely related to eels, which are teleosts. Like sharks, rays, and chimaeras, lampreys and hagfish have a skeleton made of cartilage. But unlike all other fish, lampreys and hagfish lack jaws. A lamprey's mouth consists mainly of a round sucking organ and a toothed tongue. Certain types of lampreys use their sucking organ to attach themselves to other fish. They use their toothed tongue to cut into their victim and feed on its blood (see **Lamprey** [picture: The lamprey's mouth]). Hagfish have a slitlike mouth with sharp teeth but no sucking organ. They eat the insides of dead fish.

The chief kinds of fish

WORLD BOOK illustration by Marion Pahl

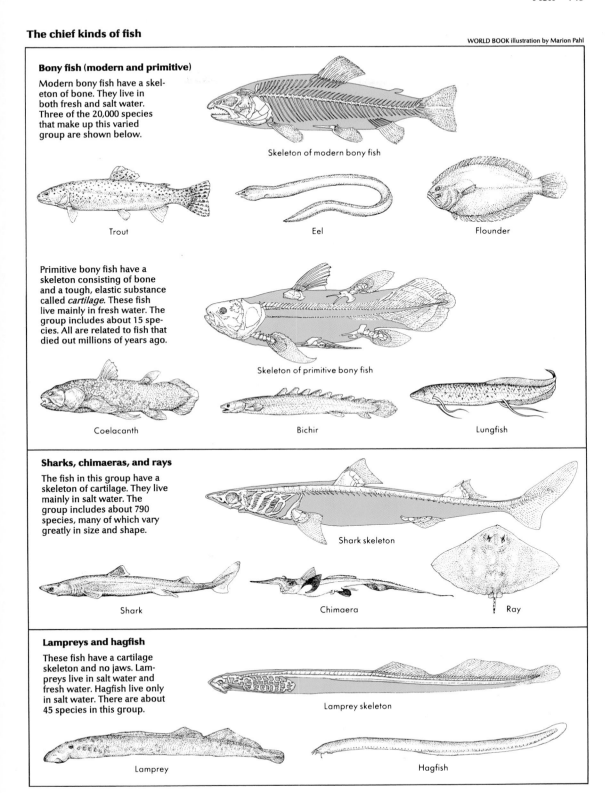

Bony fish (modern and primitive)

Modern bony fish have a skeleton of bone. They live in both fresh and salt water. Three of the 20,000 species that make up this varied group are shown below.

Skeleton of modern bony fish

Trout

Eel

Flounder

Primitive bony fish have a skeleton consisting of bone and a tough, elastic substance called *cartilage*. These fish live mainly in fresh water. The group includes about 15 species. All are related to fish that died out millions of years ago.

Skeleton of primitive bony fish

Coelacanth

Bichir

Lungfish

Sharks, chimaeras, and rays

The fish in this group have a skeleton of cartilage. They live mainly in salt water. The group includes about 790 species, many of which vary greatly in size and shape.

Shark skeleton

Shark

Chimaera

Ray

Lampreys and hagfish

These fish have a cartilage skeleton and no jaws. Lampreys live in salt water and fresh water. Hagfish live only in salt water. There are about 45 species in this group.

Lamprey skeleton

Lamprey

Hagfish

Fish live almost anywhere there is water. They thrive in the warm waters of the South Pacific and in the icy waters of the Arctic and Antarctic oceans. Some live high above sea level in mountain streams. Others live far below sea level in the deepest parts of the ocean. Many fish have adapted themselves to living in such unusual places as caves, desert water holes, marshes, and swamps. A few fish, including the African and South American lungfish, can even live for months in moist mud.

Fish thus live in many environments. But all these environments can be classified into two major groups according to the saltiness of the water: (1) saltwater environments and (2) freshwater environments. Some fish can live only in the salty waters of the ocean. Others can live only in fresh water. Still others can live in either salt water or fresh water. The sections on *The bodies of fish* and *How fish live* discuss how fish adjust to their environment. This section describes some of the main saltwater and freshwater environments. It also discusses fish migrations from one environment to another. A series of color illustrations shows the kinds of fish that live in the various environments. The illustration for each fish gives the fish's common and scientific names and the average or maximum length of an adult fish.

Saltwater environments. About 13,300 species—or about three-fifths of all known fish—live in the ocean. These saltwater, or *marine,* fish live in an almost endless variety of ocean environments. Most of them are suited to a particular type of environment and cannot survive in one much different from that type. Water temperature is one of the chief factors in determining where a fish can live. Water temperatures at the surface range from freezing in polar regions to about 86° F. (30° C) in the tropics.

Many saltwater species live where the water is always warm. The warmest parts of the ocean are the shallow tropical waters around coral reefs. More than a third of all known saltwater species live around coral reefs in the Indian and Pacific oceans. Many other species live around reefs in the West Indies. Coral reefs swarm with angelfish, butterfly fish, parrot fish, and thousands of other species with fantastic shapes and brilliant colors. Barracudas, groupers, moray eels, and sharks prowl the clear coral waters in search of prey.

Many kinds of fish also live in ocean waters that are neither very warm nor very cold. Such *temperate* waters occur north and south of the tropics. They make excellent fishing grounds. The richest fishing grounds lie off the northeast coast of North America and the northwest coast of Europe. These areas yield huge catches of cod, flatfish, herring, and other food fish.

The cold waters of the Arctic and Antarctic oceans have fewer kinds of fish than do tropical and temperate waters. Arctic fish include bullheads, eelpouts, sculpins, skates, and a jellylike, scaleless fish called a sea snail. Fish of the Antarctic Ocean include the small, perchlike Antarctic cod, eelpouts, and the icefish, whose blood is nearly transparent rather than red.

Different kinds of fish also live at different depths in the ocean. The largest and fastest-swimming fish live near the surface of the *open ocean* and are often found great distances from shore. Fish that live near the surface of the open ocean include bonito, mackerel, marlin, swordfish, tuna, and a variety of sharks. Some of these fish make long annual migrations that range from tropical to near polar waters.

Many more kinds of ocean fish live in midwater and in the depths than near the surface. Their environment differs greatly from that of species which live near the surface. Sunlight cannot reach far beneath the ocean's surface. Below about 600 feet (180 meters), the waters range from dimly lit to completely dark. Most fish that live in midwater far out at sea measure less than 6 inches (15 centimeters) long and are black, black-violet, or reddish-brown. Most of them have light organs that flash on and off in the darkness. Many also have large eyes and mouths. A number of midwater species are related to the herring. One such group includes the tiny bristlemouths. Scientists believe that bristlemouths outnumber all other kinds of fish. They estimate that bristlemouths number in the billions.

Some fish species live on the ocean bottom. Many of these fish, such as eels, flounders, puffers, seahorses, and soles, live in shallow coastal waters. But many others live at the bottom far from shore. They include rattails and many other fish with large heads and eyes and long, slender, pointed tails. Many species of rattails grow 1 foot (30 centimeters) or more long. One of the strangest bottom dwellers of the deep ocean is the tripod, or spider, fish. It has three long fins like the legs of a tripod or a three-legged stool. The fish uses its fins to sit on the ocean bottom.

Some kinds of fish live in *brackish* (slightly salty) water. Such water occurs where rivers empty into the ocean, where salt water collects in coastal swamps, and where pools are left by the outgoing tide. Brackish-water fish include certain species of barracudas, flatfish, gobies, herring, killifish, silversides, and sticklebacks. Some saltwater fish, including various kinds of herring, lampreys, salmon, smelt, and sticklebacks, can also live in fresh water.

Freshwater environments. Fish live on every continent except Antarctica. They are found in most lakes, rivers, and streams and in brooks, creeks, marshes, ponds, springs, and swamps. Some live in streams that pass through caves or flow deep underground.

Scientists have classified about 8,400 kinds of freshwater fish. They make up about two-fifths of all fish species. Almost all freshwater fish are bony fish. Many of these bony fish belong to a large group that includes carp, catfish, characins, electric eels, loaches, minnows, and suckers. In this group, catfish alone total more than 2,000 species.

Like ocean fish, freshwater fish live in a variety of climates. Tropical regions of Africa, Asia, and South America have the most species, including hundreds of kinds of catfish. Africa also has many cichlids and mormyrids. A variety of colorful loaches and minnows live in Asia. South American species include electric eels, piranhas, and tetras. Temperate regions, especially in North America, also have many freshwater species, including bass, carp, minnows, perch, and trout. Blackfish and pike live in the Arctic.

In every climate, certain kinds of freshwater fish require a particular kind of environment. Some species, including many kinds of graylings, minnows, and trout, live mainly in cool, clear, fast-moving streams. Many species of carp and catfish thrive in warm, muddy, slow-moving rivers. Some fish, such as bluegills, lake trout, white bass, and whitefish, live chiefly in lakes. Black bullheads, largemouth bass, muskellunge, northern pike, rainbow trout, yellow perch, and many other species are found both in lakes and in streams and rivers.

Like marine fish, freshwater fish live at different levels in the water. For example, many cave, spring, and swamp fish live near the surface. Gars, muskellunge, and whitefish ordinarily live in midwater. Bottom dwellers include darters, sturgeon, and many kinds of catfish and suckers.

Some freshwater species live in unusual environments. For example, some live in mountain streams so swift and violent that few other forms of life can survive in them. These fish cling to rocks with their mouth or some special suction organ. A number of species live in caves and underground streams. These fish never see daylight. Most of them have pale or white skin, and many of them are blind. A few kinds of freshwater fish live in hot springs where the temperature rises as high as 104° F. (40° C).

Fish migrations. Relatively few kinds of fish can travel freely between fresh water and salt water. They make such migrations to *spawn* (lay eggs). Saltwater fish that swim to fresh water for spawning are called *anadromous* fish. They include alewives, blueback herring, sea lampreys, smelt, and most species of salmon and shad. Freshwater fish that spawn in salt water are called *catadromous* fish. They include North American and European eels and certain kinds of gobies. Some normally anadromous fish, including large numbers of certain species of alewives, lampreys, salmon, and smelt, have become *landlocked*—that is, they have become freshwater natives. After hatching, the young do not migrate to the ocean. The section *How fish adjust to change* explains why most fish cannot travel freely between salt water and fresh water.

Many saltwater species migrate from one part of the ocean to another at certain times of the year. For example, many kinds of mackerel and certain other fish of the open ocean move toward shore to spawn. Each summer, many species of haddock and other cold-water fish migrate from coastal waters to cooler waters farther out at sea. Some freshwater fish make similar migrations. For example, some trout swim from lakes into rivers to spawn. Some other fish of temperate lakes and streams, such as bass, bluegills, and perch, live near the warm surface during summer. When winter comes, the waters freeze at the surface but remain slightly warmer beneath the ice. The fish then migrate toward the bottom and remain there until warm weather returns.

Where ocean fish live

Many kinds of saltwater fish live far from shore. There, the sea can be divided into three main levels according to the amount of sunlight that reaches various depths, *below left*. Different kinds of fish live at each level.

WORLD BOOK illustration by Marion Pahl

600 feet
(180 meters)

Upper waters
(brightest sunlight)

Midwaters
(dim sunlight)

3,000 feet
(910 meters)

Depths
(little or
no sunlight)

Fish of the upper waters include such fast swimmers as the marlin and tuna. The largest kinds of fish, including the giant manta ray, also live in this region. Many upper-water fish travel great distances and range from tropical to arctic waters. Some often swim close to shore.

Bluefin Tuna

Blue Marlin

Manta Ray

Fish of the midwaters include the oarfish, which grows as long as 50 feet (15 meters). But most midwater fish grow less than 6 inches (15 centimeters) long. The lantern fish and hatchet fish have light-producing organs, as do most midwater fish. Some kinds of midwater fish swim into upper waters to feed or lay eggs.

Oarfish

Lantern Fish

Hatchet Fish

Fish of the depths live in waters that are always cold and almost totally dark. Such waters extend from lower midwaters to the bottom. Lower-midwater fish include anglerfish and other species with large mouths and sharp teeth. The rattail and the tripod fish live near the ocean bottom.

Deep-Sea Angler

Tripod Fish

Rattail

Fish of coastal waters and the open ocean

Some saltwater fish live along the coasts of continents. Others live far from shore in the open ocean, though many of these fish also swim close to shore from time to time. Both coastal and open-ocean species are pictured in these drawings. Fish of the open ocean shown here include dolphin fish, flying fish, herring, mackerel, manta rays, marlin, ocean sunfish, sailfish, swordfish, and tuna. Most of the other fish pictured live mainly in coastal waters. Some coastal fish, such as bull sharks and sawfish, always stay close to land. Others, such as bluefish and great barracuda, sometimes swim far out to sea.

George H. Harrison from Grant Heilman

Exciting game fish, such as this striped marlin, live throughout upper ocean waters. Many saltwater game fish are also important food fish. Fishing fleets catch many far out at sea.

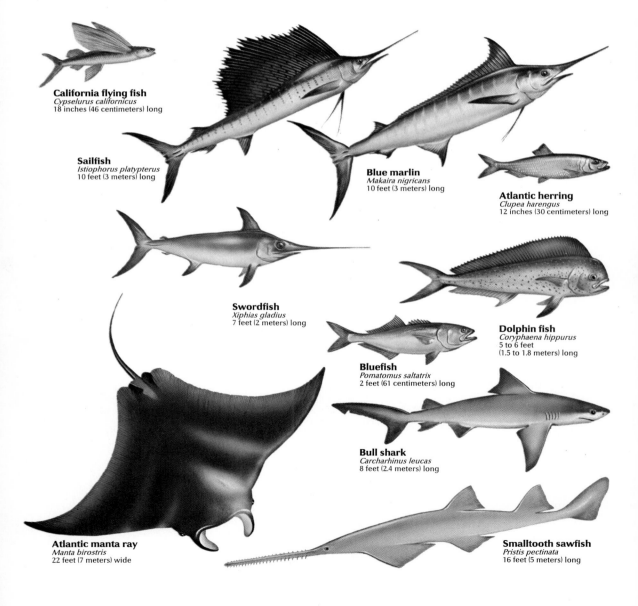

California flying fish
Cypselurus californicus
18 inches (46 centimeters) long

Sailfish
Istiophorus platypterus
10 feet (3 meters) long

Blue marlin
Makaira nigricans
10 feet (3 meters) long

Atlantic herring
Clupea harengus
12 inches (30 centimeters) long

Swordfish
Xiphias gladius
7 feet (2 meters) long

Dolphin fish
Coryphaena hippurus
5 to 6 feet
(1.5 to 1.8 meters) long

Bluefish
Pomatomus saltatrix
2 feet (61 centimeters) long

Bull shark
Carcharhinus leucas
8 feet (2.4 meters) long

Atlantic manta ray
Manta birostris
22 feet (7 meters) wide

Smalltooth sawfish
Pristis pectinata
16 feet (5 meters) long

Jim Annan

A slow swimmer, the enormous jewfish keeps close to the bottom in coastal waters. Many fish move slowly unless stirred to fast action by an approaching prey or bait.

A spotted eagle ray glides swiftly through coastal waters in search of prey. This dangerous fish has poisonous spines in its tail that can injure or even kill a human swimmer.

WORLD BOOK illustrations by Donald Moss

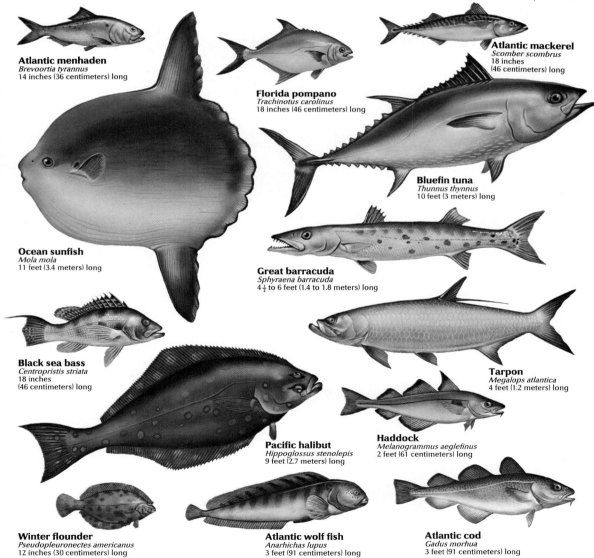

Atlantic menhaden
Brevoortia tyrannus
14 inches (36 centimeters) long

Florida pompano
Trachinotus carolinus
18 inches (46 centimeters) long

Atlantic mackerel
Scomber scombrus
18 inches
(46 centimeters) long

Bluefin tuna
Thunnus thynnus
10 feet (3 meters) long

Ocean sunfish
Mola mola
11 feet (3.4 meters) long

Great barracuda
Sphyraena barracuda
4½ to 6 feet (1.4 to 1.8 meters) long

Black sea bass
Centropristis striata
18 inches
(46 centimeters) long

Tarpon
Megalops atlantica
4 feet (1.2 meters) long

Pacific halibut
Hippoglossus stenolepis
9 feet (2.7 meters) long

Haddock
Melanogrammus aeglefinus
2 feet (61 centimeters) long

Winter flounder
Pseudopleuronectes americanus
12 inches (30 centimeters) long

Atlantic wolf fish
Anarhichas lupus
3 feet (91 centimeters) long

Atlantic cod
Gadus morhua
3 feet (91 centimeters) long

Fish of coral reefs

Hundreds of kinds of saltwater fish live in the warm, shallow waters around coral reefs. Most of these reefs are in the Indian and Pacific oceans and around the West Indies. A reef's clear, sunlit waters swarm with fish that dart in and out of the coral. Many of them are among the most beautiful in the world. Reef fish differ greatly in appearance and in many other ways. For example, some are mainly plant eaters, such as parrotfish and surgeonfish. Others, including triggerfish and trunkfish, eat small water animals as well as plants. Still others are *predators* that hunt smaller fish. Such fish include groupers and moray eels.

Ben Cropp, Tom Stack & Associates

A fierce hunter, this speckled moray eel lives in and around coral reefs and catches smaller fish as prey. The moray, a snake-like fish with sharp teeth, can attack with lightning speed.

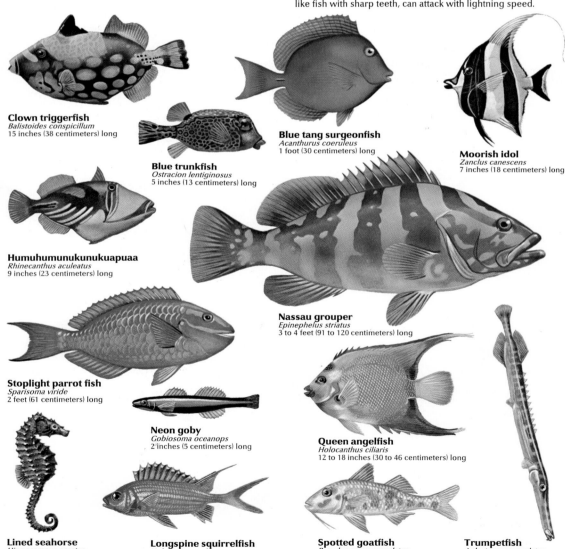

Clown triggerfish
Balistoides conspicillum
15 inches (38 centimeters) long

Blue trunkfish
Ostracion lentiginosus
5 inches (13 centimeters) long

Blue tang surgeonfish
Acanthurus coeruleus
1 foot (30 centimeters) long

Moorish idol
Zanclus canescens
7 inches (18 centimeters) long

Humuhumunukunukuapuaa
Rhinecanthus aculeatus
9 inches (23 centimeters) long

Nassau grouper
Epinephelus striatus
3 to 4 feet (91 to 120 centimeters) long

Stoplight parrot fish
Sparisoma viride
2 feet (61 centimeters) long

Neon goby
Gobiosoma oceanops
2 inches (5 centimeters) long

Queen angelfish
Holocanthus ciliaris
12 to 18 inches (30 to 46 centimeters) long

Lined seahorse
Hippocampus erectus
5 inches (13 centimeters) long

Longspine squirrelfish
Holocentrus rufus
7 to 12 inches (18 to 30 centimeters) long

Spotted goatfish
Pseudupeneus maculatus
10 inches (25 centimeters) long

Trumpetfish
Aulostomus maculatus
2 feet (61 centimeters) long

David Doubilet, Animals Animals

Small, lively swimmers, such as this school of French grunts, create almost constant movement around a reef. Some swim about hunting for food during the day, and others do so at night.

Allan Power, Bruce Coleman Ltd.

The harlequin tuskfish is one of the many brilliantly colored species that live among the coral. Dazzling colors or color patterns may help protect these fish by confusing their enemies.

WORLD BOOK illustrations by Donald Moss

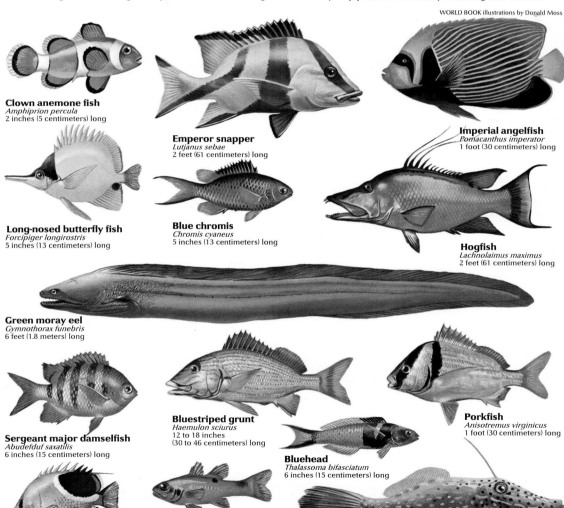

Clown anemone fish
Amphiprion percula
2 inches (5 centimeters) long

Emperor snapper
Lutjanus sebae
2 feet (61 centimeters) long

Imperial angelfish
Pomacanthus imperator
1 foot (30 centimeters) long

Long-nosed butterfly fish
Forcipiger longirostris
5 inches (13 centimeters) long

Blue chromis
Chromis cyaneus
5 inches (13 centimeters) long

Hogfish
Lachnolaimus maximus
2 feet (61 centimeters) long

Green moray eel
Gymnothorax funebris
6 feet (1.8 meters) long

Sergeant major damselfish
Abudefduf saxatilis
6 inches (15 centimeters) long

Bluestriped grunt
Haemulon sciurus
12 to 18 inches
(30 to 46 centimeters) long

Porkfish
Anisotremus virginicus
1 foot (30 centimeters) long

Bluehead
Thalassoma bifasciatum
6 inches (15 centimeters) long

Saddleback butterfly fish
Chaetodon ephippum
6 inches (15 centimeters) long

Flamefish
Apogon maculatus
4 to 5 inches
(10 to 13 centimeters) long

Scrawled filefish
Aluterus scriptus
3 feet (91 centimeters) long

Fish of the deep ocean

Fish of the deep ocean include some of the most unusual and least-known fish in the world. Many of them have large eyes, huge mouths, fanglike teeth, and light organs that flash on and off in the dark waters of the depths. Most deep-ocean fish seldom, if ever, come to the surface. Oarfish, however, sometimes swim up from the lower midwaters and create the strange appearance of a "sea serpent" as they break the surface. A number of species of deepwater fish are familiar only to scientists and have been given only scientific names. These fish include various brotulids and stomiatoids and certain species of anglers.

Ron Church, Tom Stack & Associates

A channel rockfish rests on the ocean bottom, 4,000 feet (1,200 meters) down. There, the ocean is almost totally dark. This photograph was taken from a submarine with the aid of lights.

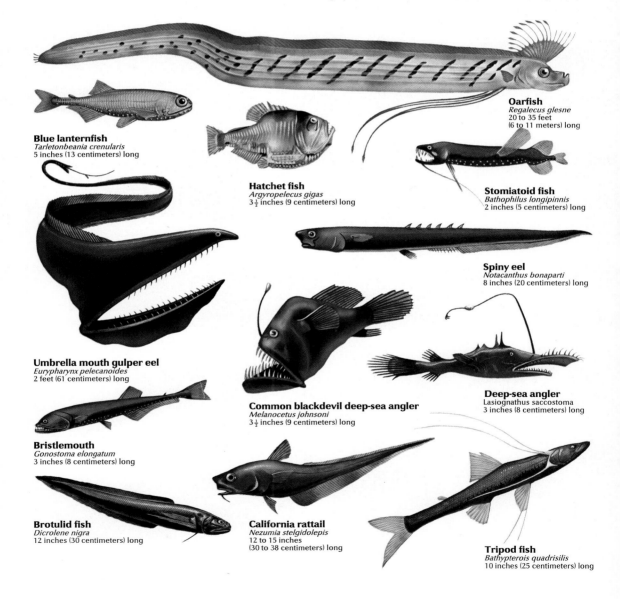

Blue lanternfish
Tarletonbeania crenularis
5 inches (13 centimeters) long

Hatchet fish
Argyropelecus gigas
3½ inches (9 centimeters) long

Oarfish
Regalecus glesne
20 to 35 feet
(6 to 11 meters) long

Stomiatoid fish
Bathophilus longipinnis
2 inches (5 centimeters) long

Spiny eel
Notacanthus bonaparti
8 inches (20 centimeters) long

Umbrella mouth gulper eel
Eurypharynx pelecanoides
2 feet (61 centimeters) long

Common blackdevil deep-sea angler
Melanocetus johnsoni
3½ inches (9 centimeters) long

Deep-sea angler
Lasiognathus saccostoma
3 inches (8 centimeters) long

Bristlemouth
Gonostoma elongatum
3 inches (8 centimeters) long

Brotulid fish
Dicrolene nigra
12 inches (30 centimeters) long

California rattail
Nezumia stelgidolepis
12 to 15 inches
(30 to 38 centimeters) long

Tripod fish
Bathypterois quadrisilis
10 inches (25 centimeters) long

Fish of tropical fresh waters

Tropical regions of Africa, Asia, and South America have a tremendous variety of freshwater fish. Many of the smaller species are popular aquarium fish. These fish include the guppies, mollies, and swordtails of North and South America and the Siamese fighting fish of Asia. Large tropical freshwater fish include the giant arapaima, which lives in jungle rivers of South America. The arapaima is one of the largest freshwater fish in the world. Some arapaimas weigh more than 200 pounds (91 kilograms). The elephant-nose mormyrid of tropical Africa uses its long snout to hunt for food under stones and in mud on river bottoms.

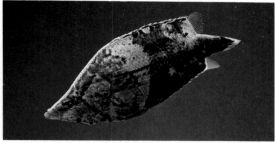

Giuseppe Mazza

The South American leaf fish is one of many unusual species that live in tropical fresh waters. By imitating a floating leaf, this fish escapes its enemies and surprises its prey.

WORLD BOOK illustrations by Donald Moss

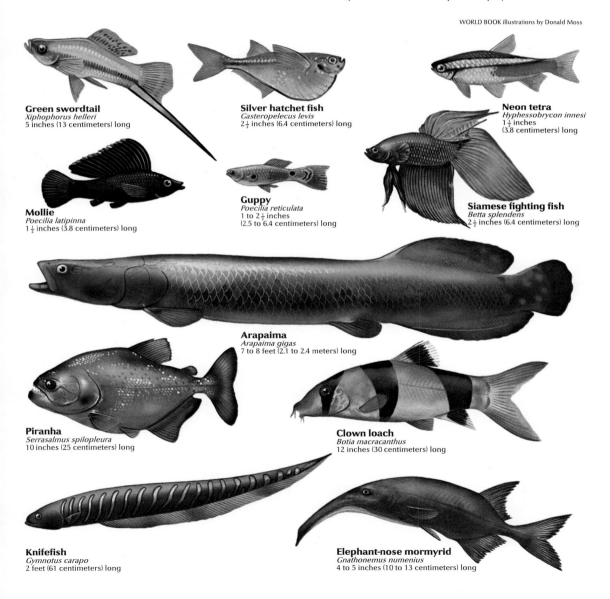

Green swordtail
Xiphophorus helleri
5 inches (13 centimeters) long

Silver hatchet fish
Gasteropelecus levis
2½ inches (6.4 centimeters) long

Neon tetra
Hyphessobrycon innesi
1½ inches
(3.8 centimeters) long

Mollie
Poecilia latipinna
1½ inches (3.8 centimeters) long

Guppy
Poecilia reticulata
1 to 2½ inches
(2.5 to 6.4 centimeters) long

Siamese fighting fish
Betta splendens
2½ inches (6.4 centimeters) long

Arapaima
Arapaima gigas
7 to 8 feet (2.1 to 2.4 meters) long

Piranha
Serrasalmus spilopleura
10 inches (25 centimeters) long

Clown loach
Botia macracanthus
12 inches (30 centimeters) long

Knifefish
Gymnotus carapo
2 feet (61 centimeters) long

Elephant-nose mormyrid
Gnathonemus numenius
4 to 5 inches (10 to 13 centimeters) long

Fish of temperate fresh waters

Unlike tropical waters, temperate waters become cold during part of the year. Fish that live in such waters must adjust their living habits to changes in water temperature. For example, in lakes that freeze over during winter, most fish move down to warmer water near the bottom and remain there until spring. The fish pictured here live in temperate lakes, rivers, and streams of North America. Many alewives, coho salmon, rainbow trout, and white sturgeon live in salt water but swim into fresh water to lay their eggs. American eels live in fresh water but swim to the ocean to lay their eggs.

Ron Church, Tom Stack & Associates

Cavefish live without seeing in the dark waters of caves and underground rivers. These Ozark cavefish have small, sightless eyes, but some other cavefish have no eyes at all.

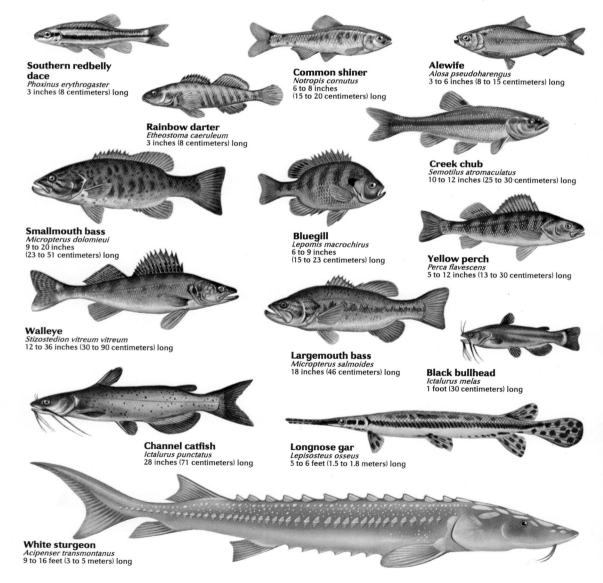

Southern redbelly dace
Phoxinus erythrogaster
3 inches (8 centimeters) long

Common shiner
Notropis cornutus
6 to 8 inches
(15 to 20 centimeters) long

Alewife
Alosa pseudoharengus
3 to 6 inches (8 to 15 centimeters) long

Rainbow darter
Etheostoma caeruleum
3 inches (8 centimeters) long

Creek chub
Semotilus atromaculatus
10 to 12 inches (25 to 30 centimeters) long

Smallmouth bass
Micropterus dolomieui
9 to 20 inches
(23 to 51 centimeters) long

Bluegill
Lepomis macrochirus
6 to 9 inches
(15 to 23 centimeters) long

Yellow perch
Perca flavescens
5 to 12 inches (13 to 30 centimeters) long

Walleye
Stizostedion vitreum vitreum
12 to 36 inches (30 to 90 centimeters) long

Largemouth bass
Micropterus salmoides
18 inches (46 centimeters) long

Black bullhead
Ictalurus melas
1 foot (30 centimeters) long

Channel catfish
Ictalurus punctatus
28 inches (71 centimeters) long

Longnose gar
Lepisosteus osseus
5 to 6 feet (1.5 to 1.8 meters) long

White sturgeon
Acipenser transmontanus
9 to 16 feet (3 to 5 meters) long

Jay Schmidt, FPG

Fighting foaming rapids, a rainbow, or steelhead, trout swims from the ocean to fresh water, where it will lay its eggs. This yearly trip makes the rainbow a popular fresh-water game fish.

Tom Myers, FPG

Kokanee salmon are a *landlocked* form of sockeye salmon. They live entirely in fresh water, unlike most other sockeye salmon, which live in the ocean but lay their eggs in fresh water.

WORLD BOOK illustrations by Donald Moss

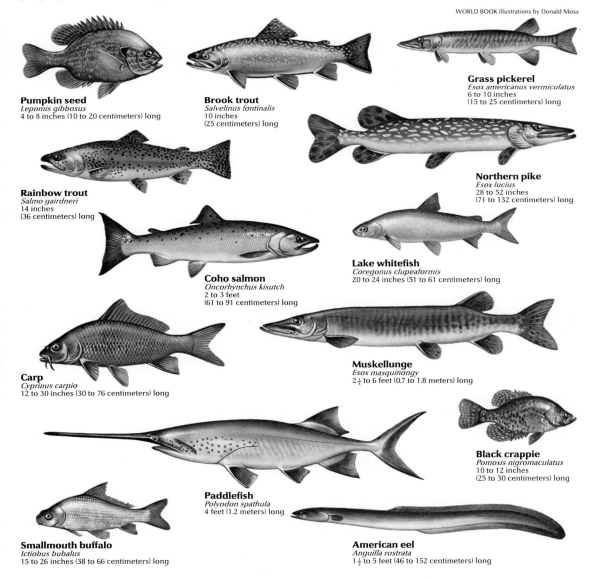

Pumpkin seed
Lepomis gibbosus
4 to 8 inches (10 to 20 centimeters) long

Brook trout
Salvelinus fontinalis
10 inches
(25 centimeters) long

Grass pickerel
Esox americanus vermiculatus
6 to 10 inches
(15 to 25 centimeters) long

Rainbow trout
Salmo gairdneri
14 inches
(36 centimeters) long

Northern pike
Esox lucius
28 to 52 inches
(71 to 132 centimeters) long

Coho salmon
Oncorhynchus kisutch
2 to 3 feet
(61 to 91 centimeters) long

Lake whitefish
Coregonus clupeaformis
20 to 24 inches (51 to 61 centimeters) long

Carp
Cyprinus carpio
12 to 30 inches (30 to 76 centimeters) long

Muskellunge
Esox masquinongy
$2\frac{1}{2}$ to 6 feet (0.7 to 1.8 meters) long

Paddlefish
Polyodon spathula
4 feet (1.2 meters) long

Black crappie
Pomoxis nigromaculatus
10 to 12 inches
(25 to 30 centimeters) long

Smallmouth buffalo
Ictiobus bubalus
15 to 26 inches (38 to 66 centimeters) long

American eel
Anguilla rostrata
$1\frac{1}{2}$ to 5 feet (46 to 152 centimeters) long

In some ways, a fish's body resembles that of other vertebrates. For example, fish, like other vertebrates, have an internal skeleton, an outer skin, and such internal organs as a heart, intestines, and a brain. But in a number of ways, a fish's body differs from that of other vertebrates. For example, fish have fins instead of legs, and gills instead of lungs. Lampreys and hagfish differ from all other vertebrates—and from all other fish—in many ways. Their body characteristics are discussed in an earlier section on *Lampreys and hagfish.* This section deals with the physical features that most other fish have in common.

External anatomy

Shape. Most fish have a streamlined body. The head is somewhat rounded at the front. Fish have no neck, and so the head blends smoothly into the trunk. The trunk, in turn, narrows into the tail. Aside from this basic similarity, fish have a variety of shapes. Tuna and many other fast swimmers have a torpedolike shape. Herring, freshwater sunfish, and some other species are flattened from side to side. Many bottom-dwelling fish, including most rays, are flattened from top to bottom. A number of species are shaped like things in their surroundings. For example, anglerfish and stonefish resemble rocks, and pipefish look like long, slender weeds. This camouflage, called *protective resemblance,* helps a fish escape the notice of its enemies and its prey.

Skin and color. Most fish have a fairly tough skin. It contains blood vessels, nerves, and connective tissue. It also contains certain special cells. Some of these cells produce a slimy *mucus.* This mucus makes fish slippery. Other special cells, called *chromatophores* or *pigment cells,* give fish many of their colors. A chromatophore contains red, yellow, or brownish-black pigments. These colors may combine and produce other colors, such as orange and green. Some species have more chromatophores of a particular color than other species have or have their chromatophores grouped differently. Such differences cause many variations in coloring among species. Besides chromatophores, many fish also have whitish or silvery pigments in their skin and scales. In sunlight, these pigments produce a variety of bright rainbow colors.

The color of most fish matches that of their surroundings. For example, most fish that live near the surface of the open ocean have a blue back, which matches the color of the ocean surface. This type of camouflage is called *protective coloration.* But certain brightly colored fish, including some that have poisonous spines, do not blend with their surroundings. Bright colors may protect a fish by confusing its enemies or by warning them that it has poisonous spines.

Most fish can change their color to match color changes that are present in their surroundings. Flatfish and some other fish that have two or more colors can also change the pattern formed by their colors. A fish receives the impulse to make such changes through its eyes. Signals from a fish's nerves then rearrange the pigments in the chromatophores to make them darker or lighter. The darkening or lightening of the chromatophores produces the different color patterns.

Scales. Most jawed fish have a protective covering of scales. Teleost fish have thin, bony scales that are rounded at the edge. There are two main types of teleost scales—*ctenoid* and *cycloid.* Ctenoid scales have tiny points on their surface. Fish that feel rough to the touch, such as bass and perch, have ctenoid scales. Cycloid scales have a smooth surface. They are found on such fish as carp and salmon. Some primitive bony fish, including bichirs and gars, have thick, heavy *ganoid* scales. Sharks and most rays are covered with *placoid* scales, which resemble tiny, closely spaced teeth. Some fish, including certain kinds of eels and fresh-water catfish, are scaleless.

Fins are movable structures that help a fish swim and keep its balance. A fish moves its fins by means of muscles. Except for a few finless species, all modern bony fish have *rayed fins.* Some primitive bony fish also have rayed fins. These fins consist of a web of skin supported by a skeleton of rods called *rays.* Some ray-finned fish have *soft rays.* Others have both soft rays and *spiny rays,* which are stiff and sharp to the touch. Some primitive bony fish have *lobed fins,* which consist of a fleshy base fringed with rays. Lobed fins are less flexible than rayed fins. Sharks, rays, and chimaeras have fleshy, skin-covered fins supported by numerous fine rays made of a tough material called *keratin.*

Fish fins are classified according to their position on

Kinds of fish scales

These drawings show examples of the four main types of fish scales and the pattern each type forms on the fish's body. Most modern bony fish have ctenoid or cycloid scales. Some catfish and a few other species have no scales at all.

WORLD BOOK illustration by Marion Pahl

Ctenoid scale (Perch)

Cycloid scale (Salmon)

Ganoid scale (Gar)

Placoid scale (Shark)

External anatomy of a fish

This drawing of a yellow perch shows the external features most fish have in common. Many kinds of fish do not have all the fins shown here, or they lack such features as gill covers or scales. For example, lampreys and hagfish have no scales and no pelvic or pectoral fins.

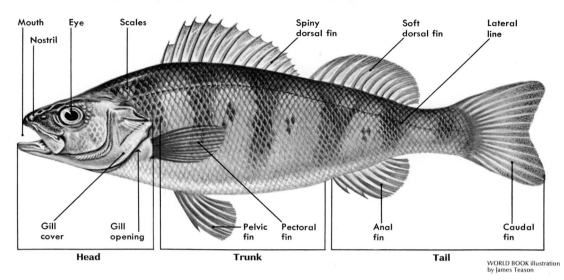

Mouth Eye Scales Spiny dorsal fin Soft dorsal fin Lateral line

Nostril

Gill cover Gill opening Pelvic fin Pectoral fin Anal fin Caudal fin

Head **Trunk** **Tail**

WORLD BOOK illustration by James Teason

the body as well as according to their structure. Classified in this way, a fin is either *median* or *paired.*

Median fins are vertical fins on a fish's back, underside, or tail. They include *dorsal, anal,* and *caudal* fins. The dorsal fin grows along the back and helps a fish keep upright. Almost all fish have at least one dorsal fin, and many have two or three. The anal fin grows on the underside near the tail. Like a dorsal fin, it helps a fish remain upright. Some fish have two anal fins. The caudal fin is at the end of the tail. A fish swings its caudal fin from side to side to propel itself through the water and to help in steering.

Paired fins are two identical fins, one on each side of the body. Most fish have both *pectoral* and *pelvic* paired fins. The pectoral, or shoulder, fins of most fish grow on the sides, just back of the head. Most fish have their pelvic, or leg, fins just below and behind their pectoral fins. But some have their pelvic fins as far forward as the throat or nearly as far back as the anal fin. Pelvic fins are also called *ventral* fins. Most fish use their paired fins mainly to turn, stop, and make other maneuvers.

Skeleton and muscles

A fish's skeleton provides a framework for the head, trunk, tail, and fins. The central framework for the trunk and tail is the backbone. It consists of many separate segments of bone or cartilage called *vertebrae.* In bony fish, each vertebra has a spine at the top, and each tail vertebra also has a spine at the bottom. Ribs are attached to the vertebrae. The skull consists chiefly of the brain case and supports for the mouth and gills. The pectoral fins of most fish are attached to the back of the skull by a structure called a *pectoral girdle.* The pelvic fins are supported by a structure called a *pelvic girdle* which is attached to the pectoral girdle or supported by

muscular tissue in the abdomen. The dorsal fins are supported by structures of bone or cartilage, which are rooted in tissue above the backbone. The caudal fin is supported by the tail, and the anal fin by structures of bone or cartilage below the backbone.

Like all vertebrates, fish have three kinds of muscles: (1) *skeletal muscles,* (2) *smooth muscles,* and (3) *heart muscles.* Fish use their skeletal muscles to move their bones and fins. A fish's flesh consists almost entirely of skeletal muscles. They are arranged one behind the other in broad vertical bands called *myomeres.* The myomeres can easily be seen in a skinned fish. Each myomere is controlled by a separate nerve. As a result, a fish can bend the front part of its body in one direction while bending its tail in the opposite direction. Most fish make such movements with their bodies to swim. A fish's smooth muscles and heart muscles work automatically. The smooth muscles are responsible for operating such internal organs as the stomach and intestines. Heart muscles form and operate the heart.

Systems of the body

The internal organs of fish, like those of other vertebrates, are grouped into various systems according to the function they serve. The major systems include the respiratory, digestive, circulatory, nervous, and reproductive systems. Some of these systems resemble those of other vertebrates, but others differ in many ways.

Respiratory system. Unlike land animals, almost all fish get their oxygen from water. Water contains a certain amount of dissolved oxygen. To get oxygen, fish gulp water through the mouth and pump it over the gills. Most fish have four pairs of gills enclosed in a *gill chamber* on each side of the head. Each gill consists of two rows of fleshy *filaments* attached to a *gill arch.*

The skeleton of a fish

The skeletons of most fish consist mainly of (1) a skull, (2) a backbone, (3) ribs, (4) fin rays, and (5) supports for fin rays or fins. The skeleton of a yellow perch is shown below.

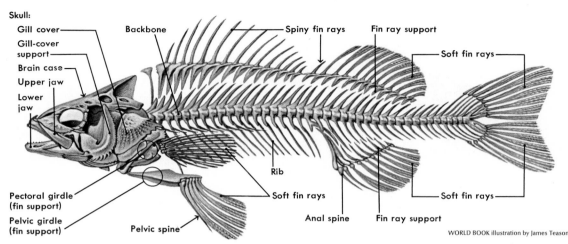

WORLD BOOK illustration by James Teason

Water passes into the gill chambers through *gill slits.* A flap of bone called a *gill cover* protects the gills of bony fish. Sharks and rays do not have gill covers. Their gill slits form visible openings on the outside of the body.

In a bony fish, the breathing process begins when the gill covers close and the mouth opens. At the same time, the walls of the mouth expand outward, drawing water into the mouth. The walls of the mouth then move inward, the mouth closes, and the gill covers open. This action forces the water from the mouth into the gill chambers. In each chamber, the water passes over the gill filaments. They absorb oxygen from the water and replace it with carbon dioxide formed during the breathing process. The water then passes out through the gill openings, and the process is repeated.

Digestive system, or *digestive tract,* changes food into materials that nourish the body cells. It eliminates materials that are not used. In fish, this system leads from the mouth to the *anus,* an opening in front of the

anal fin. Most fish have a jawed mouth with a tongue and teeth. A fish cannot move its tongue. Most fish have their teeth rooted in the jaws. They use their teeth to seize prey or to tear off pieces of their victim's flesh. Some of them also have teeth on the roof of the mouth or on the tongue. Most fish also have teeth in the *pharynx,* a short tube behind the mouth. They use these teeth to crush or grind food.

In all fish, food passes through the pharynx on the way to the *esophagus,* another tubelike organ. A fish's esophagus expands easily, which allows the fish to swallow its food whole. From the esophagus, food passes into the *stomach,* where it is partly digested. Some fish have their esophagus or stomach enlarged into a *gizzard.* The gizzard grinds food into small pieces before it passes into the intestines. The digestive process is completed in the intestines. The digested food enters the blood stream. Waste products and undigested food pass out through the anus.

How a fish's gills work

Like all animals, fish need oxygen to change food into body energy. These drawings show how a fish's gills enable it to get oxygen from the water and to get rid of carbon dioxide, a body waste.

WORLD BOOK illustration by Margaret Ann Moran

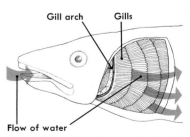

Most fish have four gills on each side of the head. Water enters the mouth and flows out through the gills. Each gill is made up of fleshy, threadlike *filaments.*

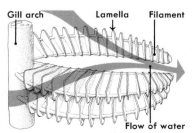

Water from the mouth passes over the filaments, which are closely spaced along a *gill arch* in two rows. Three of the many filaments of a gill are shown above.

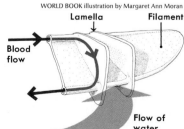

Each filament has many tiny extensions called *lamellae.* Blood flowing through a lamella takes oxygen from the water and releases carbon dioxide into the water.

Internal organs of a fish

This view of a yellow perch shows the chief internal organs found in most fish. These organs are parts of the systems that perform such body processes as breathing and digestion.

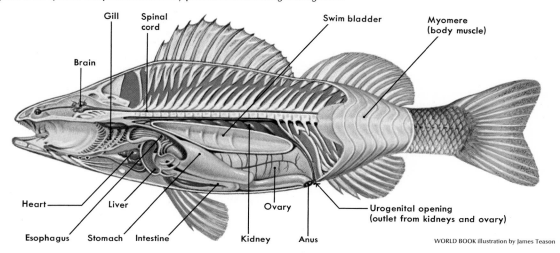

Gill · Spinal cord · Brain · Swim bladder · Myomere (body muscle) · Heart · Liver · Ovary · Urogenital opening (outlet from kidneys and ovary) · Esophagus · Stomach · Intestine · Kidney · Anus

WORLD BOOK illustration by James Teason

Circulatory system distributes blood to all parts of the body. It includes the heart and blood vessels. A fish's heart consists of two main chambers—the *atrium* and the *ventricle.* The blood flows through *veins* to the atrium. It then passes to the ventricle. Muscles in the ventricle pump the blood through *arteries* to the gills, where the blood receives oxygen and gives off carbon dioxide. Arteries then carry the blood throughout the body. The blood carries food from the intestines and oxygen from the gills to the body cells. It also carries away waste products from the cells. A fish's kidneys remove the waste products from the blood, which returns to the heart through the veins.

Nervous system of fish, like that of other vertebrates, consists of a *spinal cord, brain,* and *nerves.* However, a fish's nervous system is not so complex as that of mammals and other higher vertebrates. The spinal cord, which consists of soft nerve tissue, runs from the brain through the backbone. The brain is an enlargement of the spinal cord and is enclosed in the skull. The nerves extend from the brain and spinal cord to every part of the body. Some nerves, called *sensory* nerves, carry messages from the sense organs to the spinal cord and brain. Other nerves, called *motor* nerves, carry messages from the brain and spinal cord to the muscles. A fish can consciously control its skeletal muscles. But it has no conscious control over the smooth muscles and heart muscles. These muscles work automatically.

Reproductive system. As in all vertebrates, the reproductive organs of fish are *testes* in males and *ovaries* in females. The testes produce male sex cells, or *sperm.* The sperm is contained in a fluid called *milt.* The ovaries produce female sex cells, or *eggs.* Fish eggs are also called *roe* or *spawn.* Most fish release their sex cells into the water through an opening near the anus. The males of some species have special structures for transferring sperm directly into the females. Male sharks, for example, have such a structure, called a *clasper,* on each

pelvic fin. The claspers are used to insert sperm into the female's body.

Special organs

Most bony fish have a swim bladder below the backbone. This baglike organ is also called an air bladder. In most fish, the swim bladder provides *buoyancy,* which enables the fish to remain at a particular depth in the water. In lungfish and a few other fish, the swim bladder serves as an air-breathing lung. Still other fish, including many catfish, use their swim bladders to produce sounds as well as to provide buoyancy. Some species communicate by means of such sounds.

A fish would sink to the bottom if it did not have a way of keeping buoyant. Most fish gain buoyancy by inflating their swim bladder with gases produced by their blood. But water pressure increases with depth. As a fish swims deeper, the increased water pressure makes its swim bladder smaller and so reduces the fish's buoyancy. The amount of gas in the bladder must be increased so that the bladder remains large enough to maintain buoyancy. A fish's nervous system automatically regulates the amount of gas in the bladder so that it is kept properly filled. Sharks and rays do not have a swim bladder. To keep buoyant, these fish must swim constantly. When they rest, they stop swimming and so sink toward the bottom. Many bottom-dwelling bony fish also lack a swim bladder.

Many fish have organs that produce light or electricity. But these organs are simply adaptations of structures found in all or most fish. For example, many deep-sea fish have light-producing organs developed from parts of their skin or digestive tract. Some species use these organs to attract prey or possibly to communicate with others of their species. Various other fish have electricity-producing organs developed from muscles in their eyes, gills, or trunk. Some species use these organs to stun or kill enemies or prey.

The senses of fish

Like all vertebrates, fish have sense organs that tell them what is happening in their environment. The organs enable them to see, hear, smell, taste, and touch. In addition, almost all fish have a special sense organ called the *lateral line system,* which enables them to "touch" objects at a distance. Fish also have various other senses that help them meet the conditions of life underwater.

Sight. A fish's eyes differ from those of land vertebrates in several ways. For example, most fish can see to the right and to the left at the same time. This ability makes up in part for the fact that a fish has no neck and so cannot turn its head. Fish also lack eyelids. In land vertebrates, eyelids help moisten the eyes and shield them from sunlight. A fish's eyes are kept moist by the flow of water over them. They do not need to be shielded from sunlight because sunlight is seldom extremely bright underwater. Some fish have unusual adaptations of the eye. For example, adult flatfish have both eyes on the same side of the head. A flatfish spends most of the time lying on its side on the ocean floor and so needs eyes only on the side that faces upward. The eyes of certain deep-sea fish are on the ends of short structures that stick out from the head. These structures can be raised upward, allowing the fish to see overhead as well as to the sides and front.

A few kinds of fish are born blind. They include certain species of catfish that live in total darkness in the waters of caves and the whalefish, which lives in the ocean depths. Some of these fish have eyes but no vision. Others lack eyes completely.

Hearing. All fish can probably hear sounds produced in the water. Fish can also hear sounds made on shore or above the water if they are loud enough. Catfish and certain other fish have a keen sense of hearing.

Fish have an inner ear enclosed in a chamber on each side of the head. Each ear consists of a group of pouches and tubelike canals. Fish have no outer ears or eardrums to receive sound vibrations. Sound vibrations are carried to the inner ears by the body tissues.

Smell and taste. All fish have a sense of smell. It is highly developed in many species, including catfish, salmon, and sharks. In most fish, the *olfactory organs* (organs of smell) consist of two pouches, one on each side of the snout. The pouches are lined with nerve tissue that is highly sensitive to odors from substances in the water. A nostril at the front of each pouch allows water to enter the pouch and pass over the tissue. The water leaves the pouch through a nostril at the back.

Most fish have taste buds in various parts of the mouth. Some species also have them on other parts of the body. Catfish, sturgeon, and a number of other fish have whiskerlike feelers called *barbels* near the mouth. They use the barbels both to taste and to touch.

Touch and the lateral line system are closely related. Most fish have a well-developed sense of touch. Nerve endings throughout the skin react to the slightest pressure and change of temperature. The lateral line system senses changes in the movement of water. It consists mainly of a series of tiny canals under the skin. A main canal runs along each side of the trunk. Branches of these two canals extend onto the head. A fish senses the flow of water around it as a series of vibrations. The vibrations enter the lateral line through pores and activate certain sensitive areas in the line. If the flow of water around a fish changes, the pattern of vibrations sensed through the lateral line also changes. Nerves relay this information to the brain. Changes in the pattern of vibrations may warn a fish of approaching danger or indicate the location of objects outside its range of vision.

Other senses include those that help a fish keep its balance and avoid unfavorable waters. The inner ears help a fish keep its balance. They contain a fluid and several hard, free-moving *otoliths* (ear stones). Whenever a fish begins to swim in other than an upright, level position, the fluid and otoliths move over sensitive nerve endings in the ears. The nerves signal the brain about the changes in the position of the body. The brain then sends messages to the fin muscles, which move to restore the fish's balance. Fish can also sense any changes in the pressure, salt content, or temperature of the water and so avoid swimming very far into unfavorable waters.

The lateral line system

The lateral line system makes a fish sensitive to vibrations in the water. It consists of a series of tubelike *canals* in a fish's skin. Vibrations enter the canals through *pores* (openings in the skin) and travel to sensory organs in the canals. Nerves connect these organs to the brain.

WORLD BOOK illustrations by Marion Pahl and Zorica Dabich

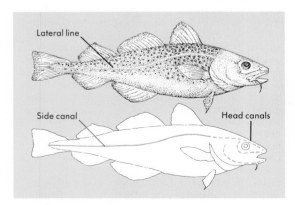

Lateral line

Side canal   Head canals

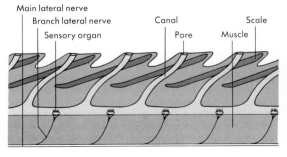

Main lateral nerve
Branch lateral nerve   Canal   Scale
Sensory organ   Pore   Muscle

Every fish begins life in an egg. In the egg, the undeveloped fish, called an *embryo,* feeds on the yolk until ready to hatch. The section *How fish reproduce* discusses where and how fish lay their eggs. After a fish hatches, it is called a *larva* or *fry.* The fish reaches adulthood when it begins to produce sperm or eggs. Most small fish, such as guppies and many minnows, become adults within a few months after hatching. But some small fish become adults only a few minutes after hatching. Large fish require several years. Many of these fish pass through one or more *juvenile* stages before becoming adults. Almost all fish continue to grow as long as they live. During its lifetime, a fish may increase several thousand times in size. The longest-lived fish are probably certain sturgeon, some of which have lived in aquariums more than 50 years. For the life spans of various other fish in captivity, see **Animal** (table: Length of life of animals).

How fish get food. Most fish are *carnivores* (meat-eaters). They eat shellfish, worms, and other kinds of water animals. Above all, they eat other fish. They sometimes eat their own young. Some fish are mainly *herbivores* (plant-eaters). They chiefly eat algae and other water plants. But most plant-eating fish probably also eat animals. Some fish live mainly on plankton. They include many kinds of flying fish and herring and the three largest fish of all—the whale shark, giant manta ray, and basking shark. Some fish are *scavengers.* They feed mainly on waste products and on the dead bodies of animals that sink to the bottom.

Many fish have body organs specially adapted for capturing food. Certain fish of the ocean depths attract their prey with flashing lures. The dorsal fin of some anglerfish dangles above their mouth and serves as a bait for other fish. Such species as gars and swordfish have long, beaklike jaws, which they use for spearing or slashing their prey. Barracudas and certain piranhas and sharks are well known for their razor-sharp teeth, with which they tear the flesh from their victims. Electric eels and some other fish with electricity-producing organs stun their prey with an electric shock. Many fish have comblike *gill rakers.* These structures strain plankton from the water pumped through the gills.

How fish swim. Most fish gain *thrust* (power for forward movement) by swinging the tail fin from side to side while curving the rest of the body alternately to the left and to the right. Some fish, such as marlin and tuna, depend mainly on tail motion for thrust. Other fish, including many kinds of eels, rely chiefly on the curving motion of the body. Fish maneuver by moving their fins. To make a left turn, for example, a fish extends its left pectoral fin. To stop, a fish extends both of its pectoral fins.

A fish's swimming ability is affected by the shape and location of its fins. Most fast, powerful swimmers, such as swordfish and tuna, have a deeply forked or crescent-shaped tail fin and sickle-shaped pectorals. All their fins are relatively large. At the other extreme, most slow swimmers, such as bowfins and bullheads, have a squared or rounded tail fin and rounded pectorals.

How fish protect themselves. All fish, except the largest ones, live in constant danger of being attacked

How a fish develops

Most fish develop from egg to adult in stages. The photographs below show three stages in the development of brook trout.

These tiny trout eggs lie among grains of sand. Curled inside each egg is an undeveloped fish called an *embryo.* The large dots are the embryo's eyes. The egg yolk nourishes the embryo.

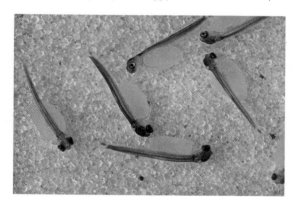

A newly hatched fish, called a *larva* or *fry,* continues to draw nourishment from the egg yolk by means of blood vessels that extend through the yolk. The yolk is contained in a *yolk sac.*

Treat Davidson, NAS

This 3-month-old trout has used its supply of yolk and now hunts for food. As it grows, it will take on the appearance of an adult trout. Most trout become adults in 2 to 5 years.

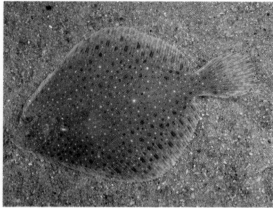

Runk/Schoenberger from Grant Heilman

A flounder, which has both eyes on one side of its body, lies on the ocean bottom with both eyes facing up. Flounders change their color pattern to match the background.

Stan Keiser from Ron Church

The electric eel stuns its enemies and prey with a powerful electric shock. The electricity-producing organs take up most of the body. The other inner organs lie just back of the head.

and eaten by other fish or other animals. To survive, fish must be able to defend themselves against predators. If a species loses more individuals each generation than it gains, it will in time die out.

Protective coloration and protective resemblance are the most common methods of self-defense. A fish that blends with its surroundings is more likely to escape from its enemies than one whose color or shape is extremely noticeable. Many fish that do not blend with their surroundings depend on swimming speed or maneuvering ability to escape from their enemies.

Fish also have other kinds of defense. Some fish, such as gars, pipefish, and seahorses, are protected by a covering of thick, heavy scales or bony plates. Other species have sharp spines that are difficult for predators to swallow. In many of these species, including scorpionfish, sting rays, and stonefish, one or more of the spines are poisonous. When threatened, the porcupine fish inflates its spine-covered body with air or water until it is shaped like a balloon. The fish's larger size and erect spines may discourage an enemy. Many eels that live on the bottom dig holes in which they hide from their enemies. Razor fish dive into sand on the bottom. A few fish do the opposite. For example, flying fish and needlefish escape danger by propelling themselves out of the water.

How fish rest. Like all animals, fish need rest. Many species have periods of what might be called sleep. Others simply remain inactive for short periods. But even at rest, many fish continue to move their fins to keep their position in the water.

Fish have no eyelids, and so they cannot close their eyes when sleeping. But while asleep, a fish is probably unaware of the impressions received by its eyes. Some fish sleep on the bottom, resting on their belly or side. Other species sleep in midwater, in a horizontal position. The slippery dick, a coral-reef fish, sleeps on the bottom under a covering of sand. The striped parrot

How fish swim

The dogfish and most other fish swim by swinging their tail from side to side, while curving the rest of their body in the opposite direction. Some fish, such as tuna, move the front of their body little in swimming. Eels and some other fish bend their body in snakelike curves.

WORLD BOOK illustration by Marion Pahl

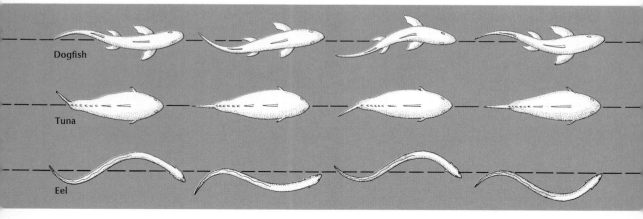

Dogfish

Tuna

Eel

Boyd Wells, Pictorial Parade

Giuseppe Mazza

A fleshy bait grows from the head of an anglerfish, *above left,* and out of the mouth of a star-gazer, *above right.* The wormlike bait attracts smaller fish. Anglerfish and stargazers snap up small fish with astonishing speed, but they move slowly at most other times.

fish, another coral-reef fish, encloses itself in an "enve-lope" of mucus before going to sleep. The fish secretes the mucus from special glands in its gill chambers.

Certain air-breathing fish, such as the African and South American lungfish, sleep out of water for months at a time. These fish live in rivers or ponds that dry up during periods of drought. The fish lie buried in hard-ened mud until the return of the rainy season. This kind of long sleep during dry periods is called *estivation.* During estivation, a fish breathes little and lives off the protein and fat stored in its body.

How fish live together. Among many species, the individual fish that make up the species live mainly by themselves. Such fish include most predatory fish. Many sharks, for example, hunt and feed by themselves and join other sharks only for mating.

Among many other species, the fish live together in closely knit groups called *schools.* About a fifth of all fish species are schooling species. A school may have few or many fish. A school of tuna, for example, may consist of fewer than 25 individuals. Many schools of herring number in the hundreds of millions. All the fish in a school are about the same size. Baby fish and adult fish are never in the same school. In some schooling species, the fish become part of a school when they are young and remain with it throughout their lives. Other species form schools for only a few weeks after they hatch. The fish in a school usually travel in close forma-tion as a defense against predators. But a school often breaks up at night to feed and then regroups the next morning. The approach of a predator brings the fish quickly back together.

Allan Power, Bruce Coleman Ltd.

Fish protected by spines include the demon stinger, *above left,* and the stonefish, *above right.* Both fish give off poison through their spines. The stonefish's poison is the deadliest of all fish poi-sons. It can kill a human being in minutes.

Ron Church, Tom Stack & Associates

Thousands of sardines make up this school. They live together most of the time but may separate at night to feed. They swim quickly back together when threatened by an enemy.

Ben Cropp, Tom Stack & Associates

A coral trout and a wrasse help each other. The small wrasse is removing parasites from the gills of the coral trout. The wrasse thus obtains food and the coral trout is cleaned.

Marineland of Florida

Three remoras ride on a lemon shark. The remoras use a sucking disk on their head to hold on to the shark. They also eat scraps of the shark's food.

Fish also form other types of relationships. Among cod, perch, and many other species, a number of individuals may gather in the same area for feeding, resting, or spawning. Such a group is only temporary and is not so closely knit as a school. Some fish, including certain angelfish and wrasses, form unusual relationships with larger fish of other species. In many such relationships, the smaller fish removes parasites or dead tissue from the larger fish. The smaller fish thus obtains food, and the other is cleaned.

How fish adjust to change. Fish sometimes need to adjust to changes in their environment. The two most common changes are (1) changes in water temperature and (2) changes in the salt content of water.

In general, the body temperature of each species of fish equals that of the water in which the species lives. If the water temperature rises or falls, a fish can adjust to the change because its body temperature changes accordingly. But the change in the water temperature must not be too great and must occur gradually. Most fish can adjust to a change in the water temperature of up to 15° F. (8° C)—if the change is not sudden. Water temperatures usually change slowly, and so there is time for a fish's body to make the necessary adjustment. But occasionally, the temperature drops suddenly and severely, killing many fish. In addition, freshwater fish are sometimes endangered by *thermal pollution,* which occurs when factories and electric power plants release hot water into rivers or lakes. The resulting increase in water temperature may be greater than most fish can adjust to.

Both fresh water and ocean water contain various salts, many of which fish need in their diet. But ocean water is far saltier than fresh water. Fish that migrate between the two must adjust to changes in the salt content of the water. Relatively few fish can make such an adjustment.

Both freshwater and saltwater fish have about the same amount of dissolved salts in their body fluids. But the body fluids of ocean fish are not so salty as the water in which the fish live. Under certain circumstances, water from a weak solution will flow into a strong solution. This natural process, called *osmosis,* takes place if the two solutions are separated by a *membrane* (thin layer) through which only the water can pass (see **Osmosis**). The skin and gill membranes of fish are of this type. For this reason, marine fish constantly lose water from their body fluids into the stronger salt solution of the sea water. To make up for this loss, they drink much water. But ocean water contains more salt than marine fish need. The fish pass the extra salt out through their gills and through their digestive tract. Saltwater fish need all the water they drink. As a result, these fish produce only small amounts of urine.

Freshwater fish have the opposite problem with osmosis. Their body fluids are saltier than fresh water. As a result, the fish constantly absorb water through their membranes. In fact, freshwater fish absorb so much water that they do not need to drink any. Instead, the fish must get rid of the extra water that their bodies absorb. As a result, freshwater fish produce great quantities of urine.

All fish reproduce sexually. In sexual reproduction, a sperm unites with an egg in a process called *fertilization.* The fertilized egg develops into a new individual. In almost all fish species, males produce sperm and females produce eggs. In a few species, the same individual produces both sperm and eggs.

The eggs of most fish are fertilized outside the female's body. A female releases her eggs into the water at the same time that a male releases his sperm. Some sperm come in contact with some of the eggs, and fertilization takes place. This process is called *external fertilization.* The entire process during which eggs and sperm are released into the water and the eggs are fertilized is called *spawning.* Almost all bony fish reproduce in this way.

Sharks, rays, chimaeras, and a few bony fish, such as guppies and mosquito fish, reproduce in a different manner. The eggs of these fish are fertilized inside the female, a process called *internal fertilization.* For internal fertilization to occur, males and females must mate. The males have special organs for transferring sperm into the females. After fertilization, the females of some species release their eggs into the water before they hatch. Other females hatch the eggs inside their bodies and so give birth to living young. Fish that bear living young include many sharks and rays, guppies, and some halfbeaks and scorpionfish.

This section discusses spawning, the method by which most fish reproduce.

Preparation for spawning. Most fish have a *spawning season* each year, during which they may spawn several times. But some tropical species breed throughout the year. The majority of fish spawn in spring or early summer, when the water is warm and the days are long. But certain cold-water fish, such as brook trout and Atlantic cod, spawn in fall or winter.

Most fish return to particular *spawning grounds* year after year. Many freshwater fish have to travel only a short distance to their spawning grounds. They may simply move from the deeper parts of a river or lake to shallow waters near shore. But other fish may migrate tremendous distances to spawn. For example, European freshwater eels cross 3,000 miles (4,800 kilometers) of ocean to reach their spawning grounds in the western Atlantic.

At their spawning grounds, the males and females of some species swim off in pairs to spawn. Among other species, the males and females spawn in groups. Many males and females tell each other apart by differences in appearance. The females of some species are larger than the males. Among other species, the males develop unusually bright colors during the spawning season. During the rest of the year, they look much like the females of their species. In some species, the males and females look so different that for many years scientists thought they belonged to different species. Among other fish, the sexes look so much alike that they can be told apart only by differences in their behavior. For example, many males adopt a special type of *courting* behavior to attract females. A courting male may swim round and round a female or perform a lively "dance" to attract her attention.

How fish reproduce

Fish reproduce *sexually*—by uniting a *sperm* (male sex cell) with an *egg* (female sex cell). In most species, the union of sex cells takes place in the water. Trout reproduction is shown below.

The female trout, *above center,* makes a nest for her eggs. She uses her tail to scoop the nest out on the gravelly bottom. The male trout, *left,* does not help make the nest.

After the nest has been made, the male moves alongside the female. As the female releases her eggs, the male releases his sperm. The sperm cells unite with the eggs in the nest.

WORLD BOOK illustration by Harry McNaught

The female then covers the nest to protect the eggs. She heads into the current and swishes her tail in the gravel to stir it up. The current carries the loosened gravel back over the eggs.

Among some species, including cod, Siamese fighting fish, and certain gobies and sticklebacks, a male claims a territory for spawning and fights off any male intruders. Many fish, especially those that live in fresh water, build nests for their eggs. A male freshwater bass, for example, uses its tail fin to scoop out a nest on the bottom of a lake or stream.

Spawning and care of the eggs. After the preparations have been made, the males and females touch in a certain way or make certain signals with their fins or body. Depending on the species, a female may lay a few eggs or many eggs—even millions—during the spawning season. Most fish eggs measure $\frac{1}{8}$ inch (3 millimeters) in diameter or less.

Some fish, such as cod and herring, abandon their eggs after spawning. A female cod may lay as many as 9 million eggs during a spawning season. Cod eggs, like those of many other ocean fish, float near the surface and scatter as soon as they are laid. Predators eat many of the eggs. Others drift into waters too cold for hatching. Only a few cod eggs out of millions develop into adult fish. A female herring lays about 50,000 eggs in a season. But herring eggs, like those of certain other marine fish, sink to the bottom and have an adhesive covering that helps them stick there. As a result, herring eggs are less likely to be eaten by predators or to drift into waters unfavorable for hatching.

A number of fish protect their eggs. They include many freshwater nest builders, such as bass, salmon, certain sticklebacks, and trouts. The females of these species lay far fewer eggs than do the females of the cod and herring groups. Like herring eggs, the eggs of many of the freshwater nest builders sink to the bottom and have an adhesive covering. But they have an even better chance of surviving than herring eggs because they receive some protection.

The amount and kind of protection given by fish to their eggs vary greatly. Salmon and trout cover their fertilized eggs with gravel but abandon them soon after. Male freshwater bass guard the eggs fiercely until they hatch. Among ocean fish, female seahorses and pipefish lay their eggs in a pouch on the underside of the male. The eggs hatch inside the male's pouch. Some fish, including certain ocean catfish and cardinal fish, carry their eggs in their mouth during the hatching period. In some species, the male carries the eggs. In other species, the female carries them.

Hatching and care of the young. The eggs of most fish species hatch in less than two months. Eggs laid in warm water hatch faster than those laid in cold water. The eggs of some tropical fish hatch in less than 24 hours. On the other hand, the eggs of certain cold-water fish require four or five months to hatch. The males of a few species guard their young for a short time after they hatch. These fish include freshwater bass, bowfins, brown bullheads, Siamese fighting fish, and some sticklebacks. But most other fish provide no protection for their offspring.

A male Siamese fighting fish blows bubbles that stick together to make a nest for eggs laid by the female. He then collects the eggs in his mouth and blows them into the nest.

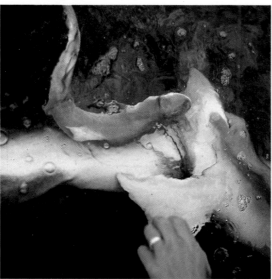

A baby lemon shark is born well-developed and attached to the female by an umbilical cord. Some shark species hatch eggs inside their bodies. Others lay their eggs in the water.

Mouthbreeding fish hold their eggs in their mouth before hatching. This male jawfish has a mouthful of eggs. Females of some species and males of others hold the eggs.

A fish that lived 58 million years ago left its "picture" in this fossil. Such fossils reveal many details about fish that are now extinct. Scientists study fossils to discover how fish developed through the ages.

Scientists learn how fish developed by studying the fossils of fish that are now extinct. The fossils show the changes that occurred in the anatomy of fish down through the ages.

The first fish appeared on the earth about 500 million years ago. These fish are called *ostracoderms.* They were slow, bottom-dwelling animals that were covered from head to tail with a heavy armor of thick bony plates and scales. Like today's lampreys and hagfish, ostracoderms had no jaws and had poorly formed fins. For this reason, scientists group lampreys, hagfish, and ostracoderms together. Ostracoderms were not only the first fish, but they were also the first animals to have a backbone. Most scientists believe that the history of all other vertebrates can be traced back to the ostracoderms. The ostracoderms gave rise to jawed fish with backbones, and they in turn gave rise to *amphibians* (vertebrates that have legs and live both on land and in water). The amphibians became the ancestors of all land vertebrates.

Ostracoderms probably reached the peak of their development about 400 million years ago. About the same time, two other groups of fish were developing—*acanthodians* and *placoderms.* The acanthodians became the first known jawed fish. The placoderms were the largest fish up to that time. Some members of the placoderm group called *Dinichthys* grew up to 30 feet (9 meters) long and had powerful jaws and sharp bony plates that served as teeth.

The Age of Fishes was a period in the earth's history when fish developed remarkably. Scientists call this age the Devonian Period. It began about 410 million years ago and lasted about 50 million years. During much of this time, dinichthys and other large placoderms ruled the seas.

The first bony fish appeared early in the Devonian Period. They were mostly small or medium-sized and, like all fish of that time, were heavily armored. These early bony fish belonged to two main groups—*sarcopterygians* and *actinopterygians.*

The sarcopterygians had fleshy or lobed fins. Few fish today are even distantly related to this group. The coelacanth and the lungfish are the only surviving sarcopterygians. In addition, certain scientists include the African bichir in this group. Some scientists believe that among fish, lungfish are the nearest living relatives of land vertebrates. The actinopterygians had rayed fins without fleshy lobes at the base. Among the first actinopterygians were the *chondrosteans,* which differed in many ways from modern ray-finned fish. The chondrosteans were the ancestors of today's ray-finned fish, which make up about 95 per cent of all fish species. The paddlefish and sturgeons are the only surviving chondrosteans, and most scientists believe the bichirs are their nearest relatives.

The first sharks appeared during the Devonian Period. They looked much like certain sharks that exist today. The first rays appeared about 200 million years after the first sharks. By the end of the Devonian Period, nearly all jawless fish had become extinct. The only exceptions were the ancestors of today's lampreys and hagfish. Some acanthodians and placoderms remained through the Devonian Period, but these fish also died out in time.

The first modern fish, or teleosts, appeared during the Triassic Period, which began about 240 million years ago. The chondrosteans of the Devonian Period had given rise to another group of primitive bony fish, the *holosteans.* The holosteans, in turn, became the ancestors of the teleosts. The only surviving holosteans are the bowfin and freshwater gars.

The teleosts lost the heavy armor that covered the bodies of most earlier fish. At first, all teleosts had soft-rayed fins. These fish gave rise to present-day catfish, minnows, and other soft-finned fish. The first spiny-finned fish appeared during the Cretaceous Period, which began about 138 million years ago. These fish were the ancestors of such highly developed present-day fish as perch and tuna. Since the Cretaceous Period, teleosts have been by far the most important group of fish.   C. Lavett Smith

Ichthyologists classify fish into various groups according to the body characteristics they have in common. They divide all fish into two superclasses: (1) *Agnatha,* meaning *jawless,* and (2) *Gnathostomata,* meaning *jawed.* The superclass *Agnatha* consists of a single class, also called Agnatha, which is divided into two orders. The much larger superclass *Gnathostomata* is divided into classes, subclasses, and orders. The orders are further divided into families, the families into genera, and the genera into species.

Superclass Agnatha.   Mouth jawless; skeleton of cartilage; no paired fins, air bladder, or scales; about 45 species in 2 orders:

> **Order Petromyzoniformes**—lampreys. Large sucking mouth; 7 pairs of external gill openings; some species parasitic; live in salt and fresh water.
> **Order Myxiniformes**—hagfish. Small nonsucking mouth; 1 to 16 pairs of external gill openings; nonparasitic; salt water.

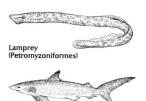

Lamprey
(Petromyzoniformes)

Superclass Gnathostomata.   Mouth jawed; most species have paired fins and scales; about 21,000 species in 2 classes:

Class Chondrichthyes.   Skeleton of cartilage; no air bladder; about 790 species in 3 orders:

> **Order Squaliformes**—sharks. Most have torpedo shape; upturned tail; 5 to 7 pairs of gill slits; no gill covers; placoid scales; mostly salt water.
> **Order Rajiformes**—rays. Most have body flattened from top to bottom; whiplike tail; 5 pairs of gill slits under pectorals rather than on sides; no gill covers; placoid scales; mostly salt water.
> **Order Chimaeriformes**—chimaeras. Short-, long-, and elephant-nosed species; pointed tail; 4 pairs of gill slits; gill covers; scaleless; salt water.

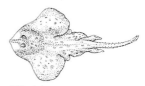

Blue shark
(Squaliformes)

Little skate
(Rajiformes)

Class Osteichthyes.   Skeleton largely or partly bone; most species have 5 pairs of gill slits, gill covers, air bladder, and cycloid or ctenoid scales; over 20,000 species in 2 subclasses:

Subclass Sarcopterygii.   Fleshy fins; skeleton partly cartilage and partly bone (primitive bony); 7 species in 2 orders:

> **Order Dipteriformes**—lungfish. Air bladder an air-breathing lung; fresh water.
> **Order Coelacanthiformes**—coelacanth. Single ancient species; salt water.

Australian lungfish
(Dipteriformes)

Subclass Actinopterygii.   Rayed fins; skeleton largely or partly bone; single dorsal and anal fins in most orders; over 20,000 species in 34 orders:

Sturgeon
(Acipenseriformes)

> **Order Polypteriformes**—bichirs. Slender body; thick ganoid scales; long dorsal fin composed of separate finlets; lunglike air bladder; fresh water.
> **Order Acipenseriformes**—paddlefish, sturgeon. Heavy body; paddlefish nearly scaleless; sturgeon have bony plates instead of scales; fresh water; some sturgeon anadromous.
> **Order Semionotiformes**—gars. Long, slender body and jaws; short, far-back dorsal fin; diamond-shaped ganoid scales; lunglike air bladder.
> **Order Amiiformes**—bowfin. Stout body; rounded tail fin; long, wavy dorsal fin; cycloid scales; bony plate under chin; single species.
> **Order Elopiformes**—bonefish, tarpon, ten-pounders. Soft fin rays; low pectorals; abdominal pelvics; deeply forked tail; silvery body; mostly salt water.
> **Order Anguilliformes**—eels. Soft fin rays; many species lack pectorals; no pelvics; some species scaleless; snakelike; mostly salt water; some catadromous.
> **Order Notacanthiformes**—spiny eels. Soft and spiny fin rays; low pectorals; abdominal pelvics; no tail fin; long, tapering body; salt water, on bottom.
> **Order Clupeiformes**—anchovies, herring, sardines, shad. Soft fin rays; low pectorals; abdominal pelvics; deeply forked tail; silvery body flattened from side to side; travel in large schools; mostly salt water.
> **Order Mormyriformes**—mormyrids. Soft fin rays; low pectorals; abdominal pelvics; many have long snout; electricity-producing organs; fresh water.
> **Order Osteoglossiformes**—bony tongues, fresh-water butterfly fish, mooneyes. Soft fin rays; low pectorals; abdominal pelvics; many have large scales and rounded tail fins; extremely varied body forms; fresh water.
> **Order Cypriniformes**—characins, gymnotid eels, loaches, minnows, suckers. Soft fin rays; most characins have a second, adipose dorsal; most species have low pectorals, abdominal pelvics; air bladder connected to inner ear by series of bones called *Weberian apparatus;* extremely varied body forms; fresh water.
> **Order Salmoniformes**—dragonfish, mudminnows, pike, salmon, viperfish. Soft fin rays; salmon have a second, *adipose* (fatty and rayless) dorsal fin; most have low pectorals; abdominal pelvics; salt and fresh water.
> **Order Myctophiformes**—lanternfish. Soft fin rays; many species have a second, adipose dorsal; fairly low pectorals; abdominal pelvics; light-producing organs; mostly deep salt water.

Longnose gar
(Semionotiformes)

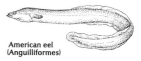

Bonefish
(Elopiformes)

American eel
(Anguilliformes)

American shad
(Clupeiformes)

Mormyrid
(Mormyriformes)

This table lists the major groups down through orders into which fish are classified. The groups are arranged according to their probable evolutionary development. One or more representative families are listed after the name of each order, along with important char- acteristics of the fish in the order. The table lists 41 orders. But some ichthyologists list fewer than 41, and others list more. Ichthyologists also disagree on the names of some orders, the way the orders should be arranged, and the species included in each.

Superclass Gnathostomata (continued)

Order Siluriformes—catfish. Soft fin rays, but some species have dorsal and pectoral spines; some have a second, adipose dorsal; low pectorals; abdominal pelvics; most scaleless; all have Weberian apparatus and barbels; mostly fresh water.

Blue catfish
(Siluriformes)

Order Gonorhynchiformes—sandfish. Soft fin rays; low pectorals; pelvics behind abdomen; slender body; beaked snout; primitive Weberian apparatus; salt water.

Order Percopsiformes—cave fish, pirate perch, trout perch. Soft fin rays except for a few spiny rays in pirate perch and trout perch; trout perch have a second, adipose dorsal; low pectorals; pelvics far forward but lacking in most cave fish; large lateral line canals in head; fresh water.

Trout perch
(Percopsiformes)

Order Batrachoidiformes—toadfish. Spiny and soft fin rays; two dorsal fins—one spiny, one soft; pectorals midway up sides; pelvics under throat; some have light-producing organs; many have poisonous spines; mostly salt water.

Order Gobiesociformes—clingfish. Soft fin rays except for single spines in pelvics; pectorals midway up sides; pelvics, under throat, form sucking disk that enables fish to cling to rocks; scaleless; small body; mostly salt water.

Order Lophiiformes—anglers, batfish, frogfish, goosefish. Spiny and soft fin rays; dorsal fin has spiny ray at front, forming dangling lure; pectorals midway up sides, forming fleshy flaps; pelvics under throat or lacking; broad, flat body; many species have light-producing organs; salt water.

Goosefish
(Lophiiformes)

Order Gadiformes—cod, eelpouts, pearlfish. Most have soft fin rays; some cod have three dorsals, two anals; high pectorals; pelvics far forward; mostly salt water.

Order Atheriniformes—flying fish, halfbeaks, killifish, needlefish, live-bearing top-minnows. Most have soft fin rays; pectorals high or midway up sides; abdominal pelvics; near surface of salt, fresh, and brackish water.

Order Polymixiformes—beardfish. Spiny and soft fin rays; pectorals midway up sides; pelvics under chest; forked tail; two chin whiskers; salt water.

Flying fish
(Atheriniformes)

Order Beryciformes—pinecone fish, squirrelfish. Spiny and soft fin rays; pectorals midway up sides; pelvics under chest; brilliantly colored; salt water.

Order Zeiformes—boarfish, dories. Spiny and soft fin rays; pectorals midway up sides; pelvics under chest; body extremely flattened from side to side; upturned mouth; salt water.

Order Lampridiformes—crestfish, oarfish, opahs, ribbonfish. Soft fin rays; many species have unusually long dorsal and anal fins; pectorals midway up sides; pelvics under chest or lacking; varied body forms; salt water.

Oarfish
(Lampridiformes)

Order Gasterosteiformes—pipefish, sea horses, sticklebacks, trumpetfish. Spiny and soft fin rays; pectorals midway up sides; pelvics under chest; slender body; tubular snout; many encased in bony plates or rings; salt and fresh water.

Order Channiformes—snakeheads. Soft fin rays; low pectorals; pelvics under chest or lacking; special air-breathing organs; fresh water.

Order Scorpaeniformes—scorpionfish, sculpins. Spiny and soft fin rays; usually two dorsals—one spiny, one soft; pectorals midway up sides; pelvics under chest; cheek covered by bony plate; many have extremely sharp, poisonous spines; varied body forms; salt and fresh water.

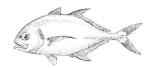

Snakehead
(Channiformes)

Order Pegasiformes—sea moths. Spiny and soft fin rays; large, spiny, winglike pectorals high on sides; small pelvics between chest and abdomen; small body encased in bony plates and rings; extended snout; salt water.

Order Dactylopteriformes—flying gurnards. Spiny and soft fin rays; two dorsal fins—one spiny, one soft; huge, winglike pectorals midway up sides; pelvics under chest; head encased in heavy bone; salt water.

Order Synbranchiformes—swamp eels. Soft fin rays; dorsal and anal fins rayless; no pectorals; pelvics under throat or lacking; gill openings under head; special air-breathing organs; eel-shaped body; fresh and brackish water.

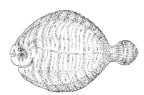

Common jack
(Perciformes)

Order Perciformes—bass, blennies, gobies, jacks, mackerel, perch. Spiny and soft fin rays; many have two dorsal fins—one spiny, one soft; pectorals midway up sides; pelvics under chest and composed of one spine and five soft rays in most species; extremely varied body forms; largest fish order, with 8,000 to 10,000 species; salt and fresh water.

Order Pleuronectiformes—flounders, soles, tonguefish. Most have soft fin rays; long dorsal and anal fins; pectorals and pelvics small or lacking; flattened body; adults have both eyes on same side of head; mostly salt water.

Order Tetraodontiformes—boxfish, ocean sunfish, puffers, triggerfish. Spiny and soft fin rays; pectorals midway up sides; pelvics under chest or lacking; scaleless or covered with spines, bony plates, or hard scales; many are poisonous to eat; varied body forms; mostly salt water.

Naked sole
(Pleuronectiformes)

Related articles in *World Book* include:

Freshwater fish

Alewife	Eel	Pike
Anableps	Electric eel	Piranha
Archerfish	Electric fish	Pupfish
Bass	Fightingfish	Roach
Bowfin	Gar	Salmon
Buffalo	Goldfish	Sculpin
Bullhead	Grayling	Smelt
Carp	Lamprey	Stickleback
Catfish	Lungfish	Sturgeon
Cavefish	Minnow	Sucker
Chub	Muskellunge	Sunfish
Crappie	Paddlefish	Trout
Darter	Perch	Whitefish
Drum	Pickerel	

Saltwater fish

Alewife	Gurnard	Salmon
Amberjack	Haddock	Sardine
Anchovy	Hagfish	Sawfish
Angelfish	Hake	Sculpin
Barracuda	Halibut	Seahorse
Bass	Herring	Shad
Blackfish	Jewfish	Shark
Bluefish	Kingfish	Skate
Bonefish	Lamprey	Smelt
Bonito	Lanternfish	Snapper
Bream	Lumpfish	Sole
Butterfish	Mackerel	Spot
Catfish	Marlin	Sprat
Cod	Menhaden	Stickleback
Coelacanth	Mullet	Stingray
Cutlassfish	Oarfish	Sturgeon
Doctorfish	Pilotfish	Swordfish
Dogfish	Pipefish	Tarpon
Dolphin	Pollock	Tilefish
Drum	Pompano	Toadfish
Eel	Porcupinefish	Torpedo
Electric fish	Porgy	Triggerfish
Eulachon	Puffer	Trout
Flatfish	Ray	Tuna
Flounder	Redfish	Turbot
Flyingfish	Remora	Wahoo
Grouper	Rosefish	Weakfish
Grunion	Sailfish	Wolffish
Grunt		

Other related articles

Animal (pictures)	Food supply	Plankton
Aquaculture	(Livestock and	Prehistoric
Aquarium	fish)	animal
Evolution	Grand Banks	Reproduction
Fish and Wildlife	Ichthyology	(Sexual repro-
Service	Instinct	duction in
Fishing	Ocean (Life in	animals)
Fishing industry	the ocean;	Sea serpent
	pictures)	Spawn
		Tropical fish

Outline

I. The importance of fish
  A. Food and game fish
  B. Other useful fish
  C. Harmful fish
  D. Fish in the balance of nature
II. Kinds of fish
  A. Bony fish
  B. Sharks, rays, and chimaeras
  C. Lampreys and hagfish
III. Where fish live
  A. Saltwater environments
  B. Freshwater environments
  C. Fish migrations
IV. The bodies of fish

A. External anatomy	C. Systems of the body
B. Skeleton and muscles	D. Special organs

V. The senses of fish
  A. Sight
  B. Hearing
  C. Smell and taste
  D. Touch and the lateral line system
  E. Other senses
VI. How fish live
  A. How fish get food
  B. How fish swim
  C. How fish protect themselves
  D. How fish rest
  E. How fish live together
  F. How fish adjust to change
VII. How fish reproduce
  A. Preparation for spawning
  B. Spawning and care of the eggs
  C. Hatching and care of the young
VIII. The development of fish
  A. The first fish
  B. The age of fishes
  C. The first modern fish
IX. A classification of fish

Questions

What kind of food do most fish eat?
How are lampreys and hagfish different from other fish?
What are *median fins*? *Paired fins*? *Chromatophores*?
How great a change in water temperature can most fish survive?
What are *fish farms*?
What is the name of the process by which most fish eggs are fertilized?
Which parts of the world have the most species of freshwater fish?
What were *ostracoderms*?
How do fish turn and make other swimming maneuvers?
What are the two main groups of jawed fish? How do they differ?

Additional resources

Level I
Fegely, Thomas D. *The World of Freshwater Fish.* Dodd, 1978.
Fletcher, Alan M. *Fishes Dangerous to Man.* Addison-Wesley, 1969. *Fishes That Hide.* 1973. *Fishes and Their Young.* 1974.
McPherson, Mark D. *Caring for Your Fish.* Troll, 1984.
Ommanney, Francis D. *The Fishes.* Rev. ed. Time-Life Books, 1980.
Overbeck, Cynthia. *The Fish Book: Introducing Tropical Fish.* Lerner, 1978.
Patent, Dorothy H. *Fish and How They Reproduce.* Holiday House, 1976.

Level II
Boschung, Herbert T., Jr., and others. *The Audubon Society Field Guide to North American Fishes, Whales, and Dolphins.* Knopf, 1983.
The Encyclopedia of Aquatic Life. Ed. by Keith Banister and Andrew Campbell. Facts on File, 1985.
Grzimek's Animal Life Encyclopedia, Vol. 4: Fishes I. Ed. by Bernhard Grzimek and others. Van Nostrand, 1973. *Vol. 5: Fishes II/ Amphibians.* 1974.
Lagler, Karl F., and others. *Ichthyology.* 2nd ed. Wiley, 1977.
Marshall, Norman B. *The Life of Fishes.* World Publishing, 1966.
Norman, John R. *A History of Fishes.* 3rd ed. by P. H. Greenwood. Halsted, 1975.
Wilson, Roberta E. and J. Q. *Watching Fishes: Life and Behavior on Coral Reefs.* Harper, 1985.

Fish is the name of a family which became prominent in American public life.

Hamilton Fish (1808-1893) was a distinguished lawyer and statesman. He was a member of the Whig Party and served as a New York representative in Congress from 1843 to 1845. He was governor of New York from 1849 to

1850, and one of New York's U.S. senators from 1851 to 1857. When the Whig Party broke up, he became a Republican. Fish served as secretary of state under President Ulysses S. Grant from 1869 to 1877. He negotiated the Treaty of Washington, which submitted the *Alabama* claims to arbitration and settled other problems with England (see **Alabama** [ship]; **Washington, Treaty of**). He was born in New York City and was graduated from Columbia College.

Hamilton Fish (1849-1936), son of Hamilton Fish, was a politician and lawyer. He served as U.S. assistant treasurer from 1903 to 1908, and as a Republican representative from New York in the United States Congress from 1909 to 1911. Fish was born in Albany, N.Y.

Stuyvesant Fish (1851-1923), another son of the first Hamilton Fish, became a banker and railroad official. He started as a clerk for the Illinois Central (now Illinois Central Gulf) Railroad in 1871 and served as its president from 1887 to 1906. While Fish was president, the Illinois Central increased its mileage by 175 per cent and became one of the most prosperous American railroads. Fish was born in New York City and was graduated from Columbia College.

Hamilton Fish (1888-   ), son of the second Hamilton Fish, served as a Republican United States representative from New York from 1920 to 1945. He was born in Garrison, N.Y., and was graduated from Harvard University.

Hamilton Fish, Jr. (1926-   ), grandson of the second Hamilton Fish, has represented New York in the U.S. House of Representatives as a Republican since 1969. He was born in Washington, D.C. He graduated from Harvard University and earned a law degree at New York University School of Law.   Nelson M. Blake

Fish and Wildlife Service is an agency of the United States government that helps conserve the nation's birds, mammals, fish, and other wildlife. It operates more than 400 wildlife refuges and many other field stations including national fish hatcheries, habitat resources field offices, and research laboratories.

The service regulates the hunting of migratory birds and conducts programs to conserve fisheries. It also studies the effects of development projects on fish and wildlife and recommends ways to prevent or minimize harmful effects. The agency runs programs to restore endangered and threatened species and works to enforce the Endangered Species Act of 1973. It also cooperates with other groups devoted to conserving wildlife.

The Fish and Wildlife Service provides funds to the states and territories for fish and wildlife conservation. It also publishes scientific reports on wildlife. The agency was established in 1940 as part of the Department of the Interior.   Critically reviewed by the Fish and Wildlife Service

See also **Bird** (Birdbanding); **National Wildlife Refuge System**.

Fish farm. See **Fish** (Food and game fish).

Fish hawk. See **Osprey**.

Fish ladder. See **Salmon** (The life of a salmon).

Fisher. See **Marten**.

Fisher, Saint John (1469?-1535), was a Roman Catholic bishop of Rochester, England. He was beheaded for saying that King Henry VIII was not the supreme head of the church in England. Fisher was born in Beverley, near Hull, and was educated at Cambridge University. He

later founded St. John's College at Cambridge. Fisher was also a learned theologian who wrote many important books. While he was awaiting death in prison, Pope Paul III made him a cardinal. His feast day is July 9.   Marvin R. O'Connell

Fisher, Vardis (1895-1968), an American author, became best known for his fictional history of the Mormons, *The Children of God* (1939). His 12-volume novel series, *The Testament of Man,* traced human thought from its beginnings to the present. The first novel in this series, *Darkness and the Deep,* was published in 1943. Fisher was born in Annis, Ida. He was graduated from the University of Utah and received a Ph.D. degree from the University of Chicago.   Bernard Duffey

Fishery is an area which supplies abundant fish for commercial purposes. Species of cod, flatfish, herring, sardines, and tuna make up the world's most important fishery resources. Many governments practice *fishery management* to conserve fish. Rules limit the size and amount of fish that may be caught, and the fishing season. The United States federal and state governments operate fish-culture stations, or *fisheries*. Here fishes are grown to be placed in various bodies of water.

See also **Fishing industry**.

Fishes, Age of. See **Devonian Period**.

Fishing is one of the most popular forms of recreation. People of all ages enjoy fishing in streams, rivers, lakes, bays, and oceans for many kinds of fish.

Some people fish with simple cane poles, but others use rods, reels, and additional equipment that requires more skill to operate. People who fish for sport are called *anglers*. They enjoy the challenge of hooking and landing fish. Many anglers try to catch certain species of fish. Some fish are especially prized for their beauty. Others are unusually strong or fast and fight hard to escape. Some species are considered crafty game that must be outwitted in order to catch them.

Some common methods of fishing include *casting, still fishing, drift fishing, trolling,* and *ice fishing*. Casting is one of the most popular methods. The angler casts

Focus on Sports

In fly fishing, the angler pulls the line off the reel by hand and casts the fly into the water with the rod.

the *lure* (artificial bait) into the water and carefully *retrieves* (gathers in) the line in an attempt to lure the fish to bite. In still fishing, the angler throws the bait into the water from a bank or anchored boat and waits for a fish to bite. When drift fishing, the angler trails the bait behind a boat, which is allowed to drift freely with the current. In trolling, the bait is trailed behind a moving boat. Ice fishing is a popular winter sport in which the angler fishes through a hole chopped in the ice.

This article discusses recreational fishing. For information on commercial fishing, see **Fishing industry.**

Fishing equipment

Manufacturers produce a wide variety of *tackle* (equipment) designed for every type of fishing. Fishing tackle includes rods, reels, lines, leaders, sinkers, floats, hooks, and bait. The choice of equipment depends chiefly on the kind of fish sought.

The two most basic fishing tools are the rod and reel. Both are available in a wide range of sizes, from those designed for freshwater *pan fish* to those made for large saltwater fish. Pan fish are small fish, such as bluegill, crappie, and yellow perch, that can fit into a frying pan. Large saltwater species include marlin, sailfish, and tuna.

Rods are tapered poles made of fiberglass, bamboo, graphite, steel, or other materials. Fiberglass and graphite rods are the most popular because they are lightweight yet strong and flexible.

All fishing rods have a handle, shaft, *reel seat,* and *guides.* The reel seat is the area on the rod where the reel is attached. On some rods, the reel is fastened below the handle, and on others it is above the handle. Guides are attachments along the shaft of the rod through which the line is strung. Some rods consist of two or more sections joined by *ferrules* (sockets and plugs) that enable them to be taken apart and carried easily.

Rods are made in many lengths, weights, and designs. Each rod is designed for use with a particular type of reel. For example, a fly rod is used with a fly reel. Rods also vary in *action* (flexibility), ranging from limber to stiff. Rods with greater flexibility are needed to catch larger fish.

Reels are used to store, release, and retrieve fishing line. Many reels have an adjustable *drag-setting device* that controls the tension of the line on the spool. There are four basic kinds of reels: (1) spinning, (2) spin-casting, (3) bait-casting, and (4) fly. Each kind of reel is manufactured in various sizes and designs. Spinning and spin-casting reels are the easiest to use and the most popular.

Spinning reels have an open-faced spool mounted on the reel seat in a vertical position parallel to the rod. The spool does not turn when the line is cast or retrieved. When cast, the line simply slips off the open end of the spool. Spinning reels have a handle for gathering in line. A device called a *bail* winds the line around the spool. The spool moves in and out of its frame so that the line is wound evenly. The spool itself turns only when a fish pulls on the line against the drag setting.

Spin-casting reels resemble spinning reels, but the spool is enclosed within a hood or cap. The line passes through a hole in the center of the cap. Most spin-

Rods and reels

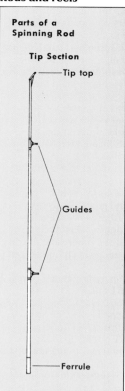

Parts of a Spinning Rod

Tip Section

- Tip top
- Guides
- Ferrule

Butt Section

- Ferrule
- Butt guide
- Foregrip
- Reel seat
- Handle
- Butt cap

Bait-casting reel

Spin-casting reel

Spinning reel

WORLD BOOK photos by Steve Spicer
Fly reel

Some basic types of lures

A popping plug floats on top of the water. When the rod is jerked, the plug's hollowed mouth goes underwater and makes popping sounds that attract fish.

A spinner has a metal blade that spins as it is drawn through the water. Spinners attract fish by their motion, vibration, and bright flashing colors.

Flies are made of feathers, hair, or other materials. A wet fly, *left,* sinks below the surface of the water. A dry fly, *right,* floats on the surface.

A floating and diving plug floats on the surface of the water until the line is *re-trieved* (gathered in). The plug then dives below the surface.

A plastic worm can be made to slide or hop along the bottom of the water by slowly retrieving the line. It does not catch on weeds as easily as other lures.

A streamer fly has a long wing made of feathers or hair. It is designed to imitate a small bait fish. Most streamer flies sink below the surface.

WORLD BOOK illustrations by James Teason

A deep diver plug dives quickly while the line is being retrieved. It may dive to a depth of 10 to 20 feet (3 to 6 meters) or more.

A jig sinks quickly after hitting the water. As the rod is jerked, a jig attracts fish by making short, rapid hops along the bottom of the water.

A spoon flutters or wobbles when pulled through the water. The action of this type of lure is designed to imitate that of a wounded bait fish.

casting reels are operated by a push button that releases the line for casting. They have a handle for gathering in the line. A device built into the hood winds the line on the spool and keeps it from tangling.

Bait-casting reels have a wide spool that lies horizontally across the reel seat. The reel has a handle that turns to release and retrieve line. For each turn of the reel handle, the spool revolves several turns. Some bait-casting reels have a device called a *level wind* that guides the line evenly on the spool.

Fly reels serve chiefly to store line and to feed line to a hooked fish. A fly reel is not designed to cast line. In fly casting, the line is pulled off the reel by hand and cast into the water with the rod.

There are two basic types of fly reels, *single-action* and *automatic.* A single-action fly reel has a handle that turns to gather in the line. An automatic fly reel has a spring mechanism that draws in the line at the push of a lever or trigger. Fly reels and rods are especially popular for trout fishing.

Lines may consist of natural fibers, such as linen or silk; or synthetic fibers, such as nylon or Dacron. Some lines are made of many fibers braided or twisted together. Others consist of *monofilaments,* which are single strands of fiber.

Monofilament lines are widely used on spinning, spin-casting, and bait-casting reels. These lines are sturdy and lightweight. Braided lines are often used with fly reels. These lines are heavier than monofilament lines. Their extra weight plays an important part in fly casting because it helps carry the line smoothly through the air.

All lines are made in a variety of thicknesses and

lengths. Lines are also rated in *pounds test,* which is the weight they can lift without breaking. They range from $\frac{1}{4}$ pound (0.1 kilogram) test to 100 pounds (45 kilograms) test. The weight and strength of the line used depends on the size of the rod and reel and the kind of fish sought.

Leaders are lengths of line made of a synthetic or metal material. A leader is connected to the end of a line and attached to a hook. Synthetic monofilament leaders are used with braided lines because they provide a less visible link between the line and the hook. Fish cannot see these leaders as well as they can see a braided line. Metal leaders are used when casting for sharp-toothed or rough-scaled fish that may break a line. Leaders range in length from 12 inches (30 centimeters) to 12 feet (3.7 meters) or longer. A leader may be attached to a line with a device called a *swivel.* A swivel allows the leader to rotate freely and thus prevents twisting of the line and leader.

Sinkers are lead weights that are attached to lines or leaders. They lower the bait and hold it in the water. An angler selects a sinker that is just heavy enough to hold the bait at the desired depth. Sinkers also provide extra weight on the line, enabling it to be cast farther. Sinkers are made in various styles designed for waters with rocky, muddy, or sandy bottoms. They range in weight from $\frac{1}{16}$ ounce (1.8 grams) to 3 pounds (1.4 kilograms).

Floats hold the bait suspended in the water. They are made of cork, plastic, or some other material that floats. The amount of line between the float and the bait determines the depth at which the bait is suspended.

Floats, which are also called *bobbers,* bob when a fish bites the hook, and so they may indicate a strike.

Some types of floats attract fish by making a popping noise when the rod is jerked. Other floats can be partially filled with water to provide additional weight for casting.

Hooks are made in many sizes and hundreds of styles. The choice depends on several factors, such as the kind of tackle used and the size of fish sought. A hook made of fine wire should be used with a light rod. A heavier wire hook can be used with heavy tackle.

Bait used to catch fish may be either natural or artificial.

Natural bait. Most freshwater and saltwater game fish feed chiefly on smaller fish. Therefore, a small live fish on a hook is one of the best kinds of natural bait. Fishes used as bait include freshwater minnows and saltwater herring, mullet, and smelt.

Fish also feed on such animals as worms, crayfish, grasshoppers, and frogs, all of which are used as live bait in freshwater fishing. Eels, clam worms, and shrimp may be used in saltwater fishing.

Many species of fish feed on dead animals as well as live ones. Such fish can be caught with *cut bait,* which consists of pieces of dead fish or other animals. Anglers also use cheese, marshmallows, fish eggs, and bread dough as bait for some freshwater fish.

Artificial bait consists of a variety of items called *lures.* Some lures look like natural bait, and others attract fish by means of their unusual color, design, motion, or sound. Lures, unlike natural bait, can be reused and can be cast farther and harder. Basic types of lures include *flies, plugs, spinners,* and *spoons.*

Flies are lightweight lures made of feathers, hair, yarn, or other materials tied onto a hook. Flies are used mainly with fly rods in fishing for trout, salmon, bass, and a variety of pan fish. Some flies look like insects, small fish, or other natural food of fish. Others attract fish by their unusual color or appearance. There are two basic types of flies, *wet flies* and *dry flies.* Wet flies sink beneath the surface of the water. Dry flies float.

Plugs are wooden or plastic lures designed to resemble small fish, frogs, and other natural bait. There are two chief kinds of plugs, *surface plugs* and *sinking plugs.* Surface plugs float on top of the water. Some sinking plugs sink when they hit the water, and others dive to various depths while the line is being retrieved. Many plugs twirl, wobble, or make popping or gurgling sounds to attract fish.

Spinners have metal or plastic blades that whirl as the spinner is retrieved through the water. They attract fish by their color, motion, and the sound they make. Spinners also work well in cloudy water, where fish might not notice silent lures. They may be used alone or with other lures or natural bait.

Spoons are rounded or dished-out metal lures that flutter when pulled through the water. Their action imitates that of wounded bait fish. Spoons are made in various sizes, shapes, and colors to catch different fish. A spoon that weighs only $\frac{1}{16}$ of an ounce (1.8 grams) may be used for pan fish. A spoon weighing 2 ounces (57 grams) or more may be used to catch muskie, lake trout, and a variety of saltwater fish.

Other equipment includes nets, tackle boxes, *stringers, creels,* and various electronic devices. Tackle boxes hold lures, hooks, and other fishing equipment. String-

Some popular bait hooks

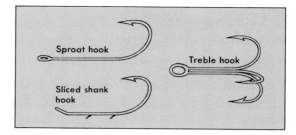

Parts of a fishhook

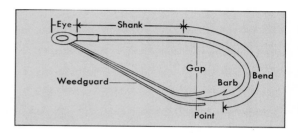

Some fishing tackle

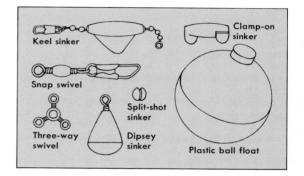

Two basic fishing knots

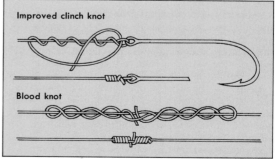

WORLD BOOK illustrations by David Cunningham

Fishing knots are used for a variety of purposes. Two important fishing knots are the *improved clinch knot* and the *blood knot.* An improved clinch knot is used to tie lines or leaders to hooks, lures, or *swivels.* Swivels are attachments that allow a line or leader to rotate freely and thus prevent twisting of the line or leader. A blood knot is used to join two lines or two leaders together.

Five ways to rig a fishing line

The illustration below shows five of the many ways of rigging a fishing line. For fly fishing, the line may be rigged with a long leader. For bottom fishing, drift fishing, and *trolling* (fishing from a moving boat), sinkers are used to hold the bait or lure at the proper depth. In *still fishing* (fishing from a shore or anchored boat), a float may be used to suspend the bait in the water.

WORLD BOOK illustration by David Cunningham

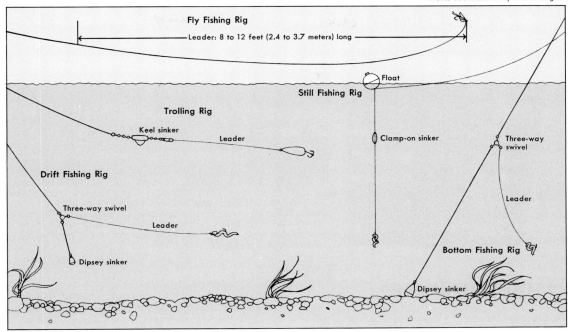

ers are cords or chains that anglers use to hold the fish they catch. A stringer is run through the mouth of the fish, which are placed in the water to keep them fresh. Creels are canvas, rattan, or willow containers used to carry fish. Some anglers use various electronic devices that measure the depth and temperature of the water or even locate fish.

Fishing tips

Successful fishing requires much practice and study. A person can learn only from experience how to hook and *play* (tire out) a fish properly. To catch a particular species of fish, an angler must study its habits—what it eats, the kinds of waters it lives in, and the water depth and temperature it prefers.

The habits of a fish influence the choice of bait, the fishing technique used, and the place chosen for fishing. For example, rainbow trout thrive in cool, clear streams with swift currents. They often feed near the surface of the water, where the current brings them insects to eat. A favorite method of catching these fish is fly fishing with a dry fly, casting upstream. On the other hand, many kinds of catfish live in muddy lakes and streams near the bottom of the water. They find their food chiefly by smell or touch. Such fish may be caught by fishing near the bottom of the lake or stream and using an odorous bait made of cheese, meat, or bread dough.

The temperature of the water influences the hunger and activity of fish. Each species prefers a certain temperature range and seeks the level of water within that range. Fish become less active when the water tempera-

ture is above or below their preferred range. Certain species may even wait until night or early dawn to feed if the water temperature near the surface is too warm. Anglers often measure the water temperature at various depths to find the level suitable for the fish they seek.

In the United States and Canada, state and provincial fishing laws regulate the times of year when certain fish can be caught and kept. These regulations, which are published by state and provincial conservation departments, also limit the number of fish that a person may catch. In addition, the departments provide information about places to fish and the best methods of catching fish in various areas.   Larry Green

See the articles on the game fish mentioned in this article. See also **Fish; Spearfishing; Eskimo** (pictures: Old and new Eskimo ways of life).

Additional resources

Level I

Arnosky, Jim. *Freshwater Fish and Fishing.* Macmillan, 1982. *Flies in the Water, Fish in the Air: A Personal Introduction to Fly Fishing.* Lothrop, 1986.

Evanoff, Vlad. *A Complete Guide to Fishing.* Rev. ed. T. Y. Crowell, 1981.

Randolph, John D. *Fishing Basics.* Prentice-Hall, 1981.

Level II

Bates, Joseph D., Jr. *Fishing: An Encyclopedic Guide to Tackle and Tactics for Fresh and Salt Water.* Rev. ed. Outdoor Life, 1985.

Johnson, Paul C. *The Scientific Angler: Using the Latest Underwater Research to Improve Your Catch.* Scribner, 1984.

Rogers, E. L. *The World's Best Fishing Holes.* Prentice-Hall, 1986.

Fishing banks. See Grand Banks.

J. R. Eyerman, Black Star

© David Falconer

Various types of fishing gear and vessels are used to catch fish. Much of the world's commercial catch is harvested with huge nets like the one being used at the left to haul in tuna. Many fishing vessels, such as the Soviet *stern trawler* above, also carry equipment on board to process fish after they have been caught.

Fishing industry

Fishing industry is an important economic activity that provides food and jobs for millions of people. The fishing industry includes all the activities involved in the commercial and recreational production of fish and shellfish. The catching, processing, marketing, and conservation of fish and shellfish are all parts of the industry. The industry also provides various other products from the sea, such as seaweeds.

Fish are an excellent source of protein, one of the chief *nutrients* (nourishing substances) that people need for a good diet. As the world's population has grown, so has the demand for food—especially food rich in protein. The fishing industry has increased its annual catch to help meet this demand. The industry markets food fish in a variety of forms. The fish are sold fresh, canned, cured, and frozen. In addition, about a third of the world's fish catch is used to produce high-quality animal feed and various industrial products.

The oceans are by far the main source of fish. Only a small portion of the world's commercial fish catch comes from such inland waters as lakes and rivers. An even smaller portion of the catch comes from *fish farms*. Fish farms are enclosures built on land, or areas in natural bodies of water where fish and shellfish are raised for food.

The fishing industry catches many kinds of fish. Such fish as anchovies, capelin, herring, mackerel, sardines, and tuna are caught near the surface of oceans. Such fish as cod, flounder, hake, and pollock are harvested near the ocean floor. Freshwater fish, such as carp, cat-

Gary D. Stauffer, the contributor of this article, is a Fishery Biologist for the United States National Marine Fisheries Service.

fish, and whitefish, are caught in inland waters.

During the early 1980's, the worldwide fish catch totaled about 85 million short tons (77 million metric tons) annually. Japan is the leading fishing country, followed by the Soviet Union, China, the United States, and Chile. United States fishing fleets harvest about 4½ million short tons (4 million metric tons) yearly. Canada ranks 16th in the world in fish production. Its annual catch totals about 1½ million short tons (1.4 million metric tons).

The fishing industry employs more than 6 million people worldwide. In the United States, about 193,000 people work on fishing boats and about 103,000 work in fish-processing plants and in other areas of the industry. The Canadian fishing industry employs a total of about 80,000 workers.

People have fished for thousands of years. Through the centuries, they have used hooks, spears, nets, and traps to capture fish. Such equipment is still used, but commercial fishing crews now harvest most of their catch with huge nets. In addition, modern fishing vessels have various devices that make fishing more efficient. For example, advanced navigational aids and fish-finding equipment enable fishing crews to range far from their home ports and to pinpoint schools of fish. Refrigeration systems aboard the vessels help prevent the catch from spoiling. These vessels can remain at sea longer than those without refrigeration.

After World War II ended in 1945, many countries expanded their fishing fleets. These fleets increased their fish catch along their home coasts as well as in distant waters. As a result, the fish harvest generally increased year after year. At the same time, however, overfishing severely reduced the stocks of some kinds of fish. Disputes also arose among countries over the ownership of fish resources. Traditionally, fish have been considered common property—that is, no one owned them until they were caught. The fish then became the property of whoever caught them. After the development of long-range fishing fleets, many nations became concerned with protecting the fish resources along their coasts from fleets of other countries. As a result, a number of international commissions were formed to promote fish conservation and to help settle disputes over fishing rights.

During the 1970's, almost all nations bordering the sea established *fishery conservation zones* in further efforts to conserve and protect their fish resources. These zones extend 200 nautical miles (370 kilometers) from a nation's coast. Countries that have adopted such zones claim authority over all fishing—and ownership of all fish—within the zones.

Where fish are caught

Areas where fish are caught commercially or recreationally are called *fisheries.* The term is also used for the act of harvesting fish. In many cases, more than one species of fish is harvested from a particular fishery. A fishery may be a small lake. Or it may extend across an enormous section of an ocean. For example, the tuna fishery that lies off the west coast of Central and South America covers about 5 million square miles (13 million square kilometers).

Ocean fisheries provide most of the world's commercial fish catch. About 75 million short tons (68 million metric tons) of fish—or about 89 per cent of the total world harvest—is taken from the oceans annually. This figure includes the production from marine fish farms. Almost all the ocean catch comes from waters near seacoasts, especially the shallow waters over the *continen-*

tal shelf. The continental shelf consists of submerged land along the coasts of the continents. In some places, the shelf extends great distances out into the ocean.

A large amount of the fish caught in waters over the continental shelf is taken from regions of *upwelling.* Upwelling occurs during certain seasons when winds blow surface waters near the coast offshore. The colder bottom waters, which are rich in nutrients, then rise to the

Worldwide fish and shellfish catch

Chief kinds	Annual catch	
	In short tons	In metric tons
Sardine and pilchard	11,205,000	10,165,000
Pollack	5,511,000	4,999,000
Jack mackerel	4,266,000	3,870,000
Anchovy and anchovetta	4,205,000	3,815,000
Mackerel	2,918,000	2,647,000
Cod	2,810,000	2,549,000
Herring	2,573,000	2,334,000
Capelin	2,042,000	1,852,000
Tuna	1,918,000	1,740,000
Shrimp and prawn	1,869,000	1,695,000
Clam	1,437,000	1,304,000
Menhaden	1,397,000	1,267,000
Hake	1,327,000	1,204,000
Squid	1,296,000	1,176,000
Oyster	1,054,000	956,000
Cutlass fish	984,000	893,000
Sand lance	881,000	799,000
Crab	844,000	765,000
Mussel	703,000	638,000
Salmon	701,000	636,000

Figures are for 1982.
Source: *Yearbook of Fishery Statistics, 1982,* FAO.

Chief commercial fishing areas

This map shows the world's major commercial fishing areas. Most lie along the *continental shelf,* the submerged land around the continents. Inland fishing areas include rivers and lakes. The map also shows the chief fish and shellfish, with the most valuable catches in boldface type.

WORLD BOOK map

Leading fishing states and provinces

Tons of fish and shellfish caught each year

Louisiana	●●●●●●●●●●●●● 900,000 short tons (817,000 metric tons)
Newfoundland	●●●●●●● 502,000 short tons (456,000 metric tons)
Alaska	●●●●●●(482,000 short tons (437,000 metric tons)
Nova Scotia	●●●●●●(469,000 short tons (426,000 metric tons)
Virginia	●●●●(376,000 short tons (341,000 metric tons)
California	●●● 264,000 short tons (240,000 metric tons)
Mississippi	●●(222,000 short tons (202,000 metric tons)
British Columbia	●●(211,000 short tons (192,000 metric tons)
Massachusetts	●● 188,000 short tons (171,000 metric tons)
North Carolina	●(144,000 short tons (133,000 metric tons)

Sources: National Marine Fisheries Service; Statistics Canada. Figures are for 1983.

Leading fishing countries

Tons of fish and shellfish caught each year

Japan	●●●●●●●●●●●●●●●● 11,878,000 short tons (10,775,000 metric tons)
Soviet Union	●●●●●●●●●●●●●(10,523,000 short tons (9,546,000 metric tons)
China	●●●●●● 5,431,000 short tons (4,927,000 metric tons)
United States	●●●●●(4,396,000 short tons (3,988,000 metric tons)
Chile	●●●● 4,049,000 short tons (3,673,000 metric tons)
Peru	●●●(3,805,000 short tons (3,452,000 metric tons)
Norway	●●(2,756,000 short tons (2,500,000 metric tons)
India	●●(2,574,000 short tons (2,335,000 metric tons)
South Korea	●●(2,515,000 short tons (2,281,000 metric tons)
Indonesia	●(2,227,000 short tons (2,020,000 metric tons)

Source: *Yearbook of Fishery Statistics, 1982*, FAO. Figures are for 1982.

surface near the coast. This upwelling of bottom waters provides nutrients for the growth of microscopic plants and animals that fish feed on, thus promoting growth of the fish population. Upwelling takes place chiefly along the coasts of Peru, western North America, northwest and southwest Africa, Somalia, the Arabian Peninsula, and Antarctica.

Atlantic Ocean fisheries. The major U.S. and Canadian fisheries in the Atlantic include the coastal waters from Newfoundland to New England and the *Grand Banks.* The Grand Banks is a stretch of shallow waters southeast of Newfoundland. The Grand Banks and the other waters of the northwest Atlantic rank among the best fishing grounds in the world. The area provides great quantities of cod and herring, as well as flounder, lobsters, and scallops.

Cod is the chief catch of the Canadian fishing industry. The nation's fishing crews harvest about 570,000 short tons (517,000 metric tons) of cod yearly in the northwest Atlantic. The area provides the U.S. fishing industry with an annual cod catch of about 52,000 short tons (47,000 metric tons). Canada also harvests about 162,000 short tons (147,000 metric tons) of herring from the northwest Atlantic each year. It leads the world in the production of Atlantic herring.

The Gulf of Mexico, an arm of the Atlantic Ocean, is another productive area for the U.S. fishing industry. It ranks as the nation's main menhaden fishery, providing about 941,000 short tons (854,000 metric tons) yearly. The Gulf of Mexico also provides large quantities of shrimp and lobsters.

The Atlantic Ocean has several other rich fishing areas. They include the northeast Atlantic near Iceland and Great Britain and the southwest Atlantic near Argentina and Brazil. Crews from a number of nations—including the Soviet Union, Norway, Denmark, Great Britain, and Iceland—fish the waters of the northeast Atlantic.

They catch herring, capelin, cod, haddock, mackerel, and many other types of fish. The chief fish caught in the southwest Atlantic Ocean include croaker, hake, and sardines.

Pacific Ocean fisheries. The major U.S. and Canadian fisheries in the Pacific include the Bering Sea, the Gulf of Alaska, and the waters off the coast of California. The chief fish caught in the Bering Sea, the Gulf of Alaska, and other areas of the North Pacific include pollock, salmon, hake, and sole. The United States is the leading salmon-fishing country. It catches about 307,000 short tons (278,000 metric tons) yearly. Canada is also a major salmon-fishing country, ranking behind the United States, Japan, and the Soviet Union. It harvests about 52,000 short tons (47,000 metric tons) a year. The waters off the California coast and to the immediate south are harvested for such fish as anchovies, herring, mackerel, and tuna.

The Pacific Ocean also has a number of other productive fisheries. They include the waters of the southeast Pacific off the coast of South America and the coastal seas of the western Pacific from Indonesia to Japan. The fisheries off the west coast of South America provide anchovettas, hake, mackerel, and sardines. The coastal seas from Indonesia to Japan are fished for anchovies, mackerel, sardines, scads, shrimp, and tuna.

Inland fisheries. About $9\frac{1}{2}$ million short tons (8.6 million metric tons) of fish—or about 11 per cent of the commercial catch worldwide—is harvested yearly from ponds, lakes, rivers, streams, and fish farms in inland waters. China and India lead all other countries in the fish catch from inland waters. China's annual inland-water catch totals about $1\frac{3}{4}$ million short tons (1.6 million metric tons). The inland-water catch by India totals approximately 983,000 short tons (892,000 metric tons). Both China and India chiefly harvest carp, tilapia, and other plant-eating fish.

The Soviet Union ranks third in the production of inland-water fish with an annual catch of about 886,000 short tons (804,000 metric tons). The Caspian Sea provides much of the nation's harvest of fish from inland waters. The main species caught in the Caspian Sea are bream, carp, salmon, and sturgeon. In addition, the rivers that flow into the Caspian yield most of the annual Soviet harvest of sturgeon. The Soviet Union produces about 28,000 short tons (25,000 metric tons) of sturgeon a year, or about 89 per cent of the world total.

The U.S. fishing industry produces about 80,000 short tons (73,000 metric tons) of fish from inland waters yearly. The major freshwater fisheries of the United States include the inland waters of the Southern States and the Great Lakes. The inland waters of the South provide buffalo fish, carp, and catfish. Much of the world's harvest of crayfish comes from Louisiana, which produces more than 4,000 short tons (3,700 metric tons) a year. The Great Lakes are fished chiefly for alewives, whitefish, smelt, and carp.

Canada harvests about 64,000 short tons (58,000 metric tons) of inland-water fish annually. The chief fish caught include alewives, northern pike, smelt, whitefish, and yellow perch. The Great Lakes are the center of the freshwater fishing industry in Canada.

Fish farms account for about 10 per cent of the world's annual commercial fish harvest. Each year, they produce about 10 million short tons (9 million metric tons) of fish, shellfish, and *aquatic plants* (plants that live in water). Fish farming is also called *aquaculture*.

Fish farms range from simple ponds or flooded rice fields to highly engineered hatcheries in which the environment is almost completely controlled. Fish farmers try to eliminate harmful environmental conditions so fish can flourish. They provide fish with proper nutrients and protect them from animals that prey on them. Aquaculture is commonly used to rebuild salmon and trout stocks that have been severely reduced.

The chief fish raised on fish farms throughout the world include carp, catfish, gourami, milkfish, salmon, tilapia, and trout. China leads all countries in aquaculture production. It has an annual harvest of about $2\frac{3}{4}$ million short tons (2.5 million metric tons), or about a fourth of the world total.

The main fish and shellfish raised on fish farms in the United States include catfish, crayfish, oysters, salmon, and trout. The nation's fish farms produce about 200,000 short tons (180,000 metric tons) of fish, shellfish, and aquatic plants yearly. Canadian fish farms raise chiefly salmon, trout, and oysters. Canada's aquaculture production totals about 6,200 short tons (5,600 metric tons) annually.

How fish are caught

Fishing vessels vary greatly in size and in the number of crew members they carry. Vessels in coastal fishing fleets are 25 to 130 feet (8 to 40 meters) long. Their crews consist of as many as 20 to 25 people or as few as 1 or 2, depending on the fishing method being used. Coastal vessels can remain at sea for several days or weeks. The fish catch is stored in holds chilled by either ice or refrigeration systems.

Long-range fishing fleets stay at sea for months at a time and travel great distances from their home ports. Many modern fleets, particularly Soviet fleets, include *processing-catcher vessels,* as well as processors, refrigerated transporters, and supply ships. Processing-catcher vessels, which measure about 260 feet (80 meters) in length, are used for both catching fish and processing the harvest into various products. Their crews have from 50 to 100 members and in most cases include a number of women.

Fishing crews use a variety of gear to catch fish. The equipment used depends on the behavior of the fish being sought and the nature of the fishing grounds. The chief types of gear include (1) nets, (2) hooks, (3) traps, and (4) harpoons.

Nets. Most of the world's commercial fish catch is taken in by huge nets. There are three main types of nets: (1) seines, (2) trawls, and (3) gill nets.

Seines (pronounced *saynz*) account for more than a third of the world's fish catch. Over half the U.S. harvest and about a seventh of the Canadian landings are hauled in with this type of net. Fishing crews use seines chiefly to catch anchovies, capelin, herring, mackerel, menhaden, sardines, tuna, and other *pelagic* schooling fish. Pelagic fish swim near the surface of the water.

The most widely used seine is the rectangular *purse*

Michael Friedel

Fish farmers raise fish in lakes, ponds, reservoirs, and similar bodies of water. The farmers help fish flourish by supplying them with nourishing foods and by protecting them from harmful environmental conditions. The men at the left are harvesting milkfish from a huge fish farm in Laguna de Bay, a lake in the Philippines.

seine. Purse seines range from about 660 to 6,600 feet (200 to 2,000 meters) in length. They have floats along the top. Weights and rings are attached along the bottom edge. A rope or cable called a *purse line* runs through the rings.

A purse seine is set into the water from a large vessel called a *seiner* with the aid of a small, high-powered boat called a *skiff.* After a school of fish is spotted, the skiff is launched from the seiner with one end of the net attached. The seiner speeds ahead, encircling the school and playing out the net as it goes. The bottom of the seine is then closed off with the purse line, capturing the school. Seiners vary from about 30 to 230 feet (10 to 70 meters) in length and carry crews of 12 to 20 people.

Trawls are funnel-shaped nets that are closed off at the tail end, where the fish collect, and open at the mouth. The most commonly used trawl is the *otter trawl.* The net has floats along the top edge of the mouth and weights on the bottom edge. The net is attached by two long towing cables to the back of a vessel called a

Common types of fishing nets

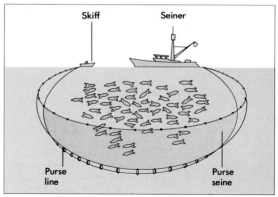

A purse seine is set from a vessel called a *seiner* by a *skiff* (small boat). Fish are caught by surrounding them with the net and then closing off its bottom with a *purse line* (rope or cable).

© David Falconer

A large Japanese *long-liner,* *above,* processes fish caught off the Aleutian Islands. Such ships are an important part of many fishing fleets that range far from their home ports.

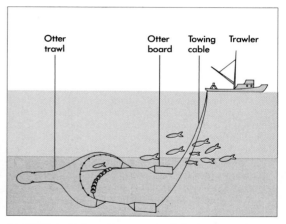

An otter trawl is towed by a vessel called a *trawler* or *stern trawler.* The towing causes two doorlike *otter boards* near the mouth of the net to hold the net open to capture fish.

C. C. Lockwood, Earth Scenes

Small U.S. shrimp boats, *above,* drag nets over the sea bottom to harvest shrimp. The catch is quickly frozen or canned on the boats or onshore to prevent it from spoiling.

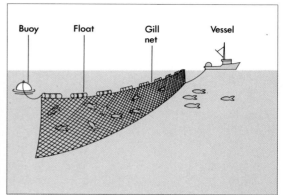

WORLD BOOK illustrations by Bill and Judie Anderson

A gill net forms a wall of webbing that entangles fish when they swim into it. The size of the open spaces of gill nets varies according to the type of fish being sought.

stern trawler or *trawler*. A large doorlike *otter board* is attached to each towing cable near the open end of the net. As the trawler tows the net, the water forces the otter boards to spread apart, holding the net open to capture the fish. The mouth of some otter trawls can be spread to a width of 120 feet (37 meters).

Trawls are used to catch cod, flounder, hake, pollock, red snapper, scallops, shrimp, and other fish and shell-fish that live on or near the ocean floor. Most trawling is done over the continental shelf in waters less than 660 feet (200 meters) deep. However, some stern trawlers fish in waters as deep as 3,300 feet (1,000 meters). Trawl-ers use sonar and other advanced equipment to locate concentrations of fish (see **Sonar**). A small trawler needs only a four-member crew. Most trawlers more than 150 feet (45 meters) long carry processing equipment. Such trawlers require larger crews.

Trawling accounts for about a third of the world's fish harvest. Trawls haul in about 20 per cent of the U.S. fish catch and about 35 per cent of Canada's catch. The otter trawl is the chief fishing gear of the distant-water fleets of European and Asian nations.

Gill nets are long rectangular nets with floats on top and weights on the bottom. They range from 50 to 1,200 feet (15 to 370 meters) in length. The nets are hung in the water near the surface or close to the ocean floor. A gill net is made of thin twine and is nearly invisible in the water. The net is set in the path of migrating fish and forms a wall of webbing that entangles fish when they swim into it. The open spaces of a gill net allow fish to thrust only their heads into the net. The entangled fish try to swim through the net, thrashing about and be-coming more entangled.

Gill nets are used to catch billfish, herring, salmon, sharks, and a number of bottom fish. However, all these fish can also be caught with other types of gear. As a re-sult, the total catch with gill nets makes up less than 5 per cent of the world harvest. Only about $4\frac{1}{2}$ per cent of the U.S. and 17 per cent of the Canadian fish catch are brought in with gill nets. Most vessels equipped with such nets measure less than 50 feet (15 meters) long and have crews of one or two people.

Hooks take advantage of the feeding behavior of fish. Bait or lures attached to a hook tempt fish to bite the hook. Hooks account for only a small percentage of the world's fish catch. The most common hooking methods used by commercial fishing crews are (1) bait fishing, (2) trolling, and (3) long-lining.

Bait fishing. In bait fishing, after a school of fish is sighted, the crew throws live bait or ground-up fish into the water from the fishing boat. The bait attracts schools of tuna or other species that feed on smaller fish to the surface near the boat. As the fish feed greedily on the bait, the crew uses bare hooks and lines to haul them in. Most bait boats have a walkway around the stern from which a crew of as many as 20 people pull in the fish.

Trolling involves towing as many as six fishing lines from two long poles. One pole extends from each side of a vessel. In many cases, metal flashers or feather lures are attached to the lines to attract fish. A large fleet of *trollers* (trolling vessels) fishes for albacore and salmon off the coasts of British Columbia and the Western United States. Billfish and tuna are also caught by troll-ing. Most trollers have crews of only two people.

Common methods of hooking and trapping

Terry Domico, Earth Images

Long-lining involves using a long *main line* like those coiled in-side the buckets. Short *dropper lines* with hooks, shown around the rims of the buckets, are attached to the main line.

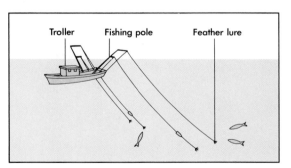

Trolling involves towing fishing lines from poles that extend from the sides of a *troller* (trolling vessel). Feather lures are often attached to the ends of the lines to attract fish.

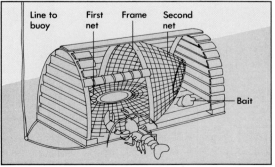

WORLD BOOK illustrations by Bill and Judie Anderson

Trapping is often used to catch lobsters and other shellfish. Traps are designed so that once a fish or shellfish reaches the bait, it has little chance of escaping.

Long-lining involves using an extremely long *main line* with attached short *dropper lines.* The main line may be stretched across the surface of the water to catch such pelagic fish as billfish, sharks, and tuna or near the ocean floor to catch such bottom fish as cod and halibut. As many as 2,000 dropper lines with baited hooks hang from the main line. Some pelagic lines may be as long as 50 nautical miles (93 kilometers). Bottom long-lines are much shorter. A small long-line vessel needs a crew of only 3 or 4 persons. Large Japanese tuna vessels carry crews of 20 to 45.

Traps depend on the migratory or feeding habits of fish. Most traps contain bait or lures to attract fish into the devices. Only a small fraction of the worldwide fish harvest is taken by means of traps.

A fish trap has an entry consisting of a funnellike tunnel or ramp. This entry directs fish through a small opening in the side of the trap. After fish are inside the trap, they have little chance of finding the opening again and escaping.

Small, baited, boxlike traps are used chiefly to capture shellfish, such as crabs, lobsters, shrimp, and crayfish. These traps are placed on the bottom of the ocean or a lake or stream. Larger, stationary traps are floated near shore in the path of migrating fish. These traps are anchored in place or fastened to wooden pilings driven into the seabed. They are used mainly to catch herring and salmon.

Harpoons are barbed spears connected by a rope to a vessel or large float. They may be shot from a cannon or hurled by a crew member. Harpoons are used mainly to kill whales. For more information on whaling and the use of harpoons, see **Whale** (Modern whaling).

How fish are processed and marketed

Methods of processing. The quality of fish declines rapidly after they die. Bacteria that can cause spoilage immediately begin to attack the fish, and enzymes start to break down the protein in fish tissues. As a result, a number of processing methods have been developed over the years to keep fish from spoiling.

Drying, salt curing, and smoking have been used to process fish for thousands of years. All three methods reduce the moisture content of fish and thus slow the growth of bacteria and the breakdown of protein.

Drying fish in the open air for six weeks or more removes most of the water from them. Drying is generally used along with salt curing or smoking.

In salt curing, processors first cut open the fish and remove the head and backbone. They then cover the fish with salt, which draws out the moisture and produces a salty solution called *brine.* Next, the fish are *dry-salted* or *pickled.* In dry-salting, the brine is drained off and the fish are hung up to dry. In pickling, the fish are stored in the brine.

To smoke fish, processors first cut up the fish and soak them in brine. They then place the fish in a large oven, where smoke and heat from smoldering wood chips dries the fish. Processors use this method chiefly to improve the flavor of fish.

© David Falconer

Processing fish aboard ship helps prevent them from spoiling. The man at the left is cleaning and cutting up fish on a Japanese factory ship shortly after they were caught. The fish are then quickly frozen and stored in freezer compartments, *right.*

Ted Spiegel, Black Star

Onshore processing of fish is done in fishing ports. These workers at a plant in Prince Rupert, Canada, are preparing deboned, meal-sized portions of fish for shipment to markets.

Canning involves sealing cut up fish in metal or glass containers and then cooking the contents under pressure. The high temperature and pressure kill bacteria and halt protein breakdown.

Freezing also prevents the growth of bacteria and protein breakdown. The quickly frozen fish are packaged in airtight wrappers or covered with a thin layer of ice. They are stored at −20°F. (−29°C) or lower. Much of the catch of such fish as cod and flounder is *filleted* (deboned) and frozen. Often, the individual fillets are frozen together in large blocks of fish. These blocks may then be made into fish sticks and meal-sized portions of breaded fish.

Other processing methods are used to produce meal and oil from fish. These industrial products are made from such species as anchovies, capelin, herring, menhaden, and sardines. To produce fish meal and fish oil, processors first cook the fish with steam. They then squeeze out most of the water and oil. The remaining solid material is dried and ground into meal. Fish oil is obtained by separating the oil from the water in a whirling device called a *centrifuge*.

Fish meal is added to livestock feed and dry pet food. It is also fed to trout and salmon raised in hatcheries. Manufacturers use fish oil to make a number of products. The most important are glue, paint, lubricants, and ink.

Marketing. Fresh fish may be sold daily in fishing ports located near fishing areas. However, fish and fish products to be sold in distant markets must first be processed to prevent spoilage.

Most fish processors operate in fishing ports. Many

fishing crews sell their catches to processors at auctions after fishing trips. The price a catch commands depends on the supply of fish at the market and the demand for it. A fishing crew does not know in advance what a harvest will earn—if it is sold at all. The uncertainty of the auction market has led some fishing crews to form *marketing cooperatives.* Cooperatives enable their members to know, before they leave port, how much fish to catch and how much the harvest will earn. Processors place orders with the cooperative for a specific quantity of fish before a fishing trip. At the same time, both sides agree on the price to be paid for the catch.

Processors sell most of their fish products to fish brokers in large cities. The brokers, in turn, sell the products to restaurants and food stores.

Fishery conservation

Countless fish die of natural causes or are eaten by animals that prey on them. Nevertheless, a rich fishery will continue to support good catches as long as the stock can produce large numbers of young annually. Problems arise chiefly as a result of overfishing and the polluting of the waters in which the fish live. Fishery conservation seeks to control the human activities that can severely reduce a fish stock.

Government regulation. Most major fishing nations have laws to conserve and protect their fish resources. The United States, Canada, and almost all other nations that border the sea have established authority over fishery conservation zones extending 200 nautical miles (370 kilometers) from their shores. These zones are intended to protect the nations' coastal fishing industries by controlling the harvest of fleets of other countries. They also enable the nations to pass conservation laws affecting the areas.

The Magnuson Fishery Conservation and Management Act of 1976 established the 200-mile fishery conservation zone off the shores of the United States. Since the passage of this act, various regulations have been adopted to conserve fish within the zone. Some regulations set quotas that limit the total catch of certain species in a fishery and in a few cases limit the number of fishing vessels permitted in an area. Other regulations restrict the areas and the time of year in which crews may fish. The size and type of fishing gear that may be used in a fishery are also regulated.

Water pollution controls also aid in fishery conservation. Such controls limit the amount of harmful materials that may be released into inland and coastal waters. These materials can kill fish or the plants and animals on which fish feed.

International commissions and treaties. Through the years, fishing nations have agreed to work together in managing fishery resources in international waters. A number of commissions have been established to protect a particular species of fish or all species in a certain area. For example, the International Pacific Halibut Commission helps regulate halibut fishing off the west coasts of Canada and the United States. The International North Pacific Fisheries Commission promotes the conservation of all fish species in the North Pacific Ocean.

Most international commissions devoted to fishery conservation operate in a similar manner. Scientists from the member nations or from the organization itself gather statistics on the size of the catch and conduct other research regarding a particular fishery or species of fish. The commissions meet annually to review the results of these studies and to recommend new ways of managing fishery resources. Each member nation then has the responsibility of passing and enforcing laws based on the recommendations.

Many nations also make *bilateral treaties* to manage fishery resources in international waters. Under such treaties, two nations agree to meet periodically to exchange information on fisheries of interest to both countries and to discuss conservation measures.

Scientific research involves many activities to improve fish harvests. Researchers determine the maximum number of fish that can be harvested annually without severely damaging the stock. Researchers often rely on records of the harvest in a fishery to check changes in the abundance of stocks from year to year. By analyzing these records, they can judge whether fishing should be increased or decreased.

Scientists study the effects of the environment on changes in fish abundance and the effects of fishing on other species. Most fish feed on other fish. Dolphins, seals, and marine birds also prey on fish. Overfishing of prey species, such as anchovies, herring, and sardines, reduces the food supply of predator species. However, overfishing of predator species, such as cod, salmon, and tuna, increases the supply of prey species.

Some researchers work to increase the rates of survival and growth of fish. Such research especially helps fish farmers. Commercially raised fish have greatly increased fish resources, chiefly in Asia and Europe. In addition, some researchers are studying unharvested types of fish to develop new products and markets. Such efforts seek to both increase the world's food supply and promote fish conservation. Through the development of new fish resources, the world's total catch can remain constant—or even be increased—without overfishing individual stocks.   Gary D. Stauffer

Related articles in *World Book.* Many articles on countries, states, and provinces have a section on fishing industry. See, for example, **Japan** (Fishing industry); **Alabama** (Fishing industry). See also:

Some food fishes

Anchovy	Haddock	Pompano	Sprat
Bass	Hake	Redfish	Sturgeon
Carp	Halibut	Rosefish	Swordfish
Catfish	Herring	Salmon	Trout
Cod	Mackerel	Sardine	Tuna
Dogfish	Menhaden	Shad	Turbot
Drum	Mullet	Smelt	Weakfish
Flounder	Perch	Snapper	Whitefish
Grouper	Pollock	Sole	

Other seafoods

Abalone	Crayfish	Oyster	Shrimp
Clam	Lobster	Scallop	Squid
Crab	Mussel		

Other related articles

Aquaculture	Food preservation	Net
Cormorant	Grand Banks	Pearl
Fish	Gulf Stream	Sponge
Fishing	Krill	Whale

Outline

I. **Where fish are caught**
  A. Ocean fisheries   C. Fish farms
  B. Inland fisheries
II. **How fish are caught**
  A. Nets   C. Traps
  B. Hooks   D. Harpoons
III. **How fish are processed and marketed**
  A. Methods of processing B. Marketing
IV. **Fishery conservation**
  A. Government regulation
  B. International commissions and treaties
  C. Scientific research

Questions

What types of fisheries provide most of the world's commercial fish catch?
Why are fish a valuable food?
What is upwelling? How does it help the fish population in an area grow?
How does the marketing cooperative method of selling a fish catch differ from the auction method?
What are fish farms?
Which are the world's leading fishing countries?
What is a purse seine? How does it work?
How may overfishing of one species of fish affect the populations of other species?
What are fish meal and fish oil? What are they used for?
How do fishery conservation zones aid in fish conservation?

Additional resources

Bell, Frederick W. *Food from the Sea: The Economics and Politics of Ocean Fisheries.* Westview, 1977.
Ferrell, Nancy W. *The Fishing Industry.* Watts, 1984. For younger readers.
Gilmour, David. *The Glass Bottom Boat: Fish Managers at Work.* NC Press(Toronto), 1987. Suitable for younger readers. Fishery management in Canada.
Idyll, C. P. *The Sea Against Hunger.* Rev. ed. Crowell, 1978.
Scarry, Huck. *Life on a Fishing Boat: A Sketchbook.* Prentice-Hall, 1983. For younger readers.
Warner, William W. *Distant Water: The Fate of the North Atlantic Fisherman.* Little, Brown, 1983.

Fishing laws. See Fishing industry (Fishery conservation).
Fishworm. See Earthworm.
Fisk, James (1834-1872), was an American financier who was involved in several business scandals in the

Michael Friedel

Scientific research can help fish farmers. This West German researcher is seeking to make carp grow faster by feeding them a high-protein diet and raising the tank's water temperature.

late 1800's. Fisk helped cause the collapse of the gold market on Sept. 24, 1869, known as *Black Friday.* He and industrialist Jay Gould had tried to monopolize the market by buying all the gold in New York City. The United States Treasury intervened, and the price of gold fell. Fisk and Gould, however, made $11 million in profit. See **Black Friday.**

Fisk was born in Bennington, Vt. During the Civil War (1861-1865), he became rich by selling cotton from areas of the South controlled by Union forces. After the war, Fisk, Gould, and Daniel Drew made huge profits by manipulating the stock of the Erie Railroad. Fisk bought an opera house in New York City and held many parties there, earning the nickname "Jubilee Jim." At the age of 37, Fisk was fatally shot by Edward Stokes, a rival for his mistress, the actress Josie Mansfield.   Peter d'A. Jones

Fiske, John (1842-1901), was an American philosopher and historian who helped promote the theory of evolution. According to this theory, all living things have *evolved* (developed gradually) from a few common ancestors. Fiske sought to bring the ideas of evolution and religion into harmony. Critics of evolution charged that it conflicted with the belief that God created all living things. Fiske rejected that argument and saw evolution simply as God's way of doing things. He developed this idea in *The Outlines of Cosmic Philosophy* (1874).

Fiske also became a popular lecturer and writer on early American history. He applied the theory of evolutionary change to history. In his book *The Beginnings of New England* (1889), Fiske stressed the European origins of United States institutions. Fiske was born in Hartford, Conn.   Robert C. Sims

Fiske, Minnie Maddern (1865-1932), was a leading American stage actress during the late 1800's and early 1900's. She was an early supporter of a natural style of acting in the United States, departing from the more exaggerated romantic style popular in the 1800's. Fiske was the chief promoter in America of the modern realistic dramas of the Norwegian playwright Henrik Ibsen. She performed in several Ibsen plays, including *A Doll's House* in 1894 and *Hedda Gabler* in 1903.

Fiske was born in New Orleans into a family of actors and actresses. Her given and family name was Marie Augusta Davey. She made her stage debut at the age of 3. In 1890, she married Harrison Grey Fiske, a newspaper editor and playwright, who wrote several plays for her. After her marriage, she performed under the name Mrs. Fiske.   Don B. Wilmeth

Fission, in physics, is the splitting of the nucleus of an atom into two nearly equal parts. This process occurs most readily in such heavy elements as uranium and plutonium. Fission can take place naturally or it can be produced artificially by striking a fissionable nucleus with a neutron or some other nuclear particle.

When a nucleus splits into two *fission fragments,* a large amount of energy is released. This energy results from the electric *repulsion* (repelling force) between the two fragments, both of which are positively charged. The fission of 1 pound (0.45 kilogram) of uranium releases as much energy as the burning of 1,140 short tons (1,030 metric tons) of coal.

A fissioning nucleus also releases several neutrons. These free neutrons may strike other nuclei and cause them to fission. A continuous series of such fissions,

called a *chain reaction,* produces the energy in atomic bombs and nuclear reactors.   J. Rayford Nix

See also **Nuclear energy; Plutonium; Uranium.**

Fistula, *FIHS chu luh,* is a tube or passage that connects two parts of the body that are not normally connected. Most fistulas connect an *abscess* (collection of pus) to the skin. A fistula also can link an artery to a vein. It can connect two internal organs, such as the bladder and the rectum.

A fistula can be present at birth, or it can be caused by shock, wounds, or infection. Surgery is usually needed to correct fistulas.   Edward J. Shahady

Fitch, Clyde (1865-1909), was a productive and successful American playwright and the first to gain international recognition. His works cover a broad range and include farces, problem plays, historical plays, and plays about high society. Several of Fitch's plays are notable for their realistic presentation of familiar scenes from life in his day. Fitch was stage manager for his plays, controlling every detail of their production.

William Clyde Fitch was born in Elmira, N.Y. From *Beau Brummell* (1890) to *The City* (1909), he wrote more than 30 original plays and 22 adaptations of novels and foreign plays. In 1901, Fitch had four plays running in New York City at the same time, *Lovers' Lane, Captain Jinks of the Horse Marines, The Climbers,* and *Barbara Frietchie.* His other plays include *The Girl with the Green Eyes* (1902), *Her Great Match* (1905), and *The Truth* (1907).   Frederick C. Wilkins

Fitch, John (1743-1798), was an American inventor. He designed the first workable steamboat in the United States. Fitch demonstrated this boat on the Delaware River near Philadelphia on Aug. 22, 1787. A steam engine powered six paddles on each side of the 45-foot (14-meter) boat. The steamboat reached a speed of about 3 miles (4.8 kilometers) per hour.

Fitch launched a 60-foot (18-meter) boat in 1788. It was propelled by paddles at the stern. A more powerful boat, launched in 1790, reached a speed of about 8 miles (13 kilometers) per hour. It operated in regular passenger service between Philadelphia and Trenton, N.J. However, there was not enough demand for passage to make this boat financially successful.

Fitch was born on a farm near Windsor, Conn. After trying out a number of trades, he became a successful brass worker and silversmith in Trenton. He gave up this

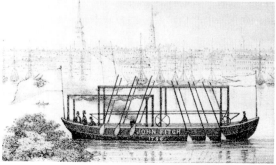

Lithograph by Henry Reigart (Brown Brothers)

One of John Fitch's earliest steamboats sailed on the Delaware River. Philadelphia can be seen on the opposite shore.

business during the Revolutionary War (1775-1783). Fitch turned his attention to the construction of a steamboat in 1785. He obtained patents on his work in the United States and France in 1791. However, he had constant trouble with his financial affairs, and never succeeded in attracting enough public support to make his boats profitable.   J. P. Hartman

See also **Fulton, Robert; Ship** (The first steamboats); **Steamboat.**

FitzGerald, Edward (1809-1883), was an English writer famous for his translation of the *Rubaiyat,* a long poetic work by the Persian poet Omar Khayyam. The poem's melancholy theme of "drink and be merry for tomorrow we die" described the mood of many people in England during the late 1800's.

FitzGerald's translation was first published anonymously in 1859. The translation was ignored until 1860, when the famous English poet Dante Gabriel Rossetti and his circle discovered the work and helped popularize it. FitzGerald prepared three revised editions that were published in 1868, 1872, and 1879. In addition to the *Rubaiyat,* FitzGerald was known for his translations of Greek and Spanish literature and for his charming letters. FitzGerald was born in Suffolk.   Jerome Bump

See also **Rubaiyat.**

Fitzgerald, Ella (1918-   ), ranks among the best and most popular jazz singers of all time. She is known for her pure and personal tone, remarkable vocal control, ability to improvise, and flawless intonation and phrasing as an interpreter of ballads.

Pablo Records
Ella Fitzgerald

Ella Fitzgerald was born in Newport News, Va. She won several amateur contests as a singer before joining Chick Webb's band in 1935. She recorded her first hit, "A Tisket A Tasket," with Webb's band in 1938. Webb died in 1939, and she took over leadership of the band for two years. In 1941, Fitzgerald began to work as a solo performer and with vocal groups. She gained world fame while working with the "Jazz at the Philharmonic" touring group of musicians and singers beginning in 1946.   Leonard Feather

Fitzgerald, F. Scott (1896-1940), was the leading writer of America's *Jazz Age,* the *Roaring Twenties,* and one of its glittering heroes. The chief quality of Fitzgerald's talent was his ability to be both a leading participant in the high life he described, and a detached observer of it. Few readers saw the serious side of Fitzgerald, and he was not generally recognized as a gifted writer during his lifetime. While he lived, most readers considered his stories a chronicle and even a celebration of moral decline. However, later readers realized that Fitzgerald's works have a deeper moral theme.

Francis Scott Key Fitzgerald was born in St. Paul, Minn., on Sept. 24, 1896. He attended Princeton University, where he wrote amateur musical comedies. He left Princeton in 1917 without a degree. Years after leaving Princeton, Fitzgerald remarked that perhaps he should have continued writing musicals, but he said, "I am too much a moralist at heart, and really want to preach at people in some acceptable form, rather than entertain them."

Fitzgerald won fame for his first novel, *This Side of Paradise* (1920). It is an immature work but was the first novel to anticipate the pleasure-seeking genera-

Bettmann Archive
F. Scott Fitzgerald

tion of the Roaring Twenties. A similar novel, *The Beautiful and Damned* (1921), and two collections of short stories, *Flappers and Philosophers* (1920) and *Tales of the Jazz Age* (1922), increased his popularity.

The Great Gatsby (1925) was less popular than Fitzgerald's early works, but it was the first of three successive novels that give him lasting literary importance. The lively yet deeply moral novel centers around Jay Gatsby, a wealthy bootlegger. *The Great Gatsby* presents a penetrating criticism of the moral emptiness of wealthy society in the United States during the 1920's.

Fitzgerald's next novel, *Tender Is the Night* (1934, revised edition by Malcolm Cowley, 1951), is a beautifully written account of the general decline of a few glamorous Americans in Europe. The book failed because readers during the Great Depression of the 1930's were not interested in Jazz Age "parties." Fitzgerald died before he completed *The Last Tycoon* (1941), a novel about Hollywood life.

Critics generally agree that Fitzgerald's early success damaged his personal life and marred his literary production. This success led to extravagant living and a need for large income. It probably contributed to Fitzgerald's alcoholism and the mental breakdown of his wife Zelda. The success also probably led to his physical and spiritual collapse, which he described frankly in the long essay *The Crack-Up* (1936). Fitzgerald spent his last years as a scriptwriter in Hollywood. A few years after his death, his books won him the recognition he had desired while alive.   Joseph N. Riddel

See also **American literature** (The "Lost Generation"); **Roaring Twenties** (Cultural trends).

Additional resources

Bruccoli, Matthew J. *Some Sort of Epic Grandeur: The Life of F. Scott Fitzgerald.* Harcourt, 1981.
Mellow, James R. *Invented Lives: F. Scott and Zelda Fitzgerald.* Houghton, 1984.

Fitzsimmons, Bob (1863-1917), held the world's heavyweight boxing championship from 1897 to 1899. Fitzsimmons also held the world's middleweight title from 1891 until he won the heavyweight championship in 1897. He was the light-heavyweight champion of the world from 1903 until 1905. Fitzsimmons gained the heavyweight title by knocking out James J. Corbett in 14 rounds. He is credited with originating the solar plexus punch in this fight (see **Solar plexus**). Fitzsimmons lost the heavyweight title to James J. Jeffries on a knockout in the 11th round.

Robert James Fitzsimmons was born in Helston, England, near Falmouth. He grew up in New Zealand and did his early fighting in Australia. Fitzsimmons moved to the United States in 1890.   Nigel Collins

Fitzsimmons, Frank Edward (1908-1981), served as president of the Teamsters union from 1971 to 1981. The Teamsters is the largest labor union in the United States. Most of the union's members are truckdrivers.

Fitzsimmons was born in Jeannette, Pa. He began his union career in 1937 as business agent of the Teamsters local in Detroit. In 1940, he became vice president of the local. The international union appointed him to a vice presidency in 1961. Fitzsimmons became acting head of the Teamsters after union president James R. Hoffa was imprisoned in 1967. Fitzsimmons succeeded as president after Hoffa resigned in June 1971. The union elected Fitzsimmons to a full term the next month. Fitzsimmons was reelected to another five-year term in 1976.   James G. Scoville

FitzSimons, Thomas (1741-1811), was a Pennsylvanian signer of the Constitution of the United States. His name is also spelled *Fitzsimmons.* At the Constitutional Convention of 1787, FitzSimons favored a strong central government that would have the power to tax imports and exports.

FitzSimons was born in Ireland. By 1760, he had immigrated to Philadelphia, where he soon became a leading merchant specializing in trade with the West Indies. During the Revolutionary War in America (1775-1783), he raised and commanded a company of militia.

FitzSimons served in the Congress of the Confederation in 1782 and 1783. He was later elected to several terms in the Pennsylvania legislature. As a Federalist Party member of the United States House of Representatives from 1789 to 1795, FitzSimons supported protective tariffs to promote American manufacturing. FitzSimons was one of the founders of the Bank of North America and the Insurance Company of North America. He lost much of his political influence after personal financial difficulties caused him to declare bankruptcy in 1805.   Richard D. Brown

Five Books of Moses. See Pentateuch.

Five Civilized Tribes is a name for the Chickasaw, Choctaw, Cherokee, Creek, and Seminole Indians. White settlers gave the tribes this name in the 1800's, after the tribes had adopted a number of European customs. Many settlers considered European ways more civilized than Indian ones.

The tribes once farmed and hunted in what is now the Southeastern United States. Most of these Indians lived in towns. Europeans, who began to explore the area in the 1500's, brought diseases that killed thousands of Indians. By the early 1700's, the Indian population had dropped by about 75 per cent.

Meanwhile, the Indians and three European powers—Great Britain, France, and Spain—fought for the land, sometimes forming alliances with one another. Britain won the struggle, but the United States took over after the Revolutionary War (1775-1783).

The tribes began to realize that they could not defeat the whites or continue living in traditional ways. Many Indians started to attend churches and send their children to schools run by missionaries. Some Indians acquired cotton plantations and slaves.

However, white settlers wanted the tribes' land. Between 1830 and 1842, the government forced most of these Indians to move to the Indian Territory, in what is now Oklahoma. Thousands died on the journey, which became known as the *Trail of Tears.* A small number of Indians stayed in the Southeast.

The United States pledged to uphold forever the Indians' land rights in the Indian Territory. However, Congress took away the western part of the Indians' land after the Civil War (1861-1865), partly to punish the tribes for helping the South fight the North. Congress began to dissolve the tribal governments gradually in 1898 and, in 1901, granted citizenship to all Indians in the territory. Today, most members of the tribes live much as other Oklahomans do.   Charles Hudson

See the separate articles on each of the five tribes. See also **Indian Territory; Oklahoma** (History).

Five-finger. See Cinquefoil.

Five-year plan is a program to increase a country's standard of living in a five-year period. The Soviet Union also uses such plans to organize the production and distribution of goods and services. It began its first five-year plan in 1928. In 1958, it replaced the five-year plan with a seven-year plan (1959-1965) aimed at surpassing the industrial progress of the United States. The Soviet Union stressed production in such industries as steel and coal. The Soviet five-year plans were reinstated beginning in 1966. China, India, and other countries have adopted five-year plans. See also **China** (The beginning of Communist rule; The Great Leap Forward); **Union of Soviet Socialist Republics** (History); **India** (Economy; History).   Richard C. Wiles

Fivepins. See Bowling (Canadian fivepins).

Fixed star is an expression often used in referring to the stars, because their places in the sky relative to one another do not seem to change. Actually, however, the stars are moving in many directions, and the pattern of the heavens is slowly changing.

But the changes are scarcely noticeable within a person's lifetime, because the stars are so far away. Even Barnard's star, the one believed to move the fastest, changes position by a distance equal only to the moon's diameter in 200 years. Compared to the planets, which can be seen constantly shifting their positions in the sky, the starry background seems "fixed."

Astronomers use photography and sighting telescopes to study the motions of all of the bright stars and many of the faint ones. In photographs taken at different times many years apart, they compare the positions of the stars and note how the stars have changed. The astronomers can then tell how the *constellations* (groups of stars) will change in the future.   C. R. O'Dell

Fixture, in law, refers to personal property that has been affixed to houses, land, or other real estate. A fixture becomes part of the real estate to which it is attached. Important factors in determining that property is a fixture are the method of attachment and the parties' intention to make the property a permanent part of the real estate. For example, if a tenant installs electric wiring in rented property, the wiring may become part of the landlord's real estate unless the tenant and landlord agree otherwise before the wiring is installed.   Linda Henry Elrod

Fjord. See Fiord.

Ewing Galloway

Flag

Whitney Smith, the contributor of this article, is Director of the Flag Research Center (Winchester, Mass.), editor of The Flag Bulletin, and author of The Flag Book of the United States and The Bibliography of Flags of Foreign Nations. Colors, sizes, proportions, and designs are all based on information supplied by official sources and checked by the Flag Research Center. Text information on the flags of countries, states, and provinces can be found in the separate articles in World Book.

Flag. A nation's flag is a stirring sight as it flies in the wind. Its bright colors and striking design stand for the country's land, its people, its government, and its ideals. A country's flag can stir people to joy, to courage, and to sacrifice. Many persons have died to protect their national flags from dishonor and disgrace. People should know how to honor their nation's flag.

There are many kinds of flags besides national ones. Some countries fly a special state flag over embassies and other government buildings at home and abroad. Presidents, kings, queens, or other government leaders have their own flags. Some flags stand for international organizations, such as the United Nations and the Red Cross. Some regional groups, such as the North Atlantic Treaty Organization (NATO) and the Council of Europe, have flags. States, provinces, and cities also have flags. Other flags represent youth groups, such as the Boy Scouts and the Girl Scouts. Still others stand for ideas, such as Christianity and peace. Some flags are even used to send messages.

The Egyptians flew the first flaglike symbols many thousands of years ago. They tied streamers to the tops of long poles. Soldiers carried these poles into battle, hoping that their gods would help them win. The people of Assyria and, later, the Greeks and Romans used symbols in the same way. Their symbols usually stood for their gods or their rulers.

Flags became important during battles. Generals watched the flags to see where their soldiers were. The flags showed which way the wind blew, and helped soldiers see the direction to aim their arrows. The flags stood for each side in a battle, and the fighting often centered around them. If the soldier who was carrying the flag was killed or wounded, others would "rally around the flag" to prevent the enemy from capturing it. If the flag was captured, many soldiers would give up the fight.

The symbols used in flags may go back thousands of years. The Shield of David, an ancient symbol of the Jews popularly known as the "Star of David," appears on the flag of Israel. The cross, a symbol of Christianity, is on the flags of many Christian nations. The crescent and star in the flags of many Muslim countries are symbols of peace and life. Generally, stars on flags stand for unity. The number of stars may show how many states are united in the country.

Most national flags use one or more of only seven basic colors. These colors are red, white, blue, green, yellow, black, and orange. The colors were all used in *heraldry,* a system of designs that grew up during the Middle Ages (see **Heraldry**). Designs on many flags follow rules of heraldry, such as a strip of white or yellow separating two colors. The Mexican flag, with white between red and green bands, follows this rule.

Years of history lie behind the colors of many flags. Denmark is said to have used the same national flag for more than 750 years. King Valdemar the Victorious of Denmark saw a white cross in the red sky just before he won a battle. Denmark has used the white cross on red since about 1219.

Popular stories often explain why flags have certain colors. The Austrian flag supposedly dates from an event in 1191, during the Third Crusade. When Duke Leopold V removed his blood-stained cloak after a battle, he found that his belt had kept a band of the cloth white. From then on, he used a red flag with a white stripe across it. Austria adopted this design in 1919.

Several nations may use the same colors in their flags. Blue and white appear in the flags of five Central American countries. These nations were once joined together in the United Provinces of Central America, which had a blue-and-white flag. Four colors—black, green, red, and white—stand for Arab unity. They appear in the flags of Iraq, Jordan, Kuwait, the Sudan, Syria, the United Arab Emirates, and Yemen (Sana).

The study of the history and symbolism of flags is called *vexillology.* The name comes from the Latin word *vexillum,* meaning a square flag or banner. Soldiers of ancient Rome carried a square military flag that hung from a crossbar fastened to a staff.

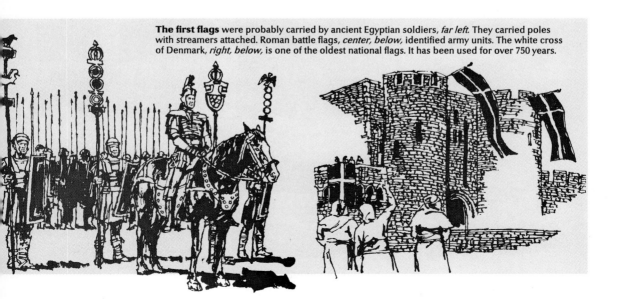

The first flags were probably carried by ancient Egyptian soldiers, *far left.* They carried poles with streamers attached. Roman battle flags, *center, below,* identified army units. The white cross of Denmark, *right, below,* is one of the oldest national flags. It has been used for over 750 years.

Flags of the Americas

Antigua and Barbuda

Argentina

Bahamas

Barbados

Belize

Bolivia

Brazil

Canada

Chile

Colombia

Costa Rica

Cuba

Dominica

Dominican Republic

Ecuador

El Salvador

Grenada

Guatemala

Guyana

Haiti

Honduras

Jamaica

Mexico

Nicaragua

Panama

Paraguay

Peru

St. Christopher and Nevis

St. Lucia

St. Vincent and the Grenadines

Suriname

Trinidad and Tobago

United States

Uruguay

Venezuela

Flags of
Europe

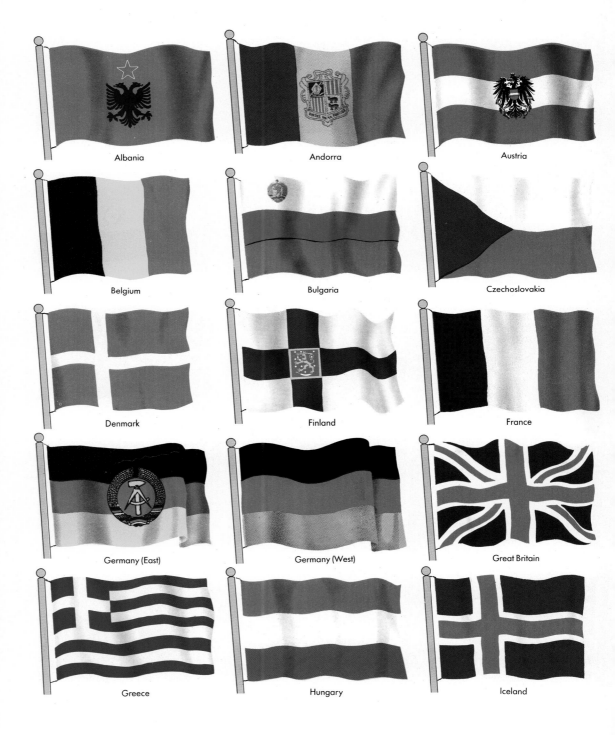

Albania

Andorra

Austria

Belgium

Bulgaria

Czechoslovakia

Denmark

Finland

France

Germany (East)

Germany (West)

Great Britain

Greece

Hungary

Iceland

Ireland

Italy

Liechtenstein

Luxembourg

Malta

Monaco

Netherlands

Norway

Poland

Portugal

Romania

San Marino

Spain

Sweden

Switzerland

Union of Soviet
Socialist Republics

Vatican City

Yugoslavia

Flags of Africa

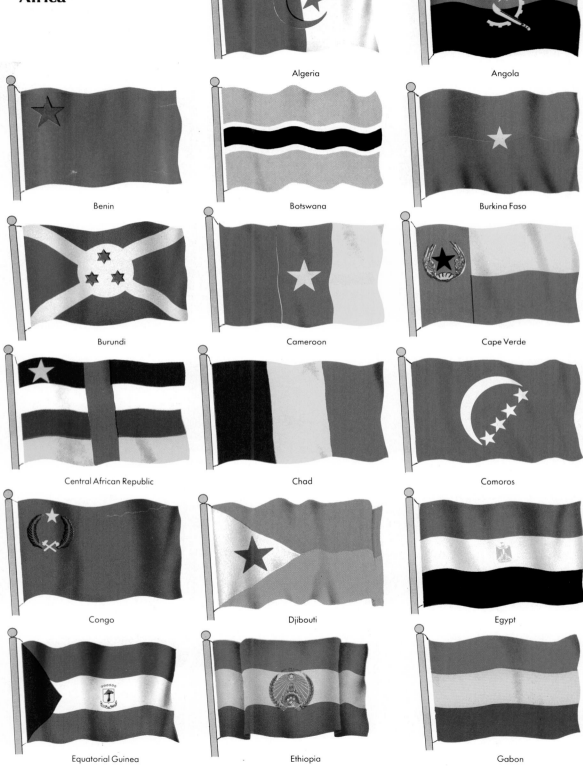

Algeria

Angola

Benin

Botswana

Burkina Faso

Burundi

Cameroon

Cape Verde

Central African Republic

Chad

Comoros

Congo

Djibouti

Egypt

Equatorial Guinea

Ethiopia

Gabon

Gambia

Ghana

Guinea

Guinea-Bissau

Ivory Coast

Kenya

Lesotho

Liberia

Libya

Madagascar

Malawi

Mali

Mauritania

Mauritius

Morocco

Mozambique

Niger

Nigeria

Flags of Africa are continued on the next page.

Flags of
Africa

continued

Rwanda

São Tomé and Príncipe

Senegal

Seychelles

Sierra Leone

Somalia

South Africa

Sudan

Swaziland

Tanzania

Togo

Tunisia

Uganda

Zaire

Zambia

Zimbabwe

Flags of Asia and the Pacific

Afghanistan

Australia

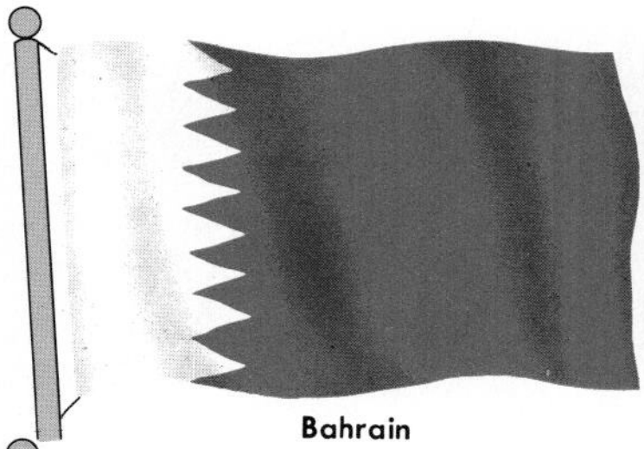

Bahrain

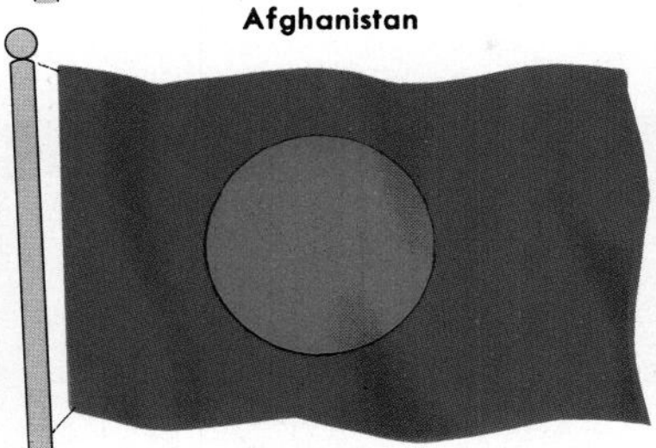

Bangladesh

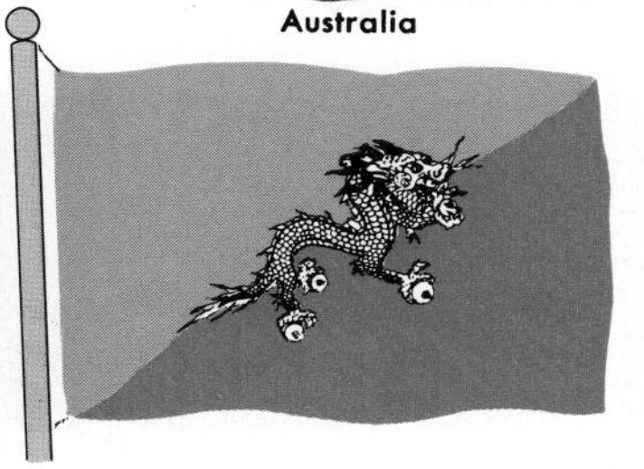

Bhutan

Brunei

Burma

China

Cyprus

Fiji

Hong Kong

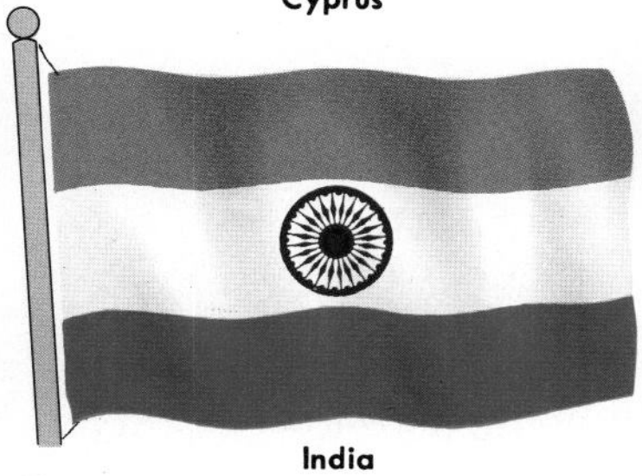

India

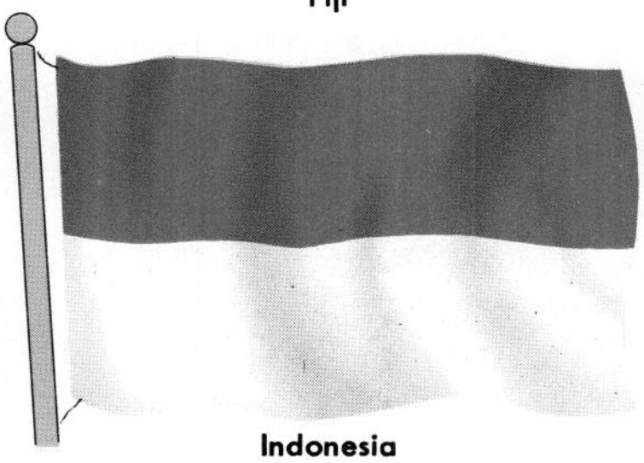

Indonesia

Iran

Iraq

Israel

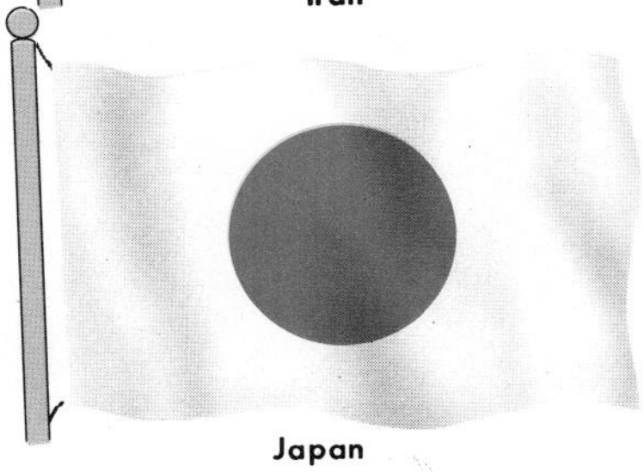

Japan

Flags of Asia and the Pacific are continued on the next page.

Flags of Asia and the Pacific

continued

Jordan

Kampuchea

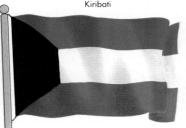

Kiribati

Korea (North)

Korea (South)

Kuwait

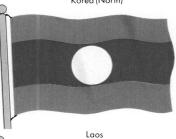

Laos

Lebanon

Malaysia

Maldives

Mongolia

Nauru

Nepal

New Zealand

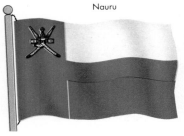

Oman

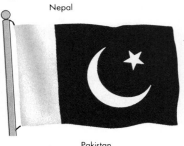

Pakistan

Papua New Guinea

Philippines

Qatar

Saudi Arabia

Singapore

Solomon Islands

Sri Lanka

Syria

Taiwan

Thailand

Tonga

Turkey

Tuvalu

United Arab Emirates

Vanuatu

Vietnam

Western Samoa

Yemen (Aden)

Yemen (Sana)

Flags of world organizations

The United Nations

North Atlantic Treaty Organization (NATO)

Organization of African Unity (OAU)

Council of Europe

Arab League

Olympic Games

Organization of American States

Red Cross

Red Crescent

Red Star of David

Flags of relief organizations. The Red Cross flag is flown in Christian countries, the Red Crescent flag in Muslim countries, and the Red Star of David flag in Israel.

Historical flags of the world

Roman flags. For years, soldiers carried the *vexillum, left.* The emperor Constantine became a Christian in the A.D. 300's, and added *XP,* meaning Christ, to the staff of the *labarum, right.*

 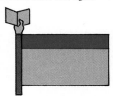

Later Roman flags bore letters standing for the Latin *senate and people of Rome.*

Muhammad's flag. The ornament on this later staff is a hand holding the Koran.

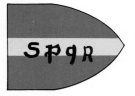

Early French flags. The French Royal Banner with three fleurs-de-lis, *left,* was used from the 1300's to the 1600's. French soldiers carried the oriflamme, *right,* between 1124 and 1415.

Early English flags. William the Conqueror's flag, *left,* first flew in England in 1066. King Richard I adopted the three lions, *right,* in 1195. They still appear on the Royal Standard.

Crusaders' flags usually had plain white crosses on red, but the Knights of St. John or Knights of Malta used a Maltese cross, *left.* The Knights Templars used a black-and-white flag.

  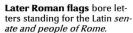

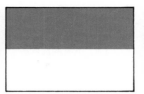

Traders' flags. Ships from Venice flew the symbol of St. Mark, patron of the city, *left.* Merchants in northern Europe flew the flag of the Hanseatic League, *right.*

Holy Roman Empire flag flew in what is now Germany from the 900's until 1806.

Crosses in the British flag. The British Union Flag, *left,* combines symbols of England, Scotland, and Ireland. The cross of St. George, *above,* was a national symbol of England as early as the

1200's. The cross of St. Andrew, *above,* had long been a symbol for Scotland, and the cross of St. Patrick, *right,* for Ireland. This Union Flag first flew in Great Britain in 1801.

Latin-American flags. Simón Bolívar's flag, *left,* first flew in Venezuela and Colombia in 1810. The Army of the Andes raised José de San Martín's flag, *center,* in Argentina in 1817. The flag of the United Provinces of Central America, *right,* flew from 1823 to 1840.

Flags of four empires disappeared in the early 1900's. The Chinese Empire flag, *left,* came down when the empire collapsed in 1912. The flag of the Russian Empire, *above,* was torn down

during the Russian Revolution of 1917. The flags of the Austro-Hungarian Empire, *above,* and German Empire, *right,* were replaced by flags of republics at the end of World War I in 1918.

Spain's Republican flag flew from 1931 to the end of the Spanish Civil War in 1939.

Flags under two dictatorships. The Germans used the Nazi swastika from 1933 to 1945. The Japanese navy flew the rising sun with rays during World War II and readopted it in 1952.

Flags in American history

The Viking flag of Leif Ericson was the first flag in North America, in the 1000's.

The Spanish flag carried by Columbus in 1492, *left,* combined the arms of Castile and Leon. Columbus' own flag, *right,* bore the initials F and Y for Ferdinand and Isabella (Ysabel).

This French flag was one of many flown in North America between 1604 and 1763.

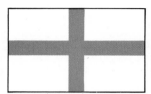

The English flag of John Cabot, *left,* flew in Canada in 1497. The British flag, *right,* adopted in 1606, flew over the British colonies in North America, beginning with Jamestown, 1607.

Dutch-East India Company flag of Henry Hudson flew in the New York area in 1609.

Russian-American Company flag flew at Russian settlements in Alaska in 1806.

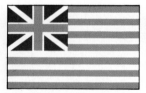

The Continental Colors served as America's first national flag from 1775 to 1777.

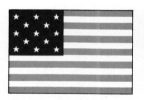

The flag of 1777 had no official arrangement for the stars. The most popular design had alternating rows of 3, 2, 3, 2, and 3 stars. Another flag with 13 stars in a circle was rarely used.

The flag of 1795 had 15 stripes, as well as 15 stars, to stand for the 15 states.

New England flags. The Taunton Flag, *left,* was raised at Taunton, Mass., in 1774. The Bedford Flag, *above,* flown in 1775, bears the words *vince aut morire,* meaning *conquer or die.* The

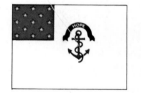

Rhode Island Flag, *above,* was carried in battle until 1781. The Bennington Flag, *right,* a variation of the original Stars and Stripes, may have flown during the Battle of Bennington in 1777.

Navy flags. American ships in New England waters flew a liberty tree flag, *left,* in 1775. Later that year, the Continental Navy began using a striped flag with a rattlesnake design.

Southern flags often had rattlesnake designs, as in the flag of Virginia's Culpeper Minutemen, 1775. William Moultrie's flag was flown by defenders of Charleston, S.C., in 1776.

Flags of the United States

The *Stars and Stripes* is the most popular name for the red, white, and blue national flag of the United States. No one knows where this name came from, but we do know the origin of several other names. Francis Scott Key first called the United States flag the *Star-Spangled Banner* in 1814 when he wrote the poem that became the national anthem (see **Star-Spangled Banner**). William Driver, a sea captain from Salem, Mass., gave the name *Old Glory* to the U.S. flag in 1824 (see **Driver, William**).

The Stars and Stripes stands for the land, the people, the government, and the ideals of the United States, no matter when or where it is displayed. Some other flags also stand for the United States, or its government, in certain situations. The *Navy Jack,* a blue flag with white stars, stands for the United States whenever it flies from a U.S. Navy ship. The stars, stripes, and colors of the U.S. flag appear in many federal and state flags.

First United States flags

At the start of the Revolutionary War, Americans fought under many flags. The first flag to represent all the colonies was the *Continental Colors,* also called the *Cambridge,* or *Grand Union, Flag.* This flag, on which the British flag appeared at the upper left, was the unofficial American flag from 1775 to 1777. It was also the first American flag to be saluted by another country. On Nov. 16, 1776, the Dutch governor of St. Eustatius in the

Today's 50-star United States flag has the following dimensions: hoist (width) of flag, 1.0 unit; fly (length) of flag, 1.9; hoist of union, .5385 (7/13); fly of union, .76; width of each stripe, .0769 (1/13); and diameter of each star, .0616.

West Indies saluted the American ship *Andrea Doria.*

But after the Declaration of Independence, the British flag was no longer appropriate as part of the U.S. flag. On June 14, 1777, the Continental Congress resolved that "the Flag of the united states be 13 stripes alternate red and white, and the Union be 13 stars white in a blue field representing a new constellation."

This American flag received its first salute from another country on Feb. 14, 1778, when French vessels in Quiberon Bay, France, saluted John Paul Jones and his ship *Ranger.*

No one knows who designed this flag, or who made

The flag of 1818 went back to 13 stripes, and had 20 stars for the 20 states. One design had four rows of five stars each. The Great Star Flag, *right,* formed the 20 stars in a large star.

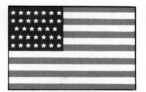

The flag of 1861, used in the Civil War, had stars for 34 states, including the South.

The 48-star flag served as the national flag the longest of any flag, from 1912 to 1959.

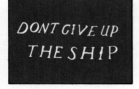

Perry's flag in 1813 bore the last words of James Lawrence, a hero of the War of 1812.

Texas flags. A Texas flag that flew when Texas was part of Mexico, *left,* bore the date of Mexico's constitution. The Texas Navy Flag, *right,* had a lone star.

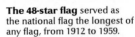

The Bear Flag flew over an independent California republic for a few months in 1846.

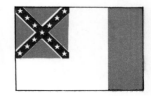

Confederate flags. The Stars and Bars, *left,* adopted in 1861, had stars for 7 seceding states. It looked too much like the U.S. flag, so troops carried a battle flag, *above.* It had stars for 11 states and for secession governments in Kentucky and Missouri, as did the flag of 1863, *above.* This looked too much like a flag of truce, so a red bar was added in 1865, *right.*

Flags of the states and territories

Alabama

Alaska

American Samoa

Arizona

Arkansas

California

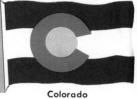

Colorado

Connecticut

Delaware

District of Columbia

Florida

Georgia

Guam

Hawaii

Idaho

Illinois

Indiana

Iowa

Kansas

Kentucky

Louisiana

Maine

Maryland

Massachusetts

Michigan

Minnesota

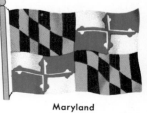

Mississippi

Missouri

Montana

Nebraska

Nevada

New Hampshire

New Jersey

New Mexico

New York

North Carolina

North Dakota

Ohio

Oklahoma

Oregon

Pennsylvania

Puerto Rico

Rhode Island

South Carolina

South Dakota

Tennessee

Texas

Utah

Vermont

Virgin Islands

Virginia

Washington

West Virginia

Wisconsin

Wyoming

Flags of the United States government

President

Vice President

Secretary of State

Secretary of the Treasury

Secretary of Defense

Attorney General

Secretary of the Interior

Secretary of Agriculture

Secretary of Commerce

Secretary of Labor*

Secretary of Health
and Human Services

Secretary of Housing
and Urban Development

Secretary of
Transportation

Secretary of
Energy*

Secretary of
Education*

Flags of the armed forces

U.S. Air Force

U.S. Army

U.S. Coast Guard

U.S. Marine Corps

U.S. Navy

*Secretary does not have a personal flag; flies the flag of the department.

Flags of cities of the United States

Baltimore

Boston

Chicago

Cleveland

Dallas

Detroit

Houston

Los Angeles

Milwaukee

New Orleans

New York

Philadelphia

Pittsburgh

Saint Louis

San Antonio

San Diego

San Francisco

Canada

Flags of Canada

Royal Union

Queen

Governor General

Armed Forces

Flags of the provinces and territories of Canada

Alberta

British Columbia

Manitoba

New Brunswick

Newfoundland

Northwest Territories

Nova Scotia

Ontario

Prince Edward Island

Quebec

Saskatchewan

Yukon Territory

the first one. Soon after the flag was adopted, Congressman Francis Hopkinson claimed that he had designed it (see **Hopkinson, Francis**).

In 1870, William J. Canby claimed that his grandmother, Betsy Ross, had made the first United States flag. Betsy Ross was a Philadelphia seamstress who made flags during the Revolutionary War. But most historians do not support the claim that Betsy Ross made the first United States flag. See **Ross, Betsy**.

The colors. The Continental Congress left no record to show why it chose red, white, and blue as the colors for the flag. But, in 1782, the Congress of the Confederation chose these same colors for the newly designed Great Seal of the United States. The resolution on the seal listed meanings for the colors. *Red* is for hardiness and courage, *white* for purity and innocence, and *blue* for vigilance, perseverance, and justice.

The stripes in the flag stand for the thirteen original colonies. The stripes were probably adopted from the

The Stars and Stripes first flew. . .

. . . **in a land battle** on Aug. 16, 1777, when troops under John Stark fought in the Battle of Bennington on the New York-Vermont border.

. . . **on a U.S. Navy ship** on Nov. 1, 1777, when John Paul Jones left Portsmouth, N.H., in the *Ranger.*

. . . **in a foreign port** on Dec. 2, 1777, when Jones sailed into Nantes, France, on the *Ranger.*

. . . **over foreign land** on Jan. 28, 1778, when John Rathbone of the sloop *Providence* captured Fort Nassau in the Bahamas.

. . . **in the Pacific Ocean** in 1784 when John Green and the *Empress of China* sailed to Macao, near Hong Kong.

. . . **around the world** from Sept. 30, 1787, to Aug. 10, 1790, on the ship *Columbia* of Boston.

. . . **over a fort in the Eastern Hemisphere** on April 27, 1805, when U.S. Marines captured Derna, Tripoli.

. . . **over a schoolhouse** in May, 1812, at a log school at Catamount Hill, Colrain, Mass.

. . . **in a naval battle in the Pacific** on March 25, 1813, when the frigate *Essex,* commanded by David Porter, captured the Peruvian cruiser *Nereyda.*

. . . **in Antarctica** in 1840 on the pilot boat *Flying Fish* of the Charles Wilkes expedition.

. . . **in a Flag Day celebration** in 1861 throughout Connecticut. An editorial in the *Hartford Courant* suggested the statewide observance.

. . . **on the moon** on July 20, 1969, after U.S. astronauts Neil A. Armstrong and Edwin E. Aldrin, Jr., landed there in their Apollo 11 spacecraft.

flag of the Sons of Liberty, which had five red and four white stripes (see **Sons of Liberty**). The British Union Jack was added to show that the colonists did not at first seek full independence.

The stars. The resolution passed by Congress in 1777 stated that the flag should have 13 stars. But Congress did not indicate how the stars should be arranged. The most popular arrangement showed the stars in alternating rows of three, two, three, two, and three stars. Another version had 12 stars in a circle with the 13th star in the center. A flag with 13 stars in a circle is often associated with the period. But there is little evidence that such a design was used. There is also no historical basis for assigning each star to a particular state.

Changes in the United States flag

By 1794, two new states had joined the Union. Congress decided to add two stars and two stripes to the flag. It ordered a 15-stripe flag used after May 1, 1795. The stars appeared in five rows, three in a row. Americans carried this flag in the War of 1812.

Five more states had come into the Union by 1817. Congress did not want the flag to have 20 stars and 20 stripes, because it would be too cluttered. Samuel Chester Reid (1783-1861), a navy captain, proposed a flag of 13 stripes, with a star for each state. Congress accepted the idea, because it could then change the stars easily. On April 4, 1818, it set the number of stripes at 13 again. It ordered a new star to be added to the flag on the July 4th after a state joined the Union.

Congress still did not say how the stars should be arranged, so flagmakers used various designs. The *Great Star Flag* of 1818 had its 20 stars arranged in the form of a five-pointed star. In the years that followed, various Presidents sometimes proclaimed new arrangements for the stars when a new state entered the Union. In some cases, the army and navy worked out the new designs. And, in some cases, no official action was ever taken. During the Civil War, President Abraham Lincoln refused to have the stars for southern states taken from the flag. Union troops fought under a 33-star flag the first three months of the war, a 34-star flag until 1863, and a 35-star flag until the war's end. No one decided on the design of the 46-star flag, used from 1908 to 1912. Presidential orders fixed the positions of the stars in 1912 (for 48 stars), in 1959 (for 49), and in 1960 (for 50).

Honoring a national flag

All citizens should know how to display their country's flag and how to salute it. Owning a flag and displaying it properly are marks of patriotism and respect.

Most countries agree that one national flag may not be flown above another. Some countries have additional rules. For example, when the U.S. flag is flown with other flags, all staff heights should be equal and the U.S. flag should be on its own right. There are two exceptions to this rule. (1) The United Nations flag flies above all flags at UN headquarters in New York City. (2) The church pennant flies above the U.S. flag while naval chaplains conduct services at sea.

Many countries have *flag codes,* or sets of rules for displaying and honoring national flags. The UN also has

a flag code. Some countries do not have such codes. They simply expect their citizens to treat their flags with respect. Congress passed the first U.S. flag code in 1942 and has amended it a number of times. The President may proclaim changes in the flag code. The following sections give the basic rules for honoring *any* national flag.

Displaying the flag

A national flag is usually displayed outdoors only in good weather, between sunrise and sunset. It may be flown at night on special occasions such as parades.

Flag customs vary from one country to another. For example, the U.S. flag flies over the White House

Displaying the flag The flag should be honored as a symbol of the nation it represents. These pictures illustrate points to remember in displaying the flag.

WORLD BOOK illustrations by Paul D. Turnbaugh

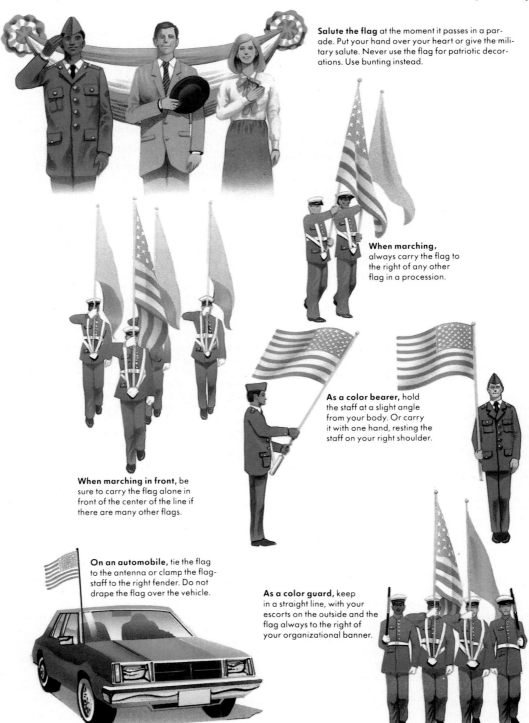

Salute the flag at the moment it passes in a parade. Put your hand over your heart or give the military salute. Never use the flag for patriotic decorations. Use bunting instead.

When marching, always carry the flag to the right of any other flag in a procession.

As a color bearer, hold the staff at a slight angle from your body. Or carry it with one hand, resting the staff on your right shoulder.

When marching in front, be sure to carry the flag alone in front of the center of the line if there are many other flags.

On an automobile, tie the flag to the antenna or clamp the flagstaff to the right fender. Do not drape the flag over the vehicle.

As a color guard, keep in a straight line, with your escorts on the outside and the flag always to the right of your organizational banner.

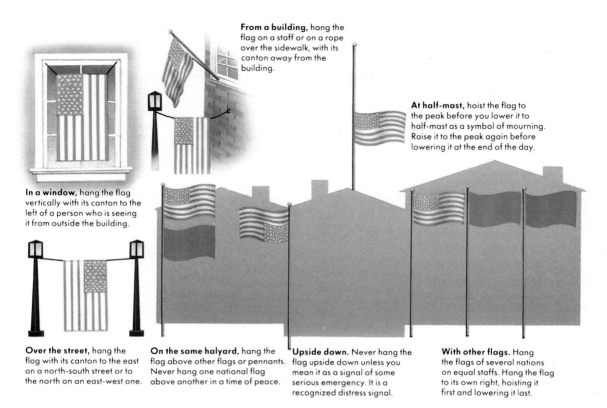

In a window, hang the flag vertically with its canton to the left of a person who is seeing it from outside the building.

From a building, hang the flag on a staff or on a rope over the sidewalk, with its canton away from the building.

At half-mast, hoist the flag to the peak before you lower it to half-mast as a symbol of mourning. Raise it to the peak again before lowering it at the end of the day.

Over the street, hang the flag with its canton to the east on a north-south street or to the north on an east-west one.

On the same halyard, hang the flag above other flags or pennants. Never hang one national flag above another in a time of peace.

Upside down. Never hang the flag upside down unless you mean it as a signal of some serious emergency. It is a recognized distress signal.

With other flags. Hang the flags of several nations on equal staffs. Hang the flag to its own right, hoisting it first and lowering it last.

With grouped staffs, place the flag at the center and highest point. With crossed staffs, put the flag on its own right, its staff on top.

On a casket, drape the flag with its canton at the head and over the left shoulder of the body. Do not lower the flag into the grave.

Behind a speaker, hang the flag flat against the wall. Do not gather or drape it on the rostrum. Use bunting for such decoration.

Beside a speaker, put the flag in the position of honor on the person's right. At a religious service, the flag should go to the right of the minister, priest, or rabbi.

In a corridor or lobby, hang the flag vertically opposite the main entrance with its canton to the left of a person coming in the door.

whether or not the President is in Washington, D.C. But the personal flag of the queen of England flies only from the building she is in at the time. The U.S. flag flies over the Capitol every day. The British flag flies over the Houses of Parliament in London only when Parliament is meeting, or on holidays and special days. The same rule applies to the Canadian flag.

In the United States, the national flag should be displayed every day except when weather conditions are severe enough to damage the flag. The flag is customarily displayed from sunrise to sunset, but it is not illegal to fly the flag 24 hours a day. When flown at night, it should be spotlighted. Congress has authorized the U.S. flag to be flown day and night at Flag House Square in Baltimore, Md., and the Battle Green in Lexington, Mass. Presidential proclamation has made the same authorization for Fort McHenry in Baltimore, the Marine Corps War Memorial in Arlington, Va., U.S. Customs ports of entry, and the Washington Monument and the White House in Washington, D.C.

The U.S. flag should be flown at polling places on election days. Legal public holidays and other special days for flying it include the following:

New Year's Day, January 1
Presidential Inauguration Day, January 20 (every 4th year)
Lincoln's Birthday, February 12
Washington's Birthday, the third Monday in February
Easter Sunday, no fixed date
Mother's Day, the second Sunday in May
Armed Forces Day, the third Saturday in May
Memorial Day, the last Monday in May
Flag Day, June 14
Independence Day, July 4
Labor Day, the first Monday in September
Citizenship Day, September 17
Columbus Day, the second Monday in October
Veterans Day, November 11
Thanksgiving Day, the fourth Thursday in November
Christmas Day, December 25

In Canada, the national flag may fly from government buildings from sunrise to sunset. It also flies on holidays and special days, including the following:

New Year's Day, January 1
Good Friday, no fixed date
Easter Monday, no fixed date
Victoria Day and *the Queen's Birthday,* the Monday before May 25
Canada Day, July 1
Labour Day, the first Monday in September
Thanksgiving Day, the second Monday in October
Remembrance Day, November 11
Christmas Day, December 25

Hanging the flag outdoors

When the flags of several countries are displayed, they should be flown from separate staffs of about equal size. The flags should also be about the same size. Almost every country requires that its own flag be given the position of honor among the flags. This position is to the left of observers as they face the main entrance to a building. The national flag may also be placed in the center of the group of flags, or at each end of a line of flags. At headquarters of international organizations, such as the UN, flags are flown in the alphabetical order of their country names in English.

From a building, a national flag should be hoisted, top first, either on a staff or on a rope over the sidewalk.

Over a street, a national flag should be suspended vertically with its top to the north on an east-west street, or to the east on a north-south street.

Hanging the flag indoors

A national flag should have a prominent place on a speaker's platform, but it should not be used to decorate the platform. Instead, bunting in the national colors should be used for decoration. In the United States, the red, white, and blue bunting should be arranged with the blue at the top. In the United States, the national flag must hang free, either flat against a wall or from a staff. In Canada, the national flag may be gathered up like bunting in a display.

If a national flag is displayed with another flag from crossed staffs against a wall, it should be on the observer's left. When a number of flags are grouped on staffs, the national flag should be in the center and at the highest point of the group.

When a national flag is displayed flat on a wall on a speaker's platform, it should be above and behind the speaker. When hung from a staff in a church or auditorium, the flag should be at the speaker's right. Any other flag that is displayed should be on the speaker's left.

Raising and lowering the flag

A national flag should be *hoisted* (run up) briskly. It is lowered slowly, and should be gathered and folded before it touches the ground. When displayed with other flags from several staffs, the national flag should be raised first and lowered last.

Breaking the flag means unfurling it dramatically at the top of the staff. The flag is folded or rolled loosely. Before it is hoisted, the halyard is tied loosely around it. When the halyard is pulled sharply, the flag unfolds.

Striking the flag means lowering it at sea, or taking it down in battle as a sign of surrender.

Dipping the flag means lowering it slightly, then immediately raising it again as a salute. In Canada and Great Britain, certain flags may be *trailed* (lowered until the peaks of their staffs touch the ground), as a salute to the queen. The U.S. flag should not be dipped to any person or thing, and should never be trailed. But when a ship from a country recognized by the United States dips its flag to a U.S. Navy ship, the naval vessel returns the salute. Most other navies follow this rule.

Flying upside down, a national flag is traditionally a signal of distress. However, it is often displayed upside down as a political protest.

Flying at half-mast, halfway up the staff, a national flag is a signal of mourning. The flag should be hoisted to the top of the staff for an instant before being lowered to half-mast. It should be hoisted to the peak again before being lowered for the day or night. On Memorial Day, the flag should be displayed at half-mast until noon only, then raised to the top of the staff. By tradition, the national flag flies at half-mast only when the entire country mourns. It is not lowered to half-mast for occasions of local mourning. If local flags are flown at half-mast, the national flag may be flown at full mast with them. Citizens may salute and pledge allegiance to the flag when it flies at half-mast.

In the United States, the U.S. flag flies at half-mast (1) for 30 days after the death of the President or a former

President; (2) for 10 days after the death of the Vice President, the Chief Justice or a retired Chief Justice, or the Speaker of the House of Representatives; and (3) from the day of death until burial of an Associate Justice, a secretary of an executive department or a military department, or the governor of a state, territory, or possession. The flag also flies at half-mast in Washington, D.C., on the day of death and the following day for a U.S. senator or representative, a territorial delegate, or the resident commissioner of Puerto Rico. The U.S. flag flies at half-mast in a state from the day the governor or one of the state's U.S. senators dies until burial. The same practice is followed in (1) a congressional district for a representative, (2) a territory for a territorial governor or delegate, and (3) Puerto Rico for the governor or resident commissioner.

In Canada, the national flag flies at half-mast only on occasions of national mourning, such as the death of the sovereign. The flag on the Parliament Buildings in Ottawa is lowered to half-mast on certain occasions. They include the day of the funeral of a member of the Senate, the House of Commons, or the Privy Council.

Carrying the flag

A national flag should always be held aloft and free, never flat or horizontal. The person who carries the flag is called the *colorbearer.*

A color guard, in military and patriotic organizations, usually includes the colorbearer, two escorts, and a bearer of an organizational flag or some other flag. The colorbearer with the national flag must be on the marching right of the other colorbearer. For this reason, a color guard cannot perform an "about face." The escorts march on each side of the two bearers. Nonmilitary color guards may include only one colorbearer and two escorts. Armed escorts may accompany the U.S. flag, but usually not the Canadian flag.

When a national flag is carried into a meeting hall, everyone in the hall should stand facing the platform. The colorbearer marches to the front and faces the audience, followed by the escorts. They stand on each side as the colorbearer puts the flag into its stand.

In a parade, when a national flag is carried with other flags, it should always be on the marching right. If there is a line of other flags, the colorbearer with the national flag marches alone in front of the center of the line.

On a float, a national flag should be hung from a staff with its folds falling free, or it should be hung flat.

On a car, a national flag should hang free and not drape over the car. It may be tied to the antenna or to a staff that is fixed firmly to the chassis or clamped to the right fender.

Saluting the flag

When a national flag is raised or lowered as part of a ceremony, or when it passes by in a parade or in review, all persons present should face it and stand at attention. A man or woman in a military uniform should give a hand salute. A man not in uniform salutes by removing his hat with his right hand and holding it at his left shoulder, with his right palm inward over his heart. A man without a hat salutes by placing his right hand over his heart. A woman also salutes by placing her right

hand over her heart. Women do not remove their hats to salute the flag. The flag should be saluted at the moment it passes by in a parade or in review. Citizens of other countries stand at attention, but need not salute.

U.S. citizens give the *Pledge of Allegiance* to the flag by holding the right hand over the heart. But civilians also show respect for the flag when the pledge is given by standing at attention and by men removing their hats. Persons in uniform should salute.

If the national anthem is played while the U.S. flag is displayed, everyone present should face it and salute in the same manner as when the flag is raised or lowered or passes by in a parade. If the flag is not displayed, all persons should stand and face toward the music. Persons in uniform should salute throughout the anthem. All others should stand at attention, and men should remove their hats.

Permitted and prohibited uses

At any funeral, a national flag may be used to cover the casket. An armed color guard may accompany the flag-draped casket of a person who served in the armed forces, but not into the church or chapel. The flag should be removed before the color guard fires a salute. It should not be lowered into the grave or allowed to touch the ground. It may be used again after the funeral.

At an unveiling of a statue or monument, a national flag should have a prominent place. But the U.S. flag should never be used as part of the covering for the monument. The Canadian flag may be used in the covering, but must be lifted off the statue.

Countries usually forbid some uses of their national flags. The United Nations flag code also lists some prohibited uses of the UN flag. A national flag should never be used for receiving, carrying, holding, or delivering anything. It should never be used as bedding, drapery, or wearing apparel, such as a costume or athletic uniform. But a flag patch may be attached to the uniform of military personnel, fire fighters, police officers, and members of patriotic organizations. A lapel flag pin should be worn on the left lapel near the heart. The national flag should not be printed on paper napkins, boxes, or other items that will be discarded. The U.S. flag should never be used for advertising purposes. It should never be marked or have anything attached to it. Advertising signs should not be fastened to the staff or halyards. Federal and state laws provide penalties for persons who use it improperly.

Caring for the flag

A national flag should be folded carefully and put away when not in use. The U.S. flag may be given a special *military fold.* It should first be folded twice lengthwise to form a long strip. Then, starting at the stripe end, it should be given a series of triangular folds. The resulting compact triangle looks like a cocked hat. If the flag is permanently attached to its staff, it should be *furled* (wrapped around the staff). It should then be *cased* (wrapped with a cover).

A national flag may be mended, dry-cleaned, or washed. An old flag, or one with an out-of-date design, may be displayed as long as it is in a respectable condition. When it is no longer fit for display, it should be destroyed in some dignified way, preferably by burning.

National flags are in many ways the most important flags in the world. They stand for all the people in a country, just as state and city flags stand for the people in smaller areas. But there are many other kinds of flags. Some flags stand for only one person, and others for one part of the government. Some flags are used only by the armed forces, and others only at sea. Some flags are used only to send messages.

Flags of individuals

Many rulers and important government leaders have personal flags. For example, the President and Vice Pres-

ident of the United States and members of the Cabinet have special flags. The queen of England and members of the royal family have special flags. The queen's flag, called the *Royal Standard,* is raised over a building as she enters it and lowered when she leaves. The queen also has a *personal standard* for use in the Commonwealth countries that have become republics. The governor general of Canada, as her personal representative, also has a special flag.

Many personal flags are older than national ones. They developed during the Middle Ages, and became especially important in battle. Noblemen flew banners of various sizes, depending on their rank. With the development of national unity in Europe, flags symbolizing the personal authority of a ruler became less important. National flags representing all the people developed.

Military flags

Flags have always been important in the armed forces. Most countries have special flags for individual units. Some countries also have separate flags for each branch of their armed forces and for top-ranking officers.

Army flags. Armies once went into combat carrying *battle flags.* Some of these army flags were quite different from the national flags of the times. However, soldiers now carry flags mostly for parades and ceremonies. Large units, such as regiments, have special *colors.* These flags often bear the names of the battles or campaigns where the unit served with distinction. United States Army units attach *battle streamers* to their flags in order to show where they have fought. Smaller units of the Army carry *guidons* in parades so that the marchers can have something to guide on.

Navy flags. Navy ships usually fly several types of flags. An ensign is displayed when a ship is at sea. It is usually flown from a flagstaff at the stern or from a *gaff* (crossbar) on the mast of the ship. In peacetime, the ensign may not be displayed if the ship is out of sight of land and no other ships are in the vicinity. In wartime, the ensign is always displayed to show the nationality of the ship.

Parts of a flag

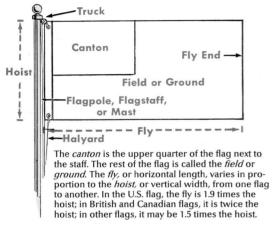

The *canton* is the upper quarter of the flag next to the staff. The rest of the flag is called the *field* or *ground.* The *fly,* or horizontal length, varies in proportion to the *hoist,* or vertical width, from one flag to another. In the U.S. flag, the fly is 1.9 times the hoist; in British and Canadian flags, it is twice the hoist; in other flags, it may be 1.5 times the hoist.

Staff ornaments

The ornaments on flagstaffs include, *left to right,* the spread eagle, halberd, ball, flat truck, star, and colors or guidon.

The shapes of flags Flags may have many shapes, including rectangular, square, and tapering. The tapering flags include triangular ones called *pennants* and ones that end in two points called *swallowtails.* Swallowtail flags may be broad or long and narrow.

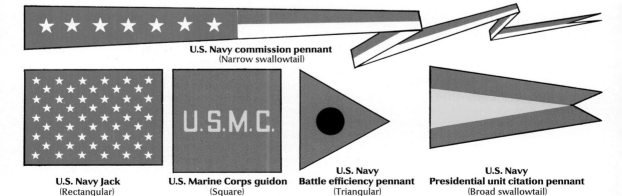

U.S. Navy commission pennant
(Narrow swallowtail)

U.S. Navy Jack
(Rectangular)

U.S. Marine Corps guidon
(Square)

U.S. Navy Battle efficiency pennant
(Triangular)

U.S. Navy Presidential unit citation pennant
(Broad swallowtail)

Flag terms

Badge is an emblem or design, usually on the fly.

Battle flag is carried by armed forces on land.

Battle streamer, attached to the flag of a military unit, names battles or campaigns where the unit served with distinction.

Bend on means to attach signal flags to a halyard.

Breadth, a measurement for flags, is 9 inches (23 centimeters) wide. A four-breadth flag is 36 inches (91 centimeters) wide. The term originated when flag cloth was made in 9-inch (23-centimeter) strips.

Bunting is cloth decorated with stripes of the national colors. The term is also used for the woolen cloth used in making flags.

Burgee is a flag or pennant that ends in a swallowtail of two points.

Canton is the upper corner of a flag next to the staff where a special design, such as a union, appears.

Color is a special flag carried by a military unit or officer. In the armed forces of many countries, regiments and larger units often carry two colors—the national flag and a unit flag.

Courtesy flag is the national flag of the country a merchant ship visits, hoisted as the ship enters port.

Device is an emblem or design, usually on the fly.

Ensign is a national flag flown by a naval ship. Some countries also have ensigns for other armed services.

Ensign staff is the staff at the stern of a ship.

Field is the background color of a flag.

Fimbriation is a narrow line separating two other colors in a flag.

Flag hoist is a group of signal flags attached to the same halyard and hoisted as a unit.

Fly is the free end of a flag, farthest from the staff. The term is also used for the horizontal length of the flag.

Garrison flag, in the U.S. Army, flies over military posts on holidays and special days. It is 20 feet (6 meters) wide by 38 feet (12 meters) long, twice as wide and long as a post flag.

Ground is the background color of a flag.

Guidon is a small flag carried at the front or right of a military unit to guide the marchers.

Halyard is a rope used to hoist and lower a flag.

Hoist is the part of the flag closest to the staff. The term is also used for the vertical width of a flag.

House flag is flown by a merchant ship to identify the company that owns it.

Jack is a small flag flown at the bow of a ship.

Jackstaff is the staff at the bow of a ship.

Merchant flag is a flag flown by a merchant ship.

National flag is the flag of a country.

Pennant is a triangular or tapering flag.

Pilot flag is flown from a ship that wants the aid of a pilot when entering port.

Post flag, in the U.S. Army, flies regularly over every army base. It is 10 feet (3 meters) wide by 19 feet (5.8 meters) long.

Reeve means to pull the halyard through the truck, raising or lowering a flag.

Staff is the pole a flag hangs on.

Standard is a flag around which people rally. Today, the term usually refers to the personal flag of a ruler, such as Great Britain's *Royal Standard.*

State flag is the flag flown by the government of a country. Many state flags are the same as national flags but with the country's coat of arms added.

Storm flag, in the U.S. Army, flies over an army base in stormy weather. It is 5 feet (1.5 meters) wide by 9 feet 6 inches (2.9 meters) long, half as wide and half as long as a post flag.

Truck is the wooden or metal block at the top of a flagpole below the *finial* (staff ornament). It includes a pulley or holes for the halyards.

Union is a design that symbolizes unity. It may appear in the canton, as the stars do in the U.S. flag. Or it may be the entire flag, as in the *Union Flag* of Great Britain.

Vexillology is the study of flag history and symbolism. The name comes from the Latin word *vexillum,* which means flag.

A family of flags

Many governments have flags for various purposes. For example, the British have a family of flags. The queen has two flags she can use: the Royal Standard, as queen, and her own standard, as head of the Commonwealth.

The Royal Standard
The queen's flag

The queen's standard
The queen's personal flag

The Union Flag
The national flag

The Red Ensign
Flown by merchant ships

The Blue Ensign
Flown by public servants

The White Ensign
Flown by naval ships

The army flag
Flown at army bases

The Royal Air Force ensign
Flown at RAF bases

Flags that talk

A U.S. Navy signalman aboard an aircraft carrier sends a message to another ship cruising alongside. He uses a system of signaling called *semaphore*. His arm positions represent letters and numbers.

U.S. Navy

When a navy ship is in port or at anchor, a small flag called the jack flies from the *jackstaff* (short flagpole at the bow), and the ensign is flown from the flagstaff at the stern. Ships of most navies fly *command flags* to show the title or command of any flag officer on board. If no officer higher than the commanding officer is on board, a flag called a *commission pennant* is flown to show the ship is in active service.

Air force flags often are flown over air bases. For example, the British air force flies a pale-blue ensign with the aircraft recognition emblem used on planes in the ensign's fly. Air force units also have their own flags and guidons.

Other government flags

Some countries have a special *state flag* that only the government uses. It flies over government buildings, embassies, and UN headquarters. Usually, a state flag is a national flag with a coat of arms added to it. Most flags in this article are national flags. State flags are shown for Andorra, Argentina, Austria, Bolivia, Costa Rica, Dominican Republic, Ecuador, El Salvador, Ethiopia, Finland, Guatemala, Haiti, Iran, Peru, Poland, San Marino, Spain, and Venezuela. Many government agencies have their own flags. Such United States units as the Foreign Service have special flags. Many British agencies fly the Blue Ensign, usually with a badge in the fly.

Flags of the sea

A merchant ship flies a *house flag* of the company that owns it. At the stern, it also flies the national flag of the country in which it is registered. The ships of some countries fly a *merchant flag* that differs from the national flag used on land. Canadian and U.S. ships fly their national flags, but British ships fly the Red Ensign. When a ship's captain wants a pilot to help the ship enter port, the captain may hoist a *pilot flag*. As a courtesy, ships also fly the flag of the country they visit.

Flags that talk

Flags are often used for signaling. Sailors may use special flags to relay orders to other ships. The National

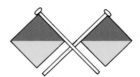 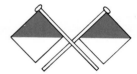

Semaphore flags are used to send messages between ships or between a ship and shore. Red-and-yellow flags, *left,* are used at sea, and red-and-white ones, *right,* on land.

Oceanic and Atmospheric Administration uses *storm warning flags* to provide weather warnings on small lakes and where its nationwide Weather Radio service is impractical.

Hand signal flags. In signaling, a *wigwag flag* is used to indicate the dots and dashes of the Morse code (see **Morse code**). A signaler uses two *semaphore flags* to spell out a message, holding them in various positions in order to indicate letters and numerals (see **Semaphore**).

The international flag code, the most complete flag signaling system, has more than 40 flags. Each flag stands for a letter of the alphabet and pennants stand for zero and the numerals 1 through 9. To send messages, sailors fly *hoists* of one to five flags that have code meanings or spell out words.

Each ship carries a code book that explains the flags in nine languages—English, French, German, Greek, Italian, Japanese, Norwegian, Russian, and Spanish. With the code book, any captain can understand messages sent to the ship. Warships fly the *code and answering pennant* when they use the international code, so other ships will know that they are not using a secret code.

Sailors use certain flags from the international code for warnings or announcements. A ship in harbor that is about to sail hoists the flag for the letter *P*, a flag once known as the *blue peter*. A ship flies the *D* if it is having difficulty steering, and the *O* if it has lost someone overboard. The flags for the letters *I* and *T* together warn that a ship is on fire; and the signal *M, A,* and *A* requests urgent medical advice.

International flag code has 36 flags and pennants for letters and numerals, a code and answering pennant, *right,* and three substitutes. A signal-receiving ship raises its answering pennant to show that the hoist has been understood. The substitutes repeat letters or numerals that precede them and make it unnecessary to carry extra sets. The North Atlantic Treaty Organization and other western navies use a fourth substitute.

International alphabet flags

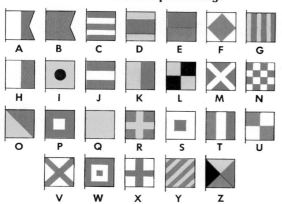

A B C D E F G

H I J K L M N

O P Q R S T U

V W X Y Z

Four groups of flags, called *flag hoists,* fly from the signal bridge of the U.S.S. *Enterprise,* a nuclear-powered aircraft carrier. Sailors clip the flags together to form messages.

Substitutes or repeaters

First   Second   Third   Fourth

International numeral pennants

1   2   3   4   5

6   7   8   9   0

U.S. Navy numeral pennants

1   2   3   4   5

6   7   8   9   0

Storm warning flags fly at shore stations to warn boats of hazardous wind and sea conditions. The red pennants for small craft and gale warnings measure 4 or 7½ feet (1.2 or 2.3 meters) wide at the mast and 7 or 15 feet (2.1 or 4.6 meters) in length. The flags for storm and hurricane warnings are 4 or 8 feet (1.2 or 2.4 meters) square. They have a black square on a red field.

Small craft advisory
Winds up to 38 mph (61 kph)

Gale warning
Winds from 39 to 54 mph (63 to 87 kph)

Storm warning
Winds from 55 to 73 mph (89 to 117 kph)

Hurricane warning
Winds at least 74 mph (119 kph)

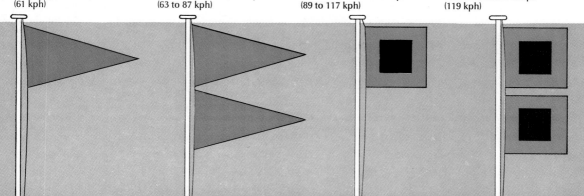

Manufacturing flags

Some governments issue specifications for the design, proportions, and colors of official flags. Many color specifications refer to the *Standard Color Card of America,* the *British Colour Council Dictionary of Colour Standards,* and other color systems. But flags are subject to variations as manufacturers standardize common colors and proportions to reduce costs.

Almost all flags are made of cloth. Most flags that fly outdoors are made with synthetic fabrics. The most commonly used fabric is nylon. Polyester and acrylics are also popular materials for flags. All of these fabrics are light, strong, and colorfast. For many years, flag makers used *bunting* in flags. This woolen cloth came in long strips called *breadths,* which were 9 inches (23 centimeters) wide. Most inexpensive flags are made of cotton, and the cotton fabric is sometimes also called bunting. Special ceremonial flags are made of rayon. Such flags look richer than those made with cotton or nylon.

Sewing is the most common method of making flags. Strips of flag material are sewn together in the proper positions and sizes to create the flag. Elaborate designs, such as the complicated seals within some flags, may be painted on cloth and then *appliquéd,* or sewn, onto the background cloth of the flag. They may also be embroidered on the flag by hand. Especially complicated flags, such as Great Britain's Royal Standard, may be painted or embroidered entirely by hand.

Many flags are printed, usually on paper or plastic materials, but sometimes on cloth. Flags and pennants are often printed on cloth by the silk-screen process. A separate silk-screen stencil is used for each color in the flag (see **Silk-screen printing**).

In making a U.S. flag, workers use machines to cut stars from white cloth and then to embroider them to the blue field of the canton. The huge machines produce hundreds of star fields at the same time. Other machines sew together long strips of red and white fabric to form the stripes. Many flag makers sew panels of six stripes for the area below the blue field and seven stripes for the area beside it, then cut the panels into the proper lengths. The blue field and panels of stripes are then sewn together. A strip of strong *heading* material is sewn along the hoist for strength. A machine punches holes at the top and bottom of the heading and inserts metal rings in them for clipping the flag to the halyard.

In making small Canadian flags, workers use silk-screen printing. With the maple leaf and red stripes as a stencil, they paint the red areas on rolls of white cloth. Then they cut up the cloth into individual flags. For large flags, three pieces of cloth, two red and one white, are sewn together and the maple leaf is appliquéd on each side of the white material.

In most countries, private firms make all the flags, although some governments make their own. Annin and Company is the world's largest flag maker. It makes millions of flags a year, including U.S. flags and flags for other countries. The company has offices in Verona, N.J., and New York City, and plants in Bloomfield and Verona, N.J. Annin produced one of the world's largest flags, a 60-by-90-foot (18-by-27-meter) Stars and Stripes for the Port Authority of New York and New Jersey. This flag hangs from the George Washington Bridge on holidays. The largest United States flag measures about 210 by 411 feet (64 by 125 meters). It is kept in the White House and brought out for display each Flag Day. The Great American Flag Fund, a nonprofit corporation, donated it to the White House in 1983.   Whitney Smith

Manufacturing U.S. flags   Flag manufacturers in the United States use skilled workers and modern equipment to produce flags of high quality. New high-speed machinery has increased the efficiency and precision of flag making. Greater use of synthetic materials has resulted in stronger, more wear-resistant flags.

Sewing white stars onto blue fabric, a huge machine produces hundreds of star fields at the same time. The modern machine embroidery is of especially high quality and precision. In the past, workers had to sew each star in place.

Sewing the stripes in long panels, automatic sewing machines join strips of red and white cloth. A worker oversees the operation and makes necessary adjustments. These high-speed machines produce stripes for thousands of flags every day.

Related articles in *World Book* include:

Flag Day	Key, Francis Scott	Semaphore
Flag officer	Navy Jack	Star-Spangled
Heraldry	Pledge of Alle-	Banner
Hopkinson, Francis	giance	Tricolor
Jones, John Paul	Ross, Betsy	Union Jack

Outline

I. Flags of the world
II. Flags of the United States
   A. First United States flags
      1. The colors
      2. The stripes
      3. The stars
   B. Changes in the United States flag
III. Honoring a national flag
   A. Displaying the flag
      1. In the United States
      2. In Canada
   B. Hanging the flag outdoors
      1. From a building
      2. Over a street
   C. Hanging the flag indoors
   D. Raising and lowering
      the flag
      1. Breaking the flag
      2. Striking the flag
      3. Dipping the flag
      4. Flying upside down
      5. Flying at half-mast
   E. Carrying the flag
      1. A color guard
      2. In a parade
      3. On a float
      4. On a car
   F. Saluting the flag
   G. Permitted and prohibited uses
   H. Caring for the flag
IV. Kinds of flags
   A. Flags of individuals

   B. Military flags
      1. Army flags
      2. Navy flags
      3. Air force flags
   C. Other government flags
   D. Flags of the sea
   E. Flags that talk
      1. Hand signal flags
      2. The international flag code
V. Manufacturing flags

Questions

What country has used the same national flag for over 750 years?
How does the *union* of a flag differ from the *canton*?
What do the stars stand for in the United States flag? What do the stripes stand for?
When is a national flag flown at half-mast?
Who flew the first flaglike emblems?
When are new stars added to the United States flag?
What is the *hoist* of a flag? The *fly*?
How are most flags made?
What is the meaning of *dipping* a flag? Of *striking*?
How can ship captains understand signals at sea?

Additional resources

Level I
Blassingame, Wyatt. *The Story of the United States Flag.* Garrard, 1969.
Desmond, Alice C. *Your Flag and Mine.* Macmillan, 1960.

Level II
Furlong, William R., and McCandless, Byron. *So Proudly We Hail: The History of the United States Flag.* Smithsonian Institution, 1981.
Matheson, John R. *Canada's Flag: A Search for a Country.* G. K. Hall, 1980.
Smith, Whitney. *The Flag Book of the United States.* Rev. ed. Morrow, 1975. *Flags and Arms Across the World.* McGraw, 1980.

Annin & Co.

Sewing the stars and stripes to-gether, a worker first stitches the short stripes to the star field. She then sews the long stripes to the field.

Inspecting sewn flags, a worker carefully checks each one to make sure there are no defects. At the same time, she trims off any extra threads.

Packaging finished flags for shipping, a worker includes booklets that outline the rules to observe in displaying and honoring the flag.

Flag Day is celebrated on June 14 in memory of the day in 1777 when the Continental Congress adopted the Stars and Stripes as the official flag of the United States. It is not an official national holiday, but the President proclaims a public Flag Day observance every year. In Pennsylvania, Flag Day is a legal holiday.

On Flag Day, people in the United States display the flag on their homes, businesses, and public buildings. Some schools honor the flag with special programs that may feature discussions of the flag's origin and meaning. Many patriotic organizations hold parades and other Flag Day demonstrations.

Flag Day was first officially observed in 1877 to celebrate the 100th anniversary of the selection of the flag. Congress requested all public buildings to fly the flag on June 14 of that year. Some people suggested that Flag Day be observed each year. Early leaders of campaigns to establish Flag Day as an annual national celebration included William T. Kerr of Pittsburgh and Bernard J. Cigrand of Waubeka, Wis. In 1897, the governor of New York proclaimed a Flag Day celebration for the first time as an annual event in that state. President Woodrow Wilson established Flag Day as an annual national celebration in his proclamation issued on May 30, 1916. In 1949, President Harry S. Truman officially recognized June 14 as Flag Day by signing the National Flag Day Bill.   Elizabeth Hough Sechrist

See also **Flag** (First United States flags).

Flag of truce is a plain white flag used by opposing sides on a battlefield when they want to discuss peace terms. It is also used to arrange for a prisoner exchange or for wounded to be rescued. Both sides stop fighting while their leaders discuss terms of the truce. All armies recognize the flag of truce.   Whitney Smith

Flag officer is the rank of the five highest officer grades in the United States Navy. These are fleet admiral, admiral, vice-admiral, rear admiral, and commodore. A flag officer usually commands a fleet or squadron. A flag officer's ship flies a flag which indicates the officer's rank.   Whitney Smith

See also **Admiral; Rank, Military.**

Flagellate. See Protozoan (Kinds).

Flagellum is the singular form of flagella. See **Protozoan** (Kinds); **Bacteria** (How bacteria move).

Flageolet, *FLAJ uh LEHT,* is a small woodwind instrument that belongs to the flute family. It consists of a wooden or metal tube with a mouthpiece at one end. The tube has four finger holes on top and two thumb holes underneath. A player holds the flageolet vertically and blows through the mouthpiece. The flageolet has a high sound similar to that of the piccolo, but somewhat softer. Sieur Juvigny, a French musician, invented the flageolet in 1581. The instrument gained its greatest popularity in the 1600's.   Thomas C. Slattery

Flagler, Henry Morrison (1830-1913), was an American businessman. He became a partner of the industrialist John D. Rockefeller and helped him organize the Standard Oil Company in 1870. Flagler remained a top executive at Standard Oil until 1911. But after the early 1880's, his main business activity was in Florida. In 1886, he helped organize what became the Florida East Coast Railroad. He later extended the railroad so that by 1912, it stretched from Jacksonville to Key West. Flagler built luxurious resort hotels in St. Augustine, Palm Beach, Miami, and other cities. He was born in Hopewell, near Canandaigua, N.Y.   Roger M. Olien

Flagstad, *FLAG stad* or *FLAHG stah,* **Kirsten,** *KUR stuhn* or *KIHSH tuhn* (1895-1962), a Norwegian operatic soprano, became famous as an interpreter of the heroines in the operas of Richard Wagner. Previously unknown to American audiences, her 1935 debut as Sieglinde in *Die Walküre* at the Metropolitan Opera House in New York City was a storybook triumph. Flagstad also became a renowned recitalist. She helped revive interest in the songs of her countryman, Edvard Grieg. Although she retired from the operatic stage in 1952, she continued to sing in concerts and to record opera and German songs. She became director of the new Norwegian State Opera in 1958. Born in Oslo, Flagstad made her operatic debut there when she was 18 years old.   Martial Singher

Flagstaff, Ariz. (pop. 34,743), is the center of a lumbering region near the colorful San Francisco Mountains in northern Arizona (see **Arizona** [political map]). Flagstaff is the home of Northern Arizona University and the Museum of Northern Arizona. Lowell Observatory, from which astronomers discovered the planet Pluto, is in Flagstaff. The city is the headquarters of the U.S. Geological Survey astrogeology division and the Navajo and

The Metropolitan Museum of Art, New York City, Crosby Brown Collection

The flageolet is played by blowing through one end and opening and closing finger and thumb holes.

© Lowell Observatory

Flagstaff is the site of Lowell Observatory, *above.* Astronomers discovered the planet Pluto from this observatory.

Hopi Indian Relocation Commission. Walnut Canyon, Sunset Crater, and Wupatki national monuments are nearby. In 1876, the nation's centennial, settlers camping in the area made a flagstaff from a pine tree and flew the American flag from it. The city's name is believed to have come from this incident. A city council and mayor govern Flagstaff. The city is the seat of Coconino County. See also **Radar** (picture: Radar mapping).
Richard N. Velotta

Flaherty, *FLA uhr tee,* **Robert Joseph** (1884-1951), was a pioneer American filmmaker. He is considered the father of documentary motion pictures. Flaherty became noted for his treatment of the lives of isolated peoples in the silent films *Nanook of the North* (1922) and *Moana* (1926) and in the sound film *Man of Aran* (1934). His short film *The Land* (1942) showed the effects of erosion. *Louisiana Story* (1948) portrayed the impact of the discovery of oil on a poor family that lived in the bayous of Louisiana.

Flaherty was born in Iron Mountain, Mich. He co-directed the feature films *White Shadows of the South Seas* (1927) with W. S. Van Dyke, *Tabu* (1931) with F. W. Murnau, and *Elephant Boy* (1937) with Zoltan Korda. Flaherty's wife, Frances Hubbard Flaherty, worked on several of his documentaries.
Rachel Gallagher

Flahiff, George Bernard Cardinal (1905-   ), archbishop of Winnipeg, Man., was appointed a cardinal of the Roman Catholic Church in 1969 by Pope Paul VI. He became the first Canadian cardinal named in a province west of Ontario. Flahiff was born in Paris, Ont. He attended the University of Toronto and universities in Strasbourg and Paris, France. He became a priest in 1930. From 1954 to 1961, Flahiff was Superior-General of the Basilian Fathers, a Canadian order. He became archbishop of Winnipeg in 1961.
Thomas P. Neill

Flail, *flayl,* is a hand implement used to thresh small grain crops such as wheat, barley, and oats. The flail was a short stick or club fastened by a leather strip to a long wooden handle. Farmers used it to beat the grain from the straw. Then they tossed the mixture of grain and straw into the air to be separated by the wind or by fanning it with a large sheet. The threshing machine and motor-operated combine replaced the flail on most farms. However, it is still used in some underdeveloped areas.

In early days, people also used flails as weapons. The flail usually consisted of a wooden bar or ball studded with metal spikes or barbs. It was joined to a short handle by a length of chain.
Melvin E. Long

Flame. See Fire.

Flame test is a way of identifying a chemical element by the color of the light it gives off when held in a flame. For most elements, the test can be made by dipping a platinum wire in a compound of the element, either powdered or in solution. The wire is then held in the flame of a Bunsen burner (see **Bunsen burner**).

An element always gives off flame of the same color. For example, compounds of barium color the flame yellowish green. Flames of calcium are orange-red. Copper gives off an emerald-green color. Lithium's flame is deep red. Sodium's flame is yellow. Strontium gives off a crimson flame. Potassium's flame is violet.
Carol P. Anderson

See also **Mineral** (Other identification tests).

Flame thrower is a weapon of war which shoots a stream of burning fuel in much the way that a fire hose squirts water. The flame belches from the nozzle of a flame gun connected by a flexible tube to two tanks of fuel on the operator's back. A tank of compressed air between the tanks of fuel provides the pressure needed to squirt the fuel through the gun. Portable flame throwers weigh a total of about 70 pounds (32 kilograms) when they are ready to fire.

The Germans introduced flame throwers during World War I (1914-1918), but they were not widely used until United States soldiers used them against the Japa-

FourByFive

A flame thrower can hurl a tongue of flame 200 feet (61 meters). The operator carries two tanks of fuel and a tank of compressed air to provide the pressure needed to squirt the fuel through the gun. When ready to fire, the portable flame thrower weighs about 70 pounds (32 kilograms).

nese in World War II (1939-1945). Soldiers used flame throwers against fortifications that could not be captured with rifle fire alone. Flame throwers became a weapon to be feared by the enemy. Soldiers who scoffed at rifle bullets often fled in panic at sight of the long, searing tongue of flame licking toward them. American soldiers called the flame thrower the *GI hot-foot.*

Fuel used in flame throwers during World War I was a mixture of gasoline and oil. During World War II, a jellied gasoline called *napalm* was developed (see **Napalm**). By using napalm, soldiers could fire portable flame throwers 200 feet (61 meters). Flame throwers that were mounted on tanks could reach targets 750 feet (230 meters) away. When the jellied fuel hit a target, it scattered into sticky blobs. These blobs bounced through small openings into fortifications. The napalm stuck to the target and was very difficult to extinguish.

Since the 1940's, flame throwers have served important functions in civilian life. For example, farmers make extensive use of flame throwers to burn away weeds and to destroy such harmful insects as tent caterpillars. Flame throwers can also be used to break rocks and melt snow.
Frances M. Lussier

Flamenco is a type of dance that originated in southern Spain. The professional flamenco dancers shown at the left are performing in a Spanish club. The colorful costumes, energetic performances, and accompaniment by guitars and hand clapping are typical of flamenco dancing.

Flamenco, *fluh MEHNG koh,* is a type of dance and music first performed by the Gypsies of southern Spain. Flamenco dancing exists both in a folk form and in a version for stage performance. In either style, a performer must improvise and add a personal interpretation to the dance. The dance may include much skillful footwork, finger snapping, and forceful but flowing arm movements.

Flamenco dances may be performed by a single person, a couple, or a larger group. The best flamenco dancers are inspired with a passionate spirit and communicate their energy to the audience. Colorful costumes and much noise contribute to the excitement of the performance.

Originally, flamenco dancers were accompanied by clapping, singing, and stamping. Later, castanets and guitars were added. The musicians provide a basic, repetitive yet varied rhythm.   Dianne L. Woodruff

See also **Spain** (picture: The flamenco).

Flamingo, *fluh MIHNG goh,* is a bird known for its long, stiltlike legs and curved bill and neck. Flamingos live in many parts of the world and spend their entire life near lakes, marshes, and seas.

Most flamingos stand from 3 to 5 feet (91 to 150 centimeters) tall. The color of a flamingo's feathers—except for some black wing feathers—varies from bright red to pale pink. For example, flamingos of the Caribbean area have coral-red feathers, and South American flamingos have pinkish-white feathers. Most flamingos eat shellfish and small, plantlike water organisms called *algae.* Hairlike "combs" along the edges of the bill strain mud and sand from the food a flamingo finds in the water. Flamingos, like ducks, have webbed feet.

Flamingos live in colonies, some of which have thousands of members. They mate once a year. Flamingos build a nest that consists of a mound of mud. Most of the females lay a single egg in a shallow hole at the top of the nest. The parents take turns sitting on the egg to keep it warm. The egg hatches after about 30 days.

Young flamingos leave the nest after about 5 days and form small groups. But the young flamingos return to the nest to feed on a fluid produced in the digestive system of the parents. The adults dribble this fluid from their mouth into the youngster's bill. After about two weeks, the young form larger flocks and start to find their own food. Flamingos live from 15 to 20 years in their natural surroundings. They live even longer in captivity.

Flamingos live in marshy areas in many parts of the world. These graceful birds feed on small organisms that they find in muddy water.

A young flamingo, *right,* lacks the large, bent bill and pinkish color of the adults. The young first leave the nest about five days after hatching.

The *lesser flamingo, left,* is a species of flamingo that lives in the Great Rift Valley of Kenya and Tanzania in Africa. The large birds feed in lakes in the valley.

Yann Arthus-Bertrand, Jacana from Photo Researchers

Most zoologists classify flamingos into four species. The *greater flamingo* lives in Africa, southern Asia and Europe, southern South America, and the West Indies. The *lesser flamingo* lives in the Great Rift Valley of Kenya and Tanzania in Africa. The other two species, the rare *Andean* and *James'* flamingos, dwell near the highland lakes of the Andes Mountains in South America. Wild flamingos once lived in southern Florida, but people killed them for their beautiful feathers faster than the birds could multiply.

Scientific classification. Flamingos belong to the flamingo family, Phoenicopteridae. The greater flamingo is *Phoenicopterus ruber.*   James M. Dolan, Jr.

See also **Bird** (How birds feed [picture: The flamingo]).

Flammarion, *FLAH MAH RYAWN,* **Camille** (1842-1925), was one of the most imaginative and colorful writers of science books. He greatly influenced the young people of many countries, and turned their interest to astronomy. His most famous work, *Popular Astronomy* (1877), became a best seller.

Flammarion was born in Montigny-le-Roi, France, and lived in or near Paris throughout his life. The poverty of his parents forced him to seek work as an engraver. He became interested in astronomy, and in 1883 founded an observatory near Paris. There he studied the moon, Mars, and double stars. Later in life, he turned to more controversial work on psychical research.

Roger H. Stuewer

Flanagan, *FLAN uh guhn,* **Edward Joseph** (1886-1948), a Roman Catholic priest, founded Boys Town near Omaha, Nebr., in 1917. He opened the community to boys of all races and religions. His work there was featured in the popular motion picture *Boys Town* (1938). Many institutions similar to Boys Town were founded in the United States and Canada, but they did not all succeed.

Father Flanagan was born in Ballymoe, near Roscommon, Ireland. He came to the United States in 1904, and studied for the priesthood. Father Flanagan completed his education at the Gregorian University in Rome and at the University of Innsbruck in Austria. Then he became a parish priest in O'Neill,

Boys Town Hall of History
Father Flanagan

Nebr. Father Flanagan's first social service was with a Workingmen's Hostel in Omaha. However, he became interested in the treatment of boys who were homeless or had broken the law.   Alan Keith-Lucas

See also **Boys Town.**

Flanders, *FLAN duhrz,* is a part of northern Europe that was a separate political unit until modern times. Two-thirds of the historic Flanders region now forms the provinces of East and West Flanders in northern Belgium and extends slightly into the Netherlands. The rest of Flanders is the northern half of the French *department* (administrative district) of Nord. Flanders is an area of rich soils, which are low lying and difficult to drain. The farms near the coast are protected by dikes and drained by canals. Farmers produce hops, fodder, wheat, flax, and sugar beets. Industries in Flanders produce coal, automobiles, textiles, and a variety of metal and electrical goods.

The early products of Flanders were wool and flax for use in the manufacture of cloth. A heavy trade in wool began, especially with England. As a result, cities developed earlier in Flanders than in most of Europe. Flanders was the market place of the continent during the 1300's and 1400's. The great trading fairs that were held in the city of Antwerp—which was then part of the historic Flanders region—brought fame and wealth to the city. Ypres, Bruges, and Ghent also grew rich through trade.

The dense population and the wealth of Flanders led to the development of a distinct Flemish culture. This culture was marked by a concern for painting, architecture, literature, and other refinements that gave Flanders

Flanders is a historic region in Europe.

WORLD BOOK map

a leading place in early European civilization.

For many years, Flanders was ruled by a succession of powerful nobles, each of whom was known as the Count of Flanders. In the early 1800's, Napoleon I made Flanders part of the French Empire. The present division of the historic Flanders region among Belgium, France, and the Netherlands was made in 1830.

Today, the name *Flanders* also refers to a Dutch-speaking region in the northern part of Belgium that has limited self-rule. This region of Belgium consists of the provinces of Antwerp, East Flanders, West Flanders, Limburg, and the northern half of Brabant (see **Flemings**). Hugh D. Clout

See also **Ghent; Painting** (The Renaissance in Flanders).

Flanders Field is a United States military cemetery near Waregem, Belgium. Buried in this cemetery are the bodies of 368 members of the armed forces who died in World War I (1914-1918). Canadian poet John McCrae wrote the famous poem, "In Flanders Fields" (see **McCrae, John**).

Flannel is a soft, warm fabric. It is made from wool and from blends that consist of wool and cotton or rayon. Manufacturers usually brush flannel to give it a *napped* (raised) surface. Most kinds of flannel are produced in the *twill weave*—that is, they have a pattern of raised, diagonal lines woven into them. Some flannels have a flat texture made by using a *plain weave*. Flannel is used chiefly in suits and coats.

A soft fabric called *flannelette* resembles flannel and is often confused with it. It has a napped surface like that of true flannel, but unlike flannel, flannelette is normally made entirely from cotton. Flannelette is used mainly for baby clothing, bed linen, nightgowns, pajamas, and shirts. Keith Slater

Flaps. See **Airplane** (The wing).

Flare, Solar. See **Sun** (Flares; The sun's brightness; Sun terms; The sun's stormy activity).

Flashbulb. See **Photography** (Lighting equipment).

Flashlight is a portable electric light in a metal, fiber, or plastic case. A typical flashlight consists of a light source, power source, case, and switch. The light source is a *lamp* (light bulb). A reflector and a lens help to focus the light into a beam. Most flashlight lamps are incandescent, but small fluorescent lamps are sometimes used (see **Electric light**). Dry-cell batteries provide the power for most flashlights. A switch mounted on the case is used to turn the flashlight on and off. The first

dry-cell flashlight was made about 1898 in New York City. See also **Battery** (How dry primary batteries work). William Hand Allen

Flat-coated retriever is considered a gamekeeper's dog in Great Britain, and is not widely known in the United States. It was bred from two North American dogs, the Labrador retriever and the St. Johns Newfoundland. The dog was first introduced in England, in 1860. It has a thick, fine, flat coat, and is usually solid black or solid *liver* (reddish-brown). The dog weighs

WORLD BOOK photo by E. F. Hoppe

The flat-coated retriever has a thick coat.

from 60 to 70 pounds (27 to 32 kilograms), and stands about 22 inches (56 centimeters) high at the shoulder. Maxwell Riddle

Flatboat is a large, raftlike barge used to haul freight and passengers. A flatboat has a flat bottom and square ends. A *keelboat,* sometimes called a flatboat, was a long narrow craft, sharp at one or both ends. It was built on a keel and ribs. These boats carried goods during the westward movement in the United States. Pioneers put their furniture and livestock on flatboats and floated to new settlements. The boats were moved by the current

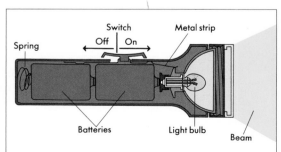

WORLD BOOK diagram by Arthur Grebetz

A flashlight shines as electric current is carried from the batteries to the light bulb by means of a metal strip.

Granger Collection

Flatboats on the Ohio River carried thousands of immigrants to new settlements in the Midwest during the early 1800's.

and by long oars which were also used for steering. A vast flatboat freight business grew on the Mississippi River and its tributaries in the 1800's.

Philip Chadwick Foster Smith

Flatcar. See **Railroad** (Freight service; Passenger and freight cars).

Flatfish is the name of a large group of valuable food fishes that includes the halibut, flounder, and sole. Flatfishes live in salt water and are found worldwide. There are more than 500 species. Flatfishes have a body that appears to be flattened horizontally. The fish actually lies on its side, with both eyes on the same side of the head. When the flatfish is first hatched, it looks like any other kind of fish. But after it has grown from $\frac{1}{2}$ to $\frac{3}{4}$ inch (13 to 19 millimeters) long, one eye begins to move closer to the eye on the opposite side of the head, and the mouth becomes twisted. The eyeless side of the fish stays under and loses its color. The upper side becomes darker. The fish then becomes colored to blend with its surroundings.   Tomio Iwamoto

See also **Flounder; Halibut; Sole; Turbot; Animal** (picture: Animal camouflage).

Flatfoot is an inherited condition in which the long arch of the foot appears to be flat or collapsed. The condition results from weak ligaments that are unable to support the arch. Many people believe that flat feet cause pain. However, this is not true because the height of the arch does not affect how the foot functions.

John F. Waller

Flattop. See **Aircraft carrier.**

Flatworm is a kind of worm. Some flatworms live freely on land or in water. Others live as parasites in human beings or other animals. Many flatworms, especially the larger species, have a flat body.

Flatworms have a simple body structure. A layer of cells called the epidermis covers the animal's body. An inner layer of cells forms an intestine in most flatworms. A tightly packed mass of cells called the *parenchyma* fills the body between the epidermis and intestine. Muscles, glands, nerves, and reproductive organs lie in the parenchyma. The only opening of the intestine is the animal's mouth. The mouth may be at the head end, the rear end, or the underside of the body.

Many flatworms have a smooth, soft body. Many have suckers or other projections on the body. Some flatworms have spines and tiny, needlelike *spicules* that serve as a kind of skeleton. Most flatworms measure less than 1 inch (2.5 centimeters) long. However, the largest flatworms, called *tapeworms,* may grow up to 100 feet (30 meters) long.

There are about 17,000 species of flatworms. They may be divided into four groups: (1) turbellarians; (2) monogeneans; (3) trematodes; and (4) cestodes, or tapeworms. Most turbellarians are free-living. They usually are found in sand and mud on the bottom of bodies of water. A few species live on land in moist soil. The other three groups of flatworms are parasites. They live in a wide variety of organisms that serve as *hosts.*

Almost all flatworms are *hermaphroditic*—that is, both male and female reproductive organs are found in the same animal. Most turbellarians lay eggs that hatch into tiny young that resemble the adults. In some turbellarians, and in all parasitic flatworms, young called *larvae* hatch from the eggs. The larvae look different from the adults and live in different habitats. For example, the larva of a monogenean has hairlike *cilia* that enable it to swim. The larva swims until it finds an appropriate fish for a host. The larva attaches to the fish and develops into an adult. The adult, which lives on the skin and gills of the fish, lacks cilia and cannot swim.

Parasitic flatworms cause disease in their hosts. Schistosomiasis, for example, is a tropical disease caused by *schistosomes* (blood flukes) living in the blood vessels of the abdomen (see **Schistosomiasis**). Adult tapeworms that live in the intestine of human beings do not usually cause much harm. However, tapeworm larvae cause serious diseases that can be fatal if not treated.

Scientific classification. Flatworms make up the phylum Platyhelminthes. The four classes of flatworms are Turbellaria, Monogenea, Trematoda, and Cestoda.   Seth Tyler

See also **Animal** (picture: Animals of the oceans); Fluke; Planarian; Tapeworm; Worm.

WORLD BOOK illustration by Zorica Dabich

The blood fluke may inhabit the blood vessels of the abdomen of human beings. This flatworm causes schistosomiasis, a disabling disease common in tropical regions.

Flaubert, *floh BAIR,* **Gustave,** *goos TAHV* (1821-1880), was a French writer whose novels contain some of the most vivid and lifelike characters and descriptions in literature. He blends precise observation with a careful attention to language and form. His *Madame Bovary* is considered perhaps the most perfect French novel.

Flaubert was born in Rouen. He lived in solitude, devoting himself to literature. His adoration of artistic beauty was paralleled by his hatred of materialism.

Flaubert tended to be a skeptic and a pessimist. His works are never sentimental or soft, but they are always deeply human. His novels show he was both a realist and a romantic. The realism can be seen in his attention to detail and his objective description of characters and events. The romanticism appears in the exotic subject matter that

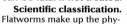

Bettmann Archive

Gustave Flaubert

Flaubert chose. *Madame Bovary* (1857) is a poetically realistic treatment of a case of adultery in a village in Normandy. *Salammbô* (1862) is a colorful historical novel about ancient Carthage. *A Sentimental Education* (1869), a kind of autobiographical novel, is an example of strict literary realism. *The Temptation of St. Anthony*

(1874) is a marvelous fantasy. *Three Tales* (1877) contains three small masterpieces, each illustrating a different style: "A Simple Heart" (contemporary realism), "Herodias" (Biblical style), and "The Legend of St. Julian the Hospitaller" (medieval style).   Thomas H. Goetz

Flavian Amphitheater. See Colosseum.

Flax is a plant raised for its fiber and seed. The fiber is made into linen fabric and a variety of other products, including rope, thread, and high-quality paper. The seeds contain *linseed oil,* which is used primarily in the production of paints and varnishes.

There are about 230 species of flax. Only one species, *Linum usitatissimum,* is grown commercially. Different varieties of this species are grown for fiber and for seed.

The flax plant stands from 3 to 4 feet (0.9 to 1.2 meters) high and has either white or blue flowers. The variety grown for fiber has a slender stem that branches near the top. Seed flax is bushier than fiber flax and bears more seeds.

Flax may be attacked by a number of fungus diseases. These diseases include *rust, wilt,* and *pasmo.* Before planting flax, farmers treat the seeds with chemicals called *fungicides* to provide protection against these diseases. Farmers also plant varieties of flax that are resistant to disease.

World production of fiber flax amounts to about 770,000 short tons (700,000 metric tons) annually. The Soviet Union accounts for more than half the world's fiber flax production. Other leading growers include France, China, Romania, Poland, and Czechoslovakia, in that order. The United States and Canada do not raise fiber flax. World flaxseed production totals about 100 million bushels, or 2,800,000 short tons (2,500,000 metric tons) yearly. Leading flaxseed-producing countries, in order of production, include Canada, Argentina, India, the Soviet Union, and the United States.

Growing and processing fiber flax. Fiber flax grows best in cool, moist climates with rainy summers. It is planted in the spring after the danger of frost has passed. It is generally grown in rotation with other crops. Rotation helps reduce the effects of diseases.

Fiber flax is harvested three to four months after

Leading flaxseed-producing states and provinces

Bushels of flaxseed produced annually

State/Province	Bushels of flaxseed produced annually
Manitoba	●●●●●●●●●●●●●●●●● 22,715,000 bushels
Saskatchewan	●●●●●●●●● 12,401,000 bushels
North Dakota	●●●● 6,008,000 bushels
South Dakota	● 1,335,000 bushels
Alberta	◖ 1,098,000 bushels

One bushel equals 56 pounds (25 kilograms). Figures are for 1985.
Sources: *Crop Production, 1985 Annual Summary,* U. S. Department of Agriculture; *Grain Trade of Canada, 1985,* Statistics Canada.

planting. If the plants are harvested too early, the fibers will be fine and silky, but weak. If the plants become too ripe, the fibers will be stiff and rough and difficult to spin into yarn. Farmers harvest fiber flax with a machine that pulls the stalks from the ground. On some farms, workers harvest the plant by hand.

After the plants have been harvested, the flax stems are soaked in water. This process, which is called *retting,* rots the stalk and exposes the fibers that lie under the woody part of the stem. There are two methods of retting—*dew retting* and *water retting.* In dew retting, farmers spread the flax in the field and allow the dew to rot the plants for several weeks. During the dew retting process, the stems are turned several times and the seeds are removed. In water retting, the seeds are removed first and the stems are then soaked in large tanks of warm water for four to eight days.

After retting, the flax stems are dried and sent through a machine that breaks them into small pieces called *shives.* Next, in a process called *scutching,* the machine separates the shives from the fibers by beating the stems with a whirling paddle or blade. In the next

Flax is valued for its seeds and its fibers. Seed flax, *left,* produces linseed oil. Fiber flax, *center,* is used to make linen. Farmers use a machine to harvest fiber flax, *right.*

Leading flaxseed-producing countries

Bushels of flaxseed produced annually

Canada	●●●●●●●●●●●●●●●●●●
	36,219,000 bushels
Argentina	●●●●●●●◖
	16,141,000 bushels
India	●●●●●●◖
	15,275,000 bushels
Soviet Union	●●●◖
	8,661,000 bushels
United States	●●●◖
	8,307,000 bushels

One bushel equals 56 pounds (25 kilograms). Figures are for 1985.
Source: *FAO Production Yearbook, 1985,* Food and Agriculture Organization of the United Nations.

step, called *hackling,* the *tow* (short) and *line* (long) fibers are straightened and separated from each other by combing. The fibers are then baled and sent to mills for processing. The seeds that were removed from the plants are processed for oil.

Growing and processing seed flax. Seed flax grows best in areas with cool climates and dry summers. Most seed flax is planted in early spring. In the fall, combines harvest the flax and separate the seeds from the rest of the plant. The seeds are then shipped to mills to be processed.

In the mill, the flax seeds are ground into a meal and steamed. The oil is then removed either by squeezing the meal in a hydraulic press or by treating the meal with chemicals called *solvents.* Flax seeds consist of about 40 per cent oil and 60 per cent water and solid matter. One bushel of seeds produces about $2\frac{1}{2}$ gallons (9.5 liters) of linseed oil. The meal that remains after processing is used as a high-protein feed for livestock.

In the United States, the unused portions of the seed flax plant are processed to remove the tow fibers. The fibers are made into yarn and into paper for cigarettes, Bibles, and other products.

History. Flax is one of the oldest cultivated crops. Flax seeds that have been found in Syria and Turkey indicate that the plant might have been grown as early as 7000 B.C. The Egyptians began cultivating flax about 5000 B.C. By about 1000 B.C., the cultivation of flax had spread to Western Europe. During the A.D. 700's, the areas that are now Belgium and France became leading producers of fine linen.

The first settlers in the United States and Canada planted fiber flax so they could make linen. But the invention of a cotton gin by Eli Whitney in 1793 made cotton yarn more economical than linen yarn. As a result, the two countries eventually abandoned fiber flax production. Flaxseed production declined in the United States and Canada in the 1950's because of the increasing popularity of latex paints over oil-based paints.

Scientific classification. Flax belongs to the family Linaceae and makes up the genus *Linum.*   David S. Seigler

See also **Linen; Linseed oil.**

Flaxman, John. See Sculpture (European).

Flea, *flee,* is a small, wingless insect that lives on mammals and birds and sucks blood for food. Fleas are dangerous pests because they can carry the germs that cause plague and typhus. They get the disease germs by biting infected rats and ground squirrels. See **Bubonic plague; Typhus.**

A flea has flat sides and a head much smaller than the rest of the body. The flea's shape and its strong, spiny legs help it glide quickly and easily through the hairs or feathers of its host. Fleas puncture the skin with their beaks to get blood.

WORLD BOOK illustration by Shirley Hooper, Oxford Illustrators Limited

Common European flea

Fleas live on human beings, cats, dogs, rats, birds, horses, poultry, rabbits, and many wild animals. A few kinds live only on certain types of animals. But most kinds pass readily from animal to human beings and from animal to animal. They leave the host as soon as it dies because they must have blood for food.

Fleas are strong and have great leaping ability for their size. Scientists have found that the flea that lives on people can jump 13 inches (33 centimeters). Fleas can be made to perform tricks such as pulling tiny wagons. *Flea circuses* feature troupes of fleas that have been "trained" to do such tricks.

Kinds of fleas. The common *European,* or *human, flea* is about $\frac{1}{8}$ inch (3 millimeters) long. It lives in the folds of clothing. It drops its eggs about the house instead of attaching them to clothing. The larvae look like maggots. When they become adults, they seek a host. Some people attract fleas more than others do, and some become sensitive to the bites. The skin around the bite becomes inflamed in such people.

The *chigoe,* another kind of flea, is native to South America. But is has spread to Africa and many temperate regions. The female chigoe burrows into the skin to lay eggs. These insects cause ulcers to form on the skin. The flea must be removed before the ulcer will heal.

Rat, cat, and dog fleas also may be serious pests. They lay many tiny oval white eggs on the animals or in their sleeping places. When the eggs hatch, the larvae crawl into bedding and into cracks in the floor. They spin their cocoons in dust and appear as adults about two weeks later.

Controlling fleas. Cleanliness and proper care of pets are the best protection against fleas. Dogs that have fleas should be scrubbed with soaps that contain an appropriate insecticide. Periodically treating pets with such soaps kills the insects. Owners can guard against fleas by changing their pets' bedding frequently. They can destroy the larvae by spraying or dusting the pets' quarters with an insecticide.

Scientific classification. Fleas make up the order Siphonaptera. The common European, or human, flea is a member of the human flea family, Pulicidae. It is classified as *Pulex irritans.*

W. Joe Lewis

Fleabane, *FLEE bayn,* is a plant often grown in rock gardens. It gets its name because people once thought

WORLD BOOK illustration by Lorraine Epstein

The garden fleabane shown above has delicate violet flowers and often grows in clusters.

that the fleabane could drive away or destroy fleas. There are over 130 different kinds of fleabane. *Canada fleabane* is also known as *horseweed, colt's-tail,* and *bloodstanch.* It grows as a common weed in Canada and the United States. A fleabane often grown in gardens has violet-colored flowers. These flowers grow in a cluster about $1\frac{1}{2}$ inches (4 centimeters) across. Another garden fleabane has brilliant orange flowers. *Blue fleabane* grows in dry areas east of the Mississippi.

The Canada fleabane can be gathered while it is flowering and carefully dried. Druggists then sell it as a drug called *erigeron,* or fleabane. Erigeron is used to treat diarrhea and dropsy and to stop the flow of blood. Lotions that repel mosquitoes often contain oil of fleabane.

Scientific classification. The fleabanes belong to the composite family, Compositae. The Canada fleabane is classified as *Conyza canadensis.* The blue fleabane is *Erigeron annuus.* The garden fleabanes are *E. speciosus* and *E. aurantiacus.*

Harold Norman Moldenke

Fleet Prison, an historic London jail, took its name from its location near Fleet stream. As early as the 1100's, it was the king's prison. In the 1500's and 1600's, it housed Puritans and victims of the Court of the Star Chamber. Later, it was a debtor's prison. In the 1700's, it became noted for cruelty. From the early 1600's until 1753, members of the clergy performed secret marriages in the prison. These ceremonies were called "Fleet marriages." The prison was abandoned in 1842, and it was later torn down.   Basil D. Henning

Fleming, Sir Alexander (1881-1955), was a British bacteriologist at St. Mary's Hospital at the University of London. In 1928, he discovered the germ-killing power of the green mold, *Penicillium notatum,* from which the life-saving antibiotic, penicillin, was first purified (see **Antibiotic; Penicillin**). For his discovery, Fleming shared the 1945 Nobel Prize in medicine with British scientists Sir Howard Florey and Ernst B. Chain. Florey and Chain helped develop the use of this drug (see **Florey, Lord; Chain, Ernst Boris**).

The discovery and development of penicillin opened a new era for medicine, and World War II (1939-1945) provided an opportune field trial for the drug. Fleming discovered penicillin accidentally when he saw that a bit of mold growing in a culture plate in his laboratory had destroyed bacteria around it. Fleming also discovered lysozyme, a substance found in human tears. Even when diluted, this agent can dissolve certain germs.

Fleming was born on a farm near Darvel, Scotland. He attended St. Mary's Medical School in London.

Audrey B. Davis

Max Ehlert, Miller Services
Sir Alexander Fleming

Additional resources

Hughes, W. Howard. *Alexander Fleming and Penicillin.* Priory Press, 1974. For younger readers.
Macfarlane, R. Gwyn. *Alexander Fleming: The Man and the Myth.* Harvard, 1984.
Maurois, André. *Life of Sir Alexander Fleming: Discoverer of Penicillin.* Dutton, 1959. An authorized biography.
Sheehan, John C. *The Enchanted Ring: The Untold Story of Penicillin.* MIT Press, 1982.

Fleming, Ian Lancaster (1908-1964), an English novelist, became one of the most popular authors of the mid-1900's. He won fame for his creation of James Bond, a British secret service agent who attracts both beautiful women and villains in his series of fantastic adventures. The sophisticated Bond, also known by the code name *007,* is the senior of three British agents who use a double-0 code number. The double-0 means that these agents are licensed to kill at their discretion.

Bond first appeared in *Casino Royale* (1953) and then in 11 other novels and two collections of short stories. The books attracted many types of readers. *Diamonds Are Forever* (1956) was a favorite of the more sophisticated readers, while *Doctor No* (1958) had a general appeal like the thrillers of the 1800's. A popular series of movies based on the Bond novels helped spread the character's fame. Fleming also wrote *Chitty Chitty Bang Bang* (1964), a children's story about an old racing car that could fly. After his death, the Bond series was continued by English author John Gardner.

Fleming was born in London. During World War II, he did espionage work as the personal assistant to the director of British Naval Intelligence.   David Geherin

Fleming, John Ambrose. See **Vacuum tube** (Development of the vacuum tube); **Electronics** (The first commercial vacuum tubes).

Fleming, Sir Sandford (1827-1915), a Canadian civil engineer, built the Intercolonial Railway across Canada and made surveys for the main line of the Canadian Pacific Railway (now CP Rail). After 1876, he played a prominent role in establishing standard time zones (see **Standard time**). He proposed the use of the 24-hour system of keeping time. He also persuaded the Canadian, Australian, and British governments to cooperate in laying the Pacific cable between Australia and Vancouver in 1902, in an attempt to have a system of communication connecting the entire British Empire.

Fleming was born in Kirkcaldy, Scotland. He moved to Canada when he was 18. He joined the engineering staff of the old Northern Railway, and in 1855 became its chief engineer. He was important in railway development for all Upper Canada. An advocate of transcontinental railroads, he became engineer in chief of the government railroads and a director of the Canadian Pacific Railway. He also paid the expense of locating a railway line in Newfoundland. He retired from active engineering in 1880.

Fleming was also interested in political affairs. He served as chancellor of Queen's University at Kingston, Ont., from 1880 to 1915.   Robert E. Schofield

Fleming valve. See Vacuum tube.

Flemings are a group of people who live in northern Belgium. The region they inhabit is called Flanders. It consists of the provinces of Antwerp, East Flanders, West Flanders, Limburg, and the northern half of Brabant (see **Belgium** [political map]). Historically, Flanders had different boundaries and included parts of France and the Netherlands. The Flemings make up about 55 per cent of the Belgian population.

The Flemings are descended from the Franks, Germanic tribes who invaded Flanders in the A.D. 400's. This invasion forced the Celtic people in the area to move south. The Celts became the ancestors of the Walloons, who now live in southern Belgium, called Wallonia.

During the Middle Ages, the Flemings dominated European trade. Agriculture, fishing, and textiles also became thriving industries in Flanders. Between the 1400's and 1600's, the region produced some of the world's greatest painters, including Jan van Eyck, Pieter Bruegel the Elder, and Peter Paul Rubens.

Language differences have long been a source of conflict between the Flemings and the Walloons. The Flemings speak Dutch, and the Walloons speak French. When Belgium gained independence in 1830, French became its only official language.

Many Flemings protested the domination of Belgium by French speakers. Dutch finally gained official recognition in the late 1800's. But the conflicts between the Flemings and Walloons continued.

The Belgian government and most businesses now use both languages. Flemings have also won the right to schools that teach in Dutch. In 1980, the Belgian government granted limited self-rule to Flanders and Wallonia.

Janet L. Polasky

See also **Belgium** (People); **Flanders; Walloons.**

Flemish language. See Belgium (Languages).

Flemish literature. See Belgium (The arts).

Flesh is the name given to the soft tissues or parts of the body of human beings and of most animals with backbones. It is made up chiefly of muscle and connective tissue, but also includes some fat. The flesh is the meaty part of the body which surrounds the skeleton and body cavity. It does not include the organs in the body cavity or the bony and liquid tissues of the body. Animal flesh, or meat, is high in essential nutrients such as fat, protein, and minerals. The word *flesh* also refers to the pulpy parts of fruits and vegetables.

Paul R. Bergstresser

Flesh-eating animal. See Carnivore.

Flesh-eating plant. See Carnivorous plant.

Fletcher, John (1579-1625), was an English playwright. For many years, Fletcher's plays were as highly praised as Shakespeare's and Ben Jonson's. Fletcher wrote many kinds of drama, but his fame centers on his skillfully theatrical tragicomedies and such comedies of manners as *The Wild Goose-Chase* (1621). Like similar Restoration plays written later, this play was meant to please a pleasure-loving, sophisticated upper-class audience.

Fletcher was born in Sussex. His success began with his famous collaboration with Francis Beaumont (about 1608-1613). But Fletcher wrote some plays independently before, and many after, this association. Many of the so-called "Beaumont and Fletcher" plays belong solely to Fletcher or to Fletcher working with others (see **Beaumont, Francis**). Shakespeare probably wrote *The Two Noble Kinsmen* and *Henry VIII* with Fletcher.

Albert Wertheim

Fletcher v. Peck, an 1810 Supreme Court case, marked the first time the Supreme Court of the United States declared a state law unconstitutional. This decision established the supremacy of the United States Constitution over state laws.

In 1795, members of the Georgia state legislature took bribes to grant land to several companies. The next legislature *revoked* (took back) the grants, but some of the land had already been sold by the companies. The new owners of the land argued that by revoking the grants Georgia had interfered with a lawful contract. The Supreme Court agreed with the landowners and declared the original sale legal. The court ruled that the Constitution prohibited a state from violating a contract.

Stanley I. Kutler

Fleur-de-lis, *FLUR duh LEE,* is a French name that literally means *flower of the lily,* but actually refers to the iris. The kings of France used an irislike design in heraldry. Some historians think this design originally represented an iris. Other historians believe the iris was once called a lily, and so the design was called *flower of the lily.* Others claim that the name originally meant *flower of Louis.*

According to legend, Clovis I used the fleur-de-lis in the early 500's after an angel gave him an iris for accepting Christianity. *Clovis* is an early form of *Louis.* King Louis VI, who reigned from 1108 to 1137, first used fleurs-de-lis for his coat of arms.   Whitney Smith

See also **Heraldry; Iris** (picture); **Flag** (picture: Historical flags of the world).

Detail of an illuminated French manuscript (1400's); Musée Condé, Chantilly, France (Laurie Platt Winfrey, Inc.)

The fleur-de-lis is an irislike design used in heraldry. Fleurs-de-lis were often associated with French royalty.

Flexner, Abraham (1866-1959), became an outstanding authority on higher education, especially in the field of medicine. In 1930, he became the first director of the Institute for Advanced Study at Princeton, N.J. (see **Institute for Advanced Study**).

Flexner's study of American medical colleges, published in 1910, caused sweeping changes in curriculum and teaching methods. He was associated with the General Education Board, an organization that provided financial assistance to United States education, from 1913 to 1928. Flexner was born in Louisville, Ky.

Galen Saylor

Flextime. See **Wages and hours** (Hours).

Flicker is a large, handsome woodpecker that lives in nearly all the wooded regions in Canada and the United States. It gets its name from its loud call, which sounds like the word "flicker."

Two of the best-known flickers are the *yellow-shafted flicker* and the *red-shafted flicker,* both of which are subspecies of the *common flicker.* The yellow-shafted flicker is a little larger than a robin. It has brownish back feathers, a conspicuous white rump patch, a black collar mark across the breast, and a small red crown patch. People often call this bird the *golden-winged woodpecker,* or *yellowhammer,* because of its golden-yellow underwings. The red-shafted flicker has bright red instead of golden colored underwings.

The flicker builds its nest in holes in trees. Because of this habit, people sometimes call it the *highhole* or *highholder.* The bird gathers wood chips with which it builds a bed for its eggs. The female flicker lays six or more white eggs.

The flicker gets much of its food on the ground. It eats worms, insects, and berries, and is especially fond of ants. It nests as far north as central Alaska, and migrates in early fall to the southern United States.

Scientific classification. The flicker belongs to the woodpecker family, Picidae. The common flicker is *Colaptes auratus.* The yellow-shafted flicker is *C. auratus auratus;* the red-shafted flicker is *C. auratus cafer.*   George J. Wallace

See also **Woodpecker; Yellowhammer; Bird** (picture: Birds of forests and woodlands).

Flickertail State. See **North Dakota.**

Flight. See **Airplane** (How an airplane flies); **Bird** (How birds move).

Flight attendant is a member of the crew on airplane passenger flights. Flight attendants serve as a personal link between the airline and its passengers during the flight. They attend to the individual needs and comforts of the passengers while performing routine flight duties. The flight attendant tries to make the passengers' trip so enjoyable that they will want to fly with the airline again. Attendants receive special training that helps them work calmly in an emergency and ensure the safety of the passengers.

The first flight attendants on United States airlines were men. But from the 1930's until the 1970's, the airlines hired only women to serve as attendants. Flight attendants were called stewardesses or hostesses. In 1971, a federal court ruled that a man could not be denied a job as a flight attendant because of his sex. Today, both men and women hold the position, but the majority of flight attendants are women.

Duties. The number of flight attendants assigned to a flight varies according to (1) the airline, (2) the length of the trip, and (3) the type of airplane. Long-distance flights may have as many as 14 flight attendants on the largest jets and 6 on other planes. Most short-run jet flights have at least 3 flight attendants. Flights on twin-engine planes may have only 1 attendant. In the United States, the Federal Aviation Administration (FAA) specifies the minimum number of flight attendants that must be carried on each type of plane.

Before the first passenger boards the plane, flight attendants perform certain duties. For example, they check on flight conditions and the flight schedule. They inspect the plane's cabin and check the food, emergency equipment, and first-aid supplies. As the passengers enter the plane, the flight attendants greet them, show them to seats, and help them put away their coats, hats, and hand luggage.

Before take-off, flight attendants give safety instructions to the passengers over the plane's public address system. They also tell the travelers about the smoking regulations and instruct them on the use of their seat belts. On jet flights, flight attendants demonstrate the use of emergency oxygen masks. If the plane takes the passengers chiefly over water, the attendants show them how to use life jackets.

The attendants make flight announcements before and after take-off. They may report on the weather en route and at the plane's destination, the altitude of the aircraft, and the flight time.

Flight attendants try to make the passengers as comfortable as possible. They provide blankets, pillows, and magazines and keep the cabin neat and clean. They help care for children and infants and give extra attention to elderly or inexperienced travelers. Attendants serve

WORLD BOOK illustration by Trevor Boyer, Linden Artists Ltd.

The red-shafted flicker has red markings on its head and underwings. Flickers live in forests throughout North America.

© David R. Frazier

A flight attendant serves at least one meal to passengers on most long flights. Attendants must be able to serve meals, snacks, and beverages in the limited space of the cabin.

© David R. Frazier

Giving safety instructions ranks as one of a flight attendant's most important duties. This flight attendant is showing a plane's passengers how to use an emergency oxygen mask.

meals, snacks, and refreshments. They also answer questions about the aircraft, the route, and travel arrangements at the flight's destination. In case of emergencies, the flight attendants must know how to give first aid. Attendants on international flights must be able to give information on foreign currency, passport regulations, customs, and international travel requirements.

After the passengers leave the plane, the flight attendants submit a flight report if their airline requires it. The attendants always prepare a report in case of an accident, injury, or unusual incident during the flight. After submitting their reports, the flight attendants are free until their next flight.

The average monthly flying time for attendants is about 77 hours, and some hold another job as well. Flight attendants must have their supervisor's approval before taking a second job. Some attendants receive promotional and nonflight assignments. Such assignments include modeling at charity fashion shows and doing other public relations work.

Requirements for flight attendant positions are the same on most United States airlines. A candidate must be at least 20 years old for most airlines, though some airlines accept candidates as young as 18 years old. A flight attendant candidate must also meet normal height and weight standards. Weight must be proportional to height. A candidate's vision, if not 20/20, must be correctable, preferably with contact lenses. A flight attendant candidate must have a pleasant appearance and must be able to pass the flight physical examination of the airline. Applicants must have at least a high school education, and most airlines require at least two years of college.

Most airlines require a candidate to be a citizen of the United States or an immigrant with a permanent resi-

dency permit. An applicant for a position with an international airline must be able to speak at least one other language besides English. Flight attendants must accept a base assignment in any city during their first six months of duty.

A person who wishes to become a flight attendant must be confident, enthusiastic, mature, and poised. Flight attendants must enjoy helping people and talking to them.

Training. Flight attendants are trained at special schools, most of which are run by the airlines. The course lasts from three to seven weeks. Most airlines house the trainees in dormitories during the instruction period.

Flight attendant training includes extensive classroom work and practical in-flight experience in a model cabin. Trainees learn to perform their duties skillfully and to handle unusual situations with poise. They study such subjects as child care, first aid, flight theory and procedures, good grooming, meal service, and psychology of passenger service. Candidates for positions on the largest jets receive special training.

Career opportunities. A career as a flight attendant combines glamour with hard work. In addition, flight attendants have many opportunities to travel and meet people.

The starting pay for flight attendants varies from airline to airline, but the minimum is about $800 a month for attendants on domestic flights. These attendants receive regular increases to a maximum of about $3,000 monthly. Attendants on international flights earn higher salaries. The minimum flying time for flight attendants is about 65 hours a month, but attendants spend at least that much time each month on duty on the ground. Attendants who fly more than 65 hours a month get paid for the extra hours that they work. The airline pays flight attendants' expenses while they are away from their base station.

Flight attendants receive excellent employee benefits. For example, they may travel as passengers at reduced fares on their own airline and on many other carriers. Most airlines also provide reduced rates for the parents, husband or wife, and children of flight attendants. Paid vacations vary from two to four weeks, depending on length of service. The airlines provide accident, health, and life insurance at reduced rates, sick leave with pay, and educational programs. Most airlines also provide maternity leave.

Many flight attendants with ability and experience have moved up to management positions. For example, a capable flight attendant may become a *purser* and have charge of a plane's cabin-service crew.

Information about a specific airline may be obtained by writing the general manager of that company's nearest office.

Critically reviewed by the Airline Flight Attendants Association

Additional resources

Morton, Alexander C. *The Official Guide to Flight Attendant Careers.* Rev. ed. International Pub. Co. of America, 1985.
Musbach, Alice, and Davis, Barbara. *Flight Attendant: From Career Planning to Professional Service.* Crown, 1980.
Nielsen, Georgia P. *From Sky Girl to Flight Attendant: Women and the Making of a Union.* ILR Press, 1982.

Flightless bird. See Bird (Birds of Australia and the Pacific Islands; How birds move).

Flin Flon, Manitoba (pop. 7,243), the province's most important mining center, lies on the Saskatchewan border. For location, see **Manitoba** (political map). The town is sprawled over bare, rocky hills around Ross Lake. Copper and zinc deposits and deposits of gold and other precious metals were discovered there in 1915, but were not fully developed until 1930. In the older part of Flin Flon, water mains and sewers lie above ground because digging through the rock terrain is too expensive. Flin Flon was founded in 1914.   Tom Dobson

Flint (pop. 159,611; met. area pop. 450,499) is Michigan's fourth largest city. Only Detroit, Grand Rapids, and Warren have more people. Flint ranks second to the Detroit area as the nation's leading producer of automobiles, automotive parts, and trucks. The city lies on the Flint River, about 60 miles (97 kilometers) northwest of Detroit (see **Michigan** [political map]).

Flint is the largest manufacturing center of the General Motors Corporation, the world's biggest automobile producer. General Motors operates 10 major manufacturing plants in the city, and three of its divisions have their headquarters there. The corporation is Flint's largest employer.

Flint is the home of the Flint Institute of Arts and the Flint Symphony Orchestra. The Flint College and Cultural Center Development Inc. includes an art gallery, concert hall, music center, planetarium, public library, and transportation museum. Schools in the city include Baker College, GMI Engineering and Management Institute, Michigan School for the Deaf, Mott Community College, and the University of Michigan-Flint.

Chippewa Indians lived in what is now the Flint area when Jacob Smith, the first white settler there, arrived in 1819. Smith, a fur trader from Detroit, built a trading

Flint Convention & Visitors Bureau

The Robert T. Longway Planetarium in Flint, Mich., is part of an educational and cultural center in the city.

post at a spot where Indians crossed the Flint River. During the 1830's, a community that became known as the Flint River settlement developed in the area. Flint was incorporated as a city in 1855. Vast white pine forests near Flint attracted lumbermen to the area during the mid-1800's, and the city became a center of lumber milling. By 1900, Flint's factories were making over 100,000 wooden road carts and carriages a year, and Flint became known as the *Vehicle City.* The Mott Foundation was founded in Flint in 1926. It has helped finance many civic improvements in the city (see **Mott Foundation, Charles Stewart**).

Flint's automobile industry began to grow rapidly after 1903, when the Buick Motor Company moved from Detroit to Flint. William C. Durant, a Flint carriage manufacturer, took control of Buick in 1904. He founded General Motors in Flint in 1908 and moved the Chevrolet Motor Company's manufacturing operations from Detroit to Flint in 1912. The automobile industry drew thousands of workers to the city, and Flint's population rose from 13,000 in 1900 to 156,000 in 1930. Flint continued to grow as the automobile industry expanded in the mid-1900's. But Flint has experienced high unemployment during periods of decline in automobile sales.

A major renewal program that began in the late 1970's has helped modernize Flint's downtown area. The program includes construction of a large hotel, a shopping plaza, and Riverbank Park. The park features fountains, walkways, and a bandstand on an island. In 1984, Six Flags AutoWorld, an amusement and educational theme park, opened in Flint.

Flint is the county seat of Genesee County. It has a mayor-council form of government.   Lawrence R. Gustin

Flint is a hard mineral that ranges in color from brown to dark gray to black. It is a form of *chalcedony* that consists of tiny crystals of quartz with extremely small pores (see **Chalcedony**). In most cases, flint occurs as small masses embedded in such rocks as chalk or limestone. Lighter colored deposits that occur as continuous layers are called *chert.*

Flint is formed by chemical action on minerals that contain a compound of silicon and oxygen called *sili-*

ca. Water dissolves the silica out of the minerals to produce a substance that resembles opal. The water in the substance then filters out, forming flint.

Most flint is so even grained that it can be chipped into smooth, curved flakes. In prehistoric times, people fashioned flint into sharp tools and weapons, such as knives, spears, and arrowheads (see **Arrowhead** [picture]). Later, people discovered that striking flint against iron or steel produces a spark, and so used flint to start fires. The flintlock firearms that were manufactured from the 1600's to the mid-1800's made use of this property.   Robert W. Charles

Flintlock was a firing mechanism used in pistols, muskets, and other firearms from about 1620 to the mid-

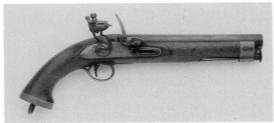

Garry James Collection (WORLD BOOK photo by Roger Fuhr)
A flintlock pistol was effective only at close range.

1800's. Flintlock weapons had a piece of flint clamped in a piece called a *cock.* When the trigger was pulled, the cock snapped forward and the flint struck a piece of steel on a pivot, creating sparks. At the same time, a small pan filled with gunpowder was exposed. The sparks caused the gunpowder to explode and ignite the main charge in the barrel. Flintlocks could be *half-cocked*—that is, in a safety position—or *fully cocked* and ready for firing. Flintlock weapons were eventually replaced by firearms that used percussion caps.

Walter J. Karcheski, Jr.

See also **Firearm; Musket.**

Flipper. See **Animal** (Wings and fins); **Seal; Whale** (Body shape).

Floatplane. See **Airplane** (Seaplanes).

Flock. See **Animal** (Animals that live together).

Flodden Field, Battle of. See **Scotland** (The House of Stuart).

Floe. See **Iceberg.**

Flood is a body of water that covers normally dry land. Most floods are harmful. They may destroy homes and other property and even carry off the topsoil, leaving the land barren. When people are not prepared, sudden and violent floods may bring huge losses. Rivers, lakes, or seas may flood the land. River floods are more common, though lake and seacoast floods can be more serious.

However, sometimes floods may be helpful. For example, the yearly floods of the Nile River built up the plains of Egypt and made the Nile Valley one of the most fertile regions in the world. These floods brought fertile soil from lands far to the south and deposited the soil on the Egyptian plains.

River floods. Most rivers overflow their normal channels about once every two years. When a river overflows land where people live, it causes a flood. When a river overflows land where people do not live, it is said to be *in flood.*

Common causes of river floods include too much rain at one time and the sudden melting of snow and ice. Under such conditions, rivers may receive more than 10 times as much water as their beds can hold. Heavy rains, sometimes from thunderstorms, can produce *flash floods* if small rivers or streams rise suddenly and overflow. Flash floods occur chiefly in mountainous areas and do not allow much time for people to be warned of danger. A flash flood at Rapid City, S. Dak., in 1972 killed 238 people along Rapid Creek. Minor causes of flooding include bridges, piers, filled land, sand bars, and other obstacles to river waters.

The Huang He (Yellow River) in China is known for its tendency to overflow its banks. This river has been called "China's sorrow" because its floods cause such great destruction. Soil carried by the Huang He has been deposited in large amounts at the bottom of the river. As a result of the soil deposits, the riverbed has been raised, increasing the chances of flooding. The worst Huang He flood ever recorded occurred in 1887. Nearly a million people died in China after the river overflowed its banks.

Three major rivers—the Brahmaputra, Ganges, and Meghna—flow through the flat plains that cover most of Bangladesh. They overflow in periodic floods and deposit fertile soil along their banks. But many of the floods cause great damage. In 1988, floodwaters covered most of Bangladesh, killing about 1,600 people and leaving about 25 million temporarily homeless.

The Mississippi-Missouri river system and the rivers that flow into it, such as the Ohio, also overflow at times. One of the greatest floods in the nation's history occurred in 1937, when the Ohio and Mississippi

© Randy Taylor, Sygma
Floodwaters can cause great damage. They have often destroyed entire communities. Floods that occur in the spring often result from melting snow and heavy rains, which combine to raise the level of rivers above their banks.

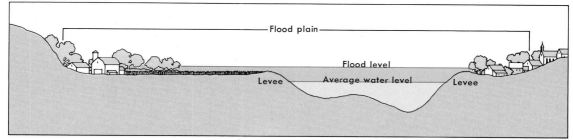

Flood plain

Flood level

Levee   Average water level   Levee

WORLD BOOK diagram by David Cunningham

A flood occurs when a river rises above its normal level and overflows its banks. People have built *levees* (dikes) along some rivers to hold back the high water, but a river may overflow even such barriers. Floodwaters generally cover only a river's *flood plain,* the nearby low-lying land. But sometimes extremely high waters flood a much larger area.

valleys were overrun by the rivers. This flood killed more than 135 people and left about a million people homeless.

The greatest flood damage in the history of the United States occurred in 1972. Heavy rain from a tropical storm caused rivers in New York and Pennsylvania to overflow. The resulting floods destroyed or damaged about $3 billion worth of property and left over 15,000 people without homes.

Seacoast floods. Most floods from the sea result from hurricanes or other powerful storms that drive water against harbors and push waves far inland. In 1970, a cyclone and a tidal wave in the Bay of Bengal, a part of the Indian Ocean, caused the greatest sea flood disaster in history. Huge waves struck the coast of Bangladesh and killed about 266,000 people. The flood also destroyed the cattle, crops, and homes of millions of other victims.

In the Netherlands, the land lies partly below the level of the sea and faces the constant danger of being flooded. The country is protected by its famous dikes, which wall off the sea. These dikes have seldom failed in modern times.

In other places, there is danger from great tidal waves which come up suddenly and unexpectedly. After the great flood of 1900, Galveston, Tex., built a sea wall. But the storms of 1913 went over the wall. Earthquakes and volcanoes also produce waves. A sea wave caused by an earthquake is called a *tsunami.* During the Good Friday earthquake in Alaska in 1964, tsunamis struck the Kodiak Islands and the southern coast of Alaska. The waves, some as high as 35 feet (11 meters), killed 122 people, including 11 in California and 4 in Oregon. Volcanic waves as high as 50 feet (15 meters) have struck Lisbon, Portugal; Messina, Sicily; and the coast of Japan. In 1883, the volcano Krakatoa in Sunda Strait, west of Java, erupted and raised the surrounding water so high that one ship was carried $1\frac{1}{2}$ miles (2.4 kilometers) inland and was left 39 feet (12 meters) above the sea. Some seacoast floods result from abnormally high tides.

Other floods. Storms and high winds also cause floods along lakeshores. Some floods occur when the water of a lake moves suddenly from side to side in rhythm. Such a movement is called a *seiche.*

The failure of artificial structures, such as dams, has caused a number of floods. In 1889, a dam near Johnstown, Pa., burst. The resulting flood killed more than

2,000 people. At least 5,000 people died in India after a dam on the Machu River collapsed in 1979.

Flood control. Flood control involves building dams to store water and channels to allow it to flow quickly to the sea. It also involves dikes, flood walls, hurricane barriers, and levees that help keep water off the land.

Continuing floods in the Mississippi Valley and other river valleys caused Congress to adopt the Flood Control Act of 1936. In 1938, Congress appropriated $376,700,000 for a five-year program of building and keeping up reservoirs, levees, and flood walls. The engineering work along the Mississippi by the U.S. Army Corps of Engineers stopped the floods of the upper Mississippi from doing damage below Cairo, Ill. Before then, the lower Mississippi had been one of the most dangerous flood areas of the world.

In 1943, the rivers that flow into the Mississippi flooded badly. More than 12 million acres (5 million hectares) of farmland were covered by water, and more than 50,000 people had to leave their homes. The

© Joe Traver, Gamma/Liaison

Flood control is often achieved through such temporary measures as sandbagging. These workers are placing sandbags along the shore of Lake Ontario to prevent its steadily rising waters from overflowing. Sandbagging is also used to control lake flooding caused by storms and high winds.

Mississippi-Missouri river system has flooded several times since then. But the flood-control system between Cairo and New Orleans has provided some protection against the flooding.

Reducing flood losses. Engineers work not only to control floods, but also to reduce flood losses. A program to decrease such losses includes regulations to control permanent construction on the *flood plain* (land that gets flooded) and to make buildings waterproof. Other programs aim to help flood victims by improving methods to warn and evacuate people from flood plains and to provide better insurance and relief aid.

The U.S. Geological Survey and the army engineers identify and map flood hazard areas in the United States. About 18,000 communities have used this information to set forth regulations for flood plain management. Many of these regulations require that a small strip of land along a waterway be left vacant. Such land is called a *floodway.* Many communities establish a wider area along the floodway for use as farmland or parkland.

Permanent buildings can be located on a flood plain and withstand flood damage. The technique of keeping water out of buildings is called *flood-proofing.* It involves raising buildings off the ground or using waterproof construction materials.

The U.S. government and the Red Cross provide relief for flood victims. Flood insurance is available in about 18,000 communities in a program administered by the U.S. government.

The National Weather Service has a network of 13 river forecast centers and 50 hydrologic service areas that provide flood warnings. Meteorologists measure the height of rivers and the amount of rain and snow to decide whether a flood may occur. They use radar to estimate how much rain or snow will fall in the near future. The National Weather Service can provide enough warning to greatly reduce loss of life and to lower property damage by as much as 15 per cent.

New technologies have improved our ability to handle floods. For example, artificial satellites in space carry instruments that can record where flooding is worst and help authorities determine where relief work should be concentrated (see **Remote sensing:** picture).

Albert Rango

Related articles in *World Book* include:

Conservation	Johnstown	Reclamation, Bureau of
Dam	Levee	
Deluge	Mississippi River	Tennessee Valley Authority
Disaster	Missouri River	
Huang He	Ohio River	

Additional resources

Berger, Melvin. *Disastrous Floods and Tidal Waves.* Watts, 1981. For younger readers.

Briggs, Peter. *Rampage: The Story of Disastrous Floods, Broken Dams, and Human Fallibility.* McKay, 1973.

Fradin, Dennis B. *Floods.* Childrens Press, 1982. For younger readers.

Ward, Roy C. *Floods: A Geographical Perspective.* Halsted, 1978.

Floor leader. See **Political party** (Organizing the government).

Flooring is the general name given to all materials used to cover floors. The most common floorings are wood, concrete, stone, and tile. The main purpose of flooring is to keep rooms clean, dry, and warm.

The first floors were probably only the leveled dirt of the land over which houses were built. For hundreds of years, the houses of poor people had only dirt floors. Log cabins of early American pioneers usually had dirt floors. But ancient peoples used floors of stone and baked clay in large public buildings and temples. The Greeks used marble in floors. The Romans learned how to make cement. Stone was the most common flooring of public buildings and churches during the Middle Ages. In the 1500's, the Venetians developed *terrazzo,* one of the oldest types of flooring. They made it of granulated marble mixed with gray or white cement.

Wood was first used as flooring in the Middle Ages. *Parquet* floors of different colored woods arranged in designs decorated early palaces. Today, flooring of highly polished hardwoods is the most popular. Other types of flooring include asphalt, cork, linoleum, rubber, plastic, and ceramic tiles (see **Linoleum; Tile**).

George W. Washa

See also **Interior decoration** (Choosing patterns).

Flora is the name given to the plant life of a particular period of time or part of the world. It corresponds to the word *fauna,* which is the term for the animal life of a certain place or time. The term *flora* is taken from the name of the mythological Roman goddess of flowers and spring. David H. Wagner

Florence (pop. 453,293) is an Italian city that became famous as the birthplace of the Renaissance. During the Renaissance, from about 1300 to 1600, some of the greatest painters, sculptors, and writers in history lived and worked in Florence.

The city lies on both banks of the Arno River in central Italy, about 60 miles (100 kilometers) east of the Ligurian Sea. For location, see **Italy** (political map). Florence is the capital of both the province of Florence and the region of Tuscany. Its name in Italian is Firenze.

Such great artists as Leonardo da Vinci, Fra Angelico, Giotto, and Michelangelo produced many of Florence's magnificent paintings and sculptures. Great writers who lived in the city included Giovanni Boccaccio, Dante, and Petrarch. Florentines also won fame in other fields. For example, the architect Filippo Brunelleschi and the political analyst Niccolò Machiavelli were born in Florence, and the astronomer Galileo did some of his work there.

Today, about a million tourists visit Florence yearly to see its splendid art galleries, churches, and museums. The people of Florence consider Michelangelo's famous statue, *David,* as the symbol of the artistic spirit of their city.

The city covers about 40 square miles (104 square kilometers) in the middle of a rich farming area. The oldest part of Florence lies in a small area divided by the Arno. Most of the city's famous buildings are on the right bank, north of the river. A broad public square called the Piazza della Signoria is a major public gathering spot and tourist attraction on the right bank. Towering over the piazza is the Palazzo Vecchio, or Palazzo della Signoria, a palace that has been the center of local government since the Middle Ages. Many old, impressive churches stand on the right bank of the Arno. The Cathedral of Florence, called the Duomo, is in the Piazza del Duomo. The eight-sided Baptistery, with its beautifully decorated bronze doors by Lorenzo Ghiberti and Andrea Pisano, is part of this piazza. The piazza also features a *campanile* (bell tower) built by Giotto and Pisano.

The tombs of Galileo, Machiavelli, Michelangelo, and other famous Florentines are in the Church of Santa Croce. This church also has frescoes by Giotto. The Church of San Marco and an adjacent museum display a collection of paintings by Fra Angelico and other artists of the 1400's. The chapel of the Church of San Lorenzo has the large stone figures carved by Michelangelo for the tombs of the powerful Medici family.

Many outstanding art galleries and museums are also on the right bank. The famous Uffizi Palace, which once housed government offices, is now an art gallery. It owns one of the world's finest collections of paintings and statues (see **Uffizi Palace**). The National Museum of the Bargello exhibits many masterpieces of Renaissance sculpture. The Galleria dell'Accademia displays medieval and Renaissance sculpture, including Michelangelo's *David*. Two copies of this statue stand elsewhere in Florence.

Florence's most elegant shopping area lies along the Via Tornabuoni, a street in the western part of the old section of the city. Some shops on this street display the kinds of clothing and leather goods that have made Florence famous for fashions.

Six bridges connect the right bank with the Oltrarno, the section of Florence south of the river. Goldsmith and jewelry shops line one of these bridges, the Ponte Vecchio, which was built in 1345. The other bridges replaced bridges destroyed during World War II (1939-1945) by retreating German troops. The present Ponte Santa Trinita is an exact reconstruction of the original bridge, which had stood since 1570.

The Oltrarno includes many antique, silver, and woodcarving shops, but its most famous attraction is the Pitti Palace. This palace—the largest in Florence—was begun in 1458 as a home for Luca Pitti, a wealthy merchant. It now displays an excellent collection of paintings (see **Pitti Palace**). The Boboli Gardens, behind the palace, are among the most beautiful gardens in Italy.

Modern apartment buildings stand in Florence's suburbs, which have developed since the 1950's. Industry is concentrated north of the city.

The people. Almost all Florentines are of Italian descent. They speak Italian and belong to the Roman Catholic Church.

Most families in the oldest part of the city live in old stone buildings that lack central heating. Large numbers of families in the suburbs make their homes in modern apartment buildings.

Florentines, like most Italians, eat their largest meal at lunchtime. This meal may include fruit, meat, vegetables, and one of several kinds of noodles called *pasta,* such as spaghetti or ravioli. Other favorites of the people include Chianti wine and beefsteak.

Florence has many public markets. Shoppers meet every morning in the market places and chat as they shop. The Mercato Nuovo, a merchandising square in the heart of Florence, attracts thousands of tourists daily.

Education and cultural life. Florence is the home of the University of Florence and several research institutes. The Academy of Fine Arts and the Luigi Cherubini Conservatory of Music are also in the city. Operas are presented at the Teatro Comunale and the Teatro Verdi. Public libraries in Florence include the Laurenziana, the Marucelliana, the Riccardiana, and one of Italy's two national central libraries.

Economy. Florentines have made fine handicrafts since the days of the Renaissance. Many of the people make or sell such handicrafts as leather products, jewelry, mosaics, pottery, and articles made of straw. Tourism is an important economic activity of Florence.

Factories in the city produce clothing, drugs, foods, glass, and plastics. Florence is a major communications and railroad center of Italy.

History. The Etruscans, a tribe that migrated to Italy from Asia, built the first settlement in what is now Florence. They arrived there about 200 B.C., but their settlement was destroyed in 82 B.C. following a Roman civil

Seymour Linden, De Wys, Inc.

The Ponte Vecchio (Old Bridge) spans the Arno River in Florence. Shops line both sides of the bridge, a historic landmark built in 1345.

Art treasures of Florence include many statues in the Piazza della Signoria, a square in the heart of the city.

war. In 59 B.C., the Roman ruler Julius Caesar established a colony on the Arno and named it Florentia. The name later became Florence.

Florence remained a small, unimportant town until about A.D. 1000. It then began to develop into a self-governing area called a *city-state*. Its population grew from perhaps 5,000 in A.D. 900 to about 30,000 in 1200.

The people of Florence developed new processes for refining wool, and the city gained importance for its woolen textiles. Florentine bankers became successful and brought much wealth to the city. The population reached about 100,000 in the early 1300's. Florence fought many wars during the 1300's and early 1400's, gaining and losing territory at various times.

During the 1300's, four Florentines introduced new styles of painting and writing that grew into great achievements of the Renaissance. Giotto painted pictures with realistic figures instead of stiff, formal subjects. In literature, Dante developed Italian as a literary language and Petrarch and Boccaccio renewed interest in the classics. For the next 300 years, Florence was a center of one of the greatest periods of cultural achievement in history.

The wealthy Medici family gained control of Florence in the early 1400's. By that time, Florence had become a strong and almost independent city-state. It controlled part of what is now central Italy. The city achieved its greatest splendor under the most famous Medici, Lorenzo the Magnificent, who ruled from 1469 to 1492. Except for brief periods, members of the Medici family governed until 1737. During their rule, Florentine literature, theater, and opera thrived in Florence and were imitated throughout Europe. See **Medici.**

Florence was the capital of Italy from 1865 to 1870, when the government moved to Rome. Many improvements were carried out in Florence during its period as the capital. For example, the tree-lined boulevards and large piazzas just outside the historical center of Florence were built at that time.

During World War II (1939-1945), several ancient palaces were destroyed during the fighting for Florence. But most of the city's art treasures escaped harm.

In 1966, a flood damaged books, manuscripts, valuable works of art, and museums and other buildings in Florence. Many nations aided in the restoration of the art works. Most of the paintings and manuscripts were saved, though some required years of careful work.

Florence has faced many problems resulting from a huge increase in the city's population. The number of Florentines has grown from about 96,000 in 1861 to more than 450,000 today. Municipal services, including electricity, have sometimes fallen short of providing enough for everyone. Pedestrians and traffic crowded the narrow streets of the old section. In 1970, private automobiles were banned from the historic center of the city.   Emiliana P. Noether

See also **Architecture** (Renaissance; picture: The dome of the Cathedral of Florence); **Painting** (The Renaissance in Florence; pictures); **Renaissance** (The Italian Renaissance); **Savonarola, Girolamo; Sculpture** (Italian Renaissance; pictures).

Flores. See **Indonesia** (table: Chief islands).

Flores Island, *FLOH ruhs* (pop. 4,367), famed for its abundant foliage, is the westernmost island of the Portuguese Azores. It covers 55 square miles (143 square kilometers). The main occupations are dairying and cattle raising. Santa Cruz is the chief town. See also **Azores.**

Florey, *FLOHR ee,* **Lord** (1898-1968), a British bacteriologist, helped develop with Ernst B. Chain the antibiotic penicillin (see **Antibiotic; Penicillin**). Sir Alexander Fleming discovered penicillin in 1928. Florey shared the 1945 Nobel Prize in medicine with Fleming and Chain (see **Fleming, Sir Alexander; Chain, Ernst Boris**). In 1940 and 1941, Florey's research team at Oxford isolated penicillin in relatively pure form, and tested it.

Howard Walter Florey was born in Adelaide, Australia. He studied at Adelaide University, and, as a Rhodes scholar, at Magdalen College, Oxford.

Audrey B. Davis

Floriculture, *FLAWR uh kuhl chuhr,* is the art, science, and business of growing ornamental plants. Some ornamental plants are grown for outdoor use, others for interior decoration and special occasions.

Raising and marketing cut flowers and decorative plants ranks as a large industry. In mild climates, people grow cut flowers and potted plants outdoors, even in winter. But in cold climates, such plants are grown in greenhouses that can be heated during cold weather. Growers can control the blossoming of flowers. For example, they arrange to have poinsettias for Christmas.

Floriculturists control the blooming of flowers by various techniques developed through research. They also control blossoming by planting the flowers on certain dates, by removing the tips of the plants, and by regulating the temperature and the periods of darkness. Sometimes they artificially lengthen or shorten the amount of light the plant receives each day. Researchers in floriculture have developed long-stemmed carnations, thornless roses, and double snapdragons. Floriculturists work in nurseries, florist shops, seed companies, public and private gardens, zoos, and environmental planning companies.   Peter H. Raven

See also **Florist; Greenhouse; Hybrid.**

David Molchos

The Florida Everglades is a fascinating region of unspoiled nature. Thousands of islands are scattered throughout the vast swamp, serving as home to a wide variety of plant and animal life.

Florida *The Sunshine State*

Florida is one of the leading tourist states in the United States. This land of swaying palm trees and warm ocean breezes attracts visitors the year around, usually about 40 million annually. Many of these vacationers enjoy Walt Disney World, an amusement park near Orlando. Miami Beach, a suburb of Miami, is one of the state's many famous resort centers. Other popular seaside resorts include Clearwater, Daytona Beach, Fort Lauderdale, Key West, Palm Beach, Panama City, and Sanibel Island.

Florida has been nicknamed the *Sunshine State* because it has many sunny days. Partly as a result of the warm, sunny climate, many older people spend their retirement years in the state. Tallahassee is the capital of

Florida. Jacksonville ranks as the state's largest city.

Florida is the southernmost state on the U.S. mainland. It is sometimes called the *Peninsula State* because it juts southward about 400 miles (640 kilometers) into the sea. The northwestern part of the state, called the *panhandle,* extends along the northern shore of the Gulf of Mexico. Florida faces the Atlantic Ocean on the east and the Gulf of Mexico on the west. The southern tip of Florida is less than 100 miles (160 kilometers) from Cuba. Florida's coastline is longer than that of any other state except Alaska.

Florida's population is growing faster than that of all but a few other states. Its economy is also expanding rapidly, especially in banking, business services, and the manufacture of computers and other electronic equipment. Florida farmers grow more than two-thirds of the nation's oranges and more than three-fourths of the nation's grapefruits. Almost all the frozen orange juice produced in the United States is processed in Florida.

In 1513, the Spanish explorer Juan Ponce de León

The contributors of this article are Arch Fredric Blakey, Associate Professor of History at the University of Florida; and Peter O. Muller, Professor and Chairman of the Department of Geography at the University of Miami.

Interesting facts about Florida

The first federal wildlife refuge in the United States was established by President Theodore Roosevelt in 1903 at Pelican Island. The island, located in the Indian River near Sebastian, was set aside for the protection of native birds such as brown pelicans, herons, and egrets. The refuge has since been enlarged, and it now covers about 4,400 acres (1,780 hectares).

Pelican Island

The lowest sea-level air pressure ever recorded in the Western Hemisphere was measured during a hurricane that struck Florida in 1935. The barometer at Matecumbe Key fell to 26.35 inches (892.3 millibars).

Florida has more "champion" trees—the largest living specimens—than any other state. Of the hundreds of trees native to the continental United States, Florida has 98 champions.

WORLD BOOK illustrations by Kevin Chadwick

The first federal savings and loan association was the First Federal Savings and Loan Association of Miami, which received its charter on Aug. 8, 1933.

The first training center for Navy pilots, the U.S. Navy Aeronautic Station, was established in Pensacola in 1914. The facility is now known as the Pensacola Naval Air Station. Today, all U.S. Navy aviators begin their training there.

U.S. Navy Aeronautic Station

Downtown Miami rises beyond the city's port, which handles passenger ships from many countries. Miami, Florida's second largest city, is a leading North American tourist center.

Steven Lucas, Southern Stock

claimed the Florida region for Spain. He named the region *Florida,* possibly for the many flowers he saw there. *Florida* is a Spanish word that means *full of flowers.* In 1565, the Spaniards established St. Augustine, the first permanent European settlement in what became the United States. Great Britain gained control of Florida in 1763 but ceded it back to Spain in 1783. After the Revolutionary War in America (1775-1783), Florida was the only part of southeastern North America that did not belong to the United States.

The United States formally obtained Florida from Spain in 1821, and Congress established the Territory of Florida the next year. Florida became a state in 1845. Shortly before the Civil War began in 1861, Florida left the Union and then joined the Confederacy. Tallahassee was the only Confederate state capital east of the Mississippi River that Union forces did not capture during the war. Florida was readmitted to the Union in 1868. The population of Florida started to swell during the early 1900's and has been growing ever since that time.

Bob Glander, Shostal

Clearwater Beach attracts many swimmers and sunbathers to its sandy shores along the Gulf of Mexico. Florida's long coastline and warm, sunny climate make it a popular vacationland.

Florida in brief

Symbols of Florida

The state flag, adopted in 1899, bears the state seal. Diagonal red bars extend from the corners of the flag over a white field. The seal was adopted in 1985. It reflects minor changes that corrected inaccuracies in the 1868 seal. The revised seal depicts a native Florida Indian maiden strewing flowers. A sabal palm, the state tree, rises in the center. A Florida steamboat sails in the background before the rising sun.

State flag

State seal

Florida (brown) ranks 22nd in size among all the states and is the 2nd largest of the Southern States (yellow).

General information

Statehood: March 3, 1845, the 27th state.
State abbreviations: Fla. (traditional); FL (postal).
State motto: *In God We Trust* (unofficial).
State song: "Old Folks at Home" ("Swanee River"). Words and music by Stephen Foster.

The State Capitol is in Tallahassee, the capital of Florida since 1824—two years after the Territory of Florida was established.

Land and climate

Area: 58,664 sq. mi. (151,939 km²), including 4,511 sq. mi. (11,683 km²) of inland water but excluding 1,735 sq. mi. (4,494 km²) of Atlantic and Gulf of Mexico coastal water.
Elevation: *Highest*—345 ft. (105 m) above sea level in Walton County. *Lowest*—sea level.
Coastline: 1,350 mi. (2,172 km)—580 mi. (933 km) along the Atlantic Ocean; 770 mi. (1,239 km) along the Gulf of Mexico.
Record high temperature: 109° F. (43° C) at Monticello on June 29, 1931.
Record low temperature: −2° F. (−19° C) at Tallahassee on Feb. 13, 1899.
Average July temperature: 81° F. (27° C).
Average January temperature: 59° F. (15° C).
Average yearly precipitation: 54 in. (137 cm).

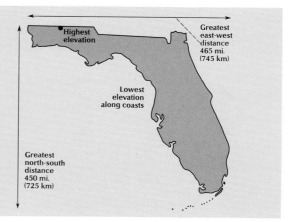

Highest elevation

Greatest east-west distance 465 mi. (745 km)

Lowest elevation along coasts

Greatest north-south distance 450 mi. (725 km)

Important dates

Pedro Menéndez de Avilés founded St. Augustine, the first permanent white settlement in what is now the United States.

Spain regained control of Florida.

| 1513 | 1565 | 1763 | 1783 |

Juan Ponce de León landed on the Florida coast and claimed the region for Spain.

Spain ceded Florida to England.

State bird
Mockingbird

State flower
Orange blossom

State tree
Sabal palm

People

Population: 9,746,421 (1980 census)
Rank among the states: 7th
Density: 166 persons per sq. mi. (74 per km²), U.S. average 67 per sq. mi. (26 per km²)
Distribution: 84 per cent urban, 16 per cent rural
Largest cities in Florida

Jacksonville	540,920
Miami	346,865
Tampa	271,523
St. Petersburg	238,647
Fort Lauderdale	153,279
Hialeah	145,254

Source: U.S. Bureau of the Census.

Population trend

Millions

(graph with vertical axis 0, 3.5, 7, 10.5, 14 and horizontal axis 1800 1820 1840 1860 1880 1900 1920 1940 1960 1980 2000)

Source: U.S. Bureau of the Census.

Year	Population*
1985	11,366,000
1980	9,746,421
1970	6,791,418
1960	4,951,560
1950	2,771,305
1940	1,897,414
1930	1,468,211
1920	968,470
1910	752,619
1900	528,542
1890	391,422
1880	269,493
1870	187,748
1860	140,424
1850	87,445
1840	54,477
1830	34,730

*All figures are census figures except 1985, which is an estimate.

Economy

Chief products

Agriculture: greenhouse and nursery products, oranges.
Manufacturing: electrical equipment, food products, printed materials, transportation equipment.
Mining: phosphate rock.

Gross state product

Value of goods and services produced in 1986, $177,729,000,000. *Services* include community, business, and personal services; finance; government; trade; and transportation, communication, and utilities. *Industry* includes construction, manufacturing, and mining. *Agriculture* includes agriculture, fishing, and forestry.

Source: U.S. Bureau of Economic Analysis.

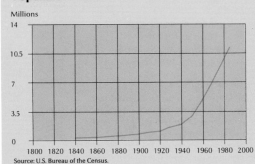

Industry 19%

Services 79%

Agriculture 2%

Government

State government

Governor: 4-year term
State senators: 40; 4-year terms
State representatives: 120; 2-year terms
Counties: 67

Federal government

United States senators: 2
United States representatives: 19
Electoral votes: 21

Sources of information

Tourism: Department of Commerce, Division of Tourism, Direct Mail, 126 Van Buren Street, Tallahassee, FL 32399-2000
Economy: Department of Commerce, Bureau of Economic Analysis, 126 Van Buren Street, Tallahassee, FL 32399-2000
Government: Department of Commerce, Division of Tourism, Direct Mail, 126 Van Buren Street, Tallahassee, FL 32399-2000
History: Department of Commerce, Bureau of Economic Analysis, 126 Van Buren Street, Tallahassee, FL 32399-2000

Florida became the 27th state on March 3.

The Walt Disney World entertainment complex opened near Orlando.

1821   1845   1961   1971

Florida formally came under United States control.

The first United States manned space flights were launched from Cape Canaveral.

Population. The 1980 United States census reported that Florida had 9,746,421 people. The population had increased 44 per cent over the 1970 figure, 6,791,418. Only Nevada and Arizona had a larger percentage of growth during this 10-year period. The U.S. Bureau of the Census estimated that by 1985 Florida's population had reached about 11,366,000.

More than four-fifths of the people of Florida live in urban areas. That is, they live in or near cities and towns of 2,500 or more. The rest live in rural areas. About 90 per cent of the people live in the state's 20 metropolitan areas (see **Metropolitan area**). These areas are Braden-ton, Daytona Beach, Fort Lauderdale-Hollywood-Pom-pano Beach, Fort Myers-Cape Coral, Fort Pierce, Fort Walton Beach, Gainesville, Jacksonville, Lakeland-Winter Haven, Melbourne-Titusville-Palm Bay, Miami-Hialeah, Naples, Ocala, Orlando, Panama City, Pensacola, Sara-sota, Tallahassee, Tampa-St. Petersburg-Clearwater, and West Palm Beach-Boca Raton-Delray Beach. For the pop-ulations of these metropolitan areas, see the *Index* to Florida's political map.

Jacksonville is Florida's largest city. Other cities over 100,000, in order of population, are Miami, Tampa, St. Petersburg, Fort Lauderdale, Hialeah, Orlando, and Hol-lywood. See the articles on Florida cities listed in the *Related articles* at the end of this article.

About 89 of every 100 Floridians were born in the United States. About 14 per cent are blacks. Many older people move to Florida from other parts of the United States after they retire. The largest groups of people from other countries now living in the state came from Great Britain, Canada, Cuba, Germany, and the Soviet Union.

Schools. Florida's earliest schools were run by Span-ish priests in the 1600's. Spanish and Indian children studied religion and the Spanish language. In the mid-1700's, English colonists provided education for the

Population density

More than 80 per cent of the people of Florida live in urban areas. Most of the biggest cities lie on or near the Atlantic or Gulf coast. Jacksonville and Miami are the state's largest cities.

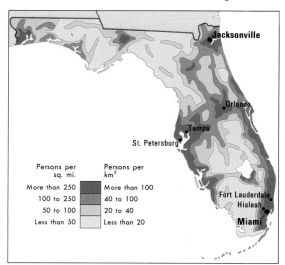

Persons per sq. mi.	Persons per km²
More than 250	More than 100
100 to 250	40 to 100
50 to 100	20 to 40
Less than 50	Less than 20

WORLD BOOK map; based on U.S. Bureau of the Census data.

Suzanne J. Engelmann, Shostal

The International Festival takes place each May in Miami. It features a parade of nations, *above,* as well as arts and crafts, in-ternational foods, and an international doll show.

Tony Arruza, Bruce Coleman Inc.

The Orange Bowl is the home of the University of Miami foot-ball team. It is also the site of the Orange Bowl football game each New Year's Day, a popular annual event in Florida.

Ned Haines, Photo Researchers

Florida Southern College, located in Lakeland, was founded in 1885. The college chapel, *above,* is a distinctive building de-signed by the famous architect Frank Lloyd Wright.

children of wealthier families. A formal system of public education began with the Constitution of 1868 and was well established by the early 1900's.

The commissioner of education heads the Florida department of education and serves as secretary of the state board of education. The governor serves as chairman of the board. Other board members include the secretary of state, attorney general, state treasurer, state comptroller, and commissioner of agriculture. The department of education coordinates the activities of public schools, community colleges, public universities, and vocational education programs. Children from age 6 through 16 are required to attend school. For the number of students and teachers in Florida, see **Education** (table).

Libraries. The St. Augustine Free Public Library is the oldest library in Florida. It opened as a subscription library in 1874. Members of this library contributed money to buy books, which they could use without charge. The state's first free, tax-supported library opened in Jacksonville in 1905.

Today, Florida has about 120 public libraries, many of which are county or regional library systems with several branches. The State Library of Florida in Tallahassee is administered by the Florida Department of State. The P. K. Yonge Library of Florida History, at the University of Florida, owns the most outstanding collection of books about the state.

Museums. The John and Mable Ringling Museum of Art, and its Circus Galleries, are located in Sarasota. They have a fine collection of about 1,000 paintings, and galleries of circus mementos. Other museums in Florida include Cummer Gallery of Art in Jacksonville; Florida State Museum in Gainesville; Henry Morrison Flagler Museum and Society of the Four Arts in Palm Beach; Museum of Fine Arts in St. Petersburg; Norton Gallery and School of Art in West Palm Beach; and Villa Vizcaya Museum and Gardens in Miami.

Universities and colleges

Florida has 36 universities and colleges that offer bachelor's or advanced degrees and are accredited by the Southern Association of Colleges and Schools. Locations shown below refer to the schools' mailing addresses. For enrollments and further information, see **Universities and colleges** (table).

Name	Location	Name	Location	Name	Location
Baptist Bible Institute	Graceville	Florida Atlantic University	Boca Raton	Rollins College	Winter Park
Barry University	Miami Shores	Florida Institute of Technology	Melbourne	St. John Vianney College	
Bethune-Cookman College	Daytona Beach	Florida International University	Miami	Seminary	Miami
Boca Raton, College of	Boca Raton	Florida Memorial College	Miami	St. Leo College	St. Leo
Central Florida, University of	Orlando	Florida Southern College	Lakeland	St. Thomas University	Miami
Clearwater Christian College	Clearwater	Florida State University	Tallahassee	St. Vincent de Paul Regional	
Eckerd College	St. Petersburg	Jacksonville University	Jacksonville	Seminary	Boynton Beach
Edward Waters College	Jacksonville	John B. Stetson University	De Land	South Florida, University of	Tampa
Embry-Riddle		Miami, University of	Coral Gables	Southeastern College of the	
Aeronautical University	Daytona Beach	North Florida, University of	Jacksonville	Assemblies of God	Lakeland
Flagler College	St. Augustine	Nova University	Fort Lauderdale	Tampa, University of	Tampa
Florida, University of	Gainesville	Palm Beach Atlantic College	West Palm Beach	Warner Southern College	Lake Wales
Florida Agricultural and		Ringling School		Webber College	Babson Park
Mechanical University	Tallahassee	of Art and Design	Sarasota	West Florida, University of	Pensacola

Photri

The John and Mable Ringling Museum of Art in Sarasota has a fine collection of about 1,000 paintings. Beautiful sculptures decorate the courtyard of the museum, *left.*

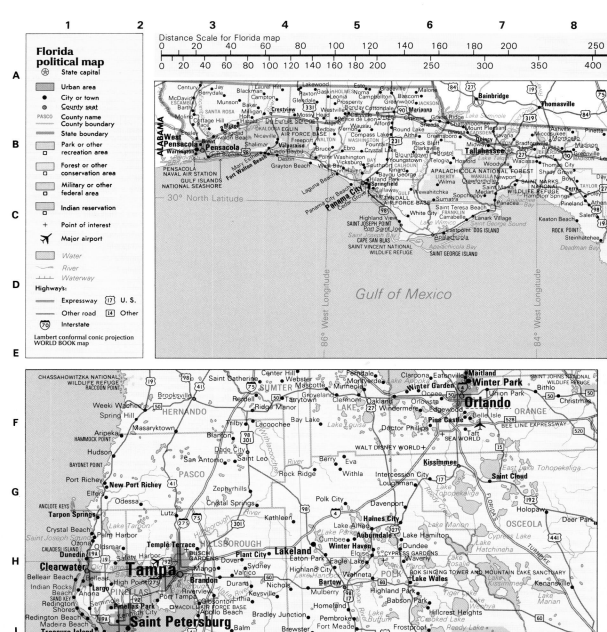
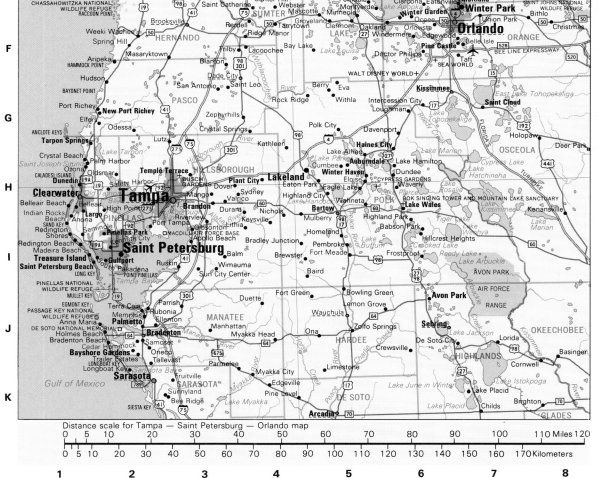

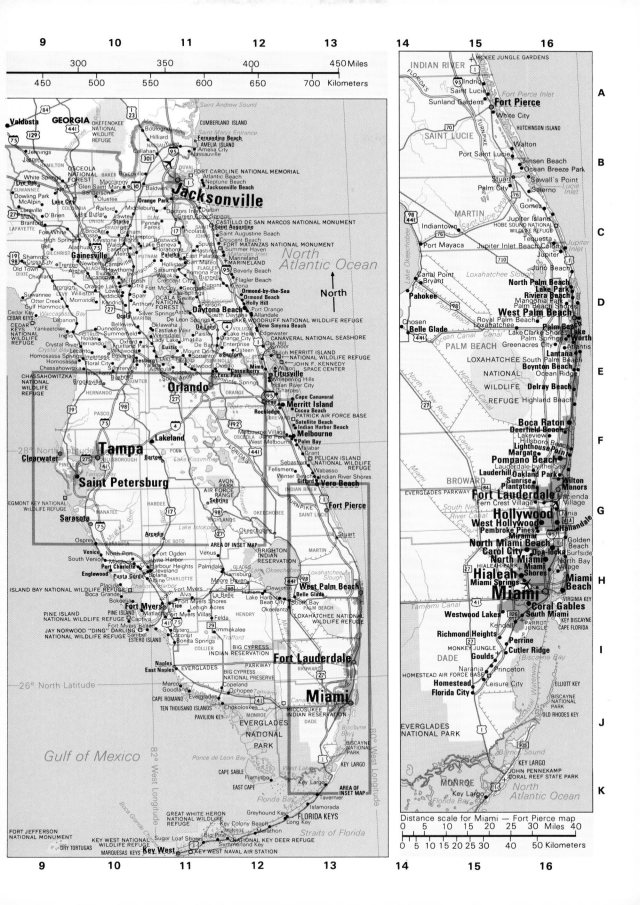

Florida map index

Metropolitan areas

Counties

Cities, towns, and villages

Downtown Jacksonville includes Hemming Plaza, *left,* a popular outdoor gathering place. Jacksonville, located in the northeastern corner of Florida, ranks as the state's largest city.

*Does not appear on the map; key shows general location.
°County seat.
Source: 1980 census. Places without population figures are unincorporated areas.

Great stretches of sandy beaches and a warm, sunny climate make Florida a year-round vacationland. About 40 million tourists come to the state annually. Southern Florida is one of the world's most beautiful resort areas. Among its many attractions are luxurious oceanfront hotels; Everglades National Park; and the Florida Keys, a chain of small islands that extends into the sea. People enjoy swimming, fishing, and water skiing in the inland and coastal waters. Visitors may see historic sites that date back to the Spanish explorers. The Orange Bowl football game in Miami on New Year's Day is one of Florida's leading annual events. Many major league baseball teams train in Florida in spring. Horse racing, greyhound racing, and jai alai games are popular.

Joachim Messerschmidt, Bruce Coleman Inc.

EPCOT Center in Walt Disney World near Orlando

David Forbert, Shostal

Spanish colonial home in St. Augustine

Places to visit

Busch Gardens, The Dark Continent, in Tampa, covers 300 acres (121 hectares) and contains African animals, rare birds, and tropical plants. Trains and a monorail carry visitors through the area.

Florida Cypress Gardens is about 5 miles (8 kilometers) southeast of Winter Haven. Tropical gardens and water shows make this one of Florida's leading attractions.

John Pennekamp Coral Reef State Park, near Key Largo, was the first underseas park in the continental United States. Visitors can see the living reef formations from glass-bottom boats or by diving underwater.

Key West, at the southern end of U.S. 1, is an old seaport and resort city. It offers a wide variety of water activities.

Lion Country Safari, near West Palm Beach, is an animal preserve where lions and other wild animals roam free. Visitors may drive through the area in cars.

Marineland of Florida, the world's first oceanarium, is between St. Augustine and Daytona Beach on Florida's Atlantic coast. Built in 1938, Marineland includes more than 100 kinds of marine creatures in their natural surroundings.

Miami Metrozoo, is a large zoo that displays animals in settings modeled after different parts of the world. The zoo also has a monorail and an aviary where exotic birds fly freely.

Ormond-Daytona Beach stretches for about 23 miles (37 kilometers) along the Atlantic coastline. Tides have beaten the beach to the hardness and smoothness of a highway. Tourists can drive their cars along the beach.

Parrot Jungle, in South Miami, has brilliantly colored parrots and cockatoos living in a jungle of cypress and live oak trees. Tricks performed by parrots and monkeys provide entertainment for visitors.

St. Augustine is the oldest permanent European settlement in the United States. Visitors may tour restored Spanish and British colonial homes.

Sanibel Island, near Fort Myers, has one of the world's finest beaches for collecting seashells. Captiva Island, a luxury resort, is nearby.

Sea World, near Orlando, features porpoise and killer whale shows. The marine center also has a colorful waterskiing show.

Spaceport U.S.A., in Cape Canaveral, is the visitor center for the John F. Kennedy Space Center. It offers bus tours of the space center and also features exhibits that deal with space travel.

Walt Disney World, near Orlando, features an amusement park, a recreational center, a storybook castle, and other attractions. It also includes EPCOT Center, which features displays that explore future technology. EPCOT Center also has re-creations of historical landmarks of the United States and other countries.

Parklands. Everglades National Park, in southern Florida, ranks among the nation's most popular tourist attractions. This park covers 1,398,800 acres (566,074 hectares) and forms the largest subtropical wilderness in the United States. Other Florida parklands managed by the National Park Service include Biscayne National Park, the Fort Jefferson National Monument, and the De Soto National Memorial. For more information on these areas and other national parklands in Florida, see the map and tables in the *World Book* article on **National Park System.**

National forests. Florida has three national forests. The largest, Apalachicola National Forest, spreads across northwestern Florida. The other two are Ocala National Forest and Osceola National Forest.

State parks. Florida has 105 state parks and historic memorials. For more information on the parks and memorials in the state, write to Division of Parks and Recreation, Florida Department of Natural Resources, 3900 Commonwealth Blvd., Tallahassee, FL 32399.

Annual events

January-March
Greek Epiphany Ceremony in Tarpon Springs (January 6); Old Island Days in Key West (January-March); Black Hills Passion Play in Lake Wales (mid-February through Easter); Florida Citrus Festival in Winter Haven (February); Florida State Fair and Gasparilla Pirate Invasion in Tampa (February); Swamp Buggy Days in Naples (February); Festival of States in St. Petersburg (March); Flying High Circus in Tallahassee (March); Motorcycle Week in Daytona Beach (March); Ringling Museum's Medieval Fair in Sarasota (March).

April-June
DeSoto Festival in Bradenton (April); Easter Week Festival in St. Augustine (April); Fiesta of Five Flags in Pensacola (May); Florida Folk Festival in White Springs (May); International Festival in Miami (May); Pensacola Shark Rodeo in Pensacola (June); "Cross and Sword" Official State Play in St. Augustine (June-July).

July-September
Rodeos in Arcadia and Kissimmee (Fourth of July weekend); Firecracker 400 Auto Race in Daytona Beach (Fourth of July); Days in Spain in St. Augustine (August).

October-December
Beaux Arts Promenade in Fort Lauderdale (November); Gator Bowl Festival and Football Game in Jacksonville (December or January); Florida Citrus Bowl Football Game in Orlando (last week in December or first week in January).

Joachim Messerschmidt, Bruce Coleman Inc.
A whale performs at Sea World near Orlando

Eric and Maureen Carle, Shostal
Cypress Gardens near Winter Haven

Stephe
John Pennekamp Coral Reef State Pa

Land regions. Florida is part of the Atlantic-Gulf Coastal Plain, a large land region that extends along the coast from New Jersey to southern Texas. Within Florida, there are three main land regions: (1) the Atlantic Coastal Plain, (2) the East Gulf Coastal Plain, and (3) the Florida Uplands.

The Atlantic Coastal Plain of Florida covers the entire eastern part of the state. It is a low, level plain ranging in width from 30 to 100 miles (48 to 160 kilometers). A narrow ribbon of sand bars, coral reefs, and islands lies in the Atlantic Ocean, just beyond the mainland. Long shallow lakes, lagoons, rivers, and bays lie between much of this ribbon and the mainland.

Big Cypress Swamp and the Everglades cover most of southern Florida. The Everglades include 2,746 square miles (7,112 square kilometers) of swampy grasslands. Water covers much of this region, especially during the rainy months.

The Florida Keys make up the southernmost part of the state. These small islands curve southwestward for about 150 miles (241 kilometers) off the mainland from Miami. Key Largo is the largest island.

The East Gulf Coastal Plain of Florida has two main sections. One section covers the southwestern part of the peninsula, including part of the Everglades and Big Cypress Swamp. The other section of Florida's East Gulf Coastal Plain curves around the northern edge of the Gulf of Mexico across the panhandle to Florida's western border.

The East Gulf Coastal Plain is similar to the Atlantic Coastal Plain. Long, narrow islands extend along the Gulf of Mexico coastline. Coastal swamps stretch inland in places. Much swampland in the region has been drained, and the land used for farming or urban development, especially in southwestern Florida.

The Florida Uplands is shaped somewhat like a giant arm and hand. A finger of the hand points down the center of the state toward the southern tip of the peninsula. The uplands separate the two sections of the East Gulf Coastal Plain from each other and separate the northern section from the Atlantic Coastal Plain.

The uplands region is higher than Florida's other land regions. But its average elevation is only between 200 and 300 feet (61 and 91 meters) above sea level. Lakes are common in the Florida Uplands. Many of these lakes were formed in *sinkholes* or *lime sinks*—cave-ins where a limestone bed near the surface has been dissolved by water action. Pine forests grow in the northern section. Citrus groves thrive in the southern part.

The northern part of the Florida Uplands extends from the northwestern corner of the state along the northern border for about 275 miles (443 kilometers). Its width varies from about 30 to 50 miles (48 to 80 kilometers). This section has fertile valleys and rolling hills of red clay. Many hardwood and softwood forests are found there. The southern part of the Florida Uplands is a region of low hills and lakes. It covers an area about 100 miles (160 kilometers) wide and about 160 miles (257 kilometers) long.

Coastline of Florida is 1,350 miles (2,173 kilometers) long. The Atlantic coast has 580 miles (933 kilometers) of shoreline. The Gulf coast is 770 miles (1,240 kilometers) long. When lagoons, bays, and offshore islands are included, the Atlantic coastline is 3,331 miles (5,361 kilometers) long and the Gulf coast is 5,095 miles (8,200 kilometers) long. Biscayne Bay, south of Miami, is the one

Shostal

The Florida Keys are a chain of small islands that stretch in a curved line about 150 miles (241 kilometers) from Biscayne Bay southwest into the Gulf of Mexico.

Land regions of Florida

WORLD BOOK map

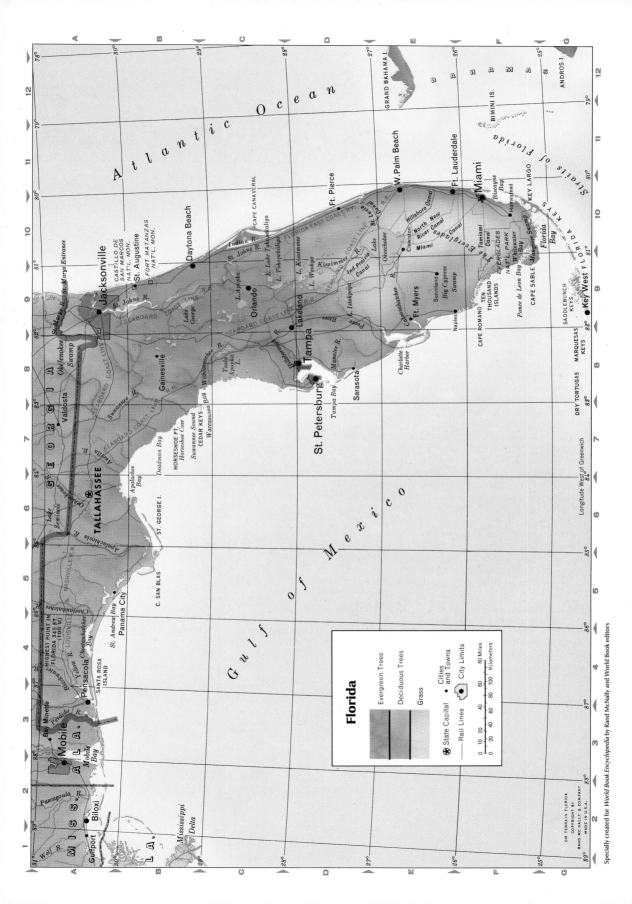

major bay on the Atlantic coast. The most important bays along the western coast include Tampa, Charlotte Harbor, San Carlos, and Sarasota. Florida Bay, beyond the southern tip of the peninsula, separates the Florida Keys from the mainland. Apalachee, Apalachicola, St. Joseph, St. Andrew, Choctawhatchee, and Pensacola bays stretch along the northern Florida shoreline of the Gulf of Mexico.

Rivers, lakes, and springs. The St. Johns River is the largest river in the state. It begins near Melbourne and flows about 275 miles (443 kilometers) northward, almost parallel to the Atlantic coastline. The St. Marys River, along the eastern Florida-Georgia border, flows eastward into the Atlantic. The Perdido River, on Florida's northwestern border, drains into the Gulf of Mexico. The Apalachicola River is northwestern Florida's most important river. It is formed where the Chattahoochee and Flint rivers join at the northern boundary of the state, and flows southward to the Gulf of Mexico. The Suwannee River flows southwestward across northern Florida and also empties into the gulf. Stephen Foster made this river famous in his song "Old Folks at Home," also known as "Swanee River." Other rivers connect many of the lakes of the uplands.

Lake Okeechobee is Florida's largest lake. It covers about 700 square miles (1,800 square kilometers) and is the second largest natural body of fresh water located wholly within the United States. Only Lake Michigan covers a larger area. About 30,000 shallow lakes lie throughout central Florida.

Florida has 17 large springs and countless smaller ones. Many of the springs contain healthful mineral waters. Wakulla Springs, near Tallahassee, is one of the nation's deepest springs. It has a depth of 185 feet (56 meters). Silver Springs, southeast of Ocala, is the largest spring in the state. Many of the springs are so clear that plant life on the bottom may be seen as deep as 80 feet (24 meters).

Plant and animal life. Forests cover about half of Florida. Common trees include ashes, bays, beeches, cypresses, gums, hickories, magnolias, mangroves, maples, oaks, palms, and pines.

Common wild flowers of Florida include irises, lilies,

David Molchos

Everglades National Park covers 1,398,800 acres (566,074 hectares) and provides a home for such swamp birds as black skimmers, *foreground,* and roseate spoonbills, *background.*

Average monthly weather

	Tallahassee					Miami				
	Temperatures				Days of rain or snow		Temperatures			Days of rain or snow
	F° High	Low	C° High	Low			F° High	Low	C° High	Low	
Jan.	65	43	18	6	8	Jan.	76	58	24	14	6
Feb.	67	44	19	7	9	Feb.	77	59	25	15	5
Mar.	72	49	22	9	9	Mar.	80	61	27	16	6
Apr.	79	56	26	13	7	Apr.	83	66	28	19	7
May	86	63	30	17	8	May	85	70	29	21	10
June	91	70	33	21	13	June	88	74	31	23	13
July	91	72	33	22	17	July	89	75	32	24	16
Aug.	90	72	32	22	14	Aug.	90	75	32	24	16
Sept.	87	69	31	21	10	Sept.	88	75	31	24	18
Oct.	81	59	27	15	5	Oct.	85	71	29	22	15
Nov.	71	47	22	8	6	Nov.	80	65	27	18	8
Dec.	65	43	18	6	8	Dec.	77	59	25	15	7

Average January temperatures
The southern portion of Florida has the warmest temperatures in wintertime. Temperatures steadily decline northward.

Average July temperatures
Florida has a warm summertime climate. Temperatures differ by only a few degrees throughout the state.

Average yearly precipitation
Florida has a rainy climate. The heaviest precipitation falls in the southeast and northwestern portions of the state.

WORLD BOOK maps

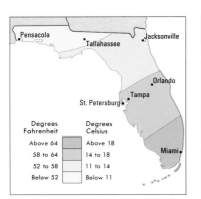

Degrees Fahrenheit	Degrees Celsius
Above 64	Above 18
58 to 64	14 to 18
52 to 58	11 to 14
Below 52	Below 11

Degrees Fahrenheit	Degrees Celsius
Above 83	Above 29
82 to 83	28 to 29
81 to 82	27 to 28
Below 81	Below 27

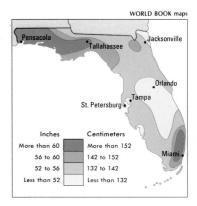

Inches	Centimeters
More than 60	More than 152
56 to 60	142 to 152
52 to 56	132 to 142
Less than 52	Less than 132

lupines, orchids, sunflowers, and such climbing vines as Carolina yellow jasmine, Cherokee rose, morning-glory, and trumpet creeper. Other flowers that grow throughout the state include azaleas, camellias, gardenias, hibiscus, oleanders, and poinsettias. The bougainvillea and the flame vine (also called golden bignonia) brighten many southern Florida gardens. Dogwoods, magnolias, and redbuds flourish in the north.

Black bears, deer, gray foxes, and wildcats live in many parts of the state. Smaller animals, such as opossums, otters, raccoons, and squirrels, are also common. Florida has the largest colonies of anhinga, egrets, herons, ibises, and pelicans north of the Caribbean Sea. Alligators live in the swamps.

More kinds of fishes may be found in Florida's waters than in any other part of the world. The freshwater lakes and rivers are filled with bass, bream, catfish, and crappies. Florida's ocean waters contain bluefish, grouper, mackerel, marlin, menhaden, pompano, red snapper, sailfish, sea trout, and tarpon. Clams, conches, crabs, crayfish, oysters, scallops, and shrimp live in Florida's coastal waters. Mullets are found in salt water and *brackish* (somewhat salty) marshes.

Climate. Most of Florida has a warm, rainy climate similar to that of the other Southern States. Florida's southern tip has a wet and dry tropical climate like that of Central America and large parts of Africa and South America.

Altantic and Gulf breezes relieve some of the summer heat near the coasts. Winters are usually mild, even in northern Florida. July temperatures are much the same in the northern and southern parts of the state. Jacksonville, in the north, has an average July temperature of 81° F. (27° C). Miami, in the south, averages 82° F. (28° C) in July. But in January, Miami averages 67° F. (19° C), and Jacksonville's average temperature drops to 55° F. (13° C). The coastal areas have slightly cooler summers and warmer winters than do inland areas. Destructive frosts rarely occur in southern Florida. But occasional cold waves damage crops as far south as the Everglades. The highest and lowest temperatures ever recorded in Florida occurred within 30 miles (48 kilometers) of each other. Tallahassee recorded the lowest temperature, −2° F. (−19° C), on Feb. 13, 1899. Nearby Monticello recorded the highest temperature, 109° F. (43° C), on June 29, 1931.

Nearly all of Florida's *precipitation* (rain, melted snow, and other forms of moisture) occurs in the form of rain. Florida has an average yearly precipitation of 54 inches (137 centimeters). An average of 32 inches (81 centimeters) falls in the rainy season, which lasts from May to October.

Florida lies along the path of many of the hurricanes that sweep across the Atlantic Ocean every summer and fall. Destructive hurricanes have struck Florida several times.

Economy

Service industries, taken together, account for about four-fifths of Florida's *gross state product*—the total value of all goods and services produced in a state in a year. The state's service industries benefit from spending by the large numbers of retired people and tourists in the state. For example, real estate companies have brought in much income by developing retirement communities and vacation resorts.

Since the 1980's, Florida's economy has been one of the fastest growing in the nation. Companies have been attracted to the state because of its warm climate and low labor costs. Jacksonville and Miami have become important financial centers. The Miami-Fort Lauderdale area, the state's leading manufacturing region, has benefited from the growth of the federal government's defense program. The state also produces equipment for government space programs.

Florida agriculture is famous for growing citrus fruits. About two-thirds of the nation's oranges and grapefruits are produced in the state. Florida also receives much income from the mining of phosphate rock, which is used to make fertilizer.

Natural resources. Florida's natural resources include sandy beaches, a sunny climate, thick forests, and rich phosphate and mineral sands deposits.

Soil. Most of Florida's soils are sandy, especially in the coastal plains. The most fertile soils are in the south, where much rich swampland has been drained and used for farming. The soils of the Florida Uplands are mostly sandy loams and clays.

Minerals. Most of Florida lies on huge beds of limestone, the state's most plentiful mineral. Florida has the

Production and workers by economic activities

Economic activities	Per cent of GSP* produced	Employed workers	
		Number of persons	Per cent of total
Community, social, & personal services	20	1,205,600	26
Wholesale & retail trade	19	1,238,800	27
Finance, insurance, & real estate	19	339,700	7
Government	12	701,900	15
Manufacturing	11	517,200	11
Transportation, communication, & utilities	9	247,400	5
Construction	7	339,500	7
Agriculture	2	102,400	2
Mining	1	9,300	†
Total	**100**	**4,701,800**	**100**

*GSP = gross state product, the total value of goods and services produced in a year.
†Less than one-half of 1 per cent.
Figures are for 1986.
Sources: *World Book* estimates based on data from U.S. Bureau of Economic Analysis, U.S. Bureau of Labor Statistics, and U.S. Department of Agriculture.

largest phosphate deposits in the United States. Most of the state's phosphate comes from mines in west-central Florida. Large stores of peat, sand, gravel, and a valuable clay called *fuller's earth* are found throughout the state. The sandy areas of the state have mineral sands including ilmenite, rutile, and zircon. Brick clays and kaolin, a pottery clay, are found chiefly in Gadsden and Putnam counties. Oil fields lie in Santa Rosa County.

Forests cover about half the state. Florida has more than 360 kinds of trees. Slash pines are the most valuable trees in Florida. The most common hardwood trees are bald cypress, black tupelo, magnolia, oak, and sweet gum. Other common trees include ash, beech, hickory, maple, and yellow pines (loblolly and longleaf). Hardwoods and pines are plentiful in the northern half of the state. Mangrove trees flourish in southern Florida's coastal marshlands.

Service industries provide 79 per cent of Florida's gross state product. Service industries are most important in the state's 20 metropolitan areas.

Community, social, and personal services make up Florida's most important service industry in terms of the gross state product. This industry consists of a variety of businesses, including doctors' offices and private hospitals, law firms, hotels and amusement parks, and repair shops. Many hotels and resorts line the state's coastal areas. Walt Disney World, an amusement park and entertainment complex near Orlando, is one of the nation's leading tourist attractions.

Next in importance among Florida service industries are (1) wholesale and retail trade, and (2) finance, insurance, and real estate. Wholesale and retail trade are the state's leading employer. Wholesale trade consists of buying goods from producers and selling the goods to other businesses. The wholesale trade of petroleum products, citrus fruits, and liquor is important in Florida. Retail trade involves selling goods directly to consumers. Major types of retail businesses include automobile dealerships, food stores, and service stations. Two of the nation's largest food-store chains, Winn-Dixie and Publix, are based in Florida.

Real estate makes up the most important part of the finance, insurance, and real estate industry. Florida's rapid population growth has benefited real estate businesses. Many homes, stores, office buildings, and other properties have been developed. The state's leading financial centers are Jacksonville and Miami. Several major U.S. banking companies are based in these cities. The Tampa-St. Petersburg area is also an important financial center. Investment firms operating in Florida receive much business from retired people.

Government is the state's fourth-ranking service industry. Government services include military activities and public schools and hospitals. The federal government operates the Kennedy Space Center on Cape Canaveral, and the Pensacola Naval Air Station.

Transportation, communication, and utilities rank last among service industries in Florida. Several shipping lines are based in the state. Telephone companies are the most important part of the communications sector. FPL Group of North Palm Beach is Florida's largest utility company. More information about transportation and communication appears later in this section.

Manufacturing accounts for 11 per cent of the gross state product of Florida. Manufactured goods have a *value added by manufacture* of about $23 billion yearly. This figure represents the increase in value of raw materials after they become finished products.

The production of electrical equipment is the leading manufacturing activity in Florida in terms of value added by manufacture. Communication equipment is the most important product of this industry. Communication

Wendell Metzen, Bruce Coleman Inc.

Workers harvest oranges in a southern Florida citrus grove. Oranges are the state's single most valuable crop. Florida produces about two-thirds of the nation's oranges and grapefruits.

equipment includes military communication systems, broadcasting devices, and telephone equipment. The Fort Lauderdale and Tampa areas produce much of the communications equipment. Other electrical equipment made in Florida includes semiconductors and other electronic components, and X ray equipment.

Food products rank second in value. Citrus fruit processing is one of the largest industries in the state. Processing plants, mostly in central Florida, produce fresh citrus fruit juices, canned juices, canned sections of fruit, and citrus by-products. Related industries make jellies and marmalades. Vegetables are quick-frozen, canned, and packaged. Florida factories also process coffee, dairy products, and seafood.

Other products manufactured in Florida, in order of value, include printed materials, transportation equipment, machinery, and chemicals. Newspapers and books are major types of printed materials. Harcourt Brace Jovanovich, one of the world's largest book publishers, is headquartered in Orlando. Aerospace and aircraft equipment are the most important type of transportation equipment made in Florida. Computers are the leading type of machinery manufactured in Florida, and fertilizer is the state's leading chemical product.

Agriculture accounts for 2 per cent of Florida's gross state product. Farmland covers about 13 million acres (5.3 million hectares), about two-fifths of the state's total area. Florida's 40,000 farms average 325 acres (132 hectares) in size.

Crops account for about 80 per cent of Florida's total farm income. Oranges are the state's single most important farm product. Other citrus fruits grown in the state

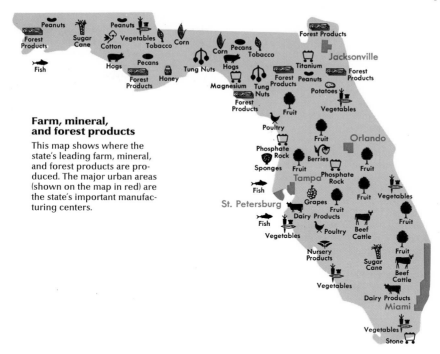

Farm, mineral, and forest products

This map shows where the state's leading farm, mineral, and forest products are produced. The major urban areas (shown on the map in red) are the state's important manufacturing centers.

WORLD BOOK map

include grapefruits, limes, tangerines, tangelos, and temples. The state's chief citrus groves lie in south-central Florida, between Orlando and Lake Okeechobee. Northern Florida is less desirable for citrus farming because of land shortages and cooler winter temperatures. Other fruits grown in the state include bananas, papayas, strawberries, and watermelons.

Tomatoes are Florida's most important vegetable and second leading crop. Most of the tomatoes come from southern Florida, the state's main vegetable-growing region. Other important vegetables produced in Florida include cabbage, celery, cucumbers, green peppers, lettuce, potatoes, snap beans, squashes, and sweet corn. Many northern states rely on Florida for fresh vegetables during cold months.

Sugar cane is another important crop in Florida. The state ranks first in sugar cane production. The Lake Okeechobee region is the center of sugar cane production. Other field crops cultivated in Florida include peanuts, soybeans, and tobacco.

Florida ranks second to California in the production of greenhouse and nursery products. Taken together these products rank as Florida's most important source of agricultural income. Florida ranks first in the production of indoor foliage plants. The state is also a major producer of potted flowers. Most of the greenhouse and nursery products are grown in the metropolitan areas of southern Florida.

Livestock and livestock products account for 20 per cent of Florida's farm income. Beef cattle and milk are the state's major livestock products. The largest cattle-raising regions are in central and south-central Florida. Okeechobee County leads in milk production. Poultry

and egg production is also important. Thoroughbred race horses are raised on farms in Marion County.

Mining provides 1 per cent of the gross state product. Phosphate rock is Florida's most valuable mineral product. The state produces about three-fourths of the nation's phosphate rock. Much of the phosphate rock is used to make fertilizers. Counties around Tampa, and Hamilton County in northern Florida, produce phosphate rock.

Petroleum ranks as the state's second leading mineral product. Santa Rosa County in northwest Florida is the chief source of petroleum. Quarries throughout the state provide limestone for use in road and building construction and in the manufacture of lime and cement. Mines in Gadsden and Marion counties supply fuller's earth, a clay used to filter petroleum. Putnam County produces large amounts of kaolin, a pottery clay. Ilmenite, monazite, thorium, and zircon are taken from sands near the St. Johns River.

Fishing industry. Florida ranks as one of the leading commercial fishing states in terms of the value of its annual fish catch. The state's annual catch is worth about $160 million. Shrimp, lobsters, and scallops are the leading catches, accounting for nearly half the total value. Florida accounts for about 10 per cent of the annual U.S. shrimp catch. The most important commercial fishes include grouper, mackerel, mullet, pompano, and red snapper. Blue and stone crabs, menhaden, oysters, and sharks are also caught in Florida's waters. Factories in Florida process menhaden into fertilizer, oil, and feed for poultry and other farm animals. The waters off Dade, Pinellas, and Monroe counties are major sponge-fishing centers in the United States.

Catfish is the chief catch in the freshwater fishing market. Lake Okeechobee and St. Johns River supply most of the catfish catch.

Electric power. Plants powered by coal, natural gas, or petroleum produce about three-fourths of Florida's electric power. Nuclear plants provide almost all the rest of the power. The state's nuclear plants operate near Crystal River, Florida City, and Fort Pierce.

Transportation. Miami International Airport handles much of the air passenger and air freight travel to and from Latin America. For this reason, Miami is often called the gateway to Latin America. Miami International and the airports at Orlando and Tampa rank among the busiest U.S. airports. Fort Lauderdale, West Palm Beach, and Jacksonville also have major airports.

Seven rail lines provide freight service in the state, and two passenger train lines link about 25 Florida cities to other cities. The state has about 93,000 miles (150,000 kilometers) of roads. Florida's Turnpike links many of the state's major cities. Four major interstate highways also cross Florida.

About 15 deepwater ports in Florida serve as ports of entry into the United States. Tampa is the main port.

Florida has a larger section of the Atlantic Intracoastal Waterway than does any other state. Florida's section of the Gulf Intracoastal Waterway winds along northwestern Florida's Gulf Coast.

Communication. Florida's first newspaper, the *East Florida Gazette,* was established in St. Augustine in 1783. Its publisher, a loyal Englishman named William Charles Wells, used his newspaper to attack Americans for fighting the Revolutionary War against England. He stopped publishing his paper and returned to England after the Spanish regained control of Florida in 1783.

Today the state has about 300 newspapers, of which about 50 are dailies. The oldest newspaper in existence is the *Florida Times-Union,* published daily in Jacksonville. It was established in 1864. Other newspapers include the Fort Lauderdale *Sun-Sentinel, Miami Herald, Orlando Sentinel, Sarasota Herald-Tribune, St. Petersburg Times, Tampa Tribune,* and the *Palm Beach Post* of West Palm Beach. Florida's first radio station, WQAM in Miami, went on the air in 1921. The first television station in Florida, WTVJ of Miami, began broadcasting in 1949. The state has about 300 radio stations and about 90 television stations.

Government

Constitution of Florida went into effect in 1969. Earlier constitutions went into effect in 1839 (before Florida became a state), 1861, 1865, 1868, and 1887.

Constitutional *amendments* (changes) must be approved by a majority of people voting on them in a general or special election. Amendments may be proposed by the Legislature. Three-fifths of each legislative house must approve the proposed amendment. Citizens also may propose amendments through the *initiative* process by presenting a petition signed by a specified number of voters. The people may also petition to call a constitutional convention. The petition must then be approved by the voters.

Executive. Florida's governor serves a four-year term and can serve more than one term, but not more than two terms in a row. Candidates for governor and lieutenant governor run as a team. Voters cast one vote for the governor and lieutenant governor.

The governor of Florida appoints the state's public service commissioners and many of its judges. Members of the Cabinet are elected to four-year terms, and may be reelected. The Cabinet consists of the attorney general, commissioner of agriculture, comptroller, secretary of state, commissioner of education, and treasurer-insurance commissioner.

Legislature consists of a 40-member Senate and a 120-member House of Representatives. Senators serve four-year terms, and representatives serve two-year terms. The Legislature's regular 60-day session opens on the first Tuesday after the first Monday in April each year. Special sessions of the Legislature may be called by the governor, by joint agreement of the leaders of each legislative house, or by a three-fifths vote of all members of the Legislature. Regular or special sessions may be extended by a three-fifths vote of each house.

In 1965, a federal court ordered Florida to *reapportion* (redivide) its Legislature to provide equal represen-

The governors of Florida

	Party	Term
William D. Moseley	Democratic	1845-1849
Thomas Brown	Whig	1849-1853
James E. Broome	Democratic	1853-1857
Madison S. Perry	Democratic	1857-1861
John Milton	Democratic	1861-1865
Abraham K. Allison	Democratic	1865
William Marvin	None	1865-1866
David S. Walker	Conservative	1866-1868
Harrison Reed	Republican	1868-1873
Ossian B. Hart	Republican	1873-1874
Marcellus L. Stearns	Republican	1874-1877
George F. Drew	Democratic	1877-1881
William D. Bloxham	Democratic	1881-1885
Edward A. Perry	Democratic	1885-1889
Francis P. Fleming	Democratic	1889-1893
Henry L. Mitchell	Democratic	1893-1897
William D. Bloxham	Democratic	1897-1901
William S. Jennings	Democratic	1901-1905
Napoleon B. Broward	Democratic	1905-1909
Albert W. Gilchrist	Democratic	1909-1913
Park Trammell	Democratic	1913-1917
Sidney J. Catts	Prohibition	1917-1921
Cary A. Hardee	Democratic	1921-1925
John W. Martin	Democratic	1925-1929
Doyle E. Carlton	Democratic	1929-1933
David Sholtz	Democratic	1933-1937
Fred P. Cone	Democratic	1937-1941
Spessard L. Holland	Democratic	1941-1945
Millard F. Caldwell	Democratic	1945-1949
Fuller Warren	Democratic	1949-1953
Daniel T. McCarty	Democratic	1953
Charley E. Johns	Democratic	1953-1955
LeRoy Collins	Democratic	1955-1961
C. Farris Bryant	Democratic	1961-1965
W. Haydon Burns	Democratic	1965-1967
Claude R. Kirk, Jr.	Republican	1967-1971
Reubin O'D. Askew	Democratic	1971-1979
Robert D. Graham	Democratic	1979-1987
Bob Martinez	Republican	1987-

The Florida Senate meets in the State Capitol in Tallahassee. The 40 members are elected to four-year terms.

Florida Division of Tourism

tation based on population. The Legislature drew up a reapportionment plan, but the Supreme Court of the United States ruled it unconstitutional. In 1967, a federal court devised its own reapportionment plan. Since 1969, the state Constitution has required that the Legislature be reapportioned every 10 years, after each federal census.

Courts. The Florida Supreme Court has seven justices, all appointed by the governor to six-year terms. The justices elect one of their members chief justice every year. Florida has five district courts of appeals. The governor appoints judges of these courts to six-year terms. In making judicial appointments, the governor chooses from among candidates selected by judicial nominating committees. Florida has 20 circuit courts and 67 county courts. Circuit court judges are elected to six-year terms, and county court judges to four-year terms.

Local government. Florida's 67 counties can vary their form of government by adopting special county charters approved by the Legislature and the people of the county. Most of the counties are governed by a board of five commissioners and are divided into five districts. County voters elect a resident from each district to serve on the county commission. Other elected county officers include the circuit court clerk, sheriff, supervisor of elections, tax assessor, and tax collector. County officials serve four-year terms.

Chartered counties and municipalities have *home rule* (self-government) to the extent that they may make laws. Counties and municipalities also have the power to *consolidate* (combine) and work as a single government. Forms of municipal government include mayor-council, mayor-commission, and commission-manager.

Revenue. Taxation provides about 70 per cent of the state government's *general revenue* (income). Most of the rest comes from federal grants and other U.S. government programs. A general sales tax accounts for more than half of the tax revenue. Other major sources of revenue include charges for government services, and taxes on motor fuels and investment transactions.

Politics. Since the Reconstruction period ended in 1877, all but three of Florida's governors have been Democrats (see **Reconstruction**). From Reconstruction through 1948, Democratic presidential candidates won the state's electoral votes every time except in 1928. Since the 1952 election, Republican candidates have won every time except in 1964 and 1976. For Florida's voting record in presidential elections, see **Electoral College** (table).

History

Indian days. Burial mounds found along Florida's western coast show that Indians lived in the region at least as long as 10,000 years ago. About 10,000 Indians lived in the Florida region when Europeans first reached its shores. The Indians belonged to at least five chief tribes. The Calusa and the Tequesta in the south and the Ais on the Atlantic coast of the central part of the peninsula hunted and fished for a living. The Timucua in the central and northeast regions and the Apalachee in the northwest were farmers and hunters.

Exploration and Spanish settlement. Legends of a fountain of youth brought the Spanish explorer Juan Ponce de León to the Florida peninsula in 1513. Ponce de León claimed the region for Spain and named it *Florida,* perhaps for the many flowers he saw there. The word *florida* in Spanish means *full of flowers.* He re-

turned to Florida in 1521 to start a colony but was severely wounded in a battle with Indians. He and his followers fled, and Ponce de León soon died.

In 1528, a Spaniard named Pánfilo de Narváez led an expedition of about 400 men to Florida's southwestern coast. He traveled northward searching for gold. But shipwrecks killed Narváez and many of his men. Another Spaniard, Hernando de Soto, landed an expedition in the Tampa Bay area in 1539. He led his men beyond the Florida region and in 1541 became the first European to reach the Mississippi River.

In 1564, a group of *Huguenots* (French Protestants) established a colony on the St. Johns River. They built Fort Caroline near what is now Jacksonville. King Philip II of Spain sent a sea captain named Pedro Menéndez de Avilés to drive the French from Florida. Menéndez and

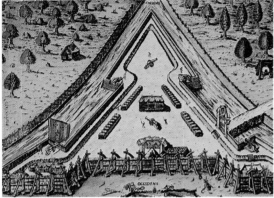

Engraving (1591) by Théodore de Bry from an illustration
by Jacques Le Moyne (Granger Collection)

Fort Caroline was built by *Huguenots* (French Protestants) in 1564 near the site of present-day Jacksonville. Spanish forces drove the French out of the Florida region in 1565.

his men arrived in Florida in 1565. They founded St. Augustine, the first permanent European settlement in what is now the United States. They massacred the French forces and ended French attempts to settle in eastern Florida.

The Spaniards spent much of the next 200 years trying to teach their way of life to the Florida Indians. Meanwhile, English colonists established settlements to the north of Florida, and France started colonies to the west. In the mid-1700's, wars broke out between the colonists of Great Britain and France. Spain sided with France. In 1762, British forces captured Cuba. In 1763, Spain gave Florida to Britain in exchange for Cuba.

The British period. Britain divided the Florida region into two separate colonies—East Florida and West Florida. West Florida included the part of the region west of the Apalachicola River. It also included parts of what are now Alabama, Mississippi, and Louisiana. East Florida included the rest of the Florida region. British control of Florida lasted until Spanish forces marched into West Florida in 1779, during the Revolutionary War in America (1775-1783). The British, already weakened by war, surrendered West Florida to Spain in 1781. Spain regained control of all Florida in 1783.

The second Spanish period lasted until 1821. In the early 1800's, Florida was the only part of southeastern North America that did not belong to the United States. Runaway slaves and prisoners and thieving Indians took refuge in the Florida region. Florida settlers fought their Spanish rulers, but Spain refused to sell Florida to the United States. In 1812, a group of eastern Florida settlers rebelled and declared their independence from Spain. But the Spaniards stopped the rebels. During the War of 1812 (1812-1815), Spain let Britain use Pensacola as a naval base. In 1814, American troops led by General Andrew Jackson stormed into Florida and seized Pensacola. During the First Seminole War (1816-1818), Jackson captured Fort St. Marks on the Gulf of Mexico. He then defeated the Seminole Indians. Finally, in the Adams-Onís Treaty of 1819, Spain agreed to turn Florida over to the United States. The United States did not actually pay any money to Spain for Florida. However, it agreed to

pay $5 million to American citizens for property damages.

Territorial days. Florida formally came under U.S. control in 1821. Andrew Jackson served as temporary governor until 1822, when Congress organized the Territory of Florida, and William P. Duval became the first territorial governor.

Thousands of American settlers poured into Florida. One of the major problems they faced was finding enough land for settlement. Seminole Indians lived in some of the territory's richest farmland. The U.S. government offered land in the Oklahoma region to the Seminole if they would leave Florida territory. Some of the Seminole accepted the offer, but others refused to leave their homes. In the Second Seminole War (1835-1842), most of the band was wiped out. This war and the Third Seminole War (1855-1858) resulted in the forced resettlement of more Seminole, but a few hundred of the band fled into the swamps and remained in Florida.

Statehood. In 1839, Florida drew up a constitution in preparation for statehood, but it had to wait for admission to the Union. Florida would be a slave state, and Congress wanted to maintain a balance between slave and free states. Florida was admitted to the Union as a slave state on March 3, 1845. The following year, Iowa was admitted as a free state. Florida had a population of about 66,500 when it entered the Union. Most of the state's farms were small, and about two-thirds of the farmers did not own slaves.

The Civil War and Reconstruction. In 1860, Abraham Lincoln was elected President. Florida and the other slave states regarded Lincoln as a threat to their way of life. On Jan. 10, 1861, Florida *seceded* (withdrew) from the Union and later joined the Confederacy.

Union forces captured most of Florida's coastal towns early in the Civil War (1861-1865). But Confederate forces won the Battle of Olustee on Feb. 20, 1864, thereby keeping control of the interior region. This region's farmers shipped cattle and hogs to the rest of the Confederacy. In March 1865, a small band of Confederate troops, helped by young boys and old men, successfully defended Tallahassee against Union forces. Tallahassee and Austin, Tex., were the only Confederate state capitals that federal troops did not capture.

During the Reconstruction period after the Civil War, Florida and the other Confederate states came under federal military rule. The defeated states had to meet certain requirements before they could be readmitted to the Union. Florida abolished slavery, but it refused to accept some of the other requirements. Republicans gained control of the Florida state government in 1868. The legislature ratified the 14th Amendment to the Constitution of the United States—guaranteeing civil rights—and, on June 25, 1868, Florida was readmitted to the Union.

Progress as a state. Florida developed rapidly during the 1880's. Geologists discovered large phosphate deposits. The state government and private investors began to drain the swamplands. Railroad lines built by tycoons Henry M. Flagler and Henry B. Plant led to the opening of new land for development. Citrus groves were planted in north-central Florida. Resort cities sprang up. People and money from Northern States poured into Florida.

Historic Florida

Juan Ponce de León of Spain landed on the Florida coast in 1513. He explored parts of the region in his search for the legendary fountain of youth. Ponce de León claimed the region for Spain.

The United States obtained Florida from Spain by the Adams-Onís Treaty of 1819. As part of the treaty, the United States agreed to pay $5 million in claims U.S. citizens made against Spain.

The Battle of Olustee on Feb. 20, 1864, was the most important Civil War battle fought in Florida. Confederate forces won the battle.

The citrus fruit industry began to develop in south-central Florida in the 1890's.

Explorer I, the first United States artificial satellite, was launched on Jan. 31, 1958, from Cape Canaveral.

Apollo 11, the first spacecraft to land astronauts on the moon, lifted off from Cape Canaveral (then called Cape Kennedy) on July 16, 1969.

Important dates in Florida

WORLD BOOK illustrations by Kevin Chadwick

1513	Juan Ponce de León landed on the Florida coast and claimed the region for Spain.
1528	Pánfilo de Narváez led an expedition into Florida.
1539	Hernando de Soto led an expedition through Florida.
1564	French Huguenot settlers built Fort Caroline on the St. Johns River.
1565	Pedro Menéndez de Avilés founded St. Augustine.
1763	Spain ceded Florida to England.
1783	Spain regained control of Florida.
1819	The U.S. obtained Florida from Spain.
1821	Florida formally came under U.S. control.
1822	Congress established the Territory of Florida.
1835	The Second Seminole War began. Most of the Seminole were wiped out during the war.
1845	Florida became the 27th state on March 3.
1861	Florida seceded from the Union and joined the Confederacy.
1868	Florida was readmitted to the Union on June 25.

1896	Henry M. Flagler's Florida East Coast Railroad reached Miami.
1906	The project of draining the Everglades started at Fort Lauderdale.
1920-1925	Land speculators poured into the state. The population increased at a tremendous rate.
1958	The country's first earth satellite, *Explorer I,* was launched on January 31 from Cape Canaveral.
1961	The first U.S. manned space flights were launched from Cape Canaveral.
1969	Florida adopted a new constitution.
1969	*Apollo 11,* the first spacecraft to land men on the moon, was launched from Cape Canaveral (then called Cape Kennedy) on July 16.
1971	The Walt Disney World entertainment complex opened near Orlando.
1977	A new state capitol was completed in Tallahassee.
1983-1985	Many of central Florida's citrus groves were destroyed by freezing weather and disease.

A severe freeze during the winter of 1894-1895 damaged much of the state's citrus crops. Citrus growers planted new groves in the south-central part of the state. This move led to the development of southern Florida. In 1896, Flagler extended his Florida East Coast Railroad line south to Miami.

The early 1900's. In 1906, the state began draining the swampland near Fort Lauderdale. This development opened up new land for farms and resorts.

Reports of fantastic profits to be made in Florida real estate swept the country. Hundreds of thousands of land speculators flocked to the state. Florida's population grew at an enormous rate. Seven new counties were formed in 1921. By 1925, Florida's economy had become a swelling bubble of progress and prosperity.

The bubble burst in 1926, when a severe depression hit Florida. Banks closed. Wealthy people suddenly lost their money. Two destructive hurricanes struck Florida's Atlantic coast in 1926 and 1928, killing hundreds of people. The state had partly recovered from these disasters by the late 1920's. Then, in 1929, the Great Depression struck the United States.

Federal and state welfare measures helped the people of Florida fight the depression. The state created jobs to develop its natural resources. The construction of paper mills by private industries led to forest conservation programs. Cooling plants were built to preserve perishable fruits and vegetables. Farmers established cooperative farm groups and cooperative markets. The state suffered setbacks in 1935 and in 1941, when severe hurricanes swept across southern Florida.

The mid-1900's. Florida's location along the Atlantic Ocean and near the Panama Canal made the state vital to the defense of the Western Hemisphere during World War II (1939-1945). Land, sea, and air bases were established in many parts of the state.

After the war, Florida's population grew rapidly. Tourism boomed and remained the state's leading source of income. But industrial expansion helped give Florida a more balanced economy. Development of industries in such fields as chemicals, electronics, paper and paper products, and ocean and space exploration provided jobs for Florida's swelling labor force.

In the 1950's, Cape Canaveral became a space and rocket center. The United States launched its first satellite from Cape Canaveral in 1958, its first manned space flights in 1961, and its first manned spaceship to the moon in 1969.

In the early 1960's, Cuba fell under Communist control. Many Cubans who opposed the Communists fled to Florida, settling mainly in Miami and Hialeah.

Like many other states, Florida faced serious racial problems during the 1950's and 1960's. In 1954, the Supreme Court of the United States ruled that compulsory segregation in public schools was unconstitutional. The Florida Constitution at that time did not permit black children and white children to attend the same schools. Integration of the state's public schools began in Dade County in 1959. By the late 1960's, every county had integrated all or most of its public schools.

In the 1960's, Florida began an ambitious program to expand its facilities for higher education. This program was partly designed to serve the future demands for personnel in the oceanographic and aerospace indus-

NASA

A space shuttle is transported to the launch facility at Cape Canaveral. The space shuttle *Columbia,* the first reusable manned spacecraft, was launched from Cape Canaveral in 1981.

tries. During the 1960's, 4 new universities, several new private colleges, and 13 new public junior colleges were established in Florida. Two other state universities opened in the early 1970's.

Recent developments. Florida grew rapidly during the 1970's and 1980's. In 1971, the Walt Disney World entertainment center opened near Orlando. Since then, the Orlando area has been the fastest growing region of the state. Other booming areas included the suburbs of Miami, Tampa, Jacksonville, Fort Lauderdale, and West Palm Beach. From 1980 to 1985, Florida's population increased by 16 per cent. By the mid-1980's, about 1,000 new residents were entering Florida each day. In 1977, a new state capitol was completed in Tallahassee. The building rises 22 stories.

During the first half of the 1980's, the number of jobs in Florida rose by 24 per cent. Many of these jobs were in electronics manufacturing and skilled services. Florida's economy continues to rely on tourism and the citrus industry. But the expansion of trade, financial, and other service industries has greatly strengthened the state's prospects for stable growth.

Florida's spectacular growth, however, has also brought problems. The increasing population requires more homes, roads, schools, sewage and water treatment plants, and health and social services. Since 1980, more than 100,000 Cuban and Haitian refugees have settled in Florida. Many of these people are poor and have few job skills, and so they cause increased demands upon social service agencies.

Uncontrolled development has also led to growing

concern for protecting and improving Florida's environment. During the 1970's, protests led to the cancellation of work on a jetport near the Everglades and a canal across northern Florida. Conservationists argued that these projects would endanger wildlife and destroy much natural beauty. In the 1960's, a canal was built to shorten the course of the Kissimmee River, which empties into Lake Okeechobee. By the mid-1980's, excess nutrients carried by the canal were causing *algae* (simple plantlike organisms) in the lake to thrive. This situation threatened other forms of life in Lake Okeechobee. In 1983, the state decided to return the Kissimmee River to its former course.

From 1983 through 1985, Florida's citrus industry suffered serious setbacks. Freezing weather and a fungal disease called *citrus canker* destroyed many of central Florida's citrus groves.

Arch Fredric Blakey and Peter O. Muller

Study aids

Related articles in *World Book* include:

Biographies

Bethune, Mary M.	Osceola
De Soto, Hernando	Ponce de León, Juan
Gorrie, John	Rawlings, Marjorie Kinnan
Mallory, Stephen R.	Smith, Edmund Kirby
Narváez, Pánfilo de	

Cities

Daytona Beach	Pensacola
Fort Lauderdale	Saint Augustine
Jacksonville	Saint Petersburg
Key West	Tallahassee
Miami	Tampa
Miami Beach	
Orlando	

History

Adams-Onís Treaty	Fort Pickens
Confederate States of America	Fountain of Youth
Electoral Commission	Seminole Indians

National parks and monuments

Biscayne National Park
Castillo de San Marcos National Monument
Everglades National Park
Fort Jefferson National Monument
Fort Matanzas National Monument

Physical features

Dry Tortugas	Lake Okeechobee
Everglades	Okefenokee Swamp
Florida Keys	Suwannee River
Gulf of Mexico	

Other related articles

Atlantic Intracoastal Waterway
Cape Canaveral
Cypress Gardens
Gulf Intracoastal Waterway
Patrick Air Force Base
Pensacola Naval Air Station
Singing Tower

Outline

I. People
  A. Population
  B. Schools
  C. Libraries
  D. Museums
II. Visitor's guide
  A. Places to visit
  B. Annual events
III. Land and climate
  A. Land regions
  B. Coastline
  C. Rivers, lakes, and springs
  D. Plant and animal life
  E. Climate
IV. Economy
  A. Natural resources
  B. Service industries
  C. Manufacturing
  D. Agriculture
  E. Mining
  F. Fishing industry
  G. Electric power
  H. Transportation
  I. Communication
V. Government
  A. Constitution
  B. Executive
  C. Legislature
  D. Courts
  E. Local government
  F. Revenue
  G. Politics
VI. History

Questions

How did Florida get its name?
What are the Florida Keys? The Everglades?
What event of 1894-1895 led to the development of southern Florida?
What is Florida's most important economic activity?
Why did Spain give Florida to Great Britain?
When was the Battle of Olustee fought?
Why did the state of Florida decide to return the Kissimmee River to its former course?
What is Florida's most plentiful mineral?
What major problems does Florida face because of its growing population?
What is Florida's leading farm product?

Additional resources

Level I
Carpenter, Allan. *Florida.* Rev. ed. Childrens Press, 1979.
Fichter, George S. *Florida in Pictures.* Sterling Publishing, 1979.
Fradin, Dennis B. *Florida in Words and Pictures.* Childrens Press, 1980.
Meltzer, Milton. *Hunted like a Wolf: The Story of the Seminole War.* Farrar, 1972.

Level II
Atlas of Florida. Ed. by Edward A. Fernald. Florida State University Foundation, 1981.
Blake, Nelson M. *Land into Water—Water into Land: A History of Water Management in Florida.* Univ. Presses of Florida, 1980.
The Florida Almanac. Ed. by Del and M. J. Marth. Pelican Pub. Co. Revised editions published frequently.
Gannon, Michael V. *The Cross in the Sand: The Early Catholic Church in Florida, 1513-1870.* 2nd ed. Univ. Presses of Florida, 1983.
Jahoda, Gloria. *Florida: A Bicentennial History.* Norton, 1976.
Milanich, Jerald T., and Fairbanks, C. H. *Florida Archaeology.* Harcourt, 1980.
Nolan, David. *Fifty Feet in Paradise: The Booming of Florida.* Harcourt, 1984. Popular economic history.
Peters, Virginia B. *The Florida Wars.* Shoe String, 1979. The Seminole Wars of the early 1800's.
Shofner, Jerrell H. *Nor Is It Over Yet: Florida in the Era of Reconstruction, 1863-1877.* Univ. Presses of Florida, 1974.
Tebeau, Charlton W. *A History of Florida.* Univ. of Miami Press, 1981. First published in 1971.

Florida, Straits of, is a channel at the southern tip of Florida. It connects the Gulf of Mexico with the Atlantic Ocean, and is sometimes called the Gulf of Florida. It was first called the New Bahama Channel. The Straits of Florida separates southeast Florida and the Florida Keys from the Bahamas on the east and from Cuba on the south. The Gulf Stream passes through the Straits of Florida, which is 300 miles (480 kilometers) long and from 50 to 150 miles (80 to 240 kilometers) wide. The main part of the channel has depths of 6,000 feet (1,800 meters). The eastern half of the straits includes the shallow waters of the Great Bahama Bank.   Peter O. Muller

Florida, University of, is a combined state and land-grant university in Gainesville, Fla. Founded in 1853, it is the state's oldest and largest university. It offers programs in accounting, agriculture, architecture, arts and sciences, building construction, business administration, education, engineering, fine arts, forest resources and conservation, journalism and communications, law, and many other fields. The university's Health Center includes colleges of dentistry, health-related professions, medicine, nursing, pharmacy, and veterinary medicine. Courses lead to bachelor's, master's, and doctor's degrees. The university also operates the Florida State Museum and several research centers. For enrollment, see **Universities and colleges** (table).

Critically reviewed by the University of Florida

Florida Keys are a group of small islands or reefs that stretch in a curved line about 150 miles (241 kilometers) long from Biscayne Bay at Miami southwest into the Gulf of Mexico. The word *keys* comes from the Spanish word *cayos,* which means *small islands.* The Florida Keys are remarkable examples of coral formation. They attract a large tourist trade. Industries include sponge and cigar manufacturing, and commercial and sport fishing. Key West, farthest from the mainland, has the most important harbor. It is joined to the mainland by U.S. Route 1, an overseas highway 128 miles (206 kilometers) long. See also **Florida** (physical map; picture: The Florida Keys); **Key West.**   Peter O. Muller

Florida Memorial College is a coeducational liberal arts school in Miami, Fla. It is affiliated with the Baptist Church. Courses lead to the bachelor's degree. The school was founded in 1879. For enrollment, see **Universities and colleges** (table).

Critically reviewed by Florida Memorial College

Florida Southern College is a coeducational liberal arts school at Lakeland, Fla. It is affiliated with the United Methodist Church, but admits students of all faiths. It has a school of music, a citrus department, and a program in international business. Many of the buildings on the campus were designed by Frank Lloyd Wright. The college is said to have the world's largest concentration of Wright's architecture. The college was chartered in 1885. For enrollment, see **Universities and colleges** (table).   Critically reviewed by Florida Southern College

See also **Florida** (picture: Florida Southern College).

Florida State University is a state-controlled coeducational school in Tallahassee, Fla. It offers programs in the arts and sciences, business, communication, criminology, education, engineering, graduate studies, home economics, law, library science, music, nursing, social sciences, social work, theater, and visual arts. The university grants bachelor's, master's, and doctor's degrees.

The school was founded in 1851. For enrollment, see **Universities and colleges** (table).

Critically reviewed by Florida State University

Florin, *FLAWR uhn,* is a type of coin first made in the Italian city of Florence in 1252. Made of pure gold, the florin weighed about an eighth of an ounce (3.5 grams). Florins became popular for trade during the economic expansion of Europe from the 1200's to the 1400's. The coin's name comes from an Italian word meaning *little flower.* It refers to a lily, the symbol of Florence. A lily appears on one side of the coin. The other side has a figure of Saint John the Baptist, the guardian saint of Florence. Many European countries produced similar versions of the Florentine florin.

Florence stopped making florins in the early 1500's. In 1849, Great Britain issued its first silver florin. This coin was valued at a tenth of a pound. In 1971, Britain adopted a florin worth 10 new pence. The Netherlands also used silver florins.   R. G. Doty

Florissant Fossil Beds National Monument, *FLAWR uh suhnt,* is near Florissant, Colo. It features fossil insects, leaves, seeds, and stumps that date back about 35 million years. Congress authorized the monument in 1969. For the area of Florissant Fossil Beds National Monument, see **National Park System** (table: National monuments). For the location of the monument, see **Colorado** (political map).

Critically reviewed by the National Park Service

Florist is a merchant who sells cut flowers and potted plants. A florist may also sell plant bulbs and seeds, potting soil, and various plant care products. Most florists employ a *floral designer,* who is specially trained in the art of arranging flowers. Others prepare floral arrangements themselves.

In the majority of florist shops, the flowers and plants come from commercial greenhouses and nurseries. However, some florists have gardens or greenhouses in which they grow many or all of the plants they sell. Customers may buy flowers or plants at the shop or call the florist and order flowers to be delivered. Many florists belong to one or more wire service associations that

WORLD BOOK photo

A florist's shop, such as the one shown above, features colorful displays of potted plants and cut flowers. A florist helps customers choose plants and flowers for various occasions.

In making a corsage, a florist uses a variety of tools and materials. The corsage shown above will consist of an orchid and such materials as ribbon, tape, and artificial leaves.

form a pool of florists in various cities throughout the United States. If a florist belonging to such an association receives an order for a delivery in another city, he or she sends the order to a member florist in that city. The order for a delivery may be transmitted either by telephone or by computer.

Special training is not required for a career as a florist. Many people prepare to become florists by studying *floriculture,* the science of growing and caring for ornamental plants. Courses that teach sales techniques and store management are also helpful. Some schools offer courses in floriculture. In addition, many florist shops have apprenticeship programs.

William Gregory Carmichael

See also **Floriculture; Flower; Greenhouse.**

Flotation process, *floh TAY shuhn,* is used to separate valuable minerals from each other or from other minerals with which they are mixed. In this process, the material that contains the minerals is first crushed and ground fine. It is then put into a tank called a *flotation cell* that contains water and certain chemicals called *flotation reagents.* These chemicals form a water-repellent film around the particles of one of the minerals, but not around the others.

To separate the minerals, the liquid in the flotation cell is stirred and air is piped in. Air bubbles cling to the water-repellent particles, causing them to rise to the top and float. For collection, the bubbles carrying the minerals must be trapped in a froth on the surface. A frothing agent, such as pine oil or eucalyptus oil, is added to create the froth. The froth with the mineral-laden bubbles can then be skimmed off. The other minerals or materials remain in the liquid. William Hustrulid

See also **Copper** (Milling).

Flotsam, *FLAHT suhm,* **jetsam,** *JEHT suhm,* **and lagan,** *LAG uhn,* are terms used to describe goods in the sea. Goods found floating in the sea are called *flotsam.* The term includes both goods cast from a vessel in distress and goods that float when a ship sinks. *Jetsam* is goods voluntarily cast overboard in an emergency, usually to lighten the vessel. Jetsam sinks and remains under water. *Lagan,* or *ligan,* is cargo which someone has sunk with the definite intention of recovering it later.

The person usually ties a buoy to lagan to mark its location.

Flotsam, jetsam, and lagan are not abandoned or derelict property. That is, the owner or master of the ship does not intend to give up the goods permanently. The owner intends to recover the goods at some later date. Under the maritime law, flotsam, jetsam, and lagan remain the property of their original owner, no matter how long they lie in the sea. The finder may only hold them for salvage, which is a legal reward the owner pays to the finder. Many courts rule that the owner must claim the goods within a year after someone else has recovered them. George P. Smith II

See also **Salvage.**

Flounder is the name of a group of saltwater flatfishes. Flounders live on the sandy and muddy bottoms of bays and along the shores of most seas. There are about 300 different types of flounders. The *winter flounder,* or *blackback,* can be found from Labrador to Cape Hatteras, and is an important food fish. The *summer flounder,* a popular game fish, ranges from Cape Cod to Florida. It also is known as the *fluke* or the *plaice.*

The flounder has a greatly compressed body with both eyes on the same side of the head. The side of the flounder facing up takes on the color of the bottom of the sea where the fish lives. The side toward the bottom is nearly white. When the flounder first hatches, it looks like a typical fish. After it grows to be about $\frac{1}{2}$ inch (13 millimeters) long, the body becomes flattened, and both eyes appear on one side of the head. The side of the head on which the eyes appear depends on the *species,* or kind, of flounder. Flounders have markings that blend with their surroundings. The fish can lie camouflaged on the bottom of the ocean. This makes it easier for them to catch the shrimp and small fish that form their basic diet. The dab, halibut, and European turbot belong to the flounder group. Flounders are also closely related to soles (see **Sole**).

Scientific classification. Flounders belong to the families Bothidae and Pleuronectidae. The winter flounder is *Pseudopleuronectes americanus.* The summer flounder is *Paralichthys dentatus.* David W. Greenfield

See also **Flatfish; Halibut; Turbot; Fish** (picture: A flounder).

The flounder is a saltwater flatfish. The starry flounder, *above,* is a popular game fish along the California coast. This fish can be identified by the colored bands on its fins. Its body is covered with sharp, thornlike spines in its skin.

Flour is a powdery food made by grinding grain. Most flour is made from wheat and is used to bake bread. Other cereal grains that are ground into flour include barley, corn, millet, oats, rice, and rye. Flour is the basic ingredient of such foods as cakes, cookies, crackers, macaroni, and pancakes.

Bread ranks as the world's most widely eaten food, and people in many countries receive more than half their nourishment from foods made with flour. Each person in the United States eats an average of about 120 pounds (54 kilograms) of flour from wheat and other grains annually. Canadians eat an average of about 135 pounds (61 kilograms) of flour per person each year.

By the 9000's B.C., prehistoric people were grinding crude flour from wild grain by crushing the grain between rocks. Later, the ancient Greeks and Romans used water wheels to power flour mills.

Types of flour. White flour made from wheat accounts for more than 90 per cent of the flour produced in the United States. There are three main types of white wheat flour: (1) bread flour, (2) cake flour, and (3) all-purpose flour. Bread flour is milled chiefly for commercial bakeries, though it is available in retail stores in some areas. Cake flour is made for commercial and home baking. All-purpose flour is used mainly at home.

The three types of flour differ primarily in their protein content. Bread flour contains at least 11 per cent protein, and cake flour contains less than $8\frac{1}{2}$ per cent protein. All-purpose flour, which is a blend of bread flour and cake flour, has a protein content of about $10\frac{1}{2}$ per cent.

When the protein in wheat flour is moistened in dough, it forms a sticky substance called *gluten*. Bread flour dough has strong gluten, cake flour dough has weak gluten, and all-purpose flour dough has a blend of strong and weak glutens. Strong gluten works well with yeast to *leaven* bread, or make it rise. Weak gluten produces tender, crumbly baked goods, but it results in poor yeast-leavened bread. Therefore, bakers use bread flour for breads and use cake flour for pastries. All-purpose flour is used for such foods as cakes, cookies, rolls, and homemade bread, and in sauces.

Bread flour is sometimes called *strong flour* because it forms strong gluten. This kind of flour is also known as *hard-wheat flour* because it comes from varieties of wheat that have hard kernels. Millers call cake flour *weak flour* because it forms weak gluten, or *soft-wheat flour* because it is produced from wheat that has soft kernels.

The term *specialty flours* is used for types of flour

How flour is milled

WORLD BOOK diagram

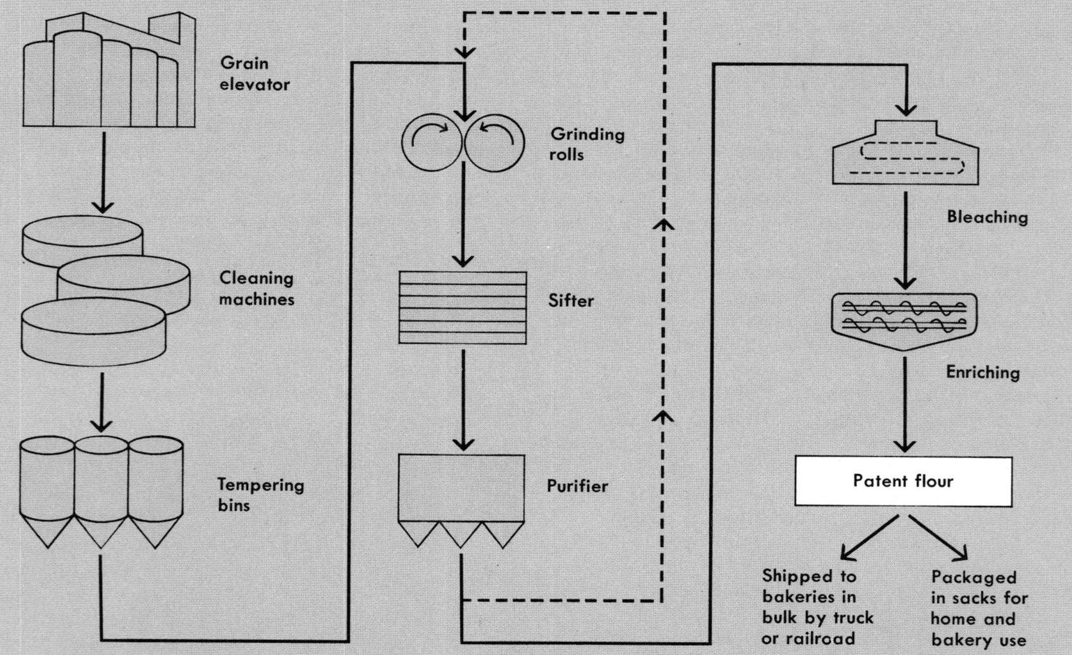

Grain elevator

Grinding rolls

Bleaching

Cleaning machines

Sifter

Enriching

Tempering bins

Purifier

Patent flour

Shipped to bakeries in bulk by truck or railroad

Packaged in sacks for home and bakery use

Preparing the wheat for milling involves cleaning and *tempering* (moistening) the kernels. Wheat consists of a covering called the *bran,* an inner part called the *endosperm,* and a tiny new plant called the *germ.*

Grinding the wheat breaks up the kernels. Sifters and purifiers then separate the endosperm from the bran and the germ. The endosperm is repeatedly ground, sifted, and purified until it forms flour.

Bleaching and enriching whitens the flour and adds iron and vitamins. This high-quality flour, called *patent flour,* is loaded into trucks or railroad cars, or packaged in sacks. Mills sell it to bakeries and groceries.

Department of Cereal Science & Food Technology, North Dakota State University

Chemists test samples of bread made from flour from different varieties of wheat. Seeds from the varieties that produce high-quality bread are distributed to farmers for planting.

other than white wheat flour. They include rye flour, whole-wheat flour, and *mixes*. Mixes consist of flour and other ingredients used to make various foods, such as cakes and pancakes.

How white flour is milled. Wheat kernels form the raw material for flour. They consist of a tough covering called the *bran,* a mellow inner part called the *endosperm,* and a tiny new wheat plant called the *germ*. To make white flour, millers separate the endosperm from the bran and germ and then grind the endosperm into flour.

Various cleaning machines first remove dirt, straw, and other impurities from the grain. Next, the wheat is *tempered* (moistened). The moisture makes the endosperm more mellow and the bran tougher.

The tempered wheat passes between a series of rough steel rollers that crush the endosperm into chunks. Pieces of bran and germ cling to the chunks of endosperm or form separate flakes. Then the crushed grain is sifted. The tiniest bits of endosperm, which have become flour, pass through the sifter into a bin. Larger particles collect in the sifter. Next, these larger particles are put into a machine called a *purifier*. There, currents of air blow flakes of bran away from the endosperm particles. The endosperm particles are then repeatedly ground between smooth rollers, sifted, and purified until they form flour. In most mills, about 72 per cent of the wheat eventually becomes flour. The rest is sold chiefly as livestock feed.

Newly milled flour is cream-colored, but some mills

bleach it to make it white. They may also add chemicals that strengthen the gluten. Some chemicals both bleach the flour and strengthen the gluten. Such treatments must be carefully controlled because the addition of too much of a chemical ruins the flour.

Wheat is rich in starch, protein, B vitamins, and such minerals as iron and phosphorus. But the vitamins and some of the minerals are chiefly in the bran and germ, which milling removes from white flour. Most millers in the United States and many other countries enrich their product by adding iron and vitamins to white flour made for home use. Most U.S. bakeries use enriched flour, or they add vitamins and minerals to dough made with unenriched white flour.

The enriching of white flour has probably helped millions of people avoid malnutrition. Diseases caused by a lack of B vitamins were common in the United States before 1941. That year, the nation's bakers and millers began enriching white-flour products. Today, few Americans suffer those diseases.

History. People probably began to make crude flour between 15,000 B.C. and 9000 B.C. They used rocks to crush wild grain on other rocks. After farming began to develop about 9000 B.C., people made flour from such cultivated grains as barley, millet, rice, rye, and wheat.

By the 1000's B.C., millers ground grain between two large, flat millstones. Later, domestic animals or groups of slaves rotated the top stone to crush the grain. By the A.D. 1100's, windmills were powering flour mills in Europe.

Few further advances in milling occurred until 1780. That year, in England, a Scottish engineer named James Watt built the first steam-powered flour mill. In 1802, Oliver Evans, a Philadelphia miller, opened the first such mill in the United States. During the late 1800's, metal rollers replaced millstones in many American and European mills. Edmund La Croix and other millers in Minneapolis, Minn., perfected the purifier in the 1870's. By the early 1900's, automation had made flour mills more productive than ever.

Today, the United States has more than 250 flour mills. They produce about 14 million short tons (12.7 million metric tons) of wheat flour annually. The top flour milling centers in the United States include Buffalo, N.Y.; Kansas City, Mo.; and Minneapolis, Minn. Canada has about 40 flour mills, and they produce about 2 million short tons (1.8 million metric tons) of wheat flour yearly. Montreal is the most important Canadian milling center. The annual world wheat flour production totals about 120 million short tons (109 million metric tons).

Mary E. Zabik

See also **Bread; Corn** (The dry-milling industry); **Gluten; Pasta; Wheat** (Food for people).

Flour beetle is any of several small, reddish, flattened beetles that breed in flour, meal, and other grain products. They often spoil the food. Adult flour beetles are about $\frac{1}{6}$ inch (4 millimeters) long. Flour beetles are found in all parts of the world, and all year long, in warm buildings.

Scientific classification. The flour beetle belongs to the family Tenebrionidae. Common species are *Tribolium confusum* and *T. castaneum*. Ellis W. Huddleston

Flow chart. See **Computer** (Preparing a program; diagram: An operations flow chart).

David Muench

Desert wild flowers thrive in the hot, dry climate of the Southwestern United States. A variety of flowering plants, such as cactuses, can survive for many months without rain. The seeds of these plants lie buried during dry periods and then sprout after the rains return.

Flower

Flower is a blossom or an entire plant that is known for its blossoms. Most plants have flowers. In some cases, however, the flowers are so small and plain that few people think of them as flowers. Most people think of flowers as being brightly colored and showy. Plants that have such blossoms include buttercups, dandelions, orchids, roses, tulips, violets, and hundreds of other garden flowers and wild flowers. Some trees, such as catal-

Peter H. Raven, the critical reviewer of this article, is Director of the Missouri Botanical Garden and Engelmann Professor of Botany at Washington University. He is also coauthor of Biology of Plants.

pas and horse chestnuts, have beautiful blossoms. But the trees themselves are never referred to as flowers. All the plants classified as either garden flowers or wild flowers are smaller than trees. Also, most of these flowering plants have soft stems rather than woody stems.

People prize flowers for their attractive shapes, gorgeous colors, and delightful fragrance. Because of their beauty, flowers are a favorite form of decoration. People also use flowers to express their deepest feelings. For more than 50,000 years, people have placed flowers on the graves of loved ones as a sign of remembrance and respect. Flowers are used at weddings to symbolize love, faithfulness, and long life. Certain flowers also have a religious meaning. Among Christians, for example, the white Easter lily stands for purity. Buddhists and Hindus regard the lotus, which is a type of water lily, as a sacred flower.

Interesting facts about flowers

Robert W. Mitchell,
Tom Stack & Associates

Yucca flowers of the American Southwest are pollinated by female yucca moths, which lay their eggs in the flowers' seed-producing organs. The eggs hatch into caterpillars, which feed on the seeds.

Werner Stoy,
Camera Hawaii

The night-blooming cereus is a climbing cactus with large, fragrant, white flowers that open only at night. The plant grows in Hawaii, the West Indies, and other areas that have a tropical climate.

Red-hot pokers have long, slender stems topped by spikes of small, brilliantly colored flowers. They belong to the lily family and may reach a height of 5 feet (1.5 meters). Most red-hot pokers grow wild in South Africa.

M. Fogden, Bruce Coleman Inc.

Stone plants of South Africa have leaves that look like the stones among which the plants grow. Each plant has two fleshy leaves. A white or yellow flower grows in a slit between the tops of the leaves.

Edward S. Ross

The fly orchid of southern Ecuador has the shape and coloring of a female tachinid fly. This resemblance attracts male tachinid flies. The males pollinate fly orchids as they travel between blossoms.

© James H. Carmichael, Jr.

Gloriosa lilies have long, graceful *stamens* (male reproductive parts) that grow outside the petals. The stems may measure up to 6 feet (1.8 meters) tall. The flowers grow in Asia and Africa.

Diana & Rick Sullivan,
Bruce Coleman Ltd.

D. Ruble from Edward S. Ross

The rafflesia is the world's largest flower. It measures up to 3 feet (91 centimeters) across. Rafflesias grow in Indonesia. They have no stems or leaves and are parasites on other plants.

William H. Allen, Jr.

Dick Keen, Acadia Multi-Image

Poinsettias have petallike leaves called *bracts, left,* that surround the plants' tiny flowers, *right.* Most poinsettias have red bracts. The plants are native to Mexico and Central America.

Originally, all flowers were wild flowers. Prehistoric people found wild flowers growing nearly everywhere, from the cold wastes of the Arctic to the steaming jungles of the tropics. In time, people learned to grow plants from seeds. They could then raise the prettiest and sweetest-smelling wild flowers in gardens. By 3000 B.C., the Egyptians and other peoples of the Middle East had begun to cultivate a variety of garden flowers, including jasmines, poppies, and water lilies. Gardeners have since developed many other kinds, and cultivated flowers are now raised in every country. Thousands of species of flowering plants still grow in the wild throughout the world. But many of these species are becoming rare as more and more wilderness areas are leveled to make room for farms and cities.

Although people admire flowers for their beauty, the function of the blossoms is to make seeds. Every blossom has male or female parts—or both male and female parts. The male and female parts together produce the seeds. The seeds develop in a female part called an *ovary,* which is a hollow structure at the base of a flower. Before the seeds can develop, however, they must be fertilized by sex cells in the pollen produced by the male parts of a flower. Among most kinds of flowering plants, the pollen is carried from the male parts of one flower to the female parts of another flower. The wind pollinates some kinds of flowers, especially those that have small, plain blossoms. Insects or birds pollinate most plants with showy or sweet-smelling flowers. In some kinds of flowering plants, the plants pollinate themselves.

Plants that have flowers are classed scientifically as *angiosperms.* The word *angiosperm* comes from two Greek words meaning *covered* and *seed.* All angiosperms bear their seeds in the protective covering. Before the seeds are fertilized, they are protected in the ovary. After the seeds are fertilized, the ovary grows into a structure called a *fruit*. The fruit encloses and protects the ripening seeds. The rest of the blossom gradually dies.

Scientists estimate that there are more than 350,000 species of plants throughout the world. About 250,000 species are flowering plants, or angiosperms. All garden flowers and wild flowers belong to this large group, as do nearly all other familiar plants. One major exception is cone-bearing plants. Like angiosperms, cone-bearing plants reproduce by means of seeds. The seeds are produced by the cones. The cones develop from structures that resemble the plain flowers of some angiosperms. But these structures lack an ovary and therefore are not considered to be flowers in the strict sense of the word.

This article describes the uses of flowers, the various kinds of garden flowers and wild flowers, and the parts of a flower. It then discusses the role of flowers in reproduction, flower hobbies, and how flowers are named and classified. For detailed information about flowering plants in general, see the *World Book* article **Plant**. *World Book* also has hundreds of articles on individual flowers and flowering shrubs. For a list of these articles, see the *Related articles* at the end of this article.

Robert H. Glaze, Artstreet

The white Easter lily is a Christian symbol for purity. In this spring display, the lilies are arranged in the form of a cross.

National flowers

A number of countries have official or unofficial national flowers. Some of these countries and their flowers are listed below.

Country	Flower	Country	Flower
Australia	Golden wattle	**Japan**	Cherry blossom, Chrysanthemum
Austria	Edelweiss		
Costa Rica	Cattleya orchid	**Malaysia**	Hibiscus
		Mexico	Dahlia
England	Rose	**Netherlands**	Tulip
Greece	Hyacinth	**Philippines**	Arabian jasmine
Guatemala	White nun orchid	**Portugal**	Carnation
India	Lotus	**Scotland**	Thistle
Israel	Almond blossom	**South Africa**	Giant protea
		Sweden	Twinflower
		Turkey	Tulip
		United States	Rose

Flowers of the states and of the Canadian provinces and territories

Apple (blossom)
  Arkansas
  Michigan
Arbutus (Mayflower)
  Massachusetts
  Nova Scotia (Trailing)
Bitter root
  Montana
Black-eyed Susan
  Maryland
Bluebonnet
  Texas
Camellia
  Alabama
Carnation (Scarlet)
  Ohio
Clover (Red)
  Vermont
Columbine (Rocky Mountain)
  Colorado
Dogwood (Flowering)
  British Columbia
  North Carolina
  Virginia
Fireweed
  Yukon Territory
Forget-me-not
  Alaska

Goldenrod
  Kentucky
  Nebraska
Hawthorn
  Missouri
Hibiscus
  Hawaii
Indian paintbrush
  Wyoming
Iris
  Tennessee
Jasmine (Carolina jessamine)
  South Carolina
Lady's-slipper
  Minnesota (Pink and white)
  Prince Edward Island
Lilac (Purple)
  New Hampshire
Lily
  Quebec (White garden lily)
  Saskatchewan (Prairie lily)
  Utah (Sego lily)
Magnolia
  Louisiana
  Mississippi

Mistletoe
  Oklahoma
Mountain avens
  Northwest Territories
Mountain laurel
  Connecticut
  Pennsylvania
Orange (blossom)
  Florida
Oregon grape
  Oregon
Pasqueflower (Wild crocus or prairie crocus)
  Manitoba
  South Dakota (American pasqueflower)
Peach (blossom)
  Delaware
Peony
  Indiana
Pine
  Maine (White pine cone and tassel)
Pitcher plant
  Newfoundland
Poppy (Golden)
  California
Rhododendron
  Washington (Coast rhododendron)
  West Virginia

Rose
  Alberta (Wild rose)
  District of Columbia (American beauty rose)
  Georgia (Cherokee rose)
  Iowa (Wild rose)
  New York
  North Dakota (Wild prairie rose)
Sagebrush
  Nevada
Saguaro (Giant cactus)
  Arizona
Sunflower
  Kansas
Syringa (Mock orange)
  Idaho
Trillium
  Ontario (White)
Violet
  Illinois (Native violet)
  New Brunswick (Purple violet)
  New Jersey
  Rhode Island (Purple violet)
  Wisconsin (Wood violet)
Yucca (flower)
  New Mexico

All flowers listed above in boldface type have separate articles in *World Book*. Pictures of the flowers appear in the various state and province articles.

Vance Henry, Taurus Photo

Tulip farms in the Netherlands, *above,* produce millions of bulbs annually. Tulip cultivation is also an important industry in Holland, Mich., and other parts of the United States. Other kinds of flowers that are commercially grown include daffodils, hyacinths, and narcissuses.

The blossoms of most flowering plants have little food value compared with other plant parts, such as the leaves and fruit. Most blossoms also lack useful chemicals or other materials that can be used in manufacturing. People use flowers mainly as decoration and in landscaping. The production and marketing of flowers for these purposes is a major industry in the United States and many other countries.

As decoration. Flowers are widely used as table decorations in homes and restaurants. In churches and other places of worship, flowers often decorate the altars. Many women wear flowers in their hair or pinned to their dress. Hawaiians often wear flower necklaces called *leis.* Flowers add beauty and color to many public festivals. One of the most famous of these festivals is the Parade of Roses held every New Year's Day in Pasadena, Calif. The parade features floats decorated with hundreds of thousands of roses and other flowers.

The flowers used as decoration may be either cut flowers or flowering house plants. Cut flowers are garden flowers that were harvested while in bloom. Cut flowers stay fresh several days if their stems are kept in water. Popular cut flowers include daisies, gladioli, irises, and roses. Flowering house plants have showy blossoms and can be grown indoors in containers. Such plants include African violets, azaleas, and wax begonias. Unlike cut flowers, flowering house plants may last almost indefinitely.

Werner Stoy, Camera Hawaii

Colorful leis, which consist of flowers strung together, are worn as necklaces in Hawaii and other Pacific islands. Favorite flowers for leis include carnations, jasmines, and orchids.

Many home gardeners grow their own cut flowers. Greenhouses and flower farms raise them commercially. Greenhouses also grow flowering house plants commercially, as do nurseries. Commercial producers sell their flowers to retail florists, who resell them to the public. Many florists—especially those who supply flowers for such occasions as weddings and funerals—are trained in the art of flower arranging. The section *Flower hobbies* discusses the art of flower arranging.

In landscaping. Flowers add greatly to the beauty of yards, gardens, parks, and other landscaped areas. The flowers may be planted in beds or borders and arranged according to size, shape, and color. Spring, summer, and fall varieties may be planted to provide a continuous display of blossoms. Some of the most popular plants used in landscaping are flowering shrubs, such as bridal wreaths, forsythias, hydrangeas, and lilacs. Flowering shrubs are especially useful in large landscaping areas because they bloom year after year and require little care.

Many public gardens and parks are noted for their beautiful displays of flowers. Bellingrath Gardens, near Mobile, Ala., are famous for their azaleas and camellias. Golden Gate Park in San Francisco has one of the world's largest collections of rhododendrons. Irises and peonies are specialties of Longwood Gardens, near Kennett Square, Pa. The Missouri Botanical Garden in St. Louis is famous for its water lilies. The Royal Botanical Gardens in Hamilton, Ont., have one of the finest collections of flowers in Canada. The gardens are especially famous for their many spring blossoms.

Other uses. In most cases, the flower buds or blossoms of flowering plants do not serve as food for people. There are some exceptions, however. The flower buds of broccoli, cauliflower, and globe artichoke plants are widely used as vegetables. Broccoli and cauliflower buds grow in thick clusters called *heads.* The heads are eaten with the stems. Artichoke buds grow singly, and only the bud is eaten. Certain seasonings also come from flower buds or flower parts. For example, cloves are the dried flower buds of the clove tree. Saffron comes from female flower parts of purple autumn crocuses. The petals of some flowers, such as roses and marigolds, have a sweet or spicy taste. They are sometimes used to flavor soups and salads, especially in Europe and Asia. Some people use dandelion and elderberry blossoms to make wine. In China, lightly fried squash flowers are a great delicacy.

Honey is made from *nectar,* a sugary liquid produced by flowers. Bees gather the nectar from the flowers. They eat some of it and store the rest in their hives. The nectar in the hives gradually turns into honey. Some flowers are better suited to honey production than others because they produce more and tastier nectar. Such flowers include alfalfa, buckwheat, clover, orange, and sage blossoms.

The petals of certain flowers contain sweet-smelling oils. Such flowers include jasmines, mimosas, and roses. The oils obtained from the petals of these flowers supply the fragrances for many high-quality perfumes. However, most perfumes are made synthetically from chemical substances.

A-Z Collection

Building a flower-covered float, *above,* requires thousands of blossoms. Elaborate floats decorated with roses, carnations, and other flowers are spectacular features of many parades.

Sabine Weiss, Photo Researchers

Perfumes made from petals are the most delicate and expensive scents. Sweet-smelling oils from the petals of such flowers as roses are extracted after the petals are aired, *above.*

© Diana Hunt from Louis Mercier

Botanical gardens display collections of flowering plants, shrubs, and trees from many parts of the world. Canada's beautiful Butchardt Gardens, *above,* near Victoria, B.C., include an English rose garden and Italian and Japanese gardens.

Garden flowers

Garden flowers are simply cultivated wild flowers. Some kinds of garden flowers are exactly like the wild species. Other kinds have been bred scientifically so that their blooms are more attractive than those of the wild variety. Garden flowers are grown on farms and in nurseries and greenhouses as well as in home gardens. Some kinds also make excellent house plants.

Garden flowers can be divided into three main groups based on how long they live: (1) annuals, (2) biennials, and (3) perennials. Annuals are plants that sprout from seed, grow to full size, bloom, produce seeds, and die—all within one year or less. Biennials are plants that live two years. They do not produce flowers and seeds until their second year of growth, after which they die. Annuals and biennials live such a short time that each generation must produce many seeds for the species to survive. Each plant uses up all its food energy in the production of flowers and seeds and so dies soon afterward. All annuals and biennials are *herbs*—that is, they have soft stems.

Perennials are plants that live at least three years. They may or may not bloom during their first year of growth. But after perennials have begun to bloom, they may do so every year almost indefinitely, depending on their species. Because perennials live longer than annuals and biennials, they do not have to produce as many seeds for the species to survive. Instead of using up all their food energy in seed production, the plants store some of it in their roots. Perennials thus go on living after their blossoms have faded and died.

Some perennials are herbs. The stems of these herbaceous perennials wither and die at the end of each summer. But their roots survive through the winter and grow new stems in spring. All other perennials, including flowering shrubs, have woody stems. Woody perennials do not wither at the end of summer. However, most of them shed their leaves in fall and rest in winter. Some kinds of herbaceous perennials grow from bulbs. Bulbs and flowering shrubs are not grown in the same way as other perennials, and so they are usually discussed separately.

The great majority of garden flowers are annuals or perennials. Only a few are biennials. However, the classification of flowers as annuals, biennials, or perennials is not always precise. For example, most perennials that are native to warm climates cannot survive cold winters. These flowers therefore cannot be grown as perennials in such places as Canada and the northern parts of the United States. But some warm-weather perennials, such as gloxinias and wax begonias, bloom during their first year of growth. They can thus be grown as annuals in northern climates.

Garden annuals

Most annuals bloom about 8 to 10 weeks after the seeds are planted. In warm climates, annuals can be planted outdoors at any time of the year. In areas with cold winters, they are usually planted in spring. Certain species can survive a light frost and so may be started outdoors from seed as soon as the ground has thawed completely. These *hardy annuals* include bachelor's buttons, morning-glories, pansies, petunias, sunflowers, sweet alyssum, and sweet peas. However, some hardy annuals, such as pansies and petunias, grow slowly. Gardeners give these flowers a head start by planting them as seedlings. Some gardeners grow their own seedlings. Others buy them from commercial greenhouses. In either case, the seeds are planted indoors in late winter or early spring. The seedlings are then ready to be transplanted outdoors as soon as the ground has completely thawed.

Some annuals, such as garden balsams and marigolds, cannot survive even a light frost. These *tender annuals* should not be planted outdoors until all danger of frost has passed. In northern regions, frosts may occur for a month or more after the ground has thawed. Gardeners in these regions almost always give tender annuals a head start by sowing the seeds indoors before the growing season begins. They then plant the seedlings outdoors in spring.

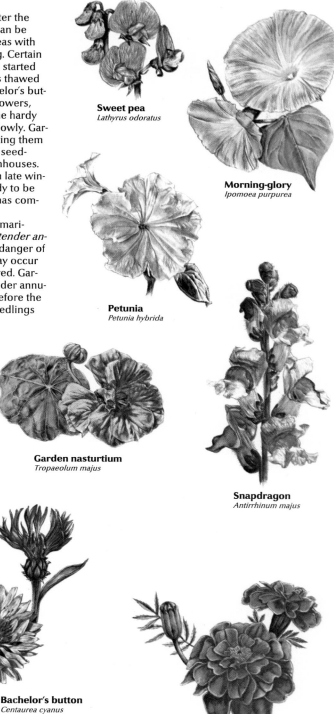

Sweet pea
Lathyrus odoratus

Morning-glory
Ipomoea purpurea

Petunia
Petunia hybrida

Garden nasturtium
Tropaeolum majus

Snapdragon
Antirrhinum majus

Zinnia
Zinnia elegans

Bachelor's button
Centaurea cyanus

French marigold
Tagetes patula

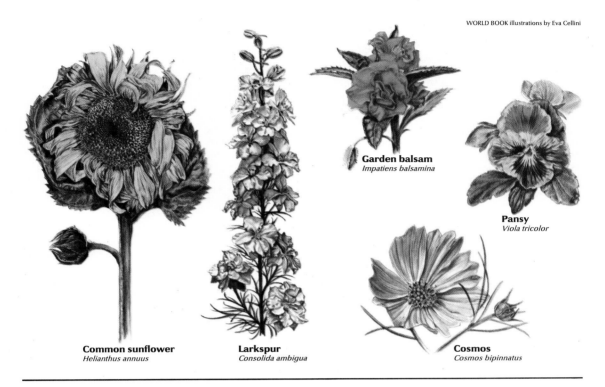

Garden balsam
Impatiens balsamina

Pansy
Viola tricolor

Common sunflower
Helianthus annuus

Larkspur
Consolida ambigua

Cosmos
Cosmos bipinnatus

Garden biennials

Gardeners who wish to start biennials outdoors usually plant the seeds in midsummer. The plants grow a stem and a few leaves by autumn. The leaves and stem then die, but the roots survive through the winter. The plants grow a new stem, bloom, produce seeds, and die during their second growing season. Instead of starting biennials outdoors, many gardeners buy them as seedlings in spring and raise them like annuals.

Hollyhock
Althaea rosea

Canterbury bells
Campanula medium

Foxglove
Digitalis purpurea

Iceland poppy
Papaver nudicaule

Sweet William
Dianthus barbatus

Garden perennials

Popular garden perennials in the United States and Canada include asters, bleeding hearts, chrysanthemums, columbines, day lilies, delphiniums, irises, lupines, peonies, phloxes, poppies, primroses, and violets. Most of these flowers need an annual cold or cool season for the growth of new buds. They therefore do not grow well in tropical climates. On the other hand, warm-weather perennials may be raised indoors in northern climates, and many of them are favorite house plants. Some of these perennials are pictured in the next section of the article under the heading *Flowers of the tropics and subtropics*. They include African violets, gloxinias, ivy geraniums, and wax begonias.

Some perennials, such as columbines and delphiniums, bloom only three or four years. Most gardeners start these plants from seeds and replace them when necessary. In most cases, longer-living perennials are started from *cuttings*—that is, pieces cut from the stems or roots of adult plants. When planted in water or soil, a cutting develops into a plant identical to the parent. Cuttings, like seedlings, should be started indoors. Some gardeners start cuttings taken from their own plants. Others buy cuttings that have already rooted.

Perennials should be set into the garden in spring or early autumn. In general, spring is the best time to plant perennials outdoors in Canada and the northern regions of the United States. Early autumn is usually the best time in warmer climates.

Most perennials spread by sending out shoots from their roots. The shoots develop into new stems. Most species produce new shoots soon after they have bloomed each year. Over several years, the offshoots from only one plant may cover a wide area. In most cases, however, the plants bloom better if they are dug up, divided, and replanted every few years.

Lily of the valley
Convallaria majalis

New York aster
Aster novi-belgii

Tall bearded iris
Iris germanica

Polyanthus primrose
Primula polyantha

Garden perennial lupine
Lupinus polyphyllus

Sweet violet
Viola odorata

Peony
Paeonia officinalis

Hardy chrysanthemum
Chrysanthemum morifolium

Christmas rose
Helleborus niger

Himalayan blue poppy
Meconopsis betonicifolia

Oriental poppy
Papaver bracteatum

Chinese delphinium
Delphinium grandiflorum

Phlox
Phlox paniculata

Tawny-orange day lily
Hemerocallis fulva

Common garden canna
Canna generalis

Bleeding heart
Dicentra spectabilis

Balloon flower
Platycodon grandiflorus

Garden perennials (Bulbs)

A bulb is an underground stem with a large bud, wrapped in starchy tissue. The bud develops into a new plant after the weather becomes favorable. The starchy tissue provides the developing plant with food.

Flowers that grow from bulbs or bulblike structures include crocuses, daffodils, fritillaries, gladioli, hyacinths, Madonna lilies, tuberous begonias, and tulips. The majority of these flowers can be grown throughout most of the United States. However, such plants as crocuses and tulips grow better in cool climates than in warm ones. The bulbs of daffodils, hyacinths, and some other flowers can be left in the ground through the winter in most parts of the United States. Certain other flowers, such as gladioli, cannot survive in extremely cold weather. In northern regions, the structures from which these plants grow should be dug up in fall, stored indoors, and then replanted outdoors in spring.

Tulip
Tulipa gesneriana

Gladiolus
Gladiolus hortulanus

Cloth-of-gold crocus
Crocus susianus

Tuberous begonia
Begonia tuberhybrida

Madonna lily
Lilium candidum

Dahlia
Dahlia pinnata

Crown imperial
Fritillaria imperialis

Daffodil
Narcissus pseudo-narcissus

Hyacinth
Hyacinthus orientalis

Garden perennials (Flowering shrubs)

Shrubs, like trees, have woody stems. But shrubs do not grow as tall as trees, and most of them have two or more thin stems rather than a single thick one. As a rule, flowering shrubs grow best in areas with fairly long summers and cool winters. Most species cannot stand very cold weather. Popular kinds of flowering shrubs include azaleas, flowering quince, forsythia, honeysuckle, hydrangeas, lilacs, redbuds, roses, roses of Sharon, and spiraeas.

Most beginning gardeners buy shrubs as young plants that are ready to set into the garden. However, gardeners can easily produce their own plants from mature shrubbery. Like herbaceous perennials, many shrubs spread by sending out shoots from their roots. Such shoots will develop into new plants if they are dug up with part of the root and replanted. Shrubs that do not send out shoots can be reproduced from cuttings.

Hybrid tea rose
Rosa dilecta

Rose of Sharon
Hibiscus syriacus

Flame azalea
Rhododendron calendulaceum

Tatarian honeysuckle
Lonicera tatarica

Bridal wreath
Spiraea prunifolia

Border forsythia
Forsythia intermedia

Big-leaved hydrangea
Hydrangea macrophylla

Lilac
Syringa vulgaris

WORLD BOOK illustrations by Allianora Rosse

Oxford Scientific Films

A carpet of wild flowers brightens a mountain meadow. Wild flowers grow almost everywhere
—in woods, fields, deserts, jungles, and swamps; on mountains and prairies; and along rivers and
seacoasts. Each environment promotes the growth of different kinds of flowers.

Each species of flowering plant grows best in a particular type of environment. The species may be unable to grow at all in a much hotter, cooler, wetter, or drier location. Gardeners can control a plant's environment to some extent. They can therefore grow certain flowers in otherwise unfavorable locations. For example, flowers that need much moisture can be raised in dry climates if the gardener supplies the flowers with the necessary water. When flowers grow in the wild, however, they do not receive such special treatment. Each of the species can survive only in the type of environment to which it is naturally suited.

There are about 250,000 kinds of flowering plants in the world. About 165,000 species are native to the tropics. The remaining 85,000 species are native to Europe, North America, and other nontropical regions. About 20,000 of these species are native to the continental United States and Canada. Roughly half of the U.S. and Canadian species have showy blossoms and so can be classed as wild flowers.

Different species of wild flowers grow in seven major wild flower environments. These environments are (1) the Arctic tundra, (2) woodlands and forests, (3) prairies and dry plains, (4) chaparrals, (5) Alpine tundras, (6) deserts, and (7) tropical and subtropical regions. In addition, a major wild flower environment may include various special environments, such as wetlands and shorelines.

These special environments have their own types of wild flowers. For example, some varieties of woodland flowers grow mainly in woodland swamps. Water flowers may be found in any environment that has lakes or rivers.

Many wild flowers have spread from their native environment to similar environments in other parts of the world. In some cases, people have introduced the flowers into new environments. In other cases, the seeds have been carried by the wind or by animals. Certain seeds easily stick to the bodies of animals and so may be carried long distances by animals that migrate. Wild flowers that have been introduced into North America from other parts of the world include bindweed, chicory, dandelions, furze, mullein, mustard, oxeye daisies, Queen Anne's lace, and yarrow. Most of these plants are now widely distributed throughout the United States and parts of Canada. In many cases, they compete with native plants and farm crops and so are regarded as weeds.

The drawings in this section illustrate typical flowers of each major wild flower environment. Except for the tropical and subtropical flowers, most of the species of flowers pictured are native to North America. In many cases, however, flowers that are closely related to these species grow in similar environments in other parts of the world.

Flowers of the Arctic tundra

The Arctic tundra extends across the extreme northern parts of North America, Europe, and Asia. It is a cold, dry, treeless grassland. Most of the region has an annual frost-free period of less than two months. The ground remains frozen all year except at the surface. The surface thaws in spring and remains soggy throughout most of the summer. Seeds tend to rot in such cool, marshy ground, and so the tundra has few annuals. However, a variety of herbaceous perennials thrive in the tundra. These hardy plants include cinquefoils, fireweeds, louseworts, poppies, and saxifrages. They come to life suddenly in spring and brighten the brief Arctic summers with their colorful blossoms.

Steve McCutcheon

WORLD BOOK illustrations by James Teason

Four-angled mountain heather
Cassiope tetragona

Lapland rosebay
Rhododendron lapponicum

Dwarf fireweed
Epilobium latifolium

Eight-petaled mountain avens
Dryas octopetala

Arctic lupine
Lupinus arcticus

Shrubby cinquefoil
Potentilla fruticosa

Purple mountain saxifrage
Saxifraga oppositifolia

Arctic poppy
Papaver radicatum

Woolly lousewort
Pedicularis lanata

Flowers of woodlands and forests

Trees need considerable moisture and a yearly frost-free period of over two months to reach full size. Woodlands and forests thus grow only in regions that meet these needs. Seedlings have difficulty competing with established plants in wooded areas, and so such areas have few annuals. Nearly all the flowers are perennials.

There are two main types of forests: (1) needleleaf and (2) broadleaf. Needleleaf forests stretch south from the Arctic tundra across most of Canada, northern Europe, and northern Asia. They also extend along lower slopes of the Rocky Mountains into the Northwestern United States. Needleleaf forests have most of the same kinds of flowers as the tundra plus such species as bog orchids, columbines, and pitcher plants.

The largest broadleaf forests outside the tropics are in the eastern half of the United States, eastern Asia, and western and central Europe. The growth of flowers in these forests is regulated largely by the amount of shade or sunlight. Many woodland flowers bloom in early spring, before the trees develop leaves and the woods become heavily shaded. These early-blooming species include bloodroots, dogtooth violets, and trilliums. After the woods become shaded, flowers bloom mainly in clearings and in meadows at the edge of the woods. Such species as spiderworts and touch-me-nots blossom in late spring or early summer. Others, such as asters and goldenrods, bloom in late summer or fall.

© Derek Fell

Needleleaf forest

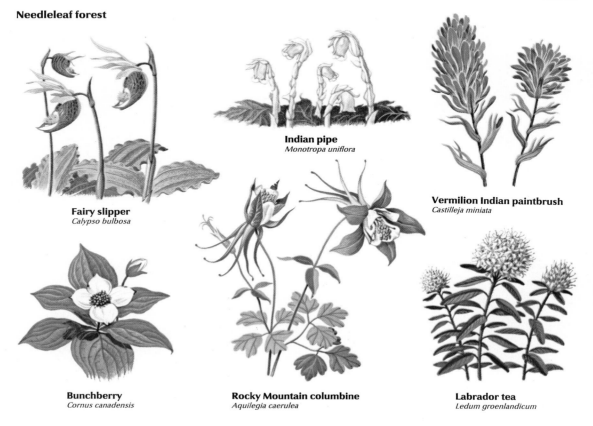

Fairy slipper
Calypso bulbosa

Indian pipe
Monotropa uniflora

Vermilion Indian paintbrush
Castilleja miniata

Bunchberry
Cornus canadensis

Rocky Mountain columbine
Aquilegia caerulea

Labrador tea
Ledum groenlandicum

Broadleaf forest

WORLD BOOK illustrations by James Teason

Tuberous water lily
Nymphaea tuberosa

Yellow dogtooth violet
Erythronium americanum

Trailing arbutus
Epigaea repens

Bloodroot
Sanguinaria canadensis

Fringed gentian
Gentiana crinita

Dutchman's-breeches
Dicentra cucullaria

Orange touch-me-not
Impatiens capensis

Round-lobed hepatica
Hepatica americana

Marsh marigold
Caltha palustris

May apple
Podophyllum peltatum

Gary goldenrod
Solidago nemoralis

Large-flowered trillium
Trillium grandiflorum

Flowers of prairies and dry plains

Prairies and dry plains are grasslands. They receive less rainfall than woodlands and have hot summers and cold or cool winters. Prairies once covered much of the central United States and south-central Canada as well as large areas of Argentina, the Soviet Union, and South Africa. Today, most of these areas are used for growing crops, especially grains. However, some prairie lands have been left in their natural state. These areas are still noted for their tall grasses and traditional spring, summer, and fall flowers. Most prairie flowers are perennials. Grasses grow so thick on prairies that few seeds can penetrate the sod. Annuals have difficulty surviving as a result. Typical kinds of prairie flowers of the United States and Canada include blazing stars, pasqueflowers, coneflowers, rattlesnake masters, sunflowers, tickseeds, and wild indigo.

The prairies of the United States and Canada give way to dry plains in the west. These plains, which are called *steppes,* receive less moisture than prairies and so are covered with short, rather than tall, grasses. Steppes also adjoin the prairies of Argentina, the Soviet Union, and South Africa. The moister areas of the steppes have many of the same kinds of flowers as the prairies. The drier sections have drought-resistant species and more annuals. Typical flowers of the North American plains include prickly pear cactuses, low townsendias, scarlet globe mallows, and sunflowers.

James P. Rowan

White evening primrose
Oenothera nuttallii

Smooth fleabane
Erigeron glabellus

Tall sunflower
Helianthus giganteus

Scarlet globe mallow
Sphaeralcea coccinea

Dotted blazing star
Liatris punctata

Prairie rose
Rosa arkansana

Prairie buttercup
Ranunculus rhomboideus

Showy gaillardia
Gaillardia pulchella

American pasqueflower
Anemone nuttalliana

Rattlesnake master
Eryngium yuccifolium

Saline shooting star
Dodecatheon pauciflorum

Prairie coneflower
Ratibida columnifera

Tickseed
Coreopsis tinctoria

Purple prairie clover
Petalostemon purpureum

White wild indigo
Baptisia leucantha

Western wallflower
Erysimum asperum

Low townsendia
Townsendia sericea

Plains prickly pear cactus
Opuntia polyacantha

Flowers of chaparrals

Chaparrals are thick growths of shrubs and scrubby trees. These areas are found along the Mediterranean Sea, in southern California, and in Australia, Chile, and South Africa. The mild, moderately dry climate of these regions is an ideal environment for the growth of wild flowers. In addition, seeds have a better chance of surviving and sprouting in such a climate than in colder, moister regions. As a result, a high percentage of chaparral flowers are annuals. The California chaparral and its neighboring oak woodlands have a tremendous variety of wild flowers. Some of them, such as fire poppies and fiddlenecks, are California natives. Other species, such as black mustard and star thistles, have been introduced into the region.

Russell D. Lamb

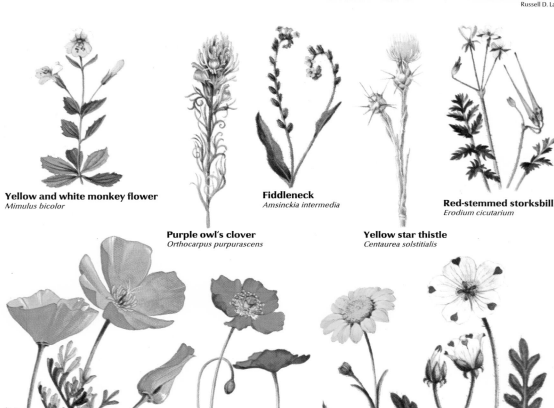

Yellow and white monkey flower
Mimulus bicolor

Fiddleneck
Amsinckia intermedia

Red-stemmed storksbill
Erodium cicutarium

Purple owl's clover
Orthocarpus purpurascens

Yellow star thistle
Centaurea solstitialis

California poppy
Eschscholzia californica

Fire poppy
Papaver californicum

Goldfields
Lasthenia chrysostoma

Five-spot
Nemophila maculata

Flowers of alpine tundras

Alpine tundras lie at high elevations in mountains throughout the world. Like the Arctic, these areas are too cold and dry for trees to grow. However, grasses, low shrubs, and a variety of wild flowers thrive. The chief alpine tundras are in the European Alps, the Himalaya of Asia, and the Rocky Mountains of North America. Most alpine flowers grow in mountain meadows, but some species are especially suited to rocky places. As in the Arctic, the yearly frost-free period is usually less than two months, and so nearly all the flowers are perennials. Most are small and grow slowly, and some do not even start to bloom until they are 10 years old or older. Many alpine and Arctic flowers are closely related, and some are identical.

Kitty Kohout

WORLD BOOK illustrations by Kate Lloyd-Jones, Linden Artists Ltd.

Alpine forget-me-not
Eritrichium elongatum

Pygmy bitterroot
Lewisia pygmaea

Club-moss ivesia
Ivesia lycopodioides

Tolmie's saxifrage
Saxifraga tolmiei

Moss campion
Silene acaulis

Arctic gentian
Gentiana algida

Alpine avens
Geum rossii

Alpine phacelia
Phacelia sericea

Sticky polemonium
Polemonium viscosum

Flowers of the desert

Deserts are extremely dry regions with a generally warm climate. Most deserts receive less than 10 inches (25 centimeters) of rainfall a year. In some cases, all the rain falls in one or two tremendous cloudbursts. Desert flowers must therefore be able to survive for many months without rain.

Some desert flowers are shrubs. These plants have vast networks of roots that absorb every available drop of moisture in the soil. Other desert flowers are herbaceous perennials with thick, spongy stems. The stems store water, which the plants use during the long dry spells. Cactuses are the best-known examples of this type of plant. Still other flowers are annuals. Annuals thrive in deserts because they have relatively few perennials to compete with. In addition, the seeds of annuals can survive even the longest dry periods. The seeds lie buried until the rains return. They then sprout, and the plants complete their entire life cycle within only a few weeks.

The deserts of southwestern North America have a wide variety of flowers, including most of the familiar kinds of cactuses. Many of the cactuses have beautiful blossoms. The North American deserts also have numerous flowering shrubs and hundreds of annuals. The shrubs include such species as brittlebushes and desert mallows. Desert marigolds, devil's claws, evening primroses, ghost flowers, and sand verbenas are only a few of the many colorful annuals.

Tim Kilby, Van Cleve Photography

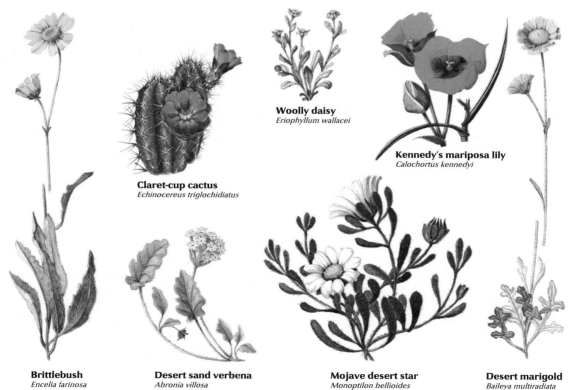

Claret-cup cactus
Echinocereus triglochidiatus

Woolly daisy
Eriophyllum wallacei

Kennedy's mariposa lily
Calochortus kennedyi

Brittlebush
Encelia farinosa

Desert sand verbena
Abronia villosa

Mojave desert star
Monoptilon bellioides

Desert marigold
Baileya multiradiata

WORLD BOOK illustrations by Kate Lloyd-Jones, Linden Artists Ltd.

Desert bluebell
Phacelia campanularia

Ghost flower
Mohavea confertiflora

Arizona poppy
Kallstroemia grandiflora

Giant four-o'clock
Mirabilis froebelii

Teddy bear cholla
Opuntia bigelovii

Desert chicory
Rafinesquia neo-mexicana

Beaver-tail cactus
Opuntia basilaris

Soapweed
Yucca glauca

Birdcage evening primrose
Oenothera deltoides

Desert mallow
Sphaeralcea ambigua

Desert lily
Hesperocallis undulata

Flowers of the tropics and subtropics

Thousands of species of wild flowers grow in the humid and warm climate of the tropics and sub-tropics. The tropical rain forests of Central and South America have the greatest variety of tropical flowers, including hundreds of rare and beautiful orchids. About 2,000 species of flowering plants are native to Hawaii. However, many have become extinct or extremely rare as a result of land development and overpicking. Southern regions of China and South Africa have the richest assortment of subtropical flowers. Southern Florida also has many species. Some of them, such as clamshell orchids, are Florida natives. Others, such as bougainvilleas, are introduced species.

David Muench
WORLD BOOK illustrations by James Teason

African violet
Saintpaulia ionantha
Tropical East Africa

Bird-of-paradise
Strelitzia reginae
South Africa

Ivy geranium
Pelargonium peltatum
South Africa

Clamshell orchid
Epidendrum cochleatum
Subtropical and tropical America

Wax begonia
Begonia semperflorens
Brazil

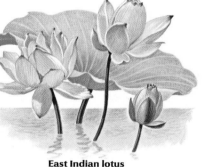

East Indian lotus
Nelumbo nucifera
Tropical Asia and Australia

Gloxinia
Sinningia speciosa
Brazil

Cape jasmine gardenia
Gardenia jasminoides
China

Torch ginger
Nicolaia elatior
Indonesia

The typical flower develops at the tip of a flower stalk. The tip is somewhat enlarged, forming a cup-shaped structure called a *receptacle*. A bud grows from the receptacle and develops into a flower.

Most flowers have four main parts: (1) the calyx, (2) the corolla, (3) the stamens, and (4) the pistils. The calyx is the outermost part of a flower. It consists of a set of leaflike or petallike structures called *sepals*. The corolla consists of a flower's petals. The stamens and pistils make up the reproductive parts of flowers. The stamens are the male parts, and the pistils are the female parts. Every flower has either stamens or pistils—or both stamens and pistils. Flowers that have all four main parts are called *complete flowers*. Flowers that lack one or more of the parts are called *incomplete flowers*. In addition to the main parts, many flowers have glands that produce nectar. These glands, which are called *nectaries,* lie near the base of the flower.

In most flowers, each main part consists of three, four, or five elements or of multiples of three, four, or five elements. In a trillium, for example, three sepals form the calyx, and three petals form the corolla. The flower has six stamens, and the pistil is composed of three equal parts. The elements may be separate from one another, like the petals of a poppy or a rose. Or the elements may be *fused* (joined together). In flowers with fused petals, for example, the corolla is shaped like a tube, bell, trumpet, pouch, or saucer. Flowers that have such corollas include morning-glories, daffodils, and petunias. In such species as evening primroses and verbenas, the petals are fused at the base and free at the tip. The corolla thus has a tubelike or bell-like base and a fringed edge.

In buttercups, morning-glories, and most other flowers, all the main parts are arranged around the center of the flower in a circular fashion. If the flower is divided in half in any direction, the halves will be alike. Such flowers are *radially symmetrical*. Orchids, snapdragons, sweet peas, and certain other flowers can be divided into identical halves only if the blossoms are cut through lengthwise. Such kinds of flowers are *bilaterally symmetrical.*

The calyx. The sepals, which make up the calyx, are the first parts to form among the majority of flowers. They protect the developing inner parts of the flower. In most cases, the sepals remain attached to the flower after it opens.

In many flowers, such as buttercups and magnolias, the sepals are greenish, leaflike structures that are on the underpart of the flower. Other flowers have sepals that look like petals. Among many members of the iris, lily, and orchid families, the sepals and the petals look so much alike that they cannot be told apart. Botanists call these petallike structures *tepals.* Certain kinds of flowers have colorful sepals in place of petals. These flowers include anemones, hepaticas, larkspurs, and marsh marigolds.

The corolla, which consists of a flower's petals, is the showy, brightly colored part of most flowers. The colors of the petals—and of colored sepals—attract insects or birds that help spread a flower's pollen. The colors come from certain chemicals in a plant's tissues. These chemicals are present in all parts of the plant, not only the petals or sepals. But they are masked in the other parts by large amounts of green or brown pigments. Many flowers also have spots, stripes, or other markings on their petals that attract insects or birds. In most cases, the odors of flowers come from oily substances in the petals. Strong odors, like bright colors, attract animals.

The stamens are the male, pollen-producing parts of a flower. They are not particularly noticeable in most flowers. In some cases, however, the stamens make up a flower's most attractive part. Male acacia flowers, for example, consist mainly of a large feathery tuft of colorful stamens.

Parts of a flower   A typical flower has four main parts. They are (1) the calyx, (2) the corolla, (3) the stamens, and (4) the pistils. The calyx forms the outermost part and consists of leaflike *sepals.* The corolla consists of the petals. The stamens and pistils make up a flower's reproductive parts.

WORLD BOOK illustration by James Teason

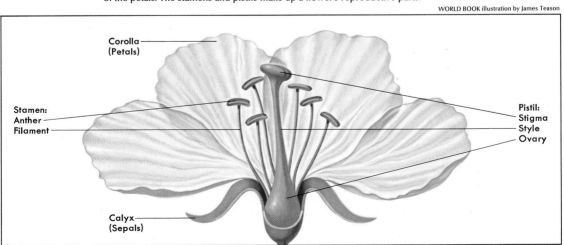

Corolla
(Petals)

Stamen:
Anther
Filament

Pistil:
Stigma
Style
Ovary

Calyx
(Sepals)

Variations in flower structure

Flowers vary in the shape, number, and color of their main parts. In addition, some species lack one or more of these parts. The examples below illustrate four variations in flower form.

WORLD BOOK illustrations by James Teason

Ray flowers

Disk flowers

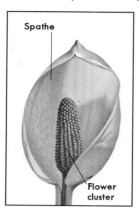

Spathe

Flower cluster

Bract

Flowers

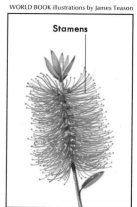

Stamens

A composite flower is many small flowers. The daisy has tiny *disk flowers* in the center and individual *ray flowers* that look like petals.

A leaflike spathe surrounds the tiny flowers of the skunk cabbage. The flowers grow in a cluster on a stalk. Some spathes have bright colors.

Large white bracts encircle the flowers of the dogwood. Many people mistakenly think that the attractive bracts are part of the flower.

Long red stamens make up the showiest part of bottlebrush blossoms. The stamens form a spike that resembles a brush used to wash bottles.

In most flowers, each stamen has two parts—a *filament* and an *anther.* The filament is a threadlike or ribbonlike stalk with an enlarged tip. The enlarged tip forms the anther. The anther consists of four tiny baglike structures that produce pollen. After the pollen is ripe, these structures split open, which releases the pollen grains.

The stamens are separate from one another in many flowers. But in such species as hollyhocks and sweet peas, some or all of the filaments are fused and form a tube around the pistil. In some flowers, the stamens are fused with one or more other flower parts. For example, the stamens of gentians are fused to the petals, and the stamens of most orchids are fused to the pistils.

The pistils are the female, seed-bearing parts of a flower. Some flowers, including all members of a pea family, have only one pistil. But most flowers have two or more. In many species, the pistils are fused into one *compound pistil.* A compound pistil is often referred to simply as a pistil. The individual pistils that make up a compound pistil are called *carpels.*

Among most flowers, each pistil or carpel has three parts—a *stigma,* a *style,* and an *ovary.* The stigma is a sticky area at the top. The style consists of a slender tube that leads from the stigma to the ovary. The ovary is a hollow structure at the base. It contains one or more structures called *ovules.*

Variations in flower structure. Many kinds of flowers grow in clusters called *inflorescences.* In some species, such as bridal wreaths and snapdragons, the individual flowers in each cluster are easy to identify as flowers. In numerous other species, however, the inflorescence looks like one flower and the individual flowers that make up the inflorescence look like petals. These species include the many members of the *composite family,* such as asters, chrysanthemums, daisies, dandelions, and sunflowers.

Among the members of the composite family, the flowers grow from a *head* at the tip of the flower stalk. Each head has several or many flowers, depending on the species. A dandelion head, for example, may have 100 or more tiny yellow flowers. Each flower, or *floret,* looks like a petal but consists of a calyx, a corolla, stamens, and a pistil. One petal makes up the corolla. The dandelion florets grow so close together that only their corollas can be seen.

The flowers of some plants grow in plain, tassellike inflorescences called *catkins.* A catkin is composed of *naked flowers*—that is, flowers that lack both petals and sepals. Plants that have catkins include alders, poplars, and willows.

Many plants that have inflorescences also have leaflike structures called *bracts* just beneath each flower cluster. In most cases, bracts are small, green, and barely noticeable. But in a few species, they are so large and showy that most people mistake them for part of the flower. The showy "petals" of bougainvilleas, dogwoods, and poinsettias are bracts. The flowers themselves are small, plain-looking inflorescences at the center of the bracts.

Among most species of flowering plants, each plant bears flowers that have both stamens and pistils. Such flowers are called *perfect flowers.* In some species, however, each plant bears flowers that have either pistils or stamens, not both. Such flowers are called *imperfect flowers.* If a flower has pistils but no stamens, it is called a *pistillate flower.* If it has stamens but no pistils, it is called a *staminate flower.* In some species, the staminate and pistillate flowers are on the same plant. Such species are known as *monoecious* species. They include begonias, oaks, and squashes. Among *dioecious* species, the male and female flowers are on different plants. Dioecious species include poplars, willows, and American holly.

Flowering plants reproduce sexually. The sexual parts of their blossoms produce male and female sex cells. The male cells, called *sperm,* are in the pollen produced by the stamens. The female cells, called *eggs,* are in the ovules produced by the pistils. The sperm and egg cells unite in the ovary at the base of a pistil and develop into seeds.

Reproduction in flowers involves two main steps: (1) pollination and (2) fertilization. Pollination is the transfer of pollen from a stamen to a pistil. Fertilization is the union of a sperm with an egg cell. Fertilization occurs in much the same way in all flowering plants. However, there are two methods of pollination: (1) cross-pollination and (2) self-pollination. Cross-pollination involves the transfer of pollen from a stamen on one plant to a pistil on another plant. In self-pollination, pollen is transferred from a stamen of one flower to a pistil of the same flower or to the pistil of another flower on the same plant.

Cross-pollination is the method of pollination in most flowering plants. The method requires an *agent* to carry the pollen from flower to flower. Insects are the most common agents of cross-pollination.

Many insects depend on flowers for food. Bees live on nectar and pollen. They also use nectar to make honey, which they feed on in winter. Butterflies and moths also live on nectar, and certain beetles and flies feed on both nectar and pollen. As an insect travels from flower to flower in search of food, pollen grains stick to its body. Some or all of these grains may brush off onto the stigmas of some flowers that the insect visits. One or more of these flowers may thus become cross-pollinated.

When searching for food, an insect could easily fail to visit a particular kind of flower unless the insect was attracted to it. Most flowers that depend on insects for pollination are brightly colored or heavily scented. Each kind of pollinating insect is attracted by certain colors or odors and so visits certain flowers rather than others. However, more than one kind of insect pollinates most insect-pollinated flowers. For example, moths and butterflies visit many of the same flowers. A few kinds of insects and flowers have developed highly specialized relationships with each other. These flowers are pollinated only by a particular kind of insect. For example, bumblebees are the type of insect that pollinates the red clover flower.

Pollination by bees. More flowers are pollinated by bees than by any other kind of insect. Bees cannot see the color red. Otherwise, they have a keen sense of sight. They also have a well-developed sense of smell. Bees are strongly attracted by yellow and blue blossoms, especially those with a sweet odor. Unlike people, bees can see ultraviolet light. Many flowers, particularly yellow ones, have elaborate ultraviolet markings. These markings attract bees to the flowers and even pinpoint the location of the nectaries.

Many of the flowers pollinated by bees have a highly complicated structure that encourages cross-pollination and discourages self-pollination. For example, a bee can reach the nectar of a snapdragon only after brushing against the stigma. It then cannot leave the flower without touching the pollen. Furthermore, the bee cannot touch the stigma after it touched the pollen.

Pollination by butterflies and moths. Butterflies and moths are attracted to flowers that produce abundant nectar. In many such flowers, the nectaries are long and tube-shaped or are at the base of a long tube-shaped corolla. Butterflies and moths have exceptionally long, tubelike mouthparts, which enable them to reach into these structures and suck up the nectar. Butterflies, like bees, prefer flowers with sweet-smelling yellow or blue blossoms.

Unlike most bees and butterflies, many moths rest during the day and search for food at night. Many of the flowers that attract moths open only at night. Most of these flowers are pale-colored or white and so are easier to see at night than dark blossoms. Many of the flowers are also heavily scented and give off their scent only at night. Flowering tobacco and various kinds of evening primroses and honeysuckles are among the plants commonly pollinated by moths.

Thomas Eisner

Yellow flowers have ultraviolet markings that attract bees and indicate where nectar is produced. The human eye cannot see these markings, *left.* But when the flowers are photographed in ultraviolet light, *right,* dark areas appear that resemble the markings seen by bees.

James P. Rowan

Pollination by butterflies usually occurs among yellow or blue flowers that produce abundant nectar. Butterflies use their long mouthparts to reach into the flower and suck up the nectar.

© Giuseppe Mazza

The structure of a hibiscus helps prevent self-pollination. The yellow stamens are shorter than the pistils, making it unlikely for pollen from a stamen to reach a pistil.

The yucca flowers of the American Southwest are pollinated only by the yucca moth. The female moth carries pollen from one yucca plant to another. She bores into the ovary of the second flower and lays her eggs inside it. She then deposits pollen from the first flower onto the stigma of the second. The moth eggs and the yucca seeds develop together. The eggs hatch into caterpillars, which feed on the seeds. But enough seeds remain to produce the next generation of yuccas.

Pollination by beetles and flies. Beetles visit flowers in which both nectar and pollen are plentiful. They prefer white or dull-colored flowers with spicy odors, such as magnolias and wild roses. Most flies do not have long enough mouthparts to suck nectar from tube-shaped flowers. These flies usually visit flowers with flat corollas, such as hawthorn blossoms and buttercups. Some flowers, such as carrion flowers and skunk cabbages, give off a foul odor that attracts flies.

Pollination by other agents. Some birds feed on nectar and so help pollinate flowers. Unlike most pollinating insects, birds have a weak sense of smell. But birds have sharp vision and see red as well as they see other colors. Most odorless red flowers are pollinated by birds. In North America, hummingbirds are the chief bird pollinators. Hummingbirds are particularly attracted to red, orange, and yellow flowers, such as columbines, fuchsias, and Indian paintbrushes. Bats pollinate certain strongly scented flowers of the tropics. The wind spreads the pollen of most plants whose flowers lack petals and sepals. These plants include oaks, ragweeds, sedges, and most wild grasses.

Self-pollination. Only a few species of plants normally pollinate themselves. Such plants include barley, oats, peas, and wheat. However, self-pollination also oc-

curs frequently in many species that depend on cross-pollination. In such cases, pollen may simply fall onto a stigma of the same plant.

Self-pollination increases the chances of transmitting undesirable characteristics to the next generation. In some cases, the seeds produced by self-pollination may be unable to *germinate* (sprout). In some other cases, the seeds may develop into plants that cannot produce seeds of their own.

Self-pollination is impossible in dioecious species because the male and female flowers are on different plants. In addition, many other plants have characteristics that discourage or prevent self-pollination. In such flowers as hibiscuses and lilies, for example, the stamens are much shorter than the pistils. Any pollen that drops from the stamens is therefore unlikely to reach a stigma of a pistil on the same plant. A few plants, such as flowering tobacco and rye, have chemicals in their cells that prevent self-pollination.

Fertilization. A pollen grain that lands on a stigma may grow a *pollen tube.* The tube pushes its way down the style to an ovule in the ovary. Sperm from the pollen grain travel down the tube to the ovule. Fertilization occurs when a sperm unites with an egg cell in the ovule. A seed then begins to develop. The ovary itself develops into a fruit that encloses the seed. For an illustration of this process, see **Plant** (How flowering plants reproduce).

An ovary may be penetrated by many pollen tubes. But the number of seeds that develop depends on the number of ovules. An ovary with one ovule develops into a single-seed fruit, such as an acorn or cherry. An ovary with many ovules develops into a fruit with many seeds, such as a milkweed pod or watermelon.

Two of the most popular flower hobbies, outdoor and indoor gardening, are discussed in the article Gardening. This section deals with three other flower hobbies: (1) studying wild flowers, (2) flower arranging, and (3) flower breeding.

Studying wild flowers. To study wild flowers scientifically, you must be able to identify them. Various handbooks help provide such identification. Most of these books deal with the flowers of a particular region, such as the Northeastern or Southwestern United States. The typical handbook divides the flowers into groups according to the color of their blossoms. Each of these groups is then subdivided according to certain other characteristics of the plants, such as the number of their petals or the arrangement of their leaves. By checking a particular flower for each of the listed characteristics, you should be able to identify it.

One way to learn about wild flowers is to study them in their natural surroundings. For example, you might try to identify all the species in a particular environment, such as a meadow or woods. By taking careful notes and revisiting the location at various times of the year, you can produce a "biography" of the common flowering plants of that environment. Another way of studying wild flowers is by collecting them. However, you must follow certain rules in picking wild flowers. After you have picked the flowers, they must be properly preserved.

Rules for picking wild flowers. About 10 per cent of all the native flowering plants of the United States are so rare that they are considered to be endangered species. Unless these plants are carefully protected in their natural surroundings, they may die out completely. For this reason, the U.S. government and most state governments have passed laws that prohibit people from picking wild flowers in public parks and forests. Such laws not only help conserve endangered species but also help preserve the blossoms so that more people can enjoy them.

In an area not protected by conservation laws, do not pick a specimen of a particular type of flower unless the species is plentiful in the area. As a general rule, wild flowers should never be uprooted. However, you may dig up one specimen by the roots, but again only if the species is abundant in the area.

Preserving wild flower specimens. The easiest way to preserve flower specimens is by pressing them. The method may be used to preserve not only the blossoms of wild flowers but also the entire plant, including the roots. While a specimen is still fresh, carefully arrange it between two sheets of newspaper. Then place the newspaper between two stacks of blotters or between the pages of an old phone book. Apply pressure by tying the blotters or phone book into a tight bundle or by using a weight. The pressure flattens the specimen and squeezes out the moisture. Change the newspaper wrapping daily and move the specimen to a dry part of the stack of blotters or phone book. After 7 to 10 days of pressing, the specimen should be dried out, unless it was especially juicy. The preserved specimen will last almost indefinitely if it is protected from moisture and insects.

How to make a dried floral arrangement

Items suitable for making a dried floral arrangement include, *left to right below*, okra pods, iris pods, silver dollar eucalyptus, eucalyptus, yellow statice, purple statice, yarrow, and safflower. The specimens should be dried in a dark, well-ventilated room for about three weeks.

Select items of various shapes, sizes, and colors.

Dry your selections by hanging them upside down.

WORLD BOOK photos by William and Stephenie Ferguson

Arrange the items artistically in a suitable container.

Tape or glue each finished specimen to a sheet of heavy paper. Then label the mounted specimen with its common and scientific names, the place where the flower was found, the date it was picked, and any interesting facts about its growing habits. An organized collection of mounted pressed flowers is called a *herbarium.* See **Herbarium.**

Flower arranging. The ancient Egyptians, Greeks, and Romans all practiced the art of making decorative arrangements of cut flowers. However, the art received its fullest development in Japan. The Japanese tradition of flower arranging dates from the 500's. At that time, Japanese Buddhists began to make floral arrangements in an elaborate style for the altars of their temples. Over the centuries, the Japanese refined and simplified this style and worked out its artistic principles. These Japanese principles have had a strong influence on the styles of flower arranging in many other countries during the 1900's.

The Japanese try above all to make each floral arrangement look natural, as if it were growing outdoors. They follow carefully worked out principles of design and color to achieve this natural effect. The Japanese use leaves and stems as major elements in many arrangements. In Western countries, on the other hand, traditional styles of flower arranging tend to emphasize only the blossoms. Although Western principles of design and color differ from those of the Japanese, they are just as important to the overall effect.

Most flower arrangements are made of fresh flowers. However, you can use dried flowers. Flowers suited to drying include chrysanthemums, goldenrods, hydran-geas, larkspurs, and pearly everlastings. You can dry any of these flowers by hanging the blossoms head downward in a dark, dry, well-ventilated room for about three weeks. You can also dry various kinds of grasses and leaves in this way and then add the specimens to the flower arrangement. A dried floral arrangement that is prepared in late summer or fall should last through the winter.

Flower breeding has become an increasingly popular hobby among gardeners. Each year, amateur gardeners in many countries produce hundreds of new varieties of flowers. Roses are especially popular for breeding, but many gardeners also work with such flowers as chrysanthemums, irises, orchids, and water lilies. Most new varieties introduce changes in the color, shape, size, or fragrance of the blossoms. For example, breeding experiments have resulted in many dwarf varieties and numerous varieties with *double flowers.* Double flowers have more than the normal number of petals. Flower breeding has also produced such improvements as greater hardiness and greater resistance to diseases and insects.

Gardeners breed flowers by crossing two related species or two varieties of the same species. Each parent is selected for a desired characteristic, such as the color or size of its blossoms. The breeder takes pollen from one parent and places it on a stigma of the other parent. Some of the resulting offspring may have the desired characteristics of both parents. Such offspring are called *hybrids.* By repeating experiments with many parents and many varieties, gardeners can produce hybrids of greater vigor and beauty.

Milt and Joan Mann, Van Cleve Photography

Japanese flower arrangers use design and color to achieve a natural effect. At the left, an arranger trims branches to form graceful lines. In the finished arrangement, *right,* the branches emphasize one large flower. The size and shape of the vase balance the arrangement.

The naming of flowers. Flowers have both common names and scientific names. Many of the common names can be traced back hundreds or even thousands of years. The practice of giving plants scientific names began during the 1700's.

Common names. The common names of many wild flowers originated in folklore. In numerous cases, a plant's name comes from a traditional belief concerning the plant. People once used many wild plants as medicines and named the plants after the ailments they were thought to cure. For example, North American wild flowers named in this way include agueweed and colicroot. People believed that agueweed cured a fever called the *ague* and that colicroot cured abdominal cramps called *colic.* In several other cases, a plant's common name simply describes a characteristic of the plant. For example, the blossoms of lady's-slippers resemble women's shoes. The leaves of pitcher plants form a pitcherlike shape. Skunk cabbages are named after their unpleasant odor.

The English names of many wild flowers end in -wort. Such flowers include birthworts, liverworts, milkworts, ragworts, and soapworts. The ending -wort comes from the Old English word *wyrt,* meaning *root* or *plant.* The first part of each name refers to some special characteristic of the plant, such as its appearance or supposed healing powers. For example, ragworts were so named because their leaves have extremely ragged edges. Birthworts provided a medicine that was believed to help women during childbirth.

The English names of many poisonous or supposedly poisonous wild flowers end in -bane. These flowers include cowbane, dogbanes, fleabanes, and henbane. The word ending comes from the Old English word *bana,* meaning *murderer.* The animal mentioned in each case was supposedly the one most affected by the poison. However, many of these plants, such as cowbane and most dogbanes, are also poisonous to other animals and to people. Some of the plants, including most fleabanes, are harmless.

The English names for many garden flowers can be traced back to Latin or ancient Greek. For example, the English name *lily* comes from the Latin name *lilium.* Peonies were called *paeoniae* in Latin, roses were *rosae,* and violets were *violae.* The English name *iris* comes from the Greek word *iris,* meaning rainbow. Hyacinths are named after Hyacinthus, a youth in Greek mythology famed for his great beauty. The names of some garden flowers come from languages other than Latin and Greek. For example, the name *tulip* comes from the Turkish word *tülbent,* meaning *turban.* Tulips are shaped somewhat like turbans and were introduced into Western countries from Turkey.

During modern times, a number of flowers have been named after people. For example, begonias were named in honor of Michel Bégon, a governor of French Canada and an amateur botanist. Dahlias were named after Anders Dahl, a Swedish botanist who introduced the flowers into Europe from Mexico. Poinsettias were named in honor of Joel R. Poinsett, a U.S. minister to Mexico, who introduced the plants into the United States from Mexico.

Scientific names. The common names of flowers are not suitable for scientific purposes. In many cases, the same flower has more than one common name. In the United States, for example, a marsh marigold is also called a kingcup, May blob, and cowslip. In other cases, the same name is used for entirely different flowers. For example, several very different species of flowers are called bluebells in various English-speaking countries. To help avoid such confusion with names, botanists refer to each species of flower by its scientific name.

The Swedish botanist Carolus Linnaeus devised the modern scientific system of plant names in the mid-1700's. In this system, each species is given a two-part Latin name. The first part of the name refers to the *genus* (group of species) to which the particular species belongs. The second part of the name refers to the species itself. Each species has only one scientific name, and each name applies to only one species. For example, the flower known as a marsh marigold, kingcup, May blob, or cowslip has the scientific name *Caltha palustris.* The genus name, *Caltha,* means *gold-colored flower* in Latin. The second part of the name, *palustris,* is a Latin word meaning *marsh loving.* No other species of plant in the world is named *Caltha palustris.* By using scientific names, botanists can identify every species of plant precisely and without confusion.

The scientific naming and the scientific classification of flowering plants are closely related. For example, newly discovered species must be classed according to genus before they can be given scientific names. However, every species keeps the second part of its name permanently, regardless of any changes that may later be made in the classification of the species. Thus, *Caltha palustris,* the marsh marigold, will always keep its specific name *palustris* even if it is someday reclassified into a different genus.

The classifying of flowers. Flowering plants make up the *division* (group) of plants called Anthophyta. This division is split into two classes: (1) *dicotyledons,* also called *dicots,* and (2) *monocotyledons,* also known as *monocots.* Plants are grouped based on the structure of their seeds. The seeds of dicots have two tiny leaves called *cotyledons.* The seeds of monocots have only one cotyledon. In addition, the petals and other flower parts of most monocots grow in threes or in multiples of three, and the veins in their leaves parallel one another. The flower parts of most dicots grow in fours or fives or in multiples of four or five, and the veins in their leaves are branched rather than parallel. Of the approximately 250,000 species of flowering plants, about 190,000 are dicots and about 60,000 are monocots.

Each of the two classes of flowering plants is divided into *orders,* each order into *families,* and each family into *genera.* The table on the following two pages lists the families that include most of the well-known garden flowers and wild flowers of the United States and Canada. These families consist mainly of herbs and shrubs, but some also include trees. The table gives (1) the approximate number of species in each family; (2) typical characteristics of most flowers in the family; and (3) the names of representative flowers.

Critically reviewed by Peter H. Raven

Representative families of flowers
Subclass Dicotyledoneae
Balsam family (Balsaminaceae)

About 450 species of annual or perennial herbs. The flowers are bilaterally symmetrical and have 3 to 5 sepals, 5 petals, and 5 stamens. One of the sepals forms a long, spur-shaped nectary at the back of the flower. Garden balsams, touch-me-nots.

Begonia family (Begoniaceae)

About 900 species. Mostly perennial herbs and shrubs, with staminate and pistillate flowers on the same plant. The staminate flowers have 2 petallike sepals, 2 petals, and many stamens. The pistillate flowers have 2 or more tepals and a compound pistil. Begonias.

Bellflower family (Campanulaceae)

About 1,800 species of annual or perennial herbs. The flowers of most species have 5 sepals, 5 petals, and 5 stamens. In most species, the petals are fused along most of their length, forming a bell-shaped corolla. Bellflowers.

Borage family (Boraginaceae)

About 2,000 species. Mostly annual or perennial herbs; some shrubs and small trees. The flowers of most species have 5 sepals fused at the base, 5 petals fused into a tubular shape at the base, and 5 stamens. Forget-me-nots, heliotropes, lungworts.

Cactus family (Cactaceae)

About 2,000 species. Perennial herbs, shrubs, and trees. Most species have numerous petals and petallike sepals and many stamens. The petals and sepals are fused at the base. Cactuses.

Composite family (Compositae)

About 20,000 species. Mostly annual, biennial, or perennial herbs and shrubs. The flowers consist of several to many florets arranged on a head. Ageratums, arnicas, asters, black-eyed Susans, blazing stars, bonesets, calendulas, chicories, chrysanthemums, compass plants, cosmos, dahlias, daisies, dandelions, fleabanes, gaillardias, goldenrods, marigolds, sunflowers, thistles, tickseeds, zinnias.

Crowfoot or buttercup family (Ranunculaceae)

About 1,800 species. Mostly annual or perennial herbs. The majority have 5 petals—or 5 showy sepals in place of petals—and many stamens and pistils. Anemones, bugbanes, buttercups, columbines, delphiniums, hepaticas, larkspurs, marsh marigold, peonies.

Evening primrose family (Onagraceae)

About 650 species. Mostly annual or perennial herbs. The majority have 4 sepals, 4 petals, and 4 or 8 stamens. The sepals are fused, in many cases forming a long tube at the base of the flower. Evening primroses, fireweeds, fuchsias, godetias.

Figwort or snapdragon family (Scrophulariaceae)

About 3,000 species. Mostly annual, biennial, or perennial herbs. Most species have 4 or 5 fused sepals, 4 or 5 petals fused at the base, and 4 stamens. Beardtongues, foxgloves, Indian paintbrushes, monkey flowers, mulleins, slipperworts, snapdragons, toadflaxes.

Gentian family (Gentianaceae)

About 800 species of annual, biennial, or perennial herbs. Most species have 4 or 5 sepals, 4 or 5 petals, and as many stamens as petals. The sepals are fused at the base, forming a cup-shaped calyx. The petals are fused into a tubular shape. Gentians.

Geranium family (Geraniaceae)

About 750 species of annual, biennial, or perennial herbs. Most species have 5 sepals, 5 petals, and 5 or 10 stamens. Crane's-bills, geraniums, pelargoniums, stork's-bills.

Mallow family (Malvaceae)

About 1,500 species. Annual, biennial, or perennial herbs; some shrubs and trees. The flowers have 5 sepals, 5 petals, and many stamens. The filaments of the stamens are fused, forming a tube around the pistil. Hibiscuses, hollyhocks, mallows, rose of Sharon.

Morning-glory family (Convolvulaceae)

About 1,800 species. Mostly annual or perennial herbaceous vines. The flowers have 5 sepals, 5 petals, and 5 stamens. In most species, the petals are fused into a bell- or funnel-shaped corolla. Bindweeds, dodders, moonflowers, morning-glories.

Mustard or cabbage family (Cruciferae)

About 3,000 species. Annual, biennial, or perennial herbs. The flowers have 4 sepals and 4 petals in the shape of a cross. Most species have 6 stamens. Candytuft, cresses, mustards, rockets, stocks, sweet alyssum, wallflowers.

Spotted Touch-Me-Not

Wax Begonia

Clustered Bellflower

Spring Forget-Me-Not

Prickly Pear

Upland Boneset

Common Buttercup

Common Evening Primrose

Snapdragon

Pine-Barren Gentian

Wild Geranium

Marsh Mallow

Common Morning-Glory

White Mustard

Subclass Dicotyledoneae (continued)

Nasturtium family (Tropaeolaceae)

About 50 species of annual or perennial herbs. The flowers of most species have 5 sepals, 5 petals, and 8 stamens. One or more of the sepals form a spur at the back of the flower. Canary creeper, nasturtiums.

Nightshade family (Solanaceae)

About 2,200 species. Mostly annual or perennial herbs; some shrubs and trees. The flowers have 5 fused sepals, 5 petals fused into the shape of a star or funnel; and 5 stamens. Belladonna, flowering tobacco, ground cherries, henbane, jimson weed, petunias.

Parsley or carrot family (Umbelliferae)

About 2,900 species. Mostly biennial or perennial herbs. In most species, the flowers are small and arranged in umbrella-shaped clusters. The florets have 5 sepals, 5 petals, and 5 stamens. Queen Anne's lace, rattlesnake masters, sweet cicely, water pennyworts.

Pea family (Leguminosae)

About 17,000 species. Annual or perennial herbs; many shrubs and trees. The flowers of most species have 5 fused sepals, 5 petals, and 10 or many more stamens. Acacias, brooms, clovers, locoweeds, lupines, mimosas, redbuds, sweet pea, wild indigos, wisterias.

Phlox family (Polemoniaceae)

About 300 species. Mostly annual or perennial herbs. The flowers have 5 fused sepals, 5 petals, and 5 stamens. The petals are fused at the base. Phloxes, polemoniums.

Pink family (Caryophyllaceae)

About 2,100 species. Mostly annual, biennial, or perennial herbs. The flowers of most species have 5 sepals, 5 petals, and 5 or 10 stamens. Baby's-breath, campions, carnations, pinks, sweet Williams.

Poppy family (Papaveraceae)

About 250 species. Mostly annual or perennial herbs. The majority have 4 petals, 2 or 3 sepals, and many stamens. Bloodroot, poppies.

Primrose family (Primulaceae)

About 800 species of annual or perennial herbs. Most species have 5 sepals, 5 petals, and 5 stamens. The petals are fused into a tubular shape at the base. The sepals are fused into a cuplike shape. Cyclamens, loosestrifes, pimpernels, primroses.

Rose family (Rosaceae)

About 3,200 species of perennial herbs, shrubs, and trees. The flowers of most species have 5 sepals, 5 petals, and numerous stamens. Agrimonies, cherry laurel, cinquefoils, cotoneasters, hawthorns, mountain avens, pyracanthas, roses, spiraeas.

Saxifrage family (Saxifragaceae)

About 1,200 species. Mostly perennial herbs and shrubs; some small trees. The flowers of most species have 5 sepals, 5 petals, and 5 or 10 stamens. Coralbells, deutzias, hydrangeas, mock oranges, saxifrages.

Violet family (Violaceae)

About 850 species. Mostly perennial herbs and shrubs. The flowers have 5 sepals, 5 petals, and 5 stamens. In many species, the petal nearest the stem is larger than the others and has a hollow sac or spur at the back. Pansies, violas, violets.

Subclass Monocotyledoneae

Amaryllis family (Amaryllidaceae)

About 1,300 species. Mostly perennial herbs. The flowers have 6 tepals and 6 stamens. All the floral parts, including the pistil, are fused at the base of the flower. Amaryllises, daffodils, jonquils, narcissuses, snowdrops.

Iris family (Iridaceae)

About 1,500 species of perennial herbs. The flowers have 3 petallike sepals, 3 petals, and 3 stamens. All the floral parts are fused at the base, forming a tube. Crocuses, freesias, gladioli, irises.

Lily family (Liliaceae)

About 4,000 species. Mostly perennial herbs. The flowers of most species have 6 tepals and 6 stamens. In some species, the tepals are fused at the base. Aloes, day lilies, dogtooth violets, hyacinths, lilies, lilies of the valley, Solomon's-seals, trilliums, tulips.

Orchid family (Orchidaceae)

More than 20,000 species of perennial herbs with bilaterally symmetrical flowers. The flowers of most species have 3 petallike sepals; 3 petals; and 1 or 2 stamens, which are fused with the style. Fairy-slippers, lady's-slippers, orchids, pogonias.

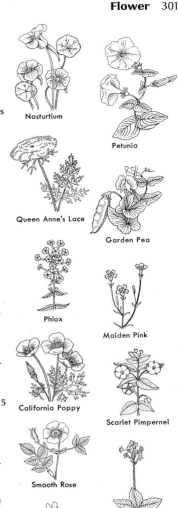

Nasturtium

Petunia

Queen Anne's Lace

Garden Pea

Phlox

Maiden Pink

California Poppy

Scarlet Pimpernel

Smooth Rose

Early Saxifrage

Round-Leafed Yellow Violet

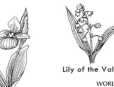

Blue Flag Iris

Daffodil

Showy Lady's-Slipper

Lily of the Valley

WORLD BOOK
illustrations by
Patricia J. Wynne

Related articles in *World Book* include:

Articles on individual flowers

World Book has hundreds of separate articles on flowering plants. Those that have showy blossoms and are not trees are listed below:

Garden flowers

Ageratum	Four-o'clock	Pink
Amaryllis	Foxglove	Plumbago
Anemone	Geranium	Poppy
Aster	Gladiolus	Portulaca
Baby's-breath	Godetia	Primrose
Bachelor's-button	Heliotrope	Pyrethrum
Balsam, Garden	Hibiscus	Salvia
Begonia	Hollyhock	Snapdragon
Belladonna	Hyacinth	Snow-on-the-
Bird's-foot trefoil	Iris	mountain
Bleeding heart	Jonquil	Star-of-Bethlehem
Calendula	Larkspur	Statice
Candytuft	Lily of the valley	Stock
Canna	Lobelia	Strawflower
Canterbury bell	Lotus	Sunflower
Carnation	Lupine	Sweet alyssum
Chrysanthemum	Marigold	Sweet pea
Cineraria	Mignonette	Sweet William
Cockscomb	Moonflower	Tansy
Cosmos	Morning-glory	Tiger lily
Crocus	Narcissus	Tuberose
Daffodil	Nasturtium	Tulip
Dahlia	Oxalis	Verbena
Day lily	Painted-tongue	Violet
Easter lily	Pansy	Viper's bugloss
Feverfew	Peony	Wallflower
Firecracker flower	Petunia	Wisteria
Flowering tobacco	Phlox	Zinnia

Wild flowers

Aconite	Clover	Indian pipe
Adonis	Cocklebur	Jack-in-the-pulpit
Agrimony	Colchicum	Jimsonweed
Amaranth	Coltsfoot	Lady's-slipper
Arbutus	Columbine	Lamb's-quarters
Arnica	Compass plant	Lily
Asphodel	Coreopsis	Locoweed
Beardtongue	Cowslip	Loosestrife
Bedstraw	Daisy	Lungwort
Beggarweed	Dandelion	Mallow
Bellflower	Devil's paintbrush	Mariposa lily
Bindweed	Dodder	Marsh mallow
Bitter root	Dogbane	May apple
Black-eyed Susan	Dogtooth violet	Milkweed
Bladderwort	Dutchman's-	Monkey flower
Blazing star	breeches	Mountain avens
Bloodroot	Edelweiss	Mullein
Bluebell	Elecampane	Mustard
Bluebonnet	Evening primrose	Oregon grape
Bluet	Fireweed	Pasqueflower
Boehmeria	Fleabane	Pimpernel
Boneset	Forget-me-not	Pitcher plant
Buckwheat	Fritillary	Pokeweed
Bugbane	Gaillardia	Prickly pear
Bunchberry	Gentian	Purslane
Buttercup	Glasswort	Pussy willow
Butterwort	Goldenrod	Ragweed
Cactus	Goldenseal	Saint-John's-wort
Calla	Heath	Sand verbena
Canada thistle	Hellebore	Saxifrage
Cardinal flower	Henbane	Sego lily
Celandine	Hepatica	Skunk cabbage
Chicory	Immortelle	Smartweed
Cinquefoil	Indian mallow	Snakeroot
Clematis	Indian paintbrush	Snowdrop

Soap plant	Sundew	Valerian
Solomon's-seal	Thistle	Venus's-flytrap
Sorrel	Toadflax	Vetch
Spring beauty	Touch-me-not	Water lily
Stickseed	Trillium	Wild carrot

Tropical and subtropical flowers

Acacia	Freesia	Pelican flower
African violet	Fuchsia	Poinsettia
Aloe	Gardenia	Rafflesia
Bird-of-paradise	Gloxinia	Slipperwort
flower	Orchid	Spiderwort
Bougainvillea	Passionflower	Water hyacinth
Cyclamen		

Flowering shrubs

Azalea	Gelsemium	Redbud
Bridal wreath	Hawthorn	Rhododendron
Broom	Honeysuckle	Rose
Camellia	Hydrangea	Rose of Sharon
Cherry laurel	Illicium	Snowball
Deutzia	Jasmine	Spiraea
Dogwood	Lilac	Twinflower
Eglantine	Mock orange	Yucca
Forsythia	Myrtle	
Furze	Ocotillo	

Other related articles

Angiosperm	Floriculture	Pollen
Botany	Florist	Seed
Breeding	Fruit	Shrub
Broccoli	Gardening	Spice
Bulb	Inflorescence	Tree
Caper	Monocotyledon	Trefoil
Cauliflower	Perfume	Vine
Dicotyledon	Plant	Weed
Duckweed		

Outline

I. The uses of flowers
  A. As decoration
  B. In landscaping
  C. Other uses
II. Garden flowers
  A. Garden annuals
  B. Garden biennials
  C. Garden perennials
  D. Garden perennials (Bulbs)
  E. Garden perennials (Flowering shrubs)
III. Wild flowers
  A. Flowers of the Arctic tundra
  B. Flowers of woodlands and forests
  C. Flowers of prairies and dry plains
  D. Flowers of chaparrals
  E. Flowers of Alpine tundras
  F. Flowers of the desert
  G. Flowers of the tropics and subtropics
IV. The parts of a flower
  A. The calyx
  B. The corolla
  C. The stamens
  D. The pistils
  E. Variations in flower structure
V. The role of flowers in reproduction
  A. Cross-pollination
  B. Self-pollination
  C. Fertilization
VI. Flower hobbies
  A. Studying wild flowers   C. Flower breeding
  B. Flower arranging
VII. How flowers are named and classified
  A. The naming of flowers
  B. The classifying of flowers

Questions

What are *annuals*? *Biennials*? *Perennials*?

What attracts insects and birds to flowers?

How do individual perennial plants spread?

What is the easiest method of preserving wild flower specimens? What steps does the method involve?

Why do annuals thrive in deserts?

What are the four main parts of a flower?

How do bees and other insects help flowering plants reproduce?

How do gardeners produce new varieties of flowers? What are such varieties called?

Why do botanists refer to flowers by their scientific names rather than by their common names?

Additional resources

Level I

Busch, Phyllis S. *Wildflowers and the Stories Behind Their Names.* Scribner, 1977.

Crowell, Robert L. *The Lore and Legends of Flowers.* Harper, 1982.

Dowden, Anne O. T. *State Flowers.* Harper, 1978. *From Flower to Fruit.* 1984.

Foster, Laura L. *Keeping the Plants You Pick.* Crowell, 1970.

Givens, Janet E. *Something Wonderful Happened.* Scribner, 1982. The story of the first flower.

Lerner, Carol. *Flowers of a Woodland Spring.* Morrow, 1979.

Milne, Lorus J. and Margery. *Because of a Flower.* Atheneum, 1975.

Rahn, Joan E. *How Plants Are Pollinated.* Scribner, 1975.

Level II

Crockett, James U. *Crockett's Flower Garden.* Little, Brown, 1981.

Diamond, Denise. *Living with the Flowers: A Guide to Bringing Flowers into Your Daily Life.* Morrow, 1982.

Gough, Tom, and Longman, David. *The Instant Guide to Healthy Flowering Houseplants.* Random House, 1985.

James, John. *Flowers When You Want Them: A Grower's Guide to Out-of-Season Bloom.* Hawthorn Books, 1977.

Kramer, Jack. *Growing Beautiful Flowers Indoors.* St. Martin's, 1980.

Meeuse, Bastiaan, and Morris, Sean. *The Sex Life of Flowers.* Facts on File, 1984.

Moggi, Guido, and Giugnolini, Luciano. *Simon and Schuster's Guide to Garden Flowers.* Simon & Schuster, 1983.

Mohlenbrock, Robert H. *Where Have All the Wildflowers Gone? A Region-by-Region Guide to Threatened or Endangered U.S. Wildflowers.* Macmillan, 1983.

Morris, Francesca. *The Flower Gardener's Answer Book.* Van Nostrand, 1978.

Okun, Sheila. *A Book of Cut Flowers.* Morrow, 1983.

Rickett, Harold W. *Wild Flowers of the United States: Vol. 1, The Northeastern States; Vol. 2, The Southeastern States; Vol. 3, Texas; Vol. 4, The Southwestern States; Vol. 5, The Northwestern States; Vol. 6, The Central Mountains and Plains.* McGraw, 1966-1973.

Flower arranging. See Flower (Flower hobbies; pictures).

Flowering maple is the common name for about 90 kinds of herbs and shrubs that grow in temperate regions of Africa, Asia, and North and South America. Flowering maples usually have heart-shaped leaves. The flowers may be a wide variety of colors. They grow singly or in clusters.

    Scientific classification. Flowering maples belong to the mallow family, Malvaceae. A common type is *Abutilon hybridum.*   Walter S. Judd

Flowering tobacco is the name of several annual and perennial plants in the nightshade family. They are grown for their sweet-scented flowers. They are also called *nicotiana.* The plants grow wild in tropical South America, but are cultivated in the United States.

WORLD BOOK illustration by Christabel King

Flowering tobacco is grown for its sweet-scented flowers. It grows wild in warm climates, but is also cultivated.

    The leaves of the flowering tobaccos are hairy and sticky. The flowers are yellow, purple, red, or white, and shaped like long tubes. The flowering tobaccos are sensitive to cold, and should be sheltered. They can be grown from seed in rich, light soil. The seeds should be planted in a hotbed or greenhouse in the early spring, and later transplanted outdoors.

    Scientific classification. Flowering tobaccos belong to the nightshade family, Solanaceae. They make up the genus *Nicotiana.*   Marcus Maxon

Floyd, William (1734-1821), was a leader in the American struggle for independence, and a New York signer of the Declaration of Independence. Floyd was born in Suffolk County, Long Island. He served in the Continental Congress from 1774 to 1777 and from 1778 to 1783.

A-Z Botanical Collection Ltd.

Bright red and yellow blossoms of a flowering maple, *above,* contrast with the plant's dark-green leaves.

The Continental Congress became the Congress of the Confederation on March 1, 1781. Floyd did committee work in the New York Congressional delegation. He was a supporter of the movement to make Thomas Jefferson President. Clarence L. Ver Steeg

FLQ. See **Canada, History of** (The Quebec separatist movement; The separatist threat).

Flu. See **Influenza.**

Flügelhorn is a brass musical instrument that resembles a large cornet and has the same general range of about $2\frac{1}{2}$ octaves. However, the flügelhorn is actually a member of the bugle family. A musician produces tones by blowing into a cup-shaped mouthpiece of the flügelhorn and vibrating the lips. The player changes notes by fingering the instrument's three valves and changing lip tension.

The flügelhorn has a mellow tone and a rich lower range. This makes it useful both as a solo instrument and as a link between the trumpet and trombone when played in ensembles. The flügelhorn is most commonly used in popular music and jazz. John Keil Richards

Fluid is any substance that flows easily. A slight pressure or force will change the form of a fluid. But fluids are also elastic, so they tend to return to their former size when the pressure is removed. Fluids include all liquids and gases. Water at ordinary temperature is a fluid and a liquid. Air is a fluid and a gas. A liquid tends always to occupy the same volume. A gas, however, readily changes its volume by expanding or contracting to fill, or fit into, any container in which it is placed.

Gases are compressible fluids and liquids are incompressible fluids. Pressure changes generally do not affect the density of a liquid (see **Density**). But in practice no liquid is completely incompressible.

A *perfect fluid* is frictionless—that is, it offers no resistance to flow except that of inertia (see **Inertia**). An *elastic fluid* has greater forces resisting changes to size or shape than forces resisting flow. A thicker, *viscous fluid,* such as molasses, is slow-flowing because of the fluid's internal friction. Raymond E. Davis

See also **Hydraulics; Mechanics.**

Fluidic engine. See Hydraulic engine.

Fluke, a fish. See Flounder.

Fluke is any one of a large group of parasitic flatworms (see **Flatworm**). Flukes live in nearly every organ—including the intestine, liver, and lungs—of human beings and other animals. They also live in the blood. Most adult flukes are flat and leaflike, but some are round or long and wormlike. They have one or two suckers that hold them to body tissue in the *host* (animal in which they live). Most flukes have both male and female reproductive organs.

Flukes have complicated life cycles involving different stages of development and from two to four hosts. The first host is usually a snail, in which the young flukes multiply. Later stages of the fluke escape from the snail and enter fish, crabs, insects, or other animals. Some attach to plants.

If a person eats an improperly cooked animal infected by flukes in their early developmental stages, the flukes may infect the person's body. The early stages of *schistosomes* (blood flukes) swim in water and burrow through the skin to reach blood vessels. The kinds of flukes that infect human beings are common in the Far

East. Blood flukes are also common in tropical parts of the Western Hemisphere and in Africa.

Scientific classification. Flukes belong to the subclass Digenea, class Trematoda, of the phylum Platyhelminthes. The liver fluke of human beings is *Clonorchis sinensis,* the lung fluke is *Paragonimus westermani,* and a common type of blood fluke is *Schistosoma mansoni.* Seth Tyler

Fluorescence, *FLOO uh REHS uhns,* is a process by which a variety of substances give off light or another form of electromagnetic radiation when they absorb energy. The term *fluorescence* also refers to the light emitted by these substances. Many gases, liquids, and solids become fluorescent when exposed to radiation or to electrically charged particles.

Fluorescent lighting is widely used in factories, offices, and schools and in some homes. Many highway lights contain fluorescent mercury vapor. TV picture tubes and electron microscopes have fluorescent screens. Biologists stain cells and tissues with fluorescent dyes to observe biological processes. Chemists detect certain air and water pollutants by using fluorescence. It also is used to detect lead poisoning and to identify minerals.

The color of fluorescing light depends on the substance involved and on the type of energy absorbed. In most cases, the wavelengths of fluorescing light are longer than those of the absorbed radiation. However, fluorescence has been observed throughout the visible portion of the electromagnetic spectrum and also in its ultraviolet and infrared regions (see **Electromagnetic waves** [The electromagnetic spectrum]).

Many kinds of energy cause fluorescence. For example, electric current produces fluorescence in neon signs. Ultraviolet rays, visible light, X rays, and various other forms of radiation also cause fluorescence.

When a fluorescent substance absorbs energy, the electrons in its atoms become *excited*—that is, their energy level increases. In some cases, the electrons re-

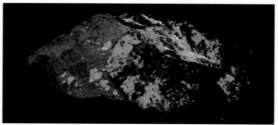

E. R. Degginger
Fluorescence occurs when certain substances absorb energy and give off electromagnetic radiation. Ultraviolet rays cause the mineral, *top,* to give off blue and green light, *above.*

main excited for only $\frac{1}{1,000,000,000,000}$ of a second. The excess energy is then emitted as light. The process stops when the energy source is removed.

Fluorescence was observed by scientists as early as the mid-1500's. It was first explained in 1852 by Sir George G. Stokes, a British physicist, who named the light.   Peter M. Rentzepis

See also **Fluorescent lamp; Fluoroscopy; Luminescence; Phosphorescence.**

Fluorescent lamp, *FLOO uh REHS uhnt,* is a tube-shaped electric light that has wide use in factories, offices, and schools. In homes, incandescent lamps are more widely used than flourescent lamps. A fluorescent lamp uses only about a fifth as much electricity as an incandescent lamp uses to produce the same amount of light. It also produces only a fifth as much heat for the same amount of light. For this reason, fluorescent lamps are sometimes called "cool" lights. In addition, fluorescent lamps last much longer than incandescent lamps.

A fluorescent lamp consists of a glass tube containing a small amount of mercury and another chemically inactive gas at low pressure. The gas in most fluorescent tubes is argon. The inside surface of the tube has a coating of chemicals called *phosphors* (see **Phosphor**). At each end of the tube is an electrode, a coil of tungsten wire coated with chemicals called *rare earth oxides.* A fluorescent circuit includes a device called a *ballast,* which provides voltage to start the lamp. The ballast also regulates the flow of current in the lamp circuit.

There are three main kinds of fluorescent lamp circuits: (1) preheat, (2) rapid-start, and (3) instant-start. Fixtures using a preheat circuit cost the least and are found in some homes. Rapid-start fixtures are more efficient than the preheat type, cheaper to operate and maintain, and widely used commercially.

When a preheat or rapid-heat lamp is turned on, electricity flows through the tungsten wire. The wire becomes heated, and the earth oxides on it give off electrons. Some of the electrons strike the argon atoms and *ionize* them—that is, the electrons give the atoms a positive or negative electric charge. When ionized, the argon can conduct electricity. A current flows through the gas from electrode to electrode, forming an *arc* (stream of electrons). Instant-start lamps start at such high voltage that the arc forms immediately. When an electron in the arc strikes a mercury atom, it raises the energy level of an electron in the atom. As this electron

returns to its normal state, it emits invisible ultraviolet rays. The phosphors on the inside walls of the tube absorb the rays, which cause the phosphors to *fluoresce* (glow), producing visible light. The color of the light produced depends on the phosphors used.

The fluorescent lamp was introduced at the New York World's Fair of 1938-1939. Since 1952, fluorescent lamps have ranked ahead of incandescent lamps in sales in the United States.   Ronald N. Helms

See also **Electric light; Fluorescence.**

Fluoridation is the addition of chemicals called *fluorides* to water supplies to help teeth resist decay. In the 1930's, researchers discovered that people who grew up where water naturally contained fluorides had up to two-thirds fewer cavities than people living in areas without fluoride in the water. Newburgh, N.Y., and Grand Rapids, Mich., began to fluoridate their water in 1945, as an experiment. By the 1950's, the tests showed that the incidence of tooth decay had decreased in these cities, and United States public health officials recommended fluoridation for all communities.

Today, about half the people of the United States drink fluoridated water. In most other countries, fluoridation is not used as widely as it is in the United States. The use of fluoride tablets and toothpastes and the application of strong fluoride solutions to the teeth by dentists can also help prevent tooth decay.

Local governments or the people of a community often must decide whether the water supply should be fluoridated. This means balancing the benefits, risks, and costs of fluoridation, as well as moral questions about its widespread use. People disagree over these issues, and fluoridation has always been controversial.

Benefits, risks, and costs. Many studies have shown that fluoridation reduces tooth decay substantially. However, large doses of fluorides can be harmful, especially to the bones and teeth. In India and other countries, for example, bone damage has occurred in people whose drinking water contained fluoride levels from 2 to 3 parts per million (ppm) or more. The level most commonly used in fluoridated water is 1 ppm. In the United States and elsewhere, *mottling* (discoloration) of the teeth becomes more common as the level of fluorides in drinking water increases. Even at the fluoride levels recommended for fluoridation, some people develop white flecks or patches on their teeth.

Some scientists believe that fluoridation involves spe-

How a fluorescent lamp works

A preheat fluorescent lamp needs a *starter* and a *ballast* to operate. The starter switches electricity through the electrodes at each end of the lamp. The current heats the electrodes so they can give off electrons. Then the ballast sends a surge of current between the electrodes to form an *arc* (stream of electrons) in the lamp. The lamp contains mercury vapor. The arc knocks electrons in the mercury atoms out of their normal position. When the electrons return to their position, the atoms give off invisible ultraviolet rays. These rays strike phosphor particles on the walls of the lamp and cause the particles to glow.

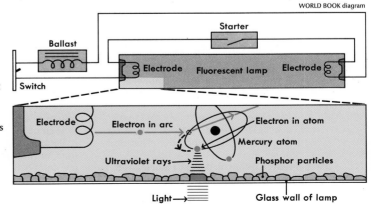

cial risks for people with kidney disease and for those particularly sensitive to toxic substances. However, ill effects from fluoridation have never been shown to be widespread. Most experts believe that the risk of harm from fluoridation is extremely small.

Most public health officials and dentists in the United States favor fluoridation. They believe it provides important benefits and involves little or no health risk. Supporters also argue that fluoridation gives the whole community fluoride protection simply, effectively, and at a small expense compared with the costs of treating tooth decay.

Moral issues. Since the 1950's, fluoridation has sparked much political controversy. Heated debates erupt when communities consider fluoridating their water supplies. Over the years, about 6 of every 10 communities voting on fluoridation have rejected it.

Many people object to fluoridation because they prefer not to take any risks associated with it, even if the risks are very small. Some people feel they have a right to make their own choices in health matters, and that a community violates this right when it adds fluorides to its water supply. On the other hand, if water is not fluoridated, people will suffer tooth decay that easily could have been prevented. Many people feel that this result is also unacceptable. Fluoridation thus produces a conflict of moral beliefs for which there is no compromise solution.   Edward Groth III

See also **Teeth** (A good diet).

Additional resources

American Dental Association. *Fluoridation Facts.* The Association, 1980.
Gotzsche, Anne-Lise. *The Fluoride Question: Panacea or Poison?* Stein & Day, 1975.

Fluoride. See Fluorine; Fluoridation.

Fluorine, *FLOO uh reen,* is a chemical element. At ordinary temperatures, it is a pale yellow gas. Fluorine combines with other elements more readily than does any other element. Compounds that contain fluorine are called *fluorides.*

The principal source of fluorine is the mineral *fluorite,* also called *fluorspar.* Fluorite consists of the compound calcium fluoride. Steelmakers use fluorite to purify steel. Chemical companies treat fluorite with sulfuric acid to produce hydrogen fluoride. Hydrogen fluoride is used to make aluminum and to produce compounds called *chlorofluorocarbons.* Chlorofluorocarbons serve as refrigerants in the cooling systems of refrigerators and air conditioners. Small amounts of fluorides applied to the teeth greatly reduce tooth decay. For this reason, fluorides are added to toothpaste, and many communities add fluorides to their drinking water.

Fluorine is the lightest of the elements known as *halogens* (see **Halogen**). It has the chemical symbol F. Fluorine's atomic number is 9, and its atomic weight is 18.9984. Fluorine may be condensed to a liquid that boils at $-188.14°$ C and freezes at $-219.62°$ C. Fluorine was first isolated in 1886 by the French chemist Henri Moissan.   Evan H. Appelman

See also **Element, Chemical** (tables); **Fluoridation; Uranium** (Ability to form compounds).

Fluorite, *FLOO uh ryt,* also called *fluorspar* or *fluor,* is a common mineral composed of calcium and fluorine.

Its chemical formula is CaF_2. In rare cases, other elements may substitute for the calcium.

Fluorite is important in the production of aluminum, steel, and hydrofluoric acid, a chemical used in manufacturing fluorine. Some lenses and prisms used in optical instruments consist of fluorite.

Fluorite crystals have a glassy luster and are cubic or eight-sided in shape. Fluorite may be transparent and colorless when pure. It also can occur in many colors due to defects in crystal structure or to impurities. Fluorite will often *fluoresce* (give off light) when exposed to ultraviolet radiation.

Fluorite occurs widely in such rocks as granite, granitic pegmatite, syenite, and in ore veins. Fluorite crystals may also line the cavity of spherically shaped, hollow stones called *geodes.* Major deposits of fluorite are found in Canada, England, Germany, Mexico, and the United States.   Robert W. Charles

See also **Fluorescence; Fluorine; Mineral** (picture).

Fluorocarbon, *FLOO uhr uh KAHR buhn,* is any of a group of synthetic organic compounds that contain fluorine and carbon. Many of these chemicals also contain chlorine, and are called *chlorofluorocarbons* (*CFC 's*). These compounds, often called *Freons,* have many uses. The two most commonly used fluorocarbons are *trichlorofluoromethane* ($CFCl_3$), also called F-11, and *dichlorodifluoromethane* (CF_2Cl_2), or F-12. They are used as refrigerants in air conditioners and refrigerators and to make plastic foams for furniture and insulation. See **Food, Frozen** (Liquid-Freon freezing).

F-11 and F-12 are nonpoisonous and nonflammable under normal conditions, and they are easily converted from liquid to gas or from gas to liquid form. These properties make the two chemicals useful as propellants in aerosol spray products (see **Aerosol**). However, scientific studies suggest that CFC's harm the environment by breaking down ozone molecules in the earth's upper atmosphere. Ozone, a form of oxygen, protects plants and animals from the harmful ultraviolet rays of the sun. As CFC's reach the upper atmosphere, ultraviolet rays cause them to break apart and release chlorine atoms. The chlorine atoms react with ozone and convert it to ordinary oxygen. In 1978, the U.S. government banned certain fluorocarbon aerosols for most uses. In 1987, 31 nations signed a treaty to limit CFC production. The next year, the Du Pont Company, the world's largest producer of CFC's, announced plans to phase out production of these chemicals.   Robert C. Gadwood

Fluoroscopy, *flu RAHS kuh pee,* is a diagnostic medical procedure that uses X rays. It enables a physician to view the internal structure and processes of the body. It produces an X-ray image of body organs actually functioning. It differs from *radiography,* a more common X-ray process that produces still images on film. Physicians use fluoroscopy to view malfunctioning organs and to observe such medical procedures as the insertion of a *catheter* (tube) in an artery and the removal of foreign objects from the lungs or stomach.

Before a fluoroscopic examination of the digestive tract, the patient drinks a liquid containing a barium compound. Barium strongly absorbs X rays, and so the digestive organs show up more clearly in the image. The patient lies on a table. An X-ray tube is mounted beneath the table and a device called an *image intensifier*

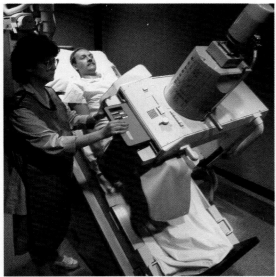

WORLD BOOK photo by Robert Frerck

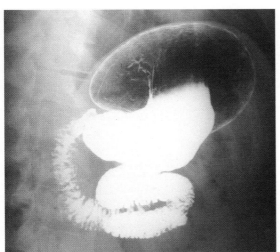

David J. Karr, M.D., Northwestern Memorial Hospital

A fluoroscope, *top,* enables doctors to view internal organs of the body while they function. The patient rests on a table with an X-ray tube beneath it. A large device called an *image intensifier* converts the X rays passing through the patient into an image that a physician can view on a TV monitor. A physician may also obtain a still picture, such as the fluoroscopic image of the stomach, *bottom.* The patient drinks a solution that causes the stomach and other organs to appear white in the image.

is suspended above the patient. X rays passing through the patient form an invisible image in the image intensifier. The image intensifier converts the X rays into a visible image that is recorded by a television camera. The physician views this image on a TV monitor.

Fluoroscopy uses relatively low doses of X rays. As a result, the risk of undesirable effects is small. The American inventor Thomas A. Edison developed the first practical fluoroscope in 1896.   Raymond L. Tanner

See also **Fluorescence; X rays.**

Fluorspar. See Fluorite.

Fluothane. See Halothane.

Flute is a woodwind instrument that serves as a soprano voice in many bands, orchestras, and woodwind groups. Most flutes are made of metal. They consist chiefly of a tube with a mouthpiece near one end. The mouthpiece has an oval hole. A musician holds the flute in a horizontal position and blows across the hole. At the same time, the player presses levers called *keys* that are positioned along the tube. The keys open and close *tone holes* to produce different notes and tones.

The *concert flute in C* is the most popular flute. It has a range of three octaves. Other members of the flute family include the *piccolo,* the *alto flute,* and the *bass flute.* The piccolo resembles a small concert flute but is pitched one octave higher (see **Piccolo**). The alto flute is pitched a fourth lower than the concert flute. The bass flute is pitched an octave below the concert flute.

Wooden flutes were played in such countries as ancient Egypt, China, and Greece. They became widely used in Europe during the mid-1700's. In the early 1800's, Theobald Boehm, a German musician, developed the first cylindrical metal flute. Boehm also developed the system of keys and tone holes used in today's flutes.
      Thomas C. Slattery

Flux, *fluhks,* in chemistry, is any substance that lowers the melting point of a substance to which it is added. A flux added to ore before melting helps to separate the impurities from the metal. In smelting iron, the flux used is generally limestone. This combines readily with the impurities to form slag, which can then be easily removed. Fluxes made of borax, soda, and potash are used to separate base metal from gold and silver. The term *flux* also refers to the rate of flow of matter or energy across a given surface.   John B. Butt

See also **Smelting.**

WORLD BOOK photo by Ralph Brunke

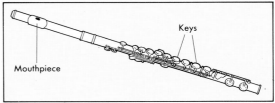

WORLD BOOK illustration by Oxford Illustrators Limited

The flute is a woodwind instrument popular in bands and orchestras. A musician plays the flute by blowing across a hole in the mouthpiece and pressing keys that cover the tone holes.

Fran Hall, N.A.S.

A horse fly's eyes act as prisms, breaking light into bands of color.

Grace A. Thompson, N.A.S.

A house fly searches for food on a crust of bread. The stiff hairs on the fly's body and legs may carry many disease germs that brush off on anything the insect touches.

Jane Burton

The greenbottle fly is named for the color of its shiny coat.

Fly is an insect with one pair of well-developed wings. The common house fly is one of the best known kinds of flies. Other kinds include black flies, blow flies, bot flies, crane flies, deer flies, fruit flies, gnats, horse flies, leaf miners, midges, mosquitoes, robber flies, sand flies, tsetse flies, and warble flies.

A number of other insects are often called flies, but they have four wings and are not true flies. These insects include butterflies, caddisflies, damselflies, dragonflies, mayflies, and scorpionflies.

Some flies are among the most dangerous pests known. They carry germs inside their bodies, on the tip of their mouthparts, or in the hair on their bodies. When a fly "bites," or when it touches any object, it may leave some of these germs behind. Flies carry germs that cause such serious diseases as malaria, sleeping sickness, filariasis, and dysentery. These insects also cause diseases in animals and plants.

Scientists have developed many ways to control flies. Some swamps are drained. Others are covered with oil or sprayed with insecticides. These treatments kill newly hatched mosquitoes and other flies that grow in water. Proper disposal of garbage, decaying plants, and animal wastes is important for control of other kinds of flies.

E. W. Cupp, the contributor of this article, is Associate Professor of Medical Entomology at Cornell University.

Some kinds of flies are helpful. They carry pollen from one plant to another, much as bees do. Others eat insect pests. Scientists use fruit flies in the study of *heredity.* These flies have provided valuable information on how characteristics are passed on from one generation to the next.

Flies live throughout the world. Among the smallest are the midges called *no-see-ums,* which are found in forests and coastal marshes. They are about $\frac{1}{20}$ inch (1.3 millimeters) long. One of the largest flies, the *mydas fly,* is found in South America. It is 3 inches (7.6 centimeters) long and also measures 3 inches from the tip of one wing to the tip of the other.

Flies are among the fastest of all flying insects. The buzzing of a fly is the sound of its wings beating. A house fly's wings beat about 200 times a second, and some midges move their wings 1,000 times a second. House flies fly at an average speed of $4\frac{1}{2}$ miles (7.2 kilo-

Facts in brief

Names: *Male,* none; *female,* none; *young,* maggots or wrigglers; *group,* swarm.
Number of newborn: 1 to 250 at a time, depending on species. As many as 1,000 a year for each female.
Length of life: Average 21 days in summer for house flies.
Where found: Throughout the world.
Scientific classification: Flies belong to the class Insecta, and make up the order Diptera.

meters) per hour. They can fly even faster for short distances to escape their enemies, which include people and many birds.

There are about 100,000 kinds of flies. They make up an *order* (chief group) of insects. The scientific name of the order is *Diptera,* which comes from Greek words that mean *two wings.* This article provides general information about flies. To learn more about various kinds of flies, see the separate *World Book* articles listed in the *Related articles* at the end of this article.

The body of a fly

A fly's body has three main parts: (1) the head, (2) the thorax, and (3) the abdomen. The body wall consists of three layers and is covered with fine hair. Many kinds of flies have dull black, brown, gray, or yellowish bodies. A few kinds, including soldier flies and hover flies, may have bright orange, white, or yellow markings. Some kinds, such as bluebottle flies and greenbottle flies, are shiny blue or green. They seem to sparkle with brassy, coppery, or golden lights.

Head. A fly has two large eyes that cover most of its head. The males of some species have eyes so large that they squeeze against each other. The eyes of most female flies are farther apart.

Like most other kinds of insects, a fly has *compound* eyes made up of thousands of six-sided lenses. A house fly has about 4,000 lenses in each eye. No two lenses point in exactly the same direction, and each lens works independently. Everything a fly sees seems to be broken up into small bits. The insect does not have sharp vision, but it can quickly see any movement.

A fly has two antennae that warn it of danger and help it find food. The antennae grow near the center of the head between the eyes. The size and shape of the antennae vary widely among different species of flies, and even between males and females of the same species. A house fly's antennae are short and thick; a female mosquito's are long and covered with soft hair; and a male mosquito's are long and feathery. The antennae can feel changes in the movement of the air, which may warn of an approaching enemy. Flies also smell with their antennae. The odor of the chemicals in rotting meat and garbage attracts house flies. The odors of certain chemicals bring vinegar flies to wine cellars.

The mouth of a fly looks somewhat like a funnel. The broadest part is nearest the head, and tubelike part called the *proboscis* extends downward. A fly uses its proboscis as a straw to sip liquids, its only food.

Flies do not bite or chew because they cannot open their jaws. Mosquitoes, sand flies, stable flies, and other kinds of "biting" flies have sharp mouthparts hidden in the proboscis. They stab these sharp points into a victim's skin and inject saliva to keep the blood from clotting. Then the flies sip the blood. Blow flies, fruit flies, and house flies do not have piercing mouthparts. Instead, they have two soft, oval-shaped parts called *labella* at the tip of the proboscis. The flies use these parts somewhat like sponges to lap up liquids, which they then suck into the proboscis. They sip liquids, or turn solid foods such as sugar or starch into liquids by dropping saliva on them.

Thorax. A fly's muscles are attached to the inside wall of the thorax. These strong muscles move the insect's

legs and wings. A fly has six legs. It uses all its legs when it walks, but often stands on only four legs. The legs of most kinds of flies end in claws which help them cling to such flat surfaces as walls or ceilings. House flies and certain other flies also have hairy pads called *pulvilli* on their feet. A sticky substance on the feet helps the insects walk on the smooth, slippery surfaces of windows and mirrors.

A fly's wings are so thin that the veins show through. The veins not only carry blood to the wings, but also help stiffen and support the wings. Instead of hind wings, a fly has a pair of thick, rodlike parts with knobs at the tips. These parts are known as *halteres.* The halteres give the fly its sense of balance. The halteres vibrate at the same rate as the wings beat when the insect is flying.

A fly is airborne as soon as it beats its wings. It does not have to run or jump to take off. In the air, the halteres keep the insect in balance and guide it so it can dart quickly and easily in any direction. A fly does not glide in the air or to a landing as do butterflies, moths, and most other flying insects. A fly beats its wings until its feet touch something to land on. If you pick up a fly, but leave the legs and wings free, the wings begin to beat immediately. Scientists sometimes do this with flies when studying wing movements.

Abdomen. A fly breathes through air holes called *spiracles* along the sides of its body. The abdomen has

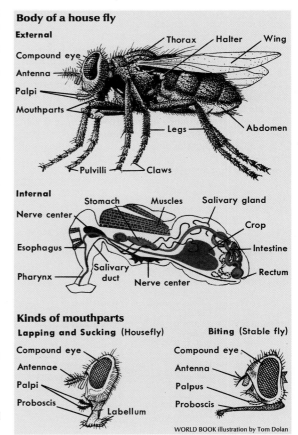

Body of a house fly

External

Thorax · Halter · Wing
Compound eye
Antenna
Palpi
Mouthparts
Legs · Abdomen
Pulvilli · Claws

Internal

Stomach · Muscles · Salivary gland
Nerve center
Crop
Esophagus
Intestine
Rectum
Pharynx · Salivary duct · Nerve center

Kinds of mouthparts

Lapping and Sucking (Housefly)
Compound eye
Antennae
Palpi
Proboscis · Labellum

Biting (Stable fly)
Compound eye
Antenna
Palpus
Proboscis

WORLD BOOK illustration by Tom Dolan

Life cycle of the house fly

Avril Ramage, Oxford Scientific Films

Eggs   **Larvae**   **Pupa**   **Newly hatched adult**

eight pairs of spiracles, and the thorax has two pairs. Air flows through the holes into tubes that carry it to all parts of the fly's body.

The life of a fly

A fly's life is divided into four stages: (1) egg, (2) larva, (3) pupa, and (4) adult. At each stage, the fly's appearance changes completely.

Egg. A female fly lays from 1 to about 250 eggs at a time, depending on the species. During her lifetime, one female may produce as many as a thousand eggs. The females of many species simply drop their eggs on water, on the ground, or on other animals. Some species stack the eggs in neat bundles.

At the tip of a female fly's abdomen is an organ called the *ovipositor,* through which the eggs are laid. The house fly usually places her ovipositor onto soft masses of decaying plant or animal material and lays her eggs there. One kind of mosquito arranges its eggs in groups that look somewhat like rafts. The eggs float on water until the larvae hatch.

The eggs of many kinds of flies are white or pale yellow, and look like grains of rice. A house fly's eggs hatch in 8 to 30 hours, but the time depends on the species of

fly. Some kinds of mosquitoes lay their eggs during late autumn, but the eggs do not hatch until spring.

Larva of a fly is often called a *maggot* or a *wriggler.* The larvae of most kinds of flies look like worms or small caterpillars. They live in food, garbage, sewage, soil, water, and in living or dead plants and animals.

A fly larva spends all its time eating and growing. It *molts* (sheds its skin and grows a new one) several times as it grows. The larval stage lasts from a few days to two years, depending on the species. The larva then changes into a pupa.

Pupa is the stage of final growth before a fly becomes an adult. The pupae of mosquitoes and some other kinds of flies that develop in water are active swimmers. Most pupae that live on land remain quiet. The larvae of some flies build a strong oval-shaped case called a *puparium* around their bodies. Black fly larvae spin a cocoon for protection. Inside, the larva gradually loses its wormlike look and takes on the shape of the adult fly. Then the adult fly bursts one end of the pupal case or splits the pupal skin down the back and crawls out. The pupal stage of a house fly lasts from three to six days in hot weather, and longer in cool weather. The length of time varies among the different species.

Adult. When the adult emerges from the pupal case, its wings are still moist and soft. The air dries the wings quickly, and blood flows into the wing veins and stiffens them. The thin wing tissue hardens in a few hours or a few days, depending on the species, and the adult flies away to find a mate.

A fly has reached full size when it comes out of the pupal case. A small fly grows no larger as it gets older, even though its abdomen may swell with food or eggs.

Adult house flies live about 21 days in summer. They live longer in cool weather, but are less active. Most adult flies die when the weather gets cold, but some hibernate. Many larvae and pupae stay alive during the winter. They develop into adults in spring.   E. W. Cupp

Some flies that spread disease

Fly	Disease	Host
Apple maggots	Bacterial rot	Apples
Black flies	Onchocerciasis (River blindness)	Human beings
Deer flies	Tularemia (Rabbit fever)	Human beings, rodents
Fly maggots	Bacterial soft rot	Potato, cabbage, other vegetables
Horse flies	Anthrax	Human beings, animals
House flies	Amebic dysentery	Human beings, animals
	Typhoid fever	Human beings
	Bacillary dysentery	Human beings
	Cholera	Human beings
Mosquitoes	Filariasis	Human beings
	Malaria	Human beings
	Yellow fever	Human beings, monkeys, rodents
	Dengue	Human beings
	Encephalitis	Human beings, horses
Olive fruit fly	Olive knot	Olives
Sand flies	Kala azar	Human beings
Tsetse flies	African sleeping sickness	Human beings

Related articles in *World Book* include:

Apple maggot	Face fly	Maggot
Bee fly	Filaria	Mediterranean
Blow fly	Fruit fly	fruit fly
Bot fly	Gnat	Midge
DDT	Hessian fly	Mosquito
Deer fly	Horse fly	Sand fly
Disease (Spread of	Insect	Tsetse fly
infectious dis-	Insecticide	Warble fly
eases)	Leaf miner	

Fly, Artificial. See Fishing (Bait).

Fly-up-the-creek. See Heron.

Flycatcher is the name of two families of birds that catch flies and other insects in the air. The flycatcher perches quietly until an insect flies past. Then it darts out quickly and seizes the victim. It closes its bill with a sharp, clicking sound. One of the families of flycatchers lives in America, and the other in Europe. Most of the American flycatchers live in warm climates. Nearly 40 species live in the United States. The most familiar ones include the *Acadian, crested, alder, scissor-tailed, olive-sided, least, yellow-bellied, vermilion, southern crested* or *yellowhammer,* and *sulfur-bellied* flycatchers. The *kingbird, phoebe,* and *wood pewee* are also flycatchers.

Flycatchers have a wide range of call notes and

WORLD BOOK illustration by Trevor Boyer, Linden Artists Ltd.

The Acadian flycatcher lives in the United States.

screams, and some of the notes sound quite musical. The crested flycatcher makes a wild, pleasant sound, somewhat like a whistle. The little alder flycatcher says "RA mee, RA mee." The olive-sided flycatcher calls "pu-pip." This bird also has an amusing call which sounds like "quick, three beers." The least flycatcher calls "che-bec" and is sometimes given that name. The sulfur-bellied flycatcher is a noisy bird that calls "kip, kip, kip, kip, squeelya, squeelya." A pair of these birds sometimes sounds like a large group of birds.

As flycatchers move about in search of food, they migrate over a wide area. They may range all the way from Canada to South America in a single year. The scissor-tailed flycatcher lives in the southern Great Plains, New Mexico, and western Texas. The Arkansas kingbird ranges from northern Canada, the Dakotas, western Minnesota, and Kansas to the Pacific Coast. The sulfur-bellied flycatcher ranges from Arizona to Bolivia.

The nesting habits of the flycatchers vary greatly. Some, like the great crested flycatcher, select holes in trees; some, like the phoebe, nest on ledges; and others, like the pewee, make dainty nests.

Scientific classification. The American flycatchers belong to the New World flycatcher family, Tyrannidae. The Acadian flycatcher is genus *Empidonax,* species *E. virescens.* The yellow-bellied is *E. flaviventris;* the least, *E. minimus;* the crested, *Myiarchus crinitus;* the olive-sided, *Nuttallornis borealis;* the scissor-

tailed, *Muscivora forficata;* the sulfur-bellied, *Myiodynastes luteiventris.* European flycatchers belong to the Old World flycatcher family, Muscicapidae.   Arthur A. Allen

See also **Bird** (pictures: Birds of the grasslands; Birds' eggs); **Kingbird; Phoebe; Wood pewee; Yellowhammer.**

Flying, in aircraft. See Aviation.

Flying buttress. See Architecture (Gothic).

Flying Doctor Service, Royal. See Australia (Transportation; picture).

Flying dragon is the name commonly given to the so-called flying lizards of southeastern Asia and the East Indies. They grow to a length of about 8 inches (20 centimeters). They do not really fly, but glide by means of folds of skin stretched over their ribs. Flying dragons live in trees and glide from tree to tree to search for food or to avoid their enemies. When resting, the lizards fold their "wings" against the sides of their bodies. During the mating season, the males spread their brightly colored "wings" to attract females.

Scientific classification. Flying dragons are members of the Old World lizard family, Agamidae. They are genus *Draco.*

Raymond B. Huey

© Tom McHugh, Photo Researchers

A flying dragon glides by spreading folds of skin.

Flying Dutchman is a ghost ship in folklore. There are many versions of the legend of the *Flying Dutchman.* The most common story involves the sighting of a phantom ship as it attempts to sail around the Cape of Good Hope in Africa. However, the captain has been cursed and his crew consists of dead men. The ship never reaches port and is doomed to sail on eternally. According to some versions of the legend, the curse resulted from an act of cruelty by the captain, perhaps aboard a ship carrying slaves. Other versions say he bargained with the Devil and lost.

The theme of the *Flying Dutchman* has been used in a number of literary and musical works. The English poet Samuel Taylor Coleridge based his poem "The Rime of the Ancient Mariner" (1798) on the legend. The German composer Richard Wagner adapted the story into his opera *The Flying Dutchman* (1843).   David J. Winslow

Flying fish. See Flyingfish.

Flying fox is a kind of large bat, not a fox. It lives in most tropical regions except South America. It is especially common in regions of the South Pacific. The head and body are about 1 foot (30 centimeters) long, and the wingspread may be over 5 feet (1.5 meters). It gets its name because its face looks like that of a fox. The flying fox eats mostly fruit, and is more properly known as a *fruit bat.* It also feeds on flower buds, nectar, and pollen. It spends the day hanging in trees, often with other fruit bats. This sometimes makes the tree look as though it is loaded with fruit. Flying foxes can travel long distances for food. Because they can damage fruit orchards, the U.S. government forbids importation of the animals without a special permit. See also **Bat.**

Scientific classification. Flying foxes make up the fruit bat family, Pteropidae. The Indian flying fox is *Pteropus giganteus.*

Clyde Jones

Flying lemur, or *colugo,* is a common mammal of Southeast Asia. It is about the size of a cat. A flying lemur looks somewhat like a lemur but is not one (see **Lemur**). Flying lemurs can glide as far as 100 yards (91 meters) from tree to tree, but they do not actually fly. Large folds of skin on the animal's sides connect its neck, legs, and tail. When it spreads its legs, this skin forms "wings" used in gliding.

John Mackinnon, Bruce Coleman Ltd.

The flying lemur does not actually fly. It has large folds of skin along its sides that connect its neck, legs, and tail. When the animal spreads its legs, this skin forms "wings" that are used in gliding from tree to tree, as shown above.

Flying lemurs have a pointed face, large eyes, and brown or gray fur with white spots. They live in rain forests and eat tropical flowers, fruits, and leaves. Most females give birth to one baby every year. Few zoos have flying lemurs, because it is hard to get their food.

Scientific classification. Flying lemurs make up the order Dermoptera. The order's single family, Cynocephalidae, has one genus, *Cynocephalus.* There are two species, *C. variegatus* and *C. volans.*   W. P. Crowcroft

See also **Mammal** (picture).

Flying lizard. See Flying dragon.

Flying saucer. See Unidentified flying object.

Flying squirrel is a squirrel that can glide through the air. A fold of skin on each side of its body connects

© J. Alsop, Bruce Coleman Inc.

The flying squirrel glides through the air by spreading its legs. Folded skin that grows between the legs stretches out to form "wings." The animal can glide more than 150 feet (46 meters).

the front and back legs. When a flying squirrel stretches out its legs, the folds of skin form "wings." It glides from tree to tree, using its broad, flat tail to guide its flight. The squirrel's path is downward, then straight, and finally upward. Glides of more than 150 feet (46 meters) have been recorded. Flying squirrels always finish lower than where they started. A high starting point makes a long glide possible. Flying squirrels live in the forests of Asia, Europe, and North America. American flying squirrels are 8 to 12 inches (20 to 30 centimeters) long, including the tail. Their coat is gray or brownish-red on the upper parts of the body and white or cream-colored on the underparts. Some Asian flying squirrels grow 4 feet (1.2 meters) long.

Flying squirrels nest in the hollows of trees. They hunt for food only at night. Other squirrels hunt by day. Flying squirrels eat berries, birds' eggs, fungi, insects, and nuts. They also eat young birds, as well as the meat of any *carcasses* (dead animals) they can find. Female flying squirrels have from two to three young twice a year. By six weeks of age, the young are "flying" on their own.

Scientific classification. Flying squirrels belong to the subfamily Petauristinae, of the squirrel family, Sciuridae. The common flying squirrel of the United States is *Glaucomys volans.* The larger *G. sabrinus* lives in Canada and the Northern United States.   Clark E. Adams

Flying Tigers was the popular name for the American Volunteer Group, a small force of volunteer U.S. aviators who became widely known as one of the most colorful groups of World War II (1939-1945). Each of its airplanes had the mouth of a tiger shark painted on it.

The American Volunteer Group was formed in 1941 to assist China in its struggle against Japanese invaders. Three squadrons of Flying Tigers fought over China and Burma from December 1941 until July 1942. Then they became part of the U.S. Army Air Forces. In their 28 weeks of combat operation, they shot down about 300 Japanese planes and lost only about a dozen of their own planes in the air. About 60 of their planes were destroyed on the ground.   James L. Stokesbury

See also **Chennault, Claire Lee.**

Flyingfish is a type of fish that throws itself from the water with the motion of its strong tail. In the air, it

WORLD BOOK illustration by Colin Newman, Linden Artists Ltd.

The flyingfish uses its tail to propel itself from the water into the air, where the fish's large fins aid in flight.

glides by spreading its large fins, which act like wings. Body muscles and the tail fin help the fish to turn in flight. The flight often covers 150 to 1,000 feet (46 to 300 meters). Flyingfish live in all warm seas. There are more than 50 species. The California flyingfish grows about 18 inches (46 centimeters) long. The sharp-nosed flyingfish lives off both coasts of tropical America. Flyingfish are excellent food.

Scientific classification. Flyingfish make up the family Exocoetidae. The California flyingfish is *Cypselurus californicus.* The sharp-nosed flyingfish is *Fodiator acutus.*   John E. McCosker

See also **Gurnard; Fish** (picture: Fish of coastal waters and the open ocean).

Flynn, Elizabeth Gurley (1890-1964), was an American labor leader. In 1961, she became the first woman to head the Communist Party in the United States.

Flynn was born in Concord, N.H. Her parents often took her to socialist meetings after the family moved to New York City in 1900. When she was 15 years old, Flynn began to speak on street corners for workers' rights. In 1906, she joined the Industrial Workers of the World (IWW), an early labor union (see **Industrial Workers of the World**). Flynn led several bloody strikes.

In 1920, Flynn helped form the American Civil Liberties Union (ACLU), an organization that works for citizens' rights. She joined the Communist Party in 1937. Flynn spent from January 1955 to May 1957 in prison for violating the Smith Act. This law makes it a crime to urge the violent overthrow of the U.S. government. During the 1950's, a period of intense anti-Communist feeling, the Smith Act was used to imprison many Communist leaders. However, the Supreme Court ruled in 1957 that teaching Communism was not, in itself, grounds for conviction.   June Sochen

Flytrap. See **Pitcher plant; Venus's-flytrap.**

Flyway. See **Bird** (Where birds migrate).

Flywheel is a heavy wheel attached to the shaft of an engine to keep its speed nearly constant. It is used where the forces driving the engine shaft are not constant. The driving forces in a gasoline engine come from a series of explosions in the engine cylinder. The driving forces produce the power needed by the engine's load. Sometimes, the driving forces become momentarily larger than necessary for the engine's load, and the engine speed increases. Then the flywheel absorbs the excess energy and prevents the speed from increasing rapidly. At other times, the driving forces from the cylin-

der become momentarily smaller than necessary. Then the flywheel's inertia keeps the speed from decreasing quickly. The action of a flywheel decreases as the number of cylinders of a gasoline engine increases. For example, less of the engine cycle energy must be temporarily stored by the flywheel with a four cylinder engine than with an eight cylinder engine.

William H. Haverdink

See also **Gasoline engine; Starter; Steam engine** (picture).

FM. See **Frequency modulation.**

Foam rubber. See **Rubber** (Sponge rubber).

Foch, *fawsh,* **Ferdinand,** *fehr dee NAHN* (1851-1929), a French military leader, was acclaimed by many as the greatest Allied general of World War I. He became supreme Allied commander in April 1918, when a powerful German drive across France seemed on the verge of victory. Foch unified Allied operations and stopped the German drive. Then he launched great counterattacks that drove German forces back into Belgium. Foch's final offensives won the war. At a meeting with Foch on Nov. 11, 1918, the German delegates signed the armistice that stopped the fighting.

Foch believed that a strong offense was the most effective way to fight a war. But his total reliance on attack early in the war almost ruined his career because he misjudged the effectiveness of German defensive firepower. He took part in disastrous offensives in August 1914 and led offensives that failed in 1915 and 1916. He was relieved of his command in December 1916, seemingly destined for minor duties. But one of Foch's great strengths lay in his ability to learn from his failures.

Foch was born in Tarbes, France. He was commissioned in the artillery in 1874. He became a professor at the *École de Guerre,* the French war college, in 1895, and he taught and wrote books on military theory. He became head of the college in 1908.

Foch commanded an army corps at the outbreak of World War I and helped drive the Germans back from the Marne River in September 1914. From the fall of 1914 to December 1916, he commanded the Northern Army Group. In 1917, Foch was made chief of the War Ministry's general staff and also served as intermediary between Henri Pétain, French commander in chief, and other Allied leaders. Foch was promoted to marshal on

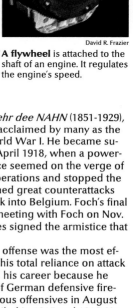

David R. Frazier

A flywheel is attached to the shaft of an engine. It regulates the engine's speed.

United Press Int.

Ferdinand Foch

Aug. 6, 1918, and was elected to the French Academy that same year.

After the war, Foch urged Premier Georges Clemenceau to demand the Rhineland at the Paris Peace Conference in 1919. When the conference denied these demands, Foch bitterly predicted a new war would occur within 20 years.   Larry H. Addington

See also **World War I** (The last campaigns).

Foehn, *fayn,* is a warm, dry wind that blows down a mountainside. The air loses its moisture as it rises to the mountaintop. It is heated by compression as it comes down the other side of the mountain. Foehns occur in mountainous regions throughout the world. They blow frequently in the Alps, where the warm wind received its name. In the Rocky Mountains, a foehn is called a *chinook* (see **Chinook**). These winds often bring rapid temperature changes. For example, the temperature at Havre, Mont., rose 33° F. (18° C) in one hour when a chinook suddenly arrived on Feb. 15, 1948. Foehns or chinooks cause snow to melt rapidly. The winds often make the climate of areas in which they occur much warmer than neighboring areas.   Richard A. Dirks

Fog is a collection of tiny water droplets that float in the air. Fog is similar to clouds, except that clouds do not touch the earth's surface, as fog does.

Fog forms from water that has evaporated from lakes, oceans, and rivers, or from moist soil and plants. This evaporated water, called *water vapor,* expands and cools as it rises into the air. Air can hold only a certain amount of water vapor at any given temperature. This amount is called the *holding capacity.* As the temperature of the air decreases, so does its holding capacity.

When the temperature drops so that the amount of water vapor in the air exceeds the holding capacity, some of the water vapor begins to *condense* (change into small droplets of water). Fog disappears when the air temperature rises and the holding capacity increases. According to international definition, fog is any condensation that reduces visibility to less than 1 kilometer (3,281 feet). Fog that does not greatly reduce visibility is called *mist* or *haze.*

There are four main kinds of fog: (1) *advection fog,* (2) *frontal fog,* (3) *radiation fog,* and (4) *upslope fog.*

Advection fog develops from air traveling over a surface of a different temperature. One kind of advection fog, called *sea fog,* occurs when warm, moist air travels over a cold surface. Sea fog is most common along seacoasts and lakeshores. Another kind of advection fog, called *steam fog,* results from cold air passing over warm water. Water vapor, evaporating continuously from the water surface, comes into contact with the cold air. When the air reaches its holding capacity, the excess water vapor condenses quickly into fog droplets that steam up from the water surface. Steam fog commonly appears on cold winter days over the Great Lakes and over warm lakes in Florida.

Frontal fog forms along a *front.* A front is a boundary between two air masses of different temperatures. Frontal fog is produced when raindrops fall from the warmer air mass into the colder one, where they evaporate. They thereby cause the water vapor in the cold air to exceed the air's holding capacity.

Radiation fog occurs on calm, clear nights as the ground loses warmth through radiation into the air. A

Kinds of fog   Fog is a mass of tiny water droplets that are suspended in the air at or near the earth's surface. Fog, which reduces visibility, forms when water vapor in the air *condenses* (returns to liquid form). The four main kinds of fog are advection fog, frontal fog, radiation fog, and upslope fog.

WORLD BOOK illustrations by Arthur Grebetz

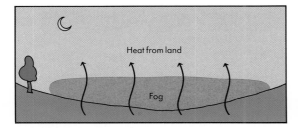

Advection fog occurs when warm, moist air travels over a cool surface, such as a seacoast or a lakeshore. It also may form when cold air passes over bodies of warm water.

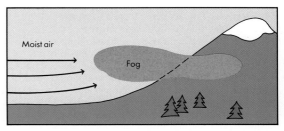

Frontal fog develops on the boundary between two air masses of different temperatures. Raindrops fall from the warmer air mass into the colder one, evaporate, and turn into fog.

Radiation fog occurs at night, when the ground gives off heat through radiation. As the land cools, so does the air above it. Because this cooler air can hold less water vapor, fog is formed.

Upslope fog forms when moist air flows upward over a sloping land surface. As the air travels up the slope, it grows cooler. This cooling of the moist air produces fog.

layer of fog forms along the ground, gradually becoming denser. Radiation fog is most common in the San Joaquin Valley in California and in other deep valleys.

Upslope fog develops when moist air moves upward along sloping terrain. The air cools as it moves up the slope until it can no longer hold the water vapor. Fog droplets then form along the slope.   T. Theodore Fujita

See also **Cloud; Dew; Smog; Water.**

Foghorn. See Siren.

Foil. See Fencing.

Fokine, *faw KEEN,* **Michel,** *mih SHEHL* (1880-1942), was a great Russian *choreographer* (dance creator). Fokine invented the one-act ballet based on music by a first-rate composer. The dance and scenery in his ballets merge with the mood and drama of the music to create a powerful theater event. Fokine composed more than 60 one-act ballets between 1905 and 1942. The best known include *The Dying Swan, Les Sylphides, Prince Igor, Scheherazade, Le Spectre de la Rose, Petrouchka,*

Photo by Emil Otto Hoppé (The Dance Collection, N.Y. Public Library)
Michel Fokine and his wife Vera danced in a 1914 revival of his ballet *Daphnis and Chloë,* based on an ancient Roman story.

L'Epreuve d'Amour, and *Firebird.*

Fokine was born in St. Petersburg (now Leningrad). There he became soloist with the Maryinsky Ballet (now the Kirov Ballet). He left Russia for Western Europe with Sergei Diaghilev's Ballets Russes in 1909. Fokine's early work with the Ballets Russes in Paris marked the beginning of his great career as a choreographer. He became a U.S. citizen in 1932.   P. W. Manchester

See also **Ballet** (Russian ballet).

Fokker, *FAHK uhr,* **Anthony Herman Gerard** (1890-1939), was a Dutch engineer, pilot, and aircraft manufacturer. He moved to Germany at the age of 20, because of the interest in aviation there. He established his first manufacturing plant near Berlin when he was 22. Fokker designed monoplanes, biplanes, and triplanes. His factories supplied many airplanes for Germany in World War I. After the war, he set up plants in the Netherlands and the United States. Fokker was born in Kediri, Java.   Robert B. Hotz

Foley, Thomas Stephen (1929-   ), a Democrat from the state of Washington, became Speaker of the United States House of Representatives in 1989. He succeeded James C. Wright, Jr., who had resigned after a House committee accused him of breaking a number of House ethics rules. Foley had served as majority *whip* (assistant leader) of the House from 1981 to 1987 and as majority leader from 1987 until he became Speaker.

Foley was born in Spokane, Wash. He graduated from the University of Washington in 1951 and the University of Washington Law School in 1957. He soon became deputy prosecutor in the Spokane County attorney's office and, later, the assistant state attorney general for Spokane.

Foley first won election to the U.S. House of Representatives in 1964. He served as chairman of the House's Agriculture Committee from 1975 to 1981 and as chairman of the House Democratic Caucus from 1976 to 1981. In the mid-1980's, Foley helped form the positions of the

Bruce Hoertel, Gamma/Liaison
Thomas Foley

House Democrats on a number of issues, including arms control, the budget, and military aid to rebels in Nicaragua.   Guy Halverson

Folger Shakespeare Library, *FOHL juhr,* in Washington, D.C., houses one of the most important collections of books on British civilization from about 1485 to 1715. It also owns the world's most important collection of books by and about William Shakespeare. The library has more than 225,000 volumes.

The library's rare books are protected in fireproof, air-conditioned vaults. An exhibition gallery displays many rare books, pictures, and objects of interest from the Elizabethan period. The library's theater is patterned after a typical playhouse of the period.

Henry Clay Folger, a former president of the Standard Oil Company of New York, founded the library in 1930. Folger left his entire fortune for the trustees of Amherst College to administer toward the development of a great research library. Scholars from all parts of the world come to the Folger Shakespeare Library for research in history and literature. The library building, a magnificent marble structure, was completed in 1932.

Critically reviewed by the Folger Shakespeare Library

Folic acid. See Vitamin (table).

Folio, *FOH lee oh,* is the name printers and publishers use for a sheet of paper folded once, making four pages, front and back. The word *folio* may also mean the page number of a book. Even-numbered pages, or folios, are always on the left. Odd-numbered folios are on the right side of the bound book or volume.

A *quarto* is a sheet folded twice, making four leaves or eight pages. An *octavo* is a sheet folded into eight leaves or 16 pages. The octavo format, or shape of the book, is the one in most common use. But folio format or octavo format tells nothing about the *size* of a book today, although formerly it did. The size today depends on the dimensions of the sheet before it was folded.

A folk painting by Edward Hicks shows a scene of Quaker farm life in Pennsylvania during the late 1700's. In several such pictures, Hicks painted his memories of his childhood home, the farm of David Twining. This painting shows Hicks as a boy standing next to Mrs. Twining, *lower right.*

Oil painting on canvas (about 1848)

Folk art is a term that refers to the work of painters, sculptors, and craftworkers who have little or no training as artists. Folk artists are ordinary people who create their works for other ordinary people, rather than for museums or wealthy collectors.

Most folk artists know nothing about the basic principles of art. For example, few of them know how to draw the human body accurately or how to use color, light, and perspective properly. Their work shows no awareness of current movements or other developments in the arts. Folk artists solve art problems as best they can. They often create a pleasing picture, carving, or household object without knowing exactly how or why they have succeeded.

Folk art has been produced in many countries for hundreds of years. This article deals with American folk art, especially during its most productive period, from about 1780 to about 1860. Most American folk artists worked in small towns in New England, New York, and Pennsylvania.

American folk artists created a wide variety of works, including paintings, sculptures, and such household objects as dishes, pots, and quilts. They also produced store signs, weather vanes, and other everyday objects. During the 1800's, sailors carved a special kind of folk sculpture called *scrimshaw.*

By 1875, the demand for folk art had declined in America because of the widespread use of machines. The machines could manufacture more goods in less

Beatrix T. Rumford, the contributor of this article, is Director of the Abby Aldrich Rockefeller Folk Art Collection in Williamsburg, Va. Unless otherwise credited, the illustrations in this article are from the Abby Aldrich Rockefeller Folk Art Collection.

time—and with fewer mistakes—than could human hands. But folk art continued in isolated rural areas, and some is still created today.

For many years, scholars and art collectors paid little attention to folk art. The first real interest in American folk art occurred in the late 1920's. At that time, a group of professional artists on vacation in Maine noticed folk art on sale in junk shops. They began to buy it because they admired its fresh, simple quality and its freedom from formal rules.

Today, much folk art is enjoyed simply for its beauty and for its skillful craftwork. In addition, folk art reflects everyday life. Much of it shows the social attitudes, political views, religious feelings, and routine habits of the people of a certain period and place. These elements make folk art a valuable source of information to historians and others who are interested in ordinary people of the past.

Kinds of folk art

Painting. Folk artists painted some subjects from memory and others from life. In many cases, folk artists copied or adapted engravings and various other kinds of prints that had originally been created by trained artists.

Many American folk painters began by making and decorating business signs. Until about 1870, many Americans could not read, and so shopkeepers used pictorial signs to advertise their products. For example, a sign showing a pig represented a butcher shop. A picture of a boot advertised a shoemaker. Most signs had bright colors and bold designs to catch the eye of passers-by.

The influence of sign painting can be seen in much early American portrait painting. Portraits were the most common type of folk painting. Artists called *limners* traveled throughout a region, painting likenesses of local residents. These portraits, like store signs, had vivid colors and simple but bold compositions.

In addition to signs and portraits, folk artists painted pictures of houses, landscapes, and ships. Many landscapes showed scenes of life on farms or in small towns. These scenes tell much about now-forgotten activities that once were so common that nobody bothered to write about them.

Sculpture. One of the earliest types of folk sculpture was the *figurehead* of a ship. A figurehead is a statue—of a woman, in most cases—that decorates the bow of a vessel. Early folk carving also included gravestones. A picture of one appears in the *World Book* article on **Sculpture** (1600-1900 [American sculpture]).

The so-called cigar store Indian was a popular subject for some sculptors. A life-sized wooden figure of an Indian warrior stood outside many shops that sold tobacco products. The Indian figures were first displayed by English merchants of the late 1600's. The merchants used this form of advertisement because Indians had introduced tobacco to the Virginia settlers.

Folk sculptors made animals and other figures for merry-go-rounds. They also carved and decorated toys and *decoys*—wooden figures of ducks and geese used by hunters to attract game birds.

Weather vanes ranked among the most important kinds of folk sculpture. Farmers and sailors needed to know about changes in the weather, and so farm build-

The Talcott Family (1832), a water color on paper

Portraits were painted by folk artists called *limners*. While in her early 20's, Deborah Goldsmith traveled throughout northern New York, painting local residents. This family ranks among her best-known compositions. The painting provides a valuable record of American clothing and furnishings of the time.

Metal weather vanes of the late 1800's were made from wood patterns carved by experienced craftworkers. A folk sculptor designed the weather vane at the right in the form of the Statue of Liberty.

Copper weather vane (after 1886)

Advertisements featured several kinds of folk art. Sculptors carved wooden Indians, *left,* which stood outside tobacco shops. Painters designed colorful signs, *below,* to advertise a store's products.

Painted wood (1800's);
Virginia Museum of
Fine Arts, Richmond

Oil painting on wood (early 1800's)

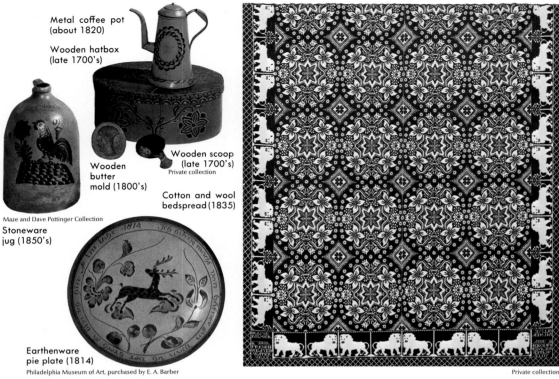

Metal coffee pot
(about 1820)

Wooden hatbox
(late 1700's)

Wooden
butter
mold (1800's)

Wooden scoop
(late 1700's)
Private collection

Cotton and wool
bedspread (1835)

Stoneware
jug (1850's)

Maze and Dave Pottinger Collection

Earthenware
pie plate (1814)

Philadelphia Museum of Art, purchased by E. A. Barber

Private collection

Household objects were carefully carved and vividly decorated to make them as attractive as possible. Craftworkers used colorful designs in painting the hatbox and kitchen utensils shown above. A weaver chose bold patterns for the bedspread on the right and added an unusual border.

A dressing table, built in 1835 by a New England craftworker, was made of cheap wood. The artist painted and decorated the table in imitation of an expensive rosewood piece.

ings and ships had weather vanes to show the direction of the wind.

Household objects. Folk art included many decorative objects used at home. Some of these objects brightened the inside of a home, and others seemed to make daily chores less boring. A number of folk artists made colorful kitchen utensils of earthenware and tin. Some homemakers specialized in sewing quilts, many of which featured bright colors and lively designs of animals, flowers, and trees.

Many pieces of useful folk art substituted for expensive furniture and utensils that most people could not afford. Some craftworkers used poor-quality wood to make such items as clocks and tables. Folk artists then painted and decorated such pieces to imitate stylish, costly furniture.

Scrimshaw. To help pass the time during long voyages, many sailors made small carvings and engravings from sperm whale teeth, whalebone, or tortoise or sea shells. Such carvings and engravings became known as *scrimshaw.*

Engravings made by American sailors during the 1800's rank as the finest examples of scrimshaw. First, the sailor smoothed and polished the object. Then he scratched a picture or design into the surface with a sharp instrument. Finally, he filled in the engraved lines with colored inks. Some sailors engraved accurate scenes of activities at sea, such as naval battles and whale hunts. Sailors also copied illustrations from books and magazines.

Many pieces of scrimshaw were useful objects, such as knitting needles and corset stays. Sailors sometimes decorated coconut shells, ostrich eggs, and other objects from nature as souvenirs of their travels.

Folk artists

Most American folk artists probably considered themselves craftworkers rather than artists. They would have used the word *artist* for those who studied and followed traditions of art created through the centuries by Europeans.

The names of most American folk artists have been lost. However, a few are known because they wrote their name on their works, developed a recognizable style, or created a large number of items. The best-known of these artists include Erastus Salisbury Field, Edward Hicks, Ammi Phillips, Eunice Pinney, and Wilhelm Schimmel.

Many folk artists were skilled craftworkers who could build houses and ships as well as paint or carve. Edward Hicks, for example, was born in Bucks County, Pennsylvania, and served a seven-year apprenticeship to a local coachmaker as a painter. Then, at the age of 21, Hicks decided to work for himself. He earned his living by lettering signs, but he is best known today for his many versions of a painting he called *The Peaceable Kingdom.*

Some folk artists were amateurs who created folk art for fun, to pass the time, or to impress their neighbors.

Still others were students, most of them teen-agers. They painted water colors, made drawings, or embroidered pieces of cloth as classroom assignments. Sometimes such schoolwork produced important pieces of folk art.

A number of folk artists had a regular job and used their artistic talent to increase their income. Schoolteachers, shopkeepers, and even physicians and lawyers earned extra money by selling objects they had created.

Some folk artists traveled throughout a region, trading pieces of their art for food and lodging. During the 1880's, Wilhelm Schimmel wandered through Cumberland County, Pennsylvania, seeking work and begging for food. In exchange for meals, Schimmel gave people animal figures he had carved and then colored with bits of paint. Today, his figures rank among the most prized American folk sculpture.

Folk art collections

Several museums in the United States exhibit only folk art or have large folk art collections. Most are in the East, where the majority of folk artists lived.

In New England, folk art can be seen at the Old Sturbridge Village in Sturbridge, Mass.; and at the Shelburne Museum in Shelburne, Vt. The Museum of Fine Arts in Boston also has a large collection.

The Pennsylvania Dutch region of southeastern Pennsylvania was an important center of folk art, and several museums there exhibit such art today. They include the Landis Valley Farm Museum in Lancaster and the

A figurehead of a giant eagle decorated the bow of the warship *Lancaster.* The sculptor designed the eagle to symbolize the power and authority of the United States wherever the *Lancaster* sailed.

Painted wood figurehead (about 1875)
by John Haley Bellamy;
Mariners Museum, Newport News, Va.

Whaling Museum, New Bedford, Mass.

Scrimshaw consisted of carvings and engravings made by sailors during long voyages. The engraving on the sperm whale tooth, *above,* shows whalers towing a dead whale to their ship.

Black folk art shows the influence of the African heritage of American slaves. A former slave probably carved this wooden figure of a boy with a bucket about 1860. The expressionless face and seated position are features of much African sculpture.

Schwenkfelder Museum in Pennsburg. The Museum of Art in Philadelphia and the Bucks County Historical Society in Doylestown, Pa., also have notable folk art collections.

The New York State Historical Association in Cooperstown exhibits folk art. The Museum of American Folk Art and the Metropolitan Museum of Art, both in New York City, have important collections. Another collection may be seen at the Henry Francis du Pont Winterthur Museum in Winterthur, Del.

The Abby Aldrich Rockefeller Folk Art Collection in Williamsburg, Va., is one of the world's largest museums devoted only to folk art. In Washington, D.C., folk art can be seen at the National Gallery of Art and the

Smithsonian Institution. In the Midwest, the Henry Ford Museum in Dearborn, Mich., has an outstanding folk art collection.   Beatrix T. Rumford

Related articles in *World Book* include:

Colonial life in	Hicks, Edward	Pennsylvania
America (Arts	Latin America	Dutch (picture)
and sciences)	(The arts; pictures)	Pickett, Joseph
Feke, Robert	Moses, Grandma	Sampler

Additional resources

American Folk Painters of Three Centuries. Ed. by Jean Lipman and Tom Armstrong. Hudson Hills, 1980.
Americana: Folk and Decorative Art. Ed. by Art & Antiques. Watson-Auptill, 1982.
Bishop, Robert, and others. *Folk Art: Paintings, Sculpture, & Country Objects*. Knopf, 1983. A guide to collecting.
Johnson, Jay, and Ketchum, W. C. *American Folk Art of the Twentieth Century*. Rizzoli, 1983.
Lipman, Jean, and others. *Young America: A Folk-Art History*. Hudson Hills, 1986.

Folk costume. See Clothing.

Folk dancing is the traditional form of social dancing of a nation or ethnic group. Throughout history, almost every culture has developed its own folk dances. These dances have been passed down from generation to generation. People have composed *dance songs,* a type of folk music, to accompany many of the dances.

Most folk dances originated as a form of celebration, religious worship, or a method of controlling mysterious forces. The form and movements of many of these dances were based on superstitious beliefs. For example, a number of early folk dances were performed in a circle because people believed this shape had magical powers. In some early cultures, circular motion was thought to bring good luck or drive away evil.

Early peoples developed dances to celebrate such events as birth, marriage, and even death. In some societies, young people conducted courtship through dances. The *Ländler* of Austria and the *fandango* of Spain are pantomime dances based on gestures of courtship.

Other folk dances were originally performed to cure disease, to obtain such favors as plentiful crops, or to celebrate success in battle. The *tarantella* of Italy originated as a method of curing the bite of the tarantula.

J. Kankel, Bavaria-Verlag

Folk dancing is an important event at folk festivals throughout the world. The dancers shown at the left in traditional costumes are performing a German folk dance on Bavarian Folk Costume Day. This annual festival is held in Bad Wiessee, West Germany, near Munich.

The Scots once celebrated victories in battle by dancing the *sword dance.*

Through the years, most folk dances lost their original meaning and came to be danced chiefly for recreation. Today, the *square dance* is perhaps the most popular folk dance in the United States. It is usually danced by four couples in a square formation. The dancers swing about, bow, change partners, and perform other lively movements as directed by a caller. Popular European folk dances include the *Irish jig,* the *flamenco* of Spain, and the *polka* of Czechoslovakia. Among black African and American Indian groups, traditional dances remain a vital part of religious ceremonies, as well as a form of entertainment.   Melvin Berger

See the pictures of dancers in the following articles: **Greece; Indonesia; Jews; Romania; Spain;** and **Yugoslavia.** See also **Dancing; Latin America** (Dancing); **Square dancing.**

Additional resources

Bambra, Audrey, and Webster, Muriel. *Teaching Folk Dancing.* Theatre Arts, 1972.
Greene, Hank. *Square and Folk Dancing: A Complete Guide for Students, Teachers, and Callers.* Barnes & Noble, 1984.
Nevell, Richard. *A Time to Dance: American Country Dancing from Hornpipes to Hot Hash.* St. Martin's, 1977.
Page, Ralph. *Heritage Dances of Early America.* Lloyd Shaw, 1976.

Folk literature. See Folklore; Literature for children (Folk literature).

Folk music consists of a people's traditional songs. No one knows who created most of the folk songs that have ever been sung or played. Folk songs deal with almost every kind of human activity. Many of these songs express the political or religious beliefs of a people or describe their history. Other folk songs simply provide amusement.

Songs written by professional composers are considered folk music if they become part of a people's traditional music. For example, the American composer Stephen Foster wrote such songs as "Oh! Susanna" and "Swanee River," which are widely accepted as folk music.

Characteristics of folk music. The melody and words of a folk song develop over a long period of time. One person makes up a song, and other people hear the song and learn to sing it. These people, in turn, sing the song for others, who also learn the words and melody. In this way, the song passes from person to person, from place to place, and from generation to generation. Through the years, the song is gradually refined and simplified. The melody becomes smoother and more expressive, and the words grow clearer and more direct. Many versions of a song also appear. In addition, the same words may be sung with different tunes, or different words may be used for the same melody.

Most American and European folk songs have a stanza form, which consists of a verse alternating with a chorus. The verses tell the story, and so each verse is different. The words of the chorus remain the same in most folk songs. Many choruses consist of nonsense words or syllables that have no meaning. Sometimes the audience joins in the singing of the chorus.

"Gee, But I Want to Go Home" is an example of a comic verse-chorus folk song. American soldiers sang it during World War I (1914-1918) and World War II (1939-1945). Here are two of its verses and the chorus:

The coffee that they give you they say is mighty fine:
It's good for cuts and bruises and tastes like iodine.

(chorus) I don't want no more of army life,
    Gee, but I want to go home.

The clothes that they give you they say are mighty fine,
But me and my buddy can both fit into mine.

(chorus) I don't want no more of army life,
    Gee, but I want to go home.

Originally, people sang folk songs with no instrumental accompaniment. Instrumental parts were later added to many tunes. Today, the guitar is the most popular instrument in folk music. Other widely used instruments include the banjo, harmonica, and violin.

Kinds of folk music. Most folk songs are ballads that tell simple stories and have simple words and music. Some ballads relate legendary incidents that occurred long ago. For example, "Barbara Allen" is a tragic love story that dates back at least to the 1600's. There are several versions of the song, some of which originated in England and others in Scotland. Some ballads are based on true events from more recent times. "Peat Bog Soldiers" describes the suffering of prisoners in Nazi concentration camps during the 1930's and 1940's. Many ballads tell about the deeds of heroes. "Casey Jones" praises a brave railroad engineer, and "John Brown's Body" honors a famous abolitionist.

Certain kinds of folk music deal with a particular activity or occupation. Laborers create *work songs* to help their long days pass more quickly. Popular work songs include "Old Chisholm Trail," sung by cowboys, and "Drunken Sailor," sung by seamen. Some *union songs* call for better conditions for workers. The execution of a famous labor organizer in 1915 inspired the union song "Joe Hill." Prisoners make up *prison songs.* "Midnight Special" tells of the loneliness of prison life. Slaves sang about their suffering in *spirituals,* such as "Go Down, Moses" and "Joshua Fit de Battle ob Jericho." In the mid-1900's, black Americans sang the spirituals "We Shall Overcome" and "Welcome Table" to emphasize their struggle for civil rights.

Some folk songs are meant only to entertain. People dance to "Buffalo Gals" and other *dance songs.* A *game song,* such as "Ring-Around-the-Rosy," gives instructions on how to play a certain game. *Nonsense songs,* among them "Arkansas Traveler" and "Frog Went a Courting," are intended to make people laugh.

American folk music is noted for its energy, humor, and emotional impact. The major influences on American folk music came from Great Britain and other European countries, and from Africa. However, the songs of American Indians also had a significant part in the heritage of American folk music. In addition, various national and racial groups preserve the folk music of their ancestors. For example, Americans of Spanish ancestry hold festivals during which traditional songs are performed.

American Indians consider their songs an extremely important part of their heritage. Traditionally, some tribes believed that gods created all the songs at the beginning of time. These songs can be revealed only in dreams or in other mystical ways. New songs cannot be composed. Indians have judged folk songs by their power, not by their beauty. For example, various tribes have songs to control the weather or to cure illness. They believe the songs must be sung correctly because errors could rob them of their power.

The early American colonists from Great Britain brought their folk music traditions with them, especially the ballad and stanza form. Later settlers from other countries also brought their own folk music, which influenced the colonial songs.

The slaves who were brought to America from Africa had a different musical tradition from that of the Europeans. However, most slaveowners did not allow the blacks to sing or play their native music. As a result, the specific words and melody of the songs were gradually forgotten. But the slaves retained the style of their music and created new songs in the African tradition. Most of these songs follow the *call-response* pattern, in which a leader sings a line and the entire group answers. Drums and other percussion instruments play a complex rhythmic accompaniment.

During the mid-1900's, a number of singers gained great popularity performing American folk songs. Some of these singers wrote songs that became part of the American folk tradition. The best known of these songs dealt with social problems, such as poverty and racial prejudice. The leading singer-composers included Bob Dylan, Woody Guthrie, Huddie Ledbetter (known as Leadbelly), and Pete Seeger.   Melvin Berger

Related articles in *World Book* include:

Baez, Joan	Folklore
Ballad	Foster, Stephen Collins
Blues	Guthrie, Woody
Burleigh, Harry Thacker	Jazz
Calypso	Latin America (Music)
Country music	Seeger, Pete
Dylan, Bob	Spiritual
Folk dancing	Western frontier life (Music)

Additional resources

Berger, Melvin. *The Story of Folk Music.* Phillips, 1976. For younger readers.
Nettl, Bruno. *Folk Music in the United States: An Introduction.* 3rd ed. Wayne State Univ. Press, 1976.
The Penguin Book of Canadian Folk Songs. Ed. by Edith Fowke. Rev. ed. Penguin (Markham, Ont.), 1987.
Stambler, Irwin, and Landon, Grelun. *The Encyclopedia of Folk, Country and Western Music.* 2nd ed. St. Martin's, 1983.

Folklore is any of the beliefs, customs, and traditions that people pass on from generation to generation. Much folklore consists of folk stories, such as ballads, fairy tales, folk tales, legends, and myths. But folklore also includes arts and crafts, dances, games, nursery rhymes, proverbs, riddles, songs, superstitions, and holiday and religious celebrations.

Folklore is as old as humanity. Written records left by the earliest peoples include examples of folklore. As soon as a people develops a writing system, they begin to record folk stories. However, folklore does not have to be written down. Much folklore is passed orally from person to person. Even today, many peoples do not have a written language, but they have folk songs, legends, myths, and other kinds of folklore. Sometimes folklore is handed down by imitation. For centuries, children have learned games, such as jump rope and mar-

bles, by watching and imitating other youngsters.

As people move from one land to another, they take their folklore with them and adapt it to their new surroundings. From the 1500's to the 1800's, for example, thousands of West Africans were transported to the Western Hemisphere as slaves. Many of the slaves enjoyed telling a number of West African folk tales about a sly spider named Anansi. Through the years, the slaves continued to tell tales of Anansi, though the stories about the spider were gradually changed to reflect life in the New World. Today, Anansi remains a popular character in black folklore, both in West Africa and in the Caribbean area.

Origins of folklore

During the 1800's, scholars believed that folklore in ancient times had been shared by all members of a society. Most ancient peoples lived in rural communities. Through the centuries, large numbers of people moved to cities and gradually lost touch with so-called "authentic" folk traditions. According to the scholars of the 1800's, those traditions were preserved by uneducated peasants called *folk,* whose way of life had changed little for hundreds of years. Two German brothers, Jakob and Wilhelm Grimm, were among the leading folklore scholars. From 1807 to 1814, they collected folk tales from peasants who lived near Kassel, in what is now West Germany. The Grimms believed that by collecting the tales, they were preserving the heritage of all Germans. The stories they collected became famous as *Grimm's Fairy Tales.* But some versions of these tales are found throughout Europe, the Near East, and Asia.

Today, scholars consider folk to be any group of people who share at least one common linking factor. This factor may be geography, as in folklore of the Ozark

Detail of *Children's Games,* an oil painting on oak panel (1560)
by Pieter Bruegel the Elder; Kunsthistorisches Museum, Vienna

Many children's games are handed down by imitation. For hundreds of years, youngsters have learned games by watching other children play. This painting of the mid-1500's shows boys and girls playing some games that young people of today enjoy.

Ethnic folklore preserves the customs of a particular national or racial group. Americans of Swedish ancestry hold an annual festival in Minneapolis that includes Swedish folk dances and songs performed in traditional costumes, *left.*

Minnesota Department of Economic Development

Mountains region; religion, as in Jewish folklore; occupation, as in cowboy folklore; or ethnic background, as in Irish-American folklore. Some scholars believe that even a family can be considered folk because many families have their own traditions and stories.

Characteristics of folklore

Folklore can be short and simple or long and complicated. Brief proverbs, such as "Time flies" and "Money talks," are famous examples of folklore. On the other hand, some Indonesian folk plays begin at sundown and end at dawn.

It is extremely difficult to make up folklore. The songs, stories, and other material that became folklore were, of course, thought up by various people. But those individuals had the rare ability to create a subject and a style that appealed to others through the years. Folklore survives only if it retains that appeal. People would not bother to retell tales or continue to follow customs that had no meaning for them. This is the reason people keep on using the same folklore over and over.

To be considered authentic folklore, an item must have at least two versions. It also must have existed in more than one period and place. For example, scholars have identified more than 1,000 versions of the fairy tale about Cinderella. These versions developed through hundreds of years in many countries, including China, France, Germany, and Turkey.

Changes in folklore often occur as it passes from person to person. These changes, called *variations,* are one of the surest indications that the item is true folklore. Variations frequently appear in both the words and music of folk songs. The same lyrics may be used with different tunes, or different words may be set to the same music. The nursery rhymes "Baa, Baa Black Sheep" and "Twinkle, Twinkle Little Star" have the same melody. Some people use the folk saying "As slow as molasses," others "As slow as molasses in January," and still others "As slow as molasses in January running uphill."

Kinds of folklore

Myths are religious stories that explain how the world and humanity developed into their present form.

Myths differ from most types of folk stories because myths are considered to be true among the people who develop them.

Many myths describe the creation of the earth. In some of these stories, a god creates the earth. In others, the earth emerges from a flood. A number of myths describe the creation of the human race and the origin of death.

Miniature (early 1300's) from the *Manesse Song Manuscript* by an unknown Swiss painter; Heidelberg University Library

Medieval folk musicians traveled throughout France and Germany. They often entertained royalty with long, elaborate songs that celebrated the heroic deeds of legendary kings and knights.

Many religious ceremonies include folk traditions. A Navajo medicine man, *right,* and his helpers create a sand painting of a sun god for use in a ritual to treat a sick child. The painting design has been handed down by generations of medicine men.

Folk tales are fictional stories about animals or human beings. Most of these tales are not set in any particular time or place, and they begin and end in a certain way. For example, many English folk tales begin with the phrase "Once upon a time" and end with "They lived happily ever after."

Fables are one of the most popular types of folk tales. They are animal stories that try to teach people how to behave. One fable describes a race between a tortoise and a hare. The tortoise, though it is a far slower animal, wins because the hare foolishly stops to sleep. This story teaches the lesson that someone who works steadily can come out ahead of a person who is faster or has a head start.

In many European fairy tales, the hero or heroine leaves home to seek some goal. After various adventures, he or she wins a prize or a marriage partner, in many cases a prince or princess. One popular kind of folk tale has a trickster as the hero. Each culture has its own trickster figure. Most tricksters are animals who act like human beings. In Africa, tricksters include the tortoise; the hare; and Anansi, the spider. The most popular trickster in North American Indian folklore is probably the coyote.

Legends, like myths, are stories told as though they were true. But legends are set in the real world and in relatively recent times.

American folklore includes many legendary heroes. David Crockett was a famous American frontiersman who was elected to the U.S. Congress from Tennessee in 1827. After Crockett died in the battle of the Alamo in 1836, he became a popular figure in American folklore. John Chapman, better known as Johnny Appleseed, planted apple trees from Massachusetts to the Midwest during the early 1800's. He was the hero of a number of legends by the time he died in the 1840's. John Henry was the black hero of many legends in the South. A famous ballad describes how he competed against a steam drill in a race to see whether a man or a machine could dig a tunnel faster. Using only a hammer, John Henry won—but he died of exhaustion.

Many legends tell about human beings who meet supernatural creatures, such as fairies, ghosts, vampires, and witches. A number of legends are associated with famous people who have died. Others tell of holy persons and religious leaders. Some legends describe how saints work miracles.

The action in myths and folk tales ends at the conclusion of the story. But the action in many legends has not been completed by the story's end. For example, a legend about a buried treasure may end by saying that the treasure has not yet been found. A legend about a haunted house may suggest that the house is still haunted.

A number of legends tell about the Loch Ness Monster, a sea serpent in Scotland; and the Abominable Snowman, a hairy beast in the Himalaya. Some people

Black folk dances in America developed from West African religious dances. From the early 1600's to the mid-1800's, thousands of West Africans were transported to the Western Hemisphere as slaves. This water-color painting of the late 1700's shows Southern plantation slaves performing a folk dance. Their musical instruments also originated in West Africa.

believe these creatures actually exist. From time to time, various expeditions have tried to find both of them.

Folk songs have been created for almost every human activity. Some are associated with work. For example, sailors sing songs called *chanteys* while pulling in their lines. Folk songs may deal with birth, childhood, courtship, marriage, and death. Parents sing folk lullabies to babies. Children sing traditional songs as part of some games. Other folk songs are sung at weddings and funerals.

Some folk songs are related to seasonal activities, such as planting and harvesting. Many are sung on certain holidays. The folk song "The Twelve Days of Christmas" is a well-known carol. Some folk songs celebrate the deeds of real or imaginary heroes. But people sing many folk songs simply for enjoyment.

Superstitions and customs are involved largely in marking a person's advancement from one stage of life to another. For example, many cultures include a custom called *couvade* to protect unborn babies. In couvade, husbands pretend that they are about to give birth. They may avoid eating certain foods considered harmful to the expected baby. They also may avoid working because such activity could injure the unborn child.

A wedding custom called *charivari* is widespread in various European societies. On the wedding night, friends of the bride and groom provide a noisy serenade by banging on pots and pans outside the couple's bedroom. The desire to avoid charivari led to the practice of leaving on a honeymoon immediately after a wedding.

A large number of superstitions and customs supposedly help control or predict the future. The people of fishing communities may hold elaborate ceremonies that are designed to ensure a good catch. Many people try to foretell future events by analyzing the relationships among the planets and stars.

Holidays are special occasions celebrated by a group, and almost all of them include folklore. Christmas is especially rich in folklore. A group may celebrate this holiday with its own special foods and costumes. Many groups have variations of the same folk custom. In a number of countries, for example, children receive presents on Christmas. In the United States, Santa Claus brings the presents. In Italy, an old woman named La Befana distributes the gifts. In some countries of Europe, the gifts come from the Christ child. In others, the Three Wise Men bring them.

Folklore and the arts

Folklore has made a major contribution to the world's arts. Many folk stories and folk songs are beautiful works of art themselves. Folklore has also inspired masterpieces of literature, music, painting, and sculpture. The English poet Geoffrey Chaucer used a number of folk tales in his famous *Canterbury Tales.* William Shakespeare based the plots of several of his plays on folk tales. These plays include *King Lear, The Merchant of Venice,* and *The Taming of the Shrew.*

Certain legends and myths have attracted artists, composers, and writers for centuries. One legend tells about a medieval German scholar named Faust who sold his soul to the devil. This legend has been the basis of many novels, plays, operas, and orchestral works. *Faust,* a drama by Johann Wolfgang von Goethe, is probably the greatest work in German literature.

Jazz developed largely from folk music of Southern blacks. Classical composers also have incorporated folk melodies into their works. For example, the Czech composer Antonín Dvořák used black spirituals in his famous symphony *From the New World.* The Austrian composer Wolfgang Amadeus Mozart used the melody of "Twinkle, Twinkle Little Star" as the basis of a work he wrote in 1778.

Folklore and society

Folklore reflects the attitudes and ideals of a society. For example, much folklore reflects how a society regards the roles of males and females in real life. In many examples of Western folklore, women are passive and uncreative. A society that produces such folklore considers men superior to women. This attitude appears in a proverb:

> A whistling maid and a crowing hen
> Are neither fit for gods nor men.

According to the proverb, a girl who whistles like a boy and a hen that crows like a rooster are unnatural. The proverb implies that women should not try to take part in activities traditionally associated with men.

A common wedding custom calls for the groom to carry his bride over the threshold of their home. This custom suggests that the woman is weak and must be carried through the doorway—and presumably through life—by the strong male. In many Western fairy tales, a female is captured by a villain and waits quietly until a heroic male rescues her.   Alan Dundes

Related articles in *World Book* include:

Kinds of folklore

Ballad	Limerick
Dancing (Folk dancing)	Mythology
Epic	Nursery rhyme
Fable	Proverb
Folk art	Riddle
Folk dancing	Romance
Folk music	Saga
Legend	Superstition

American folklore and legend

Alden (family)	Febold Feboldson	Pecos Bill
Appleseed, Johnny	Fink, Mike	Pocahontas
Bass, Sam	Frietchie, Barbara	Rip van Winkle
Billy the Kid	Henry, John	Sacagawea
Boone, Daniel	James, Jesse	Smith, John
Buffalo Bill	Jones, Casey	Song of Hiawatha
Bunyan, Paul	Kidd, William	Standish, Miles
Carson, Kit	Laffite, Jean	Stormalong,
Crockett, David	Magarac, Joe	Alfred B.
Evangeline		

British folklore and legend

Allen, Barbara	Holy Grail
Arthur, King	Lancelot, Sir
Beowulf	Launfal, Sir
Brownie	Loch Ness Monster
Bruce, Robert	Peter Pan
Brut	Rob Roy
Davy Jones	Robin Hood
Excalibur	Round Table
Galahad, Sir	Turpin, Dick
Godiva, Lady	Whittington, Dick
Guy of Warwick	

German folklore and legend

Brunhild	Munchausen, Baron
Eulenspiegel, Till	Nibelungenlied
Faust	Nix
Grimm's Fairy Tales	Pied Piper of Hamelin
Lorelei	Siegfried
Mephistopheles	Tannhäuser

Irish folklore and legend

Banshee	Cuchulainn	Giant's Causeway
Blarney Stone	Finn MacCool	Shamrock

Folklore and legend of other lands

Abominable Snowman	Fountain of Youth
Aesop's fables	Gilgamesh, Epic of
Amadis of Gaul	Jack Frost
Arabian Nights	Mother Goose
Cid, The	Roland
Don Juan	Santa Claus
Edda	Tell, William
Flying Dutchman	Winkelried, Arnold von

Other related articles

Dragon	Moon (Mythology;
Fairy	legend and folklore)
Gnome	Storytelling
Literature for children	Vampire
(Folk literature)	Werewolf

Additional resources

Afro-American Folktales: Stories from Black Traditions in the New World. Ed. by Roger D. Abrahams. Pantheon, 1985.
Explorations in Canadian Folklore. Ed. by Edith Fowke and C. H. Carpenter. McClelland (Toronto), 1985.
Favorite Folktales from Around the World. Ed. by Jane Yolen. Pantheon, 1986.
Folklore in America: Tales, Songs, Superstitions, Proverbs, Riddles, Games, Folk Drama and Folk Festivals. Ed. by Tristram P. Coffin and Hennig Cohen. Univ. Press of America, 1986. First published in 1966.
One Hundred Favorite Folktales. Ed. by Stith Thompson. Indiana Univ. Press, 1968. Suitable for younger readers.

Folkway. See Mores.

Folsom point, a type of prehistoric spearhead, was the first evidence that human beings lived in North America during the Ice Age. A cowboy first discovered the stone points near Folsom, N. Mex., during the early 1900's. In 1926, scientists found the spearheads mingled with the bones of an extinct species of bison and identified the points as prehistoric weapons. The ancient bison disappeared about 10,000 years ago, at the end of the Ice Age. The discovery of weapons with the bison bones proved that people had migrated to North America by about 8000 B.C. Before the Folsom discovery, most scientists had believed that the first people came to the Americas more recently. Most scientists today think the spearheads are 10,000 to 11,000 years old. Researchers have also discov-

P. Hollembeak and J. Beckett,
American Museum of Natural History

A Folsom point is a long, thin prehistoric spearhead.

ered Folsom points at other sites in New Mexico, Colorado, and Texas.

Folsom points differ from later spearheads in that they have a long, thin shape rather than a triangular one. The points also have a long flake removed down the center of one or both faces. The groove created by removing the flake is called a *flute,* and this type of stone point is called a *fluted* point.   Dean Snow

See also **Indian, American** (The first Americans [picture: Spear points]).

Fonda, Henry (1905-1982), was an American stage and motion-picture actor. He became famous for his portrayals of leading men of integrity and for his seemingly effortless acting style. Fonda appeared in more than 80 films. His most famous role was the title character in the comedy *Mr. Roberts,* which he played on both stage (1948) and screen (1955). He won the 1981 Academy Award as best actor for his performance in *On Golden Pond,* in which he co-starred with his daughter, Jane. He also received acclaim for his performances in *The Trail of the Lonesome Pine* (1936), *Young Mr. Lincoln* (1939), *The Grapes of Wrath* (1940), *The Lady Eve* (1941), *The Ox-Bow Incident* (1943), and *Twelve Angry Men* (1957). His son, Peter, is also a film actor and director.

Indelible, Inc.

Henry Fonda

Henry Jaynes Fonda was born in Grand Island, Nebr. He first gained recognition for his performance in the Broadway revue *New Faces* (1934). He made his motion-picture debut in *The Farmer Takes a Wife* (1935). *Fonda: My Life* (1981) is his autobiography.   Rachel Gallagher

Fonda, Jane (1937-   ), is an American motion-picture actress. She has appeared in about 35 films, many of which she co-produced through her own company. Fonda won Academy Awards as best actress for her performances in *Klute* (1971) and *Coming Home* (1978).

Jane Seymour Fonda was born in New York City. She made her film debut in *Tall Story* (1960). Her other films include *A Walk on the Wild Side* (1962), *Cat Ballou* (1965), *Barbarella* (1968), *They Shoot Horses, Don't They?* (1969), *Julia* (1977), *The China Syndrome* (1979), and *The Morning After* (1987). In 1981, she co-starred with her father, Henry Fonda, in *On Golden Pond.*

AP/Wide World

Jane Fonda

Fonda is noted for her antiwar views and her work as a political activist. She has also become known for her physical fitness workout programs.   Rachel Gallagher

Fontainebleau, *FAHN tihn BLOH* or *fawn tehn BLOH* (pop. 15,679), a small city in northern France, is famous

Lauros-Giraudon

The château of Fontainebleau is a famous French Renaissance palace. The structure is known for its diverse architectural styles, beautifully decorated interiors, and magnificent gardens.

for a magnificent *château* (castle) that stands in a nearby forest. The city lies about 35 miles (56 kilometers) southeast of Paris. For the location, see **France** (political map).

King Francis I transformed a medieval castle into the château of Fontainebleau in the early 1500's. King Louis XIII, who reigned from 1610 to 1643, was responsible for much of its construction. French kings continued to add to and remodel the château as late as the 1700's. As a result, the structure displays a number of architectural and decorative styles. It has many paintings and elegant carvings by the Italian artists Francesco Primaticcio and Fiorentino Rosso. The ballroom and the Francis I gallery feature especially impressive works of art. The château also has a small museum of Chinese art objects collected by Empress Eugénie, the wife of Emperor Napoleon III.

Many French kings used the château of Fontainebleau as a summer home. In 1814, Emperor Napoleon I gave up the throne of France at the château.   J. A. Laponce

Fontane, Theodor (1819-1898), a German author, became known for his realistic and critical novels about Prussian society during the 1800's. Many of his works vividly portray the manners, morals, and social activities of the upper classes in Prussia. In his portrayal of characters and society, Fontane blends precise observation with humor, compassion, and irony.

Most of Fontane's stories take place in Berlin and the surrounding countryside. Most of his novels deal with personal conflicts of the chief characters, many of whom are women. Fontane's masterpiece, *Effi Briest* (1895), is a realistic yet sympathetic account of marital estrangement, adultery, and divorce. Several of his other novels also deal with love and marriage in a traditional, class-conscious society, including *Trials and Tribulations* (1888), *Beyond Recall* (1891), and *Jenny Treibel* (1892). He depicts the decline of the Prussian aristocracy in *A Man of Honor* (1883) and *The Poggenpuhl Family* (1896).

Fontane was born in the province of Brandenburg. He was almost 60 years old when his first novel was published. Before that time, Fontane was known as an author of ballads and travel books.   Werner Hoffmeister

Fontanne, *fahn TAN,* **Lynn** (1887-1983), was an American actress. She and her husband, Alfred Lunt, became the most celebrated acting team of their time. Fontanne was a sophisticated, glamorous, and accomplished performer. She was best known for her leading roles in *The*

Guardsman (1924), *Strange Interlude* (1928), *Elizabeth the Queen* (1930), *Reunion in Vienna* (1931), *Design for Living* (1933), *The Great Sebastians* (1956), and *The Visit* (1958). Lunt was her co-star in all these plays except *Strange Interlude*. See **Lunt, Alfred.**

Fontanne was born near London, England. Her given first and middle names were Lillie Louise. She made her acting debut in 1905. She first visited America in 1910 and settled in the United States in 1916. She achieved her first major success in 1921 in *Dulcy*. In 1922, she married Alfred Lunt.   Daniel J. Watermeier

Fonteyn, *fahn TAYN,* **Dame Margot** (1919-   ), is generally considered the greatest British ballerina of all time. Critics have praised her precise technique and the warmth and delicacy of her style. Sir Frederick Ashton, a great English *choreographer* (dance composer), created many ballets for her, including *Daphnis and Chloe* and *Symphonic Variations*. Fonteyn gave perhaps her greatest performances in Ashton's *Ondine*. She and Ashton established a refined form of dancing that became known as the *British style*.

Margot Fonteyn was born in Reigate, England. Her

Bob Gomel, *Life Magazine* © 1965 Time Inc.

Dame Margot Fonteyn is often considered the greatest British ballerina of all time. In 1962, Fonteyn formed a partnership with Soviet-born dancer Rudolf Nureyev, *shown with her above.*

real name was Margaret Hookham. When she was 14 years old, Fonteyn began dancing with the Vic-Wells Ballet (now the Royal Ballet) in London. In 1962, she began her partnership with the Soviet-born dancer Rudolf Nureyev. She was named Dame Commander in the Order of the British Empire in 1956.   Joan Brock Pikula

See also **Ballet** (picture: *Swan Lake*).

Foochow. See Fuzhou.

An American family eating at a fast-food restaurant

A family in Senegal eating from a common bowl

Saudi Arabian men feasting on lamb and vegetables

A French couple lunching on cheeses and cold cuts

Food is a basic necessity of life. In addition, people everywhere enjoy eating. However, the kinds of food that people eat and how much food they have differ greatly around the world. There are also wide differences in the ways that people of various cultures prepare, serve, and eat food.

Food

Food is one of our most basic needs. We cannot live without it. Food gives us the energy for everything we do—walking, talking, working, playing, reading, and even thinking and breathing. Food also provides the energy our nerves, muscles, heart, and glands need to work. In addition, food supplies the nourishing substances our bodies require to build and repair tissues and to regulate body organs and systems.

All living things—people, animals, and plants—must have food to live. Green plants use the energy of sunlight to make food out of water from the soil and *carbon dioxide,* a gas in the air. All other living things depend on the food made by green plants. The food that people and animals eat comes either from plants or from animals that eat plants.

Food does more than help keep us alive, strong, and healthy. It also adds pleasure to living. We enjoy the flavors, odors, colors, and textures of foods. We celebrate

Margaret McWilliams, the contributor of this article, is Professor of Food and Nutrition at California State University at Los Angeles. She is the author of Food Fundamentals *and many other books on food and nutrition.*

special occasions with favorite meals and feasts.

Although all the food we eat comes from plants or animals, the variety of foods is incredible. Plants provide such basic foods as grains, fruits, and vegetables. Animals provide meat, eggs, and milk. These basic foods may require little or no preparation before they are eaten. Or they may be greatly changed by processing. For example, milk may be made into such foods as butter, cheese, ice cream, and yogurt.

The chief foods that people eat differ widely throughout the world. Millions of people in the Orient eat rice as their main food. People of the Pacific Islands depend heavily on fish. Most people of Turkey eat mainly cracked-wheat bread and yogurt. The people of Argentina and Uruguay eat much beef. What people eat depends chiefly on where they live and on how much money they have. It also depends on their customs, health, life style, and religious beliefs. Children learn many eating habits from their parents. But each person develops individual food preferences and prejudices. Eating habits are also influenced by how much time people have to buy, prepare, and eat food.

In developing countries of Africa, Asia, and Latin America, many families must produce all their food themselves. In the United States, Canada, and other developed countries, however, most people rely on the *food industry* for their food. The food industry includes

A Japanese family dining at a beautifully set table

Leon V. Kofod

Victor Englebert

Indians of Ecuador snacking on beans and corn

farmers, food-processing companies, researchers, shipping companies, and food stores. The growth of the food industry has greatly increased the amount and kinds of foods available in developed countries.

The supply of food has always been one of the major concerns of the human race. In many areas of the world, millions of people go hungry and many die of starvation. Food shortages and famine result from crop failures, natural disasters, overpopulation, wars, and other causes. For detailed information about food supply problems, see the articles **Food supply** and **Famine.**

Sources of food

Plants supply much of the food people eat. In many African, Asian, and Latin-American countries, the people depend on plants for more than two-thirds of their food. In Australia, Europe, North America, and parts of South America, the people eat much meat. But even in these areas, over half the diet consists of food from plants.

Some basic foods, including eggs, fruits, and vegetables, are commonly sold in their natural state. Most other foods are processed in manufacturing plants before they reach the market. All canned, dried, frozen, and pickled foods are processed. Processors also produce baked goods, frozen dinners, and many other *convenience foods,* which save work for the cook.

Food from plants. The most important foods that are obtained from plants are (1) grains and (2) fruits and vegetables.

Grains, also called *cereals,* are the seeds of such plants as barley, corn, millet, oats, rice, rye, sorghum, and wheat. The human diet has been based on grains for thousands of years. Rice or a grain product, particularly bread, is the main food in many cultures. Millers grind much of the world's grain, especially wheat, into flour. Wheat flour is used in almost all breads, in pastries, and in macaroni and other kinds of noodles. Processors also make breakfast cereals from grains.

Fruits and vegetables add a variety of colors, flavors, and textures to the diet. People enjoy fruits for their sweet or pleasantly sour flavor. Popular fruits include apples, bananas, cherries, melons, oranges, peaches, pineapples, and strawberries. Most fruits are eaten as snacks or in a salad or dessert.

Favorite vegetables include beans, broccoli, cabbage, carrots, celery, lettuce, onions, peas, potatoes, and sweet corn. Vegetables are commonly eaten during the main part of a meal. They may be served raw in a salad, cooked and served with a sauce, or added to a casserole or soup.

Other foods from plants include nuts, herbs and spices, and beverages. Coffee, cocoa, tea, and many other drinks are made from plants. Nuts are popular snacks and can be used as flavorings in other foods. Cooks also use herbs and spices to flavor foods.

Food manufacturers use plant materials to make

Interesting facts about food

Dumplings are eaten in various forms around the world. Chinese *won ton,* Italian *ravioli,* Jewish *kreplach,* and Polish *pierogi* are types of dumplings filled with meat, cheese, or vegetables.

Frankfurters were named after Frankfurt, Germany. Experts believe these sausages were first made in Germany during the Middle Ages. About 1900, an American vendor selling cooked frankfurters supposedly called them "hot dachshund sausages" because they resembled the long-bodied dog. Later, the term *hot dog* came to be used.

Hamburger was originally called *Hamburg steak.* It was named after Hamburg, Germany.

Hundred-year-old eggs, a delicacy in China, are preserved duck eggs. They are cured in the shell for about six months in a mixture of ashes, lime, salt, and tea. The curing makes the eggs taste like cheese.

Ice cream cones were first served at the St. Louis World's Fair in 1904. A thin, crisp waffle was rolled into a handy holder for a scoop of ice cream.

Pancakes are probably the oldest prepared food. The first pancakes were a mixture of pounded grain and water spread on a hot stone. Today, people enjoy such pancake variations as French *crepes,* Hungarian *palacintas,* Indian *dosai,* Italian *cannelloni,* Jewish *blintzes,* Mexican *tortillas,* and Russian *blini.*

Pizza, an international favorite, originated in Italy. *Pizza* is the Italian word for *pie.*

Pretzels were first made by monks in southern Europe as a reward for students who learned their prayers. The crossed ends of a pretzel represent praying hands.

Raw fish is a favorite food of many people. The Japanese enjoy *sashimi,* thin slices of raw seafood. *Seviche* is a popular Latin-American appetizer of raw fish in lime juice. Swedes prepare *gravad lox,* fresh salmon with dill.

Sandwiches were named after the Earl of Sandwich, an English nobleman of the 1700's. While playing cards, he ordered a servant to bring him two slices of bread with a piece of roast meat between them.

The variety of foods is amazing. This picture shows a few of the products—breads, breakfast cereals, macaroni, pancakes, pastries, and snack foods—that can be made from wheat.

cooking oils, sugar, and syrups. They also use plants to make synthetic foods. For example, they make foods that look and taste like meats from soybeans. They make nondairy creamers from vegetable fats.

Food from animals includes (1) meat, (2) eggs, and (3) dairy products. These foods cost more to produce than do foods from plants. As a result, foods from animals are eaten more in developed countries than in developing ones.

Meat consists mainly of the muscle, fat, and other parts of an animal's body. The word *meat* most commonly means the red meat of cattle, hogs, sheep, and game animals. However, the flesh of fish and poultry is also considered meat.

In the United States and Canada, popular red meats include beef and veal from cattle, pork from hogs, and lamb and mutton from sheep. Many Americans and Canadians also enjoy kidney, liver, tongue, and other *variety meats.* Favorite fish include cod, perch, salmon, trout, and tuna. Clams, crabs, lobsters, oysters, scallops, and shrimp are favorite shellfish. The most popular kinds of poultry are chicken, duck, goose, and turkey. In some countries, people enjoy the meat of caribou, goats, horses, monkeys, rabbits, or snakes. They might also eat ants, grasshoppers, snails, turtles, or certain other animals.

Much poultry is marketed as the whole animal. Many other meats are sold as *cuts,* such as chops and steaks. Ham and corned beef are *cured* (preserved) before being marketed. Meats also are processed into such products as frankfurters and cold cuts. Meat is commonly eaten during the main part of a meal.

Eggs. Farmers raise poultry, especially chickens, for their eggs as well as for their meat. Chicken eggs are popular as a breakfast or supper dish, or they can be used in custards and other cooked dishes. The eggs of certain kinds of fish are used to make a delicacy called *caviar.* In some countries, people enjoy the eggs of such birds as emus, gulls, or penguins. People of various lands also eat the eggs of alligators, crocodiles, or certain other reptiles.

Dairy products are important foods in many cultures. Cows provide most of the milk used in the United States and Canada. But such animals as camels, goats, reindeer, or sheep supply milk in other parts of the world. Milk and milk products are marketed in many forms. In addition to whole milk, people can buy buttermilk, skim milk, low-fat milk, and condensed, dried, and evaporated milk. Other products include butter, cheese, cream, ice cream, sour cream, and yogurt.

How the body uses food

Food supplies the *nutrients* (nourishing substances) that the body needs for (1) producing energy, (2) building and repairing tissues, and (3) regulating body processes. The main kinds of nutrients are carbohydrates, fats, proteins, minerals, and vitamins. Each kind of nutrient plays an important role in keeping the body healthy. Many foods are highly nourishing, but no one food supplies every necessary nutrient.

As the body digests food, the food is broken down into the various nutrients. The food eventually enters the small intestine, and the nutrients pass through the intestinal wall into the bloodstream. The blood distributes the nutrients to cells throughout the body.

In addition to nutrients, food supplies other important substances, especially water and fiber. The water in food helps dissolve nutrients and helps carry them to body cells. Water also helps carry waste products from the cells and out of the body. Fiber does not break down during digestion. Instead, fiber adds bulk to food and keeps it moving through the intestine.

People who do not get enough food to eat suffer from *undernutrition.* A person whose diet seriously lacks any nutrient is said to be *malnourished.* Some malnourished people have plenty of food available to them, but they choose to eat foods that do not supply all the necessary nutrients. Some people develop health problems because they eat too much and become overweight.

A moderate, well-balanced diet can help ensure good health. For detailed information about the foods that contribute to a healthful diet, see **Nutrition.**

Producing energy. One of the most important ways in which the body uses food is to produce energy. The proteins in food can be used to provide energy. But carbohydrates and fats serve as the major energy sources. Carbohydrates are the starches and sugars in food. Grains and potatoes are good sources of starch. Sugars include common table sugar, found in candy and other sweets, and the sugars in fruits and milk. Fats are present in eggs, meats, milk, nuts, certain vegetables, and other foods.

During digestion, carbohydrates are broken down into *simple sugars,* and fats are broken down into *fatty acids* and *glycerol.* The simple sugars, fatty acids, and glycerol are *oxidized* (burned slowly) in the body's cells. Oxidation releases the energy that we use in our daily activities and that enables the heart, lungs, and other organs to work. Oxidation also produces heat, which helps keep the body temperature at about 98.6° F. (37° C). Without this heat, the body would be unable to function properly.

Building and repairing tissues. Bones, muscles, and other body tissues constantly wear out and need to be repaired or replaced. In addition, growth depends on the formation of new tissues. The body uses the proteins in food to build and repair tissue.

All body tissues consist mainly of proteins. Proteins, in turn, are made up of chemical units called *amino acids*. The human body must obtain certain amino acids from the proteins in foods to make the proteins it needs. Digestion breaks down the proteins in foods into amino acids. The body then combines the amino acids into the kinds of proteins it requires. The protein value of foods depends on the amount and kinds of amino acids in them. Animal foods, such as meat, eggs, and dairy products, are especially rich in proteins. In addition, these proteins have all the amino acids the body needs. Grains, nuts, peanuts, and dried beans and peas are also high in protein. However, many plant foods lack one or more essential amino acids.

Some minerals help build body tissues. For example, calcium, phosphorus, and magnesium help build strong bones and teeth. Milk and other dairy products are good sources of these minerals.

Regulating body processes. The body uses proteins not only to build and repair tissues but also to help regulate various body processes. Certain proteins called *enzymes* speed up chemical reactions in the body. Enzymes help the body produce energy, digest food, and build other proteins. Many *hormones,* which regulate chemical activities throughout the body, are proteins. The *antibodies* that the body makes to fight infection are also proteins. All these proteins, like the proteins in body tissues, are made in the body from the amino acids in the food we eat.

The minerals and vitamins in food also play a major role in many body processes. People need only small amounts of minerals and vitamins. But these nutrients are just as important for good health as are carbohydrates, fats, and proteins. Unlike the other nutrients, however, minerals and vitamins can pass into a person's bloodstream without being broken down by digestion.

Minerals aid in numerous body processes. For example, iron and copper help build red blood cells. Sodium and other minerals regulate the amount of water in the body's cells. Calcium is necessary for blood clotting. Other minerals that are important to the human body include chlorine, cobalt, fluorine, iodine, magnesium, manganese, tin, and zinc.

Vitamins perform a variety of functions. They aid growth and help protect the body from disease. Vitamin A helps us see at night and promotes healthy bones, skin, and teeth. Various B vitamins help the body oxidize carbohydrates, fats, and proteins for energy. Vitamin C is necessary for healthy blood vessels and sound bones and teeth. Vitamin D helps the body use calcium and phosphorus.

Vitamins and minerals are found in a variety of foods. A well-balanced diet provides an adequate supply of all the vitamins and minerals a person needs. A shortage of certain vitamins can cause disease. For example, too lit-

tle vitamin C causes scurvy, which is marked by sore gums and bleeding under the skin. Too little vitamin D can lead to rickets, a bone disease.

Why diets differ around the world

The kinds of food that people eat vary from one country to another and even within countries. In some countries, for example, the people eat much meat. In some other countries, meat is served only on special occasions. People who are *vegetarians* eat no meat at all. Many people like certain foods that other people find very unappetizing. For example, the Chinese use the nests of birds called swifts to make bird's-nest soup. The birds build the nests of their saliva. The people of Spain enjoy fried baby eels. People in many countries consider frog legs to be a treat.

People of various cultures also prepare foods differently. In many cases, the fuel resources and cooking equipment available determine how foods are prepared. Thus, some people cook foods over an open fire. Others may use a microwave oven. Still others may eat most of their foods raw. Some people add fiery spices to their dishes. Others prefer little seasoning. Some people eat only natural, or unprocessed, foods. Others eat foods that have been highly processed.

Diets differ for a number of reasons, including (1) geographic reasons, (2) economic reasons, (3) religious reasons, and (4) customs. But differences in diet are not as great as they once were. The growth of tourism and the development of modern transportation and communication systems have led to an exchange of foods and eating habits among people throughout the world.

Geographic reasons. The location, climate, and physical features of a region help determine what the people of that region eat. In general, people who live on islands or along seacoasts depend heavily on foods from the ocean. People who live far from the sea rely mainly on livestock or grains for food. People of tropical areas can grow a variety of fruits and vegetables the year around. People who live in cool regions, which have a short growing season, depend on such crops as grains or potatoes. Terrain and soil also help determine what crops the people of a region can grow. For example, corn grows best on level, open fields with rich, well-drained soil. Rice grows best in lowland areas where the soil holds water well.

Although geography still strongly influences what people in many parts of the world eat, its importance has declined—especially in industrial countries. The development of faster transportation and of modern methods of food preservation enables many people to eat foods produced in distant lands. For example, people in numerous countries enjoy bananas from Ecuador, olives and oranges from Spain, dairy products from New Zealand, and sardines from Norway. In addition, many farmers have learned how to grow crops in unfavorable areas. Where land is hilly, for example, they might carve strips of land out of the hillsides. In dry areas, farmers might use irrigation. In areas with cold winters, they might grow certain fruits and vegetables in greenhouses during the winter.

Economic reasons. The variety and amount of food that people have to eat depend largely on their country's economy. But even in the richest countries, some peo-

Edward S. Ross

Where people live influences what foods they eat. Chinese workers harvest seaweed, *left.* It forms an important part of the diet in the Far East. Nomads of northern Africa gather and dry dates for food, *right.* The date palm grows easily in the hot, dry climate of the region.

ple cannot afford a good diet, and others simply choose to eat foods that are not nourishing. On the other hand, some people in the poorest countries have a well-balanced diet.

Most developed countries can produce all the food their people need, or the countries can afford to import the extra necessary supplies. The farmers use modern machinery and scientific methods to increase their production. Developed countries also have modern facilities to process, transport, and store food.

In highly developed countries, most families can afford to buy a variety of foods, and they are more likely to have a well-balanced diet. Their diet is rich in meat, eggs, and dairy products. They also eat large amounts of grain products and of fresh and preserved fruits and vegetables. They also enjoy the convenience of prepared or ready-to-cook foods. In addition, they often dine at restaurants or buy food from take-out restaurants to eat at home.

Most developing countries seldom produce enough food for all their people. In addition, the countries cannot afford to import the extra supplies they need. Many farmers are too poor to buy fertilizers, machinery, and other materials that would increase their output. Developing countries also lack modern facilities for processing, transporting, and storing food.

In some developing nations, many people suffer from an inadequate diet. They are too poor to buy all the food they need or a wide variety of foods. Millions of families depend on the foods they can produce themselves on small plots of land. Grains and other carbohydrates are the main foods of the majority of people in most developing countries. These foods are the least costly to produce or buy, and they require no refrigeration or other special storage. Meat, milk, and eggs are too expensive for most people. Many families bake their own bread

and make most other foods from the basic ingredients. They might even grind grain into flour to make their bread.

Religious reasons. Many religions have rules that deal with food. Some religions do not permit their members to eat certain foods. For example, the Hindu religion prohibits its members from eating beef because cattle are considered sacred. Some groups of Hindus are forbidden to eat any meat. Orthodox Jews do not eat pork, shellfish, and certain other foods. They also follow strict dietary laws regarding the storing, preparing, and serving of food.

Some religions set aside certain days for fasting and feasting. For example, Muslims may not eat or drink from dawn to sunset during Ramadan, the ninth month of the Islamic year. At the end of Ramadan, they celebrate with a feast.

Customs influence what people eat and how they prepare, serve, and eat foods. Many countries and regions have traditional dishes, most of which are based on locally produced foods. In many cases, the dishes of various cultures include the same basic ingredients. But different seasonings and cooking methods give the dish a special regional or national flavor. In the United States, for example, people enjoy such distinctively different chicken dishes as Southern-fried chicken, Louisiana chicken creole, and Texas-style barbecued chicken.

Many people consider France to be the world center of fine foods and cookery. French chefs are especially known for their elaborate dishes with rich sauces and for their fancy pastries. Perhaps the most famous English dish is roast beef and *Yorkshire pudding,* a batter pudding baked in beef juices. Italy is known for its spaghetti, macaroni, and other *pastas* and for its sauces made with tomatoes, garlic, and olive oil. Sausages, potatoes, cabbage, and beer are common in the German diet. Scandinavians enjoy herring and other fish. They also are noted for their excellent cheeses and many kinds of breads, which range from thin, crisp sheets to dark, heavy loaves.

The Spanish and Portuguese also eat much fish. Their use of onions and garlic for seasoning influenced cookery in the Caribbean islands, Mexico, and other parts of Latin America that they colonized. Caribbean cooking features such local fruits and vegetables as *plantains* (a kind of banana) and *cassava* (a starchy root). Mexican food is noted for its use of a variety of peppers. Mexicans enjoy flat corn-meal breads called *tortillas.* They may eat the tortillas plain or wrapped around bits of cheese, meat, and beans to form *tacos.*

The main food of many people in the Middle East is *pita bread,* a flat bread made from wheat. For celebrations, people of the region often prepare *shish kebab.* This dish consists of cubes of lamb, tomatoes, peppers, and onions roasted on a spikelike skewer. Rice is the main dish of many people in Japan, southern China, India, and Southeast Asia. Japanese meals commonly include vegetables, *tofu* (soybean curd), and raw or cooked fish. Chinese cookery, which many people consider among the finest in the world, varies greatly by geographical region. Cooks in southern China stir-fry chopped vegetables and meat, which they serve with a mild sauce and rice. In northern regions, people enjoy spicy fried foods served with noodles. Indians and many Southeast Asians enjoy *curry.* This stewlike dish is made of eggs, fish, meat, or vegetables and cooked in a spicy sauce.

Corn, rice, and other grains are the basic foods of many people in Africa. In Nigeria, food is often cooked in palm oil or peanut oil, and it may be sharply seasoned with red peppers. The people of Zaire serve corn and rice as a thick porridge. If they can afford it, they add meat or fish to the porridge. Many Ethiopians enjoy raw meat in a red pepper sauce.

In some cultures, the way food is served is almost as important as how it is prepared. For example, French and Japanese chefs carefully arrange food to make each dish look beautiful. In Sweden, *smörgåsbord* is a popular way to serve guests. Smörgåsbord consists of a long table set with a dazzling selection of breads, cheeses, fish, salads, and hot and cold meats.

Customs also can affect the times when people eat. In most Western cultures, for example, people commonly eat three meals a day—breakfast, lunch, and dinner. Dinner, the main meal, is usually eaten in the evening. In rural areas, however, many families eat dinner about noon and have a light supper in the evening. The British add a light, extra meal called *tea* late in the afternoon. At this meal, they serve strong tea and such foods as biscuits, cakes, or sandwiches.

In most Western cultures, people eat from individual plates and use knives, forks, and spoons. In China and Japan, the people use chopsticks. In many societies, the people eat from a common serving dish and use few utensils. Some people scoop up their food with bread or with their fingers. For example, some Hawaiian islanders use their fingers to scoop up *poi,* a pastelike food made from the tropical taro plant.

The food industry

In developing countries, many families produce their own food or buy food from local farmers. In developed countries, however, most people depend on the food industry. This section describes the food industry in the United States. However, much of the information also applies to the food industries in Canada and other developed countries.

The food industry consists of all the activities involved in producing food and getting it to consumers. The main branches of the industry include (1) production, (2) processing, (3) packaging, (4) transportation, and (5) marketing. Government regulations cover each branch and

WORLD BOOK photo

© Jonathan T. Wright, Bruce Coleman Inc.

The human diet differs greatly in rich and poor nations. In rich nations, most homemakers, such as the American woman at the left, can afford to buy a wide variety of foods. In poor countries, many families, such as the one in Nepal at the right, must produce their own food.

help assure consumers of safe, good-quality products. In addition, food companies and other organizations conduct research to increase the food supply and to improve food products.

The food industry is the fourth largest industry in the United States. About $3\frac{3}{4}$ million Americans, including self-employed farmers, work on farms to produce basic foods. Food-processing plants employ over $1\frac{1}{2}$ million workers to prepare and package foods for the market. Millions of other workers are involved in the transporting and marketing of food.

Each branch of the food industry contributes to the prices of foods in the market place. The prices reflect the cost of producing the basic food as well as the processing, packaging, transportation, and marketing costs. All these costs plus the profits each branch of the industry tries to make are paid by consumers.

Production. American farmers use modern equipment and scientific methods to produce the enormous quantities of raw materials used by food processors. The great majority of farmers specialize in raising one kind of crop or one kind of livestock.

Most U.S. farmers who specialize in crops raise a *field crop.* Field crops require a fairly large amount of land to be profitable. The chief field crops are grains, especially corn and wheat; peanuts; potatoes; soybeans; and sugar beets. Some farmers grow such produce as celery, green beans, lettuce, onions, or tomatoes. Others raise berries, grapes, nuts, or such tree fruits as apples, cherries, oranges, peaches, or pears.

Livestock farmers who raise beef cattle, hogs, and sheep produce most of the nation's meat. Many other livestock farmers keep dairy cattle or raise poultry. Some farmers raise bees, fish, goats, or rabbits.

The production of basic foods also includes the activities of commercial fishing fleets. These fleets catch huge quantities of fish and shellfish.

Processing. Most of the foods we eat have been processed. Processing changes basic foods in some way. Many processors simply add chemicals called *ad-*

ditives to foods. The various kinds of additives are intended to improve some quality of a food, such as its color, flavor, nutritional value, or storage life. However, many people consider additives to be dangerous to their health. Other processors use basic foods to manufacture entirely new food products.

Fresh eggs, fruits, and vegetables may be only washed and sorted before they reach the market. Or they may be dried or frozen. Fruits and vegetables also may be canned or pickled or used to make juice.

Meat packers slaughter cattle, hogs, and sheep. They then prepare the fresh meat for shipment to market. Meat packers also can, cure, freeze, and smoke meat, and they make it into sausages. Processors also slaughter and prepare chickens, turkeys, and other poultry for market. Large amounts of fish and shellfish are cleaned and marketed fresh. Processors also can, freeze, or pickle certain kinds of fish and shellfish. Dairy plants pasteurize and homogenize milk. Most dairies also add vitamins to milk. In addition, dairies make butter, cheese, ice cream, and yogurt from milk.

Processors manufacture many foods from basic plant and animal materials. For example, they make sugar from sugar beets and sugar cane, syrup from corn, and cooking oil from peanuts, soybeans, and various other plants. Other manufactured foods include synthetic and convenience foods. Processors developed margarine — which generally is made from corn, cottonseed, safflower, or soybean oil—as imitation butter. They make egg substitutes from real egg whites and artificial yolks. Processors use cooked meats and vegetables in canned and dried soups, frozen dinners, and canned and frozen casseroles. They combine dried eggs, flour, sugar, and other foods in packaged dessert mixes.

Packaging makes foods easy to handle and identify. It also helps protect them from spilling and from being bruised or broken. In addition, special packaging materials and methods protect foods from air, bacteria, chemicals, insects, light, moisture, and odors—all of which might spoil the food. Attractive packaging also

Jim Wood, *Cuisine* magazine

An attractive food display appeals to the eye and stimulates the appetite. This colorful assortment of dishes for an Easter celebration includes a cheese-covered ham, *center,* and red caviar, *foreground.* For many people, the way that food is served is almost as important as how it is prepared.

helps promote the sale of foods. The majority of foods, especially processed ones, are packaged. In most cases, machines pack the food into containers. Packaging is the last step in the processing of food.

Food companies use the kinds of packaging that best suit the needs and uses of their products. For example, eggs are packed in thick, sturdy cardboard or plastic cartons to protect them from breaking. Some foods, such as coffee, jelly, and peanut butter, are used a little at a time. They are packed in cans or glass jars that have a resealable lid. Plastic bags and wrap keep air away from meat, bread, potato chips, and many other foods. Such dairy products as milk and cottage cheese are packed in lightweight paper cartons that are coated with wax or plastic to prevent leakage.

Packaging may also make the home preparation or use of food easier. For example, many frozen foods can be cooked in boil-in plastic bags or in aluminum trays. Aerosol cans dispense whipped cream, and plastic squeeze bottles dispense catchup or mustard.

Transportation. Commercial shipping companies transport most of the food from producers to processors and from processors to market. Nearly all fresh foods are perishable, and must be shipped quickly. Many vegetable farmers haul their produce to nearby markets soon after it is harvested. Over longer distances, however, refrigerated trucks, railroad cars, and ships help keep perishable produce fresh. Refrigerated vehicles also haul dairy products and frozen foods. In some cases, airplanes transport highly perishable foods, such as fish, or expensive foods, such as live lobsters. Specially designed trucks and trains haul livestock.

Marketing. Some farmers sell eggs or fresh fruits and vegetables directly to consumers at roadside stands or through home deliveries. Many farmers take their produce to a *farmers' market* in a nearby city. There, food dealers and homemakers can purchase it.

Numerous grain, dairy, and other farmers sell their products directly to a food processor. Many other farmers belong to a *marketing cooperative*. A marketing cooperative collects the products of member farmers. It then sells the products to processors that offer the highest prices. Farmers sell their livestock to meat packers at large centers called *terminal markets* or at smaller *auction markets*.

Most food processors and a number of farmers sell their products to a *wholesaler*. Wholesalers buy large quantities of a product and then sell smaller amounts to *retailers*. Food retailers include supermarkets, grocery stores, delicatessens, butcher shops, restaurants, and

WORLD BOOK photo

Wholesale produce firms, *above,* buy large quantities of fruits and vegetables from farmers. The firms then sell smaller amounts to restaurants, supermarkets, and other retailers.

other businesses that sell food to consumers.

Supermarkets and groceries sell a variety of foods. Other stores sell only one line of food, such as baked goods, fish, or meat. Consumers can buy prepared meals at restaurants and cafeterias. In many office and public buildings, vending machines dispense foods.

Government regulations. In the United States, federal, state, and local government agencies supervise the food industry. These agencies help protect the health of consumers by ensuring the quality, cleanliness, and purity of foods. They also prevent food companies from making false claims about the foods they sell. Federal and state laws regulate weights, measures, and container sizes to protect buyers from being cheated.

The Food and Drug Administration (FDA) enforces standards for the food industry in general and for the truthful labeling of food products. The Department of Agriculture inspects and grades poultry, red meats, and fresh produce. The Department of Commerce supervises the production of foods made with fish. Regulations of the U.S. Postal Service and the Federal Trade

10 leading food-store chains in the United States

Company	Sales*	Assets*	Stores†	Founded	Headquarters
1. **Kroger**	$19,053,000,000	$4,614,000,000	1,317	1902	Cincinnati, Ohio
2. **American Stores**	18,478,000,000	7,010,000,000	1,529	1917	Irvine, Calif.
3. **Safeway Stores**	13,612,000,000	4,372,000,000	1,909	1902	Oakland, Calif.
4. **Great Atlantic & Pacific Tea**	9,532,000,000	2,243,000,000	1,183	1859	Montvale, N.J.
5. **Winn-Dixie Stores**	9,008,000,000	1,514,000,000	1,271	1928	Jacksonville, Fla.
6. **Southland**	7,950,000,000	4,862,000,000	8,137	1934	Dallas, Tex.
7. **Albertson's**	6,773,000,000	1,591,000,000	465	1939	Boise, Ida.
8. **Publix Super Markets**	4,804,000,000	1,173,000,000	360	1930	Lakeland, Fla.
9. **Vons**	3,917,000,000	1,673,000,000	342	1906	El Monte, Calif.
10. **Food Lion**	3,815,000,000	1,088,000,000	593	1957	Salisbury, N.C.

*May include sales and assets that are not from food stores. †Food stores, not including department and other retail stores.
Sources: "The Service 500 Directory," *Fortune,* June 5, 1989, © Time Inc.; *Moody's Industrial Manual,* 1989; company officials.

Commission (FTC) guard against false or misleading food advertisements. Local health departments set standards of sanitation for dairy farms and dairy plants and for stores, restaurants, and other establishments that sell or serve food.

Food research is conducted by food companies, food growers' associations, food institutes, government agencies, research foundations, and universities. Their efforts have led to a tremendous increase in the quantity, quality, and variety of foods available.

Agricultural researchers work to increase the food supply by developing more productive varieties of plants and livestock and more effective fertilizers and pesticides. Other researchers seek ways to improve the flavor, appearance, or nutritional value of food products. Still others study the effects of preservatives and packaging on the storage life of food.

Many food company researchers work to develop new foods, and they seek ways to make the home preparation of processed foods easier. Home economists develop new recipes, and dietitians and nutritionists look for ways in which to improve the human diet. Agricultural economists study farm management and crop and livestock production.

Food through the ages

Prehistoric times. The earliest people ate whatever plant food they could find, including wild fruits, mushrooms, nuts, roots, and seeds. They also caught fish and small land animals and ate the meat of dead animals that they found. In time, people developed weapons to hunt large animals, such as bears, bison, deer, and wild cattle. Early people probably spent much of their time searching for food. If the food supply in an area ran out, the people moved on.

The earliest people probably roasted some of their food over burning wood from fires that had started naturally. After people discovered how to make fire themselves, they could roast food more often. After they learned how to make pots, they could also boil and stew food.

By about 8000 B.C., people had begun to raise plants and animals for food. Farming assured people of a steadier food supply. It also meant settling in one area instead of traveling about in search of food. Grains were especially important crops to early farmers. Farmers also raised cattle, goats, sheep, and other animals for meat and milk.

Some groups of prehistoric people were nomadic shepherds. These groups traveled across the countryside in well-established patterns. They raised such animals as camels, goats, and sheep. Much of the nomads' diet consisted of meat and milk from their livestock.

Ancient times. Between 3500 and 1500 B.C., the first great civilizations developed in river valleys. These valleys were the Nile Valley in Egypt, the Tigris-Euphrates Valley in what is now Iraq, the Indus Valley in what is now Pakistan, and the Huang He Valley in China. All these valleys had fertile soil and a favorable climate, enabling farmers to produce abundant yields. In ancient Egypt, for example, farmers along the Nile could raise two or three crops a year on the same fields. They grew barley and wheat and such vegetables as beans, lettuce, and peas. They also raised such fruits as grapes and melons. Their livestock included cattle, goats, and sheep.

Ancient Greece and later ancient Rome could not produce enough food for their growing populations. They thus had to import large quantities of food from other countries. They also conquered and colonized lands that had plentiful food supplies. The Greeks and Romans thus enjoyed cherries from Persia; apricots, peaches, and spices from the Orient; and, most important, wheat from Egypt. By the A.D. 200's, the Roman Empire covered much of Europe, most of the Middle East, and the Mediterranean coast of Africa. Most of the empire's large farms specialized in raising wheat, which formed the basis of the Roman diet.

The Middle Ages. After the Roman Empire fell in the A.D. 400's, international trade dropped sharply. In Europe, most of the land was divided into *manors.* A manor was a large estate controlled by a lord and worked by peasants. Manors provided all the foods needed by the lords and the peasants. These foods included grains; grapes and other fruits; such vegetables as beans, cabbages, and turnips; and poultry, cattle, and other livestock.

Between 1000 and 1300, thousands of Europeans went to the Middle East to fight in the Crusades. The crusaders acquired a taste for spices and Middle Eastern foods. After they returned to Europe, their desire for different foods helped renew international trade. It also helped stimulate the exploration of new lands.

Illustration from the *Hours of the Virgin* (1500's), an illuminated manuscript by an unknown Flemish artist; the Pierpont Morgan Library, New York City.

During the Middle Ages, food was produced on *manors,* large estates controlled by lords. The peasants who lived on a manor raised livestock and grew crops.

Foods of the New World. In 1492, Christopher Columbus sailed west from Spain. He was seeking a short sea route to the spice lands of the Indies. But Columbus landed in the New World, America, not the Indies. And although Columbus did not find spices, his voyage led to a new world of food for Europeans. American Indians introduced Europeans to avocados, chocolate, corn, peanuts, peppers, pineapples, sweet and white potatoes, squashes, and tomatoes.

The American colonists enjoyed many of the Indian foods. In fact, the Indians taught them how to raise corn, which became the most important crop of the early colonial period. The Indians also taught the colonists how to cook lobsters and wild turkeys. The colonists, in turn, brought their seeds and such livestock as cattle and hogs to the New World.

Recent developments. In the United States today, people's food habits are changing in numerous ways. For example, snacks have become part of the daily diet of many Americans. At the same time, others worry about becoming overweight and watch what and how much they eat. Many health-conscious Americans believe that food additives and other chemicals used in producing and processing foods harm the body. They also are concerned that many important nutrients are lost during processing. These worries have led to the popularity of so-called *health foods.* Health foods include many unprocessed foods as well as foods grown without the use of chemical fertilizers and pesticides.

Many health-conscious people also try to include more fiber in their diet. Fiber is thought to help prevent certain intestinal diseases. Fresh fruits and vegetables and whole-grain foods supply dietary fiber. Some people avoid butter, eggs, fatty meats, and other foods high in a fatty substance called *cholesterol.* Too much cholesterol in the bloodstream may contribute to hardening of the arteries.

Another trend is the rising popularity of cooking as a hobby. In contrast, more people eat many of their meals in restaurants. Fast-food restaurants, especially, have become increasingly popular.   Margaret McWilliams

Related articles. See various country articles in *World Book* in which local foods are discussed, such as **Mexico** (Way of life). See also the following articles:

Kinds of food

Bread	Cheese	Grain	Nut	Sugar
Candy	Egg	Meat	Poultry	Vegetable
Cereal	Fruit	Milk	Spice	

Nutrition

Carbohydrate	Digestive system	Health	Protein
Diet	Fat	Lipid	Vitamin
Dietitian		Nutrition	Weight control

Preparation and processing

Artificial sweetener	Dehydrated food	Freeze-drying
Canning	Fishing industry	Meat packing
Cold storage	Food, Frozen	Packaging
Cooking	Food additive	Refrigeration
	Food preservation	

Special food dishes

Barbecue	Chili con carne	Pemmican
Bird's-nest soup	Haggis	Trepang
Caviar		

Beverages

Alcoholic beverage	Chocolate	Maguey	Soft drink
	Coffee	Maté	Tea

Other related articles

Agriculture	Flower (Other uses)	Marketing
Christmas (Christmas feasting)	Food and Agriculture Organization	Plant
Climate (Food and climate)	Food and Drug Administration	Prehistoric people (Food)
Easter (The lamb; Other foods)	Food poisoning	Restaurant
Eskimo (Food)	Food supply	Salt
Fast	Home economics	Supermarket
	Kosher	Thanksgiving Day

Outline

I. **Sources of food**
  A. Food from plants
  B. Food from animals
II. **How the body uses food**
  A. Producing energy
  B. Building and repairing tissues
  C. Regulating body processes
III. **Why diets differ around the world**
  A. Geographic reasons   C. Religious reasons
  B. Economic reasons   D. Customs
IV. **The food industry**
  A. Production   E. Marketing
  B. Processing   F. Government regulations
  C. Packaging   G. Food research
  D. Transportation
V. **Food through the ages**

Questions

What were some foods that the American Indians introduced to Europeans?
How does the physical environment help determine what the people of a region eat?
What are the most important foods from plants? From animals?
What are *food additives?* What do they do?
How does packaging help keep food from spoiling?
What is *curry? Shish kebab? Smörgåsbord?*
Why is it important to have a well-balanced diet?
What are some reasons diets differ in developed and developing countries?
What are *health foods?* Why are they popular?
Why are proteins essential to good health?

Reading and Study Guide

See *Food* in the Research Guide/Index, Volume 22, for a *Reading and Study Guide.*

Additional resources

Level I
Adler, Irving. *Food.* Day, 1977.
Burns, Marilyn. *Good for Me! All About Food in 32 Bites.* Little, Brown, 1978.
Ontario Science Centre. *Foodworks: Over 100 Science Activities and Fascinating Facts That Explore the Magic of Food.* Addison-Wesley, 1987.
Pizer, Vernon. *Eat the Grapes Downward: An Uninhibited Romp Through the Surprising World of Food.* Dodd, 1983.
U.S. Department of Agriculture. *What's to Eat? And Other Questions Kids Ask About Food: The 1979 Yearbook of Agriculture.* U.S. Government Printing Office, 1979.

Level II
Harris, Marvin. *Good to Eat: Riddles of Food and Culture.* Simon & Schuster, 1985.
Kahn, E. J., Jr. *The Staffs of Life.* Little, Brown, 1985.
Powledge, Fred. *Fat of the Land.* Simon & Schuster, 1984. Tells how food is processed and marketed in the United States.
Van Den Brul, Caroline, and Spindler, Susan. *Tomorrow's World: Food.* Parkwest Publications, 1986.
Visser, Margaret. *Much Depends on Dinner: The History and Mythology of Food.* Grove, 1986.

Food, Frozen. Freezing is one of the best ways to preserve foods. Food-processing companies freeze such foods as baked goods, orange juice, pizzas, vegetables, and complete precooked meals. Many people freeze foods at home. Freezing preserves food by preventing the growth of microbes that spoil food and by slowing down food-spoiling chemical reactions. All frozen foods should be stored at temperatures of 0° F. (−18° C) or below.

Quick-freezing preserves most foods better than slow-freezing does. Slow-freezing changes the structure of the cells of some foods in such a way that the foods leak fluids when they are later defrosted. This leakage results in undesirable changes in the food's texture. For example, leakage can make vegetables mushy, and meat tough. Also in slow-freezing, the food may not cool quickly enough to prevent spoilage by microbes or by chemical reactions. Food frozen at home is slow-frozen.

Almost all foods frozen commercially are quick-frozen. Quick-freezing causes little change in the structure of food cells and prevents spoilage by microbes and by chemical reactions.

Commercial freezing of food began in the United States before 1865. Food-processing companies originally froze food by using ice cut from ponds. In the late 1850's, such companies began making ice by using a process that involved the mechanical compression of ammonia (see **Refrigeration** [Mechanical refrigeration]). The ice was used to freeze meat and vegetables for international distribution. These early methods of freezing allowed only for slow-freezing. But in 1925, Clarence Birdseye, a Massachusetts inventor, developed a quick-freezing process for fish and vegetables. In 1929, the Postum Company (now General Foods Corporation) purchased his patents and began to produce frozen foods. Frozen foods became popular in the United States in the 1950's, when freezers became widely available.

Commercial methods of quick-freezing

There are several commercial methods of freezing foods quickly. These methods include (1) air-blast freezing, (2) indirect-contact freezing, (3) nitrogen freezing, (4) dry-ice freezing, and (5) liquid Freon freezing.

Air-blast freezing uses a steady flow of cold air at −40° to −58° F. (−40° to −50° C). The cold air is produced by passing air over coils that are cooled by a mechanical-compression system. The cold air is then blown into an insulated tunnel, and the food passes through the tunnel on a conveyor belt. In most cases, processing firms package the food before sending it through the tunnel. But for faster freezing, some processors freeze such foods as vegetables and fruit before packaging them.

Indirect-contact freezing can be done in several ways. One method uses adjustable metal plates that have hollow walls. A *refrigerant* (cooling substance) inside the plate walls cools the plate surfaces to about −28° F. (−33° C). Packaged foods are placed between the plates, which are then adjusted to make contact with the upper and lower surfaces of the packages. As the plates absorb heat, the food freezes solid. Another indirect-contact system uses a refrigerated solution of salt or of a type of alcohol called *glycol.* A mechanical conveyor moves food in cans or other packages through

Concentrated orange juice is frozen in cans. First, the juice is poured into the cans, *above.* Then the cans are sealed and immersed in a refrigerated alcohol or salt solution.

the solution. Processing companies use salt solutions and glycol solutions to freeze such products as canned fruit juices and poultry that is sealed in plastic film.

Nitrogen freezing. In this process, liquid nitrogen under pressure at −280° F. (−173° C) is first *vaporized* (turned into a misty gas). The cold nitrogen vapor then flows into a chamber, where it freezes the food. This method is expensive, but it freezes food faster and results in better products than the air-blast and indirect-contact methods do.

Dry-ice freezing resembles nitrogen freezing, except that it starts with powdered *dry ice* (solid carbon dioxide) instead of with liquid nitrogen. The dry ice vaporizes, and the cold vapor freezes the food. The dry-ice method costs even more than the nitrogen method.

Liquid-Freon freezing. In this method, unpackaged food is sprayed with, or dipped in, liquid *Freon* at −21° F. (−29° C). Freon is a chemical that contains carbon, chlorine, and fluorine (see **Fluorocarbon**). Because the Freon is in liquid form, it freezes food as fast as nitrogen vapor does, even though the nitrogen vapor is colder. The Freon evaporates completely from the food before the food is packaged. Processing companies use the liquid-Freon method to freeze such foods as shrimp and corn on the cob.

Freezing food at home

People freeze foods at home by placing them in cabinet deep-freezers or in the freezer compartments of refrigerators. Both of these kinds of freezers operate at about 0° F. (−18° C).

Freezer capacities vary considerably. A 10-cubic-foot (0.28-cubic-meter) freezer can hold up to about 25 pounds (11 kilograms) of food. Some large cabinet units hold as much as 150 pounds (68 kilograms). But regardless of a freezer's size, it is important not to overload the unit. Overloading prevents the freezer from maintaining the temperature at or below 0° F. (−18° C). In addition, a freezer should not be completely filled with unfrozen food, because the food will freeze too slowly.

Home freezers freeze food more slowly than do industrial-freezing systems. As a result, freezing food at home results in lower food quality than does industrial freezing. However, many foods make acceptable products when frozen at home. Such foods can be stored for a year at 0° F. (−18° C) if properly prepared, packaged, and frozen. Exceptions include avocados, cabbage, celery, cooked egg whites, custards, fatty fish, grapes, pears, vegetable salads, and tomatoes.

Preparing foods for freezing involves several steps. First, the foods should be washed, trimmed, and cut to the desired size. Vegetables and some fruits should then be *blanched*—that is, steamed or boiled for one to three minutes. Blanching destroys enzymes in the food. The enzymes speed up chemical changes that can give the food a disagreeable odor or flavor or a different color. Enzymes can operate even in a freezer.

Fruits may or may not be blanched, depending on their intended use. Fruits intended for cooking should be blanched. But blanching gives food a cooked flavor, and so fruits that are to be eaten uncooked should not be blanched. Fruits that are not blanched lose quality more rapidly in a freezer than do blanched fruits.

Meats need little preparation for freezing except trimming of waste parts. In general, meat, including poultry and fish, should be frozen uncooked. Cooked meat, when frozen, spoils two or three times faster than meat frozen raw. Freezing meat in a sauce slows down the spoiling. Poultry, before being frozen, must be cleaned, dressed, and thoroughly washed inside and out. Fish typically are cleaned, cut into fillets, and skinned—or cleaned, scaled, and cut into steaks.

In general, thawed foods should not be refrozen. Refreezing food and thawing it again reduces the food's quality. In addition, refreezing the food may make it unhealthful, unless it previously was thawed in a refrigerator or in a microwave oven.

Packaging is an important part of freezing food at home. Proper packaging protects the food while it is stored in the freezer. The food should be packed tightly in an airtight container to prevent evaporation. Evaporation can dry the food out. It also can cause snow called *package ice* to form inside containers that have too much air space. In addition, evaporation results in a dull or dried-out appearance called *freezer burn.* Food should be placed in small packages to speed freezing.

Problems with frozen foods

Frozen foods can cause food poisoning if they are not frozen soon enough or if they are not cooked soon enough after thawing. Food-poisoning organisms can grow in food if its temperature exceeds 45° to 50° F. (7° to 10° C) for only a few hours. If the food is cooked before it is frozen, it should immediately be put in a refrigerator or freezer. Allowing warm food to cool at room temperature permits the growth of food-poisoning microbes that may survive the freezing process.

Foods should be thawed in a microwave oven or, if such an oven is not available, in a refrigerator. Both methods prevent the growth of food-poisoning organisms. However, refrigerator thawing allows physical and chemical changes that reduce food quality.

To help prevent the loss of quality that occurs in vegetables as a result of slow thawing, processing firms package many kinds of vegetables in sealed plastic pouches. Consumers can thaw the vegetables rapidly—and cook them—by transferring the unopened pouch from a freezer directly into boiling water. The tightly packed pouches also prevent freezer burn and the formation of package ice. Many frozen foods can be cooked in a microwave oven as soon as they are removed from the freezer.

Most U.S. states require that frozen foods be stored at or below 0° F. (−18° C). However, supermarket freezer shelves are often overstocked, and many supermarket and home freezers have automatic defrost cycles that raise and lower the food's temperature repeatedly. The temperature of commercially frozen food also may repeatedly rise and fall as the food is moved from one freezer to another during distribution. As a result, some frozen foods often exceed 0° F. (−18° C). The repeated temperature changes lead to loss of food quality. For example, they cause ice crystals to form in ice cream, giving it a grainy texture. They also promote freezer burn and the formation of package ice. Theodore P. Labuza

See also **Birdseye, Clarence; Food preservation; Refrigeration.**

Food additive is any chemical that food manufacturers intentionally add to one of their products. Some additives increase a food's nutritional value. Others improve the color, flavor, or texture of foods. Still others keep foods from spoiling. Common food additives include iodine, put into salt to prevent goiter, and baking powder, added to dough to make it rise.

Some food additives come from other foods. Scientists also create many synthetic additives in the laboratory. Some people consider food additives dangerous to their health. But many of these chemicals occur naturally in foods that people have eaten for centuries.

Kinds of additives. Food manufacturers use hundreds of additives in processing various foods. These additives can be classified into six major groups: (1) preservatives; (2) nutritional supplements; (3) flavoring agents; (4) coloring agents; (5) emulsifiers, stabilizers, and thickeners; and (6) acids and alkalis.

Preservatives, such as salt, prevent the growth of bacteria that cause foods to spoil. Preservatives called *antioxidants* keep fats and oils from spoiling and prevent other foods from becoming discolored.

Nutritional supplements, such as iron, minerals, and vitamins, make foods more nourishing. A number of such supplements, including vitamin B_1 and vitamin B_2, are added to flour. These additives enrich flour and thus improve the nutritional value of bread and other products made from it. Milk with vitamin D added helps prevent rickets, a bone disease.

Flavoring agents include all spices and natural fruit flavors, as well as such artificial flavors as the vanillin used in ice cream. Some flavoring agents, such as monosodium glutamate (MSG), add no flavor of their own but improve a food's natural flavor.

Coloring agents make synthetic foods resemble real ones. Margarine manufacturers add yellow coloring to make their product look like butter. Manufacturers also add coloring to many canned foods to replace natural food colors lost in processing. Some coloring agents, such as the orange color added to the skins of oranges, improve the appearance of a food.

Emulsifiers, stabilizers, and thickeners help the ingredients in a food to mix and hold together. Algin, an emulsifier, gives ice cream its creamy texture and maintains the mixture of liquids in salad dressings. Carrageenin, the most widely used stabilizer, keeps the chocolate particles in chocolate milk from settling. Pectin and gelatin are used to thicken jams and jellies.

Acids and alkalis help maintain a chemical balance in some foods. Alkalis neutralize the high acid content of such canned foods as peas and olives. Some acids add flavor. Citric acid added to fruit juice gives it a tart taste. Carbonic acid puts the fizz in soft drinks.

Government regulations. In the United States, the Federal Food, Drug, and Cosmetic Act of 1938 sets standards for the food industry and requires truthful labeling. This law also requires a manufacturer to prove a new food additive safe before using it. The Food and Drug Administration (FDA) enforces the act. This agency tests many food additives before approving them.

The Federal Food, Drug, and Cosmetic Act prohibits the use of any food additive if that chemical causes cancer in animals. Such additives have been banned because of concern that they might also cause cancer in humans. In 1970, the FDA prohibited the sale of artificial sweeteners called *cyclamates.* Experiments had shown that cyclamates caused cancer in rats. In 1976, the FDA banned *Red No. 2,* a dye used in foods, drugs, and cosmetics.   Jean Mayer

See also **Monosodium glutamate; Pure food and drug laws.**

Food and Agriculture Organization (FAO) is a specialized agency of the United Nations. Its full name is the Food and Agriculture Organization of the United Nations. The agency works to improve the production, distribution, and use of food and other products of the world's farms, forests, and fisheries. Its goals include raising the level of nutrition and the standard of living of all people, especially the rural poor. About 160 countries belong to the FAO.

The FAO works in four ways. (1) It provides technical advice and assistance on behalf of governments and development funding agencies. (2) It collects, analyzes, and distributes information. (3) It advises governments on agricultural policy and planning. (4) It acts as a neutral forum where governments can discuss food and agricultural issues. The FAO and the United Nations co-sponsor the World Food Program. This program uses food surpluses and cash from donor nations to provide emergency relief and to stimulate development. The FAO was set up in 1945. It has headquarters in Rome.

Critically reviewed by the Food and Agriculture Organization

See also **Food supply** (Food supply programs); **United Nations** (Fighting hunger).

Food and Drug Administration (FDA) is an agency of the United States Department of Health and Human Services. The FDA administers federal laws designed to ensure the purity of food, the safeness of cosmetics, and the safety and effectiveness of biological products, drugs, and therapeutic devices. It is also concerned with the truthfulness of labels and the safety and honesty of packaging. The principal laws administered by the FDA are the Federal Food, Drug, and Cosmetic Act of 1938 and the Drug Amendments Act of 1962.

The FDA has the responsibility of promoting sanitary conditions in public eating places and interstate travel facilities. It also takes part in joint programs of the federal and state governments to ensure the safety of milk products and shellfish. In 1971, the FDA took over the enforcement of the Radiation Control for Health and

Safety Act of 1968. That law was designed to prevent unnecessary exposure to radiation from electronic products, such as television sets and X-ray equipment.

Other activities of the FDA include development of new methods for analyzing products, and research on how various substances affect human beings and animals. The FDA has laboratories and offices in over 100 cities.   Critically reviewed by the Food and Drug Administration

See also **Pure food and drug laws.**

Food chain. See Ecology; **Fish** (Fish in the balance of nature); **Sun** (Heat and light for life); **Environmental pollution** (Other kinds of pollution).

Food coloring. See Food additive (Kinds of additives).

Food for Peace is a United States government program that makes U.S. farm products available to less developed countries and needy people. Under the program, the United States sells or donates agricultural commodities—chiefly grain and grain products—to many countries in Africa, Asia, and Latin America.

Food for Peace was established in 1954. For many years, it was limited to surplus agricultural products. But in 1966, Congress removed the surplus commodities requirement and authorized the secretary of agriculture to determine which farm products were available for export under the program. Congress also directed that the program give highest priority to nations that try to solve their own problems of food shortages and economic growth. Food for Peace is administered by the Department of Agriculture, in consultation with the Department of State and other federal agencies.

Critically reviewed by the Foreign Agricultural Service

Food groups. See Nutrition.

Food poisoning results from eating food that has been contaminated by bacteria or chemicals or that is poisonous in itself. The symptoms vary widely, but in most cases they include nausea, vomiting, cramps, and diarrhea. In some types of food poisoning, muscle paralysis and even death may occur.

Most food poisoning results from bacterial contamination. Bacteria can invade almost any food, but contamination occurs chiefly in meats, seafoods, home-canned foods, and dairy products, especially creams and custards. Bacterial contamination can be prevented by using sanitary methods in preparing and storing foods.

Contamination by *staphylococcal bacteria* causes most food poisoning (see **Staphylococcus**). These bacteria release *toxins* (poisons) into the contaminated food. The toxins produce the illness. Another common type of food poisoning is *salmonellosis,* often called *salmonella* because it results from contamination by *Salmonella* bacteria. These organisms cause illness after reproducing in the digestive tract (see **Salmonellosis**). Staphylococcal and salmonella food poisoning affect the stomach and intestines, but most victims recover quickly. Still another type of food poisoning is associated with bacteria found in fried rice. *Botulism* is a far more serious, often fatal, type of bacterial food poisoning. Botulism is caused by toxins that form in improperly canned foods and is characterized by muscle paralysis (see **Botulism**).

Foods contaminated by such chemicals as lead, arsenic, and mercury cause serious forms of food poisoning. Contamination by pesticides and other organic chemicals may also lead to food poisoning.

Certain varieties of mushrooms and some kinds of fish are the best-known examples of foods poisonous in themselves. Eating such foods can lead to serious or even fatal poisoning.   James L. Franklin

See also **Food preservation; Environmental pollution** (Other kinds of pollution); **Mushroom** (Poisonous mushrooms); **Mycotoxin.**

Additional resources

Food Safety. Ed. by Howard R. Roberts. Wiley, 1981.
Richardson, Treva M. and Nicodemus, W. R. *Sanitation for Foodservice Workers.* 3rd ed. CBI, 1981. Discusses bacterial food contaminations and their prevention.

Food preservation is the term used to describe any process used to slow the normal decay of food. There are many forms of food preservation. They range from simple refrigeration to treatment with radiation. Some methods date back to prehistoric times. But others have only been developed as a result of modern advances.

Food preservation helped make today's civilization possible. Without it, most people would have to grow their own food. Food could not be transported from rural areas to urban areas without being spoiled or destroyed by pests. As a result, large cities could not exist. In addition, famines would probably be more frequent and widespread, because surpluses of food could not be stored to guard against emergencies.

How food spoils

All foods will eventually spoil if not preserved. Some, such as nuts or grains, can be stored for months with very little treatment. Others, such as milk or meat, stay fresh only one or two days without preservation.

Food spoilage results from two chief sources, *pests* and *microorganisms.* Pests include insects and rodents. Many pests destroy or severely damage crops simply by feeding on them. Some pests transmit serious diseases to foods. Pests are controlled by pesticides or by storing food in such containers as tightly sealed steel bins that prevent rodents from getting at food.

Campbell Soup Company

Food preservation helps prevent food spoilage. Canning, freezing, and a number of other methods are used to preserve a wide variety of foods, such as those shown above.

Microorganisms include bacteria, molds, and yeasts. Food spoils when enough microorganisms multiply in the food to cause changes in flavor or odor. Bacteria multiply very rapidly to produce acids, gases, and other chemicals—some of which may be poisonous to human beings. Molds are fungi that grow best on moist food surfaces at temperatures of about 90° F. (32° C). However, molds continue to reproduce at much cooler temperatures because the spores are strong and hard to kill. Mold growth is easy to see and makes food look unappetizing. Yeasts produce alcohols and certain organic compounds called *esters.* In some foods, such as wine, alcohols are desirable. But in other foods, alcohols and esters produce disagreeable flavors.

Food spoilage may occur before flavor or odor change is detectable. For example, bacteria known as *Clostridium botulinum* may not be readily noticeable in foods. However, this bacteria may cause an extremely dangerous kind of food poisoning called *botulism.* Botulism is often fatal to human beings (see **Botulism**).

How foods are preserved

The chief methods of food preservation include (1) curing, (2) canning, (3) cold storage, (4) freezing, (5) drying, (6) additives, (7) irradiation, and (8) aseptic packaging. In addition, other methods, such as pasteurization, fermentation, and controlled atmosphere storage, help preserve some foods.

Curing involves the addition of such ingredients as salt, spices, sugar, sodium nitrate, and sodium nitrite to food. It is one of the oldest methods of food preservation. Today, curing is widely used in the production of ham, pork, corned beef, and some other meats. It is also sometimes used to preserve fish, potatoes, cucumbers, and certain nuts.

Each of the ingredients that are used for curing acts on food in its own way. Salt slows the growth of microorganisms and removes part of the water from the food. Sugar counters the hardening effect of the salt. Sodium nitrate and sodium nitrite help meat keep its red color. Spices are added primarily for flavor.

Curing ingredients are applied to food in several ways. In some cases, they are rubbed onto the food. They are also applied by soaking the food in a solution of the ingredients, injecting the solution directly into the food, or mixing the ingredients with the food.

Some meat and fish are cured by smoking. Wood smoke contains chemicals that slow the growth of microorganisms. Meat to be smoked, such as ham, bacon, and other salt-cured products, is hung in a *smokehouse.* A slow-burning fire provides the smoke.

Some studies have shown that certain curing agents may be harmful. For example, too much salt in a diet may cause high blood pressure. Under certain conditions, sodium nitrite may combine with other chemicals to form nitrosamines, which can cause cancer.

Canning is the most common method of food preservation in developed countries. In this process, foods that have been sealed in airtight containers are heated to destroy microorganisms that may cause spoilage. Canning plants produce a wide variety of canned foods, including fruits, vegetables, fish, meat, poultry, and soups.

Before any food is canned, it is thoroughly cleaned. Many foods, such as fruits and vegetables, are cut,

Campbell Soup Company
Canning preserves food by heating it in airtight containers. Before any food is canned, inspectors make sure the food is properly cleaned and prepared, *above*.

sliced, or peeled before canning. After the raw food is prepared, the canning process follows five basic steps: (1) filling, (2) exhausting, (3) sealing, (4) processing, and (5) cooling.

Filling. Machines fill cans at speeds up to 1,200 containers a minute. But some filling may be done by hand. Raw foods are filled into metal or glass containers. The amount of empty space in the can, called *headspace,* is carefully controlled. Too little headspace causes cans to bulge during heating. Too much headspace results in underweight cans and shorter storage life.

Exhausting involves the removal of part of the air in the headspace to form a partial vacuum in the can. Exhausting reduces the bacteria growth in the can because most bacteria cannot survive without oxygen. This process also prevents bulging of the can during heating.

Sealing. Machines seal several hundred cans per minute. Glass containers are sealed at a somewhat slower rate. Sealed containers are airtight.

Processing. In this step, containers are heated to a carefully controlled temperature for a measured length of time. The degree of heat and length of exposure vary with the product being canned and the size of the container. During processing, microorganisms that may cause spoilage are destroyed. Containers are heated in cookers called *retorts.*

Cooling follows the processing step to prevent overcooking. Containers may be cooled by transferring them from the retort into cold water, by spraying them with cold water, or by partially cooling them in water and then air-cooling.

One of the disadvantages of canning is that the heat required for sterilization changes the food's texture, color, and flavor. In addition, some nutrients are lost in the canning process. However, canned foods are popular with consumers because of their low cost, convenience, variety, and relatively long storage life.

Cold storage, or *refrigeration,* keeps food fresh at temperatures above 32° F. (0° C). Storage at or near that temperature stops the growth and activity of most microorganisms that cause food spoilage. It also decreases enzymes that cause changes in the color, flavor, and texture of foods. Foods requiring refrigeration include fish, meats, eggs, milk, fruits, and vegetables.

Cold storage has an advantage over most other forms of preservation, because it produces few changes in food. Original color, flavor, and nutrients of food are retained with refrigeration.

Freezing removes heat from food through the use of low temperatures. Freezing slows the growth of microorganisms and stops the breakdown of nutrients. Because most foods contain large amounts of water, they freeze solidly at 32° to 25° F. (0° to −4° C).

Vegetables are among the main foods preserved by freezing. Before they are frozen, vegetables are first *blanched* (scalded). Blanching prevents enzymes, which are not killed during freezing, from changing the flavor of vegetables. Other foods preserved by freezing include meat, fish, poultry, and juices. Before freezing, food may be cleaned, peeled, or prepared in other ways. Some foods, such as those used for frozen TV dinners, are cooked before freezing.

The most common commercial freezing devices used today include (1) *plate freezers,* (2) *continuous-conveyor freezers,* (3) *air-blast freezers,* and (4) *cryogenic freezers.* Plate freezers are cabinets with shelves that have refrigeration coils beneath them. Packages of food are placed on these shelves, and the cabinet is closed for several hours until the food freezes. Continuous-conveyor freezers are large rooms with temperatures ranging from −10° to −30° F. (−23° to −34° C). Packages of food travel slowly back and forth in the room on conveyor belts until they freeze.

Air-blast freezers are similar to continuous-conveyor freezers. But air-blast freezers use a fan in the room to create a high wind. This wind, combined with temperatures as low as −30° F. (−34° C), causes quick freezing of foods. Cryogenic freezers spray liquid nitrogen or liquid carbon dioxide directly onto food to freeze it very rapidly. For example, an apple pie that takes three hours to freeze in an air-blast freezer takes only five minutes in a cryogenic freezer.

Freezing preserves nutrients better than any other preservation method. In addition, frozen vegetables contain little—if any—salt.

Drying uses heat to remove moisture from food. The microorganisms that cause food spoilage require mois-

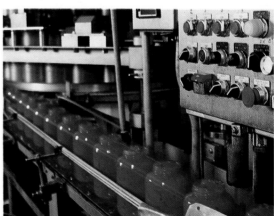

Campbell Soup Company
Filling is generally done by machines. Some machines fill up to 1,200 containers a minute. The glass containers shown above are being filled with spaghetti sauce before they are sealed.

ture to survive. Once food dries to the point where most of its water is gone, microorganisms cannot grow and cause food to spoil. Raisins, peas, soups, milk, eggs, mushrooms, and hundreds of other foods are dried. A great variety of drying techniques are used for these products, including (1) *sun drying,* (2) *tray drying,* (3) *tunnel drying,* (4) *spray drying,* (5) *pulse-combustion drying,* and (6) *drum drying.*

Sun drying consists of spreading foods in thin layers under the sun. Fruits and grains are often dried in this manner. Tray drying uses the circulation of hot air through large insulated cabinets to dry food. Tunnel drying is similar to tray drying, but the cabinet is longer. Food moves continuously through the tunnel dryer on a cart or moving belt.

Spray drying involves spraying liquids or *slurries* (mixtures of liquids and finely ground solid particles) into a large, heated chamber. Hot air is also blown into the chamber. The hot air dries the food droplets to form powders. Dried milk is one of the products obtained by this method. Pulse-combustion drying combines heat and powerful sound waves to dry food that cannot be dried by other methods. High-fructose corn syrup is one product dried in this manner. In drum drying, a thin film of food is spread onto a heated rotating cylinder called a drum. Food dries on the drum and is scraped off before the drum makes a complete rotation.

Freeze-drying. Under certain conditions, ice can change directly from a solid to a vapor without first becoming a liquid. This process, called *sublimation,* serves as the basis for the freeze-drying of food. In commercial freeze-drying, water is removed from food while the food is still frozen. Frozen food is first placed on shelves in a large vacuum chamber. The shelves are then heated to keep the food just below the melting point. As the ice vaporizes, the food maintains its shape, but becomes a spongelike, lightweight dry solid.

Freeze-drying, unlike drying, does not cause shrinkage of the food product as the water is removed. Drying produces hard, solid foods that often do not return to their original texture when *rehydrated* (have water restored). Freeze-dried foods not only retain original flavor and texture better than dried foods, but they retain nutrients better as well. However, freeze-drying is an expensive process, so it is used for only a few foods. They include instant coffee, dried soup mixes, strawberries, mushrooms, and shrimp.

Additives are chemicals added to foods to prevent spoilage or to increase nutrients. Additives are used when other methods of food preservation are unsuitable or inadequate. In the United States, additives require approval by the U.S. Food and Drug Administration (FDA). Some additives help keep foods in edible condition for as long as possible. These additives include *antioxidants* and *preservatives.* Others, such as *sequestrants* and *humectants,* help foods keep an appetizing appearance.

Many foods contain unsaturated fats, fatty acids, or oil-based vitamins. When these compounds combine with oxygen, they change into new compounds. Often this change results in the formation of harmful flavors and odors or the loss of nutrients. Antioxidants prevent the original compounds from combining with oxygen. The FDA approves the use of such antioxidants as butyl-

ated hydroxyanisol (BHA), propyl gallate, and ascorbic acid (vitamin C).

Preservatives stop microorganism growth in those foods that cannot be processed by such means as canning or freezing. Preservatives are used extensively in bread and other baked goods, pickled vegetables, fruit juices, and cheese. Some of the most common preservatives approved for use by the FDA include benzoic acid, sorbic acid, and sulfur dioxide.

Some foods contain tiny amounts of metals, such as iron or copper. These metals cause oxygen to combine with foods and produce changes in color. Sequestrants stop these metals from reacting with food. Common sequestrants include ethylenediamine tetra-acetate (EDTA) and citric acid. Humectants help retain moisture in such products as breads and cakes. These foods become unattractive and less appetizing as they dry out. Examples of humectants include glycerol and sorbitol.

Aseptic packaging sterilizes the food product and then packages it in a sterilized container. The food will keep indefinitely without refrigeration if this process is done correctly. For example, aseptic packaged milk can be stored for months in a kitchen cupboard.

Typical aseptic containers include foil-lined cartons, plastic cups, and plastic bags. These containers cost and weigh less than the metal cans or glass bottles traditionally used in packaging. Another advantage of aseptic packaging is better flavor. Cans or bottles require much longer heating time for sterilization. The longer foods are heated, the more the flavor changes. In the aseptic process, foods can be heated rapidly outside of the container. Therefore, aseptically packaged foods have a more natural flavor as well as more nutrients.

The FDA approved aseptic packaging of foods in 1981. The process is gaining popularity in the United States and other developed countries, primarily because it is cheaper and more convenient than other preservation methods.

Irradiation treats food with *ionizing radiation*—that is, radiation that produces electrically charged particles. X rays, gamma rays, and electron beams are all forms of radiation used to preserve foods. Low doses of radiation kill bacteria and inactivate enzymes with little or no chemical change in foods. Irradiation also kills insects in foods and stops the sprouting of some vegetables. In addition, it eliminates such poisonous microorganisms as salmonella or trichinae, which may cause illness.

In the United States, the FDA has approved irradiation to control the sprouting of potatoes, to kill insects in wheat and wheat flour, and to control microorganisms and insects in spices and other seasonings. Public concern over possible harmful effects of irradiation on food has caused it to have only limited use. Today, it is used commercially in the United States only for spices.

Other methods of food preservation include (1) *pasteurization,* (2) *fermentation,* (3) *fumigation,* and (4) *controlled atmosphere storage.* Pasteurization is a rapid heat treatment that destroys harmful bacteria but causes little nutrient damage. Milk is pasteurized, as are some wines and other liquids. Fermentation chemically changes foods to help preserve them. Fermentation produces such compounds as alcohol, carbon dioxide, and various acids. These agents act as preservatives on pickles, sauerkraut, salami, and some other foods.

Fumigation involves spraying foods with toxic gases to kill rats and insects. For example, methyl bromide gas is widely used to fumigate grain, dried fruits, and spices. Controlled-atmosphere storage creates conditions that help extend storage life in foods, particularly fruits. The most common controlled atmosphere consists of 92 to 95 per cent nitrogen, 3 per cent oxygen, and 2 to 5 per cent carbon dioxide.

History

Early methods. Prehistoric people probably dried grains, nuts, fruits, roots, and other plant products in the sun. People who lived in northern climates probably kept food outside their caves or huts in the winter to prevent spoilage. In more southern climates, coolness inside caves was used to store foods. After fire was discovered, cave dwellers probably dried fish and meat over a fire. Drying by fire may have led to the development of smoking as a method of preservation.

Salt curing and fermentation are two other early methods of preservation. Ancient people salted meat or fish to prevent them from spoiling. Fermentation was used by nomadic peoples in Asia to make cheese. Fermentation of fruit juice to make wine also dates back to ancient times.

Modern food preservation began in the 1700's. Lazzaro Spallanzani, an Italian naturalist, had the first recorded success with canning. He sealed meat extracts into glass flasks and heated them for an hour. Some of this food remained edible for several weeks.

By the early 1800's, Nicolas Appert, a candy maker from Paris, had worked out a canning process in which food was packed in glass jars, which were then tightly corked, and heated in boiling water. Appert also published the first book on canning, which gave specific canning methods for more than 50 foods. Although Appert had made a major contribution to canning, he did not understand why his process worked. This understanding would have to wait about 50 years until the French chemist Louis Pasteur discovered that heat killed harmful microorganisms (see **Pasteur, Louis**).

Cold storage had been used for many years to preserve foods. But a method was needed to keep food cold in hot weather. At first, ice was cut from ponds and lakes during the winter and stored in buildings called *ice houses*. Sawdust was used to cover the ice and slow its melting in the summer. In 1851, the first commercial machine for making ice was patented by John Gorrie, an American physician. This invention led to the large-scale use of refrigeration for shipping and storing foods. By 1900, there were over 400 ice plants in the United States.

Frozen foods were made possible by advances in refrigeration. In 1925, Clarence Birdseye, a Massachusetts inventor, developed the first modern quick-freezing process. He used refrigerated moving metal belts to quick-freeze fish.

Food was not dried in great volume in the United States until World War I (1914-1918), when dried food became important for feeding soldiers. The need for such food during World War II (1939-1945) led to the development of such items as instant coffee and dried milk.

Today, some people are concerned over the extent of food processing in the United States. They believe processing removes nutrients from food and that many additives are harmful to human beings. They recommend a return to natural foods that undergo a minimum amount of processing and that contain no chemical additives. However, food processors and manufacturers argue that food processing provides low-cost, nutritious foods. They also insist that chemical additives approved for use in food preservation are safe.   Jay S. Marks

Related articles in *World Book* include:

Methods of preserving food

Canning	Fumigation
Cold storage	Irradiation
Dehydrated food	Meat packing
Fermentation	Pasteurization
Food, Frozen	Refrigeration
Freeze-drying	Sterilization

Preservatives

Antibiotic	Nitrite	Sugar
Dry ice	Salt	Sulfur dioxide
Food additive	Spice	Vinegar
Nitrate		

Other related articles

Bacteria	Food poisoning
Birdseye, Clarence	Jelly and jam
Botulism	Mold
Enzyme	Pasteur, Louis
Fishing industry (Methods of processing)	Pure food and drug laws
	Spallanzani, Lazzaro
Food and Drug Administration	Yeast

Additional resources

Bailey, Janet. *Keeping Food Fresh: How to Choose and Store Everything You Eat.* Doubleday, 1985.
Bradley, Hassell, and Sundberg, Carole. *Keeping Food Safe: The Complete Guide to Safeguarding Your Family's Health While Handling, Preparing, Preserving, Freezing, and Storing Food at Home.* Doubleday, 1975.
Hertzberg, Ruth, and others. *Putting Food By.* 3rd ed. Dutton, 1982.
Trickett, Jill. *The Prevention of Food Poisoning.* Thornes & Stam, 1978.

Food service industry. See Restaurant.

Food Stamp Program is a United States government plan to help low-income households buy more and better food than they normally could afford. The program serves people receiving welfare aid and others with low incomes.

Persons apply to join the program at area welfare or public assistance offices. For a household to be eligible, it must have an income below a specified level. Its members must live together and buy food together. With certain exceptions, each adult member who is unemployed and able to work must register with the state employment service and try to find a job.

Each participating household gets a certain number of food stamps, depending on its income and size. The stamps cannot be used to buy such nonfood items as alcoholic beverages and tobacco. Grocers redeem the stamps through banks. Local banks send the stamps to federal reserve banks.

The program was established by the Food Stamp Act of 1964. It is administered by the Food and Nutrition Service of the U.S. Department of Agriculture through state and local welfare and public assistance agencies.

Critically reviewed by the Department of Agriculture

See also **Welfare.**

The food supply in poor and rich countries differs greatly, in many cases because of differences in farm output. At the left, farmers in Nepal receive a ration of rice seed, which will produce barely enough food for their needs. At the right, a U.S. farmer harvests a huge crop of soybeans.

Food supply

Food supply is the total amount of food available to all the people in the world. No one can live without food, and so the supply of food has always been one of the human race's chief concerns. The food supply depends mainly on the world's farmers. They raise the crops and livestock that provide most of our food. The world's food supply varies from year to year because the production of crops and livestock varies. Some years, terrible losses result from droughts, floods, or other natural disasters. Yet the world's population grows every year, and so the worldwide demand for food also constantly increases. Food shortages and famines occur when the food supply falls short of the amount needed.

The food supply varies not only from year to year but also from country to country. Most of the poor, *developing* nations of Africa, Asia, and Latin America seldom have enough food for most of their people. Millions of people in these countries go hungry. During years of famine, millions may die of starvation. In almost all *developed* nations, on the other hand, the majority of people have an adequate diet. But in few countries is the food supply equally distributed. In nearly every nation, some people have more than enough to eat while others live in constant hunger.

Most people in the developed countries have an ade-

Lester R. Brown, the contributor of this article, is President of Worldwatch Institute, a private, nonprofit organization that researches problems of worldwide concern, including food supply problems. He is also the senior author of the Institute's annual State of the World *reports, which review the world food situation.*

quate diet for several reasons. Almost all the developed nations lie in the world's *temperate* regions—that is, between the tropics and the polar areas. The soil and climate in temperate regions are generally well suited for farming. In addition, the developed nations have money for agricultural research and so have been able to solve various problems associated with agriculture in temperate regions. Most farmers in the developed countries can afford the fertilizers and other materials needed to produce large amounts of food. Finally, the developed countries have enough food because their population grows more slowly than their food supply.

Unlike the developed countries, most developing nations lie in or near the tropics. The soil and climate in these regions are generally not so well suited to large-scale food production as they are in temperate regions. Nor do the developing nations have much money for research. As a result, they have made relatively little progress in solving the problems of tropical agriculture. In addition, many farmers in the developing countries cannot afford to buy the fertilizers and other materials they need to produce more food. All these conditions limit food production. But the developing nations have too little food chiefly because their population grows nearly as fast as—or faster than—their food supply.

The world's population reached 5 billion in 1986 and is increasing about 1.6 per cent a year. At this rate of growth, the number of people in the world will double in 44 years. Food production must also double during this time to feed the added people.

Many experts believe that food production will be unable to keep up with population growth unless the birth rate falls sharply. This theory was first developed in detail by the British economist Thomas Robert Malthus in the late 1700's (see **Malthus, Thomas Robert**). In the past, population growth was controlled mainly by a high death rate. But during the 1900's, improved living standards and medical advances have reduced the death rate in the majority of countries. Today, most people who agree with Malthus consider family planning to be the only practical method of reducing population growth. This article discusses these and other food supply problems. It also discusses human food needs, food sources, and food supply programs.

Basic human food needs

Experts usually determine the adequacy of a person's diet by the amount of *calories* and *protein* it provides. Protein is one of the chief *nutrients* (nourishing substances) found in food. It is needed to build and maintain body cells. Other nutrients are *carbohydrates* (starches and sugars), fats, minerals, and vitamins. Calories are units of energy supplied by food. Carbohydrates and fats normally provide most of the calories in the human diet. Protein supplies the rest. People who lack sufficient calories in their diet are said to be *undernourished*. A person whose diet seriously lacks any nutrient is said to be *malnourished*. Protein malnutrition is by far the most common type of malnutrition.

The majority of people who do not get enough protein in their diet also lack sufficient calories. To make up for a continuing lack of calories, the human body changes more and more protein into energy. As a result, less protein is available to build and maintain body cells. Most malnutrition is therefore protein-calorie malnutri-

tion—an inadequate supply of both protein and calories in the diet. As many as 600 million people throughout the world—about one-ninth of the world's population—suffer from protein-calorie malnutrition. The great majority of these people live in developing countries, and most are young children. Many victims die before they are 5 years old. Many others grow up with severe mental and physical handicaps. See **Nutrition** (Protein-calorie malnutrition).

Calories. The amount of calories a person needs each day depends on the person's sex, age, body build, and degree of physical activity. A husky house painter, for example, requires far more calories than does a slightly built office worker. The United Nations (UN) estimates that a moderately active man of average weight—that is, 143 pounds (65 kilograms)—needs at least 3,000 calories a day. A moderately active woman of average weight—that is, 121 pounds (55 kilograms)—needs about 2,200. Children and young people up to 19 years of age require an average of 820 to 3,070 calories, depending on sex, weight, and age.

Daily calorie *consumption* (intake) by all people in the poorest developing countries averages under 2,000—far less than most people require. In some developed countries, daily calorie consumption averages over 3,700—far more than most people require.

Protein in the human diet consists of *animal protein* and *plant protein*. Dairy products, eggs, fish, and meat are the chief sources of animal protein. The best sources of plant protein are members of the pea family.

Per capita distribution of the world's calorie supply

This graph shows the number of food calories that would be available daily *per capita* (for each person) in the world's major regions if the calories were divided equally among all the people in the region. It also shows the average number of calories required in each region. Calorie requirements depend on the average body weight of the population, the age and sex distribution, and the level of activity.

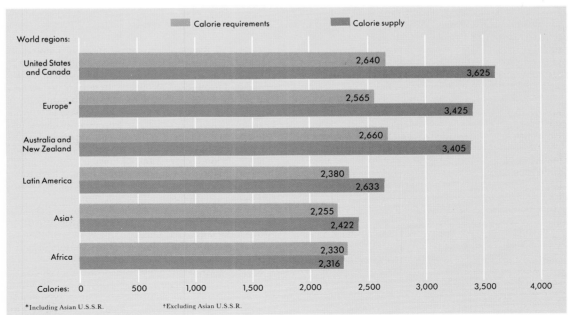

Legend: Calorie requirements | Calorie supply

World regions:

United States and Canada	requirements: 2,640	supply: 3,625
Europe*	requirements: 2,565	supply: 3,425
Australia and New Zealand	requirements: 2,660	supply: 3,405
Latin America	requirements: 2,380	supply: 2,633
Asia†	requirements: 2,255	supply: 2,422
Africa	requirements: 2,330	supply: 2,316

Calories: 0   500   1,000   1,500   2,000   2,500   3,000   3,500   4,000

*Including Asian U.S.S.R.   †Excluding Asian U.S.S.R.

Figures are 1981-1983 averages. Source: *FAO Production Yearbook 1985*, Food and Agriculture Organization of the United Nations.

These plants, which are called *legumes* or *pulses,* include beans, peas, and peanuts. *Cereal grains* also supply plant protein. The main cereal grains are barley, corn, millet, oats, rice, rye, sorghum, and wheat.

Protein is made up of molecules called *amino acids.* The human body must have certain amino acids to build and maintain body cells. Most sources of animal protein provide all the essential amino acids—and in the proportions the body requires. These food sources can thus supply all of a person's daily protein needs. On the other hand, many sources of plant protein do not supply the complete combination of amino acids. One or more of the essential amino acids are missing or insufficient. For example, cereal grains by themselves do not provide a full combination of amino acids. But if grain is eaten with certain legumes, especially protein-rich soybeans, it can meet a person's protein needs. See **Protein.**

People differ in their protein requirements, just as they do in their calorie requirements. But a person's protein needs also depend on the quality of the protein consumed. People require less protein if their diet includes some animal protein than if it includes only plant protein. The UN estimates that a man of average weight needs at least 37 grams of protein daily, if the protein is entirely animal protein. A woman of average weight needs about 29 grams. Children and young people up to 19 years of age require an average of 14 to 38 grams. In every case, a person's requirement increases if the protein is mainly plant protein.

Daily protein consumption by all people in the poorest developing countries averages as low as 33 grams. But most of the protein is plant protein. Average protein consumption in these countries therefore falls short of the minimum requirement. Also, most people in these countries have too few calories in their diet. As a result, much of the protein they consume is used to meet their energy needs rather than to build and maintain body cells. Protein consumption by all people in some developed countries averages as high as 107 to 119 grams daily. Most of the protein is animal protein and therefore far exceeds the minimum need. The extra protein provides added calories. If the calories exceed the amount required, the body stores the excess as fat.

Major sources of food

Cereal grains are the world's most important food source. Worldwide, they supply about half the calories and much of the protein that people consume. Grain is also a chief ingredient in most livestock feed and so is involved in the production of meat, eggs, and dairy products. Cereal grains are of such great importance that food experts often use the size of the grain supply as a measure of the total food supply.

Almost all the grain grown in developing countries is *food grain*—that is, people consume it directly as food. They may simply cook the grain as a main dish. Or they may use it to make bread, noodles, or some other food. People in developed countries also consume grain directly. But in addition, they use much of the grain as *feed grain,* which is fed to livestock. People consume this grain indirectly in the form of livestock products.

Grains used chiefly as feed in some countries are used chiefly as food in other countries. For example, most of the corn grown in the United States is used for

Per capita protein supply in the United States and China

In the United States, a developed country, the daily per capita protein supply is almost twice as large as in China, a developing country. In addition, the per capita supply of animal protein in the United States is nine times as large as in China.

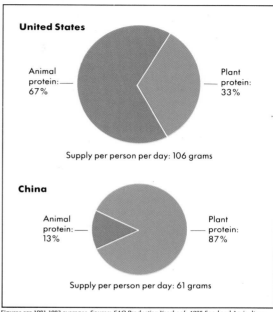

United States

Animal protein: 67%

Plant protein: 33%

Supply per person per day: 106 grams

China

Animal protein: 13%

Plant protein: 87%

Supply per person per day: 61 grams

Figures are 1981-1983 averages. Source: *FAO Production Yearbook, 1985,* Food and Agriculture Organization of the United Nations.

livestock feed. But in some African and Latin-American countries, corn is an important food grain.

Livestock and fish are the main sources of animal protein. On a worldwide basis, meat, eggs, and dairy products supply more than 80 per cent of the animal protein in the human diet. Fish provide a large percentage of the animal protein in certain countries, such as Japan, Norway, and the Philippines. But worldwide, fish supply only about 20 per cent of the animal protein people consume.

Other major food sources. In certain areas of the world, people depend heavily on food sources other than grain, livestock, or fish. Soybeans and other legumes rank second only to rice as a source of food in many Asian countries. Potatoes are a major food in parts of Europe and South America. People in some tropical areas rely largely on such native foods as bananas, *cassava* (a starchy root), and sweet potatoes or yams. Of all these foods, only legumes provide an adequate supply of essential amino acids.

Conditions that affect the food supply

The world's food supply consists mainly of food produced during the current year. But it also includes *reserves,* or *stocks,* left over from previous years. Food reserves are necessary to help prevent shortages after bad farming years. To build up reserves, the countries of the world overall must produce more food in a year than they consume. But few countries produce a surplus. The United States produces by far the largest surplus. Argentina, Australia, Canada, and New Zealand also regularly produce a food surplus.

Most countries produce either just enough food to meet their needs or not enough. If a country fails to produce enough food, it must import additional supplies or face a shortage. Most developed countries that do not produce sufficient food can afford to import the extra supplies they need. Great Britain and Japan are examples of such countries. But most developing countries cannot afford to import all the food their people require. Since the early 1950's, world food production has doubled, but so has the demand. As a result, many countries rely on food imports, chiefly from the United States.

The amount of food a country produces depends partly on its agricultural resources, such as land and water. No country has an unlimited supply of these resources. The worldwide food supply is thus affected by (1) limited agricultural resources and (2) the ever-increasing demand for food. The food supply within countries is also affected by problems of distribution.

Limited agricultural resources. Farming requires various resources—especially land, water, energy, and fertilizer. Land is the chief agricultural resource. Land used for growing crops must be fairly level and fertile.

The relation between food production and population

This graph shows the percentage contributions to world food production and world population of each major world region. Asia, Africa, and Latin America have over 75 per cent of the world's people but produce only about 50 per cent of its food.

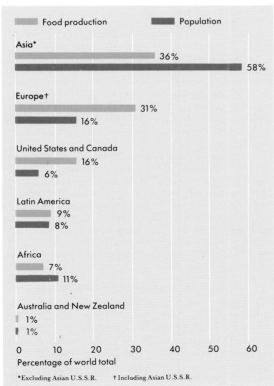

Food production   Population

Asia*
36%
58%

Europe†
31%
16%

United States and Canada
16%
6%

Latin America
9%
8%

Africa
7%
11%

Australia and New Zealand
1%
1%

0   10   20   30   40   50   60
Percentage of world total

*Excluding Asian U.S.S.R.   † Including Asian U.S.S.R.

Figures are for 1985. Source: United Nations.

But most of the world's good cropland is already in use, and most of the unused land lies in remote areas, far from markets and transportation.

All crops require water to grow, but rainfall is distributed unevenly over the earth's surface. Some farmers can depend on rainfall for all the water they need. Other farmers must use irrigation water—if it is available—because the rainfall is too light or uncertain. But the supply of irrigation water is limited, and farmers in some countries use nearly all the available supply.

Many farmers depend heavily on energy resources—particularly petroleum fuels—to operate tractors, irrigation pumps, and other farm equipment. They use fertilizers—especially nitrogen fertilizers—to enrich the soil. At present, most nitrogen fertilizers are made from natural gas. But the world's supplies of petroleum and natural gas are strictly limited. In fact, the supplies may become extremely short or nearly exhausted by the early 2000's. Farmers will therefore need other sources for energy and nitrogen fertilizers.

Meanwhile, the energy needs of farmers have greatly increased. Between 1950 and 1985, the amount of energy used to produce a ton of grain more than doubled, rising from the equivalent of less than one half barrel of oil to more than one barrel. In some countries, the energy used to produce fertilizer exceeds that used to operate tractors. In every country, the generally rising prices for energy and fertilizer add to the cost of food.

Increased use of agricultural resources can help farmers produce more food. But it can also cause environmental problems. For example, increased use of nitrogen fertilizers sometimes creates a build-up of nitrogen compounds in the soil. Rain water eventually washes these compounds into rivers and streams, where they contribute to water pollution.

Increased demand for food chiefly reflects the growth in the population of the world. To a lesser extent, it also reflects higher living standards, which allow people to eat both bigger and better meals.

The effect of population growth. Experts measure a country's food supply by the amount that would be available *per capita* (for each person) if the food were distributed equally among all the people. The food supply thus depends not only on the total amount of food but also on the number of people who must be fed.

The developed countries increased food production about 8 per cent from 1980 to 1985. During this period, the population of the developed nations grew about 3 per cent. The amount of food available per capita in these countries therefore also increased. The developing countries increased their food production by about 16 per cent, and their populations grew about 10 per cent from 1980 to 1985. Much of the increase in food production in developing countries was due to a large increase in China. Almost all of the other developing countries had little or no improvement in their per capita food production. In some developing nations, the population increases faster than the food production.

In an attempt to avoid disastrous food shortages in the future, many developing countries have promoted birth control programs (see **Birth control**). But lack of education and various other social and economic obstacles have prevented the programs from reaching or influencing most of the people.

The growth in food production and population

Developing countries have increased their food production at a faster rate than developed countries since 1970. But the population of developing countries has also increased at a faster rate. As a result, the *per capita* (per person) increase in food production has been nearly the same in the two groups of countries.

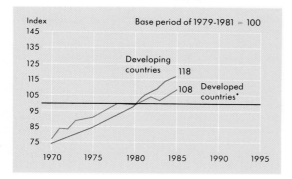

Growth of food production has been greater in developing countries than it has been in developed countries. The difference has widened since 1980 because of a large increase in production in China, a developing country.

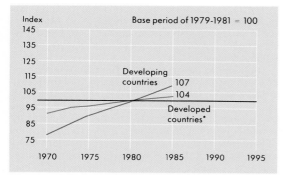

Population growth has been consistently higher in developing countries than it has been in developed countries.

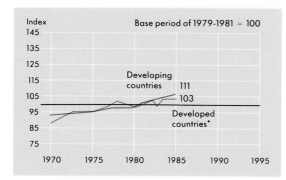

Growth in per capita food production has been nearly the same. This is because the faster growth in food production in developing countries is balanced by faster population growth.

*According to the United Nations, the developed countries are Australia and New Zealand, Canada and the United States, all European countries (including the Soviet Union), Israel, Japan, and South Africa. All other countries are developing countries.
Source: Food and Agriculture Organization of the United Nations.

The effect of higher living standards. As people improve their living standards, especially through increased personal income, they usually eat more food. In time, they also generally begin to eat more expensive foods, particularly more meat. Greater meat consumption usually calls for an increase in the amount of grain used for livestock feed. For this reason, many countries with a high standard of living also have a high per capita consumption of grain.

The people of the United States directly consume an average of about 150 pounds (68 kilograms) of grain per person annually. But about 1,500 pounds (680 kilograms) of grain per person is fed to U.S. livestock each year. Americans consume this grain indirectly in the form of meat, eggs, and dairy products. Total per capita grain consumption in the United States thus averages about 1,650 pounds (748 kilograms) annually.

Total per capita grain consumption in the developing countries averages about 400 pounds (180 kilograms) a year. Almost all this grain is consumed directly. On the average, people in the United States therefore consume more than four times as much grain as do people in the developing countries.

Distribution problems. In many developing countries, the majority of people are too poor to buy all the food they need. Much of the available supply therefore goes to the small minority of people who can afford it. The developing countries also lack modern facilities for the transportation and storage of food. In many cases, supplies cannot be delivered immediately to every area where they are needed, and they cannot be safely stored to await shipment. As a result, large quantities of food spoil or are eaten by mice, rats, and insects.

Methods to increase the food supply

Most increases in the food supply result from greater farm output. Farm output can be increased in two main ways: (1) by developing new farmland and (2) by making existing farmland more productive. Two other methods involve (1) reducing the demand for feed grain and (2) developing new sources of food.

Developing new farmland is difficult and costly. The largest areas of land that could be developed for farming lie in Africa south of the Sahara and in the Amazon River Basin of South America. Much of this land is covered with dense forests, and the tropical soil and climate are not ideal for farming. As a result, the countries that control the two regions often have difficulty getting farmers to settle and develop the land.

Making farmland more productive. Farmers have two main methods of making their land more productive. (1) They may increase their use of irrigation, energy, and fertilizer. (2) They may use improved varieties of grains and livestock, which produce higher crop yields and larger amounts of livestock products. Farmers in developed countries have used both methods during much of the 1900's. In the 1950's and 1960's, farmers in some developing countries also adopted both methods to increase their production of wheat and rice. Their effort proved so successful that it has been called the *Green Revolution.*

The development of high-yield varieties of rice and wheat made the Green Revolution possible. But the revolution also required greater use of irrigation water, energy, and fertilizer. Many farmers got the water from wells and installed electric or diesel-powered pumps to bring the water to the surface. To get the highest yields, farmers had to enrich their soil with fertilizers. During the 1960's, these methods helped such countries as India and Mexico double their wheat production.

The Green Revolution can continue to make farmland more productive. For example, if farmers in the tropics have enough water, fertilizer, and other essential resources, they can grow two or three crops a year on the same land, instead of one crop. But the Green Revolution's ability to increase the food supply is limited. As we have seen, many farmers in developing countries cannot afford the additional resources that the Green Revolution requires. But in any case, greater use of these resources makes land more productive only up to a point. Most farmers in the United States, for example, use 7 to 10 times as much fertilizer on each unit of land as do most farmers in developing countries. But U.S. grain yields are only about twice as large as those in developing countries.

Although farmland can be made more productive, the ever-rising costs of energy and fertilizer drive food prices higher and higher. And millions of people throughout the world cannot afford to buy all the food they need even at lower prices. Ways must therefore be found to expand food production at a cost that most people can afford.

The best hope for making farmland more productive lies with agricultural research. For example, research scientists are working to develop varieties of grain that not only produce higher yields but also have other improved characteristics. Such a grain might supply a more complete combination of amino acids, make more efficient use of water and fertilizer, and provide better resistance to insects and disease. But it is extremely difficult to develop a plant variety that has so many different characteristics. The necessary research therefore takes much time and money.

Reducing the demand for feed grain would increase the amount of calories and protein available for human consumption. This increase would occur because livestock consume more calories and protein than they produce. Beef cattle are especially inefficient in this respect. For every 8 to 10 pounds (3.6 to 4.5 kilograms) of grain that beef cattle consume, they produce only 1 pound (0.45 kilogram) of meat. But 8 pounds of grain supplies about 10 times as many calories and more than 4 times as much protein as a pound of beef supplies.

In the past, almost all beef cattle grazed on grass and other *forage* up to the time they were slaughtered. But since the mid-1900's, many cattle-fattening establishments called *feed lots* have opened in the United States, Canada, and certain other developed countries. A feed lot fattens cattle on grain. Today, most U.S. beef cattle are fattened on feed lots and so consume enormous quantities of grain. The demand for feed grain would lessen greatly if the cattle industry returned to its earlier practice of raising cattle chiefly on forage. But relying on forage supplies will not produce enough beef to satisfy U.S. demand. In addition, cattle raisers believe that people in the United States prefer the flavor of beef from grain-fed cattle.

The demand for feed grain would also decline if people in the developed countries ate less meat. Most people in the United States, for example, could probably reduce their meat consumption as much as 30 per cent without ill effects.

Developing new sources of food. Such oilseed crops as coconuts, cottonseed, peanuts, and soybeans are all valuable sources of protein. Soybeans have an especially high protein content and have long been an important food in Asia, where they originated. But with this exception, none of these oilseed crops is a major source of food anywhere in the world. Instead, the crops are grown mainly for their oil, which is used to make such products as margarine and salad dressing. The protein, however, remains in the meal, the part of the seed that is left after the oil has been removed. Most of the meal is used for livestock feed.

Since the mid-1900's, food processors have been working to make the protein in oilseed meal available for human consumption. They have developed a variety of inexpensive, specially flavored foods from soybean meal. Some of these products, especially those in beverage form, have been successfully marketed in developing countries in various parts of the world. Food processors are now working to convert coconut, cottonseed, and peanut meal into foods that will have a broad appeal. All three crops are widely grown in the tropics and so could provide millions of people in developing countries with inexpensive protein.

Scientists and food processors have also developed methods of enriching food. For example, scientists have produced artificial amino acids, which can be added to bread and other grain products to improve the quality of their protein.

Food supply programs

Various organizations sponsor programs to increase and improve the world's food supply. The chief interna-

Research in tropical agriculture seeks to increase food production in developing countries, most of which lie in the tropics. This researcher in India is studying tropical plant diseases.

Alain Nogues, Sygma

Emergency food supplies are provided for thousands of disaster victims annually. These Red Cross workers are distributing emergency rations to victims of a flood in Bangladesh.

tional organizations include two United Nations (UN) agencies—the Food and Agriculture Organization (FAO) and the World Bank. The World Food Council, a group of food experts appointed by the UN, helps coordinate the work of the various international organizations. Many developed nations have set up their own agencies to help increase the world's food supply.

There are a number of important food supply programs that are sponsored by religious groups and other private groups. For example, the Rockefeller Foundation, a philanthropic organization founded in the United States by the Rockefeller family, has long been one of the biggest contributors to agricultural research in developing countries.

Technical and financial programs work to expand farm output in developing countries. The Food and Agriculture Organization sponsors the chief technical assistance programs. These programs are designed mainly to train farmers in modern agricultural methods. The United Nations Development Program also sponsors technical aid programs (see **United Nations** [Economic and technical aid]).

Most financial help for agriculture in the developing countries is in the form of low-interest loans. The World Bank and various regional banks associated with the World Bank provide most of the loans. In 1976, the UN established the International Fund for Agricultural Development to obtain additional loan funds from prosperous UN members. The United States offers technical aid and loans chiefly through its Agency for International Development.

Food aid programs provide shipments of food to countries that need emergency aid. Western industrialized countries and Japan contribute most of this aid. The United States is the largest contributor. Most of the assistance given by the United States is administered

through the federal government's Food for Peace program. The World Food Program, sponsored by the UN and the FAO, channels donations from individual countries to nations in need of aid. Many private charitable organizations also supply food aid.

Research programs. Various scientific research programs seek to increase both the quality and the quantity of the food supply. For example, a variety of corn with an improved amino acid content was developed in the 1960's. But the new variety gives relatively low yields. Scientists are now working to develop a high-yield variety with the improved amino acid content.

Research scientists are also seeking ways to conserve agricultural resources. As we have seen, some of this research is aimed at developing varieties of grain that make more efficient use of water and fertilizer. Animal scientists are conducting similar experiments to develop varieties of cattle that produce more meat from the same amount of feed.

Many research projects are carried out at about 10 agricultural research institutes jointly sponsored by the FAO, the World Bank, the Ford and Rockefeller foundations, and several other organizations. The institutes have been established in developing countries, and each specializes in a particular type of research. In Mexico, for example, the International Center for the Improvement of Maize and Wheat is trying to produce improved varieties of corn, wheat, and certain other grains. Some of the institutes, such as the International Institute of Tropical Agriculture in Nigeria, are working to develop varieties of plants and livestock that are specially suited to tropical climates.

A world food reserve. In 1974, representatives from 130 countries attended a UN-sponsored World Food Conference in Rome. At the conference, the representatives adopted a plan to set up a unified world food reserve. The world's reserves now consist of the individual reserves of the major exporting countries. Each country administers its own reserve. Under the new plan, each country will continue to hold its own reserve, but it will work with participating countries in the use of the reserve. Reserve food supplies can thus be directed to parts of the world where they are needed most.

Lester R. Brown

Related articles. See **Agriculture, Food,** and **Nutrition** and their lists of *Related articles.* See also the following articles:

Outline

I. **Basic human food needs**
   A. Calories
   B. Protein
II. **Major sources of food**
   A. Cereal grains
   B. Livestock and fish
   C. Other major food sources
III. **Conditions that affect the food supply**
   A. Limited agricultural resources
   B. Increased demand for food
   C. Distribution problems

IV. Methods to increase the food supply
   A. Developing new farmland
   B. Making farmland more productive
   C. Reducing the demand for feed grain
   D. Developing new sources of food
V. Food supply programs
   A. Technical and financial programs
   B. Food aid programs
   C. Research programs
   D. A world food reserve

Questions

Why do most developing countries seldom have enough food?
What are four methods to increase the food supply?
What plants are the most important source of food?
What is protein-calorie malnutrition?
Which country produces the most surplus food?
How do higher living standards affect the food supply?
What is the Green Revolution?
How would a reduction in the demand for feed grain increase the food supply? Why?

Additional resources

Aubert, Claude, and others. *Hunger and Health: Eleven Key Questions on Farming, Food, and Health in the Third World.* Rodale, 1985.
Brown, Lester R., and others. *State of the World.* Norton. Published annually. Information about world food supplies.
Future Dimensions of World Food and Population. Ed. by Richard G. Woods. Westview, 1981.
Pringle, Laurence P. *Our Hungry Earth: The World Food Crisis.* Macmillan, 1976. For younger readers.
The World Food Book: An A-Z Atlas and Statistical Source Book. Ed. by David Crabbe and Simon Lawson. Nichols Publishing, 1981.

Food value. See Nutrition.

Food web. See Ecology (Ecosystems); **Fish** (Fish in the balance of nature).

Fool's gold. See Pyrite; **Mineral** (picture).

Foot, in poetry. See **Poetry** (Rhythm and meter).

Foot is a unit of length in the customary system of measurement used in the United States. It is equal to one-third of a yard, and contains 12 inches. One foot equals 0.3048 meter. The foot measurement was originally based on the length of the human foot. But the human foot varied in size too much to be used in measuring. When the English fixed the yard at 36 inches, they set the foot as one-third of a yard.

A *square foot* is a unit of area. It is equal to the area of a square whose sides are 1 foot long. It contains 12 x 12, or 144, square inches (929 square centimeters). A *cubic foot* is a unit of volume. It is equal to the volume of a cube 1 foot high, 1 foot wide, and 1 foot deep. It contains 12 x 12 x 12, or 1,728, cubic inches (28,327 cubic centimeters). The *board foot* is a unit measure for logs and lumber. It is 1 foot long, 1 foot wide, and 1 inch (2.54 centimeters) thick. The symbol for foot is '.   E. G. Straus

See also **Weights and measures.**

Foot is the structure at the end of the leg, on which humans and some animals stand. In animals that walk on all four legs, the ends of the front and hind limbs, or feet, are much the same. In humans, birds, and animals such as the kangaroo that walk on their hind limbs, the foot is heavier and stronger than its counterpart on the forelimb, the hand.

The bones. The human foot has 26 bones. They are (1) the seven *tarsals,* or anklebones; (2) the five *metatarsals,* or instep bones; and (3) the 14 *phalanges,* or toe bones. The tarsal bones are the *talus, calcaneus, navicu-*

lar, cuboid, and the three *cuneiform* bones. They form the heel and back part of the instep. The metatarsal bones connect the cuneiforms and the cuboid with the phalanges, and form the front part of the instep. The big toe has two phalanges. Each of the other toes has three. The ends of the phalanges meet the underside of the metatarsals to form the *ball of the foot.*

The arches. The bones of the foot form three arches, two running lengthwise and one running across the instep. The arches provide the natural elastic spring of the foot in walking or jumping. The main arch reaches from the heel bone to the ball of the foot. It is called the *long medial* or *plantar* arch. This arch touches the ground only at the heel and ball of the foot and thus acts as a shock absorber for the leg and spinal column. A thick layer of flexible cartilage covers the end of the bones of the arch (see **Cartilage**). The cartilage helps make the arch shock-absorbent. The *lateral* arch runs along the outside of the foot, and the *transverse* or *metatarsal* arch lies across the ball of the foot. The condition known as *flatfoot* may be caused by the breakdown of the arches of the foot (see **Flatfoot**).

Ligaments and muscles support the arches of the foot. The long plantar ligament, called the *plantar fascia,* is very strong. It keeps the bones of the foot in place and protects the nerves, muscles, and blood vessels in the hollow of the foot. The foot has as many muscles as the hand. But its structure permits less flexibility and freedom of movement than does that of the hand.

Tough, thick skin covers the *sole,* or bottom, of the foot. A thick pad of fatty tissue lies between the skin and the bones and the plantar ligament. This layer of fat acts like an air cushion to protect the inner parts of the foot from pressure on the foot and from jarring.

Disorders of the foot, such as corns, may result from wearing badly fitted shoes.   Leslie S. Matthews

Related articles in *World Book* include:

Achilles' tendon	Bunion	Corn
Animal (picture:	Callus	Footprinting
Kinds of feet)	Chilblain	Immersion foot
Ankle	Clubfoot	Podiatry
Athlete's foot		

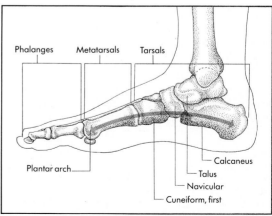

WORLD BOOK illustration by Patricia Wynne

The foot has three sets of bones—the *tarsals,* or anklebones; *metatarsals,* or instep bones; and *phalanges,* or toe bones. The *plantar arch* extends from the heel to the ball of the foot.

Foot, Michael (1913-   ), served as the leader of Great Britain's Labour Party from 1980 to 1983. He is a member of the party's left wing. The left wing calls for increased government spending on social welfare programs and for government ownership of businesses.

Foot was born in Plymouth, England, and attended Oxford University. He became a newspaper columnist and editor and a forceful left wing critic of British government policies. From 1945 to 1955, Foot represented a district of Plymouth in the House of Commons. He has represented the Ebbw Vale district of Wales since 1960. He was secretary of state for employment from 1974 to 1976. In 1976, he became deputy prime minister and leader of the House of Commons. He was named to these offices following James Callaghan's election as Labour Party leader by the party's members of Parliament. Callaghan became prime minister as a result of the election. Foot had received the second largest number of votes. His term in the offices ended in 1979, when the Conservative Party won control of the government. Callaghan resigned as Labour Party leader in 1980, and the party's members elected Foot to succeed him. Foot resigned as party leader in 1983.   Richard Rose

AP/Wide World

Michael Foot

Foot-and-mouth disease is a highly contagious disease of animals. It is also called *hoof-and-mouth disease,* though the infection does not actually involve the horny hoof, but rather the tissues around it. Foot-and-mouth disease attacks cattle, goats, hogs, sheep, and other mammals that have *cloven* (split) hoofs. It occurs among livestock in many regions of the world, particularly in Africa, Asia, Europe, and South America. The disease is rare in Australia and North America. The last outbreak of foot-and-mouth disease in the United States occurred in 1929.

Cause and symptoms. Foot-and-mouth disease is caused by a virus. Healthy livestock may contract the disease through contact with infected animals or with objects that have been contaminated by saliva or body wastes from infected animals. The virus may also be spread by wind or by birds, rats, cats, and many other animals that are not themselves affected by the disease.

Foot-and-mouth disease produces blisters in the mouth, in the tissue between the split in the hoof, and on the upper part of the foot. Infected animals also develop a high fever. They drool, have trouble walking, and lose weight rapidly. In female animals, the virus also affects the udders and the milk-producing mammary glands, causing a drop in milk production. In severe cases, the virus attacks the heart, causing death. The death rate may reach 100 per cent among young cattle and hogs, but it rarely exceeds 10 per cent among adult livestock. However, the decrease in meat and milk production of adults results in great economic losses.

Measures of control. There is no cure for foot-and-mouth disease, but countries use a variety of methods to control it. In the African, Asian, European, and South American countries where the disease is *endemic* (found regularly), it is controlled chiefly through the use of vaccines. Most vaccines protect the animals for only a short period, and so must be administered several times a year. In addition, the vaccines are expensive and, in some cases, they contain live viruses that may infect the animals. In 1981, U.S. scientists used genetic engineering techniques to develop a safer and less costly vaccine (see **Genetic engineering**).

In the United States and most other countries where the disease is not endemic, it is controlled chiefly through import restrictions and quarantine procedures. Such measures normally prevent the introduction of the virus. These countries also have policies for eliminating the disease should an outbreak occur. Most such policies call for slaughtering the infected animals, burying or burning their carcasses, and decontaminating the area in which the animals lived.   Jerry J. Callis

Foot-candle is a unit of measurement of *illumination,* the amount of light that falls on an object. The foot-candle is part of the customary, or English, system of measurement.

Two factors determine the amount of light that an object receives: (1) the *luminous intensity* (brightness) of the light source and (2) the distance between the light source and the object. As the luminous intensity of the light source increases, illumination also increases. As the distance increases, illumination decreases.

To calculate foot-candles (*fc*), scientists use the formula $fc = \dfrac{cd}{d^2}$. *Cd* is the luminous intensity of the light, measured in *candelas* (see **Candela**). *D* is the distance in feet between the light source and the object.

In the metric system, units of measurement for illumination include the *lux* and the *phot.* Distance is measured in meters to calculate luxes, and in centimeters to calculate phots.   Ronald N. Helms

See also **Light** (The brightness of light; diagram: Basic units); **Lighting** (Quantity of light).

Foot-pound is a unit of work and energy in the customary, or English, system of measurement. Physicists define *work* as the product of force and distance when a force moves an object through a distance. One foot-pound is the amount of work done when a force of 1 pound moves an object a distance of 1 foot. If a force of 2 pounds moves an object 3 feet, the work done therefore equals 6 foot-pounds. *Energy* is the ability to do work. The foot-pound is used to measure all forms of energy. One foot-pound equals the quantity of energy needed to lift a 1-pound object to a height of 1 foot. Thus, 6 foot-pounds of mechanical energy are needed to lift a 2-pound object 3 feet high.

The rate at which work is done is called *power.* To measure power, the amount of time required to do the work is considered along with force and distance. Power may be measured either in foot-pounds per second or in horsepower. One horsepower equals 550 foot-pounds per second (see **Horsepower**).

In the metric system of measurement, work and energy are measured in *joules.* One foot-pound equals 1.356 joules.   Hugh D. Young

See also **Energy** (Measuring energy); **Joule; Work.**

Foot race. See Running.

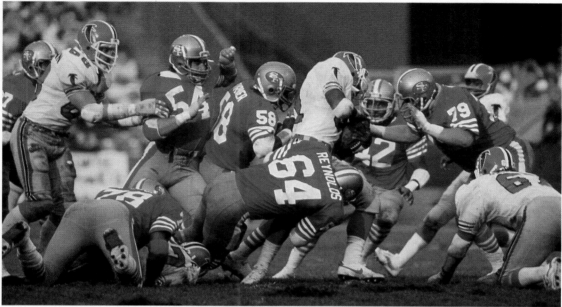

Action-packed plays make football an exciting game. On the play above, the defensive team, wearing red jerseys, tries to stop the ball carrier, wearing white, from advancing the ball.

Football

Football is an exciting team sport played chiefly in the United States and Canada. It is played by elementary school, high school, college, and professional teams. Millions of people crowd stadiums each football season to watch their favorite teams. Millions of people also watch games on television between college football teams as well as televised competition in the two major professional leagues, the National Football League (NFL) of the United States and the Canadian Football League (CFL).

In the United States, football is played by two teams of 11 players each. Canadian teams have 12 players. Each team tries to score points, mainly by running or passing *plays* (maneuvers) that move an oval ball across the opposing team's goal line. Such a run or pass scores a touchdown. During a game, possession of the ball shifts from team to team. The team with the ball is the *offensive team*. The other team is the *defensive team*. It tries to prevent the offense from scoring.

A good football team combines strength and speed. Physical contact, especially involving blocking and tackling, is a basic part of football. The sport also requires quick reactions and thorough preparation for each game. In addition, split-second teamwork is essential. All the players on a team must work together to defeat their opponents.

There are several variations of football. Two of these variations—touch football and flag football—eliminate much of the physical contact. In touch football, a play ends when a defensive player merely touches, rather than tackles, the ball carrier. In flag football, a play ends when a defensive player pulls a piece of cloth, called a *flag,* from the belt or from the back pocket of the ball carrier.

Touch and flag football are popular in high school and college *intramural* programs. In such programs, teams from the same school compete against one another. Some high schools with small enrollments have football teams with six, eight, or nine players. A few professional women's football teams have formed leagues, and a few high schools have teams for girls. However, the game is played almost entirely by men and boys, and this article concerns male football only.

Football originated in the United States. It began to develop during the mid-1800's. The sport grew out of soccer and Rugby, two kicking games that were developed in England. Soccer is called *football* in many countries, but the game differs considerably from American football.

This article deals chiefly with football as played in the United States. The game differs somewhat in Canada. The section *Canadian football* describes some of the differences.

The field and equipment

The field. Football is played on a level area 120 yards (110 meters) long and $53\frac{1}{3}$ yards (49 meters) wide. The field may have a surface of natural grass or of a synthetic material. All indoor stadiums use green synthetic surfaces that look like grass. Many outdoor stadiums also use synthetic surfaces.

The football field is marked with white lines. It is often called a *gridiron* because the pattern of lines resembles the cooking utensil used to broil foods. A *sideline* borders each of the two long sides of the field. Any player

MacGregor® Sporting Goods

The football is oval. Balls used in high school, college, and professional games have a pebble-grained leather covering. Laces along one seam provide a grip for passers and ball carriers.

who touches or crosses a sideline is ruled out of bounds. *Yard lines* cross the field every 5 yards (4.6 meters). Near each end of the field is a *goal line.* The goal lines are 100 yards (91 meters) apart. An area called an *end zone* extends 10 yards (9 meters) beyond each goal line. The yard lines are numbered from each goal line to the 50-yard line, or *midfield.*

Two rows of lines, called *hash marks,* parallel the sidelines. In college and high school games, the hash marks are 53 feet 4 inches (16.3 meters) from each sideline. In NFL games, they are 70 feet 9 inches (21.6 meters) from each sideline. All plays start with the ball between or on the hash marks. If a play ends out of bounds or between the hash marks and the sideline, the ball is placed on the nearest hash mark for the next play.

In high school and college football, two *goal posts,*

each 20 feet (6 meters) high, stand on the end line 10 yards behind each goal line. A crossbar connects the posts 10 feet (3 meters) above the ground. The posts stand 23 feet 4 inches (7 meters) apart. In the National Football League, the goal posts are $18\frac{1}{2}$ feet apart and rise 30 feet (9 meters) from the crossbar. A single post 6 feet (1.8 meters) behind the end line curves forward

Football terms

Blitz is a defensive maneuver in which one or more linebackers and defensive backs charge through the offensive line and try to tackle the quarterback before he can pass or hand off the ball.

Draw is a running play in which the quarterback fakes a pass and then hands the ball to a running back.

Field position refers to the location of the ball on the field. If the offense has the ball near its opponent's goal line, It has good field position. If the offense has the ball near its own goal line, It has poor field position.

Option is an offensive play in which the quarterback runs along the line of scrimmage with the choice of keeping the ball or tossing it to a running back.

Prevent defense refers to a defensive formation that includes extra defensive backs to provide additional protection against an expected long pass.

Rollout is a passing play in which the passer retreats a short distance behind the line of scrimmage and then runs toward a sideline before throwing the ball. The rollout maneuver helps the passer avoid tacklers, Giving him more time to find a receiver.

Sack is the tackle of a quarterback before he can throw a pass.

Screen pass is a play in which the quarterback retreats behind the line of scrimmage and then tosses a short pass to a receiver waiting behind several blockers.

Sweep means a running play around either end.

Trap is a running play in which the offensive line allows a defensive lineman into the backfield and blocks him from the side. The ball carrier then runs through the hole left by the blocked lineman.

Diagram of a U.S. football field

The football field is marked with white lines. Yard lines cross the field every 5 yards (4.6 meters). Hash marks run down the field across the yard lines. College hash marks (shown in red) divide the field into three equal sections. Professional hash marks (shown in blue) are closer to the center of the field. Goal posts stand on the end lines behind the goal lines.

WORLD BOOK diagram

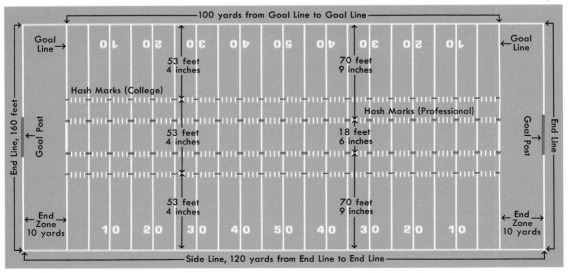

and supports the crossbar directly over the end line.

The ball is oval. It is about 11 inches (28 centimeters) long and about 7 inches (18 centimeters) in diameter at the center. Balls used in high school, college, and professional games are made of four pieces of leather stitched together. Footballs used in recreation may be made of rubber or plastic. A football has a rubber lining, which is inflated to an air pressure of $12\frac{1}{2}$ to $13\frac{1}{2}$ pounds per square inch (0.88 to 0.95 kilogram per square centimeter). The ball weighs 14 to 15 ounces (397 to 425 grams). Leather laces along one seam provide a grip for holding and passing the ball.

The uniform. A football player's uniform is made of cotton or nylon and consists of a shirt and pants. The shirt, which is called a *jersey,* has the player's number—and sometimes his name—sewn on the back and front for identification by the officials and spectators. In most cases, the players wear jerseys and pants of different colors. The uniforms fit tightly so that opposing players cannot easily grasp them when trying to block or tackle.

Protective equipment helps prevent injuries. The amount of equipment a player wears depends on his position. The section called *The players and coaches* describes the duties of the various players. Linemen wear more protective equipment than other players because they are involved in the most physical contact through blocking and tackling. Backs and ends wear less equipment so that they can run at top speed.

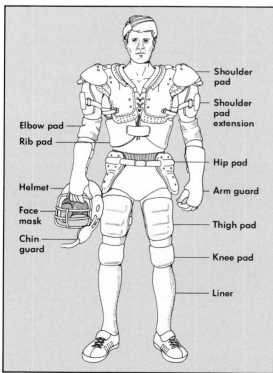

WORLD BOOK illustration by Bill and Judie Anderson

Protective equipment helps prevent injuries. The amount and type of padding depend on a player's position. Linemen wear the most padding because they do the most blocking and tackling. Backs and ends wear less so they can move more easily.

Each player wears a helmet held in place with a chin guard. The helmet has a face mask. Most players also wear a mouthpiece to help prevent injuries to their teeth. Under their uniforms, the players wear shoulder pads, hip pads, thigh pads, and knee pads. In many cases, the thigh pads and knee pads are sewn into the pants. Some players also use arm guards, elbow pads, rib pads, and liners to protect the shins.

Football players wear shoes with cleats. The cleats help prevent slipping and provide good traction when a player runs. Some players wear high-top shoes that lace up to their ankles. The lacing gives the ankles additional support and helps prevent sprains. Most backs and ends prefer low-cut shoes, which enable them to make quick *cuts* (changes in direction).

The players and coaches

Every football team has some players who play offense and others who play defense. Before each play, the offensive and defensive teams face each other along the *line of scrimmage.* This imaginary line aligns with the spot where the preceding play ended. The line of scrimmage parallels the yard lines and passes through the tip of the ball nearest each team's goal. Thus, each team has its own line of scrimmage, separated by the length of the football. The area between the two lines is called the *neutral zone.*

The offensive team consists of seven *linemen* and four *backs.* The team must have at least seven players on the line of scrimmage before a play. The linemen are divided into five *interior linemen* and two *ends.* The interior linemen consist of a *center,* two *guards,* and two *tackles.* They block for the ball carriers, passers, and pass receivers. The center also *snaps* (gives) the ball through his legs to the quarterback to begin a play.

Each of the two ends plays a position on the outside of the interior linemen. The chief job of the ends, like that of the interior linemen, is to block. However, ends may also receive passes. Occasionally, an end may even carry the ball. Many offensive *formations* (arrangements of players) have two types of ends: (1) the tight end and (2) the split end, or wide receiver. The tight end lines up near the tackle. Although the tight end serves as a pass receiver, he also has important blocking responsibilities. The split end stands on the side of the line of scrimmage opposite the tight end and several yards from the tackle. The split end is used mainly as a pass receiver.

The four backs make up the *backfield,* which generally consists of a *quarterback,* two *halfbacks,* and a *fullback.* In the standard *T-formation,* the fullback lines up 3 to 5 yards behind the quarterback and has a halfback on each side. The backs also have other names. A fullback used chiefly as a blocker is a *blocking back.* A halfback who lines up outside the tight end is called a *flanker* or a *wingback.* A halfback who usually carries the ball is a *running back.*

Most interior linemen are bigger and stronger than backs and ends because they must block against large defensive linemen. Most backs and pass receivers are smaller than linemen but faster and more agile.

The defensive team is divided into three units: (1) the line, (2) the linebackers, and (3) the secondary.

The line may have as many players as the defensive team chooses. But most teams use three, four, or five players. A three-man line consists of a *middle guard,* also called a *nose guard,* and two *ends.* A four-man line, called the *front four,* consists of two *tackles* and two *ends.* A five-man line consists of a *middle guard,* two *tackles,* and two *ends.* The defensive linemen use their size, strength, and power against offensive blockers.

The linebackers position themselves 2 or 3 yards behind the linemen. A team that uses a four-man line will normally have three linebackers. The player who lines up facing the center is the *middle linebacker.* The two other players, called *outside linebackers,* stand outside the defensive ends. Four linebackers are used with a three-man line, and two are used with a five-man line. In certain defensive formations, the linebackers will move up to the line of scrimmage with the linemen.

Linebackers, especially middle linebackers, make many tackles. They must combine strength with the ability to move quickly to wherever the ball carrier is running. They must also be good pass defenders.

The secondary is made up of two *cornerbacks* and two *safeties.* They are often called *defensive backs.* Their chief task is to defend against the offensive team's passing attacks. They also try to tackle ball carriers who have gotten by the linemen and linebackers. Defensive backs must be fast enough to cover speedy pass receivers, and they must be especially sure tacklers.

The cornerbacks stand 8 to 10 yards behind the line of scrimmage at the corners of the defensive formation. They defend against short passes thrown toward the sidelines. Safeties play 8 to 12 yards behind the line of scrimmage and defend against long passes. Sometimes, secondaries use *double coverage,* in which two defensive backs cover an especially dangerous receiver.

Many defensive teams favor *zone coverage* in the secondary, and others prefer *man-to-man coverage.* In zone coverage, each defensive back is responsible for a certain area. In man-to-man coverage, a defensive back is assigned to cover a particular receiver.

The coaches. Every team has a coaching staff made up of a *head coach* and a number of *assistant coaches.* The head coach decides which players play which positions and, often, what plays are used during a game.

Offensive and defensive formations
Before each play, the teams line up in offensive and defensive formations on the line of scrimmage. Some offensive formations are more effective for passing, and others are more effective for running. The defense selects a formation best able to stop the play it believes the offense will try.

WORLD BOOK illustrations by Arthur Grebetz

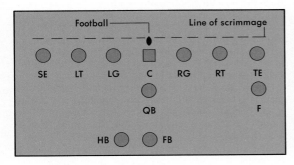

The winged T is a popular offensive formation. Two running backs line up side by side behind the quarterback. Another back, called the *flanker* or *wingback,* stands near the tight end.

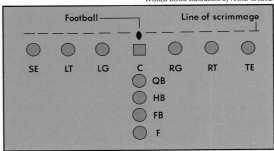

The I-formation is an offensive formation in which the running backs line up directly behind the quarterback. The players often shift before the snap so that one back becomes a flanker.

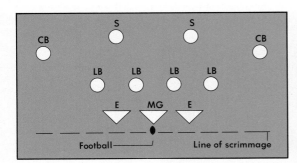

The three-four defense is often used when the defense expects a pass. It has only three linemen. The four linebackers and four defensive backs provide extra coverage of receivers.

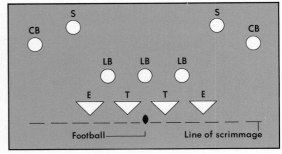

The four-three defense is the basic defense in professional football. The four linemen, three linebackers, and four defensive backs can defend well against both passing and running plays.

Key to positions
SE = Split End; LT = Left Tackle; LG = Left Guard; C = Center; RG = Right Guard; RT = Right Tackle; TE = Tight End; QB = Quarterback; F = Flanker; HB = Halfback; FB = Fullback; E = End; MG = Middle Guard; T = Tackle; LB = Linebacker; CB = Cornerback, S = Safety

The kickoff begins each half. A team also kicks off after scoring a touchdown or a field goal. The receiving team, *foreground,* places two players near its goal line to run back the kick. The kicking team lines up in a row across the field. The kicker, *top center,* kicks the ball from a tee.

Ken Kaminsky

Most assistant coaches work with particular players on the offensive and defensive teams. Some assistant coaches may perform other duties, such as scouting opposing teams for their strengths and weaknesses.

Between games, the coaches conduct *practices* to correct players' mistakes and to oversee their physical conditioning. The coaches also prepare for the next game by developing a *game plan.* A game plan is a list of offensive plays and defensive formations that the coaches believe will work against the opponent. Some coaches discuss the game plan with the quarterback and then allow him to select his own plays during the game. Other coaches prefer to choose the plays themselves. During a game, they send in their instructions for each play with a substitute player.

How football is played

The playing time in college and professional football games is 60 minutes. High school games last 48 minutes. A game is divided into *halves.* Each half, in turn, consists of two periods called *quarters.* An intermission, called *half-time,* lasts about 20 minutes between halves. There are also 1-minute or 2-minute rest periods after the first and third quarters. At the end of each quarter, teams change goals.

The official time clock is stopped only (1) after an incomplete pass, (2) if a player is injured, (3) after a team scores, (4) if a ball carrier goes out of bounds, or (5) if a player on either team or an official calls a time out. Each team may call up to three time outs each half. Time outs last 90 seconds in high school and college games and 2 minutes in NFL games. In college games, the clock is also stopped briefly after each first down to move the first down markers. During the final 2 minutes of NFL games, the clock is stopped after some plays while the ball is placed in position for the next play.

The kickoff starts each half of a football game. A team also kicks off after it scores a touchdown or a field goal. The team that kicks off to begin the game is decided by a toss of a coin at midfield. The visiting team calls "heads" or "tails." The team that wins the toss may (1) make the kickoff, (2) receive the kickoff, or (3) select the goal it wishes to defend. In most cases, teams choose to receive the opening kickoff to get the first chance at scoring. The team that loses the coin toss gets the choice of kicking, receiving, or defending either goal when the second half begins.

In high school games, the kickoff is made from the 40-yard line. Teams in college and the NFL kick off from the 35-yard line. Most kickers *place-kick* the ball. Before

Focus on Sports

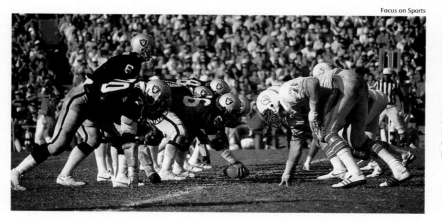

The line of scrimmage is an imaginary line that extends from the forward tip of the ball to both sidelines. Offensive and defensive players must stay on their side of the line until the center snap begins the play. If a player crosses the line of scrimmage before the snap, an official calls an *offside* penalty on that player's team.

Pete Miller, National Football League Properties, Inc.

A head coach discusses a play with his quarterback. The coach gets suggestions on strategy through headphones from assistants watching the game from a press box above the field.

kicking the ball, they stand it on an angle on a tee.

The kicker's teammates stand in a line across the field until the ball is kicked. Generally, the receiving team places two fast runners near its goal line. The runner nearest the ball catches it and runs it back toward the other team's goal. The kick returner's teammates try to block the opposing players, who are running down the field to tackle him.

After a kickoff travels 10 yards, it becomes a *free ball* —that is, either team may recover it. Normally the kicker tries to kick the ball as far down the field as possible. Occasionally, the kicker will kick the ball only a short distance to give his team a chance to recover the ball before the receiving team does. This maneuver is called an *onside kick.*

The ball is ruled *dead* if it is kicked beyond the end zone or if the kick returner catches it in the end zone and touches the ground with his knee. A *touchback* is then called, and the ball is put in play on the receiving team's 20-yard line. If the ball goes out of bounds before reaching the goal line without being touched, it must be kicked again.

The kick returner is ruled *down* if he goes out of bounds or if any part of his body except his feet or hands touches the ground. In the NFL, the kick returner must be downed by an opponent. If the returner slips and falls but is not touched by an opposing player, he may get up and advance the ball until he is tackled or goes out of bounds.

Advancing the ball. After the kick returner has been downed, the ball is placed at the point where the return ended. The offensive and defensive teams then come on the field.

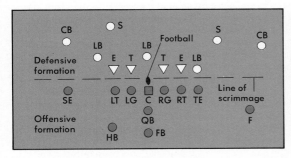

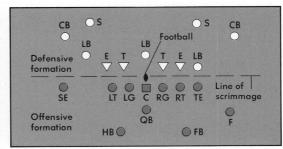

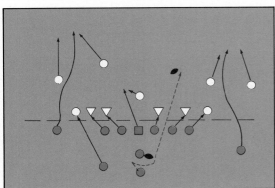

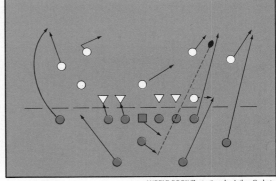

WORLD BOOK illustrations by Arthur Grebetz

A running play may go through various areas. The play above calls for the fullback to run the ball between his right guard and right tackle. The fullback gets the handoff from the quarterback and cuts back to his right. The linemen and halfback block the defensive linemen and linebackers. The flanker and split end run down-field to decoy the defensive backs into expecting a pass.

A passing play requires split-second timing. The play above calls for the linemen and halfbacks to block while the quarterback passes to the tight end. If the tight end is covered, the quarterback can pass to the split end or the flanker. Even if his blockers give him good protection from the defense, the passer has only a few seconds to select a receiver and throw the ball.

Key to positions SE=Split End; LT=Left Tackle; LG=Left Guard; C=Center; RG=Right Guard; RT=Right Tackle; TE=Tight End; HB=Halfback; QB=Quarterback; F=Flanker; FB=Fullback; E=End; T=Tackle; LB=Linebacker; CB=Cornerback; S=Safety

Focus on Sports

© Carl Skalak, Jr., OPTICOM

A pitchout is a play in which the quarterback *pitches* (tosses) the ball underhand to a back who runs around end. In the play above, another back runs ahead of the ball carrier to block.

Tackling is the chief defensive skill. The tackler usually hits with his shoulders and wraps his arms around the ball carrier, *above.* He must hold tight so the runner cannot squirm away.

The offense has four plays, called *downs,* to advance the ball at least 10 yards by running or passing. If the offense gains 10 yards, it gets a *first down.* If the team fails to make a first down, it loses possession of the ball. Each time the team gets a first down, it receives another four downs to gain 10 more yards.

Before a play begins, each team gathers in a huddle behind its side of the line of scrimmage. In the offensive huddle, the quarterback names his team's next play, the formation to be used, and the number or color he will call out to signal the center to snap the ball. In the defensive huddle, a formation is called that the team hopes will stop the offensive play.

After the teams have huddled, they line up facing each other along the line of scrimmage. The center begins the play by snapping the ball to the quarterback. The quarterback then hands or *pitches* (tosses) the ball to a running back, runs with it himself, or throws a pass. The offense directs running plays around either end, between the end and the tackle, between the tackle and the guard, or between the guard and the center.

On a passing play, the passer is usually the quarterback. Occasionally, another back or even an end will throw the ball. The passer must throw from behind the line of scrimmage. Only the ends and backs may catch a pass. The tackles, guards, and center must stay behind the line of scrimmage until the ball is thrown. They may then run down-field and block for the pass receiver.

If a defensive player catches a pass, it is called an *interception.* The defensive player may return the ball toward the opponent's goal until he is downed or goes out of bounds. His team's offensive players then come on the field and try to score.

The defense may also gain possession of the ball by recovering a fumble. A fumble occurs if an offensive player drops the ball. In high school and college games, a defensive player may run with a fumble only if he catches the ball before it hits the ground. If he recovers the ball after it hits the ground, his team gets the ball at that spot. In the NFL, a defensive player may run with a fumble after it hits the ground.

If the offensive team does not make a first down in

Michael Yada, National Football League Properties, Inc.

Passing combined with a good running attack produces a well-balanced offense. A good passer can concentrate on throwing the ball accurately even when he is about to be tackled, *above.*

Pete Miller, National Football League Properties, Inc.

A pass receiver makes a difficult catch, *above,* after maneuvering away from the defense. A good receiver can catch the ball while running swiftly and hold onto it while being tackled.

three plays, it usually punts the ball on fourth down. A punt gives possession of the ball to the other team. If the offense tries to make a first down on fourth down and fails, the other team gets the ball where the play ends. Any offensive player may punt. The kicker stands 10 to 12 yards behind the center, who snaps the ball to him for the punt. A long or well-aimed punt can force the opposing team to start its offense deep in its own side of the field.

Scoring. A team earns points by scoring (1) a touchdown, (2) a conversion, (3) a field goal, and (4) a safety.

Touchdown. A touchdown earns six points. The offense scores nearly all touchdowns. It does so by run-

ning the ball or catching a pass over the opposing team's goal line. Occasionally, the defense scores a touchdown through an interception or a fumble or by recovering a blocked punt in the end zone.

Conversion. Immediately after a touchdown, the scoring team tries for a conversion, also called the *extra point* or *point after touchdown.* Before a conversion attempt, the ball is placed on the 2-yard line in NFL games and on the 3-yard line in high school and college games. A kicker scores one point by place kicking the ball over the crossbar and between the goal posts. In high school and college games, the offense can score a two-point conversion by running or passing the ball over the goal

Official signals   Officials use a variety of hand signals during a football game. The referee usually gives the signals for various fouls. Other signals may be given by any of the officials.

WORLD BOOK illustrations by David Cunningham

First down

Touchdown, successful field goal, successful extra point

Safety

Penalty refused, incomplete pass, missed field goal, missed extra point

Time out

Personal foul

Holding

Roughing the kicker

Illegal use of hands

Clipping

Illegal forward pass

Interference

Ineligible receiver

Illegal contact

Facemasking

Offside

Illegal motion

Unsportsmanlike conduct

Illegal cut

Delay of game

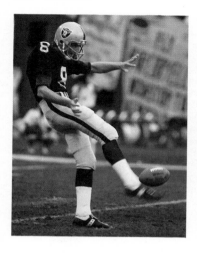

Focus on Sports

Kicking consists of punting, *left,* and place kicking, *above.* For a punt, the center snaps the ball back to the kicker, who drops it and kicks it before the ball hits the ground. For a place kick, the center snaps the ball back to a kneeling holder. The holder places the ball on one end. Unlike most place kickers, the player above is kicking barefoot.

line. In the NFL, a successful conversion scores one point whether it is kicked, run, or passed. In college games, the defensive team scores two points if it either blocks the conversion kick or intercepts the pass and then advances the ball into the opponent's end zone.

Field goal. A field goal is worth three points. It is scored by place kicking the ball over the crossbar and between the goal posts. The kick may be made from anywhere on the field.

Safety. Only the defense can score a safety, which counts two points. The defense earns a safety if it tackles the ball carrier in his own end zone, if the ball carrier steps out of the back or side of his end zone, or if a blocked punt goes out of the end zone.

The officials supervise the football game and enforce the rules. Each official has particular duties, but any of the officials may call a rule violation.

The chief official is the *referee,* who has general charge of the game. He has the final word on all rulings. The referee stands behind the offensive backfield. The *umpire* is positioned behind the defensive line and watches for violations in the line. The *head linesman* stands at one end of the line of scrimmage. He marks the forward progress of the ball and supervises the sidelines crew, which keeps track of the downs and the yardage needed for a first down. The *field judge* stands behind the defensive secondary in the middle of the field. He watches for violations on punt returns and pass plays down-field. The *back judge* is positioned behind the defensive secondary near a sideline. His job is to spot violations between the defensive backs and the offensive pass receivers. The *line judge* stands opposite of the head linesman and, like the umpire, watches for violations in the line. He is also the official timekeeper. The NFL also uses a *side judge.* He stands opposite the back judge and on the same side of the field as the head linesman. The side judge has the same responsibilities as those of the back judge.

Violations and penalties are called when players break the rules. An official signals a violation by throwing a yellow cloth, called a *flag,* in the air. In most cases, a violation occurs during a play, and the officials allow the play to be completed. The referee then explains the violation to the captain of the team that was fouled. The

captain has two choices. He may accept the penalty to be imposed on the team that committed the foul. Or he may refuse the penalty and accept the completed play. If he accepts the penalty, it is enforced and the down is usually replayed. If he accepts the play, the penalty is disregarded. A team is penalized for a violation with a loss of yardage and, in some cases, also the loss of a down. Common violations include (1) clipping, (2) holding, (3) offside, (4) interference, (5) delay of game, (6) roughing, and (7) illegal procedure.

Clipping is committed if an offensive player blocks a defensive player from behind beyond the line of scrimmage. The penalty is 15 yards.

Holding is called against an offensive player who uses his hands to block a defensive player. In high school and college games, a defensive player is penalized for holding if he uses his hands except to tackle a ball carrier. In the NFL, a defensive player may use his hands under certain conditions. The penalty is 10 yards for offensive holding and 5 yards for defensive holding. In the NFL, defensive holding also includes an automatic first down for the offense.

Offside is called if a player crosses the line of scrimmage before the ball is snapped. The penalty is 5 yards.

Interference is ruled if the pass receiver or pass defender is blocked, tackled, or shoved while the ball is still in the air. In defensive interference, the offense gets the ball at the spot of the foul and receives a first down. In offensive interference, the offense is penalized 15 yards and a down.

Delay of game. In high school and college football, the offensive team must put the ball into play within 25 seconds after the referee has signaled play to begin. In the NFL, the offense has 30 seconds. The defense may be charged with a delay penalty if it kicks the ball out of bounds on a kickoff or if it deliberately slows down the game. The penalty for delay of game is 5 yards.

Roughing is a foul committed against a kicker or passer. The defense may not tackle or bump a kicker while he is in the act of punting or place kicking. The defense may tackle a passer only while he has the ball. The player may not be hit after he throws the pass. The penalty for roughing a kicker or passer is 15 yards and an automatic first down.

Illegal procedure is called if the offense does not have seven players on the line of scrimmage or if an offensive player moves forward before the ball is snapped. Illegal procedure is also called if the offense or defense has more than 11 players on the field. The penalty is 5 yards.

Football competition

Most organized football games in the United States are played by high school, college, and professional teams. However, there are also many programs for students too young to play on school-sponsored football teams. One of the most successful of these "pee wee" programs is the Pop Warner League for boys and girls from the ages of 7 to 16. The league organizes competition according to players' ages. Games in this league follow almost the same rules used in high school and college games.

High school competition. More than 14,000 U.S. high schools have football teams. The National Federation of State High School Associations oversees most high school athletic programs, including football. In addition, each state has an organization that sets rules and policies for high school sports teams.

Most high school teams compete in classifications determined by school enrollment. They play in districts or leagues made up of schools of similar size in the same general area. Nearly all states have a play-off schedule that ends with two teams competing for the state championship in their classification.

College competition. More than 700 colleges and universities in the United States sponsor football teams. Most of the schools belong to one of over 60 conferences. Officials of each conference set standards and rules for competition among the member teams. Each season, the teams in a conference play one another for the conference championship. Some college teams,

called *independents,* do not belong to a conference. They play other independents as well as conference teams.

All conference and independent teams belong to either the National Collegiate Athletic Association (NCAA) or the National Association of Intercollegiate Athletics (NAIA). The NCAA and the NAIA set rules and supervise competition among member teams. Some teams from two-year schools, called *junior colleges* or *community colleges,* also compete against one another. They are governed by the National Junior College Athletic Association.

Most major college teams play 11 games during the regular season. After each season, a number of the teams with the best records are invited to play in *bowl games.* The games are held in such stadiums as the Rose Bowl, Cotton Bowl, and Orange Bowl. Most col-

Major collegiate bowl games

Game	Location	Year started
All-American Bowl	Birmingham, Ala.	1985
Aloha Bowl	Honolulu, Hawaii	1982
California Bowl	Fresno, Calif.	1981
Cotton Bowl	Dallas, Tex.	1937
Fiesta Bowl	Tempe, Ariz.	1971
Florida Citrus Bowl	Orlando, Fla.	1947
Freedom Bowl	Anaheim, Calif.	1984
Gator Bowl	Jacksonville, Fla.	1946
Hall of Fame Bowl	Tampa, Fla	1986
Holiday Bowl	San Diego, Calif.	1978
Independence Bowl	Shreveport, La.	1978
John Hancock Bowl	El Paso, Tex.	1936
Liberty Bowl	Memphis, Tenn.	1959
Orange Bowl	Miami, Fla.	1933
Peach Bowl	Atlanta, Ga.	1968
Rose Bowl	Pasadena, Calif.	1902
Sugar Bowl	New Orleans, La.	1935

Major college football conferences

Most major colleges and universities belong to an athletic conference. A few schools, such as Notre Dame and Miami (Fla.), do not belong to a conference and compete as *independents.* Some schools compete as independents in football but play in conferences in basketball and other sports.

Atlantic Coast Conference	Ivy League	Big Eight Conference	Western Athletic Conference
Clemson	Brown	Colorado	
Duke	Columbia	Iowa State	Air Force
Georgia Tech	Cornell	Kansas	Brigham Young
Maryland	Dartmouth	Kansas State	Colorado State
North Carolina	Harvard	Missouri	Hawaii
North Carolina State	Pennsylvania	Nebraska	New Mexico
Virginia	Princeton	Oklahoma	San Diego State
Wake Forest	Yale	Oklahoma State	Texas (at El Paso)
			Utah
			Wyoming

Pacific Ten Conference	Southeastern Conference	Big Ten Conference	Southwest Athletic Conference
Arizona	Alabama	Illinois	
Arizona State	Auburn	Indiana	Arkansas
California (at Berkeley)	Florida	Iowa	Baylor
Oregon	Georgia	Michigan	Houston
Oregon State	Kentucky	Michigan State	Rice
Stanford	Louisiana State	Minnesota	Southern Methodist
Southern California	Mississippi	Northwestern	Texas
UCLA (University of California at Los Angeles)	Mississippi State	Ohio State	Texas A&M
Washington	Tennessee	Penn State*	Texas Christian
Washington State	Vanderbilt	Purdue	Texas Tech
		Wisconsin	

*Admitted to conference in 1989 and will begin football competition against conference teams in the mid-1990's.

Heisman Trophy winners

Year	Player	School	Position	Year	Player	School	Position
1935	Jay Berwanger	Chicago	Back	1963	Roger Staubach	Navy	Back
1936	Larry Kelley	Yale	End	1964	John Huarte	Notre Dame	Back
1937	Clint Frank	Yale	Back	1965	Mike Garrett	Southern California	Back
1938	Davey O'Brien	Texas Christian	Back	1966	Steve Spurrier	Florida	Back
1939	Nile Kinnick	Iowa	Back	1967	Gary Beban	UCLA	Back
1940	Tom Harmon	Michigan	Back	1968	O. J. Simpson	Southern California	Back
1941	Bruce Smith	Minnesota	Back	1969	Steve Owens	Oklahoma	Back
1942	Frank Sinkwich	Georgia	Back	1970	Jim Plunkett	Stanford	Back
1943	Angelo Bertelli	Notre Dame	Back	1971	Pat Sullivan	Auburn	Back
1944	Les Horvath	Ohio State	Back	1972	Johnny Rodgers	Nebraska	Back
1945	Doc Blanchard	Army	Back	1973	John Cappelletti	Penn State	Back
1946	Glenn Davis	Army	Back	1974	Archie Griffin	Ohio State	Back
1947	Johnny Lujack	Notre Dame	Back	1975	Archie Griffin	Ohio State	Back
1948	Doak Walker	Southern Methodist	Back	1976	Tony Dorsett	Pittsburgh	Back
1949	Leon Hart	Notre Dame	End	1977	Earl Campbell	Texas	Back
1950	Vic Janowicz	Ohio State	Back	1978	Billy Sims	Oklahoma	Back
1951	Dick Kazmaier	Princeton	Back	1979	Charles White	Southern California	Back
1952	Billy Vessels	Oklahoma	Back	1980	George Rogers	South Carolina	Back
1953	Johnny Lattner	Notre Dame	Back	1981	Marcus Allen	Southern California	Back
1954	Alan Ameche	Wisconsin	Back	1982	Herschel Walker	Georgia	Back
1955	Howard Cassady	Ohio State	Back	1983	Mike Rozier	Nebraska	Back
1956	Paul Hornung	Notre Dame	Back	1984	Doug Flutie	Boston College	Back
1957	John Crow	Texas A&M	Back	1985	Bo Jackson	Auburn	Back
1958	Pete Dawkins	Army	Back	1986	Vinny Testaverde	Miami	Back
1959	Billy Cannon	Louisiana State	Back	1987	Tim Brown	Notre Dame	Back
1960	Joe Bellino	Navy	Back	1988	Barry Sanders	Oklahoma State	Back
1961	Ernie Davis	Syracuse	Back	1989	Andre Ware	Houston	Back
1962	Terry Baker	Oregon State	Back				

lege bowl games are played in late December or on January 1. There are also several postseason all-star games. Players who have completed their college careers may be invited to play in one or more all-star games.

Professional competition. The National Football League has been the only major professional football league in the United States since 1970. However, another league, the United States Football League, began competition in 1983. The NFL consists of 28 teams, each of which represents a city or region in the United States. The teams are divided into the American Football Conference and the National Football Conference, each with 14 teams. Each conference consists of three divisions—Eastern, Central, and Western.

Teams in the NFL play a regular season schedule of 16 games. The division champions and the next two teams in each conference with the best won-lost records advance to the play-offs. A series of play-off games determines the two conference champions. These teams then play for the NFL title in a game called the *Super Bowl.*

Each year, NFL teams obtain college players through a selection system known as a *draft.* Teams can only choose players who have completed their college playing careers. The first choice goes to the team that ended the preceding season with the worst record in the league. The Super Bowl winner picks last. No team may sign a player drafted by another team unless the player is released by the drafting team. If a college player is not drafted, he may sign with any professional team that offers him a contract.

National Football League

American Football Conference

Eastern Division	Central Division	Western Division
Buffalo Bills	Cincinnati Bengals	Denver Broncos
Indianapolis Colts	Cleveland Browns	Kansas City Chiefs
Miami Dolphins	Houston Oilers	Los Angeles Raiders
New England Patriots	Pittsburgh Steelers	San Diego Chargers
New York Jets		Seattle Seahawks

National Football Conference

Eastern Division	Central Division	Western Division
Dallas Cowboys	Chicago Bears	Atlanta Falcons
New York Giants	Detroit Lions	Los Angeles Rams
Philadelphia Eagles	Green Bay Packers	New Orleans Saints
Phoenix Cardinals	Minnesota Vikings	San Francisco 49ers
Washington Redskins	Tampa Bay Buccaneers	

Canadian football

Although hockey ranks as the favorite team sport in Canada, football is gaining increasing popularity. Football is played in Canada by high schools, more than 20 colleges and universities, and 8 professional teams that make up the Canadian Football League (CFL).

Most Canadian football is played by 12-man teams on a field 160 yards (146 meters) long and 65 yards (59 meters) wide. Eleven of the positions resemble those in U.S. football. On offense, the 12th man usually lines up in the backfield, but he may also be used as an end. On defense, the 12th man usually plays in the secondary. The offense has only three downs to make a first down.

Scoring in Canadian football differs from U.S. football in only one way. The Canadian field has a *dead-line* 25 yards (23 meters) behind each goal line. On a kickoff, the receiving team must advance the ball out of the area between the dead-line and the goal line. If it fails, the kicking team scores one point, called a *single.* The same rule applies to a punt.

Diagram of a Canadian football field

Key to positions

SE=Split end; TE=Tight end; E=End; T=Tackle; G= Guard; C=Center; F=Flanker; WB=Wingback; QB= Quarterback; RB=Running back; OLB=Outside linebacker; MLB=Middle linebacker; CB=Cornerback; HB=Halfback; S=Safety

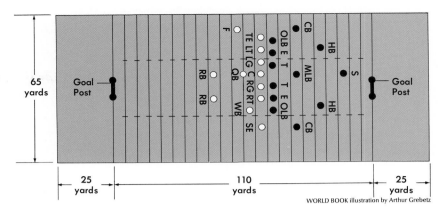

WORLD BOOK illustration by Arthur Grebetz

Nearly all Canadian colleges and universities compete in four regional conferences. The champions of each conference meet in postseason play-offs. The team that wins the play-offs is the national collegiate champion

Canadian Football League

Eastern Division	Western Division
Hamilton Tiger-Cats	British Columbia Lions
Ottawa Rough Riders	Calgary Stampeders
Toronto Argonauts	Edmonton Eskimos
Winnipeg Blue Bombers	Saskatchewan Roughriders

and receives the Vanier Cup.

The CFL is divided into an Eastern Division and a Western Division. Teams in the Eastern Division began competition in 1892, and teams in the Western Division began play in 1936. The conference champions compete for the league title. The winner receives the Grey Cup.

The history of football

Beginnings. Football began to develop during the mid-1800's, when a game similar to soccer was played in the Eastern United States. The object of the game was simply to kick a round ball across the other team's goal

Painting by William Boyd; collection of William Boyd (WORLD BOOK photo by Tom Morton)

The first college game was played between Rutgers and what is now Princeton in 1869. The contest resembled soccer rather than modern football. Teams could advance the ball only by kicking.

Football games from 1906 to 1910 were played on fields marked with a checkerboard pattern of lines. The squares measured 5 yards on each side and helped officials spot rule violations. The offense could not pass the ball within 5 yards of the center. In addition, the back receiving the snap could not cross the line of scrimmage within 5 yards of the center.

line. The football teams sometimes consisted of 30 or more players.

As the soccerlike game became popular, stricter rules were adopted and schools began to organize teams. The first college game was played on Nov. 6, 1869, in New Brunswick, N.J. In that game, Rutgers defeated the College of New Jersey (now Princeton University), 6-4.

The first game resembling present-day football was played in 1874, when a team from McGill University in Montreal, Canada, visited Harvard University. The Canadian team wanted to play the English game of Rugby, which permitted running with the ball and tackling. Harvard preferred to play its soccerlike game, in which players advanced the ball mainly by kicking. The teams agreed to play two games, the first under Harvard rules and the second under McGill rules. Harvard liked McGill's Rugby game so much that the school introduced the sport to other Eastern colleges. Running and tackling soon became as important as kicking in the U.S. game.

Shortly after the Eastern colleges began to play Rugby-style football, they began to change and improve the game. The most influential figure in modernizing football was Walter Camp, who had played for Yale University from 1876 to 1882. Under Camp's leadership, rules were adopted during the 1880's that increased the action and competition of the game. Camp was largely responsible for establishing the system of downs and yards to gain and for introducing the center snap to the quarterback. In 1889, he and sportswriter Caspar Whit-

ney began the tradition of picking an annual all-America team to honor the best college players in the country.

During the 1880's, football gained in popularity. More and more colleges played the sport, and many high schools formed teams. Numerous towns organized teams made up of players who were not in high school or college. Rivalries developed between teams from neighboring towns.

Changes in the game. By 1900, football consisted mostly of running, blocking, and tackling. The blocking and tackling became increasingly violent, and many players suffered serious injuries. The uniforms provided little protection. Players did not even wear helmets. Many games were organized fights rather than athletic contests. In 1905, President Theodore Roosevelt urged changes in the rules to make the game safer.

In 1906, college coaches and faculty members tried to find ways to eliminate some of the violence in football. One new rule permitted a back to throw the ball forward to another back or to one of the ends. According to many historians, the first forward pass was thrown in 1906 by Wesleyan University in a game against Yale University.

At first, teams ignored the forward pass. They did not consider it a logical way to advance the ball. Passing finally became popular in 1913 as a result of a game that year between Notre Dame and Army. The stronger, heavier Army team was favored to defeat the Notre Dame team. But Notre Dame quarterback Gus Dorais led his team to a 35-13 victory by throwing the ball several

The Four Horsemen formed a famous Notre Dame backfield from 1922 to 1924. They were, *left to right,* Don Miller, Elmer Layden, Jim Crowley, and Harry Stuhldreher.

Red Grange was a star running back at the University of Illinois. In a game against Michigan in 1924, *above,* Grange scored a touchdown on each of the first five times he carried the ball.

Professional football champions

National Football Conference (NFC)*

1933	Chicago Bears	**1950**	Cleveland Browns
1934	New York Giants	**1951**	Los Angeles Rams
1935	Detroit Lions	**1952**	Detroit Lions
1936	Green Bay Packers	**1953**	Detroit Lions
1937	Washington Redskins	**1954**	Cleveland Browns
1938	New York Giants	**1955**	Cleveland Browns
1939	Green Bay Packers	**1956**	New York Giants
1940	Chicago Bears	**1957**	Detroit Lions
1941	Chicago Bears	**1958**	Baltimore Colts
1942	Washington Redskins	**1959**	Baltimore Colts
1943	Chicago Bears	**1960**	Philadelphia Eagles
1944	Green Bay Packers	**1961**	Green Bay Packers
1945	Cleveland Rams	**1962**	Green Bay Packers
1946	Chicago Bears	**1963**	Chicago Bears
1947	Chicago Cardinals	**1964**	Cleveland Browns
1948	Philadelphia Eagles	**1965**	Green Bay Packers
1949	Philadelphia Eagles		

American Football Conference (AFC)†

1960	Houston Oilers	**1963**	San Diego Chargers
1961	Houston Oilers	**1964**	Buffalo Bills
1962	Dallas Texans	**1965**	Buffalo Bills

Super Bowl

The Super Bowl is played each January following the completion of the regular season and play-offs the preceding year. The 1966 NFL and AFL champions played in the first Super Bowl in January 1967. The NFL and AFL champions played through 1970, when the leagues merged. Beginning in 1971, the NFC and AFC champions played in the Super Bowl for the NFL title.

1967 Green Bay Packers (NFL) 35, Kansas City Chiefs (AFL) 10
1968 Green Bay Packers (NFL) 33, Oakland Raiders (AFL) 14
1969 New York Jets (AFL) 16, Baltimore Colts (NFL) 7
1970 Kansas City Chiefs (AFL) 23, Minnesota Vikings (NFL) 7
1971 Baltimore Colts (AFC) 16, Dallas Cowboys (NFC) 13
1972 Dallas Cowboys (NFC) 24, Miami Dolphins (AFC) 3
1973 Miami Dolphins (AFC) 14, Washington Redskins (NFC) 7
1974 Miami Dolphins (AFC) 24, Minnesota Vikings (NFC) 7
1975 Pittsburgh Steelers (AFC) 16, Minnesota Vikings (NFC) 6
1976 Pittsburgh Steelers (AFC) 21, Dallas Cowboys (NFC) 17
1977 Oakland Raiders (AFC) 32, Minnesota Vikings (NFC) 14
1978 Dallas Cowboys (NFC) 27, Denver Broncos (AFC) 10
1979 Pittsburgh Steelers (AFC) 35, Dallas Cowboys (NFC) 31
1980 Pittsburgh Steelers (AFC) 31, Los Angeles Rams (NFC) 19
1981 Oakland Raiders (AFC) 27, Philadelphia Eagles (NFC) 10
1982 San Francisco 49ers (NFC) 26, Cincinnati Bengals (AFC) 21
1983 Washington Redskins (NFC) 27, Miami Dolphins (AFC) 17
1984 Los Angeles Raiders (AFC) 38, Washington Redskins (NFC) 9
1985 San Francisco 49ers (NFC) 38, Miami Dolphins (AFC) 16
1986 Chicago Bears (NFC) 46, New England Patriots (AFC) 10
1987 New York Giants (NFC) 39, Denver Broncos (AFC) 20
1988 Washington Redskins (NFC) 42, Denver Broncos (AFC) 10
1989 San Francisco 49ers (NFC) 20, Cincinnati Bengals (AFC) 16
1990 San Francisco 49ers (NFC) 55, Denver Broncos (AFC) 10

*National Football League (NFL) until 1970.
†American Football League (AFL) until 1970.

on Aug. 31, 1895, when a team from Latrobe, Pa., defeated a team from nearby Jeannette, 12-0. In the early days, many college players played with their school teams on Saturdays and with professional teams on Sundays. Later, the rules prohibited a player from being an amateur and a professional at the same time.

Professional football had little organization until 1920, when the American Professional Football Association was founded. Jim Thorpe, the great American Indian athlete, was elected its president. In 1922, the organiza-

V. V. Rubio, Focus on Sports

Fran Tarkenton set many passing records as a quarterback in the National Football League during the 1960's and 1970's.

tion was renamed the National Football League (NFL).

In its early days, professional football was far less popular than college football. Professional football began to win support in 1925. That year, Red Grange, a famous all-American halfback from the University of Illinois, signed to play with the Chicago Bears. He played in a series of games that drew over 350,000 fans and greatly increased interest in professional football.

In 1933, the NFL split into two divisions. Later that year, the Chicago Bears, champions of the Western Division, defeated the New York Giants, champions of the Eastern Division, for the first world professional football title. The league held its first draft in 1936.

In 1944, an eight-team league called the All-America Football Conference was formed. The league began competition in 1946. Many of its players were veterans of the NFL. The All-America Football Conference and the NFL merged in 1950 into a 13-team league.

During the 1950's, professional football began to gain great popularity throughout the United States. TV networks paid millions of dollars to televise the games. In 1960, another professional league, the American Football League (AFL), was formed. The eight-team AFL competed with the NFL for fans and college players. It even tried to sign up star NFL players. In 1966, after six years of rivalry, the two leagues agreed to merge in 1970 into one league consisting of the American Football Confer-

times to his end Knute Rockne. Rockne later became head coach at Notre Dame and one of the most successful coaches in the history of college football. By the 1920's, the forward pass had become a basic part of football and helped make the game more exciting. Meanwhile, most other basic rules had been adopted. In 1912, for example, a touchdown's value was set at six points, and the number of downs was set at four.

The rise of professional football. According to tradition, the first professional football game was played

Focus on Sports

Star NFL running backs included O. J. Simpson, *above,* and Walter Payton, *below.* In 1973, Simpson became the first professional to gain 2,000 yards in a season. Payton holds the NFL record for most yards gained rushing in a career.

Focus on Sports

ence and the National Football Conference. A new professional league, the World Football League (WFL), began play in 1974. Midway through the 1975 season, it ceased operations because of severe financial losses.

Football today. During the 1970's and 1980's, TV continued to play a major role in the popularity of football. The Super Bowl became the most popular annual televised sports event in the United States.

After the first two games of the 1982-1983 season, the NFL players went on strike. This was the first regular-season strike in NFL history. Play resumed eight weeks later with plans for a shortened regular season and a revised play-off schedule. Another professional league, the United States Football League, was organized in

1982. It began playing in 1983. The league suspended play after the 1985 season.

In 1989, Pete Rozelle resigned as NFL commissioner, a position he had held since 1960. Under Rozelle's leadership, the NFL and AFL merged in 1966, the league added several teams, and it enormously increased its income from television. Also in 1989, the NFL announced it would sponsor a new professional international football league, to consist of teams in North America and Europe. Games were to be played in the spring, and competition was to begin in 1991.   Tom Landry

Related articles in *World Book* include:

Brown, Jim	Kemp, Jack F.	Simpson, O. J.
Bryant, Paul	Lombardi, Vince	Soccer
Camp, Walter	Namath, Joe	Stagg, Amos
Grange, Red	Ohio (Places to visit)	Alonzo
Grey Cup	Payton, Walter	Tarkenton, Fran
Halas, George	Robinson, Eddie	Thorpe, Jim
Heisman Memorial	Rockne, Knute	Unitas, John
Trophy	Rugby football	Warner, Pop

Outline

I. The field and equipment
    A. The field
    B. The ball
    C. The uniform
    D. Protective equipment
II. The players and coaches
    A. The offensive team
    B. The defensive team
    C. The coaches
III. How football is played
    A. The playing time
    B. The kickoff
    C. Advancing the ball
    D. Scoring
    E. The officials
    F. Violations and penalties
IV. Football competition
    A. High school competition
    B. College competition
    C. Professional competition
V. Canadian football
VI. The history of football

Questions

What are some differences between U.S. and Canadian football?
When are most college bowl games played?
What does the *back judge* do? The *field judge?*
How does *zone coverage* differ from *man-to-man coverage?*
How does the National Football League obtain college players in its draft each year?
What are *hash marks?*
When did the forward pass become popular?
What is *clipping? Roughing?*
How does a team score a *safety?*
In what ways may the offensive team lose possession of the ball?

Additional resources

Level I
Aaseng, Nate. *College Football: You Are the Coach.* Lerner, 1984. *Football: It's Your Team.* 1985.
Dickmeyer, Lowell A. *Football Is for Me.* Lerner, 1979.
Fox, Larry. *Football Basics.* Simon & Schuster, 1981.

Level II
Barrett, Frank and Lynn. *How to Watch a Football Game.* Holt, 1980.
DeLuca, Sam. *Football Made Easy.* Jonathan David, 1983.
Treat, Roger L. *The Encyclopedia of Football.* 16th ed. A. S. Barnes, 1979.
Zimmerman, Paul. *The New Thinking Man's Guide to Pro Football.* Simon & Schuster, 1984.

Foote, Andrew Hull (1806-1863), was a Union Navy officer during the Civil War. He became the first American naval officer to command a flotilla of ironclad gunboats in battle. His fleet joined the army in attacks on Fort Henry on the Tennessee River and on Fort Donelson on the Cumberland River in February 1862. He helped break the Confederate line of defense in the surrounding area. He became a rear admiral in July 1862.

A temperance society he founded on board the U.S.S. *Cumberland* in 1843 led to the abolishment in 1862 of the serving of liquor on U.S. warships. He commanded the U.S.S. *Perry* along the coast of Africa in operations against the African slave trade from 1849 to 1851.

Foote was born in New Haven, Conn., and studied briefly at the U.S. Military Academy. He joined the navy at the age of 16.   Richard S. West, Jr.

Footnote is a note printed in small type at the bottom of a page. It is used to give information that is too long or too detailed to be included in the original statement. Footnotes sometimes explain a word or idea that might easily be misunderstood, but more often they merely cite the source or authority for what the author says. Footnotes help to keep sentences short and free of excess facts. For example, a student writing a composition about the aardvark might want to tell some fact that had been learned from *The World Book Encyclopedia.* The following sentence would be awkward:

> In an article entitled Aardvark on page 2 of Volume A of *The World Book Encyclopedia*, it is stated that in the 1600's Dutch settlers in Africa gave the aardvark its name.

When a footnote is used, however, the sentence can be quickly and easily read:

> The aardvark received its name from Dutch settlers in Africa in the 1600's.[1]

> [1]"Aardvark," *The World Book Encyclopedia*, Vol. A, p. 2.

A number in small type is commonly used to draw attention to a footnote. An asterisk (*), or a dagger (†), or a double dagger (‡) may be used instead of a number.

Footnotes referring to a book should list the name of the author first, the book title second, and the page number third. Those referring to magazine articles list the author first, the title of the article second, the name of the magazine third, the volume fourth, the date of issue fifth, and the page number sixth.   R. B. Downs

Footprinting is a system of identification similar to fingerprinting. Footprints are the impressions made by ridges on the soles of the feet. Like fingerprints, footprints remain unchanged throughout a person's lifetime. No individual's footprints have been found to be identical to those of another person. Footprints found at the scene of a crime may help identify suspects, especially in hot areas of the world where people often go barefoot. Footprints also provide a means of identification when fingerprints cannot be obtained because of severe burns or other injuries. Many hospitals footprint newborn infants for identification shortly after birth and keep the prints on file for future reference. See also **Fingerprinting.**   John I. Thornton

Forbes, Esther (1891-1967), was an American author. She won the 1943 Pulitzer Prize in American history for her brilliant historical biography, *Paul Revere and the World He Lived In.* While writing this book, she became interested in the apprentice boys of Boston, and the part they played in the Revolutionary War. After finishing the adult biography, Forbes wrote for young people the novel *Johnny Tremain,* about an apprentice in the exciting days of the Boston Tea Party. This book won the Newbery Medal in 1944. She also wrote such American historical novels as *A Mirror for Witches* (1928), *Paradise* (1937), *The General's Lady* (1938), *The Running of the Tide* (1948), and *Rainbow on the Road* (1954).

Forbes was born in Westborough, Mass. She studied at the University of Wisconsin.   Evelyn Ray Sickels

Forbes' Road. See Pennsylvania State Road.

Forbidden City. See Beijing (The city); Lhasa.

Force is any cause that changes the motion or the shape of an object. For example, when you push a cart, you apply force to make the cart move forward. When you squeeze a piece of soft clay, the force you apply changes the shape of the clay.

Many forces affect the *velocity* (speed) of a moving object. For example, when you roll a ball across a carpet, friction between the ball and the carpet acts against the motion of the ball and thus slows the ball down. Any change in velocity is called *acceleration.* A decrease in velocity is also sometimes called *negative acceleration* or *deceleration.*

There are several kinds of forces. *Mechanical forces* act when objects touch each other. Your body applies mechanical force when you pedal a bicycle or kick a football. However, electricity, gravitation, and magnetism are forces that act without contact among objects. Instead, they act through a distance, and arise from a *field* of force. For instance, the electric fields around charged particles cause these particles either to attract or repel one another. This article deals mainly with mechanical forces.

Measuring force

The *mass* of an object and the acceleration of the object must be known in order to measure force. The mass

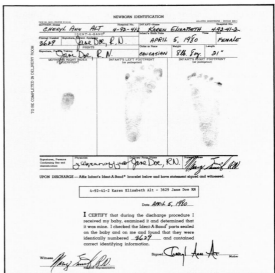

University of Illinois Hospital

Footprints of a newborn baby are recorded by many hospitals for identification purposes. The baby's footprints appear on a certificate along with the mother's fingerprint.

of an object is the amount of matter it has. Mass is measured in pounds or kilograms (see **Mass**). Acceleration describes how much the velocity of an object changes. It is usually expressed by a distance divided by a time squared. For example, an object may change its velocity at a rate of 1 foot per second every second. The acceleration would then be 1 foot per second squared. This quantity can also be expressed as an acceleration of 1 foot per second per second.

Units in the metric system and in the customary, or English, system of measurement are used to measure force. In the metric system, force is expressed chiefly in terms of *newtons*. One newton is the force required to accelerate a 1-kilogram object by 1 meter per second squared. In the English system, the basic unit of force is the *poundal*. One poundal is the force needed to accelerate a 1-pound body 1 foot per second squared.

The relationship among force, mass, and acceleration was first described by the English physicist Sir Isaac Newton in the 1600's. He stated that large forces produce greater acceleration than do small forces, and that heavy objects accelerate less rapidly than do light objects. Newton expressed the relationship among acceleration, force, and mass in the equation $F = ma$. In this equation, F equals the force applied to the object, m equals the object's mass, and a equals the acceleration produced in the object. Newton's description of the relationship among these quantities is known as his second law of motion (see **Motion** [Newton's laws of motion]).

How forces interact

In many cases, more than one force acts on an object at the same time. Such *concurrent forces* produce a single net force, also called a *resultant force*.

Concurrent forces that produce motion when they interact are called *unbalanced forces*. For example, when two people push a stalled car forward, the combined forces they apply overcome the friction between the road and the tires. As a result, the car rolls forward.

Forces that do not produce motion when they interact are called *balanced forces*. For example, when you sit in a chair, the force of gravity pulls you toward the earth. At the same time, the chair pushes you upward, away from the earth. The force of the chair cancels out the force of gravity, and you remain stationary. A person or object acted upon by balanced forces in this way is said to be *in equilibrium*.

Calculating resultant force

To calculate the resultant force, a person needs to know the direction and magnitude of the concurrent forces. If the concurrent forces act in the same direction, then the resultant force also acts in that direction. The magnitudes of the concurrent forces are simply added to determine the magnitude of the resultant force. If two concurrent forces operate in opposite directions and have unequal magnitudes, then the resultant force acts in the direction of the stronger force. The magnitude of the resultant force equals the difference in magnitudes between the two concurrent forces.

Many concurrent forces act at an angle to each other. Quantities called *vectors* are used to calculate the resultant of such forces. A vector tells the magnitude of a force and the direction in which it operates. It can be represented by an arrow—also called a vector—that points in the direction of the force. The length of the arrow indicates the magnitude of the force. Any scale may be chosen when drawing vectors. The point of the arrow is called its *head* and the opposite end, its *tail*.

There are three main methods of using vectors to determine resultant force: (1) the parallelogram method, (2) the polygon method, and (3) the analytic method.

The parallelogram method is used for calculating the resultant force of only two concurrent forces at a time. In this method, the vectors that represent the concurrent forces are used to construct a parallelogram. For example, suppose that two forces act at an angle to each

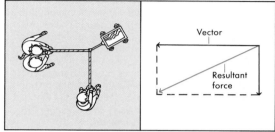

The parallelogram method is a technique for determining the *resultant force* (net force) of two forces acting on an object. In the diagram at the left above, three children exert two forces on a wagon by pulling on two ropes. In the diagram at the right, arrows called *vectors* show the direction and size of the two forces. These vectors are then used to construct a parallelogram. The diagonal of the parallelogram represents the resultant force applied to the wagon.

other. After choosing a scale, draw these forces as vectors whose tails join at a single point. This point represents the object upon which the forces act. Next, construct a parallelogram, using the two vectors as two sides of the figure. Then draw the *diagonal* of the parallelogram—that is, draw a line from the point that represents the object to the opposite corner. Next, make the diagonal into a vector pointing away from the object. This vector represents the resultant force. To determine the magnitude of the resultant force, simply measure the length of its vector.

The polygon method is used to calculate resultant force when more than two concurrent forces interact. In

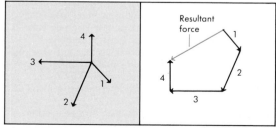

The polygon method enables physicists to analyze the interaction of three or more forces. Vectors representing these forces are used to construct a polygon. The vector drawn to complete the polygon shows the resultant force.

this method, vectors that represent concurrent forces are used to construct a polygon. These vectors are drawn one after the other, with the head of the first vector joined to the tail of the second vector, and so on. A final vector is drawn to connect the tail of the first vector to the head of the last vector. This new vector completes the polygon and represents the resultant force. It should point away from the tail of the first vector.

The analytic method is also used to find the resultant force when more than two forces interact. This method is based on the fact that any vector can be expressed as the resultant of two smaller vectors at right angles to each other. For example, a 5-newton vector can be expressed as the resultant of a 4-newton vector and a 3-newton vector that are at right angles to each other. In this example, the 5-newton vector is the *hypotenuse* of the triangle it forms with the 4-newton vector and the 3-newton vector. The square of the 5-newton vector (25) is therefore equal to the sum of the squares of the two other vectors (9 + 16). For a complete explanation of this principle, see **Pythagorean Theorem.**

With the analytic method, each concurrent force is first expressed as a vector. All but one of the vectors are then broken down into smaller vectors that act at right

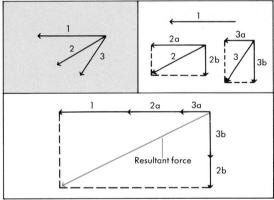

WORLD BOOK illustrations

The analytic method is used to calculate resultant force when several forces interact. The method is based on the fact that any force, such as number 2, *above,* can be expressed as the resultant force of two smaller forces, such as 2a and 2b.

angles to each other. One vector of each right angle is drawn parallel to the vector that has not been broken down. Next, those vectors pointing in the same or opposite directions are added. The addition results in a pair of vectors at right angles to each other. The resultant force for this pair of vectors can then be calculated using the parallelogram method. This force is also the resultant force of the original concurrent forces.

Fundamental forces

Physicists consider all forces in the universe to be forms of four fundamental forces. These basic forces—from the weakest to the strongest—are (1) gravitation, (2) the weak nuclear force, (3) electromagnetism, and (4) the strong nuclear force. The weak nuclear force and the strong nuclear force are also known as the *weak interaction* and the *strong interaction.*

Gravitation exerts influence over great distances in space. It works most effectively on large masses. For example, the sun's gravity holds the earth in its orbit. The electromagnetic force operates over much shorter distances than does gravitation. Electromagnetism holds molecules together. The weak and strong nuclear forces act within the nuclei of atoms.   *Gregory A. Benford*

Related articles in *World Book* include:

Antigravity	Friction	Newton
Centrifugal force	Grand unified theo-	Newton, Sir Isaac
Centripetal force	ries	Physics
Cohesion	Gravitation	Power
Dynamics	Gyroscope	Pressure
Dyne	Inertia	Statics
Electric field	Jet propulsion	Strength of materi-
Electricity	Magnet and mag-	als
Electromotive force	netism	Torque
Energy	Moment	Weight

Force bill was any of several measures passed or considered by the United States Congress that authorized the use of military power to enforce federal law. The first force bill was sometimes called the "Bloody Bill." It became a law on March 2, 1833, after South Carolina had declared the protective tariff laws of 1828 and 1832 "null, void, and no law" within the borders of the state (see **Nullification**). The bill authorized the President to use U.S. armed forces to collect the duties. A compromise tariff was passed, and bloodshed was averted.

During the period of Reconstruction, three other force bills were passed. Two of them (one signed May 31, 1870, and another Feb. 28, 1871) were designed to enforce the 15th Amendment (black suffrage). An act of April 20, 1871, known as the Ku Klux Klan Act, was intended to enforce the 14th Amendment (civil rights).

The Lodge Federal Elections Bill of 1890, which passed the House of Representatives but not the Senate, was also called a force bill. Its purpose was to use federal authority to prevent discrimination against black voters in the Southern States. It was denounced in the South as an attempt to bring back the methods of Reconstruction.   *H. Wayne Morgan*

Ford is a place where a stream or river can be crossed. During early times, people had to cross a waterway by wading through or swimming across its shallow part. During wartime, soldiers must often *ford* (cross) water where bridges have been blown up. They sometimes do this by placing *pontoons* (portable floats) in a line across the water. See also **Pontoon bridge.**

Ford, Ford Madox (1873-1939), was an English author of complex and symbolic novels which show the influence of the psychological novels of Henry James. In *The Good Soldier* (1915), his best-known work, Ford revealed with keen irony the declining influence of the upper class in English life. This novel was followed by the series called *Parade's End,* which consists of *Some Do Not* (1924), *No More Parades* (1925), *A Man Could Stand Up* (1926), and *The Last Post* (1928). The series traces changes in English society during and after World War I. Ford and Joseph Conrad wrote two novels together, *The Inheritors* (1901) and *Romance* (1903).

Ford was born Ford Madox Hueffer in Merton, England. He edited two famous literary magazines, the *English Review* and the *Transatlantic Review,* and was writer-in-residence at Olivet (Mich.) College from 1937 until his death.   *Garrett Stewart*

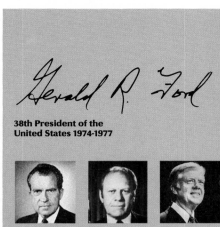

38th President of the United States 1974-1977

Nixon
37th President
1969-1974
Republican

Ford
38th President
1974-1977
Republican

Carter
39th President
1977-1981
Democrat

Nelson A. Rockefeller
Vice President
1974-1977

Gerald R. Ford Library

Ford, Gerald Rudolph (1913-   ), was the only Vice President of the United States to become President upon the resignation of a chief executive. Richard M. Nixon resigned as President on Aug. 9, 1974, and Ford took office that same day. When Nixon left the presidency, he faced almost certain impeachment because of his role in the Watergate political scandal.

Ford had been Vice President for only eight months when he took office as President. Nixon had appointed him to succeed Vice President Spiro T. Agnew, who resigned while under criminal investigation for graft. Ford was the first person to be appointed to fill a vacancy in the vice presidency. He also was the only person to serve as both Vice President and President who did not win election to either office. In the 1976 election, Ford was defeated in his bid for a full term as President by former Governor Jimmy Carter of Georgia, his Democratic opponent.

Ford, a Michigan Republican, had been elected to the U.S. House of Representatives 13 straight times before he replaced Agnew. He also had served as House minority leader.

The American people warmly welcomed Ford to the presidency. He had a calm, friendly manner and an unquestioned reputation for honesty. But Ford's popularity dropped sharply about a month later after he pardoned Nixon for all federal crimes that Nixon might have committed as President. Many Americans felt that Nixon should have been brought to trial in the Watergate scan-

dal. Others believed that Nixon should not have been pardoned until he admitted his role in the Watergate scandal.

Ford was challenged by major economic problems, including a recession, rapid inflation, and high unemployment. The economy began to recover in 1975, though the unemployment rate remained high. U.S. foreign policy suffered a major defeat in 1975, when the Vietnam War ended with a Communist victory.

Ford was a big, athletic man who loved sports. He often turned to the sports section of his newspaper before reading any other news. Ford starred as a football player in high school and college, and football had a major influence on his life. "Thanks to my football experience," he once said, "I know the value of team play. It is, I believe, one of the most important lessons to be learned and practiced in our lives." Ford swam regularly and also enjoyed golf and skiing.

Early life

Family background. Ford was born on July 14, 1913, in Omaha, Nebr. He was named Leslie Lynch King, Jr. His father, Leslie Lynch King, Sr., operated a family wool business there. Leslie's parents were divorced about two years after his birth. His mother, Dorothy Gardner King, then took him to Grand Rapids, Mich., where she had friends. In 1916, she married Gerald R. Ford, owner of a small paint company in the city. Ford adopted the boy and gave him his name. The stocky, blond youth, who became known as "Jerry," grew up with three younger half brothers, James, Richard, and Thomas.

Jerry's real father also remarried. Jerry had a half brother, Leslie H. King; and two half sisters, Marjorie King Werner and Patricia King.

J. F. terHorst, the contributor of this article, is a Columnist for The Detroit News-Universal Press Syndicate *and the author of* Gerald Ford and the Future of the Presidency.

Sorrow and celebration characterized two events that took place during the Ford Administration. The Vietnam War ended in a Communist victory in 1975. Thousands of South Vietnamese refugees fled from their homeland in a U.S.-sponsored airlift, *left.* In 1976, a fleet of tall ships from various nations, *below,* sailed toward New York City harbor to take part in festivities marking the bicentennial of the founding of the United States.

The world of President Ford

Ethiopian Emperor Haile Selassie was deposed by military leaders in 1974, after a 44-year reign.

The Soviet Union deported Alexander Solzhenitsyn, a Nobel Prize-winning novelist, in 1974. He later settled in the United States.

The continuing drama of the Watergate scandal reached a climax in 1975, when top members of the Nixon Administration were found guilty of perjury, conspiracy, and obstruction of justice. Former Attorney General John Mitchell and presidential aides John Ehrlichman and H. R. Haldeman were among the persons sentenced to prison.

Portugal's colonial rule in Africa ended in 1975, when it granted independence to Angola, Cape Verde, Mozambique, and São Tomé and Príncipe.

Juan Carlos I became king of Spain in 1975, following the death of Francisco Franco, Spain's dictator since 1939.

The Apollo-Soyuz Test Project accomplished its goal of cooperation in space in July 1975. A U.S. spacecraft docked with a Soviet spacecraft in space, and crew members from both vehicles conducted joint scientific experiments.

Women were admitted to the military academies of the United States Army, Air Force, and Navy for the first time in 1976.

The deaths of Chinese Communist leaders Mao Zedong and Zhou Enlai in 1976 marked the end of an era. The two men had led China since 1949.

The movement for an independent Quebec gained strength in Canada in 1976, when a separatist political party won control of the provincial government.

Boyhood. Jerry's parents encouraged him to develop pride in civic responsibility. His stepfather participated in programs to aid needy youths in Grand Rapids and took an active interest in local politics. His mother devoted much of her time to charity projects and other activities of the Grace Episcopal Church, where the Fords worshiped. Jerry joined the Boy Scouts and achieved the rank of Eagle Scout, the highest level in Scouting. He later proudly referred to himself as the nation's "first Eagle Scout Vice President."

Jerry was a strong, husky boy and excelled in sports. He first gained public attention as the star center of the South High School football team. He was selected to the all-city high school football team three times and was named to the all-state team in his senior year of high school.

At school, Jerry usually wore a suit and tie, though most boys in those days wore a sport shirt, slacks, and sweater. He studied hard and received good grades. He also won a contest sponsored by a local motion-picture theater to choose the most popular high school senior in Grand Rapids.

Important dates in Ford's life

1913 (July 14) Born in Omaha, Nebr.
1935 Graduated from the University of Michigan.
1942-1946 Served in the U.S. Navy during World War II.
1948 (Oct. 15) Married Elizabeth (Betty) Bloomer.
1948 Elected to the first of 13 successive terms in the U.S. House of Representatives.
1965 Became House minority leader.
1973 (Dec. 6) Became Vice President of the United States.
1974 (Aug. 9) Succeeded to the presidency.
1976 Lost presidential election to Jimmy Carter.

As a teen-ager, Jerry waited on tables and washed dishes at a small restaurant across the street from South High School. One day, his real father came in and introduced himself to the startled youth. Jerry knew about his natural father but had not seen him since his parents' divorce. King asked Jerry if he would like to live with the King family. Jerry said he considered the Fords his family. Later, in 1936, King helped Ford get a summer job as a ranger in Yellowstone National Park.

College student. Ford entered the University of Michigan in 1931. He earned good grades and played center on the undefeated Michigan football teams of 1932 and 1933. In 1934, his teammates named him the team's most valuable player. He played center on the

Ford's birthplace was this house in Omaha, Nebr. His parents divorced when he was 2. Ford and his mother moved to Grand Rapids, Mich., where she remarried and he spent his boyhood.

The White House

Young Jerry, shown at the age of $2\frac{1}{2}$, liked to play with his dog, Spot. He developed into a strong, husky child, who enjoyed sports and became active in the Boy Scouts.

college team that lost to the Chicago Bears, 5 to 0, in the 1935 All-Star Football Game.

Ford graduated from Michigan in 1935. The Detroit Lions and the Green Bay Packers offered him a contract to play professional football, but Ford had decided to study law. He accepted a job as assistant football coach and boxing coach at Yale University, hoping he could also study law there. Ford coached full time at Yale from 1935 until 1938, when he was accepted for admission by the Yale Law School.

While at Yale, Ford became a partner in a modeling

agency in New York City. His partner, Harry Conover, a model, operated the agency. In March 1940, Ford modeled sports clothes for an article in *Look* magazine. The modeling agency succeeded, but Ford became dissatisfied with his share of the profits and soon sold his interest.

Ford received his law degree from Yale in 1941. He ranked in the top third of his graduating class.

Grand Rapids lawyer

In June 1941, Ford was admitted to the Michigan bar. Shortly afterward, he and Philip W. Buchen, a former roommate at the University of Michigan, opened a law office in Grand Rapids. The United States entered World War II in December 1941, and Ford soon volunteered for the United States Navy.

Naval officer. Ford entered the Navy in April 1942, and became an ensign. He taught physical training at a base in Chapel Hill, N.C., for a year. Then he became the physical-training director and assistant navigation officer of the U.S.S. *Monterey,* an aircraft carrier. In 1943 and 1944, the *Monterey* took part in every big naval battle in the Pacific Ocean. Ford was discharged in January 1946 as a lieutenant commander.

Entry into politics. Ford resumed his law career in Grand Rapids and also became active in a local Republican reform group. Leaders of the organization, called the Home Front, included U.S. Senator Arthur H. Vandenberg of Michigan, who had helped establish the United Nations, and Ford's stepfather. The two men urged Ford to challenge U.S. Representative Bartel J. Jonkman in the Republican primary election of 1948.

Jonkman believed that the United States should stay out of foreign affairs as much as possible. Vandenberg and Ford had supported that policy before World War II, but the war changed their views. Ford defeated Jonkman in the primary and then beat Fred Barr, his Democratic opponent in the November election. The voters of

AP/Wide World

Ford starred as center on the University of Michigan football team. His teammates named him most valuable player in 1934. He later coached football and boxing at Yale University.

The White House

The Ford family in 1948. Seated are, *left to right,* Gerald's half brother James, Mrs. Dorothy Ford, and Gerald. Standing are half brother Thomas, Gerald R. Ford, Sr., and half brother Richard.

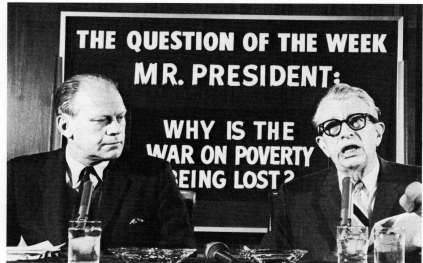

THE QUESTION OF THE WEEK MR. PRESIDENT: WHY IS THE WAR ON POVERTY BEING LOST?

United Press Int.

As House minority leader, Ford appeared with Senate Minority Leader Everett M. Dirksen in a series of televised press conferences in the late 1960's.

Michigan's Fifth Congressional District reelected Ford 12 straight times.

Marriage. In 1947, Ford met Elizabeth (Betty) Bloomer (April 8, 1918-   ). She was born in Chicago and moved to Grand Rapids with her family when she was 3 years old. Her father, William S. Bloomer, was a machinery salesman. Her mother, Hortense, took an active interest in Grand Rapids community affairs.

As a child, Betty became interested in dancing. She continued to study the dance and, during the 1930's, joined a New York City group directed by the noted dancer Martha Graham. Betty also worked as a fashion model. In 1942, she returned to Grand Rapids and married William Warren, a local furniture salesman. They were divorced in 1947.

When Ford met Betty, she was working as a fashion coordinator for a Grand Rapids department store. They were married on Oct. 15, 1948, just before Ford first won election to the U.S. House of Representatives. Ford campaigned on the day of his wedding and arrived late for the ceremony. The Fords had four children, Michael Gerald (1950-   ), John Gardner (1952-   ), Steven Meigs (1956-   ), and Susan Elizabeth (1957-   ).

Career in Congress

Rise to power. Ford gained a reputation as a loyal Republican and a hard worker during his early terms in Congress. He was named to the defense subcommittee of the House Appropriations Committee in 1953 and became known as a military affairs expert. Some Republican leaders mentioned Ford as a possible candidate for the vice presidential nomination in 1960. But the nomination went to Henry Cabot Lodge, Jr., the U.S. ambassador to the United Nations.

During the early 1960's, Ford became increasingly popular among young Republican members of Congress. In 1963, they helped elect him chairman of the Republican Conference of the House. In this position, his first leadership role in the House, Ford presided at meetings of the Republican representatives.

In November 1963, President Lyndon B. Johnson established the Warren Commission to investigate the assassination of President John F. Kennedy. Johnson appointed Ford as one of the seven members of the commission. Ford and a member of his staff, John R. Stiles, later wrote a book about Lee Harvey Oswald, *Portrait of the Assassin* (1965).

House minority leader. In 1965, Ford was chosen House minority leader. As minority leader, he urged Republican members of the House to do more than just criticize the proposals of Democrats, who held a majority in the House. Ford worked for Republican alternatives to Democratic programs.

Ford attracted national attention when he appeared with Senate Minority Leader Everett M. Dirksen on a series of televised Republican press conferences. The series, which reporters called the "Ev and Jerry Show," drew increased attention to Republican views.

Ford supported President Johnson's early policies in the Vietnam War. But by 1967, with no end of the war in sight, Ford began to strongly attack U.S. military strategy in Vietnam. That year, he gave a speech entitled "Why Are We Pulling Our Punches in Vietnam?" The speech encouraged Republicans to oppose Johnson's war policies. In addition, Republicans and Southern Democrats joined under Ford's leadership in opposing many of Johnson's social programs. Ford considered these programs either too costly or unnecessary.

In 1968, Richard M. Nixon was elected President. The Democrats kept control of both houses of Congress, but Ford helped win approval of a number of Nixon's policies concerning the Vietnam War and inflation.

In 1970, Ford led an effort to impeach William O. Douglas, a liberal associate justice of the Supreme Court of the United States. Ford strongly criticized Douglas' vote in a case involving Ralph Ginzburg, the editor of a magazine that had paid the justice $350 for an article. Ford also objected to Douglas' encouragement of political dissent in various writings. The matter ended after a House investigating committee reported that there was a lack of evidence to support Douglas' impeachment.

As Vice President, Ford went on a nationwide speaking tour and expressed his faith in President Richard Nixon, who came under severe criticism as a result of the Watergate scandal.

The resignation of Agnew. In 1972, Nixon and Vice-President Spiro T. Agnew won reelection in a landslide. That same year, Ford won election to his 13th successive term in the House.

Early in 1973, federal investigators uncovered evidence that Agnew had accepted bribes. The charges covered the period that Agnew had served as Baltimore County Executive and then as governor of Maryland, and later as Vice President. As a result of the investigation, Agnew resigned from the vice presidency on Oct. 10, 1973. Nixon nominated Ford to replace Agnew. The nomination required the approval of both houses of Congress under procedures established in 1967 by the 25th Amendment to the United States Constitution. Previously, vacancies in the vice presidency had remained unfilled until the next presidential election.

The Senate approved Ford's nomination by a 92 to 3 vote on November 27. The House approved it, 387 to 35, on December 6, and Ford was sworn in as the 40th Vice President later that day. He became the first appointed Vice President in the nation's history.

Vice President (1973-1974)

Shortly before Ford became Vice President, the House of Representatives started impeachment proceedings against Nixon. Some members of Congress believed that Nixon was hiding evidence related to the Watergate scandal, which had begun in June 1972. The scandal arose after Nixon's reelection committee became involved in a burglary at Democratic national headquarters in the Watergate building complex in Washington, D.C. Later, evidence linked several top White House aides with the burglary or with an effort to conceal information about it.

Speaking tour. The Watergate scandal shook public confidence in Nixon, even though he insisted he had no part in it. As Vice President, Ford went on a nationwide speaking tour and expressed his faith in Nixon. He ad-

dressed business, civic, and youth groups in cities throughout the country. Ford also took part in many Republican fund-raising activities and campaigned for Republican candidates. By mid-1974, the Vice President had visited about 40 states and made several hundred public appearances.

The resignation of Nixon. In July 1974, the House Judiciary Committee recommended that Nixon be impeached. It voted to adopt three articles of impeachment for consideration by the full House of Representatives. The first article accused the President of interfering with justice by acting to hide evidence about the Watergate burglary from federal law-enforcement officials. The other articles charged that Nixon had abused presidential powers and illegally withheld evidence from the judiciary committee.

Ford continued to defend Nixon, arguing that the President had committed no impeachable offense. Ford also predicted that the House of Representatives would not impeach Nixon.

Then, on August 5, Nixon released transcripts of taped White House conversations that clearly supported the first proposed article of impeachment. Almost all of Nixon's remaining support in Congress collapsed immediately. The Republican leaders of both the House and the Senate warned Nixon that he faced certain impeachment and removal from office.

Nixon resigned as President on the morning of August 9. At noon that day, Ford took the oath of office as the 38th President of the United States. Warren E. Burger, chief justice of the United States, administered the presidential oath of office to Ford in the East Room of the White House. Ford became the only President in the nation's history who had not been elected to either the presidency or the vice presidency.

Ford's Administration (1974-1977)

Ford kept all of Nixon's Cabinet officers at the start of his Administration. He nominated Nelson A. Rockefeller, former governor of New York, as Vice President. Rockefeller took office in December 1974, after both the Senate and the House confirmed his nomination.

Early problems. When Ford became President, he was challenged at home by soaring inflation and a loss of public confidence in the government. Inflation was causing hardship among many Americans, especially the poor and the elderly. Sharp rises in prices also threatened to cause a severe business slump.

Public faith in government had plunged to its lowest level in years, largely because of the Watergate scandal. In addition, the Nixon impeachment crisis had slowed the work of many federal agencies and created confusion about various government policies.

Fighting on the Mediterranean island of Cyprus provided the first foreign crisis for the new President. In August 1974, Turkish troops invaded Cyprus and took control of a large part of the island. The take-over occurred after Turkish Cypriots strongly protested the formation of a new government by Greek Cypriots. Angry Greeks, Greek Cypriots, and Americans of Greek ancestry charged that the United States should have used its influence to stop the Turks.

The national scene. Relations between Ford and the Democratic-controlled Congress were strained. Con-

Ford was sworn in as President on Aug. 9, 1974, in the East Room of the White House. Mrs. Betty Ford watched Chief Justice Warren Burger administer the oath of office.

gress passed few of his major proposals. Ford vetoed over 50 bills. He believed most of these bills would have increased the rate of inflation.

The Nixon pardon severely hurt Ford's early popularity. On Sept. 8, 1974, he pardoned Nixon for all federal crimes the former President might have committed as chief executive. Ford said he took the action to end divisions within the nation and to "heal the wounds that had festered too long." But the pardon angered millions of Americans. Many of them believed that the government should have brought Nixon to trial if it had enough evidence to do so. Many others felt that Ford should not have granted the pardon until Nixon had admitted his involvement in the Watergate scandal.

The amnesty program was announced by Ford eight days after he pardoned Nixon. The new President of-

fered amnesty to draft dodgers and deserters of the Vietnam War period. The program required most of these men to work in a public service job for up to two years. About 22,000 of the approximately 106,000 eligible men applied for amnesty under the program. Most of the rest objected to the work requirement and refused to apply.

The economy. At the beginning of his Administration, Ford called inflation the nation's "public enemy Number 1." With quick congressional approval, he established the Council on Wage and Price Stability to expose any inflationary wage and price increases.

Ford also proposed tax increases for corporations, families, and individuals. But he dropped these plans later in 1974 after a recession struck the nation. Ford then introduced legislation to create public service jobs

The Turkish invasion of the island of Cyprus was Ford's first foreign crisis. Critics felt he should have used U.S. influence to stop the Turks.

Vice President and Cabinet

Vice President	*Nelson A. Rockefeller
Secretary of state	*Henry A. Kissinger
Secretary of the treasury	*William E. Simon
Secretary of defense	James R. Schlesinger
	*Donald H. Rumsfeld (1975)
Attorney general	William B. Saxbe
	Edward H. Levi (1975)
Secretary of the interior	*Rogers C. B. Morton
	Stanley K. Hathaway (1975)
	Thomas S. Kleppe (1975)
Secretary of agriculture	Earl L. Butz
	John A. Knebel (1976)
Secretary of commerce	Frederick B. Dent
	*Rogers C. B. Morton (1975)
	*Elliot L. Richardson (1975)
Secretary of labor	Peter J. Brennan
	John T. Dunlop (1975)
	W. J. Usery, Jr. (1976)
Secretary of health,	
education, and welfare	*Caspar Weinberger
	F. David Mathews (1975)
Secretary of housing and	
urban development	*James T. Lynn
	*Carla A. Hills (1975)
Secretary of transportation . .	Claude S. Brinegar
	*William T. Coleman, Jr. (1975)

*Has a biography in *World Book.*

for the unemployed and to lower federal income taxes. Congress passed both measures.

Early in 1975, inflation slowed and the economy began to recover. But in May that year, more than 9 per cent of the nation's labor force had no jobs—the highest level of unemployment since 1941. The unemployment rate dropped slowly during the recovery. In October 1976, it stood at about 8 per cent.

Two attempted assassinations of Ford occurred in California during September 1975. The first attempt, by Lynette Alice Fromme, a follower of a convicted murderer named Charles Manson, took place on September 5 in Sacramento. A Secret Service agent saw Fromme pointing a pistol at Ford and grabbed the gun before it was fired. On September 22, Sara Jane Moore, who had been associated with groups protesting United States government policies, shot at Ford in San Francisco but missed. Both women were convicted of attempted assassination of a President and sentenced to life imprisonment.

Foreign affairs. Ford relied heavily on the guidance of Secretary of State Henry A. Kissinger, who had also been Nixon's chief adviser on foreign policy. In 1975, Ford and Kissinger helped Egypt and Israel settle a territorial dispute that had resulted from a war between the two nations in 1973. Ford also worked to continue Nixon's program to improve U.S. relations with China and the Soviet Union.

The Vietnam War ended in April 1975, after Communist North Vietnam conquered South Vietnam. That same month, Communist troops also took over Kampuchea, which borders Vietnam on the west. Shortly before South Vietnam fell, Ford asked Congress to give that nation more than $700 million in emergency military aid. But Congress felt the aid could not save South Vietnam and rejected the request. Ford arranged for the

evacuation of refugees from South Vietnam. About 100,000 of them came to the United States.

The Mayagüez seizure. In May 1975, Kampuchean Communist troops seized the *Mayagüez,* a U.S. merchant ship, in the Gulf of Thailand. Ford sent 200 U.S. Marines to the area, and they quickly recaptured the ship and rescued its 39 crew members.

Life in the White House was relaxed and informal during Ford's presidency. The Fords impressed visitors with their personal warmth and friendly hospitality. They liked to entertain and invited over 900 guests to a White House Christmas Party for members of Congress in 1974. The Fords especially enjoyed dancing.

Susan Ford was the only one of the four Ford children who lived in the White House during most of Ford's presidency. She entered Mount Vernon College in Washington in 1975. Susan's Siamese cat, Shan, was one of the family pets. Another was the President's dog, a golden retriever named Liberty.

Betty Ford underwent surgery for breast cancer about a month after Ford became President. She won the admiration of millions when she resumed her busy schedule of activities after recovering from the operation. Mrs. Ford also became noted for her support of women's rights. She campaigned for adoption of the Equal Rights Amendment to the U.S. Constitution. This amendment was designed to give women the same rights men had in business and other fields.

The 1976 election. Former Governor Ronald Reagan of California challenged Ford for the 1976 Republican presidential nomination. The two fought a close, bitter contest in the state primary elections. Ford narrowly won nomination on the first ballot at the Republican National Convention in Kansas City. At his request, the con-

Gerald R. Ford Library

The President's family in the White House. Standing behind President and Mrs. Ford are, *left to right,* daughter Susan, sons Steven, John, and Michael, and Michael's wife, Gayle.

vention nominated Senator Robert J. Dole of Kansas for Vice President. Their Democratic opponents were former Governor Jimmy Carter of Georgia and Senator Walter F. Mondale of Minnesota.

During his campaign against Carter, Ford pledged to continue policies that he believed had brought about the economic recovery and the slowdown in the inflation rate. Carter charged that Ford had mismanaged the economy. He argued that Ford's policies had contributed to the continuing high rate of unemployment. The campaign included the second series of nationally televised debates between presidential candidates in U.S. history. The first series took place in 1960 between John F. Kennedy, the Democratic candidate, and Nixon, then the Republican nominee. In the 1976 election, Carter defeated Ford by 1,678,069 popular votes out of over $81\frac{1}{2}$ million. Ford carried 27 states, while Carter carried 23 states and the District of Columbia. However, Carter received 297 electoral votes compared to Ford's 240. Reagan received one electoral vote. See **Electoral College** (table).

Later years

After Ford left the White House, he served on the board of directors of several companies. He also spent much time lecturing at colleges and universities and speaking to organizations. In 1979, he published his autobiography, *A Time to Heal.* He handled some assignments for Ronald Reagan after Reagan became President in 1981. Also in 1981, the Gerald R. Ford Museum opened in Grand Rapids and the Gerald R. Ford Library opened in Ann Arbor, Mich.   J. F. terHorst

Related articles in *World Book* include:

Agnew, Spiro T.	Republican Party
Constitution of the United	Rockefeller, Nelson A.
States (Amendment 25)	United States, History of the
Nixon, Richard M.	Vice President of the U.S.
President of the U.S.	Watergate
Presidential succession	

Outline

I. Early life
  A. Family background   C. College student
  B. Boyhood
II. Grand Rapids lawyer
  A. Naval officer   C. Marriage
  B. Entry into politics
III. Career in Congress
  A. Rise to power
  B. House minority leader
  C. The resignation of Agnew
IV. Vice President (1973-1974)
  A. Speaking tour
  B. The resignation of Nixon
V. Ford's Administration (1974-1977)
  A. Early problems
  B. The national scene
  C. Foreign affairs
  D. Life in the White House
  E. The 1976 election
VI. Later years

Questions

Who first encouraged Ford to seek public office?
What national problems did Ford face when he became President?
What new approach did Ford develop for the Republicans in the House after he became minority leader?
What high honor did Ford earn as a Boy Scout?

What influence did football have on Ford's life?
Under what provision of the United States Constitution did Ford become Vice President?
Why was Ford's succession to the presidency unique?
What action severely hurt Ford's early popularity?
What recreational activities did Ford enjoy?
What was the "Ev and Jerry Show"?

Additional resources

Ford, Gerald R. *A Time to Heal: The Autobiography of Gerald R. Ford.* Harper, 1979.
The Great Debates: Carter vs. Ford, 1976. Ed. by Sidney Kraus. Indiana Univ. Press, 1979.
Hartmann, Robert T. *Palace Politics: An Inside Account of the Ford Years.* McGraw, 1980.
MacDougall, Malcolm D. *We Almost Made It.* Crown, 1977. Discusses how Ford's campaign was created and executed.
Osborne, John. *The White House Watch: The Ford Years.* New Republic Books, 1977.
Reichley, A. James. *Conservatives in an Age of Change: The Nixon and Ford Administrations.* Brookings, 1981.

Ford, Hannibal Choate (1877-1955), an American inventor and engineer, developed equipment to control the range and accuracy of gunfire. He perfected the method that allowed guns to aim accurately from the rolling decks of a ship at sea.

Ford formed the Ford Instrument Company in 1915 and became its first president. Later it became a division of the Sperry Rand Corporation (now part of Unisys Corporation). He helped make many improvements on typewriters and also invented an automatic bombsight. Ford was born in Dryden, N.Y.   Robert P. Multhauf

Ford, Henry (1863-1947), was the leading manufacturer of American automobiles in the early 1900's. He established the Ford Motor Company, which revolutionized the automobile industry with its assembly line method of production. The savings from this technique helped Ford sell automobiles at a lower price than anyone had before. From 1908 to 1927, more than half the cars sold in the United States were Fords.

Early life. Ford was born on a farm in what is now Dearborn, Mich. He became a machinist at the age of 16 and later worked as an engineer at a Detroit electric company. As a young man, Ford became interested in automobiles, which were then a new invention. He built his first successful gasoline engine in 1893 and his first automobile in 1896.

Industrial accomplishments. In 1903, Ford organized the Ford Motor Company. At first, the company produced only expensive cars, as its competitors did. However, Ford soon began working to make a simple, sturdy car that large numbers of people could afford. He achieved one of the first such cars with the Model T, which appeared in 1908. In 1909, Ford decided to produce only Model T's.

The Model T's original price of $850 was too high for many customers. To lower the price, Ford and his executives tried new ways to reduce production costs. For example, the company created an assembly

Ford Motor Company
Henry Ford

line method in which conveyor belts brought automobile parts to workers. Each worker performed a particular task, such as adding or tightening a part. This system helped reduce the assembly time of a Ford automobile from about $12\frac{1}{2}$ worker-hours in 1912 to about $1\frac{1}{2}$ worker-hours in 1914.

Ford Motor Company began to produce its own parts instead of buying them from independent suppliers at a higher price. Ford also shipped automobile parts, rather than assembled automobiles, to market areas, where assembly plants put the parts together. Parts cost less to ship than whole automobiles did. In addition, the company began to make its own glass and steel.

As the company's production costs fell, Ford passed much of the savings on to his customers. The price of a Model T dropped to $500 in 1913, $390 in 1915, and $260 in 1925, putting the automobile within reach of the average family.

In 1914, Ford raised the minimum wage to $5 a day for his employees 22 years of age and over. This rate was more than twice what most wage earners received. Ford also reduced the workday from 9 to 8 hours. Workers flocked to Ford plants seeking jobs, and Ford could choose the hardest-working and smartest ones. To encourage productivity, Ford introduced a profit-sharing plan, which set aside part of the company's profits for its employees.

During the late 1920's, Ford continued to produce the Model T even though its popularity had declined. Meanwhile, the General Motors Corporation (GM) gained an increasing share of the U.S. automobile market. GM offered a wide variety of models equipped with many luxuries. GM also introduced new designs yearly and advertised its cars as symbols of wealth and taste. Ford, however, continued to offer only basic transportation at a low cost. The Model T changed little from year to year, and until 1926 it came in only one color, black.

Ford finally introduced a new design, the Model A, in

Oil painting on canvas (early 1950's) by Norman Rockwell; Henry Ford Museum and Greenfield Village, Dearborn, Mich.

Henry Ford's first automobile was built in a workshop in Detroit. The automobile, completed in 1896, is now on display at the Henry Ford Museum in Dearborn, Mich.

1927, after more than 15 million Model T's had been sold. In 1932, Ford introduced the first low-priced car with a *V-8 engine,* a powerful engine that had eight cylinders arranged in a V. By that time, however, GM had taken the lead from Ford Motor in U.S. auto sales. Ford Motor declined throughout the 1930's, and some people began to question Henry Ford's management skills. In 1945, Henry Ford II, one of Ford's grandsons, took over the company.

Political and charitable activities. Ford had long taken an interest in political affairs. In 1915, during World War I, he and about 170 other people traveled to Europe at his expense to seek peace. The group, which lacked the approval of the United States government, failed to persuade the warring nations to settle their differences.

In 1918, the year the war ended, Ford ran as a Democrat for a Senate seat from Michigan. He lost the election and did not seek public office again, but he continued to speak out on political issues. He made many statements critical of Jews. He also opposed labor unions. He fought attempts by the United Automobile Workers (UAW) to organize his employees.

Ford devoted much time and money to educational and charitable projects. He established Greenfield Village and the Henry Ford Museum, both in Dearborn. The village is a group of restored historical buildings. The museum includes exhibits in science, industry, and art. In 1936, Ford and his son, Edsel, set up the Ford Foundation, the world's largest foundation, which gives grants for education, research, and development.

Ford wrote four books with author Samuel Crowther. They are *My Life and Work* (1922), *Today and Tomorrow* (1926), *Edison As I Know Him* (1930), and *Moving Forward* (1931).   Robert Sobel

See also **Automobile** (Henry Ford); **Ford, Henry, II; Ford Foundation; Ford Motor Company; Greenfield Village.**

Additional resources

Harris, Jacqueline L. *Henry Ford.* Watts, 1984.
Lacey, Robert. *Ford, the Men and the Machine.* Little, Brown, 1986.
Lewis, David L. *The Public Image of Henry Ford: An American Folk Hero and His Company.* Wayne State Univ. Press, 1976.
Nevins, Allan, and Hill, F. E. *Ford.* 3 vols. Scribner, 1954-1963.

Ford, Henry, II (1917-1987), was an American automobile manufacturer who reorganized the Ford Motor Company during the 1940's and rescued it from near bankruptcy. He was a grandson of Henry Ford, who organized the company in 1903.

Henry Ford II was born in Detroit. During World War II (1939-1945), he served in the United States Navy at Great Lakes Naval Training Center. In 1943, he was released from the Navy to help Ford Motor, which produced military vehicles and other supplies.

Ford became vice president of the company in 1943 and took over the presidency from his grandfather in 1945. At that time, the company was losing about $9 million a month. Ford hired a team of expert managers to help him reorganize the company. He also introduced new marketing methods and automobile designs to meet the changing tastes of the American public. In 1949, after the reorganization, the company earned about $177 million.

An assembly line in 1914 was used to build Model T automobiles in Highland Park, Mich.

During the 1950's and 1960's, such successful models as the Thunderbird, Falcon, Mustang, and Maverick helped keep the company strong. In 1960, Ford became chairman of the board and chief executive officer of Ford Motor. He retired as chief executive officer in 1979 and as chairman in 1980.

Ford helped establish a number of social welfare organizations. In 1967, for example, he helped found the Urban Coalition, which works to solve urban problems. It became the National Urban Coalition in 1970. In 1968, he helped organize the National Alliance of Business to find jobs for the unemployed.   Robert Sobel

See also **Ford, Henry; Ford Motor Company.**

Ford, John (1586-1640?), was an English playwright. Such critics of the 1900's as T. S. Eliot have ranked Ford as the finest English playwright in the period after the death of William Shakespeare.

Ford wrote in collaboration with other playwrights, but created several distinguished plays of his own. The most famous are two sensational tragedies, *The Broken Heart* (1629) and *'Tis Pity She's a Whore* (1632?); and the historical drama *Perkin Warbeck* (1633), about a man who claims to be the rightful heir to the English throne.

Ford was strongly influenced by the idea of *melancholy,* a name given in his time to a disease of the mind. Individuals afflicted with melancholy in modern times might be called *neurotic.* This modern psychological aspect of Ford's plays has contributed greatly to their success with audiences and readers of the 1900's. Ford was born in Devonshire.   Albert Wertheim

Ford, John (1895-1973), became the first motion-picture director to win Academy Awards for four movies. He won the awards for *The Informer* (1935), *The Grapes of Wrath* (1940), *How Green Was My Valley* (1941), and *The Quiet Man* (1952). Ford became famous for staging outdoor motion pictures with a keen sense of back-

ground and deep feeling for people. His major outdoor and western movies include *The Iron Horse* (1924), *The Hurricane* (1937), *Stagecoach* (1939), *Fort Apache* (1948), *She Wore a Yellow Ribbon* (1949), *Wagonmaster* (1951), *Mogambo* (1952), *The Horse Soldiers* (1959), and *Cheyenne Autumn* (1964).

Ford was born in Portland, Me. His real name was Sean Aloysius O'Feeney. Ford began his directing career in 1914 and directed more than 200 movies. In 1973, President Richard M. Nixon awarded Ford the Presidential Medal of Freedom.   Howard Thompson

Ford Foundation is the world's largest foundation. It seeks to advance human welfare by contributing money to help solve national and international problems. The foundation mainly grants funds to institutions and organizations that show promise of producing significant achievement. The Ford Foundation was established in 1936. Since then, the foundation has given or pledged more than $6 billion to more than 8,000 institutions and organizations in the United States and other countries.

Programs. The foundation supports programs in six areas: (1) urban poverty, (2) rural poverty and resources, (3) human rights and social justice, (4) government and public policy, (5) education and culture, and (6) international affairs. It also assists work on several population-related issues, such as teen-age pregnancy and population policy in developing countries.

The urban poverty program grants funds to aid community renewal, prevent arson, improve inner-city secondary schools, fight youth unemployment, and combat crime. Other funds go toward seeking alternatives to dependency on welfare relief, improving the health of children, and resettling refugees and migrants.

The rural poverty and resources program has five goals. These objectives are to improve land and water management, strengthen policymaking in rural areas, increase agricultural production in developing countries, develop community organizations, and expand job opportunities for the poor, especially women.

The human rights and social justice program helps promote and protect civil and political liberties. It also grants funds to help increase economic and social opportunities for minorities, women, and other disadvantaged groups. In addition, the program supports efforts to defend human rights and protect the rights of refugees and migrants.

The government and public policy program assists experiments to improve the structure and functions of governments. It encourages local initiatives and civic participation in government. This program also helps finance research on the impact of public policies on minorities, the poor, and social insurance and welfare programs.

The education and culture program supports efforts to improve teaching and learning in higher education and to encourage scholarship and strengthen scholarly resources. The program also grants money to develop talent and resources in the creative and performing arts, preserve and restore traditional cultures and art forms, and analyze major policy issues affecting higher education and the arts.

The international affairs program aids research, training, policy analysis, and the spread of information on five major global issues. These issues are the movement of refugees and migrants, the maintenance of international peace, the changing world economy, U.S. foreign policy, and international studies and relations.

History. Automobile manufacturer Henry Ford and his son, Edsel, established the Ford Foundation. Most of its grants went to charitable and educational institutions in Michigan until 1950. That year, the foundation became a national organization.

The foundation has headquarters at 320 E. 43rd Street, New York, NY 10017. It also has offices in other countries. For assets, see **Foundations** (table).

Critically reviewed by the Ford Foundation

Ford Motor Company ranks as one of the giants of American industry. The company manufactures various models of Ford, Lincoln, and Mercury automobiles. It also makes Ford trucks and tractors, farm machinery, and industrial engines and accessories. The company also manufactures advanced products for space and military use. Ford Motor Company wholly owns the Ford Aerospace & Communications Corporation, Ford Motor Credit Company, The American Road Insurance Company, the Ford Land Development Corporation, and Rouge Steel Company.

Ford has about 75 assembly and manufacturing plants in the United States. The largest Ford manufacturing center is the Rouge complex near Detroit, Mich. The plant covers 1,200 acres (486 hectares) and employs 27,000 people. The Rouge plant has its own dock for lake freighters.

Ford also has manufacturing subsidiaries in Great Britain, Canada, Belgium, Germany, Australia, Argentina, Brazil, and Mexico, and maintains other sales and assembly facilities in Europe, South America, and New Zealand. Ford is a joint owner of manufacturing companies in Malaysia, South Africa, Taiwan, and Turkey. For the sales, assets, and number of employees of the Ford

Motor Company, see **Manufacturing** (table: 50 leading U.S. manufacturers).

Henry Ford organized the company in 1903. The success of the Model N, brought out in 1906, led to the introduction of the famous Model T in 1908. Affectionately known as the "Tin Lizzie," this simple and inexpensive car became very popular. All but the body of the Model T could be assembled in 93 minutes on an assembly line established at the Ford factory in Highland Park, Mich., in 1913. The Model T finally gave way to the Model A in 1927. In 1932, Ford brought out the V-8 engine.

Ford family interests controlled the company until 1956. In January 1956, the Ford Foundation sold 10,200,000 shares of its Ford company stock to the public. This was the largest single stock issue ever offered to the public up to that date. With this sale, the Ford Motor Company became a publicly owned company. It has about 285,000 stockholders.

Critically reviewed by the Ford Motor Company

See also **Ford, Henry; Ford, Henry, II; Ford Foundation.**

Ford's Theatre. See Lincoln, Abraham (Assassination); **National Park System** (table: National historic sites).

Forearm. See Arm.

Forecasting, Weather. See Weather (with pictures); Meteorology; Weather Service, National.

Foreclosure. See Mortgage.

Forefathers' Day. See December (Special days).

Foreign Agricultural Service is an agency of the United States Department of Agriculture. Its main purpose is to develop markets in other countries for farm products from the United States. The Foreign Agricultural Service also acts as an information agency to tell American farmers and trade groups what is happening in agriculture throughout the world. The service performs these duties through a staff in Washington, D.C. It also has agricultural experts stationed at diplomatic posts and special trade offices in other countries.

The Foreign Agricultural Service tries to reduce or eliminate unreasonable foreign tariffs or other trade barriers erected against United States agricultural products. Much of this work is done through the General Agreement on Tariffs and Trade (GATT), of which the United States is a member. The service also works with private trade groups to increase the foreign demand for United States farm products.

Critically reviewed by the Foreign Agricultural Service

Foreign aid refers to the money, goods, or services that governments and private organizations give to help other nations and their people. Both private groups and governments give aid to help less developed nations fight poverty, disease, and ignorance. But since the start of the Cold War in the 1940's, foreign aid has also become an important part of foreign policy for many nations.

The governments of many countries give aid to support three foreign policy goals: (1) to promote national security; (2) to increase international trade; and (3) to achieve political objectives, including humanitarian goals. The nations giving aid try to strengthen their own national defenses by strengthening friendly or neutral governments. They also give aid to create or maintain trade and investment ties with other nations. And when they give aid, they expect the receiving nations to support, or at least not oppose, their political policies.

Kinds of foreign aid

Foreign aid takes many forms. It may be CARE packages of food or clothing for needy people, or Peace Corps volunteers working in villages. It could be technicians who teach others such things as modern farming methods or how to operate heavy construction machinery. Foreign aid could also take the form of long-term loans to help developing countries build roads and power plants.

Foreign aid includes money, supplies, and technical assistance aimed at helping another country build up its economic and military power. But foreign aid does not include military forces sent to help another country. Nor does it include international trade, private international investment, or diplomatic efforts to help other countries.

Private aid is offered by voluntary nongovernment organizations, such as CARE and the Red Cross. Governments give *official* aid, also known as *public* aid. Official aid given by one country to another is called *bilateral* aid. Aid given by a group of countries through the United Nations (UN) or other institutions is called *multilateral* aid.

About three-fourths of all official aid is bilateral. In the late 1980's, such aid amounted to about $42 billion a year. In the late 1980's, the United States gave the largest amount of economic aid. Other leading contributors included France, Great Britain, Japan, the Soviet Union, Saudi Arabia, and West Germany.

United States aid programs

Large-scale foreign aid began during World War II (1939-1945). From the early 1940's to the mid-1960's, the United States gave or lent about $140 billion in foreign aid. At one time or another, almost every country in the world has received U.S. aid. Since World War II, about a third of all U.S. aid has gone to help other nations build up their armed forces. The rest has gone to teach people new skills, to provide emergency aid for people who lacked food or homes, and to build up national wealth and income in poor countries. Changes in types of aid and in the countries receiving aid reflect changes in U.S. interests since 1940.

World War II aid. From 1940 through 1945, the United States gave over $50 billion in supplies and

© Joe Viesti
Aid in solving food shortages includes technical assistance. United States farm experts teach modern farming methods to increase production. This expert from the United Nations is advising a Haitian sesame seed farmer.

equipment to its allies, especially Great Britain and the Soviet Union. It gave much of this aid through the Lend-Lease Program. The United States also started a technical and development assistance program for Latin America and gave funds to war relief programs.

Relief and reconstruction. One of the most pressing needs at the end of World War II was to provide food and shelter for millions of people in Europe and Asia. Another was to help the people rebuild their war-torn countries. The United Nations Relief and Rehabilitation Administration (UNRRA), an organization financed largely by U.S. grants, helped meet these needs. So did U.S. loans to Great Britain and other nations. But these were only temporary measures. In 1948, the United States began the first broad reconstruction program, the Marshall Plan (European Recovery Program). The plan gave the countries of Western Europe about $13 billion for rebuilding over a period of four years.

Economic development and mutual security. After the Marshall Plan, U.S. interests turned to promoting the economic development and military security of developing countries in Africa, Asia, and Latin America. In 1950, the U.S. Congress authorized $35 million for President Harry S. Truman's proposed Point Four Program to give technical assistance to these countries.

The threat of Communism changed the emphasis in

© Abbas, Gamma/Liaison

Aid to education provides funds and teachers for schools and universities in many countries, including Ethiopia, *left.* The Agency for International Development administers most of the economic and foreign aid programs sponsored by the U.S. government.

foreign aid. Americans were concerned about the Communist take-over in China in 1949, the Korean War in the 1950's, and increasing Cold War tensions between the United States and the Soviet Union. To stop the spread of Communism, the United States helped found the North Atlantic Treaty Organization (NATO), and pledged military aid to NATO members. It gave military and economic aid to developing countries facing Soviet or Chinese pressure. These countries included Greece, Laos, South Korea, South Vietnam, Taiwan, and Turkey. The United States has also given mutual security aid to India, Pakistan, Yugoslavia, and other developing countries it has considered to be of major political importance.

In 1957, the United States set up a Development Loan Fund. It lent money on easy terms to developing countries so that they could build up their economies. Countries could also get bilateral help from the Export-Import Bank, another agency of the U.S. government.

In the 1960's, Presidents John F. Kennedy and Lyndon B. Johnson strongly supported technical assistance and economic development programs. In 1961, Congress established the Agency for International Development (AID) to administer all U.S. bilateral aid programs, and Kennedy established the Peace Corps. Thousands of American Peace Corps volunteers have lived and worked with people in developing countries to help them improve their living conditions. In 1961, the United States and 19 Latin American countries formed the Alliance for Progress to promote economic development and social reform in Latin America. Under the Food for Peace Program, which was set up in 1954, food shipments to needy nations averaged about 1\frac{1}{2}$ billion a year during the 1960's.

But in the early 1970's, the United States reduced its foreign aid program. Public support for foreign aid weakened. The United States felt it needed the money more for military and domestic programs. It also had to end a balance of payments deficit caused by the nation spending more money abroad than foreigners spent in the United States. In the mid-1970's, U.S. foreign aid began to rise again, especially to Egypt and Israel.

Other countries' aid programs

Other nations besides the United States give economic aid to developing countries. France gives much aid to its overseas territories and to its former colonies in Africa. Belgium, Great Britain, and other former colonial powers also give aid to their former colonies.

The Soviet Union has given large amounts of military and economic aid to several countries, including Afghanistan, Cuba, Egypt, India, North Korea, and Vietnam. But in the 1970's, Soviet leaders began to reduce economic assistance to other countries. They believed that such aid brought the Soviet Union few benefits and that the receiving countries did not appreciate the aid.

Other countries have been less concerned than the Soviet Union and the United States with aid for security purposes. They are more interested in promoting trade, cultural, or diplomatic ties.

France gives the most technical assistance because most of its aid goes to Africa, which lacks trained people. Belgium, Great Britain, Italy, and West Germany also supply much technical assistance.

The non-Communist countries coordinate their bilat-

Leading contributors of foreign aid

Contributor	Aid (In millions of U.S. dollars)	Aid as per cent of GNP*
United States	$9,403	0.24 %
France	3,995	0.78
Japan	3,797	0.29
Soviet Union	3,002	0.28
West Germany	2,942	0.47
Saudi Arabia	2,646	2.88
Canada	1,631	0.49
Great Britain	1,531	0.34
Netherlands	1,135	0.91
Italy	1,098	0.31
Sweden	840	0.86
Kuwait	749	3.16
Australia	749	0.49
Norway	575	1.03
Denmark	440	0.80
Belgium	438	0.54

Leading recipients of foreign aid

Recipient	Aid (In millions of U.S. dollars)	Aid as per cent of GNP*
India	$2,078	1.06 %
Israel	2,042	9.66
Egypt	1,951	6.06
Vietnam	1,393	7.53
Bangladesh	1,202	8.14
Sudan	1,136	15.46
China	963	0.30
Pakistan	960	2.65
Ethiopia	900	19.44
Morocco	890	6.65
Indonesia	868	1.00
Syria	746	4.37

*GNP = gross national product. The gross national product is the total value of goods and services produced by a country in a year.
Figures are for 1985. Sources: Organization for Economic Cooperation and Development; U.S. Central Intelligence Agency; World Bank.

eral aid through the Organization for Economic Cooperation and Development (OECD). The countries providing aid often negotiate as a group with aid-receiving countries to determine the size and use of aid programs.

Multilateral aid programs

About a fourth of all official foreign aid is multilateral. A large part of this aid is channeled through the United Nations and United Nations agencies. Most multilateral aid goes for development and technical assistance, and disaster relief. Multilateral agencies do not offer military aid.

Technical assistance and relief. United Nations technical assistance, refugee, and relief programs are financed mostly by contributions from member governments. A large share of these contributions goes to the United Nations Development Program (UNDP). The UNDP selects aid projects and distributes funds to various agencies to carry out the projects. Each agency also receives funds directly from member countries.

Five agencies carry out much of the UN's technical assistance work in developing countries. (1) The Food and Agriculture Organization of the United Nations (FAO) promotes agricultural development. (2) The United Nations Educational, Scientific and Cultural Organization (UNESCO) gives educational and scientific assistance. (3) The World Health Organization (WHO) helps countries improve their health services. (4) The United Nations

Children's Fund (UNICEF) helps fight children's diseases, and aids needy children and mothers. (5) The International Labor Organization (ILO) conducts labor training programs. Other agencies also give technical assistance to developing countries. The United Nations Industrial Development Organization (UNIDO) was formed in 1966 to give advice on industrial development. Other agencies aid refugees.

The United Nations Conference on Trade and Development (UNCTAD) does not give aid. But it serves as a forum for its members to frame aid and trade policies to benefit developing countries. For more information on most of the UN's specialized agencies, see **United Nations** (Specialized agencies).

Worldwide lending programs help developing countries finance development projects. The International Bank for Reconstruction and Development (World Bank), an independent UN agency, makes long-term loans to member governments at reasonable interest rates. The International Development Association (IDA), a World Bank affiliate, makes loans to the least developed member countries, allowing 50 years to repay at very low interest. Another World Bank affiliate, the International Finance Corporation (IFC), invests in private enterprises in developing countries.

Regional development programs aid poor countries in particular areas. The Inter-American Development Bank (IDB) makes long-term development loans to Latin American countries. Founded in 1959, the IDB is financed mainly by the U.S. government. Headquarters are in Washington, D.C. The Asian Development Bank, established in 1965, lends money to governments and private enterprises in Asia. The bank's original financing came mainly from the United States, Japan, India, and Australia. Headquarters are in Manila, the Philippines. The African Development Bank, financed by over 25 African countries, makes loans to promote economic and social development in Africa. Founded in 1964, the bank has headquarters in Abidjan, Ivory Coast.

Two agencies of the European Economic Community (EEC) aid developing countries. The Overseas Development Fund provides grants to associate members of the EEC in Africa. The EEC-sponsored European Investment Bank makes development loans to the African associates, and to Greece and Turkey.   W. Scott Thompson

Related articles in *World Book* include:

<table>
<tr><td>Agency for International Development</td><td>International Labor Organization</td></tr>
<tr><td>Alliance for Progress</td><td>International trade</td></tr>
<tr><td>Asian Development Bank</td><td>Lend-Lease</td></tr>
<tr><td>Developing country</td><td>Marshall Plan</td></tr>
<tr><td>European Community</td><td>Peace Corps</td></tr>
<tr><td>Export-Import Bank of the United States</td><td>Point Four Program</td></tr>
<tr><td>Food and Agriculture Organization</td><td>Technical assistance</td></tr>
<tr><td></td><td>UNESCO</td></tr>
<tr><td>Food for Peace</td><td>United Nations (Specialized agencies; Working for progress)</td></tr>
<tr><td>Foreign policy</td><td></td></tr>
<tr><td>International Development Association</td><td>World Bank</td></tr>
<tr><td></td><td>World Health Organization</td></tr>
<tr><td>International Finance Corporation</td><td></td></tr>
</table>

Additional resources

Mee, Charles L. *The Marshall Plan.* Simon & Schuster, 1984.
Rostow, Walt W. *Eisenhower, Kennedy, and Foreign Aid.* Univ. of Texas Press, 1985.

U.S. Foreign Assistance: Investment or Folly? Ed. by John Wilhelm and Gerry Feinstein. Praeger, 1984.
White, John A. *The Politics of Foreign Aid.* St. Martin's, 1974.

Foreign bill of exchange. See Economics (World finance).

Foreign correspondent reports the news from important places in other countries. Such reporters may work for a newspaper, magazine, press association, or radio or television network in their own country.

Increasing interest in international affairs has assured foreign correspondents a permanent place in American journalism. Their stories provide the most reliable public report of affairs in other nations. The press associations, Associated Press and United Press International, employ many of the foreign correspondents who report to American readers. Others are heard through major radio and television networks.

Foreign correspondents who have become best known are those who served during wars. Richard Harding Davis covered the Spanish-American War, the Boer War, the Russo-Japanese War, and the early part of World War I (see **Davis, Richard Harding**). In World War II, Ernie Pyle's columns from Great Britain, Africa, and Europe appeared in many papers. His columns were written in a simple, folksy style, and became highly popular (see **Pyle, Ernie**).

In early American newspapers, foreign news was copied from papers brought from other countries, mostly England. Merchant ships brought these papers. But there was little opportunity for really effective foreign correspondence until ocean cables became available after 1858. The invention of the wireless and the development of radio increased the demand for fast reporting of events abroad.   John Eldridge Drewry

See also **War correspondent.**

Foreign exchange. See Money (table: Exchange rates); **International trade** (Financing international trade); **Economics** (World finance).

Foreign language study. See Language (Learning a foreign language).

Foreign Legion is one of the world's most colorful and gallant fighting forces. The Legion is a unit of the French government and is called the *Légion Étrangère* in French. It consists of volunteers. Most Legionnaires come from countries other than France. Frenchmen are forbidden to join the Legion, but some enlist by giving false nationalities.

Men who apply for duty in the Legion must be between 18 and 40 years old. They must pass a strict physical examination to be accepted. Legionnaires enlist for five years.

The Legion does not make its records public, and an atmosphere of mystery, exaggeration, and glamor surrounds it. Some men join the Legion to escape political punishment, and others to seek adventure. Still others join to avoid punishment for crime. However, the Legion accepts no known criminals, and the number of criminals in the unit has been exaggerated in many fictional accounts. Doctors, lawyers, merchants, and priests have served in the Legion. Whatever their reasons for joining the force, the Legionnaires rank among the world's best soldiers.

Discipline in the Legion is harsh. But the unit never lacks recruits. About 350,000 men have served in the Legion. Today, it has about 8,000 members. Headquarters are in Aubagne, France, just outside Marseille.

Louis Philippe created the Legion in 1831, for service outside France. Its original purposes were to offer a haven for foreign mercenaries serving in the Swiss Guard, and to assist in the conquest of Algeria. A total of 4,000 men, most of them Poles, Spaniards, Germans, and Italians, were organized into nationalistic battalions. Each group spoke its own language. The Legion's flag then, as now, was the tricolor, on which appears a globe marked *France* and the words: "The King of the French to the Foreign Legion."

The Legion's most famous uniform consisted of baggy red trousers and a high-collar blue coat. During World War I, the Legion wore the blue of the French army. Shortly after the war, it adopted the present khaki uniform. The Legion's insignia is a small red grenade that spouts seven flames.

The Legion has served most frequently in colonial wars. But it has also participated in France's major wars. After its work in Algeria, it fought for Spain in the Carlist War of 1835. Only 500 men survived the three years in Spain and returned to Algeria. For the next 50 years, the Legion was involved in subduing and making peace with the people of Algeria and Morocco. When it was not fighting, it was erecting buildings. Legionnaires constructed the first European-style buildings in almost every city in North Africa. During these 50 years, the Legion also fought elsewhere, and underwent organizational changes.

In 1854, two regiments fought in the Crimean War. About 450 Legionnaires were killed in the war. In 1859, two regiments fought the Austrians in Italy, in an attempt to revive France's empire. Nearly 150 Legionnaires died in the campaign. In 1863, Napoleon III involved the Legion in another desperate and hopeless cause. The Legion formed part of the French army sent to Mexico to support Maximilian's attempt to seize authority in that country. In that campaign, which lasted until 1867, the Legion lost about 470 men.

A handful of Legionnaires bravely fought the Battle of Camerone in Mexico on April 30, 1863. The date of that battle is considered the sacred date of the corps, and Legionnaires throughout the world observe it each year. They conduct memorial services, and retell the story of the men who withstood the assaults of 2,000 enemy soldiers and refused to surrender. Of the last six Legionnaires who made a final bayonet charge, three survived and were captured. The officer in charge lost his wooden hand. It now rests in a place of honor in the Legion's Hall of Fame in Aubagne, France.

When Germany invaded France in 1870, the Legion sent help to the mother country. Their capture of Orléans was the only bright spot in the tale of French resistance. In 1885, four battalions went to Indochina to protect that colony against local uprisings. After successfully accomplishing this mission, the units were organized into the Fifth Regiment, and stationed permanently in Indochina.

During World War I (1914-1918), the first two regiments of the Legion supplied four other regiments for service in France. About 45,000 Legionnaires fought Germany. Of these, nearly 31,000 were killed, wounded, or missing in action. As a result of its gallant actions, the Legion became one of the most decorated French military units of World War I.

In World War II (1939-1945), Legionnaires served in many parts of the world. At first, they fought the Japanese in Indochina, and against Nazi Germany in France and Norway. Later, some units fought for Vichy France. But most units joined General Charles de Gaulle and served in North Africa, France, and Germany.

After World War II, the Legion again became a haven for political refugees and former soldiers, particularly Germans. With up-to-date equipment, it was again called upon to fight in Indochina from 1946 to 1954, this time against Communist rebels. The Legion sparked the final heroic resistance at Dien Bien Phu. When Algeria became independent in 1962, Legion headquarters moved from Sidi Bel Abbès, Algeria, to Aubagne, France. Through the years, most of the Legion's units moved out of Africa. In 1984, one unit serving in Lebanon was the target of Muslim terrorist attacks. Today, the majority of the units are stationed in France and the Pacific islands controlled by France.   Charles Mercer

Additional resources

Wellard, James H. *The French Foreign Legion.* Little, Brown, 1974.
Young, John R. *The French Foreign Legion: The Inside Story of the World-Famous Fighting Force.* 2nd ed. Thames & Hudson, 1985.

Foreign office. See Diplomacy.

Foreign policy refers to the relations of a nation with other nations in an attempt to achieve a set of objectives. The nation ordinarily seeks to gain these objectives by *diplomacy* (official negotiations between states). But it may also try to secure them through war. The announced aims of a nation are usually peace, security, and justice. But each country judges what these objectives mean in its own case.

A nation usually has several broad aims which remain the same even though its political parties or its form of government may change. French foreign policy has traditionally been concerned with the security of the country's northeast frontiers, often endangered by German attack. Great Britain tried to maintain a balance of power in Europe during the late 1800's and early 1900's. A cornerstone of United States foreign policy since 1823 has been the Monroe Doctrine, a policy designed to prevent European interference in the affairs of North America and South America (see **Monroe Doctrine**). After World War II ended in 1945, the containment policy of the United States tried to prevent Communist expansion (see **Cold War**).

Influences on foreign policy

Broad national objectives have to be supported by specific actions. Shaping foreign policy involves a series of choices among a variety of alternative possible courses. Foreign policy is a continuous process, because each new step depends on former action and the changes it causes in the behavior of other nations.

Alliances. All countries need the cooperation of other nations. They continually modify their own policies in order to obtain and preserve allies. For example, after World War II, the United States needed the cooperation of European nations in trying to "contain" the Soviet Union. It tried to strengthen countries which shared the American interest in halting the spread of Soviet Communism. The United States offered economic aid to war-devastated Western Europe through the Marshall Plan and other programs of foreign aid. The United States also entered an alliance of western democracies, the North Atlantic Treaty Organization (NATO). The Soviet Union in turn reacted to the joint activities of the Western nations, and Soviet moves then required shifts in American policies.

The foreign policies of allies may conflict with each other when put into practice. For instance, the traditional American attitude against colonialism sometimes created tensions when the United States had to work with other powers that had colonies.

Domestic policies sometimes interfere with foreign policy. For example, United States farm programs have unintentionally produced great surpluses of some commodities. The United States has disposed of some surpluses abroad at far below the world market price. This action has caused friction between the United States and some of its allies whose economies depend on the export of the same commodities.

Historical and social traditions in a country play a large part in its foreign policy. For example, Canadian foreign policy differs from that of the United States, even though both are English-speaking democracies with a long record as good neighbors. Until 1931, Canada was a part of the British Empire. Therefore, Canadians have been more concerned about European affairs, and less interested in the Far East than have Americans. Social relations in a country also make a difference in its foreign policy. Canada has two peoples, English- and French-speaking. Its government must act so as not to antagonize the large French minority, which is traditionally more "isolationist."

Economic factors also enter into foreign policy. Canada's economy depends greatly on the export of products from its fields, forests, and mines. When Canada was still in the process of industrializing, trade questions were more important in Canadian foreign policy than in that of the United States. But by the 1970's, with many countries industrializing and competing with the United States, trade questions once again became prominent in U.S. foreign policy. This was particularly evident in U.S.-Japan relations during the 1980's.

Shaping foreign policy

The executive takes the initiative in shaping a nation's foreign policy because the state must speak with one voice. The chief executive receives advice from the foreign minister and the foreign office. The Department of State aids the President of the United States. The Ministry of External Affairs serves this function in Canada. The foreign service of the executive branch provides information and carries out the policy. Other executive departments, such as defense and treasury, participate in foreign policy to some extent.

The legislature can usually approve or disapprove of actions already taken by the administration. The American governmental system is based on a separation of powers. For this reason, policymaking is more difficult in the United States than in many other democracies. The United States Senate must agree by a two-thirds vote to treaties concluded by the President. The

House of Representatives, as well as the Senate, must approve of expenditures made to carry out foreign policy.

Public opinion plays a role in both democratic and totalitarian societies. In dictatorships, the person or persons heading the government can make rapid decisions without immediate need to secure popular consent. Americans historically favored a policy of isolationism. Such a policy worked during the 1800's because European nations were too occupied with conflicts among themselves to be able to threaten North America. But after U.S. involvement in two world wars, American leaders were able to convince the American people that the United States should abandon isolationism and act as a great power. Since World War II, American public opinion has generally supported worldwide foreign commitments. An exception was the Vietnam War (1957-1975), which cooled popular support for foreign commitments for about 10 years after it ended.

Many nations try to reach beyond foreign governments directly to the people. A country's information services carry out such programs. The United States Voice of America broadcasts to many countries, including the Soviet Union. Economic aid and technical assistance programs, student and teacher exchanges, and the Peace Corps program are other means used by the U.S. government to build good will overseas.

Other factors directly or indirectly shape foreign policy. No government can long uphold a foreign policy that does not balance with the nation's capabilities. Its power to carry out a policy depends on resources and geographical location, and on the education, skills, and loyalty of the people. Policymakers must also consider a country's military strength, its experience in diplomacy, and its ability to win support from the governments of other nations.   Michael P. Sullivan

Related articles. See the *History* section of the country articles, such as **France** (History). See also **Canada, History of; United States, History of the.** See also:

Council on Foreign Relations	Foreign Service
Diplomacy	International law
Foreign aid	International relations
Foreign Policy Association	International trade

Foreign Policy Association (FPA) is a national organization whose purpose is to increase the interest and understanding of Americans in world affairs. The FPA works independently of the government and of political parties. It sponsors the annual *Great Decisions* program, in which participants study and discuss eight major foreign policy issues.

The FPA publishes *Headline Series* five times a year. Each of these booklets contains analyses of major foreign policy problems and world areas written by experts. The association also publishes "Foreign Policy Briefs" for candidates and voters during presidential election years. The briefs discuss the foreign policy issues of special concern to the nation.

The FPA was founded in 1918. It is financed by individuals, corporations, and foundations, and by the sale of its publications and services. It has national headquarters at 205 Lexington Avenue, New York, NY 10016.

Critically reviewed by the Foreign Policy Association

Foreign relations. See Foreign policy; International relations.

Foreign Service is the principal organization through which the international affairs of the United States government are conducted. The Foreign Service is administered by the U.S. Department of State and other American government agencies that are directly involved in foreign affairs. The service provides trained personnel for United States embassies and consulates in other countries. Members of the Foreign Service also fill many positions in the Department of State in Washington, D.C.

Service

Foreign Service posts abroad fall into two categories—*diplomatic* and *consular.* Chiefs of diplomatic missions, or embassies, are appointed by the President and accredited to the chief of state of the host country. An ambassador heads the embassy. He or she is a personal representative of the President of the United States. Consular officers assist American citizens abroad and handle United States business and commercial affairs overseas. Consular officers are not accredited to the host government and cannot represent the President.

Members of the Foreign Service perform administrative work in U.S. embassies, mission, and consulates; negotiate with government officials of other countries; report to the U.S. Department of State on economic, political, and social conditions; issue passports and visas; protect the interests and welfare of U.S. citizens abroad; and interpret U.S. policies to governments and citizens of other countries. Some members of the Foreign Service perform specialized tasks in economics, international commercial and labor affairs, and administration.

Most newly appointed Foreign Service officers receive orientation at the Foreign Service Institute (FSI) in Washington, D.C., before they are sent abroad. The institute teaches the languages and customs of other countries, gives advanced instruction in foreign affairs, and provides training in specialized activities of the Foreign Service. Senior Foreign Service officers often go back to the institute for special training before starting new assignments. The institute also offers courses for the spouses and dependents of Foreign Service officers and other government officials who work overseas.

Foreign Service personnel serving overseas may receive allowances for living expenses if government-owned quarters are not available. They may also receive allowances for travel and official entertainment. The government may provide additional living expenses for personnel in cities where the cost-of-living index is higher than in Washington, D.C. Most Foreign Service employees serve overseas for periods of five to seven years out of every ten years. On assignments of this length, the government provides home leave at its own expense after two to three years.

Personnel

There are approximately 14,000 persons in the Foreign Service. About 8,000 work in the United States. Many of them work at the Department of State in Washington, and many others work for such agencies as the Agency for International Development, the Department of Agriculture, and the Department of Commerce. The rest serve in other countries. Foreign Service personnel receive their appointments on a merit basis. Consideration is also given to geographic distribution and to the recruitment of women and members of minority groups so that the work force of the Foreign Service is broadly representative of the American people.

There are three main classifications of Foreign Service personnel: (1) Foreign Service Officers, (2) Senior Foreign Service Officers, and (3) Foreign Service Specialists.

Foreign Service officers are appointed by the President with the advice and consent of the U.S. Senate. They are assigned positions both in the United States and abroad. These positions are in administrative, consular, economic, and political fields. They are graded from Class 6, the entry level position, up to Class 1. Salary ranges for each class increase at higher grades. After teaching Class 1, Foreign Service officers are considered for promotion into the Senior Foreign Service.

Applicants to the Foreign Service must be United States citizens. They also must be at least 21 years old—or 20, if they have already completed their junior year of college. There is no upper age limit, but applicants must be able to complete at least one tour of duty before the required retirement of 65. A tour of duty lasts about two or three years.

Appointments to the Foreign Service are made on a competitive basis. Candidates must first take a written examination. The test is given once each year in December in about 150 cities in the United States and at U.S. embassies and consulates. Candidates who pass the written examination qualify for a one-day *assessment* (evaluation). During the assessment, candidates are judged on their creativity and communication skills, and on their ability to work with others and analyze ideas and problems. Candidates given further consideration go through a background investigation and medical examination. Dependents who would accompany selected candidates abroad must also pass a medical examination.

After completing these steps, the candidates receive a final evaluation. The names of the candidates who pass are listed in order of their scores. Candidates ordinarily receive appointments according to their rank on the list and as vacancies occur. They generally start at the Class 6 or 5 levels.

The secretary of state at times appoints new Foreign Service officers to meet special needs. Such appointments cannot last more than five years. Salaries of the specialists appointed by the secretary of state follow the same structure as the salaries of other Foreign Service officers.

Senior Foreign Service officers are also appointed by the President with the advice and consent of the Senate. There are three regular classes of Senior Foreign Service personnel—counselor, minister-counselor, and career minister. Officers in these classes all rank above Foreign Service officers in Class 1. Members of the Senior Foreign Service excel in management and the development of policy. They also have wide knowledge in the culture, economics, history, and language of various nations.

Foreign Service specialists are appointed by the secretary of state. They include secretaries, clerks, security officers, and other service employees in the Foreign Service and agencies that deal with international affairs.

History

Beginnings. In the early years of the United States, many people took seriously the advice of President George Washington to avoid foreign entanglements, and opposed having any representation abroad. This opposition was so great that even the highest-ranking American diplomats sent abroad held only the rank of minister, instead of ambassador. Such a diplomat often carried only the title of *chargé d'affaires.*

Early diplomats of the United States included Benjamin Franklin, Thomas Jefferson, John Adams, John Jay, and James Monroe. In those early years, ministers had to pay their own travel expenses, provide their own living quarters, and hire their own secretaries. However, in spite of the low respect diplomats received, four of the first six United States presidents had a diplomatic background.

The *spoils system,* or appointment and promotion on a political basis, dominated the Foreign Service throughout the 1800's and the early 1900's. United States representation abroad consisted mainly of untrained personnel. Diplomatic positions served as rewards for service, and frequently went to unqualified political associates and wealthy people who were campaign contributors.

The Rogers Act. World War I imposed new responsibilities on the Foreign Service, and brought about substantial reforms. In 1924, John Jacob Rogers, a Massachusetts congressman, succeeded in legislating improvements in the Foreign Service through the Rogers Act, the basis of the present U.S. Foreign Service. This act combined the consular and diplomatic branches of the Foreign Service. The act also established difficult competitive examinations for Foreign Service career officers, and put promotion on a merit, rather than a political, basis. The act established the first retirement and disability pay system. It also installed the system of extra allowances so that competent people without private fortunes could accept overseas appointments in the Foreign Service.

After World War II, greater changes occurred in the Foreign Service. Many stemmed from the Foreign Service Act of 1946. This legislation gave ambassadors and ministers their first pay raises in nearly 100 years. It raised pay levels generally, and set up a new class system for the Foreign Service.

The Foreign Service Act of 1980 led to other significant changes. It established the Senior Foreign Service and increased Foreign Service salaries to bring them in line with those of the same classes in the United States Civil Service. In addition, the act set up an office to improve job placement for spouses of Foreign Service members, and improved retirement and survivors benefits for such spouses.

Many top-ranking ambassadors still receive appointments on political grounds. But at least two-thirds of the chiefs of overseas posts have advanced through the Foreign Service ranks.

Critically reviewed by the Department of State

See also **Consul; Diplomacy; Diplomatic corps; State, Department of.**

Foreign trade. See **International trade.**

Foreign trade zone is an area in the United States where importers may store, exhibit, and process foreign goods without paying *customs duties* (import taxes). The zones are policed by the U.S. Customs Service. Customs officials collect duty only if the goods entering the United States are to be used or sold. If the goods are exported directly from the foreign trade zones, no duty is paid. In other countries, foreign trade zones are sometimes called *free trade zones* or *free ports* (see **Free trade zone**).

The United States has foreign trade zones in about 30 of its almost 300 *ports of entry.* Ports of entry are cities with customs facilities where goods may enter the country legally. The Foreign-Trade Zones Board—made up of the secretaries of commerce, the treasury, and the army—administers the zones. The board was established in 1934. An executive secretary in the Department of Commerce directs the program for the Foreign-Trade Zones Board.   Robert M. Stern

Foreman, George (1949-   ), an American boxer, was the world heavyweight champion from January 1973, to October 1974. He won the title with an upset victory over Joe Frazier, the previous champion. Foreman lost the title when he was knocked out by Muhammad Ali. The defeat was Foreman's first after 40 straight victories, 37 of them by knockout, since he turned professional in 1969.

George Edward Foreman was born in Marshall, Tex. He dropped out of high school in Houston and, in 1965, joined the Job Corps, a government program for training unemployed youths. He learned how to box in the Job Corps. Foreman first became famous for winning the heavyweight championship at the 1968 Olympic Games. Foreman retired from boxing in 1977, but resumed his fighting career in 1987.

Wide World

George Foreman

Herman Weiskopf

Forensic ballistics. See **Ballistics** (Forensic ballistics).

Forensic science. See **Crime laboratory.**

Foreordination, *FAWR awr duh NAY shuhn,* is the belief that every event is *foreordained,* or decreed beforehand, by God. Supporters of this doctrine argue that if God does not ordain every event, He cannot be said to be all-powerful. Foreordination in its extreme form teaches that, by God's mysterious choice, some people are destined for hell and other people are destined for heaven.

Many religious traditions have taught some form of foreordination. But it is most often associated with John Calvin, whose ideas influenced the Congregationalists, Baptists, Presbyterians, and Episcopalians (see **Calvin, John**). In recent years, most churches have moderated or ceased to emphasize the doctrine of foreordination.

Jonathan Z. Smith

See also **Predestination.**

Jerry Frank, DPI

Robert Frerck, Dimensions

Jacques Jangoux

Tropical rain forest　　　　　**Tropical seasonal forest**　　　　　**Savanna**

Different kinds of forests grow in different parts of the world. Many scientists divide the world's forests into the six main *formations* (types) shown in the photographs above and on the next page. The forests that make up each formation have similar plant and animal life.

Forest

Forest is a large area of land covered with trees. But a forest is much more than just trees. It also includes smaller plants, such as mosses, shrubs, and wild flowers. In addition, many kinds of birds, insects, and other animals make their home in the forest. Millions upon millions of living things that can only be seen under a microscope also live in the forest.

Climate, soil, and water determine the kinds of plants and animals that can live in a forest. The living things and their environment together make up the forest *ecosystem.* An ecosystem consists of all the living and nonliving things in a particular area and the relationships among them.

The forest ecosystem is highly complicated. The trees and other green plants use sunlight to make their own food from the air and from water and minerals in the soil. The plants themselves serve as food for certain animals. These animals, in turn, are eaten by other animals. After plants and animals die, their remains are broken down by bacteria and other organisms, such as protozoans and fungi. This process returns minerals to the soil, where they can again be used by green plants to make food.

Although individual members of the ecosystem die,

Paul F. Maycock, the contributor of this article, is Professor of Botany at Erindale College, University of Toronto.

the forest itself lives on. If the forest is wisely managed, it provides us with a continuous source of wood and many other products.

Before people began to clear the forests for farms and cities, great stretches of forestland covered about 60 per cent of the earth's land area. Today, forests occupy about 30 per cent of the land. The forests differ greatly from one part of the world to another. For example, the steamy, vine-choked rain forests of central Africa are far different from the cool, towering spruce and fir forests of northern Canada.

This article provides general information on the importance of forests and describes their structure. It also discusses the major kinds of forests in the world and in the United States and Canada. Finally, the article describes how forests function as an ecosystem and how they have changed and developed through the ages. For detailed information on forest products and forest management, see the articles **Forest products** and **Forestry.**

The importance of forests

Forests have always had great importance to human beings. Prehistoric people got their food mainly by hunting and by gathering wild plants. Many of these people lived in the forest and were a natural part of it. With the development of civilization, people settled in towns and cities. But they still returned to the forest to get timber and to hunt.

Today, people depend on forests more than ever, especially for their (1) economic value, (2) environmental value, and (3) enjoyment value. The science of forestry is

Jen and Des Bartlett, Bruce Coleman Inc.

Ray Atkeson, DPI

Jacques Jangoux

Temperate deciduous forest   **Temperate evergreen forest**   **Boreal forest**

concerned with increasing and preserving these values by careful management of forestland.

Economic value. Forests supply many products. Wood from forest trees provides lumber, plywood, railroad ties, and shingles. It is also used in making furniture, tool handles, and thousands of other products. In many parts of the world, wood serves as the chief fuel for cooking and heating.

Various manufacturing processes change wood into a great number of different products. Paper is one of the most valuable products made from wood. Other processed wood products include cellophane, plastics, and such fibers as rayon and acetate.

Forests provide many important products besides wood. Latex, which is used in making rubber, and turpentine come from forest trees. Various fats, gums, oils, and waxes used in manufacturing also come from trees. In some primitive societies, forest plants and animals make up a large part of the people's diet.

Unlike most other natural resources, such as coal, oil, and mineral deposits, forest resources are renewable. As long as there are forests, people can count on a steady supply of forest products.

Environmental value. Forests help conserve and enrich the environment in several ways. For example, forest soil soaks up large amounts of rainfall. It thus prevents the rapid runoff of water that can cause erosion and flooding. In addition, rain is filtered as it passes through the soil and becomes *ground water.* This ground water flows through the ground and provides a clean, fresh source of water for streams, lakes, and wells.

Forest plants, like all green plants, help renew the atmosphere. As the trees and other green plants make food, they give off oxygen. They also remove carbon dioxide from the air. People and nearly all other living things require oxygen. If green plants did not continuously renew the oxygen supply, almost all life would soon stop. If carbon dioxide increases in the atmosphere, it could severely alter the earth's climate.

Forests also provide a home for many plants and animals that can live nowhere else. Without the forest, many kinds of wildlife could not exist.

Enjoyment value. The natural beauty and peace of the forest offer a special source of enjoyment. In the United States, Canada, and many other countries, huge forestlands have been set aside for people's enjoyment. Many people use these forests for such activities as camping, hiking, and hunting. Others visit them simply to enjoy the scenery and relax in the quiet beauty.

The structure of forests

Every forest has various *strata* (layers) of plants. The five basic forest strata, from highest to lowest, are (1) the canopy, (2) the understory, (3) the shrub layer, (4) the herb layer, and (5) the forest floor.

The canopy consists mainly of the *crowns* (branches and leaves) of the tallest trees. The most common trees in the canopy are called the *dominant* trees of the forest. Certain plants, especially climbing vines and epiphytes, may grow in the canopy. *Epiphytes* are plants that grow on other plants for support but absorb from the air the water and other materials they need to make food.

The canopy receives full sunlight. As a result, it produces more food than does any other layer. In some forests, the canopy is so dense it almost forms a roof over the forest. Fruit-eating birds, and insects and mammals that eat leaves or fruit, live in the canopy.

The understory is made up of trees shorter than those of the canopy. Some of these trees are smaller species that grow well in the shade of the canopy. Others are young trees that may in time join the canopy layer. Because the understory grows in shade, it is not as productive as the canopy. However, the understory provides food and shelter for many forest animals.

The shrub layer consists mainly of shrubs. Shrubs, like trees, have woody stems. But unlike trees, they have more than one stem, and none of the stems grows as tall as a tree. Forests with a dense canopy and understory may have only a spotty shrub layer. The trees in such forests filter out so much light that few shrubs can grow beneath them. Most forests with a more open canopy and understory have heavy shrub growth. Many birds and insects live in the shrub layer.

The herb layer consists of ferns, grasses, wild flowers, and other soft-stemmed plants. Tree seedlings also make up part of this layer. Like the shrub layer, the herb layer grows thickest in forests with a more open canopy and understory. Yet even in forests with dense tree layers, enough sunlight reaches the ground to support some herb growth. The herb layer is the home of forest animals that live on the ground. They include such small animals as insects, mice, snakes, turtles, and ground-nesting birds and such large animals as bears and deer.

The forest floor is covered with mats of moss and with the wastes from the upper layers. Leaves, twigs, and animal droppings—as well as dead animals and plants—build up on the forest floor. Among these wastes, an incredible number of small organisms can be found. They include earthworms, fungi, insects, and spiders, plus countless bacteria and other microscopic life. All these organisms break down the waste materials into the basic chemical elements necessary for new plant growth.

Kinds of forests

Many systems are used to classify the world's forests. Some systems classify a forest according to the characteristics of its dominant trees. A *needleleaf forest,* for example, consists of a forest in which the dominant trees have long, narrow, needlelike leaves. Such forests are also called *coniferous* (cone-bearing) because the trees bear cones. The seeds grow in these cones. A *broadleaf forest* is made up mainly of trees with broad, flat leaves. Forests in which the dominant trees shed all their leaves during certain seasons of the year, and then grow new ones, are classed as *deciduous forests.* In an *evergreen forest,* the dominant trees shed old leaves and grow new ones continuously and so remain green throughout the year.

In some other systems, forests are classified according to the usable qualities of the trees. A forest of broadleaf trees may be classed as a *hardwood forest* because most broadleaf trees have hard wood, which makes fine furniture. A forest of needleleaf trees may be classed as a *softwood forest* because most needleleaf trees have softer wood than broadleaf trees have.

Many scientists classify forests according to various *ecological systems.* Under such systems, forests with similar climate, soil, and amounts of moisture are grouped into *formations.* Climate, soil, and moisture determine the kinds of trees found in a forest formation.

The structure of the forest

Every forest has various *strata* (layers) of plants. The five basic strata, from highest to lowest, are (1) the canopy, (2) the understory, (3) the shrub layer, (4) the herb layer, and (5) the forest floor. This illustration shows the strata as they might appear in a temperate deciduous forest.

WORLD BOOK illustration by Jean Helmer

Canopy

Understory

Shrub Layer

Herb Layer

Forest Floor

One common ecological system groups the world's forests into six major formations. They are (1) tropical rain forests, (2) tropical seasonal forests, (3) temperate deciduous forests, (4) temperate evergreen forests, (5) boreal forests, and (6) savannas.

Tropical rain forests grow near the equator, where the climate is warm and wet the year around. The largest of these forests grow in the Amazon River Basin of South America, the Congo River Basin of Africa, and throughout much of Southeast Asia.

Of the six forest formations, tropical rain forests have the greatest variety of trees. As many as 100 species—none of which is dominant—may grow in 1 square mile (2.6 square kilometers) of land. Nearly all the trees of tropical rain forests are broadleaf evergreens, though some palm trees and tree ferns can also be found. In most of the forests, the trees form three canopies. The upper canopy reaches about 150 feet (46 meters) high. A few exceptionally tall trees, called *emergents,* tower above the upper canopy. The understory trees form the two lower canopies.

The shrub and herb layers are thin because little sunlight penetrates the dense canopies. However, many climbing plants and epiphytes crowd the branches of the canopies, where the sunlight is fullest.

Most of the animals of the tropical rain forests also live in the canopies, where they can find plentiful food. These animals include such flying or climbing creatures as bats, birds, insects, lizards, mice, monkeys, opossums, sloths, and snakes.

Tropical seasonal forests grow in certain regions of the tropics and subtropics. These regions have a definite wet and dry season each year or a somewhat cooler climate than that of the tropical rain forest. Such conditions occur in Central America, central South America, southern Africa, India, eastern China, and northern Australia and on many islands in the Pacific Ocean.

Tropical seasonal forests have a great variety of tree species, though not nearly as many as the rain forests. They also have fewer climbing plants and epiphytes. Unlike the trees of the rain forest, many tropical seasonal species are deciduous. The deciduous trees are found especially in regions with distinct wet and dry seasons. The trees shed their leaves in the dry season.

Tropical seasonal forests have a canopy about 100 feet (30 meters) high. One understory grows beneath the canopy. Bamboos and palms form a dense shrub layer, and a thick herb layer blankets the ground. The animal life resembles that of the rain forest.

Temperate deciduous forests grow in eastern North America, western Europe, and eastern Asia. These regions have a *temperate* climate, with warm summers and cold winters.

The canopy of temperate deciduous forests is about 100 feet (30 meters) high. Two or more kinds of trees dominate the canopy. Most of the trees in these forests are broadleaf and deciduous. They shed their leaves in fall. The understory, shrub, and herb layers may be dense. The herb layer has two growing periods each year. Plants of the first growth appear in early spring, before the trees have developed new leaves. These plants die by summer and are replaced by plants that grow in the shade of the leafy canopy.

Large animals of the temperate deciduous forests include bears, deer, and, rarely, wolves. These forests are also the home of hundreds of smaller mammals and birds. Many of the birds migrate south in fall, and some of the mammals hibernate during the winter.

Some temperate areas support mixed deciduous and evergreen forests. In the Great Lakes region of North America, for example, the cold winters promote the growth of heavily mixed forests of deciduous and evergreen trees. Forests of evergreen pine and deciduous oak and hickory grow on the dry coastal plains of the Southeastern United States.

Temperate evergreen forests. In some temperate regions, the environment favors the growth of evergreen forests. Such forests grow along coastal areas that have mild winters with heavy rainfall. These areas include the northwest coast of North America, the south coast of Chile, the west coast of New Zealand, and the southeast coast of Australia. Temperate evergreen forests also cover the lower mountain slopes in Asia, Europe, and western North America. In these regions, the cool climate favors the growth of evergreen trees.

The strata and the plant and animal life vary greatly from one temperate evergreen forest to another. For ex-

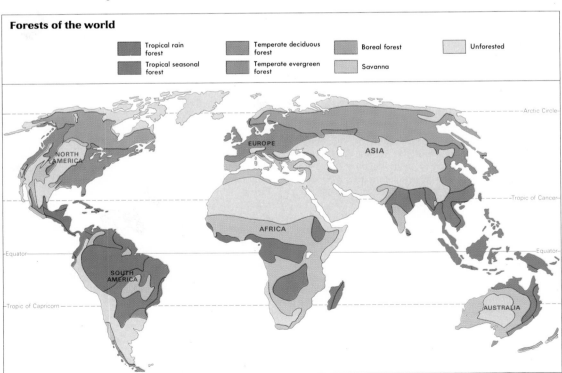

Forests of the world

Tropical rain forest • Temperate deciduous forest • Boreal forest • Unforested

Tropical seasonal forest • Temperate evergreen forest • Savanna

WORLD BOOK map: adapted from *Physical Elements of Geography* by Trewartha, Robinson, and Hammond. Copyright © 1967 by McGraw-Hill, Inc. Used with permission of McGraw-Hill Book Company.

ample, the mountainous evergreen forests of Asia, Europe, and North America are made up of conifers. The coastal forests of Australia and New Zealand, on the other hand, consist of broadleaf evergreen trees.

Boreal forests are found in regions that have an extremely cold winter and a short growing season. The word *boreal* means *northern.* Vast boreal forests stretch across northern Europe, Asia, and North America. Similar forests also cover the higher mountain slopes on these continents.

Boreal forests, which are also called *taiga,* have the simplest structure of all forest formations. They have only one uneven layer of trees, which reaches up to about 75 feet (23 meters) high. In most of the boreal forests, the dominant trees are needleleaf evergreens—either spruce and fir or spruce and pine. The shrub layer is spotty. However, mosses and lichens form a thick layer on the forest floor and also grow on the tree trunks and branches. There are few herbs.

Many small mammals, such as beavers, mice, porcupines, and snowshoe hares, live in the boreal forests. Larger mammals include bears, caribou, foxes, moose, and wolves. Birds of the boreal forests include ducks, loons, owls, warblers, and woodpeckers.

Savannas are areas of widely spaced trees. In some savannas, the trees grow in clumps. In others, individual trees grow throughout the area, forming an uneven, widely open canopy. In either case, most of the ground is covered by shrubs and herbs, especially grasses. As a result, some biologists classify savannas as grasslands. Savannas are found in regions where low rainfall, poor soil, frequent fires, or other environmental features limit tree growth.

The largest savannas are tropical savannas. They grow throughout much of Central America, Brazil, Africa, India, Southeast Asia, and Australia. Animals of the tropical savannas include giraffes, lions, tigers, and zebras.

Temperate savannas, also called *woodlands,* grow in the United States, Canada, Mexico, and Cuba. They have such animals as bears, deer, elk, and pumas.

Forests of the United States and Canada

The United States and Canada are rich in forests. Before the first white settlers arrived in the 1600's, forests covered most of the land from the Atlantic Ocean to the Mississippi River. Altogether, nearly 40 per cent of the land north of Mexico was forested at that time. More than half this forestland was in Canada and Alaska, where only a small portion has been cleared. Even in the lower United States, forests still grow on much of the original forestland. Today, the United States, excluding Hawaii, has about 753 million acres (305 million hectares) of forests. Canada has about 796 million acres (322 million hectares). In both countries, forests cover about a third of the land area.

The forests of the United States and Canada include all the major formations discussed in the previous section, except for tropical rain forests. The U.S.-Canadian forests can be divided into many smaller formations. One common system recognizes nine U.S.-Canadian formations. They are (1) subtropical forests, (2) southern deciduous-evergreen forests, (3) deciduous forests, (4) northern deciduous-evergreen forests, (5) temperate savannas, (6) mountain evergreen forests, (7) Pacific coastal forests, (8) boreal forests, and (9) subarctic woodlands.

Subtropical forests thrive along the coasts of the Atlantic Ocean and the Gulf of Mexico in the Southeastern United States. In these regions, the climate stays hot and humid throughout the year.

In southern Florida, raised areas of the swampy Everglades support forests of live oak, mahogany, and sabal palm. These forests have a dense undergrowth of ferns, shrubs, and small trees. Epiphytes and vines crowd the branches of the taller trees. Broadleaf-evergreen forests grow farther north, along the edges of the Atlantic and Gulf coasts. The dominant trees in these forests are bay, holly, live oak, and magnolia. Thick growths of Spanish moss, an epiphyte that looks like long gray hair, hang from the branches.

Southern deciduous-evergreen forests grow on the flat, sandy coastal plains of the Southeastern United States. The forests extend along the Atlantic Coastal Plain from New Jersey to Florida and along the Gulf Coastal Plain from Florida to Texas. These regions have long, hot summers and short winters.

Most of the forests consist of evergreen pine and deciduous oak. Pitch pine is the most common evergreen in the northern part of these forests. Going southward, pitch pine is replaced, in order, by loblolly, longleaf, and slash pine.

Deciduous forests occupy a region bounded by the coastal plains on the south and east, the Great Lakes on the north, and the Great Plains on the west. This region has dependable rainfall and distinct seasons. Severe frosts and heavy snows occur during winter in the northern parts of this formation.

The northern part of the deciduous forest region was once covered by glaciers. But the glaciers did not reach the southern portion, which has the oldest and richest deciduous forest in North America. This forest lies in the central Appalachian Mountains region. The dominant trees of the forest include ash, basswood, beech, buckeye, cucumber magnolia, hickory, sugar maple, yellow poplar, and several kinds of oaks.

In most deciduous forests outside the central Appalachians, fewer species of trees dominate. For example, various kinds of oaks dominate the forests from southern New England to northwestern Georgia. Hickory and tulip trees—and in drier areas several species of pine—grow among the oak trees. Beech and sugar maple trees dominate the northeastern and north-central deciduous forests. However, these forests also have many other kinds of trees, such as black cherry, red maple, red oak, and white elm. The northwestern deciduous forests are dominated by basswood and maple. Some oak trees also grow in these forests.

Northern deciduous-evergreen forests stretch from the Great Lakes across southeastern Canada and northern New York and New England. In this region of cold winters and warm summers, deciduous trees of the south are mixed with conifers of the north.

The dominant evergreens throughout much of this region include white-cedar, hemlock, and jack, red, and white pine. The chief broadleaf species include basswood, beech, sugar maple, white ash, and yellow birch. In moist areas, hemlock and white-cedar grow in mixed stands with black ash and white elm. Drier areas have forests of red and white pine, which is mixed with some

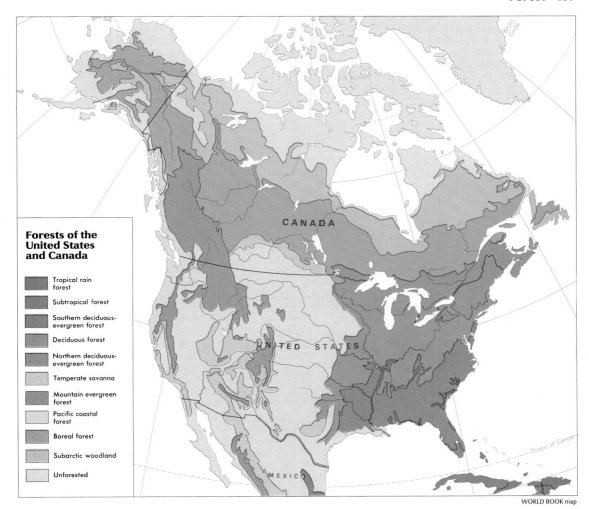

Forests of the United States and Canada

- Tropical rain forest
- Subtropical forest
- Southern deciduous-evergreen forest
- Deciduous forest
- Northern deciduous-evergreen forest
- Temperate savanna
- Mountain evergreen forest
- Pacific coastal forest
- Boreal forest
- Subarctic woodland
- Unforested

CANADA

UNITED STATES

MEXICO

WORLD BOOK map

ironwood and red oak. Areas that are neither especially dry nor moist support maple or beech forests. The region's swamps are covered with black spruce and larch.

Temperate savannas are found in areas of Canada and the United States that have fairly light annual rainfall and a long season of dryness. Temperate savannas dominated by aspen grow in North Dakota, Manitoba, Saskatchewan, and Alberta. Outside this region, oak, pine, or both oak and pine dominate the temperate savannas of North America. Savannas of bur oak, mixed in some areas with other oaks or hickory, extend in a belt from Manitoba through Texas. Coniferous savannas of juniper and piñon pine cover the dry foothills of the mountainous regions of the Southwestern United States from Texas to Arizona, and the southern half of Mexico. In California, the foothills of the Sierra Nevada have similar savannas of blue oak and digger pine. Along the coast of southern California, the climate supports a broadleaf savanna of various species of oaks.

Mountain evergreen forests grow above the foothill savannas of the mountains of the western United States and Canada. In general, the climate in the mountains becomes colder, wetter, and windier with increas-

ing altitude. The forests of the lower and middle slopes are called *montane forests.* Those of the upper slopes are known as *subalpine forests.*

In the Rockies, the lower montane forests consist of unmixed stands of ponderosa pine. At higher elevations, Douglas-fir becomes dominant. Douglas-fir is mixed with grand fir in the northern Rockies and with blue spruce and white fir in the southern Rockies. Above this zone lie the cold, snowy subalpine forests, which are dominated by Engelmann spruce and subalpine fir. Lodgepole pine is also common in both the montane and subalpine zones, especially in areas that have been affected by fire. The highest elevation at which trees can grow is called the *timber line.* Beyond this point, the climate is too severe for tree growth. In the timber-line regions, the trees grow in a scattered, savannalike way. The timber-line regions are dominated by bristlecone pine in the southern Rockies, by limber pine in the central Rockies, and by Lyall's larch and whitebark pine in the northern Rockies.

In the Sierra Nevada, incense-cedar grows in moist areas of the lower montane forests. Douglas-fir, Jeffrey pine, ponderosa pine, and sugar pine thrive on drier slopes. In central California, magnificent stands of giant sequoia trees grow on the western slopes of the Sierra Nevada. The sequoias are the bulkiest, though not the tallest, of all the world's trees. The largest sequoias measure about 100 feet (30 meters) around at the base. White fir dominates the upper montane forests of the Sierra Nevada. At subalpine elevations, the mountains support forests of red fir mixed with lodgepole pine and mountain hemlock. These subalpine forests thin out into savannas of bristlecone and whitebark pine at elevations near the timber line.

Pacific coastal forests extend along the Pacific Ocean from west-central California to Alaska. The warm currents of the Pacific help give this region a mild climate the year around. Warm, moisture-filled winds from the ocean bring heavy annual precipitation.

Huge conifers dominate the Pacific coastal forests. Forests of redwood, one of the world's tallest trees, grow along a narrow coastal strip from central California to southern Oregon. Many of these giants tower more than 300 feet (91 meters). Inland from the redwoods and to the north, grow magnificent forests of Douglas-fir, Sitka spruce, western hemlock, and western redcedar. Along the coast of northern Washington and southern British Columbia, the high annual precipitation supports thick temperate rain forests. These forests, with their moss-covered Douglas-fir, Sitka spruce, and Pacific redcedar, make up a damp, green wilderness found nowhere else in North America.

Boreal forests sweep across northern North America from northwestern Alaska to Newfoundland. In this region of severe cold and heavy snowfall, winter lasts seven to eight months. However, the short growing season has dependable rainfall and many hours of daylight each day. The boreal forests are dominated by coniferous evergreens, chiefly balsam fir, black spruce, jack pine, and white spruce. Some areas support stands of larch, which is a deciduous conifer. Such deciduous broadleaf trees as balsam poplar, trembling aspen, and white birch grow in areas that have been burned over by forest fires. The boreal forests have many *bogs* (areas of wet, spongy ground). Some of the bogs are treeless. Other bogs, called *muskegs,* are covered by a deep mat of moss on which dwarfed conifers grow.

Subarctic woodlands lie along the northern edge of the boreal forests. The climate in this region is bitterly cold, with low precipitation and an extremely short growing season. These conditions force the trees to grow in a widely spaced, savannalike fashion. Black spruce dominates most of the region. Other boreal trees, such as aspen, larch, white birch, and white spruce, grow in some places. North of the woodlands lies the Arctic tundra, where trees cannot survive.

The life of the forest

Forests are filled with an incredible variety of plant and animal life. For example, scientists recorded nearly 10,500 kinds of organisms in a deciduous forest in Switzerland. The number of individual plants and animals in a forest is enormous.

All life in the forest is part of a complex ecosystem, which also includes the physical environment. Ecologists study forest life by examining the ways in which the organisms interact with one another and their environment. Such interactions involve (1) the flow of energy through the ecosystem, (2) the cycling of essential chemicals within the ecosystem, and (3) competition and cooperation among the organisms.

The flow of energy. All organisms need energy to stay alive. In forests, as in all other ecosystems, life depends on energy from the sun. However, only the green plants in the forest can use the sun's energy directly. Through a process called *photosynthesis,* they use sunlight to produce food.

All other forest organisms rely on green plants to capture the energy of sunlight. Green plants are thus the *primary producers* in the forest. Animals that eat plants are known as *primary consumers* or *herbivores.* Animals that eat herbivores are called *secondary consumers* or *predators.* Secondary consumers themselves may fall prey to other predators, called *tertiary* (third) *consumers.* This series of primary producers and various levels of consumers is known as a *food chain.*

In a typical forest food chain, tree leaves (primary producers) are eaten by caterpillars (primary consumers). The caterpillars, in turn, are eaten by shrews (secondary consumers), which are then eaten by owls (tertiary consumers). Energy, in the form of food, passes from one level of the food chain to the next. But much energy is lost at each level. Therefore, a forest ecosystem can support, in terms of weight, far more green plants than herbivores and far more herbivores than predators.

The cycling of chemicals. All living things are made up of certain basic chemical elements. The supply of these chemicals is limited, and so they must be recycled for life to continue.

The *decomposers* of the forest floor play a vital role in chemical recycling. The decomposers include bacteria, earthworms, fungi, some insects, and certain single-celled organisms. Decomposers obtain food by breaking down dead plants and the wastes and dead bodies of animals into their basic chemicals. The elements pass into the soil, where they are absorbed by the roots of growing plants. Without decomposition, the supply of such essential elements as nitrogen, phosphorus, and potassium would soon be exhausted.

Some chemical recycling does not involve decomposers. Green plants, for example, release oxygen during photosynthesis. Animals—and plants as well—need this chemical to *oxidize* (burn) food and so release energy. In the oxidation process, animals and plants give off carbon dioxide, which the green plants need for photosynthesis. Thus the cycling of oxygen and carbon dioxide works together and maintains a steady supply of the two chemicals.

Competition and cooperation. Every forest animal and plant must compete with individuals of its own and similar species for such necessities as nutrients, space, and water. For example, red squirrels in a boreal forest must compete with one another—and with certain other herbivores—for conifer seeds, their chief food. Similarly, the conifers compete with one another and with other types of plants for water and sunlight. This competition helps ensure that the organisms best adapted to the forest will survive and reproduce.

Cooperation among the organisms of the forest is common. For many species, cooperation is necessary for survival. For example, birds and mammals that eat

How a forest develops

A forest develops through a series of changes in the kinds of plants and animals that live in an area. This process is called *ecological succession.* The pictures below show how a forest might develop and succession occur on abandoned farmland in the Southeastern United States.

WORLD BOOK illustrations by Jean Helmer

A grassy meadow develops during the first few years. Pine seedlings appear throughout the meadow.

An evergreen forest gradually develops. Young pines need full sun, so deciduous trees form the understory.

A deciduous-evergreen forest develops as the old pines die. Deciduous trees fill in the gaps in the canopy.

A wholly deciduous forest finally develops. This forest is the *climax* (final) stage in the succession.

fruit rely on plants for food. But the plants, in turn, may depend on these animals to help spread their seeds. Similarly, certain microscopic fungi grow on roots of trees. The fungi obtain food from the tree, but they also help the tree absorb needed water and nutrients.

For a diagram of a forest ecosystem, see **Ecology.**

Forest succession

In forests and other natural areas, a series of orderly changes may occur in the kinds of plants and animals that live in the area. This series of changes is called *ecological succession.* Areas undergoing succession pass through one or more *intermediate* stages until a final *climax* stage is reached. Forests exist in intermediate or climax stages of ecological succession in a great number of places.

To illustrate how a forest develops and succession occurs, let us imagine an area of abandoned farmland in the Southeastern United States. The abandoned land will first support communities of low-growing weeds, insects, and mice. The land then gradually becomes a meadow as grasses and larger herbs and shrubs begin to appear. At the same time, rabbits, snakes, and ground-nesting birds begin to move into the area.

In a few years, young pine trees stand throughout the meadow. As the trees mature, the meadow becomes an intermediate forest of pines. The meadow herbs and shrubs die and are replaced by plants that grow better in the shade of the pine canopy. As the meadow plants disappear, so do the food chains based on them. New

herbivores and predators enter the area, forming food chains based on the plant life of the pine forest.

Years pass, and the pines grow old and large. But few young pines grow beneath them because pine seedlings need direct sunlight. Instead, broadleaf trees—particularly oaks—form the understory. As the old pines die, oaks fill the openings in the canopy. Gradually, a mixed deciduous-evergreen forest typical of the Southeastern United States develops.

But the succession is still not complete. Young oaks grow well in the shade of the canopy, but pines do not. Therefore, a climax oak forest may eventually replace the mixed forest. However, pine wood is much more valuable than oak wood. For this reason, foresters in the Southeastern United States use controlled fires to check the growth of oaks and so prevent the climax forest from developing.

Different successional series occur in different areas. In southern boreal regions, for instance, balsam fir and white spruce dominate the climax forests. If fire, disease, or windstorms destroy one of the coniferous forests, an intermediate forest of trembling aspen and white birch may develop in its place. These deciduous trees grow better in direct sunlight and on unprotected, bare ground than do fir and spruce.

The aspen-birch forest provides the protection young boreal conifers need, and soon spruce and fir seedlings make up most of the understory. In time, these conifers grow taller than the aspen and birch trees. The deciduous species cannot reproduce in the shade of the new

Early forests

Forests evolved throughout the various periods of the earth's history. At the beginning of the Carboniferous Period—about 360 million years ago—tree-sized club mosses and horsetails were dominant forest plants. By the start of the Jurassic Period—about 205 million years ago—conifers had become widespread. During the Tertiary Period, which lasted from about 63 million to 5 million years ago, flowering broadleaf trees became common.

WORLD BOOK illustrations by Paul D. Turnbaugh

Carboniferous forest

Jurassic forest

Tertiary forest

canopy, and gradually the climax forest of fir and spruce trees is reestablished.

The history of forests

The first forests developed in marshlands about 365 million years ago, toward the end of the Devonian Period. They consisted of tree-sized club mosses and ferns, some of which had trunks nearly 40 feet (12 meters) tall and about 3 feet (1 meter) thick. These forests became the home of early amphibians and insects.

By the beginning of the Carboniferous Period—about 360 million years ago—vast swamps covered much of North America. Forests of giant club mosses and horsetails up to 125 feet (38 meters) tall grew in these warm swamps. Ferns about 10 feet (3 meters) tall formed a thick undergrowth that sheltered huge cockroaches, dragonflies, scorpions, and spiders. In time, seed ferns and primitive conifers developed in the swamp forests. When plants of the swamp forests died, they fell into the mud and water that covered the forest floor. The mud and water did not contain enough oxygen to support decomposers. As a result, the plants did not decay but became buried under layer after layer of mud. Over millions of years, the weight and pressure on the plants turned them into great coal deposits.

Later forests. As the Mesozoic Era began, about 240 million years ago, severe changes in climate and in the earth's surface wiped out the swamp forests. In the new, drier environment, gymnosperm trees became dominant. *Gymnosperms* are plants whose seeds are not enclosed in a fruit or seedcase. Such trees included seed ferns and primitive conifers like those that grew in the swamp forests. They also included cycad and ginkgo trees, which became widespread. Gymnosperm trees formed forests that covered much of the earth. Amphibians, insects, and large reptiles lived in these forests.

The first flowering plants appeared during the early Cretaceous Period, sometime after 138 million years ago. Flowering plants, which are called *angiosperms,* produce seeds enclosed in a fruit or seedcase. Many angiosperm trees became prominent in the forests. They included magnolias, maples, poplars, and willows. Flowering shrubs and herbs became common undergrowth plants.

At the start of the Cenozoic Era, about 63 million years ago, the earth's climate turned cooler. Magnificent temperate forests then spread across North America, Europe, and Asia. The forests included a wealth of flowering broadleaf trees and needleleaf conifers. Many birds and mammals lived in these forests.

Modern forests. The earth's climate continued to turn colder. By about 2.4 million years ago, the first of several great waves of glaciers had begun to advance over much of North America, Europe, and Asia. Since the development of agriculture began about 11,000 years ago, the ice sheets had destroyed large areas of the temperate forests in North America and Europe. Only the temperate forests of southeastern Asia remained largely untouched.

The forests of the world took on their modern distribution after the last of the glaciers retreated. For example, the great boreal forests developed across northern Europe and North America. But the world's forest regions are not permanent. Today, for instance, temperate forests are invading the southern edge of the boreal region. Another ice age or other dramatic environmental changes could greatly alter the world's forests.

Deforestation

Human activities have had tremendous impact on modern forests. Since agriculture began about 10,000 years ago, large forest areas have been cleared for farms and cities. During the 1800's and 1900's, great expanses of forests have been eliminated because of logging activities and industrial pollution. The destruction of forests is called deforestation.

Today, severe deforestation occurs in tropical areas, primarily as a result of the clearing of land for agriculture and industry. Until the late 1940's, tropical rain forests covered about 6 million square miles (16 million square kilometers) of the earth's land. In the late 1980's, they covered only about 4 million square miles (10 million square kilometers). About 39,000 square miles (100,000 square kilometers) of tropical rain forests are destroyed each year. Most of this destruction occurs in Latin America and Southeast Asia.

In other parts of the world, industrial pollution is a chief cause of deforestation. Factories often release poisonous gases into the air and dangerous wastes into lakes and rivers. Air pollutants may combine with rain, snow, or other precipitation and fall to earth as *acid rain* (see **Acid rain**). These pollutants can restrict plant growth in a region and eventually kill most plants there. In parts of Europe, forest areas set aside long ago for continuous timber production have been seriously damaged by industrial pollution. Pollution also threatens forests in eastern North America.

Deforestation has many far-reaching effects. For example, as forest areas decrease, the amount of oxygen released into the air through photosynthesis also decreases. Renewal of the oxygen supply is vital to the continuing survival of oxygen-breathing organisms. Also, as less carbon dioxide is taken up by photosynthesis, the amounts of carbon dioxide released into the air increases. As a result, more heat from the sun is trapped near the earth's surface instead of being reflected back

into space. Many scientists believe that this *greenhouse effect* is causing a steady warming that could lead to threatening climatic conditions (see **Greenhouse effect**). The destruction of forests also destroys the habitats of many living creatures. Countless species of animals and plants have been wiped out by deforestation.

Paul F. Maycock

Related articles in *World Book.* See **Tree** and its list of *Related articles.* See also the *Economy* section of the various country, state, and province articles. Other related articles include:

Conservation	Forestry	Petrified forest
Ecology	Jungle	Tropical rain
Forest products	National forest	forest
Forest Service		

Outline

I. The importance of forests
    A. Economic value   C. Enjoyment value
    B. Environmental value
II. The structure of forests
    A. The canopy   D. The herb layer
    B. The understory   E. The forest floor
    C. The shrub layer
III. Kinds of forests
    A. Tropical rain forests
    B. Tropical seasonal forests
    C. Temperate deciduous forests
    D. Temperate evergreen forests
    E. Boreal forests
    F. Savannas
IV. Forests of the United States and Canada
    A. Subtropical forests   E. Temperate savannas
    B. Southern deciduous-   F. Mountain evergreen forests
        evergreen forests   G. Pacific coastal forests
    C. Deciduous forests   H. Boreal forests
    D. Northern deciduous-   I. Subarctic woodlands
        evergreen forests
V. The life of the forest
    A. The flow of energy
    B. The cycling of chemicals
    C. Competition and cooperation
VI. Forest succession
VII. The history of forests
VIII. Deforestation

Questions

How do forests help conserve and enrich the environment?
Where is the oldest deciduous forest in North America?
How does an *intermediate* forest differ from a *climax* forest?
Which layer of the forest produces the most food? Why?
Where do forests of the world's bulkiest trees grow? What are these trees?
When did the first forests develop? What did they consist of?
How do deciduous and evergreen forests differ?
How does the forest food chain work?
What is the *timber line*?
Which kind of forest has the greatest variety of trees?

Additional resources

Level I
Brown, Vinson. *Reading the Woods: Seeing More in Nature's Familiar Faces.* Macmillan, 1973. First published in 1969.
List, Albert, Jr. and Ilka. *A Walk in the Forest: The Woodlands of North America.* Crowell, 1977.

Level II
McCormick, Jack. *The Life of the Forest.* McGraw, 1966.
Mohlenbrock, Robert H. *The Field Guide to U.S. National Forests.* Congdon & Weed, 1984.
Walker, Laurence C. *Trees: An Introduction to Trees and Forest Ecology for the Amateur Naturalist.* Prentice-Hall, 1984.

© Glyn Davies, International Centre for Conservation Education

Deforestation of a tropical rain forest destroys the habitat of many plants and animals. This photograph shows loggers clearing part of a rain forest in Malaysia.

Forest conservation. See **Conservation** (Forest conservation); **Forestry.**
Forest fire. See **Forestry** (Fire).

Forest products have long provided people with food, shelter, clothing, and fuel. Prehistoric people ate berries and nuts that grew in forests. They built shelters from the branches of trees and wore clothing made of plant materials. By about 500,000 B.C., they used wood as a fuel to make fire.

Today, wood is one of our most important raw materials. It is used in making thousands of products, from building materials to plastics and photographic film. Wood is the source of paper for books, newspapers, and packaging materials. In the United States and Canada, most houses are built of wood. Despite its usefulness as a raw material, the chief use of wood throughout the world is as a fuel.

There are thousands of forest products. Most can be classified into one of four main groups: (1) wood products, (2) fiber products, (3) chemical products, and (4) fuel products. Wood products are made from solid wood or from pieces that are large enough to be readily identified as wood. Fiber products such as paper are made from wood fibers. Chemical products are manufactured by breaking down wood and wood fibers and chemically treating them. Such chemical products as cellophane, lacquer, and rayon do not feel or look like wood. But all are made from it. Fuel products include logs, wood pellets, and charcoal. Other forest products come from the bark, fruit, gum, leaves, and sap of trees.

Jim L. Bowyer, the contributor of this article, is Head of the Department of Forest Products at the University of Minnesota, Twin Cities Campus.

This article describes different forest products. For information about logging, see **Lumber.**

Wood products

Wood has many characteristics that make it an important construction material. It can be easily shaped with tools and fastened with nails, screws, staples, and adhesives. It is light but strong. Wood provides insulation against electricity, heat, cold, and sound. It can hold paint and other finishes, and it does not rust. Unlike metal construction materials, wood is a *renewable resource*—that is, a new supply grows after the timber has been harvested. Some of the chief wood structural materials are round timbers, lumber, plywood, veneer products, and particle board.

Round timbers include pilings, poles, and posts. Pilings are driven into the ground as foundations for buildings, wharves, and other heavy structures. Poles link overhead telephone wires and power lines. Posts are used chiefly to build fences. Round timbers are simply trees that have been stripped of their branches and bark, and cut into logs. The logs are dried and treated for protection against decay and insect attack.

Lumber includes boards and larger pieces of wood that have been sawed from logs. The construction industry uses about 50 per cent of the lumber manufactured in the United States. The rest is used in making crates, furniture, railroad ties, sporting goods, toys, and thousands of other products. See **Lumber.**

Wood scientists classify lumber as *softwood* or *hardwood,* depending on the kind of tree. This classification

Some kinds of forest products   Trees provide thousands of wood, chemical, and other products that people use every day. Wood products include lumber and plywood. Chemical products, such as charcoal and paper, are made from wood by chemical processes. Other forest products include nuts and turpentine.

WORLD BOOK illustrations by David Cunningham

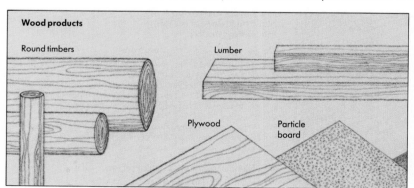

Wood products

Round timbers   Lumber   Plywood   Particle board

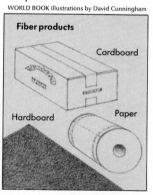

Fiber products

Cardboard   Hardboard   Paper

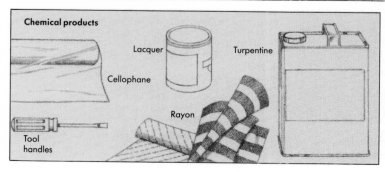

Chemical products

Lacquer   Turpentine   Cellophane   Rayon   Tool handles

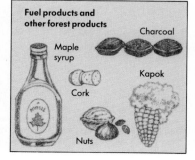

Fuel products and other forest products

Charcoal   Maple syrup   Kapok   Cork   Nuts

does not always indicate the hardness of the wood. Various softwoods produce harder lumber than do some hardwoods. Softwood lumber comes from needleleaf trees that are also called *evergreens* or *conifers.* It is used primarily for structural work because of its straightness and length. Softwoods include pine, larch, fir, hemlock, redwood, cypress, cedar, and Douglas-fir.

Hardwood lumber comes from trees that lose their leaves every autumn. Many hardwoods are known for their beautiful grain patterns. For this reason, they are widely used for cabinets, flooring, furniture, and paneling. Popular hardwoods include birch, maple, oak, sweet gum, walnut, and mahogany.

Plywood consists of a number of thin sheets of wood called *veneers* that are glued together. The veneers are arranged so that the grain direction in each layer is at a right angle to the grain direction of the next layer. This arrangement gives plywood several advantages over lumber. Plywood shrinks, swells, and warps less than lumber, and it can be easily nailed near the edges without splitting. A very thin veneer of expensive hardwood can be applied to a core of less expensive wood, producing plywood that has the look of expensive wood but not the cost. Plywood and veneers are widely used in the construction and furniture industries.

Veneer products are made of thin veneers. These veneers may be cut into long strips or other shapes. Veneer products include beams that support ceilings and floors, matches, tongue depressors, and toothpicks.

Particle board is made from wood shavings, flakes, wafers, splinters, or sawdust left over in sawmills and paper mills. This wood is mixed with an adhesive and pressed at a high temperature and pressure to form large sheets or panels. Particle board shrinks and swells very little in length and width. It may be used as a base for flooring and furniture. Some particle board has the strength of plywood and many of the same uses.

Fiber products

Wood is made up of many tiny fibers. Manufacturers produce paper and paperboard, hardboard, and insulation board from wood fibers. Wood fiber is also used as attic insulation, as a protective soil covering called *mulch,* and even as a dietary fiber in breakfast cereals.

Paper and paperboard are made from wood chips that have been reduced to a fiber pulp by chemicals, heat, or other treatment. The pulp is then formed into a mat, filtered, drained, and pressed. Paper products include bags, books, cartons, packaging materials, and tissue.

Hardboard is manufactured by pressing wood fibers into flat sheets at a high temperature and pressure. Hardboard is used chiefly in furniture, siding, and paneling.

Insulation board is manufactured from wood fibers that are formed into a mat, pressed lightly, and dried. It weighs less than hardboard. Insulation board is used for acoustical tile and under siding in construction.

Chemical products

Many wood products are made from wood or bark that has been broken down into such basic chemical

Some uses of forest products

Wood products		Veneer products		Naval stores	
		Baskets	Paneling	Adhesives	Printing inks
Lumber		Boxes	Tongue depres-	Cleaners	Rosin
Barrels	Laminated	Cabinets	sors	Disinfectants	Synthetic
Baseball bats	beams	Furniture	Toothpicks	Linoleum flooring	rubber
Boats	Mine timbers	Matches		Lubricants	Turpentine
Bowling pins	Molding				Varnishes
Boxes	Musical	**Fiber products**			
Cabinets	instruments			**Fuel products**	
Caskets	Paneling	**Hardboard**			
Crates	Pencils	Automobile interiors	Paneling	Charcoal	Sawdust
Doors	Railroad ties	Cabinets	Siding	Fireplace logs	Wood chips
Fencing	Shingles	Furniture	Signs	Pulverized fuel	
Flooring	Structural timber	Garage doors			
Furniture	Window frames			**Other forest products**	
		Insulation board			
Particle board		Ceiling tile	Sheathing	**Bark**	
Cabinet tops	Furniture			Adhesives	Fuel
Doors	Paneling	**Paper and paperboard**		Cork	Soil mulch
Drawer sides	Roof decking	Bags	Newspaper	Dyes	Tannic acid
Floor under-	Sheathing	Books	Packaging	**Fruit and seeds**	
layment	Siding	Cartons	Tissue	Beechnuts	Hickory nuts
				Black walnuts	Kapok
		Chemical products		Blueberries	Pecans
Plywood				Cranberries	Pine nuts
Airplanes	House foun-	**Cellulose products**			
Boats	dations	Acetate	Lacquers	**Gum**	
Concrete forms	Paneling	Adhesives	Photographic	Pine oil	Tall oil
Containers	Roof decking	Cellophane	film	Rosin	Turpentine
Floor under-	Sheathing	Ceramics	Plastics		
layment	Siding	Detergent additives	Rayon	**Leaves**	
Furniture	Structural beams		Tire cords	Holly	Pharmaceu-
		Lignin products		Household	ticals
Round timbers		Animal feeds	Cement	cleaner	Soap
Bridges	Pilings	Artificial	Dyes	Perfumes	Wreaths
Fence posts	Utility poles	vanilla	Plastics	**Sap**	
Log homes		Ceramics	Printing inks	Maple sugar	Maple syrup
			Textile binder		

parts as cellulose and lignin. Cellulose is the main ingredient of wood fibers. Lignin, found in and between wood fibers, holds the fibers together.

Cellulose products. Cellulose may be chemically treated to change its properties and to produce such compounds as *cellulose acetate* and *cellulose nitrate*. Both of these compounds are used in adhesives, lacquers, and plastics. Plastic items molded from cellulose compounds include piano keys, tool handles, and table tennis balls. Cellulose nitrate is also an ingredient in explosives. Other cellulose compounds have specialized uses in such products as paint, foods, and textiles.

Manufacturers process cellulose to produce rayon and acetate fibers, which are used for clothing, draperies, and upholstery. Rayon cords strengthen tires. Other materials made from cellulose include cellophane and photographic film. See **Cellulose; Rayon.**

Lignin products. Lignin has far fewer uses than cellulose. It is used in making printing inks, dyes, and concrete. Manufacturers use it to *bind* (hold together) animal food pellets and textiles. Artificial vanilla is used as a flavoring in many foods. It also is made from lignin.

Naval stores include turpentine and rosin—materials once essential to the operation of wooden sailing ships. Almost all naval stores come from the processing of pine pulp.

Fuel products

In many developing countries, wood has long served as the primary fuel for cooking and heating. In industrialized countries, wood has been burned mainly in fireplaces and charcoal grills. After petroleum prices rose in the 1970's, wood became a popular fuel in communities near forested areas. Fuel products made from wood include split, dried logs; compressed wood pellets; charcoal; and sawmill by-products. In addition, the forest products industry burns the thick liquid that results from pulping wood.

Other forest products

Although most forest products are made from wood, some come from the bark, fruit and seeds, gum, leaves, and sap of trees. By-products from sawmills include wood chips, shavings, and sawdust. These by-products

10 largest forest products companies in the United States

Company	Forest products sales	Total sales*	Total employees	Year founded	Headquarters
1. Georgia-Pacific Corporation	$8,565,000,000	$8,603,000,000	42,000	1927	Atlanta
2. International Paper Company	6,647,000,000†	7,763,000,000	45,500	1898	New York City
3. Weyerhaeuser Company	6,407,315,000	6,989,829,000	39,800	1900	Tacoma, Wash.
4. James River Corporation	5,097,978,000	5,097,978,000	39,000	1969	Richmond, Va.
5. Kimberly-Clark Corporation	4,809,100,000†	4,884,700,000	37,400	1872	Dallas
6. Champion International Corporation	4,614,719,000	4,614,723,000	30,700	1937	Stamford, Conn.
7. Scott Paper Company	4,122,000,000	4,122,000,000	25,400	1879	Philadelphia
8. Stone Container Corporation	3,232,919,000	3,232,919,000	18,800	1926	Chicago
9. Boise Cascade Corporation	3,076,616,000	3,820,810,000	20,200	1931	Boise, Ida.
10. Mead Corporation	2,579,925,000	4,208,800,000	20,500	1846	Dayton, Ohio

*Includes all sales and services.   †Includes intercompany sales.   Source: Standard and Poor's Compustat Services, Inc., 1987 figures.

Leading countries in forest products

Wood removed from forests in a year

United States	586,600,000 cu. yds. (448,490,000 m³)
Soviet Union	465,240,000 cu. yds. (355,700,000 m³)
China	344,480,000 cu. yds. (263,370,000 m³)
India	320,490,000 cu. yds. (245,030,000 m³)
Brazil	295,470,000 cu. yds. (225,910,000 m³)
Canada	224,060,000 cu. yds. (171,310,000 m³)
Indonesia	194,900,000 cu. yds. (149,010,000 m³)
Nigeria	124,100,000 cu. yds. (95,570,000 m³)
Sweden	69,760,000 cu. yds. (53,340,000 m³)
Tanzania	59,560,000 cu. yds. (45,540,000 m³)

Figures are for 1985. Source: *Yearbook of Forest Products, 1985*, Food and Agriculture Organization of the United Nations.

Leading states and provinces in forest products

Wood removed from forests in a year

British Columbia	97,520,000 cu. yds. (74,560,000 m³)
Oregon	68,250,000 cu. yds. (52,180,000 m³)
Georgia	53,590,000 cu. yds. (40,970,000 m³)
Washington	52,450,000 cu. yds. (40,100,000 m³)
Quebec	47,770,000 cu. yds. (36,520,000 m³)
Alabama	38,780,000 cu. yds. (29,650,000 m³)
Ontario	36,790,000 cu. yds. (28,130,000 m³)
Mississippi	32,960,000 cu. yds. (25,200,000 m³)
California	31,730,000 cu. yds. (24,260,000 m³)
Louisiana	24,520,000 cu. yds. (18,750,000 m³)

Figures are for 1984. Sources: state forestry officials; U.S. Forest Service; Statistics Canada.

Plywood, *left,* is a widely used wood product. Workers in this manufacturing plant in Vancouver, Canada, are stacking finished pieces of plywood.

© Bill Staley, West Stock

may be used in making particle board and other products, in bedding for animals, and in floor-sweeping compounds.

The bark from the cork oak tree provides cork for such products as bottle stoppers, bulletin boards, and insulation. The bark of the hemlock and other trees furnishes tannic acid used in processing animal hides. Bark is sometimes used as fuel, ground cover, or mulch.

Fruit and seeds harvested from forest trees include many kinds of nuts. The seedpods of the kapok, or silk-cotton, tree provide kapok fibers. Kapok is widely used as a filler in jackets and sleeping bags.

Latex is a milky substance produced by plants and trees of the sapodilla family. Latex is the source of natural rubber, which is used to make balloons, hoses, tires, and other items.

The leaves of some forest trees furnish ornamental greenery for Christmas wreaths and similar products. The leaves of certain evergreens and eucalyptus species are distilled to produce oil used in perfumes, household cleaners, soaps, and certain drugs. Sap from certain kinds of maple trees can be made into maple syrup and maple sugar.

The forest products industry

The manufacture of forest products is a major industry in the United States and Canada. The U.S. forest products industry employs more than 1 $\frac{1}{2}$ million people and produces $120 billion worth of goods annually. The industry has about 50,000 manufacturing plants. United States forest products companies own about 70 million acres (28 million hectares) of commercially valuable forestland. They also harvest timber in state and national forests under government leases. In addition, they buy logs from the owners of small wooded areas.

Canada's forest products industry is a leading source of export income. About 270,000 Canadians work for companies that make forest products. These firms produce about $22 billion worth of goods yearly. Canada is the world's leading producer of *newsprint,* the paper on which newspapers are printed. It produces about a third of the world's total supply each year.   Jim L. Bowyer

Related articles in *World Book.* See **Wood** and its list of *Related articles.* See also the following articles:

Bark	Cork	Fiberboard	Lacquer
Charcoal	Creosote	Gum	Lumber

Naval stores	Resin	Sap	Turpentine
Paper	Rosin	Tannic acid	Veneer
Rayon	Rubber	Tar	

Forest ranger. See Forestry; Forest Service.

Forest Service is an agency of the United States Department of Agriculture. It has the task of promoting the best use of forestland. It manages about 191 million acres (77 million hectares) of national forests and other lands. Forest Service rangers try to protect these forests against insects, disease, and fire. The rangers preserve wildlife and supervise grazing. They see that no more timber is cut in any one year than a single year's growth can replace. They keep a cover of plants on sloping land to guard against rapid soil erosion and floods. The rangers also supervise camping and picnic areas, and keep up a system of lookout stations, telephone lines, two-way radio communication, and roads and trails. They often help to rescue people who are lost or injured.

The agency cooperates with state and local governments and private landowners. For example, it advises and assists them in protecting and planting forests.

The Forest Service carries on research programs at eight experimental stations and at the Forest Products Laboratory in Madison, Wis. It also conducts research projects at sites throughout the United States. Founded as the Bureau of Forestry, the agency became the Forest Service in 1905.   Critically reviewed by the Forest Service

See also **National forest.**

Forester. See Forestry; Forest Service.

Forester, Cecil Scott (1899-1966), was an English novelist who won fame for his fictional creation of Horatio Hornblower, a British naval hero of the 1800's. Hornblower's exciting adventures, his coolness and inventiveness under stress, and his weakness for women endeared him to a large reading public. Hornblower rises from midshipman to admiral in a series of novels that includes *Beat to Quarters* (1937), *Flying Colours* (1938), *A Ship of the Line* (1939), and *Lord Hornblower* (1946). His adventure novel *The African Queen* (1935) was made into a popular motion picture in 1951.

Forester believed his other novels, especially *The General* (1936), were equal to the Hornblower books. But his readers overwhelmingly favored the naval hero. Forester was born in Cairo, Egypt, and was educated in England. He lived in the United States from 1945 until his death.   Garrett Stewart

Weyerhaeuser Co.

Georgia-Pacific Corp.

Harvesting and planting trees mechanically contributes to efficient management of timber resources. The powerful jaws of tree shears, *left,* fell trees in a fraction of the time of a saw. A planting gun, *right,* digs a hole, inserts a seedling, and pats down the soil in one operation.

Forestry is the science of managing forest resources for human benefit. The practice of forestry helps maintain an adequate supply of timber for the manufacture of lumber, plywood, paper, and other wood products. It also includes the management of such valuable forest resources as water, wildlife, grazing areas, and recreation areas.

In general, forests provide the greatest benefits when they are managed with the goal of providing several benefits at once. This concept, called *multiple use forest management,* is applied in the national forests of the United States and in most state forests. These forests furnish about a third of the timber harvested annually in the United States. They also provide water for communities; food and shelter for wildlife; grazing land for livestock; and recreation areas for campers, hikers, and picnickers.

In some forests, however, the importance of one resource may outweigh that of others. For example, companies that manufacture paper or other wood products manage their forests primarily for maximum timber production. The U.S. forest products industry owns about 67 million acres (27 million hectares) of forestland. This acreage equals about half that of the forestland owned

George R. Parker, the contributor of this article, is Associate Professor of Forestry at Purdue University.

and managed for timber production by the federal, state, and local governments. However, industrial forests produce about as much commercial timber yearly as do government forests. Private individuals own about 300 million acres (120 million hectares) of small woodland areas, but few of these forests are well managed.

This article discusses the scientific management of forest resources. For information on the various products made from trees, see **Forest products.** For a discussion of forest ecology, see **Forest.**

Managing timber resources

The goal of managing timber resources is to achieve an approximate balance between the annual harvest and growth of wood. This balance, called a *sustained yield,* ensures a continuous supply of timber. It is achieved by managing forests so they have areas of trees of equal yield for each age group, from seedlings to mature trees. The science of harvesting and growing crops of trees for sustained yield is called *silviculture.* The practice of silviculture requires that foresters know how various species of trees grow in different climates and soils, and how much sunlight and water the trees need. Foresters also use the science of genetics to breed trees that have improved growth rates and greater resistance to diseases and pests.

Harvesting. There are four chief methods of harvesting timber: (1) clearcutting, (2) seed tree cutting, (3) shelterwood cutting, and (4) selection cutting. Each cutting method is also a way of replacing the crop. New trees grow from seeds produced by the remaining or surrounding trees, from sprouting stumps, or from seeds or seedlings that foresters plant.

Clearcutting is the removal of all the trees in a certain area of a forest. Clearcut areas range in size from a few acres to 600 acres (243 hectares) or more. The areas must be large enough to prevent surrounding forests from affecting them. Clearcutting is generally used to re-establish a *stand* (large group of trees) that is more even in age, by removing a mature one. It is also the method generally used when a forest is to be replaced by planting or by sprouting stumps.

Seed tree cutting resembles clearcutting, but foresters leave a few trees widely scattered in the harvested area to provide a natural source of seeds. These seed trees are removed after the new stand is established. Seed tree cutting can be used with loblolly pine, longleaf pine, and other southern pines.

Shelterwood cutting involves harvesting timber in several stages over a period of 10 to 20 years. Foresters establish a new stand as the old one is removed. Shelterwood cutting can be used with such trees as oak, ponderosa pine, and white pine, which require shade during their first few years of growth. It also allows the growth of some trees in a stand to continue after the majority of the trees have ceased growing well.

Selection cutting is the harvesting of small patches of mature trees to make room for younger trees and new growth. The trees are removed on the basis of their size and nearness to other trees. However, foresters leave many larger trees standing to produce seeds. Selection cutting leaves only small openings in a forest, and so it works best with trees that grow well in shade. Such trees include American beech, hemlock, and sugar maple. Forests may be harvested by selection cutting every 5 to 30 years.

Planting. Foresters plant new timber crops by a process called *artificial reforestation.* They either plant seeds directly in the harvested land, or they raise seedlings in a nursery and transplant these young trees in the forest. The process is called *afforestation* when these methods are used to plant trees on land that was never covered by a forest.

Direct seeding works best on cultivated land or on land where a timber crop has been destroyed by fire. The seeds are treated with a chemical repellent, which discourages animals from eating them, and they are sown sometime between late autumn and early spring. Airplanes or helicopters are generally used to scatter the seeds, but seeds may also be placed in the ground with hand tools. About 30,000 seeds per acre (74,000 seeds per hectare) are usually sown to assure an adequate crop of trees.

Forests are planted with seedlings in late winter or early spring, before the buds of the seedlings have opened for the growing season. Seedlings grow in a nursery for a period of one to four years before being transplanted in the forest. Foresters generally plant approximately 800 trees per acre (1,976 trees per hectare), using hand tools or various kinds of planting machines. A person can plant approximately 1 acre (0.4 hectare) a day by hand—about as much land as a machine can plant in an hour.

Tree improvement involves breeding trees for superior growth rates and increased resistance to diseases and pests. Foresters begin this process by searching forests for the straightest and fastest-growing trees of the species. Such trees, sometimes called *supertrees,* must also have high-quality wood and be healthy and free of harmful insects and other pests. Tree improvement programs have been used for species such as black walnut, Douglas fir, and loblolly pine.

After foresters find a superior tree, they take cuttings, called *cions,* from its branches. The cions are brought to a nursery and *grafted* (joined) to the roots of 2-year-old trees (see **Grafting**). The cions receive nutrients through the roots of the young trees but keep the characteristics of the tree from which they were cut. Foresters then take pollen from the male cones of the cions and pollinate the female cones of cions from other superior trees. The foresters keep careful records of the cions used for each pollination.

How timber is harvested

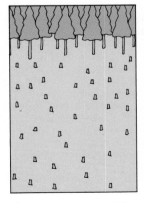

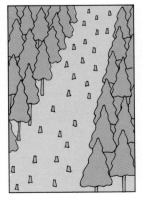

WORLD BOOK diagrams by David Cunningham

Clearcutting removes all the trees in a large area. It provides full sunlight in which new seedlings can develop.

Seed tree cutting leaves a few scattered trees in the area to provide a source of seeds for a new crop.

Shelterwood cutting, which is used for trees that require shade to develop, removes trees in several stages.

Selection cutting involves harvesting small patches of mature trees to make room for new and younger trees.

After pollination, the female cones produce seeds that are planted in the nursery and grown into seedlings. Foresters transplant the seedlings into special plantations and closely measure the growth of the trees. If the trees from a particular set of parents appear to be developing into supertrees, the seeds from those parents may be produced commercially for reforestation.

Managing other forest resources

Water. Nearly all forests serve as *watersheds*—that is, sources of water for rivers and streams. The soil of forests collects water by soaking up rain and melted snow. Watershed management largely involves keeping the forest soil porous so it can absorb a maximum amount of water.

The soil of a forest is covered by a spongy layer of leaves and twigs, called *litter*. The action of earthworms, insects, rodents, and decaying roots creates spaces within the soil. When rain or snow falls, the water is absorbed by the litter and these spaces in the soil. Much of the water is used by plants, and some flows underground and then into rivers, streams, and wells. If forest soil becomes too hard and nonporous, water flows over the surface of the ground, carrying mud and other materials into nearby streams. This runoff damages other soil, pollutes the water of the streams, and may even cause flooding.

Foresters help keep soil porous in several ways. They plant trees or shrubs in open areas in the forest to assure a continuous supply of litter. They regulate livestock grazing to maintain a good cover of grass and to prevent the animals from packing down the earth. Foresters also make sure that truck roads built for logging

© John Running, Stock, Boston

Artificial reforestation involves planting new trees in bare areas. This forester is planting pine seedlings in an area where trees were burned out in a forest fire.

© Terry Wild

A forest campground may provide cooking facilities, electrical outlets, and plumbing. Foresters plan recreation areas to meet the needs of campers without harming the environment.

operations are carefully designed to prevent damage to the soil.

Wildlife. Forests provide homes for a wide variety of wildlife, including bears, birds, deer, fish, foxes, and rodents. Wildlife management involves maintaining a balance between the number of animals in a forest and the supply of food, water, and shelter.

Forests that consist of a mixture of young and old trees generally support the greatest variety of wildlife. Dense forests of old, tall trees provide good homes for birds, insects, and such climbing mammals as raccoons and squirrels. But the shade in such forests prevents the growth of enough herbs, shrubs, and small trees to feed deer and other large animals that live on the ground. However, openings made in the forest during the timber harvest allow more sunlight to reach the forest floor. Hollow trees may also be left in large openings to serve as dens and nesting places. New plants soon begin to sprout in the clearings, providing food for wildlife. The animals tend to feed along the edges of the clearings, near the protective cover of the trees.

Wildlife management also involves controlling animal populations by regulating hunting. During food shortages caused by overpopulation of wildlife, animals may damage trees by feeding on bark, buds, and twigs.

Grazing land. Many forests in dry areas have widely spaced trees with heavy growths of grass and shrubs inbetween. Farmers who own small woodlands in such areas often let their livestock graze there. In the Western United States, thousands of ranchers use the wide grasslands of the national forests as a source of feed for cattle and sheep. However, the use of rangeland must be carefully regulated to prevent overgrazing, which can damage watersheds.

Foresters preserve grasslands—and protect watersheds—chiefly by making sure that livestock roam over the entire range. Also, they control the number of livestock placed in a given area. The foresters thus prevent the animals from using up the grass or packing down the soil too much in any one area. Foresters sometimes fence off rangeland into many pastures and rotate the grazing among them. To keep livestock moving on open ranges, watering holes may be developed at scattered locations. Placing salt licks away from the water also contributes to better use of the range.

In addition to controlling overgrazing, foresters maintain grasslands through cultivation. For example, they kill brush, weeds, and poisonous plants with chemicals and then sow the area with seeds. Foresters also may restrict grazing on some land for a year or more to allow new grass to grow there.

Recreation areas. The scenic beauty and natural resources of forests provide opportunities for many recreational activities, including camping, hiking, fishing, and hunting. In the United States, millions of people visit the state and national forests annually. Many forest products companies also open areas of their woodlands to the public, chiefly for hunting and fishing. Privately owned wooded areas also provide recreational benefits.

Many areas of state and national forests are managed primarily for recreation. Government foresters carefully plan these areas to provide maximum benefits to visitors with minimum harm to the forests. Before developing a campground, for example, foresters study such factors as the terrain, the amount of shade, and the availability of water in the area. They can then install picnic tables, cooking equipment, electrical outlets, plumbing, roads and trails, and parking areas without seriously upsetting the ecological balance of the forest.

Protecting forest resources

The full benefits of forest resources can be obtained only if timber is protected from fires, diseases, and insect pests. Fire is a great threat to forests because it can cause tremendous damage in a short time. In the United States, fires destroy about 3 million acres (1.2 million hectares) of timber annually. But the destruction caused by diseases and pests is even greater—nearly seven times that of fire.

Fire. About 90 per cent of the forest fires in the

© Liane Enkelis, Stock, Boston

Fighting a forest fire involves removing the fuel from the path of the flames. Fire fighters may clear leaves, wood, and other material from the forest floor with axes and shovels, *above.*

United States are caused by human beings. Most of the rest start when lightning strikes trees. Little can be done to avoid fires caused by lightning, but fires caused by people can be prevented. Smokers start many fires by carelessly dropping lighted matches and cigarettes in forests. Other forest fires are set deliberately. Forest fires can best be prevented by educating people to understand the value of forests and the importance of protecting them. During dry seasons, when fires can easily start, foresters may close a forest to the public to reduce the danger of fire.

Foresters may watch for fires from lookout towers in a forest. These towers have binoculars, direction finders, and other equipment to locate fires, and a telephone or short-wave radio to call fire fighters to a burning area. However, most lookout towers have been replaced by airplane patrols.

Forest fires feed on fallen leaves, twigs, and other decaying material on the forest floor. The task of extinguishing a forest fire largely involves removing this blanket of fuel. Fire-fighting crews spray water or chemicals on the burning area to cool the fire and slow its progress. They then can get close enough to the flames to dig a *fireline.* The fire fighters start a fireline by clearing all brush, logs, and trees from a wide strip around the fire. Then they scrape away the litter and some of the soil with axes, shovels, or bulldozers. Fire fighters called *smoke jumpers* may parachute from airplanes or helicopters to dig a fireline in an area that is difficult to reach by land.

After creating a fireline, the fire fighters may set *backfires* to burn the area between the line and the forest fire itself. Backfires remove additional fuel and widen the fireline to help stop the spread of the flames. After a fire dies, the fire fighters clear any flammable material from the edge of the burned area. This action prevents the material from smoldering and starting new fires.

Fire is sometimes used as a tool to benefit the forest. In a process called *prescribed burning,* foresters may set small fires in the litter on the forest floor to reduce the potential fuel for a fire. Prescribed burning also kills diseases, insect pests, and the seedlings of unwanted trees. This technique must be used with extreme caution.

Diseases and pests. Most tree diseases are caused by fungus infections. Diseases attack trees chiefly by clogging the flow of sap, killing the leaves, or rotting the roots or wood. Some of the most destructive tree diseases in the United States include beech bark disease, chestnut blight, Dutch elm disease, oak wilt, and stem blister rusts that affect pines.

Insects that damage trees include bark beetles, sucking insects, and *defoliators.* Bark beetles feed on a tree's inner bark. Sucking insects suck the fluid from trees. Defoliators eat leaves. Various kinds of bark beetles destroy thousands of evergreens yearly in the Southern and Western United States. Defoliators, which include spruce budworms and tussock moths, also attack evergreens. One defoliator, the gypsy moth, is especially harmful to oak trees. Sucking insects, such as aphids and scales, feed on all types of trees.

Foresters control diseases and pests by three chief methods: (1) biological controls, (2) silvicultural controls, and (3) direct controls. Biological controls fight diseases and pests with natural enemies. For example, foresters might increase the number of birds in a forest to reduce the insect population. Silvicultural controls use methods of timber management to make a forest undesirable for diseases and pests. Foresters follow such silvicultural practices as removing old, weak trees that are easy prey for fungi and insects. Direct controls include the use of chemical pesticides to kill fungi and insects. The chemicals can upset the ecological balance of a forest, and so pesticides are generally used only if other controls fail to stop pests and diseases.

History

People have used forest resources since prehistoric times. Throughout history, the use of forests has been regulated when shortages of timber have occurred. During the Middle Ages, forest wildlife was protected to ensure a sufficient supply of game for the nobility to hunt. Forest management developed as a science during the 1800's in Europe, chiefly in France, Germany, and the Scandinavian countries.

In the United States, the early settlers treated the nation's vast timberland as though it would last forever. They cleared much more land than they needed for their homes and crops. Lumbermen destroyed large areas of forestland by wasteful logging methods, and few people worried about abandoned, cutover forests. Some of this land still lies barren.

By 1891, a conservation movement had started, and Congress authorized the President that year to set aside wooded areas called *forest reserves.* The U.S. Forest Service was established in 1905, with Gifford Pinchot as its first chief (see **Pinchot, Gifford**). The Forest Service was given control of the forest reserves, which in 1907 became known as national forests. Today, national forests cover about 187 million acres (75.7 million hectares).

In 1911, Congress passed the Weeks Law, which authorized the government to purchase forests that serve as watersheds for important rivers and streams. The Clarke-McNary Act of 1924 expanded the Weeks Law to cover the purchase of land necessary for timber production and to make government funds available to the states to protect all forests from fire. In 1947, Congress passed the Forest Pest Control Act. This law provided for federal cooperation with states and owners of private forests to control insect pests and diseases.

The Multiple Use-Sustained Yield Act was passed in 1960. It directed that the national forests be managed to produce a sustained yield of timber and an adequate supply of other forest resources. In 1964, Congress passed the Wilderness Act, which provided for the preservation of *wilderness areas* in national forests and on other federal lands. No roads or buildings may be built in wilderness areas, and timber harvesting is forbidden there. In the mid-1980's, wilderness areas in the United States covered about 90 million acres (36 million hectares).

During the 1970's, a long-standing controversy deepened over the emphasis on timber production in the national forests compared with the management of other resources. The use of clearcutting came under especially severe criticism by some conservationists, who charged that the practice leaves ugly patches of barren land. The Forest and Rangeland Renewable Resources Planning Act was passed in 1974 to establish procedures for continually reviewing the management of American forests.   George R. Parker

Related articles in *World Book.* See **Forest** and **Forest products** and their lists of *Related articles.* See also the following articles:

Aphid	Gypsy moth	Tree farming
Conservation	National forest	Tussock moth
Dutch elm	Nursery	Wildlife
disease	Scale insect	conservation
Forest service		

Additional resources

Level I

Abrams, Kathleen S. and L. F. *Logging and Lumbering.* Messner, 1980.
Blatchford, Noel. *Your Book of Forestry.* Faber & Faber, 1980.
Paige, David. (pseud. of Richard Whittingham). *A Day in the Life of a Forest Ranger.* Troll, 1979.

Level II

Frome, Michael. *The Forest Service.* 2nd ed. Westview, 1984.
The International Book of the Forest. Simon & Schuster, 1981.
MacKay, Donald. *Heritage Lost: The Crisis in Canada's Forests.* Macmillan (Toronto), 1985.

Forfeiture, *FAWR fuh chuhr,* is a legal punishment or penalty by which a person who is guilty of wrongdoing or who has breached a contract or condition loses some right or possession. People who drive too fast may have their licenses taken away and thus *forfeit* the right to drive. A corporation may forfeit its charter if it abuses its privileges. Ordinarily, in the United States, forfeitures of this type can be made only by court action or by administrative action which is later subject to review by a court. *Civil,* or *contractual,* forfeiture may occur when a person fails to perform certain duties required under a contract. For example, if a person fails to make payment for an automobile purchased on credit, he or she may forfeit ownership of the automobile.   Joel C. Dobris

Forge. See **Forging** (Hand forging; picture); **Blacksmith.**

Forgery, *FAWR juhr ee,* is deliberately tampering with a written paper for the purpose of deceit or fraud. Common kinds of forgery include fraudulently signing another person's name to a check or document, changing the figures on a check to alter its amount, and making changes in a will or contract. The punishment for forgery is usually imprisonment. Intent to defraud must be proved before a person can be convicted of forgery. Literary forgers have tried to pass off forged documents as rare manuscripts.   Charles F. Wellford

Forget-me-not is a plant that belongs to the borage family. It grows in both wild and cultivated forms in temperate regions. Many forget-me-nots are European varieties that have been brought to the United States as garden plants. These forget-me-nots have hairy stems and soft, hairy leaves. The small flowers are light-blue with yellow centers and grow in clusters. Several kinds of forget-me-nots have white or pink flowers. Almost all kinds have pink flower buds.

Most forget-me-nots grow best in shady, moist places. The most popular kinds are *perennials,* which means they live for more than one year. They are grown by breaking up clumps of existing plants and transplanting them. Several common varieties are *annuals* that live only one year. They are grown from seed and bloom in autumn.

The forget-me-not grows clusters of light-blue flowers.

The forget-me-not is a symbol of friendship and of true love. The flower appears in many legends. In German legend, *forget me not* were the last words a lover spoke before he drowned trying to get the flower for his sweetheart. According to another legend, all the plants and animals shrank away from Adam and Eve when the two were expelled from the Garden of Eden, except for one tiny blue flower that said, "Forget me not!"

Scientific classification. Forget-me-nots belong to the borage family, Boraginaceae. The common forget-me-not is *Myosotis scorpioides.* The annual or garden forget-me-not is *M. sylvatica.* Myosotis means *mouse ear,* and refers to the leaves.

James S. Miller

See also **Flower** (picture: Flowers of Alpine tundras).

Forging is a process in which metal is shaped by being heated and then hammered or pressed. Almost any metal can be forged, but the most commonly forged ones include steel and aluminum, and alloys of nickel and titanium. *Forgings* (objects made by forging) range in size from small hand tools to huge engine shafts weighing hundreds of tons. They include such products as wrenches, crankshafts, axles, and aircraft landing gear supports.

Metals are composed of crystals. The hammering or pressing of metal bends the crystals and makes their structure less stable. But the heat used in forging enables new crystals to form in place of the deformed ones. This process is called *recrystallization.* In most cases, the new crystals are smaller and the metal is tougher than before. For this reason, forging is used in manufacturing many metal products that must withstand great stress.

Metal can be forged either by hand, using a handheld hammer, or by machine. Hand forging, which is probably the oldest method of shaping metal, has been practiced since prehistoric times. Today, however, nearly all forging is done by machine.

Hand forging is used primarily for small forgings and in repair work. It is practiced by blacksmiths, who forge horseshoes and other small iron objects. Blacksmiths first heat iron in a *forge* (open furnace) until it becomes red-hot. Then they remove the iron with tongs and hammer it into shape while holding it against an anvil. See **Blacksmith.**

Machine forging enables forgings to be mass-produced. Forging machines vary greatly in size and can handle objects that are far too heavy to forge by hand. Large cranes must be used to turn some of the heaviest forgings on the anvils.

There are two kinds of forging machines, *forging hammers* and *forging presses.* Both use hollow tools called *dies* to help shape metal. The metal is forced into the die and takes the shape of the die's cavity.

Forging hammers shape metal by striking it repeatedly in rapid succession. The power to raise the hammer is provided by steam, hydraulic energy, or electricity. In some forging hammers, the power also lowers the hammer. In other machines, called *drop hammers,* the hammer falls of its own weight. Forging hammers are used to shape most small forgings.

© Wardene Weisser, Berg & Associates

Blacksmiths, *above,* forge horseshoes and other small iron objects by hand. Blacksmiths heat the iron to a red glow in a *forge* (open furnace) before they hammer it into shape.

© Stacy Pick, Stock, Boston

A huge steel forging emerges from a forging press at a steel mill. Forging presses squeeze red-hot metal into a desired shape by forcing it into a die.

Forging presses squeeze metal into shape. Pressing is a much slower process than hammering, but only a press can provide the force necessary to make the most massive forgings. Pressing also causes less shock to the machine and the building that houses it than hammering does. Most forging presses are powered by hydraulic energy.

Dies that help shape forgings may be paired or single. Paired dies are used to make tools, engine parts, and other forgings that have complex shapes. The upper die is attached to the hammer or the moving part of the press, and the lower die to the anvil. Items produced by paired dies are called *closed die forgings* or, if a drop hammer is used, *drop forgings.*   Gordon H. Geiger

See also **Die and diemaking; Steam hammer.**

Formaldehyde is probably most familiar as the active ingredient in the solution used to preserve insects and other biological specimens. This solution, called *formalin,* is a water solution containing 35 to 40 per cent formaldehyde by weight. Formaldehyde itself is a colorless gas which is the simplest member of the class of organic chemicals called *aldehydes.*

Formaldehyde was discovered in 1867 by August Wilhelm von Hofmann, a German chemist. It is made commercially by the oxidation of methanol (methyl alcohol). Formaldehyde is used for disinfecting, for embalming, and for preserving grains and vegetables. It is also used in the manufacture of pharmaceuticals, urea resins, and dyes. The plastics industry prepares Bakelite from formaldehyde and phenol.

Formaldehyde has a stifling odor and can irritate membranes of the eyes, nose, and throat. In addition, laboratory tests have shown that formaldehyde probably causes cancer. The chemical formula of formaldehyde is CH_2O. It boils at $-21°$ C.   Robert C. Gadwood

See also **Aldehyde; Methanol.**

Formalin. See Formaldehyde.

Formic acid is an important industrial chemical. Leather manufacturers use formic acid for tanning and for removing hair from animal skins. It is also used in the manufacture of dyes, rubber, and many other products.

Formic acid has the chemical formula CH_2O_2. In its pure form, the acid is a strong-smelling, colorless liquid. It is highly corrosive and can cause severe burns if it comes in contact with a person's skin.

Formic acid gets its name from *Formica rufa,* the scientific name for a species of red ants. The acid was originally obtained by the destruction and distillation of these ants. Today, formic acid is produced in a two-step process. First, carbon monoxide and sodium hydroxide are heated under pressure to form sodium formate. This salt is then treated with hydrogen chloride to liberate the formic acid.   Robert J. Ouellette

Formosa. See Taiwan.

Formula. See Baby (Feeding procedures); in science, see Algebra (Writing formulas); **Chemistry.**

Formula One racing. See Automobile racing (Formula One racing).

Forrest, Edwin (1806-1872), was probably the first important actor in the history of American theater. Forrest was the most popular actor of his time. He dominated the American stage from the mid-1820's until his death.

Forrest's style reflected the romantic school of acting, which was vigorous, passionate, and seemingly unrestrained. Forrest's muscular physique made him an impressive figure on stage. Although some people considered his acting coarse and excessively emotional, Forrest was a disciplined, conscientious performer. He earned his early reputation in such plays by William Shakespeare as *King Lear, Othello,* and *Richard III.* But he also encouraged native drama in the United States by offering prizes for new plays written by Americans. Forrest was born in Philadelphia.   Stanley L. Glenn

Forrest, Nathan Bedford (1821-1877), was a Confederate general in the Civil War. He was a brilliant cavalry leader. He enlisted as a private in the Confederate Army in June 1861, and became a lieutenant colonel in command of a troop of cavalry by October. Forrest had no military education, but he enjoyed amazing success as a strategist and tactician.

Forrest escaped with his men from the Battle of Fort Donelson and fought at Shiloh in 1862 (see **Civil War** [Raids]). General Forrest then developed raiding tactics that made his cavalry a fearsome striking force. At Brice's Cross Roads, Miss., in June 1864, Forrest won a battle that was a model for cavalry warfare. When asked the secret of his victory, he is said to have replied, "To git thar fustest with the mostest men."

Forrest became a lieutenant general in February 1865. He was beaten by the Union Army at Selma, Ala., in April 1865. After the war, Forrest served as the first leader of the Ku Klux Klan, a white-supremacist organization that attempted to deny blacks their civil rights. Forrest was born in Bedford County, Tennessee.   Frank E. Vandiver

Forrestal, *FAWR ihst uhl,* **James Vincent** (1892-1949), was the first United States secretary of defense. He served from September 1947 until March 1949. He also served as secretary of the Navy from 1944 to 1947, and helped build the U.S. fleet into the largest in the world. In 1954, the Navy named a class of aircraft carriers the *Forrestal* in his honor.

When Congress passed the National Security Act in 1947 to unify the armed forces, it created a civilian secretary of national defense. President Harry S. Truman appointed Forrestal to the post. Forrestal resigned in 1949 due to mental and physical exhaustion. The strain of his job was blamed by many for his suicide two months later.

Forrestal was born in Beacon, N.Y. In World War I, he served as a naval aviator and then turned to a financial career in New York City.   Harvey Wish

Forster, E. M. (1879-1970), was an English novelist, essayist, and literary critic. His novels show his interest in personal relationships and in the social, psychological, and racial obstacles to such relationships. His fiction stresses the value of following generous impulses.

Forster's most highly praised novels are *Howards End* (1910) and *A Passage to India* (1924). *Howards End* is a social comedy with tragic overtones about several English middle-class characters. It reflects Forster's ideal of an "aristocracy of the sensitive, the considerate, and the plucky." *A Passage to India* describes the clash between English and traditional Indian cultures in India. Forster's other four novels are *Where Angels Fear to Tread* (1905), *The Longest Journey* (1907), *A Room with a View* (1908), and *Maurice* (completed in 1914, published in 1971, after the author's death).

For the last 46 years of his life, Forster produced only nonfiction. But he wrote his essays, biographies, and literary criticism in a masterly style noted for the same grace, polish, and elegant wit that characterized his novels. Edward Morgan Forster was born in London.

Garrett Stewart

See also **Bloomsbury Group.**

Forsythia, *fawr SIHTH ee uh,* is a shrub that belongs to the olive family. It grows as high as 9 feet (2.7 meters) and has spreading, arched branches. People sometimes

W. Atlee Burpee Co.
The forsythia is a hardy, spreading shrub. It blooms in early spring and has tiny bell-shaped yellow flowers.

call the forsythia the *golden bell* because its yellow flowers look like tiny, golden bells. One to six flowers grow in clusters. Forsythias produce many blossoms, which open in early spring before the leaves appear. The leaves grow 3 to 5 inches (8 to 13 centimeters) long and are egg-shaped. They usually have jagged edges. Forsythias grow well in any garden soil and can withstand cold temperatures. The forsythia is named for the British botanist William Forsyth.

Scientific classification. Forsythias belong to the olive family, Oleaceae. Different forsythias are *Forsythia suspensa* and *F. viridissima.*   Fred T. Davies, Jr.

See also **Flower** (picture: Garden perennials).

Fort originally was a fortified building or place that provided defense against attack. On the American frontier, many forts also served as trading posts. Many cities that grew up around forts bear their names, including Fort Wayne, Ind. The term *fort* now applies to permanent United States army posts. For information on various forts, see the articles and cross-references following this article. See also **Blockhouse; Castle.**

Hugh M. Cole

Fort Beauséjour National Historic Park. See Canada (National historic parks and sites).

Fort Belvoir, *BEHL vawr,* Virginia, is the site of the United States Army Defense Systems Management College. It also houses National Guard and Army reserve units. The fort covers about 8,700 acres (3,500 hectares) along the Potomac River, and lies 18 miles (29 kilometers) south of Washington, D. C. The Army established Camp Belvoir in 1912. It was named after the ruins of

Belvoir, the home of Colonel George William Fairfax, a friend and neighbor of George Washington. The fort once housed the United States Army Engineer Center.

Steve E. Dietrich

Fort Benjamin Harrison, Indiana, is the home of the United States Army Finance and Accounting Center and the Soldier Support Center. It also houses The Adjutant General's School and is headquarters of the 123rd Army Reserve Command. The post lies 12 miles (19 kilometers) northeast of Indianapolis, and covers about 2,500 acres (1,000 hectares). It was founded in 1903 and named for President Benjamin Harrison.

Steve E. Dietrich

Fort Benning, Georgia, is the site of the United States Army Infantry Center. This command includes the infantry school and the Army School of the Americas. The infantry school also conducts airborne and ranger training courses. The post covers 182,000 acres (73,650 hectares). It lies 9 miles (14 kilometers) south of Columbus on the Chattahoochee River. The Army established Camp Benning in 1918. The post was named after Brigadier General Henry L. Benning who served in the Confederate Army in the Civil War (1861-1865).   Thomas S. Grodecki

Bill C. Walton, U.S. Army
Paratroop trainees practice parachute jumping at Fort Benning, the chief training center for U.S. airborne troops.

Fort Bliss, Texas, houses the United States Army Air Defense Artillery Center and School. Troops train there to operate antiaircraft artillery and guided missiles. The post's firing ranges cover about 1,200,000 acres (486,000 hectares) in Texas and New Mexico. The post opened in 1854 and was named for Lieutenant Colonel William Bliss, a Mexican War hero.   Thomas S. Grodecki

Fort Bragg, North Carolina, is the home of airborne combat units of the United States Army. It also houses the Special Warfare Center, which trains troops in psychological and guerrilla warfare. The post lies 9 miles (14 kilometers) northwest of Fayetteville, and covers about 149,000 acres (60,000 hectares). It was founded in 1918, and named for Braxton Bragg, a Confederate Army general in the Civil War.

The Army trained its first two airborne divisions, the 82nd and the 101st, at Fort Bragg during World War II. After the war, the post became the headquarters of the 82nd Airborne Division and the XVIII Airborne Corps.

Thomas S. Grodecki

Fort Condé. See Alabama (Exploration).

Fort Crèvecoeur. See Hennepin, Louis.

Fort Dearborn was built near the mouth of the Chicago River, close to the site of Chicago's present Michigan Avenue Bridge. Soldiers under the command of Captain John Whistler built the fort in 1803. It was named after General Henry Dearborn. The double stockade had blockhouses on two corners, enclosed log barracks, stables, and an Indian agency.

A garrison of soldiers at Fort Dearborn protected the few Americans on the frontier from attacks by Indians. Soon after the War of 1812 began, the troops and settlers were ordered to move to Fort Wayne for greater safety. The soldiers feared Indian attacks on the way, and urged Captain Nathan Heald to stay within the stockade. The captain insisted on obeying orders. He destroyed all ammunition that could not be carried and left the post with about 100 troops and settlers on Aug. 15, 1812.

A band of 500 Potawatomi and allied Indians attacked the Americans near the fort (at the eastern end of Chicago's present Eighteenth Street). They killed more than half of the Americans, captured the rest, and burned the fort the next day. Fort Dearborn was rebuilt about 1816, and torn down in 1836. By then the danger of Indian attack in the area had passed. Walker D. Wyman

See also **Dearborn, Henry.**

Fort-de-France, *FAWR duh FRAHNS* (pop. 99,844), is the capital of Martinique, an island in the West Indies that is an overseas department of France. It lies on the west coast of the island. For location, see **West Indies** (map).

Fort-de-France has palm-lined streets, brightly colored buildings, and a waterfront park. It is a shipping center for sugar, rum, fruit, and other products of Martinique. It is also Martinique's financial center. The city attracts many tourists. A French naval base is located there.

Fort-de-France was founded in 1675. It was called Fort Royal until the late 1700's, when it received its present name. The city has been the capital of Martinique since 1692. The city was partially destroyed by an earthquake in 1839 and by a fire in 1890. Gustavo A. Antonini

See also **Martinique.**

Fort Des Moines. See Des Moines (Government).

Fort Dix, New Jersey, is a center of U.S. Army basic training. It covers about 31,000 acres (13,000 hectares) and lies 17 miles (27 kilometers) southeast of Trenton. An Army Personnel Center processes troops for overseas duty there. The center also discharges or releases soldiers from the Army. The fort, founded in 1917, was named after John A. Dix, a Union major general in the Civil War (1861-1865). Many of the activities at Fort Dix are scheduled to be transferred to other bases by 1995, according to an act passed by Congress in 1988.

Steve E. Dietrich

Fort Donelson. See Civil War (Battles of Fort Henry and Fort Donelson); **National Park System** (table: National battlefields).

Fort Duquesne, *doo KAYN,* was built by the French in 1754 at the fork of the Monongahela and Allegheny rivers. French forces had driven Virginian frontiersmen from this site. The French named the fort after the Marquis Michel-Ange Duquesne, governor general of Canada. The Battle of the Great Meadows took place near the fort in 1754. The French defeated a band of militiamen led by George Washington. This battle marked the beginning of the French and Indian War.

In 1755, the French defeated General Braddock in another battle near Fort Duquesne. Three years later, the French burned the fort and fled northward when they learned that a British force was approaching. The British

Chicago Park District

A replica of Fort Dearborn was built in 1933 for Chicago's Century of Progress Exposition, and later dismantled. It contained articles used by settlers at the time the original fort was built.

built Fort Pitt nearby on the Monongahela. Pittsburgh later rose on this site.   Walker D. Wyman

See also **French and Indian wars.**

Fort Eustis, *YOO stihs,* Virginia, houses the United States Army Transportation Center. It covers about 8,200 acres (3,300 hectares), and lies 11 miles (18 kilometers) south of Williamsburg. Other activities at the fort include the Aviation Logistics School, the Training Support Center, and aviation matériel laboratories. Fort Eustis has the nation's only all-military-operated railway system. The post was set up as a Coast Artillery training area in 1918, and named for Brigadier General Abraham Eustis, an artillery officer of the early 1800's.

Steve E. Dietrich

Fort Frederica National Monument, *frehd uh REE kuh,* is on Saint Simons Island in Georgia. The monument contains the ruins of a fort built in the 1700's. James Edward Oglethorpe, founder of the colony of Georgia, had the fort built as a defense against the Spaniards. For the fort's area, see **National Park System** (table: National monuments).

Critically reviewed by the National Park Service

Fort George G. Meade, Maryland, houses the headquarters of the First United States Army and the National Security Agency. The fort covers about 13,000 acres (5,300 hectares) and lies about 15 miles (24 kilometers) northeast of Washington, D.C. The post was established in 1917 to house troops drafted during World War I (1914-1918). It was originally named Camp Meade for Major General George Gordon Meade, a Union Army commander during the Civil War (1861-1865). In 1928, the post was renamed Fort Leonard Wood. The Army gave the post its current name in 1929. The U.S. government plans to reduce the base to 4,700 acres (1,900 hectares) by 1995.   Thomas S. Grodecki

Fort Gordon, Georgia, is the home of the United States Army Signal School and the Dwight D. Eisenhower Medical Center. It lies 15 miles (24 kilometers) southwest of Augusta and covers about 56,000 acres (23,000 hectares). It was founded in 1941 as an infantry training center and named for Lieutenant General John B. Gordon, a Confederate Army officer and former governor of Georgia. The Signal Corps Training Center was established at the post in 1948.   Thomas S. Grodecki

Fort Henry, Battle of. See Civil War (Battles of Fort Henry and Fort Donelson).

Fort Hood, Texas, houses some of the armored units of the United States Army. It lies 2 miles (3 kilometers) west of Killeen, and covers about 217,000 acres (88,000 hectares). The post was founded in 1942 as Camp Hood, and named for John B. Hood, a Confederate Army general who commanded the Texas Brigade. It became a permanent fort in 1950. North Fort Hood lies 17 miles (27 kilometers) to the north.   Thomas S. Grodecki

Fort Jefferson National Monument is located on the Dry Tortugas Islands, 68 miles (109 kilometers) west of Key West, Fla. The fort was established in 1846. It was a federal prison from 1863 to 1873. Scientists find unusual bird and marine life in the area. Fort Jefferson National Monument was established in 1935. For its area, see **National Park System** (table: National monuments).

Critically reviewed by the National Park Service

Fort Knox, Kentucky, houses the United States Army Armor Center. This command includes the armor

Karl Kummels, Shostal

The gold depository at Fort Knox contains more than $6 billion of the gold owned by the United States government.

school, armor board, bullion depository, and armor training center. The post covers 110,000 acres (44,500 hectares), and lies 35 miles (56 kilometers) south of Louisville. The government took over part of the present post for army maneuvers in 1918. Camp Knox was established in 1918, and named for Major General Henry Knox, the first secretary of war. Its name became Fort Knox in 1933. The post has been called "the Home of Armor," because the Army created its first armored force here in 1940. Four combat armored divisions were trained at Fort Knox during World War II (1939-1945).

The U.S. Treasury Department completed its gold depository there in 1936. The depository contains more than $6 billion worth of gold. During World War II, the Constitution, Declaration of Independence, Gutenberg Bible, Lincoln's Gettysburg Address, and Magna Carta were placed in the depository at Fort Knox for safekeeping.   Critically reviewed by Fort Knox

Fort-Lamy. See N'djamena.

Fort Langley. See Canada (Historic parks).

Fort Lauderdale, *LAW duhr DAYL* (pop. 153,279), is a major resort city and a leading vacation and retirement center in Florida. It lies on the Atlantic Ocean, about 25 miles (40 kilometers) north of Miami. For the location of Fort Lauderdale, see **Florida** (political map). Fort Lauderdale's location and warm climate have made it one of the fastest growing cities of the United States. The city's population increased from about 18,000 in 1940 to about 153,000 in 1980. Fort Lauderdale, Hollywood, and Pompano Beach form a metropolitan area with a population of 1,018,200.

During the 1800's, Seminole Indians lived in what is now Fort Lauderdale. White settlers, most of whom farmed and fished for a living, first arrived in the area in the 1890's. They named their settlement after a fort that Major William Lauderdale had built there in 1838, during the Second Seminole War.

Description. Fort Lauderdale, the county seat of Broward County, covers about 32 square miles (83 square kilometers). This area includes 3 square miles (8

square kilometers) of inland water. Fort Lauderdale has about 85 miles (137 kilometers) of navigable canals and waterways. Fort Lauderdale is sometimes called the *Venice of America,* though it does not have canals instead of streets, as does the city of Venice, Italy. Fort Lauderdale also has about 6 miles (10 kilometers) of ocean beaches, where people can go boating, fishing, and swimming.

Cultural attractions in the city include the Museum of Art and the Parker Playhouse. Fort Lauderdale has a ballet company and an opera guild. The city is also the headquarters of the Philharmonic Orchestra of Florida. Nova University is located near Fort Lauderdale. Three other area schools share facilities and offer advanced courses at the nine-story University Tower in downtown Fort Lauderdale.

Construction and tourism rank as Fort Lauderdale's leading sources of income. The Fort Lauderdale metropolitan area has about 1,700 manufacturing firms. Their chief products, in order of value, are computers and communications equipment, electrical equipment, printed materials, and machinery.

Port Everglades, at the south end of Fort Lauderdale, serves as a major port for cargo ships and passenger cruisers. Major airlines use Fort Lauderdale-Hollywood International Airport.

Government and history. Fort Lauderdale has a commission-manager form of government. The voters in the city elect the five commissioners to a three-year term. The candidate who receives the most votes becomes mayor. The commissioners hire a city manager to serve as the chief administrator of Fort Lauderdale's local government.

The city had a population of only about 150 when it was incorporated in 1911. After World War II ended in 1945, a tourist boom resulted in a rapid population growth. Fort Lauderdale received national attention during the 1960's, when thousands of college students began to spend their spring vacation there. Today, about 3 million tourists visit the city yearly.

William H. Bates

Fort Leavenworth, *LEHV uhn WUHRTH,* Kansas, is the home of the U.S. Army Combined Arms Center. It also houses the Army Command and General Staff College, the Army's senior tactical school. The fort covers about 5,600 acres (2,300 hectares) on the Missouri River, about 30 miles (50 kilometers) northwest of Kansas City. The Army operates a military prison there, the U.S. Disciplinary Barracks. The fort was named for Brigadier General Henry Leavenworth, who founded it in 1827.

Steve E. Dietrich

See also **Kansas** (Places to visit).

Fort Lee, Virginia, is the home of the United States Army Quartermaster Center and School, the Army Logistics Center, and the Army Logistics Management College. It lies 3 miles (5 kilometers) east of Petersburg, and covers about 5,600 acres (2,300 hectares). The post was founded in 1917 and named for Confederate General Robert E. Lee. After World War I (1914-1918), it served as a wildlife sanctuary until it reopened during World War II (1939-1945). It became a permanent fort in 1950.

Steve E. Dietrich

Fort Lennox National Historic Park. See Canada (National historic parks and sites).

Fort Leonard Wood, Missouri, is the home of the United States Army's Engineer Center and School. It covers about 65,000 acres (26,000 hectares) and lies in the Mark Twain National Forest, 135 miles (215 kilometers) southwest of St. Louis (see **Missouri** [map]). The post was built in 1941 and named for Major General Leonard Wood, who was Army chief of staff from 1910 to 1914. Fort Leonard Wood provides basic and advanced training for Army recruits in the Midwestern United States.

Thomas S. Grodecki

Fort Loudoun Dam. See Tennessee Valley Authority (The dams).

Fort Louis. See Alabama (Exploration).

Fort Malden National Historic Park. See Canada (National historic parks and sites).

Fort Marion National Monument. See Castillo de San Marcos National Monument.

Fort Massachusetts. See Mississippi (Places to visit).

Fort Matanzas National Monument, *muh TAN zuhs,* is near St. Augustine, Fla. The Spanish built the fort in the early 1740's. It served as a defense for St. Augustine against French colonizers. St. Augustine is the oldest permanent settlement established in the United States by Europeans. Fort Matanzas National Monument was established in 1924. For area, see **National Park System** (table: National monuments).

Critically reviewed by the National Park Service

Fort McClellan, *muh KLEHL uhn,* Alabama, is the home of the United States Army Chemical School, the Military Police School, and the Department of Defense Polygraph Institute. It also houses a basic combat training brigade. The fort was a training site for the U.S. Women's Army Corps (WAC) from 1952 until 1978, when the corps was dissolved. The fort covers about 47,000 acres (19,000 hectares) northeast of Anniston. It was established in 1917 and named for Major General George B. McClellan, who served as commander of Union forces during the early years of the Civil War (1861-1865).

Steve E. Dietrich

Fort McHenry National Monument and Historic Shrine is in Baltimore, Md. Francis Scott Key composed "The Star-Spangled Banner" as he watched a battle at the fort during the War of 1812. The fort was named for James McHenry, a signer of the United States Constitution from Maryland. The monument was established in 1939. For area, see **National Park System** (table: National monuments). See also **Maryland** (picture: The Fort McHenry National Monument).

Critically reviewed by the National Park Service

Fort McPherson, *muhk FUHR suhn* or *muhk FEER suhn,* Georgia, serves as the headquarters of the United States Army Forces Command. This command supervises the combat readiness of all the Army's active and reserve forces. The fort covers about 480 acres (190 hectares) and lies within the city limits of Atlanta. The Army made it a permanent post in 1889, and named it after Maj. Gen. James B. McPherson, a Union Army commander killed in the Civil War (1861-1865).

Steve E. Dietrich

Fort Monmouth, *MAHN muhth,* New Jersey, is the headquarters of the United States Army Communications-Electronics Command. It also houses the U.S. Military Academy Preparatory School, the Chaplain Center and School, and electronics research and development laboratories. The fort covers 1,550 acres (630 hectares), and lies about 40 miles (65 kilometers) south of New York City. The post was established in 1917 and received its present name in 1925.   Steve E. Dietrich

Fort Monroe, Virginia, is the headquarters of the United States Army Training and Doctrine Command. This command controls all Army individual schooling and training and manages the Army ROTC program. The post lies on Old Point Comfort at the mouth of the James River, about 11 miles (18 kilometers) north of Norfolk. It overlooks the entrance to Hampton Roads and covers about 1,100 acres (450 hectares).

Engineers began building a fort there in 1819, although the site had been fortified as early as 1609. In 1832, the post was named Fort Monroe, after President James Monroe. Poet Edgar Allan Poe served at Fort Monroe before he entered West Point. Robert E. Lee supervised construction of the walled fort in the early 1830's. Jefferson Davis, President of the Confederacy, was imprisoned at Fort Monroe for two years after the Civil War ended in 1865. The original fort is still surrounded by a moat.   Steve E. Dietrich

Fort Moultrie, *MOOL tree,* or *MOHL tree,* is a fort on Sullivan's Island at the main entrance to Charleston Harbor, S.C. Settlers first called it Fort Sullivan. In 1776, the fort withstood a British attack designed to capture Charleston and make it a base of British operations in the South. The attack included 10 British ships under Sir Peter Parker, carrying a strong force of British troops under Sir Henry Clinton. They withdrew after 10 hours. The American forces at Charleston numbered 6,500 men, of whom 435 were stationed at Fort Sullivan. They were commanded by Colonel William Moultrie, for whom the fort was renamed. This defense saved the South temporarily from invasion. Clinton again tried to conquer South Carolina later in the war, and Fort Moultrie fell on May 7, 1780.

Just before the Civil War, a United States garrison occupied Fort Moultrie. It was abandoned by its commander, Major Anderson, who moved his troops to Fort Sumter on Dec. 26, 1860. During the bombardment of Sumter the following April, Fort Moultrie served as Confederate headquarters.

Edgar Allan Poe was once a sergeant major at Fort Moultrie. He wrote "Israfel" there.   Walker D. Wyman

See also **Flag** (picture: Flags in American history); **Fort Sumter; Moultrie, William.**

Fort Necessity was a fortification built by George Washington in 1754. It was located in southwestern Pennsylvania. Washington surrendered it to the French in 1754. The French allowed his army to march out of the fort and return home. The site became a national battlefield site in 1931 and a national battlefield in 1961. For area, see **National Park System** (table: National battlefields). See also **Washington, George** (Surrender of Fort Necessity).

Fort Niagara was built by the French in 1726 on land bought from the Seneca Indians. It stood on the eastern shore of the Niagara River and guarded a narrow passage which led to the rich fur lands west of the river. British forces captured the fort during the French and Indian War. They used it during the Revolutionary War as a starting point for raids against western settlers. Fort Niagara remained in British hands until 1796, when the

Jay Treaty finally gave it to the United States. The British captured the fort again during the War of 1812. It remained in British hands until 1815.

Fort Little Niagara was the name of another fort in the same region. The French built this fort in 1751, and destroyed it during the French and Indian War to prevent the British from taking it.   Walker D. Wyman

Fort Peck Dam, on the Missouri River in northeastern Montana, is one of the largest earth-fill dams in the world. It contains about 125,600,000 cubic yards (96,050,000 cubic meters) of earth. Fort Peck Dam was completed in 1937. It stretches for nearly 4 miles (6 kilometers) across the Missouri. The main section is 10,578 feet (3,224 meters) long, and a dike section on the west riverbank is 10,448 feet (3,185 meters) long. The dam is 250 feet (76 meters) high. The reservoir holds 19.1 million acre-feet (23.6 billion cubic meters) of water. See also **Dam** (picture).   Edward C. Pritchett

Fort Pickens was a U.S. military post on Santa Rosa Island near Pensacola, Fla. It remained under federal control throughout the Civil War. When Florida *seceded* (withdrew) from the Union in January, 1861, Lieutenant Adam J. Slemmer moved a small body of federal soldiers into Fort Pickens. Union and Confederate authorities agreed that the Union would not reinforce the fort, and the Confederate States would not attack it. But after Confederate forces fired on Fort Sumter, S.C., on April 12, 1861, and the war began, the Union rushed reinforcements to Fort Pickens. The defenders of the fort withstood a surprise attack on Oct. 9, 1861.
      Frank L. Klement

Fort Prince of Wales. See **Canada** (National historic parks and sites); **Manitoba** (Places to visit).

Fort Pulaski National Monument, *puh LAS kee* or *pyoo LAS kee,* is on the coast of Georgia. It includes a brick fort which Union forces captured in 1862. The fort could not withstand the Union Army's cannon attack. The monument was established in 1924. For the area of Fort Pulaski National Monument, see **National Park System** (table: National monuments).

Fort Randall Dam is part of a large-scale federal program for the development of the Missouri River basin. The dam lies in south-central South Dakota near Lake Andes above old Fort Randall. United States Army engineers began building this electric-power and navigation project in 1946. They completed it in 1956. The dam is 160 feet (49 meters) high and 10,700 feet (3,261 meters) long. The earth-fill dam contains 50,200,000 cubic yards (38,380,000 cubic meters) of earth. Its reservoir can store 6.1 million acre-feet (7.5 billion cubic meters) of water. The power plant has a capacity of 320,000 kilowatts, and began operating in 1954.   Edward C. Pritchett

Fort Recovery. See **Ohio** (Places to visit).

Fort Riley, Kansas, is the home of the United States Army's First Infantry Division. It lies about 100 miles (160 kilometers) west of Kansas City and covers about 100,000 acres (40,000 hectares). The Army set up the post in 1853 and later named it for Major General Bennett Riley, who fought in the Mexican War (1846-1848). Fort Riley is known as "the cradle of the cavalry" because many cavalry regiments were organized there, including Lieutenant Colonel George A. Custer's Seventh Cavalry.
      Thomas S. Grodecki

See also **Kansas** (Places to visit).

Fort Rucker, Alabama, houses the United States Army Aviation Center. The center trains pilots and maintenance workers for the Army's own air force of small fixed-wing airplanes and helicopters. Also located at the post are the Army Safety Center, the Aviation Development Test Activity, and the Army Aeromedical Center. The post lies 25 miles (40 kilometers) northwest of Dothan and covers about 64,000 acres (26,000 hectares). It was established in 1942 and named for Colonel Edmund W. Rucker, a Confederate Army cavalry leader.

Thomas S. Grodecki

Fort Sainte Marie. See Ontario (Early settlement).

Fort Sam Houston, Texas, houses the headquarters of the Fifth United States Army. The fort covers 3,160 acres (1,280 hectares) within the city limits of San Antonio and about 28,000 acres (11,000 hectares) at Camp Bullis, 20 miles (32 kilometers) northwest of the city. Also located at the post is the Academy of Health Science, one of the world's largest medical training centers. The post was established in 1876 as the Military Post of San Antonio. In 1890, its name was changed to honor Samuel Houston, the first president of the Republic of Texas.

Thomas S. Grodecki

Fort Shafter, Hawaii, serves as the headquarters of the United States Army Western Command. It covers 1,300 acres (530 hectares) northwest of Honolulu's main urban area. The post was set up as Kahauiki Military Reservation in 1899. In 1907, it was named for Major General William R. Shafter, who fought in the Civil War (1861-1865) and the Spanish-American War (1898).

Steve E. Dietrich

Fort Sill, Oklahoma, is the site of the United States Army Field Artillery Center and School. The post covers 94,220 acres (38,000 hectares) near Lawton. The Army established the post in 1869 to keep watch over the Comanche and Kiowa tribes. The post was named after Brigadier General Joshua W. Sill, a Union commander killed at the Battle of Stones River during the Civil War (1861-1865). The grave of the Apache leader Geronimo is located at Fort Sill.   Thomas S. Grodecki

Fort Smith (pop. 71,626; met. area pop. 162,813) is the most important manufacturing center in Arkansas and the state's second largest city. Only Little Rock has more people. Fort Smith is a transportation center on the western border of Arkansas. It lies at the foot of the Boston Mountains in the Arkansas River Valley (see **Arkansas** [political map]). Part of its metropolitan area lies in Oklahoma. The Fort Smith area includes coal and natural gas deposits and small farms. Large national forests lie to the city's north, southwest, and south. Fort Smith factories produce about 100 different products, including furniture, home refrigerators, and heating and air-conditioning units.

Downtown Fort Smith includes the courtroom of the famous frontier "hanging judge," Isaac C. Parker. The courtroom is a national historic site. The downtown section also includes a historical museum, an art center-community theater complex, and a civic center.

Fort Smith began as a fort that was established by the United States Army in 1817 to keep peace between the Osage and Cherokee Indians. The fort was named for General Thomas A. Smith, commander of the military district in which the fort stood. Fort Smith grew into a town, which was incorporated in 1842. It was incorpo-

rated as a city in 1885. The discovery of natural gas near the city about 1900 gave the growing Fort Smith industries a cheap source of power. In 1969, a federal navigation project on the Arkansas River made it possible for barges to reach Fort Smith. The city became an important port on the Arkansas River Navigation System.

Debbye Hughes

See also **Arkansas** (Interesting facts about Arkansas).

Fort Stanwix National Monument, in Rome, N.Y., was authorized in 1935 as a memorial to the Revolutionary War (1775-1783) and United States colonial history. For area, see **National Park System** (table: National monuments).

Fort Sumter was the first Union fort captured by the Confederates in the Civil War (1861-1865). In 1860, South Carolina seceded from the Union and prepared to seize the United States forts in the harbor at Charleston, S.C. Major Robert Anderson (1805-1871) directed the harbor defenses. He made his headquarters in Fort Moultrie. Anderson realized that South Carolina troops would soon attack Fort Moultrie and that it would be difficult to defend his position. He moved his headquarters to Fort Sumter.

In April 1861, Pierre Beauregard, the Confederate general, demanded the surrender of the fort. Anderson refused. The vigorous bombardment that followed began the Civil War. On April 14, Union troops evacuated the fort. The Confederates permitted Anderson and his command to leave with their weapons and their flag. The Confederates held Fort Sumter until February 1865.

John Donald Hicks

See also **Beauregard, Pierre G. T.; Civil War** (Opening battles; picture: Fort Sumter); **Fort Moultrie; South Carolina** (picture: Fort Sumter); **Ruffin, Edmund.**

Fort Sumter National Monument lies in Charleston Harbor, South Carolina. It was authorized in 1948 as a Civil War memorial. For area, see **National Park System** (table: National monuments). See also **Fort Sumter; National Park System** (picture).

Fort Supply Dam is a federal flood-control project located in northwestern Oklahoma. It is on Wolfe Creek near its junction with the North Canadian River. Fort Supply Dam is an earth-fill structure 11,865 feet (3,616 meters) long and 85 feet (26 meters) high. The reservoir has a storage capacity of 106,100 acre-feet (131 million cubic meters) of water. The dam was completed in 1942.

Edward A. Pritchett

Fort Ticonderoga, on Lake Champlain in New York State, was an important stronghold during the Revolutionary War. It commanded the invasion route by water from Canada. When hostilities began, a group of Americans organized an expedition to seize the fort. The group included Ethan Allen, a Vermont colonial leader. On May 10, 1775, Allen and Benedict Arnold led the *Green Mountain Boys* (Vermont soldiers) in a surprise attack and captured the fort without loss of life. The British recaptured the fort in 1777, but abandoned it in 1780 when they gave up hope of using the invasion route.

In 1908, the fort was rebuilt, and a museum was opened there. The museum contains articles used by soldiers of the revolution.   Walker D. Wyman

Fort Union National Monument is near Watrous, N. Mex. The army built the fort in 1851 as a defensive point on the Santa Fe Trail. It became a national monument in 1954. For area, see **National Park System** (table: National monuments).

Critically reviewed by the National Park Service

Fort Wayne (pop. 172,349; met. area pop. 354,156) is a commercial and industrial center in northeastern Indiana. It is the second largest city in the state. Only Indianapolis has more people. Fort Wayne lies about 130 miles (209 kilometers) northeast of Indianapolis. For location, see **Indiana** (political map).

Fort Wayne, the county seat of Allen County, covers about 62 square miles (161 square kilometers). The St. Marys and St. Joseph rivers join within the city to form the Maumee River.

Cultural attractions in Fort Wayne include the Fort Wayne Philharmonic Orchestra. The Community Center for the Performing Arts is the home of the Fort Wayne Ballet, the Civic Theater, and other fine-arts groups. The city's museums include the Lincoln Library and Museum of the Lincoln National Life Foundation, the Allen County-Fort Wayne Historical Museum, the Museum of Art, and the Diehm Museum of Natural History.

A campus of Indiana University-Purdue University is located in Fort Wayne. Other institutions of higher education include the Indiana Institute of Technology, St. Francis College, and Fort Wayne Bible College. Fort Wayne's biggest tourist attraction, the Three Rivers Festival, is a spectacle of parades and historical displays that is held in July.

The Fort Wayne area has about 450 manufacturing plants. The chief products include machinery, electronic parts and equipment, and transportation equipment. Major airlines and freight and passenger trains serve the city.

The Miami Indians settled in what is now the Fort Wayne area before white settlers arrived. A United States Army officer, Major General "Mad Anthony"

Wayne, built a fort there in 1794. The fort and the town that grew up around it were named in his honor. Fort Wayne was incorporated as a city in 1840.

Fort Wayne was a fur-trading center until the 1830's. In 1832, construction began at Fort Wayne on the Wabash and Erie Canal, which linked Lake Erie with the Wabash River. Fort Wayne was nicknamed *The Summit City* because it stands on the highest point between the waterways leading to the Atlantic Ocean and those leading to the Gulf of Mexico. The city's population grew as Irish and German immigrants came to work on the canal and in related industries. A railroad built through the city in 1854 helped attract industry. By 1900, the population had grown to over 45,000.

A number of construction projects were completed in downtown Fort Wayne in the early 1980's. They included an office complex, a convention center, and an art museum. Fort Wayne has a mayor-council form of government.   Richard A. Battin

See also **Indiana** (picture: Historic Fort Wayne).

Fort William, Ontario. See **Thunder Bay.**

Fort Worth, Tex. (pop. 385,164; met. area pop. 973,138), is a major industrial city and one of the nation's chief aircraft producers. It is a leader among Southwestern cities as a market for grain and oil. Fort Worth lies about 30 miles (48 kilometers) west of Dallas in north-central Texas. For location, see **Texas** (political map).

Major Ripley A. Arnold founded Fort Worth in 1849 as an Army post to protect settlers from Indian attacks. The post was named for Major General William J. Worth, a hero of the Mexican War. Fort Worth is still occasionally called "Cowtown." The city got this early nickname because of its history as a cattle-marketing center.

The city. Fort Worth occupies about 251 square miles (650 square kilometers) in the center of Tarrant County. The Fort Worth metropolitan area covers three counties and occupies a total of 2,539 square miles (6,576 square kilometers).

Fort Worth's main business district lies on the south bank of the Trinity River, which runs through the center of the city. The tallest buildings in Fort Worth include City Center II, the Continental Plaza, and the InterFirst Bank Tower. Each of these buildings is 40 stories high. At the southeast end of the downtown area, the Fort Worth Convention Center covers 14 city blocks between Houston and Commerce streets.

About 23 per cent of the people of Fort Worth are black. People of Mexican ancestry make up about 12 per cent of the population.

Economy of Fort Worth is based on manufacturing, which employs about one-fourth of the workers in the area. The area has about 1,800 manufacturing firms. Fort Worth's largest industries make airplanes, helicopters, and electronic equipment. Its aircraft plants are among the largest in the nation. Other products include food products, mobile homes, oil-well equipment, and shipping containers. Fort Worth is also one of the Southwest's leading grain-milling and storage centers.

Fort Worth lies in the center of a rich oil-producing region, and about 35 oil companies have offices in the city. About 40 insurance firms have their headquarters in Fort Worth. The city ranks as a major wholesale outlet for the Southwest. It is served by railroad passenger trains, rail freight lines, and bus and truck lines. Two in-

Artstreet

Fort Ticonderoga, a military stronghold on Lake Champlain during the Revolutionary War, has been rebuilt as a museum.

terstate highways intersect in the downtown area. The Dallas-Fort Worth International Airport lies about midway between the two cities.

Education and cultural life. Fort Worth is the home of the Southwestern Baptist Theological Seminary, Texas Christian University, and Texas Wesleyan College. A campus of the University of Texas is in nearby Arlington. Tarrant County Junior College has four campuses in Fort Worth. The city's public school system consists of 115 elementary and high schools. Fort Worth also has about 50 private schools, about 30 of which are church-supported schools.

The *Star-Telegram* is the only daily newspaper in Fort Worth. Ten television stations and about 40 radio stations serve the city.

Fort Worth has a ballet company, an opera company, and a symphony orchestra. Many people enjoy summer musicals at the Casa Mañana theater-in-the-round. The William Edrington Scott Theatre features plays and motion pictures. Fort Worth's annual Southwestern Exposition and Fat Stock Show is one of the nation's largest livestock shows. The Texas Rangers of the American League play their home baseball games in Arlington Stadium, which is in nearby Arlington.

The Fort Worth Museum of Science and History, one of the largest children's museums in the United States, has live animals in some exhibits. The Amon Carter Museum of Western Art displays paintings and sculpture of the American West by the American artists Frederic Remington and Charles M. Russell. The Fort Worth Art Center also exhibits works by American artists. The Kimbell Art Museum includes a large collection of European paintings.

In Forest Park, 3 miles (5 kilometers) west of downtown, the Fort Worth Zoological Park has more than 600 kinds of animals. The park also has the actual homes of early Fort Worth settlers in a log cabin village. The nearby Botanic Gardens features about 150,000 plants.

Government. Fort Worth has a mayor-council form of government. Voters elect the mayor and eight council members to two-year terms. The mayor and council members all serve without salary. The council employs a city manager as the administrative head of the government. The city manager carries out policies established by the council, prepares the budget, and appoints and dismisses department heads. The Fort Worth city government gets most of its income from property and sales taxes.

History. On June 6, 1849, Major Ripley A. Arnold established an Army post called Fort Worth to protect settlers from attacks by Indians. The soldiers left in 1853, and many settlers moved into the Army buildings. Fort Worth became the county seat of Tarrant County in 1860. During the 1860's and 1870's, the people traded with cowboys driving cattle to markets in Kansas. Fort Worth was incorporated as a city in 1873.

In 1876, the Texas and Pacific Railroad reached Fort Worth, allowing cattle to be shipped directly from the city. Fort Worth's first flour mill opened in 1882. As the cattle and grain industries developed, the city's population grew from 500 in 1870 to 26,688 in 1900.

In 1902, the Swift and Armour companies built large meat-packing plants in Fort Worth. The meat industry helped Fort Worth's population reach 73,312 by 1910. The discovery of several oil fields in West Texas about 1915 brought more people to Fort Worth. By 1930, the city's population had climbed to 163,447. The Great Depression almost stopped Fort Worth's growth during the 1930's. Only 14,000 new residents settled there between 1930 and 1940.

During World War II (1939-1945), Fort Worth became a center for the manufacture of airplanes, helicopters, and other military products. Jobs created by defense industries caused a sharp population rise during and after the war. The city had 356,268 people by 1960.

Fort Worth's growth slowed during the 1960's, and the population of the city declined in the 1970's as many people moved to the suburbs. Unemployment in the defense and oil industries contributed to the population slowdown and decline.

Fort Worth's development has been affected by a traditional rivalry with Dallas, which has a larger population and a stronger economy. Efforts toward greater cooperation led to construction of the Dallas-Fort Worth International Airport, which opened in 1974.

In the 1980's, Fort Worth's population began to grow, largely because of an increase in national defense spending in the area. About a fourth of the city's work-

Lee Angle Photography

Fort Worth is one of the largest industrial cities in Texas. The Tarrant County Convention Center, *right,* stands at the edge of the city's main business district.

ers are employed in manufacturing, and so Fort Worth needs industrial jobs for steady growth and a strong economy. The city depends heavily on jobs in defense plants, especially in the General Dynamics factory. General Dynamics is the city's leading employer.

To help slow and offset the movement of people and trade away from the city into the suburbs, city leaders began major urban renewal programs in the late 1970's. Four downtown office buildings, each 35 to 40 stories high, were completed in the early 1980's. In 1986, voters approved a $165-million bond issue—the largest in the city's history—for street improvements and new parks and recreation facilities. Kyle O. Thompson

Fortaleza, *FAWR tuh LAY zuh* (pop. 648,815; met. area pop. 1,581,588), is a city on the northeast coast of Brazil. For the location of Fortaleza, see **Brazil** (political map). Fortaleza is the capital of the state of Ceará. The Metropolitan Cathedral, a large Gothic church, is a major landmark of the city. Fortaleza's economy depends largely on the activities of the state and city governments and on the processing and export of such products as cotton and carnauba wax.

Fortaleza was first settled in the early 1600's, when the Portuguese built a fort there. Fortaleza received the status of a town in 1711. In 1799, it became the capital of Ceará. Fortaleza has experienced rapid growth since the mid-1900's. The city now has more than five times as many people as it had in 1950. J. H. Galloway

Fortas, *FAWR tuhs,* **Abe** (1910-1982), was appointed an associate justice of the Supreme Court of the United States by President Lyndon B. Johnson in 1965. In 1968, Johnson nominated Fortas for the position of chief justice. Johnson withdrew the nomination at Fortas' request after a Senate filibuster prevented a vote on the nomination. Fortas resigned from the court in 1969 following widespread criticism of his association with the Wolfson Family Foundation. Financier Louis E. Wolfson had been convicted of stock manipulation in 1967. After joining the court, and at a time when Wolfson was under federal investigation, Fortas had agreed to perform services for the Wolfson Foundation. He was to receive $20,000 a year for life from the foundation, but he later canceled the agreement.

Fortas was born in Memphis, Tenn. He graduated from Southwestern College and Yale Law School. From 1933 to 1937, he was an assistant professor of law at Yale. Fortas held many government posts. He became undersecretary of the interior in 1942. He entered private law practice in Washington, D.C., in 1947. He became known as an outstanding appeals lawyer and a defender of civil liberties. Carl T. Rowan

Forten, James (1766-1842), was a black American businessman who won fame as an abolitionist during the early 1800's. He believed that most American blacks wanted to live as free people in the United States. He opposed efforts being made at the time to help blacks move to Africa.

Forten was born in Philadelphia, the son of free parents. He was a powder boy on an American ship during the Revolutionary War in America (1775-1783). Forten was captured in the war at the age of 15 and spent seven months on a British prison ship. In 1786, he worked in a Philadelphia sailmaking shop. Forten rose to the position of foreman two years later and became owner of

the business in 1798. About that time, he invented a device that helped crew members handle heavy sails. The invention greatly aided his business, and Forten became wealthy.

During the War of 1812, Forten helped recruit about 2,500 blacks as part of a force to defend Philadelphia against a British invasion. In 1817, he presided over a meeting of Philadelphia blacks who protested the American Colonization Society's attempts to resettle free blacks in Africa. During the 1830's, he contributed much money to the noted abolitionist William Lloyd Garrison and to Garrison's antislavery newspaper, *The Liberator.* Forten also helped runaway slaves seeking freedom in the North. See also **Abolition movement** (In the United States). Otey M. Scruggs

Fortress of Louisbourg. See **Canada** (National historic parks and sites).

Fortuna, *fawr TOO nuh* or *fawr TYOO nuh,* was the goddess of luck in Roman mythology. Fortuna was associated only with good fortune in early Roman religion. However, after she became identified with Tyche, the Greek goddess of chance, she was also considered a giver of bad luck. Fortuna often is shown with a wheel that she turned to bring success or failure. She also appears with a rudder, symbolizing her power to steer people's lives. The word *fortune* comes from her name. Elaine Fantham

Fortunetelling is the practice of predicting future events by methods generally considered illogical and unscientific. Persons who claim to foretell the future are called *fortunetellers.*

Some fortunetellers say they possess a form of *clairvoyance* that makes them aware of events before they occur. Clairvoyance is the knowledge of events, objects, or people without using any known senses. Scientists do not know whether clairvoyance actually exists. Most fortunetellers do not claim to have clairvoyant powers. Instead, they use special systems of prediction. Some of these systems are complicated, and fortunetellers often say they are scientific. But most scientists consider such systems to be *pseudosciences* (false sciences).

Fortunetelling has been especially popular during certain periods of history. For example, the ancient Greeks and Romans believed the gods spoke to them through prophets called *oracles.* Many persons went to oracles for advice about the future. In later times, the Christian church discouraged fortunetelling. However, an ancient type of fortunetelling called *astrology* became extremely popular in Europe during the Renaissance, the period from about 1300 to about 1600. Some forms of fortunetelling remain popular today, especially in primitive societies and underdeveloped countries. Most Americans regard fortunetelling as a form of amusement, but many believe in it sincerely.

Methods of fortunetelling. Throughout history, hundreds of different fortunetelling methods have been used. One of the most famous methods involves gazing into a crystal ball. Many methods of fortunetelling seem to depend entirely on chance. For example, fortunetellers have made predictions based on the order in which a rooster ate grains of wheat placed on letters drawn on the ground. Predictions also have been based on the shape taken by oil poured on water, or on segments of writing chosen from a book at random.

However, fortunetellers claim that mysterious causes and relationships, not chance, make their predictions possible. For example, astrology is based on the belief that the sun, moon, planets, and stars control people's lives. Therefore, the positions and movements of these bodies supposedly can be used to predict the future.

Other fortunetelling systems include *numerology* and *palmistry*. In numerology, a fortuneteller makes predictions through numbers based on a person's name and birth date. In palmistry, a fortuneteller tries to foresee an individual's future by studying the lines, markings, shape, and the size of the person's hand.

Some fortunetellers only pretend to rely on special systems. For example, a fortuneteller may investigate a client's background and then impress the client by relating many things from this background information. A fortuneteller also may rely on a broad knowledge of human nature. The fortuneteller knows what most people want to hear and so makes statements about the future that could apply to almost anyone. The fortuneteller then observes the client's reactions to these statements and develops a more detailed prediction on the basis of these reactions.

Dangers of fortunetelling. Most fortunetelling is based on the idea that mysterious forces control human life. Therefore, a belief in fortunetelling may rob people of trust in their own ability to control the future. Also, some individuals have lost large sums of money to dishonest fortunetellers.

Some people argue that honest fortunetellers may give harmless—and even sensible—advice to troubled persons who cannot afford psychiatric help. However, businesses and marriages have been wrecked because a person acted on bad advice given by a fortuneteller. Some states and cities have laws against fortunetelling. In general, however, these laws are poorly enforced, and Americans spend millions of dollars annually on fortunetelling.   Marcello Truzzi

Related articles in *World Book* include:

Astrology	Magic	Omen
Augur	Necromancy	Oracle
Clairvoyance	Nostradamus	Palmistry
Divination	Numerology	Superstition
Graphology	Occultism	

Forty-Niner was a gold-seeker who rushed to California after gold was discovered there in 1848. The first Forty-Niners reached San Francisco on the steamer *California* on Feb. 28, 1849. Ships from all parts of the world carried other gold-seekers there. But the greatest number arrived in covered wagons by way of the Oregon Trail and the California Trail. Gold seekers increased California's population from about 15,000 early in 1848 to over 100,000 by the end of 1849. The Forty-Niners were the first of still heavier migrations to California during the following years. See also **California** (The gold rush); **Gold rush** (picture).   Oscar O. Winther

Forum, Roman, was the section of ancient Rome that served as the center of government. It was the administrative, legislative, and legal center of the Republic and of the Roman Empire. Many important buildings and monuments stood there, including the *Curia* (Senate House), the temples of Concord and Saturn, the Basilica Julia and Basilica Aemilia, the Arch of Septimius Severus, and the *Tabularium* (Hall of Records).

Events in the Roman Forum often affected the rest of the known world. Marcus Tullius Cicero's stirring speeches on the floor of the Curia in the 60's B.C. saved the Republic from a rebellion led by Catiline. Also at the Forum, in 27 B.C., the senate gave Augustus the powers that made him the first emperor of Rome. Romans went to the Forum to hear famous orators speak and to see the valuables seized after distant battles.

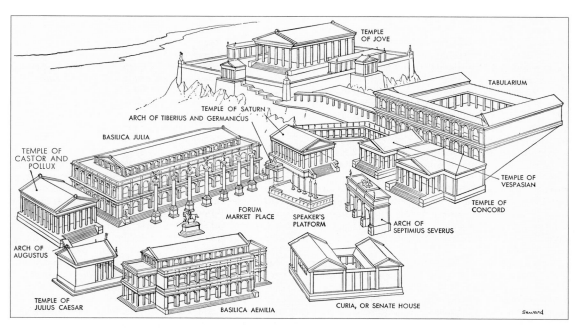

The early Roman Forum had this arrangement during the period of its greatest magnificence.

In Rome's earliest days, the Forum area was a swamp used as a cemetery by the people of surrounding villages. The Etruscans turned these villages into the city of Rome and drained the marshes, probably during the 500's B.C. Residents built shops and temples around the edges of the Forum area. The Forum became the civic and legal center of Rome by the mid-100's B.C., and the merchants moved their shops to other parts of the city.

The barbarians who invaded Rome in the A.D. 400's did not destroy the Forum. But its buildings gradually crumbled after the fall of Rome, and people came to call it *Cow Plain* because it had become so desolate. Excavations have since uncovered many of the ancient columns and arches. Rome had other forums, some with architecture as outstanding as that of the Roman Forum. Several emperors named forums in their own honor. But only the first forum was called *Forum Romanum* (Roman Forum).   D. Brendan Nagle

See also **Rome** (Forums; picture: Roman Forum); **Rome, Ancient** (picture).

Foscolo, Ugo (1778-1827), was an Italian author. His *Le ultime lettere di Jacopo Ortis* (1802, revised in 1817), is sometimes considered the first modern Italian novel. It is the tragic story of a young student's love for Teresa, a woman whose hand has been promised to another man, Odoardo. The story is told in the form of letters, and shows the influence of Johann Wolfgang von Goethe's *The Sorrows of Young Werther.* Many of Foscolo's odes and sonnets tell in a lyrical yet classical style about his personal sufferings and disappointments. His best-known poem, *The Sepulchers* (1806-1807), is an ode that stresses the importance of graves as living reminders of one's ancestors.

Foscolo was born on the island of Zákinthos in the Ionian Sea. His early poetry is filled with his desire to see Italy unified. In 1815, Foscolo left Italy for England, where he spent the rest of his life teaching Italian and writing essays for periodicals and newspapers.
          Richard H. Lansing

Fosdick, Harry Emerson (1878-1969), became one of the best-known Protestant preachers in the United States. He devoted his entire career as a preacher, professor, and author to the conflict between science and religion. He preached the right of science to its place in the world. Fosdick opposed the views held by the Fundamentalists (see **Fundamentalism**).

Fosdick was pastor of the First Baptist Church in Montclair, N.J.; and the First Presbyterian Church, Park Avenue Baptist Church, and the nondenominational Riverside Church, all located in New York City. He was professor of preaching at Union Theological Seminary in New York City from 1915 to 1946. He served with the Y.M.C.A. in England, Scotland, and France during World War I.

Fosdick's many books include *The Meaning of Prayer, The Manhood of the Master, The Modern Use of the Bible, On Being a Real Person,* and an autobiography, *The Living of These Days.*

Fosdick was born in Buffalo, N.Y. He graduated from Colgate University. Fosdick also studied at Union Theological Seminary and at Columbia University.
          L. J. Trinterud

Foss, Joseph Jacob (1915-   ), was a leading United States fighter pilot in the South Pacific during World War II. He also served as Republican governor of South Dakota from 1955 to 1959. During the war, Foss led a United States Marine Air Force unit known as *Joe's Flying Circus.* The unit shot down 72 Japanese planes. Foss destroyed 26 of them. He received the Congressional Medal of Honor, Bronze Star, Silver Star, and the Purple Heart. He was the director of operations for the Central Air Defense Force in the Korean War. Foss was commissioner of the American Football League from 1959 to 1966. He was born near Sioux Falls, S. Dak. See also **War aces.**   Everett W. Sterling

Fossey, Dian (1932-1985), was an American zoologist who studied the mountain gorillas of the Virunga Mountains in east-central Africa. She founded the Karisoke Research Center in Rwanda and lived there in near-

© Veit/Watkins from Sipa
Dian Fossey studied and photographed mountain gorillas in Africa. She won their trust by imitating their sounds and habits.

isolation for almost 18 years. Fossey's research on wild mountain gorillas led to efforts to protect this rare and endangered species. She was mysteriously murdered at her camp in Rwanda in December 1985.

Fossey was born in San Francisco. She received a bachelor's degree in occupational therapy from San Jose State College (now San Jose State University) in 1954. In 1963, inspired by a book about mountain gorillas by American zoologist George Schaller, Fossey borrowed money and traveled to Africa to see the animals. There, Fossey visited the camp of British anthropologist Louis Leakey. In 1966, Leakey picked Fossey to begin a long-term field study of the animals. Fossey received a doctorate for her gorilla research from Cambridge University in Cambridge, England, in 1974.

To gain acceptance by the mountain gorillas, Fossey imitated their habits and sounds. She studied them daily and came to know each animal individually. After several of her favorite mountain gorillas were killed, Fossey focused on protecting the animals from poachers and from the destruction of their mountain habitat. Some United States officials believe Fossey may have been murdered by poachers angered by her strong attempts to protect the animals. Fossey described her research in the book *Gorillas in the Mist* (1983). A motion picture about her with the same title was released in 1988.
          Randall L. Susman

Fossils, such as these dinosaur skeletons, help museum visitors visualize ancient species. Scientists study fossils to learn about the development and ways of life of prehistoric organisms.

Fossil

Fossil is the mark or remains of a plant or animal that lived thousands or millions of years ago. Some fossils are leaves, shells, or skeletons that were preserved after a plant or animal died. Others are tracks or trails left by moving animals.

Most fossils are found in *sedimentary rocks.* These fossils formed from plant or animal remains that were quickly buried in *sediments*—the mud or sand that collects at the bottom of rivers, lakes, swamps, and oceans. After thousands of years, the weight of upper layers of sediment pressing down on the lower layers turned them into rock (see **Sedimentary rock**). A few fossils are whole plants or animals that have been preserved in ice, tar, or hardened sap.

The oldest fossils are microscopic traces of bacteria that scientists believe lived about $3\frac{1}{2}$ billion years ago. The oldest animal fossils are remains of *invertebrates* (animals without a backbone) estimated to be about 700 million years old. The oldest fossils of *vertebrates* (animals with a backbone) are fossil fish about 500 million years old.

Steven M. Stanley, the contributor of this article, is Professor of Earth and Planetary Sciences at The Johns Hopkins University. He has written several books on paleontology.

Fossils are more common and easier to find than many people realize. For example, fossils are plentiful in nearly every state in the United States. Even so, scientists believe that only a small portion of the countless plants and animals that have lived on earth have been preserved as fossils. Many species are thought to have lived and died without leaving any trace whatsoever in the fossil record.

Although the fossil record is incomplete, many important groups of animals and plants have left fossil remains. These fossils help scientists discover what forms of life existed at various periods in the past and how these prehistoric species lived. Fossils also indicate how life on earth has gradually changed over time. This article explains how fossils provide information on ancient life. For a description of animals of the past, see **Prehistoric animal;** for a description of early human beings, see **Prehistoric people.**

How fossils reveal the past

In the distant past, when most fossils formed, the world was different from today. Plants and animals that have long since vanished inhabited the waters and land. A region now covered with high mountains may have been the floor of an ancient sea. Where a lush tropical forest thrived millions of years ago, there may now be a cool, dry plain. Even the continents have drifted far from the positions they occupied hundreds of millions of years ago. No human beings were present to record these changes. But *paleontologists* (scientists who study prehistoric life) have pieced together much of the story of the earth's past by examining its fossil record.

Understanding ancient plants and animals. By studying fossils, paleontologists can learn a great deal about the appearance and ways of life of prehistoric organisms. One way paleontologists learn about a fossil animal or plant is by comparing it to living species. In many cases the comparisons show that the fossil species has close living relatives. Similarities and differences between the fossil species and its living relatives can provide important information. For example, fossils show that *Homo erectus*—a species that lived from $1\frac{1}{2}$ million to 300,000 years ago—was an ancient ancestor of modern human beings. Its fossilized pelvis, leg, and foot bones are similar in structure to modern human bones. Paleontologists know that the bones of modern humans are designed for walking upright. From this evidence, they have determined that *Homo erectus* also walked upright (see **Homo erectus**).

Fossil plants and animals that do not have close living relatives are more difficult to understand. One way to learn how they lived is to compare their fossils to unrelated living species that have similarly shaped structures. For example, fossils show that about 210 million to 63 million years ago there lived a group of reptiles with one long, slender finger extending from each front limb. This bone structure does not resemble that of any living reptile. It appears, however, similar to the wings of modern birds. Since modern birds use their wings for flying, paleontologists conclude that these ancient creatures also flew. Paleontologists call them *pterosaurs,* which means *winged lizards.*

The conditions under which fossil creatures died and were buried can also reveal how they lived. Paleontologists have found fossil nests of partially grown baby dinosaurs. These fossils indicate that certain species of dinosaurs fed and cared for their young in nests, much as today's birds do.

Fossils of tracks, trails, or burrows—called *trace fossils*—provide information on the behavior of prehistoric animals. Groups of dinosaur tracks, for example, suggest that some species of dinosaurs traveled in herds. Other trace fossils show that primitive worms lived in simple tubes dug in the sea floor.

Tracing the development of life. The fossil record provides important evidence of the history of life. Fossils indicate that over hundreds of millions of years life on earth has *evolved* (developed gradually) from simple, one-celled bacteria and algae into a tremendous variety of complex organisms. Fossils also indicate that certain species changed dramatically, giving rise to entirely new forms of life.

The location of fossils in the *strata* (layers) of sedimentary rock can show how living things increased in complexity through time. As sediment was deposited, new layers settled on top of older ones. When the sediment turned to stone, these layers were preserved in the order in which they were laid down. In undisturbed strata, fossils in the lower—and thus older—layers are more primitive than those in the younger strata found nearer the surface.

The fossils preserved in the strata of the Grand Canyon in Arizona provide a good example of the increasing complexity of living things. Strata near the bottom are about 1 billion years old and contain only primitive fossil algae. Strata dating from 600 million to 500 million years ago contain fossils of invertebrates, including those of extinct sea animals called *trilobites.* Remains of fish first appear in strata about 400 million years old. Some of the upper strata, which formed between 330 million and 260 million years ago, contain tracks of such early land animals as amphibians and small reptiles.

Certain fossils indicate that particular groups of plants or animals evolved from others. These *transition fossils* combine characteristics of two major groups. For example, fossil skeletons of *Ichthyostega,* a creature that lived about 360 million years ago, provide evidence that amphibians evolved from fish. Paleontologists classify

Donald Baird

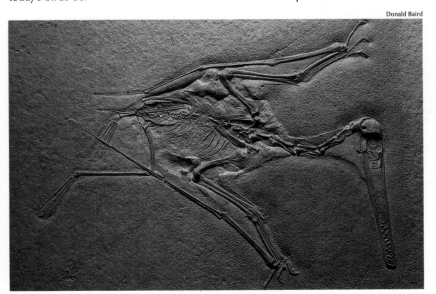

A fossil *Pterodactylus,* a type of pterosaur, provides information on the animal's behavior. The long, slender finger bones, which are similar to birds' wings, indicate that *Pterodactylus* flew. Its tapered snout and sharp teeth suggest that it fed on worms and other burrowing creatures, plucking them out of the earth as some modern birds do.

Tracing the history of life

In the Grand Canyon, many *strata* (layers) of sedimentary rock are exposed, *left*. Fossils in the strata show how living things increased in complexity over time. The oldest strata in the diagram at the right contain only simple fossil algae. Primitive sea animals—trilobites and brachiopods—appear in the next oldest strata. Younger strata, by contrast, contain fossils of more complex organisms, including traces of plants, fish, and reptiles.

Tom Algire, FPG

World Book diagram by Paul D. Turnbaugh

286-245 million years old
- Late trilobites
- Shark teeth
- Clams
- Reptile tracks
- Scorpion tracks
- Insect wings
- Ferns
- Land plants related to present-day horsetails

360-286 million years old
- Snails
- Later brachiopods
- Bark from tree-sized club mosses
- Coral

570-360 million years old
- Early trilobites
- Plates from bony fish
- Early brachiopods

More than 570 million years old
- Algae
- Fossils not shown to scale

Ichthyostega as one of the first amphibians because it had legs and lungs, enabling it to live on land. *Ichthyostega's* leg bones, however, were similar to the fin bones of fish. It also had fishlike teeth and a broad, finned tail for swimming. Fossils indicate that later amphibians lost these fishlike traits and became better adapted to life on land.

Fossils also show how groups of plants and animals became more diverse after they originated. Fossil leaves and pollen grains of the first flowering plants date from the early Cretaceous Period, sometime after 138 million years ago. These fossils record only a small number of species. Fossils from the mid-Cretaceous, about 90 million years ago, include a wide variety of flowering plants from many different environments.

Recording changes in the earth. Paleontologists use fossils to determine how the earth's climate and landscape have changed over millions of years. For instance, they have found fossils of tropical palm trees in Wyoming, an area that has a cool climate today. These fossils indicate that the climate in that area has cooled. Paleontologists have found fossil oysters in Kansas and other areas that are far inland today. Such fossils reveal that a shallow sea once spread over these areas.

Fossils also provide evidence supporting the theory of *continental drift*—the idea that the positions of the continents have changed over hundreds of millions of years. Paleontologists have found similar kinds of fossil dinosaurs on all of the modern continents. It is unlikely that similar species could have evolved on separate continents. As a result, most earth scientists believe that when the dinosaurs first appeared—about 240 million years ago—nearly all the earth's land mass was united as

E. R. Degginger, Animals Animals

Barry L. Runk from Grant Heilman

Fossils reveal ancient environments. A fossil palm, *left,* suggests that Wyoming once had a tropical climate. Fossil oysters, *right,* indicate that a sea once covered part of Texas.

a single supercontinent. In contrast, fossils of mammals show complex differences from continent to continent. This indicates that after about 200 million years ago, when mammals were beginning to develop and spread, the supercontinent was breaking apart. The continents were drifting slowly to the positions they occupy today. See **Continental drift.**

How fossils form

The great majority of plants and animals die and decay without leaving any trace in the fossil record. Bacteria and other microorganisms break down such soft tissues as leaves or flesh. As a result, these tissues rarely leave fossil records. Even most hard parts, such as bones, teeth, shells, or wood, are eventually worn away by moving water or dissolved by chemicals. But when plant or animal remains have been buried in sediment, they may become fossilized. These remains are occasionally preserved without much change. Most, however, are altered after burial. Many disappear completely, but still leave a fossil record in the sediment.

Fossils may be preserved in several ways. The main processes of fossilization are (1) the formation of impressions, molds, and casts; (2) carbonization; and (3) the action of minerals.

Formation of impressions, molds, and casts. Some fossils consist of the preserved form or outline of animal or plant remains. Impressions, also called *prints* or *imprints,* are shallow fossil depressions in rock. They form when thin plant or animal parts are buried in sediment and then decay. After the sediment has turned to stone, only the outline of the plant or animal is preserved. Many impressions consist of small grooves left by the bones of fish or the thick-walled veins found inside leaves. Sometimes even delicate soft parts, such as feathers or leaves, are preserved as impressions.

Molds form after hard parts have been buried in mud, clay, or other material that turns to stone. Later, water dissolves the buried hard part, leaving a mold—a hollow space in the shape of the original hard part—inside the rock. A cast forms when water containing dissolved minerals and other fine particles later drains through a mold. The water deposits these substances, which eventually fill the mold, forming a copy of the original hard part. Many seashells are preserved as molds or casts.

Carbonization results when decaying tissues leave behind traces of carbon. Living tissues are made up of compounds of carbon and other chemical elements. As decaying tissues are broken down into their chemical parts, most of the chemicals disappear. In carbonization, a thin, black film of carbon remains in the shape of the organism. Plants, fish, and soft-bodied creatures have been preserved in precise detail by carbonization.

The action of minerals. Many plants and animals became fossilized after water that contained minerals soaked into the pores of the original hard parts. This action is called *petrifaction.* In many such fossils, some or all of the original material remains, but it has been strengthened and preserved by the minerals. This process is called *permineralization.* The huge tree trunks in the Petrified Forest of Arizona were preserved by permineralization.

In other cases, the minerals in the water totally re-

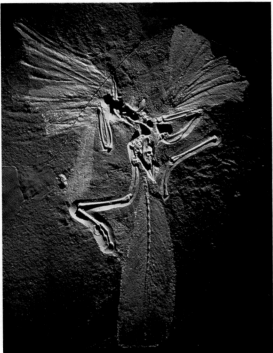

American Museum of Natural History

An impression of an archaeopteryx began to form when the bird was buried in soft silt. The silt turned to limestone, preserving the delicate outlines of the bird's wing and tail feathers.

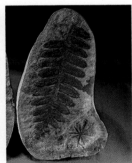

American Museum of Natural History   Runk/Schoenberger from Grant Heilman

A mold preserved the three-dimensional form of a trilobite after its body decayed.

A carbonized fossil of a fern consists of traces of carbon in the shape of the leaf.

placed the original plant or animal part. This process, called *replacement,* involves two events that happen at the same time: The water dissolves the compounds that make up the original material, while the minerals are deposited in their place. Replacement can duplicate even microscopic details of the original hard part.

Other processes. Occasionally, animal and plant structures are fossilized with little or no change. In *mummification,* an animal's skin and other tissues are preserved by drying or by the action of chemicals. Mummification may occur when a dead animal is buried

© William E. Ferguson

Petrified wood formed after dissolved minerals were deposited in the pores of dead tree trunks. The structure of the wood, including bark and growth rings, is visible in these specimens.

in a dry place, such as a desert, or in asphalt or some other oily substance.

Some processes fossilize whole animals. Insects sometimes are preserved whole in *amber,* the hardened sap of ancient pines or other trees. Such insects were trapped in the sticky sap and then sealed when it turned to amber. In Alaska and in Siberia, a region in northern Asia, woolly mammoths thousands of years old have been found frozen in the ground. Their hair, skin, flesh,

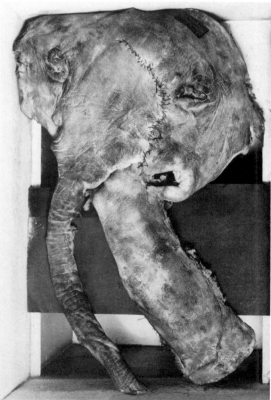

American Museum of Natural History

A baby woolly mammoth was unearthed from the frozen ground in Alaska. Scientists can learn a great deal from such frozen fossils because much of their tissue is preserved intact.

and internal organs have been preserved as they were when the mammoths died.

Studying fossils

Discovering fossils. Fossils can be found wherever sedimentary rocks are exposed. In moist regions, these rocks are usually buried under a layer of soil and plant life, but they become exposed by water erosion in river valleys. Sedimentary layers also become uncovered during highway construction and other building projects. In deserts and other arid regions, erosion exposes sedimentary rocks over broad areas. And oil-well drilling often brings up fossil-bearing sedimentary rocks from deep within the earth.

Paleontologists search in specific areas for particular types of fossils. In North America, for example, most fossil mammals are found west of the Mississippi River. Paleontologists hunt for fossil ancestors of human beings in eastern and southern Africa. Canada and Australia have deposits of well-preserved ancient marine invertebrates.

Collecting fossils. Different fossils require different collecting techniques. Fossils of shells, teeth, and bones preserved in soft sand or mud are easiest to collect. Paleontologists can dig out these fossils with a trowel or shovel or remove them by hand. Fossils preserved in hard rock are most easily found and collected when they have become exposed by natural *weathering.* Weathering refers to the chemical and physical processes that break down rock at the surface of the earth. Fossils that are more resistant to weathering than the surrounding rocks stand out on exposed rocky surfaces. Most such fossils can be collected by breaking loose the rock with a chisel, hammer, or pick. Paleontologists collect fossils that are hidden in solid rock by breaking the rock with a sledge hammer or a hammer and chisel. Rocks containing fossils often break along the surfaces of the fossils.

Fragile fossils must be protected before they are broken out of rock. Paleontologists wrap the exposed parts of such fossils in layers of cloth soaked with wet plaster. After the plaster hardens, the fossils can be safely chipped from the rock and transported to a laboratory, where the plaster is removed.

In the laboratory, paleontologists use electric grinding tools, fine picks, or even needles to remove any remaining rock. Fossils enclosed in limestone may be soaked in a weak acid solution, which dissolves the limestone but not the fossil. Paleontologists may decide to leave a fossil attractively exposed but still partly hidden in the rock.

Working with fragments. Many fossils are collected in fragments, which must be assembled like pieces of a jigsaw puzzle. In general, the first time a fossil species is reconstructed in this manner, the fragments must represent the complete specimen. Later reconstructions can be made from incomplete fragments by comparing them to the complete fossil and replacing the missing parts with artificial materials.

Vertebrate fossils can be reconstructed as *free mounts,* in which the skeleton seems to stand by itself. Paleontologists first make a small model of the finished skeleton. They then construct a framework of steel, plastic, or other strong material to support the skeleton. Fi-

© William E. Ferguson

Albert Dickson

Removing fossils from rock requires patience and the proper tools. The fossil collectors in the photo above employ hammers and chisels to chip huge dinosaur bones from an exposed rock wall. In the laboratory, *right,* a technician uses a small, handheld jackhammer called an *air scribe* to remove rock from fragile fossil fragments.

nally, they fasten the bones to the outside of the framework to hide it.

Classifying fossils. Like living plants and animals, fossil species are classified according to how closely related they are to one another. In general, scientists determine how closely related various species are by comparing their many biological features (see **Classification, Scientific**). For fossil groups, these features are primarily the shapes of hard parts, such as shells, teeth, and skeletons, because these are the features that are preserved. For example, paleontologists may look at skull shape and tooth size when determining the different species of saber-toothed cat.

Dating fossils. Through many years of research, paleontologists have come to understand the order in which most kinds of fossils occur in the geological record. When a fossil species is first discovered, it is usually found along with other species. If paleontologists know the position of the other species in the history of life, they can determine the position of the new species. This type of dating only indicates whether one fossil is older or younger than another fossil. It does not provide a fossil's age in years.

Paleontologists determine how old a fossil is by measuring the *radioactive isotopes* in the rocks that contain the fossil. Radioactive isotopes are forms of chemical elements that break down, or *decay,* to form other materials. Scientists know the rates of decay of various radioactive isotopes. By comparing the amount of a radioactive isotope in a rock to the amount of the material produced by its decay, scientists can calculate how long the decay has been taking place. This length of time represents the age of the rock and the fossils it contains.　Steven M. Stanley

Related articles in *World Book* include:

Andrews, Roy Chapman
Ant (picture: Fossils of ants)
Anthropology (picture)
Coal (picture: Fossil ferns)
Cuvier, Baron
Dinosaur

Earth
Evolution
Geology
Insect (picture: Fossil imprint of a dragonfly)
Osborn (Henry F.)
Paleontology
Plant (Early plants)

Rock (Organic sediments)
Teilhard de Chardin, Pierre

Tree (Fossil trees; picture)

Outline

I. How fossils reveal the past
　A. Understanding ancient plants and animals
　B. Tracing the development of life
　C. Recording changes in the earth

II. How fossils form
　A. Formation of impressions, molds, and casts
　B. Carbonization
　C. The action of minerals
　D. Other processes

III. Studying fossils
　A. Discovering fossils
　B. Collecting fossils
　C. Working with fragments
　D. Classifying fossils
　E. Dating fossils

Questions

How are fossils formed by permineralization?
How do paleontologists remove fossils from rocks?
What are the oldest fossils?
How do fossils support the theory of continental drift?
What are trace fossils?
How do paleontologists date fossils?
Why do most fossils consist of preserved hard parts?
What is a free mount?
What do fossils reveal about the evolution of living things?
What features do paleontologists use in classifying fossil species?

Additional resources

Level I
Gallant, Roy A. *Fossils.* Watts, 1985.
Lauber, Patricia. *Dinosaurs Walked Here: And Other Stories Fossils Tell.* Bradbury, 1987.
Rhodes, Frank H., and others. *Fossils: A Guide to Prehistoric Life.* Golden Press, 1962.

Level II
Arduini, Paolo, and Teruzzi, Giorgio. *Simon & Schuster's Guide to Fossils.* Simon & Schuster, 1986.
Fortey, Richard A. *Fossils: The Key to the Past.* Van Nostrand, 1982.
MacFall, Russell P., and Wollin, J. C. *Fossils for Amateurs: A Guide to Collecting and Preparing Invertebrate Fossils.* 2nd ed. Van Nostrand, 1983.
Simpson, George G. *Fossils and the History of Life.* Scientific American Books, 1983.

Fossil Butte National Monument, *byoot,* an area of rare fish fossils, is in southwestern Wyoming. The fossils date from the Paleocene and Eocene epochs, two periods in the earth's history from 40 million to 65 million years ago. The site became a national monument in 1972. For its area, see **National Park System** (table: National monuments).

Critically reviewed by the National Park Service

Fossil fuel. See Energy supply; Fuel.

Foster, Sir George Eulas (1847-1931), was an outstanding Canadian statesman. He was minister of trade and commerce from 1911 to 1921 during the administrations of Sir Robert L. Borden and Arthur Meighen. From 1882 to 1900 and from 1904 to 1921, Foster served in the Canadian House of Commons. He served in the Canadian Senate from 1921 until his death.

Foster was born in Carleton County, N.B. He was educated at the University of New Brunswick and served as a professor of classics there from 1873 to 1879. Foster was knighted in 1914. He was a member of the Canadian delegation to the Paris Peace Conference in 1919. He also served as a delegate to the League of Nations in 1920, 1921, 1926, and 1929. Robert Craig Brown

Foster, Stephen Collins (1826-1864), was one of America's best-loved songwriters. The best of Foster's songs have become part of the American cultural heritage. Some of them became so popular during Foster's lifetime that they were adapted (with suitable words) for Sunday school use. Foster's songs are frequently moving in their sincerity and simplicity. His most popular works include "Old Folks at Home," which he wrote in 1851, (also known as "Swanee River," see **Suwannee River**); "My Old Kentucky Home, Good Night" (1853); and "Massa's in de Cold, Cold Ground" (1852). He also wrote such rollicking songs as "Oh! Susanna" (1848), and "Camptown Races" (1850), and such romantic songs as "Beautiful Dreamer" (1864), and "Jeanie with the Light Brown Hair" (1854). He wrote more than 200 songs, and wrote the words and the music for most of them.

Foster was born on July 4, 1826, near Lawrenceville, Pa. (now part of Pittsburgh). He had little musical training, but he had a great gift of melody. At the age of 6, he taught himself to play the clarinet, and he could pick up any tune by ear. He composed "The Tioga Waltz" (1841) for piano at 14. Three years later, his first song, "Open Thy Lattice, Love," was published.

Foster wrote his first minstrel melodies, called "Ethiopian songs," in the 1840's. These were "Lou'siana Belle" (1847) and "Old Uncle Ned" (1848). Blackface minstrel shows, in which white entertainers blackened their faces, were becoming popular in the United States (see **Minstrel show**). Foster decided to write songs for the minstrels and to improve the quality of their music.

He went to Cincinnati in 1846 to work as a bookkeeper for his brother. That year he wrote "Oh! Susanna." Soon it became the favorite song of the "Forty-

University of Pittsburgh
Stephen Foster

Niners" in the California gold rush of 1849. He married Jane McDowell in 1850, and settled in Pittsburgh to work as a composer. He arranged with the minstrel leader, E. P. Christy, to have his new songs performed on the minstrel stage. Foster was a poor businessman, and he sold many of his most famous songs for very little money. He lived in New York City from 1860 until his death, struggling against illness, poverty, and alcoholism. Richard Jackson

Additional resources

Austin, William W. *"Susanna," "Jeanie," and "The Old Folks at Home": The Songs of Steven C. Foster from His Time to Ours.* 2nd ed. Univ. of Illinois Press, 1987.

Howard, John T. *Stephen Foster, America's Troubadour.* T. Y. Crowell, 1962. Reprint of 1953 revised edition.

Stephen Foster Song Book. Ed. by Richard Jackson. Dover, 1974. Includes reprints of original or early editions of his sheet music.

Foster parent is a person who provides care for children who are unable to live with their natural, or biological, parents. In some cases, the natural parents have deserted, abused, or neglected the children. The children are called foster children and are under the supervision of a public or private social service agency. These agencies find foster parents who can provide the love and care that children need to grow and develop.

Few children remain in foster homes until they reach adulthood. Most return to their natural parents, are placed with other relatives, or are adopted. Some foster parents adopt foster children whose parents have lost the right to care for them. Canada and the United States have similar foster parent systems.

To take children into their homes, foster parents must be approved or licensed by the state or province in which they live. License requirements include good health, adequate housing, and certain qualities of personality and family life. Social service agencies generally pay foster parents for part of the clothing and food and for all of the medical care the children require. Foster parents receive training relating to their role as substitute parents. Such training focuses on parenting skills, child management techniques, and the special roles and relationships involved in foster care. Foster parents who care for children with moderate mental or physical handicaps receive specialized training plus an extra service fee.

The foster parent's role requires understanding of children who are separated from their families and adjusting to a new environment. Foster parents work with the social service agency to help the child and his or her parents maintain contact with each other and, if possible, to return the child to the parents.

Many foster parents belong to local, state, or provincial foster parent associations. In the United States, some foster parents are members of the National Foster Parent Association. Canadian foster parents may belong to the Canadian Foster Parents Association. Helen D. Stone

See also **Children's home.**

Foucault, *foo KOH,* **Jean Bernard Léon,** *zhahn behr NAR lay AWN* (1819-1868), a French physicist, used a revolving mirror to measure the speed of light. Some types of measuring apparatus still use adaptations of his method. Foucault proved in 1850 that light travels more slowly in water than in air, and that the speed varies inversely with the index of refraction. He also made improvements in the mirrors of reflecting telescopes.

Foucault demonstrated the rotation of the earth on its axis with a pendulum experiment, and also by using a gyroscope that maintained its axis in a fixed direction while the earth turned relative to that direction (see **Gyroscope; Pendulum** [picture: A Foucault pendulum]). Foucault also discovered the existence of eddy currents, which are produced in a conductor moving in a magnetic field. Foucault was born in Paris.   Richard G. Olson

Foundation. See Building construction; House.

Foundations are organizations that aid research, cultural progress, and human welfare. Gifts of money from wealthy people and groups help establish and finance most foundations.

Many foundations are called *corporations, endowments, funds,* or *trusts.* There are more than 24,000 foundations in the United States, not including privately endowed colleges, hospitals, and learned societies. These foundations have assets of about $68 billion. Americans give about $80 billion to charity every year. The foundations give about $4 $\frac{1}{2}$ billion, or about 6 per cent of this amount. Much of it is given in the form of grants to organizations and individuals. Canada, Great Britain, and the nations of Western Europe have a much smaller number of foundations than the United States has.

How foundations are organized

A foundation can be organized as a *trust* or as a *nonprofit corporation* (see **Corporation**). It is easier to set up a trust than a nonprofit corporation, because there are fewer legal formalities. A nonprofit corporation can operate with greater freedom, however, because the law does not restrict its powers so narrowly. Both trusts and nonprofit foundations are governed by a *trustee* or *trustees,* or legally appointed administrators. The trustees may administer the foundation by themselves, or they may hire executives to manage the work of the foundation.

Foundations are also organized according to the way they spend their funds. A *perpetuity* can spend only the income from its assets. For example, its assets may consist of stocks that pay regular dividends. A *liquidating foundation* must spend all its money within a specified period of time. An *optional foundation* can spend either its income or both the income and the assets. The Carnegie Corporation of New York is a perpetuity. The Julius Rosenwald Fund was self-liquidating. The Rockefeller Foundation is an optional foundation.

Kinds of foundations

Foundations may be either public or private. Private foundations include *independent, company-sponsored,* and *operating* foundations. The only type of public foundation is the *community* foundation. Each type of foundation distributes funds in different ways and for different purposes.

Independent foundations often bear their founders' names and are usually the best known to the public. They include the Carnegie Corporation of New York, the Ford Foundation, and the Rockefeller Foundation. Many independent foundations have charters that allow them to operate freely in such fields as education, health, and welfare. However, some people organize foundations for more specific purposes. If foundations of this kind are organized as perpetuities, they often outlive their original aim. For example, the Bryan Mullanphy Fund, which was established in St. Louis in 1851, furnished "relief to all poor emigrants and travelers coming to St. Louis on their way . . . to settle in the West." By 1900, it became impossible to find enough people who could qualify.

Company-sponsored foundations are established by companies and corporations. Although legally separate from the profit-making businesses that provide their funds, foundations often concentrate their work in areas of interest to the founding firms. Since about 1950, company-sponsored foundations have grown significantly both in number and in the average size of their individual endowments. Some of the larger company-sponsored foundations include the AT&T Foundation, Alcoa Foundation, and the General Motors Foundation.

Operating foundations generally employ their own staffs to directly operate programs determined by their charter and governing body. Thus, their programs are tailored to specific purposes. They award few or no grants to outside individuals or organizations. For example, the Norton Simon Foundation devotes its funds primarily to the purchase and display of works of art.

Community foundations or trusts have usually been established in urban areas by gifts from individuals living in those areas. Frederick H. Goff, a Cleveland banker, established the first community foundation, the Cleveland Foundation, in 1914. Since then, such foundations have been set up in most major cities of the United States. The people of these various communities control the foundations. Community foundations have usually given money to local welfare programs. However, many of the larger community foundations now often contribute to more general projects.

The work of foundations

There are a number of chief areas of foundation interest. These areas include education, welfare, health, science, and the humanities.

Education has always been a main area of foundation interest. For example, the General Education Board, a Rockefeller charity, worked to raise the level of secondary and higher education in the Southern States. The Independence Foundation provides support for secondary education in the United States. The Ford Foundation gave money to raise the salaries of teachers in private colleges and universities in the United States. The Ford Foundation has the largest assets of any foundation (see **Ford Foundation**). The Ford Foundation and the Carnegie Corporation of New York together established the National Merit Scholarship Corporation in 1955. The scholarship corporation provides college and university scholarships. The National Merit scholarships are awarded to outstanding high school students (see **Scholarship**).

Welfare. For many years, various foundations have given money to help needy people. But in the 1950's, research programs designed to solve specific social problems began to replace gifts to charity. For example, the Field Foundation, Inc., and the Russell Sage Foundation have sponsored important programs dealing with the psychological, health, and social problems of youth and the aged (see **Field Foundation, Inc.**).

Health and medicine attract much foundation aid. For example, the Carnegie Corporation sponsored a study of medical education by Abraham Flexner that resulted in a vast improvement in medical schools in the United States (see **Flexner, Abraham**). The Rockefeller Foundation aids medical research, and has sponsored valuable campaigns against hookworm, malaria, and yellow fever (see **Rockefeller Foundation**). The Robert Wood Johnson Foundation sponsors programs to improve the quality of health care in the United States and the public's access to it. The John and Mary R. Markle Foundation offers scholarships and fellowships for medical study and research. The Albert and Mary Lasker Foundation gives several grants in medical research each year. Several community and private foundations aid the handicapped, such as victims of defective hearing, sight, and speech. The Foundation for Child Development supports this work.

Science. Foundations often support scientific projects. The Mary Flagler Cary Trust provides funds for the ecological and plant sciences. A number of foundations provide aid to the National Research Council, an agency devoted to science research. The Research Corporation, founded in 1912, has supported research in many scientific areas. The National Science Foundation, a federal government agency, also encourages science research. But this foundation depends on Congress for funds (see **National Science Foundation**).

Literature and the fine arts are helped by the foundations that award scholarships and fellowships to talented people. The John Simon Guggenheim Memorial Foundation has been one of the leaders in giving this kind of aid. The Ford Foundation has helped the American Council of Learned Societies, which uses part of these funds for scholarships and fellowships. The Ford Foundation also has given money to universities and colleges for the publication of scholarly books. The Carnegie Corporation of New York helps strengthen liberal arts programs in universities and colleges. It also has contributed to art and music appreciation by providing universities and colleges with reproductions of art works and recordings of music. The A. W. Mellon Educational and Charitable Trust gave about $20 million to build and maintain the National Gallery of Art in Washington, D.C. (see **National Gallery of Art**).

Religion. A few large foundations aid specific religious institutions and groups, and many small foundations make such gifts. Several foundations have given large sums to interdenominational programs and religious education. The Aurora Foundation has made numerous grants for a variety of missionary activities. The Raskob Foundation for Catholic Activities supports Roman Catholic institutions.

Civic affairs have interested many foundations. The Gannett Foundation has helped a number of communities in the United States and abroad deal with various civic issues. The John D. and Catherine T. MacArthur Foundation conducts a Special Grants Program that is primarily concerned with civic affairs in the Chicago metropolitan area. The Ford Foundation and one of the organizations it created, The Fund for the Republic, have made many large grants to support education in citizenship and democracy.

International affairs. Many foundations support programs in the United States and in other countries to improve international relations. The Ford Foundation, the W. K. Kellogg Foundation, Rockefeller Foundation, and others support *exchange programs.* These pro-

Leading United States foundations

Name	Assets	Total giving†	Founded	Headquarters
1. **Ford Foundation***	$4,758,862,000	$169,719,000	1936	New York City
2. **Getty Trust, J. Paul**	3,690,834,000	159,141,000	1953	Los Angeles
3. **Kellogg Foundation, W. K.***	3,108,333,000	74,600,000	1930	Battle Creek, Mich.
4. **MacArthur Foundation, John D. and Catherine T.***	2,271,000,000	105,000,000	1970	Chicago
5. **Lilly Endowment***	1,913,568,000	56,585,000	1937	Indianapolis
6. **Johnson Foundation, Robert Wood***	1,803,866,000	94,675,000	1936	Princeton, N.J.
7. **Rockefeller Foundation***	1,605,603,000	45,439,000	1913	New York City
8. **Pew Memorial Trust***	1,550,025,000	90,246,000	1948	Philadelphia
9. **Mellon Foundation, Andrew W.***	1,477,000,000	66,808,000	1969	New York City
10. **Kresge Foundation***	1,047,074,000	42,480,000	1924	Troy, Mich.
11. **Duke Endowment***	797,525,000	40,033,000	1924	Charlotte, N.C.
12. **Mott Foundation, Charles Stewart***	733,290,000	20,428,000	1926	Flint, Mich.
13. **Carnegie Corporation of New York***	715,333,000	26,715,000	1911	New York City
14. **McKnight Foundation**	711,300,000	29,731,000	1953	Minneapolis, Minn.
15. **Keck Foundation, W. M.**	647,221,000	36,532,000	1954	Los Angeles

Leading Canadian foundations

Name	Assets	Total giving†	Founded	Headquarters
1. **McConnell Family Foundation, J. W.**	$280,806,000	$11,956,000	1937	Toronto
2. **Vancouver Foundation**	120,400,000	12,241,000	1943	Vancouver
3. **CRB Foundation**	100,000,000	600,000	1985	Montreal
4. **Hospital for Sick Children Foundation**	81,989,000	9,390,000	1972	Toronto
5. **Donner Canadian Foundation**	69,000,000	2,957,000	1950	Toronto

*Has a separate article in *World Book.*
†Total giving includes grants, matching amounts, program amounts, and scholarships.
Figures for U.S. foundations are for 1986 and 1987. Figures for Canadian foundations are in Canadian dollars and are for 1985 and 1986.
Sources: The Foundation Center, New York City; The Canadian Centre for Philanthropy, Toronto.

grams help Americans study and teach in other countries, and bring people from other countries to study and teach in the United States.

Other interests. Foundations have many special interests. For example, the Ford Foundation established Resources for the Future, Inc., an organization interested in the conservation of natural resources. The Twentieth Century Fund conducts public policy research programs. The Atlantic Foundation concentrates on support for marine science and ocean engineering projects.

Canadian foundations

Canadian foundations do not have the same freedom as United States foundations. The Canadian government carefully regulates their growth. Canada does not have as many foundations as the United States, nor are they so large.

Outstanding Canadian foundations include the J. W. McConnell Family Foundation, the Vancouver Foundation, and the Hospital for Sick Children Foundation. The J. W. McConnell Family Foundation, Canada's largest charitable organization, has its headquarters in Montreal. It distributes its funds to institutions in the fields of conservation, culture, education, health, and welfare. A large percentage of its contributions are given to institutions in Quebec. The Vancouver Foundation is a community foundation that supports projects in Vancouver and British Columbia. The Hospital for Sick Children Foundation helps support the Hospital for Sick Children in Toronto.

History

The earliest foundations appeared in ancient Egypt and the city-states of ancient Greece. The Greek philosopher Plato established a fund to support his academy. Many Roman emperors set up municipal foundations for the relief of the poor. During the Middle Ages, the Roman Catholic Church administered many private funds used to support hospitals, schools, and other charitable causes.

The United States had few foundations before the Civil War. In 1790, Benjamin Franklin's will established funds for the poor in Boston and Philadelphia. In 1846, the Smithsonian Institution was founded with funds left by the scientist James Smithson, "for the increase and diffusion of knowledge among men."

The Peabody and Slater funds became the first modern foundations in the United States. George Peabody, an American banker, founded the Peabody Fund in London in 1867. John Fox Slater, a manufacturer, founded the Slater Fund in New York in 1882. They created the funds to aid education in the South after the Civil War.

Andrew Carnegie, one of the greatest steel manufacturers in the United States, spread the idea in the early 1900's that people with large fortunes should devote part of their wealth to the betterment of humanity. Carnegie established many foundations, including the Carnegie Endowment for International Peace and the Carnegie Corporation of New York. Many other wealthy people, such as Edward S. Harkness and Andrew W. Mellon, followed Carnegie's example.

The number of foundations in the United States has increased steadily in recent years. High income and in-heritance taxes have been a significant factor in promoting this growth.   Joseph C. Kiger

Related articles in *World Book* include:

Biographies

Carnegie, Andrew	Kellogg, W. K.	Rockefeller,
Duke, James B.	Mellon, Andrew	John D.
Field (family)	Peabody, George	Smithson, James
Ford, Henry		

Foundations

See the separate articles on some of the U.S. foundations in the *table* with this article. See also the following articles:

Carnegie Foundation for the   Field Foundation
Advancement of Teaching   Rosenwald Fund, Julius

Other related articles

Brookings Institution	Rhodes Scholarship
Endowment	Scholarship
Fellowship	

Founding Fathers were statesmen of the Revolutionary War period, particularly those men who wrote the Constitution of the United States. The Founding Fathers included Benjamin Franklin, Alexander Hamilton, James Madison, Gouverneur Morris, George Washington, and other delegates to the Constitutional Convention of 1787. See also **Constitution of the United States.**

Foundry is a plant where workers make molded metal products called *castings*. Products made in foundries range from engine blocks to toy soldiers. The process of pouring melted metals into molds is called *founding*. The metals commonly used include iron, steel, brass, bronze, aluminum, lead, zinc, and magnesium (see **Cast and casting**). Dies can also be made in foundries (see **Die and diemaking**).

Foundries that turn out heavy castings often do their founding in large pits in the floor. Overhead cranes ease the work of lifting and carrying the heavy molds and castings from place to place. Some foundries are highly automated. In such foundries, machines are used to make the molds, pour the metal, and clean the castings.
          Gordon H. Geiger

See also **Forging; Heat** (picture: People use heat).

Fountain is a jet or stream of water that rises naturally or artificially as a result of pressure. In a natural fountain, this pressure comes from the weight of water collected in a reservoir, its temperature, or both. The water flows through an underground passage until it can discharge, as in a spring, or shoot out, as in a geyser. In artificial fountains, pumps supply the pressure. This article deals with artificial fountains.

Artificial fountains can be both decorative and practical. They help keep pools and ponds clean and can reduce excess flow of water. Decorative fountains are frequently found in plazas, parks, and malls. In such fountains, water may flow from or over sculptures of people, mythical creatures, or natural objects. People enjoy watching and hearing the water's movement.

Fountains have existed for thousands of years. In ancient Greece, people built fountains above springs thought to have magical powers. The Greeks added beautiful statues of Greek gods and goddesses to the flowing waters. The ancient Romans built hundreds of fountains in Rome, copying Greek designs.

Some of the most complicated and beautiful fountains in Europe were built during the Renaissance and

© Adam Woolfitt, Woodfin Camp, Inc.

A fountain at the Palace of Versailles, near Paris, is one of several beautiful fountains on the palace ground. Begun in 1661, the Versailles fountains had elaborate pumping systems that were characteristic of many fountains built in Europe from the 1500's to the 1700's.

baroque periods, from the 1500's to the 1700's. Elaborate pumping systems created wide cascades of water, channeled water down steps, or forced it to shoot up in powerful jets. Many famous fountains were built during the 1600's and 1700's. These include the Fountain of the Four Rivers (1651) and the Trevi Fountain (1762), both in Rome. The fountains at the Palace of Versailles (begun in 1661), near Paris, are also well known.

During the late 1800's and early 1900's, many fountains that imitated classical designs were built in city parks and public squares and on private estates in the United States. Beginning in the 1960's, many U.S. landscape architects introduced fresh ideas into fountain design. Today, architects use computers to control lights and water flow in public fountains. These fountains are as elaborate and beautiful as those of any previous era.

Craig S. Campbell

See also **Artesian well; Geyser; Rome** (picture: Rome's Piazza Navona); **Taft, Lorado** (picture); **Versailles** (picture).

Fountain of Castalia. See Parnassus.

Fountain of Youth was an imaginary spring. Many legends were told about it in both Europe and America. Its waters were supposed to make old persons young, and to heal all kinds of sickness. Tribes of Indians in Central America and the West Indies thought the spring was in the Bahama Islands. Spanish explorers searched for it throughout the area. Ponce de León searched for the fountain in Florida, but he never found it. A spring in St. Augustine, Fla., is shown today as one that he discovered.   Walter C. Langsam

See also **Ponce de León, Juan** (Early career).

Fountain pen. See Pen.

Four Corners is the only place in the United States where four states meet. Arizona, Colorado, New Mexico, and Utah come together at this point (see **United States** [political map]). A monument marks the site. It is surrounded by a concrete platform which bears the seals of the four states.

Four-eyed fish. See Anableps.

Four freedoms. President Franklin D. Roosevelt, in a message to Congress on Jan. 6, 1941, said that any settlements made after World War II should be based on "four freedoms." He defined these four freedoms as freedom of speech, freedom of worship, freedom from want, and freedom from fear.

He asked Congress for laws allowing him to lend or lease war materials to countries fighting the Axis, or to any country whose defense was important to the United States (see **Lend-lease**). President Roosevelt's words were as follows:

"In the future days, which we seek to make secure, we look forward to a world founded upon four essential human freedoms.

"The first is freedom of speech and expression—everywhere in the world.

"The second is freedom of every person to worship God in his own way—everywhere in the world.

"The third is freedom from want—which, translated into world terms, means economic understandings which will secure to every nation a healthy peaceful life for its inhabitants—everywhere in the world.

"The fourth is freedom from fear—which, translated into world terms, means a worldwide reduction of armaments to such a point and in such a thorough fashion that no nation will be in a position to commit an act of physical aggression against any neighbor—anywhere in the world."

4-H is an educational program that helps young people develop new skills, explore possible career choices, and serve their communities. It is the largest informal educational program for young people in the United States.

The 4-H slogan is "Learn by Doing." Members of 4-H acquire useful skills and knowledge by working on various projects and activities. These projects and activities deal with the environment, health and safety, leadership, nutrition, plants and animals, science and technology, and many other subjects. Members also learn to make decisions, deal with stress, build a good self-image, and develop other skills that help them become responsible and productive citizens.

The four H's stand for *head, heart, hands,* and *health.* Members show their high ideals with their motto, *To Make the Best Better,* and with this pledge:

> I pledge
> My *Head* to clearer thinking,
> My *Heart* to greater loyalty,
> My *Hands* to larger service, and
> My *Health* to better living,
>   for my club, my community, my country, and my world.

More than 80 countries have 4-H or similar programs. About 5 million young people in the United States, Puerto Rico, Guam, and the Virgin Islands belong to 4-H. Canadian 4-H clubs have about 50,000 members. In the United States, approximately 500,000 adults work with 4-H members as volunteer leaders. About 150,000 teenagers who have completed several years of 4-H work also serve as leaders.

In the United States, anyone 9 through 19 years old may become a member of 4-H. In Canada, the ages for membership vary depending on the province. Young people may participate in 4-H through a variety of programs. Many young people belong to 4-H clubs. However, youths also may form a 4-H special interest group. Members of a special interest group work on a joint project or workshop. The 4-H program also provides teachers with project materials for classroom use. These materials allow young people to participate in 4-H as a

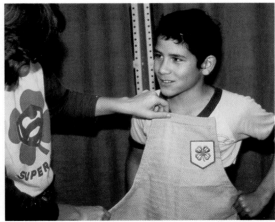

National 4-H Council

Clothing projects give 4-H members the opportunity to learn sewing skills and to display completed items in a fashion show.

part of their schoolwork. In addition, 4-H offers membership through individual study programs and 4-H instructional television programs.

Members of 4-H serve their communities with one or more special projects a year. For example, a 4-H club might plant trees or conduct a bicycle safety program. Many clubs and groups prepare educational exhibits for community fairs.

There is no official 4-H uniform. However, many members wear 4-H pins or clothing with the 4-H emblem or other identification. The 4-H emblem is a green four-leaf clover that has a white H on each leaf.

The 4-H movement began in the United States during the early 1900's. At first, only farm children participated in the 4-H program. They worked on such projects as canning, raising livestock and poultry, and growing crops. Many city youngsters began to join 4-H after clubs added projects of more interest to them, such as career studies and automobile care and safety.

Today, only about a sixth of the 4-H members in the

National 4-H Council

National 4-H Council

Exhibiting livestock at a county fair, *left,* is part of a 4-H project. The 4-H emblem, *above,* is a four-leaf clover with an *H* on each leaf. The four *H's* stand for *head, heart, hands,* and *health.*

United States live on farms. The rest of the organization's members live in other rural areas and in cities, towns, and suburbs.

The Cooperative Extension System, a joint project of the federal, state, and county governments, guides 4-H work in the United States. The extension system works in cooperation with state land-grant universities (see **Land-grant university**). An extension office in nearly every county in the United States employs one or more agents. The agents recruit and assist local 4-H volunteer leaders and help members with their projects.

Projects and activities

Individual projects. Each 4-H member carries out at least one project a year. In most states, he or she may select the project from a list of 50 to 100 choices. Members may also design their own projects. A 4-H project may involve almost any subject that encourages the young person to learn and to use the imagination.

Some subjects have several project levels, and so members may continue working in these subject areas over a number of years. Other projects are for certain age groups. For example, projects for older members include studies of possible career choices and of such health issues as drug abuse and physical fitness.

Many 4-H members who live in rural areas choose projects that deal with crops and livestock, forestry, and marketing. Both city and rural members enjoy projects involving clothing, computers, home improvement, nutrition, public speaking, and the conservation of natural resources.

Various 4-H projects that were once limited to farm youngsters have been developed to serve members in cities as well. A rural youngster, for example, may choose a project in raising and caring for a horse. A city youth who does not own a horse may select a project in horsemanship. Projects that once helped rural youths learn how to raise crops have also been made more flexible for city members. For example, suburban youths may learn how to plant large gardens. Inner city mem-

bers, who have limited space, may learn how to tend backyard plots, window boxes, or indoor plants.

Each 4-H member receives a booklet that explains the requirements of the selected project. The booklet also contains information and questions to make the member think and learn about the subject. For example, a booklet for a food, nutrition, and fitness project might include information on consumer choices, food groups, and physical fitness.

The county extension office provides visual aids and other teaching materials to 4-H members. County agents and volunteer leaders visit members at home to review their projects.

Many 4-H members finish a year's project by preparing an educational exhibit about their subject for a local or county fair. Other members finish their project work by taking part in computer program demonstrations, public speaking contests, or other special activities related to their projects. Some members prepare talks and demonstrations to share what they have learned. Members may earn medals, certificates, ribbons, trophies, and scholarships for their work.

Group activities. Teen-agers interested in a particular subject, such as leadership skills or coping with stress, may organize a joint project or workshop dealing with that subject. Members of such 4-H special interest groups need not belong to a local 4-H club. After completing a project or workshop, the group may start another one. Or the members may join other special interest groups.

Most 4-H clubs and groups carry on community service activities. For example, they may assist when bloodmobiles visit their neighborhood, or they may lead community beautification programs. Many 4-H clubs and groups fight such problems as drug abuse and pollution. Members may help the aged, the blind, the mentally retarded, and the poor.

Members of 4-H get together for all kinds of recreation. They hold picnics and sporting events and go on hikes. Some clubs organize music and drama programs.

National 4-H Council

Conservation and environmental pollution are topics of interest to many 4-H members. These 4-H'ers are removing weeds and debris to beautify their community.

Camping is a favorite 4-H activity, and about 400,000 members attend 4-H camps each summer.

Older 4-H members may join county senior clubs and councils or county junior leader groups. Members of these organizations are especially active in community service programs. Older 4-H members also develop leadership abilities as they help younger members with their projects.

Organization

In the United States, the federal, state, and county governments contribute funds to 4-H work through the Cooperative Extension System. They also cooperate in employing the county extension agents. The state land-grant universities and the United States Department of Agriculture supply educational materials for 4-H members. They also help organize national and state 4-H events.

The 4-H program in Canada receives support from the federal and provincial governments. The Provincial Extension Service, an agency similar to the U.S. Cooperative Extension System, has offices in each province. Business and nonprofit organizations also support 4-H in both the United States and Canada.

Young people may join a 4-H program already in their community, or they may organize a new club or group. In the United States, members join through their county extension office. In Canada, they enroll through the provincial 4-H agencies. The United States has about 153,000 local clubs, and Canada has about 5,000 local clubs.

Volunteers are essential to the success of the 4-H program. Most 4-H clubs choose their own adult volunteer leaders. Many select a parent or other relative of a club member. Adult volunteer leaders donate their time, provide transportation, and purchase some teaching materials. They help members with their projects and activities and also may lead a project group. Teen-agers may become junior or teen leaders after several years of 4-H work. They assist adult leaders and help younger members with their work and with their project records.

County extension agents help organize 4-H programs within the county. They also help train local volunteer leaders.

Each state has a 4-H leader at the state land-grant university. State leaders and their staffs choose the 4-H projects their state will offer and organize statewide 4-H events. They also help prepare aids and materials for members and volunteer leaders. At the national level, 4-H is directed by an assistant deputy director and a staff for 4-H and youth programs in the U.S. Department of Agriculture.

4-H sponsors. In the United States, the National 4-H Council, a nonprofit corporation, supports 4-H work on a nationwide basis. The National 4-H Council helps arrange and conduct 4-H activities and events, operates public information services, and develops educational materials.

The council publishes project handbooks, leaders' guides, and the *4-H Leader,* which is written for adult and junior 4-H leaders. The council also organizes sponsored programs in which outstanding 4-H members receive awards for their work. These awards include medals of honor, scholarships, and free trips to national 4-H events. In addition, the council operates the National 4-H Supply Service, a mail-order house that offers more than 2,000 items bearing the 4-H emblem.

The National 4-H Center in Chevy Chase, Md., is managed by the council. Members of 4-H may attend summer courses on leadership and citizenship at the center. The council also holds leader-training and professional improvement sessions at the center and at other locations throughout the United States.

The council sponsors the International Four-H Youth Exchange and other international programs. About 1,000 adults and young people annually participate in the council's international 4-H programs.

The National 4-H Council was established in 1976. The council resulted from the merger of two previous 4-H sponsors—the National 4-H Service Committee and the

Food projects teach 4-H members cooking skills. They learn the principles of nutrition and how to prepare balanced meals.

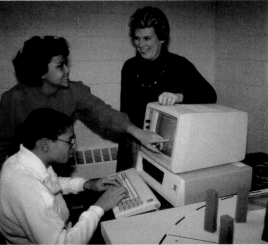
Projects for older members may help them choose a career. These volunteers are teaching a 4-H'er how to use a computer.

National 4-H Foundation. A 25-member board of trustees administers the National 4-H Council. Its work is supported by contributions from corporations, foundations, and individuals. The council has its office at 7100 Connecticut Avenue, Chevy Chase, MD 20815.

In Canada, most 4-H programs are administered by the provincial departments of agriculture. Two national groups—the Canadian 4-H Council and the Canadian 4-H Foundation—provide educational support. The council coordinates 4-H programs and events in Canada, and the foundation raises funds for 4-H. Members of both groups represent business and nonprofit organizations and the national and provincial governments. The council and foundation have their headquarters at 323 Chapel Street, Ottawa, ON K1N 7Z2.

National, state, and county events. Soon after Thanksgiving each year, about 1,600 American 4-H members meet in Chicago for the National 4-H Congress. Most delegates receive free trips to the congress as winners of state, sectional, or national 4-H contests in such areas as 4-H projects or citizenship. The congress also honors individuals and business firms for their services to 4-H. Delegates discuss problems that affect young people in the United States and hear speeches by leaders in agriculture, government, industry, and science.

Each spring, about 325 delegates from the United States and Canada attend the weeklong National 4-H Conference in Washington, D.C. These delegates include both young people and adults. They tour the city and attend workshops to discuss contemporary issues and plan future 4-H programs.

The United States observes National 4-H Week each year during the first full week of October. Newspaper and magazine articles and radio and television programs stress the educational values of 4-H. During National 4-H Week, clubs review their work and plan new programs.

Many states sponsor meetings similar to the national conferences. Other events sponsored by states as well as counties include fairs, workshops, camps, and exhibitions.

Each November, the Canadian 4-H Council sponsors a weeklong National 4-H Conference in Toronto. About 80 Canadian and 10 American 4-H members participate in the conference. The members tour Toronto, meet with government and business officials, discuss current social and economic issues, and exchange ideas about 4-H work.

History

The 4-H movement started in the United States in many places at about the same time. During the 1890's and early 1900's, educators in several states began programs to teach farm children useful skills. In 1896, Liberty Hyde Bailey, a naturalist at Cornell University, began to publish nature study leaflets for country schools and to organize nature study clubs.

Corn, canning, and poultry clubs that stressed learning by doing started in several Southern and Midwestern states in the early 1900's. Schoolteachers and school superintendents were responsible for organizing most of these clubs.

In 1902, A. B. Graham, a township school superintendent in Ohio, began one of the first clubs similar to today's local 4-H clubs. Graham's club held regular meetings with planned programs. Members worked on projects dealing with corn and other vegetables, flowers, and soil testing.

In 1902, the University of Illinois helped O. J. Kern, a county school superintendent, organize local agricultural clubs in Winnebago County, Illinois. In 1904, Will B. Otwell, an Illinois agricultural leader, encouraged 8,000 Illinois farm boys to exhibit their corn projects at the Louisiana Purchase Centennial Exposition (also called the St. Louis World's Fair) in St. Louis. W. H. Smith, a county school superintendent, began to organize local corn clubs in Holmes County, Mississippi, in 1907. Girls' canning clubs started in South Carolina in 1910.

The U.S. Department of Agriculture encouraged the formation of the clubs. It appointed Seaman A. Knapp, who had established a cotton demonstration farm in Texas in 1903, to direct club work. Southern land-grant colleges joined with the Agriculture Department in sponsoring the clubs.

In 1914, the Smith-Lever Act established what is now the Cooperative Extension System. The Smith-Lever Act also granted states federal funds to organize boys' and girls' agricultural clubs, and each state soon set up a club department. Gradually, boys and girls began joining the same clubs, as they do today.

During the early 1920's, agricultural clubs throughout the United States adopted the 4-H emblem and the name 4-H Club. Clubs in Iowa had begun to use a clover emblem with white H's about 1910.

Agricultural clubs grew more slowly in Canada. The first clubs began in 1913. But they were not organized nationally until 1931, when the government formed the Canadian Council on Boys' and Girls' Clubs (now called the Canadian 4-H Council). Most Canadian clubs have both boys and girls.

Today, more than 80 nations have 4-H or similar programs. In a number of countries, the groups have not adopted all parts of the 4-H program. But all the groups

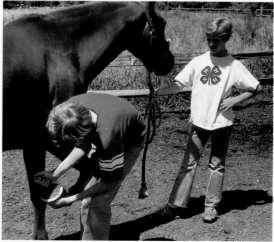

National 4-H Council

Horsemanship projects may involve raising horses. Many rural and suburban 4-H'ers exhibit their horses at shows.

work to help young people develop useful skills and become productive citizens.

Critically reviewed by the National 4-H Office

See also **Agricultural education; County agricultural extension agent; County extension home economist.**

Four horsemen of Notre Dame. See Football (picture).

Four Horsemen of the Apocalypse, *uh PAHK uh lips,* are beings mentioned in the sixth chapter of the last book of the New Testament of the Bible, The Revelation of St. John the Divine. The chapter tells of a scroll in God's right hand that is sealed with seven seals. When the first four of these seals are opened, four horsemen appear. Their horses are white, red, black, and pale (literally, greenish-yellow). The horsemen represent various hardships that the human race must endure before

WORLD BOOK illustration by Lorraine Epstein

The four-o'clock has colorful, fragrant flowers.

What seem to be the flowers are actually colorful *involucres* (modified bracts) surrounding the tiny true flowers. The four-o'clock gets its name because the plant's flowers open late in the afternoon and close in the morning.

The four-o'clock grows well in almost any kind of soil. The plant can be started from seeds, or from its roots, saved for planting in the spring. The four-o'clock makes an attractive, bushy border plant.

Scientific classification. Four-o'clocks are in the four-o'clock family, Nyctaginaceae. The marvel-of-Peru is *Mirabilis jalapa.* Robert W. Schery

See also **Flower** (picture: Flowers of the desert).

Fourdrinier machine. See Paper (How paper is made).

Fourier, *FOO ree ay,* **Charles** (1772-1837), was an important French socialist. He criticized the social conditions of his times, and held that society could be improved if private property were eliminated.

Fourier thought society could be improved through an economic and social regrouping of people. He wanted to create small, self-sufficient farm communities of about 1,600 people each. Each person would own a share of the property in these communities. All people in the community would be required to work, but they could choose their own type of work. Fourier's ideas attracted many followers. However, he could not put together enough money to start such a venture. Fourier was born François Marie Charles Fourier in Besançon, France. Brison D. Gooch

Fourteen Points were a set of principles proposed by President Woodrow Wilson as the basis for ending World War I (1914-1918) and for keeping the peace. On Jan. 8, 1918, in an address before both houses of Congress, Wilson stated these proposals, which became famous as the *Fourteen Points.* The proposals included "open covenants openly arrived at," removal of economic barriers, and "adjustment of all colonial claims." The Fourteen Points also proposed arms reductions, territorial readjustments, and the formation of a "general association of nations."

Wilson never offered any detailed explanation of how the Fourteen Points might be made to work. In spite of

Woodcut (about 1496) by Albrecht Dürer; the Metropolitan Museum of Art, Gift of Junius S. Morgan, 1919

The Four Horsemen of the Apocalypse symbolize the forces of destruction and war in the New Testament Book of Revelation. They represent Conquest, War, Famine, and Death.

the end of the world, specifically Conquest, War, Famine, and Death.

The four horsemen are often featured in art and literature. The German artist Albrecht Dürer included a picture of them in a series of woodcuts illustrating the Book of Revelation. Terrance D. Callan

Four-o'clock, also called the *marvel-of-Peru,* is an attractive perennial from tropical America. It is easy to grow, and is cultivated as an annual in North America. The four-o'clock grows from 2 to 4 feet (61 to 120 centimeters) high. It has fragrant flowers that may be white, pink, red, yellow, or a mixture of several of these colors.

this vagueness, millions of people hailed the principles as the basis for a free world, united in peace. However, at the Paris Peace Conference in 1919, Wilson encountered much opposition to the Fourteen Points. Wilson's principles were almost lost in the compromises he was forced to make in negotiating the peace treaties.

Norman D. Palmer

For a summary of the text of the Fourteen Points, see **Wilson, Woodrow** (The Fourteen Points).

Fourteenth Amendment to the Constitution of the United States forbids the states to deny any citizen the rights granted by federal law. It also defines how citizenship is acquired and declares that all citizens are entitled to equal protection of the law. The original purpose of the amendment was to provide citizenship for former slaves and give them full civil rights. Amendment 14 took effect on July 9, 1868.

Through the years, the Supreme Court of the United States has interpreted the 14th Amendment in different ways. In 1905, the court used it in *Lochner v. New York* to strike down state laws regulating working hours. Later courts reversed this decision.

The court has applied the equal protection clause many times. In 1954, in *Brown v. Board of Education of Topeka,* the court ruled that racial segregation in public schools is unconstitutional. In 1971, the court declared in *Reed v. Reed* that no person may be denied equality before the law because of sex. In 1973, in *Roe v. Wade,* the court ruled that states may not prohibit a woman, under certain conditions, from having an abortion. In 1978, the court ruled in *Regents of the University of California v. Allan Bakke,* that university admissions programs may not use quotas to achieve racial balance.

June Sochen

See also **Bakke case; Brown v. Board of Education of Topeka; Constitution of the U.S.** (Amendment 14); **Government** (The role of state government); **Lochner v. New York; Roe v. Wade.**

Fourth dimension. We usually think of space as having three dimensions: length, width, and height. A box that is 6 feet long, 4 feet wide, and 2 feet high can be described by the ordered set of numbers (6,4,2). Such a set may also be used to describe the position of a point in space—for example, the position of an airplane. But three numbers cannot represent the location of a *moving* plane. To indicate when a plane in flight is at a particular location, such as (6,4,2), we need a fourth dimension—time.

The path of a flying plane can be plotted in four dimensions as shown in the graph to the right, where the plane takes off from point O and travels southeast. The position on the x-axis shows its distance south of point O; the position on the y-axis, its distance east of point O; and the position on the z-axis, its altitude. Curve P represents the path of the plane through space. The points along curve P indicate the location of the plane at four different times, called t_0 to t_4.

The fourth dimension need not always represent time, however. It may represent anything that we can measure, including temperature and weight.

In the early 1900's, the mathematician Hermann Minkowski realized that the special relativity theory proposed by physicist Albert Einstein described a universe with four dimensions. According to Minkowski, time

combines with the three dimensions of space to form *space-time.* Mathematicians afterward began to study geometries of four or more dimensions. See **Relativity.**

Thomas J. Brieske

Fourth estate is a name often given to the newspaper profession. Among the members of the fourth estate are those who gather, write, and edit the news for the press. The phrase *fourth estate* is believed to have first been used in writing by Thomas Babington Macaulay. In 1828, he wrote in an essay that "The gallery in which the reporters sit has become a fourth estate of the realm."

Macaulay was adding a term to those already used for the three estates, or classes, of the English realm. These were lords spiritual, lords temporal, and commons. The three estates later came to stand for government, while reference to a fourth estate described any other influential body in English political life, such as the army or the press.   Earl F. English

Fourth of July. See Independence Day.

Fourth Republic. See France (History; Government).

Fovea centralis. See Eye (Focusing; diagram: Parts of the eye).

Fowl. See Poultry; Chicken.

Fox is a bushy-tailed, sharp-snouted member of the dog family. True foxes include the arctic fox, the gray fox, and the red fox. Several foxlike animals are also called foxes. Foxes and foxlike animals live throughout the world, except in Antarctica and Southeast Asia and on some islands. They may be found in farmlands and forests, on deserts, and even in wooded areas of some cities and suburbs.

Foxes are quick, skillful hunters. The red fox can easily catch a dodging rabbit. This fox can also creep silently toward a bird, then rush up and pounce on it.

Some kinds of foxes, especially the arctic fox and the red fox, have long, soft fur that is valued highly. People trap foxes for their fur and also raise the animals on fur farms (see **Fur**).

Some people hunt the red fox because of its skill in trying to avoid capture. Many hunters seek only the excitement of the chase and do not kill the fox. The hunters use hounds to follow the scent of the fox. But the fox may double back on its trail or run into water, making its scent difficult to follow.

Most foxes are about the same size. Gray foxes and red foxes, the commonest kinds in the United States and

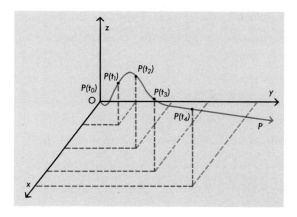

G. Ronald Austing, Bruce Coleman, Inc.

The gray fox is the only member of the dog family that frequently climbs trees. It may scamper into the branches to escape an enemy or, apparently, for no reason at all.

Canada, grow from 23 to 27 inches (58 to 69 centimeters) long. The tail measures an additional 14 to 16 inches (36 to 41 centimeters). Most of these animals weigh from 8 to 11 pounds (3.6 to 5 kilograms).

The body of a fox

Most species of foxes resemble small, slender dogs. But unlike most dogs, foxes have a bushy tail. Foxes also have large, pointed ears and a long, sharp snout.

A fox has keen hearing and an excellent sense of smell. It depends especially on these two senses in locating prey. A red fox can hear a mouse squeak over 100 feet (30 meters) away. Foxes quickly see moving objects, but they might not notice objects that are motionless.

A fox has four toes and a toelike *dewclaw* on each front foot. The animal's dewclaw is actually a nonmovable thumb and does not reach the ground. Each hind foot has only four toes. When a fox walks or trots, its

Facts in brief

Names: *Male,* dog; *female,* vixen; *young,* pup or cub.
Gestation period: 49 to 79 days, depending on species.
Length of life: Up to 14 years.
Where found: Throughout the world except Antarctica, Southeast Asia, and some islands.
Scientific classification: Foxes belong to the dog family, Canidae. The bat-eared fox is *Otocyon megalotis.* The gray fox is *Urocyon cinereoargenteus.* The kit fox is *Vulpes velox.* The red fox is *Vulpes fulva.* The maned wolf is *Chrysocyon brachyurus.* The raccoon dog is *Nyctereutes procyonoides.*

hind paws step into the tracks of the front paws.

Most foxes carry their tails straight backward when running. The tail droops when the animal walks. A fox may sleep with its tail over its nose and front paws. Many foxes have a scent gland on the tail. Scent from this gland gives foxes a distinctive odor.

The life of a fox

Most knowledge about foxes comes from studies of the red fox. The information in this section refers mostly to the red fox, but other species of foxes do not differ greatly.

Foxes live in family groups while the young are growing up. At other times, they live alone or in pairs. They do not form packs as wolves do. A male and a female mate in early winter. They play together and cooperate in hunting. If one of a pair of foxes is chased by an enemy, its mate may dash out of a hiding place and lead the pursuers astray.

Foxes communicate with one another with growls, yelps, and short yapping barks. A fox also makes *scent stations* by urinating at various spots. The scent stations tell foxes in the area that another fox is present.

Young. A female fox gives birth to her young in late winter or early spring. A young fox is usually called a *pup,* but may also be called a *cub.* Red foxes have from four to nine pups at a time, and gray foxes have from three to five. Both the *vixen* (female) and the *dog* (male) bring their pups food and lead enemies away from them.

A newborn fox weighs about 4 ounces (110 grams)

© Kojo Tanaka, Animals Animals

Jane Burton, Bruce Coleman Ltd.

Red foxes live in family groups. An adult male and female, *above,* stay together after mating until their pups mature. The same pair may mate year after year. The eyes of all fox pups, *right,* do not open until about nine days after the animals are born.

J. Simon, Bruce Coleman Inc.

Dens of various kinds of foxes may be underground, in a hollow log or tree, in a cave, or among rocks. Most red foxes enlarge burrows of other animals, but some dig their own dens.

and has a short muzzle and closed eyes. Its eyes open about nine days after birth. Pups drink the mother's milk for about five weeks. Then they begin to eat some solid food and leave their den for short periods. Later, the pups wrestle with one another and pounce on insects, leaves, sticks, and their parents' tails. The adults also bring live mice for the young to pounce on. Later, the adults show the pups how to stalk prey. The pups start to live on their own in late summer and may wander far from their place of birth. The parents may separate then or in early fall and rejoin during the winter.

Dens. Foxes settle in dens after mating. A fox den may be underground, in a cave, among rocks, or in a hollow log or tree. Some red foxes dig their own dens, but most use burrows abandoned by such animals as woodchucks. The foxes may enlarge a burrow if necessary. An underground den may be as long as 75 feet (23 meters) and have several entrances. A main tunnel leads to several chambers that the animals use for nests and for storing food. Two pairs of red foxes may share one burrow. Gray foxes dig less than red foxes. Most gray foxes live in caves, rock piles, logs, or tree holes.

Many kinds of foxes live in dens only while raising pups. After the pups have grown old enough to hunt for themselves, the adults and the pups both sleep in the open most of the time.

Food. Foxes eat almost any animal they can catch easily, especially mice and other kinds of rodents. They also hunt birds, frogs, insects, lizards, and rabbits. Foxes also eat many kinds of fruit and the remains of dead animals. Most species hide the uneaten parts of their prey. They dig a shallow hole, drop the meat in, and spread dirt over it. A fox returns to the stored food, both to feed and, apparently, to check on it.

Foxes may prey on farmers' chickens if the birds roam freely or if the chicken coops are not closed tightly. But foxes help farmers by eating mice and rats. In some areas where foxes had been killed off, rodents increased so much that farmers brought in other foxes.

Hunting. Foxes hunt mostly at night and remain active the year around. They often roam grassy meadows and listen for the squeaks of mice. The grass conceals the mice, but if a fox sees a slight movement of blades of grass, it jumps onto the spot. Foxes sometimes stand on their hind legs to get a better view in tall grass. A fox

also may lie in wait and pounce on a ground squirrel or a woodchuck as the victim leaves its burrow.

Kinds of foxes

Red foxes live throughout most of Asia, Europe, and northern North America. They are the most common foxes of Canada and the northern United States.

The majority of red foxes have bright rusty-red or red-orange fur, with whitish fur on the belly. They have blackish legs and a white tip on the tail. But not all red foxes have red coats. Some, called *silver foxes,* have coats of black fur tipped with white. Silver foxes may appear blackish, gray, or frosty silver, depending on the length of the white tips. Silver foxes with black fur are called *black foxes.* Other red foxes, called *cross foxes,* have rusty-red coats with a large black cross at the shoulders. The cross extends down the middle of the back. Silver foxes, cross foxes, and typical red foxes may be born at the same time to the same parents.

Kit foxes, also called *swift foxes,* roam the grasslands and deserts of western North America. The kit fox has sandy yellow-gray fur with a black tip on the tail. This fox, a close relative of the red fox, measures from 15 to 20 inches (38 to 51 centimeters) long, not including a tail 11 inches (28 centimeters) long. It weighs from 4 to 6 pounds (1.8 to 2.7 kilograms). This animal got its name because its small size is like that of a kitten. See **Animal** (Animals of the desert [picture]).

Gray foxes live throughout most of the United States, Mexico, and Central America, and in part of northern South America. Some live in the far southern parts of Canada. They are the most common foxes of the southern United States. The gray fox's back is the color of salt and pepper mixed together. Its underparts are whitish. The sides of the neck, shoulders, and legs, and the tail's underside are rust-colored. The tail has a black tip. This fox is also called the *tree fox* because it climbs trees.

Arctic foxes live in the far northern regions of Asia, Europe, and North America. The long fur of the arctic fox's coat protects the animal from the extreme cold. The arctic fox has shorter, more rounded ears than most other foxes. These small ears let less body heat escape than larger ears would. Arctic foxes are about the same size as red foxes. See **Arctic fox.**

The skeleton of a fox

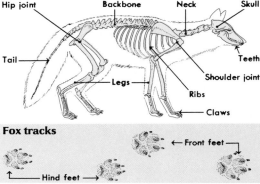

Hip joint   Backbone   Neck   Skull

Tail

Teeth

Shoulder joint

Legs

Ribs

Claws

Fox tracks

← Front feet →

↑ — Hind feet →

WORLD BOOK diagram by Marion Pahl

E. R. Degginger

The Arctic fox lives in the polar region of the Arctic Ocean. Its long fur coat protects the animal from the extreme cold. The fur turns from brown or gray in summer to white in winter.

E. R. Degginger

The raccoon dog is a small foxlike animal that lives throughout eastern Asia. The animal has a chunky body, a grayish fur coat, and a masked face that makes it look like a raccoon.

Fennecs, the smallest kind of foxes, live in the deserts of North Africa and Arabia. A fennec grows only about 16 inches (41 centimeters) long and weighs 2 to 3 pounds (0.9 kilogram to 1.4 kilograms). It has pale sandy fur with whitish underparts. Its ears are 4 to 6 inches (10 to 15 centimeters) long. Fennecs have a large surface area through which they can lose body heat to keep from becoming overheated. See **Fennec.**

Bat-eared foxes, also called *big-eared foxes,* live in dry areas of eastern and southern Africa. A bat-eared fox has large ears that resemble those of a fennec. It has a gray-brown back and sandy underparts. This animal is about the size of a red fox. Bat-eared foxes feed mostly on insects, especially termites. They also eat fruits and such rodents as mice and rats. Bat-eared foxes can change direction sharply while running at full speed, and this ability helps them catch rodents.

South American "foxes" are not true foxes, but they resemble foxes. They include several grayish or brownish animals of various sizes. The largest one, the *maned wolf,* grows as long as 4 feet (1.2 meters) and may weigh 50 pounds (23 kilograms). It is called a wolf because of its large size, but it looks like a long-legged red fox. It has long, yellowish-orange fur that grows especially long and manelike along the middle of its back. The maned wolf has such long legs in proportion to its body that it is often called the "fox that walks on stilts." It feeds on insects, small animals, and fruits.

Raccoon dogs, which live in eastern Asia, have chunky, grayish bodies and masked faces that make them look like raccoons. But these animals are closely related to foxes, not raccoons. A raccoon dog measures about 22 inches (56 centimeters) long, not including a tail 6 inches (15 centimeters) long. It weighs up to 18 pounds (8 kilograms). Raccoon dogs that live in places with bitter cold winters sleep during much of the winter. Joseph A. Davis

Fox, Charles James (1749-1806), a brilliant English statesman and speaker, was a friend of the American Colonies in their fight for freedom. He also defended the French Revolution when most British leaders, including Edmund Burke, opposed it. He was sympathetic, had a warm personality, and was an eloquent speaker.

Fox was born in Westminster. In 1768, he entered Parliament as a Tory, but later joined the Whig Party. Because of his support in Parliament of the American Colonies during the Revolutionary War, King George III became his enemy. His career was also disturbed by the opposition of William Pitt. Fox had a major role in the preliminaries of the impeachment of Warren Hastings (see **Hastings, Warren**). Fox became England's secretary for foreign affairs in 1806. André Maurois

Fox, George (1624-1691), an English religious leader, founded the Society of Friends, or Quakers, about 1647. He taught that the presence of the "Inner Light" in the individual should guide that person's faith and actions. His followers were first called *Quakers* because Fox once told a British judge "to tremble at the word of the Lord." See **Quakers.**

As a young man, Fox believed that he had received a divine call, and began going from place to place preaching his ideas of religion. Fox advised people to give up their worldly pleasures. He was imprisoned several times for his teachings. Fox made missionary journeys through Ireland, Scotland, the West Indies, North America, and the Netherlands, and attracted many followers. He was born in Leicestershire, England. Peter W. Williams

Lithograph by Leopold Grozelier; Chicago Historical Society

George Fox

Fox, Paula (1923-), an American author, won the 1974 Newbery Medal for her children's novel *The Slave Dancer.* This story describes the experiences of a white boy and a black slave aboard an American ship carrying slaves from Africa in 1840.

Paula Fox was born in New York City. Her other children's books include *How Many Miles to Babylon?* (1967), *The Stone-Faced Boy* (1968), *Portrait of Ivan* (1969), *Blowfish Live in the Sea* (1970), *A Place Apart* (1980), *One-Eyed Cat* (1984), *The Moonlight Man* (1986), and *Lily and the Lost Boy* (1987). She has also written several books for adults. Virginia L. Wolf

Fox, Terry (1958-1981), was a courageous young Canadian athlete. Fox had only one leg but attempted to run

Canapress
Terry Fox, a bone cancer victim, raised about $25 million for cancer research during a run across Canada in 1980, *above*.

across Canada in 1980 to help raise money for cancer research.

Terrance Stanley Fox was born in Winnipeg, Man. He grew up in Port Coquitlam, B.C. Fox's right leg was amputated above the knee because of bone cancer in 1977, and he was given an artificial leg. The suffering he witnessed in the cancer wards where he was treated inspired Fox to make his run. He trained for 15 months and began the run in April 1980 at St. John's, Nfld. Fox called it the "Marathon of Hope" and averaged nearly a marathon, or about 26 miles (42 kilometers), a day for 143 days. He traveled through snow, hail, and intense heat. Fox ran 3,339 miles (5,374 kilometers). He was forced to stop near Thunder Bay, Ont., on September 1 after learning that cancer had spread to his lungs. Fox was hospitalized, and he died about 10 months later. His run raised about $25 million for cancer research.

Before Fox died, he was awarded the Order of Canada, the nation's highest civilian honor. Runs in his memory are held yearly in Canada to raise money for cancer research. Fox's run inspired Steve Fonyo, another Canadian who had lost a leg to cancer. In 1985, at the age of 19, Fonyo completed a 14-month, 4,924-mile (7,920-kilometer) run across Canada.   Leslie Scrivener

Fox hunting, also called *riding to hounds,* is a sport that originated in England in about the middle 1700's. The sport consists of finding a wild fox, and hunting it by scent with a pack of hounds especially trained for the purpose. The fox hunters, mounted on horses bred and trained for the sport, follow the hounds across the countryside, over fences, ditches, and streams. This group of mounted followers is called the *field.* It is led by the

master of foxhounds. The pack of hounds is managed in the hunting field by the *huntsman.*

The first packs of hounds used only for fox hunting were established in England. Colonial settlers in Virginia, Maryland, and Pennsylvania brought the sport to America. There are now more than 150 organized packs of foxhounds in the United States and Canada.

Critically reviewed by the Masters of Foxhounds Association of America

See also **American foxhound; English foxhound; Virginia** (picture).

Fox Indians. See Sauk Indians.

Fox terrier. See Smooth fox terrier; Wire fox terrier.

Fox trot is a ballroom dance that first became popular in the United States about 1914. The dance combined slow, gliding walking steps with fast walking steps. At first, the dance was performed to ragtime. Its special quality was created by *syncopation* (accenting normally unaccented beats). Later, people danced the fox trot to any popular tune in $\frac{4}{4}$ time.

The fox trot probably got its name from Harry Fox, a vaudeville performer. Fox performed a frantic trotting dance in a vaudeville show. Ballroom dancers adopted and modified the steps into a smoother, less jerky dance for couples. At first, the fox trot was danced to very fast music, but it later became much slower. The fox trot was very popular in the 1920's.   Dianne L. Woodruff

Foxfire. See Will-o'-the-wisp.

Foxglove is the name for a group of plants native to Europe, northern Africa, and western and central Asia. The foxglove gets its name from its flowers, which are shaped somewhat like fingers of a glove. The leaves of the purple foxglove and the Grecian foxglove contain a powerful poison used to make the drug *digitalis.* In rare cases, children and animals have died from this poison after eating foxgloves. Physicians use small amounts of digitalis to treat certain heart diseases (see **Digitalis**).

The foxglove grows from 2 to 5 feet (60 to 150 centimeters) tall. The long oval leaves grow along the stem. The bell-shaped flowers are purple, pink, lilac, yellow, or white—the deeper-colored ones more or less spotted. They grow along one side of a wandlike cluster.

WORLD BOOK illustration by Robert Hynes
The foxglove produces richly colored flowers. The bell-shaped blossoms grow in a cluster along one side of the stem.

The plants are biennials or short-lived perennials, usually dying after the second season. New seed should be planted yearly for continual bloom.

Scientific classification. Foxgloves belong to the figwort family, Scrophulariaceae. The purple foxglove is *Digitalis purpurea*. The Grecian foxglove is *D. lanata*.

Donna M. Eggers Ware

See also **Superstition** (The role of superstitions).

Foxhound is a medium-sized hound. Packs of hounds hunt foxes by following their scent on the ground. The American Kennel Club recognizes two distinct breeds, American and English. See **American foxhound; English foxhound.**   Olga Dakan

Foxx, Jimmie (1907-1967), became one of the leading home run hitters in baseball history. A strong right-handed batter, Foxx hit 534 home runs during 21 seasons in the major leagues.

A first baseman, Foxx played for the Philadelphia Athletics under manager Connie Mack from 1925 through 1935. He also played for the Boston Red Sox (1936-1942), the Chicago Cubs (1942-1944), and the Philadelphia Phillies (1945). He had a .325 lifetime batting average in the major leagues. He was elected to the National Baseball Hall of Fame in 1951. James Emory Foxx was born in Sudlersville, Md.   Dave Nightingale

Fra Angelico, *frah an JEHL uh кон* (1400?-1455), was an Italian painter. He helped pioneer Renaissance methods of art in the city of Florence. His strong, plain figures in measured space reflected the newer ideas of his time, but he continued to use the bright, unshadowed colors that were traditional. He had many imitators who added sentimental flavor to his style. Such work has been credited to him.

Fra Angelico was a Dominican friar. When the great new monastery of San Marco in Florence was established about 1435, he became a member and remained one until his death. He covered the walls of the monastery with religious images. Many of Fra Angelico's other paintings are now collected at the monastery as a museum of the artist's work. One of his paintings, *The Annunciation,* appears in the **Painting** article. Fra Angelico's other works include *The Coronation of the Virgin* and *The Nativity.*

Fra Angelico was born in Vecchio, Italy. He became a monk in Fiesole when he was 19, and was known as Fra Giovanni da Fiesole. Later, his admirers called him Fra Angelico (angelic brother).   Creighton Gilbert

See also **Aquinas, Saint Thomas** (picture).

Fractal, *FRAK tuhl,* is a complex geometric figure made up of small-scale and large-scale structures that resemble one another. Fractals represent mathematical equations and may be used for illustrating the regular features of complex objects and patterns.

There are two main types of fractals—*regular fractals* and *random fractals*. Regular fractals, also called *geometric fractals*, consist of large and small structures that, except for their size, are exact copies of one another. For example, a regular fractal known as the *Koch snowflake* is made up entirely of small triangles added to the sides of larger triangles.

In random fractals, the large-scale and small-scale structures are mathematically related, but may differ in detail. Many random fractals represent irregular patterns found in nature. For example, Brownian motion—the random motion of a particle suspended in a fluid—can be represented by a random fractal.

Scientists have used fractals to understand rainfall trends, the distribution of vegetation, and patterns formed by clouds and ocean waves. Artists use fractals to create computer-generated art.

Harold M. Hastings

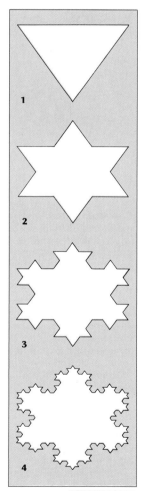

WORLD BOOK diagram
by Linda Kinnaman

A Koch snowflake is a fractal that is formed by adding small triangles to the sides of larger triangles. The diagram above shows the formation of a Koch snowflake in four steps.

Oil painting on wood panel; National Gallery of Art, Washington, D.C., Andrew W. Mellon Collection

The *Madonna of Humility* by Fra Angelico shows the artist's skill in combining delicate colors with simple, graceful figures.

$$\frac{1}{3} + \frac{2}{3} = \frac{3}{3} = 1$$

Students learn to add fractions. The four basic operations of arithmetic—addition, subtraction, multiplication, and division—can all be performed using fractions.

Fraction

Fraction is a part of something. When objects are measured, often the measurements do not come out in whole units. A book may weigh between 2 and 3 pounds. The amount over 2 pounds is a fraction of a pound. A board may measure between 10 and 11 inches long. It is 10 inches plus a fraction of an inch long. The word *fraction* comes from *frangere,* a Latin word meaning *to break.* Fractions result from breaking a unit up into a number of equal parts. A unit can be broken into any number of parts. If you break a stick into two pieces, however, you do not necessarily have two halves of the stick. In order to have two halves of the stick, you must break it into two pieces of equal length.

Fractions are written in numerical form as two numerals separated by a line.

$$\frac{2}{5} \text{ or } 2/5$$

In arithmetic, a fraction generally stands for the number of equal parts into which something has been divided and the number of those parts that are being considered. For example, the fraction $\frac{2}{5}$ represents two parts of something that has been divided into five equal parts.

The fraction form is also used for (1) expressing division, (2) representing a ratio, and (3) stating a rate. In ex-

pressing division, the fraction $\frac{2}{5}$ may indicate two divided by five—for example, dividing two candy bars equally among five people. A ratio is a comparison of two quantities that are both measured in the same units. A ratio may compare a part to a whole or a part to another part. For example, if there are two girls and three boys on a debating team, the ratio of girls (a part) to team members (the whole) is two to five $\left(\frac{2}{5}\right)$. The ratio of girls (a part) to boys (another part) on the team is two to three $\left(\frac{2}{3}\right)$. In mathematics, any number that can be written as the ratio of two whole numbers is called a *rational number* (see **Ratio**). Rate is the relation between two quantities that are measured in different units. For example, a basketball team may score at the rate of two goals per every five minutes of play.

The different uses and meanings of fractions are closely related. Often, understanding one of the meanings of fractions will help make understanding other uses easier. This article concentrates on the meaning of fractions as parts of a whole and examines the use of fractions in arithmetic.

Expressing fractions

In words. The names for fractions come from the number of equal parts into which a whole unit has been divided. In English, there are special names for the fractional parts formed when a unit is divided into two, three, or four equal parts. When a unit is broken into two equal parts, each part is called a half. When it is broken into three equal parts, each part is called a third. And when it is broken into four equal parts, each part is called a quarter or a fourth. The names for other fractional parts are made by adding *-th* to the end of the

Karen Connors Fuson, the contributor of this article, is Associate Professor of Education at Northwestern University.

Fraction terms

Cancellation involves dividing a numerator and a denominator by the same number.

Common, in arithmetic, means *shared* or *the same.* Fractions with the same denominator, such as $\frac{1}{5}$ and $\frac{2}{5}$, have a *common denominator.*

Complex fraction has a fraction in its numerator, its denominator, or both. The fraction $\frac{\frac{7}{12}}{\frac{5}{9}}$ is a complex fraction.

Converting a fraction means changing its form but not its value. For example, $\frac{4}{6}$ can be converted to $\frac{8}{12}$ by multiplying both the numerator and the denominator by two: $\frac{4}{6} \times \frac{2}{2} = \frac{8}{12}$. The fraction $\frac{2}{2}$ is a form of one.

Decimal fractions have denominators of 10 or of 10 multiplied by itself a number of times.

Denominator is the number written below the line in a fraction. In the fraction $\frac{2}{3}$, the denominator is 3. The denominator tells into how many parts a whole has been divided.

Equivalent fractions have different numerators and denominators, but still express the same part of a whole.

For example, the fractions $\frac{1}{2}$ and $\frac{2}{4}$ are equivalent.

Improper fraction has a numerator that is equal to, or larger than, the denominator. For example, $\frac{3}{3}$ and $\frac{5}{3}$ are improper fractions.

Mixed number is a combination of a fraction and a whole number. For example, $2\frac{1}{4}$ is a mixed number.

Numerator is the number written above the line in a fraction. In the fraction $\frac{2}{3}$, the numerator is 2. The numerator tells how many parts are being considered.

Proper fraction is a fraction whose numerator is smaller than its denominator. For example, $\frac{3}{4}$ is a proper fraction, because 3 is smaller than 4.

Reducing a fraction means converting it to an equivalent fraction with a smaller numerator and denominator. But the new fraction has the same value as the old.

Term refers to either the numerator or the denominator of a fraction.

Value of a fraction is the number that the fraction stands for. Equivalent fractions, such as $\frac{2}{3}$ and $\frac{6}{9}$, have the same value and stand for the same number.

---

word that tells the number of equal parts into which the unit has been broken. For example, the fractional parts made by breaking a mile into 10 equal parts are called *tenths* of a mile.

As a unit is broken into more and more equal parts, each part gets smaller and smaller. But the fraction names make it sound as though the parts were getting larger and larger. The *-th* in *sixth,* for instance, means that each part is one of six equal parts of a whole unit. If the same unit were broken into 12 equal parts, each part would be a twelfth. Although a twelfth may sound larger than a sixth, each twelfth actually is only half as big as each sixth. The larger-sounding fraction name means that the original unit has been broken into more—and thus smaller—parts.

The number word before the fraction name tells how many of the fractional parts are being considered. For example, five-sixths represents five of the sixths into which something has been broken. Six-sixths means that

a unit has been divided into six equal parts, and all six parts are being considered. Therefore, six-sixths equals one whole unit. Similarly, seven-sevenths, eight-eighths, nine-ninths, and so on all equal one.

In symbols. When fractions are written in numerical form, the bottom, or second, numeral is called the *denominator* (namer). It provides the name of the fraction, telling the number of equal parts into which the unit has been broken. The top, or first, numeral is called the *numerator* (numberer). It tells how many of the fractional parts are being considered. The numerator and the denominator are called the *terms* of a fraction.

Fractions such as $\frac{4}{10}$, $\frac{7}{100}$, and $\frac{5}{1,000}$ are called *decimal fractions*. Decimal fractions have denominators of 10 or 10 multiplied by itself a number of times. Decimal fractions can be written without a denominator by using the decimal system. In this system, the value of each decimal place in a figure is 10 times smaller than that of the place to its left. For example, the first place to the right

---

Different meanings of the fraction notation $\frac{2}{5}$

Kind of meaning	Meaning:	Words for fraction notation
Fractional part	*One* (of something) broken into *five* equal parts and then *two* of the parts taken	two-fifths
Division-sharing	*One* share when *two* somethings are shared among (divided equally among) *five* people	two divided by five or $2 \div 5$ or $5\overline{)2}$
Ratio	The amount in one quantity compared to the amount in another quantity that is measured in the same way	the ratio two to five
Rate	The amount in one quantity for each amount in another quantity measured by a different unit	
	The measuring units for each quantity need to be given:	two *liters* of gas per every five *miles*
	Sometimes the measuring unit is in fraction notation:	two and a half liters per mile $2\frac{1}{2}\ \frac{\text{liters}}{\text{mile}}$

Expressing fractions in words When a unit is divided into two equal parts, each part is called *one-half.* Each of three equal parts of a unit is *one-third.* The names for other fractions are made by adding *-th* to the number of parts.

One unit

One-*half* of a unit — Broken (divided) into *two* equal parts

One-*third* of a unit — Broken (divided) into *three* equal parts

One-*fourth* of a unit — Broken (divided) into *four* equal parts

One-*fifth* of a unit — Broken (divided) into *five* equal parts

One-*sixth* of a unit — Broken (divided) into *six* equal parts

One-*seventh* of a unit — Broken (divided) into *seven* equal parts

One-*eighth* of a unit — Broken (divided) into *eight* equal parts

One-*ninth* of a unit — Broken (divided) into *nine* equal parts

One-*tenth* of a unit — Broken (divided) into *ten* equal parts

One-*eleventh* of a unit — Broken (divided) into *eleven* equal parts

of the decimal point is the $\frac{1}{10}$'s (tenths) place. The second place to the right of the decimal point is the $\frac{1}{100}$'s (hundredths) place. When decimal fractions are written using the decimal system, the number of parts into which the unit has been divided is indicated by the number of decimal places used. The numerals that are in the decimal places used represent the number of parts that are being considered. For example, the fraction $\frac{7}{10}$ may be written as 0.7 in the decimal system. Twenty-seven hundredths is written as 0.27. For information on changing fractions to decimals and changing decimals to fractions, see **Decimal system** (Decimals and fractions).

Equivalent fractions

When two fractions have different numerators and denominators but still express the same part of a whole, they are called *equivalent fractions.* The chart on the following page shows several equivalent fractions.

If you compare the part of the whole unit formed by $\frac{1}{2}$ with the part formed by two $\frac{1}{4}$'s, you can see that they have the same length. When $\frac{1}{2}$ of the original unit is broken into two equal parts, each of those new parts is $\frac{1}{4}$ of the whole unit. The chart also shows that three $\frac{1}{6}$'s are the same as $\frac{1}{2}$ broken into three equal parts, four $\frac{1}{8}$'s are $\frac{1}{2}$ broken into four equal parts, and so on.

Breaking each part of a fraction into more equal parts is the same as multiplying the numerator and the denominator of that fraction by the same number. Multi-

plying the numerator and denominator of a fraction by the same number produces an equivalent fraction that has larger numbers in both the numerator and denominator.

To make an equivalent fraction with smaller numbers in both numerator and denominator, divide the numerator and denominator by the same number.

$$\frac{6 \div 2 = 3}{12 \div 2 = 6} \qquad \frac{5 \div 5 = 1}{10 \div 5 = 2}$$

Finding an equivalent fraction with smaller numbers in

Multiplying to find equivalent fractions is like breaking a fractional part into smaller parts. For example, multiplying both the numerator and denominator of $\frac{1}{2}$ by 3 gives $\frac{3}{6}$, which expresses the same part of the whole as $\frac{1}{2}$. This operation is the same as breaking $\frac{1}{2}$ into three equal parts.

1/2

3/6

$$\frac{1}{2} = \frac{1 \times 3}{2 \times 3} = \frac{3}{6}$$

1/4 1/4 1/4

9/12

$$\frac{3}{4} = \frac{3 \times 3}{4 \times 3} = \frac{9}{12}$$

the numerator and the denominator is called *reducing the fraction*. When no number except 1 can be used to divide both the numerator and denominator evenly, the fraction is said to be *reduced to its lowest terms*.

Comparing fractions

When two fractions have the same denominator, it is easy to tell which fraction is larger. The fraction with the larger number in the numerator is larger, because more parts of the unit are being considered. For instance, $\frac{5}{7}$ of something is larger than $\frac{3}{7}$ of that same thing.

When two fractions have different denominators, it is more difficult to find out which fraction is larger. To compare fractions with different denominators, change the fractions into equivalent fractions. This process is called finding a *common denominator*. An easy way of finding a common denominator is to multiply the two original denominators and use that product as the common denominator. Then, multiply the numerator and denominator of each of the fractions by the number that will give the common denominator. For example, to find out which fraction is larger, $\frac{1}{2}$ or $\frac{3}{7}$, multiply the denominators to find the common denominator: $2 \times 7 = 14$.

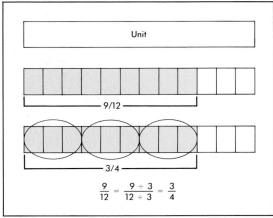

WORLD BOOK illustration

$$\frac{9}{12} = \frac{9 \div 3}{12 \div 3} = \frac{3}{4}$$

Dividing to find equivalent fractions is called *reducing fractions*. For example, dividing the numerator and denominator of $\frac{9}{12}$ by 3 gives $\frac{3}{4}$. This is like grouping nine $\frac{1}{12}$'s into three groups of three $\frac{1}{12}$'s. Each group of three $\frac{1}{12}$'s equals $\frac{1}{4}$.

Equivalent fractions   Fractions may have different numerators and denominators and still express the same part of a whole unit. Such fractions are called *equivalent fractions*. The chart below shows a unit that has been divided into different fractional parts. It also shows several groups of fractional parts that are equivalent to $\frac{1}{2}$, $\frac{1}{3}$, or $\frac{1}{4}$. For example, $\frac{1}{2}$ expresses the same part of the unit as a group of two $\frac{1}{4}$'s ($\frac{2}{4}$) or of five $\frac{1}{10}$'s ($\frac{5}{10}$). For this reason, $\frac{1}{2}$, $\frac{2}{4}$, and $\frac{5}{10}$ are equivalent fractions.

WORLD BOOK chart

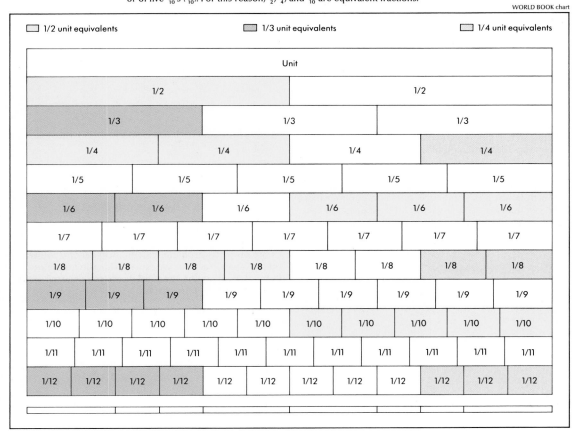

Fourteen will be the common denominator. To change $\frac{1}{2}$ to an equivalent fraction with 14 in the denominator, multiply both the numerator and the denominator by seven. To change $\frac{3}{7}$ to an equivalent fraction with a denominator of 14, multiply the numerator and the denominator by two, because $7 \times 2 = 14$.

$$\frac{3}{7} \times \frac{}{?} = \frac{}{14} \qquad 7 \times 2 = 14, \text{ so } \frac{3}{7} \times \frac{2}{2} = \frac{?}{14} = \frac{6}{14}$$

$$\frac{1}{2} \times \frac{}{?} = \frac{}{14} \qquad 2 \times 7 = 14, \text{ so } \frac{1}{2} \times \frac{7}{7} = \frac{?}{14} = \frac{7}{14}$$

So, $\frac{3}{7}$ is equal to $\frac{6}{14}$ and $\frac{1}{2}$ is equal to $\frac{7}{14}$. Because $\frac{7}{14}$ is larger than $\frac{6}{14}$, $\frac{1}{2}$ is larger than $\frac{3}{7}$. This method of finding a common denominator may be thought of as multiplying both the numerator and the denominator of each fraction by the denominator of the other fraction.

Calculations using fractions

Addition and subtraction of fractions can be performed only when the fractions have the same denominator. When the denominators are the same, they name the same sized parts of the whole. You can add sevenths to sevenths to get sevenths. You can subtract thirds from thirds to get thirds. But you cannot add sevenths and thirds, or subtract thirds from sevenths.

To add or subtract fractions that already have the same denominator, add or subtract the numerators, but do not change the denominator. The denominator in the answer will be the same as the denominator of the fractions in the problem. When fractions are added or subtracted, the total number of fractional parts changes, but the size of each of those parts does not change.

$$\frac{2}{6} + \frac{3}{6} = \frac{5}{6} \qquad \frac{7}{8} - \frac{5}{8} = \frac{2}{8}$$

To add or subtract fractions that have different denominators, first rename each fraction to an equivalent fraction so that the new fractions have a common denominator. Then add or subtract.

$$\frac{2}{3} - \frac{1}{2} = \frac{2 \times 2}{3 \times 2} - \frac{1 \times 3}{2 \times 3} = \frac{4}{6} - \frac{3}{6} = \frac{1}{6}$$

Multiplication of fractions is similar to multiplication of whole numbers. One meaning for multiplication is that of repeated addition.

3×4 means $4 + 4 + 4$, or three groups of 4.
$3 \times \frac{1}{2}$ means $\frac{1}{2} + \frac{1}{2} + \frac{1}{2}$, or three groups of $\frac{1}{2}$, or three $\frac{1}{2}$'s.

When positive whole numbers are multiplied, the product is *larger* than either of the original numbers. But when a fraction is multiplied by a fraction, the product is *smaller* than the original fraction because you are just taking a part of it.

$\frac{2}{3} \times \frac{4}{5}$ means $\frac{2}{3}$ of $\frac{1}{5} + \frac{2}{3}$ of $\frac{1}{5} + \frac{2}{3}$ of $\frac{1}{5} + \frac{2}{3}$ of $\frac{1}{5}$, or $\frac{2}{3}$ of a group of four $\frac{1}{5}$'s, or $\frac{2}{3}$ of $\frac{4}{5}$.

The fraction $\frac{4}{5}$ stands for four of the parts formed when a unit is divided into five equal parts. The problem $\frac{2}{3} \times \frac{4}{5}$ means taking $\frac{2}{3}$ of each of those four $\frac{1}{5}$'s. We can find $\frac{2}{3}$ of $\frac{1}{5}$ by breaking $\frac{1}{5}$ into three equal parts and taking two of them. When a unit has been divided into five equal parts ($\frac{1}{5}$), and each of these five parts has been fur-

ther divided into three equal parts ($\frac{1}{3}$), the result is that the original whole unit has been divided into 15 equal parts, or $\frac{1}{15}$'s. Therefore, $\frac{1}{3}$ of $\frac{1}{5}$ is $\frac{1}{15}$. If we take two $\frac{1}{15}$'s from each of four $\frac{1}{5}$'s, we have $\frac{2}{3}$ of $\frac{4}{5}$, or $\frac{8}{15}$.

To multiply two fractions, multiply their two numerators to get the new numerator. Then multiply their two denominators to get the new denominator.

$$\frac{1}{2} \times \frac{1}{4} = \frac{1 \times 1}{2 \times 4} = \frac{1}{8} \qquad \frac{5}{6} \times \frac{3}{4} = \frac{5 \times 3}{6 \times 4} = \frac{15}{24}$$

Another meaning of multiplication is that of area—length times width. A card that measures 3 inches wide and 5 inches long, or 3 *by* 5 (3×5) inches, has a total area of 15 square inches. The multiplication of fractions may also be thought of as the expression of area. For example, $\frac{2}{3} \times \frac{4}{5}$ may indicate the area of a rectangle that measures $\frac{2}{3}$ unit wide by $\frac{4}{5}$ unit long. The area formed by $\frac{2}{3}$ unit by $\frac{4}{5}$ unit includes eight of the 15 equal parts of the whole square unit. The rectangle therefore has an area that is $\frac{8}{15}$ of the area of the whole square unit. This answer is the same as that found by multiplying the numerators and multiplying the denominators of the two fractions.

Often, multiplication of fractions can be made easier by first performing *cancellation*. Cancellation involves dividing both a numerator and a denominator by the same number. This is the same as dividing a fraction by one, and so it does not alter the answer. When canceling, cross out the old terms and write in the new terms. In the following problem, the 7's can be canceled by dividing a numerator and a denominator by 7, and the 6 and the 8 can be canceled by dividing by 2.

$$\overset{1}{\underset{4}{\cancel{7}}} \times \overset{3}{\underset{1}{\cancel{6}}} = \frac{3}{4}$$

For more information on canceling, see the article on **Cancellation.**

Division. A division problem can be rewritten as a multiplication problem.

$63 \div 9$ means "how many 9's in 63?" or $9 \times ? = 63$.

$\frac{9}{20} \div \frac{3}{4}$ means "how many $\frac{3}{4}$'s in $\frac{9}{20}$?" or $\frac{3 \times ?}{4 \times ?} = \frac{9}{20}$.

The second problem can be rewritten as:

$$\frac{9 \div 3}{20 \div 4} = \frac{?}{?}$$

Comparing this problem with the original one, we see that to divide fractions we must divide the numerators to get the new numerator and divide the denominators to get the new denominator.

$$\frac{9}{20} \div \frac{3}{4} = \frac{9 \div 3}{20 \div 4} = \frac{3}{5}$$

However, many division problems do not come out even.

$$\frac{2}{5} \div \frac{3}{7} = \frac{2 \div 3}{5 \div 7}$$

Two cannot be divided evenly by three, and five cannot be divided evenly by seven. Using the division meaning of fractions, we can rewrite the original problem as a

Two ways of multiplying fractions

The diagram on the left expresses the problem $\frac{2}{3} \times \frac{4}{5}$ by dividing a whole unit into smaller parts and then taking a fraction of those parts. The diagram on the right shows how multiplying fractions can be thought of in terms of area. The yellow rectangle represents a fraction of the larger rectangle. One side is $\frac{2}{3}$ the length of the large rectangle, and the other is $\frac{4}{5}$ of its width.

WORLD BOOK illustrations

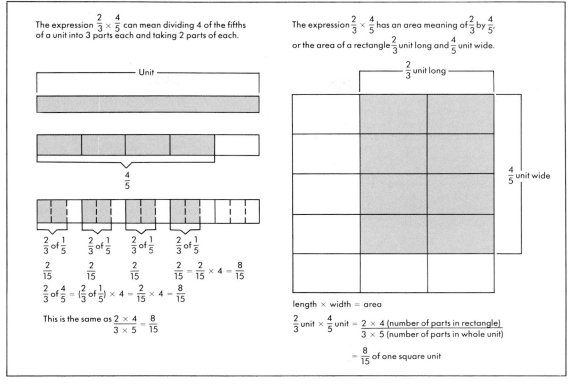

The expression $\frac{2}{3} \times \frac{4}{5}$ can mean dividing 4 of the fifths of a unit into 3 parts each and taking 2 parts of each.

Unit

$\frac{4}{5}$

$\frac{2}{3}$ of $\frac{1}{5}$ $\frac{2}{3}$ of $\frac{1}{5}$ $\frac{2}{3}$ of $\frac{1}{5}$ $\frac{2}{3}$ of $\frac{1}{5}$

$\frac{2}{15}$ $\frac{2}{15}$ $\frac{2}{15}$ $\frac{2}{15} = \frac{2}{15} \times 4 = \frac{8}{15}$

$\frac{2}{3}$ of $\frac{4}{5} = (\frac{2}{3}$ of $\frac{1}{5}) \times 4 = \frac{2}{15} \times 4 = \frac{8}{15}$

This is the same as $\frac{2 \times 4}{3 \times 5} = \frac{8}{15}$

The expression $\frac{2}{3} \times \frac{4}{5}$ has an area meaning of $\frac{2}{3}$ by $\frac{4}{5}$, or the area of a rectangle $\frac{2}{3}$ unit long and $\frac{4}{5}$ unit wide.

$\frac{2}{3}$ unit long

$\frac{4}{5}$ unit wide

length $\times$ width $=$ area

$\frac{2}{3}$ unit $\times \frac{4}{5}$ unit $= \frac{2 \times 4 \text{ (number of parts in rectangle)}}{3 \times 5 \text{ (number of parts in whole unit)}}$

$= \frac{8}{15}$ of one square unit

complex fraction. A complex fraction has a fraction in its numerator, in its denominator, or in both.

$$\frac{2}{5} \div \frac{3}{7} = \frac{\frac{2}{5}}{\frac{3}{7}}$$

We can simplify this problem by multiplying the fractions in the numerator and the denominator by the *inverse* of the denominator. The inverse of a fraction is formed by putting its numerator in the denominator and its denominator in the numerator. The inverse of $\frac{3}{7}$ is $\frac{7}{3}$. The product of any fraction and its inverse is one.

$$\frac{3}{7} \times \frac{7}{3} = \frac{3 \times 7}{7 \times 3} = \frac{21}{21} = 1$$

Multiplying both the numerator and the denominator of a complex fraction by the inverse of its denominator is the same as multiplying the complex fraction by one. This operation forms a simpler equivalent fraction with a denominator of 1.

$$\frac{2}{5} \div \frac{3}{7} = \frac{\frac{2}{5}}{\frac{3}{7}} = \frac{\frac{2}{5} \times \frac{7}{3}}{\frac{3}{7} \times \frac{7}{3}} = \frac{\frac{2}{5} \times \frac{7}{3}}{\frac{21}{21}} = \frac{\frac{2}{5} \times \frac{7}{3}}{1} = \frac{2}{5} \times \frac{7}{3}$$

So, $\frac{2}{5} \div \frac{3}{7} = \frac{2}{5} \times \frac{7}{3}$, or $\frac{2}{5}$ times the inverse of $\frac{3}{7}$. Divid-

ing by a fraction is the same as multiplying by the inverse of that fraction.

$$\frac{2}{5} \div \frac{3}{7} = \frac{2}{5} \times \frac{7}{3} = \frac{2 \times 7}{5 \times 3} = \frac{14}{15}$$

Improper fractions

A fraction that has a numerator that is smaller than its denominator is called a *proper fraction.* A fraction in which the numerator is equal to or larger than the denominator is called an *improper fraction.* All improper fractions have a value that is equal to or greater than one. For example, the fraction $\frac{27}{20}$ stands for 27 of the parts formed when a unit is divided into 20 equal parts. Since one whole unit contains only 20 of 20 equal parts, $\frac{27}{20}$ must be larger than one unit. It is $\frac{7}{20}$ more than 1.

The value of the improper fraction $\frac{27}{20}$ may also be written as $1\frac{7}{20}$. Such a number, combining a whole number and a fraction, is called a *mixed number.* Thinking of the division meaning of fractions helps us understand how to change improper fractions to mixed numbers. For example, $\frac{26}{3}$ may be rewritten as 26 divided by 3.

$$\frac{26}{3} = 3\overline{)26} = 8\frac{2}{3}$$
$$\underline{24}$$
$$2$$

To change a mixed number to an improper fraction, first write the mixed number as an addition problem. For example, the mixed number $5\frac{2}{3}$ has the same value as $5 + \frac{2}{3}$. The next step is to write the whole number as a fraction. Any whole number can be written in fraction form by using the whole number as the numerator and using 1 as the denominator. Therefore, 5 is written as $\frac{5}{1}$. After writing the whole number in fraction form, find a common denominator and add.

$$5\frac{2}{3} = \frac{5}{1} + \frac{2}{3} = \frac{5 \times 3}{1 \times 3} + \frac{2}{3} = \frac{15}{3} + \frac{2}{3} = \frac{17}{3}$$

A short cut is to multiply the whole number by the denominator of the fraction. Then add this product to the numerator of the fraction and write the sum as the new numerator. The denominator remains the same.

$$6\frac{7}{8} = \frac{(6 \times 8) + 7}{8} = \frac{48 + 7}{8} = \frac{55}{8}$$

When adding or subtracting mixed numbers, you can write the mixed numbers as addition problems first. Then the whole numbers may be added or subtracted separately from the fractions.

$$9\frac{3}{8} + 4\frac{2}{5} =$$

$$9\frac{3}{8} = 9 + \frac{3}{8} = 9 + \frac{3 \times 5}{8 \times 5} = 9 + \frac{15}{40}$$
$$+$$
$$4\frac{2}{5} = 4 + \frac{2}{5} = 4 + \frac{2 \times 8}{5 \times 8} = 4 + \frac{16}{40}$$
$$\overline{13 + \frac{31}{40} = 13\frac{31}{40}}$$

However, some problems that involve subtraction of mixed numbers are more complicated.

$$8\frac{1}{3} - 4\frac{2}{5} =$$

$$8\frac{1}{3} = 8 + \frac{1}{3} = 8 + \frac{1 \times 5}{3 \times 5} = 8 + \frac{5}{15}$$
$$-$$
$$4\frac{2}{5} = 4 + \frac{2}{5} = 4 + \frac{2 \times 3}{5 \times 3} = 4 + \frac{6}{15}$$

Normally, the next step would be to subtract the whole numbers and then subtract the fractions. But $\frac{6}{15}$ cannot be subtracted from $\frac{5}{15}$. To subtract these fractions, we must make the top fraction larger. This can be done by borrowing 1 from the 8. If we do so, the whole number becomes 7. Then, we can add the borrowed 1, in the form of $\frac{15}{15}$, to $\frac{5}{15}$ and subtract the fractions.

$$8 + \frac{5}{15} = 7 + 1 + \frac{5}{15} = 7 + \frac{15}{15} + \frac{5}{15} = 7 + \frac{20}{15}$$
$$-$$
$$4 + \frac{6}{15} = 4 + \frac{6}{15}$$
$$\overline{3 + \frac{14}{15} = 3\frac{14}{15}}$$

To multiply or divide mixed numbers, change them to improper fractions. Then multiply or divide as usual.

History

More than 4,000 years ago, ancient Babylonian astronomers used fractions made by dividing a unit into 60 parts, then dividing each of these parts into 60 parts, and so on. This system is still used for telling time and for measuring angles in minutes and seconds. The ancient Chinese developed decimal fractions made by dividing units over and over again by 10.

Egyptian mathematicians who helped build the pyramids more than 4,000 years ago used only fractions with 1 in the numerator. Such fractions are called *unit fractions.* The use of only unit fractions made it necessary to express other fractional parts as sums. For example, $\frac{3}{4}$ is expressed in unit fractions as $\frac{1}{2} + \frac{1}{4}$.

About 2,000 years ago, the ancient Greeks wrote fractions with the numerator on the bottom and the denominator on the top. They did not separate the numerator and denominator by a line. Later, they began writing fractions with the numerator on the top and the denominator on the bottom. Hindu mathematicians in India adopted this method of writing fractions from the ancient Greeks.

During the A.D. 700's, Arabs conquered parts of India. There, the Arabs learned the decimal system and this method of writing fractions. During the 300 years that followed, the Arabs spread this knowledge through western Asia, across northern Africa, and into Spain.

During the late 1400's, several arithmetic books that explained the use of fractions and the decimal system were published in Europe. Following the publication of these books, large numbers of Europeans began to use fractions to perform everyday calculations.

Today, fractions are used mostly in connection with inches, cups, pounds, and other measurements in the English system of measurement. However, almost all countries other than the United States use the metric system of weights and measures. The metric system of measurement uses decimal fractions that are written with a decimal point rather than with a numerator and a denominator (see **Metric system**).

Also, many problems that were once done with fractions using paper and pencil are now done on electronic calculators. These calculators express fractions in the decimal form. As a result of these changes, there are fewer and fewer uses for the fraction form. However, the fraction form continues to be an important means of expressing rates, ratios, and division. The fraction form also continues to be important in algebra and in other special areas of mathematics as a method of writing rational numbers. Karen Connors Fuson

Related articles in *World Book* include:

Outline

Practice fraction examples

1. Bill is $62\frac{1}{2}$ inches tall. Mary is $56\frac{1}{4}$ inches tall. How much taller is Bill than Mary?

2. Sandy's house stands on a quarter-acre plot. Her father bought the three-eighths acre plot next to it. What is the size of the combined plots of land?

3. Mrs. Barry uses $\frac{3}{4}$ of a teaspoon of instant coffee to make one cup. How many teaspoons of instant coffee should she use to make six cups?

4. John wants to saw a board into four equal pieces. He finds that the board is 7 feet $3\frac{5}{8}$ inches long. How long should he make each piece?

5. Lisa can "step off" distances. The average length of her step is $2\frac{1}{2}$ feet. The length of her room measures 7 steps, and the width of her room measures 6 steps. How long is Lisa's room? How wide?

Answers to the practice examples

1. $6\frac{1}{4}$ inches	3. $4\frac{1}{2}$ teaspoons	5. $17\frac{1}{2}$ feet; 15 feet
2. $\frac{5}{8}$ acre	4. 1 ft. $9\frac{29}{32}$ in.	

Fractional distillation. See Distillation; Petroleum (Refining petroleum).

Fracture is a broken bone. There are many kinds of fractures. Common types include closed, open, multiple, comminuted, greenstick, and spiral fractures. In a *closed,* or *simple, fracture,* a bone breaks, but the skin over it does not. In an *open,* or *compound, fracture,* both the bone and skin break, and there is danger of infection. *Multiple fracture* means there is more than one break in a bone. A *comminuted fracture* occurs when a bone breaks into three or more major fragments or as many as hundreds of tiny pieces. In a *greenstick fracture,* the break cuts only part way through the bone. A *spiral fracture* results when a bone is broken by a twisting force.

People of all ages break bones. But the bones of old people are more fragile than those of young people. They break more easily and need more time to heal.

A physician can detect a fracture in several ways. Usu-

ally, there is pain, soreness, or tenderness in a fracture area. Swelling and discoloration also occur. Sometimes, there is movement of the bone under the skin and obvious deformity. *Crepitus* often signals a broken bone. Crepitus is a harsh grating sound caused when the broken ends of the bone rub together. In some cases, only an X ray will reveal a fracture. Fractures should be treated only by physicians. The injured part should be kept motionless until a physician arrives.   James A. Hill

See also **First aid** (Fractures and dislocations).

Fragmentation, *FRAG muhn TAY shuhn,* is the breaking of any material into small pieces. The fragmentation bomb or shell is used against troops, trucks, and grounded aircraft. It has a heavy case that breaks into thousands of small *fragments* (pieces) when it explodes.

Some fragmentation bombs are cases containing hundreds of small bombs, or *bomblets.* These bombs vary in size. Fragmentation shells fired from artillery guns usually set so the shells burst in the air just above the enemy troops.   Norman Polmar

See also **Bomb** (Fragmentation bombs).

Fragonard, *fra gaw NAR,* **Jean Honoré,** *zhahn aw naw RAY* (1732-1806), was a French artist who painted in the delicate, decorative style known as rococo. Fragonard's favorite subjects were courtship and flirtation among the upper classes. He also became known for his portraits, especially of famous entertainers, and for his charming paintings of children. In addition, he was one of the leading landscape painters in French art. *The Swing* (1766), Fragonard's most famous painting, illustrates the rococo style at its peak. The painting appears in the **Painting** article.

Fragonard was born in Grasse. He studied with Jean Chardin and François Boucher, two noted French painters. Boucher, a leading rococo artist, strongly influenced Fragonard's style. Early in his career, Fragonard produced traditional paintings of historical subjects. He then began to paint the witty, romantic scenes that were typical of the rococo style. During the 1770's, Fragonard painted a series of pictures, called *The Progress of Love,* that are masterpieces of rococo art.   Willard E. Misfeldt

See also **Painting** (Rococo); **Rococo.**

Frambesia. See Yaws.

Frame construction. See Building construction; House.

Franc, *frangk,* is the standard coin of France. The franc is also used in Belgium, Luxembourg, Switzerland, and many other countries. For the franc's value in each country, see **Money** (table: Exchange rates).

Some common kinds of fractures

WORLD BOOK illustrations by Patricia Wynne

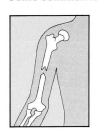 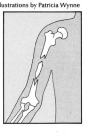

Closed   **Open**   **Multiple**

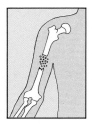 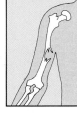 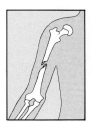

Comminuted   **Greenstick**   **Spiral**

WORLD BOOK photo by James Simek

The French franc. On one side are the words "République Française" ("French Republic"), *left.* The other has the motto, "Liberté, Égalité, Fraternité" ("Liberty, Equality, Fraternity").

The Arc de Triomphe in Paris is a symbol of French patriotism. Napoleon Bonaparte began the stone arch as a monument to his troops in 1806, and King Louis Philippe completed it in 1836. Under the arch lies the tomb of France's Unknown Soldier of World War I.

France

France is the largest country of Western Europe in area. It ranks second to the Union of Soviet Socialist Republics (U.S.S.R.) in area among all the European nations.

Paris, the capital and largest city of France, is one of the world's great cities. For hundreds of years, Paris has been a world capital of art and learning. Many great artists have produced their finest masterpieces there. Every year, millions of tourists visit such famous Paris landmarks as the Cathedral of Notre Dame, the Eiffel Tower,

The contributor of this article is William M. Reddy, Professor of History at Duke University and author of Money and Liberty in Modern Europe.

and the Louvre—one of the largest art museums in the world.

There is much more to France than just Paris, however. The snow-capped Alps form the border between France and Italy. Sunny beaches and steep cliffs stretch along the French coast on the Mediterranean Sea. Fishing villages dot the Atlantic coast of northwestern France. The peaceful, wooded Loire Valley has many historic *châteaux* (castles). Colorful apple orchards, dairy farms, and vineyards lie throughout much of the countryside. Many regions of France have fields of golden wheat.

The French are famous for their enjoyment of life. Good food and good wine are an important part of eve-

The French countryside has many picturesque villages. This village lies in the Périgord region of southwestern France. Many French villagers farm the land or work in nearby cities.

Fashion styles from Paris are copied by clothing manufacturers throughout the world. This model wears an evening ensemble by French designer Jean-Louis Scherrer at a fashion show.

Open-air markets spill out onto the sidewalks of many French cities and towns. These shoppers are selecting fresh fruits and vegetables. The French value good food and skillful cooking.

ryday living for most French people. The wines of France are considered the best in the world. Almost every restaurant and area has at least one special recipe of its own. The delicious breads, appetizers, sauces, soups, and desserts of France are copied by cooks in most parts of the world.

France has a long and colorful history. Julius Caesar and his Roman soldiers conquered the region before the time of Christ. Then, after Rome fell, the Franks and other Germanic tribes invaded the region. France was named for the Franks. By the A.D. 800's, the mighty Charlemagne, king of the Franks, had built the area into a huge kingdom.

In 1792, during the French Revolution, France became one of the first nations to overthrow its king and set up a republic. A few years later, Napoleon Bonaparte seized power. He conquered much of Europe before he finally was defeated. During World Wars I and II, France was a bloody battleground for Allied armies and the invading German forces.

France is not only a beautiful and historic country, it is also rich and powerful. France has great automobile, chemical, and steel industries. It is a leader in growing wheat, vegetables, and many other crops. France stands fifth among the countries of the world in its trade with other nations, as measured by exports. France also plays an important part in world politics. Its foreign policies affect millions of people in other countries.

France in brief

General information

Capital: Paris.
Official language: French.
Official name: République Française (French Republic).
National anthem: "La Marseillaise."
National motto: *Liberté, Égalité, Fraternité* (Liberty, Equality, Fraternity).

Largest population centers (1982 census)

Cities	Metropolitan areas
Paris (2,176,243)	Paris (8,706,963)
Marseille (874,436)	Lyon (1,236,096)
Lyon (413,095)	Marseille (1,115,697)
Toulouse (347,995)	Lille (945,572)
Nice (337,085)	Bordeaux (650,123)

The French flag is called the *tricolor*. In 1789, King Louis XVI first used its three colors to represent France. France has no official coat of arms.

Land and climate

Land: France lies in western Europe, with coastlines on the Atlantic Ocean and Mediterranean Sea. The country borders Spain, Italy, Switzerland, West Germany, Belgium, and Luxembourg, and lies across the English Channel from Great Britain. The Pyrenees Mountains separate France from Spain. The Alps border Italy; the Alps and Jura Mountains border Switzerland. The Central Highlands occupies south-central France. Most of northern, western, and north-central France is flat or has rolling hills. Major rivers include the Loire, Seine, and Rhône.

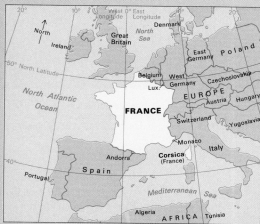

Area: 210,026 sq. mi. (543,965 km²), including mainland France and Corsica. *Greatest distances*—east-west, 605 mi. (974 km); north-south, 590 mi. (950 km). *Coastline*—2,300 mi. (3,701 km).
Elevation: *Highest*—Mont Blanc, 15,771 ft. (4,807 m). *Lowest*—below sea level at the Rhône River delta.
Climate: Warm summers and cool winters, except on the Mediterranean coast, which is warmer in all seasons. Typical daytime summer high about 75° F. (24° C) in the north; 82° F. (28° C) on the Mediterranean coast. Winter daytime highs about 43° F. (6° C) in the north; about 54° F. (12° C) on the Mediterranean coast. Moderate precipitation year-round, except for dry summers along the Mediterranean.

Government

Form of government: Parliamentary democracy.
Head of state: President (elected by people to 7-year term).
Head of government: Prime minister.
Legislature: Parliament of two houses—the National Assembly (577 members) and the Senate (319 members). The National Assembly is more powerful than the Senate.
Executive: Prime minister and president each have some executive powers.
Judiciary: Highest court is the Court of Cassation.
Political subdivisions: 22 regions, containing 96 metropolitan departments.

People

Population: *1990 estimate*—56,236,000; *1982 census*—54,334,871. *1995 estimate*—57,370,000.
Population density: 268 persons per sq. mi. (103 per km²).
Distribution: 74 per cent urban, 26 per cent rural.
Major ethnic/national groups: About 93 per cent French (including Basques, Bretons, and others who have long lived in France). About 7 per cent recent immigrants and their descendants—mostly from Algeria, Morocco, Tunisia, Italy, Portugal, Spain, Turkey, and Indochina.
Major religions: 75 per cent Roman Catholic, 3 per cent Muslim, 2 per cent Protestant, 1 per cent Jewish.

Population trend

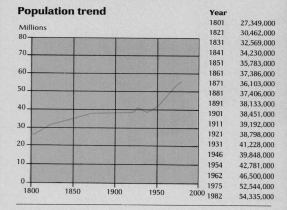

Year	
1801	27,349,000
1821	30,462,000
1831	32,569,000
1841	34,230,000
1851	35,783,000
1861	37,386,000
1871	36,103,000
1881	37,406,000
1891	38,133,000
1901	38,451,000
1911	39,192,000
1921	38,798,000
1931	41,228,000
1946	39,848,000
1954	42,781,000
1962	46,500,000
1975	52,544,000
1982	54,335,000

Economy

Chief products: *Agriculture*—beef cattle, milk, wheat, grapes, sugar beets, potatoes, apples, hogs, chickens and eggs. *Manufacturing*—iron and steel, chemicals, automobiles, electronic goods, textiles and clothing, aerospace equipment, processed foods and beverages, railway equipment. *Mining*—iron ore.
Money: *Basic unit*—franc. For value in U.S. dollars, see Money (table: Exchange rates).
Gross national product: *1987 total GNP*—$714,994,000,000. *1987 GNP per capita*—$12,860.
Foreign trade: *Major exported goods*—chemicals, machinery, electrical and electronic equipment, automobiles, aircraft, weapons, wine, grains, iron and steel. *Value of exported goods and services*—$219,645,000,000 (1987). *Major imported goods*—petroleum, machinery, chemicals, automobiles. *Value of imported goods and services*—$223,722,000,000 (1987). *Main trading partners*—West Germany, Italy, Belgium, Great Britain, United States, Netherlands, Spain.

The political importance of France today resulted partly from the leadership of Charles de Gaulle, who served as president of the country from 1958 to 1969. De Gaulle established a strong French republic. He looked on France as a world power and followed a policy that was independent of both the United States and the Communist nations. De Gaulle ended France's close military ties with the United States and tried to improve relations with Communist countries. De Gaulle's actions angered many other nations, but to the proud people of France he was a symbol of their nation's greatness.

Government

France is a parliamentary democracy with a strong national government. Its present government, called the *Fifth Republic,* has been in effect since 1958. The First Republic was established in 1792. Between 1792 and 1958, the structure of the French government changed many times.

France's national government has three branches. They are (1) an executive branch headed by a president and a prime minister, (2) a legislative branch consisting of a Parliament, and (3) a judicial branch, or system of courts. The French constitution provides each branch of government with certain powers, but the branches' functions sometimes overlap.

National government. The president of France is elected to a seven-year term by voters aged 18 or older. The president can serve an unlimited number of terms. The president appoints the prime minister (also called premier). The prime minister chooses the other ministers who make up the *Council of Ministers* (cabinet). The president is considered the *head of state* and the prime minister is *head of the government.* The president manages the nation's foreign affairs. The prime minister directs the day-to-day operations of the government.

France's Parliament consists of two houses, the National Assembly and the Senate. The National Assembly consists of 577 *deputies,* elected by the voters for five-year terms, unless an election is called earlier. The president has the power to dissolve the National Assembly and call for new elections. The Senate has 319 members. Senators are elected to nine-year terms by regional and city electoral colleges. The National Assembly is more powerful than the Senate. For example, if the two houses disagree on the text of a proposed law, the National Assembly makes the final decision. In addition, the Council of Ministers must have the support of a majority of members in the National Assembly. Without such a majority, the ministers must resign, and the president appoints a new prime minister.

Local government. The basic unit of local government in France is the *commune.* France has about 36,500 communes, which vary in size from small villages to large cities. Each commune is governed by a mayor and a local council.

Mainland France and the island of Corsica are divided into 96 *metropolitan departments.* Each department is administered by a locally elected council. Each also has a commissioner (formerly a prefect), who is appointed by the national government and who represents the government. Each department is part of one of France's 22 regions. Each region has a regional council, elected by the people, and a president elected by the council members. The region of Corsica has a special status with more local independence.

France has nine inhabited overseas possessions: Guadeloupe and Martinique, both in the West Indies; Reunion and Mayotte, both in the Indian Ocean; New Caledonia, French Polynesia, and the Wallis and Futuna Islands, all in the South Pacific Ocean; French Guiana in South America; and Saint-Pierre and Miquelon in the North Atlantic Ocean. These possessions are considered part of France. Their people vote for the president of France and send representatives to both houses of the French Parliament.

Politics. France has several political parties. The Socialist Party and the French Communist Party hold liberal or radical views. In theory, both parties support public ownership or control of most of the nation's factories, machines, and other basic means of production. In practice, however, the Socialists have cooperated with private business since the 1930's. Both the Socialists and Communists support strong, government-financed social security and medical benefits. The chief conservative political parties in France are the Union for French Democracy (UDF) and the Rally for the Republic (RPR). The UDF has called for removing government regulations that restrict individuals and companies from operating freely in the French economy. The RPR supports the policies of former French President Charles de Gaulle. It favors a strong national government and an aggressive foreign policy. The National Front, an extremely conservative political party, opposes immigration and favors the death penalty.

Courts are in the major cities of each department. Appeals from civil and criminal courts may be taken to *Courts of Appeal.* The *Courts of Assizes* hear cases involving murder and other serious crimes. The decisions of the Courts of Appeal and Assizes are generally final. But the *Court of Cassation,* the highest court of France, may review them. It can return cases to the lower courts for new trials. A minister of justice controls appointments and promotions of judges. Judges are appointed for life.

Armed forces. Men between the ages of 18 and 35 must serve one year of active duty in the French armed forces. About 550,000 men and women serve in the army, navy, and air force. The French government spends about 20 per cent of its national budget on the military.

People

Among the people of France, there are notable regional differences in language and traditions. As a result, many people in France have a strong sense of regional identity. In the regions of Corsica and Brittany, some people have organized to work for independence from France. However, most people in the various regions of France feel comfortable having both a regional identity and a national "French" identity.

Population. France has a population of about 56 million. About a sixth of the French people live in the Paris metropolitan area, one of the largest metropolitan areas in the world. France has 36 cities with populations of over 100,000. Five of the cities have more than 300,000 people. In order of size, they are Paris, Marseille, Lyon, Toulouse, and Nice. See the articles on French cities

France map index

Cities and towns

      (Index continued on page 458.)

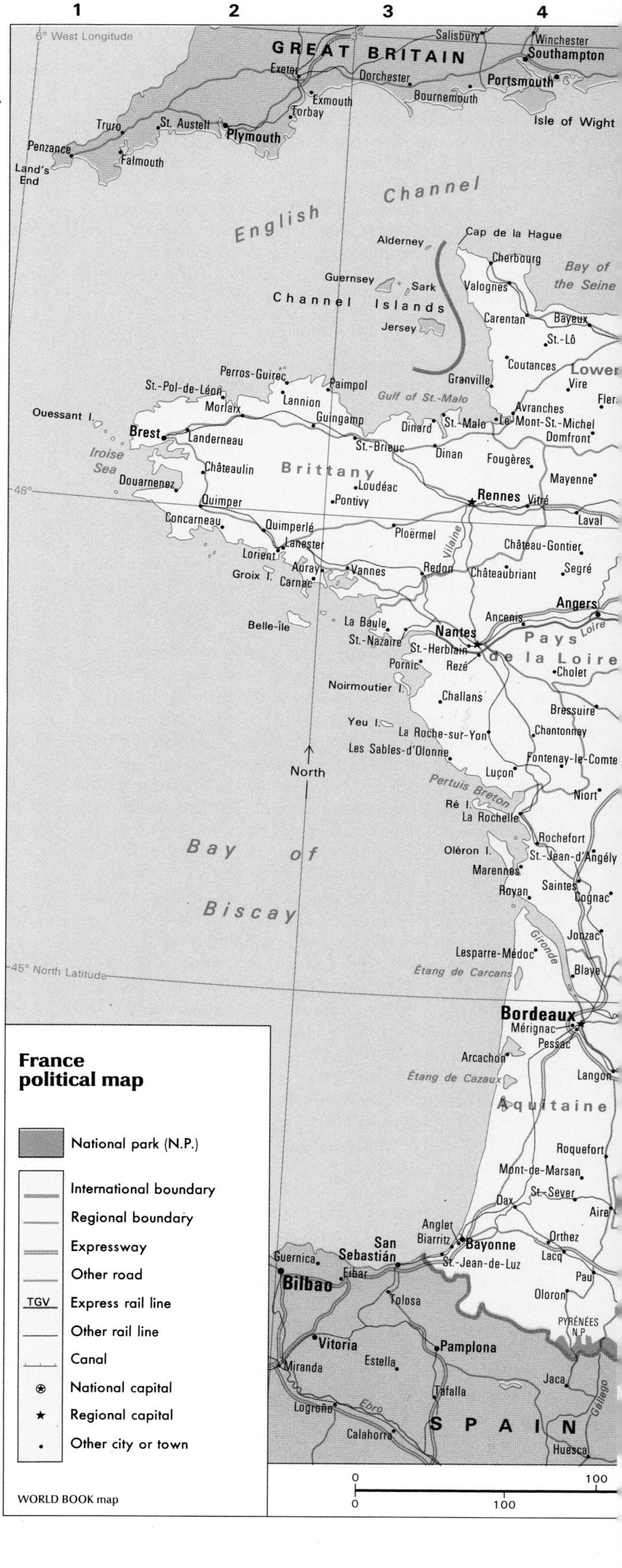

France political map

▨	National park (N.P.)
──	International boundary
──	Regional boundary
──	Expressway
──	Other road
TGV	Express rail line
──	Other rail line
──	Canal
⊛	National capital
★	Regional capital
•	Other city or town

WORLD BOOK map

0 ———— 100
0 ———— 100

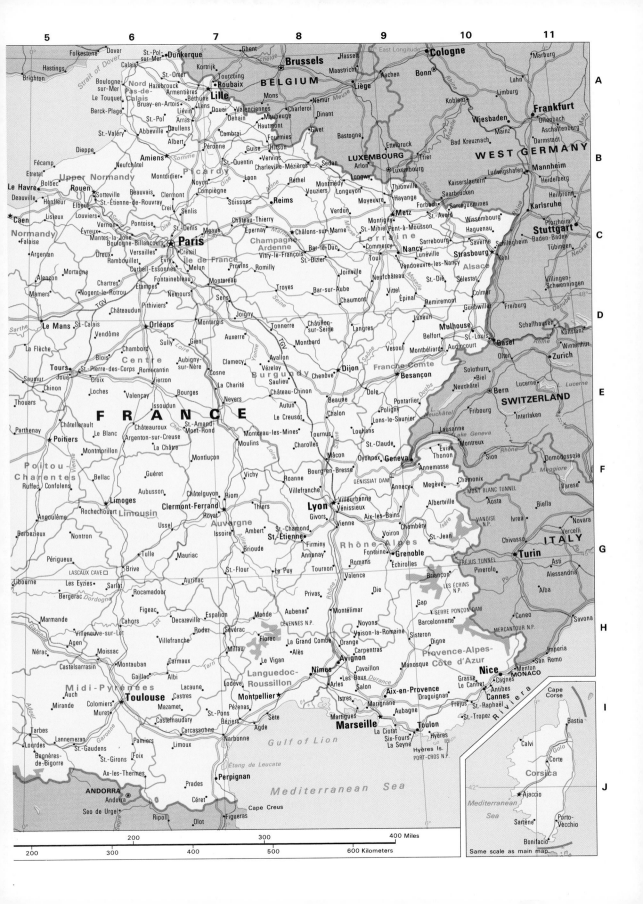

Lons-le-Saunier	20,105	.E	9
Lorient	62,554	.D	2
Lourdes	17,425	.I	5
Lunéville	21,468	.G	9
Lyon	413,095		
	†1,236,096	.F	8
Mâcon	38,404	.F	8
Maisons-Altort*	51,065	.C	6
Malakoff*	32,553	.C	6
Mantes-la-Jolie	43,564	.C	6
Marcq-en-Baroeul*	35,278	.A	7
Marignane*	31,109	.I	9
Marseille	874,436		
	†1,115,697	.I	9
Martiques	42,037	.I	9
Massy*	40,135	.C	6
Maubeuge	36,061	.A	8
Meaux	45,005	.C	7
Melun	35,005	.C	7
Menton	25,072	.I	11
Mérignac*	51,306	.G	4
Metz	114,232		
	†194,792	.C	9
Meudon*	48,450	.C	6
Meyzieu*	26,776	.G	9
Millau	21,695	.H	7
Mons-en-Baroeul*	26,638	.B	7
Montargis	16,110	.D	7
Montauban	50,682	.H	6
Montbéliard	31,836		
	†129,936	.D	10
Montceau-les-Mines	26,925	.E	8
Mont-de-Marsan	27,326	.I	4
Montélimar	29,161	.H	8
Montereau	19,413	.D	7
Montfermeil*	22,926	.C	6
Montgeron*	22,039	.C	7
Montigny	22,114	.C	9
Montluçon	49,912	.F	7
Montmorency*	20,798	.C	6
Montpellier	197,231		
	†225,292	.I	8
Montreuil*	93,368	.C	7
Montrouge*	38,517	.C	6
Morlaix	18,348	.C	2
Moulins	25,159	.F	7
Mulhouse	112,157		
	†222,726	.D	10
Nancy	96,317		
	†314,163	.C	9
Nanterre*	88,578	.C	6
Nantes	240,539		
	†474,068	.E	3
Narbonne	41,565	.I	7
Neuilly-sur-Marne*	31,195	.C	7
Neuilly-sur-Seine*	64,170	.C	6
Nevers	44,020	.E	7
Nice	337,085		
	†451,467	.I	10
Nimes	124,220		
	†138,051	.I	8
Niort	58,203	.F	4
Noisy-le-Grand*	40,585	.C	7
Noisy-le-Sec*	36,880	.C	6
Orange	26,499	.H	8
Orléans	102,710		
	†225,019	.D	6
Orly*	23,766	.C	6
Orsay*	14,071	.C	6
Oullins*	27,168	.F	8
Oyonnax	22,739	.F	9
Palaiseau*	28,369	.C	6
Pantin*	43,553	.C	6
Paris	2,176,243		
	†8,706,963	.C	6
Pau	83,790		
	†135,622	.I	5
Périgueux	32,916	.G	5
Perpignan	111,669		
	†139,956	.J	4
Pessac	50,267	.H	4
Poissy	36,389	.C	6
Poitiers	79,350	.F	5
Pontoise	28,434	.C	6
Puteaux*	36,117	.C	6
Quimper	56,907	.D	2
Reims	177,234		
	†204,149	.C	8
Rennes	194,656		
	†241,320	.D	4
Rezé	33,562	.E	4
Rillieux*	31,799	.G	8
Roanne	48,705	.F	8
Rochefort	26,167	.F	4
Rodez	24,368	.H	7
Romainville*	25,363	.C	6
Romans	33,152	.G	9
Rosny-sous-Bois*	36,970	.C	7
Roubaix	101,602	.A	7
Rouen	101,945		
	†385,807	.B	5
Royan	17,540	.G	4
Rueil-Malmaison*	63,412	.C	6

St.-Brieuc	48,563	.C	3
St.-Chamond	40,267	.G	8
St.-Cloud*	28,561	.C	6
St.-Denis*	90,829	.C	6
St.-Dié	23,759	.D	10
St.-Dizier	35,189	.C	8
St.-Étienne	208,159		
	†319,524	.G	8
St.-Étienne-du-Rouvray	32,444	.C	6
St.-Germain-en-Laye*	38,499	.C	6
St.-Herblain	41,958	.E	3
St.-Lô	23,212	.C	4
St.-Malo	46,347	.C	3
St.-Martin-d'Hères*	35,188	.G	9
St.-Maur*	80,811	.C	6
St.-Nazaire	68,348		
	†131,793	.E	3
St.-Ouen*	43,606	.C	6
St.-Pol-sur-Mer*	23,055	.A	6
St.-Priest*	42,677	.G	8
St.-Quentin	63,567	.B	7
St.-Raphaël	24,118	.I	10
Ste.-Geneviève-des-Bois*	30,439	.D	6
Saintes	26,602	.G	4
Salon	34,846	.I	9
Sarcelles*	53,630	.C	6
Sarreguemines	24,763	.C	10
Sartrouville*	46,197	.C	6
Saumur	32,149	.E	5
Savigny*	32,502	.C	6
Schiltigheim	29,574	.C	10
Sedan	23,477	.B	8
Sens	26,602	.D	7
Sète	39,545	.I	8
Sevran*	41,809	.C	7
Sevres*	20,208	.C	6
Six-Fours	25,526	.I	9
Soissons	30,213	.C	7
Sotteville	30,558	.B	6
Stains*	36,079	.C	6
Strasbourg	248,712		
	†378,478	.C	10
Suresnes*	35,187	.C	6
Talence*	34,692	.H	4
Tarbes	51,422	.I	5
Thiais*	26,637	.C	6
Thionville	40,573		
	†139,066	.B	9
Thonon	27,161	.F	10
Toulon	179,423		
	†418,617	.I	9
Toulouse	347,995		
	†550,526	.I	6
Tourcoing	96,908	.A	7
Tours	132,209		
	†268,647	.E	5
Trappes*	29,763	.C	6
Tremblay-lès-Gonesse*	29,644	.C	7
Troyes	63,581		
	†127,146	.D	8
Tulle	18,880	.G	6
Valence	66,356	.G	9
Valenciennes	40,275		
	†350,560	.A	7
Vandoeuvre-lès-Nancy	33,682	.C	9
Vannes	42,178	.D	3
Vanves*	22,868	.C	6
Vaulx-en-Velin*	44,160	.F	8
Vénissieux	64,804	.G	8
Verdun	21,516	.C	8
Vernon	22,243	.C	6
Versailles	91,494	.C	6
Vesoul	18,412	.D	9
Vichy	30,527	.F	7
Vienne	28,294	.G	8
Vierzon	34,209	.E	6
Vigneux-sur-Seine*	24,462	.C	6
Villefranche	28,881	.F	8
Villejuif*	52,448	.C	6
Villemomble*	26,499	.C	6
Villenave-d'Ornan*	21,073	.H	4
Villeneuve-d'Ascq*	59,527	.A	7
Villeneuve-la-Garenne*	23,906	.C	6
Villeneuve-le-Roi*	20,512	.C	6
Villeneuve-St.-Georges*	28,119	.C	6
Villeneuve-sur-Lot*	23,045	.H	5
Villeurbanne	115,960	.F	8
Villiers*	22,022	.C	7
Villiers-le-Bel*	24,808	.C	6
Vincennes*	40,384	.C	6
Viry-Châtillon*	30,224	.C	6
Vitry-le-François	18,261	.C	8
Vitry-sur-Seine*	85,263	.C	6
Voiron	18,911	.G	9
Wattrelos*	44,626	.A	7
Yerres*	25,715	.C	6

*Does not appear on map; key shows general location.
†Population of metropolitan area, including suburbs.
Source: 1982 census.

Population density

The population distribution of mainland France is fairly even. Paris is the most heavily populated urban area. On Corsica, pictured in the bottom right-hand corner of the map, most people live near the coast.

Persons per sq. mi.	Persons per km2
More than 250	More than 100
125 to 250	50 to 100
60 to 125	25 to 50
Less than 60	Less than 25

WORLD BOOK map

listed in the *Related articles* at the end of this article.

About 7 per cent of France's population consists of foreign residents. The largest foreign groups are people from Algeria, Morocco, Tunisia, Italy, Portugal, Spain, Turkey, and Indochina. In recent years, hundreds of thousands of refugees from former French colonies in Africa and Indochina have moved to France. The status of these immigrants is a controversial issue in the country. For example, Algerian immigrants represent a large work force that the country has not yet absorbed. Algerian workers are often the first to be laid off during periods of slow economic activity. Because they send most of their earnings home, many of them live in poor neighborhoods. Some immigrants from Morocco, Portugal, Tunisia, and Turkey are in similar situations. On the other hand, many Vietnamese refugees have become more fully integrated into French society.

Ancestry. In ancient times, peoples called *Gauls* lived in what is now France (see **Gaul**). The Gauls were a Celtic people related to the Welsh and the Irish. Roman, Germanic, and then Norse invaders came from the south, east, and north. The Romans brought peace to the warring Gallic tribes, and Roman law became the basis of modern French law. The name of France came from Germanic conquerors called *Franks*. Many people of northeastern France have Germanic ancestors. Some people from Normandy trace their ancestry back to the Norse people who settled there.

Language. By about the 1500's, the language that is

now called French was spoken only in the area around Paris. The rest of the people living in what is now France spoke Basque, Breton, Dutch, or German, or dialects related to modern French, such as Walloon, Picard, or Provençal. The building of the modern French nation is closely tied to the standardization and increased use of the local dialect of Paris beginning in the 1500's. For a detailed discussion of the French language, including its development, see **French language.**

On the island of Corsica, the majority of the population speaks a dialect similar to Italian. A group of people living along the Pyrenees Mountains speaks Basque. The region of Brittany has a significant number of people who speak Breton. Along the border with Belgium, many people speak the Flemish dialect of Dutch. The region of Alsace has many German-speaking people. In all of these regions, however, French is taught in the schools and the number of people who speak the regional tongue has dwindled from one generation to the next. In Corsica, Brittany, and the Pyrenees, people have formed groups to promote the use of the local language.

Way of life

City life. Almost three-fourths of the French people live in cities and towns of at least 2,000 people. The Paris metropolitan area has more than $8\frac{1}{2}$ million people. In the larger cities, most people live in apartments. Many Parisians live in old apartment buildings. In general, the older a building is, the more prestigious it is. Many French city dwellers tolerate buildings with old plumbing and appliances so they may enjoy antique fireplaces and ceiling beams.

Strict zoning regulations help protect and enhance the center of many French cities. Such regulations may prohibit traffic on certain city streets or limit high-rise construction in the center of a city. The regulations are designed to ensure a high quality of life for urban residents. Such urban problems as overcrowding and high

Apartment buildings, such as these in Lyon, are home to many French city dwellers.

© Guy Marche, FPG

© Howard Friedman, Photo Researchers

Villages set amid well-tended fields typify much of rural France. About a fourth of the French live in rural areas. Most enjoy the same comforts and conveniences as city dwellers.

crime rates are more likely to occur in the outskirts of cities or in nearby suburbs.

While city living is generally pleasant, it is also expensive. Many poor city residents live outside the city centers in run-down apartments or in housing complexes built by the government. Many middle-class people cannot afford to live in Paris, and instead live in a suburb as a second choice. Mass transit systems carry people from the suburbs to a variety of jobs and recreational and cultural activities in the city.

Rural life. Only about a fourth of the French people live in rural areas. However, France traditionally has been an agricultural society. The French people are thus more familiar with—and more respectful of—such rural activities as farming and hunting than are people in many urbanized countries.

Most rural residents enjoy the same comforts and conveniences as city dwellers. Most of them live in single-family houses in villages or on farms. They own a car and a television set and have such modern appliances as a refrigerator and a washing machine.

Farm families make up much of the rural population in France. Most farmers own their land. Some rent all or part of their land. A few French farmers are wealthy. But many farmers require other sources of income to support their families. A spouse or another family member may hold a job as a factory worker, office worker, or teacher. In poorer areas such as Brittany, some farmers earn barely enough to support themselves.

One problem for rural France is that most of its farms are too small to compete with the farms of many other Western European countries. For this reason, French farms cannot support all those born and raised on them. Since 1959, the rural population of France has dropped by almost half.

Food and drink. The French consider cooking an art. French *haute cuisine* (gourmet cooking) has set a standard accepted in many parts of the world since the 1700's. French chefs have created many delicious sauces and fancy appetizers. French appetizers include *escargots* (snails) in garlic butter sauce, scallops and mushrooms in a creamy wine sauce, and puff pastries filled with chicken in cream sauce. Sausages and *pâtés* (chopped meat cooked with spices) also serve as appetizers. Goose liver pâté with black mushroomlike *truffles* is considered a special delicacy. French cooks put tasty fillings of cheese, vegetables, shrimp, ham, or bacon into omelets, *crêpes* (thin, rolled pancakes), and *quiches* (custard baked in a pastry shell). These dishes are served as appetizers or light meals.

A typical French main meal has several courses. It starts with an appetizer or onion or potato soup. Popular main courses include steaks, chops, and roast chicken, served with French fried potatoes. A green salad often follows the main course, then cheese or fresh fruit. Crusty French bread accompanies most courses. A very special meal might add a light fish course before the main course and a dessert after the cheese course. Desserts include fancy pastries, fruit tarts, and crêpes filled with whipped cream or cooked fruit.

Such hearty French specialities as *bouillabaisse* and *cassoulet* make a full meal and need few extras. Bouillabaisse is a chunky chowder with six or more kinds of fish and shellfish. Cassoulet is a casserole of beans, sausage, poultry, and pork.

The French eat light breakfasts. A typical breakfast consists of such soft rolls as *croissants* and *brioches,* served with butter and jam, plus coffee.

Some French people drink wine at lunch and dinner, sometimes different wines for different courses. Beer, cider, or mineral water may substitute for wine. Coffee is served at breakfast, and after other meals.

Recreation. The greatest national sporting event in France is the Tour de France, a bicycle race. Every sum-

mer, more than a hundred professional cyclists race around almost the entire country. They ride daily for nearly a month, and finish in Paris. Thousands of spectators line the route and cheer them along.

France's most popular team sport is *soccer,* a form of football. Almost every area and region in France has its own team. The French also enjoy such sports as *boules* (a form of bowling), fishing, ice skating, rugby, skiing, swimming, and tennis.

All French workers are entitled to receive five weeks of paid vacation every year. In July and August, automobiles filled with vacationers crowd the highways leading south to the Mediterranean Sea and the mountains. To accommodate vacationers, there are thousands of special camps and inexpensive resorts that organize activities for children and adults. Many French people have second homes in the country. Vacation festivals in many southern cities feature music, theater, parades, and folk dancing.

Throughout the year, city dwellers take daily walks through public parks. They may stop at one of the sidewalk cafes that dot many city boulevards. Many French people also enjoy watching television and listening to the radio. TV programs made in the United States have become especially popular.

Holidays. Most French holidays and festivals are closely connected with the Roman Catholic Church. Many cities celebrate Shrove Tuesday, the last day before Lent, with a merry festival called *Carnaval.* The Carnaval celebration in Nice includes a colorful parade, and attracts many tourists. Most villages honor their local patron saints with a festival in July.

On *Noël* (Christmas), French families hold reunions and the children receive gifts (see **Christmas** [In France]). The people also exchange gifts on *Le Jour de l'An* (New Year's Day). On *Pâques* (Easter), the children receive colored candy eggs and chocolate chickens.

© Bernard Hermann, Gamma/Liaison
Sidewalk cafes provide a pleasant place for French people to stop to eat or drink and visit with friends. The cafes are popular spots in most French cities and towns.

AP/Wide World
The Tour de France is the greatest national sporting event in France. Each summer, more than 100 of the world's top cyclists compete in the nearly monthlong race.

The French national holiday is Bastille Day, July 14. It marks the capture of the Bastille, a fortified prison, by the people of Paris in 1789, during the French Revolution. A large military parade is held in Paris on Bastille Day. At night, the people watch fireworks and dance in the streets until dawn. The French celebrate Labor Day on May 1, and Armistice Day on November 11.

Religion. About 75 per cent of the French people are Roman Catholics. About 3 per cent are Muslims, and about 2 per cent are Protestants. About 1 per cent are Jews. France has more Jews than any other European country. From 1801 to 1905, the French government recognized Roman Catholicism as the religion of the majority of the people. Bishops and priests were state officials, and were paid by the government. This church-state connection, established by Napoleon and Pope Pius VII, was broken by French law in 1905.

Education. French children between the ages of 6 and 16 must go to school. About 85 per cent of the children attend public schools. The others attend private schools, most of which are operated by the Roman Catholic Church.

Children from ages 2 through 6 may attend free nursery schools. Reading is taught during the last year of these schools. Children from ages 6 through 11 attend elementary schools. Formerly, boys and girls went to separate schools. But since the 1970's, they have attended school together. After five years of elementary school, children enter a *collège*. A collège is a four-year school that resembles a junior high school.

After collège, students enter either a vocational high school or a general high school. Both kinds of high schools are called *lycées*. Vocational high schools offer job training in business, crafts, farming, and industry.

General high schools provide a three-year course that prepares students to enter universities. The last year of general high school is a period of specialized study in

© Peter Vadnal, Art Resource

French museums are among the best in the world. The Orsay Museum, *above*, occupies a restored former railway station in Paris. It displays art from the 1800's and 1900's.

one of five areas. These areas are philosophy, experimental sciences, mathematics, mathematics and technology, and economics and social sciences. A *baccalauréat* examination completes this program. This examination is so difficult that about a third of the students fail to pass it.

France has about 75 universities. Each university selects its courses and teaching methods. Students have a voice in university administration. The government provides financial support to students.

France also has schools of higher education called *Grandes Écoles* (Great Schools). They prepare students for high-ranking careers in the civil and military services, commerce, education, industry, and other fields.

Museums and libraries. France has many excellent museums. The best known, the Louvre in Paris, is one of the largest art museums in the world (see **Louvre**). Many old castles and palaces, once the homes of kings and emperors, are national historical museums. They include the palace at Versailles, built by King Louis XIV (see **Versailles**). The Orsay Museum in Paris, located in a beautifully restored former railway station, exhibits paintings from the 1800's and 1900's—including many impressionist works. The Georges Pompidou National Center of Art and Culture in Paris includes a museum of modern art, a major public reference library, and a museum of industrial design. The Museum of Man has important scientific exhibits.

Public libraries are in all large French cities. France's national library, the Bibliothèque Nationale in Paris, is one of the largest libraries in Western Europe (see **Bibliothèque Nationale**). Other important libraries include the Mazarine Library of the Institute of France, the

© Claudia Parks, The Stock Market

Bastille Day, July 14, is France's national holiday. The people of France celebrate the holiday with parades, fireworks, and dancing. These dancers are performing at a celebration in Arles.

country's major learned society. The University of Paris also has fine libraries.

Arts

Since the Middle Ages, French artists, composers, architects, and writers have been among the cultural leaders of Europe. During many periods of history, French styles in painting, music, drama, and other art forms served as models for other Western countries. This section discusses the major art movements in France. For more information, see **French literature, Architecture, Sculpture, Painting,** and **Classical music** with their lists of *Related articles.*

The Middle Ages. The greatest works of medieval French art were magnificent Gothic cathedrals built from about 1150 to 1300. The finest examples include the Cathedral of Notre Dame in Paris and cathedrals in the cities of Amiens, Chartres, Reims, and Rouen. Much of the finest French sculpture of the time was created as decoration for the Gothic cathedrals.

Poetry was the most important literary form among medieval French writers. Musician-poets called *troubadors* wrote love songs in the Provençal dialect of southern France. Poets called *trouvères* carried this poetry to northern France. Other medieval poets wrote epic poems and long fictional works called *romances.*

The Renaissance was an important cultural period that reached its height during the 1400's and 1500's. François Rabelais was the most important French fiction writer of the French Renaissance. His satirical *Gargantua and Pantagruel* (1532-1564) is a masterpiece of Western literature. Seven French poets called the Pléiade wanted to create a new kind of French poetry based on ancient Greek and Roman models. Pierre de Ronsard and Joachim du Bellay were the group's major poets. Michel de Montaigne was the last great writer of this period. He created the personal essay as a literary form.

The finest French Renaissance architecture appeared as magnificent castles called *châteaux.* The best examples include those at Fontainebleau, Chambord, and Azay-le-Rideau. All were built in the early 1500's.

Baroque and rococo art developed in France during the 1600's and 1700's. Baroque art was large in scale and dramatic. Perhaps the greatest monument to baroque art in France is the spectacular palace at Versailles (begun about 1661).

The major French baroque composers were Jean Baptiste Lully and Jean Philippe Rameau, both known for their operas. François Couperin was an important composer of music for a keyboard instrument called the *harpsichord.*

Rococo art was smaller in scale and more delicate than that of the baroque style. The leading rococo artists were three painters—François Boucher, Jean Honoré Fragonard, and Antoine Watteau.

French classical art spanned the 1600's and 1700's as well. It stressed order, balance, and harmony, and placed heavy emphasis on the role of the intellect in analyzing human behavior. François de Malherbe was the first and greatest classical poet. His clear, rational, and sober poems became the basic style for classical verse. In prose, the leaders were two philosophers, René Descartes and Blaise Pascal.

The greatest expression of French classical literature was in drama. The major figures were Pierre Corneille, Jean Racine, and Molière. Corneille and Racine wrote tragedies. Molière ranks as the greatest writer of comedy in French drama.

In painting, classical ideals were best represented by Claude. His landscapes illustrate the classical admiration for balance, harmony, and order.

The Age of Reason, also called the *Enlightenment,* was a period of intellectual achievement in the 1600's and 1700's dominated by philosophical literature. Writers of this period emphasized reason and observation as the best methods of learning truth. The crucial figures in this movement were Voltaire, Jean Jacques Rousseau, and Denis Diderot.

Romanticism began in the late 1700's and flourished until the mid-1800's. It was partly a reaction against the attitudes of classicism and the Age of Reason. For example, romantic art and literature stressed emotions and

Castles called *châteaux* were the high point of French Renaissance architecture. Many of these magnificent castles stand in the Loire Valley. At Chenonceaux, near Tours, a château spans the River Cher, *left.* It was built in the 1500's.

Monument to Balzac (1897), a bronze statue; Museum of Modern Art, New York City

Sculptor Auguste Rodin created many expressive figures. One of his finest works is a statue of French author Honoré de Balzac.

the imagination over reason and self-discipline.

Jean Jacques Rousseau was a major personality in romanticism even though he was also a leader of the Enlightenment. The greatest romantic writer was the novelist, poet, and playwright Victor Hugo. Honoré de Balzac, Stendhal, and George Sand were also outstanding romantic novelists, though their work was more realistic than that of the typical romantic novelist.

Romantic painting was colorful and dramatic. It is best represented in the painting of Théodore Géricault and Eugène Delacroix. Auguste Rodin is recognized as the greatest romantic sculptor, though he worked later in the 1800's than most other romantic artists.

Hector Berlioz was the greatest French romantic composer. He gained fame for his large-scale orchestral works. Georges Bizet wrote the romantic *Carmen* (1875), probably the most popular opera ever written.

Realism and naturalism were movements of the middle and late 1800's that tried to portray life accurately and objectively. Gustave Flaubert was the major representative of realism, notably for his novel *Madame Bovary* (1857). Guy de Maupassant gained recognition for his realistic short stories. Naturalism, an extreme form of realism, was led by novelist Émile Zola.

Impressionism was a movement of the late 1800's and early 1900's centered on French painting. The impressionists tried to capture the immediate impression of an object or event. The leading impressionist painters included Edouard Manet, Camille Pissarro, Edgar Degas, Claude Monet, and Pierre Renoir. A movement called *postimpressionism* developed out of impressionism. The key French postimpressionists were Paul Cézanne, Paul Gauguin, Georges Seurat, and Henri de Toulouse-Lautrec. The movement produced two great composers, Claude Debussy and Maurice Ravel.

The 1900's. Paul Claudel, Andre Gide, Marcel Proust, and Paul Valery were the leading French writers of the early 1900's. Claudel wrote works that reflect his deep

St. John on Patmos, a manuscript painting from *The Hours of Etienne Chevalier* (1450-1455); Musée Conde, Chantilly (Giraudon/Art Resource)

The Table (1925), an oil painting on canvas; Tate Gallery, London (Art Resource)

Detail of a room (late 1600's) in the palace of Versailles (© Triarchou, Gamma/Liaison)

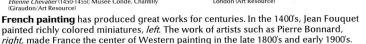

French painting has produced great works for centuries. In the 1400's, Jean Fouquet painted richly colored miniatures, *left*. The work of artists such as Pierre Bonnard, *right*, made France the center of Western painting in the late 1800's and early 1900's.

Masterpieces of French decorative art include beautiful tapestries and carpets, and richly carved furniture.

Roman Catholic faith. Gide and Proust were major novelists. Valery wrote classical poetry.

Philosophers Jean-Paul Sartre and Albert Camus wrote important drama and essays in the mid-1900's. Major French writers of the late 1900's include Alain Robbe-Grillet, Claude Simon, and Marguerite Duras.

Such painters as Georges Braque, Pablo Picasso (who was born in Spain), Georges Rouault, and Fernand Léger helped shape modern art. Sculptors Aristide Maillol, Jean Arp, and Antoine Pevsner were also important. The Swiss-born French architect Le Corbusier had a great influence on architecture with his *International Style.*

Composers Pierre Boulez and Olivier Messiaen were leaders in experimental music. Boulez became known for his work in electronic music.

The land

France has wide differences in geography. The northern and western regions consist mainly of flat or rolling plains. Hills and mountains rise in the eastern, central, and southern parts of France. France has 10 main land regions. They are (1) the Brittany-Normandy Hills, (2) the Northern France Plains, (3) the Northeastern Plateaus, (4) the Rhine Valley, (5) the Aquitanian Lowlands, (6) the Central Highlands, (7) the French Alps and Jura Mountains, (8) the Pyrenees Mountains, (9) the Mediterranean Lowlands and Rhône-Saône Valley, and (10) Corsica.

The Brittany-Normandy Hills have low, rounded hills and rolling plains. This region consists of ancient rock covered by poor soils, with some fertile areas along the coast. Apple orchards, dairy farms, and grasslands crisscross the land. In some areas, thick hedges separate the fields. Many bays indent the rugged coast and have important fishing harbors.

The Northern France Plains have highly fertile soils and productive industries. The plains are flat or rolling, and are broken up by forest-covered hills and plateaus.

This heavily populated region includes Paris. The Paris Basin, also called the Île-de-France, is a large, circular area drained by the Seine and other major rivers. East of Paris, a series of rocky ridges resembles the upturned edge of a huge saucer. Coal is mined near the Belgian border.

The Northeastern Plateaus share the Ardennes Mountains with Belgium. This wooded region becomes a little more rugged to the southeast in the Vosges Mountains. It has great deposits of iron ore, and produces iron and steel. Farmers raise livestock and a variety of crops on the lower slopes and in the valleys. Lumberers operate in the large forests.

The Rhine Valley has steep slopes and flat bottom lands. Trees and vines cover the slopes, and rich farmlands lie along the Rhine River. This river, which forms part of France's boundary with Germany, is the main inland waterway in Europe. Important roads and railways follow its course.

The Aquitanian Lowlands are drained by the Garonne River and the streams that flow into it. Sandy beaches lie along the coast. Inland, the region has pine forests, rolling plains, and sand dunes. Its many vineyards supply grapes for France's important wine industry. Oil and natural gas fields are in the Landes area, a forested section south of the major seaport of Bordeaux.

The Central Highlands, or *Massif Central,* is thinly populated. The soils in the region are poor, except in some valleys where rye and other crops are grown. Cattle and sheep graze on the lower grasslands, and forests cover the higher slopes. The Loire River, about 650 miles (1,050 kilometers) long, rises in the Cévennes, a mountain range. The Loire is the longest river in France. See **Loire River.**

The French Alps and Jura Mountains border on Italy and Switzerland. Snow-capped Mont Blanc, the highest point in France, rises 15,771 feet (4,807 meters). Many

© Victor Englebert, Photo Researchers

The cliffs of Normandy rise along the English Channel, in the Brittany-Normandy Hills of northwestern France. Most of this region consists of ancient rock covered by poor soils. However, some fertile areas lie near the coast.

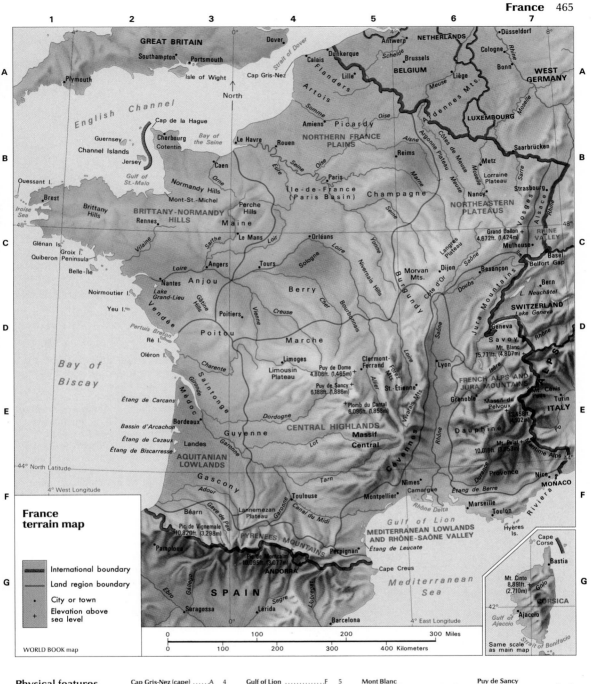

France terrain map

- ▨ International boundary
- — Land region boundary
- • City or town
- + Elevation above sea level

WORLD BOOK map

0   100   200   300 Miles

0   100   200   300   400 Kilometers

Mt. Cinto
8,891ft.
(2,710m) +

Same scale as main map

In Alsace, on the Northeastern Plateaus, vineyards spread over the rolling valleys and lower slopes of the Vosges Mountains. The region also has large forests and many potash deposits.

© Luis Villota, The Stock Market

Mont Blanc, in the French Alps, is the highest peak in France, rising 15,771 feet (4,807 meters). A thick blanket of snow always covers most of the top half of the mountain.

© D. Phillipe, FPG

The sunny Riviera is warmed by breezes from the Mediterranean Sea. The Alps shield the area from cold north winds. The Riviera's ideal climate attracts vacationers throughout the year.

© Michele Burges, The Stock Market

tourists visit nearby Chamonix and other ski resorts in the mountains. Mountain streams provide much hydroelectric power. See **Alps; Mont Blanc.**

The Pyrenees Mountains extend along France's border with Spain. Many peaks in this range rise more than 10,000 feet (3,000 meters). The rugged mountains have poor soils and are thinly populated. See **Pyrenees.**

The Mediterranean Lowlands and Rhône-Saône Valley region has productive farming areas, and irrigation is used widely. Fruits, vegetables, and wine grapes are important products. Marseille, on the Mediterranean Sea, is the leading seaport of France. The coast also includes the Riviera, a famous resort area. See **Rhône River; Riviera.**

Corsica is a Mediterranean island about 100 miles (160 kilometers) southeast of mainland France. It has hills and mountains similar to those of the Central Highlands. The island has generally poor soils and a steep, rocky coastline. Crops are grown in the valleys, and sheep graze in the mountains. See **Corsica.**

Climate

The climate varies widely among the various regions of France. The differences in climate are closely related to the distance of the land from the Atlantic Ocean or the Mediterranean Sea. Westerly winds that blow in from the Atlantic strongly influence the climate of western France. The coastal regions there have a rainy climate with cool winters and mild summers.

To the east, away from the Atlantic, the climate changes sharply between seasons. These inland regions have hot summers and cold winters, with medium rainfall throughout the year. The mountainous regions receive the most *precipitation* (rain, melted snow, and other forms of moisture), most of it in summer. Heavy winter snows fall in the Alps and Jura Mountains, and huge glaciers are found in the Alps.

Average January temperatures

Inland regions of France have cold winters. The country's coastal regions have milder winters.

Average July temperatures

Along the Atlantic coast and in most inland regions, summers are mild. The Mediterranean coast has hot summers.

Average yearly precipitation

Mountainous regions receive the most precipitation. Inland regions and the Mediterranean coast receive the least.

WORLD BOOK maps

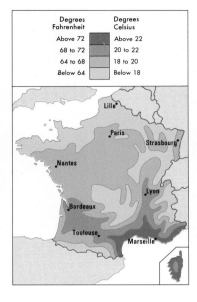

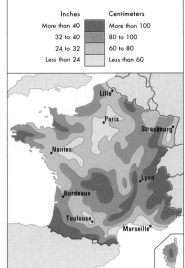

Average monthly weather

	Paris						Marseille					
	Temperatures				Days of rain or snow			Temperatures				Days of rain or snow
	F°		C°					F°		C°		
	High	Low	High	Low				High	Low	High	Low	
Jan.	42	32	6	0	15		Jan.	53	38	12	3	10
Feb.	45	33	7	1	13		Feb.	52	37	11	3	9
Mar.	52	36	11	2	15		Mar.	55	38	13	3	8
Apr.	60	41	16	5	14		Apr.	59	41	15	5	10
May	67	47	19	8	13		May	65	46	18	8	10
June	73	52	23	11	11		June	72	52	22	11	9
July	76	55	24	13	12		July	78	58	26	14	6
Aug.	75	55	24	13	12		Aug.	83	61	28	16	4
Sept.	69	50	21	10	11		Sept.	82	61	28	16	5
Oct.	59	44	15	7	14		Oct.	76	57	24	14	7
Nov.	49	38	9	3	15		Nov.	67	50	19	10	10
Dec.	43	33	6	1	17		Dec.	59	43	15	6	11

Along the Mediterranean Sea, the lowlands have hot, dry summers and mild winters with some rainfall. Swift, cold north winds called *mistrals* sometimes blow over southern France and cause crop damage. The Alps shield the sunny Riviera from the cold north winds during much of the year.

Economy

France is a prosperous nation and its people have a high standard of living. The prosperity resulted largely from sweeping economic changes that have been made since the 1940's. Before World War II, the French economy was based chiefly on small farms and business firms. After the war ended in 1945, the French government worked to modernize the economy. New methods of production and trade were developed through a series of national plans. These improvements have brought ever-increasing production.

Most French businesses are privately owned. But the government has long owned all or part of some businesses. For example, it has had complete ownership of France's three largest banks and of Renault—the largest French automobile manufacturer. The government has also had partial ownership of two steel companies. Socialists gained control of the presidency and Parliament in 1981 and increased government ownership of businesses. The Socialist government bought controlling interest in several manufacturers of technical and military equipment, and some banks and other financial institutions. When Conservatives gained control of Parliament in 1986, they began to sell the government-owned businesses to private owners. But after the national elections in 1988, the government became more heavily Socialist again, and Conservatives lost much of their effectiveness in reversing Socialist policies.

Natural resources play an important part in France's prosperity. Fertile soils are the country's most important natural resource. More than 90 per cent of France's total land area is fertile. The richest farmlands lie in the north and northeast, where wheat and sugar beets are the chief crops. The rainier northwest consists mainly of grasslands, used for grazing cattle and sheep, and orchards. Many of the drier areas of southern France have good soils for growing grapes. Soils are generally poor in the Central Highlands and on Corsica.

France has major deposits of iron ore and *bauxite* (aluminum ore). Coal, petroleum, natural gas, and potash are also found. France has large areas of forests.

Service industries are those economic activities that produce services, not goods. About 60 per cent of the workers are employed by service industries. Service industries are especially important to the Paris area.

Community, government, and personal services form the most important type of service industry. This industry employs about a third of all workers. It includes such economic activities as education and health care, government and the military, and data processing.

Trade, hotels, and restaurants form the second most important type of service industry in terms of employment. Paris is a major world center for the wholesale trade of automobiles and chemicals. Marseille, France's main seaport, is the center of the country's foreign trade. Lyon is a leading city in the wholesale trade of textiles. Retail trade, hotels, and restaurants are greatly aided by the large numbers of tourists that visit France.

Other service industries include finance, insurance, and real estate; transportation and communication; and utilities. Transportation and communication are discussed later in this section.

Manufacturing. France ranks as one of the world's leading manufacturing nations. The Paris area is the country's chief manufacturing center, but there are factories in cities and towns throughout the country.

France's gross national product

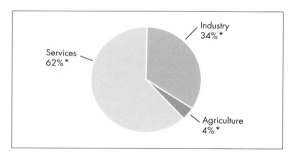

Services
62%*

Industry
34%*

Agriculture
4%*

The gross national product (GNP) is the total value of goods and services produced by a country in a year. The GNP measures a nation's total economic performance and can also be used to compare the economic output and growth of countries. France's GNP was $714,994,000,000 in 1987.

Production and workers by economic activities

Economic activities	Per cent of GDP* produced	Employed workers† Number of people	Employed workers† Per cent of total
Manufacturing	27	4,647,000	22
Community, government, & personal services	23	6,686,000	31
Finance, insurance, & real estate	19	1,759,000	8
Trade	12	3,449,000	16
Construction	6	1,577,000	7
Transportation & communication	5	1,297,000	6
Agriculture, forestry, & fishing	4	1,595,000	8
Utilities	3	193,000	1
Mining	1	107,000	1
Total	100	21,310,000	100

*Based on gross domestic product (GDP) in 1984. GDP is the total value of goods and services produced within a country in a year.
†Figures are for 1987.
Sources: International Labor Organization; United Nations; World Bank.

© Louis Goldman, Photo Researchers
Tourism contributes significantly to the French economy. A *bateau-mouche* (excursion boat), *above*, carries tourists along the Seine River in Paris. Millions of tourists visit Paris every year.

France is the fourth largest producer of automobiles in the world, after Japan, the United States, and West Germany. French cars include Renaults and Peugeots. Automobile plants are in the Paris Basin and near Lyon, Rennes, and Douai. France also makes railroad equipment and has developed the world's fastest trains.

France is a major manufacturer of sophisticated military and commercial airplanes. Toulouse is the center of aircraft production. France has a successful space program, and has launched rockets and several communications satellites. The country also produces aerospace equipment, electronic defense systems, and many kinds of weapons. France has a fast-growing commercial electronics industry that produces computers, radios, television sets, and telephone equipment.

The chemical industry produces a variety of products, from industrial chemicals to medicines and cosmetics. French plants make high-quality glass and tires.

The French iron and steel industry uses imported iron ore as well as ore mined in France. The aluminum industry uses much of the bauxite taken from French mines. Local and imported wood goes into the production of furniture, lumber, and pulp and paper. The famous French perfume industry, based in Paris, uses flowers that are grown in southeastern France.

France is a major producer of industrial machinery, and also ranks as a leader in designing new machines. French firms perform engineering services and also construct industrial and transportation projects in many countries. France also produces machine tools and *robotic* machines that perform repeated tasks in factories.

Cotton and silk textiles have long been important French products. French plants also produce nylon and other artificial fibers. The Lyon area, long a center for manufacturing silk, also has artificial-fiber factories. Paris, the fashion capital of the world, produces much of the nation's clothing.

Food processing employs many French people. Famous French foods include breads, meats, fruit preserves, and especially wines and cheeses. France ranks as the world's second largest wine-producing country, after Italy. The wines are aged in deep cellars or caves. France produces butter and about 400 kinds of cheeses, including Brie, Camembert, and Roquefort. France also is among the leading producers of sugar.

Agriculture. France is Western Europe's largest agricultural producer and one of the world's leading exporters of farm products. Almost all French farms have electricity, and most have modern farm machinery. French farms average 68 acres (28 hectares) in size. About two-thirds of French farm income comes from meat and dairy animals. About a fourth of the land consists of grassland used for grazing. Beef cattle are the chief meat animals, and lambs and sheep are also important. Much of the milk produced on dairy farms is used in making butter and cheese. French farmers have always raised some chickens and hogs, and specialized, large-scale production of these animals is expanding rapidly.

Crops grow on more than a third of France's land. Large farms in the Paris Basin and the north grow most of the wheat, France's leading single crop. Most grapes used in making wine are grown in southern France. Grapes for high-quality wines come from several regions, including Alsace, Bordeaux, Burgundy, Champagne, and the Loire Valley. The Mediterranean region produces grapes used for cheaper wines. Each region

© Chip Hires, Gamma/Liaison

Automobile production is one of France's leading industries. Workers build engines in a Renault factory, *above.*

produces grapes that have their own special flavor. Grapes from southwestern France are used in brandy.

Apple orchards dot many areas of northern France, especially Normandy. Potatoes, sugar beets, and such livestock-feed crops as barley, corn, oats, and rapeseed are major crops. Other important crops grown in France include beans, carrots, cauliflower, cherries, flowers, peas, peaches, pears, sunflower seeds, and tomatoes.

Economy of France

This map shows the economic uses of land in France. It also indicates the country's main farm products, its chief mineral deposits, and its most important fishing products. Major manufacturing centers are shown in red.

Mostly cropland

Cropland mixed with grazing land

Mostly grazing land

Forest land

Generally unproductive land

Fishing

•   Manufacturing center

•   Mineral deposit

WORLD BOOK map

France produces more wine than any other country except Italy. Wooden barrels hold the wine for aging, *above.* A wine tester, at the left, uses a *wine thief* to draw a sample.

© Bruce Thomas, The Stock Market

Forestry. Forests cover about a fourth of France. Heavily forested sections include the Northeastern Plateaus, the Central Highlands, the southwest coastal areas, and the slopes of the Alps, Juras, Pyrenees, and Vosges. Many forests have been planted in the Landes area of southwestern France for use by the pulp and paper industry. Cork oaks, pine trees, and olives grow along the dry Mediterranean coast and on Corsica. Forest fires are common in these regions. Other trees of France include ashes, beeches, and cypresses.

Mining. Iron ore is France's most important mineral deposit. Most of it comes from Lorraine, and is used in the region's steel industry. Deposits of bauxite, from which aluminum is made, are found in southeastern France. Bauxite was named after the town of Les Baux in the producing area. Alsace has much potash, a substance used in making fertilizers. Discoveries of natural gas at Lacq, in southwestern France, have attracted many industries. French mines also yield gypsum, salt, sulfur, tungsten, and uranium.

Fishing. French commercial fishing brings in a yearly catch of about 750,000 short tons (680,000 metric tons). Fishing crews work off the French coasts, or sail to the waters of Iceland and Newfoundland. Many fleets operate from Brittany and Normandy. Seafood taken includes cod, crabs, lobsters, monkfish, mussels, oysters, pollock, sardines, scallops, tuna, and whiting.

Energy sources. Nuclear power plants provide more than half of France's electricity. France is a world leader in nuclear energy technology and in the production of nuclear fuels. Most of the rest of France's electric power is generated by coal-burning plants or by hydroelectric power. The Alps and the Jura Mountains have many hydroelectric plants.

In 1966, the French government began operating the world's first tidal power plant. It uses the tides in the mouth of the Rance River in Brittany. These tides are among the highest in the world, and may reach a height of 44 feet (13 meters). A solar power plant operates in the Pyrenees.

Foreign trade of France, as measured by exports, ranks fifth in the world after the United States, West Germany, Japan, and Great Britain. The value of France's imports is slightly higher than the value of its exports. France's major imports are petroleum products. Its major exports include chemical products, machinery, electrical equipment, and automobiles. France belongs to the European Community, also called the European Common Market (see **European Community**). About half of France's trade is with Common Market countries, chiefly West Germany. Major trade partners outside the Common Market include Saudi Arabia, the Soviet Union, Switzerland, and the United States.

Transportation. Since the 1700's, France has had more road mileage in relation to its size than any other European country. Today, it has a fine highway system, including many multilane expressways. Most French households own at least one automobile. Two of the world's longest highway tunnels link France and Italy. One, 8.1 miles (13.0 kilometers) long, cuts through Fréjus Peak. The other, 7.3 miles (11.7 kilometers) long, cuts through Mont Blanc. In 1987, construction began on a tunnel beneath the English Channel that will link France and Great Britain by rail (see **English Channel**).

The French railway system, owned and operated by the government, provides excellent passenger and freight service. The rail network forms a cobweb pattern with Paris as the hub. A railroad tunnel, 8.5 miles (13.7 kilometers) long, through Fréjus Peak links France with Italy. In 1981, a high-speed electric train began operating between Paris and Lyon. Called the TGV (*train à grande vitesse,* or high-speed train), it reaches speeds of 167 miles (269 kilometers) per hour. In 1989, a faster TGV began operation between Paris and cities in western France. A top speed of 186 miles (300 kilometers) per hour makes it the world's fastest passenger train.

Charles de Gaulle and Orly airports, both near Paris, rank among the world's busiest airports. Other major airports include Marseille, Nice, and Lyon. Air France, an airline jointly owned by the French government and private investors, serves about 75 countries. Another airline, Air Inter, provides service among the large cities of France. Air Inter is fully owned by the government.

© S. Kanno, FPG

France's TGV (*train à grande vitesse,* or high-speed train) began operating between Paris and Lyon in 1981.

Ships and barges operate on navigable rivers and canals throughout France. These rivers include the Rhine, Rhône, and Seine. Northern and eastern France have well-developed canal systems. Oceangoing ships dock at many fine French seaports. The country's busiest seaports are Marseille, Le Havre, and Dunkerque.

Communication. France has about 85 daily newspapers, representing a wide range of political opinions. The largest newspaper, *Ouest-France* of Rennes, prints about 45 different editions, each with local news. Other major daily newspapers include *Le Figaro, France-Soir, Le Monde, Libération,* and *Le Parisien Libéré* of Paris; *Sud-Ouest* of Bordeaux; *La Voix du Nord* of Lille; *Le Progrès* of Lyon; *Le Provençal* of Marseille; and *Le Dauphiné Libéré* of Grenoble. Major weekly news magazines include *L'Express* and *Le Nouvel Observateur.*

France has several television and radio networks, most of which are operated by independent government agencies. The broadcasting system's income is largely provided by annual taxes on radios and television sets. Almost all French households own at least one radio and most own a television set.

A government agency supervises France's motion-picture industry. The agency's activities include giving financial aid to producers, especially of experimental films and movies of serious dramatic value. The annual Cannes Film Festival, in Cannes, is the world's largest international film event. France has about 4,700 motion-picture theaters.

History

Early days. In ancient times, tribes of Celts and other peoples lived in what is now France. The Romans called the region *Gallia* (Gaul). Roman armies began to invade Gaul about 200 B.C. By 121 B.C., Rome controlled the Gallic land along the Mediterranean Sea and in the Rhône Valley. Julius Caesar conquered the entire region between 58 and 51 B.C. The people, called *Gauls,* soon adopted Roman ways of life. They used the Latin language of the invaders. Gaul prospered under Roman rule for hundreds of years, in spite of barbarian invasions during the A.D. 200's and 300's. See **Celts; Gaul.**

Victory of the Franks. The border defenses of the West Roman Empire began to crumble in the A.D. 400's. Germanic tribes from the east, including Burgundians, Franks, and Visigoths, crossed the Rhine River and entered Gaul. They killed many Gauls and drove others west into what is now Brittany. Clovis, the king of the Salian Franks, defeated the Roman governor of Gaul in 486 at Soissons. Clovis then defeated other Germanic tribes in Gaul, and extended his kingdom. He founded the Merovingian *dynasty* (a series of rulers from the same family), and adopted Christianity. See **Clovis I; Franks; Merovingian.**

The rise of manorialism and feudalism. From the 600's to the 1000's, during the chaotic years of the early Middle Ages, manors covered much of France. Manors were large estates governed by owners called *landlords* or *lords,* who offered military protection to peasants called *serfs.* Manorialism was a system of organizing agricultural labor. See **Manorialism; Serf; Middle Ages.**

A political and military system called feudalism began to appear in the 700's. A feudal lord gave his subjects land in return for military and other services. Both the lord and his subjects, called *vassals,* were aristocrats. The land granted by a lord was called a *fief.* Some small fiefs supported only one vassal. Other fiefs were quite large, such as the province of Normandy. Manorialism and feudalism thrived until the 1100's. See **Feudalism.**

The Carolingian dynasty. By the mid-600's, the Merovingian kings had become weak rulers, interested chiefly in personal pleasures. Pepin of Herstal, the chief royal adviser, gradually took over most of the royal powers. His son, Charles Martel, extended the family's power. Charles received the title of *Martel* (the Hammer) after defeating an invading Arab army in 732. The battle began near Tours and ended near Poitiers. Charles Martel became king of the Franks in all but title. See **Charles Martel.**

Charles Martel's son, Pepin the Short, overthrew the last Merovingian ruler and became king of the Franks in 751. He founded the Carolingian dynasty, and enlarged the Frankish kingdom. Pepin also helped develop the political power of the pope by giving Pope Stephen II a large gift of land north of Rome. See **Papal States; Pepin the Short.**

Pepin's son, Charlemagne, was one of the mightiest conquerors of all time. After Charlemagne became king of the Franks, he went on more than 50 military campaigns and expanded his kingdom far beyond the borders of what is now France. He also extended the pope's lands. In 800, Pope Leo III crowned Charlemagne Emperor of the Romans. For the story of Charlemagne and a map of his empire, see **Charlemagne.**

Charlemagne died in 814, and his three grandsons later fought among themselves for control of his huge empire. They divided it into three kingdoms in 843. In the Treaty of Verdun, one grandson, Charles the Bald, received most of what is now France. The second kingdom consisted of much that is now Germany. The third kingdom lay between the other two. It consisted of a strip of land extending from the North Sea to central

Kings and emperors of France

Ruler	Reign	Ruler	Reign
* Hugh Capet	987-996	* Louis XI	1461-1483
Robert II	996-1031	* Charles VIII	1483-1498
* Henry I	1031-1060	* Louis XII	1498-1515
Philip I	1060-1108	* Francis I	1515-1547
Louis VI	1108-1137	* Henry II	1547-1559
Louis VII	1137-1180	* Francis II	1559-1560
* Philip II	1180-1223	* Charles IX	1560-1574
Louis VIII	1223-1226	* Henry III	1574-1589
* Louis IX	1226-1270	* Henry IV	1589-1610
Philip III	1270-1285	* Louis XIII	1610-1643
* Philip IV	1285-1314	* Louis XIV	1643-1715
Louis X	1314-1316	* Louis XV	1715-1774
John I	1316	* Louis XVI	1774-1792
Philip V	1316-1322	* Napoleon I	1804-1814
* Charles IV	1322-1328	* Louis XVIII	1814-1815
* Philip VI	1328-1350	* Napoleon I	1815
John II	1350-1364	* Louis XVIII	1815-1824
* Charles V	1364-1380	* Charles X	1824-1830
* Charles VI	1380-1422	* Louis Philippe	1830-1848
* Charles VII	1422-1461	* Napoleon III	1852-1870

*Has a separate biography in *World Book.*

Silver and gold statue encrusted with emeralds and rubies by an unknown sculptor (about 1349);
Aachen Cathedral (Art Resource)

Charlemagne was the most famous ruler of the Middle Ages.
He became king of the Franks in 768. He went on to conquer
much of western Europe and unite it under one great empire.

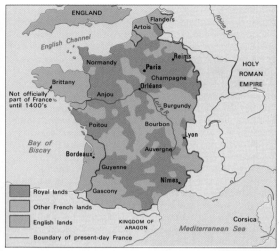

WORLD BOOK map

Capetian France in 1328 consisted of royal lands—those that
were the personal holdings of the king—and lands held by
French nobles who were vassals of the king.

Italy. The middle kingdom north of Italy was divided between the other two in 870. See **Verdun, Treaty of.**

The Capetian dynasty. By the late 900's, the Carolingian kings had lost much power, and the strength of the
nobles had increased. The kings became little more than
great feudal lords chosen by the other feudal nobles to
lead them in war. But in peacetime, most of their authority extended only over their personal estates. In 987, the
nobles ended the Carolingian line of kings and chose
Hugh Capet as their king. He started the Capetian
dynasty. Many historians mark the beginning of the
French nation from the coronation of Hugh Capet. See
Capetian dynasty; Hugh Capet.

Important dates in France

58-51 B.C. Julius Caesar conquered Gaul.
A.D. 486 Clovis, a king of the Franks, defeated the Roman governor of Gaul.
800 Charlemagne became emperor of the Romans.
987 Hugh Capet was crowned king of France.
1302 Philip IV called together the first Estates-General, the ancestor of the French Parliament.
1309-1377 The popes lived in Avignon.
1337-1453 France defeated England during the Hundred Years'
War.
1598 Henry IV issued the Edict of Nantes, which gave limited
religious freedom to Protestants.
1643-1715 Louis XIV ruled France, and consolidated the absolute authority of the French king.
1789-1799 The French Revolution took place. It ended absolute
rule by French kings.
1792 The First Republic was established.
1799 Napoleon seized control of France.
1804 Napoleon founded the First Empire.
1814 Napoleon was exiled; Louis XVIII came to power.
1815 Napoleon returned to power, but was defeated at Waterloo. Louis XVIII regained the throne.
1848 Revolutionists established the Second Republic.
1852 Napoleon III founded the Second Empire.
1870 -1871 Prussia defeated France in the Franco-Prussian War.
The Third Republic was begun.

1914-1918 France fought on the Allied side in World War I.
1939-1940 France fought on the Allied side in World War II
until defeated by Germany.
1940-1942 Germany occupied northern France.
1942-1944 The Germans occupied all France.
1946 France adopted a new constitution, establishing the
Fourth Republic.
1946-1954 A revolution in French Indochina resulted in France's
giving up the colony.
1949 France joined the North Atlantic Treaty Organization
(NATO).
1954 Revolution broke out in the French territory of Algeria.
1957 France joined the European Community, also called the
European Common Market.
1958 A new constitution was adopted, marking the beginning
of the Fifth Republic. Charles de Gaulle was elected president.
1962 France granted independence to Algeria.
1966 De Gaulle withdrew French troops from NATO.
1969 De Gaulle resigned as president.
1981 Socialist victories in presidential and parliamentary elections resulted in France's first leftist government since
1958.
1987 Construction of a railroad tunnel under the English Channel between France and Great Britain began.

For many years, the Capetian kings controlled only their royal *domain* (land), between Paris and Orléans. The great feudal nobles ruled their own domains almost independently. The dukes of Normandy were the most powerful of these nobles. Normandy became the most unified and best administered feudal state in Europe. In 1066, the Norman Duke William, later called William the Conqueror, invaded England and became king. See **Norman Conquest; William** (I, the Conqueror).

Growth of royal power. The Capetian kings gradually added more territory to their personal lands, and became stronger than any of their rivals. In addition, every Capetian king for over 300 years had a son to succeed him on the throne. As a result, the nobles' power to select kings died out. The nobles were further weakened because many of them left France between 1100 and 1300 on crusades to capture the Holy Land from the Muslims. See **Crusades.**

Philip II, called Philip Augustus, was the first great Capetian king. After he came to the throne in 1180, he more than doubled the royal domain, and tightened his control over the nobles. Philip built up a large body of government officials, many of them from the middle classes in the towns. He also developed Paris as a permanent, expanding capital. See **Philip** (II) of France.

The handsome Philip IV, called Philip the Fair, rebelled against the pope's authority. He taxed church officials, and arrested a bishop and even Pope Boniface VIII. Philip won public approval for his actions in the first Estates-General, a body of Frenchmen that he called together in 1302. This group was the ancestor of the French Parliament. In 1305, through Philip's influence, a French archbishop was elected pope and became Pope Clement V. In 1309, Clement moved the pope's court from Rome to Avignon, where it remained until 1377. See **Philip** (IV); **Pope** (The troubles of the papacy).

Social conditions in Capetian France. By the 1100's, an economic revival in Europe had put money back into use. Towns, which had lost their importance under manorialism and feudalism, sprang up near main trade routes. At first, towns were self-governing. Merchants and craftworkers settled in the towns and formed organizations called *guilds.* Guilds played an important role in town government (see **Guild**). As royal government grew, towns became judicial and administrative centers, as well as manufacturing and trading centers.

Although many people moved to the towns in search of jobs, much of the population stayed in the countryside. Agricultural methods were too primitive to support more than a very small nonagricultural population. Thus, people were still needed on farms to produce food. In both towns and in the country, life expectancy was short. Most children died before reaching the age of 5.

A period of wars. The last king of the Capetian dynasty, Charles IV, died in 1328 without a male heir. A cousin succeeded him as Philip VI and started the Valois dynasty. King Edward III of England, a nephew of the last Capetian king, also claimed the French throne. In 1337, Edward landed an army in Normandy. This invasion started a series of wars between France and England known as the Hundred Years' War (1337-1453). The English won most of the battles. But the French, after their victory at Orléans under Joan of Arc, drove the English

out of most of France. See **Hundred Years' War; Joan of Arc, Saint; Valois.**

Louis XI laid the foundations for absolute rule by French kings. During the Hundred Years' War, the kings had lost much of their power to the French nobles. Louis regained this power. His greatest rival was Charles the Bold, Duke of Burgundy. Charles died in battle in 1477 while trying to conquer the city of Nancy, and Louis seized most of his vast lands. See **Louis** (XI).

Francis I invaded northern Italy, and captured Milan in 1515. In a later Italian campaign, Francis was defeated by Charles V of the Holy Roman Empire. French wars against the Holy Roman Empire continued into the reign of Henry II. The Empire and England were allies. In 1558, this alliance gave Henry an excuse to seize the port city of Calais, England's last possession in France. See **Francis** (I) of France; **Henry** (II) of France.

Religious wars. During the early 1500's, a religious movement called the Reformation developed Protestantism in Europe. Many French people became Protestants. They followed the teachings of John Calvin, and were called *Huguenots.* After 1540, the government persecuted the Huguenots severely, but they grew in number and political strength. In the late 1500's, French Roman Catholics and the Huguenots fought a series of civil wars that lasted over 30 years. In 1572, thousands of Huguenots were killed during the Massacre of Saint Bartholomew's Day. See **Calvin, John; Huguenots.**

Henry III died in 1589 without a male heir. He was followed by Henry of Navarre, who became Henry IV and started the Bourbon dynasty. But Roman Catholic forces prevented him from entering Paris because he was the leader of the Huguenots. In 1593, Henry became a Roman Catholic to achieve peace. He entered the capital the next year. In 1598, Henry signed the Edict of Nantes, which granted limited freedom of worship to the Huguenots. See **Bourbon; Henry** (III and IV) of France.

The age of absolutism. The power of the kings and their *ministers* (high government officials) grew steadily from the 1500's to the 1700's. France became a strong nation, largely through the efforts of these ministers. The first important minister was Maximilien de Béthune, Duke of Sully, who served Henry IV. Sully promoted agriculture and such public works as highways and canals. He reduced the *taille,* the chief tax on the common people. The actual ruler behind Louis XIII was his prime minister, Armand Jean du Plessis, Cardinal Richelieu. Richelieu increased royal power more than any other individual. See **Richelieu, Cardinal.**

Louis XIV was the outstanding example of the absolute French king. He is said to have boasted: "I am the State." After his prime minister died in 1661, Louis declared that he would be his own prime minister. In 1685, Louis canceled the Edict of Nantes and began to persecute the Huguenots savagely. About 200,000 Huguenots fled France, which weakened the country's economy. Louis' minister of finance, Jean Baptiste Colbert, promoted a strong economy. But the construction of Louis' magnificent palace at Versailles and a series of major wars drained France's finances. Louis tried to rule supreme in Europe. He was stopped by military alliances that included England, Spain, the Holy Roman Empire, and other nations. See **Grand Alliance; Louis XIV; Succession wars** (The war of the Spanish succession).

The gathering storm. By the 1700's, a government bureaucracy had developed to manage a large standing royal army, as well as to collect taxes. Royal courts upheld law and order. Lawyers and jurists of the courts bought their offices from the king at very high prices. The king allowed those who bought the highest judicial offices to call themselves nobles, and he granted them tax exemptions.

This burdensome system worked well enough to allow remarkable economic and population growth in the 1700's. But the population growth exceeded agriculture's production capacities, and food shortages and famines became common. Such growth also strained the guild system that governed the activities of merchants and craftworkers in the towns.

Burdened by the needs of the military and unable to tax nobles or church lands, the government was forced to borrow heavily. In 1786, the government proposed a new land tax in order to avoid bankruptcy. Many urban lawyers, merchants, clerks, and craftworkers, as well as some aristocrats, opposed any new taxes. The French Revolution was born out of this crisis.

The French Revolution. To win support for new taxes, King Louis XVI called a meeting of the Estates-General. The Estates-General was made up of representatives from the three *estates,* or classes—the clergy, the nobility, and the commoners. It opened on May 5, 1789, at Versailles, near Paris. In June 1789, members of the third estate—the commoners—declared themselves a National Assembly, with full power to write a new constitution for France. The third estate had as many representatives as the other two estates combined.

At first, Louis XVI delayed taking action and began gathering troops around Paris to break up the Assembly. However, many French people organized an armed resistance movement in Paris. On July 14, 1789, a huge crowd of Parisians captured the royal fortress called the Bastille. Louis XVI was forced to give in. By September 1791, the Assembly had drafted a new constitution that made France a constitutional, or limited, monarchy, with a one-house legislature.

The new government did not last long. In April 1792, France went to war against Austria and Prussia. These nations wished to restore the king to his position. In the summer of 1792, as foreign armies marched on Paris, revolutionaries imprisoned Louis XVI and his family and overthrew the monarchy. A national convention elected by all adult French males opened on Sept. 21, 1792, and declared France a republic.

Civil and foreign wars pushed the new republican government to extreme and violent measures. Radical leaders such as Maximilien Robespierre gained power. They said that terror was necessary to preserve liberty. Thus, while the revolution survived under radical leadership, it also sentenced many "enemies of the republic" to death. Thousands of people were executed. In time, the radicals began to struggle for power among themselves. Robespierre was condemned by his enemies and executed. His death marked the end of the period called the Reign of Terror. See **Robespierre.**

In 1795, a new constitution was adopted that formed a government called the Directory. The Directory, a five-man board, governed France from 1795 to 1799, during the last half of the French Revolution. For more details on the causes, violence, and reforms of the French Revolution, see **French Revolution.**

Napoleon. During the French Revolution, a young officer named Napoleon Bonaparte rose through the ranks of the army. He was named a general in 1793, and his power grew rapidly. In 1799, Napoleon overthrew the revolutionary French government and seized control of France. Napoleon was an excellent administrator. He created a strong, efficient central government and revised and organized French law. He was also a military genius with great ambition. By 1812, Napoleon's forces had conquered most of western and central Europe. But maintaining control over this vast empire eventually overextended French power, and Napoleon was forced to give up his throne in 1814. He returned to rule France again for about three months in 1815 before his final defeat at Waterloo. For the story of Napoleon's life and a map of his empire, see **Napoleon I.**

The revolutions of 1830 and 1848. The Bourbon dynasty returned to power after Napoleon's downfall. Charles X, who became king in 1824, tried to reestablish the total power of the earlier French kings. He was overthrown in the July Revolution of 1830. See **Charles** (X) of France; **July Revolution; Louis** (XVIII).

The revolutionists placed Louis Philippe on the throne. He belonged to the Orléans branch of the Bourbon family. France was peaceful and prosperous during Louis Philippe's reign. But the poorer classes became dissatisfied because only the wealthy could vote or hold public office. The February Revolution of 1848 overthrew the government and established the Second Republic. All Frenchmen received the right to vote. See **Louis Philippe; Revolution of 1848.**

The voters elected Louis Napoleon Bonaparte, a nephew of Napoleon, to a four-year term as president in 1848. He seized greater power illegally in 1851, and declared himself president for 10 years. In 1852, he estab-

Storming of the Bastille (about 1800), an oil painting on canvas by an unknown artist; Château Versailles (Giraudon/Art Resource)

The storming of the Bastille on July 14, 1789, was an early event in the French Revolution. A huge crowd of Parisians captured the fortress, forcing royal troops to withdraw from Paris.

lished the Second Empire and declared himself Emperor Napoleon III. See **Napoleon III**.

The Franco-Prussian War. During the 1860's, France became alarmed over the growing strength of Prussia. France feared that a united Germany under Prussian leadership would upset Europe's balance of power. After a series of disputes, France declared war on Prussia in 1870. Prussia defeated France the next year. In the peace treaty following the war, France was forced to give almost all of Alsace and part of Lorraine to the new German Empire. See **Franco-Prussian War**.

The Third Republic. After Prussian victories in 1870, the French revolted against Napoleon III. They established a *provisional* (temporary) republic, which became known as the Third Republic, and in 1871 elected a National Assembly. In 1875, the Assembly voted to continue the republic, and wrote a new constitution.

French strength and prosperity grew until World War I began in 1914. French explorers and soldiers won a vast colonial empire in Africa and Asia. Only Great Britain had a larger overseas empire. France strengthened its army, and formed a military alliance with Russia in 1894 and the *Entente Cordiale* (cordial understanding) with Great Britain in 1904. French industries expanded steadily, especially after 1895.

By the 1890's, most French people were reconciled to the Third Republic, but few were deeply committed to it. An incident known as the Dreyfus affair finally forced the nation to take sides on this issue. On Oct. 15, 1894, Alfred Dreyfus, a Jewish French army officer, was arrested on suspicion of spying for Germany. In December, a military court found him guilty. Evidence of his innocence slowly trickled out and eventually attracted much attention. Many people began to rally to Dreyfus' side. They included Socialists representing the French working class, moderate republicans, and other people with no political background.

These people believed that the French army had acted arbitrarily in convicting Dreyfus and feared that the republic was endangered. They made Dreyfus a symbol of civil liberties and republican virtues and worked to get him a new trial. Opponents of republican government and army supporters came together and denounced Dreyfus and his supporters as antipatriotic. A fight followed that resulted in a strengthening of support for the republic. In 1906, France's highest court reviewed the Dreyfus case and declared Dreyfus innocent. See **Dreyfus, Alfred**.

World War I. During the early 1900's, France and Germany had disagreements over colonial territories, and each country feared an attack by the other. In 1907, France established a diplomatic agreement called the Triple Entente with Great Britain and Russia. The French prepared for war. Soon after the start of World War I (1914-1918), Germany invaded France. The Germans hoped to defeat France quickly. But by late 1914, the French army had halted the German advance. For $3\frac{1}{2}$ years, the opposing forces fought from trenches that stretched across northeastern France and Belgium.

The worst fighting faced by the French army during the war took place around the city of Verdun in 1916. In February, the German army launched a major attack to take Verdun. For five months, intense fighting involved hundreds of thousands of troops. At first, the Germans

made rapid progress. But they were slowly rolled back. In July, the Germans halted their unsuccessful attack.

The Battle of Verdun became a symbol of the French nation's will to resist. But the battle had also drained the nation. From the middle of 1917, France's allies began handling most of the war's major battles. The war produced enormously high casualties, partly as a result of the destructive powers of new weapons such as the machine gun and poison gas. Millions of French servicemen were killed or wounded. For more on the story of France in the war, see **World War I**.

Between World Wars. In the Treaty of Versailles, signed in 1919, France recovered Alsace and the German part of Lorraine from Germany. France and other Allied nations also were awarded *reparations* (payments for war damages) from Germany. Germany fell behind in making these payments. As a result, French and Belgian troops occupied the Ruhr Valley of Germany in 1923. After Germany agreed to keep up the payments, the troops were withdrawn in 1925. See **Alsace-Lorraine; Ruhr** (History); **Versailles, Treaty of**.

The French did much to reestablish good relations with Germany. France joined other Allied nations and Germany in the Rhineland Security Pact of 1925. This agreement in part guaranteed the security of the French-German border. France reduced Germany's reparations, and dropped various controls over Germany set up by the Treaty of Versailles. Suggestions by Aristide Briand, the French foreign minister, led to the Kellogg-Briand Peace Pact of 1928 (see **Kellogg-Briand Peace Pact**). It was signed by France, Germany, and 13 other nations. But in 1929, France began building the Maginot Line as a fortified defense against Germany.

During the 1930's, the worldwide economic depression and the rise of fascist leader Adolf Hitler in Germany caused serious political unrest in France. In 1936, at a time of widespread strikes, a government called the Popular Front came to power in France. It made many promises to striking workers and tried to establish a strong position against fascism. But in 1938, the government began to give in to the demands of Nazi Germany. As part of this policy of *appeasement,* France signed the Munich Agreement, which forced Czechoslovakia to give territory to Germany (see **Munich Agreement**).

World War II began when Germany invaded Poland on Sept. 1, 1939. Two days later, France and Great Britain declared war on Germany. On May 10, 1940, the Germans attacked Belgium, Luxembourg, and the Netherlands. They invaded France through Belgium on May 12, passing northwest of the Maginot Line. The Germans launched a major attack to the south on June 5, and entered Paris on June 14. On June 22, France signed an armistice with Germany. The Germans occupied the northern two-thirds of France, and southern France remained under French control. Southern France was governed at Vichy by Marshal Henri Philippe Pétain, who largely cooperated with the Germans. See **Pétain, Henri Philippe**.

After France fell, General Charles de Gaulle fled to London. He invited all French patriots to join a movement called *Free France,* and continue fighting the Germans. This *resistance* movement also spread throughout France. Some groups of French people called *Maquis* hid in hilly areas and fought the Germans. After Allied troops landed in French North Africa in November 1942,

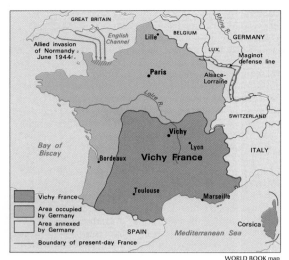

WORLD BOOK map

France in World War II. Germany occupied northern France from 1940 to 1944. Southern France remained under French control, with its capital at Vichy, until 1942, when it was occupied.

AP/Wide World

Allied troops rode through Paris on Aug. 26, 1944, the day after they freed the city from Nazi occupation in World War II. French citizens crowded the streets to welcome the troops.

German troops also occupied southern France. The Germans tried to seize the French fleet at Toulon. But the French sank most of the fleet's ships to prevent them from being captured by the Germans. See **De Gaulle, Charles; Maquis.**

On June 6, 1944, the Allies landed in France at Normandy. They landed in southern France on August 15. After fierce fighting and heavy loss of lives, the Allied troops entered Paris on August 25. De Gaulle soon formed a provisional government and became its president. In 1945, France became a charter member of the United Nations. For the story of France in the war, see **World War II.**

The Fourth Republic. In October 1945, the French people voted to have the National Assembly write a new constitution creating the Fourth Republic. In this election, French women voted for the first time. De Gaulle resigned as president in January 1946, over disagreements with the Assembly. The new constitution, much like that of the Third Republic, went into effect in October 1946. De Gaulle opposed it because it did not provide strong executive powers.

France received much aid from the United States, and rebuilt its cities and industries which had been badly damaged during the war. But political troubles at home and colonial revolts overseas slowed the nation's economic recovery. France played an important part in the Cold War between the Communist countries and the Western nations (see **Cold War**). The Communist Party was one of the largest in France after the war, and it controlled the chief labor unions. Communist-led strikes in 1947 and 1948 crippled production across the country. But in 1949, France became a charter member of the anti-Communist North Atlantic Treaty Organization (NATO).

The first revolt by a French colony began in Indochina in 1946. Indochina was eventually divided into Kampuchea (Cambodia), Laos, and North and South Vietnam. The French withdrew from Indochina in 1954 after heavy losses. See **Indochina** (French Indochina).

Later in 1954, revolution broke out in the French territory of Algeria. To prevent revolutions in Morocco and Tunisia, France made them independent in 1956. Other French colonies in Africa received independence later. But France refused to give up Algeria, the home of almost a million French settlers. France gradually built up its army in Algeria to about 500,000 men, and the war continued through the 1950's. See **Algeria** (The Algerian Revolution).

In spite of the costly colonial wars, France's economy grew rapidly. By the late 1950's, it had broken all French production records. The boom developed with U.S. aid and a series of national economic plans begun in 1946. French businessmen and government officials were determined to prove that France's greatness had not disappeared. Between 1947 and 1958, France helped form several economic organizations that were important steps toward a European confederation. For discussions of these organizations, see **Europe, Council of; European Community.**

The Fifth Republic. By 1958, large numbers of French people thought it was useless to continue fighting in Algeria. But the idea of giving up Algeria angered many French army leaders and settlers in the colony. They rebelled in May 1958 and threatened to overthrow the French government by force unless it continued fighting. In a compromise solution, de Gaulle was called back to power as prime minister, with emergency powers for six months. His government prepared a new constitution, which the voters approved on Sept. 28, 1958. This constitution, which established the Fifth Republic, gave the president greater power than ever before and sharply reduced the power of Parliament. In December, the Electoral College elected de Gaulle to a seven-year term as president.

France under de Gaulle. De Gaulle's government continued the war in Algeria, hoping the Algerians would agree to a compromise settlement that provided some French control. By 1961, however, the government realized that only Algerian independence would end the rebellion. Peace talks began in 1961 and ended with a cease-fire in March 1962. At de Gaulle's urging, French voters approved Algerian independence in April. Algeria became independent on July 3, 1962, and most French settlers there returned to France.

Algerian independence set off a wave of bombings and murders in France and Algeria by the Secret Army Organization (OAS). This group, which included many army officers, accused de Gaulle of betraying France by ending the war. The OAS tried several times to kill de Gaulle. Its leaders were eventually captured and sentenced to prison.

After the Algerian crisis, some French politicians tried to weaken de Gaulle's strong rule. They wanted to reestablish the former power of Parliament and reduce that of the president. But de Gaulle made the presidency even stronger. He declared that the president should have nationwide support and be elected by the people, not by the Electoral College. In 1962, the voters approved a constitutional amendment that provided such elections.

De Gaulle was reelected to a second seven-year term in 1965. French foreign policy became his main interest. De Gaulle declared that the French were "a race created for brilliant deeds," but that they could not achieve greatness with their "destiny in the hands of foreigners." He hoped to make France the leader of an alliance of Western European nations. This alliance would be free of U.S. or Soviet influence. Instead of relying on American protection through NATO, de Gaulle developed an independent French nuclear-weapons program. In 1966, de Gaulle removed all French troops from NATO. He also declared that all NATO military bases and troops had to be removed from France by April 1967. France

withdrew from NATO militarily, but it remained a member politically.

In 1957, France and other Western European nations formed the European Community, also called the European Common Market. De Gaulle believed France could work within this economic organization to become stronger and more influential in Western Europe. In 1963, he prevented Great Britain from joining the Common Market. He considered Britain a rival for leadership in Western Europe. He also believed Britain's ties with the United States would give America too much influence on Europe's economy.

In the late 1960's, many French people became dissatisfied with de Gaulle's government. This dissatisfaction led to a severe national crisis in May 1968. Students staged demonstrations in Paris, some of which erupted into violent clashes with the police. Demonstrations, many accompanied by violence, spread throughout France, and millions of workers joined in by going on strike. The country was paralyzed for more than two weeks, and many people expected the overthrow of de Gaulle's government and possible civil war. But de Gaulle managed to bring the situation under control by the end of May. He called a general election in June, and his supporters won more than 70 per cent of the seats in Parliament. However, de Gaulle's reputation as a leader had been seriously damaged by what the French called the "events of May." In April 1969, de Gaulle asked for minor constitutional reforms and said he would resign if the voters did not approve them. The French people voted against the reforms, and de Gaulle resigned.

France after de Gaulle. Georges Pompidou was elected president in June 1969. He had been de Gaulle's prime minister, and he promised to continue de Gaulle's policies. But Pompidou changed de Gaulle's foreign policy by cooperating more closely with the United States. He also improved relations with Great Britain. In 1971,

France's empire France's colonial empire spanned two eras. From the early 1600's to the 1760's, France built a vast empire in North America. From the 1800's to the mid-1900's, France held many colonies in Africa and Asia. The names of the remaining French overseas possessions are underscored on the map.

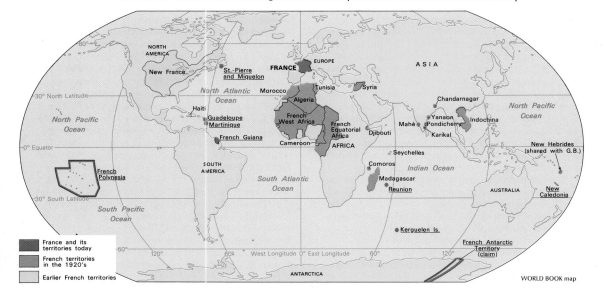

WORLD BOOK map

AP/Wide World

Charles de Gaulle served as president of France from 1958 to 1969. He greatly increased the power of the presidency, particularly in the conduct of foreign policy.

Pompidou and British Prime Minister Edward Heath agreed on Britain's entry into the Common Market.

At home, Pompidou's government faced economic problems. The nation's industrial growth began to slow down, unemployment increased, and inflation rose to a high level. Part of the economic trouble resulted from the worldwide oil crisis in 1973. Oil-producing countries raised the price of oil sharply, and France was seriously affected because it imports most of its petroleum.

Pompidou died in April 1974. The Gaullist Party, which had supported de Gaulle and Pompidou, split into a number of separate groups in the presidential election that followed in May. These groups supported various candidates. As a result, the Gaullist Party was weakened. Valéry Giscard d'Estaing, head of the Independent Republican Party, was elected president.

The Gaullists and a group of parties that supported Giscard won a majority of the seats in France's parliamentary elections held in 1978. Those parties formed a coalition government. The leftist Socialist and Communist parties were their main opponents.

France today. Like all modern nations, France has economic and social problems that remain unsolved. Large numbers of immigrants from Africa and southern Europe live in crowded city slums and in large apartment blocks on the outskirts of cities. Old people on fixed incomes, and farmers whose farms are too small to modernize, barely manage to make ends meet in times of inflation. Unemployment is a major problem. Young people suffer from unemployment more than any other

group. In addition, industrial growth has brought not only prosperity but also widespread pollution.

Despite its economic problems, however, France's overall standard of living is higher today than ever before. Most French people own such material goods as automobiles, refrigerators, telephones, and washing machines. Social security laws give workers some protection against unemployment, illness, and old age.

France ranks among the world leaders in total industrial production and in the export of agricultural products. Nuclear power plants are being built to free France from dependence on imported fuels. The army has been modernized, and France has its own nuclear weapons.

The loss of most of its colonial empire has relieved France of the cost of governing and developing the colonies. However, France still gives economic, technical, and military aid to many of its former colonies. Since the mid-1960's, France has supported the government of Chad against rebels by supplying military aid and, at times, troops. In 1982, France sent troops to Lebanon as part of a peacekeeping force. In 1983, a terrorist bombing killed 54 French troops in Beirut, Lebanon. France withdrew its troops from Lebanon in 1984.

Politically, France moved sharply to the left in 1981. The voters elected François Mitterrand of the Socialist Party president. In addition, the Socialists won a majority of the seats in parliamentary elections held in 1981. The elections gave France its first leftist government since 1958. Moderates and conservatives had controlled all the governments since then. Under the moderates and conservatives, the government owned some French businesses, including the Renault automobile company. The new Socialist leaders greatly increased government ownership of businesses. See the introduction of the *Economy* section of this article.

From the time of Napoleon I, France's departments were administered by prefects—officials appointed by, and responsible to, the national government. But the Socialist government gave locally elected councils the responsibility for the departments. In 1982, the government changed the title *prefect* to *commissioner.*

The 1981 elections resulted in a sharp decline in the number of parliamentary seats held by Communists. But the Communists had supported Mitterrand in the presidential race. He appointed Communists to 4 minor posts in the 44-member cabinet, marking the first Communist participation in the cabinet since 1947. In 1984, the Communists resigned from the cabinet, after disagreements with the government over economic policies.

The Socialists lost their parliamentary majority in the 1986 elections. Conservatives gained control of Parliament. Mitterrand remained president, but he named Jacques Chirac, a conservative, as prime minister. Chirac gained much influence in the government. In the 1988 elections, Mitterrand waged a successful campaign against Chirac and won a second term as president. Shortly after his election, Mitterrand dissolved the National Assembly. In new legislative elections, the Socialists and their allies won a slight majority. As a result, in 1988, Mitterrand appointed Michel Rocard, a Socialist, to replace Chirac as prime minister. Rocard's government has followed social and economic policies quite similar to those favored by many moderates and conservatives. These policies include cutting government spending, holding wages down, and slowing the government purchase of private corporations.

William M. Reddy

Related articles in *World Book* include:

Political and military leaders

See the table *Kings and emperors of France* with this article. Other biographies include:

Catherine de Médicis	Marat, Jean P.
Charles Martel	Mazarin, Jules Cardinal
Chateaubriand, François R. de	Mirabeau, Comte de
Claudel, Paul	Mitterrand, François Maurice
Clemenceau, Georges	Montcalm, Marquis de
Colbert, Jean B.	Murat, Joachim
Condorcet, Marquis de	Ney, Michel
Corday, Charlotte	Pétain, Henri P.
Daladier, Édouard	Poincaré, Raymond
Danton, Georges J.	Richelieu, Cardinal
De Gaulle, Charles A. J. M.	Robespierre
Eugénie Marie de Montijo	Rochambeau, Comte de
Foch, Ferdinand	Roland de la Platière, Marie
Genêt, Edmond C. É.	Sieyès, Emmanuel J.
Giscard d'Estaing, Valéry	Talleyrand
Lafayette, Marquis de	Talon, Jean B.
Lamartine, Alphonse	Thiers, Louis A.
Laval, Pierre	Tocqueville, Alexis de

Cities and towns

Amiens	Grenoble	Orléans
Avignon	La Rochelle	Paris
Bordeaux	Le Havre	Reims
Brest	Le Mans	Rouen
Calais	Lille	Strasbourg
Cannes	Lourdes	Toulon
Carcassonne	Lyon	Toulouse
Chartres	Marseille	Tours
Cherbourg	Nancy	Versailles
Dunkerque	Nantes	Vichy
Fontainebleau	Nice	

History

Agincourt, Battle of	Huguenots
Austerlitz, Battle of	Hundred Years' War
Bastille	July Revolution
Bourbon	Louisbourg
Continental System	Mississippi Scheme
Crécy, Battle of	New France
Crimean War	Poitiers, Battle of
Crusades	Reformation
Dauphin	Renaissance
Estates-General	Revolution of 1848
Feudalism	Succession wars
Franco-Prussian War	Waldenses
Franks	World War I
French and Indian wars	World War II
French Revolution	Zouaves

Overseas possessions

French Guiana	Martinique
French Polynesia	New Caledonia
French Southern and Antarctic Territories	Reunion
Guadeloupe	Saint-Pierre and Miquelon

Physical features

Aisne River	Dover, Strait of	Pyrenees
Ardennes Mountains and Forest	English Channel	Rhône River
	Loire River	Saône River
Bay of Biscay	Marne River	Seine River
Corsica	Mont Blanc	Somme River

Regions

Alsace-Lorraine	Flanders	Normandy
Brittany	Gascony	Riviera
Burgundy		

Other related articles

Architecture	Denis, Saint	Motion picture
Army (The French Army)	Doll (History)	(History)
	École des Beaux-Arts	Navy (The world's major navies)
Basques		
Bastille Day	Eiffel Tower	Normans
Bibliothèque Nationale	Fleur-de-lis	Painting
	Foreign Legion	Paris, University of
Bicycle racing (Road races)	French Academy	Premier
	French language	Salic law
Christmas (In France)	French literature	Sculpture
Classical music	Furniture	Sorbonne
Code Napoléon	Institute of France	Statue of Liberty
Democracy (French contributions to democracy)	Louvre	Theater (France)
	Maginot Line	Tuileries
	Marseillaise	Wine (Where wine comes from)

Outline

I. Government
　A. National government　　D. Courts
　B. Local government　　　E. Armed forces
　C. Politics
II. People
　A. Population　　　　　C. Language
　B. Ancestry
III. Way of life
　A. City life　　　　　　F. Religion
　B. Rural life　　　　　　G. Education
　C. Food and drink　　　H. Museums and
　D. Recreation　　　　　　libraries
　E. Holidays
IV. Arts
　A. The Middle Ages　　　F. Romanticism
　B. The Renaissance　　　G. Realism and
　C. Baroque and rococo art　　naturalism
　D. French classical art　　H. Impressionism
　E. The Age of Reason　　I. The 1900's
V. The land
VI. Climate
VII. Economy
　A. Natural resources　　G. Fishing
　B. Service industries　　H. Energy sources
　C. Manufacturing　　　I. Foreign trade
　D. Agriculture　　　　J. Transportation
　E. Forestry　　　　　K. Communication
　F. Mining
VIII. History

Questions

What major changes in French government were made by Charles de Gaulle?
How did France get its name?
What is the principal religion of France?
How did the Romans influence French ways of life?
What is France's chief crop? Chief mineral deposit?
Who seized control after the French Revolution?
What is France's cultural and economic center?
How does France rank in foreign trade?

Reading and Study Guide

See *France* in the Research Guide/Index, Volume 22, for a *Reading and Study Guide.*

Additional resources

Ardagh, John. *France in the 1980s.* Viking, 1983.
Bertier de Sauvigny, Guillaume de, and Pinkney, D. H. *History of France.* Rev. ed. Forum Press, 1983.
The Hachette Guide to France. Random House, 1985.
James, Edward. *The Origins of France: From Clovis to the Capetians.* St. Martin's, 1982.
Tuppen, John N. *The Economic Geography of France.* Littlefield, Adams, 1983.
Wright, Gordon. *France in Modern Times: From the Enlightenment to the Present.* 3rd ed. Norton, 1981.

France, *frans* or *frahns,* **Anatole,** *a na TAWL* (1844-1924), was the pen name of Jacques Anatole François Thibault, a French novelist and critic. He won the 1921 Nobel Prize for literature.

France was born in Paris, the son of a well-to-do bookseller. His childhood was filled with the magic of literature. In his autobiography, *My Friend's Book* (1885), France recalled the pleasures of those years and the mental stimulation he received from Paris, especially its libraries and bookshops.

France's first successful novel was *The Crime of Sylvester Bonnard* (1881). Beginning in 1886, he wrote a literary column for the newspaper *Le Temps*. His clear and elegant style, the subtlety of his observation, and his disinterested rejection of extreme causes gained him the reputation of being a friendly, easy-going man. France's novel *Thaïs* (1890) seemed to symbolize his ideals of pleasure and wisdom.

The famous Dreyfus affair, which shook the nation, led France to write about political and social issues (see **Dreyfus, Alfred**). His novels of the 1900's reflect his part in the struggle for social justice that took place in the country. He began to ridicule society and its institutions in *Penguin Island* (1908), his most famous novel, and in *The Gods are Athirst* (1912) and *The Revolt of the Angels* (1914). The irony of these novels has been compared to that of the works of Voltaire.   Edith Kern

Francesca, Piero della. See Piero della Francesca.

Franchise, *FRAN chyz,* is a type of business agreement. Under such an agreement, a company, individual, or governmental unit grants another company or individual the right to sell certain products or services for a particular period at a specific location. The right itself is also called a franchise. There are two main types of franchise agreements—private and public.

Private franchises are a popular way to conduct business, and there are about 500,000 franchise units in the United States. They include such business operations as Burger King, Dunkin Donuts, Baskin-Robbins, Holiday Inn, and H & R Block.

Under a franchise agreement, a *franchisee* (buyer) pays a fee to a *franchisor* (seller) to obtain the franchise. The franchisee may also pay a percentage of the firm's sales to the franchisor. In return, the franchisor provides the franchisee with such services as personnel training, financial assistance, and advertising. In addition, the franchisor often allows the franchisee to use a well-known trade name. This feature may be extremely valuable to the franchisee. For example, suppose a family is traveling through an unfamiliar town at dinnertime. The family sees just ahead three possible places to stop for dinner—Chuck's Chicken, Bill's Burgers, and a Burger King. Although people who have eaten at all three know that the food they serve is equally good, the traveling family will probably stop at the Burger King. They are likely to recognize its name because they have probably eaten at other Burger Kings in the past.

Public franchises are usually between public utilities and a city, state, or other governmental unit. For example, suppose a city and an electric company have reached an agreement about electric service for the city. Under a typical agreement of this nature, the city would grant the electric company the right to run power lines on city land and to be the only electric company in the area. In return, the electric company would have to serve all public needs for this service and to have its fees approved by a governmental body such as a public service commission. Other public services that operate under franchise agreements include telephone service, garbage collection, and cable TV.   William H. Bolen

See also **Chain store** (Franchise chain stores); **Public utility; Restaurant** (Chains and franchises).

Francis was the name of two kings who ruled France in the 1500's.

Francis I (1494-1547) became king in 1515, succeeding Louis XII, who was both his cousin and his father-in-law. He was intelligent, fond of pleasure, and devoted to the arts. He was also ambitious, inconstant, and somewhat dishonest. He began his reign brilliantly with the great victory of Marignano in 1515. This victory gave him a foothold in northern Italy.

It soon became clear, however, that the interests and ambitions of France clashed with the Holy Roman Empire, which included Spain and Germany. Francis and the Holy Roman Emperor Charles V carried on a bitter struggle for years (see **Charles** [V] Holy Roman emperor). Francis was captured and imprisoned in 1525, in another Italian campaign. He won his freedom in 1526 by making false promises. The last war between Francis I and Charles V ended in 1544 without having made great changes. Francis had shown himself greedy for power and indifferent about how he obtained it.

Francis persecuted the Protestants, but not so severely as some of his successors. Possibly the king would have been more savage against them if he had not given most of his attention to other affairs. He enjoyed beautiful surroundings, took an interest in new art and literature, and spent money lavishly. Such activities gave him a reputation as a patron of the Renaissance.

Francis II (1544-1560), grandson of Francis I, became king in 1559, but died the next year. Mary, Queen of Scots, was his wife. In his reign began the long, bitter rivalry between the noble houses of Guise and Bourbon, which cost France so much during the religious wars between Catholics and Huguenots.   William C. Bark

See also **Catherine de Médicis; France** (A period of wars); **Huguenots; Mary, Queen of Scots.**

Francis II (1768-1835) was the last Holy Roman emperor. He also reigned as Emperor Francis I of Austria. He strongly opposed revolutionary movements generated in Europe by the French Revolution (1789-1799).

Francis was born in Florence, Italy, and belonged to the Habsburg (or Hapsburg) family. He succeeded his father, Leopold II, as ruler of Austria in 1792 and was elected Holy Roman emperor that same year. In 1804, Francis adopted the additional title of emperor of Austria. By 1806, Emperor Napoleon I of France had forced Francis to resign as Holy Roman emperor, and the Holy Roman Empire ended. After 1809, Francis allowed his shrewd foreign minister, Prince von Metternich, to direct Austria's foreign affairs. Under Metternich's guidance, Austria in time joined Great Britain, Prussia, and Russia to fight Napoleon. The united European powers defeated Napoleon in 1814 and 1815.

As emperor of Austria, Francis blocked all efforts aimed at even modest political reform. These efforts included growing demands for local self-government by Bohemians, Croatians, Hungarians, Italians, and other groups. At the end of his reign, Francis urged his successor to "Rule and change nothing." Peter N. Stearns

See also **Aix-la-Chapelle, Congress of; Holy Alliance; Marie Louise; Metternich.**

Francis, Dick (1920-   ), is a British author of mystery novels, most with horse-racing backgrounds. Francis' books feature ordinary, middle-aged men who are called upon to be heroes. They are not detectives, but are cast into roles in which they must solve mysteries. Francis' thrillers have won acclaim for their crisp, clear prose and expert handling of character and suspense.

Francis was born near Tenby, Wales. He was a leading English steeplechase jockey from 1948 to 1957. He was racing correspondent for the London Sunday Express from 1957 to 1973. His first mystery novel, *Dead Cert,* appeared in 1962. Some of Francis' later mysteries have explored such subjects as photography (*Reflex,* 1981), banking (*Banker,* 1983), and the distillery business (*Proof,* 1985). *The Sport of Queens* (1957) is an autobiographical account of Francis' racing career.

David Geherin

Francis de Sales, *saylz,* **Saint** (1567-1622), was a French nobleman. He was educated at the College of Clermont in Paris. There he became so devoted to the Blessed Virgin Mary that he took a vow of chastity and dedicated himself to her service. After becoming a doctor of law in Padua, he entered the priesthood in 1593. In 1602, he became bishop of Geneva. He and Saint Jane de Chantal established the Visitation Order for the purposes of teaching and caring for the sick. Francis wrote many spiritual books, the most popular of which is *An Introduction to the Devout Life.* He was born in Thorens in Savoy. His feast day is January 29. Marvin R. O'Connell

Francis Ferdinand, archduke of Austria. See **World War I** (The assassination of an archduke); **Austria** (Austria-Hungary).

Francis Joseph (1830-1916), also spelled *Franz Josef,* was the aged ruler of the dual monarchy of Austria-Hungary at the beginning of World War I. Francis Joseph ruled as emperor of Austria for 68 years. His popularity, as well as military force, held the widely different elements of the dual monarchy together. When his heir and nephew, Archduke Francis Ferdinand, was assassinated in 1914, Francis Joseph declared war on Serbia. This led to World War I (see **Serbia; World War I**).

Francis Joseph became Emperor of Austria in 1848, a year of national revolutions. He was a member of the ancient ruling family of Habsburg (see **Habsburg, House of**). During his long reign Austria prospered, although it suffered several military defeats. In the war against Sardinia and France in 1859, Austria lost the province of Lombardy (see **Sardinia, Kingdom of**). Prussia defeated Austria and three smaller German states in the Seven Weeks' War of 1866. As a result, Austria lost much of its influence in Germany (see **Seven Weeks' War**). Francis Joseph then adopted more liberal internal policies, allowing the Hungarians equal rights. This brought about the Austro-Hungarian empire, and Francis Joseph took the additional title of king of Hungary in 1867 (see **Austria-Hungary**).

Francis Joseph's only son, Rudolph, killed himself in 1889. An Italian anarchist killed Francis Joseph's wife, Elizabeth. A nephew, Charles I, succeeded him as emperor (see **Charles I**). Gabriel A. Almond

Francis of Assisi, *uh SEE zee,* **Saint** (1181?-1226), founded the Franciscan religious order of the Roman

St. Francis in Ecstasy (about 1480), a tempera and oil painting on a wood panel; © The Frick Collection, New York City.

Saint Francis of Assisi was one of the most popular saints of the Middle Ages. This painting by the Italian artist Giovanni Bellini shows Francis about to receive the *stigmata*—wounds resembling those that Jesus received at the Crucifixion. The gentle animals and peaceful landscape symbolize the saint's love of nature and all living things.

Catholic Church. His simple life of poverty inspired many people during the Middle Ages. Today, many people admire Francis because of his love of peace and his respect for all living creatures.

Francis, the son of a prosperous textile merchant, was born in Assisi, Italy. As a young man, he took an active part in the city's commercial, political, and social life. Francis was captured while fighting in a war between Assisi and the nearby city of Perugia. He spent most of 1202 and 1203 in an enemy prison. The suffering he saw during the war caused him to think about the meaning and purpose of his life.

In 1205, after seeing a vision of Jesus Christ, Francis changed his way of life. He disowned his father, rejected his inheritance, and began to devote his life to rebuilding churches and serving the poor. Francis adopted absolute poverty as his ideal. He tried to pattern his life after the life of Christ by preaching the Gospel and healing the sick. Soon, Francis started to attract followers.

In 1209, Francis founded the Franciscan order. Although many of his followers became priests, Francis remained a layman. See **Franciscans.**

In 1212, while traveling to Syria to convert the Muslims, Francis was shipwrecked on the coast of Yugoslavia. He tried to go to Morocco as a missionary but became ill in Spain and could not continue. In 1219, Francis accompanied the crusaders to Egypt. There, he tried to convert the sultan but failed.

Francis returned to Italy in 1220. He continued to preach but let others administer the Franciscans. In 1224, while Francis prayed on Mount Alvernia near Florence, the *stigmata* appeared on his body. The stigmata are five wounds resembling those suffered by Jesus on His hands, feet, and side during the Crucifixion. Two years later, Francis died near Assisi in the Portiuncula chapel, his favorite church and the first headquarters of the Franciscans. Francis was *canonized* (declared a saint) in 1228. His feast day is celebrated October 4.

Francis expressed his religious ideals in poems as well as through his ministry. In "Canticle of the Sun," he showed his love for all living things. His poems also contributed to the development of Italian literature. About 100 years after Francis' death, a Franciscan collected stories about the saint and his companions in *The Little Flowers of Saint Francis.* William J. Courtenay

Additional resources

Chesterton, G. K. *St. Francis of Assisi.* Arden Library, 1979. First published in 1923.
De Paola, Tomie. *Francis: The Poor Man of Assisi.* Holiday House, 1982. For younger readers.

Francis turbine. See Turbine (Water turbines).
Francis Xavier. See Xavier, Saint Francis.
Franciscans, *fran SIHS kuhnz,* are members of a variety of Roman Catholic religious orders that take their inspiration and *rule* (program of life) from Saint Francis of Assisi. In 1209, Francis founded the Order of Friars Minor to reform the church around the spirit of poverty based on the Gospels. Between 1212 and 1214, Francis and his friend Saint Clare founded an order for women called the Second Order of St. Francis or the Poor Clares.

The order's expansion led to an overly complex organization and a consequent need to revise the rule. A split occurred between the Spirituals or *zelanti* and the main body, later called the Conventuals. The Spirituals wanted strict observance of Francis' original rule. The Conventuals advocated moderation. Pope John XXII settled the dispute in favor of the Conventuals in 1317. In 1415, a reform movement within the Conventuals resulted in the formation of another group called the Observants. In 1897, Pope Leo XIII issued a unification decree that produced today's three independent families of Franciscan orders for men—the Friars Minor, Friars Minor Conventuals, and Friars Minor Capuchins.

The early Franciscans devoted themselves to preaching and to caring for the spiritual needs of the people. But the order soon branched out into educational, missionary, and social work. David G. Schultenover

See also **California** (History); **Capuchins; Francis of Assisi, Saint; Friar; Mission life in America.**

Francium, *FRAN see uhm,* is a radioactive element produced in certain nuclear reactions. It is the heaviest member of the group of elements called the *alkali metals.* The group also includes lithium, sodium, potassium, rubidium, and cesium. Like the other alkali metals, francium takes the form of singly charged positive ions in its compounds. Its chemical properties closely resemble those of cesium. See **Alkali; Cesium.**

The most stable isotope of francium has a half-life of 21 minutes (see **Radioactivity** [Half-life]). Because of this great instability, scientists have not been able to produce weighable quantities of the element.

The French scientist Marguerite Perey discovered francium in 1939 as a product of the radioactive decay of actinium. It was formerly known as *virginium.* Francium has an atomic number of 87, and its chemical symbol is Fr. Duward F. Shriver

Franck, *frahngk,* **César** (1822-1890), was a French composer, organist, and teacher. His compositions are a synthesis of the strict Viennese forms of sonata, symphony, and quartet and the late romantic harmonies of composers Franz Liszt and Richard Wagner.

Franck wrote several oratorios and operas, but he achieved his greatest success with his instrumental works. The Symphony in D minor (1889) is his most frequently performed piece, followed by the Sonata in A major (1887) for violin and piano. Franck's other major compositions include the Quintet in F minor (1880) for piano and strings, the String Quartet in D major (1890), the complex *Symphonic Variations* (1886) for piano and orchestra, and the *Prelude, Chorale, and Fugue* (1885) for piano.

César Auguste Jean Guillaume Hubert Franck was born in Liège, Belgium, and moved to Paris with his family in 1835. He was the organist at the Basilica of Ste.-Clotilde from 1858 until his death. Franck gave many acclaimed organ concerts following services at the church. His *Six Pieces* (1868) for organ emerged from those concerts. Franck taught organ at the Paris Conservatory from 1872 until his death, exerting a strong influence on such composers as Paul Dukas, Vincent d'Indy, and Henri Duparc. Vincent McDermott

Franck, James. See Nobel Prizes (Nobel Prizes for physics—1925).

Franco, Francisco (1892-1975), was dictator of Spain from 1939 until his death in 1975. He came to power at the end of the Spanish Civil War. In that war, he led the rebel Nationalist Army to victory over the *Loyalist* (Republican) forces. After the war ended in 1939, Franco held complete control of Spain. His regime was similar to a Fascist dictatorship. He carried out the functions of chief of state, prime minister, commander in chief, and leader of the Falange, the only political party permitted (see **Falange Española**). He adopted the title of *El Caudillo* (The Leader). In the early years of his regime, Franco tried to eliminate all opposition. He later eased restrictions.

His early life. Franco was born Francisco Franco Bahamonde in El Ferrol del Caudillo, in the province of La Coruña. His father was a naval officer. Young Franco was trained as an army officer at the Infantry Academy of Toledo. Between 1912 and 1927, he held important command posts in Spanish Morocco. His troops there helped put down a long rebellion against Spanish rule. He was made a general at the age of 34.

In 1931, Spain became a republic. During the next five years, disputes involving Spanish political groups became increasingly severe. At first, Franco avoided becoming involved in the disputes. But when the moderate conservatives won the election of 1933, Franco became identified with

Black Star

Francisco Franco

them. In 1934, Franco helped put down a revolt by *leftists,* who wanted sweeping changes in Spain's way of life. In 1935, he became army chief of staff. The following year, the leftists won the election and sent Franco to a post in the Canary Islands.

Military leaders plotted to overthrow the leftist government in 1936. Franco delayed taking part in the plot, but he was promised command of the most important part of the army. The revolt began in July 1936 and it started a total civil war. Two and a half months later, the rebel generals named Franco commander in chief and dictator. Franco's forces, called Nationalists, received strong support from Italy and Germany. On April 1, 1939, after 32 months of bitter fighting, the Nationalists gained complete victory. Franco then became dictator without opposition.

As dictator, Franco kept Spain officially neutral during World War II. But he sent "volunteers" to help Germany fight the Soviet Union. After the war, the victorious Allies would have little to do with Spain because of Franco's pro-Fascist policies.

The Western powers became more friendly toward Franco during the Cold War with the Soviet Union, because he was against Communism. In 1953, Franco signed an agreement with the United States. He permitted the United States to build air and naval bases in Spain in exchange for economic and military aid. This aid helped bring about industrial expansion. Spain's living standard rose dramatically during the 1960's. By the mid-1970's, Spain had become a relatively modern, industrialized country.

In the early 1960's, opposition to Franco became more

outspoken. Miners and other workers went on strike, though strikes were illegal. Opposition groups organized in secret. Franco relaxed police controls and economic restriction somewhat. In 1966, strict press censorship was relaxed.

Franco declared, in 1947, that Spain would be ruled by a king after he left office. In 1969, Franco named Prince Juan Carlos to be king and head of state after Franco's death or retirement. Juan Carlos is the grandson of King Alfonso XIII, who left Spain in 1931. Franco died in November 1975, and Juan Carlos became king (see **Juan Carlos I**).   Stanley G. Payne

See also **Spain** (Government; History).

Additional resources

Fusi, J. P. *Franco: A Biography.* Harper, 1987.
Garza, Hedda. *Francisco Franco.* Chelsea House, 1987. Suitable for younger readers.
Payne, Stanley G. *The Franco Regime: 1936-1975.* Univ. of Wisconsin Press, 1987.

Franco-Prussian War began in 1870 as a result of a dispute between France and Prussia, a German state. All the other German states joined Prussia, and the conflict became one between France and Germany.

Events leading up to the war. Prussia had defeated Austria in the Seven Weeks' War and had replaced it as the leading German power. Emperor Napoleon III of France allowed himself to be influenced by patriots who wanted to humiliate Prussia. Otto von Bismarck, Prussia's prime minister, was equally anxious for a struggle. Bismarck hoped to strengthen the unity of the German states by having them fight a war against France.

An excuse for war was easily found. Prince Leopold of Hohenzollern-Sigmaringen, a Roman Catholic relative of the Prussian king, had been offered the Spanish crown. The French felt that if Leopold ruled Spain, the Hohenzollern family would become too powerful. Leopold's father refused the crown on his behalf, but France insisted on a Prussian guarantee that Leopold would be forbidden from ever accepting the Spanish throne.

Count Benedetti, the French ambassador, presented this demand to Wilhelm I of Prussia at Ems, in Prussia. Wilhelm received Benedetti politely, but refused the French demand. He then sent a telegram to Bismarck telling what had happened. Bismarck condensed this "Ems dispatch" in such a way that it aroused great fury when it was published in France on July 14, 1870. The French declared war on July 19.

Progress of the war. Both countries entered the struggle with enthusiasm. General Helmuth Karl von Moltke, head of the Prussian Army, had made careful preparations for war with France. The French were largely unprepared.

The Germans defeated the French at Wissembourg, Woerth, and Spicheren, and inflicted severe losses. The French armies under Marshal MacMahon and Marshal Bazaine were separated and kept apart by the Germans. Bazaine was surrounded at Metz. MacMahon, who had been ordered to march to the relief of Bazaine, met the Germans in a great battle near Sedan. The French were overwhelmed, MacMahon's army surrendered, and the Emperor Napoleon III was taken prisoner. Bazaine later surrendered at Metz.

The end of the war. When the news of the defeat at Sedan reached Paris, the French deposed Napoleon and prepared to defend the city. The army and the citizens of Paris fought bravely, but they had to yield the city to the Germans early in 1871. The war ended with the Treaty of Frankfurt, which was signed on May 10, 1871. The treaty provided that France would give most of Alsace and part of Lorraine to Germany, pay Germany one billion dollars, and support a German army of occupation until the sum was paid. Germany expected the huge debt to handicap France for many years. But the French miraculously paid it off in less than three years. The French government, with the financial help of the French people, secured loans that enabled it to pay off the debt.

Results. The Franco-Prussian War abolished the North German Confederation and created a new German Empire. It helped set the stage for World War I by increasing French and German hostility.

Charles W. Ingrao

Related articles in *World Book* include:

Alsace-Lorraine	Napoleon III
Balloon (Balloons in war)	Prussia
Bismarck, Otto von	Seven Weeks' War
Germany (History)	Thiers, Louis Adolphe
Hohenzollern	Wilhelm (I) of Germany
Moltke, Helmuth Karl von	

Additional resources

Howard, Michael. *The Franco-Prussian War: The German Invasion of France, 1870-1871.* Methuen, 1981. First published in 1961.
Ollivier, Émile. *The Franco-Prussian War and Its Hidden Causes.* Ayer, 1970. First published in 1912.
Oncken, Hermann. *Napoleon III and the Rhine: The Origin of the War of 1870-1871.* Russell & Russell, 1967. First published in 1928.
Steefel, Lawrence D. *Bismarck, the Hohenzollern Candidacy, and the Origins of the Franco-German War of 1870.* Harvard, 1962.

Francolin, *FRANG kuh lihn,* is a kind of partridge. It grows about 1 foot (30 centimeters) long, and may be richly barred or spotted. The male francolin generally is black and white, with a handsome black head and white ear patch. The female francolin is brownish. The *common francolin* lives in parts of southern Asia and southern Europe. Other francolins may be much more plainly colored. They live throughout the whole of Africa, and in southern Asia and Europe. See also **Partridge; Quail.**

Scientific classification. Francolins belong to the partridge, pheasant, and quail family, Phasianidae. The common francolin is *Francolinus francolinus.* Joseph J. Hickey

Frank. See Franks.

Frank, Anne (1929-1945), a German-Jewish girl, wrote a vivid, tender diary while hiding from the Nazis during World War II. Anne was born in Frankfurt, Germany. She and her family moved to the Netherlands in 1933 after the Nazis began to persecute Jews. In 1942, during the Nazi occupation of the Netherlands, the family hid in a secret annex behind the Amsterdam office of her father's business. Anne recorded her experiences in a diary. Two years later, the family was betrayed and ar-

Wide World
Anne Frank

rested. Anne died in the Nazi concentration camp at Belsen. Her diary was published in 1947, and later was made into a play and a film, both called *The Diary of Anne Frank.* Alison Leslie Gold

Additional resources

Frank, Anne. *The Diary of a Young Girl.* Rev. ed. Doubleday, 1967.
Anne Frank's Tales from the Secret Annex. Rev. ed. 1984.
Schnabel, Ernst. *Anne Frank: A Portrait in Courage.* Harcourt, 1958.

Frankenstein is a famous horror novel written by the English author Mary Shelley. The novel was published in 1818 under the title *Frankenstein, or the Modern Prometheus.* It tells the story of Victor Frankenstein, a scientist who tries to create a living being for the good of humanity but instead produces a monster.

Frankenstein creates his monster by assembling parts of dead bodies and activating the creature with electricity. The monster, which has no name in the book, is actually a gentle, intelligent creature. But everyone fears and mistreats him because of his hideous appearance. Frankenstein himself rejects the monster and refuses to create a mate for him. The monster's terrible loneliness drives him to seek revenge by murdering Frankenstein's wife, brother, and best friend. Frankenstein dies while trying to find and kill the monster, who disappears into the Arctic at the end of the novel.

Many motion pictures have been based on the character of Frankenstein's monster. Most of them are simply tales of horror and have little to do with the serious themes of Shelley's novel. These themes include the possible dangers involved in scientific experimentation with life and the suffering caused by judging people by their appearance. James Douglas Merritt

See also **Shelley, Mary W.**

Frankenthaler, Helen (1928-), is a leading American painter. In the 1950's, working in the abstract expressionist style, Frankenthaler developed a painting technique called *soak-stain.* Frankenthaler poured very thin paint directly onto the raw canvas. As the paint soaked into the canvas, staining it with color, texture was eliminated and the flatness in the canvas surface was emphasized.

The lyrical interaction of forms and colors in Frankenthaler's paintings illustrates the physical process of their creation. Colors run into one another and forms seem to overlap through the different stainings. Some areas of Frankenthaler's harmonious, well-balanced compositions remain unstained, which further illustrates the lack of separation between the paint and canvas surface.

Most of Frankenthaler's paintings have a narrative title, such as *Pre-Dawn,* which is reproduced in the **Painting** article. Frankenthaler is also a printmaker. She was born in New York City. Deborah Leveton

Frankfort (pop. 25,973) is the capital of Kentucky. The city lies in north-central Kentucky, at the western edge of the state's Bluegrass Region. For the loca-

Cora Kelley Ward
Helen Frankenthaler

tion of Frankfort, see **Kentucky** (political map).

Frankfort's chief industry is government. The Kentucky state government ranks as the city's largest employer. Whiskey distilling is an important private industry in Frankfort. Other products include clothing, appliance parts, and automobile wheels.

Landmarks of Frankfort include the State Capitol, which resembles the United States Capitol in design; and the Old State House, now a museum. Many tourists visit the Frankfort Cemetery to see the graves of Daniel Boone and his wife, Rebecca. Other attractions include tours of local distilleries, which produce Kentucky bourbon whiskey, and the Corner of Celebrities historic district in downtown Frankfort. Kentucky State University is in Frankfort.

Like many cities, Frankfort has had to deal with the flow of business to suburban shopping centers. Since the 1960's, urban renewal efforts have eliminated slums and restored part of downtown Frankfort. The renewal program included construction of Capital Plaza, a 28-story modernistic civic center and office complex.

In 1751, Christopher Gist became the first white person to reach what is now Frankfort. In 1773, Hancock Taylor made the first survey of the land. The Virginia legislature established Frankfort as a town in 1786, before Kentucky became a state. Kentucky achieved statehood in 1792, and Frankfort was selected as its capital. Frankfort is the seat of Franklin County and has a council-manager form of government.   Ron Herron

See also **Kentucky** (pictures).

Frankfurt, *FRANGK fuhrt* or *FRAHNGK furt* (pop. 595,348), is the transportation hub of West Germany. It stands on the banks of the Main River in the German state of Hesse. For the location of Frankfurt, see **Germany** (political map). A network of railroads and highways links the city with all parts of Western Europe. Frankfurt has one of the largest airports in Europe. A river and canal system links the city with the North Sea. Frankfurt has three harbor areas, and ranks as one of the busiest inland ports in Germany. The full name of the city is Frankfurt am Main.

The city is a world center of commerce and banking. The Rothschild family opened its first bank there in 1798 (see **Rothschild**). Frankfurt holds two great trade fairs a year. The fair held in September opened first in 1240 and the February fair started in 1330. Frankfurt also holds many specialized trade fairs, including its famous annual book fair. Factories in Frankfurt produce chemicals, machinery, and electrical equipment.

Frankfurt is an important center of West German intellectual and cultural life. The city is the birthplace of famous German writer Johann Wolfgang von Goethe, whose home is now a museum. Frankfurt's attractions include the Römer town hall, a building that dates from the 1400's. The building contains the *Kaisersaal,* the meeting room at one time of the German emperors and princes. Also in the city is the Paulskirche, a church where leaders of the unsuccessful Revolution of 1848 met to draft a German national constitution.

Frankfurt's geographical position made it important from the time of the Roman Empire. The shallow ford in the Main River provided the easiest north-south river crossing in all Germany. The Franks forded the river in early times, and the city's name means *ford of the Franks*

(see **Franks**). Merchants traveling between Mediterranean countries and northern Europe naturally passed through Frankfurt. In about A.D. 500, the Franks seized a Roman fort at the crossing and founded a settlement. Allied bombers leveled nearly half of Frankfurt during World War II (1939-1945), but the city was rebuilt after the war. The U.S. Air Force still maintains the Rhein-Main air base just outside Frankfurt.   Peter H. Merkl

Frankfurter. See Sausage.

Frankfurter, Felix (1882-1965), served as an associate justice of the Supreme Court of the United States from 1939 until he retired in 1962. Before that time, Frankfurter spent 25 years as professor of law at Harvard University, and was an influential adviser to Presidents Woodrow Wilson and Franklin D. Roosevelt.

As a Supreme Court justice, Frankfurter was independent, forward-looking, and judicial-minded. His writings include *The Case of Sacco and Vanzetti; The Public and Its Government; The Commerce Clause Under Marshall, Taney and Waite;* and *Mr. Justice Holmes and the Supreme Court.*

Frankfurter was born in Vienna, Austria, and came to the United States in 1894. He was graduated from the College of the City of New York and Harvard Law School. He held several posts in Washington, D.C., during World War I, and went to the Versailles Peace Conference in 1919, where he served as a legal aide to President Wilson.   Merlo J. Pusey

Frankincense is a fragrant gum resin obtained from certain trees that grow in Africa and Asia. It is also called *olibanum.* Since ancient times, frankincense has been burned as an incense during religious services. The Bible says that one of the wise men brought Jesus a gift of frankincense (Matt. 2).

Frankincense is the hardened resin from the bark of trees of the genus *Boswellia.* The resin hardens into pale-colored drops called *tears.* These tears are used as incense in religious services. Perfumers dissolve the natural resin in alcohol to get a product called *olibanum absolute.* When steam is passed through olibanum absolute, it yields an oil perfumers call *essential oil.* This essential oil is added to perfumes to give a long-lasting, spicy fragrance.   Paul Z. Bedoukian

Franking and penalty privileges are ways of sending official matter through the United States mails without prepayment of postage. The Vice President, members of and delegates to Congress, and certain other officials of Congress use the *franking privilege.* They use it to mail official correspondence, public documents, the Congressional Record, seeds, and agricultural reports. The mailer puts his or her signature or its facsimile on each piece of mail instead of a postage stamp. Widows of former Presidents may frank all their domestic mail. Congress appropriates money to pay the U.S. Postal Service for the postage involved in these franking privileges.

Departments, offices, and agencies of the executive branch of the government use the *penalty privilege* without prepayment of postage for mailing official matter. Each item bears a printed clause citing the penalty for private use of this privilege. Each division pays the Postal Service the amount of postage chargeable on its penalty mail at regular postal rates.

Critically reviewed by the United States Postal Service

Detail of a pastel portrait (1783) by Joseph-Sifrède Duplessis; New York Public Library (Bettmann Archive)

Franklin served his nation as a statesman, scientist, and public leader.

Benjamin Franklin

Franklin, Benjamin (1706-1790), was a jack-of-all-trades and master of many. No other American, except possibly Thomas Jefferson, has done so many things so well. During his long and useful life, Franklin concerned himself with such different matters as statesmanship and soapmaking, book-printing and cabbage-growing, and the rise of tides and the fall of empires. He also invented an efficient heating stove and proved that lightning is electricity.

As a statesman, Franklin stood in the front rank of the people who built the United States. He was the only person who signed all four of these key documents in American history: the Declaration of Independence, the Treaty of Alliance with France, the Treaty of Peace with

Great Britain, and the Constitution of the United States. Franklin's services as a diplomat in France helped greatly in winning the Revolutionary War. Many historians consider him the ablest and most successful diplomat that America has ever sent abroad.

Franklin was the leader of his day in the study of electricity. As an inventor, he was unequaled in the United States until the time of Thomas A. Edison. People still quote from Franklin's *Sayings of Poor Richard* and read his *Autobiography.* Franklin helped establish Pennsylvania's first university and America's first city hospital.

Franklin's fame extended to Europe as well as America. Thomas Jefferson hailed him as "the greatest man and ornament of the age and country in which he lived." A French statesman, Count Honoré de Mirabeau, referred to Franklin as "the sage whom two worlds claimed as their own."

Early life

Benjamin Franklin was born in Boston, Mass., on Jan. 17, 1706. He was the 15th child and youngest son in a family of 17 children. His parents, Josiah and Abiah Franklin, were hard-working, God-fearing folk. His father made soap and candles in his shop "at the sign of the Blue Ball" on Milk Street.

Student and apprentice. Benjamin attended school in Boston for only two years. He proved himself excellent in reading, fair in writing, and poor in arithmetic. Josiah Franklin decided that he could not afford further education for his youngest son. He kept Benjamin home after the age of 10 to help cut wicks and melt tallow in the candle and soap shop.

Franklin's schooling ended, but his education did not. He believed that "the doors of wisdom are never shut," and continued to read every book that he could get. He worked on his own writing style, using a volume of the British journal *The Spectator* as a model. His prose became clear, simple, and effective. The boy also taught himself the basic principles of algebra and geometry, navigation, grammar, logic, and the natural and physical sciences. He studied and partially mastered French, German, Italian, Spanish, and Latin. He eagerly read such books as *Pilgrim's Progress,* Plutarch's *Lives,* Cotton Mather's *Essays to Do Good,* and Daniel Defoe's *Robinson Crusoe.* Franklin made himself one of the best-educated persons of his time.

Franklin did not care much for the trade of candle-making. When the boy was 12, his father persuaded him to become an apprentice to his older brother James, a printer. James proved to be a good teacher, and Benjamin a good pupil. He soon became a skilled printer. He wrote several newspaper articles, signed them "Mrs. Silence Dogood," and slipped them under the printshop door. James admired the articles, and printed several of them. But he refused to print any more when he discovered that Benjamin had written them. The brothers quarreled frequently, and Benjamin longed to become his own master. At 17, Franklin ran away to Philadelphia, which was then the largest city in the American Colonies. The story of his arrival there has become a classic of American folklore. Many tales describe the runaway apprentice trudging bravely up Market Street with a Dutch dollar in his pocket, carrying one loaf of bread under each arm and eating a third.

Printer. From 1723 to 1730, Franklin worked for various printers in Philadelphia and in London, England, where he was sent to buy printing presses. He became part owner of a print shop in 1728, when he was 22. Two years later, he became sole owner of the business. He began publishing *The Pennsylvania Gazette,* writing much of the material for this newspaper himself. His name gradually became known throughout the colonies. Franklin had a simple formula for business success. He believed that successful people had to work just a little harder than any of their competitors. As one of his neighbors said: "The industry of that Franklin is superior to anything I ever saw . . . I see him still at work when I go home from the club; and he is at work again before his neighbors are out of bed."

Later in 1730, Franklin married Deborah Read, the daughter of his first Philadelphia landlady. Deborah was not nearly so well educated as her husband. Her letters to him have many misspelled words. The Franklins were a devoted couple. He addressed his letters to "my dear Debby," and she signed her replies, "your afeckshonet wife."

Franklin had three children, two boys and a girl. One of the boys, William, became governor of New Jersey.

The first citizen of Philadelphia

Publisher. Franklin's printing business prospered from the start. He developed *The Pennsylvania Gazette* into one of the most successful newspapers in the colonies. He always watched carefully for new ideas. Historians credit him as the first editor in America to publish a newspaper cartoon, and to illustrate a news story with a map. He laid many of his projects for civic reform before the public in his newspaper. Franklin published *The Pennsylvania Gazette* from 1729 until 1766.

But Franklin achieved even greater success with *Poor Richard's Almanac* than with his newspaper. He wrote and published the almanac for every year from 1733 to 1758. The fame of the almanac rests mainly on the wise and witty sayings that Franklin scattered through each issue. Many of these sayings preach the virtues of industry, frugality, and thrift. "Early to bed and early to rise, makes a man healthy, wealthy, and wise." "God helps them that help themselves." "Little strokes fell great oaks." Other sayings reflect a shrewd understanding of human nature. "He's a fool that makes his doctor his heir." "He that falls in love with himself will have no rivals." See **Poor Richard's Almanac.**

Civic leader. Franklin never actively sought public office, although he was interested in public affairs. In 1736, he became clerk of the Pennsylvania Assembly. The poor service of the colonial postal service disturbed him greatly. Hoping to improve matters, he agreed to become Philadelphia's postmaster in 1737. He impressed the British government with his efficiency in this position, and in 1753 he became deputy postmaster general for all the colonies. Franklin worked hard at this job, and introduced many needed reforms. He set up the first city delivery system and the first Dead-Mail Office. He speeded foreign mail deliveries by using the fastest packet ships available across the Atlantic Ocean. To speed domestic mail service, he hired more post riders, and required his couriers to ride both night and day. Franklin also helped Canada establish its first regu-

Printer and publisher

As an apprentice, Franklin began his lifelong career in printing and publishing at the age of 12.

Bettmann Archive

As a printer, Franklin bought a press with Hugh Meredith in 1728. He became sole owner two years later.

lar postal service. He opened post offices at Quebec, Montreal, and Trois Rivières in 1763. He also established messenger service between Montreal and New York.

Franklin was public-spirited, and worked constantly to make Philadelphia a better city. He helped establish the first subscription library in the American Colonies. The members of this library contributed money to buy books, and then used them free of charge. The original collection still exists. Fire losses in Philadelphia were alarmingly high, and Franklin organized a fire department. He reformed the city police when he saw that criminals were getting away without punishment. City streets were unpaved, dirty, and dark, so he started a program to pave, clean, and light them. Philadelphia shamefully neglected the sick and insane during Franklin's time. He raised money to help build a city hospital, the Pennsylvania Hospital, for these unfortunates. Scholars in the American Colonies had no professional organization, so Franklin helped establish the American Philosophical Society, with headquarters in Philadelphia. The city had no school for higher education, so Franklin helped found the academy that grew into the University of Pennsylvania. As a result of projects such as these, Philadelphia became the most advanced city in the 13 colonies.

The scientist

Experiments with electricity. Franklin was one of the first persons in the world to experiment with electricity. He conducted his most famous electrical experiment at Philadelphia in 1752. He flew a homemade kite during a thunderstorm, and proved that lightning is electricity. A bolt of lightning struck a pointed wire fastened to the kite and traveled down the kite string to a key fastened at the end, where it caused a spark. Then he tamed lightning by inventing the lightning rod (see **Lightning rod**). He urged his fellow citizens to use this device as a sure "means of securing the habitations and other buildings from mischief from thunder and lightning." When lightning struck Franklin's own home, the soundness of his invention became apparent. The lightning rod saved the building from damage. Franklin's lightning rod demonstrated his saying that "An ounce of prevention is worth a pound of cure." Authorities generally agree that Franklin created such electrical terms as *armature, condenser,* and *battery.* See **Electricity** (History).

Franklin's experiments with electricity involved some personal risk. He knocked himself unconscious at least once. He had been trying to kill a turkey with an electric

Poor Richard, 1733.

AN

Almanack

For the Year of Chrift

1733,

Being the Firft after LEAP YEAR.

And makes fince the Creation Years
By the Account of the Eaftern *Greeks*   7241
By the Latin Church, when ☉ ent. ♈   6932
By the Computation of *W.W.*   5742
By the *Roman* Chronology   5682
By the *Jewifh* Rabbies.   5494

Wherein is contained

The Lunations, Eclipfes, Judgment of the Weather, Spring Tides, Planets Motions & mutual Afpects, Sun and Moon's Rifing and Setting, Length of Days, Time of High Water, Fairs, Courts, and obfervable Days.

Fitted to the Latitude of Forty Degrees, and a Meridian of Five Hours Weft from *London,* but may without fenfible Error, ferve all the adjacent Places, even from *Newfoundland* to *South-Carolina.*

By *RICHARD SAUNDERS,* Philom.

PHILADELPHIA:

Printed and fold by *B. FRANKLIN,* at the New Printing-Office near the Market.

Bettmann Archive

As an author, Franklin signed the pen name Richard Saunders to his famous *Poor Richard's Almanac.*

shock, but something went wrong and Franklin, not the bird, was stunned. Franklin later said: "I meant to kill a turkey, and instead, I nearly killed a goose."

Other studies. Franklin's scientific interests ranged far beyond electricity. He became the first scientist to study the movement of the Gulf Stream in the Atlantic Ocean. He spent much time charting its course and recording its temperature, speed, and depth. Franklin was the first to show scientists and naval officers that sailors could calm a rough sea by pouring oil on it. He favored daylight-saving time in summer. It struck him as silly and wasteful that people should "live much by candle-light and sleep by sunshine."

Franklin gave the world several other valuable inventions in addition to the lightning rod. The Franklin stove proved most useful to the people of his day. By arranging the flues in his own stove in an efficient way, he could make his sitting room twice as warm with one fourth as much fuel as he had been using. People everywhere appreciate his invention of bifocal eyeglasses most of all. This invention allowed both reading and distant lenses to be set in a single frame. Franklin discovered that disease flourishes in poorly ventilated rooms. Franklin also showed Americans how to improve acid soil by using lime. He refused to patent any of his inventions, or to use them for profit. He preferred to have them used freely as his contribution to the comfort and convenience of everyone.

Franklin quickly appreciated the inventive efforts of other people. He once said that he would like to return to earth a hundred years later to see what progress humanity had made. The first successful balloon flight took place in 1783, during Franklin's stay in Paris. Many bystanders scoffed at the new device and asked, "What good is it?" Franklin retorted, "What good is a newborn baby?"

Franklin's scientific work won him many high honors.

The Royal Society of London elected him to membership, a rare honor for a person living in the colonies. Publishers translated his writings on electricity into French, German, and Italian. The great English statesman William Pitt told the House of Lords that Franklin ranked with Isaac Newton as a scientist. He called Franklin "an honor not to the English nation only but to human nature."

The public servant

The Plan of Union. In the spring of 1754, war broke out between the British and French in America (see **French and Indian wars**). Franklin felt that the colonies had to unite for self-defense against the French and Indians. He printed the famous "Join or Die" cartoon in his newspaper. This cartoon showed a snake cut up into pieces that represented the colonies.

Franklin presented his Plan of Union at a conference of seven colonies at Albany, N.Y. This plan tried to bring the 13 colonies together in "one general government." The Plan of Union contained some of the ideas that were later included in the Constitution of the United States. The delegates at the Albany Congress approved Franklin's plan, but the colonies failed to ratify it. Said Franklin: "Everyone cries a union is absolutely necessary, but when it comes to the manner and form of the union, their weak noddles are perfectly distracted." See **Albany Congress.**

The war forced Franklin to turn his attention to the unfamiliar field of military matters. Early in 1755, General Edward Braddock and two British regiments arrived in America with orders to capture the French stronghold of Fort Duquesne, at the point where the Allegheny and Monongahela rivers met. The British had trouble finding horses and wagons for the expedition, and Franklin helped provide the necessary equipment. However, the French and Indians ambushed the British on the banks

Public-minded citizen

Postal service improved when Franklin became deputy postmaster general in 1753.

A subscription library Franklin helped set up in 1731 was the first of its kind in America.

The academy he helped found, *left,* later became the University of Pennsylvania.

The city hospital he organized, *right,* was the first in America.

of the Monongahela River. Braddock was killed, and the British army was almost destroyed. In the meantime, Franklin raised volunteer colonial armies to defend frontier towns, and supervised construction of a fort at Weissport in Carbon County, Pennsylvania.

A delegate in London. In 1757, the Pennsylvania legislature sent Franklin to London to speak for the colony in a tax dispute with the *proprietors* (descendants of William Penn living in Great Britain). The proprietors controlled the governor of the colony, and would not allow it to pass any tax bill for defense unless their own estates were left tax-free. In 1760, Franklin finally succeeded in getting the British Parliament to adopt a measure that permitted the taxation of both the colonists and the proprietors. Franklin remained in Great Britain during most of the next 15 years as a sort of unofficial ambassador and spokesman for the American point of view.

A serious debate developed in Great Britain in the early 1760's at the end of the French and Indian War. The French, who lost the war, agreed to give the British ei-

pledged his entire fortune to pay for the tea destroyed in the Boston Tea Party if the British government would agree to repeal its unjust tax on tea (see **Boston Tea Party**). The British ignored his proposal. Franklin realized that his usefulness in Great Britain had ended, and sadly sailed for home on March 21, 1775. Franklin had done everything possible to keep the American Colonies in the empire on the basis of mutual respect and good will.

The statesman

Organizing the new nation. Franklin arrived in Philadelphia on May 5, 1775, about two weeks after the Revolutionary War began. The next day, the people of Philadelphia chose him to serve in the Second Continental Congress. Franklin seldom spoke at the Congress, but became one of its most active and influential members. He submitted a proposed Plan of Union that contained ideas from his earlier Albany Plan of Union. This plan laid the groundwork for the Articles of Confederation. Franklin served on a commission that went to Canada in

Scientist and inventor

Franklin and his kite, *left,* showed the world that lightning is actually electricity.

Franklin's glasses. He invented bifocal lenses for distance and reading use.

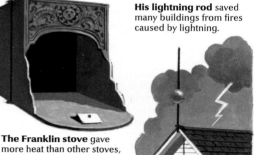

WORLD BOOK illustrations by Robert Addison

His lightning rod saved many buildings from fires caused by lightning.

The Franklin stove gave more heat than other stoves, and used much less fuel.

ther the French province of Canada or the French island of Guadeloupe in the West Indies. At the height of the argument, Franklin published a pamphlet that shrewdly compared the boundless future of Canada with the relative unimportance of Guadeloupe. Europeans and Americans read it carefully. Some historians believe that it influenced the British to choose Canada.

Franklin also took part in the fight over the Stamp Act (see **Stamp Act**). He seems to have been rather slow to recognize that the proposed measure threatened the American Colonies. But once he realized its dangers, he joined the struggle for repeal of the act. This fight led to one of the high points of his career. On Feb. 13, 1766, Franklin appeared before the House of Commons to answer a series of 174 questions dealing with "taxation without representation." Members of the House threw questions at him for nearly two hours. He answered briefly and clearly. His knowledge of taxation problems impressed everyone, and his reputation grew throughout Europe. The Stamp Act was repealed a short time later, and he received much of the credit.

Political relations between Great Britain and the colonies grew steadily worse. Franklin wanted America to remain in the British Empire, but only if the rights of the colonists could be recognized and protected. He

an unsuccessful attempt to persuade the French Canadians to join the Revolutionary War. He worked on committees dealing with such varied matters as printing paper money, reorganizing the Continental Army, and finding supplies of powder and lead.

The Continental Congress chose Franklin as postmaster general in 1775 because of his experience as a colonial postmaster. The government directed him to organize a postal system quickly. He soon had mail service from Portland, Me., to Savannah, Ga. He gave his salary to the relief of wounded soldiers.

Franklin helped draft the Declaration of Independence, and was one of the document's signers. During the signing ceremonies, according to tradition, John Hancock warned his fellow delegates, "We must be unanimous; there must be no pulling different ways; we must all hang together." "Yes," Franklin replied, "we must indeed all hang together, or assuredly we shall all hang separately."

Serving in France. Shortly after the Declaration of Independence was adopted in July 1776, Congress appointed Franklin as one of three commissioners sent to represent the United States in France. The war was not going well, and Congress realized an alliance with France might mean the difference between victory and

Benjamin Franklin served as minister to France from 1778 to 1785. The picture above shows Franklin in 1778 at the court of King Louis XVI and Queen Marie Antoinette, *seated right.*

Franklin represented Pennsylvania at the Constitutional Convention in 1787. Poor health prevented him from taking an active part. But his presence held the convention together.

defeat. Late in 1776, at the age of 70, Franklin set forth on the most important task of his life.

Franklin received a tremendous welcome in Paris. The French people were charmed by his kindness, his simple dress and manner, his wise and witty sayings, and his tact and courtesy in greeting the nobility and common people alike. Crowds ran after him in the streets. Poets wrote glowing verses in his honor. Portraits and busts of him appeared everywhere.

In spite of Franklin's popularity, the French government hesitated to make a treaty of alliance with the American Colonies. Such a treaty would surely mean war between France and Great Britain. So with tact, patience, and courtesy, Franklin set out to win the French government to the American cause. His chance came after British General John Burgoyne's army surrendered at Saratoga. The French were impressed by this American victory, and agreed to a treaty of alliance. The pact was signed on Feb. 6, 1778. Franklin then arranged transportation to America for French officers, soldiers, and guns. He managed to keep loans and gifts of money flowing to the United States. Many historians believe that without this aid the Americans could not have won their independence.

In 1778, Franklin was appointed minister to France. He helped draft the Treaty of Paris, which ended the Revolutionary War. France, Great Britain, and Spain all had interests in the American Colonies, and Franklin found it difficult to arrange a treaty that satisfied them all. The treaty gave the new nation everything it could reasonably expect. Franklin was one of the signers of the Treaty of Paris in 1783.

The twilight years

Franklin returned to Philadelphia in 1785. For the next two years, he served as president of the executive council of Pennsylvania. This office resembled that of a governor today. In 1787, Pennsylvania sent the 81-year-old Franklin to the Constitutional Convention. The delegates met in Independence Hall and drafted the Constitution of the United States. Age and illness kept Franklin from

taking an active part. But his wisdom helped keep the convention from breaking up in failure. Franklin was the oldest delegate at the convention.

Franklin also helped the convention settle the bitter dispute between large and small states over representation in Congress. He did this by supporting the so-called Great Compromise. The compromise sought to satisfy both groups by setting up a two-house Congress. In his last formal speech to the convention, Franklin appealed to his fellow delegates for unanimous support of the Constitution.

Franklin's attendance at the Constitutional Convention was his last major public service. However, his interest in public affairs continued to the end of his life. He rejoiced in Washington's inauguration as the first President of the United States. He hoped that the example of the new nation would lead to a United States of Europe. In 1787, he was elected president of the first antislavery society in America. Franklin's last public act was to sign an appeal to Congress calling for the speedy abolition of slavery.

Franklin died on the night of April 17, 1790, at the age of 84. About 20,000 people honored him at his funeral. He was buried in the cemetery of Christ Church in Philadelphia beside his wife, who had died in 1774. Franklin accomplished much in many fields, but he began his will with the simple words: "I, Benjamin Franklin, printer . . ." Franklin left $5,000 each to Boston and Philadelphia, part to be used for public works after 100 years, and the rest after 200 years. Part of this money has been used to establish the Franklin Technical Institute, a trade school in Boston, and the Franklin Institute, a scientific museum in Philadelphia.

His place in history

Franklin led all the people of his time in his lifelong concern for the happiness, well-being, and dignity of humanity. George Washington spoke for a whole generation of Americans in a letter to Franklin in 1789: "If to be venerated for benevolence, if to be admired for talents, if to be esteemed for patriotism, if to be beloved for philanthropy, can gratify the human mind, you must have the pleasing consolation to know that you have not lived in vain."

Franklin's name would almost certainly be on any list of the half-dozen greatest Americans. His face has appeared on postage stamps, and on the coins and paper money of the United States. Two Presidents of the United States proudly bore his name: Franklin Pierce and Franklin D. Roosevelt.

Philadelphia has also revered the memory of its most famous citizen. The University of Pennsylvania named its athletic field in his honor. One of the show places of the city is the spacious Benjamin Franklin Parkway. Midway along the Parkway stands the Franklin Institute, dedicated to popularizing the sciences that Franklin loved so well. This building contains the Benjamin Franklin National Memorial, with its great statue of the seated philosopher by James Earle Fraser. The Franklin Institute has also set up a reconstruction of Franklin's printing shop, with his own printing presses (see **Franklin Institute**).   James H. Hutson

Related articles in *World Book* include:

American literature (Politics)	Harmonica	Rebus
Cartoon (Early cartoons; picture)	Kite	Stamp collecting (picture: The first stamps)
Electricity (History)	Philadelphia	
	Poor Richard's Almanac	

Outline

I. Early life
  A. Student and apprentice
  B. Printer
II. The first citizen of Philadelphia
  A. Publisher
  B. Civic leader
III. The scientist
  A. Experiments with electricity
  B. Other studies
IV. The public servant
  A. The Plan of Union   B. A delegate in London
V. The statesman
  A. Organizing the new nation
  B. Serving in France
VI. The twilight years
VII. His place in history

Questions

How did Franklin happen to become a printer?
What famous newspaper did Franklin establish?
In what ways did Franklin help Philadelphia become the most advanced city in the 13 colonies?
How did Franklin become one of the best-educated men of his time?
Why did Franklin run away to Philadelphia?
What was Franklin's formula for business success?
What is considered to be Franklin's greatest contribution as a colonial statesman?
What did Franklin do with his salary as postmaster general?
How many years did Franklin attend school?
What was Franklin's last major public service?

Reading and Study Guide

See *Franklin, Benjamin,* in the Research Guide/Index, Volume 22, for a *Reading and Study Guide.*

Additional resources

Bowen, Catherine D. *The Most Dangerous Man in America: Scenes from the Life of Benjamin Franklin.* Little, Brown, 1974. Five dramatic episodes in Franklin's life.
Clark, Ronald W. *Benjamin Franklin: A Biography.* Random House, 1983.
Donovan, Frank R. *The Many Worlds of Benjamin Franklin.* American Heritage, 1964. For younger readers.
Franklin, Benjamin. *Autobiography.* Many editions of this work are available.
Lopez, Claude-Anne, and Herbert, E. W. *The Private Franklin: The Man and His Family.* Norton, 1985. First published in 1975.
Sandak, Cass R. *Benjamin Franklin.* Watts, 1986. For younger readers.
Schoenbrun, David. *Triumph in Paris: The Exploits of Benjamin Franklin.* Harper, 1976. His diplomatic achievements during the American Revolution.
Van Doren, Carl C. *Benjamin Franklin.* Greenwood, 1973. First published in 1938. Pulitzer Prize winner.

Franklin, Sir John (1786-1847), pioneered English exploration in the Arctic area. He lost his life during an expedition to find a northern water route across North America, called the Northwest Passage.

Franklin was born in Lincolnshire, England, and joined the British Navy at the age of 15. He was a midshipman on Matthew Flinders' voyage around Australia in 1803. In 1819, Franklin explored the mouth of the Coppermine River while leading his first Arctic expedition. He led his second expedition to the Arctic in 1825 and 1826.

In 1845, Franklin led the best-equipped expedition to enter the Arctic up to that time. He discovered a Northwest Passage, but he and his crew died during the expedition. When no one returned from the voyage, Lady Franklin sponsored many trips to search for her husband. A full exploration of the Arctic region resulted. A search party led by Sir Robert McClure crossed the Northwest Passage during an expedition from 1850 to 1854. Later, explorers found evidence of Franklin's party and reconstructed his voyage.   James G. Allen

See also **Northwest Passage.**

Franklin, John Hope (1915-   ), an American historian, has written many books about black Americans. His book *From Slavery to Freedom* (1947) is a widely praised account of blacks in America.

Franklin was born in Rentiesville, Okla. He earned a bachelor's degree at Fisk University, and master's and doctor's degrees at Harvard University. Franklin taught at colleges in North Carolina from 1939 to 1947, and then at Howard University until 1956. He served as a professor at Brooklyn College from 1956 to 1964, at the University of Chicago from 1964 to 1982, and at Duke University from 1982 to 1985.

University of Chicago
John Hope Franklin

His books include *The Free Negro in North Carolina* (1943), *The Militant South* (1956), *Reconstruction After the Civil War* (1961), and *The Emancipation Proclamation* (1963). He is coauthor of a junior high school textbook, *Land of the Free* (1966).   Edgar Allan Toppin

Franklin, Rosalind Elsie (1920-1958), was a British chemist and molecular biologist. She made important X-ray studies of *deoxyribonucleic acid,* commonly called *DNA,* which transmits genetic information from one generation to the next (see **Cell**). Franklin's work contributed greatly to the construction in 1953 of a model of the structure of DNA. This model was built by the biologists James D. Watson of the United States and Francis H. C. Crick of Great Britain. Franklin's research also helped verify the accuracy of the model.

Franklin made other important contributions to chemistry and molecular biology through her use of X-ray diffraction techniques (see **X rays** [In scientific research]). Her structural analysis of coals and chars promoted a better understanding of their properties. She also determined the complex structure of the tobacco mosaic virus, which attacks tobacco plants.

Franklin was born in London and graduated from Cambridge University in 1941. She died of cancer at the age of 37.　　　Marjorie C. Caserio

Franklin, State of, was never admitted to the Union. It was organized as a state between 1784 and 1788, and had its own constitution and governor. In 1784, North

State of Franklin

WORLD BOOK map

Carolina ceded part of its western lands to the federal government. Before Congress could vote to accept the region, North Carolina withdrew the offer. The people of the region set up a separate state because they were left without state or federal protection. They named it for Benjamin Franklin, probably in hopes of gaining his support. John Sevier was elected governor of the region. Representatives of North Carolina and other congressmen opposed admitting the state of Franklin to the Union.

Franklin, however, governed itself as a state for four years. Because money was scarce, people received furs, whiskey, and tobacco as salaries. North Carolina gained control of the area in 1788, and pardoned its leaders. The voters elected Sevier to the North Carolina Senate. In 1789, North Carolina once again ceded its western lands to the United States. Franklin became part of eastern Tennessee in 1796, and Sevier became the first governor of Tennessee.　　　Marshall Smelser

See also **Sevier, John; Tennessee** (Territorial years).

Franklin Institute, in Philadelphia, is a nonprofit scientific and educational institution. It includes the Science Teaching Museum, the Fels Planetarium, the Franklin Institute Policy Analysis Center, the Bartol Research Foundation, and a library. The institute's rotunda is the Benjamin Franklin National Memorial.

The Science Teaching Museum has exhibits that demonstrate the fundamentals and applications of the sciences. The Fels Planetarium projects a replica of the stars and the planets. The Franklin Institute Policy Analysis Center conducts studies specializing in health related issues. The Bartol Research Foundation performs basic research in astronomy, astrophysics, cosmic radiation, and nuclear physics.

The institute, founded in 1824, was named for Benjamin Franklin. In 1826, it first published its *Journal of the Franklin Institute,* a leading scientific publication in the United States. The institute grants certificates and awards, including the Franklin Medal, to individuals or organizations for their work in the sciences. The Franklin Institute is located at 20th and Benjamin Franklin Parkway, Philadelphia, PA 19103.

　Critically reviewed by the Franklin Institute

See also **Franklin, Benjamin** (The twilight years).

Franklin stove. See **Range** (History).

Franklin's gull is not a sea bird like most gulls. It lives on the prairies during the summer. Franklin's gull is also called the *prairie pigeon.* It breeds from southern Canada to Oregon and east to Iowa. It spends the winter from Louisiana to South America. Franklin's gull is about 14 inches (36 centimeters) long. It is white, with a bluish-gray back. Its head and neck are dark gray in the summer, but turn white in winter. It has a red bill tipped with black.

Flocks of these birds fly over the prairies, giving flute-like cries. Franklin's gull makes its nest of rushes among the reeds of marshy lakes. Thousands of the birds build colonies of many nests fairly close together. By the end of May, the female has laid 2 or 3 eggs, dull white to olive, with brown blotches. Franklin's gull helps the farmer by eating many harmful insects.

　Scientific classification. Franklin's gull is in the gull and tern family, Laridae. It is *Larus pipixcan.*　　　Alfred M. Bailey

See also **Gull.**

Franks were members of a confederation of Germanic peoples that attacked the Roman Empire beginning in the A.D. 200's. The Franks were divided into two branches, the Salians and the Ripuarians. The Salians settled in the Low Countries on the lower Rhine, near the North Sea. The Ripuarians moved into the region around what are now the cities of Trier and Cologne, Germany, on the middle Rhine.

Clovis, a king of the Salian Franks, began a massive invasion of Roman Gaul (now France) in 486. He defeated Gauls, Romans, Visigoths, and others to create a kingdom stretching from east of the Rhine River to the Pyrenees Mountains. Clovis was the first great Germanic ruler to adopt orthodox Christianity, in place of the heresy called *Arianism* practiced by the East Germanic peoples (see **Arianism**). When Clovis died in 511, the Franks,

WORLD BOOK map

The Frankish kingdom in A.D. 768

though outnumbered by their Gallo-Roman neighbors 20 to 1, had such a firm hold on Gaul that the region was called France after them.

Frankish history is divided into two periods. These periods are the *Merovingian,* from about 481 to 751, and the *Carolingian,* 751 to 987. Charlemagne, who was king of the Franks from 768 to 814, created a vast empire. In 800, Pope Leo III crowned him emperor of the Romans. After the time of Charlemagne, the Frankish empire began to break up into what later became the kingdoms of France, Germany, and Italy.   William G. Sinnigen

See also **Charlemagne; Charles Martel; Clovis I; Feudalism; Merovingian.**

Franz Josef. See Francis Joseph.

Franz Josef Land is a group of about 85 islands in the Arctic Ocean, north of Novaya Zemlya. The islands are the most northerly land of the Eastern Hemisphere. They cover about 8,000 square miles (21,000 square kilometers) and are part of the Soviet Union. No one lives on most of the islands. The largest islands in the group include Alexandra Land, George Land, Wilczek Land, and Graham Bell Island. In July, the mean temperature of this ice-covered land ranges from 8.2° to 10° F. (−13.2° to −12° C). In winter, the mean temperature is −22° F. (−30° C). But gales may force the temperature as low as −50° F. (−46° C).

An Austro-Hungarian expedition discovered the islands in 1873 and named them for Emperor Franz Josef (also spelled Francis Joseph). The Soviet Union claimed the islands in 1926.   Theodore Shabad

Fraser, Douglas Andrew (1916-   ), was an American labor leader. He served as president of the United Automobile Workers (UAW), one of the largest labor unions in the United States, from 1977 to 1983.

Fraser was born in Glasgow, Scotland, and moved to Detroit with his family when he was 6 years old. In 1934, he went to work as a metal finisher for the De Soto division of the Chrysler Corporation. He joined the UAW shortly after the union was founded in 1935. In 1943, at the age of 27, Fraser became president of one of the UAW's local unions in Detroit.

During the 1950's, Fraser served eight years as an administrative assistant to Walter P. Reuther, who was then president of the UAW. From 1970 to 1977, Fraser served as vice president of the union and as director of several UAW departments.   James G. Scoville

Fraser, James Earle (1876-1953), was an American sculptor. His works reflect his love for the American West and his admiration for American Indians and animals of the Great Plains.

Fraser's most famous work, *The End of the Trail* (1915), shows an exhausted Indian on horseback. Fraser also designed the buffalo nickel (1913), a coin with a buffalo on one side and the head of an Indian on the reverse side. Fraser created large works for parks and government buildings, such as the statue of Alexander Hamilton (1921) in front of the United States Treasury in Washington, D.C. Fraser was born in Chicago.   Bess L. Hormats

See also **Oklahoma** (picture: Cowboy Hall of Fame in Oklahoma City).

Fraser, Malcolm (1930-   ), served as prime minister of Australia from 1975 to 1983. Fraser, then the leader of Australia's Liberal Party, succeeded Labor Party leader Gough Whitlam as prime minister.

Whitlam's government was dismissed in November 1975 by Australia's governor general, Sir John Kerr, after the Senate rejected the national budget. Kerr appointed Fraser prime minister and instructed him to form a temporary government until an election could be held. The Liberal and National Country (now National) parties combined forces to win the election in December, and Fraser continued as prime minister. Fraser again led the combined Liberal and National Country parties to victory in 1977 and in 1980. As prime minister, Fraser worked to limit government spending, reduce unemployment, and strengthen ties with the United States and Britain. Inflation and unemployment helped the Labor Party win the 1983 elections, ending his term as prime minister.

Australian Information Service
Malcolm Fraser

Fraser was born near Melbourne. His full name is John Malcolm Fraser. Fraser received a master's degree from Oxford University in England. In 1955, he was elected to the Australian House of Representatives. From 1966 to 1971, Fraser served successively as minister for the army, minister for education and science, and minister for defence.   C. M. H. Clark

Fraser, Simon (1776-1862), was a fur trader and explorer in what is now the Canadian province of British Columbia. He worked for the North West Company, a Montreal fur-trading firm. In 1805, he was put in charge of the company's operations west of the Rocky Mountains. He built that area's first trading posts and explored many of its rivers. In 1808, Fraser explored what is now called the Fraser River. Fraser was born in Bennington, Vt. He moved with his family to Canada when he was a young child.   P. B. Waite

Fraser River is a waterway in British Columbia that is famous for its salmon fisheries. It flows across the southern part of the province, from the Rocky Mountains to the Strait of Georgia near Vancouver, B.C. For location, see **British Columbia** (physical map).

The Fraser River is about 850 miles (1,370 kilometers) long. The Chilcotin, Nechako, and Thompson rivers are its chief tributaries. The river drains a basin of about 92,000 square miles (238,000 square kilometers)—almost two-thirds of southern British Columbia. Highways and railroads follow the Fraser. Sawmills and pulp and paper mills are important in the river valley towns of Prince George, Kamloops, and Quesnel. Sir Alexander Mackenzie, an explorer and fur trader, traveled the middle section of the river in 1793. The river was named for Simon Fraser, a fur trader who followed it to the sea in 1808. The Fraser was the scene of a gold rush in 1858.   Graeme Wynn

Fraternal Order of Eagles. See Eagles, Fraternal Order of.

Fraternal society is an association of persons drawn together by common interests. The society may be organized chiefly to provide companionship and pleasure for its members, or it may be set up to furnish its members with certain benefits such as life, accident, and health insurance. Fraternal societies sometimes take part in civic programs or social work.

Many fraternal societies are secret lodges, with passwords, ceremonies, and initiation rites. Each society adopts its own constitution and bylaws, and sets up its own rules of procedure. Most societies restrict their membership. Some fraternal societies admit only men as members, while a few limit their membership to women. Many fraternal societies for men have auxiliary chapters or organizations to which mothers, wives, daughters, and sisters of members can belong. A few fraternal societies are limited to a single state, but almost all have national or even international membership.

Governing methods. Fraternal societies elect representatives from local chapters to serve on a governing board within the limit of a district usually covering a state. Each society elects delegates to its national convention from the memberships of the various lodges or from the governing boards of the various states or districts. The delegates in turn elect the officers who make up the supreme governing body. These officers serve until the next national convention is held.

History. Early fraternal societies were somewhat like the English *friendly societies* which first appeared in the 1500's. Working people organized these clubs to provide sickness and death benefits for members. Several fraternal societies founded branches in the United States and Canada during the early 1800's.

The Ancient Order of United Workmen, founded by John Upchurch in 1868, was the first fraternal society in the United States to pay substantial death benefits in the form of insurance to a deceased member's family. Other groups organized fraternal societies on the model of the Ancient Order of United Workmen. Many of these societies in later years merged with other groups to form the present fraternal societies. Early fraternal societies performed a genuine service by furnishing life insur-

ance to members whose incomes were so low they could not otherwise have enjoyed insurance benefits.

The National Fraternal Congress was formed in 1886 to provide state regulation and uniform legislation for fraternal benefit societies. In 1901, certain fraternal societies formed the Associated Fraternities of America. The two associations united in 1913 to form the National Fraternal Congress of America.

Critically reviewed by the National Fraternal Congress of America

Related articles in *World Book* include:

B'nai B'rith	Knights of Columbus
De Molay, Order of	Knights of Pythias
Eagles, Fraternal Order of	Masonry
Eastern Star	Moose, Loyal Order of
Elks, Benevolent and Protective Order of	Odd Fellows, Independent Order of
Good Templars, International Organization of	Rainbow for Girls
	Rosicrucian Order
Job's Daughters	Tammany, Society of

Fraternity is a society of college or university students and alumni. Fraternities are often called *Greek-letter societies* because most fraternities form their names by combining two or three letters of the Greek alphabet. The word *fraternity* comes from the Latin word *frater,* meaning *brother.* Members pledge to keep the group's ceremonies and mottoes secret.

The best-known kind of fraternity is the *general* or *social fraternity. Professional fraternities* are made up of people preparing for, or working in, such professions as education, law, medicine, and science. Fraternities called *honor societies* select their members for exceptional academic records. *Recognition societies* are for people with superior achievement in a specific area. A student may join only one general fraternity. But a general fraternity member may also join a professional fraternity, an honor society, or both.

Many fraternities admit both men and women, but most general fraternities are for men. Women's organizations for college students and alumnae are discussed in the **Sorority** article.

Fraternities in the United States

Name	Members	Chapters*	Year founded	Where founded	National headquarters
General fraternities					
Acacia	40,000	42	1904	University of Michigan	Indianapolis
Alpha Chi Rho	16,528	42	1895	Trinity College (Conn.)	Neptune, N.J.
Alpha Delta Gamma	7,859	12	1924	Loyola University of Chicago	Fort Mitchell, Ky.
Alpha Delta Phi	43,000	31	1832	Hamilton College	Morton Grove, Ill.
Alpha Epsilon Pi	49,810	85	1913	New York University	Omaha, Nebr.
Alpha Gamma Rho	40,800	55	1904	Ohio State University	Kansas City, Mo.
Alpha Gamma Sigma	12,456	8	1922	Ohio State University	Ava, Mo.
Alpha Kappa Lambda	15,888	19	1914	University of California	Indianapolis
Alpha Phi Alpha	70,000	175	1906	Cornell University	Chicago
Alpha Phi Delta	9,000	24	1914	Syracuse University	West Cape May, N.J.
Alpha Sigma Phi	46,230	54	1845	Yale University	Delaware, O.
Alpha Tau Omega	141,000	151	1865	Virginia Military Institute	Champaign, Ill.
Beta Sigma Psi	5,665	10	1925	University of Illinois	Florissant, Mo.
Beta Theta Pi	130,259	113	1839	Miami University	Oxford, O.
Chi Phi	39,841	47	1824	Princeton University	Atlanta
Chi Psi	17,500	32	1841	Union College (N.Y.)	Ann Arbor, Mich.
Delta Chi	51,272	77	1890	Cornell University	Iowa City, Ia.
Delta Kappa Epsilon	60,000	44	1844	Yale University	New York City
Delta Phi	12,400	16	1827	Union College (N.Y.)	Ithaca, N.Y.
Delta Psi	6,000	8	1847	Columbia University	New York City
Delta Sigma Phi	69,129	98	1899	City University of New York	Indianapolis
Delta Tau Delta	110,287	118	1858	Bethany College (W.Va.)	Indianapolis

*College chapters.

Fraternities in the United States (continued)

Name	Members	Chapters*	Year founded	Where founded	National headquarters
General fraternities—continued					
Delta Upsilon	88,000	87	1834	Williams College	Indianapolis
FarmHouse	15,064	30	1905	University of Missouri	St. Joseph, Mo.
Kappa Alpha Order	94,825	118	1865	Washington and Lee University	Lexington, Va.
Kappa Alpha Psi	63,000	294	1911	Indiana University	Philadelphia
Kappa Alpha Society	7,922	8	1825	Union College (N.Y.)	Ithaca, N.Y.
Kappa Delta Rho	15,914	33	1905	Middlebury College	Greensburg, Pa.
Kappa Sigma	160,142	200	1869	University of Virginia	Charlottesville, Va.
Lambda Chi Alpha	173,162	214	1909	Boston University	Indianapolis
Omega Psi Phi	80,000	306	1911	Howard University	Washington, D.C.
Phi Beta Sigma	65,000	450	1914	Howard University	Washington, D.C.
Phi Delta Theta	164,363	162	1848	Miami University	Oxford, O.
Phi Gamma Delta	118,102	123	1848	Washington and Jefferson College	Lexington, Ky.
Phi Kappa Psi	77,256	89	1852	Washington and Jefferson College	Indianapolis
Phi Kappa Sigma	41,000	59	1850	University of Pennsylvania	Valley Forge, Pa.
Phi Kappa Tau	58,235	81	1906	Miami University	Oxford, O.
Phi Kappa Theta	41,026	50	1889	Brown and Lehigh universities	Indianapolis
Phi Lambda Chi	10,000	7	1925	Arkansas State University	Jonesboro, Ark.
Phi Mu Delta	8,000	8	1918	University of Massachusetts	State College, Pa.
Phi Sigma Kappa	100,000	112	1873	University of Massachusetts	Indianapolis
Pi Kappa Alpha	140,275	175	1868	University of Virginia	Memphis, Tenn.
Pi Kappa Phi	47,382	102	1904	College of Charleston	Charlotte, N.C.
Pi Lambda Phi	29,300	46	1895	Yale University	Norwalk, Conn.
Psi Upsilon	39,000	33	1833	Union College (N.Y.)	Paoli, Pa.
Rho Psi	500	12	1916	Cornell University	Cherry Hill, N.J.
Sigma Alpha Epsilon	199,000	201	1856	University of Alabama	Evanston, Ill.
Sigma Alpha Mu	37,295	53	1909	City University of New York	Carmel, Ind.
Sigma Chi	180,000	192	1855	Miami University	Evanston, Ill.
Sigma Nu	150,000	186	1869	Virginia Military Institute	Lexington, Va.
Sigma Phi Epsilon	150,251	246	1901	University of Richmond	Richmond, Va.
Sigma Phi Society	9,525	10	1827	Union College (N.Y.)	Royal Oak, Mich.
Sigma Pi	49,739	109	1897	Vincennes University	Vincennes, Ind.
Sigma Tau Gamma	44,533	73	1920	Central Missouri State University	Warrensburg, Mo.
Tau Delta Phi	13,000	14	1910	City College (New York City)	Newark, N.J.
Tau Epsilon Phi	42,000	49	1910	Columbia University	Atlanta
Tau Kappa Epsilon	157,050	300	1899	Illinois Wesleyan University	Indianapolis
Theta Chi	108,191	149	1856	Norwich University	Trenton, N.J.
Theta Delta Chi	33,814	31	1847	Union College (N.Y.)	Boston
Theta Kappa Omega	9,000	8	1872	California Military Academy	Laurel, Miss.
Theta Xi	49,387	56	1864	Rensselaer Polytechnic Institute	St. Louis
Triangle	17,756	35	1907	University of Illinois	South Bend, Ind.
Zeta Beta Tau	96,000	90	1898	City College (New York City)	New York City
Zeta Psi	41,405	52	1847	New York University	White Plains, N.Y.
Largest professional fraternities					
Delta Sigma Pi (Business)	122,774	163	1907	New York University	Oxford, O.
Phi Delta Kappa (Education)	119,000	560	1906	Indiana University	Bloomington, Ind.
Phi Delta Phi (Law)	114,000	146	1869	University of Michigan	Washington, D.C.
Phi Alpha Delta (Law)	112,000	150	1902	South Haven Mich.	Granada Hills, Calif.
Alpha Kappa Psi (Business)	110,000	200	1904	New York University	Indianapolis
Beta Alpha Psi (Accounting)	100,000	154	1919	University of Illinois	Lincoln, Nebr.
Largest honor societies					
Phi Kappa Phi (Scholarship)	500,000	239	1897	University of Maine	Baton Rouge, La.
Phi Beta Kappa (Scholarship)	380,000	279	1776	College of William and Mary	Washington, D.C.
Phi Eta Sigma (Freshmen)	352,901	222	1923	University of Illinois	Auburn, Ala.
Alpha Lambda Delta (Freshmen)	309,637	205	1924	University of Illinois	Muncie, Ind.
Tau Beta Pi (Engineering)	257,000	236	1885	Lehigh University	Knoxville, Tenn.
Beta Gamma Sigma (Business)	200,000	220	1913	University of Wisconsin	St. Louis
Eta Kappa Nu (Engineering)	170,000	171	1904	University of Illinois	Urbana, Ill.
Psi Chi (Psychology)	149,313	613	1929	Yale University	Arlington, Va.
Pi Gamma Mu (Social Science)	148,331	180	1924	Southwestern College	Winfield, Kans.
Sigma Xi (Scientific)	125,000	499	1886	Cornell University	New Haven, Conn.
Largest recognition societies					
Alpha Phi Omega (Service)	185,000	350	1925	Lafayette College	Kansas City, Mo.
Scabbard and Blade (Military)	127,403	96	1904	University of Wisconsin	Stillwater, Okla.
Beta Beta Beta (Biology)	95,000	309	1922	Oklahoma City University	Unadilla, N.Y.
Blue Key (Leadership)	94,000	141	1924	University of Florida	Metairie, La.
Kappa Pi (Art)	53,000	120	1911	University of Kentucky	Birmingham, Ala.

*College chapters.

Sources: *Encyclopedia of Associations*, Gale Research Co., Detroit, 1987; National Interfraternity Conference.

Most fraternities have *chapters* (local units) in several schools in the United States and Canada. Intercollegiate, national, and international fraternities of all kinds have about 23,000 chapters and about 11,700,000 members. Local fraternities serve a single school.

Fraternities began in the United States. Phi Beta Kappa was the first fraternity. It was founded in 1776 at William and Mary College as a general fraternity. It later became an honor society. The Kappa Alpha Society was founded in 1825 at Union College in Schenectady, N.Y. It is the oldest continuing general fraternity. Theta Xi, the first professional fraternity, was founded in 1864 at Rensselaer Polytechnic Institute. It became a general fraternity in 1926. Phi Delta Phi, founded in 1869 at the University of Michigan for law students, is the oldest continuing professional fraternity.

General fraternities

Membership. To join a social fraternity, a student must be invited by its members. The invitation to join, called a *bid,* must be approved by the chapter members. Bids are made following a period called *rush*. During rush, students who are interested in joining a fraternity attend events to learn about various fraternities and meet their members. Students who accept bids are called *pledges* or *associates*. They must prove their ability to live, study, and work with fraternity members before they are finally accepted for membership. A pledge or associate who fills all requirements is initiated and receives a *fraternity pin* (badge).

Activities. Fraternities are well known for social activities, such as dances and parties. But they also play an important role in other aspects of college life. Fraternities encourage members to work for good grades, and they stress participation in athletic, cultural, political, social, and other activities. Most fraternities maintain a fraternity house, where their members live. Fraternity life provides experience in self-government and develops skills in cooperation, leadership, and relations with other people. Fraternities aid charity programs, extend hospitality to students from other countries, and provide funds for scholarships to fellow students and for summer camps for children. Most fraternities have alumni chapters and associations that advise chapters in financial affairs.

Organization. Each general fraternity chapter is a self-governing unit. But they are regulated by college officials, their own interfraternity council, and the national or international headquarters of the fraternity.

Most colleges have an interfraternity council. The council consists of representatives from all fraternities on campus. It promotes joining a fraternity, settles interfraternity disputes, and enforces conduct codes.

Representatives from each chapter of a national fraternity meet every year or two years in a national convention to decide fraternity policy. National officers, usually alumni, are elected at the conventions. Most national fraternities have a permanent staff and publish a magazine.

The National Interfraternity Conference, Inc., established in 1909, provides a forum for its 58 member fraternities. The NIC provides services in the areas of government affairs and university and public relations. It also sponsors an annual meeting. The National Interfraternity Conference has headquarters at 3901 W. 86th Street, Suite 280, Indianapolis, IN 46268.

Professional fraternities

Professional fraternities are similar to general fraternities in many ways. But professional fraternities are made up of persons with a common academic or occupational interest. Some professional groups require higher academic standing than do general fraternities. Members may not pledge other fraternities in the same profession, but they may pledge a general fraternity. There are over 75 intercollegiate professional fraternities for men and women, with more than 3,100 chapters and about 1,700,000 members. Most of these fraternities belong to the Professional Fraternity Association.

Honor and recognition societies

Honor societies are either *departmental* or *general.* A departmental honor society selects men and women who have excellent academic records in a specific area of study. A general honor society selects members from all fields of study. A recognition society selects those who have done outstanding work in an area such as retailing or community service.

Critically reviewed by the National Interfraternity Conference

See also **Phi Beta Kappa.**

Fraud is an intentional untruth or a dishonest scheme used to take deliberate and unfair advantage of another person or group of persons. It includes any means, such as surprise, trickery, or cunning, by which one cheats another. *Actual fraud* includes cases of misrepresentation designed specifically to cheat others, as when a company sells lots in a subdivision that does not exist. Actual fraud includes something said, done, or omitted with the design of continuing what a person knows to be a cheat or a deception. *Constructive fraud* includes acts or words that tend to mislead others, as when a person sells an automobile without telling the purchaser that the car stalls often.

Usually, the victim of fraud may sue the wrongdoer and recover the amount of damages caused by the fraud or deceit. But the victim must be able to prove damages.

Statute of Frauds, enacted in England in 1677, required certain common types of contracts, such as those dealing with real estate, to be in writing. The states of the United States and the provinces of Canada have laws based on this statute.   George T. Felkenes

Fraunces Tavern, *FRAWN sehz,* is famous as the place where George Washington said farewell to his officers on Dec. 4, 1783. It is at the corner of Broad and Pearl streets in New York City and is one of the city's oldest houses. Long Room, where this event took place, has Revolutionary War flags and many relics. Étienne de Lancey, a rich Huguenot, built it as a home in 1719. In 1762, Samuel Fraunces, a West Indian, bought the house and opened it as the Queen's Head Tavern. The Sons of the Revolution bought the building and restored it between 1904 and 1907.   Marshall Smelser

Frazer, *FRAY zuhr,* **Sir James George** (1854-1941), a Scottish anthropologist, wrote the famous *Golden Bough.* This book traces the development of the world's religions from their earliest forms. Frazer also wrote *Totemism and Exogamy; Folklore in the Old Testament; Superstition in the Growth of Institutions;* and *Anthologia*

Anthropologica. Frazer was born in Glasgow and was educated at Glasgow and Cambridge universities. He taught social anthropology at the University of Liverpool.   David B. Stout

See also **Mythology** (How myths began).

Frazier, *FRAY zhuhr,* **Edward Franklin** (1894-1962), a sociologist, was a leading authority on black life in the United States. His writings prompted studies of how such forces as slavery and the prejudices of whites affected the black family. His best-known book is *The Negro Family in the United States* (1939).

Frazier was born in Baltimore. He attended Howard and Clark universities before earning a doctor's degree from the University of Chicago in 1931. He taught at several schools from 1916 to 1934. He headed the sociology department at Howard University from 1934 to 1959. He was president of the American Sociological Society in 1948. His books include *The Free Negro Family* (1932), *The Negro in the United States* (1949), *Black Bourgeoisie* (1957), and *The Negro Church in America* (published in 1964, after his death).   Edgar Allan Toppin

Freckles. See **Skin** (Skin color).

Frederic, *FREHD uhr ihk* or *FREHD rihk,* **Harold** (1856-1898), played an important part in the rise of realism in American fiction. His literary reputation has grown significantly since the mid-1900's. Frederic believed that writers should describe realistically the life they had experienced. His best novels portray the narrow, grim small-town life of his native upstate New York in the late 1800's. Frederic also was interested in the impact of controversial ideas and of the developing political and industrial forces of the day.

Frederic's best novel, *The Damnation of Theron Ware* (1896), describes the influence of controversial social and religious ideas on a rigid small-town congregation. In *Seth's Brother's Wife* (1887), Frederic portrayed the mingling of politics and journalism in a small town. *The Market Place* (1899) depicts a greedy American inventor whose financial and social successes feed his ambitions for political power in England. Frederic was born in Utica, N.Y.   Alan Gribben

Frederick I (1121?-1190), called *Barbarossa* or *Red Beard,* succeeded his uncle Conrad III as king of Germany in 1152. He became Holy Roman emperor in 1155. The German people admired and respected him as a great national hero. In 1180, he defeated his great rival for power in Germany, Henry the Lion, Duke of Saxony and Bavaria. He enforced his authority in Germany and the Slavic borderlands to the east.

He was less successful in a bitter struggle against Pope Alexander III and the Lombard League of North Italian cities. The league defeated Frederick at the Battle of Legnano in 1176. It was in this battle that foot soldiers recorded their first great victory over feudal cavalry. The Lombard cities forced Frederick to grant them self-government in the Peace of Constance in 1183. The emperor started on the Third Crusade to the Holy Land in 1189, but drowned the next year while crossing a river. A German legend, however, says that Barbarossa never really died but instead is sleeping beside a huge table in the Kyffhäuser Mountains. When his beard grows completely around the table, the legend says, Barbarossa will arise and conquer Germany's enemies.

Charles W. Ingrao

Frederick II (1194-1250), called *Stupor Mundi* (The Amazement of the World), was one of the most brilliant rulers of the Middle Ages. He was an excellent administrator, an able soldier, and a leading scientist of his time. He understood several languages and encouraged the development of poetry and sculpture. His book on falcons is still consulted by experts.

Frederick belonged to the royal Hohenstaufen family (see **Hohenstaufen**). He was the son of the Holy Roman Emperor Henry VI and grandson of Frederick I. Frederick II was crowned German king when he was 2 years old, and king of Italy when he was 4. He became Holy Roman emperor in 1215, and made himself king of Jerusalem in 1229. Frederick governed his Sicilian kingdom well. He established the University of Naples in 1224 and made the University of Salerno the best school of medicine in Europe. Throughout his life, Frederick was in conflict with the popes and the rising towns of Germany and Italy. See **Gregory IX**.   Charles W. Ingrao

Frederick II (1712-1786), the third king of Prussia, became known as Frederick the Great. He started his reign in May 1740 and a few months later invaded Silesia, one of the richest provinces of Maria Theresa of Austria. This attack caused the War of the Austrian Succession. It also led to the Seven Years' War, in which Frederick held off the armies of three major powers, Austria, France, and Russia. He kept most of Silesia and expanded Prussia more when he joined with Austria and Russia and took a part of Poland (see **Poland** [The partitions]). Frederick built a strong government and army. He encouraged industry and agriculture. He also made Prussia a rival to Austria for control of other German states.

Frederick has been called an "enlightened despot" because he supported the progressive ideas and reforms of the period of history called the *Enlightenment* or *Age of Reason* (see **Age of Reason**). The French writer Voltaire lived at Frederick's court as a guest from 1750 to 1753. The German people remember Frederick as a strong king and a great military hero. He was born in Berlin. He was the son of Frederick William I of Prussia and Princess Sophia Dorothea of Hanover, the sister of King George II of Great Britain.   Charles W. Ingrao

See also **Frederick William I; Maria Theresa; Prussia** (Frederick the Great); **Seven Years' War; Succession wars.**

Frederick III (1831-1888), the only son of Wilhelm I, became king of Prussia and German emperor in 1888. He died of cancer just three months after he succeeded his father. He believed in parliamentary government and took an important part in political affairs during his father's reign. Bismarck, the chancellor of Imperial Germany, opposed Frederick's liberal views (see **Bismarck, Otto von**). Frederick was born in Potsdam. He married the Princess Royal Victoria, daughter of Queen Victoria of England. Their oldest son was Wilhelm II (See **Wilhelm** [II]). See also **Prussia**.   Charles W. Ingrao

Frederick the Great. See **Frederick II** (of Prussia).

Frederick William (1620-1688), often called the Great Elector, ruled the German state of Brandenburg from 1640 to 1688. Brandenburg later became the heart of the powerful Prussian kingdom.

During his rule, Frederick William laid the foundations for the future military greatness of Prussia. He was only 20 years old when he succeeded his father as *elec-*

tor (ruler). He ruled Brandenburg during the last eight years of the Thirty Years' War, which brought great ruin to Brandenburg (see **Thirty Years' War**). After the war ended in 1648, Frederick William began to send people to towns that had been deserted. He also won the power to raise and collect taxes and used money to build a standing army.

Frederick William fought against both King Louis XIV of France and King Charles XI of Sweden. He defeated Swedish troops in an important battle at Fehrbellin, Germany, in 1675.

Throughout his reign, he devoted much of his time to improving his territory. He encouraged industries, opened canals, and established a postal system. He reorganized the universities of Frankfurt and Königsberg and founded the Royal Library in Berlin. At his death, Frederick William left to his son Frederick III of Brandenburg (later King Frederick I of Prussia) a prosperous state and an enlarged army.   Charles W. Ingrao

Frederick William I (1688-1740) served as king of Prussia from 1713 until his death. He developed the most efficient government in Europe and made Prussia a leading military power.

Frederick William I was born in Berlin. He was a member of the Hohenzollern royal family and the son of Frederick I, the first king of Prussia. After becoming king, he established a merit system for hiring and promoting government officials and eliminated corruption in the government by placing spies to observe employees at all levels. Frederick William I also sharply reduced the number of government officials and cut government expenses.

The king used the money saved through his cost-cutting measures to improve the Prussian Army. Frederick William I doubled the size of the army to over 80,000 men and made it the best-trained army in Europe. He was called the "sergeant king" because he spent a great deal of his time with his soldiers. He paid large sums of money to recruit a "Giants Regiment," made up of soldiers more than 6 feet (180 centimeters) tall. Despite the strength of his army, Frederick William I was a timid statesman who kept Prussia out of war for almost his entire reign.

Unlike his father and his son, who later became known as Frederick the Great, Frederick William I had little interest in the arts or education. He publicly ridiculed the young Frederick for preferring poetry, music, and philosophy to military affairs.   Charles W. Ingrao

Fredericksburg, Va. (pop. 15,322), is one of the most historic cities in the United States. It lies on the Rappahannock River, about midway between Richmond, Va., and Washington, D.C. (see **Virginia** [political map]). The city grew as a trading post because of its river location. Today, interstate highways make the area a distribution center for corporations serving East Coast businesses. The homes of George Washington's mother and sister are in Fredericksburg. Across the river is Ferry Farm, where Washington spent part of his boyhood. The former law offices of the nation's fifth President, James Monroe, are in Fredericksburg. Several Civil War battlefields lie in or near the city. Fredericksburg is the home of Mary Washington College.   David C. Lyne

Fredericksburg, Battle of. See **Civil War** (Battle of Fredericksburg; table: Major battles).

Fredericton (pop. 44,352) is the capital of the Canadian province of New Brunswick. The city lies on the St. John River, in the southwestern part of the province. For the location of Fredericton, see **New Brunswick** (political map).

Fredericton's industries include meat processing, shoe manufacturing, and steel fabrication. The provincial and federal governments are the major employers. The city has many craftworkers. The workers' products include jewelry, leather goods, pottery, and wooden toys. Fredericton is the home of the Beaverbrook Art Gallery and Christ Church Cathedral, one of the finest examples of Gothic architecture in North America. The city is also the home of the University of New Brunswick and St. Thomas University.

Maliseet and Micmac Indians once lived in what is now the Fredericton area. The British founded Fredericton in 1762 on the site of an abandoned French settlement. They named the settlement in honor of Prince Frederick, the second son of King George III. After the Revolutionary War in America ended in 1783, about 6,000 people from the United States moved to Fredericton because they wanted to remain British subjects. The city became the capital of New Brunswick in 1785. The provincial legislative building was built in downtown Fredericton in 1880 (see **New Brunswick** [picture: The Legislative Building]).

In 1974, several surrounding communities united with Fredericton, and the city's population rose from 24,254 to about 44,000. The area of the city increased from 23 to 51 square miles (60 to 132 square kilometers). An urban renewal project called Kings Place opened in Fredericton in 1974. It includes business offices and a shopping center. Fredericton has a mayor-council form of government.   Sterling Kneebone

Frederik, also spelled *Frederick,* is the name of two kings of Denmark who were members of the House of Schleswig-Holstein-Sonderburg-Glücksburg.

Frederik VIII (1843-1912) ruled Denmark for six years after the death of his father, Christian IX, in 1906. Frederik was born in Copenhagen. He was the brother of Queen Alexandra of England and of King George I of Greece. His second son, Charles, became King Haakon VII of Norway, and his oldest son, Christian X, succeeded him.

Frederik IX (1899-1972), the oldest son of Christian X, was king from 1947 until his death. He had served as crown prince for 35 years and as regent during World War II when his father was injured. He married Princess Ingrid of Sweden in 1935. His oldest daughter, Margrethe, succeeded him.   Raymond E. Lindgren

Free city is an independent city-state with its own government. Such city-states developed in Italy and Germany during the Middle Ages. The German free cities received their independence in the 1100's as a reward for helping the German emperor against the nobles. The free cities included Hamburg, Lübeck, and Bremen. They became states in the German Empire in 1871, but kept special tariff privileges until 1888. Danzig (now Gdańsk, Poland) and Fiume (now Rijeka, Yugoslavia) were free cities for a time under the League of Nations. See also **City-state; Gdańsk.**   J. Salwyn Schapiro

Free enterprise system. See **Capitalism; Business** (Business in a free enterprise system).

Free Methodist Church is a religious denomination. It follows the Methodist teachings of John Wesley and the free will doctrine of the Arminians (see **Arminius, Jacobus**). The church was founded in 1860 by ministers and members of the laity who had been excluded from the Genesee Conference of the Methodist Episcopal Church because they tried to restore historic Wesleyan principles to the church. They believed in simplicity of life and worship; rent-free seats; abolition of slavery; and freedom from secret societies. See **Methodists.**

The church maintains a strong missionary program. Headquarters are in Winona Lake, Ind. The church's full name is the Free Methodist Church of North America.

Critically reviewed by the Free Methodist Church

Free-piston engine, sometimes called a *gasifier,* generates hot gases usually used to run a turbine. It can burn nearly any liquid fuel, from kerosene to peanut oil. Most free-piston engines have one or more pairs of pistons mounted facing each other in a cylinder. These pistons work much the same way as the pistons in a diesel engine, except they are not connected to a crankshaft.

Burning fuel makes the pistons bounce back and forth against cushions of air trapped in the ends of a compressor cylinder. As the pistons move toward each

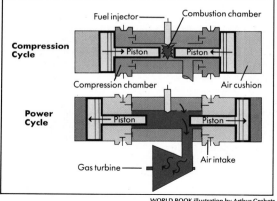

WORLD BOOK illustration by Arthur Grebetz

A free-piston engine works by bouncing pistons off cushions of air. As the pistons move inward, *top,* they compress air between them. Fuel explodes in the combustion chamber, driving the pistons apart, *bottom.* Hot gases escape to drive a turbine.

other, they compress air, raising it to a high temperature. When fuel is injected, it explodes, drives the pistons apart, and produces hot gases. After the explosion, this air forces the gases through the turbine. Some of these engines have only one piston used as an air compressor or a pile driver.

Pateras Pescara, a Spanish engineer, is credited with inventing the engine in the 1920's.   David E. Cole

See also **Diesel engine; Turbine (Gas).**

Free port. See **Free trade zone.**

Free school. See **Alternative school.**

Free silver was a plan to put more money in circulation in the United States by coining silver dollars. The plan was backed chiefly by farmers and silver miners in the late 1800's, when the United States government usually used gold coins to redeem paper money.

Supporters of the free-silver plan wanted all silver that was brought to the mint made into coins on a standard that made 16 ounces of silver equal to 1 ounce of gold. The 16-to-1 standard had existed before the U.S. Treasury stopped making silver dollars in 1873.

Farmers believed the plan would help them get higher prices for crops. Miners and silver producers also favored it as a market for their silver. The Populist Party supported the free-silver plan in the 1892 elections, and Democrat William Jennings Bryan urged the adoption of the plan when he ran for President in 1896. The issue died after Alaskan gold discoveries in 1896 increased the supply of money.   H. Wayne Morgan

See also **Populism; Bryan, William Jennings.**

Free Soil Party was a political group organized in Buffalo, N.Y., in 1848. The party opposed the extension of slavery into the territories and the admission of new slave states to the Union. Many members of the party had once belonged to the Liberty Party (see **Liberty Party**). The Free Soil Party was joined and strengthened by a discontented faction of the Democratic Party in New York that was known as the Barnburners.

Martin Van Buren became the Free Soilers' candidate for President in 1848. Their campaign slogan was "Free Soil, Free Speech, Free Labor, and Free Men." The party did not carry any state, but it polled over 291,000 votes. Thirteen Free Soil candidates were elected to the House of Representatives. A coalition of the Free Soil and Democratic parties elected Salmon P. Chase to the Senate in 1848, and Charles Sumner in 1851.

The Free Soil Party lost the support of the Barnburners before the presidential election of 1852. This loss cut the party strength far below what it had been in the preceding election, but the Free Soil candidate for the presidency, John P. Hale, still polled 156,000 votes. Before the election of 1856, the remnants of the Free Soil Party had joined forces with the newly formed Republican Party.   Donald R. McCoy

See also **Barnburners.**

Free trade is the policy of permitting the people of a country to buy and sell where they please without restrictions. A nation that follows the policy of free trade does not prevent its citizens from buying goods produced in other countries, or encourage them to buy at home.

The opposite of free trade is *protection,* the policy of protecting home industries from outside competition. This protection may be provided by placing *tariffs,* or special taxes, on foreign goods; by restricting the amounts of goods that people may bring into the country; or by many other practices.

The theory of free trade is based on the same reasoning as the idea that there should be free trade among the sections of a country. Consumers in Indiana gain by buying oranges from California, where the fruit can be grown less expensively. They would also gain by buying woolen goods from Great Britain if the goods could be produced there at less cost than in the United States.

Free-trade thinking is based on the principle of *comparative advantage* (see **International trade**). According to this principle, market forces lead producers in each area to specialize in the production of goods on which their costs are lower. Each area imports goods that are costlier for it to produce. Such a policy leads to the greatest total worldwide production, so that consumers receive the largest possible supply of goods at the lowest prices.

Objections to free trade. Despite superior efficiency under free trade, most countries favor some protection. One reason is the unsettled state of world affairs. Many people believe that so long as there is risk of war, a nation should not be too dependent on foreign supplies. Another reason is to support the incomes of those workers and firms that may be harmed by cheaper imports. Today, many less developed countries use protection to encourage their "infant" industries, more or less as the United States did in the 1800's.

Those people who favor free trade argue that protection can be harmful to a country's welfare and can lead to national isolation, national jealousies, and threats of war, which in turn necessitate even greater protection. They believe that free trade leads to understanding and world peace.   Robert M. Stern

Related articles in *World Book* include:

Customs union	Exports and imports
European Community	Free trade zone
European Free Trade Association	Smith, Adam
	Tariff

Free trade zone is an area in a country where goods can be imported without paying *customs duties* (import taxes). Foreign traders may store, exhibit, assemble, or process products in these zones before shipping them elsewhere for sale or use. Free trade zones are located near such transportation centers as seaports and airports. A free trade zone must operate in a city that is a *port of entry.* Such a city has customs centers through which goods enter a country. A free trade zone differs from a *free port,* which is an entire city or territory where no customs duties are collected.

Free trade zones encourage foreign trade by enabling merchants to conduct their trade more cheaply than would otherwise be possible. If goods are imported directly from a free trade zone, traders pay duties only to the country where the goods will be sold or used. No duty is paid to the country in which the zone is located. The zone also enables traders to exhibit their goods at a site near the intended market without paying duties before the items are sold.

There are about 275 free trade zones in the world. The United States has about 70 free trade zones, which are called *foreign trade zones.* In 1934, Congress established the Foreign-Trade Zones Board to authorize and administer the zones. The board is an agency of the U.S. Department of Commerce.   Roma Dauphin

Free verse is a style of poetry that does not follow traditional rules of poetry composition. In writing free verse, poets avoid such usual elements as regular meter or rhyme. Instead, they vary the lengths of lines, use irregular numbers of syllables in lines, and employ odd breaks at the end of each line. They also use irregular accents and rhythms and uneven rhyme schemes. But free verse is not free from all form. It does use such basic poetic techniques as alliteration and repetition.

Free verse first flourished during the 1800's when the romantic poets adopted the style. The American poet Walt Whitman is often considered the father of free verse, using the style effectively in his "Song of Myself"

(1855). In the early 1900's, a movement in poetry called *imagism* began using free verse. Such imagist poets as the American-born T. S. Eliot and Ezra Pound used free verse to create poetry based on the placement of precise images next to personal commentary. E. E. Cummings, a highly unorthodox American poet, experimented with unusual punctuation and typography. By the mid-1900's, free verse had become the standard verse form in poetry, especially in the works of such American poets as Robert Lowell, Theodore Roethke, and William Carlos Williams.   Samuel Chase Coale

Each poet mentioned in this article has a biography in *World Book.* For an example of free verse, see Theodore Roethke's poem under *Forms* in the **Poetry** article. See also **Meter.**

Free will is a term for the free choice most of us assume we have in making decisions. Our moral and legal systems, which praise, blame, reward, and punish, seem to assume that people have free will. If people lack free will, it seems unreasonable to hold them responsible for their decisions and actions. It would be difficult justifying the rewarding or punishing of people for actions they could not help doing.

The idea that there is free will has been questioned because it seems to conflict with the widely held belief in *determinism.* Determinism is the view that every event is already determined by previously existing conditions or causes. According to this view, the present state of the world determines everything that will happen in the future. Then human decisions and actions, like all other events, would be determined by causes that precede them. Critics of free will maintain that our choices are not really free if they are already determined before we make them.   Ivan Soll

Free World. See **Cold War** (introduction).

Freebooter. See **Pirate.**

Freedmen's Bureau was an agency created by the United States Congress to help the slaves freed at the end of the Civil War (1861-1865). It provided food and shelter for poor persons and supervised contracts between former slaves and their employers. The bureau protected the rights of blacks, provided opportunities for education, and helped them in many other ways.

In March 1865, Congress created the Bureau of Refugees, Freedmen, and Abandoned Lands. The bureau, better known as the Freedmen's Bureau, was part of the War Department. Its commissioner, General Oliver O. Howard, directed its agents.

Northern missionary and charity groups helped the Freedmen's Bureau finance and set up more than 4,300 schools for blacks. These schools included Atlanta, Fisk, and Howard universities and Hampton Institute. The agency built many hospitals and provided millions of meals for poor blacks and whites. It also supervised the distribution of abandoned lands to former slaves.

President Andrew Johnson criticized the bureau's work as unconstitutional meddling in the affairs of the Southern States. Johnson blocked the agency's distribution of abandoned lands to freed blacks. He vetoed two bills to renew the bureau, but Congress repassed one of them and expanded the powers of the bureau in 1866. Democrats charged that the agency used blacks to gain more power for the Republican Party. The bureau was disbanded in 1872.   Alton Hornsby, Jr.

Freedom is the ability to make choices and to carry them out. The words *freedom* and *liberty* mean much the same thing. For people to have complete freedom, there must be no restrictions on how they think, speak, or act. They must be aware of what their choices are, and they must have the power to decide among those choices. They also must have the means and the opportunity to think, speak, and act without being controlled by anyone else. However, no organized society can actually provide all these conditions at all times.

From a legal point of view, people are free if society imposes no unjust, unnecessary, or unreasonable limits on them. Society must also protect their rights—that is, their basic liberties, powers, and privileges. A free society tries to distribute the conditions of freedom equally among the people.

Today, many societies put a high value on legal freedom. But people have not always considered it so desirable. Through the centuries, for example, many men and women—and even whole societies—have set goals of self-fulfillment or self-perfection. They have believed that achieving those goals would do more to make people "free" than would the legal protection of their rights in society. Many societies have thought it natural and desirable for a few people to restrict the liberty of all others. This article discusses the ways that governments and laws both protect and restrict freedom.

Kinds of freedom

Most legal freedoms can be divided into three main groups: (1) political freedom, (2) social freedom, and (3) economic freedom.

Political freedom gives people a voice in government and an opportunity to take part in its decisions. This freedom includes the right to vote, to choose between rival candidates for public office, and to run for office oneself. Political freedom also includes the right to criticize government policies, which is part of free speech. People who are politically free can also form and join political parties and organizations. This right is part of the freedom of assembly.

In the past, many people considered political freedom the most important freedom. They believed that men and women who were politically free could vote all other freedoms for themselves. But most people now realize that political liberty means little unless economic and social freedom support it. For example, the right to vote does not have much value if people lack the information to vote in their own best interests.

Social freedom includes freedom of speech, of the press, and of religion; freedom of assembly; academic freedom; and the right to due process of law.

Freedom of speech is the right of people to say publicly or privately what they believe. Political liberty depends on this right. People need to hold free discussions and to exchange ideas so they can decide wisely on political issues. Free speech also contributes to political freedom by making government officials aware of public opinion. See **Freedom of speech.**

Freedom of the press is the right to publish facts, ideas, and opinions without interference from the government or private groups. This right extends to radio, television, and motion pictures as well as to printed material. Freedom of the press may be considered a special type of freedom of speech, and it is important for the same reasons. See **Freedom of the press.**

Freedom of religion means the right to believe in and to practice the faith of one's choice. It also includes the right to have no religion at all. See **Freedom of religion.**

Freedom of assembly is the right to meet together and to form groups with others of similar interests. It also means that people may associate with anyone they wish. On the other hand, no one may be forced to join an association against his or her will.

Academic freedom is a group of freedoms claimed by teachers and students. It includes the right to teach, discuss, research, write, and publish without interference. It promotes the exchange of ideas and the spread of knowledge. See **Academic freedom.**

Due process of law is a group of legal requirements that must be met before a person accused of crime can be punished. By protecting an individual against unjust imprisonment, due process serves as a safeguard of personal freedom. Due process includes people's right to know the charges against them. The law also guarantees the right to obtain a legal order called a *writ of habeas corpus.* This writ orders the police to free a prisoner if no legal charge can be placed against the person. It protects people from being imprisoned unjustly. See **Due process of law; Habeas corpus.**

Economic freedom enables people to make their own economic decisions. This freedom includes the right to own property, to use it, and to profit from it. Workers are free to choose and change jobs. People have the freedom to save money and invest it as they wish. Such freedoms form the basis of an economic system called *capitalism* (see **Capitalism**).

The basic principle of capitalism is the policy of *laissez faire,* which states that government should not interfere in most economic affairs. According to laissez faire, everyone would be best off if allowed to pursue his or her own economic interests without restriction or special treatment from government.

Since the 1930's, economic freedom has come to mean that everyone has the right to a satisfactory standard of living. This concept of economic freedom, sometimes called "freedom from want," often conflicts with the principle of laissez faire. For example, government has imposed minimum-wage laws that limit the smallest amount of money per hour an employer can pay. Laws also protect workers' rights to reasonable hours, holidays with pay, and safe working conditions. And if people cannot earn a living because of disability, old age, or unemployment, they receive special aid.

Limits on freedom

The laws of every organized society form a complicated pattern of balanced freedoms and restrictions. Some people think of laws as the natural enemies of freedom. In fact, people called *anarchists* believe that all systems of government and laws destroy liberty (see **Anarchism**). Actually, the law both limits and protects the freedom of an individual. For example, it forbids people to hit others. But it also guarantees that people will be free from being hit.

Reasons for limits on freedom. The major reason for restricting freedom is to prevent harm to others. To achieve the goal of equal freedom for everyone, a government may have to restrict the liberty of certain individuals or groups to act in certain ways. In the United States, for example, restaurant owners no longer have the freedom to refuse to serve people because of race.

Society also limits personal freedom in order to maintain order and keep things running smoothly. When two cars cannot cross an intersection at the same time without colliding, traffic regulations specify which should go first.

Also, every person must accept certain duties and responsibilities to maintain and protect society. Many of these duties limit freedom. For example, a citizen has the duty to vote, pay taxes, and serve on a jury. The idea of personal freedom has nearly always carried with it some amount of duty to society.

Limits on political freedom. Democracies divide political power among the branches of government, between government and the citizens, and between the majority and minority parties. These divisions of power restrict various liberties. For example, citizens have the right to vote. As a result, elected officials must respect voter opinion. They are not free to govern as they please. A system called the *separation of powers* divides authority among the three branches of government—executive, legislative, and judicial. Each branch is limited by the others' power. Majority rule does not give the majority party the liberty to do whatever it wants. No matter how large the majority, it can never take away certain rights and freedoms of the minority.

Limits on social freedom prevent people from using their liberty in ways that would harm the health, safety, or welfare of others. For example, free speech does not include the right to shout "Fire!" in a crowded theater if there is no fire. Freedom of speech and of the press do not allow a person to tell lies that damage another's reputation. Such statements are called *slander* if spoken and *libel* if written.

The law also prohibits speeches or publications that would endanger the nation's peace or security. Under certain conditions, it forbids speeches that call on people to riot. It also outlaws *sedition* (calling for rebellion).

In addition, many governments limit freedom of speech and of the press to protect public morals. For example, many states of the United States have laws against *pornography* (indecent pictures and writings). See **Obscenity and pornography.**

The government limits freedom of religion by forbidding certain religious practices. For example, it prohibits human sacrifice. It also bans *polygamy* (marriage to more than one person at a time), though Islam and other religions permit the practice.

Most other social freedoms can be restricted or set aside to protect other people or to safeguard the nation. For example, people may not use freedom of assembly to disturb the peace or to block public streets or sidewalks. The writ of habeas corpus may be suspended during a rebellion or an invasion.

Limits on economic freedom. In the past, most governments put few limits on economic freedom. They followed a policy of not interfering in economic affairs.

But since the 1800's, the development of large-scale capitalism has concentrated wealth in the hands of relatively few people. This development has convinced many people that government must intervene to protect underprivileged groups and promote equality of economic opportunity. Such beliefs have led to increased restrictions on big business and other powerful economic groups. For example, the Supreme Court of the United States once ruled that minimum-wage laws violated the "freedom of contract" between employer and employee. But today, laws regulate wages, hours, and working conditions; forbid child labor; and even guarantee unemployment insurance. Most people believe these laws protect economic freedom rather than violate it.

Economic freedom is also limited when it conflicts with other people's rights or welfare. For example, no one is free to cheat others. The right of hotelkeepers to do what they choose with their property does not allow them to refuse a room to people of a certain race or religion. The freedom of manufacturers to run their factories as they wish does not allow them to dump industrial wastes into other people's drinking water.

History

In ancient Greece and Rome, only the highest classes had much freedom. By about 500 B.C., Athens and several other Greek city-states had democratic governments. Citizens could vote and hold office, but they made up a minority of the population. Women, slaves, and foreigners did not have these rights.

During Rome's years as a republic, from 509 to 27 B.C., the highest classes had many liberties. But the lower classes could not hold public office or marry into upper-class families. Lowest of all were the slaves, who, as a form of property, had no legal rights.

The Middle Ages produced a political and economic system called *feudalism.* Under feudalism, the peasants known as *serfs* had little freedom, but nobles had much. Lower-ranking noblemen furnished troops and paid taxes to a higher-ranking nobleman called their *lord.* The lower-ranking noblemen were known as the lord's *vassals.* Vassals had many important rights. For example, a lord had to call his vassals together and get their permission before he could collect extra taxes. Another custom called for disputes between a vassal and his lord to be settled by a court of the vassal's *peers*—men of the same rank as he.

In 1215, King John of England approved a document called Magna Carta. This document made laws of many customary feudal liberties. For example, it confirmed the tradition that the king could raise no special tax without the consent of his nobles. This provision brought about the development of Parliament. In addition, the document stated that no freeman could be imprisoned, exiled, or deprived of property, except as provided by law. The ideas of due process of law and trial by jury developed from this concept. Most important of all, Magna Carta established the principle that even the king had to obey the law. See **Magna Carta.**

In the Middle Ages, the Christian church restricted freedom of thought in Europe. The church persecuted Jews, Moslems, and others who disagreed with its beliefs. It restricted writings it considered contrary to church teachings. But church teachings also acted as a check on the unreasonable use of political power.

The Renaissance and the Reformation emphasized the importance of the individual. As a result, people began to demand greater personal freedom. Anabaptists and other Protestant groups elected their own ministers and held free and open discussions. These practices carried over into politics and contributed to the growth of democracy and political freedom. In 1620, for example, the Puritans who settled in Massachusetts signed a document called the Mayflower Compact, in which they agreed to obey "just and equal laws."

During the Age of Reason, many people began to regard freedom as a natural right. Parliament passed the English Bill of Rights in 1689. This bill eliminated many powers of the king and guaranteed the basic rights and liberties of the English people.

At the same time, the English philosopher John Locke declared that every person is born with natural rights that cannot be taken away. These rights include the right to life and to own property; and freedom of opinion, religion, and speech. Locke's book *Two Treatises of Government* (1690) argued that the chief purpose of government was to protect these rights. If a government did not adequately protect the citizens' liberty, they had the right to revolt.

In 1776, the American colonists used many of Locke's ideas in the Declaration of Independence. For example, the declaration stated that people had God-given rights to "Life, Liberty and the pursuit of Happiness."

As the Industrial Revolution spread during the 1700's, the free enterprise system became firmly established. The Scottish economist Adam Smith argued for the laissez faire policy in his book *The Wealth of Nations* (1776).

During the 1700's, three important French philosophers—Montesquieu, Jean Jacques Rousseau, and Voltaire—spoke out for individual rights and freedoms. Montesquieu's book *The Spirit of the Laws* (1748) called for representative government with separation of powers into executive, legislative, and judicial branches. Rousseau declared in his book *The Social Contract* (1762) that government draws its powers from the consent of the people who are governed. Voltaire's many writings opposed government interference with individual rights.

The writings of these three men helped cause the French Revolution, which began in 1789. The revolution was devoted to liberty and equality. It did not succeed in making France a democracy. But it did wipe out many abuses and limit the king's powers.

The Revolutionary War in America (1775-1783) won the colonies independence from Great Britain. In 1789, the Constitution of the United States established a democratic government with powers divided among the President, Congress, and the federal courts. The first 10 amendments to the Constitution took effect in 1791. These amendments, now known as the Bill of Rights, guaranteed such basic liberties as freedom of speech, press, and religion; and the right to trial by jury.

The 1800's brought into practice many beliefs about freedom that had developed during the Age of Reason. In 1830, and again in 1848, revolutionary movements swept over much of Europe. Many European monarchs lost most of their powers. By 1848, the citizens of many nations had won basic civil liberties and at least the beginnings of democratic government. These nations included Belgium, Denmark, and the Netherlands. Most

European nations also ended slavery during the 1800's. In 1865, the 13th Amendment to the Constitution abolished slavery in the United States. The 15th Amendment, adopted in 1870, gave former slaves the right to vote.

Workers also gained many important rights during the 1800's. Many nations, including Great Britain and the United States, passed laws that regulated working conditions in factories. Workers in several countries won the right to form labor unions.

The 1900's. After World War I ended in 1918, many European nations established representative democracies. A number of them also gave women the right to vote. The United States did so in 1920 with the 19th Amendment. By 1932, 16 European nations had become republics governed by elected representatives.

By the 1930's, many people no longer believed that the simple absence of restrictions could make them free. Instead, the idea of freedom expanded to include employment, health, and adequate food and housing. In 1941, President Franklin D. Roosevelt reflected this broad view in his "four freedoms" message. He called for four freedoms—freedom of speech, freedom of religion, freedom from want, and freedom from fear—to be spread throughout the world. For the text of Roosevelt's message, see **Four freedoms.**

In 1948, the United Nations General Assembly adopted the Universal Declaration of Human Rights. This declaration listed rights and freedoms that the UN thought should be the goals of all nations.

In the 1960's, the civil rights struggle by blacks resulted in much important legislation in the United States. The 24th Amendment to the Constitution, adopted in 1964, banned poll taxes in federal elections. The Civil Rights Act of 1964 forbade employers and unions to discriminate on the basis of color, national origin, race, religion, or sex. The act also prohibited hotels and restaurants from such discrimination in serving customers.

In 1972, Congress passed the Equal Rights Amendment to the Constitution. The amendment would have guaranteed equality of rights under the law to all persons regardless of sex. However, it never took effect because it failed to win ratification from the states.

Critically reviewed by William C. Havard

Related articles in *World Book* include:

Academic freedom	Freedom of religion
Bill of rights	Freedom of speech
Censorship	Freedom of the press
Civil rights	Privacy, Right of
Communism (Personal freedom)	Voting
Democracy	

Additional resources

Barth, Alan. *The Rights of Free Men: An Essential Guide to Civil Liberties.* Random House, 1983.
Bergmann, Frithjof. *On Being Free.* Harper, 1977.
Fromm, Erich. *The Sane Society.* Random House, 1977. First published in 1955. An examination of freedom in the United States.
Gastil, Raymond D. *Freedom in the World: Political Rights and Civil Liberties.* Greenwood. Published annually.
Handlin, Oscar and Mary. *The Dimensions of Liberty.* Harvard, 1961.

Freedom, Academic. See Academic freedom.

Freedom Day, National, falls on February 1. It commemorates the day a resolution was signed proposing an amendment to the Constitution to outlaw slavery. Congress adopted the resolution, and President Abraham Lincoln signed it on Feb. 1, 1865. Amendment 13 was ratified by the states and was proclaimed on Dec. 18, 1865 (see **Constitution of the United States**). It freed all slaves in the North. Lincoln's Emancipation Proclamation of Jan. 1, 1863, had freed only the slaves in territories that were in rebellion against the United States (see **Emancipation Proclamation**).

In 1948, Congress authorized the President to proclaim the first day of February in each year as National Freedom Day. President Harry S. Truman made Feb. 1, 1949, the first such day.   Elizabeth Hough Sechrist

Freedom of Information Act is a law that authorizes anyone to examine most of the records of agencies in the executive branch of the United States government. Records can be obtained by presenting an agency with a written request for specific documents. Some agencies charge a small fee for providing copies of such records. Congress passed the law, often called the FOIA, in 1966 in an effort to discourage secrecy in government.

The FOIA states that only certain documents can be withheld. These include records relating to national security, personnel files of government employees, and records of criminal investigations. Confidential information about business companies, including sales records and patent applications, also can be withheld. The FOIA enables a person to challenge the government in court if an agency refuses to release information covered by the act.

The FOIA was strengthened in 1974 by amendments that require federal agencies to respond more quickly to requests for information. One amendment requires the agencies to answer an FOIA inquiry within 10 working days. Another provides for disciplinary action against any government official who withholds documents illegally. A later law, the "Government in the Sunshine Act" of 1976, put additional limits on government secrecy by requiring most meetings of federal agencies to be open to the public.   Jethro K. Lieberman

See also **Sunshine laws.**

Freedom of religion is the right of a person to believe in and practice whatever faith he or she chooses. It also includes the right of an individual to have no religious beliefs at all.

Like most rights, freedom of religion is not absolute. Most countries prohibit religious practices that injure people or that are thought to threaten to destroy society. For example, most governments forbid human sacrifice and *polygamy,* the practice of having more than one wife or husband at the same time.

Throughout most of history, many people have been persecuted for their religious beliefs. The denial of religious liberty probably stems from two major sources—personal and political. Religion touches the deepest feelings of many people. Strong religious views have led to intolerance among various faiths. Some governments have close ties to one religion and consider people of other faiths to be a threat to political authority. A government also may regard religion as politically dangerous because religions may place allegiance to God above obedience to the state.

The question of morality has caused many conflicts between church and state. Both religion and government are concerned with morality. They work together if the moral goals desired by the state are the same as those sought by the church. But discord may result if they have different views about morality. An example is the disagreement of many religious people with governments that allow abortion.

In the United States. The desire for religious freedom was a major reason Europeans settled in America. The Puritans and many other groups came to the New World to escape religious persecution in Europe.

The First Amendment of the United States Constitution guarantees that "Congress shall make no law respecting an establishment of religion, or prohibiting the free exercise thereof . . . ." This provision originally protected religious groups from unfair treatment by the federal government only. Until the mid-1800's, New Hampshire and some other states had laws that prohibited non-Protestants from holding public office. Several states, including Connecticut and Massachusetts, even had official state churches. Since the 1940's, however, the Supreme Court of the United States has ruled that all of the states must uphold the First Amendment's guarantees of religious freedom.

Today, freedom of religion remains an issue in the United States. Various court rulings have interpreted the First Amendment to mean that the government may not promote or give special treatment to any religion. Judges have struck down plans that called for the government to give financial aid to religious schools. The courts have also ruled unconstitutional a number of programs to teach the Bible or recite prayers in public schools. These rulings are highly controversial. See **Religious education.**

But church and state are not completely separated in the United States. The nation's motto is *In God We Trust.* Sessions of Congress open with prayers, and court witnesses swear oaths on the Bible. Several court decisions support such practices.

Christian moral views have had a predominant influence on U.S. laws because most of the nation's people are Christians. In 1878, for example, the Supreme Court upheld a federal law against polygamy, even though this law restricted the religious freedom of one Christian group, the Mormons. At that time, the Mormon faith included belief in polygamy. But the laws and the courts agreed with the view of most Americans that polygamy is harmful to society.

In other countries. Religion has been discouraged or even forbidden in countries ruled by dictators. For example, the governments of China, the Soviet Union, and other Communist nations have persecuted religion on a large scale. A person's highest allegiance, they believe, belongs to Communism, not to a Supreme Being. Communist dictators consider religion a competitor for such allegiance. Although they do not forbid religion entirely, they make it difficult for people to practice any faith. Communist authorities have imprisoned religious leaders and have closed churches. The Soviet Union has conducted intensive propaganda campaigns to persuade people not to attend church. China has imprisoned or expelled foreign missionaries.

In some countries that have an official state church, or where most of the people belong to one church, other faiths do not have religious freedom. For example, many Muslim nations discriminate against Christians and Jews. Even in countries that do not have a state church, members of minority religions may have economic or social disadvantages. Roman Catholics in Northern Ireland, which is mostly Protestant, complain of such unfair treatment.

Other countries, including Great Britain and Sweden, have state churches. But the governments of these nations grant freedom of worship to other religious groups. In some countries, the government provides equal support for all religions.

History. Many ancient peoples permitted broad religious freedom. These peoples worshiped many gods and readily accepted groups with new gods. Jews and, later, Christians could not do so because they worshiped only one God. They also believed that allegiance to God was higher than allegiance to any ruler or state. Some ancient peoples did not accept these beliefs, and they persecuted Christians and Jews.

During the Middle Ages, from about the A.D. 500's to the 1500's, the Roman Catholic Church dominated Europe and permitted little religious freedom. The Catholic Church persecuted Jews and Muslims. The church also punished people for any serious disagreement with its teachings. In 1415, the Bohemian religious reformer John Hus was burned at the stake for challenging the authority of the pope.

The Reformation, a religious movement of the 1500's, gave birth to Protestantism. The Catholic Church and Catholic rulers persecuted Protestant groups. Many Protestant denominations persecuted Catholics and other Protestant groups as well. But by the 1700's and 1800's, the variety of religions that resulted from the Reformation had led to increased tolerance in many countries. These countries included Great Britain, the Netherlands, and the United States. But intolerance remained strong in some countries. Poland and Russia, for example, severely persecuted Jews. One of the most savage religious persecutions in history occurred in the 1930's and 1940's, when Nazi Germany killed about 6 million Jews.   Richard E. Morgan

Additional resources

Cord, Robert L. *Separation of Church and State: Historical Fact and Current Fiction.* Lambeth Press, 1982.
Maddox, Robert L. *Separation of Church and State: Guarantor of Religious Freedoms.* Crossroad, 1987.
Miller, William L. *The First Liberty: Religion and the American Republic.* Knopf, 1988. First published in 1986.
Neuhaus, Richard J. *The Naked Public Square: Religion and Democracy in America.* Eerdman's, 1984.
Smith, Elwyn A. *Religious Liberty in the United States: The Development of Church-State Thought Since the Revolutionary Era.* Fortress, 1972.

Freedom of speech is the right to speak out publicly or privately. The term covers all forms of expression, including books, newspapers, magazines, radio, television, and motion pictures. Many scholars consider freedom of speech a natural right.

In a democracy, freedom of speech is a necessity. Democratic constitutions guarantee people the right to express their opinions freely because democracy is government of, by, and for the people. The people need information to help them determine the best political and social policies. The governments need to know what

most people—and various minorities—believe and want.

Most nondemocratic nations deny freedom of speech to their people. The governments of these countries operate under the theory that the ruler or governing party "knows best" what is good for the people. Such governments believe that freedom of speech would interfere with the conduct of public affairs and would create disorder.

Limitations. All societies, including democratic ones, put various limitations on what people may say. They prohibit certain types of speech that they believe might harm the government or the people. But drawing a line between dangerous and harmless speech can be extremely difficult.

Most democratic nations have four major restrictions on free expression. (1) Laws covering *libel* and *slander* prohibit speech or publication that harms a person's reputation (see **Libel; Slander**). (2) Some laws forbid speech that offends public decency by using obscenities or by encouraging people to commit acts considered immoral. (3) Laws against spying, treason, and urging violence prohibit speech that endangers life, property, or national security. (4) Other laws forbid speech that invades the right of people not to listen to it. For example, a city ordinance might limit the times when people may use loudspeakers on public streets.

In the United States. Freedom of speech was one of the goals of the American colonists that led to the Revolutionary War (1775-1783). Since 1791, the 1st Amendment to the United States Constitution has protected freedom of speech from interference by the federal government. Since 1925, the Supreme Court of the United States has protected free speech against interference by state or local governments. The court has done this by using the *due process* clause of the 14th Amendment (see **Due process of law**).

The government restricts some speech considered dangerous or immoral. The first major federal law that limited speech was the Sedition Act of 1798 (see **Alien and Sedition Acts**). It provided punishment for speaking or writing against the government. The law expired in 1801 and was not renewed.

In the late 1800's, Congress passed several laws against obscenity. But during the 1900's, court decisions generally have eased such restrictions. For example, judges lifted the bans on such famous books as *Ulysses* by James Joyce, in 1933, and *Lady Chatterley's Lover* by D. H. Lawrence, in 1960. See **Obscenity and pornography**.

The Espionage Act of 1917 and the Sedition Act of 1918, passed during World War I, forbade speeches and publications that interfered with the war effort. Since 1919, the Supreme Court has suggested that speech presenting "a clear and present danger" to the nation may be restricted. In 1940, Congress passed the Smith Act, which made it a crime to urge the violent overthrow of the United States government.

Most periods of increased restrictions on speech occur when threats to individuals, national security, or social morality seem grave. During such times of stress, the courts have provided little protection for individual freedom. In the early 1950's, for example, fear of Communism was strong in the United States because of the Korean War and the conviction of several Americans as

Soviet spies. In 1951, the Supreme Court upheld the Smith Act in the case of 11 leaders of the Communist Party convicted for advocating the overthrow of the government. Since the mid-1950's, however, the courts have become more concerned about personal rights and have provided greater protection for freedom of speech.

In other countries. The development of freedom of speech in most Western European countries and English-speaking nations has resembled that in the United States. In various other countries, this freedom has grown more slowly or not at all.

Some major powers, including Great Britain and France, have severe restrictions on free expression in the interests of national security. Such smaller countries as Denmark and Switzerland have less concern about security and, consequently, fewer restrictions. Ireland perhaps has stricter controls over freedom of expression than does any other Western nation. These controls are based on the moral teachings of the Roman Catholic Church, to which about 95 per cent of the Irish people belong.

The rulers of some countries have simply ignored or have taken away constitutional guarantees of freedom of speech. For example, the rulers of China, Iran, and South Africa severely limit freedom of speech. These dictators believe they alone hold the truth. Therefore, they say, any opposition must be based on falsehood and regarded as dangerous.

History. Throughout history, people have fought for freedom of speech. During the 400's B.C., the city-state of Athens in ancient Greece gave its citizens considerable freedom of expression. Later, freedom of speech became closely linked with many struggles for political and religious freedom. These struggles took place during the Middle Ages, from about the A.D. 500's to the 1500's. They also played an important part in the Reformation, a religious movement of the 1500's that gave rise to Protestantism.

In the 1600's and 1700's, a period called the Age of Reason, many people began to regard freedom of speech as a natural right. Such philosophers as John Locke of England and Voltaire of France based this idea on their belief in the importance of the individual. Every person, they declared, has a right to speak freely and to have a voice in the government. Thomas Jefferson also expressed this idea when he wrote the Declaration of Independence.

During the 1800's, democratic ideas grew and increasing numbers of people gained freedom of speech. At the same time, however, the growth of cities and industry required more and more people to live and work in large groups. To some people, such as the German philosopher Karl Marx, the interests of society became more important than those of the individual. They thought nations could operate best under an intelligent central authority, rather than with democracy and individual freedom.

In the 1900's, a number of nations have come under such totalitarian forms of government as Communism and fascism. All these nations have abolished or put heavy curbs on freedom of speech.

Technological advances have helped create a centralization of both power and communications in many industrial nations. In such nations, a government can use this power to restrict speech, so that the ordinary person with an idea to express may find it difficult to reach an audience. On the other hand, the same technological advances have produced new methods of communication. These new methods could lead to increased freedom of speech. Jethro K. Lieberman

See also **Censorship; Freedom; Freedom of the press; Public opinion.**

Additional resources

Berger, Melvin. *Censorship.* Watts, 1982. Suitable for younger readers.
Haiman, Franklyn S. *Speech and Law in a Free Society.* Univ. of Chicago Press, 1981.
Hentoff, Nat. *The First Freedom: The Tumultuous History of Free Speech in America.* Delacorte, 1980.
Kalven, Harry. *A Worthy Tradition: Freedom of Speech in America.* Harper, 1988.

Freedom of the press is the right to publish facts, ideas, and opinions without interference from the government or from private groups. This right applies to the printed media, including books and newspapers, and to the electronic media, including radio and television.

Freedom of the press has been disputed since modern printing began in the 1400's, because words have great power to influence people. Today, this power is greater than ever because of the many modern methods of communication. A number of governments place limits on the press because they believe the power of words would be used to oppose them. Many governments have taken control of the press to use it in their own interests. Most publishers and writers, on the other hand, fight for as much freedom as possible.

Democratic constitutions grant freedom of the press to encourage the exchange of ideas and to check the power of the government. Citizens of democracies need information to help them decide whether to support the policies of their national and local governments. In a democracy, freedom of the press applies not only to political and social issues but also to business, cultural, religious, and scientific matters.

Most democratic governments limit freedom of the press in three major types of cases. In such cases, these governments believe that press freedom could endanger individuals, national security, or social morality. (1) Laws against *libel* and *invasion of privacy* protect people from writings that could threaten their reputation or privacy (see **Libel**). (2) Laws against *sedition* (urging revolution) and treason work to prevent publication of material that could harm a nation's security. (3) Laws against *obscenity* (offensive language) aim at the protection of the morals of the people.

Dictatorships do not allow freedom of the press. Dictators believe they alone hold the truth—and that opposition to them endangers the nation.

In the United States, freedom of the press is guaranteed by the First Amendment to the Constitution. All state constitutions also include protection for press freedom. Court decisions help make clear both the extent and the limits of this freedom. In general, the First Amendment prohibits censorship by the government before publication.

The U.S. press regulates itself to a great extent. For example, most publishers do not print material that they know is false or that could lead to crime, riot, or revolution. They also avoid publishing libelous material, obscenities, and other matter that might offend a large number of readers. In addition, because the press in the United States depends heavily on advertising income, it sometimes does not publish material that would displease its advertisers.

Freedom of the press was one goal of the American Colonies in their struggle for independence from Great Britain. The libel trial of John Peter Zenger in 1735 became a major step in the fight for this freedom. Zenger was the publisher of the *New-York Weekly Journal,* which criticized the British government. A jury found Zenger innocent after his attorney argued that Zenger had printed the truth and that truth is not libelous. See **Zenger, John Peter.**

The severest restrictions on the press in the United States—and in all other countries—are imposed during times of stress, especially wartime. During World War II (1939-1945), for example, Congress passed laws banning the publication of any material that could interfere with the war effort or harm national security.

During the late 1960's and early 1970's, criticism by the U.S. press of the nation's involvement in Vietnam became increasingly widespread. This criticism helped broaden public opposition to the Vietnam War and probably influenced the government's change in policy toward the war. In 1971, the government tried to stop *The New York Times* and *The Washington Post* from publishing parts of a secret study of the Vietnam War. The government claimed that publication of the so-called *Pentagon Papers* could harm national security. But the Supreme Court blocked the government's action.

Also in the 1960's and 1970's, many judges issued rulings frequently referred to as *gag orders.* The orders forbade the press to publish information that judges thought might violate a defendant's right to a fair trial. Such information might include confessions made by defendants or facts about their past. The press argued that gag orders violated the First Amendment. In 1976, the Nebraska Press Association challenged a Nebraska gag order before the Supreme Court. The court ruled that such orders are unconstitutional, except in extraordinary circumstances.

In other countries. Freedom of the press exists largely in the Western European countries, the English-speaking nations, and Japan. It is present to a limited extent in some Latin-American countries.

Press restrictions vary greatly from country to country. In Great Britain, for example, the press restricts itself on what it prints about certain aspects of the private lives of members of the royal family. In Italy, the press restricts itself on what it prints about the pope. Such nations as Australia and Ireland have strict obscenity laws. But the obscenity laws in such countries as Norway and Sweden are not strict. Denmark dropped all its obscenity laws during the 1960's. In South Africa, which has strict racial separation policies, the press is generally free. But the government there restricts press discussion of racial conflict.

The governments of many countries have strict overall controls on the press. A number of nations in Asia, Latin America, and the Middle East have censorship boards that check all publications. The censors make sure newspapers and other publications follow government guidelines and agree with official policy. The governments of China, Romania, and certain other Communist nations own and operate the press themselves. The Communist Party in each of these countries makes sure that the press follows party policies. The governments use the press largely to spread propaganda.

History. Rulers and church leaders restricted the writing and distribution of certain material even before there was a press. In those days, when everything was written by hand, books considered offensive were banned or burned. Since the A.D. 400's, the Roman Catholic Church has restricted material that it considers contrary to church teachings.

Early printers had to obtain a license from the government or from some religious group for any material they wanted to publish. In 1644, the English poet and political writer John Milton criticized such licensing in his pamphlet *Areopagitica.* This essay was one of the earliest arguments for freedom of the press. In time, Great Britain and other nations ended the licensing system. By the 1800's, the press of many countries had considerable freedom.

Freedom of the press led to some abuses. In the late 1800's, for example, some U.S. newspapers published false and sensational material to attract readers. Some people favored government regulation to stop such abuses by the so-called "yellow press." But in most cases, such regulation would have been unconstitutional.

During the 1900's, the U.S. press has grown to accept its responsibility to the public. Journalists and other media professionals have become far more careful and conscientious in checking facts and reporting the news. In many other countries, however, the press has lost its freedom. For example, the Fascists in Italy and the Nazis in Germany destroyed press freedom before and during World War II and used the press for their own purposes. Civilian or military dictatorships have ruled many countries in the years since World War II ended in 1945. All these governments have censored the press heavily.

Jethro K. Lieberman

See also **Freedom; Freedom of speech; Journalism** (Restrictions on freedom of the press); **Censorship.**

Additional resources

Adams, Julian. *Freedom and Ethics in the Press.* Rosen, 1983. Suitable for younger readers.

Friendly, Fred W. *Minnesota Rag: The Dramatic Story of the Landmark Supreme Court Case That Gave New Meaning to Freedom of the Press.* Random House, 1981.

Georgetown Law Journal. *Media and the First Amendment in a Free Society.* Univ. of Massachusetts Press, 1973.

Zerman, Melvyn B. *Taking on the Press: Constitutional Rights in Conflict.* Crowell, 1986.

Freedom rider. See Black Americans (The growing movement); **Kennedy, John F.** (Civil rights).

Freehold. See Estate.

Freeholder. See Colonial life in America (Land ownership).

Freeman, Douglas Southall (1886-1953), a United States historian and editor, became a leading authority on the history of the Confederacy. He won a Pulitzer Prize in 1935 for *R. E. Lee,* a biography he worked on for 19 years. He also shared a Pulitzer Prize with John A. Carroll and Mary W. Ashworth for *George Washington.* Many historians consider this work the most authoritative Washington biography. Freeman also wrote *Lee's Lieutenants,* which was published in three volumes; *The South to Posterity;* and *Virginia—A Gentle Dominion.* He wrote vividly about military history and problems.

Freeman served as editor of the *Richmond* (Va.) *News Leader* from 1915 to 1949. He also worked as a radio commentator from 1925 until his death. He was born in Lynchburg, Va., the son of a Confederate veteran. He graduated from Richmond College and received a Ph.D. from Johns Hopkins University.   Merle Curti

Freeman, Mary Eleanor Wilkins (1852-1930), was an American author. She became known for her short stories, which accurately and sensitively describe New England village life during the late 1800's. Freeman's works reflect her Puritan religious background and often deal with matters of conscience. Her stories also vividly portray the economic hardships of rural New England life. The central character in several stories is an older woman in conflict with her family, village society, or a suitor.

Freeman's best stories were published in the two collections *A Humble Romance* (1887) and *A New England Nun* (1891). In addition to short stories, Freeman wrote children's stories, a play, poems, and 12 novels. She was born in Randolph, Mass.   Bert Hitchcock

Freeman, Orville Lothrop (1918-   ), served as secretary of agriculture from 1961 to 1969, under Presidents John F. Kennedy and Lyndon B. Johnson. He was governor of Minnesota from 1955 to 1961.

Freeman graduated from the University of Minnesota in 1940. During World War II, he served with the U.S. Marine Corps. Freeman was wounded in action and received the Purple Heart. After the war, he earned his law degree and was a member of a Minneapolis law firm from 1947 to 1955. Freeman was chairman of the Minnesota Democratic-Farmer-Labor Party from 1948 to 1950. He was born in Minneapolis.   Eric Sevareid

Freeman-Thomas, Freeman. See **Willingdon, Marquess of.**

Freeman's Farm, Battles of. See **Revolutionary War in America** (Victory at Saratoga; table: Major battles).

Freemasonry. See **Masonry.**

Freeport Doctrine. See **Lincoln, Abraham** (The debates with Douglas).

Freer Gallery of Art, in Washington, D.C., is a government museum famous for its collections of Asian art. These include paintings, sculpture, bronzes, ceramics, glass, jade, lacquer, and metalwork from the Near and Far East. The gallery has important Biblical manuscripts in Greek, Aramaic, and Armenian. It also has many works by James Whistler and other American painters of the late 1800's.

The library at the Freer Gallery of Art contains 40,000 volumes. The museum staff carries on research in the arts and cultures represented in the collections. The Smithsonian Institution administers the building and endowment fund. Charles Lang Freer, a Detroit industrialist, gave his collections and an endowment to the Smithsonian by deed of gift executed in 1906.

Critically reviewed by the Smithsonian Institution

Freesia, *FREE zhuh,* is a fragrant, attractive plant belonging to the iris family. It is a native of South Africa, but gardeners throughout the world cultivate it in greenhouses. It has a *corm* (bulblike stem) and long, narrow leaves shaped like swords. Most freesias have white or yellow flowers, but many colors are possible. The flowers grow in clusters that look like spikes. Many

WORLD BOOK illustration by Christabel King

The freesia has lovely, fragrant flowers. Gardeners grow freesias in greenhouses because these plants bloom in winter.

people plant the freesia because the flowers bloom in winter. They plant the corm indoors about mid-August. It grows better in a cool greenhouse where the night temperature is not above 50° F. (10° C). When the flowers appear, the plant should be watered freely.

Scientific classification. The freesia belongs to the iris family, Iridaceae. It is *Freesia refracta.*   Alfred C. Hottes

Freestone. See **Limestone.**

Freethinker is a person who refuses to accept the authority of a church or the Bible. A freethinker insists on the freedom to form religious opinions on the basis of his or her own reasoning powers.

The name *freethinker* dates back to the 1700's. The English philosopher Anthony Collins used the term in his *Discourse of Freethinking* (1713). Collins and his friend John Toland argued against the authority of the Christian Church. Later, Lord Bolingbroke and David Hume were among the leading English Freethinkers. In France, Voltaire was the leader of a group of people who argued for "natural" religion, as against revealed religion. Freethinking became fashionable in Germany during the reign of Frederick the Great. At the present time, few freethinkers belong to organized groups. Modern freedom of religion has made such organized bodies unnecessary.   David E. Klemm

Freetown (pop. 469,776) is the seaport capital of Sierra Leone. It stands on the estuary of the Sierra Leone River, and has an excellent harbor. The city has a tropical climate. Temperatures average 80° F. (27° C), and rainfall totals about 150 inches (381 centimeters) a year. For the location of the city, see **Sierra Leone** (map).

Industries in Freetown include fish processing and soap factories and ship repair yards. Exports include chromite, diamonds, ginger, gold, kola nuts, palm oil and kernels, and platinum. British philanthropists founded the city in 1787 as a home for freed slaves.

James W. Fernandez

Freeway. See **Road** (Primary highways).

Freeze-drying, also called *lyophilization, ly AHF uh luh ZAY shuhn,* is a process that removes water from a substance to preserve the substance for future use. Drug companies use freeze-drying in preparing many medicines. Biologists use it in preparing animal specimens for display, or parts of organisms for microscopic study. The process is used to preserve some foods and beverages and to restore valuable papers damaged by water.

Freeze-drying differs from other drying methods because the substance is frozen before being dried. The item is then placed in a refrigerated vacuum chamber. There, any water in the product changes from ice to water vapor. Unlike other drying processes, freeze-drying does not shrink the substance or lessen its ability to dissolve in a liquid. For this reason, freeze-drying is useful for certain drugs and for coffee and tea, all of which must dissolve rapidly. The low temperature at which the process takes place allows serums and other drug solutions to retain their original characteristics.

Hikers and military personnel often carry freeze-dried foods because these products are light and compact. However, freeze-drying is not widely used for the preservation of food because the difficulties of freeze-drying animal and plant cells make it uneconomical.

Harold T. Meryman

See also **Coffee** (Instant coffee); **Dehydrated food; Food preservation** (Freeze-drying).

Freezing point is the temperature at which a substance changes from a liquid to a solid. The freezing points of different substances vary greatly. Mercury, for example, freezes at −38.87° C. However, gold has a freezing point of 1063° C.

The freezing point of a pure substance is identical to its *melting point* (see **Melting point**). For example, water freezes at 0° C, and its solid form, ice, melts at the same temperature. After a pure substance reaches its freezing point, the liquid and solid forms of the substance exist in *equilibrium* (a state of balance) with each other. Unless heat is added or removed, they will remain in that state indefinitely because for each amount of liquid that freezes, an equal amount of solid melts. The heat that must be added to melt a given substance, or be removed to freeze it, is called the *heat of fusion.*

The composition of a substance affects its freezing point. Pure substances, such as a pure element or a simple compound, freeze at one specific temperature. In contrast, mixtures, which consist of several chemically uncombined substances, freeze over a range of temperatures. Bronze, an alloy of copper and tin, solidifies as the temperature falls from 1000° to 800° C.

The freezing point of most liquids can be lowered by adding another substance. This fact is the basis for using antifreeze in automobile radiators during the winter. Antifreeze contains ethylene glycol, which has a freezing point of −13° C. A mixture of equal parts of ethylene glycol and of water freezes at about −37° C.

A significant increase in pressure can affect the freezing point. The application of pressure raises the freezing point of gold, mercury, and other substances that con-

tract upon freezing. As these substances solidify, their volume decreases. Pressure promotes this decrease, and so the substances freeze at a temperature above their normal freezing point.

An increase in pressure lowers the freezing point of a few substances, such as antimony, bismuth, and water. These substances increase in volume and expand as they begin to freeze. Added pressure prevents this volume change and expansion from occurring at the normal freezing point. As a result, the substances can freeze only at a lower temperature.   S. E. Babb, Jr.

See also **Ice.**

Freight is manufactured goods or raw materials transported from one place to another. In the United States, railroads carry the greatest amount of freight. Truck freight is second in importance and continues to increase because of improved road networks and vehicles. Truck trailers are sometimes loaded onto flat railroad cars or on barges in order to eliminate the need for loading, unloading, and reloading goods. Shipping by water provides the least expensive way to send freight. Shipping freight by air has increased. However, it is still relatively unimportant in moving freight because the cost remains high. Pipelines are used to move such products as natural gas and crude oil in an economical manner.

The Interstate Commerce Commission sets rates for all interstate carriers except airplanes. A state commerce commission sets rates for freight carried within the state.   Jay Diamond

Related articles in *World Book* include:

Barge	Railroad (What makes up a
Bill of lading	railroad)
Containerization	Ship
Interstate commerce	Transportation
Pipeline	Truck

Freighter. See **Ship** (Classification of cargo ships; General cargo ships).

Fréjus Tunnels, *fray ZHOOS,* are two tunnels—one a railroad tunnel and the other a motor-traffic tunnel—that connect the Italian province of Turin with the French province of Savoy. The tunnels run through Fréjus Peak in the Alps. The railroad tunnel, which was built between 1857 and 1871, was the first tunnel to be cut through the Alps. The power drill and air compressor were used for the first time in building this tunnel. The railroad tunnel is 8.5 miles (13.7 kilometers) long. It was formerly called Mont Cenis Tunnel, after the name of the railroad for which it was built. The motor-traffic tunnel was completed in 1980 and is 8.1 miles (13 kilometers) long.   Edward W. Fox

Fremantle, Charles. See **Australia** (Exploring the new land).

Frémont, *FREE mahnt,* **John Charles** (1813-1890), sometimes called "The Pathfinder," explored much of the area between the Rocky Mountains and the Pacific Ocean. In 1856, he was the first Republican candidate for President of the United States, but he lost to James Buchanan, a Democrat. He served in the Army and Navy, and as a United States senator.

As a second lieutenant in the Army Topographical Corps, Frémont worked as a surveyor in the Carolina mountains. He made his first important independent survey to the Wind River chain of the Rockies in 1842.

During this trip, he met the frontiersman Kit Carson, who became the guide for his expeditions. Frémont's *Report of the Exploring Expedition to the Rocky Mountains* described this trip, and established his reputation.

Frémont explored part of the Oregon region in 1843. He visited Fort Vancouver, and then moved to the Carson River in Nevada early in 1844. From there he went to California, which was then a Mexican province. After exploring the Southwest, he returned to St. Louis, Mo., in August 1844. Frémont helped produce the first scientific map of the American West.

The third expedition, in 1845, was organized with the Mexican War (1846-1848) in prospect. Frémont aroused the suspicions of the Mexican authorities in California, and they ordered him to leave. However, by the summer of 1846 he was inspiring discontented Americans in the Sacramento Valley to organize the Bear Flag Revolt (see **California** [Mexico surrenders]).

Commodore Robert Stockton of the Navy and General Stephen W. Kearny of the Army became involved in a dispute over conflicting orders, and Frémont sided with Stockton. When Kearny won, he had Frémont court-martialed for insubordination (see **Kearny, Stephen W.**). The Army dismissed Frémont from the service. President James K. Polk overruled the dismissal, but Frémont then resigned from the Army. He made a fourth expedition in 1848, searching unsuccessfully for a possible route for a transcontinental railroad. He then settled in California and served as a U.S. senator from September 1850 until March 1851. In a fifth expedition in 1853, he again failed to find a railroad route.

In June 1856, Frémont became the presidential candidate of the newly formed Republican Party. He had been asked to be the Democratic presidential candidate, but declined because that party supported slavery. One Republican slogan was "Free Speech, Free Press, Free Soil, Free Men, Frémont, and Victory!" During the campaign, Democrats argued that Frémont's election would cause the Southern States to separate from the Union and possibly lead to civil war. Frémont carried 11 states in the election of 1856. Buchanan, his Democratic rival, carried 19 and won the election.

Early in the Civil War (1861-1865), President Abraham Lincoln gave Frémont command of the Union Army's Western Department. But Frémont issued a proclamation taking over the property of rebelling Missouri slaveowners, and freeing their slaves. His act aroused the public and angered Lincoln, who transferred him to western Virginia. Later, he served from 1878 to 1883 as territorial governor of Arizona.

Frémont was born in Savannah, Ga., and studied at Charleston (S.C.) College. In 1841, he married Jessie Benton, the daughter of the powerful Missouri senator Thomas Hart Benton. Mrs. Frémont, who had helped her husband write stirring accounts about his Rocky Mountain expeditions, became a regular

Engraving by J. C. Fry; Chicago Historical Society
John Charles Frémont

magazine writer after her husband lost his wealth in the 1870's. She also wrote several books describing her own experiences.   William H. Goetzmann

See also **Lincoln, Abraham** (Election of 1864).

French, language. See **French language.**

French, Daniel Chester (1850-1931), was one of the most famous American sculptors of his time. His best-known works include the large statue of Abraham Lincoln (1922) in the Lincoln Memorial in Washington, D.C., and *The Minute Man* (1875), a Revolutionary War memorial in Concord, Mass. Another important work is *Death Staying the Hand of the Sculptor* (1892), which is part of a large memorial in Boston. French also completed many portraits and sculptures for government buildings. He was born in Exeter, N.H., and studied in the United States and Italy.   Bess L. Hormats

See also **Lincoln Memorial.**

French, John Denton Pinkstone (1852-1925), Earl of Ypres, commanded the first units of British soldiers sent to France in World War I. French returned to Great Britain in December 1915 to lead the home forces. He served as chief of Great Britain's General Staff from 1912 to 1914. After World War I, he was lord lieutenant, or British governor, of Ireland from 1918 to 1921. French became a navy midshipman when he was 14 years old, but joined the army four years later.   Alfred F. Havighurst

French Academy is a French organization of intellectuals. It is called *L'Académie Française* in French. Its activities include awarding literary prizes and publishing a dictionary of the French language.

The academy has 40 members, known as the *Forty Immortals.* Once elected, they are members for life. Most are writers, but others have been scientists, sociologists, philosophers, and doctors. In general, a seat in the academy becomes vacant only when a member dies. Individuals who wish to be considered for membership contact academy members to declare their candidacy. The members vote on which person to accept. Until 1894, all members were French-born male citizens of France. Since then, the academy has included men and women of other nationalities who write in French.

Cardinal Richelieu, a French statesman, founded the French Academy in 1635. It was suppressed in 1793, during the French Revolution. Napoleon I reorganized the academy in 1803 as part of the Institute of France, a group of learned societies that are supported by the government.   Catharine Savage Brosman

See also **Institute of France.**

French and Indian wars were four wars fought one after another in North America between 1689 and 1763. The wars were fought mainly between France and England, which became part of Great Britain during the second war. In each of the four wars, both sides fought with the support of Indian allies. The French and Indian wars resulted in Britain's gaining almost all of France's territory in North America.

Causes of the French and Indian wars. In 1689, England's colonies in North America were located along the Atlantic coast. French settlements lay north of the English colonies, along the shores of the St. Lawrence River and the Great Lakes. France also had outposts to the south, in the Mississippi River Valley. England claimed all the territory that stretched inland from its own colonies. The French also claimed much of this land. Until about 1750, however, various Indian tribes actually controlled the inland territory. Both the English and the French traded with the Indians for furs.

At first, the French and English struggled with each other for control of the fur trade. Later, they also fought for the land between the Appalachian Mountains and the Mississippi River. In addition, they disputed each other's claims to fishing grounds off the coast of Newfoundland. Religious hostility added to the tension. Almost all the French were Roman Catholics, and most of the English were Protestants.

King William's War (1689-1697) was named for King William III of England. It grew out of the struggle in Europe called the War of the League of Augsburg (see **Grand Alliance**). The war began when Indians allied to the English raided French settlements near Montreal. The French and their Indian allies struck back against New York and the New England colonies, attacking Schenectady, N.Y., and Salmon Falls, N.H., in 1690. The English responded in the same year by seizing Port Royal, the seat of the government of the French territory of Acadia (see **Acadia** [map]). They also launched two unsuccessful assaults on the province of Quebec, one each in 1690 and 1691. The war ended in 1697 with the signing of the Treaty of Ryswick. This treaty gave back to England and France all the American land they had lost during the war.

Queen Anne's War (1702-1713), named for Queen Anne of Great Britain, grew out of the conflict in Europe known as the War of the Spanish Succession (see **Succession wars**). Spain also took part in Queen Anne's War, which centered in New England, South Carolina, and Florida. The war began when the French and their Indian allies raided English frontier settlements in New England. One of these settlements, Deerfield, Mass., was destroyed by the Indians and French in 1704. The English attacked Acadia later that year and again in 1707. Also in 1707, England became part of Great Britain (see **Great Britain** [History]). In 1710, Britain captured Port Royal. In the South, the British briefly took control of the town of St. Augustine in the Spanish territory of Florida.

Spanish and French forces attacked Charleston, S.C., but failed to capture the city.

Queen Anne's War ended in 1713 with the signing of the Treaty of Utrecht. By the terms of the treaty, France gave Great Britain Newfoundland, the Nova Scotia region of Acadia, and the French territory around Hudson Bay. The treaty did not clearly define the boundaries of the land won by Britain, and thus led to more fighting.

King George's War (1744-1748), named for King George II of Britain, grew out of the struggle in Europe known as the War of the Austrian Succession (see **Succession wars**). The fighting in North America began when the French tried unsuccessfully to regain Nova Scotia. The greatest battle of the war occurred in 1745, when New England colonial troops under William Pepperrell captured the French fortress of Louisbourg on Cape Breton Island. The Treaty of Aix-la-Chapelle, which ended the war, gave back to Britain and France the territory each side had lost in the war.

The French and Indian War (1754-1763) was the last and most important conflict in North America before the Revolutionary War in America (1775-1783). The French and Indian War broke out in America, and then spread to Europe in 1756. It was called the Seven Years' War in Europe and Canada (see **Seven Years' War**).

After King George's War, territorial rivalries between Britain and France had become stronger as the two countries' settlements expanded. In addition, the Iroquois Indians had begun to permit some British settlement in the Ohio River Valley. Formerly, the Iroquois had barred both French and British settlers from the region. The French, who feared the loss of the Ohio country's fur trade, responded by trying to strengthen their own claim to the area. In 1753, they built a chain of forts along the Allegheny River in Pennsylvania, at the eastern end of the Ohio River Valley.

The British colony of Virginia also claimed the land along the Allegheny. Virginia's lieutenant governor, Robert Dinwiddie, sent 21-year-old Major George Washington to demand that the French abandon their new forts and return to Canada. The French refused to

English engraving by Laurie and Whittle (Granger Collection)

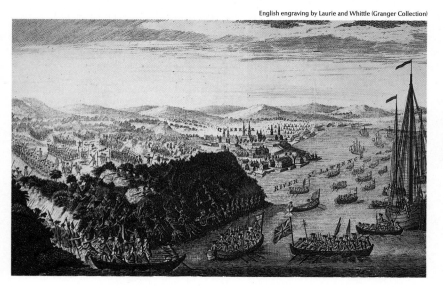

The Battle of Quebec in 1759 ended in victory for Great Britain. This engraving shows British troops led by General James Wolfe storming the Plains of Abraham, above the city.

The French and Indian War

The French and Indian War led to the end of France's colonial empire in North America. The war also established British dominance over most of the French possessions there. The map at the right shows where the major battles of the war took place.

	British possession
	French possession
——	Colonial boundary
✳	Major battle
▪	Fort
・	City

0   200 Miles
0   200 Kilometers

WORLD BOOK map

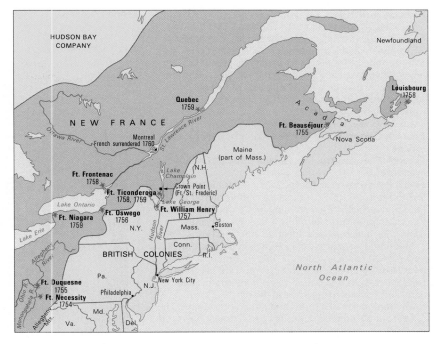

leave. In 1754, Washington led a small band of colonial troops to the disputed territory to force the French to withdraw. The French defeated Washington at Fort Necessity, in the first battle of the French and Indian War. Meanwhile, representatives of seven of the British colonies met in Albany, N.Y., to plan further military action (see **Albany Congress**).

French successes. In 1755, General Edward Braddock led a band of British and colonial soldiers, including George Washington, against Fort Duquesne (now Pittsburgh). Braddock was unfamiliar with North American methods of warfare, which often involved ambush. He also had few Indians to act as scouts. As a result, when Braddock's troops encountered a French and Indian force near Fort Duquesne, Braddock and many of his men were killed. Washington led the survivors to safety.

The British also failed to take Crown Point and Fort Niagara. However, they succeeded in seizing Forts Beauséjour and Gaspereau in what is now New Brunswick.

In 1756, the Marquis de Montcalm took charge of the French forces in North America and captured Britain's Fort Oswego. The next year, the French and their Indian allies destroyed Fort William Henry.

British victories. In 1756, William Pitt became the political leader of Great Britain. His leadership, and that of the vigorous young officers he sent to North America, gave new life to the British cause. In 1758, British forces captured Louisbourg and Forts Frontenac and Duquesne. In 1759, the British took Crown Point and Forts Niagara and Ticonderoga. Meanwhile, General James Wolfe began attacking French forces near the city of Quebec, which was held by troops under General Montcalm. After nearly three months of occasional fighting, Wolfe's army defeated the French on the Plains of Abraham, outside the city (see **Quebec, Battle of**). The

fall of Quebec crippled the French war effort, but the struggle continued until British troops under General Jeffery Amherst captured Montreal in 1760.

The war ended in 1763 with the signing of the Treaty of Paris. The treaty gave Britain almost all French land in Canada and, to the south, all of France's holdings east of the Mississippi River except New Orleans. Great Britain also received the territory of Florida from Spain, which had become France's ally in 1762. In return, Spain was given New Orleans and all French lands west of the Mississippi. France kept two tiny islands south of Newfoundland—St.-Pierre and Miquelon—and the Caribbean islands of Martinique and Guadeloupe.

Fred W. Anderson

Related articles in *World Book* include:

Acadia	Montcalm, Marquis de
Amherst, Lord Jeffery	Pontiac
Braddock, Edward	Rogers' Rangers
Coureurs de bois	Washington, George (Messenger
Fort Duquesne	to the French)
Fort Niagara	Wolfe, James
Franklin, Benjamin (The Plan of Union)	

Reading and Study Guide

See also *French and Indian wars* in the Research Guide/Index, Volume 22, for a *Reading and Study Guide.*

Additional resources

Donaldson, Gordon. *Battle for a Continent: Quebec, 1759.* Doubleday (Toronto), 1973.
Kopperman, Paul E. *Braddock at the Monongahela.* Univ. of Pittsburgh Press, 1976. The campaign of 1755.
Lawson, Don. *The Colonial Wars: Prelude to the American Revolution.* Abelard-Schuman, 1972. For younger readers.
Leach, Douglas E. *Arms for Empire: A Military History of the British Colonies in North America, 1607-1763.* Macmillan, 1973.
Peckham, Howard H. *The Colonial Wars, 1689-1762.* Univ. of Chicago Press, 1964. A standard work.

French bulldog is a strong, heavy little dog. It weighs from 18 to 28 pounds (8 to 13 kilograms). This bulldog has a more pleasant face than the English one. It has a large, square head, rounded ears, and a short nose. Its chunky body is broader in front than in back. It has soft, loose skin that usually is wrinkled on its face and shoulders. Its coat may be white, yellowish, or brownish, often with darker-colored patches. See also **Dog** (picture: Nonsporting dogs).

Critically reviewed by the French Bulldog Club of America

French Canada. See Quebec; Canada; Canada, History of.

French Canadians. See Canada (People); Canadian literature.

French Equatorial Africa was a federation of four territories in central Africa that was administered by France. It included what are now four independent nations: Central African Republic, Chad, Congo, and Gabon. Each nation has a separate article in *World Book.*

The region formerly called French Equatorial Africa covers 969,114 square miles (2,509,994 square kilometers). Nearly all the people in the region are black Africans. Bantu-speaking peoples live in the south. Fulah, Sara, and Toubou groups live in the north.

The region has vast forest and mineral resources. The richest known mineral deposits lie in Gabon. Chief products include cotton, rice, meat, peanuts, cacao, coffee, timber, manganese, and oil.

The first French colonists arrived in Equatorial Africa in 1839, and settled on the Gabon River. In 1849, they founded Libreville as the capital of the colony. The capital was later moved to Brazzaville. The four territories of French Equatorial Africa were offered the chance to become independent republics in November 1958. All chose to become self-governing states. They became independent nations in August 1960.   James W. Fernandez

French Foreign Legion. See Foreign Legion.

French Guiana, *gee AH nuh* or *gee AN uh,* is an overseas *department* (administrative district) of France on the northeastern coast of South America. It covers about 35,135 square miles (91,000 square kilometers) and has a population of about 73,000. Cayenne is the capital and largest city.

Almost all the people of French Guiana are blacks or *Creoles* (people of mixed black and white ancestry). Most of the people live along the coast. The interior of French Guiana is largely wilderness. The interior has important mineral and forest resources, but they have not been developed. French Guiana depends heavily on France for financial support.

Historically, French Guiana has been known for its penal colonies. For about 150 years, France sent convicts to French Guiana. Political prisoners were kept on Devils Island, an offshore isle. Other convicts were kept in prison camps at Kourou and Saint-Laurent. The prison camps were widely known for their cruelty. The French finally closed them in 1945 and sent the prisoners back to France. In the 1960's, France turned the camp at Kourou into a space research center.

Anthony P. Maingot, the contributor of this article, is Associate Professor of Sociology at Florida International University.

French Guiana

⊛ **Capital**

• Other City or Town

—— **Road**

▲ Highest Known Elevation

〜 *River*

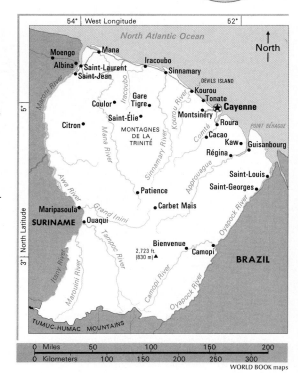

WORLD BOOK maps

Government. French Guiana was made an overseas department of France in 1946. Its government is like that of France's mainland departments. French Guiana is administered by an elected general council made up of 16 members. The members of the general council elect the president of the department. French Guiana has one representative in each house of the French Parliament. The court system in French Guiana is much like the court system of France (see **France** [Courts]).

People. About 90 per cent of the people of French Guiana are blacks or Creoles. Most are descendants of slaves who were brought to French Guiana during the 1600's and 1700's. Many are Haitians who moved to French Guiana in the 1980's. The rest of the people are American Indians, Chinese, Europeans, Indochinese, Lebanese, and Syrians. The Indians were the first people to live in French Guiana. Today, they live in the interior. Most of the rest of the people live along the coast.

Most French Guianans speak French, the department's official language. Many Creoles also speak a dialect that is a mixture of French and English. Most of the people are Roman Catholics.

Children are required by law to attend school. French

Guiana has both public and private elementary schools, a high school, and two vocational schools. About 75 per cent of the people can read and write.

After French Guiana became an overseas department of France in 1946, the French government built hospitals and clinics there. The French government has also waged campaigns to wipe out leprosy, malaria, and tuberculosis in the department.

The land and climate. French Guiana has three land regions—a coastal plain in the north, a hilly plateau in the center, and the Tumuc-Humac Mountains in the south. Rain forests cover most of the country. More than 20 rivers flow north through French Guiana to the Atlantic Ocean. The most important rivers are the Maroni and the Oyapock. The Maroni forms part of the border between French Guiana and Suriname. The Oyapock flows along French Guiana's border with Brazil.

French Guiana has a tropical climate. Temperatures average about 80° F. (27° C) throughout the year. About 130 inches (330 centimeters) of rain falls annually, most of it from December to June.

Economy. French Guiana's economy is not well developed. The department depends on France for money to operate its government, to help support its industries, and to pay for health care and other services. Most of the workers are employed by the government.

French Guiana's chief industries include gold mining and the processing of agricultural and forest products. A shrimp industry is being developed. The leading farm products include bananas, cattle, corn, pineapples, rice, sugar cane, and yams. The farmers do not raise enough food to feed the people, and so much food must be imported.

The interior of French Guiana has rich, well-watered soil; valuable timberland; and large deposits of bauxite, an ore used in making aluminum. But these resources have not been developed.

History. The French were the first Europeans to settle in what is now French Guiana. They came in the early

Sebastiao Salgado, Magnum

Cayenne, the capital of French Guiana, lies on an island at the mouth of the Cayenne River. About half the French Guianan people live in the city.

1600's, when many European nations were building colonial empires in the Americas. French Guiana became a French colony in 1667. Since then, the region has been under French control, except for a short period in the early 1800's when it was ruled by British and Portuguese military forces.

France began to send political prisoners to French Guiana during the French Revolution in the 1790's. In 1854, a formal prison system was established in the colony. About 70,000 people were held in the prisons from 1852 to 1945, when France closed them.

French Guiana became an overseas department of

Victor Englebert

Devils Island, a small isle off the French Guianan coast, was for many years a brutal prison camp for political prisoners of France. The camp was closed in 1945.

France in 1946. Since then, French Guiana has worked, with the help of France, to develop its economy and improve the life of its people. In the 1980's, a strong movement for independence from France developed in French Guiana. But most of the people want French Guiana to remain an overseas department of France.

Anthony P. Maingot

See also **Cayenne; Penal colony.**

French Guinea. See Guinea (country); French West Africa.

French horn is a brass musical instrument. It consists largely of a metal tube about 12 feet (3.7 meters) long. The tube is coiled into a circular shape and ends in a

The French horn is a metal tube coiled into a circular shape. The instrument ends in a flared bell. A musician uses one hand to press the key levers in various combinations to produce notes. The other hand is placed inside the bell to control the horn's tone.

Northwestern University (WORLD BOOK photo by Ted Nielsen)

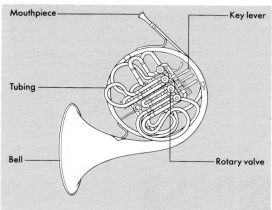

Mouthpiece — Key lever

Tubing

Bell — Rotary valve

WORLD BOOK illustration by Zorica Dabich

large flared bell. The musician produces tones by vibrating the lips in a funnel-shaped mouthpiece. The instrument has three or more valves. The musician fingers the valves with the left hand and places the right hand in the bell for special effects. The player changes notes by moving the valves and changing lip tension. The hand in the bell creates additional pitches and varies the tone qualities. The French horn produces a warm sound that blends well with other instruments.

The French horn is descended from the hunting horn, a coiled valveless instrument sometimes worn around the player's neck. The French composer Jean Baptiste Lully is credited with introducing the French horn into the orchestra about 1664.   John Keil Richards

See also **Mellophone.**

French language is the official language of France, its overseas territories, and associated states. It is also an official language of Belgium, Canada, Haiti, Luxembourg, Switzerland, and the United Nations. More people speak such languages as Chinese, English, Russian, or Spanish than speak French. However, French is so widely spoken that it ranks with English as an international language. More than 90 million people speak French as their mother tongue, and millions of others use it as a second language.

French is a beautiful and harmonious language. It has served for hundreds of years as the language of diplomats. Its clear style and regular *syntax* (arrangement of words) make it especially suitable for diplomatic, legal, and business use, and for literature.

Many of the words in the English language come from French. English began to absorb French words after the Norman conquest of England in 1066. The king's court and courts of justice used French, but the common people continued to speak English. French words gradually became part of English. For example, the words *mouton, boeuf,* and *porc,* which the nobility used instead of *sheep, ox,* and *swine,* became *mutton, beef,* and *pork* in English. Thousands of French terms have been adopted, in whole or in part, into English. They include *art, dress, faith, prison,* and *theater.*

French grammar

Nouns and adjectives. Few French nouns have *inflections,* which are changes of form (see **Inflection**). All nouns are either masculine or feminine. For example, *the book (le livre)* is masculine, and *the chair (la chaise)* is feminine. In most cases, adjectives are made feminine by adding *e.* For example, the feminine of *petit* (small) is *petite.* Plurals are most commonly formed by adding *s* to the singular. The plural of *le petit livre* is *les petits livres.* The plural of *la petite chaise* is *les petites chaises. Le* and *la* are the masculine and feminine singular forms of the definite article *the. Les* is both the masculine plural form and the feminine plural form.

Verbs. French has 14 tenses, 7 simple and 7 compound (see **Tense**). The *simple* tenses are formed by adding endings to the infinitive or to the stem of the verb. The *compound* tenses are made up of the past participle of the verb and an appropriate form of one of the auxiliary verbs *avoir* (to have) or *être* (to be).

In written French, verbs are classified according to the endings of their infinitives. They fall into three groups: *-er* verbs, such as *donner* (to give); *-ir* verbs, such as *finir* (to finish); and *-re* verbs, such as *vendre* (to sell). French has many irregular verbs.

Word order in French is similar to that of English in many cases. A sentence is made negative by placing *ne* before the verb and *pas* after it. A question is formed by inverting the order of the subject and verb or by placing the phrase *est-ce que* (is it that) before the sentence. The following are the affirmative, negative, and interrogative forms of the sentence *John gives the books to my friends:*

Affirmative: *Jean donne les livres à mes amis.*
Negative: *Jean ne donne pas les livres à mes amis.*
Interrogative: *Jean donne-t-il les livres à mes amis?* or *Est-ce que Jean donne les livres à mes amis?*

In the perfect tense, a past tense, the forms are:
Affirmative: *Jean a donné les livres à mes amis.*
Negative: *Jean n'a pas donné les livres à mes amis.*
Interrogative: *Jean a-t-il donné les livres à mes amis?* or *Est-ce que Jean a donné les livres à mes amis?*

Pronunciation of French is often difficult for English-speaking people. The French do not pronounce final consonants, except for the letters *c, f, l,* and *r.* For example, *lits* (beds) is pronounced *lee,* and *et* (and) is pronounced *ay.* French vowels are sharp, clear, single sounds. A few do not occur in English. For example, there is no exact equivalent for the *u* of *lune* (moon). It is a sound that combines *ee* and *oo* and is made with the lips rounded. Syllables that end in *n* or *m* have a nasal sound. The French *r* is pronounced by vibrating the *uvula,* a piece of flesh that hangs from the back of the roof of the mouth. The French *r* sounds harsher than the English *r.* The French often link words together. For example, *les hommes* (the men) is pronounced *lay ZOHM.*

Development

Beginnings. French is one of the Romance languages, which developed from Latin (see **Romance languages**). When the Roman emperor Julius Caesar conquered Gaul (France) in the 50's B.C., he found the people speaking a language called *Gaulish.* The Gauls gradually adopted the language of the Roman soldiers. This language, called *vernacular* (common) *Latin,* differed from the Latin used by educated people. The Gauls did not learn to speak popular Latin as the soldiers spoke it. They changed the vocabulary on the basis of the way the words sounded. For example, a Gaul hearing the stressed syllables *bon* and *ta* of the word *bonitatem* (kindness) shortened the word to *bonta.* This word has become *bonté* in modern French.

Only about 350 Gaulish words have become part of modern French. The Franks, who invaded Gaul during the A.D. 400's and renamed the country France, contributed about 1,000 words to French. Danish Vikings, who occupied northern France in the 800's, added about 90

words. A number of French words have also come from Greek. As French has developed, its grammar has changed. For example, the language originally had six cases of nouns, as did Latin. French now has two cases. The number of tenses in French has also decreased.

Old French. By the 700's, vernacular Latin had evolved so completely into *la langue romane,* also called Romance, that few could read Latin without a dictionary. The new language first appeared in written form in the Oaths of Strasbourg, a treaty signed by two descendants of the Frankish king Charlemagne in 842.

Beginning in the 900's, Romance developed in France into *Old French,* which had two distinct dialects, each with many minor dialects. The *langue d'oc* flourished in the south, and the *langue d'oïl* prevailed in the north. These terms came from the word for *yes,* which was *oc* in the south and *oïl* in the north. The most famous dialect of the langue d'oc was *Provençal,* the language of the troubadours (see **Troubadour**). A dialect of the langue d'oïl spoken in the area around Paris became the accepted tongue throughout France because of the political influence of the capital.

Modern French. During the Renaissance, a period in European history between about 1300 and 1600, more Greek and Latin words were added to French. In the 1500's, the French people had many contacts with the Spaniards and Italians and adopted a number of Spanish and Italian words.

During the 1600's, writers and scholars began to standardize the structure of French. In 1784, the French author Antoine Rivarol could boast *"Ce qui n'est pas clair n'est pas français"* ("What is not clear is not French"). Today, speakers of French consider it one of the most precise languages.   Fred M. Jenkins

See also **French literature; French Academy.**

French words and phrases

(Pronunciations are approximate)

Numbers

un, *uhn,* one	**trente,** *trawnt,* thirty		
deux, *duh,* two	**quarante,** *kah RAWNT,* forty		
trois, *trwah,* three	**cinquante,** *sang KAWNT,* fifty		
quatre, *KAH truh,* four	**soixante,** *swah SAWNT,* sixty		
cinq, *sangk,* five	**soixante-dix,** *swah sawnt DEES,* seventy		
six, *sees,* six			
sept, *seht,* seven	**quatre-vingts,** *kah truh VANT,* eighty		
huit, *weet,* eight			
neuf, *nuhf,* nine	**quatre-vingt-dix,** *kah truh vant DEES,* ninety		
dix, *dees,* ten			
vingt, *vant,* twenty	**cent,** *sawnt,* one hundred		

Days of the week

lundi, *luhn DEE,* Monday	**vendredi,** *vawn druh DEE,* Friday
mardi, *mahr DEE,* Tuesday	
mercredi, *mair kruh DEE,* Wednesday	**samedi,** *sahm DEE,* Saturday
jeudi, *jhuh DEE,* Thursday	**dimanche,** *dee MAWNSH,* Sunday

Months of the year

janvier, *jhawng VEEAY,* January	**août,** *oo,* August
février, *fay VREEAY,* February	**septembre,** *sehp TAWM bruh,* September
mars, *mahrs,* March	**octobre,** *ohk TOH bruh,* October
avril, *ah VREEL,* April	**novembre,** *noh VAWM bruh,* November
mai, *may,* May	**décembre,** *day SAWM bruh,* December
juin, *jhwan,* June	
juillet, *jhwee YEH,* July	

Common words

après, *ah PREH,* after	**jaune,** *jhohn,* yellow
aujourd'hui, *oh jhoor DWEE,* today	**joli,** *zhoh LEE,* pretty
blanc, *blawnk,* white	**madame,** *mah DAHM,* madam
bleu, *bluh,* blue	**mademoiselle,** *mahd mwah ZEHL,* miss
chose, *shohz,* thing	**maison,** *may ZOHN,* house
court, *koor,* short	**mauvais,** *moh VAY,* bad
dans, *dawn,* in, into	**mère,** *mair,* mother
de, *duh,* of, from	**monsieur,** *muh SYUH,* Mr., sir
enfant, *awn FAWN,* child	**où,** *oo,* where
être, *EH truh,* to be	**père,** *pair,* father
femme, *fahm,* woman	**pour,** *poor,* for
fermer, *fehr MAY,* to close	**rouge,** *roozh,* red
frère, *frair,* brother	**sans,** *sawn,* without
garçon, *gahr SOHN,* boy, waiter	**soeur,** *suhr,* sister
gris, *gree,* gray	**vert,** *vair,* green

Common expressions

au revoir, *oh ruh VWAHR,* good-by
bonjour, *bohn JHOOR,* hello
comment allez-vous? *koh mawnt ah lay VOO,* how are you?
merci beaucoup, *MAIR see boh KOO,* thank you very much
parlez-vous français? *par lay voo frawn SAY,* do you speak French?
quelle heure est-il? *kehl ur eh TEEL,* what time is it?
qu'est-ce que c'est? *kehs kuh SAY,* what is it?
s'il vous plaît, *seel voo PLAY,* please
très bien, *tray BYEHN,* very well

French literature is one of the world's richest and most influential national literatures. French writers have contributed to every major literary form, excelling in epic poetry, lyric poetry, drama, and fiction and other types of prose.

French literature has strongly influenced the work of writers in many countries. During the 1600's, the French cultural movement called *classicism* had a major impact on most other European literatures. French writers of the 1700's dominated the intellectual life of Europe. During the 1800's and early 1900's, French literary movements called *realism* and *symbolism* helped shape the work of many British and American writers.

Most French writers have placed special importance on form, language, style, and tradition. They have followed rules and models more closely than writers in other literatures. In general, *rationalism* has been an essential element in French writing. Rationalism emphasizes reason as the governing principle in human conduct. The impact of rationalism has produced writing that is clear, self-controlled, and artistically well-crafted.

Although rationalism has played a vital part in French literature, a strong experimental quality has also appeared in French writing at various times. This experimental writing is often emotional, passionate, and expressed in unorthodox literary forms.

Early French literature

French literature began in the A.D. 800's during the Middle Ages. Poetry dominated medieval French literature. Much poetry was intended to be sung or recited to largely illiterate audiences by traveling entertainers

called *jongleurs.* Gradually, two main kinds of poetry emerged—*lyric* and *narrative.*

Lyric poetry flourished from the 1100's to the 1400's. It began in southern France, where musician-poets called *troubadours* wrote love songs in the Provençal dialect. Some of this poetry was carried to northern France, where it was imitated by poets called *trouvères.* Both the troubadours and trouvères composed lyric poems that praised women and the ideal of love.

The greatest French lyric poet of the Middle Ages was François Villon. He composed ballades and long poems that dealt with the themes of love, failure, and death. His masterpiece is a 2,000-line autobiographical poem called the *Grand Testament* (1461).

Narrative poetry includes four important types: (1) epic poems, (2) romances, (3) lais and contes, and (4) fabliaux. All were written for aristocratic audiences except fabliaux, which were more for the middle class.

Epic poems were tales of warfare and heroic deeds in battle. They were called *chansons de geste* (epic songs). Trouvères composed the chansons to be chanted to musical accompaniment. The most famous was *The Song of Roland* (about 1100). It describes an incident during a campaign led by the famous ruler Charlemagne.

Romances were long fictional works, often filled with fantastic adventures. There were several kinds. *Romans antiques* (classical romances) were based on ancient subjects, such as the Trojan War between Greece and Troy, probably during the 1200's B.C. *Romans bretons* (Breton romances) told stories about King Arthur and his Knights of the Round Table in medieval Britain.

One of the greatest French romances is the *Romance*

French literature

Masters of French literature from the 1100's to the present rank among the greatest literary figures in the world. This table lists the leading French writers in chronological order. The table also includes a number of works and groups of poets important in the history of French literature during the Middle Ages.

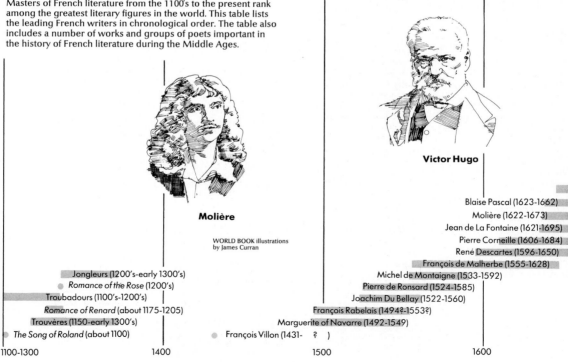

Molière

WORLD BOOK illustrations by James Curran

Victor Hugo

Jongleurs (1200's-early 1300's)
Romance of the Rose (1200's)
Troubadours (1100's-1200's)
Romance of Renard (about 1175-1205)
Trouvères (1150-early 1300's)
The Song of Roland (about 1100)

François Villon (1431-　?　)

Marguerite of Navarre (1492-1549)
François Rabelais (1494?-1553?)
Joachim Du Bellay (1522-1560)
Pierre de Ronsard (1524-1585)
Michel de Montaigne (1533-1592)
François de Malherbe (1555-1628)
René Descartes (1596-1650)
Pierre Corneille (1606-1684)
Jean de La Fontaine (1621-1695)
Molière (1622-1673)
Blaise Pascal (1623-1662)

1100-1300　　　　　　1400　　　　　　　1500　　　　　　1600

of the Rose. Guillaume de Lorris wrote the first part in the early 1200's as an *allegory* (symbolic story) about love. Jean de Meung continued the poem from about 1275 to 1280 as a satire on the society of his time.

Lais and contes were short verse tales about chivalry, love, and the supernatural. Lais were based on Celtic sources. Contes were generally based on Latin sources. The poet Marie de France wrote many important lais in the late 1100's.

Fabliaux were short, usually humorous stories that were often satiric and sometimes very coarse. The collection of fabliaux *Romance of Renard* (about 1175 to 1205) uses animal characters to satirize human society.

Early prose included romances that appeared later than verse romances and often told the same stories. Historical chronicles became a major form of prose literature. The best-known historical writers were Philippe de Commines, Jean Froissart, Jean de Joinville, and Geoffroy de Villehardouin.

Early drama was composed primarily in verse and dealt with religious themes. Religious dramas can be grouped into three types. *Mystery plays* dramatized scenes from the Scriptures. *Miracle plays* portrayed the intervention of the Virgin Mary or saints in human affairs. *Morality plays* were symbolic dramas intended to educate. *Secular* (nonreligious) comedies called *farces* developed as interludes during the performance of religious dramas.

The Renaissance

The Renaissance was a period of European cultural history that began in Italy about 1300 and spread to other parts of Europe. In French literature, the Renaissance extended from the early 1500's to about 1600.

The French Renaissance was a flowering of learning and literature inspired by ancient Greek and Latin models and by Italian literature. Writers and scholars called *humanists* played a major role in the Renaissance. Humanists combined scholarship with an increased interest in the individual and in worldly, rather than religious, concerns. See **Humanism.**

From 1494 to 1525, French armies invaded Italy. These invasions led to increased contact with Italian art and literature and with Greek humanist scholars. These contacts helped stimulate the Renaissance in France. During the early 1500's, King Francis I and his sister Marguerite of Navarre served as patrons of humanists and other writers in their courts. Marguerite herself was a learned author. She based her collection of tales called the *Heptaméron* (1558) on *The Decameron* by the Italian Renaissance writer Giovanni Boccaccio in the mid-1300's.

François Rabelais was the most important fiction writer of the French Renaissance. His major work is *Gargantua and Pantagruel.* This exuberant, often bawdy, narrative in five parts was published between 1532 and 1564. The work satirizes the legal, political, religious, and social institutions of Rabelais' time.

The Pléiade was a group of seven poets who wanted to create a new kind of French poetry based on ancient Greek and Roman models. Pierre de Ronsard was the leader of the group. His subjects were such common Renaissance themes as love, the passage of youth, and the immortality of the poet.

Françcis-René de Chateaubriand (1768-1848)
Madame de Staël (1766-1817)
André Chénier (1762-1794)
Pierre de Beaumarchais (1732-1799)
Denis Diderot (1713-1784)
Jean-Jacques Rousseau (1712-1778)
Abbé Prévost (1697-1763)
Voltaire (1694-1778)
Montesquieu (1689-1755)
Pierre Marivaux (1688-1763)
Alain René Lesage (1668-1747)
François de Fénelon (1651-1715)
Jean de La Bruyère (1645-1696)
Jean Racine (1639-1699)
Nicolas Boileau-Despréaux (1636-1711)
Madame de La Fayette (1634-1693)
Jacques Bossuet (1627-1704)

André Breton (1896-1966)
Jean Cocteau (1889-1963)
Jean Giraudoux (1882-1944)
Guillaume Apollinaire (1880-1918)
Paul Valéry (1871-1945)
Marcel Proust (1871-1922)
André Gide (1869-1951)
Paul Claudel (1868-1955)
Arthur Rimbaud (1854-1891)
Guy de Maupassant (1850-1893)
Paul Verlaine (1844-1896)
Stéphane Mallarmé (1842-1898)
Émile Zola (1840-1902)
Alphonse Daudet (1840-1897)
Jules de Goncourt (1830-1870)
Hippolyte Taine (1828-1893)
Alexandre Dumas fils (1824-1895)
Edmond Goncourt (1822-1896)
Gustave Flaubert (1821-1880)
Charles Baudelaire (1821-1867)
Alfred de Musset (1810-1857)
George Sand (1804-1876)
Charles Sainte-Beuve (1804-1869)
Victor Hugo (1802-1885)
Alexandre Dumas père (1802-1870)
Honoré de Balzac (1799-1850)
Alfred de Vigny (1797-1863)
Alphonse de Lamartine (1790-1869)
Stendhal (1783-1842)

Michel Butor (1926-)
Alain Robbe-Grillet (1922-)
Marguerite Duras (1914-)
Claude Simon (1913-)
Albert Camus (1913-1960)
Eugène Ionesco (1912-)
Jean Anouilh (1910-1987)
Simone de Beauvoir (1908-1986)
Samuel Beckett (1906-1989)
Jean-Paul Sartre (1905-1980)

1700   1800   1900   2000

Joachim du Bellay was the second most important Pléiade poet. He was the first French poet to use extensively the sonnet form, which he borrowed from Italian Renaissance poets. Du Bellay wrote an important prose essay called *Defense and Glorification of the French Language* (1549). In the essay, du Bellay "defended" French as a suitable language for poetry against those who favored Latin, the language used by Roman poets. Du Bellay also urged poets to enrich the French vocabulary with technical words, dialect, and words from Greek and Latin.

Étienne Jodelle was a dramatist as well as a Pléiade poet. He wrote the first original French comedy, *Eugéne* (1552), and the first tragedy, *Cleopatra Prisoner* (1552).

Michel de Montaigne was the last great writer of the French Renaissance. Montaigne created the personal essay as a literary form. A personal essay is written in an informal, conversational style. Montaigne's essays were loosely organized meditations on such topics as education, travel, death, customs, knowledge, and the author himself. A strong sense of skepticism about human nature runs through Montaigne's writings.

The classical age

The reigns of King Louis XIII and especially King Louis XIV are known as the *classical age* in French literature. This period, from about 1600 to the early 1700's, is generally considered the high point in French literature.

The classical writers did not reject the ideals of the Renaissance. However, the period developed a greater spirit of order and refinement. French writers especially emphasized reason and the intellect in analyzing ideas and human behavior. See **Classicism.**

Classical poetry. François de Malherbe was the first important classical poet and the most influential. During the early 1600's, Malherbe wrote clear, rational, sober poetry that became the basic style for classical verse. Jean de La Fontaine and Nicolas Boileau-Despréaux were also leading classical poets. La Fontaine wrote a famous collection of animal tales in verse called *Fables* (1668-1694). Boileau wrote *The Art of Poetry* (1674). In this critical work in verse, the author described the literary principles of moderation and nobility of style that characterized classical poetry of his time.

Classical drama was the greatest expression of French classicism. The masters of classical drama were Pierre Corneille, Jean Racine, and Molière.

Corneille was the first great classical writer of tragedy. His plays present noble characters involved in conflicts of duty, loyalty, and love. Corneille stressed the importance of the will, self-control, honor, and freedom. His major tragedies include *The Cid* (1636 or 1637), *Horace* (1640), *Cinna* (1640), and *Polyeucte* (1642).

Racine was the greatest writer of classical tragedy. His plays show characters in the grip of passions they cannot control. A somber religious pessimism colors his works. Racine adapted ancient Greek and Roman subjects in such masterpieces as *Andromaque* (1667) and *Phèdre* (1677).

Molière was the greatest writer of comedy in French drama. His best plays are satires and present strong characters in conflict with social conventions. Molière wrote his finest comedies in the mid-1660's. They include *Tartuffe, Don Juan,* and *The Misanthrope.*

Classical prose. Two philosophers wrote works that rank as masterpieces of French classical prose. René Descartes wrote *Discourse on Method* (1637), an influential example of rationalist thought. Blaise Pascal wrote outstanding prose works that reveal his deep Christian faith. Pascal's best-known religious work is a collection of reflections called *Pensées.* The collection was first published in 1670, though a complete edition was not issued until 1844.

A group of writers called *moralists* described human conduct and manners in letters, sayings called *maxims,* and other prose forms. The satire *The Characters of Theophrastus* (1688) by Jean de La Bruyère is an example of moralist literature. It combines maxims with literary portraits of the people and social types of the day.

Madame de La Fayette wrote one of the first important novels in French literature, *The Princess of Cleves* (1678). The novel has been praised for its psychological analysis and skillful construction.

Jacques Bossuet was a historian and Roman Catholic bishop known for his eloquent and moving sermons. François Fénelon was a Roman Catholic archbishop. His literary reputation primarily rests on *Telemachus* (1699), a romance filled with the author's ideas on education, morals, politics, and religion.

The Age of Reason

The 1700's in France are often called the *Age of Reason,* or the *Enlightenment.* During this century, philosophers emphasized reason as the best method for learning truth. Much of the literature was philosophical, produced by such important thinkers as Voltaire, Denis Diderot, and Jean Jacques Rousseau. See **Age of Reason.**

Voltaire was the most famous literary figure of his time. He used his literary skills to fight intolerance and bigotry and to promote rationalism. Voltaire's most famous work is the satirical novel *Candide* (1759). He also wrote tragedies, partly influenced by the plays of William Shakespeare. In addition, Voltaire helped develop the principles of modern historical writing through his many works on European and world history.

Denis Diderot is chiefly known as the editor of the French *Encyclopédie* (1751-1772), one of the great intellectual achievements of the Age of Reason. The *Encyclopédie* was a collection of learned articles contributed by writers in many fields. The work attempted to explain rationally the latest scientific discoveries. It also attacked religious authority, economic inequality, and abuses of justice.

Jean Jacques Rousseau proposed changes in French society in his novel *The New Heloise* (1761) and in education in the novel *Emile* (1762). Rousseau's autobiographical *Confessions* (published in 1782 and 1789, after his death) helped create the modern literature of self-analysis. Rousseau's sensitivity to nature reintroduced a meditative and lyrical feeling into French literature. This sensitivity appears most prominently in *Reveries of the Solitary Stroller* (1782).

Several other major writers contributed to the Age of Reason. Montesquieu wrote witty social criticism in his *Persian Letters* (1721). Alain René Lesage produced a famous satirical novel, *Gil Blas* (1715-1735). The Abbé Prévost composed a popular sentimental novel, *Manon*

Lescaut (1731). Pierre Marivaux wrote novels about middle-class society and delicate comedies about problems of love as seen by women. Pierre Beaumarchais wrote the satirical comedies *The Barber of Seville* (1775) and *The Marriage of Figaro* (1784). Both plays deal with the irrational nature of aristocratic privilege and contributed to the ideas that led to the French Revolution (1789-1799).

Romanticism

Romanticism was a movement that had its roots in the late 1700's and flourished during the early and mid-1800's. Romanticism was partly a reaction against classicism and the Age of Reason. Romantic writers rejected what they considered to be the excessive rationalism and lifeless literary forms of previous periods. The romantics emphasized the emotions and the imagination over reason, and they promoted freer forms of literary expression. Romantic writers were extremely self-centered. The writer's personality was often the most important element in a work. See **Romanticism.**

The preromantics. French romanticism was influenced by earlier romantic movements in England, Germany, and Spain. A number of French writers, called *preromantics,* also helped shape the movement during the late 1700's and early 1800's.

Jean Jacques Rousseau is identified with the Age of Reason. However, he was also an important forerunner of romanticism because he prized feeling over reason and spontaneity over self-discipline. Rousseau also influenced the romantics with his lyrical prose style, his introduction of passionate love into the French novel, and his sensitivity to the beauties of nature.

François-René de Chateaubriand exerted a tremendous influence through his fiction. The feelings of boredom, loneliness, and grief that dominate his writings became essential elements of romantic literature. Chateaubriand created a basic character in romantic writing—the solitary, passionate, and misunderstood hero. Chateaubriand had strong religious feelings, and his works helped revive interest in the Christian Middle Ages, a period scorned by writers of classicism and the Age of Reason.

Madame de Staël made a major impact on French romantic critical theory with *On Literature* (1800). She introduced German romanticism into France in *On Germany* (1810). The poet André Chénier incorporated several technical elements into his verse that were adopted by romantic poets.

Romantic poetry began in 1820 with the publication of *Poetic Meditations* by Alphonse de Lamartine. His melancholy poems dealt with nature, love, and solitude.

Victor Hugo was the greatest figure in French romanticism, excelling as a poet, dramatist, and fiction writer. Hugo's *Odes and Diverse Poems* (1822) have a colorful, exotic quality. His later collections, such as *Autumn Leaves* (1831), are more personal and meditative.

Alfred de Vigny is best known for *Antique and Modern Poems* (1826). The poems are philosophical and often dramatic, stressing human unhappiness and the loneliness of the superior individual.

Alfred de Musset had great lyrical gifts. His melancholy and musical poems concern love, suffering, and solitude. In his lyrics called *Nights* (1835-1837), Musset described the anguish he suffered over a lost love.

Romantic drama dealt with historical subjects and melodramatic situations, often mixing comedy with tragedy. The dramas emphasized color and spectacle, unlike the more controlled dramas of classicism and the Age of Reason. Victor Hugo wrote the first significant romantic play, the historical drama *Hernani* (1830). Vigny and Musset also contributed to romantic drama. Vigny's *Chatterton* (1835) featured a popular character in romantic literature, the neglected artist. Musset wrote sophisticated comedies noted for their verbal brilliance.

Romantic fiction. Many romantic authors wrote historical novels modeled on the works of the Scottish novelist Sir Walter Scott. Alexandre Dumas père (the elder) wrote the famous historical novel *The Three Musketeers* (1844), set during the reign of King Louis XIII in the 1600's. Victor Hugo's *The Hunchback of Notre Dame* (1831) showed the romantic taste for the Middle Ages.

Some romantic writers moved toward a more realistic style of fiction. Such authors as Honoré de Balzac, George Sand, and Stendhal retained many romantic characteristics in their work. But they modified their romanticism with a more faithful observation of life.

Beginning in 1829, Balzac wrote almost 100 novels and stories that were collected as *The Human Comedy* (1842-1848). In this series, the author attempted to describe the entire French society of his time. Balzac portrayed a wide range of human types, with their motivations and interactions. He also explored the influence of social institutions and values, especially society's attitudes toward money.

George Sand was the pen name of a Frenchwoman who began her literary career by writing novels of love and passion, such as *Indiana* (1832) and *Lélia* (1833). Later, she turned to rural subjects, especially in her novel of country life, *The Haunted Pool* (1846).

Stendhal was a rationalist, but he liked passionate, strong characters and melodramatic situations. A master psychologist, Stendhal used a clear and ironic style to portray the struggle between passion and calculating ambition. His two masterpieces are *The Red and the Black* (1830) and *The Charterhouse of Parma* (1839).

Realism

Realism was a literary doctrine that emerged partly as a reaction against romanticism. The realists believed that art should reproduce life accurately, honestly, and objectively. By the mid-1800's, realism was dominating French literature. See **Realism.**

Gustave Flaubert was the major representative of French realism. He followed Balzac in his love of detail and his careful observation of facts. For his novel *Madame Bovary* (1857), Flaubert deliberately chose an ordinary subject—a dull country doctor and his shallow wife. This portrait of French provincial life ranks among the masterpieces of French literature.

Guy de Maupassant became known for his realistic short stories. De Maupassant was an expert at observing human behavior. Many of his stories portray provincial life in Normandy or the tedious existence of petty civil servants in Paris.

There were two main types of realistic drama in France. One was the *well-made play,* which emphasized plot and suspense. The comedies of Eugène Scribe were the best examples. The other type was the *problem,* or *thesis, play.* Most dealt with social problems, such as divorce and legal injustice. The leading writers of problem plays were Émile Augier, Eugène Brieux, and Alexandre Dumas fils (the younger).

Literary criticism played a major role in realistic literature and greatly influenced later literary criticism. The leading realistic critic was Charles Sainte-Beuve. He believed that a literary work should be studied through the author's life and personality. He also placed importance on the social environment and historical background in which the work was created.

Naturalism

During the late 1800's, a movement called *naturalism* emerged as an extreme form of realism. Naturalistic writers emphasized the sordid and coarse aspects of human conduct. The typical naturalistic work is pessimistic and often criticizes social injustice. The movement followed a philosophy called *determinism,* which taught that a person's character is determined by environment and heredity rather than free will. See **Naturalism.**

Émile Zola was the leading French naturalistic writer. He proposed to treat fiction as a "laboratory" in which the laws of human behavior could be discovered. Zola created masterpieces of description and social criticism in his series of 20 novels called *The Rougon-Macquart* (1871-1893). The novels were named after the family that occupies a central place in the stories.

The brothers Edmond and Jules de Goncourt collaborated on *Germinie Lacerteux* (1864), a somber novel about a servant girl who leads a life of vice. But the brothers were better known for their *Journal,* which recorded the literary and social life of Paris from 1851 to 1896.

Henri Becque was the most important naturalistic playwright. His drama *The Vultures* (1882) is a bitter exploration of ruthless human conduct.

Hippolyte Taine was the leading naturalistic literary critic. Taine developed a deterministic view of literature that can be summarized as *race, milieu, and moment.* Race referred to the author's heredity. Milieu was the author's environment, and moment was the state of the artistic tradition in which the author worked. According to Taine, these three factors governed literary creativity.

Symbolism

French symbolism was a literary movement of the late 1800's. The term *symbolism* has also been applied to the work of a number of French writers who did not belong to the specific movement. See **Symbolism.**

The key figures in the symbolist movement were the poets Charles Baudelaire, Stéphane Mallarmé, Paul Verlaine, and Arthur Rimbaud. They wanted to liberate the techniques of poetry from traditional styles to create freer verse forms. The symbolists believed poetry should suggest meanings through impressions, intuitions, and sensations rather than describe objective reality. Much of their poetry was personal and obscure.

Charles Baudelaire was the forerunner of symbolism. His *Flowers of Evil* (1857) is a collection of about 100 related poems. The work reflects Baudelaire's somber view of humanity and its vices. However, he wrote that

humanity had the potential to create poetic beauty.

Stéphane Mallarmé was the first great symbolist poet. Mallarmé hoped that poetic language could approach absolute truth. His works are difficult to understand because of their unusual syntax, learned words, elaborate metaphors, and abstract subject matter. His most famous poem is *The Afternoon of a Faun* (1876).

Paul Verlaine wrote simple, melodious verse that is delicate, graceful, and musical. In *Songs Without Words* (1874), he tried to create a sense of music in verse.

Arthur Rimbaud was a boy genius. He was producing highly original poetry at the age of 16. At the age of about 19, Rimbaud composed *A Season in Hell* (1873), an autobiographical collection of prose and verse that describes his tortured spiritual experiences.

No symbolist novelist or dramatist equaled the poets. However, the dreamy symbolist plays of Maurice Maeterlinck gained some attention. Maeterlinck was a Belgian author, but he wrote in French.

The 1900's

The four masters. Four authors dominated French literature during the early 1900's. They were Paul Claudel, André Gide, Paul Valéry, and Marcel Proust. All were born about 1870, and all passed through a symbolist phase in their early careers. By 1920, each was recognized as a master of French literature.

Claudel wrote drama, poetry, criticism, and religious commentary that reflected his strong Roman Catholic beliefs. Claudel's poetry is filled with bold metaphors, violent emotions, and flowery language. However, his best-known works are his religious plays, notably *Break of Noon* (written in 1906) and *The Tidings Brought to Mary* (1912).

Gide was a novelist who became controversial because of his unorthodox views on religion and morality. Gide's fiction has been praised for its style and psychological insights into character. In 1909, he helped found *The New French Review,* the leading French literary journal of the early 1900's.

Proust was perhaps the greatest French novelist since Balzac. His monumental autobiographical novel *Remembrance of Things Past* was published in seven parts from 1913 to 1927. The novel is a highly personal and poetic work as well as a brilliant study of social manners and character psychology.

Valéry wrote poetry that shows the influence of the rational tradition in French literature. Valéry stressed emotional control and classical forms in his poetry. His major works include the long poem *The Young Fate* (1917) and the lyrics collected in *Charms* (1922). Valéry was also an outstanding literary critic.

Surrealism was a movement founded in 1924 by a group of writers and painters in Paris. The surrealists wanted to revolutionize society. They explored unconscious thought processes, especially dreams, which they believed would yield ultimate truth. See **Surrealism.**

The poet Guillaume Apollinaire was a major influence on surrealism. His *Alcools* (1913) is a collection of beautiful lyrics that celebrate the imagination. The chief theorist and leader of the surrealists was André Breton. The leading poets were René Char, Paul Éluard, and Louis Aragon. However, all three wrote their finest poetry after they left the movement in the late 1930's. Their main themes were love and patriotism.

Existentialism was a philosophy that strongly influenced French literature after World War II (1939-1945). Jean-Paul Sartre, the leading existential writer, became famous for such plays as *No Exit* (1944) and *Dirty Hands* (1948) as well as for philosophical writings and criticism. His works explore moral and political topics, especially the problems of freedom and commitment. Simone de Beauvoir helped popularize existentialist ideas in such works as *For a Morality of Ambiguity* (1947). Albert Camus was not strictly an existentialist. But, like Sartre, he explored ethical and moral problems in several works, including the novels *The Stranger* (1942) and *The Plague* (1947) and the long essay *The Myth of Sisyphus* (1942).

French drama of the mid-1900's. Several novelists and poets contributed to French drama in the mid-1900's, including Sartre and Camus. Other leading playwrights were Jean Anouilh, Jean Giraudoux, and Jean Cocteau. Anouilh explored questions of illusion and reality, the individual against society, and the nature of duty. He often used mythological and historical subjects. Giraudoux wrote in a witty, elaborate, artificial style. His best-known plays investigate the nature of love or protest against war and greed. Cocteau became known for his fantasies on mythological subjects.

Recent French literature. Since the 1950's, there have been two major developments in French literature. One was the emergence of the Theater of the Absurd. Playwrights in this movement tried to dramatize what they believed was the essentially meaningless nature of life. The leading absurdists were Samuel Beckett and Eugène Ionesco. Beckett was Irish and Ionesco was Romanian, but they both wrote in French, and their most significant works were first staged in Paris.

The other major development was the New Novel. Its chief representatives included Alain Robbe-Grillet, Michel Butor, Nathalie Sarraute, and Claude Simon. These writers moved away from traditional approaches to the novel, such as realistic storytelling and plots. Instead, their novels concentrate on descriptions of events and objects as experienced or seen by the characters.

In the 1970's, a feminist movement appeared in French literature. A number of critics, mostly women, turned their attention to women writers of the past. They also analyzed female characters in fiction and the expression of feminist concerns in modern literature. Marguerite Duras and Hélène Cixous are among the leading French feminist writers.   Catharine Savage Brosman

Related articles in *World Book* include:

Early French literature

Chrétien de Troyes	Roland	Trouvère
Froissart, Jean	Troubadour	Villon, François

The Renaissance

Du Bellay, Joachim	Rabelais, François de
Humanism	Renaissance
Marot, Clement	Ronsard, Pierre de
Montaigne, Michel de	

The classical age

Boileau-Despréaux, Nicolas	Corneille, Pierre
Bossuet, Jacques	Cyrano de Bergerac, Savinien
Classicism	de

Descartes, René	Malherbe, François de
Fénelon, François de S.	Molière
La Bruyère, Jean de	Pascal, Blaise
La Fayette, Madame de	Perrault, Charles
La Fontaine, Jean de	Racine, Jean
La Rochefoucauld, Duc de	

The Age of Reason

Age of Reason	Montesquieu
Bayle, Pierre	Philosophes
Beaumarchais, Pierre de	Rousseau, Jean-Jacques
Diderot, Denis	Sade, Marquis de
Lesage, Alain René	Voltaire
Marivaux, Pierre	

Romanticism

Balzac, Honoré de	Romanticism
Chateaubriand, François de	Rostand, Edmond
Dumas, Alexandre, *pere*	Rousseau, Jean-Jacques
Hugo, Victor	Sand, George
Lamartine, Alphonse de	Staël, Madame de
Mérimée, Prosper	Stendhal
Musset, Alfred de	Vigny, Alfred
Nerval, Gérard de	

Realism and naturalism

Brieux, Eugène	Naturalism
Daudet, Alphonse	Realism
De Maupassant, Guy	Sainte-Beuve, Charles
Dumas, Alexandre, *fils*	Scribe, Augustin Eugène
Flaubert, Gustave	Taine, Hippolyte
France, Anatole	Verne, Jules
Goncourt	Zola, Émile
Mistral, Frédéric	

Symbolism

Baudelaire, Charles	Rimbaud, Arthur
Gautier, Théophile	Sully-Prudhomme, René
Maeterlinck, Maurice	Symbolism
Mallarmé, Stéphane	Verlaine, Paul

The 1900's

Anouilh, Jean	Colette	Perse, Saint-John
Apollinaire, Guillaume	Existentialism	Prévert, Jacques
	Genet, Jean	Proust, Marcel
Beauvoir, Simone de	Gide, André	Rolland, Romain
Beckett, Samuel	Giraudoux, Jean	Romains, Jules
Breton, André	Ionesco, Eugène	Saint-Exupéry, Antoine de
Camus, Albert	Malraux, André	
Céline, Louis-Ferdinand	Martin du Gard, Roger	Sartre, Jean-Paul
Claudel, Paul	Mauriac, François	Surrealism
Cocteau, Jean	Maurois, André	Valéry, Paul

Other related articles

Drama	French language	Philosophy
Epic	Novel	Poetry
French Academy		

Outline

VIII. **Symbolism**
IX. **The 1900's**

Questions

What were the characteristics of *naturalism*?
When did *existentialism* influence French literature?
Who wrote *Cinna*? *Lélia*? *Flowers of Evil*?
What was the *Pléiade*?
Who were the two leading novelists of the early 1900's?
How did the preromantics influence *romanticism*?
What were *contes*? *Fabliaux*?
When did French literature begin?
Who was the most influential classical poet?
What were the two main types of realistic drama?

Reading and Study Guide

See *French Literature* in the Research Guide/Index, Volume 22, for a *Reading and Study Guide.*

Additional resources

Bradby, David. *Modern French Drama, 1940-1980.* Cambridge, 1984.
Brée, Germaine. *Twentieth-Century French Literature.* Univ. of Chicago Press, 1983.
Cazamian, Louis F. *A History of French Literature.* Oxford, 1967. First published in 1955.
Hicks, Benjamin E. *Plots and Characters in Classic French Fiction.* Shoe String, 1981.
The Oxford Companion to French Literature. Ed. by Paul Harvey and J. E. Heseltine. Oxford, 1959.
The Random House Book of Twentieth-Century French Poetry. Ed. by Paul Auster. Random House, 1982.

French Morocco. See Morocco (History).

French Polynesia, *PAHL uh NEE zhuh,* is an overseas territory of France. It lies in the Pacific Ocean, about 2,800 miles (4,500 kilometers) south of Hawaii. For location, see **Pacific Islands** (map). The territory is made up of about 120 islands scattered over an area about the size of Western Europe. These islands consist mainly of the Austral, Gambier, Marquesas, Society, and Tuamotu island groups. Papeete, on Tahiti—one of the Society islands—is the territory's capital.

Most of the territory's people are Polynesians. Tourism, agriculture, and fishing are important economic activities. The chief products include coconuts, pearls, and tropical fruits. French Polynesians elect representatives to the French Parliament and vote in French presidential elections.   Robert Langdon

See also **Marquesas Islands; Society Islands; Tahiti; Tuamotu Islands.**

French Quarter. See New Orleans (Downtown New Orleans).

French Revolution brought about great changes in the society and government of France. The revolution, which lasted from 1789 to 1799, also had far-reaching effects on the rest of Europe. It introduced democratic ideals to France but did not make the nation a democracy. However, it ended supreme rule by French kings and strengthened the middle class. After the revolution began, no European kings, nobles, or other privileged groups could ever again take their powers for granted or ignore the ideals of liberty and equality.

The revolution began with a government financial crisis but quickly became a movement of reform and violent change. In one of the early events, a crowd in Paris captured the Bastille, a royal fortress and hated symbol of oppression. A series of elected legislatures then took control of the government. King Louis XVI and his wife, Marie Antoinette, were executed. Thousands of others met the same fate in a period called the Reign of Terror. The revolution ended when Napoleon Bonaparte, a French general, took over the government.

Background. Various social, political, and economic conditions led to the revolution. These conditions included dissatisfaction among the lower and middle classes, interest in new ideas about government, and financial problems caused by the costs of wars.

Legal divisions among social groups that had existed for hundreds of years created much discontent. According to law, French society consisted of three groups called *estates.* Members of the clergy made up the first estate, nobles the second, and the rest of the people the third. The peasants formed the largest group in the third estate. Many of them earned so little that they could barely feed their families. The third estate also included the working people of the cities and a large and prosperous middle class made up chiefly of merchants, lawyers, and government officials.

The third estate resented certain advantages of the first two estates. The clergy and nobles did not have to pay most taxes. The third estate, especially the peasants, had to provide almost all the country's tax revenue. Many members of the middle class were also troubled by their social status. They were among the most important people in French society but were not recognized as such because they belonged to the third estate.

The new ideas about government challenged France's *absolute monarchy.* Under this system, the king had almost unlimited authority. He governed by *divine right*— that is, the monarch's right to rule was thought to come from God. There were checks on the king, but these came mainly from a few groups of aristocrats in the *parlements* (high courts). During the 1700's, French writers called *philosophes* and philosophers from other countries raised new ideas about freedom. Some of these thinkers, including Jean Jacques Rousseau, suggested that the right to govern came from the people.

The financial crisis developed because the nation had gone deeply into debt to finance fighting in the Seven Years' War (1756-1763) and the Revolutionary War in America (1775-1783). By 1788, the government was almost bankrupt. The Parlement of Paris insisted that King Louis XVI could borrow more money or raise taxes only by calling a meeting of the Estates-General. This body, also called States-General, was made up of representatives of the three estates, and had last met in 1614. Unwillingly, the king called the meeting.

The revolution begins. The States-General opened on May 5, 1789, at Versailles, near Paris. Most members of the first two estates wanted each of the three estates to take up matters and vote on them separately by estate. The third estate had as many representatives as the other two estates combined. It insisted that all the estates be merged into one national assembly and that each representative have one vote. The third estate also wanted the States-General to write a constitution.

The king and the first two estates refused the demands of the third estate. In June 1789, the representatives of the third estate declared themselves the National Assembly of France. They gathered at a tennis court and pledged not to disband until they had written a constitution. This vow became known as the Oath of the Tennis Court. Louis XVI then allowed the three estates to join together as the National Assembly. But he began to gather troops around Paris to break up the Assembly.

Meanwhile, the masses of France also took action. On July 14, 1789, a huge crowd of Parisians rushed to the Bastille. They believed they would find arms and ammunition there for use in defending themselves against the king's army. The people captured the Bastille and began to tear it down. At the same time, leaders in Paris formed a revolutionary city government. Massive peasant uprisings against nobles also broke out in the countryside. A few nobles decided to flee France, and many more followed in the next five years. These people were called *émigrés* because they emigrated. The uprisings in town and countryside saved the National Assembly from being disbanded by the king.

The National Assembly. In August 1789, the Assembly adopted the Decrees of August 4 and the Declaration of the Rights of Man and of the Citizen. The decrees abolished some feudal dues that the peasants owed their landlords, the tax advantages of the clergy and nobles, and regional privileges. The declaration guaranteed the same basic rights to all citizens, including "liberty, property, security, and resistance to oppression" as well as representative government.

The Assembly later drafted a constitution that made France a limited monarchy with a one-house legislature. France was divided into 83 regions called departments, each with elected councils for local government. But the right to vote and hold public office was limited to citizens who paid a certain amount of taxes.

The Assembly seized the property of the Roman Catholic Church. The church lands amounted to about a tenth of the country's land. Much of the church land was sold to rich peasants and members of the middle class. Money from the land sales was used to pay some of the nation's huge debt. The Assembly then reorganized the Catholic Church in France, required the election of

priests and bishops by the voters, and closed the Church's monasteries and convents. Complete religious tolerance was extended to Protestants and Jews. The Assembly also reformed the court system by requiring the election of judges. By September 1791, the National Assembly believed that the revolution was over. It disbanded at the end of the month to make way for the newly elected Legislative Assembly.

The Legislative Assembly. The new Assembly, made up mainly of representatives of the middle class, opened on Oct. 1, 1791. It soon faced several challenges. The government's stability depended on cooperation between the king and the legislature. But Louis XVI remained opposed to the revolution. He asked other rulers for help in stopping it, and plotted with aristocrats and émigrés to overthrow the new government. In addition, public opinion became bitterly divided. The revolution's religious policy angered many Catholics. Other people demanded stronger measures against opponents of the revolution.

The new government also faced a foreign threat. In April 1792, it went to war against Austria and Prussia. These nations wished to restore the king and émigrés to their positions. The foreign armies defeated French forces in the early fighting and invaded France. Louis XVI and his supporters clearly hoped for the victory of the invaders. As a result, angry revolutionaries in Paris and other areas demanded that the king be dethroned.

In August 1792, the people of Paris took custody of Louis XVI and his family and imprisoned them. Louis's removal ended the constitutional monarchy. The Assembly then called for a National Convention to be elected by all the people, and for a new constitution.

Meanwhile, French armies suffered more military defeats. Parisians feared that the invading armies would soon reach the city. Parisians also feared an uprising by the large number of people in the city's prisons. In the first week of September, small numbers of Parisians took the law into their own hands and executed more than 1,000 prisoners. These executions, called the September Massacres, turned many people in France and

Destruction of the Symbols of the Monarchy, Place de la Concorde, August 10, 1793,
an oil painting on canvas by Pierre-Antoine Demachy; Musée Carnavalet, Paris

Hatred of the monarchy in France increased because of King Louis XVI's efforts to end the revolution. Louis was executed on Jan. 21, 1793, and the revolution became more extreme. About seven months later, a crowd in Paris burned a crown and a throne that had belonged to the king, *left.*

Europe against the revolution. A victory by the French Army at Valmy on September 20 helped end the crisis.

The National Convention. The king's removal led to a new stage in the revolution. The first stage had been a liberal middle-class reform movement based on a constitutional monarchy. The second stage was organized around principles of democracy. The National Convention opened on Sept. 21, 1792, and declared France a republic. The republic's official slogan was "Liberty, Equality, Fraternity."

Louis XVI was placed on trial for betraying the country. The National Convention found him guilty of treason, and a slim majority voted for the death penalty. The king was beheaded on the guillotine on Jan. 21, 1793. The revolution gradually grew more radical—that is, more open to extreme and violent change. Radical leaders came into prominence. In the Convention, they were known as the Mountain because they sat on the high benches at the rear of the hall. Leaders of the Mountain were Maximilien Robespierre, Georges Jacques Danton, and Jean Paul Marat. Their bitter opponents were known as the Gironde because several came from a department of that name. The majority of the deputies in the Convention, known as the Plain, sat between the two rival groups. The Mountain dominated a powerful political club called the Jacobin Club.

Growing disputes between the Mountain and the Gironde led to a struggle for power, and the Mountain won. In June 1793, the Convention expelled and arrested the leading Girondists. In turn, the Girondists' supporters rebelled against the Convention. Charlotte Corday, a Girondist sympathizer, assassinated Jean Paul Marat in July 1793. In time, the Convention's forces defeated the Girondists' supporters. The Jacobin leaders created a new citizens' army to fight rebellion in France and a war against other European nations. A military draft provided the troops, and rapid promotion of talented soldiers provided the leadership for this strong army.

Terror and equality. The Jacobin government was dictatorial and democratic. It was dictatorial because it suspended civil rights and political freedom in the emergency. The Convention's Committee of Public Safety took over actual rule of France, controlling local governments, the armed forces, and other institutions.

The committee governed during the most terrible period of the revolution. Its leaders included Robespierre, Lazare Carnot, and Bertrand Barère. The Convention declared a policy of terror against rebels, supporters of the king or the Gironde, and anyone else who publicly disagreed with official policy. In time, hundreds of thousands of suspects filled the nation's jails. Courts handed down about 18,000 death sentences in what was called the Reign of Terror. Paris became accustomed to the rattle of two-wheeled carts called *tumbrels* as they carried people to the guillotine. Victims of this period included Marie Antoinette, widow of Louis XVI.

The Jacobins, however, also followed democratic principles and extended the benefits of the revolution beyond the middle class. Shopkeepers, peasants, and other workers actively participated in political life for the first time. The Convention authorized public assistance for the poor, free primary education for boys and girls, price controls to protect consumers from rapid inflation, and taxes based on income. It also called for the

The Death of Marat (1793), an oil painting on canvas by Jacques Louis David; The Royal Museum of Fine Arts, Brussels, Belgium (SCALA/Art Resource)

The death of Marat spurred on the Reign of Terror. Charlotte Corday, a Girondist sympathizer, fatally stabbed the Jacobin leader while he took a bath, *above.*

abolition of slavery in France's colonies. Most of these reforms, however, were never fully carried out because of later changes in the government.

The revolution ends. In time, the radicals began to struggle for power among themselves. Robespierre succeeded in having Danton and other former leaders executed. Many people in France wished to end the Reign of Terror, the Jacobin dictatorship, and the democratic revolution. Robespierre's enemies in the Convention finally attacked him as a tyrant on July 27 (9 Thermidor by the French calendar), 1794. He was executed the next day. The Reign of Terror ended after Robespierre's death. Conservatives gained control of the Convention and drove the Jacobins from power. Most of the democratic reforms of the past two years were quickly abolished in what became known as the Thermidorian Reaction.

The Convention, which had adopted a democratic constitution in 1793, replaced that document with a new one in 1795. The government formed under this constitution was called the Directory, referring to the five-man executive directory that ruled along with a two-house legislature. France was still a republic, but once again only citizens who paid a certain amount of taxes could vote.

Meanwhile, France was winning victories on the battlefield. French armies had pushed back the invaders and crossed into Belgium, Germany, and Italy.

The Directory began meeting in October 1795. But it was troubled by war, economic problems, and opposition from supporters of monarchy and former Jacobins.

In October 1799, a number of political leaders plotted to overthrow the Directory. They needed military support and turned to Napoleon Bonaparte, a French general who had become a hero in a military campaign in Italy in 1796 and 1797. Bonaparte seized control of the government on Nov. 9 (18 Brumaire in the revolutionary calendar), 1799, ending the revolution.

The French Revolution brought France into opposition with much of Europe. The monarchs who ruled the other nations feared the spread of democratic ideals. The revolution left the French people in extreme disagreement about the best form of government for their country. By 1799, most were probably weary of political conflict altogether. But the revolution created the long-lasting foundations for a unified state, a strong central government, and a free society dominated by the middle class and the landowners.   Isser Woloch

Related articles in *World Book* include:

Biographies

Corday, Charlotte	Mirabeau, Comte de
Danton, Georges Jacques	Napoleon I
Du Barry, Madame	Robespierre
Lafayette, Marquis de	Roland de la Platière, M. J.
Louis (XVI)	Sieyès, Emmanuel Joseph
Marat, Jean Paul	Talleyrand
Marie Antoinette	

Background and causes

Bastille	Rights of Man, Declaration
Divine right of kings	of the
Estates-General	Rousseau, Jean J.
	Versailles

The revolution

Émigrés	Guillotine	Marseillaise
Girondists	Jacobins	

Other related articles

Clothing (The 1700's)	Tricolor
Swiss Guard	Tuileries

See also *French Revolution* in the Research Guide/ Index, Volume 22, for a *Reading and Study Guide.*

Additional resources

Bosher, J. F. *The French Revolution.* Norton, 1988.
Doyle, William. *Origins of the French Revolution.* 2nd ed. Oxford, 1988.
Lefebvre, Georges. *The French Revolution.* 2 vols. Columbia Univ. Press, 1962-1964.
Paxton, John. *Companion to the French Revolution.* Facts on File, 1988.
Voices of the French Revolution. Ed. by Richard Cobb and Colin Jones. Salem House, 1988.

French Somaliland. See Djibouti (country).
French Southern and Antarctic Territories are overseas possessions of France. They include the Kerguelen and Crozet *archipelagos* (groups of islands) and Amsterdam and Saint Paul islands, all in the Indian Ocean. The islands cover about 3,000 square miles (7,770 square kilometers). The territories also include Adélie Coast, an area in Antarctica, south of Australia. A High Administrator and Consultative Council, both appointed by the French government, govern the territories.

Kerguelen Island, the largest island of the territories, covers 2,577 square miles (6,674 square kilometers). It is about 2,100 miles (3,380 kilometers) southeast of Madagascar. The Crozet Archipelago lies about 850 miles

(1,370 kilometers) west of the Kerguelen group. Both groups of islands are cold, damp, and windy. Penguins, whales, and elephant seals live in the region. Amsterdam and Saint Paul lie about 800 miles (1,300 kilometers) northeast of the Kerguelen group. These islands have a milder climate, and lobster and cod are caught in the surrounding waters.

Only scientists who are studying the region live in the French Southern and Antarctic Territories. Their studies include the region's weather, geology, and animal and plant life.   Ian W. D. Dalziel

French West Africa was a federation of eight territories in western Africa. France administered the territories from 1895 to 1958. Dakar, now the capital of Senegal, was the capital. French West Africa included eight territories that are now independent countries: Dahomey (now Benin), French Guinea (now Guinea), French Sudan (now Mali), Ivory Coast, Mauritania, Niger, Senegal, and Upper Volta (now Burkina Faso). For more detailed information on these countries, see their separate articles in *World Book.*

The land. French West Africa spread over 1,789,186 square miles (4,633,970 square kilometers). It covered most of the great bulge of Africa that juts into the Atlantic Ocean. French West Africa occupied about one-seventh of the African continent. An area of rolling plains, it has tropical rain forests along the southern coasts, a belt of thick grasslands across the center, and the barren Sahara in the north.

History. Before Europeans took control of what became French West Africa, the people of the region were divided into many groups. Some of the groups were loose associations of families that lived in small areas without centralized authority. Other groups formed more elaborate states, with central governments and large populations.

Several great empires bordered the Sahara. The Ghana Empire was strongest during the A.D. 1000's. The Mali Empire reached its height in the 1300's. The Songhai Empire flourished in the 1500's.

The Portuguese were the first Europeans to explore the west African coast. They arrived in the mid-1400's.

WORLD BOOK map

French West Africa, *shown in yellow,* was a federation of eight territories in western Africa until 1958. But now eight separate and independent countries cover this region.

Then came the French, the Dutch, and the English. The English were mainly interested in buying slaves they could sell in the West Indies and America. In 1624, King Louis XIII of France granted a French company a charter to trade in Senegal. The French established St. Louis, now a city in Senegal, as a fortified trading post at the mouth of the Sénégal River in 1658.

Throughout the 1700's, Britain and France fought for control of this area. In 1815, Britain finally recognized French control of St. Louis and Gorée at the tip of Cape Verde peninsula. But France did not seriously extend its control throughout French West Africa until the late 1800's. In 1895, France grouped its colonies in western Africa under the authority of a governor general. Dakar became the governor general's headquarters in 1902.

France proclaimed a constitution for the Federation of West Africa in 1904. But many areas were far from being completely controlled. Some remained under military authority until after 1945.

French West Africa became a federation of eight overseas territories within the French Union in 1946. France extended citizenship rights to the Africans, but gave only some of them the right to vote. In 1947, France started an economic development program for the federation. In 1956, France gave all Africans in the federation the right to vote.

When France adopted a new constitution in 1958, French Guinea voted to leave the French Union and became an independent country. The other seven territories voted to remain associated with France within the new French Community. But by the end of 1958, these territories had voted to become autonomous republics.

In 1959, French Sudan and Senegal united to form the Federation of Mali. They negotiated with France for full independence, but agreed to remain in the French Community. The Federation of Mali broke up in August 1960, and French Sudan became the Republic of Mali. The other five republics then asked for complete independence. All of them had received their freedom by the end of 1960. The republics all became members of the United Nations.   Immanuel Wallerstein

Related articles in *World Book* include:

Arabs	Guinea	Niger
Benin	Ivory Coast	Niger River
Berbers	Mali	Senegal
Burkina Faso	Mauritania	

French West Indies consist of several small islands at the eastern end of the Caribbean Sea (see **West Indies** [map]). They are part of the Lesser Antilles island chain. The French West Indies cover 1,083 square miles (2,805 square kilometers) and have a population of 657,000. They make up two overseas departments of France. The departments are Guadeloupe, which consists of the island of Guadeloupe and several smaller islands; and Martinique, which consists of the island of Martinique. The French West Indies enjoy a higher standard of living than many of the other Caribbean islands because they receive financial assistance from the French government. The chief industries are tourism and the production of sugar cane. See also **Guadeloupe; Martinique.**   Gary Brana-Shute

Freneau, *fruh NOH,* **Philip** (1752-1832), was an American poet and journalist. He became known as the "Poet of the American Revolution" for the poetry he wrote at-

tacking the British during the Revolutionary War (1775-1783). Freneau also wrote descriptive and imaginative poetry about nature. They include "The Wild Honey Suckle" (1786) and "The Indian Burying Ground" (1788).

Philip Morin Freneau was born in New York City. He was a sailor during the Revolutionary War and suffered greatly after being captured by the British. His experiences as a prisoner inspired the poem "The British Prison Ship" (1781). Freneau was active in politics during much of his life. From 1791 to 1793, he edited the *National Gazette,* a newspaper that opposed the Federalist Party led by Alexander Hamilton.   Edward W. Clark

Freon. See Fluorocarbon.

Frequency. See Electric generator (A simple generator); Sound (Frequency and pitch).

Frequency band, also called *waveband,* is a range of radio frequencies set aside for a single broadcasting station. A station's transmitter produces a certain constant *carrier frequency.* But the information being transmitted, such as sound or a TV picture, slightly *modulates* (changes) the carrier frequency. Because of this modulation, each station must use a range of frequencies for its broadcasts. For example, most amplitude modulation (AM) stations require a frequency band of 5 *kilohertz* above and below the carrier frequency of their transmitters. One kilohertz equals 1,000 *hertz* (cycles per second). The use of frequency bands keeps nearby stations from interfering with one another's broadcasts.

Frequency band also refers to any group of radio frequencies used for one purpose, such as commercial, ship-to-shore, amateur, airplane, or police broadcasting. In the United States, the Federal Communications Commission (FCC) assigns frequency bands. For example, in commercial broadcasting, the frequency band for AM stations ranges from about 500 to 1,600 kilohertz. The range for frequency modulation (FM) stations is from 88 to 108 *megahertz.* One megahertz equals 1 million hertz. TV stations use several bands in the *very high frequency* (VHF) and *ultrahigh frequency* (UHF) ranges (see **Very high frequency waves; Ultrahigh frequency waves**).   Hugh D. Young

See also **Radio** (How radio works).

Frequency modulation, *FREE kwuhn see MAHJ uh LAY shuhn,* usually called simply FM, is a method of sending sound signals on radio waves. Frequency modulation and *amplitude modulation* (AM) are the two chief means of transmitting music and speech.

A radio wave has a fixed *frequency,* the number of times the wave vibrates per second. It also has a definite *amplitude* (size). In frequency modulation, the frequency of the transmitting radio wave is made higher or lower to correspond with the vibrations of the sound to be sent. But the amplitude of the wave is not varied. In contrast, amplitude modulation keeps the frequency of the transmitting wave constant. But it changes the wave's amplitude in accordance with the vibrations of the sound signal being transmitted.

FM has some advantages over AM. It is relatively free of static from thunderstorms and of other types of interference that affect AM broadcasts. FM also provides a more faithful reproduction of music and speech.

One of the main uses of frequency modulation is FM radio broadcasting. The transmission of stereophonic programs ranks as an important development in this area. In FM stereo broadcasting, sound signals from two microphones or from both *channels* (transmission paths) of a stereo record are sent on the same radio wave. Transmitting a program by this method is called *multiplexing.* For the best results, a listener needs a special receiver that can "decode" the sounds from the two channels and send them through two separate speakers.

A commercial FM station can transmit special programs of uninterrupted music in addition to its regular or stereo broadcasts. Such programs provide pleasant background music for offices, restaurants, and stores.

Frequency modulation also has other uses. For example, television stations transmit the audio portion of their programs by this method. Telephone companies also use FM in *microwave radio relaying,* a system designed to send long-distance phone calls.

Edwin H. Armstrong, an American electrical engineer, invented frequency modulation in 1933. FM became widely used in the 1940's.   Richard W. Henry

See also **Radio** (How radio works); **High fidelity system.**

Fresco, *FREHS koh,* is a painting made on fresh plaster, using pigments mixed with water. *Fresco* is the Italian word for *fresh.* To make a fresco, the artist usually first makes a drawing, called a *cartoon,* that is the exact size of the proposed picture. A smaller sketch in colors is also made. Then, fresh lime plaster—as much as can be painted in one day—is laid on the surface of the wall or ceiling that is to be decorated. The artist places the

Frescoes (1474) in the Ducal Palace of the Gonzaga family (SCALA/Art Resource)
Colorful frescoes decorated many palaces and public buildings of the Italian Renaissance. The Italian painter Andrea Mantegna painted the frescoes shown above in the palace of a duke.

cartoon on the surface, traces the outline, and then is ready to begin painting.

After mixing the dry pigments with water, the painter brushes them onto the damp plaster. As the plaster sets, it binds the colors permanently to its surface. Work must proceed rapidly because the plaster will not hold colors that are applied after it has dried. At the end of the day, any unpainted plaster is cut away, making a clean edge for the next day's work.

The lime in the plaster bleaches many pigments that are suitable for other painting techniques. Only pigments that can resist the action of the lime can be used in fresco painting. Most are earth colors, whose tones are not as bright as those used in oil painting.

Fresco painting reached its height during the Italian Renaissance of the 1400's and 1500's. Among the most celebrated frescoes of that period are Michelangelo's decorations of the Sistine Chapel in the Vatican. Two Mexican artists, Diego Rivera and José Clemente Orozco, inspired a revival of fresco painting in the United States in the 1930's.   Reed Kay

Related articles in *World Book* include:

Cartoon	Masaccio	Renaissance (pictures)
Easter (picture: The Resurrection)	Michelangelo	Rivera, Diego
Fra Angelico	Mural	Simone Martini
Ghirlandajo, Domenico	Orozco, José Clemente	Vatican City (picture: The Sistine Chapel)
Giotto	Painting	
	Raphael	

Fresno, *FREHZ noh* (pop. 217,129; met. area pop. 514,621), is the main marketing, distribution, and financial center of central California. It lies in Fresno County, in the middle of the fertile San Joaquin Valley. For location see **California** (political map).

Irrigation from the nearby Kings and San Joaquin rivers helps Fresno County lead the nation's counties in agricultural products sold. Farmers there grow over 200 crops. Grapes and cotton rank as the chief crops. The largest fig orchards in the United States flourish near Fresno. About 80 per cent of the nation's raisins, which are dried grapes, are produced there. Fresno is often called the raisin-growing capital of the world.

The packing, processing, and shipping of agricultural products is Fresno's chief industry. Other industries include oil and gas production; tourism and convention business; and the manufacturing of ceramics, chemicals, farm machinery, glass, and vending machines.

Downtown Fresno includes a civic center, a convention center, and the William Saroyan Theater. The city is the home of the Metropolitan Museum, the Fresno Opera Association, and the Fresno Philharmonic Orchestra. Universities and colleges in Fresno include California School of Professional Psychology, Fresno; California State University, Fresno; Fresno City College; Fresno Pacific College; Mennonite Brethren Biblical Seminary; and West Coast Christian College.

Yokut Indians lived in what is now the Fresno area when Mexican ranchers acquired land there in the 1840's. The United States captured the California territory from Mexico during the Mexican War (1846-1848).

The gold rush of 1849 attracted thousands of people to California. By 1860, investors were buying land in the Fresno area. Leland Stanford and others realized the area had farm potential. Stanford, a founder of the Central Pacific Railroad, built a rail line into the San Joaquin

Valley. In 1872, the railroad company built the town of Fresno Station (now Fresno). Several irrigation canals were constructed during the 1870's and 1880's, and the town became a booming farm community. Fresno was incorporated as a city in 1885.

Since the mid-1900's, the development of industries related to agriculture has helped create a population boom in Fresno. The city's population jumped from 60,685 in 1940 to 217,129 in 1980. Fresno is the county seat of Fresno County and has a council-manager form of government.   Scott E. Tompkins

Fret. See Guitar.

Freud, *froyd,* **Anna** (1895-1982), was an Austrian-born leader in the field of child psychoanalysis, the treatment of children's mental illnesses. Her work was influenced by the psychoanalytic theories of her father, the Austrian physician Sigmund Freud (see **Freud, Sigmund**).

Anna Freud believed children go through various normal stages of psychological development. She maintained that psychoanalysts must have knowledge of these stages to diagnose and treat mental illness in children. According to her, such knowledge can be obtained only through research involving the direct observation of children.

Freud was born in Vienna. She conducted most of her research at the Hampstead Child Therapy Course and Clinic, which she established in London in 1938. The clinic's activities include the treatment of mentally ill children, helping handicapped youngsters, and training workers in child therapy.   George H. Pollock

Freud, *froyd,* **Sigmund** (1856-1939), was an Austrian physician who revolutionized ideas on how the human mind works. Freud established the theory that unconscious motives control much behavior. He thus greatly advanced the field of psychiatry. His work has helped millions of mentally ill patients. His theories have brought new approaches in child rearing, education, and sociology and have provided new themes for many authors and artists. Most people in Western society view human behavior at least partially in Freudian terms.

His life

Freud was born on May 6, 1856, in Freiberg, Moravia, a region that is now part of Czechoslovakia. He was the oldest of eight children, and his father was a wool merchant. When Freud was 4 years old, his family moved to Vienna, the capital of Austria. He graduated from the medical school of the University of Vienna in 1881. Freud later decided to specialize in *neurology,* the study and treatment of disorders of the nervous system.

In 1885, Freud went to Paris to study under Jean Martin Charcot, a famous neurologist. Charcot was working with patients who suffered from a mental illness now called *hysteria.* Some of these people appeared to be blind or paralyzed, but they actually had no physical defects. Charcot demonstrated that their real problem was mental, and that the physical symptoms could be relieved through hypnosis.

Freud returned to Vienna in 1886 and began to work extensively with hysterical patients. He gradually formed ideas about the origin and treatment of mental illness. Freud used the term *psychoanalysis* for both his theories and his method of treatment. When he first presented his ideas in the 1890's, other physicians reacted

with hostility. But Freud eventually attracted a group of followers, and by 1910, he had gained international recognition.

During the following decade, Freud's reputation continued to grow. But two of his early followers, Alfred Adler and Carl Jung, split with Freud and developed their own theories of psychology (see **Adler, Alfred; Jung, Carl**). Freud was constantly modifying his own ideas, and in 1923, he published a revised version of many of his earlier theories. That same year, he learned he had cancer of the mouth. He continued his work, though the cancer made working increasingly difficult. In 1938, the Nazis gained control of Austria. Under their rule, Jews were persecuted. Freud, who was Jewish, went to England with his wife and children to escape persecution. He died there of cancer in 1939.

Freud wrote many works. However, his most important writings include *The Interpretation of Dreams* (1900), *Three Essays on the Theory of Sexuality* (1905), *Totem and Taboo* (1913), *General Introduction to Psychoanalysis* (1920), *The Ego and the Id* (1923), and *Civilization and Its Discontents* (1930).

His theories

On behavior. Freud observed that many patients behaved according to drives and experiences of which they were not consciously aware. He thus concluded that the unconscious plays a major role in shaping behavior. He also concluded that the unconscious is full of memories of events from early childhood—sometimes as far back as infancy. Freud noted that if these memories were especially painful, people kept them out of conscious awareness. He used the term *defense mechanisms* for the methods by which individuals did this. Freud believed that patients used vast amounts of energy in forming defense mechanisms. Tying up energy in defense mechanisms could affect a person's ability to lead a productive life, causing an illness that Freud called *neurosis.*

Freud also concluded that many childhood memories dealt with sex. He theorized that sexual functioning begins at birth, and that a person passes through several psychological stages of sexual development. During this passage from infant sexuality to adult sexuality, an individual makes many self-discoveries and learns to control his or her sexual impulses. Freud believed that the normal pattern of sexual development is interrupted in some individuals. These people become *fixated* at an earlier, immature stage. He felt that such fixation could contribute to mental illness in adulthood.

On the mind. Freud divided the mind into three parts: (1) the *id,* (2) the *ego,* and (3) the *superego.* He recognized that each person is born with various instincts, such as the drive to satisfy hunger and the drive to satisfy sexual needs. The id is the mental representation of these biological instincts. The id does not distinguish be-

Dr. W. Hoffer

Sigmund Freud

tween the internal mind and the outside environment. For example, the id stimulates the eating drives, but it makes no distinction between a mental image of food and the food itself.

The ego distinguishes between the internal mind and external reality. It controls behavior that bridges the gap between mental images and the outside world. For example, the ego directs a hungry person to look for and to eat real food.

The superego governs moral behavior. It is the mental representation of society's moral code. The superego seeks to limit behavior based on the drives of the id.

In mentally healthy individuals, the three parts of the mind work in harmony. But in others, the parts may conflict. For example, the superego might oppose all sexual behavior, thus preventing fulfillment of the id's sexual drives. If the parts of the mind oppose one another, psychological disturbance can result.

On treatment. At first, Freud treated neurotic patients by using the hypnotic techniques he had learned from Charcot. But he modified this approach several years later and simply had patients talk about whatever was on their minds. He called this technique *free association*. By free associating—that is, by speaking freely— the patient sometimes came upon earlier experiences that contributed to the neurosis.

Often, however, the painful memories that caused the neurosis were held in the unconscious through defense mechanisms. Freud then analyzed the random thoughts that had been expressed during free association. He did this in an effort to penetrate the patient's defense mechanisms. He also interpreted the patient's dreams, which he believed were symbolic clues to unconscious memories. After he felt he understood the root of the problem, Freud talked with the patient about the person's earlier experiences. He paid particular attention to the painful feelings—hostility or love, for example—that the patient directed at Freud himself. Through this *transference* of past feelings to the present, the patient could be relieved of the painful memories. The symptoms of the neurosis might then disappear.

His influence

Freud ranks as one of the most influential thinkers in history. His research and writings changed the way many people thought about human nature. The strongest impact of Freud's theories occurred in psychiatry and psychology. Some psychiatrists and psychologists disagree with certain of his ideas. However, Freud's work on the origin and treatment of mental illness helped form the basis of modern psychiatry. In psychology, Freud especially influenced the field of abnormal psychology and the study of the personality.

Freud's theories on sexual development led to open discussion and treatment of sexual matters and problems. His stress on the importance of childhood helped teach the value of giving children an emotionally nourishing environment. His insights also influenced the fields of anthropology and sociology. Most social scientists accept his concept that an adult's social relationships are patterned after early family relationships.

Attitudes toward antisocial behavior have also been influenced by Freud. Many parents and teachers believe that behavior problems can be caused by a child's emo-

tional conflicts. Similarly, many criminologists are convinced that large numbers of people commit crimes because of unconscious drives. Many such people can be helped more effectively by psychiatric care than by a prison sentence.

In art and literature, Freud's theories encouraged understanding of *surrealism* (see **Surrealism**). Like psychoanalysis, surrealistic painting and writing explores the inner depths of the unconscious mind. Freudian concepts have provided subject matter for many authors and artists, and critics frequently analyze art and literature in Freudian terms.   George H. Pollock

See also **Dream; Libido; Oedipus complex; Psychoanalysis.**

Additional resources

Clark, Ronald W. *Freud: The Man and the Cause.* Random House, 1980. Biography and criticism.
Jones, Ernest. *Life and Work of Sigmund Freud.* 3 vols. Basic Books, 1953-1957. The standard biography.
Stevens, Richard. *Freud and Psychoanalysis: An Exposition and Appraisal.* St. Martin's, 1983.

Frey, *fray,* also called Freyr, *frayr,* was the god of agriculture and fertility in Norse mythology. He was the son of the god Njord and the giantess Skadi. Frey's twin sister, Freyja, was the Norse goddess of love and marriage. Both belonged to the *Vanir,* a special group of peaceloving gods.

Myths tell how Frey flew over the earth in a chariot pulled by a golden boar that lit up the sky. These myths also tell how Frey sailed the seas in a ship large enough to hold all the gods. When Frey was not using his ship, he folded it up and carried it in his pocket.

In ancient times, farmers traveled with an image of Frey in their wagons. They believed this practice made their crops thrive. Many ancient Scandinavian families claimed to be descended from Frey because they thought his presence guaranteed a plentiful harvest and world peace.   C. Scott Littleton

See also **Freyja.**

Freyja, *FRAY uh,* was the goddess of love and marriage in Norse mythology. She was also associated with human fertility and childbirth. Freyja was the daughter of the god Njord and the giantess Skadi. Her twin brother, Frey, was the Norse god of agriculture and fertility. Both Freyja and Frey belonged to a group of peace-loving gods called the *Vanir.* Freyja was known as the Bride of the Vanir because she had many love affairs. According to Norse myths, Freyja originated a powerful kind of witchcraft called *seithr.* In seithr, certain women communicated with spirits to learn about the future. Freyja, as the leader of seithr, traveled in a wagon pulled by cats. See also **Frey.**   C. Scott Littleton

Friar is the title applied to a member of one of the Roman Catholic religious orders of men who originally lived as *mendicants* (beggars). The term friar comes from a Latin word that means *brother.* The mendicant orders differ from monastic orders in that they were founded for active ministry in the world, such as preaching and missionary or social work. Thus friars are more mobile than monks, who generally spend most of their lives in monasteries. Friars live in houses called *friaries.*

Mendicant orders were first officially recognized by the church in the early 1200's. They multiplied rapidly until the second Council of Lyons (1274) suppressed all but four major ones. They were the Dominicans (called Black Friars or Preaching Friars), Franciscans (Gray Friars or Friars Minor), Carmelites (White Friars or Brothers of the Blessed Virgin Mary of Mount Carmel), and an order of Augustinians (Austin Friars or Hermits of St. Augustine). A few other lesser orders survived the suppression or were founded later. At first, mendicants renounced all possessions held in common and depended on *alms* (charity). However, the Council of Trent (1545-1563) authorized the orders to hold goods in common.

David G. Schultenover

See also **Capuchins; Carmelites; Dominicans; Franciscans.**

Friars Minor. See Franciscans.

Friction is the property that objects have which makes them resist being moved across one another. If two objects with flat surfaces are placed one on top of the other, the top object can be lifted without any resistance except that of gravity. But if one object is pushed or pulled along the surface of the other, there is a resistance caused by friction.

Friction has many important uses. It makes the wheels of a locomotive grip the rails of the track. It allows a conveyor belt to turn on pulleys without slipping. You could not walk without friction to keep your shoes from sliding on the sidewalk. This is why it is hard to walk on ice. The smooth surface of the ice produces less friction than a sidewalk, and allows shoes to slip.

Friction also has disadvantages. It produces heat that may cause objects to wear. This is why oil and other lubricating liquids are used to fill spaces between moving machinery parts. The lubricating liquid reduces friction and makes the parts move more easily and produce less heat.

Kinds of friction. There are three chief kinds of friction. *Sliding* or *kinetic* friction is produced when two surfaces slide across each other, as when a book moves across a table. *Rolling friction* is the resistance produced when a rolling body moves over a surface. The friction between an automobile tire and a street is rolling friction. *Fluid friction* or *viscosity* is the friction between moving fluids or between fluids and a solid. Thinner fluids have less viscosity than thicker fluids, and usually flow faster. See **Viscosity.**

Laws of friction. The basic law of friction says that the force needed to overcome friction is proportional to the total *normal,* or perpendicular, force pressing one surface against the other. That is, when the weight of a box being pulled across a floor is doubled, the force necessary to pull it must be doubled. When the box weighs four times as much, four times as much force must be used to pull it. The ratio between the weight being moved and the force pressing the surfaces together is called the *coefficient of friction* (*C.F.*). The value of *C.F.* depends on the type of surfaces moving against each other. The coefficient of friction equals the force needed to move an object divided by the force pressing the surface together. This can be written $C.F. = \dfrac{F}{P}$.

For example, suppose a force of 30 pounds (*F*) is needed to pull a block weighing 80 pounds (*P*) across a flat surface. The coefficient of friction (*C.F.*) equals 30 divided by 80, or 0.375. In a similar example using the metric system, the force would be measured in units called *newtons.* Suppose a force of 45 newtons is needed to slide a block weighing 12.2 kilograms. The block presses down with a force of 120 newtons. This is because gravity at the earth's surface pulls with a force of 9.8 newtons for every kilogram an object weighs, and 9.8 times 12.2 equals 120. The coefficient of friction equals 45 divided by 120, or 0.375.

The coefficient of friction varies with the different materials used. The *C.F.* of wood sliding on wood is between 0.25 and 0.50. Metal sliding on metal has a *C.F.* between 0.15 and 0.20. The frictional force due to rolling friction is about $\frac{1}{100}$ as much as that due to sliding friction. But various conditions, including hardness, smoothness, and diameter of the materials, affect rolling friction. To design machines, engineers must know the various coefficients of friction.

Oil reduces friction. The *C.F.* for iron rolled on oiled wood, for example, would be much less than .018. The kind of surface has almost no effect when it is covered with oil or other liquids. The friction then depends on the viscosity of the liquid and the relative speed between the moving surfaces.   Gregory Benford

See also **Bearing; Fire** (Methods of starting fires); **Heat** (Friction).

Friday is the sixth day of the week. The name comes from the Anglo-Saxon word *Frigedaeg,* which means *Frigg's day.* Frigg was a goddess of love in Norse mythology. The Scandinavians considered Friday their luckiest day. But people today associate Friday the 13th with bad luck. One explanation for this belief is that Christ was crucified on Friday, and 13 men were present at the Last Supper. People have called Friday *hangman's day* because it once was the day for the execution of criminals. In memory of the crucifixion, some Christians fast on Fridays, except on a feast day, such as Christmas. Christians observe *Good Friday* two days before Easter in memory of Christ's suffering. The Jewish Sabbath begins at sunset on Friday. Friday is also a holy day among Muslims. Muslims also celebrate the creation of Adam on Friday.   Grace Humphrey

See also **Black Friday; Good Friday; Week.**

Friedan, *free DAN,* **Betty** (1921-   ), is considered the founder of the women's liberation movement in the United States. She first gained fame from her book *The Feminine Mystique* (1963). In this book, she protested that society puts pressure on women to be housewives only and not to seek a career.

In 1966, Friedan helped found the National Organization for Women (NOW) to fight for equal rights for women. She led a nationwide protest called the Women's Strike for Equality on Aug. 26, 1970. That date marked the 50th anniversary of the granting of the vote to U.S. women. In 1971, Friedan helped form the National Women's Political Caucus, which encourages women to seek political office.

Betty Naomi Goldstein

Jack Lenahan, *Chicago Sun-Times*
Betty Friedan

Friedan was born in Peoria, Ill. She graduated from Smith College in 1942.   Cynthia Fuchs Epstein

See also **National Organization for Women.**

Friedman, *FREED muhn,* **Milton** (1912-   ), is an American economist whose controversial theories sparked widespread debate. He was awarded the 1976 Nobel Prize in economics.

Friedman argued against government intervention in the economy, claiming that the forces of a free market will efficiently solve most economic problems. He rejected the theories of John Maynard Keynes and his followers. Keynesian economists call for short-term changes in government spending to control the economy. Instead, Friedman urged a gradual, continuous increase in the money supply to promote economic growth. He set forth these theories in his book *A Monetary History of the United States, 1867-1960* (1963). Friedman and other economists who support such theories are called *monetarists.* In his book *Capitalism and Freedom* (1962), Friedman proposed a *negative income tax.* Under this plan, families with incomes below a certain level would receive cash payments from the government.

Friedman was born in New York City and received a Ph.D. degree from Columbia University. He taught economics at the University of Chicago from 1946 to 1977. He then moved to Stanford University's Hoover Institution on War, Revolution, and Peace.   Leonard S. Silk

Friends, Religious Society of. See Quakers.

Friendship 7. See Glenn, John Herschel, Jr.

Frietchie, *FREECH ee,* **Barbara,** is the heroine of John Greenleaf Whittier's poem "Barbara Frietchie" (1864). The poem describes a supposed incident during the Civil War when the Confederate General Stonewall Jackson and his troops marched through Frederick, Md. Ninety-year-old Barbara Frietchie was the only resident of the town who risked the anger of the Confederate troops by flying a Union flag. Jackson saw the flag and ordered it shot down. But she grasped the flag as it fell, and waving it defiantly:

> "Shoot, if you must, this old gray head,
> But spare your country's flag," she said.

Jackson was moved by the old woman's bravery and permitted her to fly the flag as the troops marched through town.

No one knows for sure whether the incident related in Whittier's poem actually occurred. But a woman named Barbara Fritchie (1766-1862), also spelled Frietchie, actually lived in Frederick. A reproduction of her home stands on the supposed site of the incident (see **Maryland** [Places to visit; picture]).   B. A. Botkin

Frigate, *FRIHG iht,* is a warship used chiefly to escort amphibious and merchant ships. Frigates are used for patrol duty as well. These ships can launch rockets and torpedoes against submarines. Some frigates have guided missiles for use against aircraft and surface ships. Some larger frigates can carry one or two antisubmarine helicopters. Frigates have radar and sonar to detect enemy aircraft, surface ships, and submarines.

Most frigates of the United States Navy belong to the *Knox* and *Oliver Hazard Perry* classes. The *Knox* type is used mostly for antisubmarine warfare. Knox frigates measure 438 feet (131 meters) long, and steam turbines propel them at speeds of more than 27 knots (nautical miles per hour). In addition to their antisubmarine weapons, these frigates have a 5-inch (127-millimeter) gun and short range missiles for use against enemy planes. Each *Knox* class frigate also carries a helicopter.

Frigates of the *Oliver Hazard Perry* class, launched since 1976, can fire missiles against ships and aircraft. They also carry a 3-inch (76-millimeter) gun, torpedoes, and a helicopter. These frigates measure 445 feet (133 $\frac{1}{2}$ meters) long, and gas turbines propel them at over 28 knots.

In 1794, frigates became the first warships authorized by the United States Congress. The frigate *Constitution,* nicknamed *Old Ironsides,* ranks as one of the nation's most famous ships. It is docked at the Charlestown Navy Yard in Boston (see **Constitution** [ship]).

During World War II (1939-1945), the U.S. Navy had a class of escort ships called frigates. After the war, the Navy used the term *frigate* for large destroyer-type ships. In 1975, the Navy reclassified most of these ships as cruisers.   Norman Polmar

See also **Cruiser.**

Frigatebird, *FRIHG iht burd,* is a sea bird with a large wingspread and unusually great powers of flight. People sometimes speak of it as the most graceful bird of the seas. It is a relative of the pelican, and is also called *man-of-war bird.*

Frigatebirds live in the tropics throughout the world. They are about 40 inches (100 centimeters) long, but their wings spread to about 8 feet (2.4 meters). Black feathers with a metallic sheen cover the upper part of their bodies. The females, or both sexes of some spe-

WORLD BOOK illustration by George Suyeoka

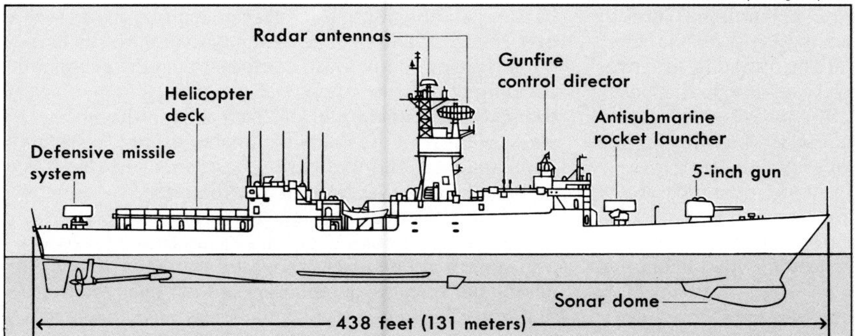

Frigates serve as patrol ships and as escorts for amphibious and merchant ships. Those of the *Knox* class, such as the frigate shown at the left, are used largely for antisubmarine warfare.

Radar antennas

Gunfire control director

Helicopter deck

Antisubmarine rocket launcher

Defensive missile system

5-inch gun

Sonar dome

438 feet (131 meters)

WORLD BOOK illustration by Trevor Boyer, Linden Artists Ltd.

Frigatebirds live in the tropics. The male, *bottom,* grows a reddish pouch during the nesting season.

cies, have white feathers on the underside. The young birds have white heads. In nesting season, the male grows a reddish pouch under its bill. It can blow up this pouch like a balloon.

Frigatebirds breed in colonies and build their nests on rocks, high cliffs, or trees on uninhabited islands. They eat fish, which they catch from the surface of the sea or steal from other birds.

Scientific classification. Frigatebirds form the frigatebird family, Fregatidae. The frigatebird of the coast of the southeastern United States is *Fregata magnificens.* The species *F. minor* and *F. ariel* are most common in the Pacific and Indian oceans.

James J. Dinsmore

See also **Bird** (picture: Birds of the ocean and the Antarctic).

Friml, *FRIHM uhl,* **Rudolf** (1879-1972), was one of the most popular composers of operettas of the early 1900's. Friml wrote more than 20 operettas, gaining immediate fame with his first production, *The Firefly* (1912). His operetta *Rose-Marie* (1924) became the most popular international hit of the 1920's. It features the famous ballad "Indian Love Call." Friml's *The Vagabond King* (1925) contains the well-known "Song of the Vagabonds." Friml composed one of his most popular melodies for the *Ziegfeld Follies of 1923.* After lyrics were added, it became known as "The Donkey Serenade."

Friml was born in Prague, Czechoslovakia, and studied with the famous Czech composer Antonín Dvořák. In 1901, Friml became the piano accompanist for the noted Czech violinist Jan Kubelik. Friml performed in America with Kubelik and as a piano soloist, settling in the United States in 1906. He became a citizen of the United States in 1925. Friml wrote light instrumental pieces for orchestra until he began composing operettas. In the early 1930's, musical tastes changed and the romantic European style of Friml's compositions seemed outdated. He therefore gave up the theater and spent the rest of his life composing privately and performing piano concerts.

Gerald Bordman

Fringe benefits. See Labor movement (Arranging contracts).

Fringe tree is a small tree or large shrub named for its threadlike or fringelike white flower petals. It is also called *old man's beard.* The fringe tree grows up to 35 feet (11 meters) high. Its delicate flowers bloom in early spring.

Fringe trees grow wild in the United States from New Jersey and southern Pennsylvania south to Florida and west to southern Missouri. They thrive on rich, well-drained soil along the banks of rivers and streams. Gardeners plant fringe trees as ornamentals as far north as

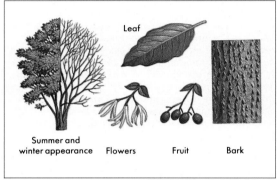

WORLD BOOK illustration by John D. Dawson

The fringe tree is named for its delicate threadlike or fringelike white flower petals that bloom in the early springtime. The tree's bark contains substances that can be used as medicines.

southern New England. Fringe trees have hard, heavy, pale-brown wood. The bark contains substances that can be used as medicines. A smaller kind of fringe tree grows wild in China.

Scientific classification. The fringe tree belongs to the olive family, Oleaceae. The common fringe tree is *Chionanthus virginica.*   T. Ewald Maki

Frisbee, *FRIHZ bee,* is a plastic, saucer-shaped disk that skims through the air when flipped with the hand. It is used both in recreation and in organized sporting events. The word *Frisbee* is a trademark for a popular brand of the disk. Most disks measure from 8.5 to 11 inches (21 to 27 centimeters) in diameter, and weigh between 3.5 and 6.2 ounces (100 to 175 grams).

The disk can be thrown in many different ways to provide both rotational spin and forward motion. By controlling the angle of release, a player can make a disk curve, skip, hover, or travel in a straight line. Skilled players can catch a disk between the legs, behind the back, or on one finger. An experienced player can toss a disk 230 feet (70 meters) or farther. Several events have been developed involving competition in throwing and catching the disk.   Daniel McCulloch Roddick

Frisch, Karl von (1886-1982), an Austrian zoologist, was a pioneer in the field of animal behavior. Frisch and two naturalists—Konrad Lorenz of Austria and Nikolaas Tinbergen, who was born in the Netherlands—won the 1973 Nobel Prize for physiology or medicine.

Frisch's best-known work dealt with the communication system of bees. He discovered that bees "dance" in certain patterns to tell members of their hive where to find food. These patterns can indicate the distance and direction of food from the hive (see **Bee** [Swarming;

Finding food; diagram: A field worker]). Frisch also showed that fish can see colors. Scientists had previously thought fish were color-blind.

Frisch was born in Vienna. He studied at the Universities of Munich and Vienna and received a Ph.D. degree from the latter institution in 1910. From 1910 to 1958, he taught at several European universities. Frisch wrote many books, including *Bees: Their Vision, Chemical Senses, and Language* (1971) and *A Biologist Remembers* (1967), an autobiography.   John A. Wiens

Frisch, Max (1911-   ), a Swiss author, became one of the leading writers in the German-speaking world after World War II. His novels and plays concern the problem of identity and the question of how individuals can find their true self.

According to Frisch, the images imposed on us by others, and the images we in turn impose on others, falsify and destroy the authenticity of human personality and individual existence. In his novels *I'm Not Stiller* (1954), *Homo Faber* (1957), and *Wilderness of Mirrors* (1964), Frisch shows the shallowness of how individuals view others and the inability to understand one's own identity. Frisch's plays, notably *Don Juan and the Love for Geometry* (1953), *The Firebugs* (1957-1958), and *Andorra* (1961), deal with the same themes. Frisch was born in Zurich.   Peter Gontrum

Frisch, Ragnar, *RANG nair* (1895-1973), a Norwegian economist, shared the 1969 Nobel Prize in economics with Jan Tinbergen of the Netherlands. The two men received the award for their work on the development of mathematical models used in *econometrics* (mathematical analysis of economic activity). The Nobel Prize in economics was awarded for the first time in 1969.

Frisch was born in Oslo and graduated from Oslo University. He served as a professor in social economy and statistics at the university from 1931 until his retirement in 1965. Frisch led a number of theoretical investigations concerning production, economic planning, and national accounting. He helped establish the Econometric Society in 1930 and was chief editor of its journal, *Econometrica,* until 1955. Frisch also served as an adviser to various developing countries, including Egypt and India.   Leonard S. Silk

Fritillary, *FRIHT uh LEHR ee,* is the common name for a *genus* (group) of herbs that belong to the lily family. This group is made up of nearly a hundred different species of plants that grow throughout the North Temperate Zone. Fritillaries have nodding, bell-shaped flowers. All fritillaries bloom in the spring. Most fritillaries are hardy plants, and grow well in good garden soil. Popular kinds of fritillaries include the *crown imperial* and the *checkered lily,* or *snakes-head.* The crown imperial has brick or yellow-red flowers. The checkered lily has checkered or veined purple-colored flowers.

Scientific classification. The fritillary belongs to the lily family, Liliaceae. The crown imperial fritillary is *Fritillaria imperialis.* The checkered lily is *F. meleagris.*   Theodor Just

Fröbel, *FRU buhl,* **Friedrich Wilhelm August,** *FREE drihkh VIHL helm OW gust* (1782-1852), was a German educator who founded the kindergarten movement. Fröbel, whose name is also spelled Froebel, started his first kindergarten in 1837. Other educators had established schools for very young children, but Fröbel was the first to use the word *kindergarten* for

such schools. This word comes from two German words meaning *garden of children.* By 1900, kindergartens had spread throughout Europe, Canada, and the United States.

Fröbel designed the kindergarten to help children learn naturally. His program included free play, games, and such activities as clay modeling, paper cutting, and weaving. Fröbel designed instructional materials that remained standard equipment for many years.

Fröbel believed in the unity of God, nature, and humanity, and this belief guided his philosophy of education. He thought education should promote the natural development of a person's spiritual being. His book *The Education of Man* (1826) explains his philosophy.

Fröbel was born in Oberweissbach, near Erfurt, in what is now East Germany. He began to teach in 1805. He opened his first school, an institution for older children, in 1816.   Douglas Sloan

See also **Kindergarten** (Early kindergartens).

Frobisher, *FROH bih shuhr,* **Sir Martin** (1535?-1594), was one of the first English navigators to search for a Northwest Passage to India and the East. He became known as one of the greatest seamen of the reign of Queen Elizabeth I. He fought against the Spanish Armada, and was knighted for his services.

His three attempts to reach Asia by sailing west extended geographic knowledge. On the first voyage in 1576, he rounded the southern end of Greenland, visited Labrador, and became the first European to sail into the bay on Baffin Island. This bay now bears his name. Frobisher took back to England rock that some persons thought was gold ore. This touched off a scramble to join in his second voyage in 1577. Frobisher annexed the country to England on this trip, and returned with 200 short tons (180 metric tons) of rock. On his third voyage, in 1578, he sailed with 15 ships and 41 miners. He entered what later became Hudson Strait, but made no further attempts at discovery. This time he brought back some 1,300 short tons (1,180 metric tons) of the rock. But it proved valueless, and interest in the Northwest Passage declined. Frobisher was born in Altofts, Yorkshire.

James G. Allen

WORLD BOOK illustration by Lorrain Epstein

Fritillaries are lilies with bell-shaped flowers. The checkered lily, *above,* has checkered or veined purple-colored flowers.

E. R. Degginger

Harold Hungerford

Frogs vary greatly in color and size. The spotted, brownish-green leopard frog, *above,* measures from 2 to 3½ inches (5 to 9 centimeters) long. The colorful arrow poison frog, *top right,* grows from 1 to 2 inches (2.5 to 5 centimeters) long. The green tree frog, *bottom right,* is less than 2 inches long.

Frog

Frog is a small, tailless animal with bulging eyes. Almost all frogs also have long back legs. The strong hind legs enable a frog to leap distances far greater than the length of its body. Frogs live on every continent except Antarctica. But tropical regions have the greatest number of species. Frogs are classified as *amphibians.* Most amphibians, including most frogs, spend part of their life as a water animal and part as a land animal.

Frogs are related to toads but differ from them in several ways. The section *Kinds of frogs* describes the basic differences between frogs and toads.

The first frogs appeared on earth about 180 million years ago. About 2,700 species of frogs and toads have developed from these early ancestors. Some species spend their entire life in or near water. Others live mainly on land and come to the water only to mate. Still other species never enter the water, not even to mate. Many kinds are climbers that dwell in trees. Others are burrowers that live underground.

Throughout history, frogs have been the source of superstitions. One old myth says that frogs fall from the sky during a rain. Actually, many species that live underground leave their burrows during or after a rain at the start of the mating season. Because people seldom see these frogs the rest of the year, they imagine the animals fell from the sky with the rain.

The body of a frog

The giant, or Goliath, frog of west-central Africa ranks as the largest frog. It measures nearly a foot (30 centime-

Don C. Forester, the contributor of this article, is Associate Professor of Biology at Towson State University.

ters) long. The smallest species grow only ½ inch (1.3 centimeters) long. Frogs also differ in color. Most kinds are green or brown, but some have colorful markings.

Although different species may vary in size or color, almost all frogs have the same basic body structure. They have large hind legs, short front legs, and a flat head and body with no neck. Adult frogs have no tail, though one North American species has a short, taillike structure. Most frogs have a sticky tongue attached to the front part of the mouth. They can rapidly flip out the tongue to capture prey.

Like higher animals, frogs have such internal organs as a heart, liver, lungs, and kidneys. However, some of the internal organs differ from those of higher animals. For example, a frog's heart has three chambers instead of four. And although adult frogs breathe by means of lungs, they also breathe through their skin.

Legs. A few burrowing species have short hind legs and cannot hop. But all other frogs have long, powerful hind legs, which they use for jumping. Many frogs can leap 20 times their body length on a level surface. Frogs also use their large hind legs for swimming. Most water-dwelling species have webbed toes on their hind feet. The smaller front legs, or arms, prop a frog up when it sits. The front legs also help break the animal's fall when it jumps. Frogs that live in trees have tiny, sticky pads on the ends of their fingers and toes. The pads help the animal cling to the tree trunk as it climbs.

Skin. Most frogs have thin, moist skin. Many species have poison glands in their skin. The poison oozes onto the skin and helps protect the frog. If an enemy grabs a frog, the poison irritates the enemy's mouth and causes the animal to release the frog. Frogs have no hair, though the males of one African species, the so-called hairy frog, look hairy during the mating season. At that time, tiny, blood-rich growths called *papillae,* which resemble hair, grow from the sides of the frog's body.

Skeleton of a grass frog

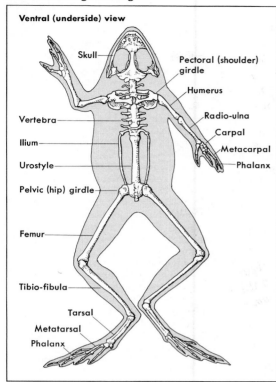

Ventral (underside) view

Skull
Pectoral (shoulder) girdle
Humerus
Radio-ulna
Carpal
Metacarpal
Phalanx
Vertebra
Ilium
Urostyle
Pelvic (hip) girdle
Femur
Tibio-fibula
Tarsal
Metatarsal
Phalanx

These structures provide males with extra oxygen during a period when they are very active.

Some species of frogs change their skin color with changes in the humidity, light, and temperature. Frogs shed the outer layer of their skin many times a year. Using their forelegs, they pull the old skin off over their head. They then usually eat the old skin.

Senses. Frogs have fairly good eyesight, which helps them in capturing food and avoiding enemies. A frog's eyes bulge out, enabling the animal to see in almost all directions. Frogs can close their eyes by pulling the eyeballs deeper into their sockets. This action closes the upper and lower eyelids. Most species also have a thin, partly clear inner eyelid attached to the bottom lid. This inner eyelid, called the *nictitating membrane,* can be moved upward when a frog's eyes are open. It protects the eyes without completely cutting off vision.

Most frogs have a disk of skin behind each eye. Each disk is called a *tympanum,* or eardrum. Sound waves cause the eardrums to vibrate. The vibrations travel to the inner ear, which is connected by nerves to the hearing centers of the brain.

Most frogs have a delicate sense of touch. It is particularly well developed in species that live in water. The tongue and mouth have many taste buds, and frogs often spit out bad-tasting food. The sense of smell varies among species. Frogs that hunt mostly at night or that live underground have the best sense of smell.

Voice. Male frogs of most species have a voice, which they use mainly to call females during the mating season. In some species, the females also have a voice. But the female's voice is not nearly so loud as the male's.

Internal organs of a male grass frog

A frog's internal anatomy resembles that of higher animals in many ways. In addition, frogs are small and easily available. For these reasons, frogs have long been used for dissection in basic biology classes. The drawing at the left shows the organs that are visible when the frog's belly is cut open. The drawing at the right shows the structures behind the first layer of organs.

WORLD BOOK illustrations by Marion Pahl

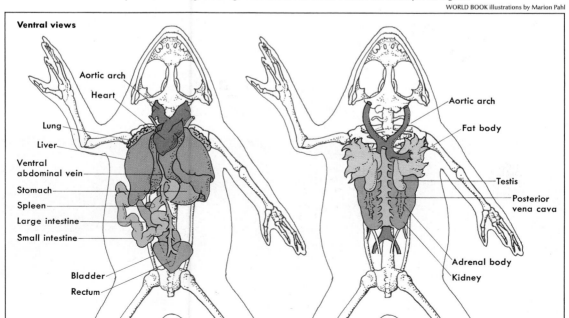

Ventral views

Aortic arch
Heart
Lung
Liver
Ventral abdominal vein
Stomach
Spleen
Large intestine
Small intestine
Bladder
Rectum

Aortic arch
Fat body
Testis
Posterior vena cava
Adrenal body
Kidney

Grant Heilman

Anthony Bannister, NHPA

A male frog, *above,* sounds a mating call by puffing out its throat and forcing air over its vocal cords. It uses this call to attract a female.

A frog's sticky tongue is used to capture prey. The green frog shown at the left is about to eat a fly. The disk behind its eye is an eardrum.

A frog produces sound by means of its *vocal cords.* The vocal cords consist of thin bands of tissue in the *larynx* (voice box), which lies between the mouth and lungs. When a frog forces air from its lungs, the vocal cords vibrate and give off sound.

Among many species, the males have a *vocal sac,* which swells to great size while a call is being made. Species that have a vocal sac produce a much louder call than do similar species that have no sac. Some species have a vocal sac on each side of the head. Others have a single sac in the throat region.

The life of a frog

Frogs, like all other amphibians, are *cold-blooded—*that is, their body temperature tends to be the same as the temperature of the surrounding air or water. Frogs that live in regions with cold winters hibernate. Some species hibernate in burrows. Others spend the winter buried in mud at the bottom of a pond or stream, breathing through their skin. During hibernation, a frog lives off materials stored in its body tissues.

Mating. Most frogs that live in tropical and semitropical regions breed during the rainy season. In other regions, most species of frogs breed in spring or in early summer.

The majority of frogs, including most species that live on land, mate in water. The male frogs usually enter the water first. They then call to attract mates. Their call also helps direct other males to a pool suitable for mating. Each species has its own mating call. Naturalists can identify many kinds of frogs more easily by their call than by their appearance. Female frogs respond only to the call made by males of their own species. In certain species, individual differences in the mating call may determine which male the female chooses to mate with. Males of some species also have a territorial call. This call warns other males of the same species that a certain area is occupied and that intruders are not welcome.

After a female frog enters the water, a male grasps her and clings to her back. In this position, the male fertilizes the eggs as they leave the female's body. The eggs hatch within 3 to 25 days, depending on the species and the water temperature. Higher water temperatures speed up development, and lower temperatures slow it down. Among most species, a tiny, tailed animal known as a *tadpole* or *polliwog* hatches from the egg.

Eggs. The eggs of different species vary in size, color, and shape. A jellylike substance covers frog eggs, providing a protective coating. This jelly also differs from species to species.

Some species of frogs lay several thousand eggs at a time. But only a few of these eggs develop into adult frogs. Ducks, fish, insects, and other water creatures eat many of the eggs. Even if the eggs hatch, the tadpoles also face the danger of being eaten by larger water animals. In addition, the pond or stream in which the eggs were laid sometimes dries up. As a result, the tadpoles die.

Certain tropical frogs lay their eggs in rain water that collects among the leaves of plants or in holes in trees. Other tropical species attach their eggs to the underside of leaves that grow over water. When the eggs hatch, the tadpoles fall into the water.

Treat Davidson, NAS

In water, a frog uses its strong hind legs for swimming. Many water-dwelling species, such as the North American bullfrog, *above,* have webbed toes on their hind feet as well.

Stephen Dalton, NHPA

On land, the frog's muscular hind legs are used for jumping. The legs of the large edible frog, *above,* have still another use. People throughout Europe eat them.

The life of a frog   A frog's life has three stages: (1) egg, (2) tadpole, and (3) adult frog. Most female frogs lay a clump of several hundred eggs in water. A male frog clings to the female's back and fertilizes the eggs as she lays them. Tiny fishlike tadpoles hatch from the eggs. As the tadpoles grow, they develop legs and a froglike body. In time, they become adult frogs and can live out of water.

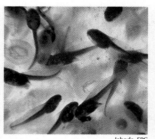

Jahoda, FPG

Newly hatched tadpoles

Jane Burton, Bruce Coleman Inc.   E. S. Ross   Giuseppe Mazza

Frog eggs and egg laying   **Older tadpole, with legs**   **Frog near completion of metamorphosis**

Among some species, one of the parents carries the eggs until they hatch. For example, the female of certain South American tree frogs carries the eggs on her back. Among another species of frog, the midwife toad, the male carries the eggs wound around his hind legs. Males of another species, Darwin's frog, carry the eggs in their vocal pouch.

Some tropical frogs lay their eggs on land. They lay them under logs or dead leaves. These frogs have no tadpole stage. A young frog hatches from the egg and begins life as a land animal.

Tadpoles are not completely developed when they hatch. At first, the tadpole clings to some support in the water, using its mouth or a tiny sucker. A tadpole has no neck, and so its head and body look like one round form. The animal has a long tail and resembles a little fish. It breathes by means of gills, which are hidden by a covering of skin.

A tadpole's form changes as the animal grows. The tail becomes larger and makes it possible for the animal to swim about to obtain food. Tadpoles eat plants and decaying animal matter. Some tadpoles eat frog eggs and other tadpoles.

In time, the tadpole begins to grow legs. The hind legs appear first. Then the lungs begin to develop and the front legs appear. The digestive system changes, enabling the frog that develops to eat live animals. Just before its *metamorphosis* (change) into a frog, the tadpole loses its gills. Finally, a tiny frog, still bearing a stump of a tail, emerges from the water. Eventually, the animal absorbs its tail and assumes its adult form.

Some tadpoles are so small they can hardly be seen. But a fully developed bullfrog tadpole may measure 6 to 7 inches (15 to 18 centimeters) long. It may take two or even three years for a bullfrog tadpole to develop into a frog. But among most species, the tadpoles change into adults within a few months. In a few species that breed in temporary ponds, this process may take less than two weeks.

Adult frogs. After a frog becomes an adult, it may take a few months to a few years before the animal is mature enough to breed. The green frog and the pickerel frog mature in about three years. In captivity, a bullfrog may live more than 15 years. But few species of frogs live longer than 6 to 8 years in the wild. Many are eaten by such enemies as bats, herons, raccoons, snakes, turtles, and fish.

Adult frogs eat mainly insects and other small animals, including earthworms, minnows, and spiders. Most frogs use their sticky tongue to capture prey. The tongue is flipped out of the mouth in response to movement by the prey.

Most frogs have teeth only on their upper jaw. Toads lack teeth altogether. As a result, frogs and toads swallow their prey in one piece. To aid in the swallowing process, the frog's eyes sink through openings in the skull and force the food down the throat.

Kinds of frogs

Frogs and toads make up the order Anura, or Salientia, one of the three main groups of amphibians. Most zoologists divide this order into at least 19 families of living frogs and toads.

One family of anurans consists of *true frogs. True toads* make up another family. Most true toads have a broader, flatter body and darker, drier skin than do most true frogs. True toads are commonly covered with warts, but true frogs have smooth skin. Unlike most true frogs, the majority of true toads live on land. The adults go to water only to breed. For more information on true toads, see **Toad.**

Of the other families in the order Anura, some closely resemble true frogs, and others closely resemble true toads. Still others have features of both true frogs and true toads. Certain anuran families other than the true toads also have the word *toad* as part of their common name.

Some of the most common frogs in the United

States and Canada belong to the true frog and tree frog families.

True frogs live on every continent except Antarctica. They are most common in Africa. The majority of true frogs live in or near water. They have long hind legs, smooth skin, a narrow waist, and webbed hind feet.

More than 20 kinds of true frogs live in the United States. Many of these frogs also live in Canada. A group of related species known as leopard frogs are the most widespread. Leopard frogs range from the Atlantic coast to eastern California and from northern Canada to the Mexican border. The bullfrog, which may grow up to 8 inches (20 centimeters) long, ranks as the largest American and Canadian frog. Other common true frogs of the United States and Canada include the green frog, the pickerel frog, and the wood frog. Unlike most other true frogs, the wood frog spends much of its time away from water. It lives in damp wooded areas of Alaska, Canada, and the Midwestern and Eastern United States.

Tree frogs, like true frogs, live on all continents except Antarctica. Most tree frogs measure less than 2 inches (5 centimeters) long and dwell in trees.

About 25 species of tree frogs live in the United States. Some of these species are also found in Canada. Common species in the Eastern United States include the green tree frog, the gray tree frog, and the spring peeper. Western tree frogs include the California tree frog, the canyon tree frog, and the Pacific tree frog. Some North American tree frogs, called chorus frogs and cricket frogs, live mainly on the ground.

Other frogs of the United States include leptodactylid frogs, narrow-mouthed toads, spadefoot toads, and tailed frogs.

Leptodactylid frogs make up a large family of frogs that live mainly in Australia and South America. Those found in the United States include the barking frog, the cliff frog, and the white-lipped frog. The barking frog and the cliff frog live on rocky cliffs in Texas. These frogs lay their eggs under rocks. Tiny frogs hatch from the eggs, without going through the tadpole stage. The white-lipped frog lives in the southern Rio Grande Valley area of Texas. The female white-lipped frog lays her eggs in a hole near water. She then beats the egg jelly into a foam. The tadpoles live in the foam nest until rain washes them into the nearby water.

Narrow-mouthed toads live throughout most tropical and subtropical regions. As their name suggests, these frogs have an extremely narrow mouth. The eastern narrow-mouthed toad, the Great Plains narrow-mouthed toad, and the sheep frog are the only members of this family that live in the United States. All three species live in burrows and eat ants and termites.

Spadefoot toads live in Asia, Europe, North America, and northwestern Africa. These frogs are called spadefoots because most of them have a sharp-edged spadelike growth on each hind foot. They use this growth as a digging tool.

Spadefoot toads live throughout much of the United States. They dwell underground and are usually seen only after a rain. Several species live in dry regions of the Great Plains and the Southwest. These spadefoots may remain in their burrows for weeks at a time to stay moist. They breed following heavy rains, often laying their eggs in temporary ponds. The tadpoles develop rapidly. If enough food is available, tiny adults may emerge in only 12 days.

Tailed frogs live in swift mountain streams of the northwestern United States and southwestern Canada. The moving water makes external fertilization of the eggs difficult. Instead, the male uses a taillike structure to fertilize the eggs while they are inside the female. Tadpoles of tailed frogs have a large sucker that enables them to hold on to rocks even in the strongest current.

Frogs and human beings

Frogs benefit us in many ways. They eat large numbers of insects, which might otherwise become serious pests. Frogs also provide us with food. The meaty hind legs of larger frogs are considered a delicacy in many countries. In the United States, people mainly eat the legs of bullfrogs, green frogs, and leopard frogs. Frogs also are used widely in the laboratory. Medical researchers use frogs to test new drugs, and students dissect frogs to learn about anatomy.

Human beings are, in fact, the frog's worst enemy. People obtain most of the frogs used for food and in the laboratory from the wild. Furthermore, people destroy the homes and breeding places of frogs by replacing natural areas with cities and farms. They also pollute and so poison the waters in which frogs dwell.

Scientific classification. True frogs make up the family Ranidae. All North American true frogs are in the genus *Rana*. Tree frogs make up the family Hylidae. Leptodactylid frogs make up the family Leptodactylidae; narrow-mouthed toads, the family Microhylidae; and spadefoot toads, the family Pelobatidae. The tailed frog belongs to the family Leiopelmatidae.

Don C. Forester

Outline

I. **The body of a frog**
   A. Legs
   B. Skin
   C. Senses
   D. Voice
II. **The life of a frog**
   A. Mating
   B. Eggs
   C. Tadpoles
   D. Adult frogs
III. **Kinds of frogs**
   A. True frogs
   B. Tree frogs
   C. Other frogs
IV. **Frogs and human beings**

Questions

How many species of frogs are there?
Which is the most widespread frog in the United States and Canada?
How do tadpoles breathe? How do adult frogs?
In what ways do frogs benefit us?
What do tadpoles eat? What do adult frogs eat?
How did spadefoot toads get their name?
Why are some frogs able to climb trees?
What is the function of a male frog's territorial call?
What are some of the changes a tadpole undergoes during its metamorphosis into a frog?
What is the function of the *nictitating membrane*?

Additional resources

Level I

Cole, Joanna. *A Frog's Body.* Morrow, 1980.
Lane, Margaret. *The Frog.* Dial, 1981.
Petty, Kate. *Frogs and Toads.* Watts, 1985.
Webster, David. *Frog and Toad Watching.* Messner, 1986.

Level II

Blassingame, Wyatt. *Wonders of Frogs and Toads.* Dodd, 1975.
Frogs. Ed. by Gerald Donaldson. Van Nostrand, 1980. A collection of stories, poems, facts, and fancies about frogs.
Mattison, Christopher. *Frogs and Toads of the World.* Facts On File, 1987.

Froissart, *FROY sahrt* or *frwah SAHR,* **Jean,** *zhahn* (1337?-1410?), a French poet and historian, wrote *The Chronicles of France, England, Scotland, and Spain.* This four-volume work describes events from 1325 to 1400, especially the Hundred Years' War (see **Hundred Years' War**). *The Chronicles* are based partly on what Froissart actually witnessed and partly on research. His history is not always accurate, but he described vividly the manners and personalities of the times. One critic said, "Froissart's whole business was to live in the fourteenth century, and tell us what he saw there." William Morris and other writers of the 1800's drew materials for some of their narrative poems from *The Chronicles.* Froissart also wrote of his school days and early love affairs in "L'Espinette Amoureuse."

During the 1360's, Froissart served five years as secretary to Queen Philippa of England. He studied to be a priest, but preferred writing of chivalry and adventure. Froissart was born in Valenciennes, France.

Francis J. Bowman

Fromm, *frahm,* **Erich** (1900-1980), was a German-born social psychoanalyst. He became a leading supporter of the idea that most human behavior is a learned response to social conditions. In adopting this concept, Fromm rejected much of the theory of the noted Austrian psychiatrist Sigmund Freud. Freud maintained that instincts determine most human behavior.

Fromm applied the ideas of sociology to psychoanalysis. He studied the social and cultural processes by which people come to learn and act out the behavior expected of them by their society.

Fromm wrote numerous books that reflect his many fields of interest, such as philosophy, psychology, religion, and sociology. His major works include *The Sane Society* (1955), *The Art of Loving* (1956), and *The Heart of Man* (1964).

Fromm was born in Frankfurt. He earned his Ph.D. degree from the University of Heidelberg in 1922. In 1933, Fromm came to the United States to lecture at the Institute for Psychoanalysis in Chicago. He became a United States citizen in 1940. Fromm held various positions in psychoanalytical institutions in the United States and taught at universities in the United States and Mexico.

George H. Pollock

Frond. See Fern.

Fronde, *frawnd,* was a revolt of nobles against the French monarchy. The word means *sling,* a popular game among French boys. Historians do not know how the revolt got its name. In 1648, the Parlement of Paris rebelled against French tax policies. The Prince of Condé led armies that crushed the rebellion in 1649. Condé himself then led a new revolt in 1650. It failed in 1652, and the monarchy became stronger than it had been before the revolt.

Front. See Weather (Fronts; illustrations).

Frontal bone. See Head.

Frontenac, *FRAHN tuh nak* or *frawnt NAHK,* **Comte de,** *kaunt duh* (1620-1698), was governor general of New France, the French empire in North America, in the late 1600's. He helped establish France's power in North America so firmly that it lasted for more than 50 years after his death.

Frontenac was appointed governor general in 1672. His stern, military ways and hot temper often got him into trouble with the civil authorities in New France. But Frontenac knew when to be tactful and when to be masterful with the Indians. The colony prospered under his rule.

Frontenac encouraged exploration of the west, and aided the expeditions of Robert Cavelier, Sieur de la Salle; Louis Jolliet; and Father Marquette. But he quarreled constantly with Bishop Laval and the priests, mainly about using brandy in the Indian trade. The church objected to this. He was recalled to France in 1682.

Seven years later, however, he was again appointed governor general, as New France needed his stern rule. The French planned to drive the English out of North America, or hold them in a narrow strip of land along the Atlantic. Frontenac began campaigns against the Iroquois Indians, whom the English encouraged in their attacks on New France. Warfare followed on the New York and New England frontiers. Frontenac's bands of

Detail of a water color by J. H. de Rinzy; Public Archives of Canada

The Comte de Frontenac served two terms as governor general of New France during the late 1600's. This water color shows Frontenac, seated in a canoe, on his way to Fort Cataraqui, which he built on Lake Ontario in 1673.

French fighters and Algonquian Indians were not able to make permanent conquests. In 1690, Frontenac defended Quebec against an attacking English fleet. Six years later, Frontenac's forces laid waste the villages and lands of the Iroquois. The Treaty of Ryswick, in 1697, stopped the war for a time. Frontenac died less than a year later.

Frontenac became a soldier as a boy, and was made a brigadier general at the age of 26. He served in Flanders, Germany, Italy, Hungary, and Crete before he became governor general of New France. His given and family name was Louis de Buade.   Ian C. C. Graham

See also **Canada, History of** (The royal province).

Frontier. See **Pioneer life in America; Western frontier life; Westward movement.**

Frost is a pattern of ice crystals formed from water vapor on grass, windowpanes, and other exposed surfaces near the ground. Frost occurs mainly on cold, cloudless nights when the air temperature drops below 32° F. (0° C), which is the freezing point of water.

Frost and dew form in much the same way. During the day, the earth's surface absorbs heat from the sun. When the sun sets, the earth begins to cool. The drop in temperature is greater on clear nights than on cloudy nights because there are no clouds to reflect the heat given off from the earth's surface. As the cooling continues, the water vapor in the air condenses to form dew-

drops on objects. Some of these dewdrops freeze when the temperature falls below 32° F. The frozen droplets increase in size, becoming frost crystals when the surrounding dewdrops evaporate and deposit water vapor on the crystals. At temperatures below freezing, water vapor sometimes changes directly into ice crystals without first forming dewdrops.

Frost crystals, also called *hoarfrost,* occur in two basic forms—platelike and columnar. The *platelike* crystals are flat and resemble snow crystals. The *columnar* crystals are six-sided, hollow columns of ice.

The term *frost* also refers to below-freezing temperatures harmful to plants. At such temperatures, the fluids in plant cells freeze and expand, causing the cell walls to rupture. Farmers protect their crops from this type of killing frost by warming cold surface air with oil-burning heaters. They also use large fans to mix the surface air with the warmer air above it. Artificial fog may also be produced to reduce the loss of heat from the surface.

Norihiko Fukuta

Frost, Robert Lee (1874-1963), became the most popular American poet of his time. He won the Pulitzer Prize for poetry in 1924, 1931, 1937, and 1943. In 1960, Congress voted Frost a gold medal "in recognition of his poetry, which has enriched the culture of the United States and the philosophy of the world." Frost's public career reached a climax in January 1961, when he read

Platelike frost crystals are flat and closely resemble snow crystals. Frost crystals of this type commonly form delicate, lacy patterns on windowpanes, *above.*

Columnar frost crystals are six-sided, hollow columns of ice. They may resemble thick needles when they grow on such exposed objects as blades of grass or leaves of plants, *above.*

his poem "The Gift Outright" at the inauguration of President John F. Kennedy.

His life. Frost was born in San Francisco on March 26, 1874. After the death of his father in 1885, his family moved back to New England, the original family home. Frost attended schools in Lawrence, Mass., and later briefly attended Dartmouth and Harvard colleges. In the early 1890's, he worked in New England as a farmer, an editor, and a schoolteacher, absorbing the materials that were to form the themes of many of his most famous poems. His first volume of poetry, *A Boy's Will,* appeared in 1913. His final collection, *In the Clearing,* appeared in 1962. Frost died on Jan. 29, 1963.

Wide World

Robert Frost

His poems. Frost's poetry is identified with New England, particularly Vermont and New Hampshire. Frost found inspiration for many of his finest poems in the region's landscapes, folkways, and speech mannerisms. His poetry is noted for its plain language, conventional poetic forms, and graceful style. Many of his earliest poems are as richly developed as his later poems.

Frost is sometimes praised for being a direct and straightforward writer. While he is never obscure, he cannot always be read easily. His effects, even at their simplest, depend upon a certain slyness for which the reader must be prepared. In "Precaution," Frost wrote:

> I never dared be radical when young
> For fear it would make me conservative
> When old.

In his longer, more elaborate poems, Frost writes about complex subjects in a complex style.

Frost tends to restrict himself to New England scenes, but the range of moods in his poetry is rich and varied. He assumes the role of a puckish, homespun philosopher in "Mending Wall." In such poems as "Design" and "Bereft," he responds to the terror and tragedy of life. He writes soberly of vaguely threatening aspects of nature in "Come In" and "Stopping by Woods on a Snowy Evening." In the latter poem, he wrote:

> My little horse must think it queer
> To stop without a farmhouse near
> Between the woods and frozen lake
> The darkest evening of the year.

"Precaution" and the second stanza from "Stopping by Woods on a Snowy Evening" from *The Poetry of Robert Frost* edited by Edward Connery Lathem. Copyright 1923, © 1969 by Holt, Rinehart and Winston. Copyright 1936, 1951 by Robert Frost. Copyright © 1964 by Lesley Frost Ballantine. Reprinted by permission of Henry Holt and Company and Jonathan Cape Limited.

A similar varied pattern can be found in Frost's character studies. "The Witch of Coos" is a comic account of the superstitions of rural New England. In "Home Burial," this same setting is the background of tragedy centering around a child's death. In "The Hill Wife," Frost shows the loneliness and emotional poverty of a rural existence driving a person insane.

By placing people and nature side by side, Frost often appears to write the kind of romantic poetry associated with England and the United States in the 1800's. There is, however, a crucial difference between his themes and those of the older tradition. The romantic poets of the 1800's believed people could live in harmony with nature. To Frost, the purposes of people and nature are never the same, and so nature's meanings can never be known. Probing for nature's secrets is futile and foolish. Humanity's best chance for serenity does not come from understanding the natural environment. Serenity comes from working usefully and productively amid the external forces of nature. Frost often used the theme of "significant toil"—toil by which people are nourished and sustained. This theme appears in such famous lyrics as "Birches," "After Apple-Picking," and "Two Tramps in Mud Time." Clark Griffith

Additional resources

Burnshaw, Stanley. *Robert Frost Himself.* Braziller, 1986.
Poirier, Richard. *Robert Frost: The Work of Knowing.* Oxford, 1977. Interpretation and criticism.
Pritchard, William H. *Frost: A Literary Life Reconsidered.* Oxford, 1984.
Thompson, Lawrance R., and Winnick, R. H. *Robert Frost: A Biography.* Holt, 1981. The authorized biography of the poet, condensed into one volume.

Frostbite is an injury that results from exposure of the skin to extreme cold. Frostbite occurs when ice crystals form in the skin and—in more severe cases—in the tissue beneath the skin. Frostbite most commonly affects the ears, nose, hands, and feet. A frostbitten area may turn red or unnaturally white. Early symptoms include feelings of coldness, tingling, pain, and numbness.

Frostbite should be treated by restoring circulation and warmth to the affected part. Rubbing frostbite with snow or ice is dangerous because it might remove skin and damage the tissue. It is safest to warm the frostbitten part rapidly in warm, but not hot, water. The water temperature should be between 102° and 105° F. (39° and 41° C). Intense pain may occur during the rapid rewarming. The victim should be kept in a warm room, with the affected part slightly raised. If frostbite is not treated quickly, *gangrene* (tissue death) may develop. Healed tissue may show such long-term complications as increased sensitivity to cold and disturbances of sensation. Charles J. McDonald

See also **Chilblain; First aid** (Frostbite); **Immersion foot.**

Frozen food. See Food, Frozen.

FRS. See Federal Reserve System.

Fructose is a sugar produced by nearly all fruits and by many vegetables. Fructose, also known as *levulose* and *fruit sugar,* is nearly twice as sweet as *sucrose* (table sugar). Fructose is used to sweeten such food products as diet foods, gelatin desserts, jellies, soft drinks, and syrups. It is the chief sweetener in honey.

Foods that contain fructose taste as sweet as similar foods made with sucrose, but they may have fewer calories. Fructose gives ice cream and candies a smooth texture. It also absorbs moisture readily and so helps keep baked goods from becoming stale.

Fructose is produced commercially as a liquid, powder, or tablet. Food processors use fructose primarily in the form of *high-fructose corn syrup,* which is obtained from cornstarch. Kay L. Franzen

See also **Corn syrup; Sugar** (Kinds of sugar).

Fruit is the part of a flowering plant that contains the plant's seeds. Fruits include acorns, cucumbers, tomatoes, and wheat grains. However, the word *fruit* commonly refers to the juicy, sweet or tart kinds that people enjoy as desserts or snacks. The word comes from the Latin word *frui,* meaning *enjoy.* Popular fruits include apples, bananas, grapes, oranges, peaches, pears, and strawberries.

Many fruits are nutritious as well as appetizing. For example, oranges and strawberries contain large amounts of Vitamin C. Most fruits have a high sugar content, and so they provide quick energy. Fruits alone cannot provide a balanced diet, however, because the majority of them supply little protein.

The world's fruit growers raise millions of tons of fruit annually. Fruit growing is a branch of *horticulture,* a field of agriculture that also includes the raising of nuts, vegetables, flowers, and landscape crops. Most nuts are actually fruits, as are such vegetables as cucumbers, green peppers, and tomatoes. To prevent confusion, horticultural scientists define a fruit as an edible seed-bearing structure that (1) consists of fleshy tissue and (2) is produced by a *perennial.* A perennial is a plant that lives for more than two years without being replanted. The horticultural definition of a fruit excludes nuts and vegetables. Nuts are firm rather than fleshy. Most vegetables are *annuals*—that is, the plants live for only one season.

In some cases, the horticultural definition of a fruit conflicts with the definition used by botanists and with common usage. For example, watermelons and muskmelons are fruits, and most people regard them as such. But they grow on vines that must be replanted annually, and so horticulturists regard melons as vegetables. Rhubarb is sometimes considered a fruit. But people eat the leafstalk of the rhubarb plant, not the seed-bearing structure. Therefore, horticulturists classify rhubarb as a vegetable.

This article discusses fruits chiefly from a horticultural point of view. The last section tells about fruits from a botanical viewpoint.

How horticulturists classify fruits

Most of the fruits that are widely raised in North America today were originally brought from other regions. For example, apples, cherries, and pears originated in Europe and western Asia. Apricots and peaches first came from China, and lemons and oranges from China and Southeast Asia. All these fruits are now grown in any part of the world that has a favorable climate.

All fruits need at least some moisture, and most require considerable amounts. Dates and olives are among the few fruits that can be grown in dry regions without irrigation.

Horticulturists classify fruits into three groups, based on temperature requirements for growth: (1) temperate fruits, (2) subtropical fruits, and (3) tropical fruits.

How horticulturists classify fruits Any seed-bearing structure produced by a flowering plant is a fruit. But the word *fruit* has a more limited meaning in common usage and in horticulture, the branch of agriculture that includes fruit growing. Thus, the word usually refers to the edible sweet or tart fruits that are popular foods and widely grown farm crops. Horticulturists classify these fruits into three groups, based on temperature requirements for growth: (1) temperate fruits, (2) subtropical fruits, and (3) tropical fruits. Some examples of each of these types are shown below.

WORLD BOOK illustrations by James Teason

Temperate fruits must have an annual cold season. They are raised mainly in the Temperate Zones, the regions between the tropics and the polar areas.

Subtropical fruits need warm or mild temperatures throughout the year but can survive occasional light frosts. They are grown chiefly in subtropical regions.

Tropical fruits cannot stand frost. They are raised mainly in the tropics. Large quantities of some species, especially bananas and pineapples, are exported.

Temperate fruits must have an annual cold season to grow properly. They are raised chiefly in the Temperate Zones, the regions between the tropics and the polar areas. Most temperate fruits come from Europe and North America, but Asia and Australia also have major producing areas.

The principal temperate fruits are apples, apricots, cherries, peaches, pears, and plums. In addition, most *small fruits,* which grow on plants smaller than trees, are raised mainly in the Temperate Zones. They include blueberries, cranberries, grapes, raspberries, and strawberries.

Subtropical fruits require warm or mild temperatures throughout the year but can survive an occasional light frost. They are grown chiefly in subtropical regions.

The most widely grown subtropical fruits are the citrus group, which includes grapefruit, lemons, limes, and oranges. Oranges, the leading citrus crop, are grown throughout the subtropics, from southern Japan to southern Europe. In the United States, Florida produces by far the most oranges. Citrus crops are also raised on some farms in the tropics, but the somewhat cooler climate of the subtropics produces better-tasting and more attractive fruit. Other subtropical fruits include dates, figs, olives, pomegranates, and certain types of avocados.

Tropical fruits are raised mainly in the tropics and cannot stand even a light frost. Bananas and pineapples, the best-known tropical fruits, are grown throughout the tropics, and much of each crop is exported. The majority of other tropical fruits are consumed locally for the most part. They include acerolas, cherimoyas, litchis, mangoes, mangosteens, and papayas.

Growing fruit

Almost all species of fruits grow on plants that have a woody stem. Such plants are trees, bushes, or woody vines. Fruits that grow on trees include apples, cherries, lemons, limes, oranges, and peaches. Most small fruits grow on bushes, but grapes come from woody vines. Bananas and strawberries grow on plants that have a soft, rather than a woody, stem.

Fruit crops, unlike most other crops, are not grown from seeds. Plants grown from seeds may vary in many ways from generation to generation. But growers strive to produce plants that will bear fruits of uniform type, appearance, and quality. Such fruits bring the highest prices when marketed. Fruit plants produce fruits of uniform quality if grown *vegetatively*—that is, from certain parts of desirable plants, such as stems, buds, and roots. The part that is grown develops new tissues and new parts identical to those of the parent plant.

Fruit plants are produced vegetatively in three main ways: (1) by grafting, (2) from cuttings, and (3) from specialized plant structures. Most fruit trees are reproduced by grafting. In this process, a bud or piece of stem from one tree is joined to a *rootstock* from another. A rootstock is a root or a root plus its stem. The resulting tree will have most of the same characteristics as the tree from which the bud or stem was taken. However, the rootstock may determine such characteristics as the size and productivity of the new tree.

Some fruit plants are produced from *cuttings* or from specialized structures. Most cuttings are pieces of stem that grow roots when placed in water or moist soil. Specialized structures called *runners* are used to grow strawberry plants. Runners are long, slender shoots that mature strawberry plants send out along the ground. A runner placed in soil develops into a new plant.

Some fruit growers produce their own plants from grafts, cuttings, or specialized structures. But most growers buy plants from nurseries that specialize in producing them.

The branch of horticulture that deals with fruit growing is called *pomology.* Pomologists have developed highly efficient methods of planting and caring for fruit crops, and most fruit farms use these techniques.

There are three main steps in growing fruit: (1) planting, (2) caring for the crop, and (3) harvesting.

Planting. Fruit crops are perennials, and so they do not have to be replanted annually as do most other crops. After the original planting, a fruit farmer need only replace plants that become unproductive. Many fruit plants remain productive for 30 to 50 years or even longer. In mild climates, farmers generally plant trees, bushes, and vines in fall. In cold climates, planting usually takes place in spring.

Most bushes are planted from 3 to 5 feet (0.9 to 1.5 meters) apart in rows that are 6 to 10 feet (1.8 to 3 meters) apart. Rows of grapevines are spaced about 10 feet (3 meters) apart. In the past, farmers almost always grew full-sized fruit trees. In most cases, the trees were planted from 20 to 40 feet (6 to 12 meters) apart to allow room for growth. Today, many farmers prefer to grow dwarf trees, which are planted close together. The branches of each tree may grow up a supporting framework called a *trellis.* The trellis enables all the fruit to receive the maximum amount of sunlight, and so the crop ripens better and faster than it otherwise would. Fruit is also easier to harvest from dwarf trees than from full-sized trees.

Caring for the crop. Most fruit growers use special machinery to fertilize, cultivate, and otherwise care for their crops. Fruit crops must be fertilized at least once a year. Some fertilizers are applied to the soil, and others are sprayed on the plants. Many fruit growers cultivate the soil around young fruit plants periodically. This practice helps control weeds and thus encourages the growth of the crop. Most fruit crops grown in extremely dry regions must be irrigated. Farmers use various methods, such as ditches and sprinklers, to distribute irrigation water.

In many cases, the branches of a young fruit tree must be *trained* so that the tree develops a uniform shape and a sturdy structure. Training may involve propping the trunk or tying the branches, or it may consist entirely of pruning. Pruning strengthens a plant by ridding it of unproductive branches. Nearly all fruit plants have to be pruned at least once annually. In addition, most fruit farmers remove some of the crop from the trees during the early stages of the fruit's growth. This practice, called *thinning,* helps increase the size of the remaining fruit.

The majority of fruit growers use chemical pesticides to protect their crops against diseases and insect pests. Most pesticides are sprayed or dusted on crops by tractor-driven machinery or specially equipped light airplanes or helicopters. Plant breeders have also devel-

A mechanical cherry picker shakes a cherry tree to loosen the fruit. The cherries drop onto outstretched cloths, roll onto a conveyor, and are deposited in a tank of salt water. The fruit floats in the water and thus is protected from being bruised.

oped varieties of fruit plants that resist certain diseases and harmful insects.

Sudden spring frosts can endanger fruit crops in temperate or subtropical regions. Farmers use water distributed by sprinklers to protect small-fruit crops from frosts. Water releases heat as it freezes. If it is sprinkled onto the crops continuously, it keeps the tender flowers and young fruits from freezing. Farmers use heaters to protect tree crops from spring frosts.

Harvesting. Fruits are bruised more easily than most other crops, and so they must be harvested with greater care. Most are picked by hand. However, the increasing cost of hand labor has encouraged the use of fruit-harvesting machines. Some of these machines have arms that shake the fruit loose from the plants. The loosened fruit drops onto outstretched cloths. Other mechanical fruit pickers have fingers that "comb" the fruit from the plants.

Marketing fruit

The United States is the leading fruit-producing country in the world. It raises more than 10 per cent of all the apples, pineapples, and plums; about 20 per cent of the lemons, oranges, peaches, and strawberries; and about 55 per cent of the grapefruit. California is the nation's chief fruit-growing state. Other leading states include Florida, Michigan, New York, Oregon, and Washington.

Most fruit scheduled to be sold fresh is taken from the orchard or field by truck and delivered to a packing house. Many large fruit farms have their own packing facilities. Commercial packing houses are centrally located in fruit-growing regions. Most large packing houses are fully mechanized. Machines wash the fruit, sort it according to size and quality, and pack each batch into containers. The fruit is then shipped to market or stored for future delivery. Railroads and trucks carry most overland shipments of fruit. Most overseas shipments travel by ocean freighter.

Fruits can be stored for varying lengths of time under controlled conditions. Temperate tree fruits must be stored at temperatures near freezing. Some kinds of apples can be kept fresh for about a year under such con-

ditions. On the other hand, most small fruits remain fresh only a few days or weeks in cold storage. Tropical and subtropical fruits can be stored for a few weeks or months under temperature-controlled conditions. The temperatures, though cool, must be well above freezing. The amount of oxygen ordinarily present in the air promotes spoilage of fruit. The storage time for all fruits can be lengthened by reducing the oxygen supply.

Much fruit is shipped directly from farms to food processors. Processing plants preserve fruit by such methods as canning, drying, and freezing. See **Food, Frozen; Food preservation.**

Developing new varieties of fruit

Occasionally, an individual plant develops an unexpected characteristic. For example, a fruit tree may suddenly start to bear fruit of a different color. Such a plant is called a *sport.* Growers have used sports to develop many new cultivated varieties of fruit. Cultivated varieties are also known as *cultivars.* The trees of Delicious apples originally produced only pale-colored, striped fruit. Then, some of the branches on individual trees began to bear solid-red apples. By grafting these branches onto appropriate rootstocks, growers produced the attractively colored varieties of Delicious apples available today.

Sports often play an important role in the development of new varieties of fruit. But the majority of new varieties are produced by a process called *selection.* In selection, plants grown from seed are examined for various desirable qualities. An individual plant may thus be singled out for high productivity or for the superior color, texture, or flavor of its fruit. By reproducing this plant vegetatively, the desirable characteristic is preserved from one generation to the next. If the characteristic persists, the fruit may be classed as a new variety.

In addition to selection, modern fruit growers also use a technique called *crossing* or *hybridization.* In this process, pollen is taken from a plant that has been selected for a particular desirable trait. The pollen is placed in the flower of a plant selected for another desirable quality. Some of the plants grown from the resulting seed may have the desirable characteristics of both parents. Occasionally, one of these plants may prove worthy of being classed as a new variety. In most cases, however, the entire process of selection and hybridization must be repeated many times to produce a new variety. Hybridization is a highly useful technique because it enables growers to produce varieties with more and more desirable qualities.

How botanists classify fruits

Fruit, the seed-bearing structure of a flowering plant, develops from the *ovaries* of the flowers. An ovary is a hollow structure near the base of a flower. It may hold one seed or more than one, depending on the species of the plant. See **Tree** (diagram: How most trees reproduce [Fruit-bearing trees]).

The wall of an ovary of mature fruit, in which the seed is fully developed, has three layers. The outer layer is called the *exocarp,* the middle layer is known as the *mesocarp,* and the inner layer is the *endocarp.* The three layers together are called the *pericarp.*

Botanists classify fruits into two main groups: (1) sim-

Simple fruits Simple fruits are classified into two main groups, depending on whether their tissue is fleshy or dry. Fleshy simple fruits include most of the seed-bearing structures that are commonly called fruits. They are divided into three main types: (1) berries, (2) drupes, and (3) pomes. The drawings below show some examples of each of these types and of several dry simple fruits.

WORLD BOOK illustrations by James Teason

Berries consist entirely of fleshy tissue, and most species have many seeds. The seeds are embedded in the flesh. This group includes only a few of the fruits that are commonly known as berries.

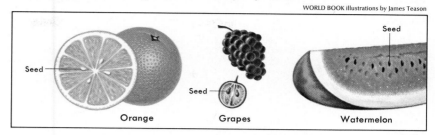

Orange — Grapes — Watermelon

Drupes are fleshy fruits that have a hard inner stone or pit and a single seed. The pit encloses the seed.

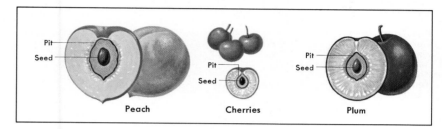

Peach — Cherries — Plum

Pomes have a fleshy outer layer, a paperlike core, and more than one seed. The seeds are enclosed in the core.

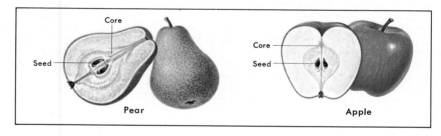

Pear — Apple

Dry simple fruits are produced by many kinds of trees, shrubs, garden plants, and weeds. The seed-bearing structures of nearly all members of the grass family, including corn and wheat, belong to this group.

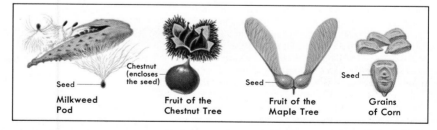

Milkweed Pod — Fruit of the Chestnut Tree — Fruit of the Maple Tree — Grains of Corn

Compound fruits A compound fruit consists of a cluster of seed-bearing structures, each of which is a complete fruit. Compound fruits are divided into two groups, (1) aggregate fruits and (2) multiple fruits.

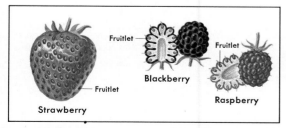

Strawberry — Blackberry — Raspberry

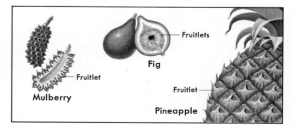

Mulberry — Fig — Pineapple

Aggregate fruits include most of the fruits that are commonly called berries. Each fruitlet of a blackberry or raspberry is a small drupe. Each "seed" of a strawberry is a dry fruitlet.

Multiple fruits include mulberries, figs, and pineapples. Mulberry fruitlets are small drupes. Each "seed" in a fig and each segment of a pineapple is a fruitlet.

Leading fruits in the United States

Value and quantity of utilized production

Fruit	Value	Short tons	Metric tons	Leading states in quantity of production
Oranges	$1,074,078,000	7,512,000	6,815,000	Florida, California
Apples	1,028,039,000	3,936,000	3,571,000	Washington, New York, Michigan, Pennsylvania, California
Grapes	712,761,000	3,175,000	2,880,000	California, New York, Washington
Strawberries	503,641,000	510,000	463,000	California, Florida, Oregon
Raisins	395,520,000	1,970,000	1,787,000	California
Grapefruit	335,056,000	2,349,000	2,131,000	Florida, California, Arizona, Texas
Peaches	326,810,000	1,119,000	1,015,000	California, South Carolina, Georgia, New Jersey, Pennsylvania
Lemons	218,125,000	697,000	632,000	California, Arizona
Pears	210,640,000	754,000	684,000	Washington, California, Oregon
Cranberries	194,606,000	179,000	162,000	Massachusetts, Wisconsin
Plums and prunes	178,239,000	294,000	267,000	California, Oregon, Michigan, Washington
Avocados	176,416,000	189,000	171,000	California, Florida
Cherries	162,905,000	246,000	223,000	Michigan, Washington, Oregon
Pineapples	100,658,000	646,000	586,000	Hawaii
Nectarines	75,720,000	172,000	156,000	California
Blueberries	67,000,000	65,000	59,000	Michigan, New Jersey, Maine
Olives	53,290,000	111,000	101,000	California
Tangerines	48,313,000	149,000	135,000	California, Florida, Arizona
Apricots	22,029,000	55,000	50,000	California
Limes	21,017,000	64,000	58,000	Florida
Tangelos	19,012,000	133,000	121,000	Florida
Kiwifruit	16,800,000	21,000	19,000	California
Temples	15,909,000	133,000	121,000	Florida
Dates	13,218,000	18,000	16,000	California

Figures are for 1986. Source: U.S. Department of Agriculture.

ple fruits and (2) compound fruits. A simple fruit develops from a single ovary, and a compound fruit develops from two or more ovaries.

Simple fruits are by far the largest group of fruits. They are divided into two types, depending on whether their pericarp is fleshy or dry.

Fleshy simple fruits include most of the seed-bearing structures that are commonly called fruits. There are three main kinds of these fruits: (1) berries, (2) drupes, and (3) pomes.

Berries have an entirely fleshy pericarp. Botanists classify bananas, blueberries, grapes, green peppers, muskmelons, oranges, tomatoes, and watermelons as berries. Some berries, including watermelons and muskmelons, have a hard rind. Such fruits are called *pepos.* Other berries, including the citrus fruits, have a leathery rind. They are called *hesperidiums.* Raspberries, strawberries, and most of the other fruits commonly known as berries are actually compound fruits.

Drupes have an exocarp that forms a thin skin. The endocarp develops into a stone or pit, and only the mesocarp is fleshy. Such fruits include apricots, cherries, peaches, and plums.

Pomes are fleshy fruits with a paperlike core. Apples and pears are pomes.

Dry simple fruits include the pods of the bean plant, the milkweed, the pea plant, and the locust tree; the grains of the corn, rice, and wheat plants; and nuts. Botanists regard nuts as single-seed fruits with a hard pericarp called a shell. The seed is the edible part. Acorns, chestnuts, and hazelnuts are true nuts. But many so-called nuts are classed otherwise by botanists. For example, almonds are the seeds of drupes.

Compound fruits consist of a cluster of ripened ovaries. There are two main types of compound fruits, *aggregate fruits* and *multiple fruits.* Aggregate fruits develop from single flowers, each of which has many ovaries. Blackberries and raspberries are aggregate fruits. The strawberry is a special type of aggregate fruit. Each "seed" in a strawberry is actually a complete fruit. The flesh surrounding the seeds develops from the base of the flower rather than from the ovaries. Multiple fruits develop from a cluster of flowers on a single stem. Figs, mulberries, and pineapples are multiple fruits.

Jules Janick

Related articles in *World Book* include:

Temperate fruits

Apple	Cranberry	Nectarine
Apricot	Currant	Oregon grape
Beach plum	Dewberry	Peach
Blackberry	Gooseberry	Pear
Blueberry	Grape	Plum
Boysenberry	Huckleberry	Quince
Casaba	Loganberry	Raspberry
Cherry	Melon	Strawberry
Crab apple	Muskmelon	

Subtropical fruits

Avocado	Kumquat	Orange
Citron	Lemon	Persimmon
Citrus	Lime	Pomegranate
Date palm	Loquat	Tangelo
Fig	Mandarin	Tangerine
Grapefruit	Olive	Tangor
Kiwi fruit		

Tropical fruits

Acerola	Coconut palm	Mango	Pineapple
Banana	Guava	Mangosteen	Sapodilla
Cherimoya	Litchi	Papaya	Tamarind

Other related articles

Berry	Grafting	Raisin
Bramble	Horticulture	Rose (The rose
Burbank, Luther	Hybrid	family)
Canning	Jelly and jam	Vegetable
Drupe	Nut	(Fruits)
Espalier	Pectin	Vitamin
Food, Frozen	Prune	Wine
Food preservation	Pruning	

Fruit bat. See Flying fox.

Fruit fly is any of several kinds of flies whose larvae eat their way through different fruits. Fruit flies include some of the most harmful agricultural pests.

Members of one family of these insects are called *peacock flies* because of their habit of strutting on fruit. They are small insects

WORLD BOOK illustration by Shirley Hooper, Oxford Illustrators Limited

Fruit fly

with many colors and beautiful wings. They lay their eggs in fruits, berries, nuts, and other parts of plants. Larvae that hatch from the eggs are small white maggots that tunnel their way through the fruit. This family of fruit flies includes the destructive *Mediterranean fruit fly, Oriental fruit fly, Mexican fruit fly,* the various cherry fruit flies, and the apple maggot. Quarantine laws prevent bringing infested fruit into the United States. Control methods include applying chemical sprays and introducing the flies' natural enemies. Another control technique involves releasing large numbers of sterilized male flies. A female fly that mates with one of the sterilized males cannot produce fertile eggs.

The *pomace,* or *vinegar, flies* also are called fruit flies. Their maggots feed chiefly on decaying fruit and on crushed grapes in wineries. Scientists often use one species of pomace fly, *Drosophila melanogaster,* in heredity studies. This species is especially useful in such studies because the *chromosomes* (parts of a cell containing hereditary material) of its salivary glands are large. The species also reproduces rapidly.

Scientific classification. Peacock flies belong to the family Tephritidae, or Trypetidae. The pomace flies form the family Drosophilidae.   Sandra J. Glover

See also **Apple maggot; Compound eye** (picture: The compound eye of a fruit fly); **Heredity** (Science project); **Mediterranean fruit fly.**

Fruit sugar. See Fructose.

Frustration tolerance. See **Child** (Aggressive and antisocial behavior); **Baby** (From 1 to 6 months).

Fry, Christopher (1907-   ), is an English playwright. Fry has written primarily in verse, trying to re-create the beauty and eloquence of Elizabethan drama. Fry achieved his greatest popularity during the late 1940's and early 1950's. However, his attempt to revive drama in verse never became a trend.

Fry's most popular plays were the witty verse comedies *The Lady's Not for Burning* (1948), his best-known play; *A Phoenix Too Frequent* (1946); and *Venus Observed* (1950). He also made adaptations of modern French plays. *The Lark* (1955), based on a drama by Jean Anouilh, deals with the life of Joan of Arc. *Tiger at the Gates* (1955), adapted from a drama by Jean Giraudoux, is an antiwar play set during the Trojan War. Fry wrote religious dramas such as *The Boy with a Cart* (1938) and *The Firstborn* (1948). He has also written screenplays for films, including *Ben-Hur* (1959) and *The Bible* (1966). Fry was born in Bristol.   Gerald M. Berkowitz

Fry, Elizabeth Gurney (1780-1845), a British reformer, was among the first to insist that prisoners need help rather than punishment in becoming good citizens. Her work aroused the conscience of officials, and led to

many reforms. She was horrified by conditions in Newgate Prison in London, particularly among the women. Many women had their children with them in prison. Although it was considered dangerous to go among the prisoners, she visited them, found work for them, started schools for their children, and insisted on better living conditions. She also began a simple form of nurses' training and a free school at her home. Elizabeth Fry was born in Norfolk, England.   Alan Keith-Lucas

Fu-chou. See Fuzhou.

Fuchs, *fyooks,* **Sir Vivian Ernest** (1908-   ), is a British geologist and Antarctic expert. He headed the British Commonwealth Trans-Antarctic Expedition in 1957 and 1958. Sir Edmund Hillary led the New Zealand party. The expedition, the first known party to cross Antarctica, covered 2,158 miles (3,473 kilometers) in 99 days, and made geophysical observations. Fuchs became director of the British Antarctic Survey in 1958. See also **Antarctica** (International cooperation; picture: The first Antarctic crossing).   John Edwards Caswell

Fuchsia, *FYOO shuh,* is a house and garden plant that is widely cultivated in North America and Europe. There are about 100 species of fuchsias. Some grow as shrubs or trees. Others are trailing, climbing, or hanging vinelike plants. Fuchsias are native to Central and South America, Tahiti, and New Zealand.

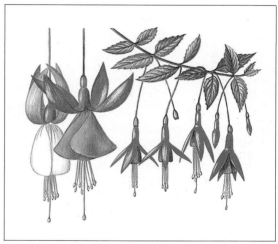

WORLD BOOK illustration by Christabel King

Fuchsia flowers resemble dangling earrings. Some fuchsias grow wild. Others are cultivated in gardens and greenhouses.

Fuchsias are commonly called *lady's eardrops.* The cultivated species usually have showy hanging flowers. The flower parts are often fleshy and in contrasting bright colors. These fuchsias have trailing stems and are popularly grown in hanging baskets.

Gardeners use cuttings of fuchsias to develop new plants. The cuttings are often stored in cool greenhouses and then planted in the spring. The fuchsia is named after the German botanist Leonhard Fuchs.

Scientific classification. Fuchsias belong to the evening primrose family, Onagraceae. The fuchsias most commonly planted in greenhouses and gardens are *Fuchsia coccinea; F. fulgens;* and *F. hybrida.*   Melinda F. Denton

Fuel is a material that provides useful energy. Fuels are used to heat and cool buildings, cook food, power engines, and produce electricity. Some fuels occur naturally and others are artificially created. Such natural fuels as coal, petroleum, and natural gas are obtained from underground deposits that were formed millions of years ago from the remains of plants and animals. These fuels, which are called *fossil fuels,* account for about 90 per cent of the energy people use today.

Synthetic fuels can be made from fossil fuels, certain types of rock and sand, and *biomass.* Biomass is the name given to such replaceable organic matter as wood, garbage, and animal manure that can be used to produce energy. Some fuels are made from chemicals.

Most fuels release energy by burning with oxygen in the air. But some—especially chemical fuels used in rockets—need special *oxidizers* in order to burn. Oxidizers are compounds that contain oxygen. Nuclear fuels do not burn but release energy through the *fission* (splitting) or *fusion* (joining together) of atoms.

Since the 1970's, shortages of some fuels and concerns about the environmental effects resulting from the burning of fuels have led people to explore other sources of energy. This article discusses five groups of fuels—(1) solid fuels, (2) liquid fuels, (3) gas fuels, (4) chemical fuels, and (5) nuclear fuels—and their uses. For information on the availability of fuels, their effect on the environment, and alternative energy sources, see **Energy supply** and **Environmental pollution.**

Solid fuels

Coal is used chiefly to produce electricity. It is burned to create heat to turn water into steam. The steam is then used to rotate *turbines,* machines that generate electricity (see **Turbine**). Some coal is made into *coke,* a charcoallike solid that is an essential raw material in the production of iron and steel. Coal is also used to heat buildings and to provide energy for industrial machinery.

There are four forms of coal: (1) *lignite,* or *brown coal,* (2) *subbituminous coal,* (3) *bituminous coal,* and (4) *anthracite.* Bituminous coal is the most plentiful and important coal used by industry. It contains more carbon and produces more heat than either lignite or subbituminous coal. It is also the coal best suited for making coke. Anthracite is the least plentiful and hardest coal. It contains more carbon and produces more heat than other coals. But it is difficult to ignite and burns slowly.

Peat is partially decayed plant matter found in swamps called *bogs.* It is used as a fuel chiefly in areas where coal and oil are scarce. In Ireland and Scotland, for example, peat is cut, formed into blocks, and dried. The dried blocks are then burned to heat homes.

Biomass. Wood has been used as a fuel since prehistoric times—longer than any other material. Today, it is an important fuel chiefly in developing countries, where it is used for cooking and heating. In the United States and other industrialized nations, it is not a major source of energy. But some paper and pulp factories, which make wood products, obtain the energy for their manufacturing processes by burning bark, sawdust, and other wood waste. Wood is also used to make charcoal.

Biomass materials other than wood are also used as fuel. For example, heat produced by burning nutshells, rice and oat hulls, and other by-products of food processing is often used to operate plant equipment.

Liquid fuels

Liquid fuels are made mainly from petroleum, but some synthetic liquid fuels are also produced. Liquid fuels are easy to store and transport. They are the major source of energy for automobiles, airplanes, and other vehicles, and they are also used to heat buildings.

Petroleum, also called *crude oil,* ranges from clear yellow-brown oils to thick, black tars. Some crude oil is burned as fuel in stoves and boilers without processing. However, most petroleum is refined to produce such fuels as *gasoline, diesel oil,* and *kerosene.* Gasoline is used by most motor vehicles and piston-engine airplanes. Diesel oil powers most trains, ships, and large trucks. Kerosene provides energy for jet airplanes.

Other fuel oils obtained by refining petroleum include *distillate oils* and *residual oils.* Distillate oils are light oils, which are used chiefly to heat homes and small buildings. Residual oils are heavy, thick oils. They provide energy to power utilities, factories, and large ships. They are also used to heat large buildings.

Synthetic liquid fuels include fuels made from coal, natural gas, biomass, *oil shale* (a rock that contains oil), and *bituminous sands* (sands that contain a substance from which oil can be obtained). Such fuels are processed mainly in areas where one type of fuel is abundant, but other vital fuels are scarce. For example, South Africa has several large plants that make gasoline from coal. In this way, South Africa—with its abundance of coal and scarcity of petroleum—is able to provide its own motor fuel. In the Canadian province of Alberta, plentiful bituminous sands are processed to yield oil. In Brazil, such biomass as sugar cane pulp and cassava plants are used to produce fuel for automobiles. Some motorists in the United States use a similar fuel, called *gasohol,* in their cars. Gasohol consists of a mixture of gasoline and alcohol. The alcohol in gasohol is often produced from such grains as corn and wheat.

Gas fuels

Gas fuels include natural and manufactured gases. Such fuels flow easily through pipes and are used to provide energy for homes, businesses, and industries. In many countries, vast networks of pipelines bring gas fuels to millions of consumers.

Natural gas is used to heat buildings, cook food, and provide energy for industries. It consists chiefly of methane, a colorless and odorless gas. Natural gas is usually mixed with compounds of the foul-smelling element sulfur so gas leaks can be detected.

Butane and propane, which make up a small proportion of natural gas, become liquids when placed under large amounts of pressure. When pressure is released, they change back into gas. Such fuels, often called *liquefied petroleum gas* (*LPG*) or *liquefied natural gas* (*LNG*), are easily stored and shipped as liquids. They provide energy for motor homes and can serve as fuel for people who live far from natural gas pipelines.

Manufactured gas, like synthetic liquid fuels, is used chiefly where certain fuels are abundant and others are scarce. Coal, petroleum, and biomass can all be converted to gas through heating and by chemical procedures. Gas can also be produced by treating such bio-mass as animal manure with bacteria called *anaerobes.* The bacteria expel methane as they digest the waste.

Chemical fuels

Chemical fuels, which are produced in solid and liq-uid form, create great amounts of heat and power. They are used chiefly in rocket engines. Chemical rocket pro-pellants consist of both a fuel and an oxidizer. A com-mon rocket fuel is the chemical hydrazine. The oxidizer is a substance, such as nitrogen tetroxide, that contains oxygen. When the propellant is ignited, the oxidizer pro-vides the oxygen the fuel needs to burn. Chemical fuels are also used in some race cars.

Nuclear fuels

Nuclear fuels provide energy through the fission or fusion of their atoms. Uranium is the most commonly used nuclear fuel, though plutonium also provides nu-clear energy. When the atoms of these elements un-dergo fission, they release tremendous amounts of heat. Nuclear fuels are used mainly to generate electricity. They also power some submarines and ships. Nuclear energy can also be produced through the fusion of hy-drogen atoms. But scientists have not yet developed the technology needed to harness such energy.

Geoffrey E. Dolbear

Related articles in *World Book* include:

Alcohol	Fission	Kerosene
Biomass	Fusion	Methane
Bituminous sands	Gas	Nuclear energy
Butane and propane	Gasohol	Oil shale
Carbon	Gasoline	Peat
Charcoal	Heat	Petroleum
Coal	Heating (Sources of	Plutonium
Coke	heat)	Rocket (Kinds of
Coke oven gas	Hydrocarbon	rocket engines)
Fire	Hydrogen	Uranium

Fuel cell is a device that produces electricity from a fuel and an *oxidizer,* a substance that combines with the fuel. The fuel and oxidizer react chemically at two sepa-rate *electrodes* (electrical terminals) to produce the di-rect electric current. A battery produces electricity in a similar way. But in a battery, the electrodes themselves are the fuel and oxidizer and are used up in the reaction. In a fuel cell, the fuel and oxidizer are added from out-side, and the electrodes remain largely unchanged.

Today, fuel cells are used only to supply electricity for special uses. For example, fuel cells provide electricity for the U.S. space shuttle. These cells use hydrogen as the fuel and oxygen as the oxidizer. They produce about $1\frac{1}{2}$ kilowatts of power.

Scientists and engineers hope to lower the cost and increase the reliability of fuel cells. They are working to produce cells that can be run directly on low-cost fuels, such as diesel fuel, gasoline, or natural gas. Oxygen in the air would be the oxidizer in these cells. Future uses for fuel cells may include furnishing electricity and heat for homes and powering military vehicles or civilian electric cars.

The main advantage of fuel cells over other methods of generating electricity is their high efficiency. Most electric power today is generated by machines that use heat. The efficiency of these machines is limited. In the-ory, fuel cells can change chemical energy into electric-ity without any change in temperature. However, today's fuel cells do produce some waste heat.

In a fuel cell, the fuel is oxidized at the fuel electrode and gives up electrons at a relatively high energy level (see **Oxidation**). These electrons make up the electricity produced by the cell. The electrons flow through an out-side circuit and then back to the oxidizer electrode at a lower energy level. There, a reaction with the oxidizer occurs, and *ions* (electrically charged atoms or groups of atoms) are formed. These ions flow through the *elec-trolyte* (current-carrying solution) between the elec-trodes and complete the electric circuit.

There are three types of fuel cells. *Low-temperature fuel cells* use water-based electrolytes, and *medium-*

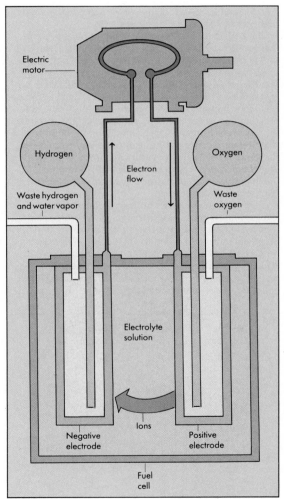

WORLD BOOK diagram by Arthur Grebetz

A fuel cell has two electrical terminals called *electrodes.* In the fuel cell above, hydrogen is pumped through the negative elec-trode into a solution called an *electrolyte.* The hydrogen reacts with electrically charged atoms called *ions,* forming water. This reaction causes the hydrogen to give up electrons. The elec-trons flow around a circuit to the positive electrode, powering the motor in the process. At the positive electrode, oxygen re-acts with the water in the electrolyte and renews the ions.

temperature fuel cells use *molten* (melted) salts. *High-temperature fuel cells,* which are the most efficient type, use solid ceramic electrolytes. This type of fuel cell can operate at 1832° F. (1000° C).   Jack Winnick

Fuel injection is a system for squirting fuel into the cylinders of gasoline and diesel engines. It replaces the carburetor when used on gasoline engines.

On most gasoline engines that use fuel injection, a pump forces fuel under high pressure to a nozzle at each cylinder. The nozzles then spray the fuel into an *intake port* (chamber) near each cylinder. There the fuel partially mixes with air before a valve opens to admit the mixture into the cylinder. The fuel may be injected into the intake port in a continuous stream or periodically. Some automotive gasoline engines use a system called *single point* or *throttle body* fuel injection. This system has only one or two fuel injection nozzles. Each nozzle delivers fuel to several cylinders.

Fuel injection overcomes several disadvantages of carburetors. A carburetor mixes air and fuel. Heat from the engine vaporizes this mixture to help it burn properly. The expansion of the heated air reduces the amount of air going to the cylinders. The cylinders can get differing amounts of the fuel vapor. The amount varies according to the design of the *manifold* (pipe connecting the carburetor and cylinders) and the distance of a cylinder from the carburetor. Poor distribution of the fuel-air mixture can prevent some of the fuel from burning, resulting in lower fuel economy and higher exhaust emissions. The engine also may flood or ice up during the winter, or develop *vapor lock* during the summer (see **Vapor lock**).

Fuel injection includes both an air-flow system and a fuel system. Electronic or mechanical controls link the two systems so that the proper ratio of fuel to air is maintained in each cylinder. The nozzles help break the fuel into a fine spray so that it burns almost completely. The control of the fuel-air mixture also prevents vapor lock and enables cold engines to start quickly and run smoothly. Fuel injection can also improve the engine's

WORLD BOOK diagram by Arthur Grebetz
A fuel injection system pumps gasoline to a nozzle, which sprays the fuel into a chamber. There, the fuel is mixed with air before a valve opens to admit the mixture into the cylinder.

response to changes in the position of the gas pedal.

All diesel engines use fuel injection. In most of these engines, the nozzles spray the fuel directly into the engine cylinders. A pump compresses the fuel to a much higher pressure than for gasoline fuel injection. In some cases, a single pump is located centrally on the engine and a distributor system directs the high-pressure fuel to the cylinders. In other cases, each cylinder has a separate pump.   David E. Cole

See also **Diesel engine** (How a diesel engine works).

Fuel shortage. See **Automobile** (The gasoline shortage); **Transportation** (Problems of modern transportation).

Fuentes, *FWEHN tays,* **Carlos** (1928-   ), is Mexico's best-known fiction writer and an important figure in Spanish-American literature. Fuentes writes imaginative and complex narratives that reflect a keen intellectual awareness of history and the workings of power. He has experimented with many varieties of construction in his novels, particularly those involving shifts in place, time, and the identity of characters.

Fuentes' first novel, *Where the Air is Clear* (1958), is set in Mexico City and shifts back and forth between the city's past and present. *The Death of Artemio Cruz* (1962) also moves backward and forward in time as it presents a revolutionary's rise to power and his later moral deterioration. *Change of Skin* (1967) emphasizes the instability of personal identity. Fuentes' most ambitious novel is *Terra Nostra* (1975), which goes beyond the known facts of history to offer an alternate version of how events might have unfolded.

Fuentes' later work incorporates elements of popular culture. *The Hydra's Head* (1977) resembles a thriller full of political intrigue. *Distant Relations* (1982) is similar to a Gothic novel. *The Old Gringo* (1985) resembles a Western and includes special insights into relations between the United States and Mexico. Fuentes' essays were collected in *Myself with Others* (1988).

Fuentes was born in Mexico City. He was Mexico's ambassador to France from 1975 to 1977.

Naomi Lindstrom

Fugard, *FOO gahrd,* **Athol,** *ATH uhl* (1932-   ), is a South African playwright. Many of his plays explore the destructive effects of *apartheid,* the policy of racial segregation enforced by the government of South Africa. Fugard, who is white, has directed and acted in many of his own plays.

Fugard's first play to gain recognition was *The Blood Knot* (1961). The drama tells the story of two half brothers, one with light skin and the other with dark skin. *Boesman and Lena* (1969) concerns two impoverished people of mixed race and their struggle for survival. Fugard joined black South African actors John Kani and Winston Ntshona in writing the comedy *Sizwe Banzi Is Dead* (1972), in which a black man trades identity papers with a corpse. *"Master Harold" . . . and the Boys* (1982) deals with the relationship between a white boy and a black waiter, showing how racism disrupts their friendship. His other dramas include *Hello and Goodbye* (1965), *A Lesson from Aloes* (1978), and *The Road to Mecca* (1987). Harold Athol Lannigan Fugard was born in Middleburg, Cape Province.   Mardi Valgemae

Fugitive slave laws were laws that provided for the return of runaway slaves who escaped from one state to another. A clause in the Northwest Ordinance of 1787 provided for the return of slaves who had escaped to the free Northwest Territory. In 1793, Congress passed a fugitive slave law which allowed owners to recover their slaves merely by presenting proof of ownership before a magistrate. An order was then issued for the arrest and return of the escaped slaves, who were allowed neither a jury trial nor the right to give evidence in their own behalf. Under this law, free blacks living in the North were sometimes kidnapped and taken South as slaves. For this reason, some Northern states gave orders not to help recover fugitive slaves.

The Compromise of 1850 included a provision that imposed heavy penalties on people who aided a slave's escape or interfered with a slave's recovery. Some Northern states passed *personal liberty laws,* which sometimes prohibited state and local officers from obeying national fugitive slave laws.　　John Donald Hicks

Fugue, *fyoog,* is a musical composition in which several voices or instruments repeat a number of melodies with slight variations. A fugue is based on *counterpoint,* a composing technique in which two or more melodies are combined (see **Counterpoint**).

A fugue begins with a section called the *exposition,* in which the melodies are first stated. The basic melody is called the *subject.* It is followed by a melody called the *answer.* The answer resembles the subject but it is performed in a different but related key. A third melody, called the *countersubject,* accompanies the answer. The other melodies then enter in sequence. After all the performers state the subject, the exposition is complete. The term *fugue* comes from the Latin word *fuga,* meaning *flight.* The subject seems to be "fleeing" from the other melodies that chase it.

After the exposition, the subject is repeated in different but related keys. In most fugues, brief passages called *episodes* link the entrances of the subject. Fugues generally end in *stretto,* in which the subject and answer are performed closer together than in the exposition.

The fugue as a type of independent composition began in the 1600's. The German composer Johann Sebastian Bach became noted for his fugues.

R. M. Longyear

Fuji, Mount. See Mount Fuji.

Fujiyama. See Mount Fuji.

Fulani, *foo LAH nee,* are a people of the grassy regions of western Africa. The more than 5 million Fulani live as far west as Senegal and as far east as Cameroon. For hundreds of years, most Fulani have been cattle herders and have lived as minority groups among various agricultural peoples. The Fulani are known as *Fula, Foulah,* or *Peul* in some African nations.

The Fulani originated in what are now Senegal and Guinea. A group of Fulani called the Tukulor (also spelled *Toucouleur*) built a powerful empire there during the A.D. 600's. Descendants of these Fulani often intermarried with those they conquered. The Fulani gradually spread eastward and reached Nigeria and Cameroon in the early 1800's.

Many Fulani became Muslims in the early 1700's and conquered a number of their neighbors in holy wars. Between 1804 and 1809, Uthman Dan Fodio, a Muslim religious leader, conquered most of the Hausa states of

Peter Marlow, Magnum

Fulani girls often wear earrings and necklaces. The Fulani are one of the largest ethnic groups in Nigeria.

Northern Nigeria. He then established an empire consisting of several Fulani states. Uthman's empire remained powerful until the British conquered Northern Nigeria in 1903. Many Fulani still live in the northern part of Nigeria.　　T. O. Beidelman

Fulbright, J. William (1905-　　), an Arkansas Democrat, served in the United States Senate from 1945 to 1974. He was chairman of the Senate Foreign Relations Committee from 1959 to 1974. Fulbright became a leading critic of U.S. involvement in the Vietnam War (1957-1975). During the 1960's and early 1970's, Fulbright was a spokesman for those who wanted Congress to have more control over presidential warmaking powers. He sponsored the Fulbright Act of 1946, which provides funds for the exchange of students between the United States and other countries (see **Fulbright Scholarship**).

James William Fulbright was born in Sumner, Mo., and entered the University of Arkansas at the age of 16. He graduated from Arkansas in 1925 and from the George Washington University Law School in 1934. From 1925 to 1928, he studied at Oxford University in England as a Rhodes scholar. Fulbright served as president of the University of Arkansas from 1939 to 1941 and was elected to the United States House of Representatives in 1942. He criticized U.S. foreign policy in his books, including *Old Myths and New Realities* (1964) and *The Arrogance of Power* (1967).　　William J. Eaton

Fulbright Scholarship is an award by the United States government for research, teaching, or graduate study. The scholarship program was begun under the Fulbright Act of 1946, named for its sponsor, Senator J. William Fulbright of Arkansas. It seeks to promote better understanding between the peoples of the United States and other countries.

The annual awards allow U.S. citizens to study or work in other lands and permit people of other countries to study or work in the United States. About 110 countries participate in the program annually, and more than 155,000 scholarships have been awarded, about 55,000 of them to U.S. citizens.

Money for the awards came at first from the sale of surplus World War II equipment to other countries. The U.S. government and participating countries and universities now fund the program. The U.S. Information

Agency (USIA) administers it. The Board of Foreign Scholarships selects the award winners. Interested persons may contact one of the following agencies.

For graduate study: The Institute of International Education, 809 United Nations Plaza, New York, NY 10017.

For secondary-school teaching: Teacher Exchange Branch, Bureau of Educational and Cultural Affairs, U.S. Information Agency, Washington, DC 20547.

For university lecturing and post-doctoral research: The Council for International Exchange of Scholars, 11 Dupont Circle NW, Suite 300, Washington, DC 20036.

Critically reviewed by the United States Information Agency

Fulcrum. See Lever.

Fuller, Buckminster (1895-1983), was an American engineer and inventor who sought to express the tech-

Dennis Stock, Magnum

Buckminster Fuller became famous for designing large, lightweight prefabricated enclosures called *geodesic domes.*

nology and needs of modern life in buildings and enclosures of space. He had an intense interest in expanding people's ability to control large areas of their environment and still have a close relationship with nature. Fuller believed that solutions should be comprehensive rather than particular. His designs show the influence of such natural molecular structures as the tetrahedron.

Fuller solved many design problems in such diversified fields as automobiles, buildings, and cities. His influence was spread through his lectures, teaching, and writings. A collection of essays he wrote discussing his theories and designs was published as *Ideas and Integrities* (1963). The title of Fuller's book *Synergetics* (1975) was the word he used for the cooperation of nature and design.

Richard Buckminster Fuller was born in Milton, Mass. He gained international attention in 1927 by designing an all-metal prefabricated home called a *Dymaxion house.* After World War II (1939-1945), he concentrated on designing large, lightweight prefabricated enclo-

sures that he called *geodesic domes.*   Nicholas Adams

Fuller, Margaret (1810-1850), was an American journalist and reformer. She became a leader of a philosophical movement called *transcendentalism* (see **Transcendentalism**).

Sarah Margaret Fuller was born in Cambridgeport, Mass., near Boston. She began her journalistic career by serving from 1840 to 1842 as editor in chief of the transcendentalist magazine *The Dial.* Under her guidance, *The Dial* became one of the most important periodicals in American literary history. From 1844 to 1846, she wrote literary criticism for the *New York Tribune.* Her book *Papers on Literature and Art* (1846) grew out of her contributions to the *Tribune.*

As a reformer, Fuller campaigned for women's rights. Her most important book, *Woman in the Nineteenth Century* (1845), explores the political, economic, social, and intellectual status of women. She was far ahead of her time in her criticism of discrimination against women because of their sex.

Fuller went to Europe in 1846. The next year, she married the Marchese Angelo Ossoli, a follower of the Italian patriot Giuseppe Mazzini. The couple participated in the Italian revolution of 1848 and 1849. During a voyage to the United States, they and their son drowned when their ship sank.   John Clendenning

Fuller, Melville Weston (1833-1910), served as chief justice of the United States from 1888 to 1910. He was a capable Supreme Court administrator. But he clung to the doctrine of states' rights in a time of problems that required increasing federal regulation. His two best-known decisions declared the national income tax unconstitutional, and, by interpretation, greatly weakened the 1890 Sherman Antitrust Act (see **Antitrust laws**).

Fuller was born in Augusta, Me. He graduated from Bowdoin College and studied law at Harvard University. He was a Chicago corporation lawyer from 1856 to 1888. He served as a member of the Illinois constitutional convention in 1862, and later was a member of the Illinois legislature. He was an arbitrator of the Anglo-Venezuelan dispute and a member of the Permanent Court of Arbitration at The Hague, from 1900 to 1910.

Jerre S. Williams

Fuller's earth is a claylike material that bleaches and purifies fats and oils. It consists of 50 to 80 per cent silica. Bleaching and purifying occur when particles of fuller's earth remove asphalt and resin from fatty or oily substances. The particles do this by *adsorbing* (collecting and holding) the asphalt and resin (see **Absorption and adsorption**). Petroleum companies use fuller's earth to purify crude oil and to lighten its color. Fuller's earth is also used to purify animal and vegetable oils. People once used a powdered form of it to remove grease from cloth and wool. Fuller's earth gets its name from this process, called *fulling.*   Walter E. Reed and Barrie Wall

Fulmar, *FUL muhr,* an ocean bird, is one of the petrels. The northern fulmar is the size of a duck. Its yellow bill is nearly as long as its head. The feet of the fulmar are webbed. The hind toe is reduced to a claw.

This bird breeds on rocky shores and makes a shallow nest in high, rocky places. It lays one egg in the nest. The fulmar feeds on any animal matter, but prefers fatty substances like whale blubber. The fulmar is valuable for its feathers, down, and oil. The people of Saint

Kilda, an island near Scotland, eat the bird's flesh and eggs.

The fulmar lives in far northern seas from Melville Island to Greenland and Svalbard. In winter, it goes south to the Massachusetts coast and the southern coasts of Great Britain. It is common around Saint Kilda Island, the Outer Hebrides, and Scotland.

Scientific classification. The fulmar belongs to the family Procellariidae. The northern fulmar is *Fulmarus glacialis.*

James J. Dinsmore

See also **Petrel.**

Fulton, Robert (1765-1815), was an American inventor, mechanical and civil engineer, and artist. He is best known for designing and building the *Clermont,* the first commercially successful steamboat. The *Clermont* ushered in a new era in the history of transportation. In addition to his work with steamboats, Fulton made important contributions to the development of the submarine and to canal transportation.

Early years. Fulton was born Nov. 14, 1765, on a farm near Little Britain in Lancaster County, Pennsylvania. He spent his boyhood in Lancaster, and showed inventive talent at an early age. He turned out lead pencils, household utensils for his mother, and skyrockets for a town celebration. Fulton developed a hand-operated paddle wheel for use on a rowboat. He also built a rifle that had sight and bore of original design.

Fulton went to Philadelphia at the age of 17, and was apprenticed to a jeweler. He soon began to win fame as a painter of miniatures and portraits. He saved enough money to buy a farm for his mother.

At the age of 21, Fulton went to England to study with the fashionable American artist Benjamin West. In London, Fulton was able to make a moderate living as an artist. But he became increasingly interested in scientific and engineering developments. After 1793, he gave his full attention to this field, and painted only for amusement.

The inventor. Fulton's first enthusiasm was for canal development. He designed new types of canal boats, and a system of inclined planes to replace canal locks. Other mechanical problems challenged him. He invented a machine for making rope and one for spinning flax. He made a labor-saving device for cutting marble, and invented a dredging machine for cutting canal channels. In 1796, Fulton published *A Treatise on the Improvement of Canal Navigation.*

About 1797, Fulton turned his attention to the submarine. In 1801, he built a diving boat, the *Nautilus,* which could descend 25 feet (7.6 meters) under water. His work with submarines claimed most of his energies until 1806. He realized the dangers which submarines would bring to naval warfare, but thought that they might serve to limit sea war and piracy, for that very reason. Fulton's experimental submarines were able to dive and surface, and he succeeded in blowing up anchored test craft. But the problem of propulsion under water was

Detail of an oil portrait (about 1806 to 1810) by John Vanderlyn; Detroit Institute of Arts, gift of the Ford Foundation

Robert Fulton

never satisfactorily solved. Fulton's ideas interested both Napoleon Bonaparte and the British Admiralty, but neither ever adopted them wholeheartedly.

In 1802, Robert R. Livingston, the United States minister to France, interested Fulton in turning his attention to the steamboat. Fulton had been interested for many years in the idea of steam propulsion for a boat. An experimental boat, launched on the Seine River in Paris in 1803, sank because the engine was too heavy. But a second boat, which was built in the same year, operated successfully. Fulton ordered an engine from the British firm of Boulton & Watt, and returned to the United States in 1806.

Builds the *Clermont.* Fulton directed the construction of a steamboat in New York in 1807. This boat, which Fulton registered as the *North River Steam Boat,* became famous as the *Clermont.* On Aug. 17, 1807, the steamboat started on its first successful trip up the Hudson River from New York City to Albany. After some alterations, the boat began to provide regular passenger service on the Hudson.

The *Clermont* was not the first steamboat to be built, but it was the first to become a practical and financial success. Part of Fulton's success was due to his concern for passenger comfort. His handbills announced: "Dinner will be served at exactly 2 o'clock . . . Tea with meats . . . Supper at 8 in the evening" and "A shelf has been added to each berth, on which gentlemen will please put their boots, shoes, and clothes, that the cabin will not be encumbered."

After the success of the *Clermont,* Fulton became occupied with building and operating other boats. He also

Courtesy of the New York Historical Society, New York

The *Clermont,* invented by Robert Fulton, was the first commercially successful steamboat. The ship made its first successful trip up the Hudson River. Fulton made this watercolor sketch of the *Clermont* in 1808.

defended the monopolies that state legislatures had granted to him and Robert Livingston.

Fulton designed and built a steam-powered warship, *Fulton the First,* for the defense of New York harbor in the War of 1812, but he died before the completion of this remarkable craft. The statue of Fulton in Statuary Hall, Washington, D.C., honors his achievements.

J. Paul Hartman

See also **Clermont; Fitch, John; Livingston, Robert R.; Steamboat; Ship** (The *Clermont*).

Additional resources

Flexner, James T. *Steamboats Come True: American Inventors in Action.* Rev. ed. Little Brown, 1978.
Parsons, William B. *Robert Fulton and the Submarine.* AMS, 1967. First published in 1922.
Philip, Cynthia O. *Robert Fulton: A Biography.* Watts, 1985.

Fumarole, *FYOO muh rohl,* is a hole or vent in the ground that gives off volcanic gases. Most fumaroles occur in volcanic regions, such as Yellowstone National Park. The gases given off usually are steam mixed with carbon dioxide, hydrogen, hydrogen sulfide, hydrogen chloride, and nitrogen. Some of the gases are poisonous. Others cause choking. Fumaroles that give off sulfurous gases are called *solfataras.*   Gordon A. Macdonald

See also **Hot springs.**

Fumigation, *FYOO muh GAY shuhn,* is a method of killing pests that involves the use of toxic gases. It is widely used to eliminate weeds, *nematodes* (roundworms), and other pests from cropland. It is also used to protect such foods as grains, nuts, and spices from rats and insects during storage. Goods shipped between countries often are fumigated to prevent pests and diseases from spreading from one country to another. Houses, apartments, and other buildings are sometimes fumigated to kill cockroaches, termites, and other insects.

The chemicals used in fumigation are called *fumigants.* They work well only in an enclosed area. For example, stored foods commonly are covered with plastic sheets during fumigation. The sheets trap the gases beneath them, enabling the foods to absorb the fumigants. Some farmland is treated to kill nematodes by injecting fumigants into the soil, which acts as a cover. Plastic sheets are generally used as an additional cover for fields fumigated against weeds, insects, and plant diseases. The sheets are removed about 24 to 48 hours after the fumigants are applied. The fields can be safely planted about one to two weeks later. By then, the gases have been *dissipated* (released) from the soil.

Fumigants are poisonous to people and must be handled with care. They are usually applied by trained, licensed professionals. Commonly used fumigants include cyanide, formaldehyde, and methyl bromide. Foods that have been fumigated are safe to eat only after the fumigant has been dissipated.   Walter A. Skroch

See also **Insecticide; Pesticide.**

Funafuti, *FYOO nuh FYOOT ee* (pop. 900), is the capital of Tuvalu, a small island country in the South Pacific Ocean. Funafuti is one of the world's smallest and most unusual national capitals. It is the largest islet of an *atoll* that is also called Funafuti. An atoll is a ring-shaped coral reef that surrounds a lagoon. The Funafuti atoll consists of 30 islets that have a total area of 689 acres (279 hectares).

All the people live in Fongafale village on the islet of Funafuti. The main government offices of Tuvalu, and a hospital, a hotel, and a jail, are on the islet. A wharf and an airport are located nearby. Funafuti was the site of a military base during World War II (1939-1945).

Robert Langdon

See also **Tuvalu.**

Funchal, *fun SHAHL* (pop. 48,638), is the capital, largest city, and chief port of the Madeira Islands. The Madeiras belong to Portugal and lie in the Atlantic Ocean off the northwest coast of Africa. Funchal is on the southern coast of the island of Madeira. The city's pleasant climate makes it a popular resort.

Portuguese settlers founded Funchal in 1421. The city has many beautiful gardens and a cathedral that dates from the 1400's. Funchal's economy is based on the tourist trade and the export of sugar and the famous Madeira wines. The city also produces ceramics and linen embroidery. Funchal has a modern airport, and airlines connect the city with western Europe.

Douglas L. Wheeler

See also **Madeira Islands** (picture: The harbor of Funchal).

Function, in mathematics. See **Algebra** (Functions); **Calculus** (Functions).

Functional illiteracy. See **Illiteracy.**

Fundamental Orders. See **Connecticut** (introduction; English settlement).

Fundamentalism, *FUHN duh MEHN tuh lihz uhm,* is a broad movement within Protestantism in the United States. The fundamentalist movement tries to preserve what it considers the basic ideas of Christianity against criticism by liberal theologians.

At the end of the 1800's, many liberal religious scholars challenged the accuracy of the Bible. They also used historical research to question previously accepted Christian beliefs. The liberals attempted to adjust Christian theology to then new discoveries in the sciences, particularly in biology and geology. Many Christians believed the work of the liberals threatened the authenticity and even the survival of Christianity.

From 1910 to 1915, anonymous authors published 12 small volumes titled *The Fundamentals.* Fundamentalism got its name from these booklets. The authors tried to explain what they felt were basic Christian doctrines that should be accepted without question. These doctrines included the *infallibility* (absolute accuracy) of the Bible, including the story of creation and accounts of miracles. Other doctrines included the Virgin Birth of Jesus, Christ's atonement for the sins of humanity through His Crucifixion, and His Second Coming.

Fundamentalism began in the North, but it has gained its greatest strength in Southern areas. Baptists and Presbyterians have been most directly affected by the theological debates between liberal and conservative Protestants. Fundamentalism, however, has had an influence on all Protestant denominations, particularly such groups as the Church of God, Assemblies of God, and Pentecostal churches. Television evangelism has also been influenced by conservative fundamentalist beliefs. Organizations within a movement called the New Religious Right have adopted social and political positions based on a literal use of Biblical texts. The infallibility of the Bible remains an important fundamentalist issue today.

The term *fundamentalism* is also used to describe conservative trends in other religious denominations, notably Judaism and Islam.   Robert L. Ferm

See also **Bob Jones University; Scopes trial.**

Additional resources

Hill, Samuel S., and Owen, D. E. *The New Religious/Political Right in America.* Abingdon, 1982. Balanced account of the impact and influence of modern fundamentalism.
Marsden, George M. *Fundamentalism and American Culture: The Shaping of Twentieth Century Evangelicalism, 1870-1925.* Oxford, 1980.
Russell, Charles A. *Voices of American Fundamentalism: Seven Biographical Studies.* Westminster, 1976.

Funeral customs are special ceremonies performed after a person dies. Throughout history, humankind has developed such customs to express grief, comfort the living, and honor the dead.

Nearly all religions include the belief that human beings survive death in some form. For many people, a funeral symbolizes a passage from one life to another, rather than the end of a person's existence. Such a ceremony, which is associated with the completion of one phase of life and the beginning of another, is called a *rite of passage.* Other rites of passage include baptism, initiation into adulthood, and marriage.

Funeral customs vary from society to society, but many of the same practices are found throughout the world. These practices include public announcement of the death; preparation of the body; religious ceremonies or other services; a procession; a burial or other form of disposal; and mourning.

Preparation of the body varies among peoples. Typically, however, the corpse is laid out and washed. Sometimes it is painted or anointed with oils. It is then dressed in new or special garments or wrapped in a cloth called a *shroud.* In most societies, the body is put in a coffin, also called a casket, or other container.

Many peoples hold an all-night watch called a *wake* beside the corpse. They may do so in the belief that the wake comforts the spirit of the dead or protects the body from evil spirits. In the past, another reason for a wake was to watch for signs of life. Before modern tests were developed, an unconscious person might be mistaken for dead.

In the United States and Canada, funeral directors preserve most bodies by a process called *embalming.* An embalmer removes the blood and injects a chemical solution into the veins to retard decay. The embalmer also uses cosmetics to restore a more natural appearance to the dead person, who may have been disfigured by a long illness or an accident. Such treatment is common in North America because most bodies are kept several days or more before the funeral. During this period, relatives and friends come to view the body. Embalming is not required by law except in special circumstances, such as if a body is to be transported or stored. In other countries, embalming is rare because most people are buried within a day or two after death.

The funeral may include prayers, hymns and other music, and speeches called *eulogies* that recall and praise the dead person. In the United States, many funeral services take place at a funeral home with the embalmed body on display. After the service, a special vehicle called a *hearse* carries it in a procession to the cemetery or crematory. A final brief ceremony is held before the body is buried, or cremated in a special furnace. After many funerals, the mourners return with the bereaved family to their house and share food. Later, a tombstone or other monument is erected to record the dead person's life and mark the place of burial.

Burial is the most common method of disposal in Christian, Jewish, and Muslim countries. Human burial developed from the belief that the dead rise again. Like a seed, according to this belief, a body is planted in the earth to await rebirth.

Cremation is customary in Buddhist and Hindu nations and is increasing in the United States and Canada. However, Orthodox Jews, Roman Catholics, and some Protestant groups oppose this practice. They believe the body is the temple of the soul or of the Holy Spirit and should not be destroyed. Other religions do not object to cremation.

Some societies dispose of their dead in other ways. For example, the Sioux Indians of North America place their dead on high platforms. Some groups of Aborigines, the original inhabitants of Australia, leave dead bodies in trees. In Tibet, bodies are sunk in water. The Parsis, a religious group who live mainly in India, take their dead to special enclosures called *towers of silence.* There, birds pick the bones clean. The Parsis believe the earth and fire are sacred and must not be violated by burying or burning a corpse.

Mourning is the expression of grief after a death. People in mourning may deny themselves amusement, avoid certain foods, or wear special clothing. Until the 1940's, Americans and Europeans wore black armbands and hung funeral wreaths on their doors while in mourning. Some societies regard a period of mourning as a time of uncleanliness. They believe death contaminates the survivors and makes them *taboo* (set apart as cursed or sacred). See **Taboo.**

History. As early as 60,000 years ago, prehistoric people observed special ceremonies when burying their dead. Neanderthal graves, for example, contain tools, weapons, and evidence of flowers. The ancient Egyptians and other early peoples placed food, jewels, and other goods in tombs. Such provisions showed the belief that a person continued to exist after death and had the same needs as in life. The Egyptians also developed embalming into an advanced technique called *mummification.* They believed the spirit would someday return to inhabit the body. Therefore, it had to be preserved to prevent the soul from perishing.

During the 1900's, traditional funeral and mourning practices have declined in the United States. Ideas about death and the treatment of the dead are changing. Criticism of North American funeral practices as needlessly elaborate and expensive has led many people to seek alternatives. For example, some families prefer to hold a memorial service at their home or church.

However, the funeral fills important emotional needs. It focuses attention on the grief of the survivors and provides a public ceremony that helps them acknowledge and accept their loss. In addition, a funeral helps survivors express their feelings and discharge grief.

Robert Fulton

Related articles in *World Book* include:
Catacombs   Cremation

Crypt
Death
Embalming
Epitaph
Funeral director
Mask (Burial masks and death
    masks; picture)
Mummy
Necropolis
Potter's field
Pyramids
Sarcophagus
Tomb
Wake

Additional resources

Mitford, Jessica. *The American Way of Death.* Fawcett, 1978. First published in 1963.
Rosenblatt, Paul C., and others. *Grief and Mourning in Cross-Cultural Perspective.* HRAF Press, 1976.

Funeral director is a person who prepares the dead for burial or for other forms of disposition. The funeral director also performs other services at the time of death. A funeral director is also called a *mortician.* In some states, a person who is licensed to provide funeral services is called an *embalmer.*

Responsibilities. An important service of a funeral director is to supervise the embalming of the body for temporary preservation. Embalming is done by removing the blood and body fluids and injecting a preserving fluid into the arteries. Embalming may also include restoring facial features that were disfigured by an accident or prolonged illness.

A funeral director organizes the kind of funeral or other arrangement desired by the family or friends of the dead person. The director obtains a burial permit, notifies relatives and the press, and plans with the clergy for services. Services may be held in the home, a church, or the funeral home, and at the grave or crematory. Services may also be nonreligious.

Most funeral homes have such facilities as a chapel, a casket-selection room, and a preparation room. A funeral director's equipment may include a hearse, also called a funeral coach; a flower car; limousines; and an ambulance.

Funeral directors are in a position to offer experienced and sympathetic advice to the mourners. In some cases, they assist families for several months following the funeral. They may help relatives of the dead person collect insurance and death benefits from social security, from unions, or from fraternal and veterans' organizations.

History. Throughout history, people in all societies have regarded the disposal of the dead as a solemn act requiring group concern and accompanied by certain ceremonies. Patterns of conduct have developed out of a sense of loss, grief, and mystery caused by death. Religious beliefs and practices have been the most important of these patterns of conduct. Funeral directors help people perform ceremonies that follow their beliefs and customs. By the mid-1800's, the functions performed by a funeral director had become a service occupation in the United States. By 1900, funeral directors were required by law to have certain training and to meet other qualifications.

As a career. In the United States, about 20,000 funeral homes employ about 60,000 people. Most funeral directors have both a funeral director's and an embalmer's license or a combination license.

Each state establishes its own licensing requirements, but nearly all the states require a high school diploma. About 20 states require up to two years of college.

Nearly every state also requires at least a year of study in funeral-service education, plus an apprenticeship of from one to three years. The most common apprenticeship is for one year. All applicants for a license must pass a state board examination. The American Board of Funeral Service Education has approved 40 funeral-service education schools.

Information about a career in funeral direction may be obtained from the National Funeral Directors Association, 11121 W. Oklahoma Avenue, Milwaukee, WI 53227.

Critically reviewed by the National Funeral Directors Association

See also **Embalming; Funeral customs.**

Fungal disease, *FUHNG guhl.* Many kinds of fungi live and feed on the tissues of living plants and animals (see **Fungi**). These *parasites* often cause diseases in the plants and animals they infect.

Diseases of plants. The most important fungi that live on plants include smuts, rusts, and mildews. They affect many kinds of plants. One kind of fungal disease, chestnut blight, has destroyed American chestnut trees. Dutch elm disease, caused by a fungus, threatens to eliminate the elm trees of the United States. Fungal diseases in plants sometimes spread rapidly. To avoid crop losses, farmers may use *fungicides,* chemicals that kill fungi (see **Fungicide**). Breeders try to develop plants that will resist fungus attacks.

Diseases of human beings and animals. Fungi that infect people and animals may cause skin disorders or serious illness. *Actinomycosis,* or lumpy jaw, is a fungal disease of cattle and other animals. But it may also affect people. Other fungal diseases of human beings include *blastomycosis, coccidioidomycosis,* and *moniliasis.* These diseases often attack the lungs. *Thrush,* a fungal disease of the throat, is found mainly in infants. *Tinea* (ringworm) affects parts of the skin.

Various bacteria that live on the skin and mucous membranes help prevent fungal infections. The use of certain antibiotics to treat bacterial infections sometimes results in the destruction of the body's helpful bacteria as well. In such cases, a fungal infection may set in. Physicians can effectively treat many fungal infections with antibiotics that fight fungi.   William F. Hanna

Related articles in *World Book* include:

Actinomycosis	Histoplasmosis
Athlete's foot	Mildew
Blight	Ringworm
Damping-off	Rot
Dutch elm disease	Rust
Ergot	Smut
Fungi	Thrush (disease)
Fungicide	Wilt

Fungi, *FUHN jy,* are organisms that lack chlorophyll, the green coloring matter that many plants use to make food. Fungi cannot make their own food. Instead, they absorb food from their surroundings.

According to *mycologists* (scientists who study fungi), there are over 100,000 species of fungi. Yeasts and other one-celled fungi are too small to be seen without a microscope. But most types can be seen with the unaided eye. Some of the most common fungi include mildews, molds, mushrooms, and plant rusts.

Parts of a fungus. Except for yeasts and other one-celled fungi, the main part of a fungus consists of thousands of threadlike cells called *hyphae.* These tiny,

Black bread mold   Black bread mold is one of the most common fungi. A 10-day growth of this mold covers the slice of bread shown at the left. The tiny fruiting bodies of the mold can be seen in the photograph in the center. The diagram at the right shows the structure of the mold in more detail.

Runk/Schoenberger from
Grant Heilman

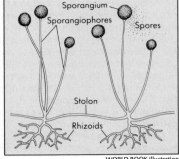

WORLD BOOK illustration
by Sarah Woodward

branching cells form a tangled mass called a *mycelium*. In many kinds of fungi, the mycelium grows beneath the surface of the material on which the organism is feeding. For example, the mycelium of a mushroom often grows just beneath the surface of the soil. The umbrella-shaped growth known as a mushroom is actually the *fruiting body* of the fungus. The fruiting body produces cells called *spores,* which develop into new hyphae. Spores are smaller and simpler than the seeds of plants, but both enable an organism to reproduce.

Some bread molds and microscopic species of fungi bear spores in tiny structures called *sporangia.* In black bread mold, the sporangia form at the tips of upright hyphae called *sporangiophores.* Other hyphae called *stolons* spread over the surface of the bread. They are anchored by *rhizoids* (rootlike structures). Groups of sporangia usually form above the rhizoids.

How a fungus lives. Fungi live almost everywhere on land and in water. Some fungi are parasites that feed on living plants and animals. Other fungi, called *saprophytes,* live on decaying matter. Still other fungi live together with other organisms in ways that are mutually beneficial. Such a relationship is called *symbiotic.* For example, a fungus and an organism called an *alga* may live together symbiotically to form a *lichen* (see **Lichen**).

Some fungi also live with the roots of plants in a symbiotic relationship known as a *mycorrhiza.* The fungus takes carbohydrates from the plant. In return, the fungus helps supply the plant with water and such important minerals as phosphorus, potassium, iron, copper, and zinc. Most species of trees, shrubs, and herbs have mycorrhizal relationships with fungi.

Fungi cannot produce their own food because they do not contain chlorophyll. They take carbohydrates, proteins, and other nutrients from the animals, plants, or decaying matter on which they live. Fungi discharge chemicals called *enzymes* into the material on which they feed. The enzymes break down complex carbohydrates and proteins into simple compounds that the hyphae can absorb.

Most kinds of fungi reproduce by forming spores. Some spores are produced by the union of *gametes* (sex cells). Others, called *asexual* or *imperfect* spores, are produced without the union of gametes. Many fungi produce spores both sexually and asexually. Many spores are scattered by the wind, and others are transported by water or by animals. Mushrooms and some other fungi forcefully discharge their spores. A spore that lands in a favorable location *germinates* (starts to grow) and eventually produces a new mycelium.

Yeasts can reproduce by forming spores, but many kinds of yeasts reproduce by *budding.* When a yeast buds, a bulge forms on the cell. A cell wall grows and separates the bud from the original yeast cell. The bud then develops into a new cell. Budding produces a large number of yeast cells rapidly.

The importance of fungi. Fungi break down complex animal and plant matter into simple compounds. This process of *decomposition* enriches the soil and makes essential substances available to plants in a form they can use. Through decomposition, fungi also return carbon dioxide to the atmosphere, where green plants reuse it to make food.

Fungi play a major role in a number of foods. For example, mushrooms and truffles are considered delicacies by many people (see **Truffle**). Cheese manufacturers add molds to Camembert and Roquefort cheeses to ripen them and provide their distinctive flavors. Yeasts cause the *fermentation* that produces alcoholic beverages. In the fermentation process, yeasts break down

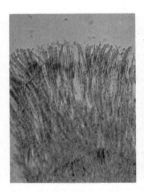

Some penicillium molds, such as the one shown above, cause citrus fruits to spoil. Others ripen certain cheeses.

Grant Heilman

Corn smut has infected this corn plant. Smuts and other parasitic fungi cause great damage to grain crops.

sugar into carbon dioxide and alcohol. Baker's yeast causes bread to rise by producing carbon dioxide from the carbohydrates in the dough. The carbon dioxide gas bubbles up through the dough and causes it to rise. Someday, yeasts may become an important new source of food. Some people already eat yeasts as a rich source of protein and B vitamins.

Some molds produce important drugs called *antibiotics*. Antibiotics weaken or destroy bacteria and other organisms that cause disease. Penicillin, the first and most important antibiotic, was discovered in 1928 by Sir Alexander Fleming, a British bacteriologist. *Penicillium notatum* is one of several green molds that produce penicillin, which physicians use in treating many diseases caused by bacteria.

Some fungi cause great damage. Parasitic fungi destroy many crops and other plants. Important parasitic fungi that attack plants include mildews, rusts, and smuts. Others produce diseases in animals and people. Some mushrooms are poisonous and can cause serious illness or death if eaten. Molds spoil many kinds of food. In damp climates, mildews and other fungi can ruin clothing, bookbindings, and other materials. Fungi may also cause wood to decay or rot.

Scientific classification. Botanists traditionally classified fungi in the plant kingdom. Today, however, most biologists consider fungi to be a separate kingdom called Fungi.

Joe F. Ammirati

Related articles in *World Book.* See **Fungal disease** and its list of *Related articles.* See also the following articles:

Mold	Parasite	Saprophyte
Mushroom	Puffball	Yeast

Fungicide, *FUHN juh syd,* is a chemical substance used to kill growths called *fungi* that are harmful to human beings and plants. Diseases caused by fungi can destroy or seriously damage food crops. A fungal disease destroyed the potato crop in Ireland, resulting in the Irish potato famine, which caused about 750,000 people to starve in the 1840's. Fungus also caused the chestnut blight that killed thousands of American chestnut trees in the United States during the early 1900's.

Great quantities of fungicides are sold each year to protect plants and human beings from fungal diseases. Fungicides are sprayed or dusted on plants to kill fungal diseases called *rusts, mildews, smuts,* and *molds.* They are used to protect potatoes, apples, and other crops from fungal diseases called *blight* and *scab.* Many kinds of seeds are dipped in a fungicide to prevent *damping-off,* a disease that kills young plants.

Human beings use preparations containing a fungicide to prevent such diseases as *athlete's foot.* Fabrics are treated with fungicides to prevent rotting.

Inorganic fungicides are made from metal compounds. Copper compounds have been widely used to protect against mildew on fruit trees, grapevines, and vegetables, and to treat seeds. Among the copper compounds is Bordeaux mixture, which contains copper sulfate and lime. Other compounds contain carbonate, chloride, hydroxide, and sulfate. Sulfur and lime-sulfur are used to control scab and another fungal disease called *brown rot,* which attack fruit.

Organic fungicides are chemical compounds that contain carbon, hydrogen, and oxygen atoms. Most organic fungicides are *synthetic* (artificially created). Form-

aldehyde and chloranil are used to treat seeds and potatoes. Maneb, nabam, and zineb are sprayed on the leaves of fruit trees and on vegetables and cereal grasses to kill rusts and fungi that cause blight. Other organic fungicides are used to prevent rot in wood, rope, tents, and some paints.

Fungicides must be poisonous to fungi. But they must not be harmful to the plants or animals they are supposed to protect. Fungicides should be used with care, because many will be harmful to plants if they are applied too heavily. Many fungicides are poisonous to humans. They should be stored where small children, livestock, and pets cannot get them. Some fungicides also leave poisonous deposits on food crops. The deposits must be cleaned off before these crops are used.

Harold D. Coble

Related articles in *World Book* include:

Fungal disease	Mildew	Pesticide (Types)
Fungi	Mold	Rust
Insecticide		

Funj Sultanate, *funj SUHL tuh nayt,* was a Muslim empire in what is now Sudan in northeastern Africa. The empire began in the early 1500's and fell in 1821. It reached its height between 1600 and 1650 when Funj armies conquered neighboring peoples. The Funj became greatly feared in the region between the Red Sea and the Nile River.

The origin of the black-skinned Funj people is uncertain. They may have descended from Shilluk raiders from the White Nile region. In the early 1500's, the Funj adopted Islam, the Muslim religion. In 1504, they founded their capital, Sennar, south of the present-day city of Wad Madani. The sultanate went on to conquer the northern region of Sudan and nearly all the area between the Blue Nile and White Nile, south of the present-day city of Khartoum. From 1600 to 1650, the Funj used a slave army built by the sultan Badi II Abu Daqn to further extend their empire.

Between 1650 and 1750, the Funj nobles became jealous of the sultans' power and revolted frequently. Finally, in 1761, a group of officers deposed the ruling sultan. A period of decline followed, and the empire fell in 1821 after Egypt invaded it. Leo Spitzer

Funny bone is not a bone, but a sensitive place at the bend of the elbow. In this area, the *ulnar nerve* lies between the skin and bone. The nerve is relatively unprotected because it lies near the surface. Even a slight blow on this area stimulates the nerve. This stimulation produces pain and a tingling sensation that travels into the ring finger and little finger. Sometimes the funny bone is referred to as "the crazy bone." Delmas J. Allen

Funston, *FUHN stuhn,* **Frederick** (1865-1917), was a major general in the United States Army. He won the name "Fighting Bantam of the Army" because he was only 5 feet 5 inches (165 centimeters) tall.

Funston joined the rebel forces in Cuba against the Spaniards in 1896. During the Spanish-American War, he commanded troops in the Philippine Islands. In 1901, he helped capture Emilio Aguinaldo, the Philippine guerrilla leader. After the San Francisco earthquake in 1906, he was placed in charge of the city to restore order. He commanded U.S. forces at Veracruz, Mexico, in 1914. Funston was born in New Carlisle, Ohio.

H. A. DeWeerd

Fur is the thick growth of hair that covers the skin of many kinds of animals. People make coats and other warm clothing from fur. They value fur for its beauty as well as for the warmth that it provides.

Fur consists of a combination of stiff, oily *guard hair* on top and thick *underfur* beneath. The guard hair sheds moisture, and the underfur acts as an insulating blanket that keeps the animal warm.

Because fur comes from wild animals, it cannot be flawless like cloth, which is manufactured from fibers. The work involved in repairing imperfect pelts and then sewing them together into clothing contributes to the high cost of fur garments. In some years, the scarcity of fur-bearing animals makes prices rise even higher.

Fur that comes from animals is called *natural fur.* It accounts for about 99 per cent of the dollar value of fur garment sales in North America. Manufacturers also produce *artificial fur,* which looks like many kinds of natural furs but costs far less and is not as warm.

Prehistoric people wore animal skins for warmth and protection. They also used fur skins for blankets, rugs, and wallhangings. During the 400's B.C., an active fur market operated in Athens, Greece. Fur became a luxury during medieval times, when only kings and princes wore such expensive furs as ermine and sable. The desire for furs stimulated much of the early exploration of North America. In the 1600's, fur trading became the most important industry in Canada. See **Fur trade.**

Today, the fur industry plays an important role in the economies of many nations. Most of the world's fur supply comes from fur ranches, where fur-bearing animals are raised in pens. The rest comes from trapping wild animals. During the 1960's and 1970's, some wildlife protection groups and animal rights groups began to protest the trapping of animals for fur.

The Soviet Union produces more fur than any other

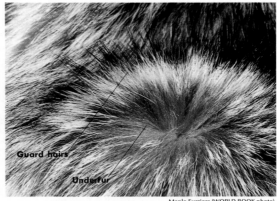

Maple Furriers (WORLD BOOK photo)

Fur consists of long *guard hairs* and thick *underfur.* The guard hairs shed moisture, and the underfur keeps the animal warm.

nation. The United States ranks as the second largest producer, followed by Canada. The fur garments produced annually in the United States have a total retail value of about $1 $\frac{3}{4}$ billion. The retail value of Canadian fur garment production is about $450 million yearly. The United States and Canada export millions of dollars worth of fur pelts yearly. Major importers of fur include France, Great Britain, Greece, Italy, Japan, Switzerland, the United States, and West Germany.

Kinds of fur

Natural fur. Popular natural furs used for clothing include beaver, coyote, fox, mink, muskrat, rabbit, and raccoon. Chinchilla, mink, Persian lamb, and sable are some of the most fashionable and expensive furs.

Furs vary greatly in color, texture, and value. Colors

Some important furs

Fur	Fur family	Animal's main habitat	Description
* **Beaver**	Rodent	North America	Dark brown; short, thick fur.
* **Chinchilla**	Rodent	Fur ranches	Blue-gray; long, branched, fine fur.
* **Coyote**	Dog	North America	Gray, yellow-gray, tan; long, thick fur.
* **Ermine**	Weasel	Soviet Union	White, black; short, thick fur.
Fisher	Weasel	Canada	Dark brown; short, soft fur.
Fitch	Weasel	Europe, Soviet Union	Yellow, beige, brown, black; long, silky fur.
* **Fox**	Dog	Asia, Europe, North America	Red, blue, silver, white; long, soft fur.
* **Lynx**	Cat	North America, Soviet Union	Beige, white; long, silky fur.
* **Marten**	Weasel	Asia, North America	Blue-brown; soft, thick fur.
* **Mink**	Weasel	Fur ranches, North America, Soviet Union	Brown, gray, white; long, silky fur.
* **Mole**	Mole	Netherlands, Scotland	Blue, gray; soft, thick fur.
* **Muskrat**	Rodent	North America, Soviet Union	Brown; long, silky fur.
* **Nutria**	Rodent	South America	Dark brown; short, soft fur.
* **Opossum**	Opossum	South America, United States	Creamy; short, rough fur.
* **Otter**	Weasel	North America, South America	Brown; short, thick fur.
Persian lamb	Sheep	Afghanistan, Soviet Union, Namibia	Black, brown, gray; woolly, tightly curled fur.
* **Rabbit**	Rodent	Australia, Europe, Japan, North America	White, brown, gray; short, fluffy fur.
* **Raccoon**	Raccoon	North America	Silver gray, dark gray, black; long, coarse fur.
* **Sable**	Weasel	Canada, Soviet Union	Dark brown; long, silky fur.
* **Seal**	Seal	Alaska, Canada, Soviet Union, Namibia, Uruguay	Gray, salmon, silver, white; short, silky or stiff fur.
* **Skunk**	Weasel	North America	Black; long, silky fur.
* **Squirrel**	Rodent	Asia, Europe, North America	Gray; short, soft fur.

*Has a separate article in *World Book.*

Some kinds of fur

Mink ranges in color from white to many shades of gray and brown.

Fox fur is long and soft. The most popular shades include red, white, and silver.

Muskrat fur is light brown. Some is dyed to resemble other kinds of fur.

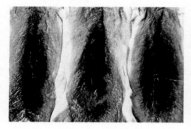

Chinchilla is highly prized for its luxurious softness and unusual coloration.

Sable, one of the most beautiful and expensive furs, has a brown color.

Maple Furriers (WORLD BOOK photos)

Beaver is prized for both its soft underfur, *left,* and its outer guard hair, *right.*

range from jet-black to snow-white, with many shades of brown, blue, gray, red-orange, and tan. Fur texture varies from the velvety softness of beaver to the coarseness of raccoon. In the late 1980's, the price of a fur pelt in the United States ranged from about $1.00 for a squirrel skin to $1,700 for a ranched sable from the Soviet Union.

Rodents provide more skins for furs than any other group of animals. Beavers, muskrats, and other rodents make up more than three-fourths of the total wild fur catch in the United States and Canada. The weasel family supplies the greatest number of pelts from fur ranches. Weasels include ermines, minks, and sables.

Artificial fur consists of synthetic fibers that have been processed to look like real fur. Artificial furs serve as an alternative for people who choose not to wear natural fur. The most popular "fake furs" are imitation lamb, mink, muskrat, and seal.

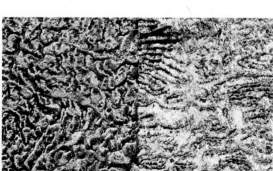

Maple Furriers (WORLD BOOK photo)

Natural and artificial Persian lamb differ in appearance, as a close-up photograph shows. The natural fur is on the left.

Manufacturers make artificial furs by weaving and knitting synthetic fibers into *pile fabrics.* Pile consists of soft, clipped fiber ends. Pile is treated to make it look like real fur. Natural fur fibers are sometimes woven into the pile to make it feel more like genuine fur.

How fur is obtained

Fur ranching. Millions of foxes and minks are raised yearly on ranches in the United States, Canada, and many European countries. Ranches in Afghanistan, the Soviet Union, and Namibia (South West Africa) raise Karakul sheep, whose fur is called *Persian lamb* (see **Karakul**). Ranchers raise chinchillas in Europe, North America, South Africa, South America, and Zimbabwe. Most of the furs produced in the United States and Canada come from ranches.

The first fur ranches were established in the 1880's in Prince Edward Island, Canada. Today, fur ranchers conduct breeding programs based on the principles of genetics. Skilled ranchers breed their animals to produce offspring of particular colors and sizes or with other special characteristics.

Trapping. Most fur trapping occurs in winter, when furs are thickest, longest, and shiniest. Each trapper sets a series of traps called a *trap line* along riverbanks and at other spots the animals visit frequently.

Some wildlife protection groups and animal rights groups oppose the trapping of animals for fur. These groups especially object to the use of *leg-hold traps.* The jaws of such traps snap shut on an animal's leg and hold the animal until the trapper arrives to kill it. The U.S. and Canadian fur industries have worked to create more humane traps. *Padded traps,* also called *soft-catch traps,* have been developed. The jaw of such a trap, which grips the animal's paw, has a rubberized lining.

Government conservation programs regulate fur trapping in every state of the United States except Hawaii, which has no fur-bearing animals. Government conservation programs also operate in every Canadian province. Each state and province issues trapping licenses and determines when and where trapping may take place. Regulations also set limits on the number of animals that may be trapped at one time. The United States and many other nations prohibit the import of furs of animals that are in danger of becoming extinct. These animals include cheetahs, leopards, tigers, and wolves. See **Wildlife conservation.**

Skinning. Two main methods are used for skinning animals—*cased* and *open.* Ermines, minks, and other small animals are skinned by the cased method. The rancher or trapper slits a line across the rump from leg to leg and peels the pelt off inside out. Beavers and other larger animals are skinned by the open method. A line is slit up the animal's belly and the pelt is peeled off from side to side. After removing the pelts, ranchers and trappers scrape them clean of all fat and tissue, dry them, and ship them to market.

Marketing fur

Most ranchers and trappers ship their furs to one of the great auction houses in the major fur-trading centers of the world. In the United States, the chief auction houses operate in Greenville, S.C.; Minneapolis, Minn.; New York City; and Seattle. Major Canadian auction houses are in Montreal; North Bay, Ont.; Regina, Sask.; Vancouver, B.C.; and Winnipeg, Man. Leading European fur auction centers include Leningrad, the Soviet Union; London; and Oslo, Norway. The Hudson's Bay Company in Canada is the world's largest fur-trading firm.

Representatives of auction houses visit trappers and ranchers to arrange the shipment of pelts to market. The largest cargoes of furs come to market from November through February. Fur dealers, manufacturers, and retailers attend the auctions. Buyers may examine several hundred thousand pelts in the warehouses on *examin-*

David R. Frazier

A mink rancher raises his animals in pens in a long barn. More than half the world's fur comes from animals raised on ranches.

ing days. The furs are auctioned off on *sales days.* Buyers must pay for their purchases on or before the *prompt day,* which is usually about a month after the sales day. On the prompt day, the furs are shipped according to the buyers' instructions.

Processing fur

Dressing. Pelts bought at fur auctions must be cleaned and made flexible by a process called *dressing.* First, the pelts are softened in a salt solution that removes all excess tissue and grease. Excess skin that is still attached to the pelt is then removed, either by hand or by machine. Next, the processors apply a special grease to the leather and put the skins into a machine called a *kicker.* The kicker has wooden feet that pound the grease into every pore of a skin. The pelts are then placed in revolving drums, where they are cleaned and dried with special sawdust and compressed air. Later, the processors may pluck out the long guard hairs, leaving only the thick fur fibers. The fur may also be sheared shorter to give it a plush effect.

David R. Frazier

Fur buyers inspect pelts at a fur merchant's storeroom and decide which ones to purchase. The storeroom contains pelts of various fur-bearing animals from many parts of the world.

David R. Frazier

Pelts are matched according to color, luster, thickness, and other features. Matched pelts enable a manufacturer to produce a garment that has the same color and texture throughout.

How a fur coat is made   Making a fur coat requires the labor of many highly skilled workers. The illustrations below show some of the important steps involved in converting raw pelts into a finished garment.

Photographs by David R. Frazier

Dressing includes the removal, by hand or by machine, of any bits of flesh that are still attached to the pelts.

Trimming. Workers trim off the heads, paws, bellies, rumps, and tails, which are used to make cheaper garments.

Letting-out is one of many techniques used by fur cutters. It involves cutting the pelts into long diagonal strips.

Sewing. An operator sews the strips together to form lengthened, narrow pelts. The pelts are sewn into a sheet of fur.

Blocking consists of shaping the sheet of fur by stapling it to a large board on which the coat pattern has been drawn.

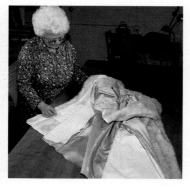

Finishing. The sheet of fur is made into a coat, which is then cleaned. Finally, workers sew in the lining of the coat.

Dyeing. Many furs are dyed to improve their appearance or to make them look like other types of fur. Processors may put furs into a vat of dye, or they may dye entire coats by hand. Sometimes dark fur is bleached and then dyed a pale shade. In a special dyeing process called *tipping,* only the tips of the fur fibers are dyed. This process makes furs resemble darker pelts of the same variety. Tipping helps the manufacturer match several pelts to be used in the same coat.

Cutting and sewing. Furs differ in quality and appearance, and so manufacturers must carefully grade and match processed skins. A manufacturer makes the pattern for a garment and then selects the skins to be used. Workers stretch the skins and trim off the heads, paws, bellies, rumps, and tails. These parts are used to make cheaper garments.

A worker called a *cutter* trims and shapes the skins to make the best use of the material. An *operator* then sews the skins together to form a sheet of fur that approximately matches the shape of the pattern. Next, a worker called a *blocker* applies small amounts of water to the skin to make it stretch just enough to cover the edges of the pattern. Then the fur is *blocked,* or stapled,

to a large pine board and left to dry. Later, any surplus material is trimmed from the skin and the fur is sewn into a garment. Finally, the garment is cleaned and the lining is sewn in.

In the United States, a law called the *Fur Products Labeling Act* requires manufacturers to place a label in a conspicuous place on all fur garments. This label must provide certain information, including: (1) the name in English of the animal that produced the fur; (2) the country of origin, if the fur is imported; and (3) whether the fur is natural or dyed. If the fur contains paws, bellies, or other scrap parts, that fact must also appear on the label. In addition, the label on a used garment must clearly indicate that the item is second-hand.   Sandy Blye

Related articles in *World Book.* See the articles on the animals marked by an asterisk in the table *Some important furs* in this article. See also the following articles:

Alaska (Fur industry)
Animal (pictures)
Astor (John Jacob)

Canada (Fur industry)
Pribilof Islands
Trapping

Fur trade was one of the earliest and most important industries in North America. The fur trading industry played a significant role in the development of the

United States and Canada for more than 300 years.

The fur trade began in the 1500's as an exchange between Indians and Europeans. The Indians traded furs for such goods as tools and weapons. Beaver fur, which was used in Europe to make felt hats, became the most valuable of these furs (see **Beaver**). The fur trade prospered until the mid-1800's, when fur-bearing animals became scarce and silk hats became more popular than felt hats made with beaver. Today, most trappers sell their pelts. But some Eskimo and Indian trappers in Canada still trade furs to fur companies for goods.

The early fur trade. The earliest fur traders in North America were French explorers and fishermen who arrived in what is now Eastern Canada during the early 1500's. Trade started after the French offered the Indians kettles, knives, and other gifts as a means to establish friendly relations. The Indians, in turn, gave pelts to the French. By the late 1500's, a great demand for fur had developed in Europe. This demand encouraged further exploration of North America. The demand for beaver increased rapidly in the late 1500's, when fashionable European men began to wear felt hats made from beaver fur. Such furs as fox, marten, mink, and otter also were traded.

In 1608, the French explorer Samuel de Champlain established a trading post on the site of the present-day city of Quebec. The city became a fur-trading center. The French expanded their trading activities along the St. Lawrence River and around the Great Lakes. They eventually controlled most of the early fur trade in what became Canada. The French traders obtained furs from the Huron Indians and, later, from the Ottawa. These tribes were not trappers, but they acquired the furs from other Indians. The French also developed the fur trade along the Mississippi River.

During the early 1600's, English settlers developed a fur trade in what are now New England and Virginia. English traders later formed an alliance with the Iroquois Indians and extended their trading area from Maine down the Atlantic Coast to Georgia.

European business companies handled a large number of the furs shipped from North America during the 1600's and 1700's. The most famous of these firms, the Hudson's Bay Company, was established in 1670. It was founded by a group of English merchants, with the help of two French fur traders, Sieur des Groseilliers and Pierre Esprit Radisson. The English government gave the company sole trading rights in what is now the Hudson Bay region. See **Hudson's Bay Company; Groseilliers, Sieur des; Radisson, Pierre E.**

During the 1700's, French and British fur traders competed bitterly over trading rights in the region between the Allegheny Mountains and the Mississippi River. This competition, plus other conflicts between the two nations, led to the French and Indian War in 1754. Great Britain won the war in 1763 and took over France's colonial empire in North America.

During the late 1770's, merchants in Montreal founded the North West Company to compete with the Hudson's Bay Company. Members of the new firm were called "Nor'Westers." The company's traders led many daring expeditions in search of fur in far western Can-

The fur trade in North America

The fur trade played an important role in the development of Canada and the United States from the 1500's to the mid-1800's. This map shows the chief areas of the fur trade in North America. The groups that controlled these areas and the periods in which the trade flourished under each group are shown below.

French
1500's to 1763

Colonial American
1600's to late 1700's

Hudson's Bay Company
1670 to 1850's

North West Company
1770's to 1821

Russian
1790's to 1850's

American
1820's to 1850's

→ Fur export route

• Trading post

• City

0		1,000 Miles
0		1,000 Kilometers

WORLD BOOK map

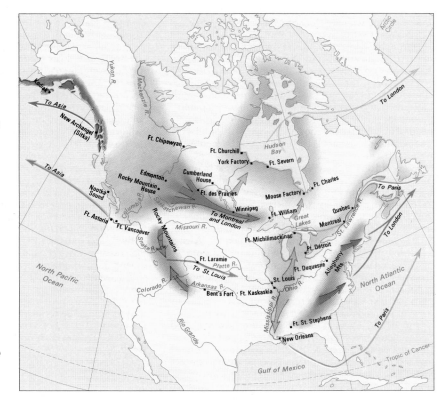

Water color by William Henry Jackson; Denver Public Library, Western History Department

The annual rendezvous, *above,* was a center of Western fur trading in the 1800's. Trappers assembled at these gatherings in the Rocky Mountains to trade or sell their pelts to fur companies.

ada. However, the company failed financially and, in 1821, merged with the Hudson's Bay Company. See **North West Company.**

During the late 1700's, Russia began to develop the fur trade in the area that is now Alaska. The Russian-American Company was established there in 1799.

The 1800's. The Lewis and Clark expedition to the Pacific Ocean in 1804 and 1805 led to the development of fur trading in the West. Several companies competed heavily for this western trade. They included firms headed by John Jacob Astor, William H. Ashley, Pierre Chouteau, and Manuel Lisa. See **Astor** (John Jacob); **Chouteau** (family).

Many Indians of the West had little interest in trapping, and so the fur-trading companies hired white frontiersmen to obtain pelts. These trappers became known as "mountain men" because they roamed through wild areas of the Rocky Mountains in search of fur. Such mountain men as Kit Carson, John Colter, and Jedediah Smith gained fame for their roles in settling the West.

Ashley, the head of the Rocky Mountain Fur Company, began to hold an annual trappers' gathering in the Rocky Mountains in 1825. At each gathering, called a *rendezvous,* trappers sold their furs and bought supplies for the next year. The rendezvous saved them from traveling long distances to various trading posts.

The fur trade started to decline in the Eastern United States by the late 1700's. The decline resulted chiefly from the clearing of large areas for settlement. As more and more land was cleared, fur-bearing animals became increasingly scarce. Overtrapping of fur-bearing animals hurt the fur trade in the Western United States and

Western Canada. In addition, the value of beaver fur dropped sharply in the 1830's, when European hat manufacturers began to use silk instead of felt. By 1870, most fur-trading activity had ended.

Effects of the fur trade. The fur trade contributed to the development of British and French empires in North America. During the 1600's, the prospect of wealth from the fur trade attracted many Europeans to the New World. Traders and trappers explored much of North America in search of fur. They built trading posts in the wilderness, and settlements grew up around many of the posts. Some of these settlements later became such major cities as Detroit, New Orleans, and St. Louis in the United States; and Edmonton, Montreal, Quebec, and Winnipeg in Canada.

The fur trade led to conflict between France and Great Britain in America. Rivalries over trading alliances also arose among Indian tribes that wanted to obtain European goods. The fur trade promoted friendly relations between the Indians and traders. But it also brought Indian hostility toward white settlers because the clearing of land threatened the supply of fur-bearing animals.

The claims of fur traders played a part in establishing the border between the United States and Canada. For example, the areas of trade controlled by U.S. and British traders helped determine the border in the region of the Great Lakes.   John Elgin Foster

Related articles in *World Book* include:

Fraser, Simon
Fur
Hearne, Samuel
Henry, Alexander

Mackenzie, Sir Alexander
Mackenzie, Roderick

McKay, Alexander
Simpson, Sir George
Trading post

Additional resources

De Voto, Bernard A. *Across the Wide Missouri.* Houghton, 1964. First published in 1947. Chronicles the Rocky Mountain fur trade from its peak years to its decline.

Francis, Daniel. *Battle for the West: Fur Traders and the Birth of Western Canada.* Hurtig (Edmonton), 1982. Suitable for younger readers.

Innis, Harold A. *The Fur Trade in Canada: An Introduction to Canadian Economic History.* Rev. ed. Yale, 1962.

Newman, Peter C. *Company of Adventurers.* Viking, 1985. *Caesars of the Wilderness.* 1987. Two volumes which tell the story of the Hudson's Bay Company.

Furfural, *FUR fuh ral,* is a liquid chemical that is used in many industries. Manufacturers use it in making nylon, plastics, and other products. Furfural changes from colorless to yellow and finally dark brown when it is exposed to the air. Its vapor irritates the eyes, nose, and throat.

Furfural is used in the production of the chemical tetrahydrofuran (THF). Butadiene, a material used in *synthetic* (artificial) rubber, can be made from THF. THF is also used as a solvent to dissolve other substances in industry.

Furfuryl alcohol, another compound made from furfural, is used in making resins which protect metals from *corroding* (being eaten away). Many synthetic resins are made with furfural. Manufacturers use these synthetic resins to make plastic products. Because furfural kills various fungi, germs, and insects, it is used in fungicides, germicides, and insecticides. Rubber manufacturers use furfural to speed up the vulcanization process used to make rubber harder and more durable.

Chemists call furfural a selective solvent because it will dissolve some materials in a mixture and not others. Petroleum refineries use furfural to dissolve the harmful carbon and sulfur compounds found in impure lubricating oils. Furfural is also used to refine other petroleum products such as diesel fuel.

Chemical manufacturers prepare furfural by mixing acid with waste plant materials such as corncobs or the hulls of cottonseeds, oats, or rice. Furfural is also found in some natural oils. Johann Döbereiner, a German chemist, reported his discovery of furfural in 1832. He accidentally obtained the chemical by treating sugar with sulfuric acid and manganese dioxide. American chemists discovered the methods now used to manufacture furfural in the early 1920's.

Furfural is an organic chemical with the formula C_4H_3OCHO. It belongs to the aldehyde chemical family and is sometimes called *furfuraldehyde* (see **Aldehyde**). Furfural freezes at $-37.6°$ F. ($-38.7°$ C) and boils at $323°$ F. ($161.7°$ C). It is about 1.16 times as dense as water.

Geoffrey E. Dolbear

Furies, *FYUR eez,* were the terrible goddesses of vengeance in Roman mythology. The Greeks called them *Erinyes* or *Eumenides.* The Roman poet Virgil wrote of three Furies in his epic poem the *Aeneid.* He called them Alecto, Tisiphone, and Megaera. They carried whips and had snakes in their hair.

The Furies punished people for committing crimes. The Furies were especially vengeful against anyone who had killed a member of his or her family. In his tragedy *The Eumenides,* the Greek playwright Aeschylus describes how they drove Orestes insane for killing his mother, Clytemnestra. Elaine Fantham

See also **Orestes.**

Furlong is an English unit of measurement of length equal to 40 rods, or $\frac{1}{8}$ mile (0.2 kilometer). Furlong originally meant the length of one furrow in a plowed field. This was indefinite because farmers plowed many different lengths of furrows. Gradually the furlong became a standard length.

Among the old English writers, the furlong was one-eighth of a mile in each of the world's different standards for a mile. In the 800's, the word meant the same as the Latin *stadium,* which was one-eighth of the Roman mile. The furlong is seldom used today except on horse-race tracks. E. G. Straus

See also **Weights and measures.**

The Furies were avenging goddesses in classical mythology. This painting shows them in a scene from a Greek tragedy by Aeschylus. They were usually shown with brass wings and snakes on their bodies.

Detail from Greek vase painting of the late 300's B.C.; The British Museum, London

Furnace is a device in which heat is produced. Some furnaces heat the air in people's homes. Others produce steam to run electric power plants. Furnaces are necessary in the manufacture of iron and steel, glass, pottery, and other products. They also are used in petroleum refining. This article deals with both industrial and home heating furnaces. For detailed information on home heating systems, see the article on **Heating.**

Furnaces range in size from kitchen ovens to the huge furnaces used in steel production. Most industrial furnaces are built of *refractory* (heat-resistant) bricks, which are able to withstand great variation in temperature without weakening. The walls and roofs of some modern furnaces are made of refractory fiberglass cloth that is mounted on metal frames. The combustion chamber in most home heating furnaces is made of stainless steel or some other refractory material.

Sources of heat. Most furnaces generate heat by burning fuel. These furnaces are called *combustion furnaces.* Early combustion furnaces burned wood or charcoal. In the 1600's, coal began to replace these fuels. During the mid-1900's, many industrial furnaces were converted to burn oil. Today, most industrial combustion furnaces burn natural gas. This fuel causes almost

no air pollution, and it is easy to control. Most home heating furnaces burn gas or oil.

There are two basic types of combustion furnaces—*direct fired* and *indirect fired.* In direct-fired furnaces, the flame is in the same compartment as the *charge* (the material to be heated). In an indirect-fired furnace, also called a *muffle furnace,* the flame is contained in a separate chamber from the charge. This chamber, called a *muffle,* may be a cavity in the furnace wall or a steel tube that runs through the furnace. Indirect-fired furnaces are used when the charge may be harmed by the gases produced during combustion.

Combustion furnaces can be heated to the temperature required to perform a wide variety of jobs simply by burning the fuel. Some jobs, however, such as smelting iron ore or melting glass, need a higher temperature than the combustion of fuel alone can produce. In such cases, the flame is made hotter by heating air before it is mixed with the fuel. For example, air is drawn into a glassmaking furnace through a pile of bricks that has been heated by hot gases leaving the furnace.

Not all furnaces are heated by the combustion of fuel. For example, electric furnaces use electricity to produce heat. Nuclear reactors get their heat from the energy released when the nuclei of uranium or plutonium atoms split. The high temperatures produced in solar furnaces are obtained through the use of mirrors that focus the sun's rays. See **Electric furnace; Nuclear reactor; Solar energy** (Capturing solar energy).

Heating the charge. There are two basic types of furnaces, based on the way they heat a charge: (1) *batch furnaces* and (2) *continuous furnaces.*

Batch furnaces heat materials singly or a group at a time. Clay pots, for instance, are baked in batches in *kilns* (ovens). After baking, all the pots are removed before the next batch is placed in the kiln.

Handling the hot charges is often a problem in batch processing, because of the high temperatures required in industrial furnaces. A number of solutions have been developed. Workers use steel tongs to remove small articles from batch furnaces, and large mechanical arms and cranes are used to handle larger items. In a *car bottom furnace,* a type of batch furnace, the floor and door are on wheels and can be pulled out like a drawer to reach the charge. A *top hat furnace* can be lifted off its base to be loaded or unloaded. Batches of steel and copper are heated in large pot furnaces. Once the materials are melted, the whole furnace is tilted and the glowing hot liquid pours out a spout.

Continuous furnaces heat a steady flow of material that passes through them. This material may be rolled through the furnace on carts, pushed through by hydraulic rams, or carried on conveyor belts. Crude oil and water are carried through furnaces in pipes. Some furnaces rely upon gravity to move the material through them. For example, iron ore is fed in at the top of a blast furnace and molten iron flows out from the bottom. Cement is produced by roasting crushed limestone in a *rotary kiln,* a slightly inclined, long steel tube lined with refractory brick. The pieces of limestone are fed in at the higher end and slowly tumble to the lower end as the kiln rotates.   Robert H. Essenhigh

See also **Boiler; Iron and steel** (How iron is made; How steel is made).

A home heating furnace is a typical combustion furnace. Gas is piped into the furnace and burned, warming a heat exchanger, which works like a radiator. A blower forces air through the heat exchanger, where the air is warmed before traveling to the rooms. The blower also draws cool air into the furnace, where it is warmed again and recirculated.

WORLD BOOK diagram by Arthur Grebetz

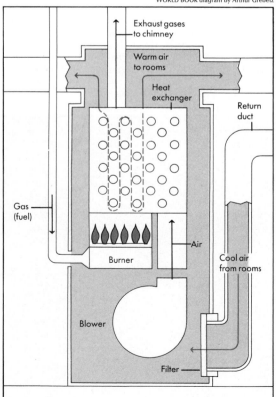

Exhaust gases to chimney

Warm air to rooms

Heat exchanger

Return duct

Gas (fuel)

Air

Burner

Cool air from rooms

Blower

Filter

Well-designed furniture contributes beauty and comfort to daily life. The chairs, sofas, and tables in this living room reflect the clean, simple lines of modern furniture styles.

Furniture

Furniture consists of chairs, tables, beds, and other pieces that provide comfort and convenience in our daily lives. Many kinds of furniture are used in homes, schools, and offices. We relax on comfortable couches, and we store various belongings in chests, dressers, and bookcases. Desks provide a place for study and paperwork. Numerous television sets and phonographs have handsome cabinets, and so they also serve as pieces of furniture. In many homes, a piano is an impressive piece of furniture.

In addition to being useful, furniture is attractively designed to make our surroundings more pleasant. Furniture works with other decorative and useful objects to beautify a room. Such items, including rugs and carpets, curtains, draperies, lamps, and pictures, are called *furnishings.*

Most furniture is made of wood or wood products. But furniture makers also use glass, metal, plastics, and a variety of other materials.

Certain pieces of the finest furniture rank among the world's greatest works of art. Over the years, expert designers and *artisans* (skilled craftworkers) have created richly decorated furniture in various styles. Many of these artisans were regarded as artists equal to the most famous painters and sculptors of their day. Today, museums display examples of their furniture as masterpieces of art.

People who study the history of furniture have given names to the different styles. Some styles are named for important people. For example, Louis XIV furniture is named for King Louis XIV of France. Other styles are named for historical periods. Thus, the Federal style of American furniture recalls the beginning of the federal system of government in the United States. Still other styles, such as art nouveau, take their name from an art movement.

The history of furniture can be seen as a series of styles that become popular for a time and then fall from fashion. Designers then revive earlier styles, adapting them to fit the taste of the time.

The history of furniture is closely related to the history of human culture. For thousands of years, all fine furniture was designed to accommodate the tastes of royalty and the nobility and other wealthy people. These people considered furniture a symbol of their power and rank rather than a practical necessity. Beginning in the A.D. 1500's, a middle class of people gradually developed in Western countries. People of this class wanted furniture that was comfortable and suited to their homes. By the 1800's, the tastes of middle-class buyers set the standard for furniture styles. Most furniture made today is still designed to be practical, comfortable, and easy to maintain.

This article describes the history of furniture from its earliest period to the present time. For a discussion of the importance of furniture in interior decoration, see the *World Book* article **Interior decoration.**

John W. Keefe, the contributor of this article, is the Curator of Decorative Arts at the New Orleans Museum of Art.

Early furniture

The ancient Egyptians created the first known fine furniture about 3000 B.C. Later, the Greeks and then the Romans developed outstanding furniture in their own characteristic styles. The age of Greek and Roman culture was followed by the Middle Ages, a period that in general produced little important furniture.

Ancient Egypt (3100 B.C.-1070 B.C.). The ancient Egyptians considered the ownership of furniture a mark of social rank. The best-made and most beautiful furniture decorated the palace of the Egyptian king. Members of the nobility, wealthy officials, and landowners also possessed fine furniture. The common people had only one piece of furniture—a three-legged stool—in their simple homes.

Egyptian furniture makers did some of their best work in designing beds. Most beds had legs shaped like the legs of an animal, usually a lion. These beds led to the development of couches in the shape of an animal, such as a lion or a leopard.

Egyptian artisans also made fine chairs. The finest chairs had a seat of woven cord covered with a removable cushion. The development of the armchair was probably the most lasting Egyptian contribution to furniture design. Other Egyptian furniture included boxes, cabinets, and small tables.

Ancient Greece (about 1100 B.C.-A.D. 400). In ancient Greece, as in ancient Egypt, only persons of the highest social rank possessed much furniture. Most Greek citizens owned only a three-legged stool and perhaps a crudely made table.

The Greeks borrowed many furniture forms, including the bed and the couch, from the Egyptians. Beds became major pieces of household decoration in ancient Greece because they were used for dining as well as for sleeping. During a meal, a person would lie on the bed on his or her side, leaning on one elbow for support.

Greek artisans produced a variety of seating furniture. The most important were the thrones made for people of high rank. Some thrones had a low back decorated with one or more carvings of animal heads. Others had a high back with flowerlike carvings. The arm supports were in the form of rams' heads. The most common type of Greek chair, called the *klismos,* had curved legs. The front legs curved forward, and the rear legs curved to the back.

The Greeks used tables more than the Egyptians did. Most Greek tables had three legs that ended in feet shaped like hoofs or paws. Greek artisans decorated the finest furniture with inlaid patterns of fine wood, silver, gold, and gems. They either carved ivory to form the feet or cast them in silver or bronze.

Ancient Rome (700's B.C.-A.D. 400's). The Romans borrowed many furniture forms from the Greeks but gave them a distinctly Roman character. For example, the Romans used more bronze and silver in their furniture than did the Greeks. Romans used the Greek klismos but made it heavier and larger. They also covered it with upholstery. Roman furniture makers adopted a Greek stool design and developed it into a stool called a *curule.* The curule had two pairs of legs. The delicate,

Egyptian Museum, Cairo, Egypt
(Metropolitan Museum of Art/Lee Boltin)

An ancient Egyptian throne, *above,* which belonged to King Tutankhamen, is decorated with carvings of lion heads and paws.

Relief from a gravestone (about 400 B.C.); Archaeological Museum, Athens, Greece (Raymond V. Schoder, S.J.)

A simply built chest, *right,* is typical of the furniture of the Middle Ages. Carvings were a common form of furniture decoration during this period.

Church of St. Mary, Stoke D'Abernon, England (Hanford Photography)

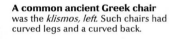

A common ancient Greek chair was the *klismos, left.* Such chairs had curved legs and a curved back.

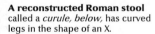

A reconstructed Roman stool called a *curule, below,* has curved legs in the shape of an X.

Rijksmuseum, Nijmegen, the Netherlands

curved legs in each pair were crossed in the form of an X.

Tables were very popular among the Romans. Many tables had three or four legs connected by crossbars. The *slab table* was a major Roman contribution to table design. The tabletop consisted of a large slab of marble or wood, which rested on carved upright marble slabs. Artisans sculptured various designs into the upright slabs, including animals, flowers, fruits, and vines.

The Middle Ages (400's-1300). During the period of European history called the Middle Ages, skillful furniture making generally became a lost art. Most furniture of the Middle Ages was coarse and unrefined by the standards of ancient Greece and Rome. Furniture makers painted or *gilded* (coated with gold) most pieces to disguise their crude construction. As in earlier times, people of high rank owned the best furniture.

Landowners and church officials of the Middle Ages traveled frequently. They usually took their furniture and other possessions with them on their journeys. Much furniture thus was designed to be portable. Large pieces were put together in such a way that they could be taken apart and carried easily. Chests were used for storage as well as for seats.

During the 1200's, a new Western European art style called *Gothic* influenced the design of furniture. Artisans decorated their furniture, especially chests and cupboards, with arches, columns, and other features of Gothic architecture.

Oriental furniture

In the Oriental countries, as in Egypt and Europe, only high-ranking officials and wealthy people owned finely crafted furniture. The artisans of China, Japan, and India produced the most noteworthy Oriental furniture. The earliest high-quality Oriental furniture was produced in China during the 200's B.C.

China. By the time of the Han dynasty (202 B.C.-A.D. 220), the Chinese had developed several furniture forms. The most characteristic was the *kang,* a platform on which a person could lie to sleep or rest. The Chinese of this period grouped a variety of small stools and tables around the kang.

Later Chinese furniture falls into two categories: household furniture and the furniture used in royal palaces. Chinese household furniture was simple and practical. Palace furniture was larger, heavier, and more richly decorated than household furniture.

A notable characteristic of all Chinese furniture was the skillful manner in which artisans joined the parts. They used no pegs or nails and seldom used glue. Instead, they carved the edges of parts so expertly that the parts fitted together tightly.

By the early 1400's, the Chinese were using low dining tables supported by gracefully curved legs now known as *cabriole* legs. A cabriole leg has S-shaped curves, and it ends with a decorative foot. Beginning in the 1700's, this design became an important feature of Western furniture and was given the French name *cabriole.* The best-known Chinese chair design had a single vertical *splat*—a piece of wood that formed the center of the chair's back.

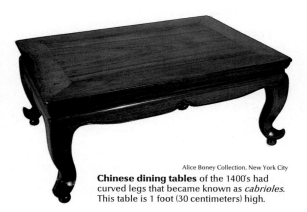

Alice Boney Collection, New York City

Chinese dining tables of the 1400's had curved legs that became known as *cabrioles.* This table is 1 foot (30 centimeters) high.

R. Hatfield Ellsworth Collection, New York City (Lee Boltin)

A typical Chinese chair of the 1500's had a single vertical *splat* that formed the center of the chair's back.

Mary and Jackson Burke Collection, New York City (Lee Boltin)

A Japanese cabinet of the early 1600's is made of lacquered wood. The doors and shelves have grapevine designs.

Japan. Japanese architectural styles largely determined that country's furniture styles. Earthquakes occurred frequently in Japan, which resulted in the building of light, one-story buildings. In both home and palaces, the Japanese used small, lightweight cabinets, chests, and writing tables rather than large, heavy pieces. The Japanese customarily sat and slept on floor mats, and so they used no chairs or beds. Their furniture was simple in shape, but it was beautifully decorated with colorful designs of flowers, animals, and scenes from Japanese literature. Japanese artisans lacquered the furniture to give it a glossy finish. This use of lacquer gave the furniture a distinctive quality. Japanese furniture makers also beautified their work with shell inlays and rich fabrics.

India. The earliest important pieces of Indian furniture were chairs designed to be used by members of the nobility. Such thrones later developed into four-legged platforms on which a person sat with legs folded. Many of these thrones had the shape of a flower blossom. A person sat on cushions and used pillows for a backrest. Indian beds were covered with luxuriously upholstered cushions and mattresses.

© The Frick Collection, New York City

An Italian Renaissance chest called a *cassone, above,* is made of fine wood and beautifully carved. Such chests were the most popular type of furniture in Italy during the Renaissance.

The Renaissance

The Renaissance was a period of European history that lasted from about 1300 to 1600. A major characteristic of the period was a revival of interest in *classical* cultures—that is, the cultures of ancient Greece and Rome. Classical art thus had a strong influence on furniture designed during the Renaissance. Italian artisans created the first important Renaissance furniture. Their work attracted much attention in other European countries, especially France, England, and Spain.

Italy. During the Renaissance, the palaces of Italian nobles became famous for their luxurious interiors, which included fine furniture and magnificent paintings. Actually, these palaces contained few pieces of furniture by today's standards. The best-furnished room in a palace was the *studio,* a library in which the owner kept books, manuscripts, gems, medals, and small sculptures. These items rested on shelves in beautifully ornamented cupboards.

Chests continued to be important articles of furniture, as they were in the Middle Ages. During the early 1500's, a large type of chest called a *cassone* was carved, gilded, and painted with scenes from classical history and mythology. A new form of chest called the *cassapanca* developed from the cassone. The cassapanca had a backrest and arms, and it was used as a sofa as well as a chest. Large cupboards called *sideboards* or *credenzas* became popular pieces of Italian furniture. Artisans decorated them with columns and other features of classical architecture.

France. French Renaissance furniture can be divided into two important styles, called Francis I and Henry II. Each style was named after a French king. Francis I ruled from 1515 to 1547. Henry II ruled from 1547 to 1559.

Before the reign of Francis I, French furniture reflected the Gothic style of the late Middle Ages. A new style developed after Francis brought leading Italian artists to France to remodel the royal *château* (castle) at

Château de Beauregard, Blois, France (P. Hinous, Agence TOP)

A French Renaissance cabinet, *above,* was designed in the Henry II style, which became popular during the mid-1500's. Such cabinets had a small upper section that rested on a larger base. Furniture makers decorated these pieces with carvings of human figures and scenes from Greek and Roman mythology.

English furniture of the Renaissance was solid and sturdy, as this picture indicates. The picture shows the drawing room of Hardwick Hall, an English estate, as it looked in the 1590's. The room has a new and distinctly English furniture form, a dining table called a *draw-table, foreground.* The length of the table could be increased by drawing its halves apart and adding leaves. Carvings of mythical winged beasts support the tabletop.

Fontainebleau. In redesigning the château, the Italian artisans introduced decorative *motifs* (designs) that revolutionized French art of the period. These motifs included the use of columns; carved human heads surrounded by scrolls; carved bands, called *strapwork,* which imitated tooled leather bookbindings; and *niches* (hollowed-out areas in walls).

The Italian-inspired Francis I style of furniture lasted until the mid-1500's. The Henry II style, which was more varied and more identifiably French, then replaced it. Carved human figures still played an important decorative role, as did carved animals. Columns and arches served as supports for tables. But the new style gave furniture a lighter appearance. For example, French artisans refined the traditional cabinet form by placing a small upper section on a larger base.

England. The Italian Renaissance influenced England largely because of the encouragement of King Henry VIII, who ruled England from 1509 to 1547. Henry invited Italian artists and artisans to work in England. English furniture makers then blended the Italian ornamental style with traditional English designs to create an English Renaissance style.

A number of distinctly English furniture forms appeared during the reign of Queen Elizabeth I, who ruled from 1558 to 1603. One of these forms was the *draw-table,* a large oak dining table made in halves that could be drawn apart. The length of this table could be increased by adding one or two top sections called *leaves* after drawing the halves apart. Another fashionable English design was the *court cupboard,* which had open shelves for displaying valuable plates and silverware. The cupboard had legs that were decorated with classical and Italian Renaissance motifs. Perhaps the most impressive pieces of English Renaissance furniture were beds, which featured handsome carvings and expensive fabrics.

Spain developed a Renaissance style that combined Spanish, Italian, and Moorish influences. The Moors

were North African Muslims who had invaded Spain in the A.D. 700's. The Moorish impact on Spanish furniture appeared in an emphasis on gilding and the use of geometric designs that were made with ivory and wood inlays.

A major contribution of Spanish artisans was the design of a portable cabinet called a *vargueno.* The vargueno's door was hinged at the lower edge. When opened, the door served as a writing desk. The vargueno had many small drawers and a central cupboard.

A portable cabinet called a *vargueno* was a contribution of Spanish artisans. Varguenos had a door that could serve as a desk. This vargueno, made about 1600, rests on another cabinet.

The 1600's

An Italian tabletop of the 1600's is decorated with semiprecious stones in a technique called *pietre dure.* Other popular tabletops of the period were made of marble or inlaid wood.

Museo dell' Opificio
delle Pietre Dure,
Florence, Italy (SCALA)

The early 1600's were years during which most of Europe was engaged in political and religious wars. This warfare hindered the development of the arts in many European countries. Only Italy and the Netherlands enjoyed peace, and Italian artisans especially became an important source of new furniture design. Dutch furniture makers achieved excellence in creating beautiful floral designs with inlays of tropical woods and *mother-of-pearl* (the lining of certain sea shells).

In France, King Henry IV established royal furniture workshops in the Louvre in Paris. He financed the workshops and brought leading artisans from other countries to work in them.

Italy led in furniture development largely because many rich Italian merchants were building great palaces during the period. The merchants wanted the finest furniture for their palaces, and Italian artisans supplied it.

Many Italian tables had a base modeled on the slab tables of ancient Rome. Other tables had a top made of marble or inlaid wood on a base sculptured in the form of mythical creatures, shells, floral designs, and human figures. Sculptured human figures also supported cabinets, candlestands, and some chairs.

Italian artisans created fashions for chests, cabinets, and cupboards that spread throughout Europe. The cassone of the 1500's developed into a long credenza with a number of doors. The credenza, in turn, gradually

Château of Vaux-le-Vicomte (1661) near Melun, France; (R. Guillemot, Agence TOP)

The Louis XIV style was known for its luxury. Louis Le Vau, the French architect who designed this room, combined beautiful furniture with works of art and architectural decorations to achieve an elegant effect. The sofa and high-backed chairs are typical of the Louis XIV style.

State beds, which featured a carved canopy and luxurious drapings, were important pieces of furniture among the nobility and the wealthy during the late 1600's. Daniel Marot, an influential French furniture maker, designed this state bed for the royal bedroom in Hampton Court Palace, near London.

developed into two new forms. One form was a tall two-door cabinet. The other was a tall chest of drawers that rested on a stand.

Many people of the early 1600's considered the quality of upholstery to be a measure of a householder's social rank. As a result, beds—which were richly decorated with silk, velvet, and other luxurious fabrics—became major pieces of furniture. Such large *state beds* were placed in the main room of a palace or large house as well as in the bedrooms.

Louis XIV furniture was the most notable furniture of the late 1600's. Louis XIV had become king of France in 1643, when he was only 4 years old. He took control of the French government in 1661, after the death of France's chief minister, Jules Cardinal Mazarin. Louis, who was then 23 years old, devoted himself to making France the cultural and political center of the Western world. He considered furniture making and the decorative arts to be politically important because he could use them to glorify his position as king. He bought a building on the outskirts of Paris, turned it into workshops, and staffed the shops with expert artisans. He commissioned them to create furnishings for his residences. These furnishings created a new national style of art.

Actually, the artisans worked almost entirely on a single project in Versailles, where they converted a royal hunting lodge into a luxurious royal palace. The noted French architect Charles Le Brun supervised the huge Versailles project and hired artisans from other countries. The decorating and furnishing of the Versailles palace became such a large undertaking that many foreign artisans took up permanent residence in France. Many of them married French women and had children who became furniture makers, creating a native French group of artisans.

The remarkable style of the furnishings made for the Versailles palace became known as the *Louis XIV* style.

This luxurious style was particularly notable for two important characteristics. One was a *veneer* technique invented by a French cabinetmaker, André Charles Boulle. In this technique, artisans "sandwiched" a *veneer* (thin layer of material) between two veneers of a contrasting material. Artisans used such materials as brass, ebony, and a dull silvery metal called pewter. They cut through the layers to create contrasting scrolled patterns. Veneers were applied to Louis XIV cabinets, writing tables, and other furniture. Le Brun and Louis himself were responsible for the second characteristic—furniture of solid silver made for the main rooms at Versailles.

The French influence spreads. The furnishings of the Versailles palace set the standard for other royal palaces, and soon French styles were imitated in palaces throughout Europe. But there were also political and religious reasons for the spread of French influence.

The national religion of France was Roman Catholicism, but most French artisans were Protestants. The French Protestants, called *Huguenots,* enjoyed religious freedom under the Edict of Nantes, which was issued by King Henry IV in 1598. In 1685, Louis XIV took away the Huguenots' freedom by canceling the edict. Most of the artisans then fled to the Netherlands or to England. There, they worked among the nobles and wealthy merchants and so established a taste for French design in the two countries.

Daniel Marot became one of the most influential Huguenot artisans both in the Netherlands and in England. Marot worked for William III, who was a Dutch prince before he became king of England in 1689. Marot also designed the interiors and furniture for Hampton Court Palace, near London. His designs created a demand in the late 1600's for high-backed chairs with French-style upholstered seats and backs. Marot's work also led to a fashion for state beds with drapery even more luxurious than that used in France.

Stavros S. Niarchos Collection (Josse)

A low chest of drawers called a *commode* became a popular furniture form of the 1700's. The commode above has curves of bronze. Curved decorations were basic to the *rococo* style of the early 1700's.

The French neoclassical style of the late 1700's, *right,* featured light, graceful furniture with straight lines. The influence of ancient Roman art can be seen in the decorations on the furniture and walls.

Queen's Salon (1781), Versailles, France (Lauros, Giraudon)

Artisans in France and England dominated furniture design during the 1700's. Furniture makers in other countries interpreted the French and English designs and developed them into individual national styles.

French styles

The Régence Style of the early 1700's received its name because a *regent* (temporary ruler) governed France during the period. After Louis XIV died in 1715, his 5-year-old grandson became King Louis XV. Because of the king's youth, his uncle, the Duke of Orléans, was appointed regent. The duke disliked the formality of Versailles and moved the royal court to Paris. There, a less ceremonial life style developed among the people of the court. They lived in residences called *town houses,* which were smaller and more intimate than the palace at Versailles. The style of furniture created for these town houses became known as the Régence style.

Régence furniture had a lighter, more graceful quality than Louis XIV furniture, emphasizing curves and delicate floral designs. Perhaps its most important characteristic was the use of the cabriole leg, which was inspired by Chinese furniture.

During the Régence period, the French cabinetmakers André Charles Boulle and Charles Cressent developed a low chest of drawers called a *commode.* This form became one of the most popular of the 1700's and was made with regional variations throughout Europe.

The rococo style. During the 1730's, the Régence style took on the features of a new style called *rococo.* The leading designer of rococo furniture was Juste-Aurèle Meissonnier. His motifs stressed swirling curves, *asymmetrical* (irregular) designs, and carvings in the form of rocks and shells. The name *rococo* came from the word *rocaille,* which was used to describe the rock-

European Room by Mrs. James Ward Thorne, Art Institute of Chicago

French provincial furniture was a comfortable style favored by middle-class people in the French provinces. This bedroom of the 1700's includes a tall cupboard and a bed set into the wall.

and-shell designs. The rococo style was also called the *Louis XV* style.

Rococo furniture was designed to blend with the overall architectural plan of a room. For example, artisans designed tables, mirrors, benches, and beds so that they could be set into wall niches provided by the architect. Oriental furniture styles also influenced rococo design. A style called *chinoiserie,* loosely based on Chinese motifs, became especially popular. Oriental lacquer also became fashionable.

The neoclassical style, called the *Louis XVI* style in France, replaced the rococo style by the late 1750's. The word *neoclassical* is a combination of the prefix *neo,* which means *new,* and the word *classical.* Neoclassical design thus reflected a renewed interest in the furniture motifs of ancient Greece and Rome. Neoclassical designers gradually eliminated the numerous curves of the rococo style in favor of the straight outlines of classical furniture. In place of elaborate rococo decorations, neoclassical artisans used thin pieces of plain wood arranged in geometric designs.

Much neoclassical furniture was inspired by classical motifs that were discovered in the mid-1700's by archaeologists in two ancient Roman cities, Pompeii and Herculaneum. The cities had been buried by an eruption of Mount Vesuvius in A.D. 79.

Art Institute of Chicago

The Queen Anne style of the early 1700's featured splat-backed upholstered chairs and large desks called *secretaries*. The style introduced the cabriole leg into English furniture.

Art Institute of Chicago

The Chippendale style dominated English and American furniture of the mid-1700's. The three chairs in the room shown above have carved mahogany legs, which are characteristic of the style. The influence of Chinese furniture design appears in the splat-backed chair on the left.

Dining room at Osterley Park House (about 1770); the National Trust, London

The English neoclassical style was begun by Robert Adam, a Scottish architect, in the 1760's. His light, harmonious designs can be seen in this dining room. A mirror in a richly carved frame hangs above a table called a *sideboard*. Carved plaster ornaments decorate the walls and ceiling.

English styles

The Palladian style was popular in England during the early 1700's. It was named after Andrea Palladio, an Italian architect of the 1500's. English artisans adopted elements of Palladio's style, which was based on the style of Roman architecture. For example, they decorated chests and cupboards with such architectural features as columns, ornamental moldings called *cornices,* and triangular top sections called *pediments.*

Henry Francis DuPont Winterthur Museum, Wilmington, Del.

Early American furniture was simple and sturdy. Most of the designs were based on English styles. The room at the left dates from about 1670. The cupboard, with its open shelves and a closed cabinet, reflects the influence of a type of English furniture called a *court cupboard.*

The Queen Anne style. The Palladian style was so expensive to produce that only wealthy people could afford it. The English middle class used a less expensive—and more comfortable—style. It was called the Queen Anne style after the queen who ruled England from 1702 to 1714. The Queen Anne style introduced the cabriole leg into English furniture design.

Chippendale furniture. In 1754, the English cabinetmaker and furniture designer Thomas Chippendale published a book of furniture designs called *The Gentleman and the Cabinet-Maker's Director.* It was the first book dealing entirely with furniture to be published in England, and it had a tremendous influence. In the book, Chippendale did not introduce any new styles. But he portrayed existing styles, especially the rococo, with such freedom and vigor that his designs were widely copied. His influence became so widespread that the name Chippendale has come to mean almost any English and American rococo furniture of the mid-1700's.

English neoclassical furniture. Robert Adam, a Scottish architect and furniture designer, introduced the neoclassical style into England in the 1760's. Adam borrowed some of his ideas from the French neoclassical style, but he also contributed many original elements. For decoration, he used delicate floral motifs, ram and ox heads, and other features inspired by ornaments on Roman buildings and tombs. Adam introduced the sideboard, or credenza, into English furniture. He also became known for skillfully blending furniture into the architectural plan of a room.

A number of English furniture makers adopted Adam's neoclassical style during the late 1700's. Two of the best known, George Hepplewhite and Thomas Sheraton, prepared design books that popularized the style. The furniture made according to Adam's original designs was very expensive. Hepplewhite, Sheraton, and other furniture makers simplified the designs to reduce the cost of the furniture for middle-class buyers.

Early American furniture

In the English colonies of North America, furniture design generally reflected the styles that were popular in England at the time. However, colonial artisans developed variations of the English styles. Starting about 1790, the most common early American style was a neoclassical variation called the *Federal* style. This style took its name from the young nation's new federal form of government. Duncan Phyfe, the leading American furniture designer of the period, worked in New York City and helped make it the manufacturing center for the Federal style. High-quality furniture was also produced by artisans in Boston; Philadelphia; and Newport, R.I.

The Federal style of American furniture began about 1790. It was influenced by the straight lines of English neoclassical furniture. The pieces in the bedroom shown above were largely based on designs by such English furniture makers as George Hepplewhite and Thomas Sheraton.

Until the early 1800's, furniture fashions were set largely by the tastes of nobles and other wealthy people. But beginning in the early 1800's, the tastes of the middle class set the standard for furniture fashions. People of the middle class wanted variety and novelty in furniture design. As a result, a great number of styles became popular for a short time and were then replaced by new styles.

During the 1800's, many furniture expositions were held in major cities in the United States and Europe. At these expositions, furniture makers from many countries displayed their own designs and viewed the designs of others. These designs greatly influenced public taste. The expositions thus had the effect of establishing international furniture styles. The United States and European countries adopted the same major styles, with some regional differences.

The furniture of the 1800's falls into two categories: (1) furniture based on historical styles and (2) furniture intended to be truly original. Some furniture makers simply copied earlier styles. Others used earlier styles as models but changed them to give them freshness and new vigor. The invention of new furniture-making machines during the 1800's helped designers develop new styles. With these machines, designers could use materials in new ways. For example, they could use such materials as cast iron and wire in ways that had been impossible.

The Empire style, the first major style of the 1800's, originated while Emperor Napoleon I ruled the French empire. Like Louis XIV, Napoleon wanted to use furniture as a symbol of political greatness. As a result, Empire furniture was impressive—large and heavy.

Empire artisans borrowed designs from Egyptian, Greek, and Roman furniture. They made chairs with curved rear legs shaped like those on the Greek klismos. They decorated furniture with such classical subjects as lions, sphinxes, and sculptured female figures called *caryatids.* Empire commodes, writing tables, and desks called *secretaries* were designed to fit into the overall plan of a room.

The Regency style, a neoclassical style, was fashionable in England and the United States along with the Empire style. The Regency style was named after the period from 1811 to 1820, when the Prince of Wales served as regent for King George III of England. Most Regency furniture combined Egyptian, Chinese, and Gothic motifs with neoclassical elements. The style featured couches with ends shaped like scrolls, and chairs loosely modeled on the klismos. Stools based on the Roman curule also were popular.

Regency artisans used little carved ornamentation. They often used a decorative technique called *penwork,* in which artists inked designs on light-colored wood or a painted white surface. Regency artisans also decorated furniture with brass inlays.

The Biedermeier, or Restoration, style. After the fall of Napoleon I in 1815, the majestic Empire style went out of fashion. A more informal style favored by middle-class people replaced it. This new style was called either by its German name, *Biedermeier,* or by its French name, *Restoration.* The name Biedermeier came from a comic character in German popular literature (see **Biedermeier**). The term Restoration refers to the restora-

An Empire-style dressing table, *above,* features a round mirror and built-in candleholders. The table also has a marble top and curved, crossed legs like the legs of the Roman curule.

Biedermeier furniture of the early 1800's had an informal, practical style. The chair and drop-front desk shown above illustrate the appealing simplicity of the style.

tion of the French monarchy after the fall of Napoleon's empire. The style produced comfortable, practical furniture that had simple lines and simple decoration. The most important forms were desks, display cabinets, small work tables, and pianos.

Historical revivals. From the 1830's to the late 1800's, a number of earlier styles were revived. The most important styles, in the order in which they appeared, were the Gothic, rococo, and Renaissance revivals. People used each style in a particular room. They placed Gothic furniture in the library, rococo in the *drawing room* (parlor) and bedroom, and Renaissance in the dining room.

Most Gothic revival furniture consisted of neoclassical forms with Gothic ornaments. These ornaments included pointed arches and decorative patterns called *tracery.* The style was particularly popular in England, where a variation called the *Elizabethan revival* became fashionable. In France, Gothic revival was known as the *cathedral* or *troubadour* style.

The rococo revival replaced the Gothic revival in the 1840's. Chairs and sofas in this style had cabriole legs and oval backs based upon the Louis XV style of the 1700's. Artisans decorated pieces with rocaille carving and introduced large pieces, such as mirrored wardrobes, sideboards, and display cabinets. Such pieces remained popular throughout the 1800's.

The Renaissance revival began in the court of the French emperor Napoleon III, who ruled from 1852 to 1870. It achieved the greatest popularity in the late 1870's and the 1880's. Artisans of this period tried to reproduce the furniture designs of the 1400's and 1500's. Designers emphasized angular forms and richly upholstered chairs, sofas, and stools.

Art nouveau was an art movement that developed as a revolt against the historical revival styles. It began in the 1800's and lasted until the early 1900's. Art nouveau

Parlor furniture in the rococo revival style, *above,* has cabriole legs and oval backs edged with fine wood carvings.

furniture featured design elements based on natural forms, such as blossoms, roots, stalks, and vines. Artisans combined these forms with a graceful motif called a *whiplash* curve. Art nouveau decorations also included female heads surrounded by flowing hair.

Middle-class buyers could not afford the handmade and expensive art nouveau furniture. After wealthy buyers tired of the style's specialized designs, it fell from fashion. But the popularity of art nouveau and its rejection of traditional styles greatly contributed to design developments in furniture of the 1900's.

Art nouveau was a decorative style characterized by a graceful curve known as a *whiplash* curve. This feature appears in both the furniture and the wall and ceiling decorations in the dining room shown at the left.

During the 1900's, many designers have rejected traditional furniture styles. The designers of this period have made use of new manufacturing methods and new materials to revolutionize both the appearance and the function of furniture.

A variety of modern furniture styles has appeared during the 1900's, but most of the styles share a number of characteristics. The chief characteristic of modern furniture is its *abstract* form—that is, its appearance is not based on recognizable forms, such as animals or human figures. Most modern furniture has little decoration. Designers have used as few materials as possible and have selected materials that are lightweight, hard, and smooth. They have reduced the number of parts in a piece of furniture. For example, modern tables and chairs may have only one support instead of the traditional four legs. Such reductions in materials and parts have made manufacturing simpler and less costly.

Modern designers have also reduced the number of furniture forms used in a room. For example, some designers have eliminated traditional cabinets and cupboards and replaced them with sets of drawers and shelves called *storage units.* Some storage units are built into walls and become part of a room's architecture. Others are *modular units,* which can be moved and combined in various ways to fit a particular setting or to rearrange space in an area.

Early styles

De Stijl (The Style) was an art movement that began in the Netherlands about 1917. Led by the Dutch architect and furniture designer Gerrit Rietveld, the De Stijl movement produced furniture that emphasized abstract, rectangular forms. Rietveld used only the three primary colors—blue, red, and yellow. The pure geometric

forms of De Stijl furniture and the lightness and clarity of the design influenced most later styles of the 1900's.

The Bauhaus was a school of design founded by the German architect and educator Walter Gropius in 1919. Perhaps the most important Bauhaus contribution to furniture design was the development of the use of *tubular steel.* Tubular steel is steel tubing that can be bent and shaped to form furniture frames and supports. This use of tubular steel reduced the number of expensive joints in a piece of furniture and the amount of upholstery needed to cover the piece.

Marcel Breuer, a Bauhaus instructor, introduced tubular steel in his *Wassily* chair in 1925. Breuer made this light, elegant, and comfortable chair of chrome-plated tubular steel and canvas. In 1929, Ludwig Mies Van der Rohe, a director of the Bauhaus, created his famous *Barcelona* chair of curved steel bars and leather cushions. The chair's curved, X-form legs recalled the style of the curule stools of ancient Rome.

Organic design is the name often given to the work of the American architect Frank Lloyd Wright. Wright believed that furniture should fit naturally into its surroundings. Like other pioneers of modern furniture design, Wright reduced his forms to basic geometric outlines. But, unlike De Stijl and Bauhaus furniture, which could be used interchangeably in most homes or offices, each piece of Wright furniture was an original design intended to blend into a specific setting.

Art deco was a popular art movement during the 1920's and 1930's. It showed the influence of art nouveau but eliminated the curves and naturalistic carvings common in that earlier style. Art deco designers created streamlined shapes that stressed geometric proportions and emphasized the fine quality of the materials. Unlike most other modern styles, which were undecorated, art

The David and Alfred Smart Gallery, University of Chicago

Organic design—a creative technique promoted by the American architect Frank Lloyd Wright—results in furniture that closely matches its architectural setting. The photograph at the left shows the dining room furniture Wright designed for his famous Robie House, which was built in Chicago in 1909.

Classics of modern furniture design

The chairs shown below rank among the furniture masterpieces of the 1900's. Their designs, as in Mies Van der Rohe's Barcelona chair and Eero Saarinen's tulip chair, have a light, airy appearance that is typical of most modern furniture. The caption beneath each picture gives the name of the designer, the date the chair was created, and the chair's most important materials.

Atelier International

Gerrit Rietveld (1917)
Painted wood

Knoll International

Marcel Breuer (1928)
Cane and steel tubing

Knoll International

Mies Van der Rohe (1929)
Steel and leather

I C F, Inc.

Alvar Aalto (1934)
Molded plywood

Herman Miller, Inc.

Charles Eames (1946)
Plywood and metal

Knoll International

Hans Wegner (1949)
Wood and cane

Knoll International

Harry Bertoia (1952)
Metal rods and wire

Knoll International

Eero Saarinen (1957)
Plastics and aluminum

deco used various decorative motifs, notably lightning bolts, wheels and circles, pyramids, and waterfalls.

Modern Scandinavian design originated in the 1920's in the Scandinavian countries—Denmark, Sweden, and Norway—and in Finland. Kaare Klint, a Danish architect, is considered the first of several leaders of the modern Scandinavian style. Most Scandinavian furniture was made with native hardwoods, notably birch. The use of wood gave the style a warmer, more natural quality than modern furniture that relied on steel.

Recent developments

The United States became a major furniture design center during the 1940's, largely through the activities of the Museum of Modern Art in New York City. In 1940, the museum established a department of industrial art, which held furniture exhibitions and sponsored competitions in furniture design. Several of the designs entered in these competitions had great international impact. The museum brought worldwide attention to many American designers, notably Charles Eames and Eero Saarinen. Many experts consider Eames the first internationally important American furniture designer.

In 1940, Eames and Saarinen won a museum competi-

tion for their design for an armchair. The arms, back, and seat of the chair were joined in one molded plywood form. In 1946, Eames designed a chair in which the plywood seat was attached to a thin frame of chrome-plated rods by rubber disks. The disks allowed the parts of the chair to shift with the weight of the sitter, thus providing extra comfort. In 1957, Saarinen crated the *tulip suite,* a cluster of curved chairs and a table, all made of fiberglass and mounted on single, slender aluminum supports. The suite consisted only of chairs and a table because Saarinen wanted to eliminate other forms of furniture.

During the 1900's, large companies have been formed that design and manufacture furniture. One of the most famous is Knoll International, founded in New York City in 1938 by Hans Knoll. This company produces furniture created by many leading modern designers. Milan, Italy, became notable among several design centers that have also appeared since the mid-1900's.

Although designers of the 1900's have revolutionized furniture, most buyers still purchase furniture made in traditional styles. The French and English styles of the 1700's and 1800's are especially fashionable and are manufactured by modern furniture makers.

During the 1700's and early 1800's, furniture making in America was a craft rather than an industry. All the furniture made during this period was produced in small woodworking shops.

The manufacture of furniture became an important industry in the United States in the mid-1800's. Large factories were built to serve the demands of middle-class people, who wanted a wide variety of furniture. The Midwest became the chief furniture-producing region because it had an abundant supply of hardwoods and was close to water transportation routes. Chicago, Cincinnati, and St. Louis became important furniture-manufacturing cities.

During the 1800's, Grand Rapids, Mich., was the most famous furniture center in the United States. William Haldane, a cabinetmaker, built the first furniture factory in Grand Rapids in 1848. Later, other furniture factories opened in that city. Artisans and designers from England, the Netherlands, Sweden, and Switzerland settled in Grand Rapids. The expertise and ideas that these Europeans brought with them added to the quality of furniture produced there.

Since the end of World War II (1939-1945), the South has replaced the Midwest as the leading U.S. furniture-making region. Today, factories in the South manufacture furniture worth about a third of the value of all the furniture made in the United States. The Midwest now produces about a fourth of the value of all furniture made in the United States.

More than 5,000 manufacturers make furniture in the United States. They employ about 400,000 people. During the mid-1980's, Americans spent more than $15 billion annually on commercially produced furniture, making it one of the leading consumer industries in the country.   John W. Keefe

Baker Furniture

Furniture making often requires much handwork in addition to work done by machines. This worker applies a coloring substance to get a matching finish on all parts of a chest.

Study aids

Related articles in *World Book* include:

Biographies

Adam (family)
Chippendale, Thomas
Eames, Charles
Hepplewhite, George

Morris, William
Phyfe, Duncan
Sheraton, Thomas

Styles

Art deco
Art nouveau
Bauhaus
Biedermeier

Rococo
White House (pictures)

Other related articles

Antique
Architecture
Art and the arts (picture: The
 useful arts)
Bed
Colonial life in America (Furnishings)
Folk art
Inlay
Interior decoration
Ironwork, Decorative
Lamp
Mahogany
Mount Vernon

Museum (picture)
Pioneer life in America (Furnishings)
Rhode Island (picture: Gold
 Room in the Marble House
 in Newport)
Shakespeare, William (picture:
 A bedroom in the Birthplace)
Wicker
Williamsburg
 (picture)
Wood

Outline

I. Early furniture
  A. Ancient Egypt   C. Ancient Rome
  B. Ancient Greece   D. The Middle Ages
II. Oriental furniture
  A. China   B. Japan   C. India
III. The Renaissance
  A. Italy   B. France   C. England   D. Spain
IV. The 1600's
  A. The early 1600's   C. The French influence
  B. Louis XIV furniture   spreads
V. The 1700's
  A. French styles   C. Early American furniture
  B. English styles
VI. The 1800's
  A. The Empire style   D. Historical revivals
  B. The Regency style   E. Art nouveau
  C. The Biedermeier, or
     Restoration, style
VII. The 1900's
  A. Early styles
  B. Recent developments
VIII. The furniture industry

Questions

Who was the leading designer of the Federal style in American furniture?
What was a *klismos*? A *curule*?
How did the Bauhaus influence furniture design in the 1900's?
What is a *cabriole* leg?
How did classical art influence Italian Renaissance furniture?
What were the two main characteristics of the Louis XIV style?
How did Japanese architecture influence Japanese furniture?
What were some characteristics of the Regency style? The Régence style?
Who was Kaare Klint? Eero Saarinen?
How did the rococo style differ from the neoclassical style?

Additional resources

Aronson, Joseph. *The Encyclopedia of Furniture.* Rev. ed. Crown, 1965.
Boger, Louise A. *The Complete Guide to Furniture Styles.* Scribner, 1982. Reprint of 1969 revised edition.
Butler, Joseph T. *Field Guide to American Antique Furniture.* Facts on File, 1985.
Furniture. Time-Life Books, 1987. A guide to furniture repair.

Lucie-Smith, Edward. *Furniture: A Concise History.* Thames & Hudson, 1985. First published in 1979.

Mang, Karl. *History of Modern Furniture.* Abrams, 1979.

Furtwängler, *FOORT vEHNG lur,* **Wilhelm,** *VIHL hehlm* (1886-1954), was a noted German musical conductor. He conducted orchestras in Lübeck, Mannheim, Vienna, Berlin, and other European cities from 1911 to 1922. He succeeded Arthur Nikisch as permanent conductor of both the Berlin Philharmonic Orchestra and the Leipzig Gewandhaus Orchestra in 1922. Furtwängler made his debut in the United States with the New York Philharmonic Symphony in 1925. He was born in Berlin, Germany.   David Ewen

Furze is a spiny shrub native to Europe and Africa. It is sometimes called *gorse* or *whin.* The plant has many dark green branches that are covered with spines. It grows to a height of 4 feet (1.2 meters) or more and has fragrant, yellow flowers. It is used as an ornamental plant or for ground cover in North America and grows wild in some areas. See also **Legume.**

Scientific classification. Furze is in the pea family, Leguminosae, or Fabaceae. It is *Ulex europaeus.*   Ronald L. Jones

Fuse is a device used to cause an explosion. There are two general types, *safety fuse* and *detonating fuse.* The safety fuse allows the person setting off the explosion to reach safety before the blast occurs. A safety fuse is made of black powder enclosed in jute, cotton yarns, and waterproofing materials. When lit, the black powder burns slowly until the flame reaches the explosive. The flame sets off the charge. A blasting cap must be attached to the fuse if dynamite is to be exploded. A detonating fuse has a core of high explosive. It explodes with great violence and is used principally to set off dynamite in quarry blasting. Either a combination of safety fuse and blasting cap, or an electric blasting cap explodes this fuse. In military use, the word is usually spelled *fuze.* It is used to refer to a mechanical device for triggering an explosion by means of electricity, impact, or pressure. See also **Ammunition; Dynamite; Explosive.**

James E. Kennedy

Fuse is a device that protects an electric circuit against damage from excessive current. A fuse contains a short piece of wire made of an alloy that melts readily. The flow of current through a fuse causes the wire to heat up. The wire melts when excessive current passes through the fuse. This action burns out the fuse and breaks the circuit. It also interrupts the flow of electricity because a fuse is always connected *in series* with the circuit it protects (see **Electric circuit** [Series circuits]). A burned-out fuse—commonly called a "blown" fuse—must be replaced for the circuit to function.

Fuses are manufactured in a variety of *current ratings.* The current rating indicates how much electricity the fuse can carry without burning out. The rating is determined by the diameter of the wire used in the device. Some fuses can carry only a fraction of an ampere, but others carry hundreds of amperes.

A type of fuse called a *plug fuse* is used in many homes. A plug fuse has a "window" of glass or mica over its wire. This feature makes it possible to quickly check whether a fuse has burned out. Another type of fuse, the *cartridge fuse,* is used in circuits that require large amounts of electricity, such as those for air conditioners and electric ranges. Miniature cartridge fuses are used

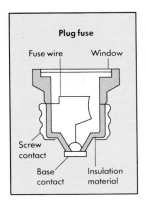 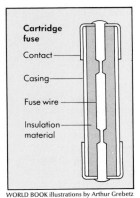

WORLD BOOK illustrations by Arthur Grebetz

Two types of fuses that protect electric circuits in the home are the plug fuse, *above left,* and the cartridge fuse, *above right.*

in automobiles and in amplifiers, television sets, and other electronic equipment. Some fuses are specially designed to withstand a current overload for a limited time. These *time-delay fuses* are useful for electric motors that need a large surge of current during start-up.

Many new homes are equipped with automatic *circuit breakers* instead of fuses (see **Circuit breaker**). These devices can be reset and so they do not have to be replaced after a current overload.   Douglas M. Lapp

Fusion, *FYOO zhuhn,* in physics, is the joining of the nuclei of two atoms to form the nucleus of a heavier element. It occurs most readily with hydrogen and other light elements. Fusion reactions, also called *thermonuclear reactions,* release a great amount of energy. The sun and other stars derive their energy from fusion reactions, as does the hydrogen bomb.

Fusion occurs when two nuclei that are moving at extremely high speeds collide with each other. High speeds are required to overcome the electric *repulsion* (repelling force) between the two nuclei, both of which are positively charged. Nuclei move at these speeds when heated to temperatures higher than 90,000,000° F. (50,000,000° C). They can also reach these speeds in a *particle accelerator* (see **Particle accelerator**).

The fusion of 1 pound (0.45 kilogram) of light nuclei produces as much energy as the burning of about 9,000 short tons (8,200 metric tons) of coal. Scientists are still conducting experiments on ways of harnessing the energy of fusion. The fuel used in most fusion experiments consists of a gaseous mixture of *deuterium* and *tritium,* two heavy isotopes of hydrogen.   J. Rayford Nix

See also **Hydrogen bomb; Nuclear energy** (Nuclear fusion; Present-day research); **Star** (Why stars shine).

Fusion bomb. See Nuclear weapon.

Future Farmers of America (FFA) is an organization for high school students who study vocational agriculture. It helps them prepare for careers in agriculture and *agribusiness* (business involving agriculture). It also trains them to become responsible citizens and leaders in their communities. FFA forms part of the agricultural education program in many public schools. Members gain practical experience through FFA activities while they study school courses in agriculture. They also develop leadership and learn to cooperate with others. Both boys and girls may join the FFA. The U.S. Department of Education sponsors the FFA nationally.

The official motto of the FFA expresses its program:

Learning to do,
Doing to learn;
Earning to live,
Living to serve.

In *learning to do,* FFA members study practical and scientific agriculture to become good farmers or prepare themselves for other careers in agriculture.

In *doing to learn,* members work on projects from which they gain practical experience.

In *earning to live,* FFA members manage farms or agribusiness enterprises that produce income.

In *living to serve,* members develop qualities of competent leadership and responsible citizenship, and work to improve their school and community.

The FFA slogan is "FFA . . . Leaders for the New Fields of Agriculture." The FFA emblem has an owl, a plow, and a rising sun within the cross section of an ear of corn. An American eagle appears above this design. The owl represents wisdom and knowledge, and the plow stands for labor and tilling the soil. The rising sun symbolizes the new day that will dawn when all farmers learn to work together. The corn stands for the agricultural interest that is common to all FFA members, and the eagle stands for the national scope of the FFA.

About 400,000 students belong to the Future Farmers of America in about 8,000 high school chapters in the United States, Puerto Rico, and the Virgin Islands. A school must have a full-time vocational agriculture teacher before it can form an FFA chapter. Only boys and girls who are studying vocational agriculture may join the organization. They may continue their membership for three years after they leave high school, or until they reach the age of 21, whichever is longer. Members wear distinctive blue corduroy jackets. The emblems and names on the jackets are embroidered in gold and blue, the FFA colors.

What FFA members do

Training. Each FFA member carries out a project over several years called the Supervised Occupation Experience (SOE) program. The SOE program is designed to put into practice the knowledge gained in vocational agriculture classes. Members usually start with small programs when they are freshmen in high school. They increase the scope of the program as they advance in their agriculture classes. The FFA adviser visits each student to supervise and help with the program. Members conduct SOE programs in such areas as production agriculture, forestry, agriculture sales and service, and horticulture.

FFA chapters often help members start a program. The FFA occasionally lends money to students whose families cannot give them the money for a good start in farming, or helps them obtain needed credit. In some areas, an FFA chapter or a school may own a farm or greenhouse where members who do not have land at home can work on their programs. The organization encourages members to expand their farming programs or agribusiness experiences so that, by the time they complete high school, they will be prepared to farm on a full-time basis, or to be employed in an agribusiness.

FFA members study career opportunities in agriculture. With their teachers, they go on field trips to nearby farms to observe good farming practices and farm management. They also visit agricultural experiment stations and agribusinesses to see the development and results of new agricultural methods. They study farm economics, marketing, computers, and soil conservation and improvement, and learn how to keep accurate, complete financial records. The FFA also trains members in farm mechanics. It teaches them how to select, use, care for, and repair farm machinery. Members also study horticulture.

By participating in chapter meetings, FFA members learn to follow parliamentary procedure, to speak in public, and to cooperate with their fellow students in programs to improve themselves and their communities. The organization recommends that chapters meet regularly at least once a month.

Activities. FFA members exhibit the animals and crops they have raised in local, county, and state fairs. Chapters participate in contests at the local, state, and national levels. Contests are held in livestock, dairy, and poultry judging; agricultural mechanics skills; dairy foods and meats evaluation; forestry; nursery and landscape; and farm management. The contests teach students judging and technical skills, and instill a spirit of competition among FFA members. The members also participate in dairy herd improvement associations, livestock breeders' groups, business associations, and other organizations that work to improve agriculture.

Local chapters sponsor recreational activities and organize educational tours. They conduct safety campaigns and home-improvement projects, and hold annual parent-member banquets. FFA chapters sometimes organize and manage community fairs. Through the FFA *Building Our American Communities* program, FFA chapters across the nation have participated in community improvement activities.

FFA members enjoy camping during the summer. Many states have FFA leadership centers that provide summer fun and offer leadership training courses.

Bill Stagg, Future Farmers of America

A livestock judging contest enables FFA members to apply knowledge gained in agriculture classes. FFA chapters participate in such contests at the local, state, and national levels.

Horticulture is a popular area of study in the FFA program. Students may prepare for occupations in such fields as greenhouse operations, *left.* The FFA emblem is shown above.

Degrees. FFA members are awarded various degrees for their achievements in agricultural projects, community service, cooperation, leadership, and scholarship. When a student joins the FFA, he or she becomes a *Greenhand,* and may buy and wear a small bronze pin bearing the FFA emblem.

After one year, Greenhands receive the *Chapter Farmer* degree if their participation in the FFA has been satisfactory. They may now wear a silver FFA pin. Most FFA members receive the Chapter Farmer degree.

A third degree, the *State Farmer,* is much harder to attain. State associations of the FFA award this degree for outstanding achievement in agricultural career development, leadership, and scholarship. They present it at annual state conventions. Among other things, a State Farmer must have worked at least 600 hours, or earned at least $500 and deposited it in a bank or invested it productively. Each state association awards the degree to no more than 3 of every 100 members a year. A State Farmer wears a gold emblem pin.

The *American Farmer* degree is the highest FFA rank.

A computer course helps Future Farmers learn how to keep accurate, complete financial records. Members also study farm economics, marketing, and soil conservation.

The national organization presents it each year to members nominated by the state associations. Each state may nominate one candidate for each 667 members. In order to encourage students to maintain their interest in agriculture, only FFA members who have been out of high school for at least one year may be nominated. Each American Farmer receives a gold key and partial travel expenses to the national convention.

The FFA also presents honorary degrees to men and women who perform exceptional service to the organization. These individuals receive *Honorary Chapter, State,* or *American Farmer* degrees and pins.

Awards are designed to encourage FFA members to do better work in areas ranging from farm business management to computer technology. The Future Farmers of America Foundation, Inc., sponsors 29 proficiency awards for FFA members, including awards for agricultural mechanics, agricultural processing, agricultural sales and service, horticulture, natural resources, and production agriculture. This foundation, organized in 1944, is supported by donations from more than 1,000 businesses. It presents four Star Farmer and four Star Agribusinessman awards each year at the national FFA

Purposes of the FFA

1. To develop competent, aggressive, rural, and agricultural leadership.
2. To create and nurture a love of country life.
3. To strengthen the confidence of members in themselves and their work.
4. To create more interest in the intelligent choice of agricultural occupations.
5. To encourage members to develop individual farming programs and to become established in agricultural careers.
6. To encourage members to improve the farm home and its surroundings.
7. To participate in worthy undertakings for the improvement of agriculture.
8. To develop character, train for useful citizenship, and foster patriotism.
9. To participate in cooperative effort.
10. To encourage and practice thrift.
11. To encourage improvement in scholarship.
12. To provide and encourage the development of organized rural recreational activities.

convention to winners chosen from among the American Farmer candidates. Other national awards are made for group achievements in chapter activities and to winners of the national FFA public speaking contest.

Individual states present awards at state FFA conventions. Local chapters award medals to outstanding members during their annual parent-member banquets or at special school assemblies. They offer the awards in various fields, including farm mechanics, electrification, horticulture, soil and water management, and farm safety. The chapters present awards to more than 80,000 students each year.

Organization

Local chapters of the FFA are sponsored by the vocational agriculture departments of local high schools. The chapters elect their own officers, choose committees, and hold regular business meetings. Chapter officers usually serve as delegates to state conventions. The vocational agriculture teacher in each high school is the adviser for the local chapter.

State associations in the individual states aid the local chapters. A state board for vocational education sponsors each state association, and the state supervisor of vocational agriculture is its adviser. State associations elect officers at an annual state convention. The state president and other state officers usually serve as delegates to the annual national convention in Kansas City, Mo.

National organization. Delegates to the national convention each year elect a Board of National Officers made up of a president, a secretary, and four vice presidents. Each vice president represents one of the FFA's four administrative regions. The regions are Central, Eastern, Southern, and Western. The FFA also has an adult Board of Directors made up of five members of the Office of Vocational and Adult Education of the Department of Education, and four state supervisors of agricultural education. State supervisors hold regional conferences and choose their four board members.

The Board of National Officers meets three times a year with the Board of Directors to conduct the business of the national organization. The Board of Directors has final authority, but in most cases it accepts the recommendations of the Board of National Officers. The two boards may refer questions of policy to the national convention.

The national FFA adviser is the head of Agricultural, Agribusiness, and Natural Resources Occupations within the Department of Education. A member of the adviser's staff serves as national FFA executive secretary. The state boards for vocational education and the local high school departments of vocational agriculture help carry out FFA programs. Part of the funds to operate the FFA come from annual dues paid by each member. Members pay $3.00 a year in national dues. The organization's headquarters are at the National FFA Center, P.O. Box 15160, Alexandria, VA 22309.

History

In 1917, Congress passed the Smith-Hughes Act, which gave the federal government the power to establational program of vocational education. It also ted the government to pay half the cost of a voca-

tional agriculture program in each state. The government now pays only about a sixth of the cost. The states and local communities pay the rest. A Federal Board for Vocational Education administered the Smith-Hughes Act at first. Later, the Department of Health, Education, and Welfare took over the management of the program. In 1980, the program was transferred to the newly created Department of Education.

In the early 1920's, vocational-agriculture students formed clubs in many communities throughout the country. In some states, the local clubs joined in statewide associations. One of these state associations, the Future Farmers of Virginia, which was formed in 1926, became the model for the Future Farmers of America. In November 1928, representatives from the state associations met in Kansas City, Mo. They adopted a constitution and founded the Future Farmers of America. Congress granted it a charter in 1950.

In 1955, the FFA began a program to improve international understanding. The FFA has helped set up Future Farmers organizations in Colombia, Costa Rica, Japan, Mexico, Peru, and the Philippines. The FFA also operates an international exchange program. It provides opportunities for members to gain work experience on farms and in agribusinesses in more than 30 countries.

FFA maintains a supply service that sells jackets, jewelry, and other items bearing its emblem. The FFA publishes a *National FFA Calendar* and *The National FUTURE FARMER* magazine. The magazine is sent every other month to members as part of their membership dues.

Critically reviewed by the Future Farmers of America

Related articles in *World Book* include:

Agricultural education	4-H
Agricultural experiment station	Future Homemakers
Agriculture	of America
Fair	Smith-Hughes Act
Farm and farming	

Future Homemakers of America is a national vocational organization for junior high and high school students enrolled in home economics subjects. Members participate in activities to help prepare themselves for roles as wage earners, community leaders, and caring family members. More than 315,000 students belong to the organization. About 11,500 local chapters operate in the United States and its territories.

Future Homemakers of America is a private, nonprofit organization supported partly by dues. It is also supported by foundation grants and corporate contributions raised by the Future Homemakers of America Foundation.

The organization has two types of chapters—Future Homemakers of America (FHA) chapters and Home Economics Related Occupations (HERO) chapters. FHA chapters emphasize homemaking education and activities related to child development, clothing production, consumer concerns, family living and parenthood, foods and nutrition, and household management. HERO chapters stress preparation for careers involving home economics skills, such as in the food service industry, clothing or textile business, and child care.

Local projects. Chapters have many different activities based on their local needs or interests. Chapter members plan and carry out projects that focus on the family, school, and community.

Future Homemakers of America helps prepare students to be homemakers, wage earners, and community leaders. The student at the left is working with youngsters in a child-care project. The organization's emblem is shown in the photo above.

Future Homemakers of America, Inc.

Projects focusing on the family relate to such issues as child abuse, divorce, and teen-age suicide. Chapters may prepare directories of family service agencies in the community, give workshops on preventing teen pregnancy, or sponsor programs to increase communication among family members. Projects that benefit the school deal with such areas as career exploration, citizenship, drug abuse, nutrition for athletes, and teen-age stress. In community projects, chapter members raise funds for charities and work with the elderly and handicapped. Members also may volunteer for other public service.

Future Homemakers of America, Inc.

HERO chapters of Future Homemakers of America stress careers involving home economics skills. These students are learning about food service by operating a restaurant.

National programs. Future Homemakers of America also has several programs conducted by chapters throughout the nation. Two of these programs deal with issues that concern teen-agers. These programs are based on the concept of *peer education*—for example, teens teaching teens. They use the powerful influence of peer pressure in a positive way to encourage young people to develop good attitudes and habits. For example, the Families and Futures program involves the exchange of facts among young future parents so that they can make responsible decisions about individual and family health. This program is co-sponsored by the March of Dimes Birth Defects Foundation. The Student Body program helps teen-agers develop good eating habits, physical fitness, and self-confidence.

Other national programs have different focuses. Future Homemakers of America co-sponsors the Japanese Exchange Program together with Youth For Understanding. Members of Future Homemakers of America receive scholarships to spend eight weeks living with the family of a member of Future Homemakers of Japan (FHJ) in Japan. FHJ members spend a year in the United States. The national STAR Events program enables members to demonstrate achievement in chapter projects, leadership skills, and occupational preparation. The term *STAR* stands for *Students Taking Action for Recognition.* Members plan, conduct, evaluate, and participate in competitive events.

Organization. Future Homemakers of America was founded in 1945. It has three levels—national, state, and local. The national level includes an executive council of student members, a board of directors made up of adults and teen-agers, and a national staff. These leaders set general policies for the organization. The official magazine, *Teen Times,* is published at the National Headquarters and Leadership Center, 1910 Association Drive, Reston, VA 22091.

State associations consist of an adult adviser and student officers. They assist local chapters, plan state workshops, and introduce national programs to the local level. Local chapters are organized through school home economics departments. Advisers are home economics teachers. Local chapter officers are students.

Critically reviewed by Future Homemakers of America

Future Nurses. See Nursing (Career information).

Futures. See Commodity exchange.

Futurism was an Italian art movement that flourished from 1909 to about 1916. It was the first of many art movements that tried to break with the past in all areas of life. Futurism glorified the power, speed, and excitement of the machine age. From the French cubist painters and multiple-exposure photography, the Futurists learned to break up realistic forms into multiple images and overlapping fragments of color. By such means, they tried to show the energy and speed of life. In literature, Futurism demanded the abolition of traditional sentence structures and verse forms.

Futurism was created by the poet Filippo Marinetti. In 1909, Marinetti issued the first of many defiant proclamations published by the Futurists. He was soon joined by the painters Giacomo Balla, Carlo Carrà, Luigi Russolo, and Gino Severini, and the painter and sculptor Umberto Boccioni. A Futurist sculpture by Boccioni entitled *Unique Forms of Continuity in Space* is reproduced in the *World Book* article on **Sculpture**.

By 1916, Futurism had lost most of its vigor. Despite its short life, Futurism influenced the theories and works of such modern art movements as Dadaism, Expressionism, and Surrealism.   Marcel Franciscono

See also **Boccioni, Umberto; Painting** (Futurism); **Sculpture** (Modern international).

Additional resources

Hulten, Pontus. *Futurism and Futurisms.* Abbeville, 1986.
Kozloff, Max. *Cubism/Futurism.* Charterhouse, 1973.

Fuzhou, *foo joh* (pop. 1,129,251), also spelled *Foochow* or *Fu-chou,* is the capital of Fujian Province in China. The city lies on the Min River, about 30 miles (48 kilometers) from the river's mouth. For location, see **China** (political map).

Fuzhou was once a center of tea and camphor trade. In 1842, it became a "treaty port" in which Great Britain gained special trading rights (see **China** [Clash with the Western powers]). Fuzhou lost importance as a trading center in the late 1800's. Japanese troops occupied the city several times during World War II (1939-1945). Fuzhou is famous for its fine lacquerware. The city's products also include industrial chemicals and electronic products.   Parris H. Chang

Red Cross Train (1914), an oil painting by Gino Severini;
The Solomon R. Guggenheim Museum, New York City

Futurist paintings express the energy, speed, and excitement that the movement saw in the machine age. Most of these paintings feature multiple images and overlapping fragments of color.

THE WORLD BOOK